Finance Acts Handbook 2017

While every care has been taken to ensure the accuracy of this work, no responsibility for loss or damage occasioned to any person acting or refraining from action as a result of any statement in it can be accepted by the authors, editors or publishers.

Finance Acts Handbook 2017

Contributors

Alistair Bambridge, ACA, CPA,
CTA, EA
Rebecca Benneyworth, MBE,
BSc, FCA
Lynnette Bober, ACA,
CTA, TEP
Graham C Brearley
Laura Charkin
Richard Cherrett
Margaret Curran
Bill Dodwell
Mark Downey
Andrew Goodall
Gordon Gray
Phil Greatrex, FCA, ATII
Mark Groom
Kendra Hann
Philip Hare
John Hayward
Charlotte Haywood
Matthew Hodkin

Andrew Hubbard, BMus, PhD,
CAT (Fellow), ATT (Fellow)
Donna Huggard
Helena Kanczula, MA (Cantab), ACA
Zigurds Kronbergs, BSc, ARCS,
MA, ACA, FCCA
Anton Lane, CTA
John Lindsay, BA, FCA, FTII
Luigi Lungarella, BA (Hons), CTA,
AIIT, ATT, AFTA
Pete Miller, CTA (Fellow)
Harish Narayanan
Janet Pierce, FCA,
CTA, TEP, AIIT
Camilla Spielman
Simon Tremblett, CTA
Neil Warren, CTA (Fellow),
ATT, FMAAT
Martin Wilson, MA, FCA
Stephen Woodhouse, LLB Partner
Tracey Wright

Tolley®

Members of the LexisNexis Group worldwide

United Kingdom	RELX (UK) Limited trading as LexisNexis, 1–3 Strand, London WC2N 5JR and 9–10 St Andrew Square, Edinburgh EH2 2AF
Australia	Reed International Books Australia Pty Ltd trading as LexisNexis, Chatswood, New South Wales
Austria	LexisNexis Verlag ARD Orac GmbH & Co KG, Vienna
Benelux	LexisNexis Benelux, Amsterdam
Canada	LexisNexis Canada, Markham, Ontario
China	LexisNexis China, Beijing and Shanghai
France	LexisNexis SA, Paris
Germany	LexisNexis GmbH, Dusseldorf
Hong Kong	LexisNexis Hong Kong, Hong Kong
India	LexisNexis India, New Delhi
Italy	Giuffrè Editore, Milan
Japan	LexisNexis Japan, Tokyo
Malaysia	Malayan Law Journal Sdn Bhd, Kuala Lumpur
New Zealand	LexisNexis NZ Ltd, Wellington
Singapore	LexisNexis Singapore, Singapore
South Africa	LexisNexis South Africa, Durban
USA	LexisNexis, Dayton, Ohio

© 2017 RELX (UK) Limited

Published by LexisNexis

This is a Tolley title

ISBN 9780754554714 (ATT)

Typeset by Letterpart Limited, Caterham on the Hill, Surrey CR3 5XL

Printed and bound by CPI Group (UK) Ltd, Croydon, CR0 4YY

Visit LexisNexis at www.lexisnexis.co.uk

FOREWORD

It is entirely appropriate that this book should cover both 2017 Finance Acts; after all, the original intention was that they should have been the single largest Finance Act in recent memory.

What has been disappointing is that so little parliamentary time was devoted to debating the provisions. Just three tiny amendments were made to the second Bill, although we should acknowledge some important changes made in four areas where new draft legislation was published in July. Many of the important changes apply from April 2017, which is hardly satisfactory for a statute enacted in November. We should be pleased that this type of backdating is much less likely in future, as Finance Act 2018 is set to become law in March 2018 – just before the new tax year.

The two Acts bring significant change and complexity for almost everyone. Companies large and small must get to grips with the new system-wide limits on interest and finance costs. These new rules are backdated to 1 April 2017; those with year-ends other than 31 March will need to perform awkward split period calculations. The Government sees this as an important part of the G20/OECD Base Erosion and Profit Shifting project, with an annual yield over £1 billion. Part of this cost will fall on companies simply borrowing money from third party sources, without the complexities of intercompany loans or shareholder debt. Groups with annual interest costs below £2 million won't be affected – other than in compliance terms.

Corporate loss relief rules have suddenly become much more flexible, but at the cost of limiting offset to 50% of group profits over £5 million. Companies of all sizes will suddenly find that losses arising from 1 April 2017 are no longer trapped in individual companies in a group.

The important abolition of permanent remittance-basis opportunities for non-domiciled individuals is enacted here – although time meant that part of the anti-avoidance rules has been deferred until 2018. The new approach removes the remittance basis for income tax and capital gains tax after 14 years' UK residence. Limited inheritance tax benefits remain, alongside better ways to bring monies into the UK to make qualifying investments.

We have our first sight of some "Making Tax Digital" legislation, with clauses covering income tax and VAT, though most of the law simply enables making regulations.

There are important changes to employment taxes. The first Finance Act includes new rules aimed at the use of labour by the public sector. These apply from 6 April 2017 and specify that PAYE/NIC must be withheld from payments to personal service companies where if "… the services were provided under a contract directly between the client and the worker, the worker would be regarded for income tax purposes as an employee of the client or the holder of an office under the client". HMRC have produced an online employment status checker to aid public sector engagers work out whether or not services should be classified as employment services.

The second major change affects "optional remuneration arrangements". From April 2017, where an employee gives up earnings for a benefit in kind, the arrangement will broadly be taxed as if there had been no sacrifice. Existing arrangements are grandfathered for one or four years, depending on the type of benefit. The result is that salary sacrifice arrangements will ultimately be effective only for pension contributions, cycle to work schemes, childcare and ultra-low emission vehicles.

Employee shareholder shares are finally brought to an end. The objective was that employees joining risky start-up businesses could be offered shares in return for giving up certain employment rights. However, evidence mounted that the scheme was proving more popular in different types of companies, leading to its withdrawal.

Once again, the authors should be congratulated on producing their commentary so quickly and the publishers in getting the text into our hands so rapidly.

Bill Dodwell
Deloitte LLP
November 2017

CONTENTS

Page

Contents

RELEVANT DATES AND ABBREVIATIONS

8 March 2017	Budget Statement
20 March 2017	Finance Bill
17 April 2017	FA 2017 Royal Assent
8 September 2017	Finance Bill September
16 November 2017	F(No 2)A 2017 Royal Assent

ABV	=	alcohol by volume
ACS	=	authorised contractual schemes
ALDA 1979	=	Alcoholic Liquor Duties Act 1979
APD	=	Air Passenger Duty
AMAP	=	Approved Mileage Allowance Payment
ANGIE	=	adjusted net group-interest expense of the group
APN	=	accelerated payment notice
ATED	=	annual tax on enveloped dwellings
ATT	=	Association of Taxation Technicians
AUT	=	authorised unit trust
BCE	=	benefit crystallisation event
BIR	=	business investment relief
CA 2006	=	Companies Act 2006
CAA 2001	=	Capital Allowances Act 2001
CEMA 1979	=	Customs and Excise Management Act 1979
CGT	=	capital gains tax
Ch	=	Chapter (of a part of an Act)
CIOT	=	Chartered Institute of Taxation
CITR	=	Community Investment Tax Relief
CJA 2003	=	Criminal Justice Act 2003
CoACS	=	Co-ownership Authorised Contractual Schemes
CRS	=	Common Reporting Standard
CSOP	=	company share option plan
CTA 2009	=	Corporation Tax Act 2009
CTA 2010	=	Corporation Tax Act 2010
DOITAS	=	disclosure of indirect tax avoidance schemes
DOTAS	=	disclosure of tax avoidance schemes
EBITDA	=	earnings before interest, tax, depreciation and amortisation
EBT	=	employee benefit trust
EEA	=	European Economic Area
EIS	=	enterprise investment scheme
ESS	=	employee shareholder status
EU	=	European Union
FA	=	Finance Act
FATCA	=	US Foreign Account Tax Compliance Act
FCA	=	Financial Conduct Authority
FSMA 2000	=	Financial Services and Markets Act 2000
GAAR	=	general anti-abuse rule
HMRC	=	Her Majesty's Revenue and Customs
ICTA 1988	=	Income and Corporation Taxes Act 1988
IFS	=	Institute for Fiscal Studies
IHT	=	inheritance tax
IHTA 1984	=	Inheritance Tax Act 1984
IPT	=	insurance premium tax
ITA 2007	=	Income Tax Act 2007
ITEPA 2003	=	Income Tax (Earnings and Pensions) Act 2003
ITTOIA 2005	=	Income Tax (Trading and Other Income) Act 2005
LLPs	=	limited liability partnerships
MET	=	minimum excise tax
MPAA	=	money-purchase annual allowance
NIRE	=	Northern Ireland regional establishment

OECD	=	Organisation for Economic Co-operation and Development
OEIC	=	open-ended investment company
OpRA	=	optional remuneration arrangements
PAIF	=	property authorised investment fund
para	=	paragraph (of a Schedule to an Act)
PAYE	=	pay as you earn
PCRT	=	Professional Conduct in Relation to Taxation
PLR	=	potential lost revenue
POTAS	=	Promoters of Tax Avoidance Scheme
PPB	=	personal portfolio bonds
PRA	=	Prudential Regulation Authority
PRN	=	promoter reference number
PRT	=	petroleum revenue tax
Pt	=	part (of an Act or of a Schedule to an Act)
QNGIE	=	qualifying net group-interest expense of the group for the period
QROPS	=	qualifying recognised overseas pension scheme
R&D	=	research and development
reg	=	regulation (of an SI)
REIT	=	real estate investment trust
RGD	=	remote gaming duty
ROPS	=	recognised overseas pension scheme
RTC	=	requirement to correct
s	=	section (of an Act)
Sch	=	Schedule (to an Act)
SEIS	=	seed enterprise investment scheme
SI	=	Statutory Instrument (since 1948)
SITR	=	social investment tax relief
ss	=	sections (of an Act)
SPC	=	secondary production company
SRN	=	scheme reference number
STC	=	Simon's Tax Cases
sub-para	=	sub-paragraph
sub-s	=	subsection
SWTI	=	Simon's Weekly Tax Intelligence
TCGA 1992	=	Taxation of Chargeable Gains Act 1992
TIOPA 2010	=	Taxation (International and Other Provisions) Act 2010
TMA 1970	=	Taxes Management Act 1970
TPA 2014	=	Taxation of Pensions Act 2014
TPDA 1979	=	Tobacco Products Duty Act 1979
UK	=	United Kingdom
ULEV	=	ultra-low emission vehicle
UT	=	Upper Tribunal
VATA 1994	=	Value Added Tax Act 1994
VED	=	vehicle excise duty
VERA 1994	=	Vehicle Excise and Registration Act 1994
VCT	=	venture capital trust

ABOUT THE AUTHORS

Alistair Bambridge, ACA, CPA, CTA, EA

Alistair Bambridge is the founder and an active partner of Bambridge Accountants. Alistair specialises in the creative industries and US and Canadian expats. He is also the author of the annual US Tax Return Guide for Expats.

Alistair Bambridge has written the commentary for F(No 2)A 2017 ss 14, 16, 17, 26, and Sch 1, 2, 3.

Rebecca Benneyworth, MBE, BSc, FCA

Rebecca Benneyworth is a lecturer, writer and consultant on a variety of taxes. She lectures extensively throughout the UK, and writes regularly for a wide range of publications. She also has a small accountancy practice based in Gloucestershire, comprising personal tax clients, self-employed individuals and small companies. She has an interest in all issues affecting smaller practices and their clients, and is a member of the ICAEW Tax Faculty committee.

Rebecca Benneyworth has written the commentary for F(No 2)A 2017 ss 60–62, Sch 14.

Lynnette Bober, ACA

Lynnette is a chartered accountant, a chartered tax adviser, and a member of the Society of Trust and Estate Practitioners. Specialising in the field of personal taxation (including remittance basis issues and offshore trust planning) she advises clients on personal and trust taxation issues. She also contributes to various technical publications and journals. Lynnette is the deputy chairman of the ICAEW Tax Faculty Private Client Committee and on a number of its subcommittees and working parties.

Lynnette Bober has written the commentary for F(No 2)A 2017 ss 31, 33, Sch 9, Sch 10.

Graham C Brearley

Graham C Brearley has worked for the majority of his professional life in VAT. He started out with HM Customs & Excise back in 1974 and worked for 15 or so years in a number of different roles. He joined Grant Thornton in 1989 and has accumulated a further 28 years of experience as a VAT consultant providing VAT advice and solutions across many sectors to many varied clients.

Graham C Brearley has written the commentary for F(No 2)A 2017 ss 48 to 59 and Sch 13.

Laura Charkin

Laura Charkin is a partner in Goodwin's Tax Practice and a member of the Private Investment Funds Group. She has particular expertise in structuring private funds, PCVs, separately managed accounts, executive incentive arrangements, the structures through which funds invest, and investment management platforms. Ms. Charkin advises on a broad range of UK tax issues including VAT, employment tax, CGT in relation to partnerships, withholding taxes and tax rules relating to carried interest and executive investments into funds. She also has considerable knowledge of international tax issues arising for investment structures with a cross-border dimension and experience with multijurisdictional fund management teams. Prior to joining Goodwin in 2017, Laura Charkin was a partner at King & Wood Mallesons (formerly SJ Berwin).

Laura Charkin and Charlotte Haywood have written the commentary for F(No 2)A 2017 s 32.

Richard Cherrett

Richard Cherrett is an associate director in Deloitte's International Markets business tax advisory group, and a fellow of the ICAEW. He advises large corporate groups on complex issues, principally the application of corporate debt and derivatives rules, and the taxation of cross-border flows.

Richard Cherrett has written the commentary for F(No 2)A 2017 s 24.

Margaret Curran

Margaret Curran has worked in the field of taxation for 30 years, at both Big 4 and smaller accountancy firms. She is currently a Technical Officer at the Chartered Institute of Taxation, with responsibility for the Management of Taxes and Owner-Managed Businesses technical sub-committees, as well as the CIOT's Digitalisation and Agent Strategy Working Group. Her role involves representing the Institute in dealings with HMRC and other Government bodies, and researching and drafting technical submissions in response to consultation documents, draft legislation and other papers. She also writes regularly for Tax Adviser magazine.

Margaret Curran has written the commentary for F(No 2)A 2017 s 65 and Sch 16.

Bill Dodwell

Bill Dodwell is Head of Tax Policy at Deloitte UK. He is responsible for consultations with HM Treasury, HMRC, the OECD and the EU. Bill was the 2016–17 President of the Chartered Institute of Taxation and he chaired the CIOT's Technical Committee from 2010–16. Bill regularly speaks to the UK media on taxation matters and tweets as @BillDodwellTax

Bill Dodwell has written the Foreword to the book.

Mark Downey

Mark Downey is the Head of Tax for the UK & European business of a major listed life insurer. He has over 30 years' experience in the world of tax, 20 years of which have been spent on insurance related tax matters. Before moving into industry he worked on insurance tax matters at a Big Four firm and in the Inland Revenue so has a possibly unique view on insurance tax from the perspective of the industry, the profession and the tax authority. Mark is a regular writer and conference speaker on tax matters affecting the life insurance industry and is also the current Chair of the Life Tax Issues Working Group at the Association of British Insurers.

Mark Downey has written the commentary for F(No 2)A 2017 s 9.

Andrew Goodall

Andrew Goodall is a freelance writer and journalist specialising in tax policy, law and administration. He is a regular contributor to Tax Analysts. His work has been published by several LexisNexis titles including Tax Adviser and Tax Journal. Other publishers include the professional bodies AAT and ACCA. Andrew is a non-practising member of the Chartered Institute of Taxation.

Andrew Goodall has written the commentary for FA 2017 ss 1–5 and s 8 and F(No 2)A 2017 ss 1–4, 6, 8, 21, 22, 25, 70, Sch 6 and Sch 7.

Gordon Gray

Gordon Gray is a Chartered Accountant and Chartered Tax Adviser. He has worked in financial services tax for almost 20 years specialising in the taxation of insurance companies and investment funds. He has worked with a number of insurers and administrators on the launch of Co-ownership Authorised Contractual Schemes since 2013 and has had a particular focus on the practical implications for taxable investors. He has also actively contributed to discussions chaired by industry bodies and HMRC on the subject and has responded to HMRC consultations. He is based in Edinburgh.

Gordon Gray has written the commentary for F(No 2)A 2017 ss 40–42.

Phil Greatrex, FCA, ATII

Phil Greatrex is a partner in CW Energy LLP. Phil has been providing tax advice to a wide range of clients in the oil and gas sector, covering petroleum revenue tax corporation tax and supplementary charge on varied, and often complex, issues for over 30 years. He has been an active member of the UKOITC and BRINDEX tax committees for many years and has extensive experience of dealing with Treasury and HMRC in lobbying for tax changes. More recently he was a member of the expert panel advising Treasury on the options available for taxation of late life assets.

Phil Greatrex has written the commentary for F(No 2)A 2017 s 44.

Mark Groom

Mark Groom is an employment tax partner in Deloitte's Compensation and Benefits group. He is also Vice Chairman of the Employment Taxes sub-committee of the Chartered Institute of Taxation. Mark specialises in pay and incentives, employment status and intermediaries, and benefits and expenses consulting and compliance including KYC, SAO, and HMRC investigations. He is a regular speaker at seminars and contributor to articles on employment tax matters and to HMRC consultations.

Mark Groom has written the commentary for FA 2017 s 7 and Sch 2 and F(No 2)A 2017 s 5.

Kendra Hann

Kendra Hann is the UK indirect tax leader responsible for managing Deloitte's UK indirect tax practice. This includes VAT, customs and excise duties, IPT and environmental taxes. She has worked in indirect tax since 1989 in the tax authority, business and the profession. Kendra specialises in advising multi-national clients on their global indirect tax issues. Kendra is a member of the Chartered Institute of Taxation and also represents Deloitte on a number of HM Treasury and HM Revenue & Customs working parties.

Kendra Hann has written the commentary for FA 2017 ss 20–23 and F(No 2)A 2017 ss 45–47.

Philip Hare

Philip Hare is a chartered accountant and chartered tax adviser. He has specialised in the venture capital tax reliefs (Venture Capital Trusts, Enterprise Investment Scheme and Seed Enterprise Investment Scheme) since their inception. He and his team at Philip Hare & Associates advise companies, investment fund managers and investors on compliance with those schemes. Philip and his team have been awarded Best EIS Tax Advisor by the EIS Association ten times since 2006, including for 2016.

Philip Hare has written the commentary for F(No 2)A 2017 ss 11–13.

John Hayward

John Hayward is a part-time self-employed pensions author. He has written for Pensions World and Tax Journal and is a member of the latter's Editorial Board. He has contributed to Butterworth's Tax Planning Service, Robin Ellison's Pensions Law and Practice, Simon's Taxes, Tolley's Finance and Law for the Older Client, Finance Act Handbook 2004 to 2017 and the ICAEW's TAXline. His specialist topics include small self-administered pension schemes and taxation aspects of all pension schemes.

John Hayward has written the commentary for FA 2017 ss 9–10 and Schs 3–4 and F(No 2)A 2017 s 7.

Charlotte Haywood
Charlotte Haywood is an associate in Goodwin's Tax Practice. She advises on a wide range of UK tax matters, primarily those affecting the private investment funds industry, including fund structuring, executive incentive arrangements and M&A and other private equity transactions. She also has experience advising on a range of personal tax matters including residence, remittance and estate planning. Prior to joining Goodwin in 2017, Charlotte Haywood was an associate at King & Wood Mallesons (formerly SJ Berwin).

Charlotte Haywood and Laura Charkin have written the commentary for F(No 2)A 2017 s 32.

Matthew Hodkin
Matthew Hodkin is a partner in the corporate tax team in the London office of Norton Rose Fulbright LLP. He specialises in the structuring of complex corporate and financing transactions, particularly in the transport, infrastructure and energy sectors. He is a member of the Law Society's Corporation Tax Sub-Committee and a member of one of HMRC's working groups on the reform of the loan relationship rules.

Matthew Hodkin has written the commentary for FA 2017 ss 25–61 and Schs 8–11

Andrew Hubbard, BMus, PhD, CAT (Fellow), ATT (Fellow)
Andrew Hubbard is the editor-in-chief of Taxation magazine. He is a long-term contributor to Tolley's Tax Planning and Finance Act Handbook. In 2006 he won the tax writer of the year award at the Taxation Awards and is a former president of both the CIOT and the ATT. He is well known as a writer and lecturer on tax matters. He has recently retired as a partner in the Nottingham office of RSM where he specialised in tax dispute resolution and the taxation of entrepreneurial businesses. Andrew originally trained as a musician before joining the Inland Revenue as an Inspector of Taxes.

Andrew Hubbard has written the commentary for FA 2017 s 15 and Sch 6 and F(No 2)A 2017 ss 34–37, Schs 11, 12.

Donna Huggard
Donna Huggard is an Indirect Tax Associate Director in Deloitte UK's Tax Policy Group. She has worked in indirect tax in New Zealand (the tax authority and the profession) and in the UK (the profession), mainly advising on VAT issues and working on tax policy issues.

Donna Huggard has written the commentary for FA 2017 ss 20–23.

Helena Kanczula, MA (Cantab), ACA
Helena Kanczula is a corporate tax director at Blick Rothenberg Limited. She is also a member of the firm's specialist property group which advises on all aspects of property structuring including SDLT. She is a regular contributor to the tax press and recent publications include articles on the "Transactions in UK land" legislation.

Helena Kanczula has written the commentary for F(No 2)A 2017 s 39.

Zigurds Kronbergs, BSc, ARCS, MA, ACA, FCCA

Zigurds Kronbergs is an experienced writer on UK, European and international tax, and is a regular contributor to several publications, including Finance Act Handbook. A specialist in tax for over 30 years, he is also European Tax Coordinator for Moore Stephens Europe Ltd and the correspondent on Latvia for the IBFD.

Zigurds Kronbergs has written the Introductions to FA 2017 and F(No 2)A 2017.

Anton Lane, CTA

Anton Lane established Edge Tax LLP following a career at the Big 4 specialising in tax investigations. Edge Tax LLP is a bespoke tax practice specialising in the disclosure of tax irregularities to HMRC and tax risk management. Anton is the author of two Tolley's Tax Digests: Practicalities of Tax Investigations and Practical guidance: Anti avoidance legislation, offshore structures and the offshore disclosure facility. Anton is also responsible for producing many articles on the area of tax disclosures and anti-avoidance legislation.

Anton Lane has written the commentary for FA 2017 s 24 and F(No 2)A 2017 ss 63, 64, 67, 69, Sch 15, Sch 18.

John Lindsay, BA, FCA, FTII

John Lindsay is a consultant in the tax department of Linklaters LLP. He advises on all corporate taxes with a focus on the taxation of capital market and securitisation transactions. John is a contributor to Simon's Taxes, Simon's Tax Planning and Tolley's Tax Planning and is also a co-author of the Taxation of Companies and Company Reconstructions (Sweet & Maxwell, 2009). He is a member of both the CIOT Technical Committee and the CIOT Corporate Tax Sub-committee and is also a member of a number of HMRC working groups.

John Lindsay has written the commentary for F(No 2) A 2017 ss 20, 23 and Sch 5.

Luigi Lungarella, BA (Hons), CTA, AIIT, ATT, AFTA

Luigi Lungarella is a graduate in Economics, a Chartered Tax Adviser, a UK Taxation Technician and an Associate of the Federation of Tax Advisers. Luigi is an indirect tax director for PKF Littlejohn in Canary Wharf, having previously been an indirect tax consultant for Arthur Andersen, KPMG and Dawnay Day.

Luigi Lungarella has written the commentary for FA 2017 ss 17–19 and F(No 2)A 2017 s 43.

Pete Miller, CTA (Fellow)

Pete Miller is Partner of The Miller Partnership and speaks and writes regularly on tax issues. Pete has worked in tax for nearly 30 years, starting as an Inspector of Taxes in 1988, before posts in Policy Division and Technical Division. He then worked for eleven years in Big 4 firms. Pete is a member of the Editorial Boards of Taxation, Tax Journal and Simon's Taxes and a Consulting Editor to TolleyGuidance, and is General Editor of Whiteman & Sherry on Capital Gains Tax and on Income Tax. He is co-author of Taxation of Company Reorganisations (5th edition, Bloomsbury Professional) and author of Tolley's Tax Digests on Disguised Remuneration, the Substantial Shareholdings Exemption, the Patent Box and Transactions in Securities.

Pete Miller has written the commentary for F(No 2)A 2017 ss 18, 19, 27, 28, Sch 4.

Harish Narayanan

Harish Narayanan is a tax advisor in KPMG's Private Client practice, based primarily in the London office. Having previously worked in the firm's Corporate Insurance and Investment Management Tax team, he has experience of providing advisory, compliance, and audit services to a broad range of clients. With a technical background in both accountancy and tax, he specialises in transactions consulting, trusts and estates planning, and the day-to-day management of large-scale investor reporting projects in the private client and banking sphere.

Harish Narayanan has, together with Simon Tremblett, written the commentary for F(No 2)A 2017 s 10.

Janet Pierce (neé Paterson), FCA, CTA, TEP, AIIT

Janet Pierce has over ten years of specialist experience in international and property taxation matters. After nearly five years as the international tax and VAT partner with Creaseys LLP, Janet left to establish Charter Tax. As well as enjoying helping all manner of clients find tax efficient solutions, Janet is a member of the Fleet chapter of the VAT Practitioners Group, a member of the International Tax Planning Association and a member of the International Fiscal Association. Janet also regularly contributes to the tax professional press and writes for various Tolley publications.

Janet Pierce has written the commentary for F(No 2)A 2017 ss 15, 29, 30 and Sch 8.

Camilla Spielman

Camilla Spielman is a Legal Director with Eversheds and has considerable experience of the taxation of investment funds and products, both retail and institutional. She regularly advises on the mergers and conversions of authorised investment funds including many PAIF conversions and a PAIF merger. She also advises on reconstructions of offshore funds and closed-ended funds including investment trusts. Her role includes advising fund management groups on product development. Following her involvement in the landmark 1998 unit trust stamp duty case, she has taken a particular interest in stamp taxes. Camilla sits on both the IA and AREF tax committees. She has been involved in many developments in the fund space working both with the industry and HM Treasury/HMRC, including PAIFs and ACSs.

Camilla Spielman has written the commentary for FA 2017 s 11 and Sch 5.

Simon Tremblett, CTA

Simon Tremblett is a private client associate director in the London office of KPMG. After many years of advising a broad range of private clients he now specialises in technical quality and review for the private client practice.

Simon Tremblett has, together with Harish Narayanan, written the commentary for F(No 2)A 2017 s 10.

Neil Warren, CTA (Fellow), ATT, FMAAT

Neil Warren is an independent VAT consultant and author and a past winner of the Taxation Awards Tax Writer of the Year. He writes extensively on VAT for most of the leading tax publications in the UK and also acts as a technical expert on VAT for a number of publishers. He worked for Customs and Excise for 13 years until 1997.

Neil Warren has written the commentary for FA 2017 s 16 and Sch 7 and F(No 2)A 2017 ss 66, 68.

Martin Wilson, MA, FCA

Martin Wilson is Chairman of the Capital Allowances Partnership Limited, specialists in all aspects of capital allowances and related reliefs. He is the author of numerous published works on the subject, including Bloomsbury's Capital Allowances: Transactions & Planning, and the capital allowances content of Lexis®PSL, Tolley's Tax Guidance, Tolley's Tax Planning and Simon's Tax Planning.

Martin Wilson has written the commentary for F(No 2)A 2017 s 38.

Stephen Woodhouse, LLB Partner

Stephen Woodhouse is a partner in Pett, Franklin having previously been a partner at Deloitte. He has been an employment tax specialist with a particular focus on remuneration design and structuring for over 25 years. During that time he has been a regular contributor to the tax press across a range of subjects and advised clients across a range of sectors on tax structuring.

Stephen Woodhouse has written the commentary for FA 2017 ss 12–14.

Tracey Wright

Tracey Wright is a partner in the tax team at Osborne Clarke LLP. She undertakes a full range of transactional and advisory tax work. She also has many years' experience of advising on employment tax matters and has a particular focus on the tax treatment of contingent workers.

Tracey Wright has written the commentary for FA 2017 s 6 and Sch 1.

FINANCE ACT 2017

INTRODUCTION

This being a General Election year, we again have a "truncated" first Finance Act of the year, drawn from the original Finance (No 2) Bill published on 20 March. That Bill had the distinction of being the longest ever, published as one thick volume of 772 pages (including beginning and end papers) containing 135 clauses and 29 Schedules.

The Act before us has, by contrast, a "mere" 155 pages, accommodating 63 sections and 11 Schedules. Casualties include the more liberal corporate loss-relief rules and the interest-deduction restrictions as well as the new non-domicile rules. Although the Government has now announced that all the dropped measures will be reintroduced, with minor modifications and mostly the same starting dates, in an autumn Finance Bill, that Bill's smooth passage through Parliament is by no means guaranteed, given the precarious nature of the Government's majority.

Of the surviving measures, the new "sugar tax" (the Soft Drinks Industry Levy) takes up surprisingly few pages (37 sections and 4 Schedules, amounting to "just" 38 pages), whereas anti-avoidance again claims the lion's share. The new overseas pensions (and offshore transfers) legislation (ss 9 and 10 and Schs 3 and 4) take up 35 pages, for example and Schs 5 and 6 on employment income provided through third parties (introduced by s 15) comprise 26 pages.

PART 1
DIRECT AND INDIRECT TAXES

Income tax charge and rates

Section 1 simply reimposes income tax for the tax year 2017/18.

Section 2 sets the main rates of income tax (basic, higher and additional rates) at the same levels as in 2016/17. They are 20% (the basic rate), 40% (the higher rate) and 45% (the additional rate). The basic, higher and additional rates charged by this section apply in England, Wales (until ITA 2007 s 6B, which provides for the Welsh basic, higher and additional rates, comes into effect) and Northern Ireland, but do not apply to certain income of Scottish taxpayers.

For the tax year 2017/18, the Scottish Parliament has set identical rates of tax (20%, 40% and 45%) for the non-savings, non-dividend income of Scottish taxpayers.

Section 3 sets the default and savings rates of income tax for 2017/18. The default rates are payable by non-UK resident individuals on their income other than savings income, whereas a non-UK resident person other than an individual (except for trustees subject to the trust rate or the dividend trust rate) is chargeable to income tax at the default basic rate and the dividend ordinary rate. The default basic, higher and additional rates are to be the same as the main rates (20%, 40% and 45%). The savings basic, higher and additional rates are also set at 20%, 40% and 45%, respectively, for 2017/18.

Section 4 sets the starting-rate limit for savings at £5,000 for 2017/18 and subsequent tax years – the same limit as applied in 2016/17. The indexation provision in ITA 2007 s 21 is thereby disapplied as regards 2017/18 only, however.

Corporation tax charge

Section 5 simply reimposes the charge to corporation tax for the financial year 2018. Since no further amendment is made to F(No 2)A 2015 s 7(1), the main rate of corporation tax for the financial year 2017 is 19%, as previously provided.

Income tax: general

Section 6 introduces Sch 1, which imposes a new charge to income tax on the employment income of workers provided to the public sector through intermediaries. Schedule 1 replaces the charge to income tax under ITEPA 2003 Pt 2 Chs 8 and 9 (still known familiarly as "IR35") with a new charge under the new ITEPA 2003 Pt 2 Ch 10 where the client is a public authority, and makes consequential amendments. The main effect of the provisions is to transfer responsibility for making PAYE and NIC deductions from the intermediary to the public-sector client or the party paying the intermediary.

Schedule 1 consists of three parts. Part 1 (paras 1–8) contains consequential ("preliminary") amendments to ITEPA 2003; Pt 2 (para 9) inserts new ITEPA 2003 Pt 2 Ch 10; Pt 3 (paras 10–14) makes further consequential amendments to both ITEPA 2003 and other statutes, whereas Pt 4 (paras 15–17) provides for commencement.

Schedule 1 Pt 1 Paragraph 1 is introductory.

Paragraphs 2 and 3 amend ITEPA 2003 ss 48 and 49 (respectively) to exclude the application of ITEPA 2003 Pt 2 Ch 8 where the intermediary provides the worker's services to a "public authority", as defined in new ITEPA 2003 s 61L (inserted by Sch 1 para 9). Paragraph 4 amends ITEPA 2003 s 52 to include engagements to which the new ITEPA 2003 Pt 2 Ch 10 is to apply to the conditions of liability set by that section where the intermediary is a partnership. Paragraph 5 inserts the definition of an "engagement to which Ch 10 applies" to ITEPA 2003 s 61. The amendments made by paras 6 and 7 have the effect of excluding the application of ITEPA 2003 Pt 2 Ch 9 (engagements provided via managed service companies) to engagements to which new ITEPA 2003 Pt 2 Ch 10 is to apply. Paragraph 8 inserts in ITEPA 2003 s 61J the identical definition inserted by para 5 in ITEPA 2003 s 61.

Schedule 1 Pt 2 Paragraph 9 inserts new ITEPA 2003 Pt 2 Ch 10 ("these provisions"), consisting of new ITEPA 2003 ss 61K–61X. These sections broadly match the equivalent sections (ITEPA 2003 ss 48–61) in ITEPA 2003 Pt 2 Ch 8.

New **ITEPA 2003 s 61K** provides that these provisions are to apply in respect of the provision of services to a public authority through an intermediary, but are not to affect the operation of ITEPA 2003 Pt 2 Ch 7 (agency workers) nor the provisions for withholding tax at source relating to visiting performers (ITA 2007 s 966(3), (4)).

New **ITEPA 2003 s 61L** defines "public authority", primarily by reference to the definition in the Freedom of Information Act 2000 and the equivalent Scottish statute. Primary healthcare providers may also be public authorities if they meet certain defined criteria.

New **ITEPA 2003 s 61M** defines the engagements to which new these provisions are to apply. It is identically worded to ITEPA 2003 s 49, which defines the engagements to which ITEPA 2003 Pt 2 Ch 8 applies, except that it contains an additional subsection providing that references to an "office-holder" in new ITEPA 2003 s 61M exclude a statutory auditor.

New **ITEPA 2003 s 61N** provides how to identify payments to a worker where there is a payment chain beginning with the client and ending with the intermediary, where any one of three conditions is met. In such circumstances, the worker is treated as receiving a payment (to be treated as earnings from an employment) from the "fee-payer", who is the person in the chain immediately above the lowest (the intermediary). The payment is referred to as "the deemed direct payment" ("DDP" from now on in these notes) and is to be treated as made at the same time as the chain payment made by the fee-payer. It is possible for the client to be the fee-payer. The conditions under which new ITEPA 2003 s 61N is to apply are: where the intermediary is a company and further conditions set out in new ITEPA 2003 s 61O are met (Condition A); where the intermediary is a partnership of which the worker is a member, it is as such a member that the worker provides the services and further conditions set out in new ITEPA 2003 s 61P are met (Condition B); or where the intermediary is an individual (Condition C).

New **ITEPA 2003 s 61O** contains the further conditions that must be met in order for new ITEPA 2003 s 61N to apply as a result of Condition A. They are that the intermediary is not an "associated company" (as defined by CTA 2010 s 449) of the client by virtue of the fact that the intermediary and the client are both under the control of the worker (either alone or with other persons) and that the worker has a "material interest" (as defined) in the intermediary (this section is broadly similar to the existing ITEPA 2003 s 51, but without the references in the latter to payments receivable by the worker directly from the intermediary).

New **ITEPA 2003 s 61P** contains the further conditions that must be met in order for new ITEPA 2003 s 61N to apply as a result of Condition B. They are that either (a) the worker (alone or with one or more relatives) is entitled to at least 60% of the partnership's profits; or (b) that most of those profits derive from the provision to a single client alone or together with associates of the client of services to which these provisions or the existing ITEPA 2003 Pt 2 Ch 8 apply; or (c) the partnership's profit-sharing arrangements provide that the income of any of the partners is based on the amount of income generated by that partner from the provision of services to which these provisions or the existing ITEPA 2003 Pt 2 Ch 8 apply. This section is virtually identical to the existing ITEPA 2003 s 52, but (again) for the reference in the latter to payments receivable by the worker directly from the intermediary.

New **ITEPA 2003 s 61Q** provides for the calculation of the DDP to be done in three steps, starting with the amount or value of the chain payment made by the person treated under new ITEPA 2003 s 61N as making the DDP. Step 1 deducts any amount in respect of VAT. Step 2 deducts amounts representing the direct cost to the intermediary of materials used or to be used in the performance of the services. Step 3 is carried out only if the person treated as making the DDP chooses to do so, and consists of deducting any amount representing expenses met by the intermediary that would have been deductible from the taxable employment earnings if the worker had been employed by the client and had met those expenses out of those earnings. The result is the amount of the DDP (but if the result is nil or negative, there is considered to have been no DDP). Where payments have been reduced by deductions for income tax or national insurance contributions, those deductions are to be added back before Step 1 is taken.

New **ITEPA 2003 s 61R** explains how the Income Tax Acts are to apply with respect to the DDP. First, they are to apply as if the worker were employed by the person treated as making the DDP and the worker's services were or are to be performed in the course of that employment. The DDP is to be treated as taxable earnings from that employment both for the purposes of ITEPA 2003 s 232 (mileage allowance relief) and for securing that any deductions under ITEPA 2003 Pt 5 Chs 2–6 (deductions allowed from earnings) are no greater than the amount of the DDP. The worker is not to be chargeable to tax on the DDP if the services were provided outside the UK and the worker would not be so chargeable if he or she were employed by the client and the DDP were a payment of earnings from that employment by reason of non-domicile or non-residence.

New **ITEPA 2003 s 61S** provides that where the person treated as making a DDP is required by virtue of new ITEPA 2003 s 61R to pay over an amount of tax to HMRC under the PAYE regulations, that person may make a deduction of the same amount from the "underlying chain payment", which is the payment the amount of which is taken as the starting point under new ITEPA 2003 s 61Q for the calculation of the DDP. Any person in the chain other than the intermediary who receives a payment from which a deduction has been made under this section may in turn make a deduction of that amount from his chain payment.

New **ITEPA 2003 s 61T** requires the client to inform the other contracting party of its decision as to whether or not these provisions apply to the worker, and, on the other party's written request, the reasons for its decision. Failure to do so within the prescribed time will transfer the liability for accounting for income tax and national insurance contributions from the fee-payer (or other person treated as making the DDP) to the client.

New **ITEPA 2003 s 61U** requires the worker to inform "the potential deemed employer" (the fee-payer or other person who would be treated under new ITEPA 2003 s 61N(3) as making the DDP if one of those conditions is met) as to whether any of the qualifying conditions in respect of the intermediary (Conditions A to C in new ITEPA 2003 s 61N) applies. If the worker fails to do so, one of those conditions is deemed to be met nevertheless.

New **ITEPA 2003 s 61V** provides that where the "services-provider" (the worker), a person connected with the services-provider or an office-holder in the company that is the intermediary provides a fraudulent document purporting to prove that the engagement is not one to which these provisions apply or that none of Conditions A to C in new ITEPA 2003 s 61N applies, the services-provider is to be treated under that section as if he were the fee-payer, even if that results in the services-provider's being treated as both employer and employee, with some exceptions.

New **ITEPA 2003 s 61W** is intended to prevent a double charge to tax where a person who has provided services to a public authority receives a payment or benefit ("the end-of-line remuneration") from another person ("the paying intermediary"), that payment can reasonably be taken to represent remuneration for those services, and the recipient of the underlying chain payment (for which see new ITEPA 2003 s 61S), which may also reasonably be taken to have been made in respect of the same services, has borne the cost of PAYE and NIC deductions. In that case, the paying intermediary and the payee may regard the amount of the end-of-line remuneration as reduced by any one or more of (a) the deemed payment under new ITEPA 2003 s 61Q; (b) capital allowances available to the paying intermediary that the payee could have deducted if he had incurred the expenditure and been employed directly by the public authority; (c) contributions to a registered pension scheme made on behalf of the payee by the paying intermediary that would not have been chargeable to income tax if made by an employer on behalf of an employee. These deductions may not reduce the amount of the end-of-line remuneration to below zero, however. The section applies not only where the end-of-line remuneration constitutes earnings of the payee but also where it takes the form of a distribution by the paying intermediary or some other form.

New **ITEPA 2003 s 61X** defines some terms.

Schedule 1 Pt 3 (paras 10–14) makes consequential amendments to ITEPA 2003, ITTOIA 2005 and CTA 2009. In the latter two cases, new sections (ITTOIA 2005 s 164B and CTA 2009 s 141A) provide that deemed direct payments received by an intermediary in a payment chain to which new ITEPA 2003 s 61N applies are not to be taken into account when calculating the profits of the intermediary's trade.

Schedule 1 Pt 4 (paras 15–17) provide that these provisions are to have effect in relation to deemed direct payments treated as made after 5 April 2017, regardless of when the services to which they relate were provided but that the consequential amendments made by Sch 1 Pts 1 and 3 are to have effect as from the tax year 2017/18.

Section 7 introduces Sch 2, which is intended to restrict the tax advantages (both in terms of income tax and Class 1 secondary national insurance contributions) otherwise flowing from the provision of benefits-in-kind via salary-sacrifice arrangements (referred to in the legislation as "optional-remuneration arrangements"). Its overall effect is twofold. It imposes a notional cost on benefits provided through optional-remuneration arrangements where the charge to tax under existing legislation would be lower, and where benefits would otherwise be fully or partly exempt, it disapplies the exemption in most cases.

Schedule 2 consists of a single part comprising 62 paragraphs. Paragraphs 1–49 contain the substantive provisions; paras 50–61 make minor and consequential amendments; and para 62 makes commencement and transitional provisions.

Paragraph 1 inserts new ITEPA 2003 ss 69A and 69B.

New **ITEPA 2003 s 69A** defines when benefits are to be regarded as provided under "optional-remuneration arrangements". Such arrangements are of two types. Type A arrangements are of the kind under which the employee gives up a present or future right to receive an amount of earnings in return for the benefit. Type B arrangements are of the kind under which the employee agrees to receive the benefit rather than an amount of earnings but are also not Type A arrangements. Where a benefit is provided partly under optional-remuneration arrangements and partly otherwise, just and reasonable apportionment is to be used to determine the extent or amount provided under the arrangements and the table in subs (7) indicates the counterpart new section or subsection under which the appropriate amount of the benefit is to be treated.

New **ITEPA 2003 s 69B** defines the "amount foregone [sic]" NB: it is a pity that the Parliamentary draftsman seems not to be aware of the difference between "forgone" (meaning "given up" or "waived") and "foregone" (meaning "having gone before"). In these notes, the correct spelling – forgone – will be used. Thus the "amount forgone", which is to be the alternative measure of the benefit chargeable to tax, is defined as the amount of earnings the right to which is surrendered in a Type A arrangement or the amount of earnings that the employee would have received instead of the benefit in a Type B arrangement. Benefits provided to a member of an employee's family or household are to be treated as provided to the employee, as one would expect.

Paragraphs 2–48 insert the charging provisions into ITEPA 2003 Pt 3. Paragraph 2 is introductory. Paragraph 3 amends ITEPA 2003 s 81 (cash vouchers) so as to provide that where a cash voucher is provided under optional-remuneration arrangements, the amount treated as earnings is to be the greater of the cash equivalent and the amount forgone with respect to the benefit of the voucher, and not simply the cash equivalent. The cash equivalent is to be deemed zero if the benefit would have been exempt but for new ITEPA 2003 s 228A (inserted by para 49).

Paragraph 4 inserts new ITEPA 2003 s 87A, which provides for the treatment of non-cash vouchers. Existing ITEPA 2003 s 87 provides that the amount chargeable to tax ("the cash equivalent") is the difference between the cost of provision and any part made good by the employee. Where the voucher is provided under optional-remuneration arrangements, however, new ITEPA 2003 s 87A now provides that the amount chargeable to tax is either (a) the cash equivalent (where the amount forgone is less than or equal to the cost of provision); or (b) the difference between the amount forgone and any part of the cost made good by the employee before 7 July following the "relevant tax year" (where the amount forgone is greater than the cost of provision). Where the voucher is a cheque voucher, the relevant tax year is the tax year in which the voucher is exchanged for money, goods or services. Where the voucher is a non-cash voucher, the relevant tax year is the later of the tax year in which the cost of provision is incurred and the tax year in which the employee receives the voucher. The cost of provision is to be deemed zero if the benefit would have been exempt but for new ITEPA 2003 s 228A (inserted by para 49). Paragraph 5 makes consequential amendments.

Paragraph 6 inserts new ITEPA 2003 s 94A, which provides for the treatment of credit-tokens. Existing ITEPA 2003 s 94 provides, as does ITEPA 2003 s 87, that the amount chargeable to tax ("the cash equivalent") is the difference between the cost of provision and any part made good by the employee. Where the credit-token is *used* under optional-remuneration arrangements, however, new ITEPA 2003 s 94A now provides that the amount chargeable to tax on each occasion that the credit-token is so used is the amount derived by subtracting from so much of the amount forgone as can justly and reasonably be attributable to such use of the credit-token in the tax year ("AF") any part of the "relevant cost of provision" as is made good by the employee before 7 July following the tax year in which the use to which the making good relates occurs. The "relevant cost of provision" is the sum of the cost of provision with respect to each occasion in the tax year in which the employee uses the credit-token under optional-remuneration arrangements. However, if the subtraction results in a negative amount, the amount chargeable to tax ("the relevant amount") is deemed to be zero. The relevant cost of provision is to be deemed zero if the benefit would have been exempt but for new ITEPA 2003 s 228A (inserted by para 49). Furthermore, if looking at the tax year as a whole, "AF" is not greater than the relevant cost of provision, new ITEPA 2003 s 94A does not apply.

Paragraphs 7–18 deal with the provision of living accommodation. Paragraph 7 makes a consequential amendment to ITEPA 2003 s 98. Paragraphs 8–12 amend ITEPA 2003 ss 98, 99, 100, 100A and 101 so that the exemptions in those sections are not to apply when the living accommodation is provided under optional-remuneration arrangements. Paragraph 13 amends ITEPA 2003 s 102, which provides that the quantum of charge for the provision of accommodation is the "cash equivalent", so that it now provides that where the accommodation is provided under optional-remuneration arrangements, the quantum of charge is to be "the relevant amount", to be determined under new ITEPA 2003 s 103A (inserted by para 15). Paragraph 14 makes consequential amendments to ITEPA 2003 s 103.

Paragraph 15 inserts new ITEPA 2003 s 103A. This provides that the relevant amount is either (a) the cash equivalent (where the amount forgone is less than or equal to the "modified cash equivalent" of the benefit); or (b) the difference between the amount forgone and "the deductible amount" (where the amount forgone is greater than the "modified cash equivalent" and "the deductible amount"). Where the amount forgone does not exceed "the deductible amount", the relevant amount is to be zero. The "modified cash equivalent" is itself deemed to be zero if the benefit would have been exempt but for new ITEPA 2003 s 228A (inserted by para 49). "The deductible amount" has one of two values. If the cost of provision of the benefit is no more than £75,000, the deductible amount is any sum made good by the employee before 7 July following the tax year containing the "taxable period" (this is the period defined in ITEPA 2003 s 102 as the period consisting of the whole or part of a tax year and in which the accommodation is provided and during the whole of which the employee holds the employment). Where the cost of provision is greater than £75,000, the deductible amount is A + B, where A is the amount made good as just described (subject to a cap equivalent to the rental value of the property) and B is the amount of any "excess rent" (broadly, that amount (if any) of the rent paid by the employee as exceeds the rental value). "The modified cash equivalent" also has one of two values. Where the cost of provision is no more than £75,000, the modified cash equivalent is equal to the rental value of the accommodation for the taxable period (new ITEPA 2003 s 105(2A), inserted by para 16). Where the cost of provision is greater than £75,000, the modified cash equivalent is defined by new ITEPA 2003 s 106(2A), inserted by para 17, and is calculated by taking the steps specified by existing ITEPA 2003 s 106(2). Paragraph 18 makes consequential amendments to ITEPA 2003 s 109.

Paragraphs 19–41 deal with car and van benefits. Paragraph 19 makes consequential amendments to ITEPA 2003 s 114. Paragraph 20 amends ITEPA 2003 s 119 so as to restrict its application to the provision of low-emission cars. The provision of low-emission cars is not to be subject to the optional-remuneration charges, but in other cases, this section is otiose, as new ITEPA 2003 s 69A (inserted by para 1) will require a comparison to be made with the amount forgone. Paragraph 21 makes consequential amendments to ITEPA 2003 s 120. New ITEPA 2003 s 120A, inserted by para 22, provides that where a car with a CO_2 emissions figure greater than 75g per km is made available under optional-remuneration arrangements *and* the amount forgone is greater than "the modified cash equivalent" of the benefit, the charge to tax (the amount to be treated as earnings) will be on the "relevant amount", to be determined under new ITEPA 2003 s 121A, which is inserted by para 23. New ITEPA 2003 s 121A provides that the relevant amount is to be found by first deducting from the amount forgone an amount in respect of the employee's capital contributions to the cost of the car or accessories (determined in accordance with new ITEPA 2003 s 132A, inserted by para 27) and from the result (referred to as "the provisional sum") making any deductions under ITEPA 2003 s 144 (as amended by para 29) in respect of the employee's payments for the private use of the car. New ITEPA 2003 s 121B, also inserted by para 23, prescribes how to calculate the "modified cash equivalent" of the benefit. The procedure mirrors that prescribed in existing ITEPA 2003 s 121 for calculating the [unmodified] cash equivalent. Thus, to the price of the car (as found in accordance with ITEPA 2003 ss 122–124A) there is to be added: (1) the price of any accessories, arriving at the "interim sum"; (2) multiplying the interim sum by the appropriate percentage; and then (3) making any deductions for periods of unavailability. The modified cash equivalent is to be deemed zero if the benefit would have been exempt but for new ITEPA 2003 s 228A (inserted by para 49). Paragraphs 24–26 make consequential amendments.

Paragraph 27 inserts new ITEPA 2003 s 132A. This provides that where the employee makes capital contributions towards the cost of a car or its qualifying accessories provided to him or her under optional-remuneration arrangements, a deduction may be made at Step 1 when calculating the relevant amount under new ITEPA 2003 s 121A equal to the product of the "capped amount" and the appropriate percentage. The "capped amount" is the smaller of (a) the total of all capital sums contributed by the employee in the tax year concerned and previously in respect of the car in question; and (b) £5,000, subject to any modification under new ITEPA 2003 s 147A (classic cars), as inserted by para 32. Paragraphs 28–31 make consequential amendments.

Paragraph 32 inserts new ITEPA 2003 s 147A, which modifies the calculation of the relevant amount (the amount treated as earnings) when the car provided is a classic car and closely matches existing ITEPA 2003 s 147, which performs the same function for cars not subject to the optional-remuneration rules. Thus, it applies to cars that are 15 or more years old at the end of the tax year concerned and whose market value is both £15,000 or more and more than the price of the car and accessories less the employee's capital contributions (capped at £5,000). Where it applies, the modified cash equivalent is the sum arrived at by deducting capital contributions (capped at £5,000) as specified by new ITEPA 2003 s 132A from the car's market value. Paragraphs 33 and 34 make consequential amendments.

Paragraph 35 inserts new ITEPA 2003 s 149A, which provides for the calculation of the fuel benefit in respect of cars provided under optional-remuneration arrangements. The basic rule is simply that if the amount forgone is greater than the cash equivalent of the benefit, it is the amount forgone that is treated as earnings and not the cash equivalent. However, the cash equivalent of the fuel is deemed to be zero if the benefit would have been exempt but for new ITEPA 2003 s 228A (inserted by para 49). Paragraph 36 makes a consequential amendment.

Paragraph 37 inserts new ITEPA 2003 s 154A, which provides for the calculation of the van benefit in respect of vans provided under optional-remuneration arrangements, where the amount forgone is greater than the "modified cash equivalent" of the benefit. The "modified cash equivalent" is to be found by taking the cash equivalent (after taking into account any reductions under ITEPA 2003 s 156 (periods of unavailability) or 157 (shared vans)) but omitting any deductions for payments by the employee for the private use of the van. However, the modified cash equivalent of the van benefit is deemed to be zero if the benefit would have been exempt but for new ITEPA 2003 s 228A (inserted by para 49). If the amount forgone is indeed greater than the modified cash equivalent, the "relevant amount" (the amount treated as earnings) is the amount forgone less deductions in respect of payments made by the employee for the private use of the van, as prescribed by new ITEPA 2003 s 158A, inserted by para 38. New ITEPA 2003 s 158A provides that a deduction may be made in calculating the relevant amount under new ITEPA 2003 s 154A equal to any amount that the employee is required to pay as a condition of the van's provision and that is actually paid before 7 July of the following tax year. However, the amount of this deduction may not exceed the amount forgone. Paragraph 39 makes consequential amendments.

Paragraph 40 inserts new ITEPA 2003 s 160A, which provides for the calculation of the van fuel benefit in respect of vans provided under optional-remuneration arrangements. As with the car fuel benefit, the basic rule is simply that if the amount forgone is greater than the cash equivalent of the benefit, it is the amount forgone that is treated as earnings and not the cash equivalent. However, the cash equivalent of the benefit is deemed to be zero if the benefit would have been exempt but for new ITEPA 2003 s 228A (inserted by para 49). Paragraph 41 makes consequential amendments.

Paragraphs 42–46 deal with taxable cheap loans. Paragraph 42 makes a consequential amendment. Paragraph 43 amends ITEPA 2003 s 175 so that where the loan is provided under optional-remuneration arrangements *and* the amount forgone is greater than the "modified cash equivalent" of the benefit, it is not the cash equivalent but the "relevant amount" that is to be treated as earnings. New ITEPA 2003 s 175A, inserted by para 44, provides how the relevant amount and the modified cash equivalent are to be determined. The relevant amount is simply the difference between the amount forgone and the amount of any interest paid on the loan for the tax year. The modified cash equivalent is the amount of interest that would have been payable on the loan for the tax year at the official rate of interest. However, the modified cash equivalent of the benefit is deemed to be zero if the benefit would have been exempt but for new ITEPA 2003 s 228A (inserted by para 49). Paragraphs 45 and 46 make consequential amendments.

Paragraphs 47 and 48 deal with the "sweep-up" provisions of ITEPA 2003 Pt 3 Ch 10 (residual liability to charge on taxable benefits). Paragraph 47 amends ITEPA 2003 s 202 so that employment-related benefits provided under optional-remuneration arrangements are not to be excluded benefits, leaving them open to charge under new ITEPA 2003 s 203A, inserted by para 48. New ITEPA 2003 s 203A provides that where an employment-related benefit is provided under optional-remuneration arrangements, it is to be the "relevant amount" and not the cash equivalent that is to be treated as earnings. Where the amount forgone is less than or equal to the cost of the benefit, the relevant amount is the cash equivalent. Where the amount forgone is greater than the cost of the benefit, the relevant amount is the amount forgone less any part of the cost of the benefit made good by the employee before 7 July following the tax year in which the benefit is provided. However, the cost of the benefit is deemed to be zero if the benefit would have been exempt but for new ITEPA 2003 s 228A (inserted by para 49).

New **ITEPA 2003 s 228A**, inserted by para 49, excludes most exemptions (whether earnings-only exemptions or employment-income exemptions, as defined by ITEPA 2003 s 227(2), (3)) from applying to benefits provided under optional-remuneration arrangements. Only exemptions that are "special case exemptions" or "excluded exemptions" escape the exclusion (and may thus still apply to benefits provided under optional-remuneration arrangements). "Special case exemptions" are those that already contain provisions referring to optional-remuneration arrangements (or salary-sacrifice arrangements) and are listed in new ITEPA 2003 s 228A(4). "Excluded exemptions" are those that it has been considered public policy should continue to encourage, however they may be provided. They include bicycles, pension contributions and advice, childcare and counselling and outplacement services and they are listed in new ITEPA 2003 s 228A(5).

Paragraphs 50–61 make other consequential amendments to ITEPA 2003. Paragraph 62 provides that the new rules apply mainly from the tax year 2017/18. However, where benefits are provided under arrangements already in place before 6 April 2017, and the terms under which they are provided do not change, the new rules will apply from 2018/19, with two exceptions. For living accommodation and cars, vans and related benefits, the old rules will continue to apply until 2021/22, and for school fees, the old rules will also continue to apply until 2021/22, as long as they relate to the same employer, the same child and the same school.

Section 8 also deals with benefits, but is a relieving measure. It concerns assets made available for an employee's use without a transfer of ownership, so that allowance may be made in certain circumstances for days in a tax year in which the asset is not available to the employee, whereas there is none at present, and the amendments it makes are to have effect as from the tax year 2017/18. Section 8 amends ITEPA 2003 s 205 so that it now provides that an asset made available for the private use of the employee or the employee's family or household is to be treated as available throughout the tax year, unless the terms under which it is provided prohibit private use and no private use is actually made of it in the year, in which case there will be no charge to tax. In other circumstances, a deduction under new

ITEPA 2003 s 205A may now be made from the annual cost of the benefit to arrive at the amount chargeable to tax or that amount may be calculated under rules in new ITEPA 2003 s 205B.

New **ITEPA 2003 s 205A**, inserted by s 8(3), provides that an amount equal to $(U/Y \times A)$ may be deducted from the annual cost, where U is the number of days in the tax year in which the asset is unavailable for private use, Y is the number of days in the tax year and A is the annual cost of the benefit. An asset is regarded as unavailable for private use on any day in the tax year before it is first available and after it is last available, is used by the employee exclusively for the purposes of the employment, and on any day for more than 12 hours of which it is not in a fit condition, is undergoing repair or maintenance, cannot lawfully be used, is in the possession of a third party who has a lien over it, or is used in a manner beyond the control of the employee, family or household.

New **ITEPA 2003 s 205B**, also inserted by s 8(3), allows for instances where private use of the asset is shared between two or more employees at the same time. Where this is the case, the aggregate cost of the benefit for all such employees together is not to exceed the annual cost of the benefit, and is to be apportioned amongst all employees concerned on a just and reasonable basis.

Section 9 introduces Sch 3, which amends the tax treatment of funds in and payments from foreign pension schemes, with the intention of aligning the treatment of foreign and UK-based schemes and restricting the opportunities for avoidance of UK tax by the use of foreign schemes.

Schedule 3 consists of three parts. Part 1 (para 1) provides for the tax provisions in FA 2004 Pt 4 to apply in certain circumstances to registered pension schemes established outside the UK. Part 2 (paras 2 and 3) essentially imposes the charge to UK tax on 100% (instead of 90%, as previously) of UK residents' foreign pension income. Part 3 (paras 4–12) imposes a charge to UK tax on lump sums paid to UK residents from foreign pension schemes where they would not otherwise be so chargeable.

Schedule 3 Pt 1 Paragraph 1 inserts new FA 2004 ss 242C–242E in new FA 2004 Pt 4 Ch 5A (itself inserted by s 10 and Sch 4), with effect from the tax year 2017/18. New FA 2004 Pt 4 Ch 5A applies to "non-UK registered schemes", which are registered pension schemes established in a country or territory outside the UK (new FA 2004 s 242A, inserted by Sch 4 para 14). Although such schemes are established abroad, they are nevertheless registered with HMRC and must comply with the relevant rules.

New **FA 2004 s 242C** provides that where it would not already do so, FA 2004 Pt 4 is to apply to non-UK registered schemes in all of four ways:

— in relation to "UK-relieved funds" of such a scheme as it applies to the funds and assets of a UK-based registered scheme. Very broadly, "UK-relieved funds" are sums or assets that directly or indirectly represent sums or assets once held under a UK-based registered scheme or that have benefited or are deemed to have benefited from relief from UK tax (new FA 2004 s 242B, inserted by Sch 4 para 14);

— in relation to a non-UK registered scheme as it applies to a UK-based registered scheme, to the extent of the scheme's UK-relieved funds;

— in relation to the rights of members of a non-UK registered scheme as it applies to a UK-based registered scheme, to the extent those rights are represented by UK-relieved funds; and

— in relation to contributions made to a non-UK registered scheme as it applies to contributions to a UK-based registered scheme.

However, to the extent that the following provisions of new Ch 5A would conflict with the above rules, those provisions are to take precedence over those rules.

New **FA 2004 s 242D** provides that, as regards the annual-allowance charge on members of a non-UK registered scheme, a member's pension input amounts are only to be taken into account in accordance with regulations if relieved inputs are to be taken to have been made. The annual-allowance charge is imposed under FA 2004 ss 227–238A, where, broadly speaking, annual contributions (inputs) exceed the annual allowance.

New **FA 2004 s 242E** applies to "investment-regulated schemes". It provides that the property of an investment-regulated non-UK registered scheme is to be regarded as taxable property if it would be so regarded if the scheme were a UK-based registered scheme. An investment-regulated pension scheme is defined in FA 2004 Sch 29A para 1 as, broadly, a non-occupational scheme in which the member or a related person is able to exercise influence over the scheme investments.

Schedule 3 Pt 2 alters the proportion of the foreign pension income of a UK-resident individual that is chargeable to tax from 90% to 100%. Paragraph 2 effects this change by omitting ITEPA 2003 s 575(2), which provides the 10% relief with respect to foreign pensions, ITEPA 2003 s 613(3), which performs the same function with respect to foreign annuities, and ITEPA 2003 s 635(3), which does so with respect to foreign voluntary annual payments, and by making consequential amendments. Paragraph 3 amends TA 1988 s 615. This legacy provision exempts from income tax annuities paid under a special superannuation fund for persons working solely outside the UK. The amendments preserve the exemption only where a "benefit-accrual condition" is met. In the case of a money-purchase arrangement relating to a member which is not a "cash-balance arrangement", the condition is that no contributions be made after 5 April 2017. In the case of a defined-benefits arrange-ment relating to a member or a "cash-balance arrangement" relating to a member, it is that there be no increase after 5 April 2017 in the value of any person's rights under the arrangement. In the case of an arrangement relating to a member which is neither a money-purchase arrangement nor a defined-benefits arrangement, the condition is both that no contributions be made after 5 April 2017 and that there be no increase after 5 April 2017 in the value of any person's rights under the arrangement. The amendments go on to define how an increase in the value of a member's rights is to be determined. Where the benefit-accrual condition is met in respect of a money-purchase arrangement, a cash-balance arrangement or a defined-benefits arrangement relating to a member in the case of a fund, and a "disqualifying contribution" is then made or a "disqualifying increase" in rights then occurs, such a contribution or such an increase is to be treated as made to or occurring in a separate, "shadow" fund. Disqualifying contributions and disqualifying increases are contributions and increases that would otherwise cause the benefit-accrual condition not to be met. The amendments made by para 3 apply from 6 April 2017, but not in relation to contributions made (in the case of a money-purchase arrangement) or rights accrued (in the case of a defined-benefits arrangements) before that date.

Schedule 3 Pt 3 brings into the charge to income tax lump sums paid from a foreign pension scheme to or in respect of UK-resident individuals by amending ITEPA 2003. Paragraph 4 is introductory.

Paragraph 5 amends ITEPA 2003 s 395B. This currently reduces the charge to tax under ITEPA 2003 s 394 on lump sums paid to an employee or former employee from an employer-financed retirement-benefits scheme established outside the UK in respect of periods of service outside the UK ("foreign service"). If the foreign service is of sufficient duration, the lump sum is wholly exempt. ITEPA 2003 s 395B is now amended so that it limits the reduction or exemption to lump sums paid to individuals who are non-resident in the tax year of receipt, with effect from 2017/18. The definition of what constitutes "foreign service" is now to be provided by new ITEPA 2003 s 395C, inserted by para 6. For service in the tax year 2013/14 and subsequently, "foreign service" means duties performed outside the UK in respect of which earnings would not be "relevant earnings" (broadly, earnings for a tax year in which the employee is not UK-resident) or in respect of which a seafarer could claim a 100% deduction. Slightly different definitions apply to earnings in tax years before 2013/14.

Paragraph 7 performs the same function as para 5 in respect of "relevant steps" chargeable as earnings under the third-party remuneration provisions of ITEPA 2003 Pt 7A (ITEPA 2003 ss 554A–554Z21).

Paragraphs 8–10 impose a charge to income tax on "relevant lump sums" paid to UK-residents by or on behalf of a person outside the UK. Paragraph 8 amends ITEPA 2003 s 573 to extend the charge to tax under that section on foreign pensions to "relevant lump sums" (as defined in new ITEPA 2003 s 574A, inserted by para 10) paid to a non-resident recipient in respect of a member who is, or was immediately before death, resident in the UK. Paragraph 9 makes a consequential amendment. New ITEPA 2003 s 574A, inserted by para 10, defines a "relevant lump sum" as a sum paid under a pension scheme that is neither a registered pension scheme, a relevant non-UK scheme nor an employer-financed retirement-benefits scheme, excluding a payment that constitutes a "relevant step" under ITEPA 2003 Pt 7A and a payment to which the existing provisions of FA 2004 Sch 34 (member-payment charges in respect of non-UK schemes) apply. In charging the relevant lump sum to tax, certain deductions specified in new ITEPA 2003 s 574A(3) may be made. These amendments apply to lump sums paid after 5 April 2017. Paragraphs 11 and 12 extend the charge on relevant lump sums to the provisions under ITEPA 2003 s 576A in respect of temporary non-residents.

Section 10 introduces Sch 4, which continues the theme of foreign pensions by imposing a charge to tax on transfers of pension savings to qualifying recognised overseas pension schemes (QROPS) requested after 8 March 2017.

Schedule 4 consists of two parts. Part 1, which comprises paras 1–10, has the principal effect of increasing from five to 10 years the initial period of non-residence during which a previous resident may still face charges to UK tax on a payment out of foreign pension schemes that have benefited from UK tax relief. Part 2 (paras 11–24) introduces a charge on a transfer to a QROPS or between one QROPS and another.

Schedule 4 Pt 1 Paragraphs 1–8 amend FA 2004 Sch 34 (which applies so-called "member-payment charges" to certain payments to members of non-UK schemes). Paragraph 1 is introductory. FA 2004 Sch 34 para 1 currently provides that the member-payment charge applies to payments to members of a "relevant non-UK scheme". A scheme is a relevant non-UK scheme if UK tax relief has been given for contributions to the scheme and either (a) a member has benefited from exemption in respect of a retirement or death benefit after 5 April 2006 when the scheme was an "overseas pension scheme" or (b) there has been a "relevant transfer" after 5 April 2006 when the scheme was a QROPS. A "relevant transfer" is currently defined in FA 2004 Sch 34 para 1(6) as a direct or indirect transfer of sums or assets held for the purposes of, or representing accrued rights under, a registered pension scheme or a relevant non-UK scheme. Members affected may either be "relieved members" (members who have pension funds or rights that have benefited from UK tax relief) or "transfer members" (members in respect of whom a relevant [non-taxable] transfer has been made).

Paragraph 2 introduces FA 2004 Sch 34 para 1(6A)–(6F), which classify relevant transfers into one of three types. An "original relevant transfer" is a relevant transfer: (1) made after 8 March 2017 from a registered pension scheme; (2) made after 8 March 2017 of the whole or part of the UK-tax-relieved fund in respect of a relieved member of a QROPS from a relevant non-UK scheme; or (3) made from a relevant non-UK scheme after 5 April 2017 of the whole or part of the UK-tax-relieved fund in respect of a relieved member of a relevant non-UK scheme that is not a QROPS. The sums or assets transferred in an original relevant transfer constitute a "ring-fenced transfer fund". The date of the transfer is referred to as the "key date". A transfer out of a ring-fenced transfer fund creates another ring-fenced transfer fund with the same key date, consisting of the transferred sums or assets. Such a transfer is a "subsequent relevant transfer". The third type of relevant transfer is one that is neither an original relevant transfer nor a subsequent relevant transfer, and includes in particular all relevant transfers made before 9 March 2017.

FA 2004 Sch 34 para 2 currently provides that there is a member-payment charge only where the payment is made to or in respect of a member who is UK-resident or who has been UK-resident earlier in the tax year in which the payment is made or in any of the five preceding tax years. Paragraph 3 amends FA 2004 Sch 34 para 2 so that this five-year rule is now to apply in respect of "5-year-rule funds" only. "5-year-rule funds" are so much of a relieved member's UK-tax-relieved fund as represents tax-relieved contributions or tax-exempt provision made *before 6 April 2017*, or, in the case of a transfer member, (broadly) non-taxable transfers received *before 6 April 2017*. The taxable period is pushed back to 10 years in respect of "10-year rule funds". In respect of relieved members, these are so much of the member's UK-tax-relieved fund as represents tax-relieved contributions or tax-exempt provision made *after 5 April 2017*. New FA 2004 Sch 34 para 2(2), as inserted by para 3(4), therefore now provides in respect of relieved members of a relevant non-UK scheme that there is a member-payment charge so far as referable to 10-year-rule funds only where the payment is made to or in respect of a member who is UK-resident or who has been UK-resident earlier in the tax year in which the payment is made or in any of the ten preceding tax years. As regards transfer members, there is a member-payments charge so far as referable to a ring-fenced transfer fund with a key date later than 5 April 2017 only where the payment is made to or in respect of a member who is UK-resident, or who has been UK-resident earlier in the tax year in which the payment is made or in any of the ten preceding tax years, or is made within five years of the key date for that fund.

FA 2004 Sch 34 para 3 relates to relieved members and provides that the member-payments charge applies only in respect of payments referable to the member's UK-tax-relieved fund. Paragraph 4 adds extra regulation-making powers to enable HMRC to adjust the amounts treated as subject to the member-payments charge. FA 2004 Sch 34 para 4 is parallel to FA 2004 Sch 34 para 3 and relates to transfer members. It provides that the member-payments charge applies only in respect of payments referable to the member's relevant transfer fund. As amended by para 5, it now provides that the charge may also apply to payments referable to the member's ring-fenced transfer fund, but clarifies that the relevant transfer fund shall not include any sums or assets in any of the member's ring-fenced transfer funds. The same additional regulation-making powers as are added to FA 2004 Sch 34 para 3 are also added to this paragraph.

Paragraphs 6 and 7 make consequential amendments. Paragraph 8 provides for commencement. The amendments made by para 3 (introducing the 10-year charge) are to have effect for payments made after 5 April 2017. The other amendments are to be treated as having come into force on 9 March 2017.

Paragraphs 9 and 10 amend ITEPA 2003 s 576A, which provides that taxable foreign pension income under ITEPA 2003 s 573 includes "relevant withdrawals" exceeding £100,000 paid from a foreign pension fund to a person who is temporarily non-resident. However, relevant withdrawals paid to relieved and transfer members are exempt if they are not referable to the UK-tax-relieved fund or relevant transfer fund. The amendments provide that, with respect to transfer members, the exemption is to apply only if the withdrawals are referable neither to the member's relevant transfer fund nor to the member's ring-fenced transfer funds. These amendments are to apply to withdrawals after 5 April 2017.

Schedule 4 Pt 2 introduces the 25% tax charge on transfers to and between QROPSs. Paragraph 11 inserts the substantive provisions, consisting of new FA 2004 ss 244A–244N.

New **FA 2004 s 244A** provides that there shall be a charge to income tax, to be known as the "overseas transfer charge" where either a "recognised transfer" is made to a QROPS or an "onward transfer" is made between one QROPS and another during the "relevant period" for the "original transfer" and the transfer is not an excluded transfer under new FA 2004 ss 244B–244H.

A "recognised transfer" is defined by FA 2004 s 169 as a transfer of sums or assets representing accrued rights under a registered pension scheme to another registered pension scheme or, of relevance here, to a QROPS. An "onward transfer" (defined in new FA 2004 s 244A(3)) is, broadly, a transfer of sums or assets in relation to a member from a QROPS or former QROPS to another QROPS for the same member. The "relevant period" (defined in new FA 2004 s 244A(4)) for a transfer is, broadly, the period from the date of the transfer to the next 5 April and a further five years thereafter. Thus, if a transfer takes place on, say, 1 May 2017, the relevant period for that transfer will normally end on 5 April 2023. The "original transfer" in relation to an onward transfer is the most recent recognised transfer from a registered pension scheme to a QROPS; in the absence of such a recognised transfer, it is a relevant transfer from a relevant non-UK scheme to a QROPS of the whole or part of the UK-tax-relieved fund from which the sums and assets transferred by the onward transfer directly or indirectly derive (new FA 2004 s 244A(5)).

New **FA 2004 s 244B** provides for the first of the exclusions from the overseas pension charge. The charge is not to apply to a recognised transfer where during the relevant five-year period following the transfer, the member is resident in the same jurisdiction as that in which the receiving QROPS is established and there is no chargeable onward transfer for which the relevant transfer is the original transfer. Similarly, an onward transfer is excluded if for the rest of the relevant period for the original transfer, the member is resident in the same jurisdiction as that in which the new receiving QROPS is established and there is no subsequent chargeable onward transfer of sums or assets deriving directly or indirectly from the earlier transfer.

New **FA 2004 s 244C** provides for the second exclusion, which applies where, in the case of a recognised transfer, both the member and the receiving QROPS are resident in an EEA member state (not the same one, necessarily) throughout the relevant five-year period and there is no chargeable onward transfer for which the relevant transfer is the original transfer. In the case of an onward transfer, the exemption applies where the member is resident, and the new receiving QROPS is established in an EEA member state (not the same one, necessarily) and there is no subsequent chargeable onward transfer of sums or assets deriving directly or indirectly from the earlier transfer.

New **FA 2004 s 244D** provides the third exclusion, which applies to transfers to a QROPS that is an occupational pension scheme and where the member is an employee of a sponsoring employer of that QROPS.

New **FA 2004 s 244E** provides the fourth exclusion, which applies where the receiving QROPS has been established by an international organisation of which the member is an employee. New **FA 2004 s 244F** excludes a transfer where the receiving QROPS is an overseas public-service pension scheme (as defined) and the member is an employee of a participating employer.

New **FA 2004 s 244G** provides the fifth exclusion, which is intended to prevent double taxation and allow for transitional relief. In the case of recognised transfers, it excludes those made in respect of a request made before 9 March 2017. In the case of onward transfers, it excludes those transfers: (a) for which the original transfer was subject to the charge and the charge paid is not repayable; (b) for which the original transfer was made before 9 March 2017; (c) for which the original transfer was made after 8 March 2017 but in respect of a request made on or before that date; or (d) made subsequent to an earlier onward transfer made after the original transfer and in which all the sums and assets transferred derive directly or indirectly from that earlier onward transfer and where that earlier onward transfer was subject to the charge and the charge paid is not repayable.

New **FA 2004 s 244H** allows HMRC to provide by regulations for further cases of exclusion. Occasions on which a repayment may become due are given in new FA 2004 s 244M.

New **FA 2004 s 244I** overrides the exclusions in cases where the scheme member fails to comply with the regulations requiring the member to provide information.

New **FA 2004 s 244J** prescribes the persons who are to be liable to the overseas pension charge. In the case of a recognised transfer to a QROPS, the persons are the scheme administrator of the transferor registered pension scheme and the member concerned, and they are to be jointly and severally liable. In the case of an onward transfer, the persons who are to be jointly and severally liable are the scheme manager of the transferor QROPS or former QROPS and the member. However, if the charge arises in respect of a transfer originally excluded under new FA 2004 s 244B (same-jurisdiction exclusion) or new FA 2004 s 244C (EEA exclusion) because an event occurs during the relevant five-year period causing the exclusion conditions no longer to be satisfied, it is the member and the scheme manager of any QROPS or former QROPS holding any of the member's ring-fenced transfer funds at the time of the event that are to be jointly and severally liable. The scheme manager of a former QROPS is to be liable to the charge only if the former QROPS was a QROPS when the inward transfer to it to which the outward transfer relates was made; if that inward transfer was made before 9 March 2017, it is a further condition that the former QROPS was a QROPS on 9 March 2017.

New **FA 2004 s 244K** provides for the amount of the charge, which is to be 25% of the "transferred value". In the case of a transfer from a registered UK pension scheme, the transferred value is the sum of the amounts [of cash] transferred and the value of any assets transferred. Where the transfer is from a registered foreign pension scheme, the transferred value is the amount of any sums and the value of any assets transferred that are attributable to "UK-relieved funds" (as defined in new FA 2004 s 242B, inserted by para 11). Where the transferor is a QROPS or former QROPS, the transferred value is the amount of any sums and the value of any assets transferred that are attributable to the member's ring-fenced transfer funds. In each case, if a lifetime-allowance charge deductible from the transfer arises on the transfer, the transferred value is to be net of the lifetime-allowance charge. If the transfer is one originally excluded under new FA 2004 s 244B (same-jurisdiction exclusion) or new FA 2004 s 244C (EEA exclusion) but now becoming chargeable, the charge is limited to those sums and assets comprised in the transfer that are represented in any of the member's ring-fenced transfer funds at the time of the triggering event.

Where the scheme operator pays the charge but does not deduct the amount from the value of the funds to be transferred, the amount of the charge is to be grossed up at the 25% rate and itself become liable to the charge. Where the operator pays the charge and does so by deduction from the value to be transferred, the "transferred value" for the purposes of the charge is the amount before the deduction. Where the member pays the charge, the transferred value is the amount transferred without any deduction for the charge. The lifetime-allowance charge (should this arise) is to be calculated as if the overseas transfer charge had not arisen. New FA 2004 s 244L confers on HMRC the power to make regulations concerning how scheme managers are to account for the overseas transfer charge.

New **FA 2004 s 244M** provides for repayments of the charge to be made on the occurrence of an "excluding event". Such an event is one giving rise within the relevant period for the transfer to circumstances such that, had they been present at the time of the transfer in respect of which the charge was paid, one of the exclusions specified in new FA 2004 ss 244B–244F or any additional exclusions under regulations made under new FA 2004 s 244H would have applied. Should such circumstances arise, HMRC must repay amounts paid in respect of the charge, but the right to repayment is not to cancel any interest or penalties for late payment of the charge should they have been imposed. Repayment to the scheme operator is to be conditional on prior compliance with information requirements. Repayments to members are to be made only if the member lodges a repayment claim no later than one year after the end of the relevant period for the transfer concerned. Repayments do not constitute "relievable pension contributions" under FA 2004 s 188. Any transfer by a scheme administrator of a registered pension scheme of all or part of the amount repaid to a QROPS is not to be a "benefit crystallisation event 8" under FA 2004 s 216.

New **FA 2004 s 224N** allows a scheme operator to apply to HMRC to be discharged of the liability to pay the charge where either the operator reasonably believed that there was no liability to overseas transfer charge in respect of the transfer concerned or it would not be just and reasonable for the operator to be so liable given all the circumstances of the case.

Paragraphs 12–23 make consequential and further amendments to FA 2004 Pt 4 (Pension Schemes etc) and other legislation. Paragraph 12 is introductory. Paragraph 13 amends FA 2004 s 169 to add a further requirement for qualification of a recognised overseas pension scheme as a QROPS, namely that the manager must confirm that he understands his potential liability to the overseas transfer charge, and confers associated regulatory powers on HMRC.

Paragraph 14 inserts new FA 2004 Pt 4 Ch 5A, which consists of new FA 2004 ss 242A and 242B. New FA 2004 s 242A defines a "non-UK registered scheme" as a registered pension scheme established outside the UK. New FA 2004 s 242B defines "UK-relieved funds". These are sums or assets held for the purposes of, or representing accrued rights under, a non-UK registered scheme that: (a) directly or indirectly represent sums or assets that have at any time been held for the purposes of, or represented accrued rights under, a registered pension scheme established in the UK; (b) directly or indirectly represent sums or assets that have themselves at any time formed the UK-relieved fund under a "relevant non-UK scheme" (as defined in FA 2004 Sch 34 para 1) of a relieved member of that scheme; or (c) are held for the purposes of, or represent accrued rights under, an arrangement under the scheme relating to a scheme member who has been an "accruing member" (as defined in SI 2006/567 reg 14ZB) and are taken by virtue of regulations to have benefited from relief from UK tax.

Paragraphs 15–17 make consequential amendments.

Paragraph 18 amends TMA 1970 s 9(1A) to add the overseas transfer charge chargeable on a scheme manager of a QROPS or former QROPS to the taxes not within the scope of self-assessment. Paragraph 19 adds a new penalty for failure to make payments on time to FA 2009 Sch 56 para 1 Table in respect of such a failure by a scheme manager to pay the overseas transfer charge on time. Paragraph 20 adds information requirements relating to the overseas transfer charge to the Registered Pension Schemes (Accounting and Assessment) Regulations 2005 (SI 2005/3454).

Paragraph 21 makes substantial amendments (including the insertion of new regs 3AE–3AJ) to the QROPS information regulations (the Pension Schemes (Information Requirements for Qualifying Overseas Pension Schemes, Qualifying Recognised Overseas Pension Schemes and Corresponding Relief) Regulations 2006 (SI 2006/208)) to allow for matters relating to the overseas transfer charge. Paragraphs 22 and 23 amend the Registered Pension Schemes (Transfers of Sums and Assets) Regulations 2006 (SI 2006/499) and the Registered Pension Schemes (Provision of Information) Regulations 2006 (SI 2006/567), respectively.

Paragraph 24 makes commencement and transitional provisions. Except where otherwise provided, the amendments made by Pt 2 of Sch 4 apply to transfers made after 8 March 2017.

Section 11 introduces Sch 5, which removes the requirement to deduct income tax at source from payments of interest distributions made by OEICs, authorised unit trusts and investment trust companies, and from interest payments paid to investors in peer-to-peer lending transactions.

Schedule 5 is in three parts. Part 1 (paras 1 and 2) covers investment trusts, open-ended investment companies (OEICs) and authorised unit trusts, whereas Pt 2 (para 3) covers peer-to-peer lending. Part 3 (paras 4 and 5) deals with commencement and consequential amendments.

Schedule 5 Pt 1 Paragraph1 inserts new ITA 2007 ss 888B–888D into ITA 2007 Pt 15 Ch 3 (which provides for deduction of tax at source from certain payments of yearly interest). New ITA 2007 s 888B provides that the duty to deduct income tax at source under ITA 2007 s 874 is not to apply to dividends of an investment trust or prospective investment trust to the extent they are treated as a payment of yearly interest by regulations under FA 2009 s 45 (i.e. SI 2009/2034). New ITA 2007 s 888C abolishes the same duty with respect to payments of yearly interest under ITTOIA 2005 s 373 (interest distributions by certain OEICs). New ITA 2007 s 888D abolishes that duty in respect of payments of yearly interest under ITTOIA 2005 s 376, which applies to certain authorised unit trusts. Paragraph 2 makes a consequential amendment to FA 2009 s 45(2).

Schedule 5 Pt 2 Paragraph 3 inserts new ITA 2007 s 888E. This provides that the duty to deduct income tax at source under ITA 2007 s 874 is not to apply to a payment of interest on an amount of "peer-to-peer lending". Lending is peer-to-peer lending if (a) the original borrower (the person to whom the credit is originally provided) and the original lender (the person originally providing the credit) enter an agreement under which the credit is to be provided on the invitation of an "operator"; (b) the operator makes the invitation via an electronic system; (c) the operation of the electronic system is a regulated activity under the FISMA (Regulated Activities) Order 2001 (SI 2001/544); and (d) the operator has permission under FISMA 2000 Pt 4 to carry on that activity.

Schedule 5 Pt 3 Paragraph 4 makes a consequential amendment to ITA 2007 s 874(3)(a). Paragraph 5 provides that the new rules are to have effect for payments of yearly interest or amounts treated as such made after 5 April 2017.

Employee shareholder shares

Sections 12–14 remove the tax reliefs hitherto attaching to shares obtained under an employee-shareholder agreement.

Section 12 removes the relief from income tax on employee shares received in return for entering into an employee-shareholder agreement. It does so by amending ITEPA 2003 s 226A and making consequential omissions. ITEPA 2003 s 226A is amended so that it now simply provides that an amount equal to the market value of the shares acquired by the employee in consideration of an employee-shareholder agreement are to be treated as earnings from the employment (where their market value is not less than £2,000). The special computation rules formerly in ITEPA 2003 s 226A(3) are omitted, as are the following provisions: ITEPA 2003 ss 226B–226D, 479(3A), 531(3A), 532(4A) and various provisions or words in CTA 2009. The amendments are to have effect in relation to shares acquired under agreements entered into after 30 November 2016, with some transitional exceptions.

Section 13 removes the reliefs from capital gains tax. It does so by omitting TCGA 1992 ss 236B–236F and making consequential amendments. The amendments are to have effect in relation to shares acquired under agreements entered into after 30 November 2016, with some transitional exceptions.

Section 14 removes the relief from income tax for consideration received by an individual on the purchase-back from the individual of employee-shareholder shares by the company. It does so by omitting ITTOIA 2005 s 385A, with effect in relation to shares acquired under agreements entered into after 30 November 2016, with some transitional exceptions.

Disguised remuneration

Section 15 and Sch 6, which it introduces, make amendments and introduce further occasions of charge to the legislation on third-party remuneration in ITEPA 2003 Pt 7A (which was inserted by FA 2011 s 26 and Sch 2).

Schedule 6 amends the existing provisions to add new charges and exclusions and provide for double taxation relief. It consists of 16 paragraphs. Paragraphs 2–11 contain the substantive provisions, para 12 makes consequential amendments and paras 13–16 provide for commencement.

Paragraph 1 is introductory.

The provisions of ITEPA 2003 Pt 7A apply where a "relevant step" is taken by a "relevant third person" and it is reasonable to assume that in essence the relevant step is taken wholly or partly in pursuance of "relevant arrangements" connected with the provision to an individual of rewards, recognition or loans in connection with that individual's former, current or prospective employment with another person, who is not the third party. The value of the relevant step is then chargeable to income tax as earnings of the individual. The definition of "relevant step" in ITEPA 2003 s 554A(2) is extended by para 2 to include steps associated with a breach of trust even where the underlying transaction is void. There are essentially three types of relevant step: (1) earmarking (setting aside a sum that will eventually be applied to making another relevant step, such as payment of a sum of money or a transfer of assets); (2) the payment of a sum of money or a transfer of assets; and (3) making an asset available without transferring it.

Paragraph 3 amends ITEPA 2003 s 554C, which defines relevant steps that constitute a payment of money or a transfer of assets, to include the transfer or release of a loan. A relevant step is now also to occur where (a) a person acquires a right to a payment of a sum of money or to a transfer of assets and the acquisition of that right is directly or indirectly connected to a payment made by way of loan or otherwise or a transfer of assets to a "relevant person" or (b) a person releases or writes off the whole or part of a loan made to a "relevant person" or the acquired right referred to in (a). However, the release or write-off of a loan by a third party is not to give rise to a charge under these provisions where it occurs on or after the death of the beneficiary.

Paragraph 4 makes a consequential amendment.

Paragraphs 5–9 provide for new exclusions from the charge to tax. New ITEPA 2003 s 554OA, inserted by para 5, provides that there is to be no charge under ITEPA 2003 Pt 7A where an employment-related loan is transferred to a different employer (the relevant step being the acquisition by a person of the right to payment equal to the whole or part of a payment made by way of a loan to a relevant person'), provided that the amount outstanding does not exceed £10,000 (which is the *de minimis* threshold for a charge to tax under ITEPA 2003 s 180 on the benefit of a cheap loan).

Paragraphs 6 and 7 make consequential amendments.

Paragraph 8 inserts new ITEPA 2003 s 554RA, which provides an exclusion for loan repayments ("relevant repayments"). The exclusion applies where the loan was made after 5 April 2009 and the repayment is made after 8 December 2010 (which was the date on which ITEPA 2003 Pt 7A took effect) and would otherwise have given rise to a charge under these provisions.

Paragraph 9 inserts new ITEPA 2003 s 554XA, which provides an exclusion for payments in respect of a tax liability. The relevant step must either be a direct payment in respect of a liability to income tax, national insurance contributions, inheritance tax or corporation tax or an indirect payment made within 60 days of the relevant step. The liability must arise from the same arrangements that gave rise to the relevant step.

Paragraph 10 substitutes ITEPA 2003 s 554Z5. In its original form, that section provides for relief from double taxation where there is an overlap between a sum of money or an asset that is the subject of a relevant step and a sum of money or an asset that was the subject of an earlier relevant step giving rise to a charge under these provisions. In these circumstances, it provides that the value of the later relevant step is to be reduced by the value of the earlier step (but not below nil). Where the overlap is partial, the reduction is by that part of the value of the earlier step that corresponds to the part of the money or asset involved in the earlier step that is covered by the overlap. An overlap is regarded as existing where the earlier and later sums of money or assets are the same sum or asset or where the later sum or asset essentially replaces the earlier sum or asset. New ITEPA 2003 s 554Z5 applies where there is an overlap between a sum of money or an asset that is the subject of a relevant step and a sum of money or an asset by reference to which the employee became subject to a liability to income tax on a prior occasion. However, that earlier tax liability must not have derived from a step (involving earmarking) that was taken in a tax year before 2011/12 and that was (or would have been) large enough to receive relief under the transitional provisions in FA 2011 Sch 2 para 59. Where the circumstances for relief are met, the value of the relevant step is reduced by the amount of the overlap (but not beyond nil). It is also a precondition for the relief that either the earlier liability is not yet due and payable or that, having become due and payable, either it has been paid (payments on account do not suffice) or the person liable has reached a settlement agreement with HMRC.

Where there is more than one earlier liability, tax has been paid on account or has not yet been paid at all, there is the possibility of relief under new ITEPA 2003 ss 554Z11B–554Z11G, inserted by para 11. Like new ITEPA 2003 s 554Z5, new ITEPA 2003 ss 554Z11B and 554Z11C apply where there is an overlap between a sum of money or an asset that is the subject of a relevant step and a sum of money or an asset by reference to which the employee became subject to a liability to income tax on a prior occasion. However, unlike the provision in the former section, the further condition is that the whole or part of the earlier liability remains unpaid and that no settlement agreement has been reached with HMRC. Where these conditions (contained in new ITEPA 2003 s 554Z11B) are met, new ITEPA 2003 s 554Z11C provides that once all or part of the earlier liability or any associated late payment interest is paid, the amount paid is to be treated as a payment on account of the later overlap liability first, and any balance against any late payment interest on that later liability. Alternatively, if all or part of the later liability or any late payment interest thereon is paid first, that payment may be set off against the earlier liability and any associated late payment interest, in that order. Provision is also made for occasions where the later charge overlaps with two or more earlier liabilities.

New **ITEPA 2003 s 554Z11D** confirms that a provisional payment of tax (i.e. a payment on account, an accelerated payment under FA 2014 s 223 or a payment pending the determination of an appeal) is not to be regarded as a full payment for the purposes of new ITEPA 2003 ss 554Z11B and 554Z11C enabling the relief to be available, unless the payer makes a successful application under new ITEPA 2003 s 554Z11E. Where a person makes that application, the provisional payment will be treated as final for the purposes of new ITEPA 2003 s 554Z11C, enabling the relief in that section to become available. However, having been deemed final, no element of it may be repaid. New ITEPA 2003 s 554Z11F provides that a provisional payment made in respect of one of two or more overlapping charges is also to be treated as a provisional payment in respect of the other charge or charges. This has the effect of preventing simultaneous accruals of late payment charges. If that provisional payment is repaid, however, it is to be treated as never having been made when calculating late payment interest. Where the value of a relevant step (whether consisting of the payment of a sum of money or not), counts as employment income, the employer is treated under ITEPA 2003 ss 687A and 695A as having made a payment of income subject to PAYE ("the notional payment"). If the employee does not make good the PAYE tax due on this notional payment to the employer within 90 days, the tax due is also treated under ITEPA 2003 s 222 as earnings from the employment. New ITEPA 2003 s 554Z11G provides that where relief is obtained under new ITEPA 2003 s 554Z11C, the amount treated as notional earnings under ITEPA 2003 s 222 is to be limited to that part not relieved. Paragraph 12 makes consequential amendments.

Paragraphs 13–16 are commencement provisions. With certain exceptions, the amendments made by Sch 6 are to have effect in relation to relevant steps taken after 5 April 2017. New ITEPA 2003 s 554RA, the new exclusion for loan repayments, applies to relevant steps taken after 8 December 2010, whereas new ITEPA 2003 ss 554Z11B–554Z11D and 554Z11G (the double taxation reliefs) are to have effect in relation to relevant steps taken after 5 April 2011, subject to transitional provisions for earlier relevant steps taken between 9 December 2010 and 5 April 2011.

Indirect taxes

VAT

Section 16 introduces Sch 7, which amends the zero-rating provisions for motor vehicles specially adapted for the disabled. Its history dates back to Budget 2012, when the Government signalled its concern that this relief was open to abuse.

Schedule 7 consists of nine paragraphs.

Hitherto, VATA 1994 Sch 8 Group 12 item 2A has defined the qualifying supply as one of a "qualifying vehicle" to (a) a handicapped person who usually uses a wheelchair or who is usually carried on a stretcher or (b) to a charity for making available to such a person by sale or otherwise for that person's domestic or personal use. Note (5L) defines "qualifying vehicle". Paragraph 1 replaces item 2A by new items 2A and 2B and para 2 replaces Note (5L) by new Notes (5M)–(5S).

New VATA 1994 Sch 8 Group 12 item 2A now refers solely to supplies to the disabled person himself or herself and incorporates the substantially unchanged definition of "qualifying vehicle" from old Note (5L). New item 2B defines what is a qualifying supply to a charity. The substantial changes are made in new Notes (5M)–(5U). Essentially, they limit qualifying supplies to the same person to no more than one every three years, and introduce information and certification requirements. A supply of a qualifying vehicle will not qualify for zero-rating if, in the three years preceding the day on which the vehicle is made available to the person, that person received another zero-rated supply of a qualifying vehicle or made a zero-rated acquisition or importation of such a vehicle (Note (5N)). An exception is made if the earlier vehicle has been stolen, destroyed or damaged beyond repair or has ceased to be suitable for the disabled person's use due to changes in that person's condition (Note (5P)). For a supply to qualify for zero-rating, the supplier must within 12 months of the supply provide HMRC with any required information (Note (5Q)) and be in possession of a certificate of the disabled person's eligibility (Notes (5R)–(5T)). Details are to be settled by regulation.

Paragraph 3 amends VATA 1994 s 62 to provide for a penalty to be imposed on a person who gives an incorrect certificate of eligibility. Paragraphs 4 to 8 make minor and consequential amendments, including the replacement throughout of the word "handicapped" by the more socially acceptable "disabled". Paragraph 9 provides that the amendments made by Sch 7 are to apply to supplies, acquisitions and importations taking place after 31 March 2017.

Insurance premium tax

Section 17 increases the standard rate of insurance premium tax (IPT) from 10% to 12%, with effect for premiums received under a taxable insurance contract after 31 May 2017. However, if the period of cover under the contract began before 1 June 2017, the increased rate is not to apply to premiums received before 1 June 2018.

Section 18 inserts new FA 1994 ss 66A–66C, which are intended to prevent forestalling of this and other future increases in the tax rate.

New **FA 1994 s 66A** provides that where a Minister of the Crown announces a proposed increase to the rate of IPT, premiums received between the date of the announcement and the date of the change are to be deemed as received on the date of change, if the cover does not begin until on or after that date. Where the cover starts before the date of change and extends for a year or more after that date, the proportion of the premiums received between the date of the announcement and the date of the change that is attributable to the later period is to be deemed as received on the date of the change.

New **FA 1994 s 66B** provides an exception to the rule in new FA 1994 s 66A where it is normal practice to collect premiums in advance for that class of risk.

New **FA 1994 s 66C** provides for the treatment of premiums relating to more than one period of cover or chargeable at different rates of IPT.

Section 18 also omits FA 1994 ss 67 and 67A–67C, although the latter two sections are to be treated as continuing to have effect in relation to premiums received after 22 November 2016 and before 8 March 2017.

Air passenger duty

Section 19 increases the rate of air passenger duty for Band B flights from £73 to £75 for standard-class travel and from £146 to £150 for other cases. As a consequence of the increase of the standard rate, the higher rate for small aircraft etc, which is set at six times the standard rate, increases from £438 to £450. The increases are to take effect from 1 April 2017.

Vehicle excise duty

Section 20 introduces increases in some rates of vehicle excise duty and abolishes the separate rates of duty that have hitherto applied on first registration after 28 February 2001 and before 1 April 2017 of light passenger vehicles. Thus, the two Tables in VERA 1994 Sch 1 para 1B are omitted and replaced by a single new Table, which raises most graduated rates of duty by comparison with the previous Table 2, which applied to second and later licences. For first registrations after 31 March 2017, the Table already inserted as VERA 1994 Sch 1 Pt 1AA by F(No 2)A 2015 s 46(2)(c) has effect.

Alcohol duties

Section 21 increases rates of alcoholic liquor duty in line with RPI inflation for spirits, general beer duty, high-strength beer duty, cider and wine and made wine. The increases have effect from 13 March 2017.

Tobacco products

Section 22 increases the rates of tobacco products duty as set out in TPDA 1979 Sch 1 by two percentage points above the rate of RPI inflation, as is now the norm. The increases came into effect at 18:00 on 8 March 2017.

Section 23 further amends the duty on cigarettes to introduce a minimum duty of £268.63 per 1000 cigarettes, where this would exceed the existing rate of duty (as amended by s 23) of 16.5% of the retail price plus £207.99 per 1000 cigarettes.

Avoidance

Section 24 makes amendments to the POTAS (promoters of tax-avoidance schemes) regime, introduced by FA 2014 and amended by FA 2015, intended to tighten the definitions of control of a body corporate or a partnership for the purposes of the threshold condition, which triggers the issue of a conduct notice. They add the concept of exercising significant influence as an alternative to having control.

Subsection (1) replaces FA 2014 Sch 34 para 13A(6)–(8) with para 13A(6)–(12). The subparagraphs now replaced simply provided that a person controlled a partnership if the person was a "controlling member" or the "managing partner". "Controlling member" is itself defined in FA 2014 Sch 36 para 19 as, broadly, a person who either alone or with connected persons, has a right to a share of more than half the assets or of more than half the income of the partnership. "Managing partner" was defined as the member of the partnership "who directs or is on a day-to-day level in control of the management" of the partnership's business. The new provisions omit the terms "controlling member" and "managing partner" and provide separate but parallel definitions of control by one person on the one hand and by two or more persons on the other (in paras 13A(7)–(8)). Control of a partnership is now said to exist where one person or two or more persons together either (a) has or have a right to a share of more than half the assets or of more than half the income of the partnership or (b) direct(s) or is or are on a day-to-day level in control of the management of the partnership's business. A definition in respect of control by two or more persons together of a body corporate is provided by new para 13A(6): namely, where they have the power to secure that the affairs of the body corporate are conducted in accordance with their wishes in any of the ways specified in FA 2014 Sch 34 para 13A(5)(a)–(c), which are unchanged. New FA 2014 Sch 34 para 13A(10) and (11) introduce new definitions of what it means to have "significant influence" over a partnership or a body corporate: namely, where one person or two or more persons together (a) do(es) not have control of that partnership or body corporate but (b) is or are able to, or actually do, exercise significant influence over it.

Subsection (2) substitutes new versions of FA 2014 Sch 34 paras 13B–13D. The existing versions of these paragraphs define when a threshold condition is met in relation to a "relevant body", respectively, by persons under another's control; persons in control of others; and persons controlled by the same person. New FA 2014 Sch 34 paras 13B–13D rephrase these definitions and add significant influence as also meeting the threshold condition.

New **FA 2014 Sch 34 para 13B**, under the new heading "Relevant bodies controlled etc by other persons treated as meeting a threshold condition" now provides that a relevant body is treated as meeting a threshold condition at any time when any of three other conditions (A to C) is met. Condition A is that a person met the threshold condition at a time the person was a promoter and controlled or had significant influence over the relevant body at the "relevant time". Condition B is that (a) a person met the threshold condition at a time when the person controlled or had significant influence over the relevant body and the relevant body was a promoter and (b) the person controlled or had significant influence over the relevant body at the "relevant time". Condition C is that (a) two or more persons together controlled or had significant influence over the relevant body at a time when one of those persons met the threshold condition and the relevant body was a promoter and (b) those persons together controlled or had significant influence over the relevant body at the "relevant time". The "relevant time" is the time referred to in FA 2014 s 237(1A).

New **FA 2014 Sch 34 para 13C**, under the new heading "Persons who control etc a relevant body treated as meeting a threshold condition", provides that a person is treated as meeting the threshold condition at the relevant time if at a time when that person controlled or had significant influence over a relevant body, that body met a threshold condition and that relevant body or another relevant body that the person controlled or over which the person had significant influence was a promoter.

New **FA 2014 Sch 34 para 13D**, under the new heading "Relevant bodies controlled etc by the same person treated as meeting a threshold condition", provides that if a person or two or more persons together controlled or had significant influence over a relevant body at a time when it met a threshold condition and that body or another relevant body that the person or those persons together controlled or over which the person or persons together had significant influence was a promoter, any relevant body that the person or those persons together controlled or over which the person or persons together had significant influence at the relevant time is treated as meeting the threshold condition at the relevant time.

Subsection (3) makes parallel amendments to FA 2014 Sch 34A paras 20–22, which are even more recent than the provisions amended by s 25(1) and (2), as FA 2014 Sch 34A was only inserted by FA 2016 with effect from 15 September 2016. That Schedule refers back to FA 2014 s 237A, itself inserted by FA 2016, which introduced a new threshold condition ("the section 237A condition"). Broadly, FA 2014 s 237A provides that where an authorised officer becomes aware at any time ("the relevant time") that a person who is carrying a business as a promoter meets any of three further conditions, the officer must determine whether the promoter's meeting that condition is significant so as to merit the issue of a conduct notice to that promoter. Similarly to FA 2014 Sch 34 paras 13B–13D, the existing FA 2014 Sch 34A paras 20–22 define when a section 237A condition is met in relation to a relevant body, respectively, by persons under another's control; persons in control of others; and persons controlled by the same person. The new, substituted, FA 2014 Sch 34A paras 20–22 are identically worded to new FA 2014 Sch 34 paras 13B–13D, with the substitution of "section 237A condition" for "threshold condition" and of "relevant section 237A(2) time" for "relevant time".

Subsection (4) makes consequential amendments. Subsection (5) provides that the amendments made to FA 2014 Sch 34 are to have effect for the purposes of determining whether a person meets a threshold condition in a period of three years ending after 8 March 2017 and sub-s (6) does likewise for the amendments made to FA 2014 Sch 34A, with respect to a section 237A condition.

PART 2
SOFT DRINKS INDUSTRY LEVY

Introductory

Part 3, which comprises ss 25–61 and Schs 8–11, introduces the new soft drinks industry levy, or the "sugar tax" as it is popularly known.

Section 25 is introductory and provides that HMRC is to be responsible for the collection and management of the levy.

Section 26 defines "soft drink" as a beverage of an alcoholic strength not exceeding 1.2% (a "subsection (1)(a) beverage") or a liquid that, when prepared in a "specified manner", constitutes such a beverage (a "subsection (1)(b) liquid"). [NB: the terms "subsection (1)(a) beverage" and "subsection (1)(b) liquid" are used in these notes for ease of reference but do not appear in the legislation.] Preparation in a "specified manner" is either dilution with water; combination with crushed ice or processing so as to create crushed ice; combination with carbon dioxide; or preparation using a process involving any combination of the above. "Packaging" a soft drink is also defined as canning, bottling or otherwise packaging it in a form suitable to be consumed without further preparation (in the case of a subsection (1)(a) beverage') or suitable for consumption when prepared in a specified manner and no more (in the case of a subsection (1)(b) liquid).

Section 27 defines a "prepared drink" as a subsection (1)(a) beverage or as a beverage that would result from preparing a subsection (1)(b) liquid in a specified manner and in accordance with a "relevant dilution ratio". That is either the dilution ratio stated or calculated from the information stated on the packaging. However, where there is insufficient information on the packaging or HMRC believes the stated dilution ratio or the necessary information have been deliberately stated or provided at a level designed to reduce or avoid liability to the levy, HMRC is to be given the power to determine the ratio.

Chargeable soft drinks

Section 28 defines "chargeable soft drink" as a packaged soft drink that meets the "sugar-content condition" and is not an exempt soft drink.

Section 29 provides that the "sugar-content condition" is met if the packaged soft drink contains "added sugar ingredients" and at least 5g of sugars (whether added or naturally present) per 100ml of prepared drink. "Added sugar ingredients" comprise calorific mono-saccharides or di-saccharides or a substance containing either or both of those chemicals, combined with other ingredients at any stage of the production process. However, a drink containing fruit juice, vegetable juice or milk or any combination thereof does not thereby contain added sugar ingredients.

Section 30 defines "exempt soft drinks" as milk-substitute drinks, alcohol-substitute drinks and soft drinks of a specified description intended for use for medicinal or other specified purposes.

Charging of the soft drinks industry levy

Section 31 provides that the levy is to be charged on the occurrence after 5 April 2018 of a "chargeable event" (subject to the "small-producer exemption" in s 37). "Chargeable events" may occur in relation to soft drinks packaged in the UK or on importation into the UK.

Section 32 deals with packaging in the UK. It provides that a chargeable event occurs when a chargeable soft drink is removed from the packaging premises, unless secondary warehousing is involved. Where chargeable soft drinks are being stored in a "compliant warehouse" or are being transported from the packaging premises to a compliant warehouse or between compliant warehouses, the chargeable event occurs when the drinks are effectively removed from the compliant warehouse without being transferred to another (i.e. when they leave the warehouse regime). However, where a chargeable soft drink is made available for sale or consumption free of charge before the occurrence of a chargeable event, the chargeable event is to be treated as occurring at the time it is made so available.

Section 33 deals with the importation of chargeable soft drinks into the UK. In this situation, a chargeable event occurs on the "first receipt" of the soft drinks by a "first recipient", who is a person carrying on a business involving the sale of chargeable soft drinks. A "first receipt" is the first occasion on which the soft drinks are delivered to a place in the UK which is the first recipient's place of business. "Sale" can be sale by wholesale, retail or sale for consumption on or near premises where the drinks are sold. However, if the first receipt involves the delivery of the soft drinks to a place of business that is a compliant warehouse, the chargeable event is deferred until the drinks are effectively removed from the compliant-warehouse regime or made available for sale or consumption by the "first seller", if earlier.

Section 34 empowers HMRC to make regulations in relation to compliant warehouses.

Section 35 defines who is the person liable to pay the levy. Where the chargeable event occurs in respect of soft drinks packaged in the UK, the person liable is the person who packages the soft drinks. Where the chargeable event occurs in respect of soft drinks imported into the UK, the person liable is the first recipient. However, if imported soft drinks are made available for sale or consumption free of charge by the first seller, it is the first seller who is liable.

Section 36 sets the rates of soft drinks industry levy at 24p per litre of prepared drink on drinks meeting the "higher sugar threshold" and at 18p per litre of prepared drink on drinks not meeting that threshold. The higher sugar threshold is met if the drink contains at least 8g of sugar per 100ml of prepared drink.

Exemption etc

Section 37 introduces the "small-producer exemption". No charge to the levy arises on a chargeable event in relation to imported chargeable soft drinks "produced" by a person who is on that day a "small producer". In the case of chargeable soft drinks packaged in the UK, the exemption applies in relation to a "qualifying small producer". Drinks are "produced" by a person where they are packaged for marketing under that person's name or business name or under another name used in accordance with a licence granted to that person. A "qualifying small producer" is defined by sub-s (5) as a small producer who has voluntarily registered under s 45 as a small producer or is unable to register because he fails to meet the condition in s 45(2)(c).

Section 38 defines "small producer" by reference to two conditions, A and B, which must both be met on the day in question. Condition A is that the aggregate of (1) the producer's chargeable soft drinks that are "subsection (1)(a) beverages" in respect of which a "relevant event" has occurred in the 12 months ending with the end of the month immediately preceding the month in which that day falls and (2) the amount of prepared drink that would result from the producer's chargeable soft drinks that are "subsection (1)(b) liquids" in respect of which a "relevant event" has occurred during that same period does not exceed 1 million litres. Condition B is that there are reasonable grounds for believing that the aggregate of the producer's chargeable soft drinks that are "subsection (1)(a) beverages" in respect of which a "relevant event" will occur in the 30 days beginning with the day in question and (2) the amount of prepared drink that would result from the producer's chargeable soft drinks that are "subsection (1)(b) liquids" in respect of which a "relevant event" will occur during that same period does not exceed 1 million litres. A "relevant event" in this connection is the removal of the chargeable soft drinks from the premises on which they are packaged. There is again a deferment of the relevant event if secondary warehousing is involved. Soft drinks produced by a person connected with the producer fall to be included in the producer's chargeable soft drinks.

Section 39 empowers HMRC to make regulations providing for tax credits to be available where after a charge to the levy has arisen, the soft drinks are either exported from the UK or are lost or destroyed.

Registration

Section 40 requires HMRC to maintain a register of information it thinks necessary for the proper performance of its collection and management duties in relation to the levy.

Section 41 imposes a liability on packagers to register at the end of any month in which they have packaged any chargeable soft drinks in relation to which a chargeable event under s 32 has occurred (past obligation to register) or on any day on which there are reasonable grounds for believing that such a chargeable event will occur in the next 30 days (future obligation to register), unless they are already "registrable" in either case. If the packager is also a producer, the liability to register is under s 42. A person who is already "registrable" is a person who is already registered under ss 41,42 or 43, or is subject to a "relevant notification requirement" under s 44, or would be registered if the person had complied with such a requirement.

Section 42 imposes a liability on producers to register at the end of any month if the "qualifying amount" of their (and any connected person's) chargeable soft drinks in relation to which a chargeable event under s 32 has occurred in the immediately preceding 12 months exceeds 1 million litres (past obligation to register) or on any day on which there are reasonable grounds for believing that the "qualifying amount" of their (and any connected person's) chargeable soft drinks in relation to which such a chargeable event will occur in the next 30 days will exceed 1 million litres (future obligation to register), unless they are already "registrable" in either case. The "qualifying amount" is the aggregate of chargeable soft drinks that are "subsection (1)(a) beverages" in relation to which a chargeable event occurs and of chargeable soft drinks that are "subsection (1)(b) liquids" in respect of which a chargeable event occurs.

Section 43 imposes a liability on a person to register in relation to imported chargeable soft drinks. The liability arises at the end of any month during which a chargeable event under s 33 has occurred on the first receipt or on the making available by that person of chargeable soft drinks or during which chargeable soft drinks have left the secondary warehousing regime and of which that person is the first recipient. The liability also arises on any day if there are reasonable grounds for believing that, in the next 30 days such a chargeable event will occur in the same circumstances. Neither liability arises if the person is already registrable.

Section 44 provides that a person who becomes liable to be registered under any of ss 41–43 shall inform HMRC to that effect within the period of 30 days beginning with the day on which the liability arises. Where HMRC is satisfied that a person is liable to be registered (whether or not that person has given the required notice), it shall register that person with effect from the day on which the liability arises.

Section 45 permits certain small producers who are not required to register nevertheless to do so (as with voluntary registration for VAT). Voluntary registration is open to persons who produce chargeable soft drinks but are not liable to register as producers under s 42 and some or all of whose chargeable soft drinks are packaged on premises in the UK by another person. Persons who are already registered under either s 41 or s 43 may also register under s 44.

Section 46 provides for the cancellation of a compulsory registration under any of ss 41–43 upon the relevant person's request if that person satisfies HMRC that none of the circumstances requiring registration is any longer present. Cancellation is to take place with effect from the day on which the request is made or on such later date as may be agreed. HMRC must also unilaterally cancel a registration without a request from the person concerned if it becomes satisfied that none of the circumstances requiring registration is any longer present. The cancellation is then to take effect from the day on which the person's liability to register ceased to exist or on such later date as may be agreed. HMRC may also cancel a registration if it is satisfied that the person was never liable to be registered either at the time of registration or subsequently.

Section 47 provides for the cancellation of a voluntary registration under s 45 if either the registered person requests it or HMRC is satisfied that the person did not meet the conditions for voluntary registration in the first place.

Section 48 confers on HMRC the power to make regulations covering the correction of entries in the register and requiring persons to notify HMRC of any relevant change in their circumstances.

Section 49 paves the way for regulations concerning notification of the liability to register and associated matters.

Offences

Section 50 creates an offence of being knowingly concerned in, or in the taking of steps with a view to, the fraudulent evasion of the soft drinks industry levy. "Evasion" includes for this purpose obtaining tax credits under s 39 or repayments of the levy under Sch 8 (introduced by s 52) to which there is no entitlement. A person found guilty of an offence under s 50 shall be liable on summary conviction in England and Wales to imprisonment for no more than 12 months (but see below) or to a fine not exceeding the greater of £20,000 and three times the total of levy that it was intended to evade or to both. On summary conviction in Scotland, the guilty party shall be liable to imprisonment for no more than 12 months or to a fine not exceeding the greater of the statutory maximum and three times the total of levy that it was intended to evade or to both. In Northern Ireland, imprisonment may not exceed six months but otherwise the same penalties apply as in Scotland. Conviction on indictment renders the person liable to imprisonment for no more than seven years or to a fine or to both. In England and Wales, the maximum term of imprisonment is six months, until the commencement of CJA 2003 s 154(1).

Section 51 creates an offence of failing to notify liability to register, subject to a reasonable-excuse defence. The same penalties apply as under s 50, except that the maximum term of imprisonment on conviction on indictment is to be three years and monetary fines are measured by reference to the "potential lost revenue".

Administration and enforcement

Section 52 empowers HMRC to make regulations concerning the payment, collection and recovery of the levy, and introduces Sch 8, which deals with recovery and overpayment.

Schedule 8 consists of three parts. Part 1 comprises paras 1–7 and provides for recovery; Pt 2 comprises paras 8–15 and provides for overpayments; Pt 3 comprises paras 16 and 17 and provides for the service of notices.

Schedule 8 Pt 1 Paragraph 1 provides that the levy shall be recoverable as a debt due to the Crown.

Paragraph 2 provides for HMRC to make an assessment where an amount of the levy has become due in respect of an accounting period but the amount cannot be ascertained and the person liable has committed a "relevant default". These are (a) failure to notify liability to register under s 44 or to notify a correction under s 48; (b) failure to make a return under regulations under s 52; (c) failure to keep documents or provide facilities for verification of returns; (d) the making of an incomplete or incorrect return in purported compliance with regulations; (e) failure to comply with record-keeping regulations under s 53; or (f) unreasonable delay in complying with a requirement failure to comply with which would be a default under any of (a) to (e) above.

Where an assessment has been made as a result of failure to make a return, the levy assessed has been paid but the proper return has still not been made, and due to a failure to make a return for another, later, period, HMRC has made a second assessment, the amount assessed under that second assessment may, as provided by para 3, be greater than it would have been in the absence of the earlier default.

Paragraph 4 enables HMRC to make an assessment where an amount of levy in respect of an accounting period has become due and the amount is ascertainable.

Paragraph 5 enables HMRC to make a supplementary assessment where it appears to HMRC that the amount that ought to have been assessed by the original assessment is less than the amount of levy actually due. Under paragraph 6, an amount assessed under paras 2, 4 or 5 shall be recoverable as if it were an amount of levy due from the relevant person but not to the extent that the assessment has been withdrawn or reduced.

Paragraph 7 provides that the normal time limit for making an assessment shall be four years from the end of the accounting period to which the assessment relates.

However, where there is a loss of levy due to a person's deliberate action or attributable to failure by the person to comply with a requirement under s 44 to notify liability to registration or under regulations under s 48 to correct an entry in the register, the time limit is extended to 20 years.

Schedule 8 Pt 2 Paragraph 8 mandates HMRC to repay any amount of levy that has been paid but was not due upon receipt of a repayment claim and empowers HMRC to make regulations to that effect.

Paragraph 9 places limits on the duty to repay. First, there is to be no liability to repay levy paid more than four years before the repayment claim is made. Second, a defence of unjust enrichment is provided. This is supplemented by para 10, which provides that in determining whether a person has been unjustly enriched, any loss or damage incurred by the person claiming repayment is to be disregarded to the extent that any part of the cost of the original payment of levy by that person was borne by another person.

Paragraph 11 enables HMRC to make regulations providing for it to disregard any arrangement for part of a repayment to be passed to another person except as provided in the regulations. Where an excessive amount has been repaid, HMRC may make an assessment under para 12 to recover the excess. Excessive-repayment assessments may be combined in a single assessment with recovery assessments. Furthermore, where it appears to HMRC that an excessive-repayment assessment ought to have been for an amount greater than that actually assessed, HMRC may make a supplementary assessment under para 13.

Paragraph 14 provides that amounts assessed under paras 12 or 13 shall be recoverable as if they were an amount of levy due from the relevant person but not to the extent that the assessment has been withdrawn or reduced. The time limit for assessments under paras 12 or 13 is set by para 15 at two years after evidence of facts sufficient for HMRC to conclude that such an assessment should be made came to HMRC's knowledge.

Schedule 8 Pt 3 Paragraph 16 provides that a notice of assessment under paras 2, 5, 12 or 13 given to a person's representative shall be treated as given to the person for whom the representative acts. Finally, para 17 provides that notices of assessment may be given to a person by sending them by post to that person's last known address.

Section 53 empowers HMRC to make regulations requiring persons to keep specified records and to preserve them for a specified period or to direct them to do so. It also introduces Sch 9, which provides for penalties for failure to comply with the requirements imposed under regulations or directions under this section.

Schedule 9 consists of two parts. Part 1 comprises paras 1–4 and imposes the penalties, whereas Pt 2, comprising paras 5–10 provides for assessments.

Schedule 9 Pt 1 Paragraph 1 imposes a penalty on a person for failure to comply with a requirement imposed by regulations under ss 48(2) (correction of register entries) or 53(1)(a) (record-keeping requirement). The amount of the penalty appears to vary according to the number of occasions in the two years preceding the failure in question on which the person has previously failed to comply with the same requirement (NB: the legislation is obscure on this point). Where there has been no such occasion, the penalty is £5 for every day for which the failure continues. Where there has been one such occasion, the penalty is £10 per day. The penalty is £15 per day where there have been two or more such failures. However, no more than 100 days of failure are to be taken into account for this purpose, and there is also a minimum penalty of £50. Failure to comply with a requirement under regulations made under s 53(1)(b) to preserve records for a specified period is to give rise to a fixed penalty of £500. However, there shall be no penalty under para 1 where the conduct that gives rise to the penalty also renders the person liable to a penalty for a deliberate inaccuracy under FA 2007 Sch 24.

Paragraph 2 imposes a penalty for failure to comply with a direction under s 53(2)(a) (record-keeping direction) of £200 for every day the failure continues, up to a maximum of 30 days. Failure to comply with a direction under s 53(3)(b) to preserve records for a specified period, however, gives rise to a fixed penalty of £500. As under para 1, there shall be no penalty under para 2 where the conduct that gives rise to the penalty also renders the person liable to a penalty for a deliberate inaccuracy under FA 2007 Sch 24.

Paragraph 3 empowers HMRC to alter the penalty amounts specified in paras 1 or 2 by regulations. Paragraph 4 establishes a reasonable-excuse defence against a penalty under paras 1 or 2.

Schedule 9 Pt 2 Paragraph 5 provides for HMRC to make assessments to recover penalties under Sch 9. However, no such assessment may be made for a penalty under para 1 unless HMRC has first given the person in default written notice of the consequences of a continuing failure to comply within the two years preceding the assessment. A further assessment may be made where the failure continues after the date to which the penalty in the earlier assessment was calculated.

Paragraph 6 provides for HMRC to make supplementary assessments if it appears to HMRC that the original assessment was for an insufficient amount.

Paragraph 7 provides that amounts assessed under paras 5 or 6 shall be recoverable as if they were an amount of levy due from the relevant person but not to the extent that the assessment has been withdrawn or reduced.

Paragraph 8 provides that the normal time limit for making an assessment under para 5 shall be four years from the end of the accounting period to which the assessment relates. However, where there is a loss of levy due to a person's deliberate action or attributable to failure by the person to comply with a record-keeping or preservation requirement under s 53, the time limit is extended to 20 years.

Paragraph 9 provides that a notice of assessment under paras 5 or 6 given to a person's representative shall be treated as given to the person for whom the representative acts.

Finally, para 10 provides that notices of assessment may be given to a person by sending them by post to that person's last known address.

Section 54 enables HMRC to make further regulations concerning enforcement, including entry, search and seizure provisions and apply any provision of CEMA 1979.

Section 55 introduces Sch 10, which provides for appeals and reviews.

Schedule 10 consists of three parts. Part 1, which comprises para 1, specifies what decisions are capable of appeal. Part 2, which comprises paras 2–8, provides for reviews, whereas Pt 3, comprising paras 9–15, provides for appeals.

Schedule 10 Pt 1 Paragraph 1 lists those HMRC decisions (15 in all) relating to soft drinks industry levy against which a person may appeal.

Schedule 10 Pt 2 Paragraph 2 provides that HMRC shall offer a person a review of a decision within para 1 that has been notified to the person. Under para 3, any other person who has the right of appeal under para 1 may require HMRC to review that decision within 30 days of the day on which that person becomes aware of the decision, unless the person has already appealed to the appeal tribunal against that decision.

Paragraph 4 provides that HMRC must review a decision if it has offered such a review under para 2 and the person has accepted that offer within 30 days of the offer date. The person may not do so, however, if the person has already appealed to the appeal tribunal. HMRC must also review a decision if required to do so under para 3, unless an appeal has already been made to the appeal tribunal against that decision. Under para 5, HMRC may, within the 30-day period for notifying acceptance of a review offer or requiring a review to be undertaken, extend that period by a further 30 days at a time. Nevertheless, para 6 allows for an out-of-time review if HMRC has received a written request to do so and it is satisfied that the person concerned had a reasonable excuse for not accepting the review offer or requiring a review within the time permitted, unless an appeal has already been made to the appeal tribunal in relation to the decision concerned.

Paragraph 7 provides that HMRC shall undertake a review of the nature and extent that appear appropriate, and that the review shall conclude that the decision is to be upheld, varied or cancelled. HMRC must give notice of its conclusion and its reasoning to the person concerned within 45 days (or an agreed longer period) of receiving notification accepting the offer or requiring the review or deciding to undertake an out-of-time review. Where HMRC does not give notice of its conclusions within the specified period, the decision is to be taken as upheld.

Paragraph 8 provides that notices under Sch 10 may be given to a person by sending them by post to that person's last known address.

Schedule 10 Pt 3 Paragraph 9 defines "appeal tribunal" as the First-tier Tribunal or the Upper Tribunal. Paragraph 10 provides that an appeal under para 1 shall be made within 30 days of the receipt by the person of the notice of the decision or, in the case of an appeal by another person under para 3, within 30 days of that person's becoming aware of the decision or until the end of an extended review period. However, if HMRC has been required under para 4 to undertake a review, an appeal may not be made until the date of HMRC's notice of its conclusions and then within 30 days of that date. Where a request has been made to HMRC under para 6 to undertake an out-of-time review, an appeal may not be made unless HMRC has notified the relevant person whether or not it will undertake the review and, if HMRC agrees to do so, until the date HMRC notifies its conclusions and then within 30 days of that date. However, where HMRC declines to undertake the review, an appeal may only be made with the appeal tribunal's permission.

Paragraph 11 provides that an appeal relating to an amount of levy that is due shall not be considered by the appeal tribunal until payment or deposit of that amount has been made, unless HMRC is satisfied or the appeal tribunal decides that payment or deposit of that amount would cause the appellant to suffer hardship.

Paragraphs 12–15 provide that, depending on the nature of the decision under appeal, the appeal tribunal shall either affirm or cancel that decision, vary it or substitute for it another decision that HMRC could have made in relation to the matter or require HMRC to undertake another review.

Section 56 introduces Sch 11.

Schedule 11 makes supplementary and consequential amendments and consists of seven paragraphs.

Paragraph 1 amends FA 2008 Sch 36 para 10 to clarify that the power to inspect business premises in order to check a person's tax position under that paragraph does not extend to that person's position as regards the levy.

Paragraph 2 amends FA 2008 Sch 41 to include failure to comply with the obligation under s 44 to give notice of liability to register as one of the failures listed in the Table in FA 2008 Sch 41 para 1 giving rise to a penalty under that paragraph. It also amends FA 2008 Sch 41 para 4 to provide that a penalty shall be payable by a person who, after a charge to the levy has arisen in respect of chargeable soft drinks, acquires possession of those drinks or becomes concerned with carrying, removing etc or otherwise dealing with them at a time when the payment of the levy is due or payable but has not been paid. Consequential amendments to other provisions of FA 2008 Sch 41 are also made.

Paragraph 3 amends FA 2007 Sch 24 so as to include an error in a return under regulations made under s 52 as a default giving rise to a penalty under FA 2007 Sch 24 para 1.

Paragraph 4 amends FA 2009 Sch 55 so as to include a failure to make a return under regulations made under s 52 as a failure giving rise to a penalty under FA 2009 Sch 55 para 1 and makes a consequential amendment.

Paragraph 5 amends FA 2009 Sch 56 to include a failure to make a payment on time of an amount payable under regulations made under s 52 or Sch 8 paras 6 or 14 as a failure giving rise to a penalty under FA 2009 Sch 56 para 1 and makes a consequential amendment.

Paragraph 6 inserts new FA 2011 Sch 23 para 24A to include as relevant data-holders any persons producing, packaging, or carrying on a business involving the sale of, chargeable soft drinks, and makes a consequential amendment.

Finally, para 7 inserts new FA 2009 Sch 53 para 11C, which provides that late payment interest in respect of an amount of levy due from a person who ought to be registered but is not shall begin to run from the date that would have been the appropriate date had the person concerned registered when first liable to do so.

Miscellaneous

Section 57 empowers HMRC to make regulations for the purposes of the levy in relation to cases where a person carries on the business of an individual who has died or become incapacitated or of a person who is subject to an insolvency procedure.

Section 58 amends PCTA 1968 s 1 to include soft drinks industry levy as a tax in respect of which a House of Commons resolution shall have temporary statutory effect.

General

Section 59 provides for interpretation.

Section 60 provides HMRC with further regulatory powers with respect to the soft-drinks industry levy.

Section 61 provides that the levy is to come into force on a day to be appointed by HMRC regulations, but that the amendment made to FA 2007 Sch 24 para 1 Table by

Sch 11 para 3 is to have effect from a day to be appointed by Treasury regulations. Different days may be appointed for different purposes.

PART 3
FINAL

Section 62 provides a key to interpretation of abbreviations of enactments used in the Act and **s 63** gives the short title.

Zigurds Kronbergs
June 2017

FINANCE ACT 2017

2017 Chapter 10

ARRANGEMENT OF SECTIONS

PART 1

DIRECT AND INDIRECT TAXES

Income tax charge and rates

Corporation tax charge

Income tax: general

Employee shareholder shares

Disguised remuneration

Indirect taxes

Avoidance

PART 2

SOFT DRINKS INDUSTRY LEVY

Introductory

Chargeable soft drinks

Charging of the soft drinks industry levy

PART 3

FINAL

SCHEDULES

An Act to grant certain duties, to alter other duties, and to amend the law relating to the national debt and the public revenue, and to make further provision in connection with finance.

[27th April 2017]

PART 1
DIRECT AND INDIRECT TAXES

Income tax charge and rates

1 Income tax charge for tax year 2017–18

Income tax is charged for the tax year 2017–18.

GENERAL NOTE

Income Tax Act 2007 s 4 provides that income tax is an annual tax – it is charged for a year only if an Act so provides. Finance Act 2017 s 1 imposes the charge for 2017/18.

2 Main rates of income tax for tax year 2017–18

For the tax year 2017–18 the main rates of income tax are as follows—

   (a) the basic rate is 20%;
   (b) the higher rate is 40%;
   (c) the additional rate is 45%.

GENERAL NOTE

Section 2 sets out the main rates at which income tax for 2017/18 is charged in accordance with ITA 2007 s 6. The basic rate is 20%, the higher rate is 40% and the additional rate is 45%.

These three rates are subject to an "income tax lock" for tax years 2016/17 and 2017/18. The effect of the lock is that the basic rate cannot exceed 20%, the higher rate cannot exceed 40% and the additional rate cannot exceed 45%.

Finance (No 2) Act 2015 s 1 provided that the lock applied to a tax year beginning after the day on which that Act was passed (18 November 2015) but before the date of the first parliamentary general election after that day. That election was held on 8 June, 2017, so the lock will not apply to 2018/19 unless it is re-enacted.

The other rates at which income tax is charged for 2017/18 are set out in ITA 2007 s 6(3), (4) and are:

– the default basic, higher and additional rates (ITA 2007 ss 6(3)(zc) and 6C, inserted by FA 2016 s 6). See FA 2017 s 3 below;
– the starting rate for savings (ITA 2007 ss 6(3)(a) and 7);
– the savings nil rate (ITA 2007 ss 6(3)(a) and 7, as amended by FA 2016 s 6);
– the savings basic, higher and additional rates (ITA 2007 ss 6(3)(aa) and 7A, inserted by FA 2016 s 6). See FA 2017 s 3 below;

– the dividend nil rate, dividend ordinary rate, dividend upper rate and dividend additional rate (ITA 2007 ss 6(3)(b) and 8, as amended by FA 2016 s 5);
– the trust rate and the dividend trust rate (ITA 2007 ss 6(3)(c) and 9);
– Scottish rates of income tax on non-savings and non-dividend income (ITA 2007 ss 6(4) and 11A, as amended by Scotland Act 2016 s 14); and
– Welsh rates of income tax (ITA 2007 ss 6(3)(zb), 6B and 11B, to be inserted by Wales Act 2014 s 9 with effect from a date to be appointed).

3 Default and savings rates of income tax for tax year 2017–18

(1) For the tax year 2017–18 the default rates of income tax are as follows—
   (a) the default basic rate is 20%;
   (b) the default higher rate is 40%;
   (c) the default additional rate is 45%.
(2) For the tax year 2017–18 the savings rates of income tax are as follows—
   (a) the savings basic rate is 20%;
   (b) the savings higher rate is 40%;
   (c) the savings additional rate is 45%.

GENERAL NOTE

Income tax rates for savings and dividend income are not devolved, and will continue to be set by the UK Parliament. FA 2016 s 6 renamed the income tax rates applicable to savings and dividend income in order to distinguish them from the rates applying to other income, and introduced a "default rate".

These changes were intended to ensure that, now that the Scottish Parliament has the power to set rates and thresholds for the non-savings, non-dividends income of Scottish taxpayers, English, Welsh and Northern Irish MPs are able to vote under the English votes for English laws procedure for the UK rates that have not been devolved.

New ITA 2007 s 9A provides in table form an overview of the new rates structure set out in ss 10– 15. It does not address certain exceptions. The table shows, for example, that a non-UK resident individual pays "savings rates" on savings income; "dividend rates" on most dividend income; and "default rates" on other income.

Default rates for non-UK residents

FA 2017 s 3(1) provides that for 2017/18 the default basic rate is 20%, the default higher rate is 40%, and the default additional rate is 45%.

These "default rates" of income tax were introduced with effect from 2017/18 by ITA 2007 ss 6C and 11C, inserted by FA 2016 s 6:
– ITA 2007 s 6C provides that the default basic rate, default higher rate and default additional rate for a tax year are the rates determined as such by Parliament for the tax year.
– ITA 2007 s 11C provides that income tax on a non-UK resident individual's income is charged at the default basic, higher and additional rates as appropriate, subject to the exceptions in s 11C(4) for savings income, dividend income and any income to which any other provision providing for a different rate (such as the Scottish rates) applies.

Savings rates

FA 2017 s 3(2) provides that for 2017/18 the savings basic rate is 20%, the savings higher rate is 40%, and the savings additional rate is 45%.

These "savings rates" of income tax were introduced with effect from 2017/18 by ITA 2007 ss 7A and 11D, inserted by FA 2016 s 6:
– ITA 2007 s 7A provides that the savings basic rate, savings higher rate and savings additional rate for a tax year are the rates determined as such by Parliament for the tax year.
– ITA 2007 s 11D provides that income tax on an individual's savings income is charged (i) at the savings basic rate if it would otherwise be charged at the basic rate or the default basic rate, (ii) at the savings higher rate if it would otherwise be charged at the higher rate or the default higher rate, and (iii) at the savings additional rate if it would otherwise be charged at the additional rate or the default additional rate.

This rule has effect only after ITA 2007 ss 12 and 12A, which apply the starting rate for savings and the savings nil rate, have been applied. It is also subject to any other provisions of the Income Tax Acts (other than ITA 2007 ss 10 and 11C) which provide for income to be charged at different rates in some circumstances.

ITA 2007 s 16 (savings and dividend income to be treated as highest part of total income) is applied in determining the extent to which savings income above the starting rate limit for savings would otherwise be charged at the basic, higher or additional rate or the default basic, default higher or default additional rate.

ITA 2007 s 11D is modified for Scottish taxpayers. References to income that would otherwise be charged at a particular rate are to be read as references to income that would, if the individual were not a Scottish taxpayer (but were UK resident), be charged at that rate.

4 Starting rate limit for savings for tax year 2017–18

(1) For the amount specified in section 12(3) of ITA 2007 (starting rate for savings) substitute "£5000".

(2) The amendment made by subsection (1) has effect in relation to the tax year 2017–18 and subsequent tax years.

(3) Section 21 of ITA 2007 (indexation), so far as relating to the starting rate limit for savings, does not apply in relation to the tax year 2017–18 (but this section does not override that section for subsequent tax years).

GENERAL NOTE

Section 4 disapplies the indexation rule for 2017/18 and sets the starting rate limit at £5,000 for that year. The starting rate for savings (set by ITA 2007 s 7(1)) and the starting rate limit (set by ITA 2007 s 12(3)) are not devolved matters. The starting rate limit was set at £5,000 for 2015/16 by FA 2014 s 3. Income Tax Act 2007 s 21 provides for the indexation of the starting rate limit but this did not result in an uplift for 2016/17.

Corporation tax charge

5 Corporation tax charge for financial year 2018

Corporation tax is charged for the financial year 2018.

GENERAL NOTE

Section 5 imposes corporation tax for financial year 2018, i.e. 1 April 2018 to 31 March 2019. The rate of corporation tax has been set as follows:
– 19% for the financial years 2017, 2018 and 2019 (F(No 2)A 2015, s 7(1));
– 17% for the financial year 2020 (F(No 2)A 2015 s 7(2), as amended by FA 2016 s 46).

Income tax: general

6 Workers' services provided to public sector through intermediaries

Schedule 1 makes provision about workers' services provided to the public sector through intermediaries.

GENERAL NOTE

Section 6 introduces Sch 1. which makes the aforementioned changes to ITEPA 2003. The changes are operative from tax year 2017/18 onwards and in relation to payments made from 6 April 2017.

Background

Finance Act 2017 s 6, Sch 1 amends and introduces a new regime in relation to income tax into ITEPA 2003 Pt 2 in respect of the taxation of workers working through intermediaries where the end user client is a public sector entity (often described by

HMRC as 'off-payroll working in the public sector'). It removes such arrangements from the current legislation in ITEPA 2003 Pt 2 Ch 8 (the drafting originating from IR35 and which captures arrangements using personal service companies) and ITEPA 2003 Pt 2 Ch 9 in relation to managed service companies and introduces a new set of rules via a new ITEPA 2003 Pt 2 Ch 10. The rules also take precedence over the construction industry scheme.

The aim of the changes is to place the burden of determining whether an employment relationship exists, with the end user public sector entity. Where such a relationship exists the obligation to assess and pay income tax ceases to be with the intermediary (often a personal service company). Instead the payments to the worker are treated as deemed earnings with a liability to collect and pay income tax via PAYE falling on persons in the supply chain and not the intermediary. If the end user public sector entity does not fulfil its obligations in relation to determining the employment status of the worker then the liability to operate PAYE will fall to it.

Equivalent provisions have been introduced for class 1 national insurance contributions (NIC) via the Social Security (Miscellaneous Amendments No. 2) Regulations 2017 (SI 2017/373). A guidance note for agents and a technical note have also been issued by HMRC. The changes to the NIC rules result in liability to pay class 1 secondary (employer's) NIC moving from the intermediary (which is the case when the IR35 rules in Pt 2 Ch 8 apply) to the other parties in the supply chain. This will impact on how the contracts are priced in the supply chain due to the burden of the class 1 secondary NIC passing up the chain.

7 Optional remuneration arrangements
Schedule 2 makes provision about optional remuneration arrangements.

GENERAL NOTE
Section 7 introduces Sch 2.

Optional remuneration arrangements ("OpRA") are arrangements where employees forego an amount of earnings and receive a benefit instead. They extend to arrangements based on salary sacrifice, as well as cash alternatives, flexible benefits, and benefits that can be traded up or down. The new rules commenced on 6 April 2017.

Broadly speaking, the taxable value of a benefit provided under OpRA will be the "relevant amount" where the amount of earnings foregone is higher than the cash equivalent or modified cash equivalent (as the case may be) of the benefit concerned. This is subject to the detailed rules applicable for each benefit.

Certain benefits are excluded from OpRA so their taxable value will continue to be determined under normal rules without having to calculate the relevant amount. These include: registered pensions, overseas pensions, pensions advice, childcare and childcare vouchers, ultra-low emission vehicles (ULEVs i.e. cars with CO_2 emissions not exceeding 75g/km), cycles and safety equipment and associated vouchers, payments & benefits in connection with company cars and vans, retraining courses, counselling and other outplacement services and statutory redundancy payments.

It may sound obvious but the new rules do not apply where no benefit is received by the employee. For example, "holiday purchase" is a popular feature of modern pay arrangements. But this simply amounts to working less in exchange for giving up pro rata pay. Taking additional days off work does not amount to the provision of a benefit. The rules are also not relevant where the employee takes earnings instead of a benefit (rather than the other way around).

Grandfathering rules delay the start of OpRA for arrangements already entered into before 6 April 2017, until the earliest of:
(i)   any variation of the terms of the arrangement (unless this is outside of the control of the parties or attributable to the employee's entitlement to specified statutory payments);
(ii) the renewal of the arrangement (including automatic renewal); and
(iii) a long-stop date depending on the type of benefit provided. The long-stop date is 5 April 2021 for cars (with CO_2 emissions exceeding 75g/km), vans, fuel, accommodation and school fees, and 5 April 2018 for all other benefits.

For this purpose, an arrangement must have been effectively made prior to 6 April 2017 to benefit from grandfathering; it will not be enough that an employee simply expressed a wish prior to 6 April 2017, to take part in a benefit under arrangements which actually commenced on or after that date.

The detailed rules on OpRA can be found in FA 2017 Sch 2, which makes numerous amendments to the benefits code and other parts of ITEPA 2003. These largely follow the "higher of rule" noted above, but there are some quirks. For example, see s 149A on private fuel benefits, which is inexplicably problematic for employees making good the cost of private fuel. Another is the treatment of sick pay, which appears likely to result in double taxation when provided under OpRA, subject to any further guidance from HMRC relieving such an outcome. A third is the treatment of Approved Mileage Allowance Payments paid under OpRA which may become taxable with no ability to claim relief by other means. A fourth surprise is that the new rules do not provide an explicit carve out for share incentives. OpRA will now need to be carefully considered in the case of, say, a bonus waiver for shares or options capable of being cash-settled. See Sch 2 below for further commentary on the changes to individual benefit rules.

8 Taxable benefits: asset made available without transfer

(1) ITEPA 2003 is amended as follows.

(2) In section 205 (cost of taxable benefit subject to the residual charge: asset made available without transfer)—

    (a) in subsection (1), for paragraph (a) substitute—

    "(a) the benefit consists in an asset being made available for private use, and",

    (b) after subsection (1) insert—

    "(1A) In this section and section 205A, "private use" means private use by the employee or a member of the employee's family or household.

    (1B) For the purposes of subsection (1) and sections 205A and 205B, an asset made available in a tax year for use by the employee or a member of the employee's family or household is to be treated as made available throughout the year for private use unless—

        (a) at all times in the year when it is available for use by the employee or a member of the employee's family or household, the terms under which it is made available prohibit private use, and

        (b) no private use is made of it in the year.

    (1C) The cost of the taxable benefit is—

        (a) the annual cost of the benefit determined in accordance with subsection (2), less

        (b) any amount required to be deducted by section 205A (deduction for periods when asset unavailable for private use).

    (1D) In certain cases, the cost of the taxable benefit is calculated under this section in accordance with section 205B (reduction of cost of taxable benefit where asset is shared).", and

    (c) in subsection (2), in the words before paragraph (a), for "cost of the taxable" substitute "annual cost of the".

(3) After section 205 insert—

"205A Deduction for periods when asset unavailable for private use

    (1) A deduction is to be made under section 205(1C)(b) if the asset mentioned in section 205(1) has been unavailable for private use on any day during the tax year concerned.

    (2) For the purposes of this section an asset is "unavailable" for private use on any day if—

        (a) that day falls before the day on which the asset is first available to the employee,

        (b) that day falls after the day on which the asset is last available to the employee,

        (c) for more than 12 hours during that day the asset—

            (i) is not in a condition fit for use,

            (ii) is undergoing repair or maintenance,

            (iii) could not lawfully be used,

            (iv) is in the possession of a person who has a lien over it and who is not the employer, not a person connected with the employer, not the employee, not a member of the employee's family and not a member of the employee's household, or

(v) is used in a way that is neither use by, nor use at the direction of, the employee or a member of the employee's family or household, or

(d) on that day the employee—

(i) uses the asset in the performance of the duties of the employment, and

(ii) does not use the asset otherwise than in the performance of the duties of the employment.

(3) The amount of the deduction is given by—

$(U / Y) \times A$

where—

U is the number of days, in the tax year concerned, on which the asset is unavailable for private use,

Y is the number of days in that year, and

A is the annual cost of the benefit of the asset determined under section 205(2).

(4) The reference in subsection (2)(a) to the time when the asset is first available to the employee is to the earliest time when the asset is made available, by reason of the employment and without any transfer of the property in it, for private use.

(5) The reference in subsection (2)(b) to the time when the asset is last available to the employee is to the last time when the asset is made available, by reason of the employment and without any transfer of the property in it, for private use.

205B Reduction of cost of taxable benefit where asset is shared

(1) This section applies where the cost of an employment-related benefit ("the taxable benefit") is to be determined under section 205.

(2) If, for the whole or part of the tax year concerned, the same asset is available for more than one employee's private use at the same time, the total of the amounts which are the cost of the taxable benefit for each of those employees is to be limited to the annual cost of the benefit of the asset determined in accordance with section 205(2).

(3) The cost of the taxable benefit for each employee is determined by taking the amount given by section 205(1C) and then reducing that amount on a just and reasonable basis.

(4) For the purposes of this section, an asset is available for an employee's private use if it is available for private use by the employee or a member of the employee's family or household."

(4) In section 365 (deductions where employment-related benefit provided)—

(a) in subsection (1)—

(i) omit the "and" at the end of paragraph (a), and

(ii) after that paragraph insert—

"(aa) the cost of the benefit was determined under section 204 or 206, and",

(b) in subsection (3), for "sections 204 to 206" substitute "section 204 or 206", and

(c) in the heading, for "employment-related benefit" substitute "certain employment-related benefits".

(5) The amendments made by this section have effect for the tax year 2017–18 and subsequent tax years.

GENERAL NOTE

Section 8 amends ITEPA 2003 s 205 (cost of the benefit: asset made available without transfer) for 2017/18 and subsequent tax years. New, detailed rules setting out the calculation of the cash equivalent of the benefit allow for days when the asset is not available for private use, and replace HMRC guidance.

A revised ITEPA 2003 s 205(1) applies where the benefit consists in an asset being made available for private use and there is no transfer of the property in the asset.

Section 8(2) inserts new sub-ss 1A to 1D in ITEPA 2003 s 205, and makes a minor change to ITEPA 2003 s 205(2).

– "Private use" is defined as private use by the employee or a member of the employee's family or household. The asset is to be treated as made available throughout the year for private use unless (a) at all times in the year when it is available for use, private use is prohibited, and (b) no private use is made of it in the year.

– The cost of the taxable benefit is the annual cost determined under revised ITEPA 2003 s 205(2), less any amount required to be deducted by a new ITEPA 2003 s 205A for periods when the asset was unavailable for private use. A new ITEPA 2003 s 205B applies if use of the asset is shared.

Section 8(3) inserts the new ITEPA 2003 ss 205A and 205B.

New ITEPA 2003 s 205A provides for a deduction if the asset is unavailable for private use on any day during the tax year. Section 205A(2) sets out the circumstances in which an asset is "unavailable" for private use on any day. These include the situation where for more than 12 hours during that day, the asset is not fit for use, is undergoing repair or maintenance, could not lawfully be used, or is in the possession of (or used by) an unconnected party. A day on which the employee uses the asset in the performance of the duties of the employment, and does not use it otherwise, is also treated as a day on which the asset is unavailable for private use.

The deduction is:

(U / Y) x A

where U is the number of days in the tax year on which the asset is unavailable for private use, Y is the number of days in that year, and A is the annual cost of the benefit determined under ITEPA 2003 s 205(2).

New ITEPA 2003 s 205B provides for a reduction in the cost of the benefit where the asset is made available for the private use of more than one employee. The reduction is made on a "just and reasonable" basis.

Section 8(4) makes a consequential amendment to ITEPA 2003 s 365 (deductions where employment-related benefit provided) to prevent a deduction being made under both s 365 and the new provisions.

9 Overseas pensions

Schedule 3 makes provision about—

    (a) registered pension schemes established outside the United Kingdom, and
    (b) payments made in respect of overseas pension entitlement.

BACKGROUND

In the Autumn Statement 2016 the government proposed to align more closely the treatment of foreign pensions with the UK's domestic pension regime. As a result the legislation introduced in s 9 and Sch 3 sets out the position for defined benefit specialist pension schemes for individuals employed abroad ("section 615 schemes", i.e. occupational pension schemes established under ICTA 1988 s 615(6)). A "section 615 scheme" is established under trust by an employer that operates wholly or partly outside the UK and provides retirement benefits for employees who work wholly outside the UK.

The legislation:

– clarifies that all lump sums paid out of funds built up before 6 April 2017 will be subject to existing tax treatment;
– abolishes "section 615 schemes';
– extends from five to ten years the period during which lump sums paid to non-UK residents from foreign pension plans that have benefited from UK tax relief are liable to UK tax;
– provides through regulations (SI 2017/398 subsequently promulgated) for updates to the conditions that foreign schemes must meet to obtain UK tax relief on contributions and transfers by removing the requirement for 70% of transferred funds to be used to provide members with an income for life and brings the pension age test into line with registered pension schemes; and
– taxes the full foreign pension of UK residents instead of at 90%.

The changes have effect from 6 April 2017.

In the Spring Budget 2017 the Chancellor announced legislation would be introduced to apply a 25% charge to pension transfers made to qualifying recognised overseas pension schemes (QROPS) to take effect for transfers requested on or after 9 March 2017. The tax would be introduced to ensure the generous tax relief of pension savings that the government provides is used as intended. It supports the government's objective of promoting fairness in the tax system and it continues to allow overseas pension transfers to be made free of UK tax up to the lifetime allowance when people leave the UK and take their pension savings with them to their new country of residence. The charge would not apply to funds already transferred to a QROPS before 9 March 2017 nor to transfers requested before that date. Exceptions to the charge would be made allowing tax-free transfers where people had a genuine need to transfer their pension, e.g. both the individual and the pension scheme are in countries within the EEA, or if outside the EEA, both the individual and the pension scheme are in the same country, or the QROPS is an occupational pension scheme provided by the individual's employer. If the individual's circumstances change within five years of the transfer, the tax treatment of the transfer would be reconsidered. It was also proposed to apply UK tax rules to payments from funds that have had UK tax relief and have been transferred on or after 6 April 2017 to a QROPS. Thus UK tax rules would apply to any payments made in the first five full tax years following the transfer regardless of whether the individual is or has been UK resident in that period. As a result, these proposals appeared in s 10 and Sch 4 of FA 2017.

It should be noted that there has been some speculation as to whether the changes proposed regarding the charge on pension transfers by s 10 and Sch 4 are lawful as exit charges in such circumstances where they lack the ability of deferral or the facility to fluctuate with any reduction in value may offend EU law. The question arises as to whether the proposed tax on a transfer of a pension from a UK registered pension scheme to a fund outside the EU offends the EU right of free movement of capital? That may not matter once the UK leaves the EU, but meanwhile legal advice for those contemplating such transfers may be the answer or even testing HMRC's reaction in the courts.

GENERAL NOTE

Section 9 introduces Sch 3 making changes to the UK tax charges that arise on overseas pension savings, including where foreign pensions and lump sums are paid to UK residents and making the tax treatment of foreign pensions more closely align UK and foreign pension savings thus making the system simpler. The changes will limit the inconsistencies in the remaining tax treatment of UK and foreign pension savings and, in particular, will address the gaps that arise as a result of only certain parts of the UK tax regime applying to foreign pension schemes. The legislation also provides for no new pension savings in specialist pension schemes for foreign service and aligns the tax treatment of registered pension schemes whether or not they are based in the UK. The changes ensure that the grandfathering of lump sums paid to UK residents out of specialist pension schemes for those employed overseas ('section 615 schemes') works properly, and also ensures that the entitlement under all types of "section 615 schemes" can receive this beneficial treatment.

10 Pensions: offshore transfers
Schedule 4 contains provision about charging income tax—
   (a) where payments are made in respect of overseas pensions, and
   (b) on transfers to qualifying recognised overseas pension schemes.

GENERAL NOTE

Section 10 introduces Sch 4 which makes provision for charging income tax (the "overseas transfer charge') on transfers to QROPS requested on or after 9 March 2017. The tax charge is an anti-avoidance measure and will not apply if a need for the transfer can be demonstrated, e.g. if both the individual and the QROPS are in the same country, both are within the EEA or the recipient QROPS is provided by the individual's employer. The overseas transfer charge may however apply within the period of five full tax years following a tax-free transfer if circumstances change, e.g. the QROPS is in the EEA and the individual ceases to be an EEA resident. Scheme administrators of registered pension schemes and scheme managers of QROPS are to be jointly and severally liable for the tax with the individual making the transfer. Consequently, new information requirements are being placed on the individual, the transferring scheme and, in the case of onward transfers, the transferring QROPS. The legislation ensures that amounts transferred are subject to the lifetime allowance only once.

11 Deduction of income tax at source
Schedule 5 makes provision about deduction of income tax at source.

GENERAL NOTE

Section 11 introduces Sch 5 which abolishes the requirement to deduct income tax at source from interest distributions made by investment trusts, authorised investment funds (openended investment companies and authorised unit trusts) and on peerto-peer lending. Schedule 5 consists of three Parts. Part 1 (paras 1 and 2) abolishes the duty to deduct income tax at source on interest distributions made by investment trusts or authorised investment funds (i.e. OEICS and AUTS). Part 2 (para 3) abolishes the duty to deduct income tax at source on interest payments made in the course of peertopeer lending. Part 3 (paras 4 and 5) provide for a consequential amendment and commencement.

Employee shareholder shares

12 Employee shareholder shares: amount treated as earnings

(1) In section 226A of ITEPA 2003 (amount treated as earnings)—

(a) in subsection (2), for "calculated in accordance with subsection (3)" substitute "equal to the market value of the shares";
(b) omit subsection (3);
(c) in subsection (6), omit "and sections 226B to 226D";
(d) in subsection (7), after "subsection (1)" insert "(but not subsection (2))".

(2) Omit sections 226B to 226D of ITEPA 2003 (deemed payment).

(3) In consequence of subsection (2), in ITEPA 2003 omit the following—

(a) section 479(3A);
(b) section 531(3A);
(c) section 532(4A).

(4) In consequence of subsection (2), in CTA 2009 omit the following—

(a) in section 1005, the definition of "employee shareholder share";
(b) section 1009(6);
(c) in section 1010(1), "and, in the case of employee shareholder shares, section 1038B";
(d) in section 1011(4)(b), "(but see also section 1038B of this Act)";
(e) in sections 1018(1) and 1019(1), "and, in the case of employee shareholder shares, section 1038B";
(f) sections 1022(5), 1026(5), 1027(5), 1033(5) and 1034(5);
(g) section 1038B;
(h) sections 1292(6ZA) and 1293(5A);
(i) in Schedule 4, the entry relating to "employee shareholder share".

(5) The amendments made by this section have effect in relation to shares acquired in consideration of an employee shareholder agreement entered into on or after the relevant day.

(6) The relevant day is 1 December 2016, subject to subsection (7).

(7) Where the individual entering into an employee shareholder agreement receives the advice referred to in section 205A(6)(a) of the Employment Rights Act 1996—

(a) on 23 November 2016, but
(b) before 1.30 pm on that day,

the relevant day is 2 December 2016.

BACKGROUND

Finance Act 2017 ss 12 to 14 are the provisions introduced to give effect to the abolition of tax reliefs for employee shareholder status (ESS) shares. ESS relief was introduced in 2013 to encourage and facilitate recruitment and job creation. The intention was to encourage employees to surrender certain employment rights in return for receiving shares on tax advantaged terms, namely:

(1) Receiving shares with a value of at least £2,000 with the value up to £2,000 being free of income tax and national insurance contributions.
(2) Relief from capital gains tax on gains realised on the disposal of shares with a value of up to £50,000 at the date of issue (subject to a cap of gains on £100,000 introduced in 2016).

In practice, the ESS relief was being used more extensively than expected and in different contexts. For example, the relief was being sought for management equity plans established in companies owned by private equity investors with shares having a low initial value but potentially substantial gains on realisation.

In response, it was announced that the relief was to be abolished in its entirety and ss 12 to 14 give effect to that.

GENERAL NOTE

Section 12 makes various changes, mainly to delete applicable provisions, to remove ESS relief from tax on the initial receipt of the shares for £2,000 of value.

13 Employee shareholder shares: abolition of CGT exemption

(1) TCGA 1992 is amended as follows.

(2) In section 58 (spouses and civil partners)—

(a) in subsection (2)—

(i) at the end of paragraph (a) insert "or";
(ii) omit paragraph (c) and the preceding "or";

(b) omit subsections (3) to (5).

(3) In section 149AA (restricted and convertible employment-related securities and employee shareholder shares), for subsection (6A) substitute—

"(6A) For the purposes of this section—

shares are "acquired" by an employee if the employee becomes beneficially entitled to them (and they are acquired at the time when the employee becomes so entitled);
"employee shareholder share" means a share acquired in consideration of an employee shareholder agreement and held by the employee;
"employee shareholder agreement" means an agreement by virtue of which an employee is an employee shareholder (see section 205A(1)(a) to (d) of the Employment Rights Act 1996);
"employee" and "employer company", in relation to an employee shareholder agreement, mean the individual and the company which enter into the agreement."

(4) Omit sections 236B to 236F (exemption for employee shareholder shares).

(5) In section 236G (relinquishment of employment rights is not disposal of an asset), in subsection (1), for "employee shareholder agreement" substitute "agreement by virtue of which the individual is an employee shareholder (see section 205A(1)(a) to (d) of the Employment Rights Act 1996)".

(6) The amendments made by this section have effect in relation to shares acquired in consideration of an employee shareholder agreement entered into on or after the relevant day.

(7) The relevant day is 1 December 2016, subject to subsection (8).

(8) Where the individual entering into an employee shareholder agreement receives the advice referred to in section 205A(6)(a) of the Employment Rights Act 1996—

(a) on 23 November 2016, but
(b) before 1.30 pm on that day,

the relevant day is 2 December 2016.

GENERAL NOTE

Section 13 amends various provisions in TCGA 1992 to abolish ESS relief (see background note to s 12 above) from capital gains tax.

14 Employee shareholder shares: purchase by company

(1) In ITTOIA 2005, omit section 385A (no charge to income tax on purchase by company of exempt employee shareholder shares).

(2) The amendment made by this section has effect in relation to the purchase from an individual of shares which were acquired in consideration of an employee shareholder agreement entered into on or after the relevant day.

(3) The relevant day is 1 December 2016, subject to subsection (4).

(4) Where the individual entering into an employee shareholder agreement receives the advice referred to in section 205A(6)(a) of the Employment Rights Act 1996—

(a) on 23 November 2016, but

(b) before 1.30 pm on that day,

the relevant day is 2 December 2016.

GENERAL NOTE

There was a further relief to ensure that where shares benefitting from ESS relief (see background note to s 12 above) were repurchased and cancelled, relief was provided from the legislation imposing an income tax charge by way of treating amounts received as a form of company distribution. Section 14 abolishes that relief.

Disguised remuneration

15 Employment income provided through third parties

Schedule 6 makes provision about employment income provided through third parties.

GENERAL NOTE

This section introduces Schedule 6.

Indirect taxes

16 VAT: zero-rating of adapted motor vehicles etc

Schedule 7 contains amendments of Schedule 8 to VATA 1994 (zero-rating).

GENERAL NOTE

This section introduces Schedule 7.

17 Insurance premium tax: standard rate

(1) In section 51(2)(b) of FA 1994 (standard rate of insurance premium tax), for "10 per cent" substitute "12 per cent".

(2) Subject to subsection (3), the amendment made by subsection (1) has effect in relation to a premium falling to be regarded for the purposes of Part 3 of FA 1994 as received under a taxable insurance contract by an insurer on or after 1 June 2017.

(3) That amendment does not have effect in relation to a premium falling within subsection (4), unless the premium falls to be regarded for the purposes of Part 3 of FA 1994 as received under a taxable insurance contract by an insurer on or after 1 June 2018.

(4) A premium falls within this subsection if it is in respect of a risk for which the period of cover begins before 1 June 2017.

(5) In the application of sections 66A and 66B of FA 1994 (anti-forestalling provision) in relation to the increase in insurance premium tax made by this section, the announcement relating to that increase is to be taken to have been made on 8 March 2017 (and "the change date" is to be taken to be 1 June 2017).

(6) This section is to be read with section 66C of FA 1994 (premiums relating to more than one period of cover).

GENERAL NOTE

Section 17 increases the standard rate of insurance premium tax (IPT) from 10% to 12% with effect from 1 June 2017.

The new rate applies to insurance premiums which fall to be received by insurers under taxable insurance contracts on or after 1 June 2017. A concessionary transitional period of 12 months applies between 1 June 2017 and 31 May 2018. Where premiums in respect of a period of cover incepted before 1 June 2017 are received, or are treated as being so received for the purposes of the special accounting scheme between 1 June 2017 and 31 May 2018, the applicable rate is 10%. Premiums received, or treated as being so received for the purposes of the special accounting scheme, after 1 June 2018 will be subject to the 12% rate of IPT notwithstanding the policy inception date.

The IPT applied to premium refunds will be at the rate originally applied.

Anti-forestalling tax avoidance measures apply to certain premiums received or written during the period 8 March 2017 to 31 May 2017 resulting in the rate of 12% being applied.

18 Insurance premium tax: anti-forestalling provision

(1) FA 1994 is amended as follows.

(2) After section 66 insert—

"66A Rate increases: deemed date of receipt of certain premiums

(1) This section applies where a Minister of the Crown announces a proposed increase in the rate at which tax is to be charged on a premium if it is received by the insurer on or after a date specified in the announcement ("the change date").

(2) This section applies whether or not the announcement includes an announcement of a proposed exception from the increase (for example, for premiums in respect of risks for which the period of cover begins before the change date).

(3) Subsection (4) applies where—

(a) a premium under a contract of insurance is received by the insurer on or after the date of the announcement and before the change date, and

(b) the period of cover for the risk begins on or after the change date.

(4) For the purposes of this Part the premium is to be taken to be received on the change date.

(5) Subsection (6) applies where—

(a) a premium under a contract of insurance is received by the insurer on or after the date of the announcement and before the change date,

(b) the period of cover for the risk—

(i) begins before the change date, and

(ii) ends on or after the first anniversary of the change date ("the first anniversary"), and

(c) the premium, or any part of it, is attributable to such of the period of cover as falls on or after the first anniversary.

(6) For the purposes of this Part—

(a) so much of the premium as is attributable to such of the period of cover as falls on or after the first anniversary is to be taken to be received on the change date, and

(b) so much as is so attributable is to be taken to be a separate premium.

(7) In determining whether the condition in subsection (3)(a) or (5)(a) is met, regulations under section 68(3) or (7) apply as they would apart from this section.

(8) But where subsection (4) or (6) applies—

(a) that subsection has effect despite anything in section 68 or regulations under that section, and

(b) any regulations under section 68 have effect as if the entry made in the accounts of the insurer showing the premium as due to the insurer had been made as at the change date.

(9) A premium treated by subsection (6) as received on the change date is not to be taken to fall within any exception, from an increase announced by the announcement, for premiums in respect of risks for which the period of cover begins before the change date.

(10) Any attribution under this section is to be made on such basis as is just and reasonable.

(11) In this section—

"increase", in relation to the rate of tax, includes the imposition of a charge to tax by adding to the descriptions of contract which are taxable insurance contracts;

"Minister of the Crown" has the same meaning as in the Ministers of the Crown Act 1975.

66B Section 66A: exceptions and apportionments

(1) Section 66A(3) and (4) do not apply in relation to a premium if the risk to which that premium relates belongs to a class of risk as regards which the normal practice is for a premium to be received by or on behalf of the insurer before the date when cover begins.

(2) Section 66A(5) and (6) do not apply in relation to a premium if the risk to which that premium relates belongs to a class of risk as regards which the normal practice is for cover to be provided for a period of more than twelve months.

(3) If a contract relates to more than one risk, then in the application of section 66A(3) and (4) or 66A(5) and (6)—

(a) the reference in section 66A(3)(b) or (5)(b) to the risk is to be read as a reference to any given risk,

(b) so much of the premium as is attributable to any given risk is to be taken for the purposes of section 66A(3) and (4) or 66A(5) and (6) to be a separate premium relating to that risk,

(c) those provisions then apply separately in the case of each given risk and the separate premium relating to it, and

(d) any further attribution required by section 66A(5) and (6) is to be made accordingly,

and subsections (1) and (2) and section 66A(9) apply accordingly.

(4) Any attribution under this section is to be made on such basis as is just and reasonable.

66C   Rate changes: premiums relating to more than one period of cover

(1) This section applies if any Act—

(a) makes an amendment of section 51(2)(a) or (b) which alters the higher rate or standard rate ("the relevant rate"),

(b) provides for the amendment to have effect in relation to a premium falling to be regarded for the purposes of this Part as received under a taxable insurance contract by an insurer on or after a particular date ("the change date"), and

(c) makes provision that excepts from that amendment a premium which is in respect of a risk for which the period of cover begins before the change date.

(2) Subsection (3) applies if a premium which is liable to tax at the relevant rate, and which falls to be regarded for the purposes of this Part as received under a taxable insurance contract by an insurer on or after the change date, is—

(a) partly in respect of a risk for which the period of cover begins before the change date, and

(b) partly in respect of a risk for which the period of cover begins on or after that date.

(3) So much of the premium as is attributable to the risk for which the period of cover begins on or after the change date is to be treated for the purposes of this Part and the provision mentioned in subsection (1)(c) as a separate premium.

(4) Where a premium is in respect of a relevant rate matter and also a matter that is not a relevant rate matter—

(a) for the purposes of the provision mentioned in subsection (1)(c), the premium is to be treated as in respect of a risk for which the period of cover begins before the change date if the part of it attributable to the relevant rate matter is in respect of such a risk, and

(b) the reference in subsection (2) to a premium which is liable to tax at the relevant rate is to be read as a reference to so much of the premium as is attributable to the relevant rate matter (and subsection (3) is to be read accordingly).

(5) If premiums of any description are excluded from the exception mentioned in subsection (1)(c), nothing in subsections (2) to (4) applies to a premium of that description.

(6) Nothing in subsection (4) applies to an excepted premium (within the meaning given by section 69A).

(7) Any attribution under this section is to be made on such basis as is just and reasonable.

(8) In this section a "relevant rate matter" means—

(a) where the relevant rate is the standard rate, a standard rate matter as defined by section 69(12)(c);

(b) where the relevant rate is the higher rate, a higher rate matter as defined by section 69(12)(d).

(9) In subsection (1) the reference to any Act includes a resolution which has statutory effect under the Provisional Collection of Taxes Act 1968."

(3) Omit—

(a) section 67 (spent transitional provision), and

(b) sections 67A to 67C (which are superseded by sections 66A and 66B inserted by subsection (2)).

(4) The amendments made by subsections (2) and (3)(b) have effect on and after 8 March 2017.

(5) Despite the repeal by subsection (3) of sections 67A and 67C of FA 1994, those sections continue to have effect so far as they apply to premiums received on or after 23 November 2016 and before 8 March 2017.

GENERAL NOTE

Section 18 inserts new ss 66A to 66C into FA 1994. It provides that the new rate of IPT will apply to certain premiums received, or treated to have been received, after the date that a Minister of the Crown first announces the proposed increase in IPT.

Where a premium is received (or is treated as so received under the special accounting scheme) on or after the announcement date, but before the change date, and relates to a risk where the period of cover begins on or after the change date, then the premium is treated as being received on the change date unless it is normal practice, for the class of risk concerned, for the premium to be received before inception of the period of cover.

Where a premium is received (or is treated as so received under the special accounting scheme) on or after the announcement date, but before the change date, and relates to a risk where the period of cover begins before the change date and ends after the first anniversary of the change date, then so much of the premium as is attributable (on a just and reasonable basis) to cover after the first anniversary of the change date is treated as a separate premium received on the change date. This applies unless it is normal practice, for the class of risk concerned, for the premium to be received before inception of the period of cover.

If a premium relates to more than one risk, then the various risks are treated separately under the above provisions as apportioned on a just and reasonable basis.

New s 66C puts in place similar provisions where the above scenarios apply to a future change in the rate of IPT.

19 Air passenger duty: rates from 1 April 2017

(1) In section 30 of FA 1994 (air passenger duty: rates of duty), in subsection (4A) (long haul rates of duty)—

(a) in paragraph (a), for "£73" substitute "£75";
(b) in paragraph (b), for "£146" substitute "£150".

(2) The amendments made by this section have effect in relation to the carriage of passengers beginning on or after 1 April 2017.

GENERAL NOTE

The standard and reduced rates of Air Passenger Duty (APD) on flights in Band B increased from £146 to £150 and from £73 to £75 respectively on 1 April 2017. The new rate applies to the carriage of passengers beginning on or after 1 April 2017.

The rates of APD on Band A journeys remain unchanged.

Note: Band B journeys are journeys where the destination is in a country or territory, the capital city of which is more than 2,000 miles away from London.

20 Vehicle excise duty: rates

(1) Schedule 1 to VERA 1994 (annual rates of duty) is amended as follows.

(2) In paragraph 1 (general rate of duty)—

(a) in sub-paragraph (2) (vehicle not covered elsewhere in Schedule with engine cylinder capacity exceeding 1,549cc), for "£235" substitute "£245", and
(b) in sub-paragraph (2A) (vehicle not covered elsewhere in Schedule with engine cylinder capacity not exceeding 1,549cc), for "£145" substitute "£150".

(3) In paragraph 1B (graduated rates of duty for light passenger vehicles)—

(a) in the words before paragraph (a), for "tables" substitute "table",
(b) in paragraph (a), at the end insert "and",

(c) in paragraph (b), at the end omit ", and",
(d) omit paragraph (c),
(e) for Tables 1 and 2 substitute—

"CO_2 emissions figure		Rate	
(1)	*(2)*	*(3)*	*(4)*
Exceeding	*Not exceeding*	*Reduced rate*	*Standard rate*
g/km	*g/km*	£	£
100	110	10	20
110	120	20	30
120	130	105	115
130	140	125	135
140	150	140	150
150	165	180	190
165	175	210	220
175	185	230	240
185	200	270	280
200	225	295	305
225	255	510	520
255	—	525	535"

(f) in the sentence immediately following Table 2—
(i) at the beginning, for "Table 2" substitute "The table", and
(ii) for paragraphs (a) and (b) substitute—
"(a) in column (3), in the last two rows, "295" were substituted for "510" and "525", and
(b) in column (4), in the last two rows, "305" were substituted for "520" and "535"."

(4) In paragraph 1J (VED rates for light goods vehicles), in paragraph (a), for "£230" substitute "£240".

(5) In paragraph 2(1) (VED rates for motorcycles)—
(a) in paragraph (a), for "£17" substitute "£18",
(b) in paragraph (b), for "£39" substitute "£41",
(c) in paragraph (c), for "£60" substitute "£62", and
(d) in paragraph (d), for "£82" substitute "£85".

(6) The amendments made by this section have effect in relation to licences taken out on or after 1 April 2017.

GENERAL NOTE

Section 20 amends the Vehicle Excise and Registration Act 1994 (VERA) to increase the rates of vehicle excise duty (VED) for cars, vans and motorcycles registered before 1 April 2017. The new rates apply from 1 April 2017. (**Note:** New cars registered after 1 April 2017 will be under a different VED scheme.)

21 Alcoholic liquor duties: rates

(1) ALDA 1979 is amended as follows.

(2) In section 5 (rate of duty on spirits), for "£27.66" substitute "£28.74".

(3) In section 36(1AA) (rates of general beer duty)—
(a) in paragraph (za) (rate of duty on lower strength beer), for "£8.10" substitute "£8.42", and
(b) in paragraph (a) (standard rate of duty on beer), for "£18.37" substitute "£19.08".

(4) In section 37(4) (rate of high strength beer duty), for "£5.48" substitute "£5.69".

(5) In section 62(1A) (rates of duty on cider)—
(a) in paragraph (a) (rate of duty per hectolitre on sparkling cider of a strength exceeding 5.5%), for "£268.99" substitute "£279.46",
(b) in paragraph (b) (rate of duty per hectolitre on cider of a strength exceeding 7.5% which is not sparkling cider), for "£58.75" substitute "£61.04", and

(c) in paragraph (c) (rate of duty per hectolitre in any other case), for "£38.87" substitute "£40.38".

(6) For the table in Schedule 1 substitute—

"TABLE OF RATES OF DUTY ON WINE AND MADE-WINE

PART 1
WINE OR MADE-WINE OF A STRENGTH NOT EXCEEDING 22%

Description of wine or made-wine	Rates of duty per hectolitre £
Wine or made-wine of a strength not exceeding 4%	88.93
Wine or made-wine of a strength exceeding 4% but not exceeding 5.5%	122.30
Wine or made-wine of a strength exceeding 5.5% but not exceeding 15% and not being sparkling	288.65
Sparkling wine or sparkling made-wine of a strength exceeding 5.5% but less than 8.5%	279.46
Sparkling wine or sparkling made-wine of a strength of 8.5% or of a strength exceeding 8.5% but not exceeding 15%	369.72
Wine or made-wine of a strength exceeding 15% but not exceeding 22%	384.82

PART 2
WINE OR MADE-WINE OF A STRENGTH EXCEEDING 22%

Description of wine or made-wine	Rates of duty per litre of alcohol in wine or made-wine £
Wine or made-wine of a strength exceeding 22%	28.74"

(7) The amendments made by this section are treated as having come into force on 13 March 2017.

GENERAL NOTE

Section 21 increases the rates of duty charged under the Alcoholic Liquor Duties Act 1979 (ALDA) on spirits, beer, wine and made-wine, and cider and perry. The amendments made by this section are to be treated as coming into force on 13 March 2017.

22 Tobacco products duty: rates

(1) TPDA 1979 is amended as follows.

(2) For the table in Schedule 1 substitute—

"TABLE

1. Cigarettes	An amount equal to 16.5% of the retail price plus £207.99 per thousand cigarettes.
2. Cigars	£259.44 per kilogram
3. Hand-rolling tobacco	£209.77 per kilogram

4. Other smoking tobacco and chewing tobacco	£114.06 per kilogram"

(3) The amendment made by this section is treated as having come into force at 6pm on 8 March 2017.

GENERAL NOTE

Section 22 amends the Tobacco Products Duty Act 1979 (TPDA) to increase the rates of duty on tobacco and tobacco products (cigarettes, cigars, hand-rolling tobacco, other smoking tobacco and chewing tobacco). The amendments made by this section are to be treated as coming into force at 6pm on 8 March 2017.

23 Tobacco products duty: minimum excise duty
(1) TPDA 1979 is amended as follows.
(2) In section 6(5)(a) (alteration of rates of duty), for "the amount" substitute "each amount".
(3) For the first row in the table in Schedule 1 (as substituted by section 22) substitute—

"1 Cigarettes	An amount equal to the higher of— (a)16.5% of the retail price plus £207.99 per thousand cigarettes, or (b)£268.63 per thousand cigarettes."

(4) The amendments made by this section are treated as having come into force on 20 May 2017.

GENERAL NOTE

Section 23 amends the TPDA to introduce a minimum excise tax (MET) with effect from 20 May 2017. The MET sets a minimum level of duty for cigarettes. In other words, the duty payable is the higher of the usual duty rates or the MET. The MET rate is set at £268.63 per 1,000 cigarettes.

Avoidance

24 Promoters of tax avoidance schemes: threshold conditions etc
(1) In Part 2 of Schedule 34 to FA 2014 (meeting the threshold conditions: bodies corporate and partnerships), in paragraph 13A (interpretation), for sub-paragraphs (6) to (8) substitute—

"(6) Two or more persons together control a body corporate if together they have the power to secure that the affairs of the body corporate are conducted in accordance with their wishes in any way specified in sub-paragraph (5)(a) to (c).

(7) A person controls a partnership if the person is a member of the partnership and—

(a) has the right to a share of more than half the assets, or more than half the income, of the partnership, or
(b) directs, or is on a day-to-day level in control of, the management of the business of the partnership.

(8) Two or more persons together control a partnership if they are members of the partnership and together they—

(a) have the right to a share of more than half the assets, or of more than half the income, of the partnership, or
(b) direct, or are on a day-to-day level in control of, the management of the business of the partnership.

(9) Paragraph 19(2) to (5) of Schedule 36 (connected persons etc) applies to a person referred to in sub-paragraph (7) or (8) as if references to "P" were to that person.

(10) A person has significant influence over a body corporate or partnership if the person—

(a) does not control the body corporate or partnership, but

(b) is able to, or actually does, exercise significant influence over it (whether or not as the result of a legal entitlement).

(11) Two or more persons together have significant influence over a body corporate or partnership if together those persons—

(a) do not control the body corporate or partnership, but

(b) are able to, or actually do, exercise significant influence over it (whether or not as the result of a legal entitlement).

(12) References to a person being a promoter are to the person carrying on business as a promoter."

(2) In Part 2 of Schedule 34 to FA 2014, for paragraphs 13B to 13D substitute—

"Relevant bodies controlled etc by other persons treated as meeting a threshold condition

13B (1) A relevant body is treated as meeting a threshold condition at the relevant time if any of Conditions A to C is met.

(2) Condition A is that—

(a) a person met the threshold condition at a time when the person was a promoter, and

(b) the person controls or has significant influence over the relevant body at the relevant time.

(3) Condition B is that—

(a) a person met the threshold condition at a time when the person controlled or had significant influence over the relevant body,

(b) the relevant body was a promoter at that time, and

(c) the person controls or has significant influence over the relevant body at the relevant time.

(4) Condition C is that—

(a) two or more persons together controlled or had significant influence over the relevant body at a time when one of those persons met the threshold condition,

(b) the relevant body was a promoter at that time, and

(c) those persons together control or have significant influence over the relevant body at the relevant time.

(5) Where the person referred to in sub-paragraph (2)(a) or (3)(a) or (4)(a) as meeting a threshold condition is an individual, sub-paragraph (1) only applies if the threshold condition is a relevant threshold condition.

(6) For the purposes of sub-paragraph (2) it does not matter whether the relevant body existed at the time referred to in sub-paragraph (2)(a).

Persons who control etc a relevant body treated as meeting a threshold condition

13C (1) If at a time when a person controlled or had significant influence over a relevant body—

(a) the relevant body met a threshold condition, and

(b) the relevant body, or another relevant body which the person controlled or had significant influence over, was a promoter,

the person is treated as meeting the threshold condition at the relevant time.

(2) It does not matter whether any relevant body referred to sub-paragraph (1) exists at the relevant time.

Relevant bodies controlled etc by the same person treated as meeting a threshold condition

13D (1) If—

(a) a person controlled or had significant influence over a relevant body at a time when it met a threshold condition, and

(b) at that time that body, or another relevant body which the person controlled or had significant influence over, was a promoter,

any relevant body which the person controls or has significant influence over at the relevant time is treated as meeting the threshold condition at the relevant time.

(2) If—

(a) two or more persons together controlled or had significant influence over a relevant body at a time when it met a threshold condition, and

(b) at that time that body, or another relevant body which those persons together controlled or had significant influence over, was a promoter, any relevant body which those persons together control or have significant influence over at the relevant time is treated as meeting the threshold condition at the relevant time.

(3) It does not matter whether—

(a) a relevant body referred to in sub-paragraph (1)(a) or (b) or (2)(a) or (b) exists at the relevant time, or

(b) a relevant body existing at the relevant time existed at the time referred to in sub-paragraph (1)(a) or (2)(a)."

(3) In Part 4 of Schedule 34A to FA 2014 (meeting section 237A conditions: bodies corporate and partnerships), for paragraphs 20 to 22 substitute—

"*Relevant bodies controlled etc by other persons treated as meeting section 237A condition*

20 (1) A relevant body is treated as meeting a section 237A condition at the section 237A(2) relevant time if any of Conditions A to C is met.

(2) Condition A is that—

(a) a person met the section 237A condition at a time when the person was a promoter, and

(b) the person controls or has significant influence over the relevant body at the section 237A(2) relevant time.

(3) Condition B is that—

(a) a person met the section 237A condition at a time when the person controlled or had significant influence over the relevant body,

(b) the relevant body was a promoter at that time, and

(c) the person controls or has significant influence over the relevant body at the section 237A(2) relevant time.

(4) Condition C is that—

(a) two or more persons together controlled or had significant influence over the relevant body at a time when one of those persons met the section 237A condition,

(b) the relevant body was a promoter at that time, and

(c) those persons together control or have significant influence over the relevant body at the section 237A(2) relevant time.

(5) Sub-paragraph (1) does not apply where the person referred to in sub-paragraph (2)(a), (3)(a), or (4)(a) as meeting a section 237A condition is an individual.

(6) For the purposes of sub-paragraph (2) it does not matter whether the relevant body existed at the time referred to in sub-paragraph (2)(a).

Persons who control etc a relevant body treated as meeting a section 237A condition

21 (1) If at a time when a person controlled or had significant influence over a relevant body—

(a) the relevant body met a section 237A condition, and

(b) the relevant body, or another relevant body which the person controlled or had significant influence over, was a promoter,

the person is treated as meeting the section 237A condition at the section 237A(2) relevant time.

(2) It does not matter whether any relevant body referred to sub-paragraph (1) exists at the section 237A(2) relevant time.

Relevant bodies controlled etc by the same person treated as meeting a section 237A condition

22 (1) If—

(a) a person controlled or had significant influence over a relevant body at a time when it met a section 237A condition, and

(b) at that time that body, or another relevant body which the person controlled or had significant influence over, was a promoter,

any relevant body which the person controls or has significant influence over at the section 237A(2) relevant time is treated as meeting the section 237A condition at the section 237A(2) relevant time.

(2) If—

(a) two or more persons together controlled or had significant influence over a relevant body at a time when it met a section 237A condition, and

(b) at that time that body, or another relevant body which those persons together controlled or had significant influence over, was a promoter, any relevant body which those persons together control or have significant influence over at the section 237A(2) relevant time is treated as meeting the section 237A condition at the section 237A(2) relevant time.

(3) It does not matter whether—

 (a) a relevant body referred to in sub-paragraph (1)(a) or (b) or (2)(a) or (b) exists at the section 237A(2) relevant time, or

 (b) a relevant body existing at the section 237A(2) relevant time existed at the time referred to in sub-paragraph (1)(a) or (2)(a)."

(4) In Part 4 of Schedule 34A to FA 2014, in paragraph 23 (interpretation)—

 (a) in sub-paragraph (1), for the definition of "control" substitute—
""control" and "significant influence" have the same meanings as in Part 4 of Schedule 34 (see paragraph 13A(5) to (11));
references to a person being a promoter are to the person carrying on business as a promoter;";

 (b) in sub-paragraph (2), for "20(1)(a), 21(1)(a) and 22(1)(a)" substitute "20 to 22".

(5) The amendments made by subsections (1) and (2) have effect for the purposes of determining whether a person meets a threshold condition in a period of three years ending on or after 8 March 2017.

(6) The amendments made by subsections (3) and (4) have effect for the purposes of determining whether a person meets a section 237A condition in a period of three years ending on or after 8 March 2017.

GENERAL NOTE

Part 5 (ss 234–283) FA 2014 introduced the Promoters of Tax Avoidance Scheme ("POTAS") legislation. It has been updated in each subsequent Finance Act.

The legislation targets promoters of tax avoidance schemes regarded as higher risk due to their failure to comply with duties under the disclosure of tax avoidance schemes ("DOTAS") regime introduced by FA 2004. Finance Act 2015 s 119 refers to Sch 19, which contains provisions amending FA 2014 Pt 5 in relation to the threshold conditions.

The legislation as introduced provided for a graduated series of sanctions against promoters:

– A conduct notice, which following a decision of an authorised officer may be issued by HMRC where one of the threshold conditions is met; and

– A monitoring notice which HMRC can issue following First-tier Tribunal approval where a promoter breaches a requirement in a conduct notice.

The thresholds conditions include where the promoter:

– is the subject of publication as a deliberate tax defaulter;

– is named in a report for a breach of the Code of Practice on Taxation for Banks;

– receives a conduct notice as a dishonest tax agent;

– failed either to disclose a tax avoidance scheme or to provide details of clients to HMRC;

– has been charged with a specified tax offence;

– has been found guilty of misconduct by a professional body;

– failed to comply with an information notice issued by HMRC;

– requires confidentiality;

– requires a contribution to a fighting fund;

– continues to market or make available a tax avoidance scheme after being given a notice to stop following a judicial ruling.

Finance Act 2016 s 160 introduced a further threshold condition, which, if met, identifies a person who is a promoter of tax avoidance schemes as a promoter to whom a provisional conduct notice, or where there are three defeats within three years, a conduct notice, may be given.

Broadly, a provisional conduct notice is for promoters of tax avoidance schemes which have fewer than three defeated schemes and further schemes are subject to challenge and those challenges are at least 75% defeated. Where a successful challenge results in a defeat a defeat notice is issued and a provisional conduct notice may become a full conduct notice. A full conduct notice may also be issued in circumstances where a provisional conduct notice is not complied with. Where a conduct notice is not complied with, a monitoring notice may be issued.

There is no right of appeal against a decision to give a promoter a conduct notice, which can last for up to two years. Conduct notices impose conditions about how a promoter must behave. Where a conduct notice has been issued, it opens the gateway for the further sanction of a monitoring notice, subject to the promoter's behavior. A provisional conduct notice does not itself open the gateway to enable the issue of a monitoring notice.

If a monitoring notice is issued the monitored promoter is subject to:

- publication by HMRC of information about the promoter;
- publication by the promoter of its status on the internet, in publications and correspondence;
- a duty on the promoter to inform clients it is a monitored promoter and to provide them with a promoter reference number (PRN);
- a duty on clients to put the PRN on their returns or otherwise to report the PRN to HMRC;
- enhanced information powers for HMRC supported with new penalties;
- preventing the promoter to impose confidentiality on clients in relation to disclosure to HMRC;
- limitations to the defences of reasonable care and reasonable excuse against the imposition of penalties;
- extended time limits for assessment on clients who fail to report a PRN to HMRC;
- a criminal offence of concealing, destroying or disposing of documents.

There is a right of appeal against a decision of the First-tier Tribunal to approve the issue of a monitoring notice.

Finance Act 2017, s 24 makes further amendments to ensure HMRC "can issue conduct notices as intended by the POTAS regime in specified situations where a person has, or persons together have, control or significant influence over a relevant body" (Explanatory Notes to Finance (No 2) Bill). The fact that the amendments are introduced in the fifth Finance Act since the introduction of the regime might suggest that those responsible for writing the legislation did not understand the way in which some promoters operate. The amendments, which seek to determine whether a person should be treated as meeting a threshold condition, have effect from 8 March 2017.

Section 24(1) replaces FA 2014 Sch 34 Pt 2 para 13A(6)–(8) with new sub-paras (6)–(12). The new subparagraphs define:

- when a person(s) has control:
  - over a body corporate (sub-para (6));
  - over a partnership (sub-paras (7) to (9)); and
- when a person has significant influence over a body corporate or partnership.

The definition of "control" over a body corporate is wide and defines the power to secure how the affairs are conducted in accordance with their wishes in any way:

- by means of the holding of shares or the possession of voting power;
- as a result of any powers conferred by the articles of association or other document regulating the body corporate or any other relevant body, or
- by means of controlling a partnership.

The definition of "control" over a partnership requires a person (or two or more persons) to be a member of the partnership and either:

- have the right to more than half the assets or income; or
- directs or is in control of the management.

Connected persons as defined within FA 2014 Sch 36 para 19(2)–(5) applies to a person referred to in sub-paras (7) or (8) as if references to "P" were to that person. The definition of connected persons for these purposes is wide and includes relatives, relatives of a spouse or civil partner as well as other entities controlled by P.

Subparagraphs (10) and (11) define when a person (or two or more persons) has significant influence over a body corporate or partnership and covers the situation where a person does not control although is able to or does exercise significant influence. It does not matter whether the significant influence is as a result of legal entitlement. Whether there is influence or "significant" influence is likely to be a contentious issue. It is envisaged that the definition could cover situations where a person's business, income or profitability would be significantly compromised if it were not for the other person, that person therefore would have influence and arguably significant influence.

Subparagraph (12) defines promoter as "the person carrying on business as a promoter" for the purposes of paragraph 13A. Section 235 FA 2014 provides a definition of a person carrying on business as a promoter and broadly includes those responsible for the design of proposed arrangements, those who make a firm approach to make the proposal available for implementation or makes the proposal available for implementation by others. The definition includes those *to any extent* involved in the design, organisation and management of the proposed arrangements.

Section 24(2) replaces FA 2014 Sch 34 Pt 2 paras 13B to 13D incorporating the changes brought about by the new sub-paras (6)–(11) (see above). Paragraphs 13B to 13D provide details of when a threshold condition is met for a relevant body controlled by other persons (13B), persons who control a relevant body (13C) and a relevant body controlled by the same person who meets a threshold condition. The main amendments to the conditions are to extend their meaning to include those who have significant influence over the relevant body and to provide that it does not matter that the relevant body did not exist at the relevant time (at any time an officer becomes aware the person is carrying on business as a promoter – FA 2014 s 237A(1)).

Section 24(3) replaces FA 2014 Sch 34A Pt 4 paras 20–22 incorporating the changes brought about by the new sub-paras (6)–(11) (see above). Paragraphs 20 to 22 set out the circumstances in which a relevant body or a person (other than an individual) can be treated as meeting any of the conditions in FA 2014 s 237A(11)–(13). Broadly, the conditions are that:

- in the period of three years ending with the relevant time at least three relevant defeats have occurred;
- at least two relevant defeats have occurred at times when a single defeat notice under s 241A(2) or (6) FA 2014 had effect;
- at least one relevant defeat has occurred at a time when a double defeat notice under s 241A(3) had effect.

The new paras 20–22 provide that the conditions in FA 2014 s 237A are met by:

- a relevant body by virtue of a person (or persons) who has control or significant influence;
- a person, other than an individual, by virtue of a relevant body which that person has control or significant influence over;
- a relevant body by virtue of another relevant body meeting a condition. The other relevant body must have been controlled or significantly influenced at an earlier time by the same person or persons who now control or significantly influence the relevant body.

PART 2

SOFT DRINKS INDUSTRY LEVY

Introductory

25 Soft drinks industry levy

(1) A tax called "soft drinks industry levy" is to be charged in accordance with this Part.

(2) The Commissioners are responsible for the collection and management of soft drinks industry levy.

GENERAL NOTE

Section 25 introduces a new levy on the production and import of soft drinks with added sugar content. The government's stated purpose behind the legislation is to tackle childhood obesity on the basis of evidence that soft drinks are one of the biggest sources of sugar in children's diets. The new levy is meant to encourage soft drinks producers to reduce added sugar content in their drinks.

The levy was announced in the 2016 Spring Budget and is due to come into effect on 6 April 2018, with the delay being built in in order to offer the soft drinks industry some time to adjust. At the second reading of the Finance Bill in the House of Commons in April 2017, the Financial Secretary stated that a number of major producers had already accelerated their work to reformulate some of the added sugar content out of their soft drinks and escape the "game-changing soft drinks industry levy".

26 "Soft drink" and "package"

(1) "Soft drink" means—

    (a) a beverage of an alcoholic strength not exceeding 1.2%;

(b) a liquid which, when prepared in a specified manner, constitutes a beverage within paragraph (a).

(2) A liquid is prepared in a specified manner if it is—

(a) diluted with water,

(b) combined with crushed ice, or processed so as to create crushed ice,

(c) combined with carbon dioxide, or

(d) prepared by way of a process that involves any combination of the processes mentioned in paragraphs (a) to (c).

(3) A person "packages" a soft drink if the person cans, bottles or otherwise packages the soft drink in a form in which—

(a) in the case of a soft drink within subsection (1)(a), it is suitable to be consumed without further preparation, and

(b) in the case of a soft drink within subsection (1)(b), it is suitable to be consumed when prepared in a specified manner (and without any other preparation),

and "packaged" is to be construed accordingly.

GENERAL NOTE

Section 26 provides the meaning of "soft drink". A "soft drink" means a beverage not exceeding 1.2% ABV. According to the government's summary of responses to consultation on the soft drinks industry levy (the "Summary of Responses"), this alcoholic strength limit has been adopted to align with current labelling regulations as it would be disproportionate to introduce additional labelling requirements to restrict this to alcoholic drinks that can be consumed by under 18s (where the limit is currently 0.5%). Section 26 also brings dilutables and cordials within the scope of the definition.

The section further goes on to define who is regarded as packaging a soft drink, which is relevant to the question of who is liable to account for the levy when a soft drink is packaged in the UK. This means that it may not be the legal owner of the drink that is liable for the levy.

27 Meaning of "prepared drink"

(1) In this Part a reference to "prepared drink" is a reference to—

(a) a soft drink within subsection (1)(a) of section 26;

(b) a beverage that would result from preparing a liquid within subsection (1)(b) of that section—

(i) in a specified manner (see section 26(2)), and

(ii) in accordance with the relevant dilution ratio.

(2) The "relevant dilution ratio" means—

(a) the dilution ratio stated on, or calculated by reference to information stated on, the packaging of the soft drink;

(b) where subsection (3) or (4) applies, the dilution ratio determined by the Commissioners.

(3) This subsection applies where the packaging of the soft drink states neither the dilution ratio nor information by reference to which the dilution ratio can be calculated.

(4) This subsection applies where—

(a) the dilution ratio, or information by reference to which the dilution ratio can be calculated, is stated on the packaging of the soft drink, and

(b) it is reasonable to assume that the main purpose, or one of the main purposes, of stating that particular dilution ratio or information is avoiding or reducing liability for soft drinks industry levy.

(5) The Commissioners may by or under regulations make provision about the criteria for—

(a) determining a dilution ratio for the purposes of subsection (2)(b);

(b) determining whether the main purpose, or one of the main purposes, of stating a particular dilution ratio or information is avoiding or reducing liability for soft drinks industry levy.

GENERAL NOTE

Section 27 defines "prepared drink". A "prepared drink" means a soft drink, either in its own right or once it has been prepared in a specified manner in accordance with the dilution ratio set out on the packaging. HMRC are given powers to determine the relevant dilution ratio where no information is available on the packaging or otherwise. HMRC can also make a determination as to the relevant dilution ratio if the stated dilution ratio fails a "main purpose" levy avoidance test. This is to combat concerns that cordials and dilutables are to some extent a matter of taste, but that manufacturers could simply change the ratio on the packaging in order to reduce liability to the levy.

Chargeable soft drinks

28 Meaning of "chargeable soft drink"

"Chargeable soft drink" means a packaged soft drink that—
- (a) meets the sugar content condition (see section 29), and
- (b) is not an exempt soft drink (see section 30).

GENERAL NOTE

Section 28 defines a "chargeable soft drink", which broadly means a packaged soft drink with specified levels of added sugar content that is not one of certain categories of exempt soft drink.

29 Sugar content condition

(1) A packaged soft drink meets the sugar content condition if it contains—
- (a) added sugar ingredients, and
- (b) at least 5 grams of sugars (whether or not as a result of containing added sugar ingredients) per 100 millilitres of prepared drink.

(2) A packaged soft drink contains "added sugar ingredients" if any of the following are combined with other ingredients at any stage in the production of the soft drink—
- (a) calorific mono-saccharides or di-saccharides;
- (b) a substance containing calorific mono-saccharides or di-saccharides.

(3) But a packaged soft drink does not contain "added sugar ingredients" only by reason of containing fruit juice, vegetable juice or milk (or any combination of them).

(4) The Commissioners may by regulations make provision about what is, or is not, to be treated for the purposes of this Part as fruit juice, vegetable juice or milk.

(5) Where regulations under subsection (4) contain a reference to an EU instrument or any provision of an EU instrument, the regulations may provide that the reference is to be construed as a reference to that instrument or that provision as amended from time to time.

GENERAL NOTE

Section 29(1) provides that only those packaged soft drinks that contain at least five grams of sugars per 100 millilitres of prepared drink, some of which is added sugar ingredients, will meet the sugar content condition. For these purposes, a drink contains "added sugar ingredients" if any calorific mono-saccharides or di-saccharides or a substance containing those molecules is combined with other ingredients at any stage in the process. The five grams refers to the total sugar content of the drink, not just the added sugar ingredients. Accordingly, certain types of high-sugar-content drink (such as fruit juice) may not fall within the scope of the levy if sugar has not been added during production.

Subsection (3) specifically excludes fruit juice, vegetable juice and milk from being considered an added sugar ingredient. On this basis, a drink whose sugar content is taken beyond the sugar content threshold only because it has fruit juice added to it would not fall within the scope of a chargeable soft drink. Further detail defining what constitutes fruit juice, vegetable juice and milk for these purposes will be contained in regulations to be made under subsection (4).

Subsection (5) contains a provision which is not that usual in recent UK statutes. It provides that, in regulations made pursuant to the section, references to EU instruments may be capable of being construed as references to those instruments as amended from time to time. This appears to be a substitute for part of para 1A Sch 2 to the European Communities Act 1972, which is of general application. It appears that this provision (and the other similar provisions in the legislation) is made in anticipation of the repeal of the European Communities Act 1972 once the UK leaves the European Union.

30 Exempt soft drinks

(1) The following are "exempt soft drinks"—

(a) milk-based drinks,
(b) milk substitute drinks,
(c) alcohol substitute drinks, and
(d) soft drinks of a specified description which are for use for medicinal or other specified purposes.

(2) "Milk-based drink" means a soft drink which contains at least 75 millilitres of milk per 100 millilitres of prepared drink.

(3) "Milk substitute drink" means a soft drink which—

(a) contains at least the specified quantities of calcium, and
(b) meets such other conditions as may be specified.

(4) "Alcohol substitute drink" means a soft drink which—

(a) is similar to a particular kind of alcoholic beverage, and
(b) meets such other conditions as may be specified.

(5) "Alcoholic beverage" means a beverage which is of an alcoholic strength exceeding 1.2%.

(6) The Commissioners may by regulations make further provision about the criteria for determining what is, or is not, to be treated as an exempt soft drink.

(7) Where regulations made under, or for the purposes of, this section contain a reference to an EU instrument or any provision of an EU instrument, the regulations may provide that the reference is to be construed as a reference to that instrument or that provision as amended from time to time.

GENERAL NOTE

Section 30 exempts a number of drinks from the soft drinks industry levy.

First, milk-based drinks containing at least 75 millilitres of milk per 100 millilitres of prepared drink are exempt. The reasoning behind the exclusion was the subject of some discussion during the consultation phase of the legislation, where the government noted that milk is a source of protein, potassium, phosphorous and iodine and, as such, milk forms a positive part of the government's policy on children's health. Milk and other dairy products feature on Public Health England's "Eat Well" plate of foods that should be consumed regularly. In light of this, the government stated in its Summary of Responses that the nutritional properties of milk justify a different approach in respect of milk-based drinks.

Second, milk substitute drinks containing at least the specified quantities of calcium are exempt on the basis that the government recognised that there should be parity of treatment of such drinks with dairy milk.

Third, s 30 exempts alcohol substitute drinks from the soft drinks industry levy. Such drinks are defined as soft drinks that are similar to particular kinds of beverages with alcoholic strengths exceeding 1.2% ABV. The government has made clear that this exemption is aimed at helping adults to make healthy choices and consume less alcohol by opting for low-alcohol substitutes (such as low-alcohol lager) with an ABV below 1.2%.

Finally, soft drinks used for medicinal or other specified purposes are also exempt from the levy. The government confirmed in the Summary of Responses that baby formulas and certain products used to treat dietary conditions will be out of scope of the levy. Further details will follow in regulations.

Charging of the soft drinks industry levy

31 Charge to soft drinks industry levy

(1) The charge to soft drinks industry levy arises on a chargeable event which occurs on or after 6 April 2018.

(2) Subsection (1) is subject to section 37 (small producer exemption).

GENERAL NOTE

Section 31 provides that the charge to the soft drinks industry levy will apply to chargeable events from 6 April 2018 onwards.

32 Chargeable events: soft drinks packaged in the UK

(1) This section applies where chargeable soft drinks are packaged by a person on premises in the United Kingdom (the "packaging premises").

(2) A chargeable event occurs on the removal of the chargeable soft drinks from the packaging premises.

(3) But—

(a) if, on removal from the packaging premises, the secondary warehousing condition is met in relation to the chargeable soft drinks, a chargeable event occurs at the time that the secondary warehousing condition ceases to be met in relation to those soft drinks (and not at the time mentioned in subsection (2));

(b) if the chargeable soft drinks are made available for sale or free of charge before a chargeable event in relation to the soft drinks occurs under subsection (2) or paragraph (a), a chargeable event occurs at the time the soft drinks are made available (and not at the time mentioned in subsection (2) or paragraph (a)).

(4) For the purposes of this section and section 33, the secondary warehousing condition is met, at any time, in relation to chargeable soft drinks if the chargeable soft drinks are, at that time—

(a) in storage in a compliant warehouse, or

(b) being transported—

(i) from the packaging premises to a compliant warehouse, or

(ii) between compliant warehouses,

in compliance with such conditions and requirements as may be imposed by regulations under section 34.

(5) References in this section and in section 33 to a "compliant warehouse" are references to premises—

(a) that are, or are to be, used for the storage of chargeable soft drinks, and

(b) in respect of which the conditions and requirements specified in regulations under section 34(a) are met.

GENERAL NOTE

There are broadly two separate heads of charge, which relate to soft drinks packaged in the UK and those that are imported into the UK. Section 32 deals with drinks that are packaged in the UK.

The charge is generally imposed at the packaging stage of the supply chain, rather than at the level of the consumer or retailer (other than in the case of some imports). The rationale for imposing the charge at this point in the supply chain is that the packager or bottler is best placed to know the precise volumes of liable products being produced, thus minimising additional administrative burdens in accounting for the levy correctly. The majority of added sugar drinks sold in the UK are produced domestically so this chargeable event will catch most of the soft drinks being consumed.

Section 32 applies to impose the levy on chargeable soft drinks that are packaged in the UK. The basic chargeable event is when a soft drink is removed from the packaging premises, but this can be delayed where the soft drink continues to be stored in a compliant warehouse or is being transported between the packager and the warehouse (or one warehouse and another), in which case the occasion of charge is deferred until the drinks leave the final warehouse in the chain. Further regulations will specify the conditions necessary for a warehouse to qualify as compliant for these purposes.

On the other hand, if the soft drink is made available for sale or given away for free before a chargeable event would otherwise arise, a chargeable event will arise at that point. The aim is to ensure that soft drinks that are produced but are wasted before entering circulation are not subject to the charge, but that drinks that are supplied before being packaged do not escape the levy.

33 Chargeable events: soft drinks imported into the UK

(1) This section applies where chargeable soft drinks are imported into the United Kingdom.

(2) A chargeable event occurs, in relation to imported chargeable soft drinks, on first receipt of the soft drinks by a relevant person (the "first recipient").

(3) But subsection (2) is subject to subsections (7) to (9).

(4) The "first receipt" of imported chargeable soft drinks is the first occasion on which the soft drinks are delivered to a place in the United Kingdom which is a relevant person's place of business (including where the chargeable soft drinks are delivered from a place outside the United Kingdom which is another place of business of the relevant person).

(5) "Relevant person" means a person who carries on a business involving the sale of chargeable soft drinks.

(6) The reference in subsection (5) to the sale of chargeable soft drinks includes a reference to—

    (a) sale by wholesale,
    (b) sale by retail, and
    (c) sale for consumption on or in the vicinity of premises on which the drinks are sold.

(7) Subsection (8) applies if, on first receipt of the imported chargeable soft drinks, the place of business to which the soft drinks are delivered is a compliant warehouse.

(8) Subject to subsection (9), a chargeable event occurs at the time that the secondary warehousing condition ceases to be met in relation to the imported chargeable soft drinks (and not at the time mentioned in subsection (2)).

(9) If the chargeable soft drinks are made available for sale or free of charge by a relevant person (the "first seller") before a chargeable event in relation to the soft drinks occurs under subsection (2) or (8), a chargeable event occurs at the time the chargeable soft drinks are made available (and not at the time mentioned in subsection (2) or (8)).

GENERAL NOTE

Section 33 deals with imported soft drinks. A chargeable event occurs when the soft drink is first received at a place of business in the UK of a person who carries on a business involving the sale of soft drinks (whether wholesale, retail or as part of a business of selling drinks for consumption (such as public houses)). There are similar provisions to those in s 32 which defer the chargeable event if the soft drinks are delivered to a compliant warehouse or which accelerate the chargeable event if they are made available for sale or given away at an earlier time. Because the levy only applies to packaged soft drinks, unpackaged soft drinks that are imported to the UK for packaging will fall under s 32 rather than s 33.

34 Secondary warehousing regulations

The Commissioners may by regulations make provision, for the purposes of sections 32 and 33—

    (a) specifying conditions and requirements in respect of premises on which chargeable soft drinks may be stored before the occurrence of a chargeable event (see section 32(5)(b));
    (b) specifying other conditions and requirements as to the storage of chargeable soft drinks for the purposes of the secondary warehousing condition (see section 32(4));
    (c) specifying conditions and requirements as to the transportation of chargeable soft drinks for the purposes of the secondary warehousing condition;
    (d) imposing obligations on specified persons to provide information in connection with the storage or transportation of chargeable soft drinks.

GENERAL NOTE

Regulations made under s 34 may make provisions specifying conditions for secondary warehousing requirements for the purposes of ss 32 and 33.

35 Liability to pay the levy

(1) Where the charge to soft drinks industry levy arises on a chargeable event within section 32(2) or (3), the person who packages the chargeable soft drinks is liable to pay the amount charged.

(2) Where the charge to soft drinks industry levy arises on a chargeable event within section 33(2) or (8), the relevant person who is the first recipient is liable to pay the amount charged.

(3) Where the charge to soft drinks industry levy arises on a chargeable event within section 33(9), the relevant person who is the first seller is liable to pay the amount charged.

GENERAL NOTE

Section 35 specifies who is liable to account for the levy.

Subsection (1) provides that, for UK-packaged soft drinks, it is the packager that is liable to account for the levy, unless the small producer exemption in s 37 applies.

Subsection (2) provides that, for imported soft drinks, it is the first relevant person (i.e. person whose business consists of selling soft drinks) that receives the soft drinks in the UK that is liable to account for the levy, unless the drink is earlier made available or sold, in which case it is the person who makes the drink available (or sells it) that is liable to account for the levy.

36 Levy rates

(1) Soft drinks industry levy is charged—

(a) in the case of chargeable soft drinks that meet the higher sugar threshold, at the rate of £0.24 per litre of prepared drink;

(b) in the case of chargeable soft drinks that do not meet the higher sugar threshold, at the rate of £0.18 per litre of prepared drink.

(2) A chargeable soft drink meets the higher sugar threshold if it contains at least 8 grams of sugars (whether or not as a result of containing added sugar ingredients) per 100 millilitres of prepared drink.

GENERAL NOTE

Section 36 provides the rates for the soft drinks industry levy. The levy is charged at two different rates: a higher rate of £0.24 per litre of prepared drink for those soft drinks that contain at least eight grams of sugars per 100 millilitres; or a lower rate of £0.18 per litre of prepared drink for all other chargeable soft drinks.

The levy is not expected to be a major source of revenue for the government. Even though the revenue projections have already been adjusted downwards in light of changing production methods, there is currently no indication that the government intends to increase the levy rates.

Exemption etc

37 Small producer exemption

(1) No charge to soft drinks industry levy arises—

(a) on a chargeable event within section 32 in relation to chargeable soft drinks produced by a person who is, on the relevant day, a qualifying small producer;

(b) on a chargeable event within section 33 in relation to chargeable soft drinks produced by a person who is, on the relevant day, a small producer.

(2) Chargeable soft drinks are "produced" by a person if they are packaged (by or on behalf of the person) for marketing under—

(a) the person's name or business name, or

(b) another name which is used in accordance with a licence granted to the person.

(3) For the purposes of this section and section 38, the "relevant day", in relation to chargeable soft drinks, is the day on which the charge to soft drinks industry levy on the chargeable soft drinks would (apart from this section) arise.

(4) "Small producer" has the meaning given by section 38.

(5) A person is a "qualifying small producer" if the person is a small producer who is either—

(a) registered under section 45 (voluntary registration: small producers), or

(b) ineligible for registration under that section because the person does not meet the condition in section 45(2)(c) (voluntary registration eligibility conditions: packaging by a person other than the producer).

GENERAL NOTE

Section 37 stipulates that no soft drinks industry levy arises on production or imports under ss 32 or 33 if the chargeable drinks were produced by a small producer. In order for a UK-based producer to be exempt from the levy by virtue of this section, it must register as a small producer under s 45 or be ineligible for such registration because it packages its own products and thus does not meet the requirement at s 45(2)(c).

Soft drinks are produced by a person if they are packaged for marketing under that person's name, or under another name that the person is licensed to use.

The exemption from the soft drinks industry levy applies to chargeable soft drinks that are produced by a small producer either in the UK or abroad. The legislation is drafted this way to ensure that only products imported from overseas manufacturers who would be eligible for the small operator relief on their total production will be exempt. There is no corresponding exemption for small importers or recipients of imported soft drinks, in order to avoid large producers from exploiting any such exemption by disaggregating the supply chain and bringing branded products into the UK free of the levy.

The exemption does allow for UK importers that only import chargeable soft drinks produced by small producers to make use of the exemption and thus avoid paying a levy under s 33, irrespective of the total quantities that they import.

38 Meaning of "small producer"

(1) A person ("the producer") who produces chargeable soft drinks is a "small producer" on the relevant day if Conditions A and B are met.

(2) Condition A is met if the aggregate of—

(a) the amount of the producer's chargeable soft drinks within section 26(1)(a) in respect of which a relevant event has occurred during the relevant 12 month period, and

(b) the amount of prepared drink that would result from the producer's chargeable soft drinks within section 26(1)(b) in respect of which a relevant event has occurred during the relevant 12 month period,

does not exceed the small producer threshold.

(3) Condition B is met if there are reasonable grounds for believing that the aggregate of—

(a) the amount of the producer's chargeable soft drinks within section 26(1)(a) in respect of which a relevant event will occur during the relevant 30 day period, and

(b) the amount of prepared drink that would result from the producer's chargeable soft drinks within section 26(1)(b) in respect of which a relevant event will occur during the relevant 30 day period,

will not exceed the small producer threshold.

(4) A "relevant event" occurs in respect of chargeable soft drinks on the removal of the chargeable soft drinks from the premises on which they are packaged.

(5) But—

(a) if, on removal from the premises on which the chargeable soft drinks are packaged, the secondary warehousing condition is met in relation to the soft drinks, a "relevant event" occurs in relation to those soft drinks at the time that the secondary warehousing condition ceases to be met in relation to them (and not at the time mentioned in subsection (4));

(b) if the chargeable soft drinks are made available for sale or free of charge before a relevant event in relation to the soft drinks occurs under subsection (4) or paragraph (a), a "relevant event" occurs at the time they are made available (and not at the time mentioned in subsection (4) or paragraph (a)).

(6) For the purposes of subsections (2) and (3)—

(a) the "relevant 12 month period" is the period of 12 months ending with the end of the month that immediately precedes the month in which the relevant day falls, and

(b) the "relevant 30 day period" is the period of 30 days beginning with the relevant day.

(7) The "small producer threshold" is 1 million litres.

(8) References in this section to "the producer's chargeable soft drinks" are references to chargeable soft drinks produced by the producer or a person connected with the producer.

GENERAL NOTE

Section 38 provides the meaning of "small producer". In order to be considered a "small producer", the producer must meet two criteria.

First, the producer must not have produced more than one million litres of chargeable soft drinks (including dilutable drinks at diluted volumes) over the previous 12 months.

Second, there must be reasonable grounds for believing that the producer will not produce more than one million litres of chargeable soft drinks (including dilutable drinks at diluted volumes) over the following 30 days.

This gives a similar threshold system as for VAT registration, albeit based on litres produced rather than taxable supplies. The relevant quantity of soft drink for each of the periods in question is effectively judged by reference to the amount in respect of which a chargeable event has, or is anticipated, to occur during that period.

References to the amount of chargeable drinks produced by a person includes those produced by persons connected with the producer for the purpose of CTA 2010 s 1122, preventing companies from splitting into several group companies to fall below the threshold.

39 Tax credits

(1) The Commissioners may by regulations make provision in relation to cases where, after a charge to soft drinks industry levy has arisen in relation to chargeable soft drinks—

(a) the soft drinks are exported from the United Kingdom;

(b) the soft drinks are lost or destroyed.

(2) The provision that may be made is provision—

(a) for the liable person to be entitled to a tax credit in respect of any soft drinks industry levy charged on the soft drinks that are exported or (as the case may be) lost or destroyed;

(b) for the tax credit to be brought into account when the person is accounting for soft drinks industry levy due from the person for the prescribed accounting period or periods.

(3) Regulations under this section may include provision—

(a) for any entitlement to a tax credit to be conditional on the making of a claim by the liable person, and specifying the period within which and the manner in which a claim may be made;

(b) for any entitlement to bring a tax credit into account to be conditional on compliance with prescribed requirements;

(c) specifying circumstances in which, and criteria for determining the period for which, a liable person is not entitled to a tax credit;

(d) requiring a claim for a tax credit to be evidenced and quantified by reference to prescribed records and other documents;

(e) requiring a person claiming any entitlement to a tax credit to keep, for the prescribed period and in the prescribed form and manner, those records and documents and a record of prescribed information relating to the claim;

(f) for the withdrawal of a tax credit where any requirement of the regulations is not complied with;

(g) about adjustments of liability for soft drinks industry levy in connection with entitlement or withdrawal of entitlement to a tax credit in prescribed circumstances;

(h) about the treatment of a tax credit where the liable person ceases to carry on a business involving the package or sale of chargeable soft drinks.

(4) Regulations under paragraph (a) of subsection (1) may include provision for the sale or provision of chargeable soft drinks on passenger transport operating between the

United Kingdom and a place outside of the United Kingdom to be treated as "export from the United Kingdom" for the purposes of regulations under that paragraph.

(5) Regulations under paragraph (b) of subsection (1) may include provision about the circumstances in which chargeable soft drinks are to be treated as lost or destroyed for the purposes of regulations under that paragraph.

(6) In this section—

"liable person" means the person who is liable under section 35 to pay the charge to soft drinks industry levy referred to in subsection (1);

"prescribed" means specified in, or determined in accordance with, regulations under this section.

GENERAL NOTE

Section 39 contains provision for the making of regulations to allow producers and importers to claim a credit against a liability to pay the levy in respect of chargeable soft drinks that are exported, lost or destroyed. This is intended only to operate as a credit mechanism, in order to reduce the risk of fraud, and is broadly intended to apply in circumstances where a soft drink is subject to the levy on removal from the premises of the packager (or imported, as the case may be) but is subsequently not consumed within the UK, either because it is exported or because it is lost or destroyed.

Since it would be very difficult for all soft drinks producers to reliably identify and distinguish all drinks that are to be exported at time of packaging, the relief will be provided after the goods have already been exported by way of a credit against the levy, adjusted on the tax return. Regulations may contain similar provision for soft drinks ultimately supplied for consumption on ships or aircraft leaving the UK.

Registration

40 The register

(1) The Commissioners must establish and maintain a register for the purposes of this Part.

(2) In this Part, "the register" means the register under subsection (1) and references to registration are to registration in it.

(3) The register may contain such information as the Commissioners think is required for the purposes of the collection and management of soft drinks industry levy.

GENERAL NOTE

HMRC will maintain a register of persons registered for the levy to facilitate collection and management.

Section 40(3) provides that the register may contain such information as HMRC consider necessary for the purposes of its duties of collection and management. It appears likely that this may include information about manufacturing plants where production takes place and specification of brand ownership.

41 Liability to register: packagers

(1) A person becomes liable to be registered—

(a) at the end of any month, if the person has packaged any chargeable soft drinks in respect of which a chargeable event within section 32 has occurred during that month;

(b) on any day, if there are reasonable grounds for believing that, during the period of 30 days beginning with that day, a chargeable event within section 32 will occur in respect of chargeable soft drinks packaged by the person.

(2) But subsection (1) does not apply to a person if—

(a) the chargeable soft drinks packaged by the person are also produced by the person, and

(b) the person is not liable to be registered under section 42 (liability to register: producers).

(3) Subsection (1) does not apply in relation to a person who is already registrable.

(4) In this section and in sections 42 and 43 references to "a person who is already registrable" are references to a person who—

(a) is registered under this section, section 42 or section 43,

(b) is subject to a relevant notification requirement, or

(c) would, if the person had complied with a relevant notification requirement, be registered under this section, section 42 or section 43.

(5) In subsection (4)(c) "relevant notification requirement" means a requirement under section 44(1) to notify the Commissioners of a liability to register—

(a) arising on a previous occasion, and

(b) in respect of which the notification period has expired.

(6) In this section "notification period" has the meaning given by section 44(2).

GENERAL NOTE

Packagers become liable to register if they have packaged any chargeable soft drinks in respect of which a chargeable event has occurred during the previous month or if there are reasonable grounds for believing that they will do so over the next 30 days. There is no minimum threshold as to the amount of chargeable soft drinks that must be packaged in order for the liability to arise (such that small packagers will be liable to register). However, by virtue of s 41(2), small producers that also package their own drinks will not have to register.

42 Liability to register: producers

(1) A person ("the producer") who produces chargeable soft drinks becomes liable to be registered—

(a) at the end of any month, if the qualifying amount of the producer's chargeable soft drinks in respect of which a chargeable event within section 32 has occurred during the immediately preceding period of 12 months exceeds the small producer threshold;

(b) on any day, if there are reasonable grounds for believing that the qualifying amount of the producer's chargeable soft drinks in respect of which a chargeable event within section 32 will occur during the period of 30 days beginning with that day will exceed the small producer threshold.

(2) The "qualifying amount" of chargeable soft drinks in respect of which a chargeable event occurs is the aggregate of—

(a) the amount of the chargeable soft drinks within section 26(1)(a) in respect of which the chargeable event occurs, and

(b) the amount of prepared drink that would result from the chargeable soft drinks within section 26(1)(b) in respect of which the chargeable event occurs.

(3) Subsection (1) does not apply in relation to a person who is already registrable.

(4) References in this section to "the producer's chargeable soft drinks" are references to chargeable soft drinks produced by the producer or a person connected with the producer.

GENERAL NOTE

Section 42 provides that producers become liable to register if they have produced more than one million litres of chargeable soft drinks (including dilutable drinks at diluted volumes) in respect of which a chargeable event has occurred over the previous 12 months and there are reasonable grounds for believing that chargeable events will exceed that threshold over the next 30 days. The legislation is framed so as to exempt small producers from the liability to register under s 42.

References to the amount of chargeable drinks produced includes those produced by persons connected with the producer for the purpose of CTA 2010 s 1122.

43 Liability to register: imported chargeable soft drinks

(1) A person becomes liable to be registered—

(a) at the end of any month if, during that month, a chargeable event within section 33 has occurred—

(i) on the first receipt, or on the making available, of chargeable soft drinks by the person, or

(ii) on the secondary warehousing condition ceasing to be met in relation to chargeable soft drinks in respect of which the person is the first recipient;

(b) on any day, if there are reasonable grounds for believing that, during the period of 30 days beginning with that day, a chargeable event within section 33 will occur—

(i) on the first receipt, or on the making available, of chargeable soft drinks by the person, or

(ii) on the secondary warehousing condition ceasing to be met in relation to chargeable soft drinks in respect of which the person is the first recipient.

(2) Subsection (1) does not apply in relation to a person who is already registrable.

GENERAL NOTE

Under s 43 importers become liable to register if they have received, sold or given away chargeable soft drinks during the preceding calendar month. They will also be liable to register if there are reasonable grounds for believing that they will do so during the following 30 days. There is no minimum threshold as to the amount of chargeable soft drinks that must be imported in order for the liability to register to arise.

44 Notification of liability and registration

(1) A person who becomes liable to be registered under section 41, 42 or 43 must notify the Commissioners of the liability before the end of the notification period.

(2) The "notification period" is the period of 30 days beginning with the day on which the liability arises.

(3) Where the Commissioners are satisfied that a person is liable to be registered (whether or not the person has notified liability under subsection (1)), the Commissioners must register the person with effect from the day on which the liability to register arises.

GENERAL NOTE

Under s 44 a packager, producer or importer of chargeable soft drinks that becomes liable to register must notify HMRC of its liability within 30 days of becoming liable, and the registration is backdated to the date on which the liability arose.

45 Voluntary registration: small producers

(1) The Commissioners must register a person who—

(a) meets the voluntary registration eligibility conditions, and

(b) applies to the Commissioners for registration under this section.

(2) The voluntary registration eligibility conditions are met by a person (P) if—

(a) P produces chargeable soft drinks,

(b) P is not liable to be registered under section 42 (liability to register: producers), and

(c) some or all of the chargeable soft drinks produced by P are packaged on premises in the United Kingdom by a person other than P.

(3) A person who is registered under section 41 or 43 may also be registered under this section.

GENERAL NOTE

A UK producer that seeks to benefit from the small producer levy exemption will need to apply for voluntary registration in order to be considered as a qualifying small producer and thus meet the criteria for the exemption set out in s 37, unless it packages all of its own soft drinks (or the drinks are packaged outside the UK).

UK producers some of whose chargeable soft drinks are packaged in the UK by another person will need to voluntarily register under s 45 in order to be regarded as a qualifying small producer and hence benefit from the levy exemption.

46 Cancellation of registration under section 41, 42 or 43

(1) A registration under section 41, 42 or 43 may be cancelled only in accordance with this section.

(2) For the purposes of this section, a person meets the "liability condition" at a particular time if—

    (a) at the end of the preceding month, the condition in section 41(1)(a), 42(1)(a) or 43(1)(a) is met in relation to the person, or

    (b) at that time, the condition in section 41(1)(b), 42(1)(b) or 43(1)(b) is met in relation to the person.

(3) The Commissioners must cancel a person's registration under section 41, 42 or 43 if—

    (a) the person requests the cancellation, and

    (b) the person satisfies the Commissioners that the person does not, at the time of the request, meet the liability condition.

(4) A cancellation under subsection (3) is to be made with effect from—

    (a) the day on which the request is made, or

    (b) such later day as may be agreed between the Commissioners and the person.

(5) The Commissioners may cancel a person's registration under section 41, 42 or 43 if they are satisfied that the person does not meet the liability condition.

(6) A cancellation under subsection (5) is to be made with effect from—

    (a) the day on which the person ceased to meet the liability condition, or

    (b) such later day as may be agreed between the Commissioners and the person.

(7) But the Commissioners must not cancel a registration under subsection (3) or (5) with effect from any time unless—

    (a) they are satisfied that it is not a time when the person would meet the liability condition, and

    (b) it is reasonable to believe that the person will not become liable to be registered under section 41(1)(a) or 43(1)(a) during the period of 12 months beginning with that time.

(8) The Commissioners may cancel a person's registration under section 41, 42 or 43 if they are satisfied that the person did not meet the liability condition on the day on which the person was registered, and has not at any subsequent time met the liability condition.

(9) A cancellation under subsection (8) is to be made with effect from the day on which the person was registered.

GENERAL NOTE

Section 46 provides for cancellation of registration. If a packager, producer or importer is no longer liable to be registered under ss 41, 42 or 43 (the sections requiring compulsory registration) it may request that HMRC cancels its registration. HMRC may also initiate cancellation itself. If HMRC are satisfied that the packager, producer or importer no longer meets the liability condition they must cancel the registration, unless in the case of a packager or importer it is reasonable to believe that it will become liable to be registered again within the next 12 months.

A cancellation of registration takes effect from the date when the liability condition ceased to be met or any later date agreed with HMRC.

HMRC may further cancel a registration with retrospective effect where they are satisfied that the relevant person did not meet the liability condition when the registration took effect or at any later time.

47 Cancellation of voluntary registration

(1) The Commissioners may cancel a person's registration under section 45 if they are satisfied that the person does not meet the voluntary registration eligibility conditions (see subsection (2) of that section).

(2) A cancellation under subsection (1) is to be made with effect from the day on which the person ceased to meet the voluntary registration eligibility conditions.

(3) The Commissioners must cancel a person's registration under section 45 if the person requests the cancellation.

(4) A cancellation under subsection (3) is to be made with effect from—

    (a) the day on which the request is made, or

(b) such later day as may be agreed between the Commissioners and the person.

GENERAL NOTE

Under s 47 a small producer that has been registered under s 45 may ask for its registration to be cancelled, in which case HMRC must cancel the registration from the date of the request (or a later date if agreed). HMRC may also cancel a small producer's registration if the producer is no longer eligible to be registered under the voluntary registration conditions, with effect from the point when the producer ceased to meet the conditions.

Although cancellation of registration would allow a producer to avoid potentially onerous requirements relating to record keeping that come with registration, it could also mean that the producer can no longer benefit from the qualifying small producer exemption from the levy under s 37(1)(a) unless the reason for the cancellation is that the producer has changed its model to package all of its own drinks.

48 Correction of the register

(1) The Commissioners may by regulations make provision about the correction of entries in the register.

(2) Regulations under subsection (1) may make provision for requiring persons who are, or are liable to be, registered to notify the Commissioners of changes in circumstances which are relevant to the register.

GENERAL NOTE

Section 48 sets out that regulations may make provision about the amendment or correction of the register maintained under s 40.

49 Applications, notifications etc

The Commissioners may by or under regulations make provision—

    (a) about the form and manner in which a notification under section 44 (notification of liability to register) is to be given;

    (b) about the information to be contained in or provided with a notification under that section;

    (c) about the form and manner of an application under section 45 (voluntary registration: small producers);

    (d) requiring applications, notifications and other communications with the Commissioners in connection with registration to be made electronically.

GENERAL NOTE

Under s 49 regulations may make provision about how a notification of a liability to register or voluntary registration is to be made and what information should be included by the applicant.

Offences

50 Fraudulent evasion

(1) A person commits an offence if the person is knowingly concerned in, or in the taking of steps with a view to, the fraudulent evasion (by that person or any other person) of soft drinks industry levy.

(2) The references in subsection (1) to the evasion of soft drinks industry levy include references to obtaining, in circumstances where there is no entitlement to it—

    (a) a tax credit under regulations under section 39;

    (b) a repayment of soft drinks industry levy under Schedule 8.

(3) A person guilty of an offence under this section is liable—

    (a) on summary conviction in England and Wales—

      (i) to imprisonment for a term not exceeding 12 months, or

      (ii) to a fine not exceeding £20,000 or (if greater) 3 times the total of the amounts of soft drinks industry levy that were, or were intended to be, evaded, or

      (iii) to both;
  (b) on summary conviction in Scotland—
      (i) to imprisonment for a term not exceeding 12 months, or
      (ii) to a fine not exceeding the statutory maximum or (if greater) 3 times the total of the amounts of soft drinks industry levy that were, or were intended to be, evaded, or
      (iii) to both;
  (c) on summary conviction in Northern Ireland—
      (i) to imprisonment for a term not exceeding 6 months, or
      (ii) to a fine not exceeding the statutory maximum or (if greater) 3 times the total of the amounts of soft drinks industry levy that were, or were intended to be, evaded, or
      (iii) to both;
  (d) on conviction on indictment—
      (i) to imprisonment for a term not exceeding 7 years,
      (ii) to a fine, or
      (iii) to both.

(4) For the purposes of subsection (3), the amounts of soft drinks industry levy that were, or were intended to be, evaded are to be taken as including—
  (a) the amount of any tax credit under regulations under section 39, and
  (b) the amount of any repayment of soft drinks industry levy under Schedule 8,
which was, or was intended to be, obtained in circumstances where there was no entitlement to it.

(5) In determining for the purposes of subsection (3) the amounts of soft drinks industry levy that were, or were intended to be, evaded, no account is to be taken of the extent to which any liability to levy of a person would be, or would have been, reduced by the amount of any tax credit or repayment of soft drinks industry levy to which the person was, or would have been, entitled.

(6) In relation to an offence committed before the commencement of section 154(1) of the Criminal Justice Act 2003 the reference in subsection (3)(a)(i) to 12 months is to be read as a reference to 6 months.

GENERAL NOTE

Section 50 provides a criminal offence for knowingly being involved in fraudulent evasion of the soft drinks industry levy, including obtaining a tax credit or repayment in relation to the levy.

On summary conviction, an offender risks imprisonment for up to 12 months or a fine that may depend on the amount of levy that was intended to be evaded. On conviction on indictment, an offender risks imprisonment for up to seven years and/or a fine.

51 Failure to notify registration liability

(1) A person who fails to comply with section 44(1) (obligation to notify the Commissioners of liability to be registered) commits an offence.

(2) In proceedings against a person (P) for an offence under subsection (1), it is a defence for P to prove that P had a reasonable excuse for the failure to comply.

(3) For the purposes of subsection (2)—
  (a) where P relies on any other person to do anything, that is not a reasonable excuse unless P took reasonable care to avoid the failure;
  (b) where P had a reasonable excuse for the failure but the excuse has ceased, P is to be treated as having continued to have the excuse if the failure is remedied without unreasonable delay after the excuse ceased.

(4) A person guilty of an offence under this section is liable—
  (a) on summary conviction in England and Wales—
      (i) to imprisonment for a term not exceeding 12 months, or
      (ii) to a fine not exceeding £20,000 or (if greater) 3 times the amount of the potential lost revenue, or
      (iii) to both;
  (b) on summary conviction in Scotland—

(i) to imprisonment for a term not exceeding 12 months, or

(ii) to a fine not exceeding the statutory maximum or (if greater) 3 times the amount of the potential lost revenue, or

(iii) to both;

(c) on summary conviction in Northern Ireland—

(i) to imprisonment for a term not exceeding 6 months, or

(ii) to a fine not exceeding the statutory maximum or (if greater) 3 times the amount of the potential lost revenue, or

(iii) to both;

(d) on conviction on indictment—

(i) to imprisonment for a term not exceeding 3 years,

(ii) to a fine, or

(iii) to both.

(5) For the purposes of subsection (4), the "potential lost revenue" is the amount of soft drinks industry levy (if any) for which the person who committed the offence is liable for the period—

(a) beginning with the date with effect from which the person is liable to be registered under this Part, and

(b) ending with the date on which the Commissioners received notification of, or otherwise were satisfied as to, the person's liability to be registered under this Part.

(6) In calculating potential lost revenue for the purposes of subsection (4), no account is to be taken of the fact that a potential loss of revenue from the person is or may be balanced by a potential over-payment by another person.

(7) In relation to an offence committed before the commencement of section 154(1) of the Criminal Justice Act 2003 the reference in subsection (4)(a)(i) to 12 months is to be read as a reference to 6 months.

GENERAL NOTE

Section 51 provides that for the purpose of the soft drinks industry levy, failure to notify HMRC of a liability to register for the levy under s 44 is considered grave enough to constitute a criminal offence. A potential offender would have a defence if it can prove that it had a reasonable excuse for the failure to comply. The defence does not cover situations where a potential offender relies on any other person to do anything unless the potential offender took reasonable care to avoid the failure.

On summary conviction, an offender risks imprisonment for up to 12 months or a fine that may depend on the amount of levy that was intended to be evaded. On conviction on indictment, an offender risks imprisonment for up to three years and an unspecified fine.

Administration and enforcement

52 Payment, collection and recovery

(1) The Commissioners may by regulations make provision about the payment, collection and recovery of soft drinks industry levy.

(2) Regulations under subsection (1) may—

(a) require persons who are or are liable to be registered under this Part to keep accounts for the purposes of the levy in the specified form and manner;

(b) require persons who are or are liable to be registered under this Part to make returns for the purposes of the levy;

(c) make provision for determining the periods ("accounting periods") by reference to which payments of the levy are to be made;

(d) make provision about the times at which payments of the levy are to be made and methods of payment;

(e) require the amounts payable by reference to accounting periods to be calculated by or under the regulations;

(f) make provision for the correction of errors made in accounting for the levy.

(3) Provision may be made by or under regulations under subsection (2)(b) about—

(a) the periods by reference to which returns are to be made,

(b) the information to be included in returns,

(c) timing, and

(d) the form of, and method of, making returns.

(4) Schedule 8 contains provision about recovery and overpayments.

GENERAL NOTE

Section 52 provides that regulations under that section may make provision about the payment, collection and recovery of the levy. In particular, the regulations can specify how returns should be made and which tax periods and payment dates that apply in respect of the levy. This section also introduces Schedule 8, which deals with HMRC procedures for recovery of unpaid levy and repayment of overpaid levy.

53 Records

(1) The Commissioners may by regulations require persons—

    (a) to keep, for purposes connected with soft drinks industry levy, records of specified matters, and

    (b) to preserve records for a specified period.

(2) A duty under regulations under this section to preserve records may be discharged—

    (a) by preserving them in any form and by any means, or

    (b) by preserving the information contained in them in any form and by any means, subject to any specified conditions or exceptions.

(3) The Commissioners may direct a person who is, or is liable to be, registered under this Part—

    (a) to keep such records as are specified in the direction;

    (b) to preserve those records for a specified period.

(4) The period specified in a direction under subsection (3)(b) may not exceed 6 years.

(5) The Commissioners may not give a direction under subsection (3) unless they have reasonable grounds for believing that the records specified in the direction might assist in identifying chargeable soft drinks in respect of which soft drinks industry levy might not be paid.

(6) A direction under subsection (3)—

    (a) must be given in writing,

    (b) must specify the consequences under Schedule 9 of failure to comply with a requirement imposed under subsection (3), and

    (c) may be revoked or replaced by a further direction.

(7) Schedule 9 makes provision about penalties for failure to comply with requirements imposed by regulations or directions under this section.

GENERAL NOTE

Section 53 grants HMRC the power to make regulations on record keeping. Regulations may make provision that requires registered packagers, producers or importers (including small producers) to keep and preserve records in accordance with the regulations. HMRC may give directions to a person who is or is liable to be registered ordering them to maintain specified records and preserve them for up to six years. This section also introduces Sch 9 which contains further provisions relating to penalties for failure to keep records.

54 Power to make further provision about enforcement

(1) The Commissioners may by regulations make further provision about enforcement of soft drinks industry levy, including provision conferring powers of entry, search or seizure.

(2) Regulations under this section may include provision—

    (a) conferring powers to enter and inspect premises that are used, or are reasonably believed to be used, in connection with the production, packaging, sale, import or export of chargeable soft drinks;

    (b) conferring powers to stop, board and search ships, aircraft and other vehicles entering, leaving or situated on premises referred to in paragraph (a);

    (c) conferring powers to inspect and take copies of business documents on premises referred to in paragraph (a);

    (d) conferring powers to examine and take samples of soft drinks found on premises referred to in paragraph (a);

(e) for the detention and seizure of chargeable soft drinks in respect of which a specified requirement of this Part has been contravened;

(f) requiring a person to provide such facilities as are reasonably necessary for an officer of Revenue and Customs to carry out an examination or search or exercise other powers conferred by the regulations;

(g) about reviews of, and appeals against, decisions made for the purposes of the regulations.

(3) Regulations under this section may, in particular, make provision by applying any provision of the Customs and Excise Management Act 1979.

GENERAL NOTE

Section 54 sets out HMRC's powers of enforcement in respect of the levy. Regulations may make provision about how the levy is to be enforced. By virtue of such regulations, their enforcement powers may include the right to enter and inspect premises, search transportation vehicles used in connection with production or import or take samples of soft drinks found on the premises of the producers or importers. The specific reference to the powers of HMRC to enforce other customs and excise legislation shows that this levy is intended to be administered in a similar way to many other duties.

55 Appeals etc
Schedule 10 makes provision about appeals and reviews.

GENERAL NOTE

Section 55 introduces Sch 10, which sets out the circumstances in which a decision made by HMRC in relation to the soft drinks industry levy can be appealed, including who may lodge an appeal, applicable time frames and determinations open to the tribunal.

56 Supplementary amendments
Schedule 11 contains supplementary amendments relating to administration and enforcement of soft drinks industry levy.

GENERAL NOTE

Section 56 introduces Sch 11, which contains supplementary amendments that make a number of consequential changes to existing legislation.

Miscellaneous

57 Regulations: death, incapacity or insolvency of person carrying on a business
(1) The Commissioners may by regulations make provision for the purposes of soft drinks industry levy in relation to cases where a person carries on a business of—

(a) an individual who has died or become incapacitated;

(b) a person (whether or not an individual) who is subject to an insolvency procedure (as defined in the regulations).

(2) Regulations under this section may include—

(a) provision requiring the person who is carrying on the business (P) to notify the Commissioners that P is carrying on the business and of the event that led to P carrying it on;

(b) provision allowing P to be treated for a limited time as if P and the person who has died, become incapacitated or is subject to an insolvency procedure were the same person;

(c) such other provision as the Commissioners think fit for securing continuity in the application of this Part in cases to which the regulations apply.

GENERAL NOTE

Section 57 allows HMRC to regulate in order to ensure the continuity of the imposition of the soft drinks industry levy where a registered packager, producer or importer is no longer able to pay the levy due as a result of certain circumstances. If a registered person dies, becomes incapacitated or subject to an insolvency procedure HMRC may treat a person that has taken over the business from the registered person as if the new packager, producer or importer was the registered person in order to ensure continuity.

58 Provisional collection of soft drinks industry levy

In section 1 of the Provisional Collection of Taxes Act 1968 (temporary statutory effect of House of Commons resolutions), in subsection (1), after "aggregates levy," insert "soft drinks industry levy,".

GENERAL NOTE

By virtue of s 58, the soft drinks industry levy is added to the list of taxes in respect of which the House of Commons may pass resolutions to renew taxation for a new financial year.

General

59 Interpretation of Part 2

(1) In this Part—

"accounting period" is to be construed in accordance with section 52(2)(c);

"chargeable soft drink" has the meaning given by section 28;

"the Commissioners" means the Commissioners for Her Majesty's Revenue and Customs;

"compliant warehouse" is to be construed in accordance with section 32(5);

"first recipient" and "first receipt", in relation to imported chargeable soft drinks, have the meaning given by section 33(2) and (4);

"first seller", in relation to imported chargeable soft drinks, has the meaning given by section 33(9);

"HMRC" means Her Majesty's Revenue and Customs;

"package" and "packaged" are to be construed in accordance with section 26(3);

"person who is already registrable" has the meaning given by section 41(4);

"prepared drink" has the meaning given by section 27(1);

"produce", in relation to chargeable soft drinks, is to be construed in accordance with section 37(2);

"relevant person" has the meaning given by section 33(5);

"secondary warehousing condition" has the meaning given by section 32(4);

"small producer" has the meaning given by section 38;

"small producer threshold" has the meaning given by section 38(7);

"soft drink" has the meaning given by section 26(1);

"sugars" means anything that is required to be described as "sugars" for the purposes of a designated food labelling obligation (see subsection (3)).

(2) In sections 30, 34, 52, 53(1) and (2) and 54 and in paragraph 11 of Schedule 8, "specified" means specified in regulations made by the Commissioners for the purposes of this Part.

(3) In the definition of "sugars" in subsection (1), "designated food labelling obligation" means an obligation that—

(a) relates to the provision of nutritional information on the packaging of food or drinks,

(b) is imposed by an enactment, an EU instrument or subordinate legislation, and

(c) is designated by regulations made by the Commissioners for the purposes of this Part.

(4) Section 1122 of CTA 2010 (meaning of connected person) applies for the purposes of this Part.

(5) For the purposes of this Part, a person "packages" chargeable soft drinks if—

(a) the person packages soft drinks, and

(b) the packaged soft drinks are chargeable soft drinks.

GENERAL NOTE

Section 59 sets out a range of definitions used in Pt 2 of the Act regulating the soft drinks industry levy.

60 Regulations

(1) Regulations under this Part—
    (a) may make different provision for different purposes;
    (b) may include incidental, consequential, supplementary or transitional provision.

(2) Regulations under this Part are to be made by statutory instrument.

(3) A statutory instrument containing regulations under section 54 may not be made unless a draft of the instrument has been laid before and approved by a resolution of the House of Commons.

(4) Any other statutory instrument containing regulations under this Part is subject to annulment in pursuance of a resolution of the House of Commons.

(5) But subsection (4) does not apply to a statutory instrument containing only regulations under section 61 (commencement of this Part).

GENERAL NOTE

Section 60 makes provisions about regulations that can be made in relation to the levy.

61 Commencement

(1) Subject to subsection (2), this Part comes into force on such day as the Commissioners may by regulations appoint.

(2) The amendment made by paragraph 3 of Schedule 11 comes into force in accordance with provision made by the Treasury by regulations.

(3) Regulations under this section may appoint different days for different purposes.

GENERAL NOTE

The legislation relating to the levy will come into force when appointed in regulations (although by virtue of s 31, a chargeable event will not occur before 8 April 2018).

PART 3

FINAL

62 Interpretation

In this Act the following abbreviations are references to the following Acts.

ALDA 1979	Alcoholic Liquor Duties Act 1979
CAA 2001	Capital Allowances Act 2001
CTA 2009	Corporation Tax Act 2009
CTA 2010	Corporation Tax Act 2010
FA, followed by a year	Finance Act of that year
ICTA	Income and Corporation Taxes Act 1988
IHTA 1984	Inheritance Tax Act 1984
ITA 2007	Income Tax Act 2007
ITEPA 2003	Income Tax (Earnings and Pensions) Act 2003
ITTOIA 2005	Income Tax (Trading and Other Income) Act 2005
TCGA 1992	Taxation of Chargeable Gains Act 1992
TMA 1970	Taxes Management Act 1970
TPDA 1979	Tobacco Products Duty Act 1979
VATA 1994	Value Added Tax Act 1994
VERA 1994	Vehicle Excise and Registration Act 1994

63 Short title

This Act may be cited as the Finance Act 2017.

SCHEDULE 1

WORKERS' SERVICES PROVIDED TO PUBLIC SECTOR THROUGH INTERMEDIARIES

Section 6

PART 1

PRELIMINARY AMENDMENTS

1 ITEPA 2003 is amended as follows.

2 In section 48 (scope of Chapter 8 of Part 2: workers' services provided through intermediaries)—

(a) in subsection (1), after "through an intermediary" insert ", but not where the services are provided to a public authority", and

(b) after subsection (2) insert—

"(3) In this Chapter "public authority" has the same meaning as in Chapter 10 of this Part (see section 61L)."

3 In section 49(1) (engagements to which Chapter applies), after paragraph (a) insert—

"(aa) the client is not a public authority,".

4 In section 52(2)(b) and (c) (conditions of liability under Chapter 8 where intermediary is a partnership), for "this Chapter" substitute "one or other of this Chapter and Chapter 10".

5 In section 61(1) (interpretation of Chapter 8), before the definition of "engagement to which this Chapter applies" insert—

""engagement to which Chapter 10 applies" has the meaning given by section 61M(5);".

6 In section 61A (scope of Chapter 9 of Part 2: workers' services provided by managed service companies), after subsection (2) insert—

"(3) See also section 61D(4A) (disapplication of this Chapter if Chapter 10 applies)."

7 In section 61D (deemed earnings where worker's services provided by managed service company), after subsection (4) insert—

"(4A) This section does not apply where the provision of the relevant services gives rise (directly or indirectly) to an engagement to which Chapter 10 applies, and for this purpose it does not matter whether the client is also "the client" for the purposes of section 61M(1)."

8 In section 61J(1) (interpretation of Chapter 9), before the definition of "managed service company" insert—

""engagement to which Chapter 10 applies" has the meaning given by section 61M(5),".

PART 2

NEW CHAPTER 10 OF PART 2 OF ITEPA 2003

9 In Part 2 of ITEPA 2003 (employment income: charge to tax), after Chapter 9 insert—

"CHAPTER 10

WORKERS' SERVICES PROVIDED TO PUBLIC SECTOR THROUGH INTERMEDIARIES

61K Scope of this Chapter

(1) This Chapter has effect with respect to the provision of services to a public authority through an intermediary.

(2) Nothing in this Chapter—

(a) affects the operation of Chapter 7 of this Part (agency workers), or

(b) applies to payments or transfers to which section 966(3) or (4) of ITA 2007 applies (visiting performers: duty to deduct and account for sums representing income tax).

61L Meaning of "public authority"

(1) In this Chapter "public authority" means—

(a) a public authority as defined by the Freedom of Information Act 2000,
(b) a Scottish public authority as defined by the Freedom of Information (Scotland) Act 2002 (asp 13),
(c) the Corporate Officer of the House of Commons,
(d) the Corporate Officer of the House of Lords,
(e) the National Assembly for Wales Commission, or
(f) the Northern Ireland Assembly Commission.

(2) An authority within paragraph (a) or (b) of subsection (1) is a public authority for the purposes of this Chapter in relation to all its activities even if provisions of the Act mentioned in that paragraph do not apply to all information held by the authority.

(3) Subsection (1) is subject to subsection (4).

(4) A primary-healthcare provider is a public authority for the purposes of this Chapter only if the primary-healthcare provider—

(a) has a registered patient list for the purposes of relevant medical-services regulations,
(b) is within paragraph 43A in Part 3 of Schedule 1 to the Freedom of Information Act 2000 (providers of primary healthcare services in England and Wales) by reason of being a person providing primary dental services,
(c) is within paragraph 51 in that Part of that Schedule (providers of healthcare services in Northern Ireland) by reason of being a person providing general dental services, or
(d) is within paragraph 33 in Part 4 of Schedule 1 to the Freedom of Information (Scotland) Act 2002 (providers of healthcare services in Scotland) by reason of being a person providing general dental services.

(5) In this section—

"primary-healthcare provider" means an authority that is within subsection (1)(a) or (b) only because it is within a relevant paragraph,
"relevant paragraph" means—

(a) any of paragraphs 43A to 45A and 51 in Part 3 of Schedule 1 to the Freedom of Information Act 2000, or
(b) any of paragraphs 33 to 35 in Part 4 of Schedule 1 to the Freedom of Information (Scotland) Act 2002, and

"relevant medical-services regulations" means any of the following—

(a) the Primary Medical Services (Sale of Goodwill and Restrictions on Sub-contracting) Regulations 2004 (SI 2004/906),
(b) the Primary Medical Services (Sale of Goodwill and Restrictions on Sub-contracting) (Wales) Regulations 2004 (SI 2004/1017),
(c) the Primary Medical Services (Sale of Goodwill and Restrictions on Sub-contracting) (Scotland) Regulations 2004 (SSI 2004/162), and
(d) the Primary Medical Services (Sale of Goodwill and Restrictions on Sub-contracting) Regulations (Northern Ireland) 2004 (SR (NI) 2004 No 477).

(6) The Commissioners for Her Majesty's Revenue and Customs may by regulations amend this section in consequence of—

(a) any amendment or revocation of any regulations for the time being referred to in this section,
(b) any amendment in Part 3 of Schedule 1 to the Freedom of Information Act 2000, or
(c) any amendment in Part 4 of Schedule 1 to the Freedom of Information (Scotland) Act 2002.

61M Engagements to which Chapter applies

(1) Sections 61N to 61R apply where—

(a) an individual ("the worker") personally performs, or is under an obligation personally to perform, services for another person ("the client"),
(b) the client is a public authority,
(c) the services are provided not under a contract directly between the client and the worker but under arrangements involving a third party ("the intermediary"), and
(d) the circumstances are such that—

(i) if the services were provided under a contract directly between the client and the worker, the worker would be regarded for income tax purposes as an employee of the client or the holder of an office under the client, or

(ii) the worker is an office-holder who holds that office under the client and the services relate to the office.

(2) The reference in subsection (1)(c) to a "third party" includes a partnership or unincorporated association of which the worker is a member.

(3) The circumstances referred to in subsection (1)(d) include the terms on which the services are provided, having regard to the terms of the contracts forming part of the arrangements under which the services are provided.

(4) Holding office as statutory auditor of the client does not count as holding office under the client for the purposes of subsection (1)(d), and here "statutory auditor" means a statutory auditor within the meaning of Part 42 of the Companies Act 2006 (see section 1210 of that Act).

(5) In this Chapter "engagement to which this Chapter applies" means any such provision of services as is mentioned in subsection (1).

61N Worker treated as receiving earnings from employment

(1) If one of Conditions A to C is met, identify the chain of two or more persons where—

(a) the highest person in the chain is the client,

(b) the lowest person in the chain is the intermediary, and

(c) each person in the chain above the lowest makes a chain payment to the person immediately below them in the chain.

(See section 61U for cases where one of Conditions A to C is treated as being met.)

(2) In this section and sections 61O to 61S—

"chain payment" means a payment, or money's worth or any other benefit, that can reasonably be taken to be for the worker's services to the client,

"make"—

(a) in relation to a chain payment that is money's worth, means transfer, and

(b) in relation to a chain payment that is a benefit other than a payment or money's worth, means provide, and

"the fee-payer" means the person in the chain immediately above the lowest.

(3) The fee-payer is treated as making to the worker, and the worker is treated as receiving, a payment which is to be treated as earnings from an employment ("the deemed direct payment"), but this is subject to subsections (5) to (7) and sections 61T and 61V.

(4) The deemed direct payment is treated as made at the same time as the chain payment made by the fee-payer.

(5) Subsections (6) and (7) apply, subject to sections 61T and 61V, if the fee-payer—

(a) is not the client, and

(b) is not a qualifying person.

(6) If there is no person in the chain below the highest and above the lowest who is a qualifying person, subsections (3) and (4) have effect as if for any reference to the fee-payer there were substituted a reference to the client.

(7) Otherwise, subsections (3) and (4) have effect as if for any reference to the fee-payer there were substituted a reference to the person in the chain who—

(a) is above the lowest,

(b) is a qualifying person, and

(c) is lower in the chain than any other person in the chain who—

(i) is above the lowest, and

(ii) is a qualifying person.

(8) In subsections (5) to (7) a "qualifying person" is a person who—

(a) is resident in the United Kingdom or has a place of business in the United Kingdom,

(b) is not a person who is controlled by—

(i) the worker, alone or with one or more associates of the worker, or

(ii) an associate of the worker, with or without other associates of the worker, and

(c) if a company, is not one in which—

(i) the worker, alone or with one or more associates of the worker, or

(ii) an associate of the worker, with or without other associates of the worker, has a material interest (within the meaning given by section 51(4) and (5)).

(9) Condition A is that—

    (a) the intermediary is a company, and

    (b) the conditions in section 61O are met in relation to the intermediary.

(10) Condition B is that—

    (a) the intermediary is a partnership,

    (b) the worker is a member of the partnership,

    (c) the provision of the services is by the worker as a member of the partnership, and

    (d) the condition in section 61P is met in relation to the intermediary.

(11) Condition C is that the intermediary is an individual.

(12) Where a payment, money's worth or any other benefit can reasonably be taken to be for both—

    (a) the worker's services to the client, and

    (b) anything else,

then, for the purposes of this Chapter, so much of it as can, on a just and reasonable apportionment, be taken to be for the worker's services is to be treated as (and the rest is to be treated as not being) a payment, or money's worth or another benefit, that can reasonably be taken to be for the worker's services.

61O   Conditions where intermediary is a company

(1) The conditions mentioned in section 61N(9)(b) are that—

    (a) the intermediary is not an associated company of the client that falls within subsection (2), and

    (b) the worker has a material interest in the intermediary.

(2) An associated company of the client falls within this subsection if it is such a company by reason of the intermediary and the client being under the control—

    (a) of the worker, or

    (b) of the worker and other persons.

(3) The worker is treated as having a material interest in the intermediary if—

    (a) the worker, alone or with one or more associates of the worker, or

    (b) an associate of the worker, with or without other associates of the worker,

has a material interest in the intermediary.

(4) For this purpose "material interest" has the meaning given by section 51(4) and (5).

(5) In this section "associated company" has the meaning given by section 449 of CTA 2010.

61P   Conditions where intermediary is a partnership

(1) The condition mentioned in section 61N(10)(d) is—

    (a) that the worker, alone or with one or more relatives, is entitled to 60% or more of the profits of the partnership, or

    (b) that most of the profits of the partnership derive from the provision of services under engagements to which one or other of this Chapter and Chapter 8 applies—

        (i) to a single client, or

        (ii) to a single client together with associates of that client, or

    (c) that under the profit sharing arrangements the income of any of the partners is based on the amount of income generated by that partner by the provision of services under engagements to which one or other of this Chapter and Chapter 8 applies.

(2) In subsection (1)(a) "relative" means spouse or civil partner, parent or child or remoter relation in the direct line, or brother or sister.

(3) Section 61(4) and (5) apply for the purposes of this section as they apply for the purposes of Chapter 8.

61Q   Calculation of deemed direct payment

(1) The amount of the deemed direct payment is the amount resulting from the following steps—

    Step 1

    Identify the amount or value of the chain payment made by the person who is treated as making the deemed direct payment, and deduct from that amount so much of it (if any) as is in respect of value added tax.

Step 2

Deduct, from the amount resulting from Step 1, so much of that amount as represents the direct cost to the intermediary of materials used, or to be used, in the performance of the services.

Step 3

Deduct, at the option of the person treated as making the deemed direct payment, from the amount resulting from Step 2, so much of that amount as represents expenses met by the intermediary that would have been deductible from the taxable earnings from the employment if—

(a) the worker had been employed by the client, and

(b) the expenses had been met by the worker out of those earnings.

Step 4

If the amount resulting from the preceding Steps is nil or negative, there is no deemed direct payment. Otherwise, that amount is the amount of the deemed direct payment.

(2) For the purposes of Step 1 of subsection (1), any part of the amount or value of the chain payment which is employment income of the worker by virtue of section 863G(4) of ITTOIA 2005 (salaried members of limited liability partnerships: anti-avoidance) is to be ignored.

(3) In subsection (1), the reference to the amount or value of the chain payment means the amount or value of that payment before the deduction (if any) permitted under section 61S.

(4) If the actual amount or value of the chain payment mentioned in Step 1 of subsection (1) is such that its recipient bears the cost of amounts due under PAYE regulations or contributions regulations in respect of the deemed direct payment, that Step applies as if the amount or value of that chain payment were what it would be if the burden of that cost were not being passed on through the setting of the level of the payment.

(5) In Step 3 of subsection (1), the reference to expenses met by the intermediary includes—

(a) expenses met by the worker and reimbursed by the intermediary, and

(b) where the intermediary is a partnership and the worker is a member of the partnership, expenses met by the worker for and on behalf of the partnership.

(6) In subsection (4) "contributions regulations" means regulations under the Contributions and Benefits Act providing for primary Class 1 contributions to be paid in a similar manner to income tax in relation to which PAYE regulations have effect (see, in particular, paragraph 6(1) of Schedule 1 to the Act); and here "primary Class 1 contribution" means a primary Class 1 contribution within the meaning of Part 1 of the Contributions and Benefits Act.

61R Application of Income Tax Acts in relation to deemed employment

(1) The Income Tax Acts (in particular, Part 11 and PAYE regulations) apply in relation to the deemed direct payment as follows.

(2) They apply as if—

(a) the worker were employed by the person treated as making the deemed direct payment, and

(b) the services were performed, or to be performed, by the worker in the course of performing the duties of that employment.

(3) The deemed direct payment is treated in particular—

(a) as taxable earnings from the employment for the purpose of securing that any deductions under Chapters 2 to 6 of Part 5 do not exceed the deemed direct payment, and

(b) as taxable earnings from the employment for the purposes of section 232.

(4) The worker is not chargeable to tax in respect of the deemed direct payment if, or to the extent that, by reason of any combination of the factors mentioned in subsection (5), the worker would not be chargeable to tax if—

(a) the client employed the worker,

(b) the worker performed the services in the course of that employment, and

(c) the deemed direct payment were a payment by the client of earnings from that employment.

(5) The factors are—

(a) the worker being resident or domiciled outside the United Kingdom or meeting the requirement of section 26A,

(b) the client being resident outside, or not resident in, the United Kingdom, and

(c) the services being provided outside the United Kingdom.

(6) Where the intermediary is a partnership or unincorporated association, the deemed direct payment is treated as received by the worker in the worker's personal capacity and not as income of the partnership or association.

(7) Where—

(a) the client is the person treated as making the deemed direct payment,

(b) the worker is resident in the United Kingdom,

(c) the services are provided in the United Kingdom,

(d) the client is not resident in the United Kingdom, and

(e) the client does not have a place of business in the United Kingdom,

the client is treated as resident in the United Kingdom.

61S Deductions from chain payments

(1) This section applies if, as a result of section 61R, a person who is treated as making a deemed direct payment is required under PAYE Regulations to pay an amount to the Commissioners for Her Majesty's Revenue and Customs ("the Commissioners") in respect of the payment.

(But see subsection (4)).

(2) The person may deduct from the underlying chain payment an amount which is equal to the amount payable to the Commissioners, but where the amount or value of the underlying chain payment is treated by section 61Q(4) as increased by the cost of any amount due under PAYE Regulations, the amount that may be deducted is limited to the difference (if any) between the amount payable to the Commissioners and the amount of that increase.

(3) Where a person in the chain other than the intermediary receives a chain payment from which an amount has been deducted in reliance on subsection (2) or this subsection, that person may deduct the same amount from the chain payment made by them.

(4) This section does not apply in a case to which 61V(2) applies (services-provider treated as making deemed direct payment).

(5) In subsection (2) "the underlying chain payment" means the chain payment whose amount is used at Step 1 of section 61Q(1) as the starting point for calculating the amount of the deemed direct payment.

61T Information to be provided by clients and consequences of failure

(1) If the conditions in section 61M(1)(a) to (c) are met in any case, and a person as part of the arrangements mentioned in section 61M(1)(c) enters into a contract with the client, the client must inform that person (in the contract or otherwise) of which one of the following is applicable—

(a) the client has concluded that the condition in section 61M(1)(d) is met in the case;

(b) the client has concluded that the condition in section 61M(1)(d) is not met in the case.

(2) If the contract is entered into on or after 6 April 2017, the duty under subsection (1) must be complied with—

(a) on or before the time of entry into the contract, or

(b) if the services begin to be performed at a later time, before that later time.

(3) If the contract is entered into before 6 April 2017, the duty under subsection (1) must be complied with on or before the date of the first payment made under the contract on or after 6 April 2017.

(4) If the information which subsection (1) requires the client to give to a person has been given (whether in the contract, as required by subsection (2) or (3) or otherwise), the client must, on a written request by the person, provide the person with a written response to any questions raised by the person about the client's reasons for reaching the conclusion identified in the information.

(5) A response required by subsection (4) must be provided before the end of 31 days beginning with the day the request for it is received by the client.

(6) If—

(a) the client fails to comply with the duty under subsection (1) within the time allowed by subsection (2) or (3),

(b) the client fails to provide a response required by subsection (4) within the time allowed by subsection (5), or

(c) the client complies with the duty under subsection (1) but fails to take reasonable care in coming to its conclusion as to whether the condition in section 61M(1)(d) is met in the case,

section 61N(3) and (4) have effect in the case as if for any reference to the fee-payer there were substituted a reference to the client, but this is subject to section 61V.

61U Information to be provided by worker and consequences of failure

(1) In the case of an engagement to which this Chapter applies, the worker must inform the potential deemed employer of which one of the following is applicable—

(a) that one of conditions A to C in section 61N is met in the case;

(b) that none of conditions A to C in section 61N is met in the case.

(2) If the worker has not complied with subsection (1) then, for the purposes of section 61N(1), one of conditions A to C in section 61N is to be treated as met.

(3) In this section "the potential deemed employer" is the person who, if one of conditions A to C in section 61N were met, would be treated as making a deemed direct payment to the worker under section 61N(3).

61V Consequences of providing fraudulent information

(1) Subsection (2) applies if in any case—

(a) a person ("the deemed employer") would, but for this section, be treated by section 61N(3) as making a payment to another person ("the services-provider"), and

(b) the fraudulent documentation condition is met.

(2) Section 61N(3) has effect in the case as if the reference to the fee-payer were a reference to the services-provider, but—

(a) section 61N(4) continues to have effect as if the reference to the fee-payer were a reference to the deemed employer, and

(b) Step 1 of section 61Q(1) continues to have effect as referring to the chain payment made by the deemed employer.

(3) Subsection (2) has effect even though that involves the services-provider being treated as both employer and employee in relation to the deemed employment under section 61N(3).

(4) "The fraudulent documentation condition" is that a relevant person provided any person with a fraudulent document intended to constitute evidence—

(a) that the case is not an engagement to which this Chapter applies, or

(b) that none of conditions A to C in section 61N is met in the case.

(5) A "relevant person" is—

(a) the services-provider;

(b) a person connected with the services-provider;

(c) if the intermediary in the case is a company, an office-holder in that company.

61W Prevention of double charge to tax and allowance of certain deductions

(1) Subsection (2) applies where—

(a) a person ("the payee") receives a payment or benefit ("the end-of-line remuneration") from another person ("the paying intermediary"),

(b) the end-of-line remuneration can reasonably be taken to represent remuneration for services of the payee to a public authority,

(c) a payment ("the deemed payment") has been treated by section 61N(3) as made to the payee,

(d) the underlying chain payment can reasonably be taken to be for the same services of the payee to that public authority, and

(e) the recipient of the underlying chain payment has (whether by deduction from that payment or otherwise) borne the cost of any amounts due, under PAYE regulations and contributions regulations in respect of the deemed payment, from the person treated by section 61N(3) as making the deemed payment.

(2) For income tax purposes, the paying intermediary and the payee may treat the amount of the end-of-line remuneration as reduced (but not below nil) by any one or more of the following—

(a) the amount (see section 61Q) of the deemed payment;

(b) the amount of any capital allowances in respect of expenditure incurred by the paying intermediary that could have been deducted from employment income under section 262 of CAA 2001 if the payee had been employed by the public authority and had incurred the expenditure;

(c) the amount of any contributions made, in the same tax year as the end-of-line remuneration, for the benefit of the payee by the paying intermediary to a registered pension scheme that if made by an employer for the benefit of an employee would not be chargeable to income tax as income of the employee.

(3) Subsection (2)(c) does not apply to—

(a) excess contributions paid and later repaid,

(b) contributions set under subsection (2) against another payment by the paying intermediary, or

(c) contributions deductible at Step 5 of section 54(1) in calculating the amount of the payment (if any) treated by section 50 as made in the tax year concerned by the paying intermediary to the payee.

(4) For the purposes of subsection (3)(c), the contributions to which Step 5 of section 54(1) applies in the case of the particular calculation are "deductible" at that Step so far as their amount does not exceed the result after Step 4 in that calculation.

(5) In subsection (1)(d) "the underlying chain payment" means the chain payment whose amount is used at Step 1 of section 61Q(1) as the starting point for calculating the amount of the deemed payment.

(6) Subsection (2) applies whether the end-of-line remuneration—

(a) is earnings of the payee,

(b) is a distribution of the paying intermediary, or

(c) takes some other form.

61X Interpretation

In this Chapter—

"associate" has the meaning given by section 60;

"company" means a body corporate or unincorporated association, and does not include a partnership;

"engagement to which Chapter 8 applies" has the meaning given by section 49(5)."

PART 3

CONSEQUENTIAL AMENDMENTS

10 In section 7(5)(a) of ITEPA 2003 (amounts treated as earnings by Chapters 7 to 9 of Part 2 are "employment income" and "general earnings"), for "9" substitute "10".

11 In section 49 of ITEPA 2003 (engagements to which Chapter 8 of Part 2 applies), after subsection (4) insert—

"(4A) Holding office as statutory auditor of the client does not count as holding office under the client for the purposes of subsection (1)(c), and here "statutory auditor" means a statutory auditor within the meaning of Part 42 of the Companies Act 2006 (see section 1210 of that Act)."

12 In section 339A of ITEPA 2003 (travel for employment involving intermediaries), after subsection (6) insert—

"(6A) Subsection (3) does not apply in relation to an engagement if—

(a) sections 61N to 61R in Chapter 10 of Part 2 apply in relation to the engagement,

(b) one of Conditions A to C in section 61N is met in relation to the employment intermediary, and

(c) the employment intermediary is not a managed service company.

(6B) This section does not apply in relation to an engagement if—

(a) sections 61N to 61R in Chapter 10 of Part 2 do not apply in relation to the engagement because the circumstances in section 61M(1)(d) are not met,

(b) assuming those circumstances were met, one of Conditions A to C in section 61N would be met in relation to the employment intermediary, and

(c) the employment intermediary is not a managed service company.

(6C) In determining for the purposes of subsection (6A) or (6B) whether one of Conditions A to C in section 61N is or would be met in relation to the employment intermediary, read references to the intermediary as references to the employment intermediary."

13 In Chapter 11 of Part 2 of ITTOIA 2005 (trade profits: specific trades), after section 164A insert—

"Worker's services provided to public sector through intermediary

164B Intermediaries providing worker's services to public sector

(1) This section applies for the purposes of calculating the trading profits of a person where—

(a) the person is the intermediary in a chain identified under section 61N of ITEPA 2003 (see section 61N(1)(b)),

(b) a deemed direct payment is treated as made under subsection (3) of that section, and

(c) the person receives a payment which can reasonably be taken to be in respect of the same services as those in respect of which the underlying chain payment is made.

(2) The payment mentioned in subsection (1)(c) is not required to be brought into account in calculating the profits of the trade.

(3) In this section "underlying chain payment" means the payment whose amount is used at Step 1 of section 61Q(1) of ITEPA 2003 as the starting point for calculating the amount of the deemed direct payment mentioned in subsection (1)(b)."

14 In Chapter 9 of Part 3 of CTA 2009 (trade profits: specific trades), after section 141 insert—

"Worker's services provided to public sector through intermediary

141A Intermediaries providing worker's services to public sector

(1) This section applies for the purposes of calculating the trading profits of a person where—

(a) the person is the intermediary in a chain identified under section 61N of ITEPA 2003 (see section 61N(1)(b)),

(b) a deemed direct payment is treated as made under subsection (3) of that section, and

(c) the person receives a payment which can reasonably be taken to be in respect of the same services as those in respect of which the underlying chain payment is made.

(2) The payment mentioned in subsection (1)(c) is not required to be brought into account in calculating the profits of the trade.

(3) In this section "underlying chain payment" means the payment whose amount is used at Step 1 of section 61Q(1) of ITEPA 2003 as the starting point for calculating the amount of the deemed direct payment mentioned in subsection (1)(b)."

PART 4

COMMENCEMENT

15 The amendments made in ITEPA 2003 by Parts 1 and 3 of this Schedule have effect for the tax year 2017–18 and subsequent tax years.

16 The amendment made by Part 2 of this Schedule has effect in relation to deemed direct payments treated as made on or after 6 April 2017, and does so even if relating to services provided before that date.

17 The payments to which the amendments made in ITTOIA 2005 and CTA 2009 by Part 3 of this Schedule apply include payments made before the passing of this Act.

GENERAL NOTE

Background

Finance Act 2017 s 6, Sch 1 amends and introduces a new regime in relation to income tax into ITEPA 2003 Pt 2 in respect of the taxation of workers working through intermediaries where the end user client is a public sector entity (often described by HMRC as "off-payroll working in the public sector"). It removes such arrangements from the current legislation in ITEPA 2003 Pt 2 Ch 8 (the drafting originating from IR35 and which captures arrangements using personal service companies) and ITEPA 2003 Pt 2 Ch 9 in relation to managed service companies and introduces a new set of rules via a new ITEPA 2003 Pt 2 Ch 10. The rules also take precedence over the construction industry scheme.

The aim of the changes is to place the burden of determining whether an employment relationship exists, with the end user public sector entity. Where such a relationship exists the obligation to assess and pay income tax ceases to be with the intermediary (often a personal service company). Instead the payments to the worker are treated as deemed earnings with a liability to collect and pay income tax via PAYE falling on persons in the supply chain and not the intermediary. If the end user public sector entity does not fulfil its obligations in relation to determining the employment status of the worker then the liability to operate PAYE will fall to it.

Equivalent provisions have been introduced for class 1 national insurance contributions (NIC) via the Social Security (Miscellaneous Amendments No. 2) Regulations 2017 (SI 2017/373). A guidance note for agents and a technical note have also been issued by HMRC. The changes to the NIC rules result in liability to pay class 1 secondary (employer's) NIC moving from the intermediary (which is the case when the IR35 rules in Pt 2 Ch 8 apply) to the other parties in the supply chain. This will impact on how the contracts are priced in the supply chain due to the burden of the class 1 secondary NIC passing up the chain.

Part 1 Preliminary Amendments

Part 1 introduces amendments to various sections within ITEPA 2003 Pt 2 Chs 8 and 9 which provide that:

– a new Ch 10 will apply instead of Ch 8 (Application of Provisions to Workers under Arrangements made by Intermediaries) to certain payment made in connection with services provided through an intermediary to the public sector; and
– Ch 9, the managed service company legislation, will not apply to an intermediary (where it otherwise would do so) if the relevant services of the individual are provided by an intermediary and the provision of such services gives rise to an engagement to which Ch 10 applies.

Part 2 New Chapter 10 of Part 2 of ITEPA 2003

Part 2 introduces a new ITEPA 2003 Pt 2 Ch 10 (ss 61K to 61X).

New ITEPA 2003 s 61K

Section 61K confirms that Ch 10 applies only with respect to the provision of services to a public authority through an intermediary, that the provisions do not impact on the application of the agency rules in ITEPA 2003 Pt 2 Ch 7 and that Ch 10 does not apply to payments to visiting performers.

New ITEPA 2003 s 61L

Section 61L defines "public authority" for the purposes of Ch 10. The definition uses the definition of public authority from the Freedom of Information Act 2000 (and equivalent in Scotland) and contains specific provisions about primary-healthcare providers. HMRC guidance confirms that it will include universities, local authorities, parish councils and the NHS.

New ITEPA 2003 s 61M

Section 61M sets out the engagements in respect of which Ch 10 applies. Save for the fact that this applies to clients who are public authorities, this mirrors ITEPA 2003 s 49 (which is the operative provision of the IR35 rules enshrined within ITEPA 2003 Pt 2 Ch 8). It provides that Ch 10 applies where a person (the worker) personally performs services for another person (the client); the client is a public authority; the services are not under a contract directly with the client but under arrangements with a third party (the intermediary); and where, had the services been provided directly between the worker and client, the worker would be regarded for income tax purposes as an employee or office holder of the client.

Subsection (4) is a new provision which makes it clear that position of a statutory auditor of the client does not count as an office under this provision. The equivalent drafting has also been added to ITEPA 2003 s 49.

New ITEPA 2003 s 61N

Section 61N sets out when a worker who falls within the circumstances set out in s 61M will be treated as receiving earnings from an employment and how such earnings will be taxed. For s 61N to apply one of Conditions A to C (contained within ss 61N to 61P) will need to be met in relation to the intermediary. The conditions set out tests in relation to an intermediary as a company, partnership or individual and replicate equivalent provisions in ITEPA 2003 Pt 2 Ch 8 (ss 51–53) save for the omission of the company requirement in s 51(1)(b).

Where an intermediary meets one of Conditions A to C, s 61N provides that you have to identify the "chain of two or more persons" with the worker at one end of the chain and the client at the end. This provision is recognising the fact that workers are often supplied by an intermediary through a number of agencies before working for the end user client.

Subsection (2) defines "the fee-payer" as the person immediately above the intermediary in the chain, which will be the party that the intermediary contracts with. This could be an agency or could be the end user client.

Pursuant to sub-s (3), where the arrangement is such that it falls into s 61 by reason of the fact that there is an intermediary fulfilling one of Conditions A to C and the arrangements between the worker and the client are such that absent the intermediary the worker would be treated as an employee of the client, then the "fee-payer" is treated as making a payment of earnings to the worker, the "deemed direct payment", at the point that the fee-payer makes a payment (or provides a benefit) to the intermediary in relation to the worker's services to client. The fee-payer has the obligation to deduct and collect income tax via PAYE.

Subsections (5)–(8) deal with the possibility that the fee-payer may not be within the territorial limits of PAYE. Subsection (8) defines a "qualifying person" as a person who is UK resident or has a place of business in the UK (i.e. being within the usual territorial limits of PAYE) and not controlled by the workers or associates of the workers nor a company in respect of which the worker or associates have a material interest. Where the original fee-payer is not a "qualifying-person", you look to the next person in the supply chain to determine who is a qualifying person and they are treated as the fee-payer. This ensures that the fee-payer is a person within the territorial limits of the PAYE system and is a person not connected to the worker. Where there is no person who is a "qualifying person" ahead of the client in the chain, then the client will be the fee-payer regardless of residence or connection. When the client is the fee-payer it will be liable to operate PAYE on the deemed direct payment regardless of its status as provided by s 61R(7).

New ITEPA 2003 s 61Q

Section 61Q sets out how the quantum of the deemed direct payment is calculated and ensures fairness by allowing deductions for VAT, materials and expenses that would have been deductible if the worker had been employed by the client. It also deducts amounts treated as employment income under the salaried member rules relating to limited liability partnerships and which may be applicable if the intermediary is a partnership. There is no 5% general deduction as is the case within the IR35 rules in Ch 8.

It also recognised that if the payment has been reduced in the supply chain for income tax and national insurance contributions (NIC) then these must be added back.

New ITEPA 2003 s 61R

Section 61R provides for how the PAYE provisions of ITEPA 2003 apply to the deemed direct payment. They treat the worker as being employed by the person treated as making the deemed direct payment, treat the services as services arising from such deemed employment and treat the deemed direct payment as taxable earnings for the purposes of ITEPA 2003 Pt 5 Chs 2 to 6 (deductions allowed from earnings).

The PAYE provisions do not apply if the worker would not be within them as an actual employee due to the worker performing services outside the UK and the worker and client not fulfilling UK residence or domicile requirements. It is also confirmed that partnerships are looked through to the worker when determining the application of s 61R.

Importantly, sub-s (7) provides that were the client is treated as the fee-payer and the worker is resident in the UK and provides services in the UK then the client is treated as resident in the UK, and hence obliged to operate PAYE, even if in fact it is non-UK resident. This ensures that there is always a party in the supply chain who will have an obligation to collect and pay income tax under the PAYE system.

New ITEPA 2003 s 61S

Section 61S allows the fee-payer to deduct the amount of income tax it has paid via PAYE from the payment it is obliged to make in the contractual supply chain. If the fee-payer does not have the direct contractual relationship with the intermediary (for example, because there is another non-UK resident agency below it in the chain), this section permits the fee-payer to deduct such income tax from the payment it makes to such agency. This follows on down the chain so that ultimately the intermediary will receive an amount reduced by the income tax.

New ITEPA 2003 s 61T

Section 61T is an important provision which places the burden on the client to confirm if it believes that the provisions of services of the worker via the intermediary are such that the worker would be treated as an employee of the client if the services were provided by the worker to the client under a contract directly between the two parties. For contracts entered into from 6 April 2017 onward, the client must inform the person that it contracts directly with on or before the later of the contract being entered into and the date the services begin to be performed. For contracts in existence at 6 April 2017 the obligation must be fulfilled before the first payment is made under the contract on or after 6 April 2017. This means that existing arrangements cannot be ignored and will be caught within the new rules if they continue past 6 April 2017.

The drafting suggests the notification can be in the contract, or otherwise. In practice, notification by way of inclusion of provisions in the contract may become the norm. HMRC has issued a new employment status service tool to assist relevant persons in determining the deemed employment status of the worker.

The client is also obliged to respond to any written questions that the contracting party may raise in respect of the client's determination of the worker's status. The client is subject to an obligation to respond within 31 days. If the client fails to provide the confirmation as to worker status, fails to respond to questions within the statutory time period or fails to use reasonable care in coming to its conclusions then it will be treated as the "fee-payer" and will be responsible for the operation of PAYE on the deemed direct payment. This is a significant change to the position before this new legislation when end users had no role to play in the application of ITEPA 2003 Pt 2 Ch 8 and were able to make payments gross to personal services companies and other intermediaries falling within Ch 8 without the need to consider the operation of PAYE or enquire into the arrangements between the worker and the intermediary. The new legislation places a significant burden on the end user client when it is a public authority. It now has an obligation to properly consider the status of the worker and explain its conclusions on a timely basis otherwise it will be become liable to operate PAYE where it might not otherwise be liable.

This requirement is effectively pushing some of the obligation to police the supply chain on to the public authority client.

It should be noted that whilst there is an obligation on the public authority client to make a determination about the employment status of the worker, this is only an obligation to inform the party that it contracts with. In many circumstances the notification will be directly to the intermediary. However, in a supply chain involving a number of parties, they will need to ensure, contractually, that this information is passed along the chain to the fee-payer. The fee-payer still ultimately has the obligation to determine if the arrangements fall within ITEPA 2003 Pt 2 Ch 10 and the legislation does not appear to have provisions which bind the fee-payer to follow the client's determination. Accordingly, it would be possible for a fee-payer (when such fee-payer is not the client) to decide that it did not wish to follow the determination of the public authority client. However, if it did so it would then need to be prepared to defend that decision to HMRC on enquiry and that may be difficult especially if the public authority client has used the employment status service in forming its view.

New ITEPA 2003 s 61U

Section 61U also places information obligations on the worker. It must inform the potential deemed employer (being the party that would be liable as the fee-payer) if the intermediary that provides its services is one caught within ITEPA 2003 Pt 2 Ch 10 (that one of Conditions A to C applies). If the worker does not provide this information then one of Conditions A to C will be treated as met which will result in a party in the supply chain being classed as a fee-payer. This provision will result in the need for those who are potentially fee-payers to ask the worker to confirm if Conditions A to C are fulfilled. Where there are non-UK resident persons in the supply chain, the deemed employer may be a party which does not contract directly with the intermediary. Accordingly, the parties to the supply chain will need to enforce this via contractual arrangements which may become burdensome.

New ITEPA 2003 s 61V

Section 61V addresses the issue of fraudulent information by providing that if the worker (in this section referred to as the "services provider") or a person connected with the worker or an office holder of the intermediary (if a company) provides fraudulent information which purports to show that the worker falls outside of Ch 10 or Conditions A to C within Ch 10 then the worker is deemed to be the fee-payer who makes the deemed direct payment and on which the obligation to operate PAYE falls.

Part 3 Consequential Amendments

Part 3 provides for consequential amendments arising.

Paragraph 12 ensures that the rules in ITEPA 2003 s 339A (travel for necessary attendance: employment intermediaries) also apply to engagements taxed under Ch 10 in the same way as they currently do for engagements caught within Ch 8.

Paragraphs 13 and 14 ensure that in circumstances where a person is an intermediary and there is a direct deemed payment arising in respect of which that person is the intermediary, such payment is not included in the intermediary's taxable profits of its trade.

Part 4 Commencement

Part 4 provides for the commencement date in relation to the aforementioned amendments to ITEPA 2003. Parts 1 and 3 apply for tax year 2017/18 onwards and Pt 2 to deemed direct payments made on or after 6 April 2017. It also confirms that the no double counting provisions in Pt 3 apply to payments made before FA 2017 was passed.

SCHEDULE 2

OPTIONAL REMUNERATION ARRANGEMENTS

Section 7

Optional remuneration arrangements

1 In Part 3 of ITEPA 2003 (employment income: earnings and benefits etc treated as earnings), in Chapter 2 (taxable benefits: the benefits code), after section 69 insert—

"69A Optional remuneration arrangements

    (1) Subsections (2) to (7) have effect for the purposes of the benefits code.

    (2) A benefit provided for an employee is provided under "optional remuneration arrangements" so far as it is provided under arrangements of type A or B (regardless of whether those arrangements are made before or after the beginning of the person's employment).

    (3) "Type A arrangements" are arrangements under which, in return for the benefit, the employee gives up the right (or a future right) to receive an amount of earnings within Chapter 1 of Part 3.

    (4) "Type B arrangements" are arrangements (other than type A arrangements) under which the employee agrees to be provided with the benefit rather than an amount of earnings within Chapter 1 of Part 3.

    (5) A benefit provided for an employee is to be regarded as provided under optional remuneration arrangements (whether of type A or type B) so far as it is just and reasonable to attribute the provision of the benefit to the arrangements in question.

    (6) Where a benefit is provided for an employee under any arrangements, the mere fact that under the arrangements the employee makes good, or is required to make good, any part of the cost of provision is not to be taken to show that the benefit is (to any extent) provided otherwise than under optional remuneration arrangements.

    (7) Where a benefit is provided for an employee partly under optional remuneration arrangements and partly otherwise than under such arrangements, the benefits code is to apply with any modifications (including provision for just and reasonable apportionments) that may be required for ensuring that the benefit is treated—

        (a) in accordance with the relevant provision in the column 2 of the table so far as it is provided under optional remuneration arrangements, and

        (b) in accordance with the relevant provision in column 1 of the table so far as it is provided otherwise than under such arrangements.

Column 1	*Column 2*
Section	*Section*
81(1)	81(1A)(b)
87(1)	87A(1)(a)
94(1)	94A(1)(a)
102(1A)	102(1B)(b)
120(1)	120A(1)(a)
149(1)	149A(2)(a)
154(1)	154A(1)(a)
160(1)	160A(2)(a)
175(1)	175(1A)(b)
203(1)	203A(1)(a)

69B Optional remuneration arrangements: supplementary

(1) For the purposes of the benefits code "the amount foregone"—

(a) in relation to a benefit provided for an employee under type A arrangements means the amount of earnings mentioned in section 69A(3);

(b) in relation to a benefit provided for an employee under type B arrangements means the amount of earnings mentioned in section 69A(4);

(c) in relation to a benefit provided for an employee partly under type A arrangements and partly under type B arrangements, means the sum of the amounts foregone under the arrangements of each type.

(2) Subsection (3) applies where, in order to determine the amount foregone with respect to a particular benefit mentioned in section 69A(3) or (4), it is necessary to apportion an amount of earnings to the benefit.

(3) The apportionment is to be made on a just and reasonable basis.

(4) In this section and section 69A references to a benefit provided for an employee include a benefit provided for a member of an employee's family or household.

(5) In this section and section 69A—

"benefit" includes any benefit or facility, regardless of its form and the manner of providing it;

"earnings" means earnings within Chapter 1 of Part 3 (and includes a reference to amounts which would have been such earnings if the employee had received them)."

Benefits in kind: amount treated as earnings

2 Part 3 of ITEPA 2003 (employment income: earnings and benefits in kind etc treated as earnings) is amended as follows.

3 (1) Section 81 (benefit of cash voucher treated as earnings) is amended as follows.

(2) After subsection (1) insert—

"(1A) Where a cash voucher to which this Chapter applies is provided pursuant to optional remuneration arrangements—

(a) subsection (1) does not apply, and

(b) the relevant amount is to be treated as earnings from the employment for the tax year in which the voucher is received by the employee.

(1B) In this section "the relevant amount" means—

(a) the cash equivalent, or

(b) if greater, the amount foregone with respect to the benefit of the voucher (see section 69B)."

(3) At the end insert—

"(3) For the purposes of subsection (1B), assume that the cash equivalent is zero if the condition in subsection (4) is met.

(4) The condition is that the benefit of the voucher would be exempt from income tax but for section 228A (exclusion of certain exemptions)."

4 After section 87 insert—

"87A Benefit of non-cash voucher treated as earnings: optional remuneration arrangements

(1) Where a non-cash voucher to which this Chapter applies is provided pursuant to optional remuneration arrangements—

(a) the relevant amount is to be treated as earnings from the employment for the tax year in which the voucher is received by the employee, and

(b) section 87(1) does not apply.

(2) To find the relevant amount, first determine which (if any) is the greater of—

(a) the cost of provision (see section 87(3)), and

(b) the amount foregone with respect to the benefit of the voucher (see section 69B).

(3) If the cost of provision is greater than or equal to the amount foregone, the "relevant amount" is the cash equivalent of the benefit of the non-cash voucher (see section 87(2)).

(4) Otherwise, the "relevant amount" is the difference between—

(a) the amount foregone, and

(b) any part of the cost of provision that is made good by the employee, to the person incurring it, on or before 6 July following the relevant tax year.

(5) If the voucher is a non-cash voucher other than a cheque voucher, the relevant tax year is—

(a) the tax year in which the cost of provision is incurred, or

(b) if later, the tax year in which the employee receives the voucher.

(6) If the voucher is a cheque voucher, the relevant tax year is the tax year in which the voucher is handed over in exchange for money, goods or services.

(7) For the purposes of subsections (2) and (3), assume that the cost of provision is zero if the condition in subsection (8) is met.

(8) The condition is that the non-cash voucher would be exempt from income tax but for section 228A (exclusion of certain exemptions)."

5 In section 88 (year in which earnings treated as received)—

(a) in subsection (1), after "87" insert "or 87A";

(b) in subsection (2), after "87" insert "or 87A".

6 After section 94 insert—

"94A Benefit of credit-token treated as earnings: optional remuneration arrangements

(1) If the conditions in subsections (2) and (3) are met in relation to any occasions on which a credit-token to which this Chapter applies is used by the employee in a tax year to obtain money, goods or services—

(a) the relevant amount is to be treated as earnings from the employment for that year, and

(b) section 94(1) does not apply in relation to the use of the credit-token on those occasions.

(2) The condition in this subsection is that the credit-token is used pursuant to optional remuneration arrangements.

(3) The condition in this subsection is that AF is greater than the relevant cost of provision for the tax year.

In this section "AF" means so much of the amount foregone (see section 69B) as is attributable on a just and reasonable basis to the use of the credit-token by the employee in the tax year pursuant to the optional remuneration arrangements to obtain money, goods or services.

(4) The "relevant amount" is the difference between—

(a) AF, and

(b) any part of the relevant cost of provision for the tax year that is made good by the employee, to the person incurring it, on or before 6 July following the tax year which contains the occasion of use of the credit-token to which the making good relates.

(5) But the relevant amount is taken to be zero if the amount given by paragraph (b) of subsection (4) exceeds AF.

(6) For the purposes of this section the "relevant cost of provision for the tax year" is determined as follows—

Step 1

Find the cost of provision with respect to each occasion of use of the credit-token by the employee in the tax year pursuant to the optional remuneration arrangements to obtain money, goods or services.

Step 2

The total of those amounts is the relevant cost of provision for the tax year.

(7) But the relevant cost of provision for the tax year is to be taken to be zero if the condition in subsection (8) is met.

(8) The condition is that use of the credit token by the employee in the tax year pursuant to the optional remuneration arrangements to obtain money, goods or services would be exempt from income tax but for section 228A (exclusion of certain exemptions).

(9) In this section "cost of provision" has the same meaning as in section 94."

7 In section 97 (living accommodation to which Chapter 5 applies), in subsection (1A)(b), for "the cash equivalent of" substitute "an amount in respect of".

8 In section 98 (accommodation provided by local authority), in the words before paragraph (a), for "This Chapter" substitute "In section 102 (benefit of accommodation treated as earnings) subsection (1A) (accommodation provided otherwise than pursuant to optional remuneration arrangements)".

9 (1) Section 99 (accommodation provided for performance of duties) is amended as follows.

(2) In subsection (1), for "This Chapter" substitute "In section 102 (benefit of accommodation treated as earnings) subsection (1A) (accommodation provided otherwise than pursuant to optional remuneration arrangements)".

(3) In subsection (2), for "This Chapter" substitute "In section 102 (benefit of accommodation treated as earnings) subsection (1A)".

10 In section 100 (accommodation provided as result of security threat), in the words before paragraph (a), for "This Chapter" substitute "In section 102 (benefit of accommodation treated as earnings) subsection (1A) (accommodation provided otherwise than pursuant to optional remuneration arrangements)".

11 In section 100A (homes outside UK owned by company etc), in subsection (1), for "This Chapter" substitute "In section 102 (benefit of accommodation treated as earnings) subsection (1A) (accommodation provided otherwise than pursuant to optional remuneration arrangements)".

12 In section 101 (Chevening House), in the words before paragraph (a), for "This Chapter" substitute "In section 102 (benefit of accommodation treated as earnings) subsection (1A) (accommodation provided otherwise than pursuant to optional remuneration arrangements)".

13 (1) Section 102 (benefit of living accommodation treated as earnings) is amended as follows.

(2) In subsection (1), for the words before paragraph (a) substitute "This section applies if living accommodation to which this Chapter applies is provided in any period ("the taxable period")—".

(3) The words in subsection (1) from "the cash equivalent" to the end become subsection (1A).

(4) After subsection (1A) insert—

"(1B) If the benefit of the accommodation is provided pursuant to optional remuneration arrangements—

(a) subsection (1A) does not apply, and
(b) the relevant amount is to be treated as earnings from the employment for that tax year."

(5) Omit subsection (2).

(6) At the end insert—

"(4) Section 103A indicates how the relevant amount is determined."

14 In section 103 (method of calculating cash equivalent), in subsection (3), for "102(2)" substitute "102(1)".

15 After section 103 insert—

"103A Accommodation provided pursuant to optional remuneration arrangements: relevant amount

(1) To find the relevant amount, first determine which (if any) is the greater of—

(a) the modified cash equivalent of the benefit of the accommodation (see sections 105(2A) and 106(2A)), and
(b) the amount foregone with respect to the benefit of the accommodation (see section 69B).

(2) If the amount mentioned in subsection (1)(a) is greater than or equal to the amount mentioned in subsection (1)(b), the "relevant amount" is the cash equivalent of the benefit of the accommodation (see section 103).

(3) Otherwise, the "relevant amount" is the difference between—

(a) the amount foregone with respect to the benefit of the accommodation, and
(b) the deductible amount (see subsections (7) and (8)).

(4) If the amount foregone with respect to the benefit of the accommodation does not exceed the deductible amount, the relevant amount is taken to be zero.

(5) For the purposes of subsections (1) and (2), assume that the modified cash equivalent of the benefit of the accommodation is zero if the condition in subsection (6) is met.

(6) The condition is that the benefit of the accommodation would be exempt from income tax but for section 228A (exclusion of certain exemptions).

(7) If the cost of providing the living accommodation does not exceed £75,000, the "deductible amount" means any sum made good, on or before 6 July following the tax year which contains the taxable period, by the employee to the person at whose cost the accommodation is provided that is properly attributable to its provision.

(8) If the cost of providing the living accommodation exceeds £75,000, the "deductible amount" means the total of amounts A and B where—

A is equal to so much of MG as does not exceed RV;
B is the amount of any excess rent paid by the employee in respect of the taxable period;
MG is the total of any sums made good, on or before 6 July following the tax year which contains the taxable period, by the employee to the person at whose cost the accommodation is provided that are properly attributable to its provision (in the taxable period);
RV is the rental value of the accommodation for the taxable period as set out in section 105(3) or (4A)(b) (as applicable).

(9) In subsection (8) "excess rent" means so much of the rent in respect of the taxable period paid—

(a) by the employee,
(b) in respect of the accommodation,
(c) to the person providing it, and
(d) on or before 6 July following the tax year which contains the taxable period,

as exceeds the rental value of the accommodation.

(10) Where it is necessary for the purposes of subsection (1)(b) and (3)(a) to apportion an amount of earnings to the benefit of the accommodation in the taxable period, the apportionment is to be made on a just and reasonable basis.

In this subsection "earnings" is to be interpreted in accordance with section 69B(5)."

16 (1) Section 105 (cash equivalent: cost of accommodation not over £75,000) is amended as follows.

(2) In subsection (1), after "equivalent" insert "or modified cash equivalent".

(3) After subsection (2) insert—

"(2A) The modified cash equivalent is equal to the rental value of the accommodation for the taxable period."

17 (1) Section 106 (cash equivalent: cost of accommodation over £75,000) is amended as follows.

(2) In subsection (1), after "equivalent" insert "or modified cash equivalent".

(3) After subsection (2) insert—

"(2A) To calculate the modified cash equivalent—

(a) apply steps 1 to 3 in subsection (2), as if the words "cash equivalent" in step 1 were "modified cash equivalent (for the purposes of section 105)";
(b) calculate the modified cash equivalent by adding together the amounts calculated under steps 1 and 3 as applied by paragraph (a)."

18 (1) Section 109 (priority of Chapter 5 over Chapter 1 of Part 3 of the Act) is amended as follows.

(2) In subsection (1)(a), for "the cash equivalent of the benefit of living accommodation" substitute "an amount".

(3) In subsection (2), for "of the cash equivalent" substitute "mentioned in subsection (1)(a)".

(4) In subsection (4), in the words before paragraph (a), for "cash equivalent of the benefit of the living accommodation" substitute "amount mentioned in subsection (1)(a)".

19 In section 114 (cars, vans and related benefits), in subsection (2)—

(a) in paragraph (a), for "the cash equivalent of" substitute "an amount in respect of";

(b) in paragraph (b), for "the cash equivalent of" substitute "an amount in respect of";

(c) in paragraph (c), for "the cash equivalent of" substitute "an amount in respect of";

(d) in paragraph (d), for "the cash equivalent of" substitute "an amount in respect of".

20 (1) Section 119 (where alternative to benefit of car or van offered) is amended as follows.

(2) For subsection (1) substitute—

"(1) This section applies where in a tax year—

(a) a car is made available as mentioned in section 114(1),

(b) the car's CO_2 emissions figure (see sections 133 to 138) does not exceed 75 grams per kilometre, and

(c) an alternative to the benefit of the car is offered."

(3) In the heading, before "car" insert "low emission".

21 In section 120 (benefit of car treated as earnings), after subsection (3) insert—

"(4) This section is subject to section 120A."

22 After section 120 insert—

"120A Benefit of car treated as earnings: optional remuneration arrangements

(1) Where this Chapter applies to a car in relation to a particular tax year and the conditions in subsection (3) are met—

(a) the relevant amount (see section 121A) is to be treated as earnings from the employment for that tax year, and

(b) section 120(1) does not apply.

(2) In such a case (including a case where the relevant amount is nil) the employee is referred to in this Chapter as being chargeable to tax in respect of the car in the tax year.

(3) The conditions are that—

(a) the car is made available to the employee or member of the employee's household pursuant to optional remuneration arrangements,

(b) the amount foregone (see section 69B) with respect to the benefit of the car for the tax year is greater than the modified cash equivalent of the benefit of the car for the tax year (see section 121B), and

(c) the car's CO_2 emissions figure (see sections 133 to 138) exceeds 75 grams per kilometre."

23 After section 121 insert—

"121A Optional remuneration arrangements: method of calculating relevant amount

(1) To find the relevant amount for the purposes of section 120A, take the following steps—

Step 1

Take the amount foregone with respect to the benefit of the car for the tax year.

Step 2

Make any deduction under section 132A in respect of capital contributions made by the employee to the cost of the car or accessories.

The resulting amount is the provisional sum.

Step 3

Make any deduction from the provisional sum under section 144 in respect of payments by the employee for the private use of the car.

The result is the "relevant amount" for the purposes of section 120A.

(2) Where it is necessary, for the purpose of determining the "amount foregone" under step 1 of subsection (1), to apportion an amount of earnings to the benefit of the car for the tax year, the apportionment is to be made on a just and reasonable basis.

In this subsection "earnings" is to be interpreted in accordance with section 69B(5).

121B Meaning of "modified cash equivalent"

(1) The "modified cash equivalent" of the benefit of a car for a tax year is calculated in accordance with the following steps (which must be read with subsections (2) to (4))—

Step 1
Find the price of the car in accordance with sections 122 to 124A.
Step 2
Add the price of any accessories which fall to be taken into account in accordance with sections 125 to 131.
The resulting amount is the interim sum.
Step 3
Find the appropriate percentage for the car for the year in accordance with sections 133 to 142.
Step 4
Multiply the interim sum by the appropriate percentage for the car for the year.
Step 5
Make any deduction under section 143 for any periods when the car was unavailable.
The resulting amount is the modified cash equivalent of the benefit of the car for the year.

(2) Where the car is shared the modified cash equivalent is calculated under this section in accordance with section 148.

(3) The modified cash equivalent of the benefit of a car for a tax year is to be taken to be zero if the condition in subsection (4) is met.

(4) The condition is that the benefit of the car for the tax year would be exempt from income tax but for section 228A (exclusion of certain exemptions).

(5) The method of calculation set out in subsection (1) is modified in the special cases dealt with in—

(a) section 146 (cars that run on road fuel gas), and
(b) section 147A (classic cars: optional remuneration arrangements)."

24 In section 126 (amounts taken into account in respect of accessories), in subsection (1), in the words before paragraph (a), after "121(1)" insert "and step 2 of section 121B(1)".

25 (1) Section 131 (replacement accessories) is amended as follows.

(2) In subsection (1), in the words before paragraph (a), after "applies" insert "for the purposes of sections 121(1) and 121B(1)".

(3) After subsection (1) insert—

"(1A) In the application of this section for the purposes of section 121B(1)—

(a) references to the cash equivalent of the benefit of the car for the tax year are to be read as references to the modified cash equivalent of the benefit of the car for the tax year, and
(b) references to step 2 of section 121(1) are to be read as references to step 2 of section 121B(1)."

26 In section 132 (capital contributions by employee), in subsection (1), in the words before paragraph (a), after "applies" insert "for the purposes of section 121(1)".

27 After section 132 insert—

"132A Capital contributions by employee: optional remuneration arrangements

(1) This section applies for the purposes of section 121A(1) if the employee contributes a capital sum to expenditure on the provision of—

(a) the car, or
(b) any qualifying accessory which is taken into account in calculating under section 121B the modified cash equivalent of the benefit of the car.

(2) A deduction is to be made from the amount carried forward from step 1 of section 121A(1)—

(a) for the tax year in which the contribution is made, and
(b) for all subsequent tax years in which the employee is chargeable to tax in respect of the car by virtue of section 120A.

(3) The amount of the deduction allowed in any tax year is found by multiplying the capped amount by the appropriate percentage.

(4) In subsection (3) the reference to "the appropriate percentage" is to the appropriate percentage for the car for the tax year (determined in accordance with sections 133 to 142).

(5) In this section "the capped amount" means the lesser of—

(a) the total of the capital sums contributed by the employee in that year and any earlier years to expenditure on the provision of—

(i) the car, or

(ii) any qualifying accessory which is taken into account in calculating under section 121B the modified cash equivalent of the benefit of the car for the tax year in question, and

(b) £5,000.

(6) This section is modified by section 147A (classic cars: optional remuneration arrangements)."

28 (1) Section 143 (deduction for periods when car unavailable) is amended as follows.

(2) Before subsection (1) insert—

"(A1) This section has effect for the purposes of—

(a) section 121(1) (method of calculating the cash equivalent of the benefit of a car), and

(b) section 121B(1) (optional remuneration arrangements: meaning of "modified cash equivalent")."

(3) In subsection (1), after "121(1)" insert "or (as the case may be) step 4 of section 121B(1)".

(4) In subsection (3), in the definition of "A", at the end insert "of section 121(1) or (as the case may be) step 4 of section 121B(1)".

29 (1) Section 144 (deduction for payments for private use) is amended as follows.

(2) In subsection (1), for "calculated under step 7 of section 121(1)" substitute "(see subsection (1A))".

(3) After subsection (1) insert

"(1A) In this section "the provisional sum" means the provisional sum calculated under—

(a) step 7 of section 121(1) (method of calculating the cash equivalent of the benefit of a car), or

(b) step 2 of section 121A(1) (optional remuneration arrangements: method of calculating relevant amount)."

(4) In subsection (2), for the words from "so that" to the end substitute "so that—

(a) in a case within subsection (1A)(a), the cash equivalent of the benefit of the car for the year is nil, or

(b) in a case within subsection (1A)(b), the relevant amount for the purposes of section 120A is nil."

(5) In subsection (3)—

(a) for "In any other case" substitute "Where subsection (2) does not apply," and

(b) for the words from "give" to the end substitute "give—

(a) in a case within subsection (1A)(a), the cash equivalent of the benefit of the car for the year, or

(b) in a case within subsection (1A)(b), the relevant amount for the purposes of section 120A."

30 (1) Section 145 (modification of provisions where car temporarily replaced) is amended as follows.

(2) In subsection (1), for paragraph (c) substitute—

"(c) the employee is chargeable to tax—

(i) in respect of both the normal car and the replacement car by virtue of section 120, or

(ii) in respect of both the normal car and the replacement car by virtue of section 120A, and"."

(3) After subsection (5) insert—

"(6) Where this section applies by virtue of subsection (1)(c)(ii), the condition in subsection (5)(b) is to be taken to be met if it would be met on the assumption that the cash equivalent of the benefit of the cars in question is to be calculated under section 121(1)."

31 (1) Section 146 (cars that run on road fuel gas) is amended as follows.

(2) In subsection (1), in the words before paragraph (a), after "applies" insert "for the purposes of sections 121 and 121B".

(3) In subsection (2), after "121(1)" insert "or (as the case may be) step 1 of section 121B(1)".

32 After section 147 insert—

"147A Classic cars: optional remuneration arrangements

(1) This section applies in calculating the relevant amount in respect of a car for a tax year for the purposes of section 120A (benefit of car treated as earnings: optional remuneration arrangements) if—

(a) the age of the car at the end of the year is 15 years or more,

(b) the market value of the car for the year is £15,000 or more, and

(c) that market value exceeds the specified amount (see subsection (4)).

(2) In calculating the modified cash equivalent of the benefit of the car, for the interim sum calculated under step 2 of section 121B(1) substitute the market value of the car for the tax year in question.

(3) Section 132A (capital contributions by employee: optional remuneration arrangements) has effect as if—

(a) in subsection (1)(b) the reference to calculating under section 121B the modified cash equivalent of the benefit of the car were to determining the market value of the car, and

(b) in subsection (5)(a)(ii) the reference to calculating under section 121B the modified cash equivalent of the benefit of the car for the tax year in question were to determining the market value of the car for the tax year in question.

(4) The "specified amount" is found as follows.

Step 1
Find what would be the interim sum under step 2 of section 121B(1) (if subsection (2) of this section did not have effect).

Step 2
(Assuming for this purpose that the reference in section 132(2) to step 2 of section 121(1) includes a reference to step 1 of this subsection) make any deduction under section 132 for capital contributions made by the employee to the cost of the car or accessories.
The resulting amount is the specified amount.

(5) The market value of a car for a tax year is to be determined in accordance with section 147(3) and (4)."

33 (1) Section 148 (reduction of cash equivalent where car is shared) is amended as follows.

(2) In subsection (1)—

(a) in the words before paragraph (a), after "applies" insert "for the purposes of sections 121 and 121B";

(b) in the words after paragraph (c), for "section 120" substitute "sections 120 and 120A".

(3) For subsection (2) substitute—

"(2) The amount to be treated as earnings in respect of the benefit of the car is to be calculated separately for each of those employees for that tax year (whether under section 120 or section 120A)."

(4) In subsection (2A), at the beginning insert "In the case of an employee chargeable to tax in respect of the car by virtue of section 120".

(5) After subsection (2A) insert—

"(2B) In the case of an employee chargeable to tax in respect of the car by virtue of section 120A, the modified cash equivalent (as determined under section 121B(1)) is to be reduced on a just and reasonable basis."

34 In section 149 (benefit of car fuel treated as earnings), in subsection (1)(b), at the end insert "or 120A".

35 After section 149 insert—

"149A Benefit of car fuel treated as earnings: optional remuneration arrangements

(1) This section applies if—

(a) fuel is provided for a car in a tax year by reason of an employee's employment,

(b) the employee is chargeable to tax in respect of the car in the tax year by virtue of section 120 or 120A, and

(c) the fuel is provided pursuant to optional remuneration arrangements.

(2) If the condition in subsection (3) is met—

(a) the amount foregone with respect to the benefit of the fuel (see section 69B) is to be treated as earnings from the employment for the tax year, and

(b) section 149(1) does not apply.

(3) The condition mentioned in subsection (2) is that the amount foregone with respect to the benefit of the fuel is greater than the cash equivalent of the benefit of the fuel.

(4) For the purposes of subsection (3), assume that the cash equivalent of the benefit of the fuel is zero if the condition in subsection (5) is met.

(5) The condition mentioned in subsection (4) is that the benefit of the fuel would be exempt from income tax but for section 228A (exclusion of certain exemptions).

(6) References in this section to fuel do not include any facility or means for supplying electrical energy or any energy for a car which cannot in any circumstances emit CO_2 by being driven.

(7) Where it is necessary for the purposes of subsections (2)(a) and (3) to apportion an amount of earnings to the benefit of the fuel in the tax year, the apportionment is to be made on a just and reasonable basis.

In this subsection "earnings" is to be interpreted in accordance with section 69B(5)."

36 In section 154 (benefit of van treated as earnings), after subsection (3) insert—

"(4) This section is subject to section 154A."

37 After section 154 insert—

"154A   Benefit of van treated as earnings: optional remuneration arrangements

(1) Where this Chapter applies to a van in relation to a particular tax year and the conditions in subsection (2) are met—

    (a) the relevant amount is to be treated as earnings from the employment for that tax year, and
    (b) section 154(1) does not apply.

In such a case (including a case where the relevant amount is nil) the employee is referred to in this Chapter as being chargeable to tax in respect of the van in the tax year.

(2) The conditions are that—

    (a) the van is made available to the employee or member of the employee's household pursuant to optional remuneration arrangements, and
    (b) the amount foregone with respect to the benefit of the van (see section 69B) is greater than the modified cash equivalent of the benefit of the van.

(3) To find the relevant amount for the purposes of this section take the following steps—

Step 1
Take the amount foregone with respect to the benefit of the van for the tax year.
Step 2
Make any deduction under section 158A in respect of payments by the employee for the private use of the van.
The result is the "relevant amount".

(4) In subsection (2) the reference to the "modified cash equivalent" is to the amount which would be the cash equivalent of the benefit of the van (after any reductions under section 156 or 157) if this Chapter had effect the following modifications—

    (a) omit paragraph (c) of section 155(8);
    (b) omit section 158;
    (c) in section 159(2)(b), for "155, 157 and 158" substitute "155 and 157".

(5) For the purposes of subsection (2) assume that the modified cash equivalent of the benefit of the van is zero if the condition in subsection (6) is met.

(6) The condition is that the benefit of the van would be exempt from income tax but for section 228A (exclusion of certain exemptions).

(7) Where it is necessary for the purposes of subsection (2)(b) and step 1 of subsection (3) to apportion an amount of earnings to the benefit of the van in the tax year, the apportionment is to be made on a just and reasonable basis.

In this subsection "earnings" is to be interpreted in accordance with section 69B(5)."

38 After section 158 insert—

"158A   Van provided pursuant to optional remuneration arrangements: private use

(1) In calculating the relevant amount under section 154A in relation to a van and a tax year, a deduction is to be made under step 2 of subsection (3) of that section if, as a condition of the van being available for the employee's private use, the employee—

    (a) is required in that year to pay (whether by way of deduction from earnings or otherwise) an amount of money for that use, and

(b) pays that amount on or before 6 July following that year.

(2) The amount of the deduction is—

(a) the amount paid as mentioned in subsection (1)(b) by the employee in respect of the year, or

(b) if less, the amount that would reduce the relevant amount to nil.

(3) In this section the reference to the van being available for the employee's private use includes a reference to the van being available for the private use of a member of the employee's family or household."

39 (1) Section 160 (benefit of van fuel treated as earnings) is amended as follows.

(2) In subsection (1)(b), after "154" insert "or 154A".

(3) At the end insert—

"(5) This section is subject to section 160A."

40 After section 160 insert—

"160A Benefit of van fuel treated as earnings: optional remuneration arrangements

(1) This section applies if—

(a) fuel is provided for a van in a tax year by reason of an employee's employment,

(b) the benefit of the fuel is provided pursuant to optional remuneration arrangements, and

(c) the employee is chargeable to tax in respect of the van in the tax year by virtue of section 154 or 154A.

(2) If the condition in subsection (3) is met—

(a) the amount foregone with respect to the benefit of the fuel (see section 69B) is to be treated as earnings from the employment for that year, and

(b) section 160(1) does not apply.

(3) The condition mentioned in subsection (2) is that the amount foregone with respect to the benefit of the fuel is greater than the cash equivalent of the benefit of the fuel.

(4) For the purposes of subsection (3), assume that the cash equivalent of the benefit of the fuel is zero if the condition mentioned in subsection (5) is met.

(5) The condition mentioned in subsection (4) is that the benefit of the fuel would be exempt from income tax but for section 228A (exclusion of certain exemptions).

(6) Where it is necessary for the purposes of subsections (2)(a) and (3) to apportion an amount of earnings to the benefit of the fuel in the tax year, the apportionment is to be made on a just and reasonable basis.

In this subsection "earnings" is to be interpreted in accordance with section 69B(5)."

41 In section 170 (orders etc relating to Chapter 6 of Part 3), in subsection (1)—

(a) after paragraph (c) insert—

"(ca) section 132A(5)(b) (corresponding provision with respect to optional remuneration arrangements),";

(b) omit "or" at the end of paragraph (d);

(c) after paragraph (e) insert ", or

(f) section 147A(1)(b) (classic car: minimum value: optional remuneration arrangements)."

42 In section 173 (loans to which Chapter 7 applies), in subsection (1A)(b), for the words from "provide" to the end substitute "make provision about amounts which, in the case of a taxable cheap loan, are to be treated as earnings in certain circumstances".

43 In section 175 (benefit of taxable cheap loan treated as earnings), for subsection (1) substitute—

"(A1) This section applies where an employment-related loan is a taxable cheap loan in relation to a tax year.

(1) The cash equivalent of the benefit of the loan is to be treated as earnings from the employee's employment for the tax year.

(1A) If the benefit of the loan is provided pursuant to optional remuneration arrangements and the condition in subsection (1B) is met—

(a) subsection (1) does not apply, and

(b) the relevant amount (see section 175A) is to be treated as earnings from the employee's employment for the tax year.

(1B) The condition is that the amount foregone with respect to the benefit of the loan for the tax year (see section 69B) is greater than the modified cash equivalent of the benefit of the loan for the tax year (see section 175A)."

44 (1) After section 175 insert—

"175A Optional remuneration arrangements: "relevant amount" and "modified cash equivalent"

(1) In section 175(1A) "the relevant amount", in relation to a loan the benefit of which is provided pursuant to optional remuneration arrangements, means the difference between—

(a) the amount foregone (see section 69B) with respect to the benefit of the loan, and

(b) the amount of interest (if any) actually paid on the loan for the tax year.

(2) For the purposes of section 175 the "modified cash equivalent" of the benefit of an employment-related loan for a tax year is the amount which would be the cash equivalent if section 175(3) had effect with the following modifications—

(a) in the opening words, omit "the difference between";

(b) omit paragraph (b) and the "and" before it.

(3) But the modified cash equivalent of the benefit of the loan is to be taken to be zero if the condition in subsection (4) is met.

(4) The condition is that the benefit of the loan for the tax year would be exempt from income tax but for section 228A (exclusion of certain exemptions).

(5) For the purpose of calculating the modified cash equivalent of the benefit of an employment-related loan, assume that section 186(2) (replacement loans: aggregation) and section 187(3) (aggregation of loans by close company to a director) do not have effect.

(6) Where it is necessary for the purposes of section 175(1B) and subsection (1) of this section to apportion an amount of earnings to the benefit of the loan for the tax year, the apportionment is to be made on a just and reasonable basis.

In this subsection "earnings" is to be interpreted in accordance with section 69B(5)."

45 In section 180 (threshold for benefit of loan to be treated as earnings), in subsection (1), for the words before paragraph (a) substitute "Section 175 does not have effect in relation to an employee and a tax year—".

46 In section 184 (interest treated as paid), in subsection (1), for the words from "the cash equivalent" to the end substitute "—

(a) the cash equivalent of the benefit of a taxable cheap loan is treated as earnings from an employee's employment for a tax year under section 175(1), or

(b) the relevant amount in respect of the benefit of a taxable cheap loan is treated as earnings from an employee's employment for a tax year under section 175(1A)."

47 In section 202 (excluded benefits), after subsection (1) insert—

"(1A) But a benefit provided to an employee or member of an employee's family or household is to be taken not to be an excluded benefit by virtue of subsection (1)(c) so far as it is provided under optional remuneration arrangements."

48 After section 203 insert—

"203A Employment-related benefit provided under optional remuneration arrangements

(1) Where an employment-related benefit is provided pursuant to optional remuneration arrangements—

(a) the relevant amount is to be treated as earnings from the employment for the tax year in which the benefit is provided, and

(b) section 203(1) does not apply.

(2) To find the relevant amount, first determine which (if any) is the greater of—

(a) the cost of the employment-related benefit, and

(b) the amount foregone with respect to the benefit (see section 69B).

(3) If the cost of the employment-related benefit is greater than or equal to the amount foregone, the "relevant amount" is the cash equivalent (see section 203(2)).

(4) Otherwise, the "relevant amount" is—

(a) the amount foregone with respect to the employment-related benefit, less

(b) any part of the cost of the benefit made good by the employee, to the persons providing the benefit, on or before 6 July following the tax year in which it is provided.

(5) For the purposes of subsections (2) and (3), assume that the cost of the employment-related benefit is zero if the condition in subsection (6) is met.

(6) The condition is that the employment-related benefit would be exempt from income tax but for section 228A (exclusion of certain exemptions).

(7) Where it is necessary for the purposes of subsections (2)(b) and (4) to apportion an amount of earnings to the benefit provided in the tax year, the apportionment is to be made on a just and reasonable basis.

In this subsection "earnings" is to be interpreted in accordance with section 69B(5)."

Exemptions

49 In Part 4 of ITEPA 2003 (employment income: exemptions), after section 228 insert—

"228A General exclusion from exemptions: optional remuneration arrangements

(1) A relevant exemption does not apply (whether to prevent liability to income tax from arising or to reduce liability to income tax) in respect of a benefit or facility so far as the benefit or facility is provided pursuant to optional remuneration arrangements.

(2) For the purposes of subsection (1) it does not matter whether the relevant exemption would (apart from that subsection) have effect as an employment income exemption or an earnings-only exemption.

(3) For the purposes of this section an exemption conferred by this Part is a "relevant exemption" unless it is—

(a) a special case exemption (see subsection (4)), or
(b) an excluded exemption (see subsection (5)).

(4) "Special case exemption" means an exemption conferred by any of the following provisions—

(a) section 289A (exemption for paid or reimbursed expenses);
(b) section 289D (exemption for other benefits);
(c) section 308B (independent advice in respect of conversions and transfers of pension scheme benefits);
(d) section 312A (limited exemption for qualifying bonus payments);
(e) section 317 (subsidised meals);
(f) section 320C (recommended medical treatment);
(g) section 323A (trivial benefits provided by employers).

(5) "Excluded exemption" means an exemption conferred by any of the following provisions—

(a) section 239 (payments and benefits connected with taxable cars and vans and exempt heavy goods vehicles);
(b) section 244 (cycles and cyclist's safety equipment);
(c) section 266(2)(c) (non-cash voucher regarding entitlement to exemption within section 244);
(d) section 270A (limited exemption for qualifying childcare vouchers);
(e) section 307 (death or retirement provision), so far as relating to provision made for retirement benefits;
(f) section 308 (exemption of contribution to registered pension scheme);
(g) section 308A (exemption of contributions to overseas pension scheme);
(h) section 308C (provision of pensions advice);
(i) section 309 (limited exemptions for statutory redundancy payments);
(j) section 310 (counselling and other outplacement services);
(k) section 311 (retraining courses);
(l) section 318 (childcare: exemption for employer-provided care);
(m) section 318A (childcare: limited exemption for other care).

(6) In subsection (5) "retirement benefit" has the meaning that would be given by subsection (2) of section 307 if "or death" were omitted in both places where it occurs in that subsection.

(7) In this section "benefit or facility" includes anything which constitutes employment income or in respect of which employment income is treated as arising to the employee (regardless of its form and the manner of providing it).

(8) In this section "optional remuneration arrangements" has the same meaning as in the benefits code (see section 69A).

(9) The Treasury may by order amend subsections (4) and (5) by adding or removing an exemption conferred by Part 4."

Other amendments

50 (1) Section 19 of ITEPA 2003 (receipt of non-money earnings) is amended as follows.

(2) In subsection (2), after "94" insert "or 94A".

(3) In subsection (3), after "87" insert "or 87A".

51 In section 95 of ITEPA 2003 (disregard for money, goods or services obtained), in subsection (1), in the words before paragraph (a), after "credit-token" insert "or the relevant amount in respect of a cash voucher, a non-cash voucher or a credit-token".

52 (1) In section 236 of ITEPA 2003 (interpretation of Chapter 2 of Part 4: exemptions for mileage allowance relief etc), in subsection (2)(b)—

(a) in the words before sub-paragraph (i), for "the cash equivalent of" substitute "an amount in respect of";
(b) in sub-paragraph (i), after "120" insert "or 120A";
(c) in sub-paragraph (ii), after "154" insert "or 154A";
(d) in sub-paragraph (iii), after "203" insert "or 203A".

(2) In section 236 of ITEPA 2003 (interpretation of Chapter 2 of Part 4), in subsection (2)(c), for "the cash equivalent of" substitute "an amount in respect of".

53 (1) Section 239 of ITEPA 2003 (payments and benefits connected with taxable cars and vans etc) is amended as follows.

(2) In subsection (3)—

(a) after "149" insert "or 149A";
(b) after "160" insert "or 160A".

(3) In subsection (6), for "the cash equivalent of" substitute "an amount (whether the cash equivalent or the relevant amount) in respect of".

54 In section 362 of ITEPA 2003 (deductions where non-cash voucher provided), in subsection (1)(a), for "87(1) (cash equivalent" substitute "87(1) or 87A(1) (amount in respect".

55 In section 318A of ITEPA 2003 (childcare: limited exemption for other care), in subsection (1)(b), for "cash equivalent of the benefit" substitute "amount treated as earnings in respect of the benefit by virtue of section 203(1) or 203A(1) (as the case may be)".

56 In section 363 of ITEPA 2003 (deductions where credit-token provided), in subsection (1)(a), for "94(1) (cash equivalent" substitute "94(1) or 94A(1) (amount in respect".

57 In section 693 of ITEPA 2003 (cash vouchers), in subsection (1), for "section 81(2)" substitute "subsection (2) of, or (as the case may be) referred to in subsection (1A)(b) of, section 81".

58 In section 694 of ITEPA 2003 (non-cash vouchers), in subsection (1), after "87(2)" insert "or 87A(4)".

59 In section 695 of ITEPA 2003 (benefit of credit-token treated as earnings), after subsection (1) insert—

"(1A) If the credit-token is provided pursuant to optional remuneration arrangements, the reference in subsection (1) to the amount ascertained under section 94(2) is to be read as a reference to what that amount would be were the credit-token provided otherwise than pursuant to optional remuneration arrangements.

In this subsection "optional remuneration arrangements" is to be interpreted in accordance with section 69A."

60 In Part 2 of Schedule 1 to ITEPA 2003 (index of defined expressions), at the appropriate places insert—

"amount foregone (in relation to a benefit) (in the benefits code) | section 69B"

"optional remuneration arrangements (in the benefits code) | section 69A"

61 In Part 2 of Schedule 1 to ITEPA 2003 (index of defined expressions), in the entry relating to "the taxable period", for "102(2)" substitute "102(1)".

Commencement and transitional provision

62 (1) The amendments made by paragraphs 1, 52(1)(a) and (2) and 60 of this Schedule have effect for the tax year 2017–18 and subsequent tax years.

(2) The amendments made by paragraphs 2 to 51, 52(1)(b) to (d), 53 to 59 and 61 of this Schedule have effect for the tax year 2017–18 and subsequent tax years.

(3) In relation to a benefit provided pursuant to pre-6 April 2017 arrangements, the amendment made by paragraph 49 has effect for the tax year 2018–19 and subsequent tax years.

(4) In relation to a benefit provided pursuant to pre-6 April 2017 arrangements, the amendments made by paragraphs 7 to 41, 52(1)(b) and (c), 53 and 61 (and paragraph 2, so far as relating to those paragraphs) have effect for the tax year 2021–22 and subsequent tax years.

(5) In relation to a benefit provided pursuant to pre-6 April 2017 arrangements, the amendments made by paragraphs 3 to 6, 42 to 48, 50, 51, 52(1)(d) and 54 to 59 (and

paragraph 2, so far as relating to those paragraphs) have effect for the tax year 2018–19 and subsequent tax years (but see sub-paragraph (10)).

(6) If any terms of a pre-6 April 2017 arrangement which relate to the provision of a particular benefit are varied on or after 6 April 2017, that benefit is treated, with effect from the beginning of the day on which the variation takes effect, as not being provided pursuant to pre-6 April 2017 arrangements for the purposes of this paragraph.

(7) If pre-6 April 2017 arrangements are renewed on or after 6 April 2017, this paragraph has effect as if those arrangements were entered into at the beginning of the day on which the renewal takes effect (and are distinct from the arrangements existing immediately before that day).

(8) In sub-paragraph (6) the reference to variation does not include any variation which is required in connection with accidental damage to a benefit provided under the arrangements, or otherwise for reasons beyond the control of the parties to the arrangements.

(9) In sub-paragraph (6) the reference to variation does not include any variation which occurs in connection with a person's entitlement to statutory sick pay, statutory maternity pay, statutory adoption pay, statutory paternity pay or statutory shared parental pay.

(10) In relation to relevant school fee arrangements which were entered into before 6 April 2017—

(a) sub-paragraph (5) is to be read as if it did not include a reference to paragraph 48;
(b) the amendment made by paragraph 48 has effect for the tax year 2021–22 and subsequent tax years.

(11) Relevant school fee arrangements to which an employee is a party ("the continuing arrangements") are to be regarded for the purposes of this paragraph as the same arrangements as any relevant school fee arrangements to which the employee was previously a party ("the previous arrangements") if the continuing arrangements and the previous arrangements relate—

(a) to employment with the same employer,
(b) to the same school, and
(c) to school fees in respect of the same child.

(12) Sub-paragraphs (6) and (7) do not have effect in relation to relevant school fee arrangements.

(13) If a non-cash voucher is provided under pre-6 April 2017 arrangements and is used to obtain anything (whether money, goods or services) that is provided on or after 6 April 2018 ("delayed benefits"), so much of the benefit of the voucher as it is reasonable to regard as being applied to obtain the delayed benefits is to be treated for the purposes of this paragraph as not having been provided pursuant to pre-6 April 2017 arrangements.

(14) For the purposes of this paragraph arrangements are "relevant school fee arrangements" if the benefit mentioned in section 69A(1) of ITEPA 2003 consists in the payment or reimbursement (in whole or in part) of, or a waiver or reduction of, school fees.

(15) In this paragraph—

"arrangements" means optional remuneration arrangements (as defined in section 69A of ITEPA 2003);
"benefit" includes any benefit or facility, regardless of the manner of providing it;
"non-cash voucher" has the same meaning as in Chapter 4 of Part 3 of ITEPA 2003;
"pre-6 April 2017 arrangements" means arrangements which are entered into before 6 April 2017.

GENERAL NOTE

Optional remuneration arrangements – Sch 2 para 1
Paragraph 1 inserts new ss 69A and 69B into ITEPA 2003.

New ITEPA 2003 s 69A – Introduction of optional remuneration arrangements

Subsections (1) and (2) establish the scope of the new legislation on Optional Remuneration Arrangements ("OpRA"), with some important nuances. Where OpRA applies, and subject to the detailed provisions applying to specific benefits, the taxable value of a benefit in kind will be the "relevant amount". Broadly speaking, this will usually be the higher of the cash equivalent or modified cash equivalent (as the case may be) of the benefit concerned, and the amount of earnings foregone by the employee in relation to that benefit.

Under sub-s (2) a benefit is only subject to the new rules **so far as** it is provided under a **Type A** or **Type B** arrangement. It is perfectly possible for a benefit to be provided partly within one (or both) and partly outside of such arrangements. The scope of the rules is restricted to that part of a benefit provided within such arrangements.

Subsection (3) defines **Type A** arrangements as those where the employee gives up a right (or future right) to receive an amount of earnings within ITEPA 2003 Pt 3 Ch 1 in exchange for a benefit. This would include arrangements where benefits are provided in exchange for a salary sacrifice, a bonus waiver, or the provision of a higher level of a particular benefit (a "trade-up") in exchange for giving up some pay.

Subsection (4) defines **Type B** arrangements as those where an employee agrees to be provided with a benefit rather than an amount of earnings within Pt 3 Ch 1. This would include arrangements where employers offer employees a choice between a benefit and a cash payment where the employee chooses the benefit.

A number of issues with these definitions warrant further consideration, best illustrated with several examples:

Example 1: Flexible benefit schemes

Many flexible benefit schemes operate on the basis of a "flex allowance/pot" which provides a value of benefits that can be selected by employees. Some schemes work on the basis that employees are entitled to be paid the allowance (or balance of any allowance) in cash, to the extent they don't take benefits; this will fall within a Type B arrangement, since taking benefits will then be in preference to receiving earnings. Other schemes work on the basis that employees are not entitled to be paid anything in cash i.e. if they don't take benefits they receive nothing; this will not fall within a Type B arrangement as taking benefits will not be in preference to receiving earnings. Other schemes work on the basis of a number of specific salary sacrifices for each benefit concerned and these will be Type A arrangements. Lastly, some schemes provide a benefits allowance with the ability to also sacrifice salary where the benefits allowance has been used up; this will comprise a mix of both Type A and Type B arrangements.

Example 2: Company cars with cash alternatives

Many modern company car schemes include a cash alternative option, to give employees flexibility to use their own choice of vehicle. Where an employee chooses a company car instead of the cash alternative on offer, this would be an example of a Type B arrangement. Not so obviously, arrangements which allow employees to "trade down" from a higher to lower level of a particular benefit in exchange for a cash payment, could arguably also fall within Type B assuming that without trading down, the employee agrees to forego the underlying cash amount on offer if he/she did so.

Example 3: Prospective employees

Say an employer offers a prospective employee a salary of £50,000. The candidate says, "Actually I'd like private medical insurance and life insurance and I'll accept a correspondingly reduced salary to keep the total cost of my package the same". He/she agrees a salary of £48,000, reflecting £2,000 worth of benefits to be provided.

It may be splitting hairs, but in the Type A definition, "giving up a future right" is arguably an oxymoron if at the time of this negotiation, the individual is not an employee and has no right to give up. However, given that s 69A(2) makes it clear that the arrangements can be made before or after the employment commences, it may be prudent to interpret this as including "agreeing now to give up a right in the future". The point does not arise with Type B, since a prospective employee can easily agree at the time of the negotiation to be provided in the future with additional benefits rather than £2,000 of salary, and that clearly falls within a Type B arrangement.

Example 4: Receipt of a "benefit" rather than "earnings within Chapter 1 of Part 3"

Both Type A and Type B arrangements envisage the employee being provided with a "benefit" and foregoing "earnings within Chapter 1 of Part 3". Given that OpRA seeks only to determine the taxable value of the benefit provided *"in exchange for"* or *"rather than"* earnings under ITEPA 2003 Pt 3 Ch 1, and that s 69A(1) makes it clear that OpRA is only relevant for the purposes of the benefits code, the new rules should not therefore impact anything which is provided outside of the benefits code instead of earnings. However, great care is required here, since there is more that potentially falls within the benefits code than might otherwise be assumed without proper analysis. This point is illustrated by the three following examples.

Example 4(i): Securities and interests in securities

Consider a share award made in exchange for, say, a bonus waiver, which might be a feature of some deferral arrangements.

ITEPA 2003 s 418(1) makes it clear that Ch 10 may also have effect in relation to securities and interests in securities. This is subject to s 418(1A), but this only removes the acquisition of employment-related securities options from Chs 1 and 10, together with chargeable events under s 477 in relation to such options. Note that this exemption resides in Pt 7 so is not disapplied by s2 28A which only disapplies Pt 4 exemptions.

A share award falling solely within Pt 3 Ch 1 or Pt 7 should fall outside the scope of OpRA. But if Ch 10 could apply to the award, that potentially brings this sort of arrangement within OpRA, which could in turn bring the "amount foregone" (the value of the bonus waived) into charge.

In addition, options which can be cash settled may not actually be options at all. If not, they may not benefit from s 418(1A), in which case they could also potentially fall within OpRA.

Example 4(ii): Benefits with money's worth

Say an employee agrees to sacrifice £250 of salary in exchange for the gift of a suit which, when new, retails at the same price. Say the suit has a marginal cost of £175 and a second hand value of £130 for the sake of argument.

It is sometimes overlooked that such a benefit is chargeable both under s 62, and under Ch 10 of the benefits code. The latter in conjunction with the salary sacrifice, brings this arrangement within OpRA as a Type A arrangement. But how would this then apply?

Section 64 applies where the same benefit would give rise to two amounts; A being the amount that would be chargeable as earnings under Ch 1, and B being the amount that would be treated as earnings and chargeable under the benefits code, in this case under Ch 10. Section 64(2)(a) then constitutes A as earnings and s 64(2)(b) determines that the excess of B over A (if there is an excess) is to be treated as earnings under the benefits code.

If the suit was provided as a gift without a salary sacrifice, so OpRA does not apply, A would be £130 and B would be £175. A would be chargeable under s 62 and the £45 excess of B over A would be chargeable under Ch 10. The total charge to tax would therefore be £175 (£130 under Ch 1 and £45 under Ch 10).

However, as a Type A arrangement, A remains as £130 chargeable under Ch 1, while B is now determined under the OpRA rules as the higher of the amount foregone £250 and the marginal cost of £175. So, B is now £250 and then s 64(2)(b) determines the excess of B over A is £120, which would be chargeable under Ch 10. So, under OpRA, the total chargeable is therefore £250 (£130 under Ch 1 and £120 under Ch 10).

For completeness, it is important to apply the legislation in the correct order. Note that s 64 follows *after* determining the amounts chargeable under each Chapter. It would be wrong to isolate the £130 chargeable under Ch 1, and then compare the £45 excess of marginal cost over second hand value, with the amount foregone. If you did that, the amount foregone would be £250 on top of the £130 chargeable under Ch 1, giving a total taxable benefit of £380 which is clearly wrong.

Example 4(iii): Expenses and Approved Mileage Allowance Payments (AMAPs)

Ignoring the exemption for AMAPs in ITEPA 2003 s 229, a flat rate or round sum cash payment would normally be considered to be Chapter 1 earnings. An AMAP will provide a profit for some employees, a loss for others and break-even for others depending on the type of car they use. So, given that the definition of earnings in s 62 includes any gratuity or other profit or incidental benefit of any kind if it is money or money's worth, an AMAP, if not exempt, would be taxable as earnings under Ch 1. Section 229 then removes any liability to income tax that would otherwise arise (under Ch 1 or otherwise).

However, AMAPs could also be chargeable under Ch 10 as a cash benefit. This would not be the case if AMAPs were taxable under Chs 3 to 9 of the benefits code (or would be but for an exemption – see s 202). But AMAPs are unlikely to be chargeable under s 70 in Ch 3, given their round sum nature, and s 70(5) specifically disapplies Ch 3 where expenses would be chargeable under Ch 1. Therefore, there remains the prospect of AMAPs falling under Ch 10 and so falling within the scope of OpRA, if provided under a Type A or Type B arrangement.

For example, AMAPs are sometimes paid on the basis that other Ch 1 earnings (which could be salary or a cash allowance) reduce correspondingly. Therefore, if we accept that the payment of an AMAP is a cash benefit falling under Ch 10, such an arrangement would be Type A or Type B, depending on how it is structured (both Type A and Type B are commonly used).

The consequence of this is that s 228A applies to switch off the exemption in s 229, rendering the payment of AMAPs taxable, and (when corresponding NIC legislation is enacted) subject to NIC.

There is perhaps a bigger problem if such arrangements are subject to OpRA, and that is the prospect that employees may not be able to claim Mileage Allowance Relief (MAR) under s 231. Under s 231, MAR is only available on the unpaid difference between what has been paid and the statutory maximum amount that could have been paid. Section 231 does not provide relief in cases where an AMAP has been paid but has been subject to tax. We will need to await HMRC guidance to clarify how this should be treated, but on my reading it appears that paying AMAPs under OpRA switches off all forms of tax relief – both the s 229 exemption and relief under s 231 – disaster!

This analysis is not wholly beyond doubt because the legislation envisages the provision of a benefit *rather than* an amount of earnings, which is arguably compromised to some extent if AMAPs are both earnings and a cash benefit. More detailed HMRC guidance may clarify if there are any boundaries to be drawn in such cases but otherwise, the overriding policy intention would seem to be that, apart from the short list of OpRA arrangements permitted by the legislation, everything else which falls wholly or partly within the broad definition of a "benefit" is likely to fall within reach of OpRA.

Example 5: meaning of "employee agrees" – Type B

The AMAP example above also serves to illustrate a different point in relation to Type B arrangements. If the employer's policy of AMAPs and top up payments is unilaterally determined by the employer, it might be argued that the employee has not agreed to be provided with AMAPs rather than an amount of earnings which means it would not be a Type B arrangement. However, it remains the fact that if one additional business mile is travelled in a month compared to the previous month, the employee will receive an additional 45p AMAP and 45p less cash allowance in the second month.

Although the employee may not have requested, and/or signed a specific agreement to be paid in the way prescribed by the employer, the employee's use of his/her private car for business purposes and acceptance of the payments offered by the employer, is likely to constitute the employee's agreement, bringing the arrangement in this example within Type B.

By way of comparison, many salary sacrifice schemes are predicated on the concept of employees opting-out if they do not want to participate, rather than opting-in if they do. It is a well-established principle that if an employee is offered the ability to opt-out of a salary sacrifice arrangement, the employee's participation in it and acceptance of payments/benefits under it, constitutes his/her agreement to it.

There are three remaining subsections to s 69A:

Subsection (5) deems a benefit to be provided under OpRA so far as it is just and reasonable to attribute its provision to the arrangements in question. The words "so far as" are consistent with sub-s (2) as noted above. This could have application in a typical flexible benefits scheme providing a mix of benefits, some without salary sacrifice (sometimes called "core benefits") and others in exchange for a salary sacrifice. Section 69A(5) ensures a reasonable approach is to be taken to identify the extent to which any benefits have been provided under OpRA, leaving the others unimpacted.

Subsection (6) prevents an argument that the OpRA rules cannot apply to a benefit, just because an employee makes good or is required to make good any part of the cost of providing the benefit concerned. In practice, an employee would seem unlikely to make good a benefit acquired with a salary sacrifice, but may well want to make good a benefit that is only brought within OpRA because the employer happens to offer a cash alternative. This provision means that OpRA can still apply to such arrangements, subject to the specific rules on making good specified for each benefit concerned. Noteworthy is the case of private fuel provided for a company car or van, where the employer offers a cash alternative; bizarrely, making good the cost of private fuel will not always be effective – see new ITEPA 2003 s149A below in relation to fuel provided for a company car and also new s160A in relation to fuel provided for a company van.

Subsection (7) makes provision for benefits which are provided only partly under OpRA. For example, consider a basic annual health check which is provided as a core benefit with neither a salary sacrifice nor a cash alternative attaching, and would be exempt were it not for OpRA. But if the employee is able to trade up to a more extensive health check in exchange for a salary sacrifice, this would bring the benefit within OpRA. Section 69A(7) sensibly confines the new rules to the *incremental part* of the benefit obtained through salary sacrifice, so the core benefit in this example would be unaffected (i.e. would continue to be exempt in this case), rather than the whole of the more extensive health-check becoming taxable in full.

New ITEPA 2003 s 69B – OpRA supplementary provisions

Section 69B makes several supplementary provisions including defining the "amount foregone" in s 69B(1), which is key to determining the taxable value of benefits in kind under OpRA from 6 April 2017. The amount foregone will normally be the amount of earnings an employee agrees to sacrifice under a Type A arrangement, or the amount of cash alternative not taken under a Type B arrangement.

In some cases, a benefit might be provided partly under a Type A and partly under a Type B arrangement, in which case the amount foregone is the aggregate of amounts foregone under both. For example, an employer offers an employee a company car at a specified lease rental value, or a cash alternative of £5,000. The employee chooses to take a car forgoing the £5,000. He/she also wants a better vehicle and to a higher specification, so agrees to sacrifice an additional £1,500. The amount foregone in this example is £6,500, being the aggregate of £5,000 under the Type B element of the arrangement and £1,500 under the Type A element of the arrangement.

Conversely, say the car chosen has a lease rental of only £4,000, so the employee only foregoes £4,000 of the cash alternative and is paid the difference fully taxable and subject to NIC. As the £1,000 has actually been paid, it has not been foregone; therefore the only amount that has been foregone is £4,000 in this case.

Subsections (2) and (3) allow the amount foregone to be apportioned on a just and reasonable basis where it is necessary to do so. For example, an employee takes part in a flexible benefits scheme and has a benefits allowance of £5,000 which can be used for the provision of benefits of his/her choosing from a range. He/she elects for private medical insurance, travel insurance, an annual health check, an additional £1,000 of pension contributions and some retail vouchers, using his/her benefits allowance in full.

Normally, the employer will specify how much needs to be sacrificed in relation to each benefit concerned, so, allocating the amount foregone between benefits should not be troublesome in practice. If for some reason the actual amounts attributable to each benefit are not known, the total would be apportioned on a just and reasonable basis, which will be particularly important in this example because:

 (i)   the £1,000 of pension contributions are specifically excluded from OpRA;
 (ii) the health check would have been tax free outside of OpRA, but will now become taxable to the extent of the amount foregone;
 (iii) the other benefits are all taxable anyway, but their respective taxable values under OpRA will be the higher of their cash equivalent and the amount foregone, as determined for each benefit respectively.

Conversely, say the employer and employee agree that all £5,000 was forgone solely in order to obtain the £1,000 of pension contributions. They argue that the other benefits are provided without foregoing anything so are not subject to OpRA. In this case, from HMRC's perspective it would be necessary to reallocate the amounts between the benefits on a just and reasonable basis under s 69B(2).

Finally, note that if an employee forgoes earnings in exchange for a benefit provided to a member of his/her household, this is also within OpRA, by virtue of s 69B(4). Throughout the rest of this commentary on OpRA, references to "employee" should be interpreted in this context.

Benefits in kind: amount treated as earnings – Sch 2 paras 2 to 48

Paragraphs 2 to 48 further amend ITEPA 2003 Pt 3.

Paragraph 3 inserts new s 81(1A) and (1B).

If provided under OpRA, the cash equivalent of the benefit of a cash voucher in s 81(1) is replaced by the "relevant amount" under new s 81(1A)(b).

The relevant amount is the higher of the amount foregone, and the cash equivalent of the voucher which is defined in s 81(2) as the sum of money for which the cash voucher is capable of being exchanged.

Note that this comparison does not have to be carried out if the voucher would be exempt, but for s 228A. Where previously exempt benefits are provided under OpRA, s 228A disapplies the exemptions concerned, apart from "special case exemptions" and "excluded exemptions" (as there defined). Then, when calculating the relevant amount, the cash equivalent is to be taken as zero, which in turn means that the relevant amount will be equal to the amount foregone.

Paragraph 4 inserts new s 87A.

New ITEPA 2003 s 87A – Non-cash vouchers

If provided under OpRA, the cash equivalent of the benefit of a non-cash voucher in s 87(1) is replaced by the "relevant amount" under new s 87A(1)(a),(b).

This excludes childcare vouchers which are not affected by the new rules as childcare vouchers are one of the "excluded exemptions".

The relevant amount is determined in two steps. First, take the higher of the amount foregone, and the cost of providing the non-cash voucher, as defined under s 87(3). Then:

(i) If the cost of provision is greater than the amount foregone, the relevant amount is the cash equivalent of the voucher in accordance with s 87(2). This is the cost of provision less the amount made good by the employee.

(ii) Otherwise the relevant amount should be the excess of the amount foregone over the amount made good by the employee (on or before 6 July following the tax year concerned).

A simpler construct for everyday use might be that the relevant amount will normally be:

(a) the higher of the cost of provision and the amount foregone, less;
(b) the amount made good by the employee.

Note that non-cash vouchers could potentially have been used to forestall the OpRA legislation and achieve extended grandfathering e.g. by providing a voucher before 6 April 2017 which could be exchanged for, say, a 10-year entitlement to car-parking (an extreme hypothetical example to make a point). Under s 88(1), the amount of a non-cash voucher treated as earnings is treated as received in the tax year in which the cost of provision is incurred or, if later, the tax year in which the voucher is provided. So if the car-parking was paid in advance and voucher provided to the employee prior to 6 April 2017, it is hard to see that OpRA would apply to this voucher at all.

When providing employees with third party retail vouchers, the employer will normally require employees to sacrifice an amount equal to the cost to the employer of providing those vouchers, and there will not normally be an additional "amount made good" by employees. In such a case, the benefit will be the cost of the voucher, which will normally be the same as the amount foregone.

However, there may be situations where employees make a salary sacrifice *and* make good an additional amount from net pay as illustrated below.

Example

In the case of an in-house voucher exchangeable for an employer's own goods, consider an example where the employer is a clothing retailer and provides a voucher exchangeable for its own clothing which normally retails for £150 and has a marginal cost of £100. Say the employee sacrifices £50 in exchange for the voucher. When the employee presents the voucher for the clothing, a discount of £50 is applied and the employee pays the balance of £100 from net pay to make up the full retail price.

In this case, the employee buys clothing and uses the voucher against the price of those goods. The voucher represents the profit margin on the goods which has no associated cost of provision. The relevant amount would be £50, being the higher of the zero cost of provision (ignoring any administration costs) and the amount foregone (£50).

When the clothing is acquired, this should not normally fall within OpRA as no earnings are foregone to acquire the goods. Here the cost of the goods is £100 which is made good by the cash payment of £100 and the £50 voucher, so no further benefit arises at that time. In any event, s 95 should apply to prevent a charge arising in respect of goods acquired on exchange of the voucher, where the cash equivalent of the voucher has already been treated as earnings.

The taxable relevant amount of £50 might be considered to be an odd and unfair outcome in this example. At the end of the day, the marginal cost of the goods has been paid for in full by the employee so why should there be any tax charge? Normality can be restored if the voucher is removed from the arrangement so it becomes, more simply, an agreement to acquire clothing with a marginal cost of £100 for £100 cash, in exchange for foregoing earnings of £50 representing the margin. In this case, the relevant amount should be £100 (being the higher of the £100 cost of provision and the £50 foregone). This produces the answer most would expect i.e. no tax charge because the marginal cost is then made good in full by the employee.

Finally, note that where previously exempt benefits are provided under OpRA, s 228A disapplies the exemptions concerned, apart from "special case exemptions" and "excluded exemptions" (as there defined). If the use of a non-cash voucher would be exempt, apart from s 228A, the relevant cost of provision would be taken as zero.

Paragraph 5 makes consequential amendments to s 88.

Paragraph 6 inserts new s 94A.

New ITEPA 2003 s 94A – Credit-tokens

If provided under OpRA, the cash equivalent of the benefit of a credit-token in s 94(1) is replaced by the "relevant amount" under s 94A(1)(a),(b). As the benefit of a credit-token arises for a tax year, in relation to each occasion during the year on which it is used, the rules for credit-tokens need to aggregate the amount foregone and the cost of provision respectively, for each such occasion in the year concerned where OpRA applies.

I use the word "aggregate" in this note for emphasis, though the legislation does not do so.

There is only a need to determine the relevant amount if the aggregate amount foregone in the tax year exceeds the relevant cost of provision in the same tax year.

For this purpose, the amount foregone is determined on a just and reasonable basis as the aggregate of such amounts attributable to the employee's use of the credit-token in the tax year concerned pursuant to OpRA. The relevant cost of provision is the aggregate of the cost of provision relating to each occasion the credit-token is used in the tax year.

Where the aggregate amount foregone is greater than the relevant cost of provision, the relevant amount should then be the excess of the aggregate amount foregone over any amount made good by the employee on or before 6 July following the tax year concerned.

Where previously exempt benefits are provided under OpRA, s 228A disapplies the exemptions concerned, apart from "special case exemptions" and "excluded exemptions" (as there defined). The relevant cost of provision is then taken as zero if the use of the credit-token would be exempt, apart from s 228A.

Paragraphs 7 to 12 make amendments to ITEPA 2003 ss 97 to 101. The changes to ss 98–101 make clear that exemptions applicable to accommodation:

– provided by local authorities;
– provided for the better performance of duties;
– to protect employees from security threats;
– owned overseas and used by employees; or
– Chevening House;

will only apply where the benefit is not provided under OpRA. Should the benefit be provided under OpRA, the legislation will disapply the exemptions and the taxable benefit will generally be equal to the amount foregone.

Paragraph 13 makes amendments to ITEPA 2003 s 102. If provided under OpRA, the cash equivalent of the benefit of living accommodation in s102 is replaced by the "relevant amount" under new s 102(1B)(a),(b). The relevant amount is then determined in accordance with s 103A (see para 15 below).

Paragraph 14 makes a consequential amendment to s 103.

Paragraph 15 inserts new s 103A.

New ITEPA 2003 s 103A – Accommodation: relevant amount

Section 103A provides the method for calculating the "relevant amount", being the taxable value of the benefit of accommodation when provided under an OpRA.

In short, if the modified cash equivalent is greater than the amount foregone, then the relevant amount is the cash equivalent determined under s 103.

Otherwise the relevant amount is the excess of the amount foregone over the "deductible amount" (if there is an excess). The deductible amount represents amounts made good by the employee for the use of the accommodation, on or before 6 July following the tax year, calculated in accordance with s 103A(7) where the cost does not exceed £75,000, or s 103A(8) where the cost exceeds £75,000.

The modified cash equivalent is calculated under ss 105(2A) or 106(2A) depending on the cost of the accommodation (see below).

Where accommodation is covered by an exemption under ss 98–101 but provided under an OpRA, the modified cash equivalent is to be taken as zero, which means that the taxable benefit will be equal to the amount foregone less the deductible amount.

Paragraph 16 amends s 105(1) and inserts new s 105(2A). Subsection (2A) defines the modified cash equivalent of accommodation costing £75,000 or less, as the rental value of the accommodation. Note that deductible amounts such as rents paid or amounts made good by the employee, are taken into account in the subsequent calculation of the relevant amount in accordance with ss 103 or 103A.

Paragraph 17 amends s 106(1) and inserts new s 106(2A). Subsection (2A) defines the modified cash equivalent of accommodation costing more than £75,000 applying Steps 1 to 3 of s 106(2):

– Step 1 is the rental value of the accommodation (as calculated by s 105);
– Step 2 is the "additional yearly rent" (as specified in s 106); and
– Step 3 is the rent that would have been payable if the property had been let at the additional yearly rent determined in Step 2.

The modified cash equivalent is the sum of Steps 1 and 3. Note that deductible amounts such as rents paid or amounts made good by the employee, are taken into account in the subsequent calculation of the relevant amount in accordance with ss 103 or 103A.

Paragraphs 18 to 21 amend ss 109, 114, 119 and 120.

Paragraph 22 inserts new s 120A.

New ITEPA 2003 s 120A – Cars

Where a car is made available to an employee under OpRA, the value of the taxable benefit of the car will be the "relevant amount". The relevant amount is determined in accordance with s 121A (see para 23 below).

However, this only applies if:

(a) the amount foregone exceeds the "modified cash equivalent" of the benefit of the car as calculated by s 121B; and
(b) the car's CO_2 emissions exceed 75 g/km (so it is not an "ultra-low emission vehicle" (ULEV)).

Note that s 120A(3)(c) takes cars with CO_2 emissions up to and including 75 g/km out of this measure. This recognises the role that salary sacrifice car schemes have had in promoting the use of low CO_2 cars and complements the government initiatives promoting the use of ULEVs. Therefore, ULEVs will continue to be taxed on the cash equivalent of the benefit as calculated by s 121, whether or not provided under OpRA.

Paragraph 23 inserts new ss 121A and 121B.

New ITEPA 2003 s 121A – Cars: relevant amount

The "relevant amount" only needs to be calculated where the amount foregone is greater than the modified cash equivalent of a car.

In such circumstances, the relevant amount will in effect replace the modified cash equivalent as the taxable value, and so capital and private use contributions must be deducted from the amount foregone at this stage.

The relevant amount is therefore the amount foregone less:

– any deductions for capital contributions (as calculated by s 132A); and
– any payments by the employee for the private use of the car (as calculated by s 144 as amended).

When an employee sacrifices salary or gives up a cash alternative for a company car, if they are provided with a package of benefits for example including a car, maintenance and insurance, the total amount foregone for that package will need to be apportioned on a just and reasonable basis under s 69B(2) in order to find the amount of earnings foregone relating to the car. So, say an employee has foregone £5,000 per annum for their company car package, if the relative cost of benefits provided are, say, car: £4,800; maintenance: £600; and insurance: £800 (total: £6,200), one basis of apportionment might be £4,800/£6,200 x £5,000 = £3,871. The modified cash equivalent should then be compared with the apportioned earnings foregone (£3,871) attributable to the car, not the whole amount of the earnings foregone (£5,000) for the package. The balance of £1,129 relating to the other connected benefits provided would be exempt under s239. Note that this is just one basis of apportionment that could be considered to be just and reasonable and others may be possible.

The modified cash equivalent is determined under s 121B (see below) which is similar to the calculation in s 121 for non-OpRA cars, except that no deduction is given for capital contributions at that stage of the calculation; this is deducted in the calculation of the relevant amount as noted above.

As with other benefits, where an apportionment is required to determine the amount foregone, s 121A(2) provides for this to be on a just and reasonable basis.

New ITEPA 2003 s 121B – Cars: modified cash equivalent

Section 121B sets out the steps to determine the "modified cash equivalent" of the benefit of a car made available under OpRA, where this is required for comparison against the amount foregone. For the purposes of OpRA, this amends the steps found in s 121 as noted below.

These steps exclude the deduction of capital contributions because this comes later when calculating the relevant amount in s 121A, subject to s 132A. They also exclude the deduction of private use contributions which are deducted subject to new s 144(1A) – see below.

– Step 1 calculates the list price of the car (per ss 122 to 124A);
– Step 2 adds the cost of accessories (broadly this is the cost of accessories added to the car when first provided and subsequent accessories over £100 per s 126);
– Step 3 calculates the appropriate percentage for the company car (per ss 133 to 142);
– Step 4 multiplies the list price of the car by the relevant percentage; and
– Step 5 reduces the benefit of the car for significant periods of unavailability under s 143.

The modified cash equivalent is the outcome of Steps 1–5.

Where the benefit of a car provided under an OpRA would be subject to an exemption but for s 228A, the modified cash equivalent is to be taken as zero, which means that the taxable benefit will be equal to the amount foregone.

Paragraphs 24 to 26 make consequential amendments to ss 126, 131 and 132.

Paragraph 27 inserts new s 132A.

New ITEPA 2003 s 132A – Cars: capital contributions

Section 132A provides for the deduction of an employee's capital contribution under Step 2 of s 121A, against the "amount foregone" where a company car is subject to OpRA (as opposed to the deduction at Step 3 of s 121 where it is not subject to OpRA).

The deduction is calculated as:

The capped amount (being the lower of £5,000 or the capital amounts previously contributed by the employee in respect of the provision of the car/its accessories) multiplied by the "*appropriate percentage*" as determined by ss 133 to 142.

References in s 132A(1)(b) and (5)(a)(ii) to determining the modified cash equivalent of a car are to be taken as references to determining its market value where the car is a classic car (see new s 147A below).

Paragraph 28 amends s 143. Section 143 provides a reduction to the "modified cash equivalent" after Step 4 of s 121B(1) where OpRA applies, where a car is unavailable for 30 days or more.

A similar reduction is given after Step 6 of s 121(1) where OpRA does not apply.

Paragraph 29 amends s 144. Section 144 provides a reduction for private use contributions made by an employee, to the provisional sum arising after Step 2 when calculating the relevant amount under s 121A(1) where OpRA applies.

A similar reduction is made to the provisional sum arising after Step 7 in s 121(1) where OpRA does not apply.

Paragraph 30 amends s 145. The change to s 145 has effect such that where a car provided under OpRA is temporarily replaced for less than 30 days, the temporary replacement does not give rise to an additional benefit provided the replacement car is not materially better than the normal car.

The expression "materially better" at s 145(5) means:

(a)   materially better in quality to the original car; and
(b)   the interim sum after deducting capital contributions at Step 3 of s 121(1) is materially higher than that of the normal car.

New sub-s 145(6) provides that when the normal and replacement cars are subject to OpRA, s 145(5)(b) is met, if it would be met based on the cash equivalent of the cars under s 121(1) (rather than based on the "modified cash equivalent" of the cars under s 121B).

Paragraph 31 makes consequential amendments to s 146.
Paragraph 32 inserts new s 147A.

New ITEPA 2003 s 147A – Classic cars

Section 147A modifies the "modified cash equivalent" calculation (under new s 121B) where the car is a classic car. This will be where:

–   the age of the car at the end of the tax year is over 15 years old;
–   the car has a market value of £15,000 or more; and
–   the market value exceeds the "specified amount".

Where the above conditions are met, the interim sum in the calculation of the modified cash equivalent of the car that would be found after Step 2 of s 121B(1), is replaced with the market value of the car (as calculated by s 147(3) and (4)).

In addition, references in s 132A(1)(b) and (5)(a)(ii) to determining the modified cash equivalent of a car are to be taken as references to determining its market value.

The "specified amount" above is defined in s 147A(4), given the assumptions stated, as the interim sum following Step 2 in the calculation of the modified cash equivalent under s 121B(1), less the value of capital contributions made under s 132.

Paragraph 33 amends s 148. The amendments make clear that where the car is a shared car, the modified cash equivalent of the car is reduced on a just and reasonable basis to reflect the employee's use of the car.

Paragraph 34 makes a consequential amendment to s 149.
Paragraph 35 inserts new s 149A.

New ITEPA 2003 s 149A – Car fuel

Where fuel is provided under OpRA for a company car (whether or not the company car itself is provided under OpRA), if the amount foregone is greater than the cash equivalent of the benefit, then the value of the benefit in kind is the amount foregone under sub-s (2)(a), and this replaces s 149(1).

Inexplicably, sub-s (2) does not provide full ability for employees to reduce the value of their fuel benefit to NIL by making good the cost of their private fuel. Worse still, where an employer requires an employee to reimburse the cost of private fuel and they do so, their cash equivalent will be NIL under s 150(3)(a) as the condition in s 151(2) is met. Therefore, in these circumstances, the amount foregone will always be greater than a cash equivalent of NIL. This in turn means that where private fuel is provided under OpRA but reimbursed in full, a taxable benefit will nevertheless arise and its value will be equal to the amount foregone.

In practice this may not be an issue in relation to Type A arrangements, because it would seem unusual for an employee to sacrifice salary in relation to fuel, and then to also make good the cost of fuel from net pay.

However, an employer could offer employees a cash alternative intended to encourage them to give up the benefit of private fuel, while requiring employees to make good the cost of private fuel if they retain the benefit. These are Type B arrangements. Note that if an employee reimburses the cost of private fuel in full when OpRA applies, he/she will remain taxable in full on the amount foregone.

Example 1: Fuel made good and OpRA does not apply

Say, a petrol vehicle has CO_2 emissions in the band 100–104 g/km, so the appropriate percentage for 2017/18 is 19%, and the car fuel benefit multiplier is £22,600. The cash equivalent of the fuel benefit is therefore £4,294. There are no Type A or Type B arrangements in place.

Say, the employee travels 5,000 private miles a year, at a fuel cost of 14ppm. The cost of the private fuel is therefore £700. The employer requires the employee to reimburse the private fuel in full, and the employee duly pays the employer £700, which reduces the cash equivalent of the benefit to NIL under s 150(3)(a).

Example 2: Fuel made good in full but OpRA applies

Mindful of just how out of proportion fuel benefits can be, another employer encourages its employees to give up their fuel benefits by offering a cash alternative payment instead of a fuel benefit, which is calculated as an average of £2,000 for the sake of illustration. The cash alternative offer means that if car fuel is taken as a benefit, it will fall under OpRA as a Type B arrangement.

Assume an employee of this employer has the same fact pattern as in Example 1 above.

The amount foregone is £2,000. The cash equivalent of the benefit is NIL because the employee has reimbursed the cost of fuel in full. Since the amount foregone exceeds the cash equivalent of the benefit the condition in s 149A(3) is met and s 149A(2) applies, which means a taxable benefit arises equal to the amount foregone of £2,000.

Example 3: Fuel made good in full but OpRA applies

Another employer and employee have the same fact pattern as in Example 2 except that the cash alternative offered is £5,000. The cash alternative offer means that if car fuel is taken as a benefit, it will fall under OpRA as a Type B arrangement.

Here, the amount foregone is £5,000. The cash equivalent of the benefit is NIL because the employee has reimbursed the cost of fuel in full. Since the amount foregone exceeds the cash equivalent of the benefit the condition in s 149A(3) is met and s 149A(2) applies, which means a taxable benefit arises equal to the amount foregone of £5,000.

This is not only considerably bigger than the actual cost of the employee's private fuel, it is also bigger than the fuel benefit would be under normal rules outside of OpRA, if the employee had not made good the private fuel.

So, while the experiences of three employees in Examples 1 to 3 are the same economically in terms of fuel provided and (in Examples 2 and 3) the reimbursement made, their tax treatment is wildly different, and this arises solely because of the employer's offer of a cash alternative to the private fuel.

Incidentally, if the cash equivalent is measured *before* being reduced to NIL on making good, this doesn't produce a sensible outcome either. In this case, in Example 2, the amount foregone (£2,000) would be less than the cash equivalent (£4,294) so s 149(1) would still apply and making good would reduce the benefit to NIL. However, in Example 3, the amount foregone (£5,000) would be more than the cash equivalent (£4,294) so s 149(1) would be disapplied, and a benefit of £5,000 would arise equal to the amount foregone. Again, from the employees' perspectives, they are in the same boat (or rather, car!), but one is able to make good effectively and the other is not, solely because of the level of cash alternative offered by the employer.

The position on this issue will remain unclear until HMRC issues guidance on the point.

Finally, s 149A may not always allow for a proportionate reduction where the cash equivalent of private fuel is proportionately reduced under ss 152 or 153. This may be self-adjusting in a Type A arrangement if the amount of earnings foregone is proportionately reduced, but in the case of a Type B arrangement, there may not be any express adjustment to a cash alternative.

Note that s 149A(7) is not intended to provide a proportionate reduction in the circumstances noted in Examples 1–3 above. It is only intended to apply where an employee has, for example, a cash allowance of £5,000 and only gives up part of it or allocates part to different benefits. In those circumstances, when determining the amount foregone, this section ensures that the proportionate amount is used in the comparison.

Finally, if s 228A disapplies an exemption that would otherwise apply in respect of private fuel provided under OpRA, the cash equivalent of the benefit is then taken as NIL, with the same consequence as noted above i.e. the value of the private fuel benefit will be equal to the amount foregone.

Paragraph 36 makes a consequential amendment to s 154.

Paragraph 37 inserts new s 154A.

New ITEPA 2003 s 154A – Vans

Where a van is made available to an employee under OpRA, the value of the taxable benefit of the van will be the "relevant amount" determined in accordance with sub-s (3) (see below).

However, this only applies if the amount foregone exceeds the "modified cash equivalent" of the benefit of the van.

The "relevant amount" is defined in sub-s (3) as the amount foregone with respect to the benefit of the van less any contributions made under new s 158A (see para 38 below) for the private use of the van.

The "modified cash equivalent" of the benefit of the van is defined in sub-s (4) as:
- the cash equivalent of the benefit of the van (as determined by s 155)
- less an adjustment for any periods where the van is unavailable (s 156) and
- as reduced where the van is shared on a "just and reasonable basis" (s 157).

Where the benefit of a van provided under an OpRA would be subject to an exemption but for s 228A, the modified cash equivalent is to be taken as zero, which means that the taxable benefit will be equal to the amount foregone less any payments made by the employee for private use.

Paragraph 38 inserts new s 158A.

New ITEPA 2003 s 158A – Vans: private use

This section allows a deduction for payments for private use by the employee in calculating the relevant amount under new s 154A (see above) provided they are made before 6 July following the end of the tax year.

Paragraph 39 makes consequential amendments to s 160.

Paragraph 40 inserts new s 160A.

New ITEPA 2003 s 160A – Vans: fuel

Where fuel is provided under OpRA for a company van (whether or not the company van itself is provided under OpRA), if the amount foregone is greater than the cash equivalent of the benefit, then the value of the benefit in kind is the amount foregone under sub-s (2)(a), and this replaces s 160(1).

This provision suffers from the same apparent omission noted in the case of private fuel provided for a company car under new s 149A (see above), in that it does not allow the employee full ability to reduce the benefit to NIL by reimbursing the employer in full for any private fuel provided.

Where an employer requires an employee to reimburse the cost of private fuel and they do so, their cash equivalent under s 160(2) will be NIL as the conditions in s 162 will be met. Therefore, in these circumstances, the amount foregone will always be greater than a cash equivalent of NIL. This in turn means that where private fuel is provided under OpRA but reimbursed in full, a taxable benefit will nevertheless arise and its value will be equal to the amount foregone.

In practice this may not be an issue in relation to Type A arrangements, because it would seem unusual for an employee to sacrifice salary in relation to fuel, and then to also make good the cost of fuel from net pay.

However, an employer could offer employees a cash alternative intended to encourage them to give up the benefit of private fuel, while requiring employees to make good the cost of private fuel if they retain the benefit. These are Type B arrangements. Note that if an employee reimburses the cost of private fuel in full when OpRA applies, he/she will remain taxable in full on the amount foregone.

Finally, if s 228A disapplies an exemption that would otherwise apply in respect of private fuel provided under OpRA, the cash equivalent of the benefit is then taken as NIL, with the same consequence as noted above i.e. the value of the private fuel benefit will be equal to the amount foregone.

Paragraphs 41 and 42 amend ss 170 and 173.

Paragraphs 43 substitutes sub-ss (A1) to (1B) for existing sub-s (1). Where a taxable cheap loan is provided under OpRA, if the amount foregone is greater than the "modified cash equivalent" of the benefit, then the value of the benefit in kind is the "relevant amount" determined under s 175A, and this replaces s 175(1).

It practice, it is unusual to find loans provided under OpRA because amounts sacrificed from salary cannot be taken as repayments of loan capital.

Amounts sacrificed could be used to replace interest that would otherwise be charged by employers on a loan, particularly where the benefit of the loan would have been exempt, but this is not an arrangement in widespread use in my experience.

Paragraph 44 inserts new s 175A.

New ITEPA 2003 s 175A – Beneficial loans

This section determines the relevant amount as the difference between the amount foregone and the actual interest paid. So, in cases where no interest is paid, the relevant amount would be equal to the amount foregone.

Subsection (2) determines the modified cash equivalent as the interest that would have been payable on the loan at the official rate, ignoring any interest actually paid by the employee.

If s 228A disapplies an exemption that would otherwise apply in respect of a taxable cheap loan provided under OpRA, the modified cash equivalent of the benefit is then taken as NIL. This has the consequence that the amount foregone will be greater than NIL, and in turn, the taxable value of the benefit will be the relevant amount, being the amount foregone less any interest actually paid.

Note that loans of £10,000 or less become chargeable under OpRA. This is because s 180 determines that the *cash equivalent* is not earnings where the £10,000 threshold conditions are met, but there is no corresponding provision under OpRA to determine that the *relevant amount* is not earnings where the threshold conditions are met.

Also, when calculating the modified cash equivalent of a loan under OpRA, certain loans are kept separate from others, given that they could be made under OpRA while the others may not be (or vice versa). These are replacement loans and loans made by a close company to a director which would otherwise be required to be aggregated under s 187.

Paragraphs 45 to 47 amend ss 180, 184 and 202.

Paragraph 48 inserts new s 203A.

New ITEPA 2003 s 203A – Other employment-related benefits

Section 203 determines the cash equivalent of employment-related benefits which are subject to the residual liability to charge in ITEPA 2003 Pt 3 Ch 10. Chapter 10 applies to all benefits provided to employees other than those for which specific rules exist in Chs 3 to 9 of the benefits code.

The right to receive sick pay (s 221) is also excluded from s 203 outside of OpRA, but HMRC considers that such a right will fall within the s 69B(5) meaning of benefit and so if provided under OpRA, the new rules will apply.

Sick pay

Some employers provide a basic level of company sick pay (above statutory sick pay) as a core benefit with no requirement to forego earnings and with no offer of a cash alternative in lieu of that core benefit. However, they may allow employees to increase the level of sick pay in exchange for a salary sacrifice. If the right to receive sick pay is a benefit within s 69B(5), this would be a Type A arrangement, chargeable under OpRA on an incremental basis i.e. the value of the right to receive the *additional* level of sick pay, would be taxable and would likely be equal to the amount foregone. (The core level of sick pay not attributable to any earnings foregone would continue to fall outside OpRA).

The tax treatment of receipts of sick pay is less clear and likely to be problematic. Section 221(4) dictates that the amount of any sick pay payment which is just and reasonable to attribute to an employer contribution, is treated as earnings. Under salary sacrifice the employee gives up salary and the employer makes the contributions. The consequence of this is that sick pay provided under OpRA will likely suffer double taxation, firstly in relation to the amount foregone, and secondly in relation to the sick pay payments (since these will be attributable to employer contributions, notwithstanding they are chargeable under OpRA). We will have to wait for HMRC guidance to clarify how this will be dealt with, assuming there was no intention to create a double tax charge. If that is correct, a "work around" to avoid this might be to deem any contributions taxed under OpRA as employee contributions.

The general rule for benefits chargeable under Chapter 10

The general rule for all employment-related benefits chargeable under Ch 10 and provided under OpRA, is that the "relevant amount" will be treated as earnings under s 203A(1)(a), and this replaces s 203(1).

If the amount foregone is greater than the cost of the benefit, the relevant amount is the amount foregone less any amount made good by the employee by 6 July following the tax year concerned.

But if the cost of the benefit is greater than or equal to the amount foregone, the relevant amount continues to be the cash equivalent of the benefit determined as normal under s 203(2).

If s 228A disapplies an exemption that would otherwise apply in respect of an employment-related benefit provided under OpRA, the cost of the benefit is then taken as NIL. This has the consequence that the amount foregone will be greater than NIL, and in turn, the relevant amount (the taxable value of the benefit under OpRA) will be the amount foregone less any interest actually paid.

Example 1: Use of a lap-top/tablet

Consider a tablet provided to an employee not being solely for business use. The example is equally applicable in principle to a lap-top, or indeed any other asset which is not exempt. Example 2 below illustrates the calculations for an exempt asset.

Say that the tablet has a retail value and cost to the employer of £720 and is provided to an employee under OpRA. The employee is asked to sacrifice £720 to use the tablet over three years starting in 2016/17, through 2017/18 and 2018/19; there is no transfer of ownership during this period. Say the market value of the tablet after three years is 15% (£108) of its original cost. After three years, the employer decides it doesn't want the tablet returned, and gifts it to the employee at no additional cost and for no additional salary sacrifice.

The tables below illustrate the complexity of the calculations required to determine the benefit arising in each tax year. It also provides a good all-round case study of the overall rules.

Example (1) Tablet costing £720 made available to an employee for three years

	Benefit calculation without OpRA	Salary sacrificed	Benefit calculation with OpRA	
Market value when first provided	720			
Benefit for use of asset				
2016/17	20% 144	240	**144**	(x)
2017/18	20% 144	240	**144**	(y)

2018/19		20%	**144**	240	**240** (z)
				720	

Market value when first provided less benefit values arising each year	(A) s206(5)	288			
Mark value when transferred	(B) s206(2)	108			
Benefit on transfer of the asset					
2018/19 Higher of (A) and (B)	s206(3)	**288** (w)			**288**
Total amount charged to tax		**720**			**816**

Notes:

Under OpRA, the cost of providing the benefit is replaced by the amount foregone where relevant as follows:

2016/17   pre-dates OpRA and so the benefit arising is simply 20% of the value of the tablet when first provided – the amount annotated (x).

2017/18   as the arrangement commenced prior to 6 April 2017, grandfathering should apply until 5 April 2018, assuming the conditions for grandfathering continue to be met (see below under para 62) – the benefit is the amount annotated (y).

2018/19   OpRA applies this year in relation to both the use of the asset under s 203(1) and the transfer of the asset under s 206. The benefit for use of the asset will be the higher of the amount foregone (£240) and the cost of providing the asset (£144) – so £240 – the amount annotated (z). The benefit arising on transfer of the asset will also be the higher of the amount foregone and the cost of providing the asset as determined under s 206. As no amount is sacrificed for the transfer, the higher figure will obviously be the cost of providing the asset.

   Note that the cost of providing the asset is also subject to its own "higher of" calculation under s 206(3). This compares the market value when the asset is first provided less the annual benefit values, with the market value at the time of transfer, and the highest figure applies – the amount annotated (w). An anomaly arises because in this "higher of" calculation, only the amounts calculated under the normal annual benefit values calculated under s 205 are deductible and not the (potentially higher) actual benefit in kind charge under OpRA. This can result in more than 100% of the original cost being taxed where the asset is provided under OpRA.

Summary   So, in this example, you can see that the total amount chargeable under an OpRA arrangement is £816, despite the asset only costing £720.

Example 2: Use of a Smartphone

Now consider the case where the asset is a Smartphone. Assume the figures for cost and market value and timings are the same as in Example 1.

Example (2) Smartphone costing £720 made available to an employee for three years

	Benefit calculation without OpRA	Salary sacrificed	Benefit calculation with OpRA	
Market value when first provided	720			
Benefit for use of asset				
2016/17	20%	**0**	240	**0** (x)
2017/18	20%	**0**	240	**0** (y)
2018/19	20%	**0**	240	**240** (z)
			720	

Market value when first provided less benefit values arising each year	(A) s206(5)	288			
Mark value when transferred	(B) s206(2)	108			
Benefit on transfer of the asset					
2018/19	Higher of (A) and (B)	s206(3)	**288** (w)		**288**
Total amount charged to tax			**288**		**528**

Notes:

Under OpRA, the cost of providing the benefit is replaced by the amount foregone where relevant as follows:

2016/17	pre-dates OpRA and so the benefit of the Smartphone is exempt under s 319.
2017/18	as with the laptop, the arrangement commenced prior to 6 April 2017, grandfathering should apply so the s 319 exemption should continue to apply.
2018/19	as with the laptop, OpRA applies this year and two benefit figures must be calculated – one for the use of the asset and one for the transfer as above. Note that the s 206(3) comparison still imputes a deduction for the annual 20% charges, even though these were exempt for the first two years.
Summary	So, in this example, you can see that the total amount chargeable is £528, which compares with a total of £288 where OpRA does not apply.

Exemptions – Sch 2 para 49

Paragraph 49 inserts new s 228A in ITEPA 2003 Pt 4 (employment income: exemptions).

New ITEPA 2003 s 228A – Exclusion of exemptions

The effect of sub-s (1) is to disapply exemptions conferred by Pt 4 for any benefit provided to an employee under OpRA, other than a "Special Case Exemption" or an "excluded exemption".

This has two impacts:

First, it causes benefits that would otherwise be exempt to become taxable to the extent they are provided under OpRA. A mobile phone considered in the example in new s 203A above, provides a simple example of this.

Second, this section is referenced throughout the OpRA legislation in the calculation of the relevant amount, such that where an exemption would otherwise apply, the cash equivalent or modified cash equivalent of the benefit concerned is taken as NIL. This leaves the amount foregone as the main determinant of the relevant amount, which is helpful. If that were not the case, it would be necessary to calculate the cash equivalent of amounts that would normally be exempt. Consider a workplace gym for example. The cost of provision of such a benefit would be difficult to calculate and given that the cost would be exempt if provided outside OpRA, the amount foregone is really the only variable that needs to be brought into charge under OpRA – and so it is.

Special Case exemptions (sub-s (4)) are largely (but not exclusively) exemptions which already include their own provisions relating to salary sacrifice, such as the s 289A exemption for deductible business expenses. This exemption was introduced in April 2016 and at the same time included s 289A(1)(*b*) so it would be disapplied where an expense is provided in conjunction with "relevant salary sacrifice arrangements". These are essentially Type A or Type B arrangements (albeit slightly different definitions are used in s 289A(5)).

Excluded exemptions (sub-s (5)) appear to be those which the government has decided are acceptable, for the time being at least, to be provided under OpRA. For example pension contributions, childcare and cycle to work schemes are the three most commonly provided by employers in this way.

Note s 239 (payments and benefits connected with taxable cars and vans and exempt heavy goods vehicles). This is necessary to avoid double taxation. For example, connected benefits such as insurance and maintenance are in effect already included in the company car benefit charge. If s 239 were disapplied by s 228A, these connected benefits would become taxable in addition to the car benefit charge. This is therefore welcome, but it has an unexpected computational impact when calculating the earnings foregone under Type A and Type B arrangements – see s 121A above.

Also note that s 307 is included in the list of excluded exemptions but only to the extent a benefit relates to the provision of retirement benefits. To the extent it relates to death in service, OpRA would need to be considered and the exemption for death in service would be lost where it applies. As many employers look to provide death in service arrangements under Excepted Group Life Policies to mitigate the impact of the reducing lifetime allowance, they will need to ensure these are not provided under any kind of OpRA arrangement. In particular it is common for some schemes to provide a core level of death cover (say 2x salary) with the ability for employees to flex up to a higher level of cover, say, 4x salary in exchange for a salary sacrifice. If structured in this way, it would cause the additional level of cover to become taxable, based on the usual "relevant amount" calculations. The core level of cover would continue to be unaffected by OpRA in this example.

Section 228A(1) refers to "benefit or facility" but benefit is already defined in s 68B(5) as including any benefit or facility, regardless of its form and the manner of providing it, so it is not clear why the words "or facility" are needed. Section 228A(7) then defines "benefit or facility" as including anything which constitutes employment income or in respect of which employment income is treated as arising to the employee (regardless of its form and the manner of providing it).

Note that employment related securities options are removed from the benefits code by s 418(1A) which resides in Pt 7. Section 228A does not therefore disapply this exemption which continues to have effect for such options. However, options which may be cash settled are arguably not options at all and may not benefit from this protection.

Finally, note that the Treasury can by order add to and remove items from the list of Special Case exemptions and Excluded exemptions.

Other amendments – Sch 2 paras 50 to 61

Paragraph 50 amends s 19.

Paragraph 51 amends s 95. Section 95 prevents a double tax charge arising on the receipt of money, goods or services from the use of a cash voucher, non-cash voucher or credit-token, where such use has already been treated as earnings.

Paragraphs 52 to 58 amend ss 236, 239, 362, 318A, 363, 693 and 694.

Paragraphs 59 amends s 695. Section 695 brings the use of credit-tokens within the PAYE regime, where used to obtain money or anything which would be a readily convertible asset. Section 695(1A) is inserted to ensure that, where a credit-token is provided under OpRA, the amount subject to PAYE is determined under the OpRA provisions, rather than the amount determined under s 94(2).

Paragraphs 60 to 61 amend Sch 1 Pt 2.

Commencement and transitional provision – Sch 2 para 62

The commencement and transitional provisions contained in para 62 include the highly valued "grandfathering provisions".

Grandfathering delays the start of OpRA for arrangements already entered into before 6 April 2017, until the earliest of:

(i) any variation of the terms of the arrangement (para 62(6));
(ii) the renewal of the arrangement (including automatic renewal) (para 62(7));
(iii) a long-stop date which depends on the type of benefit provided (paras 62(3),(4),(5)).

Subject to any further guidance on grandfathering provided by HMRC, the following points will be important:

(i) Terms of an arrangement

Note that it is a variation of *the terms* of a pre-6 April 2017 arrangement that brings grandfathering to an end. The terms of the arrangement could be varied in writing or by conduct.

An arrangement is an Optional Remuneration Arrangement as defined in s 69A i.e. Type A or Type B arrangements. The parties to the arrangement are not explicit, but given that the arrangements involve employees giving up earnings and benefits are usually provided by employers, the parties to such arrangements will usually be the employee and the employer. The terms which grandfathering requires not to be varied in order to preserve grandfathering should therefore be the terms agreed between the employee and employer (as opposed to the terms on which a supplier provides something to the employer, which the employer then provides to the employee).

For example, if a supplier varies the terms of a lease under which an asset is leased to the employer, but the employer makes no consequential amendment to the terms it has agreed with the employee, this should not impact on grandfathering. However, if an employer varies the terms with its employee, grandfathering will normally cease from the date of that variation. This is subject to para 62(8), which clarifies that variations required due to accidental damage or otherwise outside the control of the parties will not bring an end to grandfathering.

So, if an employee varies their contract mileage on a leased car which results in an increase of lease rentals and salary sacrifice amounts, unless this is part of the terms of the original agreement, then it is likely to be regarded as within the control of the parties and so grandfathering will cease at the time of the variation is made. On the other hand, if an employee has ordered a car to a certain specification before 6 April 2017, but the manufacturer has to change that specification which is then delivered on or after 6 April 2017, as the change was outside the control of the parties, this should not bring an end to grandfathering. This would be even clearer if the terms of the arrangement were explicit about the possibility of such amendments, in which case this would then not amount to a change in those terms, but would simply be a working out of those terms. HMRC has just updated its guidance including a number of helpful examples at EIM44030. Example 6 confirms the dividing line is between a variation of terms and the working out of terms that provide for variation. I would not expect any difficulty to arise where terms provide for variations required for commercial reasons and which are not intended to circumvent the policy intention of the legislation.

Under para 62(9), variations which occur in connection with a person's entitlement to statutory sick pay, statutory maternity pay, statutory adoption pay, statutory paternity pay or statutory shared parental pay, will not bring an end to grandfathering. During periods of such entitlement, the ability to make sacrifices of salary may be restricted and sometimes benefits provision could be suspended. Without this provision, such amendments would be variations of the terms of an arrangement, but para 62(9) ensures grandfathering continues in these circumstances.

(ii) Renewal of an arrangement

Renewal will bring an end to grandfathering whether arrangements are renewed expressly or automatically i.e. on an implied basis without the employee having to do anything. So, for any benefits year ending between 6 April 2017 and 5 April 2018, OpRA will apply from the start of the next benefits year.

Note that, with the exception of school fees, this also applies if benefits where grandfathering is extended to 2021 (see below) are renewed. For example, say the lease on a car with CO_2 emissions exceeding 75g/km expires on 31 December 2017, but is renewed on 1 January 2018. OpRA will apply to the car from 1 January 2018.

(iii) The long-stop dates

The long-stop date is 5 April 2021 for cars (with CO_2 emissions exceeding 75g/km), vans, fuel, accommodation and school fees, and 5 April 2018 for all other benefits and exemptions.

Note that in the case of school fees, a variation of the terms of a pre-6 April 2017 arrangement will not bring an end to grandfathering by virtue of para 62(12). However, the continuing arrangements and the previous arrangements for school fees must relate to:

(a) employment with the same employer;
(b) the same school;
(c) school fees in respect of the same child.

Grandfathering should then be preserved regardless of any other variation or renewal of the school fee arrangements.

The provisions in para 62(13) are anti-avoidance provisions in respect of "delayed benefits" provided under non-cash vouchers. The intention is simply to ensure no unfair advantage is gained in relation to pre-6 April 2017 vouchers exchanged for goods or services after 6 April 2018. Although this seems unlikely to be a widespread concern, nevertheless, the provision is not entirely clear and further guidance will be needed as to its operation in practice. Please see my analysis at s 87A above for further details.

SCHEDULE 3

OVERSEAS PENSIONS

Section 9

PART 1

REGISTERED PENSION SCHEMES ESTABLISHED OUTSIDE THE UK

1 (1) In Chapter 5A of Part 4 of FA 2004 (registered pension schemes established outside the UK), after section 242B (inserted by Schedule 4 to this Act) insert—

"242C Application of this Part to non-UK registered schemes

(1) This Part (so far as would not otherwise be the case) is to be read—

(a) as applying in relation to UK-relieved funds of a non-UK registered scheme as it applies in relation to sums or assets held for the purposes of, or representing accrued rights under, a registered pension scheme established in the United Kingdom,

(b) as applying in relation to a non-UK registered scheme, so far as the scheme relates to the scheme's UK-relieved funds, as it applies in relation to a registered pension scheme established in the United Kingdom,

(c) as applying in relation to members of a non-UK registered scheme, so far as their rights under the scheme are represented by UK-relieved funds of the scheme, as it applies in relation to members of a registered pension scheme established in the United Kingdom, and

(d) as applying to relevant contributions to a non-UK registered scheme as it applies in relation to contributions to a registered pension scheme established in the United Kingdom.

(2) Subsection (1) has effect subject to, and in accordance with, the following provisions of this Chapter.

(3) The Commissioners for Her Majesty's Revenue and Customs may by regulations make—

(a) provision elucidating the application of, or supplementing, subsection (1) or other provisions of this Chapter, or

(b) where relief from tax is involved, other provision for or in connection with the application of this Part where the interpretative presumption against extra-territorial application means that it would otherwise not apply.

(4) Regulations under subsection (3) may (in particular)—

(a) amend provisions of or made under—

(i) this Part, or

(ii) any other enactment related to taxation in connection with pensions, and

(b) make consequential amendments of provisions of, or made under, any enactment.

(5) See section 242B for the meaning of "UK-relieved funds" and "relevant contribution".

242D Non-UK registered schemes: annual allowance charge

(1) This section is about the application of the provisions of this Part relating to the annual allowance charge.

(2) Pension input amounts in respect of arrangements relating to an individual under a non-UK registered scheme are to be taken into account in applying the provisions for a tax year in relation to the individual only if, in accordance with regulations made by the Commissioners for Her Majesty's Revenue and Customs, relieved inputs are to be taken to have been made in respect of the individual under the scheme in the year.

242E Investment-regulated non-UK registered schemes

For the purposes of the application of the taxable property provisions in relation to a non-UK registered scheme, property is taxable property in relation to the scheme if it would be taxable property in relation to the scheme were the scheme a registered pension scheme established in the United Kingdom."

(2) The amendment made by this paragraph has effect for the tax year 2017–18 and subsequent tax years.

PART 2

INCOME TAX ON PENSION INCOME

UK residents to be taxed on 100%, not 90%, of foreign pension income

2 (1) Omit section 575(2) of ITEPA 2003 (foreign pensions received by UK residents: taxable amount is 90% of actual amount).

(2) Omit section 613(3) of ITEPA 2003 (annuities from non-UK sources: taxable amount is 90% of actual amount).

(3) Omit section 635(3) of ITEPA 2003 (foreign voluntary annual payments: taxable amount is 90% of actual amount).

(4) In consequence—

(a) in section 575 of ITEPA 2003—

(i) in subsection (1) omit ", (2)";

(ii) in subsection (1A), for "subsections (2) and" substitute "subsection";

(iii) in subsection (3), for "That pension income" substitute "The full amount of the pension income arising in the tax year, or (as the case may be) the UK part of the tax year,";

(iv) in subsection (3), for "that Act" substitute "ITTOIA 2005";

(b) in section 613 of ITEPA 2003—

(i) in subsection (2), for "subsections (3) and" substitute "subsection";

(ii) in subsection (4), for "that Act" substitute "ITTOIA 2005";

(c) in section 635 of ITEPA 2003—

(i) in subsection (2), for "subsections (3) and" substitute "subsection";

(ii) in subsection (4), for "That pension income" substitute "The full amount of the pension income arising in the tax year";

(iii) in subsection (4), for "that Act" substitute "ITTOIA 2005";

(d) in Schedule 45 to FA 2013 omit paragraph 72(4).

(5) In sections 613(5) and 635(5) of ITEPA 2003 (application of section 839 of ITTOIA 2005 in certain cases), for "condition B" substitute "conditions B1 and B2 (and the reference to them in subsection (1))".

(6) The amendments made by this paragraph have effect for the tax year 2017–18 and subsequent tax years, subject to sub-paragraph (7).

(7) The amendments in section 575 of ITEPA 2003, so far as they relate to relevant withdrawals, have effect in relation to relevant withdrawals paid in or after the tax year 2017–18; and here "relevant withdrawal" has the meaning given by section 576A of ITEPA 2003.

Superannuation funds to which section 615(3) of ICTA applies

3 (1) Section 615 of ICTA (trust funds for pensions in respect of employment outside UK) is amended as follows.

(2) In subsection (6)—

(a) in paragraph (b), omit the final "and";

(b) in paragraph (c), at the end insert "and";

(c) after paragraph (c) insert—

"(d) meets the benefit accrual condition (see subsection (6A));".

(3) After subsection (6) insert—

"(6A) The benefit accrual condition is—

(a) that, in the case of any money purchase arrangement relating to a member of the fund that is not a cash balance arrangement, no contributions are made under the arrangement on or after 6 April 2017;

(b) that, in the case of any cash balance arrangement relating to a member of the fund, there is no increase on or after 6 April 2017 in the value of any person's rights under the arrangement;

(c) that, in the case of any defined benefits arrangement relating to a member of the fund, there is no increase on or after 6 April 2017 in the value of any person's rights under the arrangement; and

(d) that, in the case of any arrangement relating to a member of the fund that is neither a money purchase arrangement nor a defined benefits arrangement—

    (i) no contributions are made under the arrangement on or after 6 April 2017, and

    (ii) there is no increase on or after 6 April 2017 in the value of any person's rights under the arrangement.

(6B) For the purposes of subsection (6A)(b)—

(a) whether there is an increase in the value of a person's rights is to be determined by reference to whether there is an increase in the amount that would, on the valuation assumptions, be available for the provision of benefits under the arrangement to or in respect of the person (and, if there is, the amount of the increase), but

(b) in the case of rights that accrued to a person before 6 April 2017, ignore increases in the value of the rights if in no tax year do they exceed the relevant percentage.

(6C) For the purposes of subsection (6A)(c)—

(a) whether there is an increase in the value of a person's rights is to be determined by reference to whether there is an increase in the benefits amount as defined by paragraph 14(7) of Schedule 18 to the Finance Act 2011, but

(b) in the case of rights that accrued to a person before 6 April 2017, ignore increases in the value of the rights if in no tax year do they exceed the relevant percentage.

(6D) For the purposes of subsection (6A)(d)(ii), regulations made by the Commissioners for Her Majesty's Revenue and Customs may make provision—

(a) for determining whether there is an increase in the value of a person's rights,

(b) for determining the amount of any increase, and

(c) for ignoring the whole or part of any increase;

and regulations under this subsection may make provision having effect in relation to times before the regulations are made.

(6E) In this section, "relevant percentage", in relation to a tax year, means—

(a) where, on 20 March 2017, the rules of the fund include provision for the value of the rights of a person to increase during the tax year at an annual rate specified in those rules, that rate, or

(b) in any other case, the percentage by which the consumer prices index for September in the previous tax year is higher than it was for the September in the tax year before that (or, if greater, 0%).

(6F) The Commissioners for Her Majesty's Revenue and Customs may by regulations make provision—

(a) so as to change, or modify the effect of, the benefit accrual condition;

(b) as to the matters to be taken into account in determining whether the benefit accrual condition is met;

(c) for a superannuation fund to be treated to any extent as meeting or not meeting the benefit accrual condition.

(6G) Provision under subsection (6D) or (6F) may be made by amending this section."

(4) In subsection (7)—

(a) for "In this section—" substitute "For the purposes of this section—

"arrangement", in relation to a member of a superannuation fund, means an arrangement relating to the member under the fund;

a money purchase arrangement relating to a member of a superannuation fund is a "cash balance arrangement" at any time if, at that time, all the benefits that may be provided to or in respect of the member under the arrangement are cash balance benefits;

an arrangement relating to a member of a superannuation fund is a "defined benefits arrangement" at any time if, at that time, all the benefits that may be provided to or in respect of the member under the arrangement are defined benefits;

an arrangement relating to a member of a superannuation fund is a "money purchase arrangement" at any time if, at that time, all the benefits that may be provided to or in respect of the member under the arrangement are money purchase benefits;

"cash balance benefits", "defined benefits" and "money purchase benefits" have the meaning given by section 152 of the Finance Act 2004, but for this purpose reading references in that section to a pension scheme as references to a superannuation fund;

"member", in relation to a superannuation fund, has the meaning given by section 151 of the Finance Act 2004, but for this purpose reading references in that section to a pension scheme as references to a superannuation fund;";

(b) at the end insert—

""the valuation assumptions" has the meaning given by section 277 of the Finance Act 2004."

(5) After subsection (10) insert—

"(11) Where the conditions in subsection (6)(a) to (c) are met in the case of a superannuation fund ("the actual fund")—

(a) any disqualifying contributions made under an arrangement relating to a member of the actual fund are treated for the purposes of the Income Tax Acts as instead made under an arrangement relating to the member under a separate superannuation fund ("the shadow fund" for the actual fund),

(b) any disqualifying increase in the value of a person's rights under an arrangement relating to a member of the actual fund is treated for the purposes of the Income Tax Acts as instead being an increase under an arrangement relating to the member under the shadow fund for the actual fund, and

(c) any reference in this or any other Act (including the reference in subsection (3) and any reference enacted after the coming into force of this subsection) to a fund, or superannuation fund, to which subsection (3) applies does not include so much of the actual fund as—

(i) represents any contribution treated as made under, or any increase in the value of any rights treated as an increase under, the shadow fund of the actual fund or the shadow fund of any other superannuation fund, or

(ii) arises, or (directly or indirectly) derives, from anything within sub-paragraph (i) or this sub-paragraph.

(12) For the purposes of subsection (11) a contribution, or an increase in the value of any rights, is "disqualifying" if it would (ignoring that subsection) cause the benefit accrual condition not to be met in the case of the actual fund.

(13) For the purposes of the provisions of this section relating to the benefit accrual condition, where there is a recognised transfer—

(a) any transfer of sums or assets to the recipient fund by the recognised transfer is to be categorised as not being "a contribution" to the recipient fund, and

(b) any increase in the value of rights under the recipient fund that occurs at the time of the recognised transfer is to be treated as not being an increase in that value if the increase is solely a result of the transfer effected by the recognised transfer.

(14) For the purposes of subsection (13), where there is a transfer such that sums or assets held for the purposes of, or representing accrued rights under, an arrangement relating to a member of a superannuation fund ("the transferor fund") are transferred so as to become held for the purposes of, or to represent rights under, an arrangement relating to that person as a member of another superannuation fund, the transfer is a "recognised transfer" if—

(a) the conditions in subsection (6)(a) to (c) are met in the case of each of the funds, and

(b) none of the sums and assets transferred—

(i) represents any contribution treated as made under, or any increase in the value of any rights treated as an increase under, the shadow fund of the transferor fund or the shadow fund of any other superannuation fund, or

(ii) arises, or (directly or indirectly) derives, from anything within sub-paragraph (i) or this sub-paragraph."

(6) The amendments made by this paragraph are to be treated as having come into force on 6 April 2017.

PART 3

LUMP SUMS FOR UK RESIDENTS FROM FOREIGN PENSION SCHEMES

Introductory

4 ITEPA 2003 is amended as follows.

Employer-financed retirement benefit schemes: ending of foreign-service relief

5 (1) Section 395B (exemption or reduction for foreign service) is amended as follows.

(2) In subsection (1) (conditions for entitlement to exemption or reduction), after paragraph (c) insert—

"(ca) the recipient is not resident in the United Kingdom in the tax year in which the lump sum is received,".

(3) In subsection (8) (meaning of "foreign service"), for "413(2)" substitute "395C".

(4) The amendments made by this paragraph have effect for the tax year 2017–18 and subsequent tax years.

6 After section 395B insert—

"395C Meaning of "foreign service" in section 395B

(1) In section 395B "foreign service" means service to which subsection (2), (3), (6) or (8) applies.

(2) This subsection applies to service in or after the tax year 2013–14—

(a) to the extent that it consists of duties performed outside the United Kingdom in respect of which earnings would not be relevant earnings, or

(b) if a deduction equal to the whole amount of the earnings from the employment was or would have been allowable under Chapter 6 of Part 5 (deductions from seafarers' earnings).

(3) This subsection applies to service in or after the tax year 2003–04 but before the tax year 2013–14 such that—

(a) any earnings from the employment would not be relevant earnings, or

(b) a deduction equal to the whole amount of the earnings from the employment was or would have been allowable under Chapter 6 of Part 5 (deductions from seafarers' earnings).

(4) In subsection (2) "relevant earnings" means earnings for a tax year that are earnings to which section 15 applies and to which that section would apply even if the employee made a claim under section 809B of ITA 2007 (claim for remittance basis) for that year.

(5) In subsection (3) "relevant earnings" means—

(a) for service in or after the tax year 2008–09, earnings—

(i) which are for a tax year in which the employee is ordinarily UK resident,

(ii) to which section 15 applies, and

(iii) to which that section would apply even if the employee made a claim under section 809B of ITA 2007 (claim for remittance basis) for that year, and

(b) for service before the tax year 2008–09, general earnings to which section 15 or 21 as originally enacted applies.

(6) This subsection applies to service before the tax year 2003–04 and after the tax year 1973–74 such that—

(a) the emoluments from the employment were not chargeable under Case I of Schedule E, or would not have been so chargeable had there been any, or

(b) a deduction equal to the whole amount of the emoluments from the employment was or would have been allowable under a foreign earnings deduction provision.

(7) In subsection (6) "foreign earnings deduction provision" means—

(a) paragraph 1 of Schedule 2 to FA 1974,

(b) paragraph 1 of Schedule 7 to FA 1977, or

(c) section 192A or 193(1) of ICTA.

(8) This subsection applies to service before the tax year 1974–75 such that tax was not chargeable in respect of the emoluments of the employment—

(a) in the tax year 1956–57 or later, under Case I of Schedule E, or

(b) in earlier tax years, under Schedule E,

or it would not have been so chargeable had there been any such emoluments."

7 In section 554Z4 (treatment of relevant step: residence issues), after subsection (6) insert—

"(7) Subsections (8) and (9) apply if—

(a) the relevant step is the payment of a lump sum,

(b) the payment of the lump sum is the provision of a relevant benefit under an employer-financed retirement benefits scheme, and

(c) the person by whom the lump sum is received is resident in the United Kingdom in the tax year in which the lump sum is received.

(8) If the lump sum is wholly in respect of rights which have accrued on or after 6 April 2017, there is no reduction under subsection (4).

(9) If the lump sum is wholly or partly in respect of rights which accrued before 6 April 2017, the amount of any reduction under subsection (4) is given by—

R x (A / LS)

> where—
>> A is so much of the lump sum as is in respect of rights which accrued before 6 April 2017,
>> LS is the amount of the lump sum, and
>> R is the amount which (ignoring this subsection) is given by subsection (4) as the amount of the reduction.

(10) In subsection (7)—

> "employer-financed retirement benefits scheme" has the same meaning as in Chapter 2 of Part 6 (see section 393A), and
> "relevant benefit" has the same meaning as in that Chapter (see section 393B)."

Lump sums under other foreign schemes

8 In section 573 (foreign pensions), after subsection (3) insert—

> "(4) This section also applies to a pension paid by or on behalf of a person who is outside the United Kingdom to a person who is not resident in the United Kingdom if—
>> (a) the pension is a relevant lump sum paid under a pension scheme to that person in respect of a member of the scheme, and
>> (b) the member is, or immediately before the member's death was, resident in the United Kingdom."

9 In section 574(1) (foreign pensions: meaning of "pension"), after paragraph (a) insert—

> "(aa) a relevant lump sum (see section 574A),".

10 (1) After section 574 insert—

"574A "Pension": relevant lump sums

(1) A lump sum paid under a pension scheme to a member of the scheme, or to a person in respect of a member of the scheme, is "a relevant lump sum" for the purposes of this Chapter if—

> (a) the scheme is none of the following—
>> (i) a registered pension scheme,
>> (ii) a relevant non-UK scheme, and
>> (iii) an employer-financed retirement benefits scheme established in the United Kingdom, and
> (b) the payment of the lump sum is not a relevant step by reason of which Chapter 2 of Part 7A applies.

(2) A lump sum paid under a relevant non-UK scheme to a member of the scheme, or to a person in respect of a member of the scheme, is "a relevant lump sum" for the purposes of this Chapter if the effect of paragraphs 1 to 7 of Schedule 34 to FA 2004 is that the member payment provisions (see paragraph 1(4) of that Schedule) do not apply in relation to the payment of the lump sum.

(3) If section 573 applies to a relevant lump sum then, for the purposes of section 575, the full amount of the pension income arising by reason of the payment of the lump sum is the amount of the lump sum, reduced as follows—

Step 1
Deduct so much of the lump sum as is payable by reason of commutation of rights to receive pension income on which no liability to tax arises as a result of any provision of Chapter 17 of this Part.

Step 2
Where the lump sum is paid under a pension scheme that was an employer-financed retirement benefits scheme immediately before 6 April 2017, deduct so much of the lump sum left after Step 1 as is deductible in accordance with subsection (6).
Where the lump sum is paid otherwise than under such a scheme, deduct so much of the lump sum left after Step 1 as is paid in respect of the value immediately before 6 April 2017 of rights, accrued by then, specifically to receive benefits by way of lump sum payments.

Step 3
If the lump sum is paid under an overseas pension scheme, deduct so much of the

lump sum left after Step 2 as would, if the scheme were a registered pension scheme, not be liable to income tax under this Part.

For the purposes of this Step—

(a) treat amounts not included in taxable pension income because of section 636B(3) as being not liable to tax;

(b) assume that all or part of the member's lifetime allowance is available.

(4) The amount given by subsection (3) is treated for the purposes of section 575 as arising when the lump sum is paid.

(5) The Commissioners may by regulations make provision (including provision amending this section) as to the assumptions to be made for the purposes of Step 3.

(6) These rules apply for the purposes of the first sentence of Step 2—

(a) "the post-Step 1 amount" means so much of the lump sum as is left after Step 1;

(b) "the relevant amount" means so much of the post-Step 1 amount as is paid in respect of rights specifically to receive benefits by way of lump sum payments;

(c) "reckonable service" means service in respect of which the rights to receive the relevant amount accrued (whether or not service in the same employment or with the same employer, and even if the rights originally accrued under a different employer-financed retirement benefits scheme established in or outside the United Kingdom);

(d) "pre-6 April 2017 reckonable service" means reckonable service that is service before 6 April 2017;

(e) "pre-6 April 2017 reckonable foreign service" means pre-6 April 2017 reckonable service that is foreign service;

(f) the deductible amount is the value immediately before 6 April 2017 of the rights then accrued to payment of so much of the relevant amount as is paid in respect of pre-6 April 2017 reckonable service if—

(i) at least 75% of pre-6 April 2017 reckonable service is made up of foreign service, or

(ii) the period of pre-6 April 2017 reckonable service exceeds 10 years and the whole of the last 10 years of that period is made up of foreign service, or

(iii) the period of pre-6 April 2017 reckonable service exceeds 20 years and at least 50% of that period, including any 10 of the last 20 years, is made up of foreign service;

(g) otherwise, the deductible amount is the appropriate fraction of the value immediately before 6 April 2017 of the rights then accrued to payment of so much of the relevant amount as is paid in respect of pre-6 April 2017 reckonable service;

(h) "the appropriate fraction" is given by—

$$F / R$$

where—

F is the period of pre-6 April 2017 reckonable foreign service, and

R is the period of pre-6 April 2017 reckonable service.

(7) In this section—

"employer-financed retirement benefits scheme" has the same meaning as in Chapter 2 of Part 6 (see section 393A),

"foreign service" has the meaning given by section 395C,

"member", in relation to a pension scheme, has the meaning given by section 151 of FA 2004,

"overseas pension scheme" has the same meaning as in Part 4 of FA 2004 (see section 150(7) of that Act),

"payment" includes a transfer of assets and any other transfer of money's worth,

"pension scheme" has the meaning given by section 150(1) of FA 2004, and

"relevant non-UK scheme" is to be read in accordance with paragraph 1(5) of Schedule 34 to FA 2004."

(2) The amendment made by this paragraph has effect in relation to lump sums paid on or after 6 April 2017.

11 (1) In section 576A (temporary non-residents), as it applies where the year of departure is the tax year 2013–14 or a later tax year, after subsection (4) insert—

"(4ZA) Payment of a relevant lump sum is also a "relevant withdrawal"."

(2) The amendment made by this paragraph applies in relation to relevant withdrawals on or after 6 April 2017.

12 (1) In section 576A, as it applies where the year of departure is the tax year 2012–13 or an earlier tax year, after subsection (4A) insert—

"(4AA) Payment of a relevant lump sum is also a "relevant withdrawal"."

(2) The amendment made by this paragraph applies in relation to relevant withdrawals on or after 6 April 2017.

Relief from tax under Part 9 of ITEPA 2003 not to give rise to tax under other provisions
13 (1) In section 393B(2)(a) (tax on benefits under employer-financed retirement benefit schemes: "relevant benefits" do not include benefits charged to tax under Part 9), after "646E" insert "or any deductions under section 574A(3)".

(2) The amendment made by this paragraph has effect in relation to benefits by way of lump sums paid on or after 6 April 2017.

GENERAL NOTE

Part 1 para 1 of this Schedule sets out how the rules in FA 2004 Pt 4 apply to registered pension schemes based outside the UK and how such schemes interact with registered pension schemes whether or not they are based in the UK. Part 2 paras 2 and 3 brings 100%, instead of 90%, of the foreign pension income of UK residents into charge for UK tax purposes. In addition it removes the facility for tax relief relating to new saving in the specialist pension schemes for those working outside the UK. Part 3 paras 4 to 13 brings into charge for UK tax purposes lump sums paid under foreign pension schemes to or in respect of UK residents. If the lump sum is paid under a pension scheme meeting the definition of an overseas pension scheme, the lump sum will receive the same tax treatment as the same payment made under a registered pension scheme.

Part 1 Registered Pension Schemes Established Outside the UK

Paragraph 1(1) amends FA 2004 Pt 4 Ch 5A by inserting new ss 242C, 242D and 242E.

New FA 2004 s 242C

Subsection (1) applies the tax provisions in FA 2004 Pt 4 to non-UK based registered pension schemes. In relation to UK-relieved funds held under non-UK registered pension schemes, the rules apply as they would to the sums or assets held under a UK-based registered pension scheme. Regarding a non-UK-based registered pension scheme, the rules apply as they would to a UK-based registered pension scheme to the extent of the scheme's UK-relieved funds. Regarding members of non-UK-based registered pension schemes, the rules apply to their rights under the scheme to the extent they are represented by UK-relieved funds in the same way as funds held under a UK-based registered pension scheme. In relation to contributions to a non-UK-based registered pension scheme, the rules apply as they do to contributions to a UK-based registered pension scheme.

Subsection (2) provides for other rules in Ch 5A to take precedence over the rules in s 242C(1).

Subsection (3) gives HMRC power to make regulations to clarify how the provisions of FA 2004 Pt 4 and tax relief apply regarding non-UK-based registered pension schemes.

Under sub-s (4) these regulations may amend provisions regarding the rules in FA 2004 Pt 4 and other Acts and make consequential amendments. For example, this would enable HMRC to provide for relief from tax on pension income paid under a non-UK-based registered pension scheme taxable under ITEPA 2003 Pt 9.

Subsection (5) explains that the terms used in s 242C(1) are defined in s 242B.

New FA 2004 s 242D

Subsection (1) provides that s 242D sets out how the annual allowance charge applies to non-UK registered pension schemes.

Subsection (2) confirms an individual's input into a non-UK registered pension scheme must be included in the calculation of the amount tested against the annual allowance only if HMRC has set out in regulations that they are taken to have been made in respect of that individual under the scheme in the year.

New FA 2004 s 242E

Section 242E provides that the taxable property provisions (defined in FA 2004 Sch 29A para 1) apply in relation to a non-UK registered pension scheme as if the scheme were established in the UK.

Paragraph 1 (2) provides that the changes in Sch 3 Pt 1 take effect for the tax year 2017/18 and subsequent years.

Part 2 Income Tax on Pension Income

UK residents to be taxed on 100%, not 90%, of foreign pension income

Paragraph 2 amends ITEPA 2003 in respect of the provisions relating to the UK taxation of foreign pension income.

Paragraphs 2(1) to (4) delete ITEPA 2003 ss 575(2), 613(3) and 635(3) respectively, and make amendments to ITEPA 2003 ss 575, 613 and 635, and to FA 2013 Sch 45 para 72(4) so that the full amount, instead of 90%, of a UK resident individual's foreign pension, including annuity payments from non-UK sources, is taxable in the UK.

Paragraph 2(5) amends ITEPA 2003 ss 613(5) and 635(5) by updating a reference to ITTOIA 2005 s 839.

Paragraph 2(6) provides that the changes made by para 2 take effect for the tax year 2017/18 and subsequent years subject to para 2(7) which provides that the changes to ITEPA 2003 s 575 are only applicable to relevant withdrawals within ITEPA 2003 s 576A (temporary non-residents) to the extent they were paid in the tax year 2017/18 or later.

Superannuation funds to which section 615(3) of ICTA applies

Paragraph 3 amends ICTA 1988 s 615 so that specialist pension schemes used to provide pension savings for individuals working solely outside the UK will only meet the requirements of ICTA 1988 s 615 where no new pension saving is made after 5 April 2017 to schemes established under that legislation.

Paragraph 3(2) makes consequential changes to ICTA 1988 s 615(6).

Paragraph 3(3) inserts new sub-ss (6A) to (6G) into ICTA 1988 s 615. New sub-s (6A) defines the benefit accrual position for money purchase, cash balance and defined benefits arrangements, and any other arrangement that is neither a money purchase nor defined benefits arrangement, so that their s 615 treatment is protected where no contributions are paid into the arrangement on or after 6 April 2017. New sub-s (6B) provides for determining whether there is an increase in an individual's rights under a cash balance arrangement and so whether the benefit accrual condition is met. New sub-s (6C) ensures that certain increases in the value of rights that accrued before 6 April 2017 are ignored for the purpose of establishing whether the benefit accrual condition is met. New sub-s (6D) provides a power for HMRC to make regulations to determine the increase in the value of an individual's rights, the amount of any increase and whether that increase can be ignored under an arrangement that is neither a money purchase nor a defined benefits arrangement. New sub-s (6E) defines "relevant percentage" for the purposes of all parts of ICTA 1988 s 615 that refer to it. New sub-s (6F) provides powers for HMRC to change or modify the benefit accrual condition to determine how that condition is met, to treat superannuation funds as meeting or not meeting that condition, and to provide treatment of these funds for tax purposes to the extent they do not meet the benefit accrual condition. New sub-s (6G) provides for all the powers in s 615(6D) to (6F) to be made by amending s 615.

Paragraph 3(4) amends ICTA 1988 s 615(7) to insert new definitions regarding the various types of arrangements.

Paragraph 3(5) amends ICTA 1988 s 615(10) by inserting new sub-ss (11) to (14). New sub-s (11) provides that any disqualifying contributions or increases in rights made to a scheme meeting the conditions to be a "section 615 scheme" will be treated as not arising under such a scheme – the actual fund. Instead, they are treated as arising under a separate superannuation fund, the shadow fund, to which s 615 does not apply. New sub-s (12) specifies that a contribution or increase is disqualifying if it would cause the benefit accrual provision not to be met, so that the excess of an increase over the relevant percentage would be a disqualifying excess. New sub-s (13) ensures that certain sums, assets or increases would not be disqualifying contributions or increases where there is a recognised transfer as defined in sub-s (14).

Paragraph 3(6) provides that the amendments made by para 3 come into effect on 6 April 2017.

Part 3 Lump Sums for UK Residents from Foreign Pension Schemes

Paragraph 4 amends ITEPA 2003 regarding lump sums for UK residents paid from foreign pension schemes.

Employer-financed retirement benefit schemes: ending of foreign-service relief

Paragraph 5 amends ITEPA 2003 s 395B. The amendment in para 5(2) removes foreign service relief for UK resident members of an employer-financed retirement benefits scheme (EFRBS) who receive a lump sum in the tax year. Paragraph 5(3) makes consequential amendments to ITEPA 2003 s 395B(8) regarding the definition of the term "foreign service". Paragraph 5(4) provides that the changes made by para 5 take effect from the tax year 2017/18.

Paragraph 6 inserts new s 395C into ITEPA 2003. New s 395C(1) sets out the meaning of "foreign service" provided by sub-ss (2), (3), (6) and (8). New s 395C(2) provides that service in the tax year 2013/14 or later tax years is foreign service only if the duties are performed outside the UK, the earnings would not be relevant earnings and a deduction equal to the whole amount of the earnings would have been allowable in relation to seafarers' earnings. New s 395C(3) provides that service in or after the tax year 2003/04, but before the tax year 2013/14, is foreign service only if the earnings were not relevant earnings and a deduction equal to the whole amount of the earnings would have been allowable in relation to seafarers' earnings. New s 395C(4) and (5) defines "relevant earnings" for the purposes of sub-ss (2) and (3). New s 395C(6) provides that service after the tax year 1973/74, but before the tax year 2003/04, is foreign service only if tax was not chargeable on the emoluments under Sch E Case 1 or a deduction equal to the whole amount of the emoluments was allowable under a foreign earnings deduction provision. New s 395C(7) defines "foreign earnings deduction" for the purposes of sub-s (6). New s 395C(8) provides that service before the tax year 1974/75 is foreign service only if tax was not chargeable on the emoluments under Sch E or Sch E Case 1.

Paragraph 7 inserts new ss 554Z4(7) to (9) into ITEPA 2003. New s 554Z4(7) specifies that sub-ss (8) and (9) apply in determining whether there is a reduction in the amount of the lump sum subject to tax in respect of foreign service when the relevant step is a lump sum relevant benefit under an EFRBS paid to a UK resident. Subsection (8) specifies there is no reduction in the amount of a lump sum subject to a tax charge in relation to employment income provided through third parties in respect of pension rights built up on or after 6 April 2017 in respect of foreign service. Subsection (9) provides for the calculation of the reduced amount of the lump sum subject to a tax charge under ITEPA 2003 Pt 7A relating to pension rights as far as they were built up before 6 April 2017 in respect of foreign service. New s 554Z4(10) defines "EFRBS" and "relevant benefit" for the purposes of sub-s (7)(b).

Lump sums under other foreign schemes

Paragraph 8 inserts new s 573(4) into ITEPA 2003. This provides for a UK tax charge on the payment of a relevant lump sum under a pension scheme established outside the UK where the member is UK resident, or if the member has died, was UK resident immediately before their death, including where the beneficiary is not UK resident.

Paragraph 9 amends ITEPA 2003 s 574A to insert "relevant lump sum" into the definition of foreign pension.

Paragraph 10(1) inserts new s 574A into ITEPA 2003. This defines a relevant lump sum as a lump sum paid from a pension scheme that is not a registered pension scheme, relevant non-UK scheme or EFRBS established in the UK and the lump sum is not a relevant step to which the disguised remuneration rules in ITEPA 2003 Pt 7A Ch 2 apply. New s 574A(2) provides that a lump sum paid under a relevant non-UK scheme is a relevant lump sum if the member payment provisions of FA 2004 Sch 34 do not apply to the lump sum. New s 574A(3) sets out three steps to calculate the amount of pension treated as arising in relation to a relevant lump sum under a foreign pension scheme that is not one of the schemes set out in new s 574A(1). The calculations allow for deductions that are available to any taxpayer under ITEPA 2003 Pt 9 Ch 17, only in relation to rights built up in a pension scheme before 6 April 2017, and in relation to a lump sum payable under an overseas pension scheme where an amount would be exempt from income tax if the lump sum were paid under a registered pension scheme. In the latter circumstances the member is assumed to have all or part of their lifetime allowance available for the purposes of determining whether or not the lump sum could be paid by a registered pension scheme. If the payment is in relation to a payment under an EFRBS before 6 April 2017, then the reduction is calculated under new s 574A(6) (see below). New s 574A(4) states that the amount calculated by following the steps at new s 574A(3) is treated as the amount of taxable pension income arising in the tax year. New s 574A(5) provides power for HMRC to amend the assumptions made for the purposes of the third step in new s 574A(3). New s 574A(6) ensures that a UK resident who receives a lump sum under an EFRBS, as far as the value of the lump sum is represented by rights built up before 6 April 2017, will be entitled to the tax treatment that would have been available if they had received the lump sum before that date. This limits the relief to the value of the rights immediately before 6 April 2017. New s 574A(7) defines the terms used in new s 574A. Paragraph 10(2) provides that the amendments made by para 10 take effect in relation to lump sums paid on or after 6 April 2017.

Paragraph 11 contains consequential amendments to ITEPA 2003 s 576A to include reference to the new relevant lump sum.

Paragraph 12 contains the same amendments as in para 10, but made to the version of ITEPA 2003 s 576A that applies where the year of departure from the UK is the tax year 2012/13 or earlier.

Relief from tax under Part 9 of ITEPA 2003 not to give rise to tax under other provisions

Paragraph 13 amends ITEPA 2003 s 393B(2)(a) to ensure that a deduction for foreign service relief under new s 574A will not lead to a lump sum paid on or after 6 April 2017 being a relevant benefit. This prevents a tax charge arising under ITEPA 2003 s 394 for the part of the lump sum reduced by foreign service relief.

SCHEDULE 4

PENSIONS: OFFSHORE TRANSFERS

Section 10

PART 1

CHARGES WHERE PAYMENTS MADE IN RESPECT OF

OVERSEAS PENSIONS

Amendments of Schedule 34 to FA 2004

1 Schedule 34 to FA 2004 (non-UK pension schemes: application of certain charges) is amended as follows.

2 (1) Paragraph 1 (application of member payment charges to relevant non-UK schemes) is amended as follows.

(2) After sub-paragraph (6) insert—

"(6A) There are three types of relevant transfer—

(a) an original relevant transfer,

(b) a subsequent relevant transfer, and

(c) any other (including, in particular, all relevant transfers before 9 March 2017).

(6B) "An original relevant transfer" is—

(a) a relevant transfer within sub-paragraph (6)(a) made on or after 9 March 2017,

(b) a relevant transfer within sub-paragraph (6)(b), made on or after 9 March 2017, of the whole or part of the UK tax-relieved fund of a relieved member of a qualifying recognised overseas pension scheme, or

(c) a relevant transfer within sub-paragraph (6)(b), made on or after 6 April 2017, of the whole or part of the UK tax-relieved fund of a relieved member of a relevant non-UK scheme that is not a qualifying recognised overseas pension scheme.

(6C) The sums or assets transferred as a result of an original relevant transfer constitute a ring-fenced transfer fund, and the key date for that fund is the date of the transfer.

(6D) Where in the case of a ring-fenced transfer fund ("the source fund") there is a relevant transfer of the whole or part of the fund—

(a) the sums or assets transferred as a result of the transfer constitute a ring-fenced transfer fund,

(b) that fund has the same key date as the source fund, and

(c) the transfer is "a subsequent relevant transfer", and is not an original relevant transfer.

(6E) Sub-paragraph (6D) applies whether the source fund is a ring-fenced transfer fund as a result of sub-paragraph (6C) or as a result of sub-paragraph (6D).

(6F) The Commissioners for Her Majesty's Revenue and Customs may by regulations provide that sums or assets identified in accordance with the regulations are not included in a ring-fenced transfer fund as a result of sub-paragraph (6C) or (6D)(a)."

3 (1) Paragraph 2 (member payment provisions apply to payments out of non-UK schemes if member is UK resident or has been UK resident in any of the preceding 5 tax years) is amended as follows.

(2) The existing text becomes sub-paragraph (1).

(3) In that sub-paragraph, after "scheme" insert "so far as it is referable to 5-year rule funds".

(4) After that sub-paragraph insert—

"(2) The member payment provisions do not apply in relation to a payment made (or treated by this Part as made) to or in respect of a relieved member of a relevant non-UK scheme so far as it is referable to 10-year rule funds unless the member—

(a) is resident in the United Kingdom when the payment is made (or treated as made), or

(b) although not resident in the United Kingdom at that time, has been resident in the United Kingdom earlier in the tax year in which the payment is made (or treated as made) or in any of the 10 tax years immediately preceding that year.

(3) The member payment provisions do not apply in relation to a payment made (or treated by this Part as made) to or in respect of a transfer member of a relevant non-UK scheme, so far as it is referable to any particular ring-fenced transfer fund of the member's under the scheme which has a key date of 6 April 2017 or later, unless—

(a) the member is resident in the United Kingdom when the payment is made (or treated as made), or

(b) although the member is not resident in the United Kingdom at that time—

(i) the member has been resident in the United Kingdom earlier in the tax year containing that time, or

(ii) the member has been resident in the United Kingdom in any of the 10 tax years immediately preceding the tax year containing that time, or

(iii) that time is no later than the end of 5 years beginning with the key date for the particular fund.

(4) In this paragraph—

"5-year rule funds", in relation to a payment to or in respect of a relieved member of a relevant non-UK scheme, means so much of the member's UK tax-relieved fund under the scheme as represents tax-relieved contributions, or tax-exempt provision, made under the scheme before 6 April 2017;

"5-year rule funds", in relation to a payment to or in respect of a transfer member of a relevant non-UK scheme, means—

(a) the member's relevant transfer fund under the scheme, and

(b) any of the member's ring-fenced transfer funds under the scheme that has a key date earlier than 6 April 2017;

"10-year rule funds", in relation to a payment to or in respect of a relieved member of a relevant non-UK scheme, means so much of the member's UK tax-relieved fund under the scheme as represents tax-relieved contributions, or tax-exempt provision, made under the scheme on or after 6 April 2017.

(5) See also—

paragraph 1(6C), (6D) and (6F) (meaning of "ring-fenced transfer fund"),

paragraph 3 (meaning of "UK tax-relieved fund", "tax-relieved contributions" and "tax-exempt provision" etc), and

paragraph 4 (meaning of "relevant transfer fund" etc)."

4 (1) Paragraph 3 (payments to or in respect of relieved members of schemes) is amended as follows.

(2) After sub-paragraph (5) insert—

"(5A) The Commissioners for Her Majesty's Revenue and Customs may by regulations provide that, in circumstances specified in the regulations, something specified in the regulations is to be treated as done by, to, in respect of or in the case of a relieved member of a relevant non-UK scheme."

(3) In sub-paragraph (6) (power to specify whether payments by scheme are referable to UK tax-relieved fund), after "payments made (or treated as made) by" insert ", or other things done by or to or under or in respect of or in the case of,".

(4) After sub-paragraph (7) insert—

"(8) Where regulations under sub-paragraph (6) make provision for a payment or something else to be treated as referable to a member's UK tax-relieved fund under a scheme, regulations under that sub-paragraph may make provision for the payment or thing, or any part or aspect of the payment or thing, also to be treated as referable to a particular part of that fund."

5 (1) Paragraph 4 (payments to or in respect of transfer members of schemes) is amended as follows.

(2) In sub-paragraph (1), after "relevant transfer fund" insert ", or ring-fenced transfer funds,".

(3) In sub-paragraph (2) (meaning of "relevant transfer fund"), before "so much of" insert ", subject to sub-paragraph (3A),".

(4) After sub-paragraph (3) insert—

"(3A) The member's relevant transfer fund under the scheme does not include sums or assets that are in any of the member's ring-fenced transfer funds under the scheme."

(5) In sub-paragraph (4) (power to specify whether payments by scheme are referable to relevant transfer fund), after "payments or transfers made (or treated as made) by" insert ", or other things done by or to or under or in respect of or in the case of,".

(6) After sub-paragraph (4) insert—

"(5) The Commissioners for Her Majesty's Revenue and Customs may by regulations provide that, in circumstances specified in the regulations, something specified in the regulations is to be treated as done by, to, in respect of or in the case of a transfer member of a relevant non-UK scheme.

(6) Regulations made by the Commissioners for Her Majesty's Revenue and Customs may make provision for determining whether payments or transfers made (or treated as made) by, or other things done by or to or under or in respect of or in the case of, a relevant non-UK scheme are to be treated as referable to a member's ring-fenced transfer funds under the scheme (and so whether or not they reduce the funds or any of them).

(7) Where regulations under sub-paragraph (6) make provision for a payment or transfer or something else to be treated as referable to a member's ring-fenced transfer funds under a scheme, regulations under that sub-paragraph may make provision for the payment or transfer or other thing, or any part or aspect of the payment or transfer or thing, also to be treated as referable to a particular one of those funds."

6 In paragraph 7(2)(c) (regulations about application of member payment provisions), after "relevant transfer fund" insert "or ring-fenced transfer funds".

7 (1) Paragraph 9ZB (application of section 227G) is amended as follows.

(2) In sub-paragraph (2), after "relevant transfer fund" insert "or ring-fenced transfer funds".

(3) After sub-paragraph (3) insert—

"(4) The reference in sub-paragraph (2) to the individual's ring-fenced transfer funds under the relevant non-UK scheme is to be read in accordance with paragraph 1."

8 The amendments made by paragraph 3 apply in relation to payments made (or treated as made) on or after 6 April 2017, and the amendments made by paragraphs 2 and 4 to 7 come into force on 9 March 2017.

Consequential amendments in ITEPA 2003

9 (1) Section 576A of ITEPA 2003, as it applies where the year of departure is the tax year 2013–14 or a later tax year, is amended as follows.

(2) In subsection (6)(b) (pension income: temporary non-residents: non-application where payment not referable to relevant transfer fund)—

(a) for "not referable" substitute "referable neither", and

(b) after "relevant transfer fund" insert ", nor to the member's ring-fenced transfer funds,".

(3) In subsection (10) (interpretation), at the end insert—

""member's ring-fenced transfer fund" (see paragraph 1(6C) and (6D))."

(4) The amendments made by this paragraph apply in relation to relevant withdrawals on or after 6 April 2017.

10 (1) Section 576A of ITEPA 2003, as it applies where the year of departure is the tax year 2012–13 or an earlier tax year, is amended as follows.

(2) In subsection (6) (pension income: temporary non-residents: non-application unless payment referable to relevant transfer fund), after "member's relevant transfer fund" insert ", or the member's ring-fenced transfer funds,".

(3) In subsection (8) (interpretation), before the definition of "scheme pension" insert—

""member's ring-fenced transfer funds" has the same meaning as in that Schedule (see paragraph 1(6C) and (6D));".

(4) The amendments made by this paragraph apply in relation to relevant withdrawals on or after 6 April 2017.

PART 2

INCOME TAX ON PENSION TRANSFERS: OVERSEAS TRANSFER CHARGE

Tax charge on transfers to qualifying recognised overseas pension schemes
11 In Part 4 of FA 2004 (pension schemes etc), after section 244 insert—

"Non-UK schemes: the overseas transfer charge

244A Overseas transfer charge

(1) A charge to income tax, to be known as the overseas transfer charge, arises where—

(a) a recognised transfer is made to a QROPS, or

(b) an onward transfer is made during the relevant period for the original transfer,

and the transfer is not excluded from the charge by or under any of sections 244B to 244H.

(2) Sections 244B to 244H are subject to section 244I (circumstances in which exclusions do not apply).

(3) In this group of sections, an "onward transfer" is a transfer of sums or assets held for the purposes of, or representing accrued rights under, an arrangement under a QROPS or former QROPS in relation to a member so as to become held for the purposes of, or to represent rights under, an arrangement under another QROPS in relation to that person as a member of that other QROPS.

(4) In this group of sections "relevant period" means—

(a) in the case of a recognised transfer made on 6 April in any year, the 5 years beginning with the date of the transfer,

(b) in the case of any other recognised transfer, the period consisting of the combination of—

(i) the period beginning with the date of the transfer and ending immediately before the next 6 April, and

(ii) the 5 years beginning at the end of that initial period,

(c) in the case of an onward transfer, the period—

(i) beginning with the date of the transfer, and

(ii) ending at the end of the relevant period for the original transfer (see paragraphs (a) and (b) or, as the case may be, paragraphs (d) and (e)),

(d) in the case of a relevant transfer that—

(i) is made on 6 April in any year, and

(ii) is the original transfer for an onward transfer,

the 5 years beginning with the date of the relevant transfer, and

(e) in the case of a relevant transfer that—

(i) is made otherwise than on 6 April in any year, and

(ii) is the original transfer for an onward transfer,

the period consisting of the combination of: the period beginning with the date of the relevant transfer and ending immediately before the next 6 April; and the 5 years beginning at the end of that initial period.

(5) In this group of sections "the original transfer", in relation to an onward transfer, means (subject to subsection (6))—

(a) the recognised transfer in respect of which the following conditions are met—

(i) it is from a registered pension scheme to a QROPS,

(ii) the sums and assets transferred by the onward transfer directly or indirectly derive from those transferred by it, and

(iii) it is more recent than any other recognised transfer in respect of which the conditions in sub-paragraphs (i) and (ii) are met, or

(b) where there is no such recognised transfer, the relevant transfer (see paragraph 1(6) of Schedule 34) in respect of which the following conditions are met—

(i) it is from a relevant non-UK scheme (see paragraph 1(5) of Schedule 34),

(ii) it is a transfer of the whole or part of the UK tax-relieved fund (see paragraph 3 of Schedule 34) of a member of the scheme,

(iii) it is to a QROPS, and

(iv) the sums and assets transferred by the onward transfer directly or indirectly derive from those transferred by it.

(6) Where apart from this subsection there would be different original transfers for different parts of an onward transfer, each such part of the onward transfer is to be treated as a separate onward transfer for the purposes of this group of sections.

(7) In this section and sections 244B to 244N—

"QROPS" means a qualifying recognised overseas pension scheme, and "former QROPS" means a scheme that has at any time been a QROPS;

"ring-fenced transfer fund", in relation to a QROPS or former QROPS, has the meaning given by paragraph 1 of Schedule 34;

"this group of sections" means this section and sections 244B to 244N.

244B   Exclusion: member and receiving scheme in same country

(1) A recognised transfer to a QROPS is excluded from the overseas transfer charge if during the relevant period—

(a) the member is resident in the country or territory in which the QROPS is established, and

(b) there is no onward transfer—

(i) for which the recognised transfer is the original transfer, and

(ii) which is not excluded from the charge.

(2) If the member is resident in that country or territory at the time of the transfer mentioned in subsection (1), it is to be assumed for the purposes of subsection (1) that the member will be resident in that country or territory during the relevant period; but if, at a time before the end of the relevant period, the transfer ceases to be excluded by subsection (1) otherwise than by reason of the member's death—

(a) that assumption is from that time no longer to be made, and

(b) the charge on the transfer is treated as charged at that time.

(3) An onward transfer to a QROPS ("transfer A") is excluded from the overseas transfer charge if during so much of the relevant period as is after the time of transfer A—

(a) the member is resident in the country or territory in which the QROPS is established, and

(b) there is no subsequent onward transfer that—

(i) is of sums and assets which, in whole or part, directly or indirectly derive from those transferred by transfer A, and

(ii) is not excluded from the charge.

(4) If the member is resident in that country or territory at the time of transfer A, it is to be assumed for the purposes of subsection (3) that the member will be resident in that country or territory during so much of the relevant period as is after the time of transfer A; but if, at a time before the end of the relevant period, the transfer ceases to be excluded by subsection (3) otherwise than by reason of the member's death—

(a) that assumption is from that time no longer to be made, and

(b) the charge on transfer A is treated as charged at that time.

244C   Exclusion: member and receiving scheme in EEA states

(1) This section applies to a transfer to a QROPS established in an EEA state.

(2) If the transfer is a recognised transfer, the transfer is excluded from the overseas transfer charge if during the relevant period—

(a) the member is resident in an EEA state (whether or not the same EEA state throughout that period), and

(b) there is no onward transfer—

(i) for which the recognised transfer is the original transfer, and

(ii) which is not excluded from the charge.

(3) If the member is resident in an EEA state at the time of the recognised transfer mentioned in subsection (2), it is to be assumed for the purposes of this section that the member will be resident in an EEA state during the relevant period; but if, at a

time before the end of the relevant period, the transfer ceases to be excluded by subsection (2) otherwise than by reason of the member's death—

　(a) that assumption is from that time no longer to be made, and

　(b) the charge on the transfer is treated as charged at that time.

(4) If the transfer is an onward transfer ("transfer B"), the transfer is excluded from the overseas transfer charge if during so much of the relevant period as is after the time of the onward transfer—

　(a) the member is resident in an EEA state (whether or not the same EEA state at all those times), and

　(b) there is no subsequent onward transfer that—

　　　(i) is of sums and assets which, in whole or part, directly or indirectly derive from those transferred by transfer B, and

　　　(ii) is not excluded from the charge.

(5) If the member is resident in an EEA state at the time of transfer B, it is to be assumed for the purposes of subsection (4) that the member will be resident in an EEA state during so much of the relevant period as is after the time of transfer B; but if, at a time before the end of the relevant period, the transfer ceases to be excluded by subsection (4) otherwise than by reason of the member's death—

　(a) that assumption is from that time no longer to be made, and

　(b) the charge on transfer B is treated as charged at that time.

244D　Exclusion: receiving scheme is an occupational pension scheme

A transfer to a QROPS is excluded from the overseas transfer charge if—

　(a) the QROPS is an occupational pension scheme, and

　(b) when the transfer is made, the member is an employee of a sponsoring employer of the QROPS.

244E　Exclusion: receiving scheme set up by international organisation

(1) A transfer to a QROPS is excluded from the overseas transfer charge if—

　(a) the QROPS is established by an international organisation and has effect so as to provide benefits for, or in respect of, past service as an employee of the organisation, and

　(b) when the transfer is made, the member is an employee of the organisation.

(2) In this section "international organisation" means an organisation to which section 1 of the International Organisations Act 1968 applies by virtue of an Order in Council under subsection (1) of that section.

244F　Exclusion: receiving scheme is an overseas public service scheme

(1) A transfer to a QROPS is excluded from the overseas transfer charge if—

　(a) the QROPS is an overseas public service pension scheme, and

　(b) when the transfer is made, the member is an employee of an employer that participates in the scheme.

(2) A QROPS is an "overseas public service pension scheme" for the purposes of this section if—

　(a) either—

　　　(i) it is established by or under the law of the country or territory in which it is established, or

　　　(ii) it is approved by the government of that country or territory, and

　(b) it is established solely for the purpose of providing benefits to individuals for or in respect of services rendered to—

　　　(i) that country or territory, or

　　　(ii) any political subdivision or local authority of that country or territory.

(3) For the purposes of this section, an employer participates in a QROPS that is an overseas public service pension scheme if the scheme has effect so as to provide benefits to or in respect of any or all of the employees of the employer in respect of their employment by the employer.

244G　Exclusions: avoidance of double charge, and transitional protections

(1) A recognised transfer to a QROPS is excluded from the overseas transfer charge if it is made in execution of a request made before 9 March 2017.

(2) An onward transfer ("the current onward transfer") is excluded from the overseas transfer charge if—

(a) the charge has been paid on the original transfer and the amount paid is not repayable, or

(b) the charge has been paid on an onward transfer ("the earlier onward transfer") in respect of which the conditions in subsection (4) are met and the amount paid is not repayable, or

(c) the original transfer was made before 9 March 2017, or

(d) the original transfer was made on or after 9 March 2017 in execution of a request made before 9 March 2017.

(3) An onward transfer is excluded from the overseas transfer charge so far as the transfer is made otherwise than out of the member's ring-fenced transfer funds under the scheme from which the onward transfer is made.

(4) The conditions mentioned in subsection (2)(b) are—

(a) that the earlier onward transfer was made before the current onward transfer,

(b) that the earlier onward transfer was made after the original transfer, and

(c) that all the sums and assets transferred by the current onward transfer directly or indirectly derive from those transferred by the earlier onward transfer.

244H Power to provide for further exclusions

The Commissioners for Her Majesty's Revenue and Customs may by regulations make provision for a recognised transfer to a QROPS, or an onward transfer, to be excluded from the overseas transfer charge if the transfer is of a description specified in the regulations.

244I Circumstances in which exclusions do not apply

(1) Subsection (2) applies if a recognised transfer to a QROPS, or an onward transfer, would (but for this section) be excluded from the overseas transfer charge by any of sections 244B to 244F.

(2) The transfer is not excluded from the charge if the member has, in connection with the transfer, failed to comply with the relevant information regulation.

(3) In subsection (2) "the relevant information regulation" means whichever of the following is applicable—

(a) regulation 11BA of the Registered Pension Schemes (Provision of Information) Regulations 2006 (SI 2006/567), or any regulation having effect in place of any of that regulation, as (in either case) from time to time amended, and

(b) regulation 3AE of the Pension Schemes (Information Requirements for Qualifying Overseas Pension Schemes, Qualifying Recognised Overseas Pension Schemes and Corresponding Relief) Regulations 2006 (SI 2006/208), or any regulation having effect in place of any of that regulation, as (in either case) from time to time amended.

244J Persons liable to charge

(1) In the case of a recognised transfer to a QROPS, the persons liable to the overseas transfer charge are—

(a) the scheme administrator of the registered pension scheme from which the transfer is made, and

(b) the member,

and their liability is joint and several.

(2) In the case of an onward transfer, the persons liable to the overseas transfer charge are—

(a) the scheme manager of the QROPS, or former QROPS, from which the transfer is made, and

(b) the member,

and their liability is joint and several.

(3) Subsections (1) and (2) are subject to subsection (4), and subsections (2) and (4) are subject to subsection (5).

(4) If a transfer is one required by section 244B or 244C to be initially assumed to be excluded by that section but an event occurring before the end of the relevant period means that the transfer is not so excluded, the persons liable to the overseas transfer charge in the case of the transfer are—

(a) the scheme manager of any QROPS, or former QROPS, under which the member has, at the time of the event, ring-fenced transfer funds in which any of the sums and assets referred to in section 244K(6) in the case of the transfer are represented, and

(b) the member,

and their liability is joint and several.

(5) The scheme manager of a former QROPS is liable to the overseas transfer charge in the case of a transfer ("the transfer concerned") only if the former QROPS—

(a) was a QROPS when a relevant inward transfer was made, and

(b) where a relevant inward transfer was made before 9 March 2017, was a QROPS at the start of 9 March 2017;

and here "relevant inward transfer" means a recognised or onwards transfer to the former QROPS (at a time when it was a QROPS) of sums and assets which, to any extent, are represented by sums or assets transferred by the transfer concerned.

(6) A person is liable to the overseas transfer charge whether or not—

(a) that person, and

(b) any other person who is liable to the charge,

are resident or domiciled in the United Kingdom.

244K Amount of charge

(1) Where the overseas transfer charge arises in the case of a transfer, the charge is 25% of the transferred value.

(2) If the transfer is from a registered pension scheme established in the United Kingdom, the transferred value is the total of—

(a) the amount of any sums transferred, and

(b) the value of any assets transferred,

but this is subject to subsections (5) to (9).

(3) If the transfer is from a registered pension scheme established in a country or territory outside the United Kingdom, the transferred value is the total of—

(a) the amount of any sums transferred that are attributable to UK-relieved funds of the scheme, and

(b) the value of any assets transferred that are attributable to UK-relieved funds of the scheme,

but this is subject to subsections (5) to (9).

(4) If the transfer is from a QROPS or former QROPS, the transferred value is the total of—

(a) the amount of any sums transferred that are attributable to the member's ring-fenced transfer funds under the scheme, and

(b) the value of any assets transferred that are attributable to the member's ring-fenced transfer funds under the scheme,

but this is subject to subsections (5) to (9).

(5) If the lifetime allowance charge arises in the case of the transfer and is to be deducted from the transfer, paragraphs (a) and (b) of subsections (2) to (4) are to be read as referring to what is to be transferred after deduction of the lifetime allowance charge.

(6) If the transfer is one initially assumed to be excluded by section 244B or 244C but an event occurring before the end of the relevant period means that the transfer is not so excluded, the sums and assets mentioned in whichever of subsections (2) to (4) is applicable include only those that at the time of the event are represented in any of the member's ring-fenced transfer funds under any QROPS or former QROPS.

(7) If the operator pays the charge on the transfer and does so—

(a) otherwise than by deduction from the transfer, and

(b) out of sums and assets held for the purposes of, or representing accrued rights under, the scheme from which the transfer is made,

the transferred value is the amount given by subsections (2) to (6) grossed up by reference to the rate specified in subsection (1).

(8) If the operator pays the charge on the transfer and does so by deduction from the transfer, the transferred value is the amount given by subsections (2) to (6) before the deduction.

(9) If the member pays the charge on the transfer, the transferred value is the amount given by subsections (2) to (6) without any deduction for the charge.

(10) The provisions of this Part relating to the lifetime allowance charge apply (whether or not in relation to the transfer) as if the overseas transfer charge did not arise in the case of the transfer.

(11) In this section—

"the operator" means—
    (a) the scheme administrator of the scheme from which the transfer is to be made if that scheme is a registered pension scheme, or
    (b) the scheme manager of the scheme from which the transfer is to be made if that scheme is a QROPS or former QROPS;

"UK-relieved funds", in relation to a registered pension scheme established in a country or territory outside the United Kingdom, has the meaning given by section 242B.

244L Accounting for overseas transfer charge by scheme managers

(1) In this section "charge" means overseas transfer charge for which the scheme manager of a QROPS or former QROPS is liable.

(2) The Commissioners for Her Majesty's Revenue and Customs may by regulations make provision for or in connection with—
    (a) the payment of charge, including due dates for payment,
    (b) the charging of interest on charge not paid on or before its due date,
    (c) notification by the scheme manager of errors in information provided by the scheme manager to the Commissioners in connection with charge or the scheme manager's liability for overseas transfer charge,
    (d) repayments to scheme managers under section 244M of amounts paid by way of charge, and
    (e) the making of assessments, repayments or adjustments in cases where the correct amount of charge has not been paid by the due date for payment of the charge.

(3) The regulations may, in particular—
    (a) modify the operation of any provision of the Tax Acts, or
    (b) provide for the application of any provision of the Tax Acts (with or without modification).

244M Repayments of charge on subsequent excluding events

(1) This section applies if—
    (a) overseas transfer charge arose on a transfer at the time the transfer was made, and
    (b) at a time during the relevant period for the transfer, circumstances arise such that, had those circumstances existed at the time the transfer was made, the transfer would at the time it was made have been excluded from the charge by sections 244B to 244F or under section 244H.

(2) Any amount paid in respect of charge on the transfer is to be repaid by the Commissioners for Her Majesty's Revenue and Customs so far as not already repaid.

(3) Subsection (2) does not give rise to entitlement to repayment of, or cancellation of liabilities to, interest or penalties in respect of late payment of charge on the transfer.

(4) Repayment under this section to the scheme administrator of a registered pension scheme, or the scheme manager of a QROPS or former QROPS, is conditional on prior compliance with any requirements to give information to the Commissioners, about the circumstances in which the right to the repayment arises, that are imposed on the prospective recipient under section 169 or 251 (but repayment is not conditional on compliance with any time limits so imposed for compliance with any such requirements).

(5) Repayment under this section is not a relievable pension contribution.

(6) Repayment under this section to the member is conditional on making a claim, and such a claim must be made no later than one year after the end of the relevant period for the transfer concerned.

(7) The Commissioners for Her Majesty's Revenue and Customs may by regulations make provision for or in connection with claims or repayments under this section, including provision—
    (a) requiring claims,
    (b) about who may claim,
    (c) imposing conditions for making claims, including conditions about time limits,
    (d) as to additional circumstances in which repayments may be made,
    (e) modifying the operation of any provision of the Tax Acts, or
    (f) applying any provision of the Tax Acts (with or without modifications).

244N Discharge of liability of scheme administrator or manager

(1) In this section "operator" means—

(a) the scheme administrator of a registered pension scheme, or

(b) the scheme manager of a QROPS or former QROPS.

(2) If an operator is liable under section 244J, the operator may apply to an officer of Revenue and Customs for the discharge of the operator's liability on the following ground.

(3) The ground is that—

(a) the operator reasonably believed that there was no liability to the overseas transfer charge on the transfer concerned, and

(b) in all the circumstances of the case, it would not be just and reasonable for the operator to be liable to the charge on the transfer.

(4) On receiving an application under subsection (2), an officer of Revenue and Customs must decide whether to discharge the operator's liability.

(5) An officer of Revenue and Customs must notify the operator of the decision on the application.

(6) The discharge of the operator's liability does not affect the liability of any other person to overseas transfer charge on the transfer concerned.

(7) The Commissioners for Her Majesty's Revenue and Customs may by regulations make provision supplementing this section, including provision for time limits for making an application under this section."

Further amendments in Part 4 of FA 2004.

12 Part 4 of FA 2004 is further amended as follows.

13 (1) Section 169 (recognised transfers, and definition and obligations of a QROPS) is amended as follows.

(2) In subsection (2) (what makes a recognised overseas pension scheme a QROPS), after paragraph (b) insert—

"(ba) the scheme manager has confirmed to an officer of Revenue and Customs that the scheme manager understands the scheme manager's potential liability to overseas transfer charge and has undertaken to such an officer to operate the charge including by meeting the scheme manager's liabilities to the charge,".

(3) After subsection (2) insert—

"(2A) Regulations may make provision as to—

(a) information that is to be included in, or is to accompany, a notification under subsection (2)(a);

(b) the way and form in which such a notification, or any required information or evidence, is to be given or provided."

(4) After subsection (4) insert—

"(4ZA) Regulations may require a member, or former member, of a QROPS or former QROPS to give information of a prescribed description to the scheme manager of a QROPS or former QROPS."

(5) In subsection (4A) (inclusion of supplementary provision in regulations under subsection (4)), after "(4)" insert "or (4ZA)".

(6) After subsection (4B) insert—

"(4C) Provision under subsection (2A)(b) or (4A)(a) may, in particular, provide for use of a way or form specified by the Commissioners."

(7) After subsection (7) insert—

"(7A) Regulations may, in a case where—

(a) any of the sums and assets transferred by a relevant overseas transfer represent rights in respect of a pension to which a person has become entitled under the transferring scheme ("the original pension"), and

(b) those sums and assets are, after the transfer, applied towards the provision of a pension under the other scheme ("the new pension"),

provide that the new pension is to be treated, to such extent as is prescribed and for such of the purposes of this Part as are prescribed, as if it were the original pension.

(7B) For the purposes of subsection (7A), a "relevant overseas transfer" is a transfer of sums or assets held for the purposes of, or representing accrued rights under, a relevant overseas scheme ("the transferring scheme") so as to become held for the purposes of, or to represent rights under—

(a) another relevant overseas scheme, or

(b) a registered pension scheme,

in connection with a member of that pension scheme.

(7C) In subsection (7B) "relevant overseas scheme" means—

(a) a QROPS, or

(b) a relevant non-UK scheme (see paragraph 1(5) of Schedule 34).

(7D) Regulations under subsection (7A) may—

(a) apply generally or only in specified cases, and

(b) make different provision for different cases."

(8) In subsection (8) (interpretation)—

(a) in the opening words, after "subsections (4) to (6)" insert ", (7A) to (7D)", and

(b) in the definition of "relevant requirement", at the end insert ", or

(c) a requirement to pay overseas transfer charge, or interest on overseas transfer charge, imposed by regulations under section 244L(2) or by an assessment under such regulations."

14 After Chapter 5 insert—

"CHAPTER 5A

REGISTERED PENSION SCHEMES ESTABLISHED OUTSIDE THE UNITED KINGDOM

242A Meaning of "non-UK registered scheme"

In this Chapter "non-UK registered scheme" means a registered pension scheme established in a country or territory outside the United Kingdom.

242B Meaning of "UK-relieved funds"

(1) For the purposes of this Chapter, the "UK-relieved funds" of a non-UK registered scheme are sums or assets held for the purposes of, or representing accrued rights under, the scheme—

(a) that (directly or indirectly) represent sums or assets that at any time were held for the purposes of, or represented accrued rights under, a registered pension scheme established in the United Kingdom,

(b) that (directly or indirectly) represent sums or assets that at any time formed the UK tax-relieved fund under a relevant non-UK scheme of a relieved member of that scheme, or

(c) that—

(i) are held for the purposes of, or represent accrued rights under, an arrangement under the scheme relating to a member of the scheme who on any day has been an accruing member of the scheme, and

(ii) in accordance with regulations made by the Commissioners for Her Majesty's Revenue and Customs, are to be taken to have benefited from relief from tax.

(2) In this Chapter "relevant contribution" has the meaning given by regulation 14ZB(8) of the Information Regulations.

(3) Paragraphs (7) and (8) of regulation 14ZB of the Information Regulations (meaning of "accruing member") apply for the purposes of this section as for those of that regulation.

(4) "The Information Regulations" means the Registered Pension Schemes (Provision of Information) Regulations 2006 (SI 2006/567)."

15 In section 254(6) (regulations about accounting for tax by scheme administrators), after paragraph (b) insert—

"(ba) repayments under section 244M to scheme administrators,".

16 In section 255(1) (power to make provision for assessments), after paragraph (d) insert—

"(da) liability of the scheme administrator of a registered pension scheme, or the scheme manager of a qualifying recognised overseas pension scheme or of a former such scheme, to the overseas transfer charge,".

17 In section 269(1)(a) (appeal against decision on discharge of liability), before "section 267(2)" insert "section 244N (discharge of liability to overseas transfer charge),".

18 In Schedule 32 (benefit crystallisation events: supplementary provision), after paragraph 2 insert—

"Avoiding double counting of refunded amounts of overseas transfer charge

2A (1) This paragraph applies where an amount of overseas transfer charge is repaid (whether or not under section 244M) to the scheme administrator of one of the relevant pension schemes.

(2) The amount crystallised by the first benefit crystallisation event that occurs in respect of the individual and a benefited scheme after receipt of the repayment is to be reduced (but not below nil) by the amount of the repayment.

(3) If the amount of the repayment exceeds the reduction under sub-paragraph (2), the excess is to be set sequentially until exhausted against the amounts crystallised by subsequent benefit crystallisation events occurring in respect of the individual and a benefited scheme.

(4) In sub-paragraphs (2) and (3) "benefited scheme" means—

(a) the scheme to which the repayment is made, and
(b) any other pension scheme if as a result of a recognised transfer, or a chain of two or more recognised transfers, sums or assets representing the repayment are held for the purposes of, or represent rights under, that other scheme."

Other amendments

19 In section 9(1A) of TMA 1970 (tax not within the scope of self-assessment), after paragraph (a) insert—

"(aa) is chargeable, on the scheme manager of a qualifying recognised overseas pension scheme or a former such scheme, under Part 4 of the Finance Act 2004,".

20 In Schedule 56 to FA 2009 (penalty for failure to make payments on time), in the Table in paragraph 1, after the entry for item 3 insert—

"3A	Income tax	Amount payable under regulations under section 244L(2)(a) of FA 2004	The date falling 30 days after the due date determined by or under the regulations"

21 (1) In regulation 3(1) of the Registered Pension Schemes (Accounting and Assessment) Regulations 2005 (SI 2005/3454), in Table 1, at the end insert—

"Charge under section 244A (overseas transfer charge).	1 The name, date of birth and national insurance number of each individual in whose case a transfer results in the scheme administrator becoming liable to the overseas transfer charge. 2 The date, and transferred value, of each transfer. 3 The reference number of the qualifying recognised overseas pension scheme to which each transfer is made. 4 The amount of tax due in respect of each transfer."

(2) In those Regulations, after regulation 13 insert—

"14 Claims for repayments of overseas transfer charge

(1) This regulation applies where the scheme administrator of a registered pension scheme becomes aware that the scheme administrator may be entitled to a repayment under section 244M of the Act in respect of overseas transfer charge on a transfer.

(2) The scheme administrator must, no later than 60 days after the date on which the scheme administrator becomes aware of that, make a claim for the repayment to the Commissioners for Her Majesty's Revenue and Customs.

(3) The claim must provide the following information—

(a) the member's name, date of birth and principal residential address,
(b) the date of the transfer and, if different, the date of the event triggering payability of the charge on the transfer,
(c) the date on which the scheme manager accounted for the charge on the transfer,
(d) why the charge on the transfer has become repayable, and

(e) the amount in respect of which the claim is made.

(4) In a case where the 60 days mentioned in paragraph (2) ends with a day earlier than 14 November 2017, paragraph (2) is to be treated as requiring the claim to be made no later than 14 November 2017."

(3) The amendment made by sub-paragraph (1) is to be treated as having been made by the Commissioners for Her Majesty's Revenue and Customs under the applicable powers to make regulations conferred by section 254 of FA 2004.

(4) The amendment made by sub-paragraph (2) is to be treated as having been made by the Commissioners for Her Majesty's Revenue and Customs under the powers to make regulations conferred by section 244M(7) of FA 2004.

22 (1) The Pension Schemes (Information Requirements for Qualifying Overseas Pension Schemes, Qualifying Recognised Overseas Pension Schemes and Corresponding Relief) Regulations 2006 (SI 2006/208) are amended as follows.

(2) In regulation 1(2) (interpretation), after the definition of "HMRC" insert—

""onward transfer" has the meaning given by section 244A;".

(3) In regulation 3(2) (duty to provide information to HMRC)—

(a) in sub-paragraph (c), after "no relevant transfer fund remains" insert "and no ring-fenced transfer funds remain", and

(b) after sub-paragraph (d) insert—

"(da) if the payment is made to a QROPS—

(i) whether the overseas transfer charge arises on the payment,

(ii) if the charge does arise, the transferred value and the amount of charge the scheme manager deducted from the payment before making it,

(iii) if the charge does not arise, why it does not, and

(iv) the total amount or value of the member's relevant transfer fund, and ring-fenced transfer funds, remaining immediately after the payment;"."

(4) In regulation 3, after paragraph (2) insert—

"(2A) Paragraphs (2B) and (2C) apply where—

(a) a recognised transfer is made to a QROPS, or

(b) an onward transfer is made by a QROPS or former QROPS.

(2B) Where an event occurring before the end of the relevant period for the transfer (see section 244A(4)) means that the transfer no longer counts as excluded from the overseas transfer charge or that entitlement to repayment under section 244M arises, the scheme manager of the QROPS or former QROPS must, within 90 days after the date the scheme manager is notified of the event, provide to HMRC notification of—

(a) the occurrence, nature and date of the event,

(b) the transferred value of the transfer,

(c) the amount of overseas transfer charge on the transfer,

(d) whether, and to what extent, the scheme manager has accounted, or intends to account, for the charge, and

(e) the total amount or value of the member's relevant transfer fund, and ring-fenced transfer funds, remaining immediately after the event.

This paragraph is subject to the qualification in paragraph (3A).

(2C) Where the scheme manager of the QROPS or former QROPS becomes aware that the member has at any time in the relevant period for the transfer acquired a new residential address that is neither—

(a) in the country or territory in which the QROPS or former QROPS is established, nor

(b) in an EEA state,

the scheme manager is to notify that address to HMRC within 3 months after the date on which the scheme manager becomes aware of it."

(5) In regulation 3(3)(a) (reporting duty under regulation 3(2) expires after 10 years from creation of relevant transfer fund), after "beginning" insert "—

(i) if the payment is in respect of one or more of the relevant member's ring-fenced transfer funds (whether or not it is also in respect of anything else), with the key date for that fund or (as the case may be) the later or latest of the key dates for those funds, and

(ii) if the payment is not to any extent in respect of the relevant member's ring-fenced transfer funds,"."

(6) In regulation 3, after paragraph (3) insert—

"(3A) No obligation arises under paragraph (2B) in relation to a transfer if the following conditions are met—

(a) at the date of the transfer more than 10 years has elapsed since the key date for the ring-fenced transfer fund arising from the transfer (see paragraph 1 of Schedule 34); and

(b) the relevant member to whom the transfer is made is a person to whom the member payment provisions do not apply."

(7) In regulation 3(6), in the definition of "relevant member", after "relevant transfer fund" insert "or any ring-fenced transfer fund".

(8) In regulation 3AB(4), for the words from "as a result" to the end substitute "as a result of—

(a) a transfer of the member's relevant transfer fund,

(b) a transfer of any of the member's ring-fenced transfer funds, or

(c) a recognised transfer,after the date of the relevant event concerned."

(9) In regulation 3AC—

(a) in paragraph (1)(a), before the "or" at the end of paragraph (i) insert—

"(ia) any of the member's ring-fenced transfer funds;", and

(b) in the title omit "relevant".

(10) In regulation 3AD—

(a) in paragraph (1)(a), before the "or" at the end of paragraph (i) insert—

"(ia) any of the member's ring-fenced transfer funds;",

(b) in paragraph (2), after sub-paragraph (a) insert—

"(aa) where any of the transferred sums or assets are referable to the member's UK tax-relieved fund, the value of so many of them as are referable to tax-relieved contributions, or tax-exempt provision, made under the scheme before 9 March 2017;

(ab) the value of so many of the transferred sums or assets as are referable to any of the member's ring-fenced transfer funds (if any);",

(c) in paragraph (2)(b) omit the "and" at the end,

(d) in paragraph (2)(c)(i), after "fund" insert "or any of the member's ring-fenced transfer funds",

(e) in paragraph (2)(c), in the words after paragraph (ii)—

(i) omit "it is", and

(ii) after "the date of that transfer" insert "and the date it was requested",

(f) in paragraph (2), after sub-paragraph (c) insert—

"(d) whether the overseas transfer charge arises on the transfer;

(e) if the charge does arise on the transfer—

(i) the transferred value of the transfer, and

(ii) the amount in respect of the charge deducted by the scheme manager from the transfer;

(f) if the transfer is excluded from the charge—

(i) the reason for its exclusion, and

(ii) where section 244G(2)(a) or (b) (charge paid on earlier transfer) is the reason for its exclusion, the date of the earlier transfer on which the charge was paid and the amount of charge paid on that earlier transfer; and

(g) the relevant period for the transfer (see section 244A(4)).", and

(g) in the title omit "relevant".

(11) After regulation 3AD insert—

"3AE Information provided by member to QROPS: onward transfers

(1) Paragraph (4) applies where a member of a QROPS or former QROPS makes a request to the scheme manager to make an onward transfer to a QROPS.

(2) But paragraph (4) does not apply if—

(a) the transfer will be excluded from the overseas transfer charge by section 244G, or

(b) the transfer will take place after the end of the relevant period (see section 244A(4)) for what would be the original transfer in relation to the requested onward transfer.

(3) In this regulation "original transfer", in relation to an onward transfer, has the meaning given by section 244A(5).

(4) The member must provide to the scheme manager—

(a) the member's name, date of birth and principal residential address,

(b) if the member is not UK resident for income tax purposes, the date when the member last ceased to be UK resident for those purposes,

(c) the member's national insurance number or, where applicable, confirmation that the member does not qualify for a national insurance number,

(d) the name and address of the QROPS to which the transfer is to be made,

(e) the country or territory under the law of which that QROPS is established and regulated,

(f) the reference number, if any, given by the Commissioners for that QROPS,

(g) whether the member knows for certain that the transfer would be excluded from the overseas transfer charge by one of sections 244D, 244E and 244F, and if the member does know that for certain—

(i) the section concerned (if known),

(ii) the name and address of the member's employer whose connection with the QROPS gives rise to exclusion of the transfer from the charge,

(iii) the member's job title as an employee of that employer,

(iv) the date the member's employment with that employer began, and

(v) if known, that employer's tax reference for that employment, and

(h) the member's acknowledgement in writing that the member—

(i) is aware that an onward transfer to a qualifying recognised overseas pension scheme may give rise to a liability to overseas transfer charge, and

(ii) is aware of the circumstances in which liability arises, in which liability is excluded from the outset and in which liability is excluded only if conditions continue to be met over a period of time.

(5) The information specified in paragraph (4) must be provided within 60 days beginning with the day the transfer request is made.

(6) The scheme manager must send the member notification of the requirements specified in this regulation within 30 days beginning with that day.

3AF Information provided by member to QROPS: inward and outward transfers

(1) Paragraph (2) applies where—

(a) a recognised transfer or onward transfer is made to a QROPS, or an onward transfer is made by a QROPS or former QROPS, and

(b) either—

(i) the overseas transfer charge arises in the case of the transfer, or

(ii) the transfer is required by section 244B or 244C to be initially assumed to be excluded from the overseas transfer charge by that section.

(2) Each time during the relevant period for the transfer that the member—

(a) becomes resident in a country or territory, or

(b) ceases to be resident in a country or territory,

the member must, within 60 days after the date that happens, inform the scheme manager of the QROPS or former QROPS that it has happened.

(3) In a case where the 60 days mentioned in paragraph (2) ends with a day earlier than 30 June 2017, paragraph (2) is to be treated as requiring the information to be given no later than 30 June 2017.

3AG Provision of information about liability for overseas transfer charge

(1) If an onward transfer is made from a QROPS or former QROPS and the overseas transfer charge arises on the transfer, the scheme manager of the QROPS or former QROPS must within 90 days after the date of the transfer provide the member with a notice stating—

(a) the date of the transfer,

(b) that overseas transfer charge arises on the transfer,

(c) the transferred value of the transfer,

(d) the amount of the charge on the transfer,

(e) whether, and to what extent, the scheme manager has accounted, or intends to account, for the charge, and

(f) where the scheme manager has accounted for the charge, the date the scheme manager did so.

(2) If an onward transfer is made from a QROPS or former QROPS and the transfer is excluded from the overseas transfer charge by or under sections 244B to 244H, the scheme manager of the QROPS or former QROPS must within 90 days after the date of the transfer provide the member with a notice stating—

(a) the date of the transfer,

(b) that the transfer is excluded from the overseas transfer charge,

(c) the provision by reason of which the transfer is excluded, and

(d) where that provision is section 244B or 244C—
    (i) when the relevant period for the transfer ends, and
    (ii) how the transfer may turn out not to be excluded as a result of the member changing country or territory of residence within the relevant period for the transfer.

(3) Paragraph (4) applies if—
    (a) a recognised transfer is made to a QROPS, or
    (b) an onward transfer is made by a QROPS or former QROPS.

(4) Where an event occurring before the end of the relevant period for the transfer (see section 244A(4)) means that the transfer no longer counts as excluded from the overseas transfer charge or that entitlement to repayment under section 244M arises, the scheme manager of the QROPS or former QROPS must, within 90 days after the date the scheme manager is notified of the event, provide the member with a notice stating—
    (a) the amount of overseas transfer charge on the transfer,
    (b) whether, and to what extent, the scheme manager has accounted, or intends to account, for the charge, and
    (c) where the scheme manager has accounted for the charge, the date the scheme manager did so.

3AH Accounting for overseas transfer charge on onward transfers

(1) Paragraph (2) applies where—
    (a) overseas transfer charge arises on an onward transfer from a QROPS or former QROPS,
    (b) the scheme manager has notified HMRC of the transfer or, where applicable, of the event triggering payability of the charge on the transfer, and
    (c) HMRC have provided the scheme manager with an accounting reference for paying the charge on the transfer.

(2) The scheme manager must pay the charge to HMRC using the accounting reference.

(3) Payment of the charge is due at the end of the 91 days beginning with the date of issue of the accounting reference.

3AI Assessments of unpaid overseas transfer charge on onward transfers

(1) Where the correct amount of overseas transfer charge due from a scheme manager under regulation 3AH on an onward transfer has not been paid by the time it is due, an officer of Revenue and Customs must issue an assessment to tax to the scheme manager.

(2) Tax assessed under this regulation is payable within 30 days after the issue of the notice of assessment.

3AJ Interest on overdue overseas transfer charge

(1) Tax which—
    (a) becomes due and payable in accordance with regulation 3AH, or
    (b) is assessed under regulation 3AI,
carries interest at the prescribed rate from the due date under regulation 3AH until payment ("the interest period").

(2) Paragraph (1) applies even if the due date is a non-business day as defined by section 92 of the Bills of Exchange Act 1882.

(3) The "prescribed rate" means the rate applicable under section 178 of the Finance Act 1989 for the purposes of section 86 of TMA.

(4) Any change made to the prescribed rate during the interest period applies to the unpaid amount from the date of the change.

3AK Adjustments, repayments and interest on overpaid charge

(1) If the correct tax due under regulation 3AH has not been paid on or before the due date, an officer of Revenue and Customs may make such adjustments or repayments as may be required for securing that the resulting liabilities to tax (including interest on unpaid or overpaid tax) whether of the scheme manager or of any other person are the same as they would have been if the correct tax had been paid.

(2) Tax overpaid which is repaid to the scheme manager or any other person carries interest at the prescribed rate from the later of the due date and the date on which the tax was paid until the date of repayment ("the interest period").

(3) The "prescribed rate" means the rate applicable under section 178 of the Finance Act 1989 for the purposes of section 824 of the Income and Corporation Taxes Act 1988.

(4) Any change to the prescribed rate during the interest period applies to the overpaid amount from the date of the change.

3AL Claims for repayments of charge on subsequent excluding events

(1) Repayment under section 244M (repayments of overseas transfer charge) to the scheme manager of a QROPS or former QROPS is conditional on making a claim to HMRC.

(2) Such a claim in respect of overseas transfer charge on a transfer—

(a) must be in writing,
(b) must be made no later than 12 months after the end of the relevant period for the transfer, and
(c) must provide the following information—

(i) the member's name, date of birth and principal residential address,
(ii) the date of the transfer and, if different, the date of the event triggering payability of the charge on the transfer,
(iii) the date on which the scheme manager accounted for the charge on the transfer,
(iv) why the charge on the transfer has become repayable, and
(v) the amount in respect of which the claim is made."

(12) In regulation 3B (information on cessation of a QROPS), after "relevant transfer fund", in both places, insert ", or ring-fenced transfer fund,".

(13) In regulation 3C (correction of information)—

(a) in paragraph (3)(a)(i), after "existence" insert "or, where the information relates to a ring-fenced transfer fund in respect of the relevant member, more than 10 years has elapsed beginning with the date on which that ring-fenced transfer fund came into existence", and
(b) in paragraph (3)(b), at the end insert "and there are no ring-fenced transfer funds".

(14) In regulation 5(1) (application of provisions providing for penalties)—

(a) after "3(2)," insert "(2B) or (2C),", and
(b) before "or 3C(1)" insert ", 3AE(6), 3AG".

(15) The amendments made by this paragraph—

(a) are, so far as they insert new regulations 3AE(1) to (5) and 3AF, to be treated as having been made by the Commissioners for Her Majesty's Revenue and Customs under the powers to make regulations conferred by section 169(4ZA) of FA 2004,
(b) are, so far as they insert new regulations 3AE(6) and 3AG and amend regulations 3 to 3AD and 3B to 5, to be treated as having been made by the Commissioners under the powers to make regulations under section 169(4) of FA 2004 (see section 169(4), (4A), (4B) and (4C) of that Act),
(c) are, so far as they insert new regulations 3AH to 3AK, to be treated as having been made by the Commissioners under the applicable powers to make regulations conferred by section 244L of FA 2004, and
(d) are, so far as they insert new regulation 3AL, to be treated as having been made by the Commissioners under the powers to make regulations conferred by section 244M(7) of FA 2004.

23 (1) The Registered Pension Schemes (Transfers of Sums and Assets) Regulations 2006 (SI 2006/499) are amended as follows.

(2) In regulation 5, the existing text becomes paragraph (1).

(3) After that paragraph insert—

"(2) In paragraph (1)(a) "administration costs" includes, in particular, payments of overseas transfer charge."

(4) The amendments made by this paragraph are to be treated as made by the Commissioners for Her Majesty's Customs and Revenue under the powers to make regulations conferred by paragraph 2(4)(h) of Schedule 28 to FA 2004.

24 (1) The Registered Pension Schemes (Provision of Information) Regulations 2006 (SI 2006/567) are amended as follows.

(2) In regulation 3(1) (provision of information by scheme administrators to HMRC), in column 2 of the entry in the Table for reportable event 9—

(a) after paragraph (g) insert—

"(ga) whether or not overseas transfer charge arises on the transfer;

(gb) if the transfer is excluded from the charge, the reason why it is excluded;

(gc) if the charge arises on the transfer—

(i) the transferred value, and

(ii) the amount in respect of the charge deducted from the transfer;", and

(b) after paragraph (h) insert—

"(ha) the reference number, if any, given by the Commissioners for the QROPS;".

(3) In regulation 3(7) (deadline for event report for reportable event 9), at the end insert "but, if the scheme administrator applies before the end of those 60 days for a repayment of overseas transfer charge on the transfer, the report must be delivered before the administrator applies for the repayment.

(4) In regulation 11BA(2) (information about transfer to be provided by member to scheme administrator)—

(a) in sub-paragraph (a), omit paragraphs (vi) and (vii), including the "and" at the end,

(b) after sub-paragraph (a) insert—

"(aa) the name and address of, and (if known) the reference number given by the Commissioners for, the qualifying recognised overseas pension scheme ("the QROPS");

(ab) the country or territory under the law of which the QROPS is established and regulated;

(ac) whether the member knows for certain that the transfer would be excluded from the overseas transfer charge by one of sections 244D, 244E and 244F, and if the member does know that for certain—

(i) the section concerned (if known),

(ii) the name and address of the member's employer whose connection with the QROPS gives rise to exclusion of the transfer from the charge,

(iii) the member's job title as an employee of that employer,

(iv) the date the member's employment with that employer began, and

(v) if known, that employer's tax reference for that employment;", and

(c) after sub-paragraph (b) insert "; and

(c) the member's acknowledgement in writing that the member—

(i) is aware that a recognised transfer to a qualifying recognised overseas pension scheme may give rise to a liability to overseas transfer charge, and

(ii) is aware of the circumstances in which liability arises, in which liability is excluded from the outset and in which liability is excluded only if conditions continue to be met over a period of time."

(5) After regulation 11BA insert—

"11BB Information provided by members to scheme administrators: overseas transfers

(1) Paragraph (2) applies where—

(a) a recognised transfer is made by a registered pension scheme to a qualifying recognised overseas pension scheme, and

(b) either—

(i) the overseas transfer charge arises in the case of the transfer, or

(ii) the transfer is required by section 244B or 244C to be initially assumed to be excluded from the overseas transfer charge by that section.

(2) Each time during the relevant period for the transfer that the member—

(a) becomes resident in a country or territory, or

(b) ceases to be resident in a country or territory,

the member must, within 60 days after the date that happens, inform the scheme administrator of the registered pension scheme that it has happened.

(3) In a case where the 60 days mentioned in paragraph (2) ends with a day earlier than 30 June 2017, paragraph (2) is to be treated as requiring the information to be given no later than 30 June 2017."

(6) After regulation 12 insert—

"12A Provision of information about liability for overseas transfer charge

(1) If a recognised transfer is made by a registered pension scheme to a qualifying recognised overseas pension scheme and the overseas transfer charge arises on the

transfer, the scheme administrator of the registered pension scheme must within 90 days after the date of the transfer provide the member with a notice stating—

(a) the date of the transfer,

(b) that overseas transfer charge arises on the transfer,

(c) the transferred value of the transfer,

(d) the amount of the charge on the transfer,

(e) whether, and to what extent, the scheme administrator has accounted, or intends to account, for the charge, and

(f) where the scheme administrator has accounted for the charge, the date the scheme administrator did so.

(2) If a recognised transfer is made by a registered pension scheme to a qualifying recognised overseas pension scheme and the transfer is excluded from the overseas transfer charge by or under sections 244B to 244H, the scheme administrator of the registered pension scheme must within 90 days after the date of the transfer provide the member with a notice stating—

(a) the date of the transfer,

(b) that the transfer is excluded from the overseas transfer charge,

(c) the provision by reason of which the transfer is excluded, and

(d) where that provision is section 244B or 244C, how the transfer may turn out not to be excluded as a result of the member changing country or territory of residence within the relevant period for the transfer.

(3) If overseas transfer charge on a transfer is repaid to the scheme administrator of a registered pension scheme, the scheme administrator must within 90 days after the date of the repayment provide the member with a notice stating—

(a) the date of the repayment,

(b) the amount of the repayment, and

(c) the reason for the repayment."

(7) After regulation 14ZC insert—

"14ZCA Further information provided by scheme administrators on recognised transfers to overseas schemes

(1) This regulation applies if there is a recognised transfer from a registered pension scheme to a qualifying recognised overseas pensions scheme.

(2) The scheme administrator of the registered pension scheme must provide the scheme manager of the qualifying recognised overseas pension scheme with a statement—

(a) stating whether or not the overseas transfer charge arose on the transfer, and

(b) stating—

(i) if the charge arose, the amount of the charge, and

(ii) if the transfer is excluded from the charge, the reason why it is excluded.

(3) The requirement under paragraph (2) is to be complied with before the end of the 31 days beginning with the date of the transfer.

(4) Paragraph (5) applies if overseas transfer charge on the transfer is repaid to the scheme administrator of the registered pension scheme.

(5) The scheme administrator of the registered pension scheme must provide the scheme manager of the qualifying recognised overseas pension scheme with—

(a) a copy of the statement under paragraph (2),

(b) a statement that the original statement is inaccurate and that the overseas transfer charge on the transfer has been repaid to the scheme administrator, and

(c) the reason why the transfer is excluded from the charge.

(6) The requirement under paragraph (5) is to be complied with before the end of the 31 days beginning with the date of the repayment."

(8) The amendments made by this paragraph are to be treated as made by the Commissioners for Her Majesty's Revenue and Customs under the applicable powers to make regulations conferred by section 251 of FA 2004.

Commencement and transitional provision

25 (1) Subject to sub-paragraphs (2) to (4), the amendments made by this Part of this Schedule have effect in relation to transfers made on or after 9 March 2017.

(2) The new section 169(2)(ba) of FA 2004—

(a) has effect on and after 9 March 2017 in the case of a recognised overseas pension scheme where—

(i) the notification mentioned in section 169(2)(a) of FA 2004 (notification that scheme is a recognised overseas pension scheme) is given on or after 9 March 2017, or

(ii) although that notification is given before 9 March 2017, the letter from the Commissioners for Her Majesty's Revenue and Customs advising the scheme of the reference number allocated to the scheme is dated on or after 9 March 2017, and

(b) has effect on and after 14 April 2017 in the case of a recognised overseas pension scheme where that letter is dated before 9 March 2017.

(3) The other amendments in section 169 of FA 2004, and the amendment in section 255 of that Act, come into force on 9 March 2017.

(4) The amendments in regulation 3(2) of the Pension Schemes (Information Requirements for Qualifying Overseas Pension Schemes, Qualifying Recognised Overseas Pension Schemes and Corresponding Relief) Regulations 2006 have effect in relation to payments made on or after 9 March 2017; and the new regulation 3AE inserted into those Regulations, and the reference to the new regulation 3AE(6) inserted into regulation 5(1) of those Regulations and the amendments in regulation 11BA of the Registered Pension Schemes (Provision of Information) Regulations 2006, have effect in relation to requests made on or after 9 March 2017.

(5) Overseas transfer charge on transfers made in the period beginning with 9 March 2017 and ending with 30 June 2017 is, for the purposes of section 254 of FA 2004, to be treated as charged in the 3 months ending with 30 September 2017 if it would otherwise be considered for those purposes as charged in an earlier period.

GENERAL NOTE

The provisions in Pt 1 paras 1 to 10 of this Schedule were published for consultation on 5 December 2016. They amend FA 2004 Sch 34 to extend from five to ten tax years the period of an individual's non-UK residence during which UK tax charges can apply to payments out of pension savings in overseas pension schemes which have enjoyed UK tax relief. Part 2 paras 11 to 25 set out how the overseas transfer charge will operate together with the exclusions from the charge, the amount of the charge and how those liable will account for the charge.

Part 1 Charges Where Payments Made in Respect of Overseas Pensions

Amendments of Schedule 34 to FA 2004

Paragraph 1 amends FA 2004 Sch 34 in relation to charges that are to apply where payments are made in respect of overseas pensions.

Paragraph 2 makes these amendments to FA 2004 Sch 34 para 1. Paragraph 2(2) inserts new sub-paras (6A) to (6F). New sub-para (6A) introduces three types of relevant transfer – an "original relevant transfer" (defined in new sub-para (6B)), a "subsequent relevant transfer" (defined in new sub-para (6D)) and any "other relevant transfer" which includes relevant transfers made before 9 March 2017. New sub-para (6B) defines an "original relevant transfer" as a transfer received from either a registered pension scheme or from another overseas pension scheme where the funds or rights under that scheme had benefited from UK tax relief (a relevant non-UK scheme) on or after 9 March 2017. New sub-para (6C) introduces the concept of a ring-fenced transfer fund comprising the sums or assets transferred in as an original relevant transfer. New sub-para (6D) defines a "subsequent relevant transfer" as one made out of an original relevant transfer forming the whole or part of a ring-fenced fund. New sub-para (6E) ensures that even where there are a number of transfers of the same funds the rules in sub-para (6D) apply so that any later transfers will also be subsequent relevant transfers. New sub-para (6F) gives HMRC power to make regulations setting out what does not constitute a ring-fenced transfer fund.

Paragraph 3 also amends FA 2004 Sch 34. Paragraph 3(2) and (3) provides that payment to or in respect of a member of a relevant non-UK scheme with pension funds or rights built up under that scheme which have benefited from UK tax relief (a relieved member) or who has transferred into that scheme from a registered or another relevant non-UK pension scheme where the transfer is not taxable as an unauthorised payment (a transfer member), will continue to be subject to UK tax charges. The UK tax charges will continue if the individual is UK resident or has been resident in any one of the previous five tax years to the extent that the contributions were made or transfers received before 6 April 2017. These funds are called "5-year rule funds" (defined in new sub-para (4)). Paragraph 3(4) inserts new FA 2004 Sch 34 para 2(2) to (5). Subparagraphs (2) and (3) extend to 10 years the period in which UK tax charging provisions can apply to payments out of funds from which individuals have benefited from UK tax relief on pension funds or rights under an overseas pension scheme or which individuals have transferred to a QROPS. This extension applies to funds or rights accruing or transferred on or after 6 April 2017 only. New sub-para (4) defines the terms "5-year rule funds" and "10-year rule funds" in relation to pension funds or rights which have benefited from UK tax relief and transfers. The extended UK tax charging provisions will apply to 10-year rule funds only. New sub-para (5) sets out that the definitions of the terms used in new sub-para 2 are provided in new sub-paras (1), (3) and (4).

Paragraph 4 amends FA 2004 Sch 34 para 3 in relation to payments to or in respect of relieved members of relevant non-UK schemes from pension funds or rights built up under such schemes which have benefited from UK tax relief (a "UK tax-relieved fund" as defined in new sub-para (5)). Paragraph 4(2) inserts new sub-para (5A) which provides power for HMRC to make regulations to determine a member's UK tax-relieved fund is reduced by a payment, event or anything else, e.g. this allows HMRC to make regulations providing that the amount calculated as being subject to UK tax charges is reduced even in cases where a payment is not made to the member, such as (but not limited to) when funds are designated into flexi-access drawdown. Paragraph 4(3) amends sub-para (6) giving HMRC power to make regulations to determine that something other than a payment can reduce a member's UK tax-relieved funds. Paragraph 4(4) inserts new sub-para (8) which provides that where HMRC makes regulations under new sub-para (6), it can also make regulations reducing a particular part of the UK tax-relieved fund.

Paragraph 5 amends FA 2004 Sch 34 para 4 relating to payments to or in respect of transfer members of relevant non-UK schemes which have received transfers. Paragraph 5(2) and (3) contains consequential amendments to include reference to the new ring-fenced transfer fund and new sub-para (3A) respectively. Paragraph 5(4) inserts new sub-para (3A) which provides that the sums and assets in a member's relevant transfer fund are distinct from those in a member's ring-fenced transfer fund. Paragraph 5(5) inserts new sub-para (4) providing HMRC with the power to make regulations to determine that something other than a payment can reduce a member's relevant transfer fund. Paragraph 5(6) inserts new sub-paras (5) to (7). New sub-para (5) makes the same provision as in new para 3(5A) (see para 4(2) above), but in relation to a transfer member of a relevant non-UK scheme. New sub-para (6) makes the same provision as in new para 3(6) (see para 4(3) above), but in relation to a transfer member of a relevant non-UK scheme and new sub-para (7) makes the same provision as in new para 3(8) (see para 4(4) above), but in relation to a transfer member of a relevant non-UK scheme.

Paragraphs 6 and 7 make consequential amendments to the powers to make regulations regarding relieved and transfer members and the annual allowance provisions in FA 2004 Sch 34 to include reference to the new ring-fenced transfer fund.

Paragraph 8 specifies that the changes made by Sch 4 para 3 apply in relation to payments made (or treated as made) on or after 6 April 2017, and by Sch 4 paras 2 and 4 to 7 come into force on 9 March 2017.

Consequential amendments in ITEPA 2003

Paragraphs 9 and 10 make amendments to the temporary non-residents provisions of ITEPA 2003 as a result of the changes made in Sch 4 Pt 1.

Paragraph 9 makes consequential amendments to ITEPA 2003 s 576A to include reference to the new ring-fenced transfer fund and para 10 makes these same amendments to the version of ITEPA 2003 s 576A which applies where the year of departure from the UK is the tax year 2012/13 or earlier.

Part 2 Income Tax on Pension Transfers: Overseas Transfer Charge

Tax charge on transfers to qualifying recognised overseas pension schemes

Paragraph 11 inserts new ss 244A to 244N into FA 2004 in relation to the overseas transfer charge.

New FA 2004 s 244A

Subsection (1) provides that the overseas transfer charge will arise when a recognised transfer is made to a QROPS or an onward transfer from a QROPS or former QROPS, except where the transfer is excluded from the charge.

Subsection (2) specifies how the exclusions are limited.

Subsection (3) defines an "onward transfer" from a QROPS or former QROPS to another QROPS. The sums or assets transferred representing the individual's accrued rights must be held under the new scheme to represent that individual's rights in that new scheme.

Subsection (4) defines "relevant period" in various circumstances.

Subsection (5) defines the "original transfer" in relation to an onward transfer as the most recent transfer from a registered pension scheme or where the transfer was from a currently-relieved scheme rather than a registered pension scheme, the most recent transfer from that scheme.

Subsections (6) and (7) provide that if a transfer is made up of different types of onward transfer, they are counted as separate transfers for the purposes of ss 244A to 244N.

New FA 2004 s 244B

Subsection (1) specifies that a transfer is excluded from the overseas transfer charge if in the five years from the date of the transfer the individual making the transfer is resident in the same country as the recipient QROPS and no onward transfer is made that is subject to the charge.

Subsection (2) provides that the position at the point of transfer is assumed to remain for five tax years, but if within those five years from the date of the transfer the individual is no longer resident in the same country as the transferred pension savings, then the overseas transfer charge will apply to the transferred funds in the QROPS at that point.

Subsection (3) provides that an onward transfer to a QROPS is excluded from the tax charge if in the remaining five tax years from the date of the original transfer the individual who made the transfer is resident in the same country as the QROPS to which the onward transfer was made and no subsequent onward transfer is made that is subject to the overseas transfer charge.

Subsection (4) provides that the position at the point of the onward transfer is assumed to be the case for the remaining five-tax-year period from the date of the original transfer. However, if within that time the individual is no longer resident in the same country as their transferred pension savings, then the overseas transfer charge applies to those funds at that point.

New FA 2004 s 244C

Subsections (1) and (2) provide for a transfer to a QROPS in an EEA state to be excluded from the overseas transfer charge if in the five tax years beginning with the date of the transfer the individual making the transfer is resident in a country within the EEA and no onward transfer is made that is subject to the charge.

Subsection (3) specifies that the position at the point of transfer is assumed to remain for five tax years, but if within the five-tax-year period from the date of the transfer the individual ceases to be resident in an EEA state then the overseas transfer charge will apply to the transferred funds in the QROPS at that point.

Subsection (4) excludes an onward transfer to a QROPS in an EEA state from the overseas transfer charge if in the five tax years from the date of the transfer the individual making the transfer is resident in a country within the EEA and no subsequent onward transfer is made that is subject to the charge.

Subsection (5) provides that the position at the point of the onward transfer is assumed to be the case for the remaining five-tax-year period from the date of original transfer. However, if within that time the individual ceases to be resident in an EEA state then the overseas transfer charge applies to the transferred funds in the QROPS at that point.

New FA 2004 s 244D

The provisions of s 244D exclude from the overseas transfer charge a transfer made to an occupational pension scheme and where the individual is an employee of a sponsoring employer of the QROPS.

New FA 2004 s 244E

The provisions of sub-s (1) also exclude from the overseas transfer charge a transfer made to a QROPS established by an international organisation and where the individual concerned is an employee of that international organisation at that time.

Subsection (2) defines an "international organisation".

New FA 2004 s 244F

Subsection (1) excludes from the overseas transfer charge a transfer made to a QROPS which is an overseas public service pension scheme and the individual making the transfer is an employee of one of the public service employers participating in the pension scheme at the time.

Subsection (2) similarly excludes from the overseas transfer charge a transfer made to a QROPS established by the law or government of the country in which it is established to provide benefits for or in respect of public service carried out by employees of the participating public service employer.

Subsection (3) specifies an employer is considered to participate in an overseas public service pension scheme that is a QROPS if it is established to provide benefits exclusively to or in respect of its employees.

New FA 2004 s 244G

Section 244G provides for the avoidance of a double charge to tax and transitional protections.

Subsection (1) excludes a transfer from the overseas transfer charge if it was requested before 9 March 2017.

Under the provisions of sub-s (2) an onward transfer is excluded from the overseas transfer charge if the charge was paid, not just at the time of the transfer, but on the "original transfer" (defined in s 244G(5) below) and has not been repaid, the charge was paid on a transfer from another QROPS to the QROPS making the transfer, certain conditions in new s 244G(4) (see below) are met and has not been repaid nor is capable of being repaid, the original transfer from a registered pension scheme to a QROPS was made before 9 March 2017, or in this latter instance was made on or after 9 March 2017 but was requested before that date.

Subsection (3) excludes an onward transfer from the overseas transfer charge where it was made from funds other than the individual's ring-fenced transfer fund.

Subsection (4) specifies that the conditions to be met for the onward transfer to be excluded from the overseas transfer charge are that the original transfer must have been made before the current transfer and the sums and assets transferred by the current transfer must derive directly or indirectly from the sums and assets transferred by the earlier onward transfer.

New FA 2004 s 244H

Section 244H gives power to HMRC to exclude further transfers from the overseas transfer charge in regulations.

New FA 2004 s 244I

Section 244I sets out the circumstances in which exclusions to the overseas transfer charge do not apply, i.e. where an individual does not provide all of the necessary information to the administrator of the registered pension scheme or scheme manager of the QROPS concerned.

New FA 2004 s 244J

The provisions of sub-s (1) make the registered pension scheme administrator and individual concerned jointly and severally liable for the overseas transfer charge when a recognised transfer is made to a QROPS.

Subsection (2) makes the scheme manager of the QROPS or former QROPS and individual jointly and severally liable for the overseas transfer charge where the transfer is an onward transfer.

Subsections (3) to (5) make the scheme manager of the QROPS or former QROPS holding the transferred funds and the individual making the transfer jointly and severally liable to the overseas transfer charge if a transfer is initially excluded from the charge because the individual and the recipient QROPS were both in the same country or both in different EEA states, but the charge arises within five tax years of the transfer as one of the conditions of the exclusion is no longer met. Subsection (5) also specifies that the scheme manager of a former QROPS is liable to the charge only if the scheme was a QROPS on or after 9 March 2017, it received a recognised transfer from a registered pension scheme or an onward transfer from another QROPS on or after that date.

Subsection (6) provides that scheme administrators and managers and individuals are liable to the charge whether or not they are resident or domiciled in the UK.

New FA 2004 s 244K

Section 244K sets out the amount of the overseas transfer charge and how it is to be calculated.

Subsection (1) specifies the rate of the new charge is 25% of the transferred value.

Subsections (2) and (3) state that the transferred value of the transfer from a registered pension scheme established in the UK is the amount of the sums and the value of the assets transferred. Where the registered pension scheme is established outside the UK the transferred value subject to the overseas transfer charge is limited to the amount of "UK-relieved funds" (defined in sub-s 244K(11) below) in the scheme.

Subsection (4) specifies that the transferred value subject to the new charge on a transfer from a QROPS or former QROPS is the amount of the sums and the value of the assets attributed to the individual's "ring-fenced transfer fund" (defined in sub-s 244K(11) below) subject to the provisions of new sub-ss (5) to (9).

Subsections (5) to (10) provide that if a lifetime allowance tax charge arises on a transfer then the transferred value subject to the overseas transfer charge is the amount after deducting the lifetime allowance tax charge and that charge is to be calculated without reference to the overseas transfer charge.

Subsection (6) provides that where the transfer was initially excluded from the overseas transfer charge because the individual and the QROPS to which they had transferred were both in the same country or both in different EEA states, but the charge later arises because the exclusion is no longer met within five tax years from the date of the transfer, the new charge applies to the funds representing the individual's ring-fenced transfer fund held in the QROPS or former QROPS.

Subsection (7) specifies that if the scheme administrator or manager pays the overseas transfer charge but does not deduct it from the value of the funds to be transferred, the amount of the charge is grossed up as defined in ITA 2007 s 998, in effect added to the value to be transferred and itself subject to the overseas transfer charge.

Subsection (8) sets out that if the scheme administrator or manager deducts the amount of the overseas transfer charge from the value to be transferred, then the transferred value is the amount given by sub-ss (2) to (6) without any deduction for the charge. If the individual pays the overseas transfer charge sub-s (9) specifies the transfer value is also the amount given by sub-ss (2) to (6) without any deduction for the charge.

Subsection (10) provides for the overseas transfer charge not to be taken into account in all cases, rather only when a lifetime allowance charge arises.

Subsection (11) provides definitions for terms used in s 244K.

New FA 2004 s 244L

Section 244L provides the rules for accounting for the overseas transfer charge by scheme managers.

Subsection (1) confirms that the charge referred to in s 244L is the overseas transfer charge for which he scheme manager of a QROPS or former QROPS is liable.

Subsection (2) gives power to HMRC to set out in regulations how scheme managers of QROPS and former QROPS should account for the overseas transfer charge. The regulations can make provision for or in connection with the payment dates when the charge is due, when interest arises on the charge paid after the due date, how scheme managers notify HMRC of errors in the information provided and the making of assessments, repayments and adjustments.

Subsection (3) provides that the operation and application of any provision of the Tax Acts can be modified and provided for in the regulations permitted by sub-s (2).

New FA 2004 s 244M

Section 244M specifies the circumstances in which a repayment of the overseas transfer charge will arise.

Subsection (1) provides that there can be a repayment of the charge only if it arose on a transfer when it was made and in "the relevant period" (defined in s 244A above) starting with the original transfer and circumstances arise that would have led to the transfer being excluded from the charge.

Subsections (2) and (3) provide that the charge can be repaid only to the extent it has not been repaid already, but any penalties or interest that were payable regarding the charge are not repayable.

Subsection (4) provides that a repayment of the charge depends on the scheme administrator or manager claiming the repayment meeting all the requirements to provide information to HMRC about the repayment. To prevent scheme administrators or managers claiming UK tax relief on a repayment of the charge, sub-s (5) specifies that such a repayment is not a relievable pension contribution.

Subsection (6) specifies that where an individual can make a claim on the basis they paid the tax charge from funds which did not come directly from the pension scheme, they must do so within a year of the end of the relevant period as defined in s 244A.

Subsection (7) gives HMRC power to make regulations to set out further detail about repayment claims and to provide additional circumstances in which claims may be made.

New FA 2004 s 244N

Section 244N sets out the circumstances in which a scheme administrator or manager liable to the overseas transfer charge may seek to be discharged from that liability.

Subsections (1) and (2) provide that the scheme administrator of a registered pension scheme or the scheme manager of a QROPS liable to the overseas transfer charge may apply to HMRC to be discharged from their liability to the charge on the ground grounds specified in sub-s (3). Subsection (3) specifies these grounds as the scheme administrator or manager reasonably believed there was no liability to the charge on a transfer and it would not be just and reasonable for them to be liable to the charge on the transfer.

Subsections (4) and (5) provide that HMRC must decide whether to discharge the liability and tell the scheme administrator or manager the decision.

Subsection (6) provides that a discharge under s 244N does not affect the liability of anyone liable to the overseas transfer charge on the transfer concerned.

Subsection (7) gives power to HMRC by regulations to obtain supplementary information from scheme administrators or managers and to set time limits for making an application to discharge their liability.

Further amendments in Part 4 of FA 2004

Paragraph 12 provides for the recognised transfer provisions of FA 2004 Pt 4 to be amended and for a new power to make provision for assessments in that Act.

Paragraph 13 amends FA 2004 s 169. Paragraph 13(2) inserts new sub-s (2)(ba) to provide a new declaration and undertaking that scheme managers must make for their scheme to be a QROPS. The legislation requires scheme managers of recognised overseas pension schemes (ROPS) to confirm they understand their potential liability to the overseas transfer charge and are willing to operate the charge, including paying the tax. Paragraph 13(3) inserts new sub-s (2A) giving HMRC power to make regulations requiring information or evidence in a particular form in relation to the notification of ROPS. Paragraph 13(4) inserts new sub-s (4ZA) giving HMRC power to make regulations to require members or former members of QROPS or former QROPS to provide information to scheme managers of QROPS or former QROPS. Paragraph 13(5) makes a consequential amendment to FA 2004 s 169(4A). Paragraph 13(6) inserts new sub-s (4C) to provide that the power to make regulations in relation to ROPS can require information in a particular form. Paragraph 13(7) inserts new sub-ss (7A) to (7D) and (8). Subsection (7A) gives HMRC power to make regulations to ensure that where a "relevant overseas transfer" (defined in sub-s (7B) below) of a pension in payment is made, the pension in the new pension scheme will be treated as the pension in the scheme under which it was formerly held. Subsection (7B) defines a "relevant overseas transfer" as one where accrued rights under a "relevant overseas scheme" (defined in sub-s (7C) below) are transferred so as to become held under another relevant overseas scheme or registered pension scheme in connection with an individual member of the scheme. Sub-s (7C) defines "relevant overseas scheme" as a QROPS which has not received a transfer or a relevant non-UK scheme which includes a QROPS which has received a relevant transfer. Subsection (7D) specifies that the regulations under sub-s (7A) may apply in different ways for different cases. Paragraph 13(8) amends the definition in FA 2004 s 169(8) of "relevant requirement" to include a requirement to pay the overseas transfer charge.

Paragraph 14 inserts new FA 2004 Pt 4 Ch 5A ss 242A and 242B providing definitions in relation to registered pension schemes established outside the UK. Section 242A defines the meaning of a "non-UK registered pension scheme" as a registered pension scheme established in a country or territory outside the UK. Subsection 242B(1) defines the meaning of "UK relieved funds" as those which have had UK tax relief that are held in a non-UK registered scheme, at any time formed the UK tax-relieved fund under a relevant non-UK scheme or represent accrued rights when the member accrued rights under the scheme and is taken to have benefited from UK tax relief. Subsections 242B(2) to (4) use definitions set out in SI 2006/567, the Registered Pension Schemes (Provision of Information) Regulations.

Paragraph 15 amends FA 2004 s 254(6) by inserting new sub-s 254(6)(ba) to include repayments to scheme administrators in the list of regulations that HMRC may make in relation to scheme administrators accounting for tax to HMRC.

Paragraph 16 amends FA 2004 s 255(1) by inserting new sub-s 255(1)(da) giving power to HMRC to make regulations regarding the liability of administrators of registered pension schemes and scheme managers of QROPS or former QROPS to assessments to the overseas transfer charge.

Paragraph 17 makes consequential amendments to FA 2004 ss 269(1)(a) regarding an appeal against a decision on the discharge of the liability to the overseas transfer charge.

Paragraph 18 inserts new FA 2004 Sch 32 para 2A to prevent a repaid amount of overseas transfer charge from being tested against an individual's lifetime allowance more than once. New sub-para 2A(1) applies in all cases where an amount of overseas transfer charge is repaid to the scheme administrator. New sub-para 2A(2) provides that when there is an amount to be tested against the individual's lifetime allowance under the scheme that received the repayment, it is reduced by the amount of the repayment. New sub-para 2A(3) specifies that if under sub-para 2A(2) the repayment exceeds the amount to be tested, then the remaining amount of the repayment is to be set against future tests against the individual's lifetime allowance under a benefited scheme. New sub-para 2A(4) defines a "benefited scheme" as either the scheme to which the repayment of overseas transfer charge is made or a pension scheme to which a recognised transfer (or chain of transfers) of sums or assets is made that represents a repayment of the charge.

Other amendments

Paragraph 19 amends TMA 1970 s 9(1A) by inserting sub-s (1A)(aa) to remove the scheme manager of a QROPS or former QROPS from the scope of self-assessment within which they would otherwise be as a consequence of their liability to the overseas transfer charge.

Paragraph 20 amends the Table in FA 2009 Sch 56 para 1 by inserting new item 3A which sets out the date on which the overseas transfer charge becomes due.

Paragraph 21(1) inserts a new entry into Table 1 in SI 2005/3454 reg 3(1) to specify when a scheme administrator accounts for an overseas transfer charge they must provide details of the individual making the taxable transfer, details of the transfer, details of the recipient QROPS and the amount of tax due. Paragraph 21(2) amends SI 2005/3454 by inserting new reg 14 to provide a time limit and the information that must be furnished when a scheme administrator receives information that an overseas transfer charge should be repaid. New reg 14(1) and (2) provide that a scheme administrator has 60 days to make a claim for a repayment of the transfer charge from the time they become aware of the entitlement to a repayment. New reg 14(3) specifies that to make a claim the scheme administrator has to provide HMRC with details of the member and the transfer, the date of payment of the transfer charge, the reason for repayment of the charge and the amount claimed. New reg 14(4) provides an extended period for the claim to be made if the scheme administrator becomes aware of the repayment before 14 November 2017, in which case the claim can be made no later than 14 November 2017. Paragraph 21(3) confirms that the amendment in para 21(1) is treated as made under the relevant powers in FA 2004 s 254. Paragraph 21(4) confirms that the amendment made by para 21(2) is treated as made under the relevant powers in FA 2004 s 244M(7) (see above).

Paragraph 22(1) amends SI 2006/208. Paragraph 22(2) brings the definition of "onward transfer" into the regulations. Paragraph 22(3) amends SI 2006/208 reg 3(2) by providing a reference to ring-fenced transfer funds in addition to a relevant transfer fund and inserts new reg 3(2)(da). The latter specifies that a scheme manager of a QROPS or former QROPS, when making a transfer to another QROPS must provide HMRC with certain information. Such information includes whether the transfer is subject to the overseas transfer charge – if so, details of the transferred value and amount of the charge deducted from the payment by the scheme manager and, if not, the reason why not. The information supplied must also include the remaining value of the individual's relevant and ring-fenced transfer funds immediately after the payment. Paragraph 22(4) also amends SI 2006/208 reg 3 by inserting new paras (2A) to (2C). New para (2A) specifies that paras (2B) and (2C) apply if a scheme manager of a QROPS or former QROPS makes an onward transfer to another QROPS out of funds initially excluded from the overseas transfer charge as the individual and the recipient QROPS were both in the same country or both in different EEA states. New para (2B) provides that if within five years from the date of the original transfer of the funds from a registered pension scheme to a QROPS, the scheme manager of the QROPS or former QROPS is notified that there is a change in circumstances such that the exclusion no longer applies, the scheme manager must tell HMRC within 90 days of being notified of the change, details of the change, the transferred value, the amount of overseas transfer charge which now arises and whether the scheme manager intends to account for the charge, and details of the funds remaining in the individual's ring-fenced transfer fund immediately after the change. New para (2C) provides that the scheme manager of a QROPS or former QROPS must notify HMRC where within five years from the date of the original transfer of the funds from a registered pension scheme to a QROPS, they become aware that an individual's principal residential address has changed such that the exclusion the individual and the recipient QROPS were both in the same country or in different EEA states no longer applies.

SI 2006/208 is further amended by para 22(5) in reg 3(3)(a) to ensure that the 10-year reporting period relating to payments out of transferred funds applies to payments out of ring-fenced funds as well as relevant transfer funds. The amendment provides that the 10-year reporting period starts on the key date of the ring-fenced transfer fund and if the payment is out of more than one such fund, then it is the later or latest of the key dates. If the payment is not in respect of a ring-fenced transfer fund then the current legislation applies, i.e. the 10-year reporting period starts on the date the relevant transfer fund came into existence. Paragraph 22(6) further amends SI 2006/208 reg 3 by inserting new para (3A) which provides that no obligation to provide information arises under para (2B) if 10 years have elapsed since the key date for the ring-fenced fund.

Paragraphs 22(7) to (9) amend SI 2006/208 regs 3(6), 3AB(4) and 3AC to refer to a ring-fenced transfer fund.

Paragraph 22(10) makes consequential amendments to SI 2006/208 reg 3AD when information is given by a QROPS or former QROPS to another QROPS. Subparagraphs 22(10)(a) to (d), and (g) amend reg 3AD paras 1(a), 2, 2(b) and 2(c)(i) to refer to a ring-fenced transfer fund. Paragraph 22(10)(e) ensures that the scheme manager making the transfer provides the date the original transfer that formed these funds was requested (if known). Paragraph 22(10)(f) ensures that the scheme manager making the transfer provides the information in connection with the overseas transfer charge or its exclusion.

Paragraph 22(11) amends SI 2006/208 reg 3 by inserting new regs 3AE to 3AL.

New reg 3AE specifies the information an individual must provide to a QROPS manager when they want to transfer their funds to another QROPS. This is similar information to that which the individual is required to provide to the administrator of a registered pension scheme when they want to transfer from that scheme to a QROPS. New reg 3AE(1) and (2) stipulate that the provisions of reg 3AD(4) do not apply when a member of a QROPS or former QROPS makes a request to transfer their rights to another QROPS if the transfer was made or formally requested before 9 March 2017 or if five tax years have passed since the date of original transfer from a registered pension scheme. New reg 3AE(3) provides the definition of "original transfer" which is the same as in FA 2004 s 244A(5). New reg 3AE(4) specifies the information individuals must provide to their QROPS or former QROPS scheme manager. This information includes the individual's details and details of the QROPS to which they wish to transfer. They must also state whether they know for certain that the transfer will be excluded from the charge as the recipient QROPS is an occupational pension scheme, an overseas public service pension scheme or the pension scheme of an international organisation and if so, details of their employment with a participating employer of the scheme. In addition they must provide written acknowledgment they are aware the transfer could mean they are liable to the overseas transfer charge and the circumstances in which a transfer which was initially excluded from the charge may become liable to the charge. New reg 3AE(5) requires the individual to provide the information in reg 3AE(4) within 60 days of making the transfer request. New reg 3AE(6) requires the QROPS or former QROPS scheme manager to notify the individual of the required information within 30 days of the transfer request.

New reg 3AF makes it clear that the member does not have to provide information to the scheme manager in relation to the transfer charge if the transfer takes place after the end of the relevant period. New reg 3AF(1) and (2) provides that where there has been a transfer from a registered pension scheme to a QROPS or between QROPS, and the transfer charge arises on the transfer or the transfer is assumed to be excluded from the charge, the member must tell the scheme manager if they change their country of residence during the "relevant period" (as defined in FA 2004 s 244A) within 60 days of the change. New reg 3AF(3) extends the reporting period to 30 June 2017 if the 60-day period for reporting a change under reg 3AF(2) ends before that date.

New reg 3AG specifies the information the QROPS or former QROPS manager must provide to the individual where an onward transfer gives rise to the overseas transfer charge. New reg 3AG (1) provides that if the overseas transfer charge arises on an onward transfer, within 90 days of that transfer the QROPS or former QROPS manager must provide the member with details of the transfer and any tax that has been paid or the scheme manager intends to pay. New reg 3AG(2) provides that if the onward transfer is excluded from the charge, within 90 days of that transfer the QROPS or former QROPS manager must provide the individual with details of the transfer and reason why the transfer is excluded from the charge. If the transfer is excluded as both the individual and the recipient QROPS are in the same country or different EEA states, the manager has to provide an explanation of how the funds could become taxable. New reg 3AG(3) and (4) provide that a QROPS or former QROPS manager, who has received a transfer that was excluded from the charge as both the individual and the recipient QROPS were in the same country or in different EEA states, must take action if notified within five tax years from the date of the original transfer from a registered pension scheme of an event which means the exclusion no longer applied. The action the manager must take within 90 days of being notified of the change or event is to provide the individual with details of the charge in relation to the transfer, whether the manager intends to account for the tax charge and confirmation of the date of payment of the charge if the manager has already paid it.

New reg 3AH sets out how the QROPS or former QROPS manager who is liable to an overseas transfer charge accounts for the tax to HMRC. New reg 3AH(1) and (2) specify the manager must pay the charge using the accounting reference provided by HMRC after the manager has notified HMRC of the liability. New reg 3AH(3) provides that the tax is due at the end of 91 days from the date the accounting reference was issued by HMRC.

New reg 3AI requires HMRC to raise a tax assessment on the manager for any overseas transfer charge not paid by the due date. The charge is payable within 30 days of the issue of the notice of assessment.

New reg 3AJ specifies that interest applies to overdue overseas transfer charges in the same way it applies to other income taxes.

New reg 3AK provides for the action HMRC may take if the correct overseas transfer charge has not been paid on or before it becomes due, including interest on unpaid or overpaid tax.

New reg 3AL(1) specifies that a scheme manager of a QROPS or former QROPS has to make a claim to receive a repayment of an overseas transfer charge. New reg 3AL(2) specifies that the claim must be in writing, made within 12 months of the end of the "relevant period" (as defined in FA 2004 s 244A) for the transfer and that the scheme manager must provide HMRC with details of the member and transfer, date of payment of the overseas transfer charge, reason for its repayment and amount claimed.

Paragraphs 22(12) and (13) make consequential amendments to SI 2006/208 reg 3B and 3C.

Paragraph 22(14) amends SI 2006/208 reg 5(1) to require a former QROPS manager to provide information regarding the overseas transfer charge to which the penalties regime applies.

Paragraph 22(15) confirms the amendments in para 22(11) above are treated as made under the relevant powers in FA 2004 ss 169(4ZA), 169(4), 244L and 244M(7).

Paragraph 23 amends SI 2006/499 reg 5 to provide that the circumstances in which scheme pension may be reduced includes payment of the overseas transfer charge. Paragraph 23(4) confirms the amendments made in para 22 are treated as made under the relevant powers in FA 2004 sch 28 para 2(4)(h).

Paragraph 24 amends SI 2006/567 regarding the provision of information. Paragraph 24(2) inserts into reg 3(1) (provision of information by scheme administrators to HMRC) in the Table of benefit crystallisation events (BCEs) at reportable event, BCE 9, "Transfers to qualifying recognised overseas pension schemes", the additional requirement for the scheme administrator to provide details of whether or not the transfer gave rise to the overseas transfer charge and, if so, details of the charge, or if not, the reason for exclusion from the charge. The scheme administrator is also required to provide the QROPS reference if known.

Paragraph 24(3) amends reg 3(7) bringing forward the deadline for the scheme administrator to provide information to HMRC in relation to a transfer to a QROPS where the administrator applies for a repayment of the overseas transfer charge before the deadline would otherwise have occurred.

Paragraph 24(4) amends reg 11BA(2) specifying the additional information relating to the overseas transfer charge that scheme administrators must obtain from the individual requesting a transfer to a QROPS. Subparagraphs 24(4)(a) and (b) amend the order of the information required about the recipient QROPS and additionally require the individual to provide the scheme administrator with information on whether the individual knows for certain that the transfer will be excluded from the charge as the recipient QROPS is an occupational pension scheme, an overseas public service pension scheme or the pension scheme of an international organisation and, if so, details of their employment with a participating employer of the QROPS. Furthermore, the individual must provide written acknowledgment that they are aware the transfer could mean they are liable to the charge and the circumstances in which a transfer that was initially excluded from the charge may become liable to the charge.

Paragraph 24(5) amends SI 2006/567 by inserting new reg 11BB providing that following a recognised transfer that is excluded from the overseas transfer charge or that have been subject to the charge as the individual and the recipient QROPS are in the same country or in different EEA states, the individual must within 60 days of the charge inform the scheme administrator making the transfer if, within five tax years of that transfer, their country of residence changes. This amendment also extends the reporting period to 30 June 2017 if the 60-day period for reporting a change under reg11BB(2) ends before 30 June 2017.

Paragraph 24(6) amends SI 2006/567 by inserting new reg 12A which provides that if an overseas transfer charge arises on a transfer from a registered pension scheme to a QROPS, the scheme administrator must within 90 days provide the individual with details of the transfer and the charge, the extent to which the administrator has paid the tax or intends to do so and if paid, the date of payment. This amendment also provides that if a transfer from a registered pension scheme to a QROPS is excluded from the charge, the administrator must within 90 days provide the individual with details of the transfer and the reason why the transfer was excluded. If the transfer is excluded as both the individual and the recipient QROPS are in the same country or in different EEA states the administrator must also provide an explanation of how the funds could become liable to the charge. New reg 12A(3) specifies that where the scheme administrator receives a repayment of an overseas transfer charge they must give the individual, within three months of receiving the repayment, details of the repayment and the reason why the charge was repaid.

Paragraph 24(7) amends SI 2006/567 by inserting new reg 14ZCA setting out the information that a scheme administrator must provide to a QROPS manager when making a recognised transfer to that QROPS. New reg 14ZCA(2) and (3) provide that the scheme administrator must within 31 days of the transfer inform the QROPS manager whether or not an overseas transfer charge arose on the transfer – if so, the amount of the charge and if not, the reason the transfer was excluded from the charge. New reg 14ZCA(4) and (5) provide that the scheme administrator must within 31 days of receiving repayment of the overseas transfer charge provide the recipient QROPS manager with a copy of the original statement regarding the transfer, confirmation that it is now inaccurate, details of the repayment and the reason why the transfer is now excluded from the charge.

Paragraph 24(8) confirms that the amendments made by para 23 are treated as made under the relevant powers in FA 2004 s 251.

Commencement and transitional provision

Paragraph 25(1) provides that except as set out in paras 25(2) and (3) below the requirements set out in Sch 4 have effect in relation to transfers made on or after 9 March 2017 even though the overseas transfer charge will only apply to transfers requested on or after that date.

Paragraph 25(2)(a) specifies that the new QROPS undertaking has effect from 9 March 2017 for a scheme that is notifying HMRC it meets the requirements to be a ROPS on or after that date or for a scheme that notified HMRC it meets the requirements to be a ROPS before that date but HMRC had not given a reference number to the scheme by that date. Paragraph 25(2)(b) provides that the new QROPS undertaking has effect from 14 April 2017 for schemes for which HMRC had issued a reference number before 9 March 2017.

Paragraph 25(3) provides that the remaining changes in FA 2004 s 169 and the amendment in FA 2004 s 255 come into force on 9 March 2017.

Paragraph 25(4) provides that the amendments in SI 2006/208 reg 3(2) have effect for payments made on or after 9 March 2017 and in reg 3AE have effect in relation to requests made on or after that date.

Paragraph 25(5) provides that when accounting for the overseas transfer charge arising in the period from 9 March 2017 and ending 30 June 2017, administrators of registered pension schemes treat the charge as being charged in the three-month period ending with 30 September 2017. This means that payment of the first overseas transfer charge by scheme administrators will not become due until 14 November 2017. The revised date for reporting overseas transfer charges applies only if the charge would be due at an earlier date.

SCHEDULE 5

DEDUCTION OF INCOME TAX AT SOURCE

Section 11

PART 1

INTEREST DISTRIBUTIONS OF INVESTMENT TRUST OR AUTHORISED

INVESTMENT FUND

1 In Chapter 3 of Part 15 of ITA 2007 (deduction of tax from certain payments of yearly interest), after section 888A insert—

"888B Designated dividends of investment trusts

The duty to deduct a sum representing income tax under section 874 does not apply to a dividend so far as it is treated as a payment of yearly interest by regulations under section 45 of FA 2009 (dividends designated by investment trust or prospective investment trust).

888C Interest distributions of certain open-ended investment companies

The duty to deduct a sum representing income tax under section 874 does not apply to a payment of yearly interest under section 373 of ITTOIA 2005 (in the case of certain open-ended investment companies, payments of yearly interest treated as made where distributable amount shown in accounts as yearly interest).

888D Interest distribution of certain authorised unit trusts

The duty to deduct a sum representing income tax under section 874 does not apply to a payment of yearly interest under section 376 of ITTOIA 2005 (in the case of certain authorised unit trusts, payments of yearly interest treated as made where distributable amount shown in accounts as yearly interest)."

2 In section 45(2) of FA 2009 (provision that regulations may make about dividends of investment trusts) omit paragraph (c) (power to disapply duty to deduct tax under section 874 of ITA 2007).

PART 2
INTEREST ON PEER-TO-PEER LENDING

3 In Chapter 3 of Part 15 of ITA 2007 (deduction of tax from certain payments of yearly interest), after section 888D (inserted by this Schedule) insert—

"888E Interest on certain peer-to-peer lending

(1) The duty to deduct a sum representing income tax under section 874 does not apply to a payment of interest on an amount of peer-to-peer lending.

(2) In subsection (1) "peer-to-peer lending" means credit in relation to which the condition in subsection (4) is met.

(3) In this section—

"original borrower", in relation to any credit, means the person to whom the credit is originally provided,

"credit" includes a cash loan and any other form of financial accommodation, and

"original lender", in relation to any credit, means the person who originally provides the credit.

(4) The condition is that—

(a) the original borrower and the original lender enter the agreement under which the credit is provided at the invitation of a person ("the operator"),

(b) the operator makes the invitation in the course of, or in connection with, operating an electronic system,

(c) the operator's operation of the electronic system is an activity specified in article 36H(1) or (2D) of the Order (operating an electronic system in relation to lending), and

(d) the operator has permission under Part 4A of FISMA 2000 to carry on that activity.

(5) For the purposes of subsection (4), it does not matter if the agreement mentioned in subsection (4)(a) is not an article 36H agreement (as defined in article 36H of the Order).

(6) The Commissioners for Her Majesty's Revenue and Customs may by regulations make such amendments of the preceding provisions of this section as they consider appropriate in consequence of—

(a) the Order, or any part of it, being replaced (or further replaced) by provision in another instrument, or

(b) any amendment of the Order or any such other instrument.

(7) In this section "the Order" means the Financial Services and Markets Act 2000 (Regulated Activities) Order 2001 (SI 2001/544)."

PART 3
FURTHER AMENDMENT AND COMMENCEMENT

Further amendment

4 In section 874(3)(a) of ITA 2007 (which refers to provisions which disapply the duty under section 874 to deduct tax from yearly interest), for "888" substitute "888E".

Commencement

5 (1) The new sections 888B to 888D of ITA 2007, and the repeal of section 45(2)(c) of FA 2009, have effect in relation to amounts treated as payments of yearly interest made on or after 6 April 2017.

(2) The new section 888E of ITA 2007 has effect in relation to payments of interest made on or after 6 April 2017.

GENERAL NOTE

Part 1 Interest distributions of investment trust or authorised investment fund

Paragraph 1 inserts three new sections (ss 888B, 888C and 888D) into ITA 2007, Pt 13, Ch 3. These each disapply the obligation to deduct a sum representing income tax imposed by s 874 of the Act from the type of payment named in the section.

New ITA 2007 s 888B

Section 888B relieves investment trusts of the duty to deduct a sum representing income tax from certain payments under s 874 of the Act from those dividends paid by investment trusts which are designated as payments of yearly interest under the Investment Trusts (Dividends) (Optional Treatment as Interest Distributions) Regulations 2009 (SI 2009/2034). The result is that all investment trust dividends designated as yearly interest will be payable gross.

New ITA 2007 s 888C

Section 888C relieves openended investment companies of the duty to deduct a sum representing income tax from certain payments under s 874 of the Act from those distributions paid (or treated as paid in the case of accumulation shares) by openended investment companies where a distributable amount is shown in its accounts as yearly interest in accordance with ITTOIA 2005 s 373. The result is that all allocations by openended investment companies and sub-funds of umbrella openended investment companies that allocate their distributable income in the form of interest distributions will be paid gross.

New ITA 2007 s 888D

Section 888D relieves authorised unit trusts of the duty to deduct a sum representing income tax from certain payments under s 874 of the Act from those distributions paid (or treated as paid in the case of accumulation units) by authorised unit trusts where a distributable amount is shown in its accounts as yearly interest in accordance with ITTOIA 2005 s 376. The result is that all allocations by authorised unit trusts and sub-funds of umbrella authorised unit trusts that allocate their distributable income in the form of interest distributions will be paid gross.

Paragraph 2 is a consequential amendment removing the enabling power in FA 2009 s 45(2) to make regulations disapplying the duty to deduct in respect of investment trusts.

Part 2 Interest on peer-to-peer lending

Paragraph 3 deals with interest on peertopeer lending. It inserts the new s 888E into ITA 2007, Pt 15, Ch 3.

New ITA 2007 s 888E

Section 888E defines peertopeer lending in subss (2)–(5) as a form of credit (which includes a cash loan but also any other form of financial accommodation) that meets certain conditions. These are that an operator in the course of, or in connection with, operating an electronic lending system (for which the operator has the appropriate permission under the Financial Services and Markets Act 2000) invites a lender (i.e. the credit provider) to enter into an agreement for the provision of the credit to a borrower (i.e. the original recipient).

Subsection (1) removes the duty under s 874 of the Act to deduct sums representing income tax from interest payments on amounts lent through peertopeer lending.

Subsections (6) and (7) empower HMRC to make appropriate amendments by regulations following any amendment or replacement of the Financial Services and Markets Act 2000 (Regulated Activities) Order 2001 (SI 2001/544).

Part 3 Further amendment and commencement

Paragraph 4 amends ITA 2007 s 874(3)(a).

Paragraph 5 provides for commencement. The amendments have effect from 6 April 2017.

Note: The new ITA 2007 s 888C provisions will also apply in the case of property authorised investment funds to PAIF distributions (interest) and the new ss 888C or 888D provisions in the case of open-ended investment companies and authorised unit trusts with tax-elected fund status to their TEF distributions (non-dividend) by virtue of the Authorised Investment Funds (Tax) Regulations 2006 reg 96.

SCHEDULE 6
EMPLOYMENT INCOME PROVIDED THROUGH THIRD PARTIES
Section 15

Introductory

1 Part 7A of ITEPA 2003 (employment income provided through third parties) is amended in accordance with paragraphs 2 to 11.

Meaning of "relevant step"

2 In section 554A(2) (meaning of "relevant") at the end insert "(including such a step where the taking of the step, or some aspect of the taking of the step, constitutes a breach of trust or is a constituent part of a breach of trust, and even if the step or aspect is void as a result of breach of trust).

Loans: transferring, releasing or writing off

3 (1) Section 554C (relevant steps: payment of sum, transfer of asset etc) is amended as follows.

(2) In subsection (1), after paragraph (a) insert—

"(aa) acquires a right to a payment of a sum of money, or to a transfer of assets, where there is a connection (direct or indirect) between the acquisition of the right and—

(i) a payment made, by way of a loan or otherwise, to a relevant person, or
(ii) a transfer of assets to a relevant person,

(ab) releases or writes off the whole or a part of—

(i) a loan made to a relevant person, or
(ii) an acquired right of the kind mentioned in paragraph (aa),"."

(3) After subsection (3) insert—

"(3A) For the purposes of subsection (1) "loan" includes—

(a) any form of credit, and
(b) a payment that is purported to be made by way of a loan.

(3B) Subsection (3C) applies where a person ("T") acquires from another person ("L") (whether or not for consideration)—

(a) a right to payment of the whole or part of a loan where T is the person liable (at the time of the acquisition of the right) to repay the loan, or
(b) a right to payment of a sum of money, or to a transfer of assets, where T is the person liable (at the time of the acquisition of the right) to pay the sum, or transfer the assets.

(3C) L is to be treated for the purposes of subsection (1)(ab) as releasing—

(a) in a case within subsection (3B)(a), the loan or the relevant part of it;
(b) in a case within subsection (3B)(b), the right or the relevant part of it."

4 In section 554A(4) (non-application of Chapter 2 where relevant step taken on or after A's death)—

(a) omit "within section 554B", and
(b) at the end insert "if—

(a) the relevant step is within section 554B, or
(b) the relevant step is within section 554C by virtue of subsection (1)(ab) of that section."

5 After section 554O insert—

"554OA Exclusions: transfer of employment-related loans

(1) Chapter 2 does not apply by reason of a relevant step taken by a person ("P") if—

(a) the step is acquiring a right to payment of an amount equal to the whole or part of a payment made by way of a loan to a relevant person (the "borrower"),
(b) the loan, at the time it was made, was an employment-related loan,
(c) at the time the relevant step is taken, the section 180 threshold is not exceeded in relation to the loan,
(d) at the time the relevant step is taken, the borrower is an employee, or a prospective employee, of P, and
(e) there is no connection (direct or indirect) between the relevant step and a tax avoidance arrangement.

(2) For the purposes of this section, the section 180 threshold is not exceeded in relation to a loan if, at all times in the relevant tax year—

(a) the amount outstanding on the loan, or

    (b) if two or more employment-related loans are made by the same employer, the aggregate of the amount outstanding on them,

does not exceed the amount specified at the end of section 180(2) (normal threshold for benefit of a loan to be treated as earnings).

    (3) Subsection (4) applies if—

    (a) two or more employment-related loans are made by the same employer, and

    (b) during the relevant tax year, a person acquires a right to payment of an amount (the "transfer amount") equal to the whole or part of the payment made by way of any of the loans.

    (4) The transfer amount is to be treated as an "amount outstanding" on that loan for the purposes of subsection (2)(b).

    (5) In this section—

    (a) "employment-related loan" has the same meaning as it has for the purposes of Chapter 7 of Part 3;

    (b) "relevant tax year" means the tax year in which the relevant step is taken."

6 In section 554Z(10)(b) (interpretation: relevant step which involves a sum of money), after "section 554C(1)(a)" insert "to (ab)".

7 In section 554Z12(1) (relevant step taken after A's death etc), after "554C" insert ", by virtue of subsection (1)(a) or (b) to (e) of that section,".

Exclusions: relevant repayments

8 After section 554R insert—

"554RA Exclusions: relevant repayments

    (1) This section applies (subject to subsection (5)) if—

    (a) a right to repayment of principal under a relevant loan (the "repayment right") is held by or on behalf of a person ("P"), and

    (b) on or after 9 December 2010, a sum of money (the "repayment sum") is acquired by or on behalf of P by way of repayment of principal under the relevant loan.

    (2) In this section "relevant loan" means a loan made on or after 6 April 1999.

    (3) Subsection (4) applies if—

    (a) on its acquisition, the repayment sum is the subject of a relevant step within section 554B taken by P, or

    (b) for the sole purpose of the acquisition, the making of the payment of the repayment sum is a relevant step within section 554C(1)(a).

    (4) Chapter 2 does not apply by reason of the relevant step if, on its acquisition, the repayment sum is held by or on behalf of P on the same basis as that on which the repayment right was held by or on behalf of P immediately before the acquisition.

    (5) This section does not apply where there is any connection (direct or indirect) between the acquisition by or on behalf of P of the repayment sum and a tax avoidance arrangement (other than the arrangement under which the relevant loan was made)."

Exclusions: payments in respect of a tax liability

9 After section 554X insert—

"554XA Exclusions: payments in respect of a tax liability

    (1) Chapter 2 does not apply by reason of a relevant step which is the payment of a sum of money if—

    (a) the payment is a relevant tax payment, or

    (b) where the payment is not a relevant tax payment—

      (i) the payment is made to a person for the purpose of the person making a relevant tax payment,

      (ii) the person makes a relevant tax payment of an amount equal to the amount of the first payment, and

      (iii) the relevant tax payment is made before the end of the period of 60 days beginning with the day on which the first payment is made.

    (2) "Relevant tax payment" means a payment made to Her Majesty's Revenue and Customs in respect of a relevant liability for—

    (a) income tax,

    (b) national insurance contributions,

    (c) inheritance tax, or

    (d) corporation tax.

(3) But a provisional payment of tax (see section 554Z11D) is not a relevant tax payment.

(4) A liability is a "relevant liability" if—

(a) under the terms of an agreement for the discharge of the liability, or

(b) by way of a decision on an application under this section,

an officer of Revenue and Customs agrees that the liability is to be treated as arising in respect of the relevant arrangement concerned.

(5) A person may make an application to Her Majesty's Revenue and Customs for a liability to be treated, for the purposes of this section, as arising in respect of the relevant arrangement concerned.

(6) An application under this section must be made in such form and manner, and contain such information, as may be specified by, or on behalf of, the Commissioners for Her Majesty's Revenue and Customs.

(7) An officer of Revenue and Customs must notify the applicant of the decision on an application under this section."

Double taxation

10 For section 554Z5 (overlap with earlier relevant step) substitute—

"554Z5 Overlap with money or asset subject to earlier tax liability

(1) This section applies if there is overlap between—

(a) the sum of money or asset ("sum or asset P") which is the subject of the relevant step, and

(b) a sum of money or asset ("sum or asset Q") by reference to which, on an occasion that occurred before the relevant step is taken, A became subject to a liability for income tax ("the earlier tax liability").

(2) But this section does not apply where—

(a) the earlier tax liability arose by reason of a step within section 554B taken in a tax year before 6 April 2011, and

(b) the value of the relevant step is (or if large enough would be) reduced under paragraph 59 of Schedule 2 to FA 2011.

(3) Where either the payment condition or the liability condition is met, the value of the relevant step is reduced (but not below nil) by an amount equal to so much of the sum of money, or (as the case may be) the value of so much of the asset, as is within the overlap.

(4) The payment condition is that, at the time the relevant step is taken—

(a) the earlier tax liability has become due and payable, and

(b) either—

(i) it has been paid in full, or

(ii) the person liable for the earlier tax liability has agreed terms with an officer of Revenue and Customs for the discharge of that liability.

(5) The liability condition is that, at the time the relevant step is taken, the earlier tax liability is not yet due and payable.

(6) For the purposes of this section there is overlap between sum or asset P and sum or asset Q so far as it is just and reasonable to conclude that—

(a) they are the same sum of money or asset, or

(b) sum or asset P directly, or indirectly, represents sum or asset Q.

(7) Subsection (8) applies where—

(a) the earlier tax liability arose by virtue of the application of this Chapter by reason of an earlier relevant step (the "earlier relevant step"), and

(b) reductions were made under this section to the value of the earlier relevant step.

(8) Where this subsection applies, sum or asset P is treated as overlapping with any other sum of money or asset so far as the other sum of money or asset was treated as overlapping with sum or asset Q for the purposes of this section.

(9) In subsection (1)(b)—

(a) the reference to A includes a reference to any person linked with A, and

(b) the reference to a liability for income tax does not include a reference to a liability for income tax arising by reason of section 175 (benefit of taxable cheap loan treated as earnings).

(10) In subsection (3) the reference to the value of the relevant step is a reference to that value—

(a) after any reductions made to it under section 554Z4, this section or 554Z7, but

(b) before any reductions made to it under section 554Z6 or 554Z8.

(11) For the purposes of subsection (4)(b)(i) a person is not to be regarded as having paid any tax by reason only of making—

(a) a payment on account of income tax,

(b) a payment that is treated as a payment on account under section 223(3) of FA 2014 (accelerated payments), or

(c) a payment pending determination of an appeal made in accordance with section 55 of TMA 1970."

11 After section 554Z11A insert—

"Double taxation: earlier income tax liability

554Z11B Earlier income tax liability: application of section 554Z11C

(1) Section 554Z11C applies if the conditions in subsections (2) and (3) are met.

(2) The first condition is that there is overlap between—

(a) the sum of money or asset ("sum or asset P") which is the subject of the relevant step, and

(b) a sum of money or asset ("sum or asset Q") by reference to which, on an occasion that occurred before the relevant step is taken, A became subject to a liability for income tax ("the earlier tax liability").

(3) The second condition is that at the time the relevant step is taken—

(a) an amount is payable by a person (the "liable person") in respect of the earlier tax liability, but the whole or part of that amount is unpaid and not otherwise accounted for, and

(b) the liable person has not agreed any terms with an officer of Revenue and Customs for the discharge of the earlier tax liability.

(4) For the purposes of this section there is overlap between sum or asset P and sum or asset Q so far as it is just and reasonable to conclude that—

(a) they are the same sum of money or asset, or

(b) sum or asset P directly, or indirectly, represents sum or asset Q.

(5) In subsection (2)(b)—

(a) the reference to A includes a reference to any person linked with A, and

(b) the reference to a liability for income tax does not include a reference to a liability for income tax arising by reason of section 175 (benefit of taxable cheap loan treated as earnings).

554Z11C Earlier income tax liability: treatment of payments

(1) In this section—

(a) "the earlier charge" means so much of the earlier tax liability as relates to the overlap between sum or asset P and sum or asset Q, and

(b) "the Chapter 2 overlap charge" means so much of the Chapter 2 tax liability as relates to the overlap between sum or asset P and sum or asset Q.

(2) The amount of a tax liability that relates to the overlap between sum or asset P and sum or asset Q is to be determined on a just and reasonable basis.

(3) Subsection (4) applies where, after the relevant step is taken, an amount (the "earlier charge paid amount") is paid in respect of all or part of—

(a) the earlier charge, or

(b) any late payment interest in respect of the charge.

(4) An amount equal to the earlier charge paid amount is treated as a payment on account of—

(a) the Chapter 2 overlap charge, or

(b) if that charge has been paid in full, any late payment interest payable in respect of the charge.

(5) Except where subsection (10) applies, subsection (6) applies where an amount (the "Chapter 2 paid amount") is paid in respect of all or part of—

(a) the Chapter 2 overlap charge, or

(b) any late payment interest in respect of the charge.

(6) An amount equal to the Chapter 2 paid amount is treated as a payment on account of—

(a) the earlier charge, or

(b) if the earlier charge has been paid in full, any late payment interest payable in respect of the charge.

(7) Subsection (10) applies where—

(a) the condition in 554Z11B(2) is met because there is overlap between sum or asset P and each of two or more items within section 554Z11B(2)(b), and

(b) an amount (the "Chapter 2 aggregate paid amount") is paid in respect of all or part of—

(i) two or more relevant Chapter 2 overlap charges, or

(ii) any late payment interest in respect of any of those charges.

(8) In subsection (7)(b), "relevant Chapter 2 overlap charge" means so much of the Chapter 2 tax liability as relates to the overlap between sum or asset P and one of those items within section 554Z11B(2)(b).

(9) For the purposes of subsection (10)—

(a) in the case of each of those items, the "earlier charge" in respect of the overlap between sum or asset P and the item is so much of the liability mentioned in section 554Z11B(2)(b) in the case of the item as relates to the overlap, and

(b) the Chapter 2 aggregate paid amount is to be allocated, in such proportions as are just and reasonable in all the circumstances, between the earlier charges given by paragraph (a).

(10) The amount allocated to an earlier charge under subsection (9) is treated as a payment on account of—

(a) the earlier charge to which it is allocated, and

(b) if the earlier charge has been paid in full, any late payment interest payable in respect of the charge.

(11) In this section—

"late payment interest" means interest payable under—

(a) section 86 of TMA 1970,

(b) section 101 of FA 2009, or

(c) regulation 82 of the Income Tax (Pay As You Earn) Regulations 2003 (SI 2003/2682);

"Chapter 2 tax liability" means the liability for income tax arising by virtue of the application of Chapter 2 by reason of the relevant step.

554Z11D Earlier income tax liability: provisional payments of tax

(1) Subsection (2) applies for the purposes of—

(a) section 554Z11B(3)(a), and

(b) section 554Z11C(3), (4)(b), (7)(b) and (10)(b).

(2) A person is not to be regarded as having paid, or otherwise accounted for, any tax by reason only of making a provisional payment of tax, except in accordance with an application granted under section 554Z11E.

(3) In this Part, "provisional payment of tax" means—

(a) a payment on account of income tax,

(b) a payment that is treated as a payment on account under section 223(3) of FA 2014 (accelerated payments), or

(c) a payment pending determination of an appeal made in accordance with section 55 of TMA 1970.

(4) The reference in subsection (3)(a) to a payment on account of income tax does not include a reference to a payment treated under section 554Z11C as a payment on account of a tax liability.

554Z11E Application for provisional payments to be treated as payment of tax

(1) A person may make an application to Her Majesty's Revenue and Customs for a provisional payment of tax to be treated for the purposes of section 554Z11C as—

(a) an earlier charge paid amount,

(b) a Chapter 2 paid amount, or

(c) a Chapter 2 aggregate paid amount.

(2) Where an application under subsection (1) is granted, the provisional payment of tax to which it relates may not be repaid.

(3) An application for approval must be made in such form and manner, and contain such information, as may be specified by, or on behalf of, the Commissioners for Her Majesty's Revenue and Customs.

(4) An officer of Revenue and Customs must notify the applicant of the decision on an application.

554Z11F Provisional payments of tax: further provision

(1) This section applies in a case to which section 554Z11C applies (see section 554Z11B(1)).

(2) If a provisional payment of tax is made in respect of an earlier charge in relation to an overlap, it is to be treated as also being made in respect of the Chapter 2 overlap charge in relation to the overlap.

(3) If a provisional payment of tax is made in respect of a Chapter 2 overlap charge in relation to an overlap, it is to be treated as also being made in respect of the earlier charge in relation to the overlap.

(4) If section 554Z11C(10) applies in a case (see section 554Z11C(7)) and a provisional payment of tax is made in respect of two or more relevant Chapter 2 overlap charges—

(a) the amount of the provisional payment of tax is to be allocated, in such proportions as are just and reasonable in all the circumstances, between those relevant Chapter 2 overlap charges, and

(b) a provisional payment of tax, equal to the amount allocated to the relevant Chapter 2 overlap charge relating to any particular overlap, is to be treated as also being made in respect of the earlier charge given by section 554Z11C(9) in respect of that overlap.

(5) Subsection (6) applies if—

(a) the provisional payment of tax is repaid, and

(b) late payment interest on the earlier charge or the Chapter 2 overlap charge would have accrued during the relevant period if the provisional payment of tax had not been made.

(6) The late payment interest mentioned in subsection (5) is treated as having accrued as if the provisional payment of tax had not been made.

(7) For the purposes of subsection (5), the "relevant period" is the period beginning on the day on which the provisional payment of tax is made and ending with the day on which the repayment is made.

554Z11G Earlier income tax liability: supplementary provision

(1) This section applies in a case to which section 554Z11C applies (see section 554Z11B(1)).

(2) Subsection (3) applies where an employer is treated by virtue of section 687A or 695A as making a payment of income ("the notional payment") by reason of the value of the relevant step, of which sum or asset P is the subject, counting as employment income.

(3) The reference in section 222 (payments by employer on account of tax where deduction not possible) to the notional payment is to be treated as a reference to that payment reduced by an amount equal to so much of the sum of money or (as the case may be) the value of so much of the asset—

(a) as is within the overlap, and

(b) in relation to which an amount is treated under section 554Z11C as a payment on account of either the earlier charge or the Chapter 2 overlap charge.

(3) Subsection (4) applies for the purposes of sections 65(5)(b) and 70(3)(b) of the Inheritance Tax Act 1984 (tax relief for payments which are income of a person for income tax purposes etc).

(4) The value of the relevant step of which sum or asset P is the subject is to be treated as reduced by an amount equal to so much of the sum of money or (as the case may be) the value of so much of the asset—

(a) as is within the overlap, and

(b) in relation to which an amount is treated under section 554Z11C as a payment on account of either the earlier charge or the Chapter 2 overlap charge."

Amendments to Schedule 2 to FA 2011

12 (1) Paragraph 59 of Schedule 2 to FA 2011 (transitional provision relating to Part 7A of ITEPA 2003) is amended as follows.

(2) In sub-paragraph (1)(f), after "554Z4" insert "and 554Z6".

(3) In the opening words of sub-paragraph (2), after "554Z4" insert "and 554Z6".

Commencement

13 Subject to paragraphs 14 to 16, the amendments made by this Schedule to Part 7A of ITEPA 2003 have effect in relation to relevant steps taken on or after 6 April 2017.

14 Section 554RA of ITEPA 2003, inserted by paragraph 8 of this Schedule, has effect in relation to relevant steps taken on or after 9 December 2010.

15 (1) Paragraph 13 does not apply in relation to the amendment made by paragraph 11 of this Schedule (new sections 554Z11B to 554Z11G of ITEPA 2003).

(2) Sections 554Z11B to 554Z11D and 554Z11G of ITEPA 2003, inserted by paragraph 11 of this Schedule, have effect in relation to relevant steps taken on or after 6 April 2011.

(3) Where—

(a) a relevant step (the "early step") is taken on or after 9 December 2010 but before 6 April 2011, and

(b) Chapter 2 of Part 7A of ITEPA 2003 would have applied by reason of the early step had it been taken on or after 6 April 2011 but before 6 April 2017,

sections 554Z11B to 554Z11D and 554Z11G of ITEPA 2003 have effect in relation to the early step as they have effect in relation to relevant steps taken on or after 6 April 2011.

16 The amendments made by paragraph 12 of this Schedule to paragraph 59 of Schedule 2 to FA 2011 have effect in relation to chargeable steps (as defined in that paragraph) taken on or after 6 April 2017.

GENERAL NOTE

Schedule 6 is the latest stage in the seemingly never-ending battle between HMRC and the designers of arrangements intended to avoid an income tax charge on what is in essence employment income. The disguised remuneration legislation in ITEPA 2003 Pt 7A (which was enacted in FA 2011) was designed to prevent the use of third party vehicles, such as trusts, to avoid an income charge on earnings. While it has undoubtedly been partly successful it has not been without its problems and has been amended several times since it was originally introduced. These latest amendment are highly technical and attempt to plug some of the gaps which have been exploited by promoters. The new rules also introduce a new and comprehensive code for cases where multiple charges may arise on what is essentially the same funds. Previously there was no such comprehensive code, only a series of ad hoc measures which didn't deal with all situations which were actually found in practice.

The 2017 Finance Bill as introduced included a number of other measures relating to disguised remuneration, principally a charge on (virtually all) loans from third parties which were outstanding on 5 April 2019. Those measures were dropped as part of the wash up process following the dissolution of parliament. It is assumed that they will be reintroduced in a new parliament.

Introductory – Sch 6 para 1

Paragraph 1 introduces amendments to ITEPA 2003 Pt 7A.

Meaning of "relevant step" – Sch 6 para 2

The concept of the relevant step is central to ITEPA 2003 Pt 7A. Where a relevant step, which is widely defined, is taken an employment income charge arises. Paragraph 2 makes it clear that even though a step which has been taken would be a breach of trust or would be void under trust law it still constitutes a relevant step for Pt 7A purposes. This paragraph has been added because a number of people have argued that where a particular course of action has been taken in breach of trust it cannot therefore be a relevant step, even though the breach of trust may not actually have been repaired.

Loans: transferring, releasing or writing off – Sch 6 paras 3 to 7

Many disguised remuneration arrangements involve loans. The making of a loan by a third party is a relevant step under ITEPA 2003 s 554C(1)(a) because it is the payment of a sum of money. However, a number of schemes have been devised under which existing loans are assigned, transferred or written off, often involving tripartite arrangements between the employer, the employee and the trust. HMRC continues to challenge these arrangements but para 3 is intended to put the position beyond doubt.

Paragraph 3(2) inserts new ITEPA 2003 s 554C(1)(aa) and (ab). Section 554C(1)(aa) extends the definition of relevant step to situations where a third party acquires the right to receive payment of a sum of money or the transfer of an asset, where there is a connection between the acquisition of the right and the payment by way of a loan (or a transfer of assets) to a relevant person, broadly speaking the employee. This would apply, for example, where there is a swapping around of indebtedness between the employer, employee and the trust so that the individual ends up with cash and a debt to the trust but where there has not actually been a payment of a sum of money from the trust to the individual. Section 554C(1)(ab) is of more general application. Hitherto the writing off of a loan has not constituted a relevant step: such a write off may have had other tax consequences but did not give rise to a Pt 7A charge. This section now brings the write off of a loan made to a relevant person, including the write off of an indirect loan of the type covered in new s 554C(1)(aa) within the definition of a relevant step.

Paragraph 3(3) inserts new ITEPA 2003 s 554C(3A) to (3C). Section 554C(3A) extends the definition of a loan to include any form of credit or a payment purported to be made by way of a loan. Section 554C(3B) introduces new s 554C(3C). It specifies that it applies where a person (T) acquires from another person (L) – whether or not for consideration – the right to payment of the whole (or part) of the loan where T is the person liable to repay the loan, or the right to payment of a sum of money or to a transfer of assets where T is the person liable to pay the sum or transfer the assets. Section 554C(3C) states that where that condition is met L is to be treated as releasing the loan. It also extends to the write off of acquired rights of the sort dealt with under new sub-s (3B) above. Again this is designed to ensure that indirect arrangements, where indebtedness is released not by the original third party but by somebody else, are still caught.

Paragraph 4 is an important relieving provision. There is no general exemption for relevant steps taken after the employee's death. Currently there is an exemption for relevant steps under ITEPA 2003 s 554B, the earmarking charge. Section 554A(4) is amended to extend the exemption to releases of loans after death which would otherwise have constituted a relevant step under the new s 554C(1)(ab). This is an important exemption which will make it easier to unwind employee trust arrangements etc. after the death of a beneficiary.

Paragraph 5 inserts new ITEPA 2003 s 554OA. One of the many problems with the disguised remuneration regime is that many legitimate remuneration arrangements involve third parties. For example, if all employees of a group are employed by one company and benefits or loans are provided by another group company those benefits would, without special provisions, be caught by Pt 7A. Much of the existing Pt 7A is thus taken up with provisions which remove what would otherwise be an employment income charge. Every time there is an extension of the Pt 7A charge to deal with avoidance arrangements further such relieving measures have to be introduced to ensure that the new provisions don't create inadvertent tax problems. New ITEPA 2003 s 554OA is one such clause. It is designed to prevent a charge arising on a transfer of an employment related loan where there is a change of employer.

New ITEPA 2003 s 554OA

Subsection (1) sets out the conditions for the exemption to apply. Essentially the requirement is that there is a transfer of the right to receive repayment of an employment related loan below the s 180 threshold where the borrower is an employee, or prospective employee, of the person who is entitled to repayment of the loan. The exemption does not apply if there is a connection between the transfer of the loan and a tax avoidance arrangement.

Subsection (2) specifies that a loan is within the s 180 threshold where through the tax year the total amount outstanding on the loan (or on all employment-related loans from the same employer) is less than the threshold in s 180(2) (currently £10,000).

Subsection (3) defines the scope of new s 554OA(4). It applies where two or more employment related loans are made by the same employer and during the year a person acquires a repayment of an amount equal to the whole of part of the payment made by loan.

Subsection (4) states that when sub-s (3) above applies the amount transferred is to be treated as an amount outstanding for the purposes of testing the s 180(2) limit. This is to prevent the abuse of the s 554OA(1) exemption by making indirect transfers of loan obligations.

Subsection (5) imports existing definitions into these new provisions.

Paragraphs 6 and 7 are consequential drafting amendments.

Exclusions: relevant payments – Sch 6 para 8

Paragraph 8 inserts ITEPA 2003 s 554RA which ensures that most repayments of loans do not themselves trigger a relevant step.

New ITEPA 2003 s 554RA

Subsection (1) sets out the conditions for the exemption. It will apply where a person (i.e. the trust or other third party) has a right to the repayment of the principal of a loan and a sum of money is acquired by that person (or on his behalf) by way of repayment of that principal.

Subsection (2) states that the loan must have been made on or after 6 April 1999. The relevance of that date is not obvious. It was the intended cut-off date for the new loan charge referred to in the introduction to this commentary section but that charge has not been enacted.

Subsection (3) applies where the repayment sum is the subject of a relevant step under s 554B – in other words if the amount received by the trust etc. was immediately earmarked, or where the sole purpose of the repayment was the making of a relevant step under s 554C(1)(a) i.e. the payment of a sum of money.

Subsection (4) exempts the above relevant steps (and only those relevant steps) from an income tax charge if the repayment sum is held on the same basis as the repayment right was held immediately before the repayment.

Subsection (5) states that the sub-s (4) exemption does not apply where there is a connection – direct or indirect – between the repayment sum and a tax avoidance arrangement (other than the arrangement under which the loan was originally made).

This is not an easy section to follow as, on the face of it, it is difficult to envisage how the repayment of a loan could give rise to a Pt 7A charge. What is intended here is perhaps the situation where a loan has been made by a trust to an employee and the loan is repaid. If the trustees earmark the amount received for the benefit of that same employee when the loan is repaid there is no relevant step at that point. There would still be a relevant step if subsequently the funds are used in a way which triggers a Pt 7A charge.

Exclusions: payments in respect of a tax liability – Sch 6 para 9

Paragraph 9 introduces new ITEPA 2003 s 554XA which is intended to cover the situation where a payment is made to HMRC in satisfaction of a liability under Pt 7A. HMRC in its 5 December 2016 consultation response said that it was unlikely that a charge would occur when making a payment to HMRC but wanted to put the position beyond doubt to ensure that there were no legislative uncertainties which would prevent settlement.

New ITEPA 2003 s 554XA

Subsection (1) sets out the basic exclusions. They apply where the relevant step is a relevant tax payment or a payment which is not itself a relevant tax payment but is used for the purpose of allowing the recipient to make a relevant tax payment. In this latter case the person must use the whole of the amount in making a relevant tax payment and must do so within 60 days of receiving the payment from the third party.

Subsection (2) defines a relevant tax payment as a payment to HMRC in respect of a liability to income tax, inheritance tax, NIC or corporation tax.

Subsection (3) states that a provisional payment of tax – i.e. a payment on account – is not a relevant tax payment. This means for example that if the trustees of an employee benefit trust (EBT) make a payment to an individual who then uses that money to make a payment on account to HMRC the exemption will not apply.

Subsection (4) says that a relevant liability is one which is made under a settlement for the discharge of a liability or by way of decision made by HMRC under an application under this new section. The liability must be linked to the Pt 7A arrangement itself. In other words relief will not be available if a payment is made by trustees to an individual to enable him or her to settle an unrelated liability.

Subsections (5)–(7) set out the mechanics of making an application to HMRC for relief under this section.

Double taxation – Sch 6 paras 10 and 11

One of the many issues which has arisen in practice with the disguised remuneration legislation is the potential for double charges. For example, an amount may be earmarked and later paid out: both of these are relevant steps. Equally HMRC may argue that there was a PAYE charge under the normal rules when an arrangement was set up and a Pt 7A charge when it structure is unwound. There may also be instances where payments on account have been made or payments made under accelerated payment notices and a subsequent liability arises. The existing legislation had some mechanisms to deal with these sorts of potential double charges but there was no comprehensive code and many problems arose in practice when negotiating settlements with HMRC. Paragraphs 10 and 11 thus introduce a wholly new code for dealing with interactions.

Paragraph 10 introduces new ITEPA 2003 s 554Z5.

New ITEPA 2003 s 554Z5 – Overlap with money or asset subject to earlier tax liability

This section applies if there is overlap between the sum or asset which is the subject of the relevant step and an earlier income tax liability which occurred by reference to an earlier sum or asset

It does not apply where the earlier liability arose because of a step taken within s 554B (typically the payment of a sum of money) taken before 6 April 2011 and the value of that relevant step was reduced by a FA 2011 Sch 2 para 59 credit. This provision is intended to cover steps taken during the transitional period from 9 December 2009, because the existing para 59 credit will cover any charges which arose on the subsequent relevant step.

Subsection (3) is an operative provision. The value of the relevant step is reduced (but not to a negative amount) by the amount of money or value of the asset which is within the overlap. Note that this relief is given in terms of the amount or value of the step. This contrasts with relief under s 554Z11B ff, which is given in terms of tax. For sub-s (3) to apply either the payment condition or the liability condition must be met.

Subsection (4) defines the payment condition. It is met where the earlier tax liability has become due and payable before the relevant step is taken and either the tax has been paid in full or payment terms have been agreed with HMRC.

Subsection (5) defines the liability condition. The liability condition is that terms have been agreed with HMRC for payment of that earlier liability. This would apply for example if a time-to-pay agreement had been entered into.

Subsection (6) defines the overlap. There is an overlap where it is reasonable to believe that the sum or asset giving rise to the earlier tax charge and the relevant step are the same, or one directly represents the other.

Subsection (7) deals with successive relevant steps. Subsection (8) below applies where the earlier tax liability was attributable to a relevant step and reductions were made to the value of the asset under this section.

Subsection (8) states that where sub-s (7) above applies the sum involved in the second relevant step is also treated as overlapping with the earlier step. The drafting here is particularly opaque, but the intention is that the principle that there are no double charges is maintained however many triggering events there might be.

Example

£1m is contributed to an EBT. It is accepted that this gives rise to a tax liability and tax is paid in full. The trustees then earmark £1m for the benefit of beneficiary. This is a relevant step and would normally give rise to a tax charge. But because tax was paid on the funds going into the EBT s 554Z5(3) reduces the value of that step to Nil. Subsequently £1m is loaned to the same individual by the trust. That is also a relevant step. But because it is attributable to the same underlying amount s 554Z5(3) continues to allow overlap and the value of this second relevant step is also reduced to Nil.

Subsection (9) is a definition provision. References to A include, as they do generally in Pt 7A, references to a person linked with A. References to a tax liability do not include references to the benefit in kind arising on a beneficial loan.

Subsection (10) is a consequential drafting amendment.

Subsection (11) makes it clear that for the purposes of sub-s 4(b)(i) a payment of tax does not include a payment on account, a payment under an accelerated payment notice or an amount of non-postponed tax paid pending an appeal. It is only tax which is finally and absolutely paid which will trigger the set off.

Paragraph 11 inserts new ITEPA 2003 ss 554Z11B to 554Z11G which, along with new s 554Z5, deal with potential double charges. Section 554Z5 covers situations where the tax has been paid on the earlier step. In such cases the *value* of the relevant step is reduced. These new sections (ss 554Z11B ff) deal with cases where tax has *not* been paid on the earlier step. In these cases relief is given by way of tax credit. The effect of this is that taxpayers do not gain an advantage where there is an increase in tax rates between steps.

New ITEPA 2003 s 554Z11B – Earlier income tax liability: application of s 554Z11C

Subsections (1) to (3) set out the conditions which must be met if the new s 554Z11C is to apply. The first condition is that there must be an overlap between the sum of money or asset which is the subject of the relevant step and a sum of money by reference to which person A became liable to income tax before the relevant step took place. The second condition is that an amount is payable by reference to the earlier tax liability but it has not been paid or accounted for and the person liable for the tax has not agreed terms with HMRC for the discharge or liability.

Subsection (4) provides that there is an overlap for the purposes of sub-s (2) above if it is reasonable to conclude that the two sums of money or assets are the same or the one directly or indirectly represents the other.

Subsection (5) provides that person A includes any person linked with A. The reference to a liability to income tax does not include a charge under the beneficial loan regime.

New ITEPA 2003 s 554Z11C – Earlier income tax liability: treatment of payments

This sets out the rule which allows set off of one payment against another.

Subsection (1) defines the terms. The "earlier charge" is the amount of the earlier tax liability which relates to the overlapping amounts. The Chapter 2 overlap charge is the liability under Pt 7A relating to the overlap amounts.

Subsection (2) provides that the liability which relates to the overlap is to be determined on a just and reasonable basis.

Subsection (3) introduces the conditions for offset under sub-s (4) to apply. It applies where the amount of tax and or late payment interest is paid in respect of the earlier charge.

Subsection (4) Where this condition is satisfied the amount paid (including any interest) is treated as a payment on account of the overlap charge. If that charge has been paid in full it is treated as a payment on account of interest due on the overlap charge.

Subsection (5) introduces the offset under sub-s (6). It applies, other than in cases dealt with under sub-s (10), where an amount of tax or interest is paid in respect of the relevant step (i.e. the Chapter 2 charge).

Subsection (6) states that where sub-s (5) above applies the amount (including interest) paid on the relevant step is treated as a payment on account of the earlier charge, or if that has been paid, interest on that charge.

Subsection (7) sets out the conditions under which sub-s (10) applies. It deals with cases where there is an overlap between the original charge and more than one charge under Pt 7A (or interest on those charges).

Subsection (8) is a definition provision.

Subsection (9) sets out a mechanism for dealing with the overlap between multiple Pt 7A charges. It requires a just and reasonable basis of apportionment.

Subsection (10) provides that any amount so apportioned is treated as a payment on account of the earlier charge to which is it allocated and, if that charge has been paid in full, any late payment interest in relation to that charge.

Subsection (11) is a definition provision.

The effect of this section is that where there is a charge under Pt 7A (or more than one charge) and an earlier tax charge the payment of tax on one is treated as a payment on account of the other, regardless of the order in which the payments are made.

Example

£1m is put into an EBT in a year in which the marginal income tax rate is 40%. A relevant step involving that same amount is taken in a later year in which the marginal income tax rate is 45%. Interest on the earlier amount to the date of payment is £40,000. Interest on the later amount is £20,000. A payment of £440,000 is eventually made in respect of the earlier liability and interest. The tax and interest on the relevant step is £470,000 (£450,000 plus £20,000). The £440,000 tax and interest paid on the first charge is treated as a payment on account of the latter, with the result that a further £30,000 is due.

New ITEPA 2003 s 554Z11D – Earlier income tax liability: provisional payments of tax

Subsection (1) introduces the section.

Subsection (2) sets out the rule that it is only final payments of tax which can be taken into account for the purposes of the offsets in ss 554Z11B and C. It states that a provisional payment of tax cannot be taken into account except where s 554Z11E applies.

Subsection (3) defines a provisional payment of tax as a payment on account of income, a payment under an accelerated payment notice or a payment of non-postponed tax pending an appeal.

Subsection (4) states that a payment on account of income tax does not include a payment treated under s 554Z11C as a payment on account of a tax liability. This exclusion is necessary because otherwise the credit offset within s 554Z11C would not operate properly.

New ITEPA 2003 s 554Z11E – Application for provisional payments to be treated as payment of tax

Subsection (1) allows a person to make an application to HMRC to treat a provisional payment of tax to be treated as a payment for the purposes of s 554Z11C.

Subsection (2) states that if the application is granted the provisional payment of tax cannot be repaid.

Subsection (3) states that an application must be made to HMRC in a form and manner to be specified by HMRC.

Subsection (4) says that an officer of HMRC must notify the applicant of the decision.

This section is an administrative convenience. Without it a person who had made a payment on account which he or she wanted to treat as a final payment would have to request repayment of the payment on account and then pay the same amount back to HMRC as a final payment. Under this provision there is no need to move the money round in a circle.

New ITEPA 2003 s 554Z11F – Provisional payments of tax: further provisions

Subsection (1) deals with cases within s 554Z11C (overlapping charges).

Subsection (2) states that a provisional payment of tax made in respect of an earlier overlap charge is also treated as being made in respect of the overlapping Pt 7A charge.

Subsection (3) is the mirror image of sub-s (2) above. A provisional payment of tax made in respect of a Pt 7A charge is also treated a being made in respect of the overlapping earlier charge.

Subsection (4) applies the same principle where there is more than one overlapping Pt 7A charge.

Subsection (5) introduces sub-s (6) which deals with interest. It applies where a provisional payment of tax is repaid and late payment interest on any of the overlapping charges would have accrued had the provisional payment not been made.

Subsection (6) provides that where sub-s (5) above applies the later payment interest mentioned in that section is treated as having accrued as if the provisional payment had not been made. This ensures that interest remains payable.

Subsection (7) says that the interest for the purposes of sub-s (5) is interest from the period when the provisional payment of tax is made and ending on the day on which the repayment was made.

New ITEPA 2003 s 554Z11G – Earlier income tax liability: supplementary provision

Subsection (1) states that the section applies in cases where s 554C11C (overlapping charges) applies.

Subsection (2) provides that sub-s (3) below applies where the employer is treated as making a notional payment of income under ss 687A or 695A because the value of the relevant step counts as employment income.

Subsection (3) treats the notional payment above as reduced by any amount within the overlap which is treated as a payment on account under s 554Z11C. This is a relieving mechanism which ensures that the system of tax credits continues to apply where the Pt 7A charge triggers a notional payment. Without this section a double charge could still occur, i.e. tax on the original payment and tax on the amount treated as a payment under s 222.

[*NB: at this point something seems to have gone wrong with the numbering of the Act as there are two sub-s (3s)*]

Subsection (3) (again) deals with the interaction with the inheritance tax relief under IHTA 1984 ss 65(5)(b) and 70(3)(b) for payment which are taxable income.

Subsection (4) provides that the value of the relevant step to which a person is subject is to be treated for IHT purposes only as reduced by the sum of money or value which is within the overlap and which is treated under s 554Z11C as a payment on account of another charge. The effect of this rule is to prevent double relief from IHT. Otherwise both the original amount charged to tax and the amount charged as a relevant step would qualify for IHT relief even though income tax would only be paid on one of those amounts.

Amendments to Schedule 2 to FA 2011 – Sch 6 para 12
Subparagraphs (1) to (3) include minor drafting amendments.

Commencement – Sch 6 paras 13–16
Paragraph 13 The amendments to Pt 7A have effect in relation to relevant steps taken on or after 6 April 2017. This is subject to the exceptions below.

Paragraph 14 New ITEPA 2003 s 554RA (loan repayments) applies to relevant steps taken on or after 9 December 2010. This is retrospective legislation but the provision is a relieving measure and is therefore unobjectionable.

Paragraph 15(1): The 6 April 2017 commencement date does not apply to the amendments made in para 11 (i.e. new ss 554Z11B to S554Z11G)

Sub-para (2): New ITEPA 2003 ss 554Z11B to D and s 554Z11G apply to relevant steps taken on or after 6 April 2011.

Sub-para (3): Where a relevant step (the early step) is taken on or after 9 December 2010 but before 6 April 2011 (i.e. during the anti-forestalling period) and Pt 7A would have applied had the step been taken on or after 6 April 2011 but before April 2017, ss 554Z11B to D and s 554Z11G have effect in relation to the early step as they have to steps taken on or after 6 April 2011. This is to ensure that the new provisions apply properly to relevant steps and resulting charges occurring during the anti-forestalling period.

Paragraph 16 The amendments in para 12 of this schedule (drafting amendments to FA 2011 Sch 2 para 59) apply to chargeable steps taken on or after 6 April 2017.

SCHEDULE 7
VAT: ZERO-RATING OF ADAPTED MOTOR VEHICLES ETC
Section 16

Adaptation of a qualifying motor vehicle

1 (1) In Schedule 8 to VATA 1994 (zero-rating), Group 12 (drugs, medicines, aids for the handicapped etc) is amended as follows.

(2) For item 2A substitute—

"**2A** (1) The supply of a motor vehicle (other than a motor vehicle capable of carrying more than 12 persons including the driver) to a person ("P") if—

    (a) the motor vehicle is a qualifying motor vehicle by virtue of paragraph (2) or (3),

    (b) P is a disabled person to whom paragraph (4) applies, and

    (c) the vehicle is supplied for domestic or P's personal use.

(2) A motor vehicle is a "qualifying motor vehicle" by virtue of this paragraph if it is designed to enable a person to whom paragraph (4) applies to travel in it.

(3) A motor vehicle is a "qualifying motor vehicle" by virtue of this paragraph if—

    (a) it has been substantially and permanently adapted to enable a person to whom paragraph (4) applies to travel in it, and

    (b) the adaptation is necessary to enable P to travel in it.

(4) This paragraph applies to a disabled person—

    (a) who usually uses a wheelchair, or

    (b) who is usually carried on a stretcher.

2B (1) The supply of a qualifying motor vehicle (other than a motor vehicle capable of carrying more than 12 persons including the driver) to a charity for making available, by sale or otherwise to a person to whom paragraph (3) applies, for domestic or the person's personal use.

(2) A motor vehicle is a "qualifying motor vehicle" for the purposes of this item if it is designed or substantially and permanently adapted to enable a disabled person to whom paragraph (3) applies to travel in it.

(3) This paragraph applies to a disabled person—

(a) who usually uses a wheelchair, or
(b) who is usually carried on a stretcher."

Three year rule, reporting and certification

2 In Schedule 8 to VATA 1994, in Group 12—

(a) omit Note (5L), and
(b) before Note (6) insert—

"(5M) For the purposes of Notes (5N) to (5S), the supply of a motor vehicle is a "relevant supply" if it is a supply of goods (which is made in the United Kingdom).

(5N) In the case of a relevant supply of a motor vehicle to a disabled person ("the new supply"), items 2(f) and 2A do not apply if, in the period of 3 years ending with the day on which the motor vehicle is made available to the disabled person—

(a) a reckonable zero-rated supply of another motor vehicle has been made to that person, or
(b) that person has made a reckonable zero-rated acquisition, or reckonable zero-rated importation, of another motor vehicle.

(5O) If a relevant supply of a motor vehicle is made to a disabled person and—

(a) any reckonable zero-rated supply of another motor vehicle has previously been made to the person, or
(b) any reckonable zero-rated acquisition or importation of another motor vehicle has previously been made by the person,

the reckonable zero-rated supply or (as the case may be) reckonable zero-rated importation or acquisition is treated for the purposes of Note (5N) as not having been made if either of the conditions in Note (5P) is met.

(5P) The conditions mentioned in Note (5O) are that—

(a) at the time of the new supply (see Note (5N)) the motor vehicle mentioned in Note (5O)(a) or (b) is unavailable for the disabled person's use because—

(i) it has been stolen, or
(ii) it has been destroyed or damaged beyond repair (accidentally, or otherwise in circumstances beyond the disabled person's control), or

(b) the Commissioners are satisfied that (at the time of the new supply) the motor vehicle mentioned in Note (5O)(a) or (b) has ceased to be suitable for the disabled person's use because of changes in the person's condition.

(5Q) In the case of a relevant supply of a motor vehicle to a disabled person, items 2(f) and 2A cannot apply unless the supplier—

(a) gives to the Commissioners, before the end of the period of 12 months beginning with the day on which the supply is made, any information and supporting documentary evidence that may be specified in a notice published by them, and
(b) in doing so complies with any requirements as to method set out in the notice.

(5R) In the case of a relevant supply of a motor vehicle to a disabled person, items 2(f) and 2A cannot apply unless, before the supply is made, the person making the supply has been given a certificate in the required form which—

(a) states that the supply will not fall within Note (5N), and
(b) sets out any other matters, and is accompanied by any supporting documentary evidence, that may be required under a notice published by the Commissioners for the purposes of this Note.

(5S) The information that may be required under Note (5Q)(a) includes—

(a) the name and address of the disabled person and details of the person's disability, and
(b) any other information that may be relevant for the purposes of that Note,

(and the matters that may be required under Note (5R)(b) include any information that may be required for the purposes of Note (5Q)).

(5T) In Notes (5N) to (5S)—

"in the required form" means complying with any requirements as to form that may be specified in a notice published by the Commissioners;

"reckonable zero-rated acquisition", in relation to a motor vehicle, means an acquisition of the vehicle from another member State in a case where—

(a) VAT is not chargeable on the acquisition as a result of item 2(f) or 2A, and

(b) the acquisition takes place on or after 1 April 2017;

"reckonable zero-rated importation", in relation to a motor vehicle, means an importation of the vehicle from a place outside the member States in a case where—

(a) VAT is not chargeable on the importation as a result of item 2(f) or 2A, and

(b) the importation takes place on or after 1 April 2017;

"reckonable zero-rated supply", in relation to a motor vehicle, means a supply of the vehicle which—

(a) is a supply of goods,

(b) is zero-rated as a result of item 2(f) or 2A, and

(c) is made on or after 1 April 2017.

(5U) In items 2A and 2B references to design, or adaptation, of a motor vehicle to enable a person (or a person of any description) to travel in it are to be read as including a reference to design or, as the case may be, adaptation of the motor vehicle to enable the person (or persons of that description) to drive it."

Penalty

3 (1) Section 62 of VATA 1994 (incorrect certificates as to zero-rating etc) is amended as follows.

(2) After subsection (1A) insert—

"(1B) Where—

(a) a person gives a certificate for the purposes of Note (5R) to Group 12 of Schedule 8 with respect to a supply of a motor vehicle, and

(b) the certificate is incorrect,

the person giving the certificate is to be liable to a penalty."

(3) In subsection (2), at the end insert—

"(c) in a case where it is imposed by virtue of subsection (1B), the difference between—

(i) the amount of the VAT which would have been chargeable on the supply if the certificate had been correct, and

(ii) the amount of VAT actually chargeable."

Minor amendments

4 Schedule 8 to VATA 1994 is amended as follows.

5 In Part 1 (index to zero-rated supplies of goods and services)—

(a) in the entry relating to Group 12, for "handicapped" substitute "disabled";

(b) in the entry relating to Group 4, for "handicapped" substitute "disabled".

6 In Group 4 (talking books for the blind and handicapped and wireless sets for the blind)—

(a) in item 1, for each occurrence of "handicapped" substitute "disabled";

(b) in the heading, for "handicapped" substitute "disabled".

7 In Group 12 (drugs, medicines, aids for the handicapped etc)—

(a) in items 2 to 19 and Notes (1) and (5B) to (9), for each occurrence of "handicapped" substitute "disabled";

(b) for Note (3) substitute—

"(3) Any person who is chronically sick or disabled is "disabled" for the purposes of this Group.";

(c) in the heading, for "handicapped," substitute "disabled,".

8 In Group 15 (charities etc)—

(a) in item 5 and Notes (1C) to (4A), (5A) and (5B), for "handicapped" substitute "disabled";

(b) for Note (5) substitute—

"(5) Any person who is chronically sick or disabled is "disabled" for the purposes of this Group."

Commencement

9 The amendments made by this Schedule have effect in relation to supplies made, and acquisitions and importations taking place, on or after 1 April 2017.

GENERAL NOTE

This measure fulfils the announcement made in the Autumn Statement 2012 that the legislation would be amended to reduce the amount of VAT fraud that is deemed to be taking place in relation to the zero-rated sale of motor vehicles for the use of disabled people. This includes both sales that are made privately to disabled people and also to charities which then make the vehicles available to a disabled person. The amendments took effect on 1 April 2017.

The amended legislation confirms that the buyer must be a disabled wheelchair or stretcher user and the vehicle must be for the person's personal or domestic use. In the case of sales to charities, the charity must make the vehicle available to a person that meets these conditions.

An important change is that a disabled person can only buy one vehicle at the zero-rate every three years, although there are sensible exceptions if the previous vehicle has been stolen or destroyed due to factors beyond the owner's control, or if there has been a change in the disability of the person which requires a vehicle with a different design.

To ensure compliance with the amended legislation, para 3 introduces a penalty charge for individuals who provide an incorrect certificate of eligibility.

SCHEDULE 8

SOFT DRINKS INDUSTRY LEVY: RECOVERY AND OVERPAYMENTS

Section 52

PART 1

RECOVERY

Recovery as debt due

1 Soft drinks industry levy is recoverable as a debt due to the Crown.

Assessments

2 (1) Sub-paragraph (2) applies where it appears to the Commissioners—

(a) that any period is an accounting period by reference to which a person is liable to account for soft drinks industry levy,

(b) that an amount of soft drinks industry levy for which that person is liable to account by reference to that period has become due (but the amount due cannot be ascertained), and

(c) that there has been a relevant default by the person (see sub-paragraph (3)).

(2) The Commissioners may—

(a) assess the amount of soft drinks industry levy due from the person to the best of their judgment, and

(b) notify the amount to the person.

(3) The following are "relevant defaults"—

(a) a failure to comply with a requirement of section 44 (notification of liability to register) or of regulations under section 48 (correction of the register);

(b) a failure to make a return required by regulations under section 52;

(c) a failure to keep documents, or provide facilities, necessary to verify returns required by those regulations;

(d) the making, in purported compliance with a requirement of the regulations, of an incomplete or incorrect return;

(e) a failure to comply with a requirement of regulations under section 53(1) (keeping and preserving records);

(f) an unreasonable delay in complying with a requirement, where the failure to comply would be a default within any of paragraphs (a) to (e).

3 (1) Sub-paragraph (2) applies where—

(a) the Commissioners have made an assessment for an accounting period as a result of a person's failure to make a return for that period,

(b) the levy assessed has been paid but no proper return has been made for that period, and

(c) as a result of a failure to make a return for a later accounting period, the Commissioners make another assessment (the "later assessment") under paragraph 2 in relation to the later period.

(2) The Commissioners may, if they consider it appropriate in the light of the absence of a return for the earlier period, specify in the later assessment an amount of soft drinks industry levy due that is greater than the amount that they would have considered to be appropriate had they had regard only to the later period.

4 (1) Sub-paragraph (2) applies where it appears to the Commissioners that—

(a) any period is an accounting period by reference to which a person is liable to account for soft drinks industry levy,

(b) an amount of soft drinks industry levy for which that person is liable to account by reference to that period has become due, and

(c) the amount due can be ascertained by the Commissioners.

(2) The Commissioners may—

(a) assess the amount of soft drinks industry levy due from the person, and

(b) notify the amount to the person.

Supplementary assessments

5 (1) Sub-paragraph (2) applies where—

(a) an assessment has been notified to a person under paragraph 2(2) or 4(2), and

(b) it appears to the Commissioners that the amount which ought to have been assessed as due exceeds the amount that has already been assessed.

(2) The Commissioners may—

(a) make a supplementary assessment of the amount of soft drinks industry levy due from the person to the best of their judgment, and

(b) notify the amount to that person.

Further provision about assessments under paragraphs 2, 4 and 5

6 (1) Where an amount has been assessed and notified to a person under paragraph 2, 4 or 5, it is recoverable on the basis that it is an amount of soft drinks industry levy due from that person.

(2) But sub-paragraph (1) does not have effect if, or to the extent that, the assessment has been withdrawn or reduced.

Time limits for assessments

7 (1) An assessment under paragraph 2, 4 or 5 may not be made after the end of the relevant period.

(2) Except in a case within sub-paragraph (3), the relevant period is the period of 4 years from the end of the accounting period to which the assessment relates.

(3) Where an assessment of an amount due from a person is made in a case involving loss of soft drinks industry levy—

(a) brought about deliberately by the person, or

(b) attributable to a failure by the person to comply with a requirement of section 44 (notification of liability to be registered) or a requirement of regulations under section 48 (correction of the register),

the relevant period is the period of 20 years from the end of the accounting period to which the assessment relates.

(4) In sub-paragraph (3)(a) the reference to loss brought about deliberately by a person includes a reference to a loss brought about as a result of the deliberate inaccuracy in a document given to HMRC by the person.

(5) In sub-paragraphs (3) and (4) references to a loss brought about by a person include references to a loss brought about by another person acting on behalf of that person.

PART 2

OVERPAYMENTS

Repayments of overpaid levy

8 (1) This paragraph applies where a person (P) has paid an amount to the Commissioners by way of soft drinks industry levy which was not levy due.

(2) The Commissioners are liable, on the making of a claim by P, to repay the amount.

(3) The Commissioners may by regulations make provision about—

(a) the form and manner of a claim;

(b) the information required in support of a claim.

(4) Except as provided by this paragraph, the Commissioners are not liable to repay any amount paid by way of soft drinks industry levy by reason of the fact that it was not levy due.

(5) This paragraph is subject to paragraph 9.

Supplementary provisions about repayment etc

9 (1) The Commissioners are not liable, on a claim for a repayment of soft drinks industry levy, to repay any amount paid more than 4 years before the making of the claim.

(2) It is a defence to any claim for repayment of an amount of soft drinks industry levy that the repayment of that amount would unjustly enrich the claimant.

10 (1) This paragraph applies where—

(a) an amount has been paid by way of soft drinks industry levy which (apart from paragraph 9(2)) would fall to be repaid to a person (P), and

(b) the whole or a part of the cost of the payment of that amount to the Commissioners has, for practical purposes, been borne by a person other than P.

(2) Where loss or damage has been, or may be, incurred by P as a result of mistaken assumptions made in P's case about the operation of any provision relating to soft drinks industry levy, that loss or damage is to be disregarded, except to the extent of the quantified amount, in the making of a relevant determination.

(3) In sub-paragraph (2) "the quantified amount" means the amount (if any) which is shown by P to constitute the amount that would appropriately compensate P for loss or damage shown by P to have resulted from the making of the mistaken assumptions.

(4) A "relevant determination" means a determination for the purposes of paragraph 9(2) as to—

(a) whether or to what extent the repayment of an amount would enrich P, or

(b) whether or to what extent an enrichment of P would be unjust.

(5) The reference in sub-paragraph (2) to provision relating to soft drinks industry levy is a reference to any provision made by or under any enactment which relates to the levy or to any matter connected with it.

Reimbursement arrangements

11 (1) The Commissioners may by regulations make provision for reimbursement arrangements to be disregarded for the purposes of paragraph 9(2) except where the arrangements—

(a) contain such provision as may be required by the regulations, and

(b) are supported by such undertakings to comply with the arrangements as may be required by the regulations to be given to the Commissioners.

(2) In this paragraph "reimbursement arrangements" means arrangements for the purposes of a claim to a repayment of soft drinks industry levy which—

(a) are made by a person for the purpose of securing that the person is not unjustly enriched by the repayment of any amount in pursuance of the claim, and

(b) provide for the reimbursement of a person who has for practical purposes borne the whole or any part of the cost of the original payment of that amount to the Commissioners.

(3) Regulations under this paragraph may include provision requiring reimbursement arrangements to contain provision—

(a) requiring a reimbursement for which the arrangements provide to be made within a specified period after the repayment to which it relates;

(b) for the repayment of amounts to the Commissioners where those amounts are not reimbursed in accordance with the arrangements;

(c) requiring interest paid by the Commissioners on any amount repaid by them to be treated in the same way as that amount for the purposes of any requirement under the arrangements to reimburse or repay the Commissioners;

(d) requiring records of a specified description relating to the arrangements to be kept and produced to the Commissioners, or to an officer of Revenue and Customs;

(e) imposing obligations on specified persons for the purposes of provision made under paragraphs (a) to (d).

(4) Regulations under this paragraph may—

(a) make provision about the form, manner and timing of undertakings given to the Commissioners in accordance with the regulations, and

(b) provide for those matters to be determined by the Commissioners in accordance with the regulations.

Assessment for excessive repayment

12 (1) Sub-paragraph (3) applies where—

(a) an amount has been paid at any time to a person by way of a repayment of soft drinks industry levy, and

(b) the amount paid exceeded the amount which the Commissioners were liable at that time to repay to that person.

(2) Sub-paragraph (3) also applies where a person is liable to pay any amount to the Commissioners in pursuance of an obligation imposed by regulations under paragraph 11(3)(b), (c) or (e).

(3) The Commissioners may—

(a) to the best of their judgment, assess the amount of the excess (in a case within sub-paragraph (1)) or the amount due (in a case within sub-paragraph (2)), and

(b) notify the amount to the person.

(4) Subject to sub-paragraph (5), where—

(a) an assessment is made on any person under this paragraph in respect of a repayment of soft drinks industry levy, and

(b) the Commissioners have power under Part 1 of this Schedule to make an assessment on that person as to an amount of the levy due from that person,

the assessments may be combined and notified to the person as one assessment.

(5) A notice of a combined assessment under sub-paragraph (4) must separately identify the amount being assessed in respect of repayments of soft drinks industry levy.

Supplementary assessments

13 (1) Sub-paragraph (2) applies where—

(a) an assessment has been notified to a person under paragraph 12, and

(b) it appears to the Commissioners that the amount which ought to have been assessed as due exceeds the amount that has already been assessed.

(2) The Commissioners may—

(a) on or before the last day on which the assessment under paragraph 12 could have been made, make a supplementary assessment of the amount of soft drinks industry levy due from the person, and

(b) notify the amount to that person.

Further provision about assessments under paragraphs 12 and 13

14 (1) Where an amount has been assessed and notified to a person under paragraph 12 or 13, it is recoverable on the basis that it is an amount of soft drinks industry levy due from that person.

(2) But sub-paragraph (1) does not have effect if, or to the extent that, the assessment has been withdrawn or reduced.

Time limits for assessments

15 An assessment under paragraph 12 or 13 may not be made more than 2 years after evidence of facts sufficient in the opinion of the Commissioners to justify making the assessment comes to their knowledge.

PART 3

FURTHER PROVISION ABOUT NOTICES ETC

Notifications to a person's representative

16 (1) A notice of an assessment under paragraph 2, 5, 12 or 13 given to a person's representative is to be treated for the purposes of this Schedule as a notice given to the person in relation to whom the representative acts.

(2) In sub-paragraph (1), "representative", in relation to a person, means—

(a) any of that person's personal representatives;

(b) that person's trustee in bankruptcy, interim or permanent trustee or liquidator;

(c) any person holding office as receiver in relation to that person or any of that person's property;

(d) any other person acting in a representative capacity in relation to that person.

Service of notices

17 A notice under this Schedule may be given to a person by sending it to that person by post, addressed to the person's last known address.

GENERAL NOTE

Schedule 8 Pt 1 sets out provisions relating to recovery of the soft drinks industry levy by HMRC. HMRC has the power to assess the amount of levy due from a taxpayer in various circumstances, including where the amount of the levy is unascertainable and where the amount of the levy is ascertainable, amongst other circumstances. If a taxpayer has failed to make a return for a previous period, HMRC may increase their assessment of the levy due for a later period if no accurate return for the prior period has yet been produced. The time limit for an assessment is four years from the end of the accounting period to which the assessment relates, except for loss of levy brought about deliberately by the taxpayer or attributable to a failure to by taxpayer to notify HMRC of its liability to be registered or to notify HMRC of relevant changes to enable HMRC to correct the register, in which case the time limit is 20 years.

Part 2 specifies how overpayments of the soft drinks industry levy should be handled. It contains provisions broadly similar to those in VATA 1994 ss 80, 80A and 80B dealing with the liability of HMRC to account for overpayments made by a taxpayer, and generally provide for a time limit of four years from the date of payment of the levy. These provisions also include similar provisions to the VAT provisions dealing with repayments in circumstances that would unjustly enrich the taxpayer. There are further provisions allowing HMRC to issue assessments reclaiming repayments for overpaid levy, which can be made within two years of HMRC receiving evidence of the facts that justify the repayment.

SCHEDULE 9
SOFT DRINKS INDUSTRY LEVY: REQUIREMENTS TO KEEP RECORDS ETC: PENALTIES

Section 53

PART 1
PENALTIES

Sections 48(2) and 53(1): requirements imposed by regulations

1 (1) A person who fails to comply with a requirement imposed by regulations under section 48(2) or 53(1)(a) is liable to a penalty.

(2) The amount of the penalty is equal to the relevant amount multiplied by the number of days on which the failure continues (up to a maximum of 100 days) or, if it is greater, to a penalty of £50.

(3) In relation to a failure by a person to comply with the requirement, the amount of the penalty is to be determined by reference to the number of occasions in the period of 2 years preceding the beginning of the failure on which the person has previously failed to comply with that requirement.

(4) But—

(a) a continuing failure to comply with a requirement is to be regarded as one occasion of failure occurring on the date on which the failure began;

(b) if the same omission gives rise to a failure to comply with more than one such requirement, it is to be regarded as the occasion of only one failure.

(5) The relevant amount is—

(a) if there has been no previous occasion of failure in the period mentioned in sub-paragraph (3), £5;

(b) if there has been only one such occasion in that period, £10; and

(c) in any other case, £15.

(6) A person who fails to comply with a requirement to preserve records imposed by regulations under section 53(1)(b) is liable to a penalty of £500.

(7) If by reason of conduct falling within sub-paragraph (1) or (6) a person is assessed to a penalty for a deliberate inaccuracy under Schedule 24 to FA 2007, that conduct does not also give rise to a penalty under this paragraph.

Section 53(2): requirements imposed by directions

2 (1) A person who fails to comply with a requirement imposed under section 53(2)(a) is liable to a penalty.

(2) The amount of the penalty is equal to £200 multiplied by the number of days on which the failure continues (up to a maximum of 30 days).

(3) A person who fails to comply with a requirement imposed under section 53(3)(b) is liable to a penalty of £500.

(4) If by reason of conduct falling within sub-paragraph (1) or (3) a person is assessed to a penalty for a deliberate inaccuracy under Schedule 24 to FA 2007, that conduct does not also give rise to a penalty under this paragraph.

Power to alter amounts specified in paragraphs 1 and 2

3 (1) If it appears to the Treasury that there has been a change in the value of money since the last relevant date, they may by regulations substitute for the sums specified in paragraph 1(2), (5)(a) to (c) and (6) and paragraph 2(2) and (3) such other sums as appear to them to be justified by the change.

(2) But regulations under sub-paragraph (1) may not apply to a failure which began before the date on which the regulations come into force.

(3) The "relevant date", in relation to a specified sum, means—

    (a) the date on which this Act is passed, and

    (b) each date on which the power conferred by sub-paragraph (1) has been exercised in relation to that sum.

Reasonable excuse

4 (1) A failure by any person to comply with any requirement mentioned in paragraph 1 or 2 does not give rise to a liability to a penalty under this Schedule if the person concerned satisfies—

    (a) the Commissioners, or

    (b) on appeal, a tribunal,

that there is a reasonable excuse for the failure.

(2) A failure for which there is a reasonable excuse is to be disregarded for the purposes of paragraph 1(5).

(3) For the purposes of this paragraph, in the case of a person (P)—

    (a) an insufficiency of funds is not a reasonable excuse unless attributable to events outside P's control;

    (b) where P relies on another person to do anything, that is not a reasonable excuse unless P took reasonable care to avoid the relevant failure;

    (c) where P had a reasonable excuse for the failure but the excuse has ceased, P is to be treated as having continued to have the excuse if the failure is remedied without unreasonable delay after the excuse ceased.

PART 2

ASSESSMENTS

Power to make assessments

5 (1) Where a person becomes liable for a penalty under this Schedule—

    (a) the Commissioners may assess the penalty, and

    (b) if they do so, they must notify the amount to that person.

(2) Where a person is liable to a penalty under paragraph 1 for failure to comply with a requirement imposed by regulations under section 48(2) or 53, no assessment of the penalty may be made under this paragraph unless—

    (a) the Commissioners have given the person written notice of the consequences of a continuing failure to comply with that requirement, and

    (b) the notice has been given during the period of 2 years preceding the assessment.

(3) A notice under sub-paragraph (1) must specify a date, being not later than the date of the notice, to which the amount of the penalty is calculated.

(4) If the penalty continues to accrue after that date, a further assessment or assessments may be made under this paragraph in respect of the accrued amounts.

(5) If, within such period as may be notified by the Commissioners to the person liable to a penalty, the failure to comply with a requirement imposed by regulations under section 48(2), or by regulations or a direction under 53, is remedied, it is to be treated as remedied on the date specified under sub-paragraph (3).

Supplementary assessments

6 (1) Sub-paragraph (2) applies where—

    (a) an assessment has been notified to a person under paragraph 5, and

    (b) it appears to the Commissioners that the amount which ought to have been assessed as due exceeds the amount that has already been assessed.

(2) The Commissioners may—

    (a) make a supplementary assessment of the amount due from the person, and

    (b) notify the amount to that person.

Further provision about assessments under this Schedule

7 (1) Where an amount has been assessed and notified to a person under paragraph 5 or 6, it is recoverable on the basis that it is an amount of soft drinks industry levy due from that person.

(2) But sub-paragraph (1) does not have effect if, or to the extent that, the assessment has been withdrawn or reduced.

Time limits for assessments

8 (1) An assessment under paragraph 5 may not be made after the end of the relevant period.

(2) Except in a case within sub-paragraph (3), the relevant period is the period of 4 years from the end of the accounting period to which the assessment relates.

(3) Where an assessment of an amount due from a person in a case involving loss of soft drinks industry levy—

   (a) brought about deliberately by the person, or
   (b) attributable to a failure by the person to comply with a requirement imposed by regulations under section 53 (records),

the relevant period is the period of 20 years from the end of the accounting period to which the assessment relates.

(4) In sub-paragraph (3)(a) the reference to loss brought about deliberately by a person includes a reference to a loss brought about as a result of the deliberate inaccuracy in a document given to HMRC by the person.

(5) In sub-paragraphs (3) and (4) references to a loss brought about by a person include references to a loss brought about by another person acting on behalf of that person.

Further provision about notices

9 (1) A notice of an assessment under paragraph 5 or 6 given to a person's representative is to be treated for the purposes of this Schedule as a notice given to the person in relation to whom the representative acts.

(2) In this paragraph "representative", in relation to a person, has the meaning given by paragraph 16(2) of Schedule 8.

10 A notice under this Schedule may be given to a person by sending it to that person by post, addressed to the person's last known address.

GENERAL NOTE

Schedule 9 Pt 1 sets out provisions relating to penalties. Penalties are imposed for failure to comply with the registration requirements of s 48(2) or the record-preservation requirements of s 53(1)(a). The penalty is at least £50 (but potentially higher depending on how long the failure continues and whether there have been other failures to comply with HMRC regulations under those sections). The penalty for failure to preserve specified records for up to six years as required under s 53(1)(b) is £500 and there may be further penalties for failure to comply with HMRC regulations relating to record keeping. HM Treasury have the authority to substitute any of the penalty amounts in light of inflation or deflation.

A person is not liable to pay a penalty if there is a reasonable excuse for the failure to update the register or maintain records, but a lack of funds is not considered a reasonable excuse.

Part 2 sets out provisions for the assessment of the penalties. Broadly, an assessment for a penalty due under Sch 9 must not be made more than four years after the end of the period to which it relates, except where a loss of levy was brought about deliberately by a person or by failure to maintain records in which case HMRC may make such an assessment up to 20 years from the end of the period to which it relates.

SCHEDULE 10

SOFT DRINKS INDUSTRY LEVY: APPEALS AND REVIEWS

Section 55

PART 1

APPEALABLE DECISIONS

Appealable decisions

1 A person may appeal against a decision of the Commissioners or an officer of Revenue and Customs in respect of any of the following matters—

(a) whether or not a person is liable to pay an amount of soft drinks industry levy;

(b) whether or not the Commissioners are liable to repay an amount to a person under paragraph 8(2) of Schedule 8 (overpaid levy);

(c) whether or not the repayment of an amount under that paragraph is excessive (see paragraph 12 of that Schedule);

(d) whether or not a person is liable to pay an amount to the Commissioners in pursuance of an obligation imposed by regulations under paragraph 11(3)(b), (c) or (e) of Schedule 8 (reimbursement arrangements);

(e) whether or not a person is liable to a penalty under paragraph 1(1) or (6) or 2(1) or (3) of Schedule 9 (requirements to keep records etc: penalties);

(f) the amount of soft drinks industry levy payable by a person;

(g) the amount that the Commissioners are liable to repay to a person under paragraph 8(2) of Schedule 8;

(h) where repayment of an amount under that paragraph is excessive, the amount of the excess;

(i) the amount that a person is liable to pay to the Commissioners in pursuance of an obligation imposed by regulations under paragraph 11(3)(b), (c) and (e) of Schedule 8;

(j) the amount of a penalty payable under paragraph 1(1) or (6) or 2(1) or (3) of Schedule 9;

(k) the determination of a dilution ratio under section 27(2)(b);

(l) the registration, or cancellation of registration, of a person under this Part for the purposes of soft drinks industry levy;

(m) the period by reference to which payments of soft drinks industry levy are to be made;

(n) a person's entitlement to a tax credit, the withdrawal of a tax credit, the amount of a tax credit or the period for which a tax credit is to be brought into account under regulations under section 39;

(o) the giving of a direction by the Commissioners under section 53(2) (keeping and preserving records).

PART 2

REVIEWS

Offer of review

2 (1) HMRC must offer a person (P) a review of a decision that has been notified to P if an appeal in respect of the decision may be brought under paragraph 1.

(2) The offer of the review must be made by notice given to P at the same time as the decision is notified to P.

(3) This paragraph does not apply to the notification of the conclusions of a review.

Right to require review

3 (1) Any person (other than P) who has the right of appeal under paragraph 1 against a decision may require HMRC to review that decision if that person has not appealed to the appeal tribunal.

(2) A notification that such a person requires a review must be made within 30 days of that person becoming aware of the decision.

Review by HMRC

4 (1) HMRC must review a decision if—

(a) they have offered a review of the decision under paragraph 2, and

(b) P notifies HMRC accepting the offer within 30 days from the date of the document containing the notification of the offer.

(2) But P may not notify acceptance of the offer if P has already appealed to the appeal tribunal under paragraph 1.

(3) HMRC must review a decision if a person other than P notifies them under paragraph 3.

(4) HMRC may not review a decision if P, or another person, has appealed to the appeal tribunal under paragraph 1 in respect of the decision.

Extensions of time

5 (1) If under paragraph 2 HMRC have offered P a review of a decision, HMRC may within the relevant period notify P that the relevant period is extended.

(2) If under paragraph 3 another person may require HMRC to review a matter, HMRC may within the relevant period notify the other person that the relevant period is extended.

(3) If notice is given the relevant period is extended to the end of 30 days from—

(a) the date of the notice, or

(b) any other date set out in the notice or a further notice.

(4) In this paragraph "relevant period" means—

(a) the period of 30 days referred to in—

(i) paragraph 4(1)(b) (in a case falling within sub-paragraph (1)), or

(ii) paragraph 3(2) (in a case falling within sub-paragraph (2)), or

(b) if notice has been given under sub-paragraph (1) or (2), that period as extended (or as most recently extended) in accordance with sub-paragraph (3).

Review out of time

6 (1) This paragraph applies if—

(a) HMRC have offered a review of a decision under paragraph 2 and P does not accept the offer within the time allowed under paragraph 4(1)(b) or 5(3), or

(b) a person who requires a review under paragraph 3 does not notify HMRC within the time allowed under that paragraph or paragraph 5(3).

(2) HMRC must review the decision under paragraph 4 if—

(a) after the time allowed, P, or the other person, notifies HMRC in writing requesting a review out of time,

(b) HMRC are satisfied that P, or the other person, had a reasonable excuse for not accepting the offer or requiring review within the time allowed, and

(c) HMRC are satisfied that P, or the other person, made the request without unreasonable delay after the excuse had ceased to apply.

(3) HMRC may not review a decision if P, or another person, has appealed to the appeal tribunal under paragraph 1 in respect of the decision.

Nature of review etc

7 (1) This paragraph applies if HMRC are required to undertake a review under paragraph 4 or 6.

(2) The nature and extent of the review are to be such as appear appropriate to HMRC in the circumstances.

(3) For the purposes of sub-paragraph (2), HMRC must, in particular, have regard to steps taken before the beginning of the review—

(a) by HMRC in reaching the decision, and

(b) by any person in seeking to resolve disagreement about the decision.

(4) The review must take account of any representations made by P, or the other person, at a stage which gives HMRC a reasonable opportunity to consider them.

(5) The review may conclude that the decision is to be—

(a) upheld,

(b) varied, or

(c) cancelled.

(6) HMRC must give P, or the other person, notice of the conclusions of the review and their reasoning within—

(a) a period of 45 days beginning with the relevant date, or

(b) such other period as HMRC and P, or the other person, may agree.

(7) In sub-paragraph (6) "relevant date" means—

(a) the date HMRC received P's notification accepting the offer of a review (in a case falling within paragraph 2), or

(b) the date HMRC received notification from another person requiring review (in a case falling within paragraph 3), or

(c) the date on which HMRC decided to undertake the review (in a case falling within paragraph 6).

(8) Where HMRC are required to undertake a review but do not give notice of the conclusions within the period specified in sub-paragraph (6), the review is to be treated as having concluded that the decision is upheld.

(9) If sub-paragraph (8) applies HMRC must notify P, or the other person, of the conclusion which the review is treated as having reached.

Service of notices

8 A notice under this Schedule may be given to a person by sending it to that person by post, addressed to the person's last known address.

PART 3

APPEALS

"Appeal tribunal"

9 In this Schedule "appeal tribunal" means the First-tier Tribunal or, where determined by or under Tribunal Procedure Rules, the Upper Tribunal.

Bringing of appeals

10 (1) An appeal under paragraph 1 is to be made to the appeal tribunal before—

(a) the end of the period of 30 days beginning with—

(i) in a case where P is the appellant, the date of the document notifying the decision to which the appeal relates, or

(ii) in a case where a person other than P is the appellant, the date that person becomes aware of the decision, or

(b) if later, the end of the relevant period (within the meaning of paragraph 5).

(2) But that is subject to sub-paragraphs (3) to (5).

(3) In a case where HMRC are required to undertake a review under paragraph 4—

(a) an appeal may not be made until the conclusion date, and

(b) any appeal is to be made within the period of 30 days beginning with the conclusion date.

(4) In a case where HMRC are requested to undertake a review by virtue of paragraph 6—

(a) an appeal may not be made to the appeal tribunal—

(i) unless HMRC have notified P, or the other person, as to whether or not a review will be undertaken, and

(ii) if HMRC have notified P, or the other person, that a review will be undertaken, until the conclusion date;

(b) any appeal where paragraph (a)(ii) applies is to be made within the period of 30 days beginning with the conclusion date;

(c) if HMRC have notified P, or the other person, that a review will not be undertaken, an appeal may be made only if the appeal tribunal gives permission to do so.

(5) In a case where paragraph 7(8) applies, an appeal may be made at any time from the end of the period specified in paragraph 7(6) to the date 30 days after the conclusion date.

(6) An appeal may be made after the end of the period specified in sub-paragraph (1), (3)(b), (4)(b) or (5) if the appeal tribunal gives permission to do so.

(7) In this paragraph "conclusion date" means the date of the document notifying the conclusions of the review.

Appeals: further provision

11 (1) An appeal relating to a decision that an amount of soft drinks industry levy is due from a person may not be considered by the appeal tribunal unless the amount which HMRC have determined to be due has been paid or deposited with them.

(2) In a case where the amount determined to be payable as soft drinks industry levy has not been paid or deposited an appeal may be considered—

(a) if HMRC are satisfied (on the application of the appellant), or

(b) if HMRC are not satisfied, the appeal tribunal decides,

that the requirement to pay or deposit the amount determined would cause the appellant to suffer hardship.

(3) Notwithstanding the provisions of sections 11 and 13 of the Tribunals, Courts and Enforcement Act 2007 (rights of appeal) the decision of the appeal tribunal as to the issue of hardship is final.

Determinations on appeal

12 On an appeal against a decision mentioned in paragraph 1(a) or (c) to (e), the appeal tribunal may affirm or cancel the decision.

13 On an appeal against a decision mentioned in paragraph 1(f) to (j), the appeal tribunal may—

(a) affirm the decision, or

(b) substitute for that decision another decision that the Commissioners had power to make.

14 Subject to paragraph 15, on an appeal against a decision mentioned in paragraph 1(b) or (k) to (o), the appeal tribunal may—

(a) affirm or cancel the decision;

(b) substitute for that decision another decision that the Commissioners, or (as the case may be) an officer of Revenue and Customs had power to make;

(c) vary the decision;

(d) direct that the decision, so far as it remains in force, is to cease to have effect from such time as the tribunal may direct;

(e) require HMRC to conduct a review, or a further review, of the decision.

15 (1) On an appeal against a decision mentioned in paragraph 1(k), (n) or (o), the appeal tribunal may allow the appeal only if it considers that—

(a) the Commissioners could not reasonably have been satisfied that there were grounds for the decision, or

(b) if information brought to the attention of the appeal tribunal had been available to the Commissioners at the time the decision was made, the Commissioners could not reasonably have been satisfied that there were grounds for the decision.

(2) Where sub-paragraph (1) applies in relation to a decision mentioned in paragraph 1(o) (giving of a direction), the direction has effect pending the determination of the appeal.

GENERAL NOTE

Schedule 10 Pt 1 provides that most decisions made by HMRC in relation to the soft drinks industry level are appealable, including whether or not a person is liable to pay the levy and the amount payable.

Part 2 contains provisions allowing a taxpayer to request an HMRC review of a decision before pursuing a formal appeal.

Part 3 contains provisions dealing with the time limits for an appeal to the tax tribunal (which is broadly within 30 days of the decision being notified to the relevant person or, if the appellant is not the person to whom the decision is notified, within 30 days of that person becoming aware of it, or later if permission is given by the tribunal). Importantly, the tribunal will not consider an appeal for a decision that an amount of soft drinks industry levy is due unless that full amount is paid to HMRC or deposited with them, unless HMRC or the tribunal consider such payment would cause hardship to the appellant. Depending on which decision is being appealed, the tribunal either has the power to affirm, cancel, substitute, vary or cease the decision.

SCHEDULE 11

SOFT DRINKS INDUSTRY LEVY: SUPPLEMENTARY AMENDMENTS

Section 56

HMRC powers to obtain information etc

1 (1) Schedule 36 to FA 2008 (powers to obtain information etc) is amended as follows.

(2) In paragraph 10 (power to inspect business premises etc), at the end insert—

"(5) In sub-paragraph (1), the reference to a person's tax position does not include a reference to a person's position as regards soft drinks industry levy."

(3) In paragraph 63(1) (meaning of "tax"), after paragraph (i) insert—

"(ia) soft drinks industry levy,".

Penalties: failure to notify etc

2 (1) Schedule 41 to FA 2008 (penalties: failure to notify etc) is amended as follows.

(2) In the Table in paragraph 1, after the entries relating to insurance premium tax, insert—

| "Soft drinks industry levy | Obligation under section 44 of FA 2017 (obligation to give notice of liability to be registered)." |

(3) In the heading before paragraph 4, at the end insert "etc".

(4) In paragraph 4, after sub-paragraph (1) insert—

"(1A) A penalty is payable by a person (P) where—

(a) after a charge to soft drinks industry levy has arisen in respect of chargeable soft drinks, P acquires possession of them or is concerned with carrying, removing, depositing, keeping or otherwise dealing with them, and

(b) at the time when P acquires possession of the chargeable soft drinks or is so concerned, a payment of soft drinks industry levy in respect of the chargeable soft drinks is due or payable and has not been paid."

(5) In that paragraph, in sub-paragraph (2)—

(a) for "sub-paragraph (1)" substitute "this paragraph";

(b) at the end insert—

"chargeable soft drinks" has the same meaning as in Part 2 of FA 2017.

(6) In paragraph 5(4), after "deferred" insert "or (as the case may be) chargeable soft drinks in respect of which a payment of soft drinks industry levy is due and payable and has not been paid".

(7) In paragraph 10, after "deferred" insert "or (as the case may be) chargeable soft drinks in respect of which a payment of soft drinks industry levy is due and payable and has not been paid".

(8) In paragraph 11(2)(d), after "deferred" insert "or (as the case may be) chargeable soft drinks in respect of which a payment of soft drinks industry levy is due and payable and has not been paid".

(9) In paragraph 21—

(a) in sub-paragraph (4), for "paragraph 4" substitute "paragraph 4(1)";

(b) after that sub-paragraph insert—

"(5) In paragraph 4(1A) the reference to P acquiring possession of, or being concerned in dealing with, chargeable soft drinks in respect of which a payment of soft drinks industry levy is payable but has not been paid includes a person who acts on P's behalf in doing so; but P is not liable to a penalty in respect of any action by P's agent where P satisfies HMRC or (on appeal) the First-tier Tribunal that P took reasonable care to avoid it."

Penalties: failure to comply with requirements relating to returns

3 In Schedule 24 to FA 2007 (penalties for errors), in the Table in paragraph 1, after the entry relating to the statement under section 1(1)(a) of the Petroleum Revenue Tax Act 1980, insert—

| "Soft drinks industry levy | Return under regulations under section 52 of FA 2017" |

4 (1) Schedule 55 to FA 2009 (penalty for failure to make returns etc) is amended in accordance with this paragraph.

(2) In paragraph 1(4), in the definition of "penalty date", for "13" substitute "13A".

(3) In the Table in paragraph 1, after item 13 insert—

| "13A | Soft drinks industry levy | Return under regulations under section 52 of FA 2017" |

(4) In subsections (2) and (4) of section 106 of FA 2009 (penalties for failure to make returns: commencement) references to Schedule 55 to that Act have effect as references to that Schedule as amended by this paragraph.

5 (1) Schedule 56 to FA 2009 (penalty for failure to make payments on time) is amended in accordance with this paragraph.

(2) In the Table in paragraph 1, after item 11 insert—

| "11ZA | Soft drinks industry levy | Amount payable under regulations under section 52 of FA 2017 or paragraphs 6 or 14 of Schedule 8 to that Act | The date determined by or under regulations under section 52 of FA 2017" |

(3) In subsections (2) and (4) of section 107 of FA 2009 (penalties for failure to pay tax) references to Schedule 56 to that Act have effect as references to that Schedule as amended by this paragraph.

6 (1) Schedule 23 to FA 2011 (data-gathering powers) is amended in accordance with this paragraph.

(2) After paragraph 24 insert—

"Chargeable soft drinks

24A (1) A person who is involved (in any capacity) in any of the following activities is a relevant data-holder—

(a) producing chargeable soft drinks;

(b) packaging chargeable soft drinks;

(c) carrying on a business involving the sale of chargeable soft drinks.

(2) For the purposes of sub-paragraph (1), "chargeable soft drinks", "producing" and "packaging" have the same meaning as in Part 2 of FA 2017."

(3) In paragraph 45(1) (meaning of "tax"), after paragraph (i) insert—

"(ia) soft drinks industry levy,".

Interest

7 In Schedule 53 to FA 2009 (late payment interest) after paragraph 11B insert—

"Soft drinks industry levy due from unregistered persons

11C (1) This paragraph applies where an amount of soft drinks industry levy is due from a person (P) in respect of a period during which P meets the liability condition (as defined for the purposes of section 46(2) of FA 2017) but was not registered.

(2) The late payment interest start date in respect of the amount is the date which would have been the late payment interest date in respect of that amount if P had been registered when P had first become liable to be registered."

GENERAL NOTE

The supplementary amendments set out in Sch 11 make a number of consequential changes to existing legislation as follows.

Paragraph 1 provides that HMRC's powers to inspect business premises under FA 2008 Sch 36 para 10 does not extend to checking the tax position regarding the soft drinks industry levy. However, for other purposes in that schedule references to "tax" should include the new levy.

Subparagraph 2(2) stipulates that breach of the obligation to give notice of liability to be registered for the soft drinks industry levy under s 44 gives rise to a penalty under FA 2008 Sch 41 para 1.

Subparagraph 2(4) provides that a person who acquires possession of chargeable soft drinks in respect of which there is outstanding levy to be paid will be required to pay a penalty by virtue of FA 2008 Sch 41 para 4, which puts the levy in a similar category to goods with unpaid excise duty.

By virtue of para 3 amending FA 2007 Sch 24 para 1, a penalty will be payable by a person that submits a return under s 52 that contains deliberate inaccuracies which lead to incorrect assessments of liability to tax. Paragraph 4 provides that a person who fails to submit a return altogether will be liable to a penalty by virtue of FA 2009 Sch 55 para 1.

Paragraph 5 provides that failure to pay soft drinks industry levy due under s 52 gives rise to a penalty under FA 2009 Sch 56 para 1.

Paragraph 6 renders a person who is involved in the production, packaging or sale of chargeable soft drinks a relevant data-holder for the purpose of FA 2011 Sch 23. HMRC may require such data-holders to provide relevant data as set out in Treasury regulations.

Paragraph 7 sets out that if an amount of soft drinks industry levy is due from a person that is not registered, the late payment interest start date for the purpose of FA 2009 s 101 will be deemed to be the date that would have applied if the person had been registered as required.

FINANCE (NO 2) ACT 2017

INTRODUCTION

Following the Government's "near-death experience" in June, we are now faced with the second Finance Act of the year, based on the second of three Finance Bills published in 2017.

This Act, the Finance (No 2) Act 2017, consists almost entirely of the measures originally appearing in the mammoth Finance Bill published on 20 March, which ran to the largest ever page total of 772, and dropped in the "wash-up" procedure to clear the decks for the dissolution of Parliament. Despite the fact that the first Finance Act was 155 pages in length, this Finance Act is almost as long (665 pages (excluding title and contents pages, comprising 72 sections and 18 Schedules) as the original.

One does wonder how long taxpayers and advisers can continue properly to absorb and understand the sheer volume of new and amended legislation that our legislators insist on producing.

In this Act, the "winners" in the sheer length stakes are the corporate loss provisions (145 pages), the corporate interest-restriction provisions (157 pages) and the deemed-domicile and associated provisions (a mere(!) 40 pages).

The Lords Bill, published on 1 November 2017 contains an unsatisfactorily high number of typographic errors of omission or commission, to which the reader's attention is drawn at the appropriate place in this Introduction.

Royal Assent was given on 16 November 2017.

PART 1 DIRECT TAXES

Income tax: employment and pensions

Section 1 amends ITEPA 2003 to introduce 6 July as the date immediately following the tax year in question by which employees must have made good all or part of the cost of benefits-in-kind in order for the taxable value of the benefit to be reduced accordingly. The existing variety of dates, and in some cases, the complete lack of a date, has been causing employers difficulty with real-time accounting for PAYE.

The benefits-in-kind in question and the sections (all of ITEPA 2003) affected are:

(1) non-cash vouchers (s 87);
(2) credit tokens (s 94);
(3) living accommodation costing £75,000 or less (s 105);
(4) living accommodation costing over £75,000 (s 106);
(5) private use of cars (s 144);
(6) car fuel (ss 151, 152);
(7) private use of van (s 158);
(8) van fuel (ss 162, 163);
(9) benefits treated as earnings (s 203).

The amendments made by s 1 have effect for calculating the charge to income tax for the tax year 2017/18 and subsequent years.

Section 2 alters the calculation of the benefit charge relating to ultra-low emission cars but only from the tax year 2020/21. Currently, the "appropriate percentage" for cars with an emissions figure below 50 g/km is 9%; is 13% for cars with emissions figures exceeding 50 g/km but not exceeding 75 g/km; and is 17% for cars with emissions figures exceeding 75 g/km but less than 95 g/km. However, these percentages are scheduled to increase both next year (2018/19) and the year after (2019/20). The equivalent percentages in 2019/20 will be 16%, 19% and 20%.

The amendments now made by s 2 will apply to cars with emissions figures of less than 75 g/km and for those cars with emissions figures above zero but not exceeding 50 g/km, there is to be a graduation based on the "electric range figure" of the car. This is defined (in ITEPA 2003 s 139(5) as prospectively amended) as the number of miles that is the equivalent of the number of kilometres which is the maximum distance the car can be driven in electric mode without recharging the battery. For cars with a zero emissions figure, the appropriate percentage is to be 2%.

It may be helpful to set out all the forthcoming changes in a table:

Emissions figure (g/km of CO_2)	Appropriate percentage			
	2017/18	*2018/19*	*2019/20*	*2020/21 et seq*
0	9	13	16	2
1 – 50 ER > 130	9	13	16	2
1 – 50 ER 70–129	9	13	16	5
1 – 50 ER 40–69	9	13	16	8
1 – 50 ER 30–39	9	13	16	12
1 – 5- ER < 30	9	13	16	14
51 – 54	13	16	19	15
55 – 59	13	16	19	16
60 – 64	13	16	19	17
65 – 69	13	16	19	18
70 – 74	13	16	19	19
75	13	16	19	formula
76 – 94	17	19	22	formula
95	18	20	23	formula

Notes

From 2020/21, emissions figures and electric-range figures are to be rounded down to the nearest whole number where the emissions figure is less than 75. Before 2020/21, rounding takes place only for cars with emissions figures of 95 g/km and more, and then down to the nearest multiple of five. The emissions figures in the table need to be interpreted in that light.

"Formula" means the appropriate percentage is the smaller of (a) 37 and (b) 20 plus one percentage point for each 5 g/km by which the emissions figure exceeds 75.

Section 2 also amends ITEPA 2003 s 140, which sets the appropriate percentage for cars without a CO_2 emissions figure and registered after 31 December 1997, with effect from 2020/21. The appropriate percentage for cars with a cylinder capacity of 1400 or less is to increase from 23% to 24% and that for cars with a cylinder capacity more than 1400 but not exceeding 2000 is to increase from 34% to 35%. However, the appropriate percentage for such cars that have zero emissions is to be reduced from 16% to 2%. The 2017/18 values for these cars are 18%, 29% and 9%, respectively. Parallel amendments are made to ITEPA 2003 s 141, which deals with cars registered before 1 January 1998.

Section 3 replaces the current exemption from the benefits charge contained in SI 2002/205 reg 5, and which applies to pensions advice and information provided to employees, with a broader and more generous exemption. The current exemption is capped at £150 per tax year. This regulation is to be revoked.

The new exemption, contained in new ITEPA 2003 s 308C, extends to "relevant pensions advice" either provided to a current, former or prospective employee or to the payment or reimbursement of costs incurred by a current, former or prospective employee in obtaining such advice.

"Relevant pensions advice" is information or advice in connection with such a person's pension arrangements or the use of the person's pension funds. One of two conditions, A or B, must be met, however. Condition A is that the advice is provided or related to all the employer's employees generally or to all employees generally at a particular location. Condition B is that the advice is provided or relates to all employees generally or to all employees generally at a particular location who are within five years of their relevant pension age or suffer from the relevant degree of ill health.

The new exemption is capped at £500 per tax year, and applies from the tax year 2017/18.

Section 4 extends the deduction available to employees for costs or expenses relating to legal advice or indemnity assurance. Under ITEPA 2003 s 346, an employee may claim a deduction for any of three related expenditures. Case A relates to payments in full or partial discharge of liabilities related to the employment. Case B relates to payment of costs or expenses in connection with a claim (or allegation) that the employee is subject to an employment-related liability or in connection with legal proceedings arising from such an allegation. Case C relates to indemnity-insurance premiums in connection to A or B.

Two further cases in which the deduction may be claimed are now added. Case BA covers costs incurred when an employee is required to give employment-related evidence in proceedings or investigations whether or not involving the employee. Case BB covers costs and expenses in connection with other proceedings or investigations related to the employment. Reasonably broad definitions of what constitutes giving evidence, proceedings etc are inserted as new ITEPA 2003 s 346(4).

The definition of eligible indemnity insurance in ITEPA 2003 s 349(2) is extended to include contracts covering costs and expenses related to the giving of evidence etc in matters related to the employment but not necessarily involving the employee's liability.

The charge to tax under ITEPA 2003 Part 6 Chapter 3 on termination payments exceeding £30,000 does not apply, by virtue of ITEPA 2003 s 409, to payments and benefits in respect of employee liabilities and indemnity insurance. The extent of the exception is limited by direct reference to the deduction available under ITEPA 2003 s 346. Accordingly, this also is now extended to include payments not only by the individual but also by the employer or former employer on the individual's behalf. A similar amendment is made to ITEPA 2003 s 410, which provides a similar exception for payments by personal representatives of a deceased employee, in order to include payments by the former employer on behalf of the personal representatives.

Finally, ITEPA 2003 ss 558 and 560 are amended to allow former employees to claim the new deductions now available under ITEPA 2003 s 346.

All amendments made by s 4 have effect from the 2017/18 tax year.

Section 5 restricts the scope of the £30,000 exemption for termination payments, principally by excluding an amount referred to as "post-employment notice pay" from the exemption. It does so by adding new ITEPA 2003 ss 402A–402E and 404B and making consequential amendments.

New ITEPA 2003 s 402A provides that payments and other benefits received in connection with the termination of an employment (now to be referred to as "termination awards") may be split between amounts not benefiting under ITEPA 2003 s 403 from the £30,000 exemption ("the threshold"), to which new ITEPA 2003 s 402B applies, and amounts that do so benefit. Awards made in connection with a change in duties or a change in earnings continue to benefit in full from the threshold under ITEPA 2003 s 403.

New ITEPA 2003 s 402B provides that amounts of a termination award that do not benefit from the threshold are to be treated as constituting part of the employee's general earnings and thus chargeable to income tax in full. It also disapplies the rule in ITEPA 2003 s 403(3) determining the time when benefits are received to those elements of an award to which new ITEPA 2003 s 402B applies.

New ITEPA 2003 s 402C provides that new ITEPA 2003 s 402B is not to apply to redundancy payments or approved contractual payments (as defined in ITEPA 2003 s 309) not exceeding the amount of redundancy payments that would otherwise have been payable; i.e. these payments are not to be treated as general earnings. The remainder of the termination award is referred to as the "relevant termination award". The section also introduces the concept of "post-employment notice pay" (abbreviated here to "PENP") as that element of the termination award that is to be taxable, and provides that where PENP is equal to or greater than the amount of the termination award, all of the relevant termination award is subject to new ITEPA 2003 s 402B and is taxable in full as general earnings.

New ITEPA 2003 s 402D prescribes how PENP is to be calculated. In respect of any termination, PENP is given by the formula:

$$PENP = \left(\frac{BP \times D}{P}\right) - T$$

where BP is the employee's basic pay from the employment in respect of the last pay period to end before the "trigger date", P is the number of days in that pay period, D is the number of days in the "post-employment notice period", and T is the total amount of the award that is otherwise chargeable to tax, is already taxable as earnings under ITEPA 2003 s 62, is not pay in lieu of pre-termination holiday entitlement and is not a termination bonus. The "trigger date" is defined in new ITEPA 2003 s 402E is the last day of the employment, unless either the employee or employer has given notice of termination to the other, in which case it is the day the notice is given. The "post-employment notice period", also defined in new ITEPA 2003 s 402E, is the period beginning at the end of the last day of the employment and ending with the earliest lawful termination date. This in turn is the last day of the period that is equal in length to the minimum notice (the minimum notice period that the employer must give to terminate the employment) and begins at the end of the trigger date. If the earliest lawful termination date falls no later than the last day of the employment, D (the number of days in the post-employment notice period) is taken to be nil. Consequently, PENP is also nil. Thus there is only a taxable element of the termination award not benefiting from the £30,000 threshold if the last day of the employment precedes the earliest lawful termination date. New ITEPA 2003 s 402D also provides a special definition of BP, P and D where there is no pay period that ends before the trigger date, defines "minimum notice" where the last pay period to end before the trigger date is a month, and defines "basic pay" for the purposes of the PENP formula.

New ITEPA 2003 s 402E provides the definitions already discussed and adapts the provisions for limited-term contracts.

New ITEPA 2003 s 404B confers on the Treasury the power to vary the £30,000 threshold by regulation.

Section 6 paves the way for the introduction of automated PAYE settlement agreements by the simple expedient of removing the requirement for agreements to be made with an "officer of Revenue and Customs". With effect from the tax year 2018/19, they are to be made with HMRC generally.

Section 7 reduces the money-purchase annual allowance (MPAA) from £10,000 to £4,000, with effect from the tax year 2017/18. The MPAA is the maximum amount an individual may contribute while benefiting from tax relief in any tax year to a money-purchase (defined-contribution) pension scheme if he has already "flexibly accessed" that scheme by withdrawals from the scheme fund.

Income tax: investments

Section 8 reduces the amount of the dividend nil-rate band from £5,000 to £2,000, with effect from the tax year 2018/19. The dividend nil-rate was introduced by FA 2016 and charges a nil rate of income tax on the specified amount of an individual's dividend income.

Section 9 introduces a measure of relief for individuals to whom strict application of the rules of ITTOIA 2005 s 507 for calculating gains on the part surrender or part assignment of chargeable life-insurance policies would result in a wholly disproportionate charge to tax. It follows a review announced in Budget 2016 after the *Lobler* case ([2015] UKUT 152), in which the taxpayer had faced an effective tax rate of 779%.

New ITTOIA 2005 s 507A, inserted by s 9(2), provides that a taxpayer may apply to HMRC for a review of a calculation under ITTOIA 2005 s 507 where the result of that calculation would be a gain that was "wholly disproportionate". The application must be made in writing no later than four years after the end of the tax year in which the gain arose (or later, if HMRC agree). When considering whether a gain is wholly disproportionate, HMRC may take into account, inter alia and apart from the gain itself, the economic gain on the rights surrendered or assigned, the amount of premiums paid and the amount of tax that would be chargeable if the gain were not recalculated. If HMRC decide that the gain was indeed wholly disproportionate, the gain is to be recalculated on a just and reasonable basis, and any necessary adjustments and repayments of income tax made.

New ITTOIA 2005 s 512A, inserted by s 9(3), allows for a parallel application where a wholly disproportionate gain has been calculated under ITTOIA 2005 s 511 and not under ITTOIA 2005 s 507. The calculation under ITTOIA 2005 s 511 occurs where there has either been a part-assignment for money or money's worth in the insurance year or a part-surrender for money or money's worth followed by an assignment otherwise than for money's worth in the same insurance year. Where there is more than one person affected, they must all make the application for a recalculation.

An amendment is also made to ITTOIA 2005 s 538 to require individuals who have recovered tax from trustees and then succeed in a recalculation application to repay the trustees the appropriate amount.

The amendments made by s 9 have effect from 16 November 2017 but apply to amounts recovered from trustees before as well as after that date.

Section 10 paves the way for a degree of flexibility in the types of property that an individual may select as investments held by his life-insurance policy without its thereby being treated as a personal portfolio bond. Currently, the permitted types of property are listed in the Table in ITTOIA 2005 s 520(2). Section 10 confers on the Treasury the power to amend the Table and make any consequential amendments by regulations.

Section 11 modifies the no pre-arranged exits requirement for EIS and SEIS investments to allow for the issue of shares convertible to another class or share exchanges by way of acquisition. ITA 2007 s 177(1)(a) (for the EIS) and ITA 2007 s 257CD(1)(a) (for the SEIS) currently exclude from qualification investments in shares for which the issue arrangements include "arrangements with a view to the subsequent repurchase, exchange or other disposal of those shares or of other shares in or securities of the issuing company". With effect for share issues after 4 December 2016, new substituted ITA 2007 s 177(2) and ITA 2007 s 257CD(2) clarify that such arrangements are not to include exchanges of shares or of shares and securities in the course of an acquisition of the issuing company (as defined in ITA 2007 s 247(1) or ITA 2007 s 257HB(1)) or arrangements for exchanges or conversions of the issued shares for or to shares of a different class.

Section 12 allows a parent company to receive a measure of follow-on funding from a VCT (venture capital trust) in prescribed circumstances. Where there is an HMRC-approved reconstruction under ITA 2007 s 326, in which a new company acquires an old company by a proportionate share-for-share exchange, new ITA 2007 s 327A, as inserted by s 12(3), provides how the permitted maximum-age condition under ITA 2007 s 280C and the permitted company-age requirement under ITA 2007 s 294A may be satisfied to enable the new company to receive VCT funding on the basis of the old company's funding history. Under ITA 2007 s 280C, a VCT investment made in a company after the "initial investing period" breaches the permitted maximum-age limits unless one of three conditions, A, B or C, is met. The initial investing period is seven years (10 years in the case of a knowledge-intensive company) from the company's first commercial sale. Condition A is met if a qualifying ("relevant") investment has already been made in the company during the initial investing period and some or all of the money raised by that investment was employed for the purposes of the same activities as the money raised by the new investment. Condition B is met if the sum of the amount of the new investment and the total amount of any other qualifying investments in a 30 consecutive-day period including the date of the new investment is at least 50% of the company's average turnover amount and the money raised by all these investments is employed for the purposes of entering a new product or geographical market. Condition C is met if condition B was previously met in respect of an investment and some or all of the money raised by the investment or investments was employed for the purposes of the same activities as the money raised by the new investment. Parallel conditions are prescribed for meeting the company-age requirement, which applies to share issues after the initial investing period.

New ITA 2007 s 327A(2) provides that if a VCT investment is made in the new company, the reference in condition A to the need for an investment in the initial investing period is to be taken to include references to qualifying investments made in the old company before the end of the initial investing period. With regard to condition C, references to qualifying investments made in the new company are to be taken as including qualifying investments made in the old company before the acquisition. New ITA 2007 s 327A(3) makes the same provision in respect of the company-age requirement in ITA 2007 s 294A.

The amendments made by s 12 have effect in relation to investments made or share issues made after 5 April 2017.

Section 13 also concerns the VCT scheme. Where a reorganisation by way of an exchange of shares takes place for genuine commercial reasons but some of the new shares or securities are non-qualifying (i.e. they do not meet the requirements stipulated for continuation of VCT relief), ITA 2007 s 330 enables the Treasury to make regulations to provide that those requirements are nevertheless to be regarded as met in specific situations. ITA 2007 s 330 is now amended to extend the regulation-making power to exchanges where the old shares or securities, as well as the new shares and securities, are non-qualifying.

Section 14 introduces Sch 1, which makes changes to the Social Investment Tax Relief (SITR) scheme (the legislation for which is found in ITA 2007 Part 5B (ss 257J–257TE)).

Schedule 1 consists of three Parts. Part 1 (paras 1–10) contains the main amendments to the SITR provisions; Part 2 (paras 11–13) makes consequential amendments and Part 3 (paras 14–16) provides for commencement.

Paragraph 1 is introductory. Paragraph 2 amends ITA 2007 s 257K to extend the life of the scheme for a further two years – qualifying investments may now be made no later than 5 April 2021.

Paragraph 3 inserts new ITA 2007 s 257LDA, introducing an "existing investments requirement" into the eligibility conditions for investors and investments. Essentially, this requires investors to be independent of the social enterprise concerned. Investors must, accordingly, not hold any shares or debentures in the social enterprise or in any qualifying subsidiary of that enterprise immediately before making the investment. An exception is made in the case of "risk-finance investments" and "permitted subscriber shares". A risk-finance investment is a share or debenture held by the investor in return for his advancing an amount of money to the enterprise which is EIS-, SEIS- or itself SITR-compliant. A permitted subscriber share is a share either (a) issued to the investor and held continuously by the investor since its issue or (b) acquired by the investor at a time when the company that issued it had issued no shares other than subscriber shares and had not begun to carry on, or been preparing to carry on, a trade or business.

Paragraph 4 inserts new ITA 2007 s 257LEA, introducing a further requirement – the "no disqualifying arrangements requirement". The new section is effectively a paraphrase, mutatis mutandis, of the equivalent provision for the purposes of EIS (ITA 2007 s 178A), SEIS (ITA 2007 s 257CF) and VCT relief (ITA 2007 s 299A). It is designed to disqualify arrangements the main purpose or one of the main purposes of which is to ensure that EIS, SEIS, SITR, VCT or share-loss relief becomes available as a result of the investment and that either all or most of the monies raised by the investment are paid to or for the benefit of any party to the arrangements or that, in the absence of the arrangements, it would be reasonable to expect those activities would have been carried on by another person also party to the arrangements. Paragraph 5 amends the information powers under ITA 2007 s 257SH to include information relating to new ITA 2007 s 257LEA.

Paragraph 6 inserts new ITA 2007 ss 257MNA–257MNE, which provide for the maximum amounts that may be invested under the SITR and replace the existing provisions to that effect (ITA 2007 ss 257MA and 257MB). Unlike the previous amendments, which are restrictive, the amendments made by para 6 increase the maximum investment to £1.5 million and bring the legislation into alignment with the European Union's General Block Exemption Regulation concerning State Aid (Regulation (EU) No 651/2014).

New ITA 2007 s 257MNA introduces a wholly new limit of £1.5 million on the qualifying investments a social enterprise may receive in the seven-year period beginning with its first commercial sale. The limit also applies to investments made after the end of that period if there has already been a prior qualifying investment within the period and some or all of the money raised by the prior investment was employed for the purposes of the same qualifying activity for which the new investment is intended.

New ITA 2007 s 257MNB is supplementary to new ITA 2007 s 257MNA. It defines qualifying ("relevant") investments to include investments made in a 51% subsidiary of the social enterprise or a former 51% subsidiary, and investments made in a trade that was later transferred to the social enterprise or to a 51% subsidiary.

New ITA 2007 s 257MNC specifies a maximum in respect of investments falling outside the seven-year period referred to in new ITA 2007 s 257MNA and which are not covered by the extension of that section beyond that period. It largely replicates the existing omitted ITA 2007 s 257MA. Thus the amount invested must be such that the overall £1.5 million limit is not breached and the investment itself must not exceed an amount given by the formula:

$$\left(\frac{€200,000 - M}{RCG + RSI} \right) - T$$

where M is the total of any de minimis aid granted to the enterprise or a 51% subsidiary in the three years immediately preceding the date of the investment, T is the total of qualifying investments made in the enterprise in that period, RCG is the highest rate of CGT during that period and RSI is the highest rate of SITR relief in that period.

New ITA 2007 s 257MND applies the overall £1.5 million limit in situations where either (a) an investment is made in a company that becomes a 51% subsidiary at any time in the "shorter applicable period" and the money raised is employed for the purposes of a trade that the company carried on before it became a 51% subsidiary or (b) all or part of the money raised by the investment is employed for the purposes of a trade that has been transferred to the social enterprise or to a current or former 51% subsidiary. The shorter applicable period is defined for the purposes of SITR in ITA 2007 s 257KC as the period beginning with the date of the investment and ending with the third anniversary of that date.

New ITA 2007 s 257MNE replaces ITA 2007 s 257MB and confers on the Treasury to vary the investment limit by regulations.

Paragraph 7 reduces the maximum number of employees that a social enterprise together with any qualifying subsidiaries may have from 500 to 250.

Paragraph 8 introduces a third new eligibility requirement, namely the "financial-health requirement" as contained in new ITA 2007 s 257MIA. This mirrors the equivalent provision for the EIS (ITA 2007 s 180B), the SEIS (ITA 2007 s 257DE) and VCT relief (ITA 2007 s 286B). It requires that the social enterprise must not, at the date of the investment, be "in difficulty", as defined by the Community Guidelines on State Aid for Rescuing and Restructuring Firms in Difficulty (2004/C 244/02).

Paragraph 9 amends ITA 2007 s 257MM to clarify that repayment of a loan does not amount to employing money for a qualifying purpose.

Paragraph 10 amends the list of excluded activities in ITA 2007 s 257MQ. It adds the following:

(1) leasing (including letting ships on charter or other assets on hire);
(2) receiving royalties or licence fees;
(3) operating or managing nursing homes or residential-care homes or managing property used as such;
(4) generating electricity, exporting electricity or making electricity-generating capacity available;
(5) generating heat;
(6) generating any other form of energy; and
(7) producing gas or fuel.

Excluded activity (4) replaces the existing narrower exclusion of the subsidised generation or export of electricity and entails the omission of ITA 2007 s 257MS, which thereby becomes superfluous. The activity of lending money to a social enterprise becomes an excluded activity. Excluded activity (3) is supplemented by new ITA 2007 s 257MQA, which provides definitions.

Part 2 (paras 11–13) makes consequential amendments to ITA 2007 s 178A, 257CF and 299A; FA 2015 Sch 6 and FA 2016 Sch 24 Part 2.

Part 3 (paras 14–16) provides for commencement. The amendments made by paras 3–9 (i.e. the new requirements, the maximum investment limits, the reduction in the number of permitted employees and the exclusion of loan repayments as a qualifying purpose) are to have effect for investments made after 5 April 2017, except that the new maximum investment limits are not to apply so as to disqualify investments made before 6 April 2017 and arrangements including transactions entered into before 6 April 2017 are not to be disqualifying arrangements under new ITA 2007 s 257LEA. As regards excluded activities, the amendments made by para 10 are to come into force on 6 April 2017 with respect to accreditation as a social-impact contractor under ITA 2007 s 257JD, and are to have effect in relation to investments made after 5 April 2017 with respect to meeting the trading requirement under ITA 2007 s 257MJ and to the definition of "qualifying trade" under ITA 2007 s 257MP.

Section 15 makes amendments intended to relax the requirements for and hence increase the take-up of Business Investment Relief (BIR), which is available under ITA 2017 ss 809VA–809VO to non-domiciled individuals taxed on the remittance basis.

Section 15(2) amends ITA 2007 s 809VC to expand the definition of a qualifying investment to include the acquisition of existing shares in a company that has already issued its shares to the investor.

Section 15(3) amends ITA 2007 s 809VD, which contains the definition of a "target company", being the type of company in which a qualifying investment may be made. First, it extends the period within which a target company may be preparing to carry on a qualifying activity from two years to five years. Second, it introduces a new type of target company, namely an "eligible hybrid company", which is neither an eligible trading company nor an eligible stakeholder company (both existing types of target company) but is a mixture of both (i.e. it carries on, or is preparing to carry on within the next five years, one or more commercial trades; and it holds one or more investments in eligible trading companies or is preparing to do so within the next five years).

Section 15(4) amends ITA 2007 s 809VE, which contains the definition of a "commercial trade" to specify that a company that is a partner in a partnership is not to be regarded as carrying on a trade that is carried on by the partnership.

Section 15(5) amends what is meant by a "potentially chargeable event" as defined in ITA 2007 s 809VH. A potentially chargeable event is an event that causes the relief to be withdrawn if the appropriate mitigation steps are not taken. Hitherto, a potentially chargeable event occurs, inter alia, if the investor or another relevant person receives a benefit from an "involved company". Such a company may be the target company; an eligible trading company in which the target company has invested or is intending to invest; an eligible trading company that is a 51% subsidiary of the target company; or a company connected with any of the above. The amendments remove references to an involved company, so that only the receipt of value in circumstances directly or indirectly attributable to the investment may trigger a potentially chargeable event. ITA 2007 s 809VH is also amended to cover potentially chargeable events in connection with an eligible hybrid company.

Section 15(6) amends ITA 2007 s 809VJ to prolong the grace period within which the non-domiciled individual may take mitigating steps to avoid the adverse conse-quences of a potential chargeable event to two years from the current 90 or 45 days, if the event is a breach of the five-year "start-up" rule in ITA 2007 s 809VH as amended by s 15(5).

Section 15(7) makes a consequential amendment to ITA 2007 s 809VN, and s 15(8) provides that all the amendments made by s 15 are to have effect in relation to events occurring after 5 April 2017.

Income tax: trading and property businesses

Section 16 introduces Sch 2, which changes the calculation of the profits of a trade, profession, vocation or property business, particularly as concerns the cash basis of computation. The new provisions simplify the treatment of capital expenditure for trades, professions or vocations using the cash basis, and make the cash basis mandatory (subject to an opt-out) for all but the largest property businesses.

Schedule 2 consists of four Parts. Part 1 (paras 1–11) amends the cash-basis rules for trades, professions and vocations in ITTOIA 2005. Part 2 (paras 12–41) intro-duces the cash basis for property businesses, also in ITTOIA 2005. Part 3 (paras 42–63) makes consequential amendments to other legislation. Part 4 (para 64) provides for commencement.

Schedule 2 para 1 is introductory. Paragraph 2 substitutes a new ITTOIA 2005 s 33A, which contains the basic provision for the treatment of capital expenditure under the cash basis. Whereas hitherto, ITTOIA 2005 s 33A has comprised just two subsections, the new section has 14. Whereas hitherto it has been the rule simply that no deduction is to be allowed under the cash basis for items of capital expenditure except for expenditure that would otherwise qualify for plant and machinery capital allowances and is not expenditure incurred on the provision of a car, the new provisions set out in detail the types of capital expenditure that are not to be deductible under the cash basis. These are items "of a capital nature" incurred on or in connection with:

(1) the acquisition or disposal of a business or part of a business;
(2) education or training;
(3) the provision, alteration or disposal of:
    (i) assets other than depreciating assets;
    (ii) assets not acquired or created for use on a continuous basis in the trade;
    (iii) cars;
    (iv) land (excluding the provision of a depreciating fixture but not in connection with the provision of a building, wall, floor, ceiling, waste-disposal system etc);
    (v) non-qualifying intangible assets;
    (vi) financial assets.

A depreciating asset is an asset of an estimated useful life at acquisition of less than 20 years or one that will within 20 years have declined in value by 90% or more. A non-qualifying intangible asset is one that must cease to exist within 20 years by virtue of having a fixed maximum duration. A financial asset is any right under or in connection with a financial instrument or an arrangement producing an economically equivalent return.

Paragraph 3 makes a consequential amendment to ITTOIA 2005 s 95A, which introduces the treatment of various items treated as receipts under the cash basis. Paragraph 4 makes substantial amendments to ITTOIA 2005 s 96A, which deals with the treatment of capital receipts under the cash basis. The section as amended is to apply in two situations, "Case 1" and "Case 2".

Case 1 is a situation in which two conditions, A and B, are met. Condition A is that a person carrying on a trade (here referred to as "the trader") receives disposal proceeds or capital refunds in respect of an asset at a time when the trader has elected for the cash basis to apply. Condition B is that an item of capital expenditure in respect of that asset has either (a) been deducted under the cash basis or (b) has qualified for capital allowances or otherwise been taken into account in computing the trader's profits in a tax year before that in which the trader last entered the cash basis and would have been deductible under the cash basis. Case 1 therefore covers traders who have incurred expenditure on the asset while under the cash basis or have entered the cash basis after incurring some or all of the expenditure on the asset.

Case 2 is a situation in which two of three conditions (condition C and one of conditions D and E) are met. Condition C is that the trader receives disposal proceeds or capital refunds in respect of an asset at a time when the trader has previously left the cash basis. Condition D is that capital expenditure, which would not have qualified for capital allowances, in relation to the asset had been paid when the trader was under the cash basis and obtained a deduction for it. The alternative condition E is that capital expenditure in relation to the asset had been brought into account (other than by means of capital allowances) in a tax year when the cash basis was not in effect and which preceded the tax year in which the trader last entered the cash basis.

Where either Case 1 or Case 2 applies, the disposal proceeds or capital refund are to be brought into account as a taxable receipt of the trade, with a proportional reduction where part only of the expenditure incurred was brought into account whether under the cash basis or the GAAP basis. The exception to this rule is where the whole of that amount is brought into account as a disposal value for capital-allowance purposes.

The provisions of ITTOIA 2005 s 96A dealing with ceasing to use the asset without disposing of it or with a material increase in non-business use (s 96A(4)–(6)) remain in force.

Paragraph 5 inserts new ITTOIA 2007 s 96B, which defines terms in ITTOIA 2007 s 96A as amended, such as "entering the cash basis". It also provides that whether and to what extent expenditure is brought into account in calculating the profits of a trade are to be determined on a just and reasonable basis.

Paragraph 6 makes a consequential amendment to ITTOIA 2005 s 106D. Paragraph 7 amends ITTOIA 2005 s 240C, which provides how unrelieved qualifying expenditure available for carry-forward is to be adjusted for under the cash basis when a trader enters the cash basis. The amendments limit the application of the section to qualifying expenditure under CAA 2001 Parts 2 (plant and machinery), 7 (know-how) and 8 (patents) and provide that, in calculating the profits of the trade for the first tax year under the cash basis, a deduction is to be allowed for any "cash-basis deductible" amount of the expenditure. This is defined as any amount of the expenditure for which a deduction would be allowed under the cash basis on the assumption that it was paid in the first cash-basis tax year. In determining what unrelieved qualifying expenditure is available for carry-forward, certain sections of CAA 2001 (ss 59(4), 461A(1) and 475A(1)) are to be disregarded.

Paragraph 8 inserts new ITTOIA 2005 s 240CA, to deal with unrelieved qualifying expenditure under CAA 2001 Part 5 (mineral-extraction allowances) where ITTOIA 2005 s 240D (assets not fully paid for) applies. Paragraph 9 amends ITTOIA 2005 s 240D to clarify that it applies in respect only of expenditure that would have been deductible under the cash basis. Paragraphs 10 and 11 make minor consequential amendments to ITTOIA 2005 ss 786(6) and 805(5).

Schedule 2 Part 2 (paras 12–41) introduce the cash basis as the default basis for most property businesses. Paragraph 12 is introductory.

Paragraph 13 inserts ITTOIA 2005 ss 271A–271D, which provide when the cash basis and when GAAP (or "the GAAP basis" as referred to here) is to apply in calculating the profits of a property business.

New ITTOIA 2005 s 271A provides that where any one of five conditions (A to E) is met, the profits of a property business must be calculated in accordance with GAAP (i.e. not on the cash basis).

Condition A is that at any time in the tax year concerned, the business is carried on by a company, a limited-liability partnership, trustees of a trust, or by a partnership in which one or more partners is not an individual.

Condition B is that the receipts of the business, computed under the cash basis, exceed £150,000 in the tax year concerned (the threshold is reduced pro rata if the business is not carried on for the whole of the tax year).

Condition C applies where the property business is carried on jointly with a spouse or civil partner, the two parties have not given notice of the particular percentages in which they share the profits, and the other party's profits are calculated under GAAP.

Condition D applies where a business-premises renovation allowance has been made at any time and a balancing event in the tax year would give rise to a balancing adjustment if the profits were calculated under GAAP.

Condition E is simply that an election has been made under new ITTOIA 2005 s 271A(10) for the GAAP basis to apply.

New ITTOIA 2005 s 271B explains that to calculate the profits in accordance with GAAP means to calculate them in accordance with generally accepted accounting practice, subject to adjustments required or authorised by law, i.e. as is generally required for all profit calculations under ITTOIA 2005, including those of a property business, unless there is an option for the cash basis in force. It also clarifies that ITTOIA 2005 s 272, which has hitherto provided that the profits of a property business are to be calculated in the same way as the profits of a trade but only insofar as the provisions mentioned in the Table in ITTOIA 2005 s 272(2) apply, is now to apply only where the profits are to be calculated in accordance with GAAP.

By contrast, as provided by new ITTOIA 2005 s 271C, unless one of the conditions for the application of GAAP in new ITTOIA 2005 s 271A is met, the profits of a property business must be calculated under the cash basis.

New ITTOIA 2005 s 271D sets out the basic rules for application of the cash basis to a property business. These are that the receipts are to be brought into account at the time they are received and expenses at the time they are paid, subject to any adjustment required or authorised by law in calculating profits for the purposes of income tax. Lease premiums are to be dealt with as provided by new ITTOIA 2005 s 276A (inserted by para 22) and Chapter 5 deductions and receipts as provided by new ITTOIA 2005 s 307A.

Paragraph 14 makes a minor consequential amendment. Paragraph 15 inserts new ITTOIA 2005 s 271E, which replaces the existing ITTOIA 2005 s 272(1). It provides that the profits of a property business are to be calculated in the same way as the profits of a trade, but subject to ITTOIA 2005 s 272, which limits the rule where profits are calculated under GAAP and to new ITTOIA 2005 s 272ZA (inserted by para 17), which limits the rule where profits are calculated under the cash basis.

Paragraph 16 amends ITTOIA 2005 s 272, omitting the previous s 272(1), replaced by new ITTOIA 2005 s 271E, and omits reference to ITTOIA 2005 s 25 (application of GAAP), which is now superfluous, from the Table.

Paragraph 17 inserts new ITTOIA 2005 s 272ZA, which serves the function for the cash basis which ITTOIA 2005 s 272 serves for GAAP-basis calculations. It provides that when calculating the profits of the business under the cash basis, the application of the trading-basis rules in ITTOIA 2005 Part 2 is limited to the provisions listed in the Table. Paragraphs 18 and 19 make minor consequential amendments.

Paragraph 20 amends ITTOIA 2005 s 274, which regulates the relationship between prohibitive and permissive rules relating to deductions, principally by enlarging the number of provisions that override the general rule that permissive rules are to have priority over prohibitive rules. Paragraph 21 makes a minor consequential amendment.

Paragraph 22 inserts new ITTOIA 2005 s 276A, which provides that in applying ITTOIA2005 Part 3 Chapter 4 (the rules on lease premiums) to cash-basis calculations, neither ITTOIA 2005 ss 291–294 (deductions for tenants under taxed leases) nor ITTOIA 2005 ss 296 and 298 (corporate property businesses previously taxed under TA 1988) are to apply.

Paragraph 23 inserts new ITTOIA 2005 ss 307A–307F in ITTOIA 2005 Part 3 Chapter 5 (other receipts and deductions; e.g. domestic-items relief). New ITTOIA 2005 s 307A provides how that Chapter is to apply to computations under the cash basis, specifically with regard to the new sections.

New ITTOIA 2005 s 307B prescribes the basic rules for how capital expenditure is to be treated for a property business under the cash basis. It is the equivalent for a property business to new ITTOIA 2005 s 33A, substituted by para 2, and not unsurprisingly, is similarly worded. Thus, it provides that no deduction is to be allowed under the cash basis for items of a capital incurred on or in connection with:

(1) the acquisition or disposal of a business or part of a business;
(2) education or training;
(3) the provision, alteration or disposal of:

    (i) assets other than depreciating assets;
    (ii) assets for use in ordinary residential property;
    (iii) assets not acquired or created for use on a continuous basis in the property business;
    (iv) cars;
    (v) non-qualifying intangible assets;
    (vi) financial assets.

A depreciating asset, a non-qualifying intangible asset and a financial asset are exactly as defined in new ITTOIA 2005 s 33A. "Ordinary residential property" means a dwelling in relation to which so much of a UK property business as does not consist of the commercial letting of furnished holiday accommodation in the United Kingdom is carried on. The exclusion of land does not encompass fixtures fixed to land other than ordinary residential property, but does exclude such fixtures involved in the provision of buildings, walls, floors, waste-disposal systems etc.

New ITTOIA 2005 ss 307C and 307D concern the deduction for loan interest and other loan costs under the cash basis. They apply where at the specified "end time", the total outstanding amount of loans for which a deduction is or would (but for ITTOIA 2005 s 272A or new s 307D itself) be allowed (L) is greater than the value of the properties comprised in the property business (V). The "end time" is normally the time immediately before the end of the tax year concerned, but where there is a permanent cessation of the business in the tax year, the end time is the time immediately before the cessation. Value is measured by the market value of the property when it was first brought into the business plus any capital expenditure on the property that has not resulted in a deduction or capital allowance ("not been brought into account in calculating the profits of the business"). The amount regarded as L is restricted to the "outstanding business amount" of the loan or loans, to cater for loans that are partly for the purposes of the property business and partly for other purposes. Where L does exceed V, new ITTOIA 2005 s 307D restricts the deduction to the fraction V/L of what it would otherwise have been.

New ITTOIA 2005 ss 307E and 307F provide for the treatment of capital receipts for businesses that are either under the cash basis or have previously been under the cash basis. They mirror the equivalent provisions for trades etc contained in ITTOIA 2005 ss 96A (as amended by para 4) and 97B (inserted by para 5). Accordingly, they apply in two cases, Case 1 or Case 2.

Case 1 is a situation in which two conditions, A and B, are met. Condition A is that a person carrying on the property business (from hereon referred to as "the landlord") receives disposal proceeds or capital refunds in respect of an asset at a time when the profits of the business are calculated under the cash basis. Condition B is that an item of capital expenditure in respect of that asset has either (a) been deducted under the cash basis or (b) has been brought into account in computing the profits of the business under GAAP either by means of a deduction under ITTOIA 2005 ss 58 or 59 as an incidental cost of obtaining finance, under ITTOIA 2005 s 311A as relief for replacement of domestic items or by means of capital allowances. Case 1 therefore covers landlords who have incurred expenditure on the asset while under the cash basis or have entered the cash basis after incurring some or all of the expenditure on the asset.

Case 2 is a situation in which two of three conditions (condition C and one of conditions D and E) are met. Condition C is that the landlord receives disposal proceeds or capital refunds in respect of an asset at a time when the GAAP basis applies but the cash basis has previously applied to the property business. Condition D is that capital expenditure, which would not have qualified for capital allowances, in relation to the asset had been paid when the landlord was under the cash basis and obtained a deduction for it. The alternative condition E is that capital expenditure in relation to the asset had been brought into account under GAAP either by means of a deduction under ITTOIA 2005 ss 58 0r 59 as an incidental cost of obtaining finance or under ITTOIA 2005 s 311A as relief for replacement of domestic items (but not by means of capital allowances) in a tax year when the cash basis was not in effect and which preceded the tax year in which the landlord last entered the cash basis.

Where either Case 1 or Case 2 applies, the disposal proceeds or capital refund are to be brought into account as a taxable receipt of the property business, with a proportional reduction where part only of the expenditure incurred was brought into account whether under the cash basis or the GAAP basis. The exception to this rule is where the whole of that amount is or has already been brought into account in computing the profits of the property business or as a disposal value for capital-allowance purposes.

Any question as to whether and to what extent expenditure is brought into account in calculating the profits of a property business is to be determined on a just and reasonable basis.

New ITTOIA 2005 s 307F replicates the provisions of ITTOIA 2005 s 96A(4)–(6) dealing with ceasing to use the asset without disposing of it and with a material increase in non-business use. It also provides for the treatment of an overseas property business when the landlord ceases to be UK-resident. In such a case, the landlord is treated as having disposed of the asset in respect of which the capital receipt was received for its market value when he ceased to be resident (or at the end of the UK part of a split year, as the case may be).

Paragraph 24 makes consequential amendments to ITTOIA 2005 s 311A, which provides for the relief for replacement of domestic items and para 25 does likewise to the esoteric sea-walls deduction under ITTOIA 2005 s 315. Paragraph 26 makes a consequential amendment to ITTOIA 2005 s 322.

Paragraph 27 inserts new ITTOIA 2005 s 329A, which provides that ITTOIA 2005 Part 3 Chapter 7 (ss 329–334), which provides for income and expense adjustments to be made to the treatment of a property business on a change of basis, is to apply (as amended by paras 28 and 29) when there is a change from the GAAP basis to the cash basis and vice versa. Paragraph 28 amends ITTOIA 2005 s 331, which has hitherto provided that tax is to be charged on the full amount of any adjustment income under Chapter 7, making it subject to new ITTOIA 2005 s 334A, which allows for spreading when leaving the cash basis.

Paragraph 29 inserts new ITTOIA 2005 s 334A and a new ITTOIA 2005 Part 3 Chapter 7A (ss 334B–334E). New ITTOIA 2005 s 334A provides that the trading-income rules of ITTOIA 2005 ss 239A and 239B, which allow for the spreading of adjustment income when leaving the cash basis, are also to apply (as modified) to persons leaving the cash basis in respect of a property business. That is to say, when the cash basis applies to the profits of a property business in one tax year (Year 0) and the GAAP basis to the next tax year (Year 1), the landlord may elect to spread the adjustment income as determined by Part 3 Chapter 7 equally over six years, beginning with Year 1. Having so elected, the landlord may then accelerate the allocation of adjustment income by electing under ITTOIA 2005 s 239B to have more than one-sixth of it treated as arising in any of the affected tax years.

New ITTOIA 2005 ss 334B–334E, which together constitute new ITTOIA 2005 Part 3 Chapter 7A, provide for the treatment of unrelieved qualifying expenditure (with respect to capital allowances) for landlords entering the cash basis. New ITTOIA 2005 s 334B defines that "entering the cash basis" refers to the situation where the profits of a property business, having been subject to the GAAP basis in the immediately previous tax year, are now subject to the cash basis in the current tax year. New ITTOIA 2005 s 334C is the equivalent for a property business of ITTOIA 2005 s 240C (as amended by Sch 2 para 7). It provides that where a landlord enters the cash basis with unrelieved capital expenditure brought forward from the GAAP year which would qualify for a deduction under the cash basis if the expenditure were paid in the current tax year ("the cash-basis deductible amount"), the landlord may make a deduction in the current tax year for the cash-basis deductible amount relating to each relevant property-business activity. This rule is subject to the exception in new ITTOIA 2005 s 334D. This rule applies equally to a UK property business, an overseas property business, a UK furnished holiday-lettings business and an EEA furnished holiday-lettings business. The exception in ITTOIA 2005 s 334D applies where the landlord has obtained capital allowances in respect of capital expenditure incurred at any time before the end of the tax year which is the last GAAP year, but not all of that expenditure was paid before the end of that tax year. Provided that a cash-basis deduction would have been allowable for that expenditure, the difference between the expenditure actually paid and the capital allowances obtained is to be treated in the current tax year as either a deduction (if the amount actually paid exceeds the capital allowance) or as a taxable receipt (if the reverse is the case). New ITTOIA 2005 s 334E provides for the situation where the landlord entering the cash basis is a successor who makes a succession election under CAA 2001 s 266 with a connected predecessor in the first cash-basis year. Where this is the case, everything done to or by the predecessor is to be treated for the purposes of Part 3 Chapter 7A as if it had been done to or by the successor, and any expenditure actually incurred by the successor in acquiring the plant or machinery is to be ignored in computing the profits of the property business for the tax year.

Paragraphs 30 and 31 amend ITTOIA 2005 ss 351 and 353, respectively, to clarify which tax years are to be treated as cash-basis tax years for the purposes of the post-cessation receipts provisions of ITTOIA 2005 Part 3 Chapter 10.

Paragraphs 32–41 make consequential amendments to ITTOIA 2005 ss 356, 786, 860, 866, 867, 868, 869, 870 and 872 and Sch 4 Part 2.

Schedule 2 Part 3 (paras 42–63) make consequential amendments to other statutes. Paragraph 42 amends TMA 1970 s 42. Paragraphs 43–46 amend TCGA 1992 ss 37, 41 and 47A. Paragraph 47 omits TCGA 1992 s 47B (disposals after leaving the cash basis), which becomes redundant after its key provisions are incorporated into TCGA 1992 s 47A by the amendments made by para 46.

Paragraphs 48–59 amend CAA 2001. Paragraph 48 is introductory. Paragraph 49 amends CAA 2001 s 1 consequentially on the insertion by para 50 of new CAA 2001 s 1A, which provides how capital allowances and charges are to be made for a chargeable period in which the cash basis applies, replacing CAA 2001 s 1(4), (5). The basic rule remains that no allowances or charges are to be made under CAA 2001 to a person for such a chargeable period, subject to the exceptions mentioned below, and that no disposal value is to be brought into account in such a chargeable period, subject to the same exceptions. The exceptions are to apply in respect of (a) cars and (b) qualifying expenditure incurred in a period before the person concerned enters the cash basis and in respect of which a deduction under the cash basis would not have been available.

Paragraph 51 amends CAA 2001 s 4 (definition of capital expenditure). Paragraph 52 amends CAA 2001 s 59 (unrelieved qualifying expenditure on plant and machinery available to be carried forward). CAA 2001 s 59(4) is clarified to provide that it is only that amount of capital expenditure that would qualify for a deduction under the cash basis ("cash-basis deductible amount") that may not be carried forward as unrelieved qualifying expenditure when entering the cash basis. This makes the exception for cars in CAA 2001 s 59(5) superfluous, so it is omitted.

Paragraph 53 amends CAA 2001 s 66A, which applies to persons leaving the cash basis, to extend its coverage to property businesses and to provide that where that person has obtained a deduction under the cash basis for an item of expenditure, and that expenditure would also have been qualifying expenditure under GAAP, the amount (if any) by which his unrelieved expenditure exceeds his relieved expenditure is to be regarded as qualifying expenditure that the person has incurred in the chargeable period in which the person leaves the cash basis.

Paragraph 54 inserts new CAA 2001 s 419A, which defines what a person's unrelieved qualifying expenditure is to be for the purposes of mineral-extraction allowances when entering the cash basis. It provides that, for the tax year in which a person enters the cash basis, only so much of the qualifying expenditure incurred before the chargeable period ending with the basis period for that tax year as would not be deductible under the cash basis ("the non-cash basis deductible portion") is to be taken into account. Paragraph 55 inserts new ITTOIA 2005 s 431D, which deals with persons carrying on a mineral-extraction trade leaving the cash basis. Where that person has obtained a deduction under the cash basis for an item of expenditure, and that expenditure would also have been qualifying expenditure under GAAP, the amount (if any) by which his unrelieved expenditure exceeds his relieved expenditure is to be regarded as qualifying expenditure that the person has incurred in the chargeable period in which the person leaves the cash basis.

Paragraph 56 inserts new CAA 2001 s 461A, which is the equivalent provision for know-how allowances of new CAA 2001 s 419A, and para 57 inserts new CAA 2001 s 462A, which is the equivalent of new ITTOIA 2005 s 431D. It is slightly differently worded in that it provides that the unrelieved qualifying expenditure in the pool for the chargeable period in which the trade leaves the cash basis is to be found by allocating the whole of the expenditure to the pool and then reducing it by the relieved portion.

Paragraph 58 and 59 insert the parallel provisions (new CAA 2001 ss 475A and 477A) for persons entering and leaving the cash basis and claiming patent allowances. New CAA 2001 s 475A is identically worded to new CAA 2001 s 461A. New CAA 2001 s 477A is practically identically worded to new CAA 2001 s 462A, except that there is no provision for defining as the relieved portion of the expenditure the higher of expenditure for which a deduction was obtained and the expenditure for which a deduction would have been obtained if it had been incurred wholly and exclusively for the purposes of the trade.

Paragraphs 60–63 amend ITA 2007. Paragraph 60 is introductory. Paragraphs 61 and 62 make consequential amendments. Paragraph 63 inserts new ITA 2007 s 127BA, which provides that there is to be no relief against general income for a property loss of a tax year in which the profits of the business are calculated under the cash basis.

Paragraph 64 provides that the amendments made by Sch 2 are to have effect from the tax year 2017/18, subject to the saving provisions in para 64(2)–(4).

Section 17 introduces Sch 3, which introduces a £1,000 allowance against trading and property income for individuals. Schedule 3 comprises three Parts. Part 1 (para 1) provides for the allowances; Part 2 (paras 2–12) makes consequential amendments; Part 3 (para 13) provides for commencement.

Schedule 3 para 1 inserts Part 6A, consisting of new ITTOIA 2005 ss 783A–783BQ (37 sections in all), divided into two Chapters – Chapter 1 (new ss 783A–783AR) provides for the trading allowance and Chapter 2 (new ss 783B–783BQ) for the property allowance.

New ITTOIA 2005 s 783A provides that an individual who carries on a "relevant trade" or who has miscellaneous income is to be entitled to either full relief, in which case the individual's "relevant income" is not to be charged to income tax, or to partial relief, in which case the individual's income is to be calculated by the alternative methods specified in new ITTOIA 2005 ss 783AI–783AK. Entitlement to relief is, however, to be subject to the exclusions in new ITTOIA 2005 ss 783AN–783AQ.

New ITTOIA 2005 s 783AA defines a "relevant trade" (the type of trade that qualifies for relief) as a trade carried on by an individual otherwise than in partnership and which is not a "rent-a-room trade". "Trade" includes professions and vocations. New ITTOIA 2005 s 783AB defines "miscellaneous income" as the income (before any deduction is made for expenses) arising to the individual which would otherwise be chargeable to income tax under ITTOIA 2005 Part 5 Chapter 8 (the "sweep-up" Chapter) but excludes rent-a-room receipts that would otherwise be chargeable under that Chapter.

New ITTOIA 2005 s 783AC defines "relevant income" of any tax year as the sum of the receipts of the individual's relevant trades and the individual's miscellaneous income for that year. New ITTOIA 2005 s 783AD provides that the individual's trading allowance for any tax year is to be £1,000, but this amount may be increased by regulations.

New ITTOIA 2005 ss 783AE–783AG provide for cases of full relief. New ITTOIA 2005 s 783AE provides that an individual qualifies for full relief for a tax year in which the individual's relevant income does not exceed the individual's trading allowance (i.e. for the time being, does not exceed £1,000), provided that the individual has not elected under new ITTOIA 2005 s 783AL for full relief not to be given for that year. In other words, the allowance will apply (and no deduction for expenses is to be given) unless the individual "opts out". There is also to be another set of circumstances in which the individual qualifies for full relief. This is where the individual's relevant income (calculated under GAAP) does exceed the trading allowance, but would not do so were the cash basis to apply (as the result of a hypothetical election under ITTOIA 2005 s 25A) in that tax year. This is subject to the further conditions that the individual would be eligible to elect for the cash basis for that year and would have been so eligible in the previous tax year (or had actually so elected).

New ITTOIA 2005 s 783AF provides that where an individual qualifies for full relief for any tax year, the profits or losses for that tax year of any relevant trade(s) that the individual carries on are to be treated as nil. Similarly, new ITTOIA2005 s 783AG provides that where an individual's relevant income for any tax year in which the individual qualifies for full relief includes any miscellaneous income, any such income and any expenses associated with that income are to be treated as nil.

New ITTOIA 2005 ss 783AH–783AK provide for cases of partial relief. New ITTOIA 2005 s 783AH provides that an individual qualifies for partial relief if the individual has relevant income that exceeds the trading allowance, and has made an election under new ITTOIA 2005 s 783AM for partial relief to apply. New ITTOIA 2005 s 783AI sets out the consequences of a partial-relief election where the individual has one or more relevant trades. In such a case, the "alternative method" of calculating the profits or losses of each relevant trade is to apply. The alternative method, which will be familiar to persons opting for rent-a-room relief whose receipts exceed the rent-a-room limit, excludes any deduction for expenses. Instead, the calculation begins with all taxable receipts of the trade and then deducts the £1,000 allowance (subject to the splitting provisions of new ITTOIA 2005 s 783AK) and finally makes any deduction for overlap profits. New ITTOIA 2005 s 783AJ prescribes the alternative method applicable to miscellaneous income, which is to deduct from that miscellaneous income (before any associated expenses) the £1,000 allowance, subject again to the splitting provisions of new ITTOIA 2005 s 783AK. What new ITTOIA 2005 s 783AK provides is that an individual with more than one relevant trade or one or more relevant trades and miscellaneous income, may choose to allocate the £1,000 trading allowance among the various trades and/or miscellaneous income as the individual sees fit, provided that the allocated portion of the allowance is not greater than the receipts or income against which it is set.

New ITTOIA 2005 ss 783AL provides for the election to opt out of full relief and new ITTOIA 2005 s 783AM for the election for partial relief (and hence the alternative method of calculation) to apply. Both elections must be made before the first anniversary of the end of the normal self-assessment filing date for the tax year to which they are to apply.

New ITTOIA 2005 ss 783AN–783AQ provide for various exclusions from the relief. New ITTOIA 2005 s 783AN excludes individuals (a) who have rent-a-room receipts under the rent-a-room limit but have elected under ITTOIA 2005 s 799 to disapply full rent-a-room relief for the year and (b) who have rent-a-room receipts exceeding the rent-a-room limit and have chosen not to make the election under ITTOIA 2005 s 800 for the alternative method of calculation of rent-a-room profits. New ITTOIA 2005 s 783AO excludes individuals whose relevant income includes payments by or on behalf of the individual's employer or by or on behalf of the employer of the individual's spouse or civil partner. New ITTOIA 2005 s 783AP excludes individuals whose relevant income includes payments by or on behalf of a firm of which the individual is a partner or is connected with a partner. New ITTOIA 2005 s 783AQ excludes individuals whose relevant income includes payments by or on behalf of a close company in which the individual is a participator or an associate of a participator.

New ITTOIA 2005 s 783AR provides for interpretation.

New ITTOIA 2005 Part 6A Chapter 2, consisting of new ss 783B–783BP, provides for the property allowance. It is subtly differently worded from the trading-allowance provisions. New ITTOIA 2005 s 783B provides that an individual is to be entitled to relief on "certain income" of a "relevant property business". Where the individual's "relevant property income" does not exceed the individual's property allowance, that income is not to be charged to income tax, unless the individual elects otherwise. Where, however, the individual's relevant property income does exceed the individual's property allowance, the individual may elect for an alternative method of calculating the income. Entitlement to relief is, however, to be subject to the exclusions in new ITTOIA 2005 ss 783BL–783BP.

New ITTOIA 2005 s 783BA defines the "relevant property business" (the type of business that qualifies for relief) as a property business that is not a "rent-a-room property business". Likewise, where an individual receives property-income distributions from a property Authorised Investment Fund or a profit distribution from a REIT, those deemed businesses are also not to qualify as a relevant property business. New ITTOIA 2005 s 783BB defines "relievable receipts" of an individual's relevant property businesses as all the amounts that would otherwise be brought into account as a receipt in calculating the profits of the businesses, excluding rent-a-room receipts and "non-relievable balancing charges". These latter are balancing charges under CAA 2001 Part 2 (plant and machinery allowances) unrelated to the property business.

New ITTOIA 2005 s 783BC defines "relevant property income" of any tax year as the relievable receipts of the individual's relevant property businesses for that year. New ITTOIA 2005 s 783BD provides that the individual's property allowance for any tax year is to be £1,000, but this amount may be increased by regulations.

New ITTOIA 2005 ss 783BE and 783BF provide for relief when the individual's relevant property income does not exceed the property allowance. New ITTOIA 2005 s 783BE provides that an individual qualifies for full relief for a tax year in which the individual's relevant property income does not exceed the individual's property allowance (i.e. for the time being, does not exceed £1,000), provided that the individual has not elected under new ITTOIA 2005 s 783BJ for full relief not to be given for that year. In other words, the allowance will apply (and no deduction for expenses is to be given) unless the individual "opts out". New ITTOIA 2005 s 783BF provides that where an individual qualifies for full relief for any tax year, in calculating the profits or losses for that tax year of the individual's relevant business or of both relevant property businesses, no account is to be taken of either the relievable receipts of the business or of any expenses associated with those receipts.

New ITTOIA 2005 ss 783BG-783BI provide for cases where relevant property income exceeds the property allowance. New ITTOIA 2005 s 783BG provides that an individual qualifies for partial relief if the individual has relevant property income that exceeds the property allowance, and has made an election under new ITTOIA 2005 s 783BK for partial relief to apply. New ITTOIA 2005 s 783BH sets out the consequences of a partial-relief election where the individual has one or two relevant property businesses. In such a case, the "alternative method" of calculating the profits or losses of one or both relevant property business or businesses is to apply. The alternative method begins by bringing into account the relievable receipts of the business and then deducts the £1,000 allowance (subject to the splitting provisions of new ITTOIA 2005 s 783BI), but does not bring into account any "relevant expenses" (those which would otherwise be brought into account as deductions in calculating the profits of the business and are associated with the relievable receipts). New ITTOIA 2005 s 783BI provides that where an individual has two relevant property businesses, the individual may choose to allocate the £1,000 trading allowance among the two businesses as the individual sees fit, provided that a loss is not thereby created in either business.

New ITTOIA 2005 ss 783BJ provides for the election to opt out of full relief and new ITTOIA 2005 s 783BK for the election for partial relief (and hence the alternative method of calculation) to apply. Both elections must be made before the first anniversary of the end of the normal self-assessment filing date for the tax year to which they are to apply.

New ITTOIA 2005 ss 783BL-783BP provide for various exclusions from the relief. New ITTOIA 2005 s 783BL excludes individuals who claim relief under ITTOIA 2005 s 274A for non-deductible loan costs on a dwelling. New ITTOIA 2005 s 783BM excludes individuals (a) who have rent-a-room receipts under the rent-a-room limit but have elected under ITTOIA 2005 s 799 to disapply full rent-a-room relief for the year and (b) who have rent-a-room receipts exceeding the rent-a-room limit and have chosen not to make the election under ITTOIA 2005 s 800 for the alternative method of calculation of rent-a-room profits. New ITTOIA 2005 s 783BN excludes individuals whose relevant income includes payments by or on behalf of the individual's employer or by or on behalf of the employer of the individual's spouse or civil partner. New ITTOIA 2005 s 783BO excludes individuals whose relevant income includes payments by or on behalf of a firm of which the individual is a partner or is connected with a partner. New ITTOIA 2005 s 783BP excludes individuals whose relevant income includes payments by or on behalf of a close company in which the individual is a participator or an associate of a participator.

New ITTOIA 2005 s 783BQ provides for interpretation.

Schedule 3 Part 2 (paras 2–12) make consequential amendments to ITTOIA 2005 (paras 3–11) and TIOPA 2010 (para 12). Paragraph 2 is introductory. Paragraph 3 amends ITTOIA 2005 s 1 and para 4 inserts new ITTOIA 2005 s 22A, which provides that the rules for calculating the profits of a trade, profession or vocation that an individual carries on are to be subject to the trading-allowance rules of new Part 6A Chapter 1, and where relief is given under those rules on relevant income, most deductions otherwise available under ITTOIA 2005 Part 2 are disallowed.

Paragraph 5 inserts new ITTOIA 2005 s 204A, which provides how the calculation of overlap profit interacts with the trading-allowance provisions. It applies where the overlap period falls within the basis period for two tax years in at least one of which the trading allowance is given. The precise rules operate by reference to the "non-adjusted overlap profit", which is the profit that would arise in the overlap period were it not for the trading-allowance rules of ITTOIA 2005 Part 6A Chapter 1 and this section itself.

The overlap profit is to be treated as nil if (a) full relief under new ITTOIA 2005 s 783AF is given is one or both of those tax years or (b) partial relief under new

ITTOIA 2005 s 783AI is given in one or both years and the £1,000 or smaller deduction ("the deductible amount") in respect of the allowance is not less than the non-adjusted overlap profit. On the other hand, the overlap profit is taken to be the non-adjusted overlap profit less the deductible amount where both (a) partial relief under new ITTOIA 2005 s 783AI is given in either year and the deductible amount is less than the non-adjusted overlap profit and (b) neither full relief under new ITTOIA 2005 s 783AF nor partial relief under new ITTOIA 2005 s 783AI is given in the other of the two tax years. Where, however, in both years concerned partial relief under new ITTOIA 2005 s 783AI is given and the deductible amount is less than the non-adjusted overlap profit, the overlap profit is taken to be the non-adjusted overlap profit less the higher of the deductible amounts in the two tax years.

Paragraph 6 makes a minor amendment to ITTOIA 2005 s 227A, and para 7 inserts new ITTOIA 2005 ss 227B and 227C, which deal with the interaction of the cash basis with the trading allowance. New ITTOIA 2005 s 227B provides that where the alternative occasion under new ITTOIA 2005 s 783AE(2) for full relief applies (cash-basis receipts would have fallen within the trading allowance had the cash basis been in operation) in any tax year, the individual is to be regarded as having made the cash-basis election for that tax year. Where this is the case, new ITTOIA 2005 s 227C disapplies certain sections of the adjustment-income provisions of ITTOIA 2005 Part 2 Chapter 17 and modifies the operation of certain others.

Paragraph 8 inserts new ITTOIA 2005 s 307G, which mirrors new ITTOIA 2005 s 22A, and provides that the rules for calculating the profits of a property business that an individual carries on are to be subject to the property-allowance rules of new Part 6A Chapter 2, and where relief is given under those rules on relevant property income, all deductions under ITTOIA 2005 Part 3 relating to that income are disallowed. Paragraphs 10 and 11 make minor amendments. Paragraph 12 makes a minor amendment to TIOPA 2010 ss 22(8) and 24(8).

Paragraph 13 provides that the amendments made by Sch 3 are to have effect from the tax year 2017/18.

Corporation tax

Section 18 introduces Sch 4, which amends the corporate loss carry-forward rules. It also provides that HMRC may make consequential amendments in relation to Sch 4 by statutory instrument. The amendments made by Sch 4 are twofold in nature. They are designed on the one hand to make relief for losses brought forward less restrictive but on the other hand restrict to 50% the total amount of profits against which losses brought forward may be set, subject to a generous de minimis safe harbour of £5 million.

Schedule 4 comprises no less than 12 Parts and runs to 145 printed pages (21.5% of the entire Act). Part 1 (paras 1–14) contains the new more flexible rules for losses brought forward, differentiating between "pre-1 April 2017" and "post-1 April 2017" losses and other deficits. Part 2 (paras 15–22) introduces the new 50% restriction on set-off of losses brought forward. Part 3 (para 23) provides for the availability of group relief for losses brought forward. Parts 4 to 8 contain rules specific to certain types of company: Part 4 (paras 24–26) covers insurance companies; Part 5 (paras 27–46) the creative industries; Part 6 (paras 47–55) oil and gas activities; Part 7 (paras 56–60) oil contractors and Part 8 (paras 61–68) transferred trades. Part 9 (paras 69–92) contains a new set of targeted anti-avoidance provisions. Part 10 (paras 93–105) contains rules specific to the Northern Ireland rate of corporation tax. Part 11 (paras 106–189) contains minor and consequential amendments and Part 12 (paras 190–194) provides for commencement and savings.

Schedule 4 Part 1 contains the new rules for carrying forward losses and other deficits, amending CTA 2009. Paragraphs 1 to 4 amend the treatment of non-trading deficits under the loan-relationships provisions of CTA 2009 Part 5.

Schedule 4 para 1 is introductory and Sch 4 paras 2 and 3 make consequential amendments. Their effect is to restrict application of the existing CTA 2009 Part 5 Chapter 16 to "pre-1 April non-trading deficits", i.e. to non-trading deficits arising in accounting periods beginning before 1 April 2017, and to charities. Schedule 4 para 4 inserts new CTA 2009 Part 5 Chapter 16A, consisting of new CTA 2009 ss 463A–463I.

New CTA 2009 s 463A provides that Chapter 16A is to apply to non-trading deficits arising to a company for any accounting period beginning after 31 March 2017, provided that it is not a charity at the end of that period, and introduces the remainder of the Chapter. The legislation refers to such deficits (somewhat inaccurately) as "post-1 April 2017 deficits".

New CTA 2009 s 463B provides that a company may make a claim for all or part of the deficit to be set off against *any* profits of the company for the "deficit period" (the period for which the deficit arises) or for it to be carried back to be set off against profits for earlier periods, to the extent that it is not surrendered as group relief (for which see Sch 4 Part 3) under CTA 2010 Part 5. New CTA 2009 s 463B has wording identical, save for section references and the omission of the exclusion of charities, to CTA 2009 s 459, which is the equivalent provision for "pre-1 April non-trading deficits".

Under new CTA 2009 s 463C, such a claim must be made within two years of the end of the deficit period (or later, if HMRC agree). Different claims may be made in respect of different parts of the deficit for any deficit period. New CTA 2009 s 463C has wording identical, save for section references, to CTA 2009 s 460, which is the equivalent provision for pre-1 April non-trading deficits.

When a claim is made under new CTA 2009 s 463B, new CTA 2009 s 463D provides that the claimant company must specify the profits against which the deficit is to be set off, and s 463B(1)(a) relief (current-period deficit relief) is to have priority over relief under CTA 2010 ss 37 or 62(1)–(3) for trade losses or property losses of the current or earlier periods and s 463B(1)(b) relief (later-period deficit carried back). No s 463B relief is to be available against oil and gas ring-fence profits or against oil-contractors' ring-fence profits. New CTA 2009 s 463D has similar wording to CTA 2009 s 461, which is the equivalent provision for pre-1 April non-trading deficits, except that there is no longer a priority for deficits brought forward from earlier periods and there is a new exclusion for the profits of oil contractors.

When a claim is made to carry the deficit back to an earlier period, new CTA 2009 s 463E provides that the available deficit must first be reduced by the amount set off in the deficit period itself, and the profits of later periods must be set off before the profits of earlier periods. New CTA 2009 s 463E has practically identical wording to CTA 2009 s 462, which is the equivalent provision for pre-1 April non-trading deficits, except for section references.

New CTA 2009 s 463F defines which profits are to be available for set-off by deficits brought back from later periods. The profits that are so available are loan-relationship profits (and not any other profits) of the period of 12 months immediately preceding the deficit period, but they must first be reduced by any reliefs in respect of:

(1) pre-1 April non-trading deficits of the current period (CTA 2009 s 459(1)(a));
(2) post-1 April non-trading deficits of the current period (new CTA 2009 s 463B(1)(a));
(3) losses or deficits incurred or treated as incurred in an earlier accounting period;
(4) charitable-donations relief under CTA 2010 Part 6; and
(5) trade losses of the same or an earlier period (CTA 2010 s 37).

In addition, if the company is a company with investment business, reliefs under CTA 2009 s 1216 (management expenses) and CAA 2001 Part 2 (plant and machinery capital allowances) also have priority. Apart from references to psot-1 April non-trading deficits of the current period, new CTA 2009 s 463F has identical wording to CTA 2009 s 463, which is the equivalent provision for pre-1 April non-trading deficits.

New CTA 2009 s 463G deals with carrying deficits forward to subsequent periods. The deficit available to be carried forward is what remains after any claim for relief against profits of the deficit period or earlier periods, and after any surrender of any part of the deficit for group relief. Special conditions apply to companies with investment business, Solvency 2 insurance companies and general insurance companies. Under new CTA 2009 s 463G, the amount thus available for set-off ("the unrelieved amount") is to be carried forward to the first accounting period after the deficit period, and set against the *total* profits of that first subsequent period. A claim must be made for the set-off to apply, but it need not be for the whole of the unrelieved amount, and must be made no later than two years after the end of the first subsequent period (or later, if HMRC agree). Special rules apply to "shock losses" (as defined in new CTA 2010 s 269ZK, inserted by para 16) of a Solvency 2 insurance company. No set-off under new CTA 2009 s 463G is to be available against oil and gas ring-fence profits or against oil-contractors' ring-fence profits. New CTA 2009 s 463G differs significantly from CTA 2009 s 457, which is the equivalent provision for pre-1 April non-trading deficits, since it is here that the main difference lies between the post-1 April rules and the pre-1 April rules.

New CTA 2009 s 463H deals with three specific special situations – a company with investment business whose investment business became small or negligible in the deficit period or subsequently; where the deficit is a shock loss (as defined in new

CTA 2010 s 269ZK, inserted by para 16) of a Solvency 2 insurance company; or, in the case of a general insurance company, where the first period after the deficit period is an excluded period. In all these cases, relief under new CTA 2009 s 463G is barred, but the unrelieved amount may then be set off against the *non-trading* profits of the first permissible subsequent period. New CTA 2009 s 463H has no equivalent in the pre-1 April rules.

So much of the unrelieved amount as is still unrelieved after any claims under new CTA 2009 s 463G may be set off under new CTA 2009 s 463I against total profits of a later period, to the extent not surrendered as group relief for carried-forward losses under new CTA 2010 Part 5A (inserted by Sch 4 Part 3), subject to the same conditions.

The main differences between the post-1 April rules (CTA 2009 Part 5 Chapter 16A) and the pre-1 April rules (CTA 2009 Part 5 Chapter 16) are these.

(1)　Under the post-1 April rules, carry-forward of the deficit to the first period after the deficit period, subject to any group-relief surrender, is no longer the default rule. Instead, only so much of the deficit as remains unrelieved in the deficit period or an earlier period is to be available for set-off in a later period.

(2)　Under the post-1 April rules, relief for a deficit brought forward from an earlier period is no longer automatic. Instead, a claim must be made for the relief, which may be for all or part of the unrelieved amount. Under the pre-1 April rules, unless a claim is made to the contrary under CTA 2009 s 458(1), or a claim is made for relief in the deficit period or carry-back to an earlier period, the whole of the deficit brought forward from the deficit period must be set against the non-trading profits of the first subsequent period, subject to the availability of those profits (and any excess carried forward to the next).

(3)　Under the pre-1 April rules, deficits carried forward may be set off against non-trading profits only (CTA 2009 s 457), whereas under the post-1 April rules, they may, with the exceptions specified in new CTA 2009 s 463H, be set off against *total* profits (new CTA 2009 ss 463G, 463I).

(4)　Under the post-1 April rules, group relief is available for deficits carried forward (under new CTA 2010 Part 5A, inserted by Sch 4 Part 3). No group relief is available for deficits carried forward under the pre-1 April rules.

Schedule 4 para 5 amends CTA 2009 s 753, which provides for the treatment of non-trading losses under the intangible fixed assets regime of CTA 2009 Part 8. Under the current ("pre-1 April") rules, a non-trading loss on intangible assets that is carried forward to a later period is treated as a non-trading debit of that later period (and hence aggregated with non-trading credits). Under CTA 2009 s 753 as amended for post-1 April deficits, the non-trading loss carried forward is to be treated as a non-trading loss of the later period, so that it is available for set-off against total profits of the later period.

Schedule 4 para 6 amends CTA 2009 s 1223 so that the treatment of post-1 April excess expenses of management carried forward is aligned with the new regime for non-trading deficits and trade losses.

Schedule 4 paras 7–11 amend the treatment of trade losses in CTA 2010 Part 4 Chapter 2. Schedule 4 para 7 is introductory. Schedule 4 paras 8 and 9 make consequential amendments to CTA 2010 s 36 and the italic heading before CTA 2010 s 37. Schedule 4 para 10 makes substantial amendments to CTA 2010 s 45, which provides for the carry-forward of trade losses against subsequent trade profits. The heading and CTA 2010 s 45(1) is now amended to reflect that it is to apply to losses incurred in an accounting period beginning before 1 April 2017 ("pre-1 April losses"). A further amendment removes the prerequisite that relief under the section may only be given if relief cannot be applied to reduce the profits of an earlier period; it may now be given to the extent that it has not been applied in reducing the profits of an earlier period. New CTA 2010 s 45(4A)–(4C) provide that the company is no longer obliged to use the whole of the unrelieved loss (to the extent of the available profits) but may claim to use only part of it or indeed none of it in any particular period. A claim to do so may only be made in relation to an accounting period beginning after 31 March 2017, and is to be made no later than two years after the end of the accounting period affected (or later, if HMRC agree).

Schedule 4 para 11 inserts new CTA 2010 ss 45A–45H, which contain the carry-forward rules for trade losses incurred in an accounting period beginning after 31 March 2017 (again, referred to with some licence as "post-1 April trade losses" – they are more correctly "post-31 March trade losses").

New CTA 2010 s 45A provides that where a company carrying on a trade in an accounting period beginning after 31 March 2017 incurs a loss in the trade, does not obtain relief for any amount of that loss under CTA 2010 s 37 in the same period ("the loss-making period") or a previous period or by means of group relief under CTA 2010 Part 5, it may carry forward the unrelieved amount to a later accounting period, provided that it is still carrying on the same trade in that later period, to set against its *total* profits. This rule is subject to a number of other conditions. Thus, relief under new CTA 2010 s 45A is not available where:

(1) The trade is an oil and gas ring-fence trade.
(2) The trade became small or negligible in the loss-making period.
(3) Relief under CTA 2010 s 37 was not available on the grounds that;
    (i) the trade was carried on wholly outside the United Kingdom;
    (ii) the trade was neither commercial nor carried on for statutory functions;
    (iii) the trade is one of farming or market gardening and a loss was also made in each of the prior five years; or
    (iv) the trade was one of dealing in commodity futures, was carried on in partnership and avoidance arrangements were in place.
(4) Relief under CTA 2010 s 37 was not available due to any of the special cultural-trades exclusions in CTA 2009 s 1209 (loss in the pre-completion period of a separate film trade), CTA 2009 s 1216DA (loss in the pre-completion period of a separate programme trade); CTA 2009 s 1217DA (loss in the pre-completion period of a separate video-game trade; CTA 2009 s 1217MA (loss in the pre-completion period of a separate theatrical trade); CTA 2009 s 1217SA (loss in the pre-completion period of a separate orchestral trade) or CTA 2009 s 1218ZDA (loss in the pre-completion period of a separate exhibition trade) (inserted by Sch 6 para 1).
(5) The loss is a shock loss (as defined in new CTA 2010 s 269ZK, inserted by para 16) of a Solvency 2 insurance company.
(6) The later period is an excluded accounting period (for which see new CTA 2010 s 269ZE, inserted by para 16) of a general insurance company.
(7) Relief under CTA 2010 s 37 is not available in the later period by virtue of CTA 2010 s 44 because there is a loss in that period when the trade is not carried on on a commercial basis.

Where relief is available under new CTA 2010 s 45A, it is not given automatically. The company must make a claim for the relief to be given for all or part of the unrelieved amount, no later than two years after the end of the later period (or later, if HMRC agree).

New CTA 2010 s 45B provides for a more restricted relief for losses carried forward where relief under new CTA 2010 s 45A is not available. Thus, where a company carrying on a trade in an accounting period beginning after 31 March 2017 incurs a loss in the trade, does not obtain relief for any amount of that loss (a) under CTA 2010 s 37 in the same period ("the loss-making period") or a previous period; (b) under CTA 2010 s 42 (extended relief period for ring-fence trades); or (c) by means of group relief under CTA 2010 Part 5, it may carry forward the unrelieved amount to a later accounting period and claim relief in that period, provided that it is still carrying on the same trade in that later period and relief is not available under new CTA 2010 s 45A because (a) one of conditions (2) to (7) above is satisfied; (b) the trade is a ring-fence trade; or (c) a restriction under CTA 2009 s 1210(5) with respect to film tax relief, under CTA 2009 s 1216DB(5) with respect to television tax relief, or under CTA 2009 s 1217DB(5) with respect to video-game tax relief.

A claim must be made for the relief to be given for all, part or none of the unrelieved amount, against the profits of the company's *trade* in the later period, no later than two years after the end of the later period (or later, if HMRC agree).

New CTA 2010 s 45C provides relief for any unrelieved amount that has been carried forward under new CTA 2010 s 45A but remains unrelieved in that first later period, and is then carried forward to subsequent periods, provided that the trade is still being carried on. The amount that is available for relief is so much of the unrelieved amount brought forward as has not been surrendered by means of group relief for carried-forward losses under new CTA 2010 Part 5A (inserted by Sch 4 Part 3). However, relief under new CTA 2010 s 45C is not available if:

(a) the trade became small or negligible in the first later period;
(b) relief under CTA 2010 s 37 would not available in the subsequent later period by virtue of CTA 2010 s 44 because there is a loss in that period when the trade is not carried on on a commercial basis; or
(c) that period is an excluded period of a general insurance company.

As under new CTA 2010 ss 45A, the claim must be made for the relief to be given for all or part of the unrelieved amount, no later than two years after the end of the later period (or later, if HMRC agree). As with new CTA 2010 s 45A (but not new CTA 2010 s 45B), relief under new CTA 2010 s 45C is given against the company's *total* profits in the subsequent later period.

New CTA 2010 s 45D applies where, as in new CTA 2010 s 45C, a loss has been carried forward under new CTA 2010 s 45A but remains unrelieved in that first later period, and is then carried forward to subsequent periods, provided that the trade is still being carried on, but relief under new CTA 2010 s 45C in that subsequent period is not available because the disqualifying conditions apply. That is to say:

(a) the trade became small or negligible in the first later period;
(b) relief under CTA 2010 s 37 would not available in the subsequent later period by virtue of CTA 2010 s 44 because there is a loss in that period when the trade is not carried on on a commercial basis; or
(c) that period is an excluded period of a general insurance company.

In these circumstances, relief is available under new CTA 2010 s 45D in that subsequent period. Again, a claim must be made for the relief to be given for all, part or none of the unrelieved amount, against the profits of the company's *trade* in the later period, no later than two years after the end of the later period (or later, if HMRC agree).

New CTA 2010 s 45E performs the same function in relation to new CTA 2010 s 45B as new CTA 2010 s 45C performs for new CTA 2010 s 45A. It provides relief for any unrelieved amount that has been carried forward under new CTA 2010 s 45B but remains unrelieved in that first later period, and is then carried forward to subsequent periods, provided that the trade is still being carried on. A claim must be made for the relief to be given for all, part or none of the unrelieved amount, against the profits of the company's *trade* in the subsequent later period, no later than two years after the end of the later period (or later, if HMRC agree).

New CTA 2010 s 45F provides for terminal loss relief. It applies where a loss has been carried forward under any of CTA 2010 ss 45, 45A or 45B to an accounting period in which the company ceases to carry on the trade ("the terminal period") and relief in the terminal period is not available for any part of the loss under any of those sections. That being the case, a claim for relief may be made under new CTA 2010 s 45F for the unrelieved amount to be set off against the company's profits of the terminal period and any previous accounting periods falling wholly or partly within the three years ending with the end of the terminal period. However, the relief is not available in any accounting period that is the loss-making period, a period before the loss-making period or a period beginning before 1 April 2017. Relief is given in a later period in priority to an earlier period. The profits against which the unrelieved amount is set are the company's total profits if the loss was carried forward to the terminal period under new CTA 2010 s 45A, but against the profits of the trade only, if the loss was carried forward under CTA 2010 s 45 (pre-1 April 2017 losses) or new CTA 2010 s 45B.

New CTA 2010 s 45G provides for a pro rata division of the profits available for terminal loss relief if the period to which they relate falls partly within and partly outside the three-year period.

New CTA 2010 s 45H is an anti-avoidance provision, which mirrors that under the pre-1 April 2017 rules in CTA 2010 s 41. No terminal loss relief is to be available under new CTA 2010 s 45F where once the trade ceases, a person who is not within the charge to UK corporation tax begins to carry on any of the activities of that trade and the cessation was part of a scheme or arrangement to obtain terminal loss relief under new CTA 2010 s 45F.

The main differences between the post-1 April rules (new CTA 2010 ss 45A–45H) and the pre-1 April rules (CTA 2010 ss 36–45) are these.

(1) Under the post-1 April rules, relief for a loss brought forward from an earlier period is no longer automatic. Instead, a claim must be made for the relief, which may be for all or part of the unrelieved amount. Under the pre-1 April rules, unless a claim is made under CTA 2010 s 37 for relief in the loss-making period or carry-back to an earlier period, the whole of the loss brought forward from the loss-making period must be set against the profits of the trade of the first subsequent period, subject to a sufficiency of those profits (and any excess carried forward to the next).
(2) Under the pre-1 April rules, losses carried forward may be set off against profits of the same trade only (CTA 2010 s 45(4)), whereas under the post-1 April rules, they may, subject to the conditions specified in new CTA 2010 s 45A(2), (3), be set off against *total* profits (new CTA 2010 ss 45A). Any amount still unrelieved (either due to insufficient profits) or a choice of partial relief may then be carried

forward further and relieved under new CTA 2010 s 45C by set-off against total profits or under new CTA 2010 s 45D by set-off against profits of the trade, if certain conditions are not satisfied.

(3) Under the post-1 April rules, to the extent relief against total profits is unavailable under new CTA 2010 s 45A, it may be claimed under new CTA 2010 s 45B against profits of the trade. Companies may specify that part only (or indeed, none) of the loss brought forward be set off in that first later period. Any amount still unrelieved may then be carried forward further and relieved under new CTA 2010 s 45E by set-off against profits of the trade in the subsequent period(s).

(4) Under the post-1 April rules, group relief is available for losses carried forward (under new CTA 2010 Part 5A, inserted by Sch 4 Part 3). No group relief is available for losses carried forward under the pre-1 April rules.

Schedule 4 paras 12–14 amend the rules for relief for losses of a property business. Schedule 4 para 12 is introductory. Schedule 4 para 13 amends CTA 2010 s 62, which provides that the losses of a property business must first be deducted against the company's total profits of the loss-making period. In the event that there is an insufficiency of profits in that period, the loss is carried forward and set against the first allowable total profits of a subsequent accounting period. As amended, the section now provides that:

(1) A property loss may be surrendered by way of group relief under CTA 2010 Part 5.

(2) To the extent that the loss is not fully relieved in the loss-making period or surrendered for group relief, the loss is carried forward to subsequent periods in turn, but relief is received in a later period only if a claim is made for it to apply, and that claim may specify that part only of the loss brought forward be set off in the later period.

(3) Such a claim must be made within two years of the end of the period in which it is to apply (or later, if HMRC agree).

(4) Losses brought forward from an earlier period may also be surrendered by way of group relief for carried-forward losses under new CTA 2010 Part 5A (inserted by Sch 4 Part 3).

Schedule 4 para 14 amends CTA 2010 s 63, which provides that where a company with investment business ceases to carry on a UK property business and has a loss in that property business, it may carry that loss forward for relief as an expense of management, provided that it still carries on the investment business. The amendments provide that the company must now make a claim for the relief, and may specify that part only of the loss is to be used in that way. Again, the claim must be made within two years of the end of the period in which it is to apply (or later, if HMRC agree). The expenses of management of the current period are no longer to have priority over losses brought forward and relieved under CTA 2010 s 63.

Having in Sch 4 Part 1 given more flexibility in the use of losses carried forward, Sch 4 Part 2 imposes an overall cap per company or group of £5 million + 50% of the excess on the amount of profits that are to be available to be set off by those losses. The provisions in Sch 4 Part 2 take as their model the existing loss restrictions on banking companies (CTA 2010 Part 7A Chapter 3).

Schedule 4 Part 2 consists of eight paragraphs (paras 15–22). Schedule 4 para 15 is introductory. Schedule 4 para 16 inserts new CTA 2010 Part 7ZA, entitled "Restrictions on obtaining certain deductions". New CTA 2010 Part 7ZA itself comprises 28 sections (new CTA 2010 ss 269ZA–269ZZB).

New CTA 2010 s 269ZA is introductory. New CTA 2010 s 269ZB provides for restrictions on deductions from trading profits. It provides that, in any particular accounting period, the total deductions that a company may make from its taxable total profits in respect of:

(1) losses under CTA 2010 s 45(4)(b) (i.e. pre-1 April 2017 losses brought forward and claimed as deductions from profits of the same trade);

(2) losses under new CTA 2010 s 45B (i.e. post-1 April 2017 uncommercial and other restricted losses brought forward, for which relief against total profits is not available under new CTA 2010 s 45A), and claimed as deductions from profits from the same trade;

(3) restricted losses under new CTA 2010 s 303B(4) (inserted by para 48) (i.e. non-decommissioning ring-fence losses from oil activities brought forward and claimed as deductions in the following accounting period from the profits from related activities); and

(4) restricted losses under new CTA 2010 s 303D(5) (inserted by para 48) (i.e.

non-decommissioning ring-fence losses from oil activities brought forward and claimed as deductions in subsequent later periods from the profits of related activities);

may not exceed "the relevant maximum". Deductions (3) and (4) clearly apply solely apply to a company with oil and gas ring-fence profits.

The "relevant maximum" is the sum of (a) the company's "trading-profits deductions allowance" for the accounting period and (b) 50% of the company's "relevant trading profits" for that accounting period.

The company's "trading-profits deductions allowance" (which may be nil) is so much of its "deductions allowance" as the company designates in its tax return as its "trading-profits deductions allowance" for the period. The "deductions allowance" (defined in new CTA 2010 ss 269ZR and 269ZW) is £5 million (in the case of a group, the £5 million is the group-wide allowance).

"Relevant trading profits" are defined in new CTA 2010 s 269ZF, but are, broadly speaking, that part of the company's trading profits that exceed the trading-profits deductions allowance.

A limit is placed on the amount that a company may designate as its trading-profits deductions allowance in any period. This limit is the difference between the company's deductions allowance for the period and to the total of amounts it has designated under (a) new CTA 2010 s 269ZC(5) as its "non-trading-profits deductions allowance" and (b) (in the case of insurance companies only) its "BLAGAB trade-profits deductions allowance (for which see under new FA 2012 s 124D, inserted by para 26).

New CTA 2010 s 269ZC provides for a parallel restriction on deductions from non-trading profits to that imposed by new CTA 2010 s 269ZB on deductions from trading profits. It provides that, in any particular accounting period, the total deductions that a company may make from its taxable total profits in respect of:

(1)   non-trading deficits under CTA 2009 s 457(3) (i.e. pre-1 April 2017 non-trading deficits brought forward and claimed as deductions from non-trading profits); and

(2)   non-trading deficits under new CTA 2009 s 463H(5) (i.e. post-1 April 2017 restricted non-trading deficits brought forward, for which relief against total profits is not available under new CTA 2009 s 463G, and claimed as deductions from non-trading profits),

may not exceed "the relevant maximum".

The "relevant maximum" in this case is the sum of (a) the company's "non-trading-profits deductions allowance" for the accounting period and (b) 50% of the company's "relevant non-trading profits" for that accounting period.

The company's "non-trading-profits deductions allowance" (which may be nil) is so much of its "deductions allowance" as the company designates in its tax return as its "non-trading-profits deductions allowance" for the period. The "deductions allowance", as already stated, is £5 million (in the case of a group, the £5 million is the group-wide allowance).

"Relevant non-trading profits" are defined in new CTA 2010 s 269ZF, but are, broadly speaking, that part of the company's non-trading profits that exceed the non-trading-profits deductions allowance.

A limit is placed on the amount that a company may designate as its non-trading-profits deductions allowance in any period. This limit is the difference between the company's deductions allowance for the period and to the total of amounts it has designated under (a) new CTA 2010 s 269ZB(7) as its trading-profits deductions allowance and (b) (in the case of insurance companies only) its "BLAGAB trade-profits deductions allowance (for which see under new FA 2012 s 124D, inserted by para 26).

New CTA 2010 s 269ZD determines how the total taxable profits of a company are to be determined when one or more deductions ("relevant deductions") are to be made in respect of losses etc carried forward. The sum of those relevant deductions may not exceed the difference between the "relevant maximum" and the sum of the following deductions:

(1)   deductions under new CTA 2009 s 269ZB (i.e. trade losses brought forward for set-off against trade profits);

(2)   deductions made under CTA 2009 s 457(3) (i.e. pre-1 April 2017 non-trading deficits brought forward for set-off against non-trading profits);

(3)   deductions made under new CTA 2009 s 463H(5) (i.e. post-1 April 2017

restricted non-trading deficits brought forward, for which relief against total profits is not available under new CTA 2009 s 463G, for set-off against non-trading profits); and

(4)   (in the case of insurance companies only) deductions made under FA 2012 124(5) and new FA 2012 ss 124A(5) and 124C(6).

These deductions therefore seem to have priority over "relevant deductions".

The "relevant maximum" in this case is the sum of the company's deductions allowance for the accounting period and 50% of its "relevant profits" for that period. The company's "relevant profits" are the sum of its relevant trading profits, relevant non-trading profits and (insurance companies only) relevant BLAGAB trade profits (as defined in new FA 2012 s 124D, inserted by para 26).

"Relevant deductions" are all of the following:

(i)   deductions under new CTA 2009 s 463G (non-trading post-1 April 2017 deficits carried forward for set-off against total profits);

(ii)   deductions under CTA 2009 s 753 (non-trading losses on intangible fixed assets carried forward and treated as losses of the subsequent period);

(iii) deductions under CTA 2009 s 1219 (in respect of both excess expenses of management carried forward under CTA 2009 s 1223 and terminal property-business losses carried forward under CTA 2009 s 63 and treated as expenses of management of the subsequent period);

(iv)   deductions under CTA 2010 s 37 (relief for trade losses against total current-period profits by virtue of CTA 2009 ss 1210 (film losses), 1216DB (TV programme losses), 1217DB (video-game losses), 1217MB (theatrical-production losses), 1217SB (orchestral losses) or new 1218ZDB (museum and gallery losses, inserted by Sch 6 para 1));

(v)   deductions under new CTA 2010 s 45A (post-1 April 2017 trade losses carried forward for set-off against total profits);

(vi)   deductions under CTA 2010 s 62 (relief for losses of a UK property business against current-period total profits);

(vii) deductions under new CTA 2010 s 303C (excess non-decommissioning losses of a ring-fence trade carried forward for set-off against total profits);

(viii) deductions under CTA 2010 Part 5 (group relief for current-period losses by virtue of CTA 2009 ss 1210 (film losses), 1216DB (TV programme losses), 1217DB (video-game losses), 1217MB (theatrical-production losses), 1217SB (orchestral losses) or new 1218ZDB (museum and gallery losses, inserted by Sch 6 para 1));

(ix)   deductions under new CTA 2010 Part 5A (group relief for losses carried forward); and

(x)   (for insurance companies only) deductions under new FA 2012 s 124B (excess BLAGAB trade losses carried forward.

New CTA 2010 s 269ZE applies to insurance companies only, and only to those insurance companies carrying on BLAGAB business and charged to corporation tax under FA 2012 s 68 on their I – E profit. In an accounting period in which the "adjusted shareholders' I – E profit" is less than the "BLAGAB-related loss capacity", the sum of the company's relevant deductions may not exceed the company's "modified loss cap". The terms "adjusted shareholders' I – E profit", the "BLAGAB-related loss capacity" and the "modified loss cap" are all defined in new CTA 2010 s 269ZE(3)–(10).

New CTA 2010 s 269ZF defines "relevant trading profits" (see under new CTA 2010 s 269ZB) and "relevant non-trading profits" (see under new CTA 2010 s 269ZC).

The "relevant trading profits" for an accounting period are the difference between A (the company's "qualifying trading profits" for that period and B (the company's trading-profits deductions allowance). Where B is greater than A, relevant trading profits are taken to be zero. The limit on deductions under pre-1 April losses carried forward (under CTA 2010 s 45) and restricted post-1 April losses carried forward (under new CTA 2010 s 45B), and, in the case of an insurance company, also under new CTA 2010 ss 303B and 303D, it will be remembered, is 50% of relevant trading profits plus the trading-profits deduction allowance. In the simple case, of a single stand-alone company with the full £5 million designated as the trading-profits deduction allowance, therefore, the maximum that may be deducted against trading profits is £5 million + RP/2, where RP is relevant profits.

The "relevant non-trading profits" for an accounting period are the difference between A (the company's "qualifying non-trading profits" for that period) and B (the company's non-trading-profits deductions allowance). Where B is greater than A, relevant non-trading profits are taken to be zero.

Qualifying trading profits and qualifying non-trading profits are determined in a five-step process.

Step 1 is to calculate the company's "modified total profits". These are its total profits modified by ignoring certain income and not making certain deductions. The income to be ignored is:

(a) company distributions dealt with under CTA 2009 Part 9A;
(b) oil and gas ring-fence profits as defined by CTA 2010 s 276 and oil contractors' ring-fence profits as defined in CTA 2010 s 356LD;
(c) any I – E profits of an insurance company.

The deductions that are not to be made are those in respect of pre-1 April trade losses carried forward under CTA 2010 s 45(4)(b) or restricted post-1 April losses carried forward under new CTA 2010 s 45B, *except* those losses that would be ignored for the purposes of new CTA 2010 s 269ZB, because they are excluded from the restriction. These are:

(1) the creative-industry losses of a film trade (CTA 2009 Part 15), a TV programme trade (CTA 2009 Part 15A), a video-game trade (CTA 2009 Part 15B), a theatrical trade (CTA 2009 Part 15C), an orchestral trade (CTA 2009 Part 15D) and a museum or gallery exhibition trade (CTA 2009 Part 15E, inserted by Sch 6 para 1);
(2) losses of a UK or EEA furnished holiday-lettings business;
(3) shock losses of an insurance company (new CTA 2010 s 269ZJ);
(4) certain excluded ring-fence losses under new CTA 2010 s 304(7) (inserted by para 49);
(5) pre-1 April 2017 oil-contractor losses under new CTA 2010 s 356NJ (inserted by para 59);
(6) the restricted deductions for non-decommissioning ring-fence losses under new CTA 2010 ss 303B and 303D (inserted by para 48), for which see under new CTA 2010 s 269ZB; and
(7) the deductions under CTA 2010 s 457(3) (pre-1 April non-trading deficits brought forward) and new CTA 2010 s 463H(5) (restricted post-1 April 2017 non-trading deficits brought forward).

These deductions must therefore *be made* in arriving at the modified total profits.

If the total modified profits as calculated under Step 1 are not greater than nil, the company's qualifying trading profits and its qualifying non-trading profits are both taken to be nil. If the total modified profits are equal to or greater than nil, one proceeds to Step 2.

Step 2 consists of calculating all the amounts that could be relieved (except those deductions already made under Step 1) against the company's total profits, but *excluding* the following ("the excluded deductions"):

(1) a current-period deduction which is a "relevant deduction" under new CTA 2010 s 269ZD (i.e. the deductions that are subject to the restriction) and are listed there as items (i) to (x);
(2) a deduction under CTA 2010 s 37 in respect of a trade loss brought back to the current period from a later period;
(3) a deduction under new CTA 2010 s 45F for terminal loss relief for post-1 April 2017 losses;
(4) a deduction under CAA 2001 s 260(3) for excess allowances in a qualifying activity of special leasing brought back to the current period from a later period; and
(5) a deduction under new CTA 2009 s 463E for excess non-trading deficits brought back to the current period from a later period.

The amount calculated under Step 2 is referred to as "the Step 2 amount". If the Step 2 amount is equal to or greater than the modified total profits from Step 1 the company's qualifying trading profits and its qualifying non-trading profits are both taken to be nil.

If this is not the case (i.e. if the modified total profits are greater than the Step 2 amount), one must proceed to Steps 3, 4 and 5.

Step 3 consists simply of dividing the company's modified total profits between the company's "trade profits" (the profits of a (or the trade) of the company) and its "non-trade profits".

Step 4 consists of taking the Step 2 amount and either:

(a) reducing the company's trade profits by the whole of that amount;
(b) reducing the company's non-trade profits by the whole of that amount; or

(c) reducing the company's trade profits by part of that amount and its non-trade profits by the remainder;

but not so as to reduce either the company's trade profits or the company's non-trade profits to below zero.

Step 5 defines the company's "qualifying trade profits" as the remainder (if any) of Steps 3 and 4 as regards the company's trade profits and its "qualifying non-trade profits" as the remainder (if any) of Steps 3 and 4 as regards the company's non-trade profits.

New CTA 2010 ss 269ZG–269ZP apply solely to general insurance companies that are insolvent or on the verge of insolvency. New CTA 2010 s 269ZG disapplies new CTA 2010 ss 269ZB-269ZE in any accounting period of the company that is an "excluded accounting period". An excluded accounting period is one in which two conditions, A and B, are met. Condition A is that at the end of the accounting period the company is subject to insolvency procedures (as defined in new CTA 2010 s 269ZH); immediately before it became subject to those procedures it was unable to pay its debts as they fell due and it met the "non-viability condition"; and the company's liabilities in respect of "qualifying latent claims" (as defined in new CTA 2010 s 269ZI) were the main contributory factor to its meeting the non-viability condition at that time. Condition B is that the company meets the non-viability condition also at the end of the accounting period and the main contributory factor to its doing so is the company's liabilities in respect of qualifying latent claims. A company meets the non-viability condition at any time that there is no realistic prospect of its subsequently writing any new insurance business.

A general insurance company is any person authorised under FSMA 2000 to effect or carry out contracts of general insurance, but friendly societies within the meaning of FA 2012 Part 3 are not to be regarded as general insurance companies, nor are insurance special-purpose vehicles under FA 2012 s 139.

The consequence of the disapplication of new CTA 2010 ss 269ZB–269ZE in an excluded period is that loss deductions may be made in full in that period, subject to a sufficiency of profits.

New CTA 2010 s 269ZH defines what are "insolvency procedures" for the purposes of new CTA 2010 s 269ZG. A company is in insolvency procedures if it is in liquidation, administration or receivership or it is undergoing a compromise or arrangement under Companies Act 2006 Part 26, the equivalent under earlier British or Northern Ireland legislation or an equivalent arrangement under foreign law. New CTA 2010 s 269ZI defines what are "qualifying latent claims".

New CTA 2010 s 269ZJ excludes shock losses from the restrictions. That is to say, when a "shock loss" is carried forward to an insurance company's accounting period, and deducted from trading profits under new CTA 2010 s 45B (as a restricted post-1 April trade loss), the deduction is not to be treated as falling within new CTA 2010 s 269ZB(3) and is hence not to be regarded as subject to the restriction on losses deductible from trading profits. Similarly, when a shock loss is carried forward to an insurance company's accounting period as a non-trading deficit, and deducted from non-trading profits under new CTA 2010 s 463H, the company is not treated for the purposes of new CTA 2010 ss 269ZC or269ZD (2)(b) as having made that deduction, and is hence not to be regarded as subject to the restriction on losses deductible from non-trading profits. Nor is a deduction for a shock loss a "relevant deduction" under new CTA 2010 s 269ZD. New CTA 2010 s 269ZK defines a shock loss as, broadly, a loss or other amount arising in a "solvency shock period" of an insurance company and designated as such by the company in a claim for the purpose. New CTA 2010 s 269ZL prescribes further conditions for making a shock-loss claim. These include a statement of the company's solvency capital requirement at the beginning of the solvency shock period and of the company's shock-loss threshold (as defined in new CTA 2010 s 269ZN), certified by the company's chief actuary or equivalent officer. New CTA 2010 s 269ZM defines a "solvency shock period" as a period of 12 months in which the company has a "solvency loss" (as defined in new CTA 2010 s 269ZO) exceeding its shock-loss threshold. New CTA 2010 s 269ZN defines the shock-loss threshold. This may be expressed by the formula:

$$90\% \times \left(MSCR - \sum DA \right)$$

where MSCR is the company's solvency capital requirement (SCR) modified for the loss-absorbing capacity of any deferred taxes (as required by the EU Solvency 2 Directive) and $\sum DA$ is the sum of the deductible amounts (DA) in respect of each of the company's relevant ring-fenced funds. The deductible amount for any fund is the smaller of (a) the "basic own funds" (as modified for these purposes by new

CTA 2010 s 269ZN(3), (4)) within that fund at the beginning of the accounting period and (b) the company's "notional solvency capital requirement". New CTA 2010 s 269ZO prescribes how to calculate the solvency loss. Broadly, the solvency loss over any 12-month period is the reduction in basic own funds over that period. New CTA 2010 s 269ZP defines terms, such as "solvency capital requirement" (by reference to the Solvency 2 Directive (2009/138/EC) Title 1 Chapter 6 Section 4), "basic own funds" (by reference to Solvency 2 Directive art 88) and "notional solvency capital requirement" (by reference to Commission Delegated Regulation (EU) 2015/35). New CTA 2010 s 269ZQ confers on HM Treasury the power to amend new CTA 2010 ss 269ZJ–269ZP and new FA 2012 ss 124A–124E (inserted by para 26).

New CTA 2010 ss 269ZR–269ZV prescribe how the deductions allowance for a company in a group is to be calculated.

New CTA 2010 s 269ZR applies in respect of the deductions allowance for an accounting period of a company that is at any time in that period a member of a group in which one or more other members are also within the charge to UK corporation tax. The company's deductions allowance in that situation is the sum (which may not exceed £5 million) of all (if any) amounts of the group's deduction allowances allocated to it for the period plus the "appropriate amount of non-group deductions allowance". The non-group deductions allowance comes into play only if the company was not a member of the group for the whole of the accounting period, but there was at least one member of the group that was within the charge to UK corporation tax. The appropriate amount is simply:

$$\frac{DNG}{DAC} \times £5,000,000$$

where DNG is the number of days in the period when the company was not a member of the group and DAC is the total number of days in the period. If the accounting period is shorter than 12 months, the non-group deductions allowance and the overall £5 million limit are reduced in proportion.

New CTA 2010 s 269ZS provides that for a group deduction allowance to be available, the group (which must contain two or more members within the charge to UK corporation tax) must nominate one of its members as the "nominated member". All the members within the charge to UK corporation tax must consent to the nomination and the nominated member must be one of their number. For each accounting period during which the nomination has effect, the group deductions allowance is £5 million, reduced pro rata both if the nomination does not have effect for the entire accounting period and if the accounting period concerned is less than 12 months. The nomination takes effect from the date specified (which may pre-date the date on which it is made) and ceases to have effect when either (a) a new group nomination takes effect; (b) one of the companies (which need not be the nominated member) gives notice of its revocation; or (c) the nominated member ceases to be within the charge to UK corporation tax or leaves the group. HMRC may make regulations to provide for how the nomination is to be made etc.

New CTA 2010 s 269ZT provides that the company that is the nominated member must submit for each accounting period in which its nomination has effect a statement ("the group-allowance allocation statement") allocating the group deductions allowance among the eligible group members. HMRC must receive the statement no later than the first anniversary of the filing date for the nominated member's company tax return for the accounting period to which the statement relates (subject to HMRC's agreement to a later date). New CTA 2010 s 269ZU allows for the submission of a revised statement. A revised statement may be made at any time no later than the latest of (a) the first anniversary of the nominated member's filing date for the company tax return for the accounting period concerned; (b) 30 days after the conclusion of an HMRC enquiry into that return; (c) 30 days after HMRC issues an amended return for that period following an enquiry; and (d) 30 days after an appeal against such an amendment is finally determined. New CTA 2010 s 269ZV provides for the contents of an allocation statement. The statement must not, inter alia, allocate to any of the eligible group companies a greater allowance than it is entitled to if it has not been a member of the group throughout the nominated member's accounting period and the total allocated among the group companies must not exceed the group deduction allowance. Where an excess allocation is made, the nominated member must submit a correct revised statement within 30 days of the occurrence of the event causing the excess, failing which HMRC may amend the allocation statement as the relevant officer thinks fit.

New CTA 2010 s 269ZW sets the deductions allowance for a company that is not a member of a group at £5 million, reduced pro rata if the company's accounting period to which the allowance relates is less than 12 months.

New CTA 2010 ss 269ZX and 269ZY provide for an increase of the deductions allowance where a company that is either insolvent or on the verge of insolvency reverses a provision for an onerous lease. New CTA 2010 s 269ZX provides that where a company brings into account a "relevant-reversal credit" in calculating its "specified profits" for an accounting period, it may increase its deductions allowance by the smaller of the amount of the relevant reversal credit and the specified profits. "Specified profits" are the company's modified total profits (as calculated under new CTA 2010 s 269ZF) for the accounting period plus (in the case of an insurance company, its I − E profit, if any). New CTA 2010 s 269ZY defines "relevant-reversal credit" as a credit or other income brought into account in respect of the "relevant reversal" of "a relevant onerous-lease provision". The latter provision is one relating to an onerous lease of land entered into at arm's length under which the company is the tenant and in respect of which a provision is required for accountancy purposes. A reversal is a "relevant reversal" if it is required for accountancy purposes as a result of an arm's length arrangement under which the company's obligations under the lease are varied or cancelled *and* either (a) it is reasonable to suppose that immediately before the arrangement was made, there was a material risk that within the next 12 months the company would be unable to pay its debts as they fell due and the sole or main purpose of the arrangement was to avert that risk; or (b) the company is in insolvent administration; or (c) the company's arrangement is part of a statutory insolvency arrangement. Special rules apply where the company and the landlord are connected.

New CTA 2010 s 269ZZ provides that a company's tax return must specify the amount of its deductions allowance for the period concerned if it makes a deduction subject to restriction (i.e. it makes a deduction under new CTA 2010 ss 269ZB(2), 269ZC(2) or 269ZD(2) or under new FA 2012 s 124D(1) (inserted by para 26)). New CTA 2010 s 269ZZA provides that if a company specifies an excessive amount as a deductions allowance in its company tax return, it must amend the return if it may still do so. HMRC retain the power to amend the return where it is considered that an excessive amount of relief has been given as a consequence.

Finally, new CTA 2010 s 269ZZB defines what is meant by a "group" for these purposes. The definition is wider than the equivalent for group relief. For the purposes of the deductions allowance, a group consists of an "ultimate parent company" and its subsidiaries. A company is the ultimate parent company of a group if it is the ultimate parent of each of the subsidiaries in the group but is not also the ultimate parent of another company outside the group. A company is an ultimate parent of another if it is the parent of the other company and there is no other company that is the parent of both. The relevant percentage shareholding for parenthood is 75% (or at least 75% of the profits available for distribution to equity holders or at least 75% of the assets available for distribution to equity holders on a winding-up).

Schedule 4 paras 17–22 amend CTA 2010 Part 7A Chapter 3, which contains the existing restrictions on the loss deductions available to banking companies. Schedule 4 para 17 amends CTA 2010 s 269C to provide that the general loss restrictions in new CTA 2010 Part 7ZA are to apply in addition to the special loss restrictions on banking companies, and makes consequential amendments. Schedule 4 paras 18–20 amend CTA 2010 ss 269CA, 269CB and 269CC to align the definitions in those sections of "relevant trading profits", "relevant non-trading profits" and "relevant profits" in those sections with the equivalent definitions in new CTA 2010 ss 269ZF and 269ZD, as the case may be. As a consequence, CTA 2010 s 269CD, which has hitherto defined "relevant profits" for the banking restrictions becomes redundant and is omitted by Sch 4 para 21. Schedule 4 para 22 makes consequential amendments to the definitions in CTA 2010 s 269CN.

Schedule 4 Part 3, which comprises a single paragraph (para 23), inserts new CTA 2010 Part 5A, which provides for group relief to be available for losses carried forward. Group relief has previously been available for current-period losses only. New CTA 2010 Part 5A, entitled "Group relief for carried-forward losses", contains 49 sections (new CTA 2010 ss 188AA-188FD) and is divided into six Chapters.

New CTA 2010 Part 5A Chapter 1 consists of a single section, new CTA 2010 s 188AA, which is introductory.

New CTA 2010 Part 5A Chapter 2 consists of 10 sections (new CTA 2010 ss 188BA–188BJ) and provides for the surrender of losses and other amounts. New CTA 2010 s 188BA is introductory, and provides that the purpose of the Chapter is to allow a company to surrender losses and other amounts that have been carried forward to a [later] accounting period ("the surrender period") of the company.

New CTA 2010 s 188BB provides that a company (provided, of course, that it is a member of a group) may surrender specified losses or other amounts that it has carried forward to a later period by way of group relief. The losses and other amounts specified are:

(1) post-1 April 2017 non-trading deficits carried forward under new CTA 2009 s 463G(6);

(2) non-trading losses on intangible fixed assets carried forward under CTA 2009 s 753(3);

(3) excess expenses of management of a company with investment business carried forward under CTA 2009 s 1223;

(4) post-1 April 2017 trade losses carried forward under new CTA 2010 s 45A(4);

(5) losses of a UK property business carried forward under CTA 2010 ss 62(5)(a) and 63(3)(a);

(6) excess non-decommissioning losses of an oil or gas ring-fence trade carried forward under new CTA 2010 s 303C (inserted by para 48).

These are all losses etc that are carried forward for set-off against total profits. Losses etc that are carried forward for set off against trading profits or non-trading profits only are not to be eligible for group relief.

In the case of BLAGAB trade losses carried forward by an insurance company, these may be surrendered in the amount (if any) that remains after priority set-off against BLAGAB trade profits of a later period.

Where losses etc carried forward are to be surrendered, this is to be done by the company's giving consent to one or more claims for group relief made under new CTA 2010 ss 188CB and 188CC.

New CTA 2010 s 188BC provides that pre-1 April 2017 losses carried forward are not to be eligible for surrender. Specifically, these are:

(1) non-trading losses on intangible fixed assets carried forward under CTA 2009 s 753(3) from an accounting period beginning before 1 April 2017;

(2) excess expenses of management of a company with investment business first deductible under CTA 2009 s 1219 for an accounting period beginning before 1 April 2017 and carried forward under CTA 2009 s 1223;

(3) losses of a UK property business carried forward under CTA 2010 ss 62(5)(a) and 63(3)(a) and incurred in an accounting period beginning before 1 April 2017;

(4) excess qualifying charitable donations of a company with investment business carried forward under CTA 2009 s 1223, whenever made.

New CTA 2010 ss 188BD–188BJ contain further restrictions on the availability of group relief. New CTA 2010 s 188BD provides that losses and expenses carried forward by a company with investment business whose investment business has become small or negligible may not surrender those losses etc in a surrender period beginning after that event. New CTA 2010 s 188BE contains the important provision that a company may surrender losses carried forward only if it cannot make use of those losses itself in the surrender period. More precisely, if the other "relevant deductions" (as defined in new CTA 2010 s 269ZD(3)) the company may make amount to less than the company's relevant maximum. New CTA 2010 s 188BF provides that a company may not surrender any losses or other amounts carried forward if at the end of the surrender period it has no assets capable of producing income. New CTA 2010 s 188BG applies to insurance companies in two different situations. Where the company is a general insurance company, and the surrender period is an excluded period (as defined in new CTA 2010 s 269ZG), none of the following losses etc may be surrendered:

(1) non-trading losses on intangible fixed assets carried forward under CTA 2009 s 753(3);

(2) excess expenses of management of a company with investment business carried forward under CTA 2009 s 1223;

(3) losses of a UK property business carried forward under CTA 2010 ss 62(5)(a) and 63(3)(a).

The second situation is that of a Solvency 2 insurance company, which may not surrender the same losses etc numbered (1) to (3) above in any surrender period in which it has that status, so far as the loss or expenses is or are a "shock loss".

New CTA 2010 ss 188BH–188BJ are intended to prevent double non-taxation. New CTA 2010 s 188BH provides that a company that was UK-resident in the loss-making period cannot surrender any part of a loss or other amount ("loss etc") that is attributable to a trade it carried on outside the United Kingdom in a foreign permanent establishment if the loss etc is, or at any time has been, deductible by any person other than the surrendering company in computing tax in the jurisdiction in which the permanent establishment is situated.

New CTA 2010 s 188BI covers the reverse situation, that in which the surrendering company was non-resident during the loss-making period and either the company was carrying on a trade of dealing in or developing UK land or carrying on a trade in the United Kingdom through a permanent establishment here (and therefore within the charge to UK corporation tax). One of two sets of restrictions apply in this situation, depending on whether the surrendering company was, or was not, established in the European Economic Area during the loss-making period. If it was EEA-established, then it may only surrender the loss etc if two conditions (A and B) are met. Condition A is that the loss etc is attributable to activities in respect of which the company was within the charge to UK corporation tax for the loss-making period and condition B is that the loss etc is not attributable to activities that are exempt from UK tax for the loss-making period under a double tax treaty. Even where these two conditions are met, the loss etc may not be surrendered if and to the extent that any amount brought into account in computing it has in any period been deducted by any person in any foreign jurisdiction. If the company was not EEA-established, it must meet a third condition if it is to be able to surrender the loss etc. That third condition is that the loss etc or any amount brought into account in calculating it is, or at any time has been, deductible in computing tax by any person in any foreign jurisdiction. New CTA 2010 s 188BJ imports the provisions of CTA 2010 s 109, which restricts the losses that a dual-resident company may surrender under current-period group relief.

New CTA 2010 Part 5A Chapter 3 consists of 11 sections (new CTA 2010 ss 188CA–188CK) and provides for the making and giving of claims for group relief for losses etc carried forward. New CTA 2010 s 188CA introduces the Chapter. Much of what the Chapter contains will be already familiar in terms of the existing group relief under CTA 2010 Part 5 ("current-period group relief").

New CTA 2010 s 188CB is similarly worded to CTA 2010 s 130 and provides that a company ("the claimant company") may, provided that three requirements are met, make a claim for group relief for the carried-forward losses of the surrendering company for an accounting period of its own ("the claim period"). The claim may be for all or part of the "surrenderable amounts" (the losses etc eligible for surrender) of the surrendering company for its surrender period. The three requirements are that:

Requirement 1: The surrendering company consent to the claim

Requirement 2: There is a period common to the claim period and the surrender period. This is referred to as "the overlapping period"

Requirement 3: At a time during the overlapping period, either the group condition, consortium condition 1 or consortium condition 2 is met

Consortium conditions 1 and 2 may only be met by a claimant company that is owned by a consortium.

New CTA 2010 s 188CC covers the situation where consortium conditions 3 or 4 must be met. Those conditions apply to surrendering companies owned by a consortium. It mirrors new CTA 2010 s 188CB but requires the claim to specify a particular loss-making accounting period of the surrendering company. Accordingly, the three requirements that must be met for a successful claim are:

Requirement 1: The surrendering company consent to the claim

Requirement 2: There is a period common to the claim period and the surrender period. This is referred to as "the overlapping period"

Requirement 3: Throughout a period beginning before the loss-making period and ending during or after the overlapping period, either consortium condition 3 or consortium condition 4 is met.

New CTA 2010 s 188CD prevents a would-be claimant company from making a claim where it still has capacity for claiming deductions in respect of its own losses etc carried forward. The four situations in which it is barred from making a claim in respect of an accounting period are:

(1) Any of its own losses etc as specified in new CTA 2010 s 188BB(1) (i.e. the losses etc numbered (1) to (6) in this Introduction under that section or an amount falling within new FA 2010 s 124B(1)(b) (excess post-1 April 2017 BLAGAB trade losses, inserted by para 26) have been carried forward to the accounting period and not been deducted in full

(2) The company makes a claim under CTA 2009 s 458(1) for any amount of the non-trading deficit carried forward not to be set off in that accounting period

(3) The company makes a claim under new CTA 2010 s 45(4A) (pre-1 April 2017 trade losses carried forward) for some or all of the loss not to be set off in that accounting period and

(4) The company makes a claim under new CTA 2010 s 45B(5) (restricted post-1 April 2017 trade losses carried forward) for some of the loss not to be set off in that accounting period.

New CTA 2010 s 188CE contains the group condition. This is identical to the equivalent provision (CTA 2010 s 131) for current-period group relief, except for section references. It is that the surrendering company and the claimant company both be members of the same group of companies and that both be "UK-related" (defined in new CTA 2010 s 188CJ).

New CTA 2010 s 188CF contains consortium condition 1, which is carved out of one "arm" of consortium condition 1 for current-period group relief, as contained in CTA 2010 s 132(3). It is that:

(1) the claimant company is a trading company or a holding company;
(2) the claimant company is owned by a consortium;
(3) the surrendering company is a member of the consortium; and
(4) both companies are "UK-related".

The condition is not met if the profit on a sale by the surrendering company of its shares in the claimant company (or, where applicable, in the holding company through which the shares in the claimant company are held) would be a trading receipt of the surrendering company.

New CTA 2010 s 188CG contains consortium condition 2, which is the equivalent of consortium condition 3 for current-period group relief, as contained in CTA 2010 s 133(2). It is that:

(1) the claimant company is a trading company or a holding company;
(2) the claimant company is owned by a consortium;
(3) the surrendering company is not a member of the consortium; but
(4) the surrendering company is a member of the same group of companies as a third company ("the link company");
(5) the link company is a member of the consortium; and
(4) both the surrendering company and the claimant company are "UK-related".

The condition is not met if the profit on a sale by the link company of its shares in the claimant company (or, where applicable, in the holding company through which the shares in the claimant company are held) would be a trading receipt of the link company.

New CTA 2010 s 188CH contains consortium condition 3, which is carved out of the other "arm" of consortium condition 1 for current-period group relief, as contained in CTA 2010 s 132(2). It is that:

(1) the surrendering company is a trading company or a holding company;
(2) the surrendering company is owned by a consortium;
(3) the claimant company is a member of the consortium; and
(4) both companies are "UK-related".

The condition is not met if the profit on a sale by the claimant company of its shares in the surrendering company (or, where applicable, in the holding company through which the shares in the surrendering company are held) would be a trading receipt of the claimant company.

New CTA 2010 s 188CI contains consortium condition 4, which is the equivalent of consortium condition 2 for current-period group relief, as contained in CTA 2010 s 133(1). It is that:

(1) the surrendering company is a trading company or a holding company;
(2) the surrendering company is owned by a consortium;
(3) the claimant company is not a member of the consortium; but
(4) the claimant company is a member of the same group of companies as a third company ("the link company");
(5) the link company is a member of the consortium; and
(6) both the surrendering company and the claimant company are "UK-related".

The condition is not met if the profit on a sale by the link company of its shares in the surrendering company (or, where applicable, in the holding company through which the shares in the surrendering company are held) would be a trading receipt of the link company.

New CTA 2010 s 188J defines the meaning of "UK-related". The definition is identical to that for current-period group relief found in CTA 2010 s 134, namely that a company is UK-related if it is either resident in the United Kingdom or carrying on a trade in the United Kingdom through a permanent establishment.

New CTA 2010 s 188CK provides for how group relief for carried-forward losses etc is to be given and is similar to the equivalent provision, CTA 2010 s 137, for current-period group relief. It provides that on a claim by the claimant company under new CTA 2010 s 188CB or 188CC, group relief for carried-forward losses is given by making a deduction from the claimant company's total profits of the claim period.

For a claim under new CTA 2010 s 188CB, the amount of the deduction is equal to the whole or part of the surrendering company's surrenderable amounts for the surrender period. For a claim under new CTA 2010 s 188CC, the amount of the deduction is equal to the whole or part of the surrendering company's surrenderable amounts for the surrender period which are attributable to the specified loss-making period.

The deduction is to be made in priority to deductions made under CTA 2010 s 37 for a loss incurred in an accounting period after the claim period, under CAA 2001 s 260(3) for capital allowances for an accounting period after the claim period, and under CTA 2009 ss 389 (an insurance company's loan-relationship deficit) carried back from a period after the claim period or new CTA 2009 s 463B (non-trading loan-relationship deficit) carried back from a period after the claim period. With these exceptions, the deduction must be made after all other deductions in Step 2 in CTA 2010 s 4(2).

Both claims under new CTA 2010 s 188CB and 188CC are subject to the restriction that relief for corporation tax is not to be given more than once for the same amount and to the loss restrictions in new CTA 2010 s 269ZD for deductions from total profits. In addition, claims under new CTA 2010 s 188CB are subject to the restrictions in new CTA 2010 Part 5A Chapter 4 and claims under new CTA 2010 s 188CC are subject to the restrictions in new CTA 2010 Part 5A Chapter 5.

New CTA 2010 Part 5A Chapter 4 consists of 12 sections (new CTA 2010 ss 188DA–188DL) and contains limitations on relief relating to claims under new CTA 2010 s 188CB. It therefore covers situations where the companies are in a group relationship, or where the claimant company is owned by a consortium and the surrendering company is a member of the consortium or a member of the same group as the link company. These limitations match but are not identical to the equivalent provisions for current-period group relief in CTA 2010 ss 138–149. New CTA 2010 s 188DA is introductory.

New CTA 2010 s 188DB places a general limitation on all claims under new CTA 2010 s 188CB. It is equivalent to CTA 2010 s 138. It provides that the amount of group relief for carried-forward losses to be given on a claim under new CTA 2010 s 188CB is to be limited to the smaller of (a) the unused part of the surrenderable amounts (as defined in new CTA 2010 s 188DC) and (b) the difference between (i) the claimant company's "relevant maximum for the overlapping period" (as defined in new CTA 2010 s 188DD) and (ii) the amount of previously claimed group relief for carried-forward losses for the overlapping period (as defined in new CTA 2010 s 188DE).

New CTA 2010 s 188DC prescribes how the unused part of the surrenderable amounts is to be calculated. It is the equivalent of CTA 2010 s 139 and is virtually identically worded. Thus, the unused part of the surrenderable amounts is the amount equal to the surrenderable amount for the overlapping period (the overlapping period is defined in new CTA 2010 s 188DG) less the amount of prior surrenders for that period. The surrenderable amount for the overlapping period is that proportion of the surrenderable amounts for the surrender period which equals the proportion of the surrender period included in the overlapping period. The amount of prior surrenders for the overlapping period is the total of "previously used amounts" (of group relief for carried-forward losses) for each prior claim. A prior claim is either (a) a claim under new CTA 2010 s 188CB by any company which relates to the same amounts as the current claim or (b) a claim under new CTA 2010 s 188CC by any company which relates to amounts included in the amounts to which the current claim relates, and which was made before the current claim and has not been withdrawn. The previously used amount for any prior claim is found by finding for each prior claim if there is any period that is common to the overlapping period for the current claim and the overlapping period for the prior claim. If there is no common period, there is no previously used amount. If there is a common period, the previously used amount is found by taking the proportion of the overlapping period for the prior claim that is included in the common period and applying it to the amount of group relief for carried-forward losses given on the prior claim.

New CTA 2010 s 188DD prescribes how the "claimant company's relevant maximum for the overlapping period" (as mentioned in new CTA 2010 s 188DB) is to be calculated. This is to be calculated in a three-step process. Step 1 is to calculate the claimant company's relevant maximum for the claim period in accordance with new CTA 2010 s 269ZD(4). Step 2 is to deduct from the Step 1 amount any deductions already made by the company for the claim period under:

(1) CTA 2010 s 45(4)(b) (pre-1 April 2017 trade losses carried forward);

(2) New CTA 2010 s 45B(4) (restricted post-1 April 2017 trade losses carried forward);

(3) New CTA 2010 s 303B or 303D by virtue of CTA 2010 s 304(5) (excess non-decommissioning losses of a ring-fence trade carried forward for set-off against profits from related activities);

(4) CTA 2010 s 457(3) (pre-1 April non-trading deficits brought forward) and new CTA 2010 s 463H(5) (restricted post-1 April 2017 non-trading deficits brought forward);

(5) FA 2012 s 124(5) or new FA 2012 ss 124A(5) or 124C(6) (excess BLAGAB trade losses carried forward); and

(6) New CTA 269ZD(3) (a)–(i), (k). These are the "relevant deductions" numbered (i)–(viii) and (x) in this Introduction under that section.

These are all deductions subject to loss restrictions. Accordingly, the deduction numbered (1) above must *exclude* those losses not subject to the restriction, namely the losses numbered (1)–(7) in this Introduction in the note to new CTA 2010 s 269ZF.

Step 3 is to take the proportion of the claim period included in the overlapping period and apply that proportion to the Step 2 amount. The result is the claimant company's relevant maximum for the overlapping period.

Step 1 is modified if the claimant company's relevant profits for the claim period, calculated under new CTA 2010 s 269ZD(5), are less than the amount of its deductions allowance for the claim period, calculated under CTA 2010 s 269ZD(6), and steps 1 and 2 are modified if the special loss cap under new CTA 2010 s 269ZE applies to an insurance company.

New CTA 2010 ss 188DE prescribes how the final special term referred to in new CTA 2010 s 188DB, namely the "previously claimed group relief for carried-forward losses for the overlapping period", is to be calculated. First, any prior claims must be identified. A "prior claim" for this purpose is a claim made under new CTA 2010 ss 188CB or 188CC by the claimant company for group relief for carried-forward losses made before the current claim and not withdrawn. For each such prior claim, there must be identified any period common to the overlapping period for the current claim and the overlapping period for the prior claim. If there is no such common period, there is no previously claimed amount in relation to the prior claim. If there is a common period, the proportion of the overlapping period for the prior claim that is included in the common period must be applied to the amount of group relief for carried-forward losses given on the prior claim. The result ("A") is the previously claimed group relief for carried-forward losses in relation to the prior claim. The amount of previously claimed group relief for carried-forward losses for the overlapping period is then the sum of the amounts A for each prior claim. New CTA 2010 s 188DF provides that where two or more claims for group relief for carried-forward losses are made at the same time, they are to be treated as made in such order as the company making them elects or companies making them jointly elect, failing which the order will be directed by HMRC.

New CTA 2010 s 188DG defines the overlapping period referred to in new CTA 2010 ss 188DC and 188DE. It closely matches CTA 2010 s 142, which is the equivalent provision for current-period group relief. This is the period that is common to the claim period and the surrender period. However, if for any part of the overlapping period the relief condition (i.e. the group condition or any of the consortium conditions) is not met, that part is to be treated neither as part of the surrender period included in the overlapping period nor as part of the claim period included in the overlapping period.

New CTA 2010 ss 188DH–188DL impose further limitations on the amount of relief in relation to consortium claims. They are the equivalent provisions to those of CTA 2010 ss 143–149 for current-period group relief inasmuch as they relate to the corresponding consortium conditions and apply solely to claims conditional on consortium conditions 1 or 2 (or both).

New CTA 2010 s 188DH relates to claims made by the claimant company under new CTA 2010 s 188CB reliant on consortium condition 1. It matches CTA 2010 s 144, with the substitution of the "relevant maximum" here for the "available total profits" there. The relief to be given is limited to the "ownership proportion" of the claimant company's relevant maximum for the overlapping period (as determined under new CTA 2010 s 188DD). The "ownership proportion" is the lowest of the following proportions prevailing during the overlapping period:

(1) the proportion of the claimant company's ordinary share capital beneficially owned by the surrendering company;

(2) the proportion of any of the claimant company's profits available for distribution to equity holders to which the surrendering company is beneficially entitled;

(3) the proportion of the claimant company's assets available for distribution to equity holders on a winding-up to which the surrendering company would be beneficially entitled; and

(4) the proportion of the claimant company's voting power that is directly possessed by the surrendering company.

If any of these proportions changes during the overlapping period, the average over the period is to be used.

Where the claimant company is owned by the consortium through a holding company, references to the claimant company are to be substituted by references to the holding company.

New CTA 2010 s 188DI relates to claims made claimant company under new CTA 2010 s 188CB reliant on consortium condition 2 (which involves a link company). It matches CTA 2010 s 145(2). The same limitation is to apply as under new CTA 2010 s 188DH, but the proportions (1) to (4) in that section are to be read by substituting references to the surrendering company by references to the link company.

New CTA 2010 s 188DJ also applies where the claimant company makes a claim under new CTA 2010 s 188CB reliant on consortium condition 2. It matches CTA 2010 s 146(4)–(7). Here, a limit is to be placed on the total amount of group relief for carried-forward losses that may be given to a claimant company for the claim period on consortium claims made in relation to losses etc surrendered by the link company and other companies in the group to which the link company belongs.

That limit is the limit that would apply under new CTA 2010 s 188DH in relation to a consortium claim made by the claimant company for the claim period in relation to losses etc surrendered by the link company, assuming that it was UK-related (which it need not be), and assuming that the accounting period of the link company was the same as the accounting period of the claimant company. The limit equates to the proportion of the claimant company's relevant maximum that it could claim in relation to the link company's surrenderable losses.

New CTA 2010 s 188DK is an anti-avoidance provision that applies under both consortium conditions 1 and 2 in order to counteract arrangements in place to prevent the surrendering company from controlling the claimant company. It mirrors CTA 2010 s 146B, and applies where:

(1) the claimant company makes a claim under new CTA 2010 s 188CB that relies on consortium condition 1 and there are arrangements in place during any part of the overlapping period which enable a person to prevent the surrendering company, either alone or together with one or more other consortium-member companies, from controlling the claimant company or

(2) the claimant company makes a claim under new CTA 2010 s 188CB that relies on consortium condition 2 and there are arrangements in place during any part of the overlapping period which enable a person to prevent the link company, either alone or together with one or more other consortium-member companies, from controlling the claimant company

and the arrangements are part of a scheme the main purpose or one of the main purposes of which is to enable the claimant company to obtain a tax advantage relating to group relief for carried-forward losses.

Where new CTA 2010 s 188DK applies, the relief to be given under the claim is to be calculated as if the claimant company's relevant maximum for the overlapping period were 50% of what it would otherwise be.

New CTA 2010 s 188DL also applies in relation to consortium conditions 1 and 2 and limits the relief where the claimant company is a member of a group of companies. It is the equivalent under this Part of CTA 2010 s 149. Where it applies, the claimant company's relevant maximum for the overlapping period is to be calculated by reducing the step 1 amount under new CTA 2010 s 188DD by the group's "potential relief", but not below zero.

The group's "potential relief" is the sum of:

(1) the maximum amount of current-period group relief (i.e. relief under CTA 2010 Part 5) that the claimant company could claim for the claim period on claims based on the group condition under Part 5 and

(2) the maximum amount of group relief for carried-forward losses (i.e. relief under this Part, new CTA 2010 Part 5A) that the claimant company could claim for the claim period on claims based on the group condition under Part 5A,

while ensuring that any claims made (whether under Part 5 or new Part 5A) before the claim in question by another member of the same group of companies as the claimant company reliant on the group condition are taken into account.

New CTA 2010 Part 5A Chapter 5 consists of 11 sections (new CTA 2010 ss 188EA–188EK) and forms the parallel set of provisions to those of new CTA 2010 Part 5A Chapter 4 but in this case limiting the relief available on a claim under new CTA 2010 s 188CC. It therefore applies only in relation to consortium conditions 3 and 4, where the surrendering company is owned by a consortium and the claimant company is either a member of the consortium (consortium condition 3) or a member of the link company's group (consortium condition 4). New CTA 2010 s 188EA is introductory.

New CTA 2010 s 188EB is the equivalent of new CTA 2010 s 188DB and places a general limitation on all claims under new CTA 2010 s 188CC. It provides that the amount of group relief for carried-forward losses to be given on a claim under new CTA 2010 s 188CC is to be limited to the smaller of (a) the unused part of the surrenderable amounts attributable to the specified loss-making period (as defined in new CTA 2010 s 188EC); (b) the difference between (i) the claimant company's "relevant maximum for the overlapping period" (as defined in new CTA 2010 s 188ED) and (ii) the amount of previously claimed group relief for carried-forward losses for the overlapping period (as defined in new CTA 2010 s 188EE); and (c) the "potential Part 5 group-relief amount" (as defined in new CTA 2010 s 188EF).

New CTA 2010 s 188EC is the equivalent of new CTA 2010 s 188DC and prescribes how the unused part of the surrenderable amounts attributable to the specified loss-making period is to be calculated. The unused part of the surrenderable amounts attributable to the specified loss-making period is to be the amount equal to the surrenderable amount for the overlapping period less the amount of prior surrenders for that period. The surrenderable amount for the overlapping period is found by taking the proportion of the surrender period included in the overlapping period and applying it to the surrenderable amounts for the surrender period that are attributable to the specified loss-making period. The amount of prior surrenders for the overlapping period is the total of "previously used amounts" (of group relief for carried-forward losses) for each prior claim. A prior claim is either (a) a claim under new CTA 2010 s 188CB by any company which relates to the same amounts to which the current claim relates or (b) a claim under new CTA 2010 s 188CC by any company which relates to the same amounts to which the current claim relates, and which was made before the current claim and has not been withdrawn. The previously used amount for any prior claim is found by finding for each prior claim if there is any period that is common to the overlapping period for the current claim and the overlapping period for the prior claim. If there is no common period, there is no previously used amount.

If there is a common period, the previously used amount for prior claims made under new CTA 2010 s 188CB is found by taking the proportion of the overlapping period for the prior claim that is included in the common period and applying it to the amount of group relief for carried-forward losses given on the prior claim, and then multiplying the result by the fraction A/B where A is the sum of the surrenderable amounts attributable to the specified loss-making period and B is the sum of all the surrenderable amounts. The previously used amount for prior claims under new CTA 2010 s 188CC, on the other hand, is found by taking the proportion of the overlapping period for the prior claim that is included in the common period and applying it to the amount of group relief for carried-forward losses given on the prior claim.

New CTA 2010 s 188ED is the equivalent of new CTA 2010 s 188DD and prescribes how the "claimant company's relevant maximum for the overlapping period" (as mentioned in new CTA 2010 s 188EB) is to be calculated. This is to be done in a three-step process. Step 1 is to calculate the claimant company's relevant maximum for the claim period in accordance with new CTA 2010 s 269ZD(4). Step 2 is to deduct from the Step 1 amount any deductions already made by the company for the claim period under:

(1) CTA 2010 s 45(4)(b) (pre-1 April 2017 trade losses carried forward);

(2) New CTA 2010 s 45B(4) (restricted post-1 April 2017 trade losses carried forward);

(3) New CTA 2010 s 303B or 303D by virtue of CTA 2010 s 304(5) (excess non-decommissioning losses of a ring-fence trade carried forward for set-off against profits from related activities);

(4) CTA 2010 s 457(3) (pre-1 April non-trading deficits brought forward) and new CTA 2010 s 463H(5) (restricted post-1 April 2017 non-trading deficits brought forward);

(5) FA 2012 s 124(5) or new FA 2012 ss 124A(5) or 124C(6) (excess BLAGAB trade losses carried forward); and

(6) New CTA 269ZD(3) (a)–(i), (k). These are the "relevant deductions" numbered (i)–(viii) and (x) in this Introduction in the note to that section.

These are all deductions subject to loss restrictions. Accordingly, the deduction numbered (1) above must *exclude* those losses not subject to the restriction, namely the losses numbered (1)–(7) in this Introduction in the note to new CTA 2010 s 269ZF.

Step 3 is to take the proportion of the claim period included in the overlapping period and apply that proportion to the Step 2 amount. The result is the claimant company's relevant maximum for the overlapping period.

Step 1 is modified if the claimant company's relevant profits for the claim period, calculated under new CTA 2010 s 269ZD(5), are less than the amount of its deductions allowance for the claim period, calculated under CTA 2010 s 269ZD(6), and steps 1 and 2 are modified if the special loss cap under new CTA 2010 s 269ZE applies to an insurance company.

New CTA 2010 s 188EE is the equivalent of new CTA 2010 s 188DE and prescribes how the element referred to in new CTA 2010 s 188EB as the "previously claimed group relief for carried-forward losses for the overlapping period", is to be calculated. First, any prior claims must be identified. A "prior claim" for this purpose is a claim made under new CTA 2010 ss 188CB or 188CC by the claimant company for group relief for carried-forward losses made before the current claim and not withdrawn. For each such prior claim, there must be identified any period common to the overlapping period for the current claim and the overlapping period for the prior claim. If there is no such common period, there is no previously claimed amount in relation to the prior claim. If there is a common period, the proportion of the overlapping period for the prior claim that is included in the common period must be applied to the amount of group relief for carried-forward losses given on the prior claim. The result ("A") is the previously claimed group relief for carried-forward losses in relation to the prior claim. The amount of previously claimed group relief for carried-forward losses for the overlapping period is then the sum of the amounts A for each prior claim.

New CTA 2010 s 188EF has no equivalent in new CTA 2010 Part 5A Chapter 4. It prescribes how the final element referred to in new CTA 2010 s 188EB, namely the "potential Part 5 group relief amount", is to be calculated. This requires a four-step process.

Step 1 is to calculate the maximum amount of group relief that the claimant company could have had under CTA 2010 Part 5 (current-period group relief) for losses etc that the surrendering company had (by reference to CTA 2010 s 99(1)) for the specified loss-making period, ignoring any insufficiency of profits of the claimant company from which the relief could have been deducted.

Step 2 is to deduct from the step 1 amount the amount of any group relief actually given to the claimant company under CTA 2010 Part 5 in relation to those losses etc of the surrendering company.

Step 3 is to multiply the step 2 amount by the fraction A/B, where A is the sum of the losses etc that the surrendering company had for the specified loss-making period (by reference to CTA 2010 s 99(1) but ignoring excess capital allowances and qualifying charitable donations) and were eligible for surrender and B is the sum of all the losses etc listed under CTA 2010 s 99(1) that were eligible for surrender.

Step 4 is to deduct from the step 3 amount any group relief for carried-forward losses that the claimant company had previously received on claims made under new CTA 2010 s 188CC which are related to the current claim (i.e. where both the surrendering company and the specified loss-making period are the same).

New CTA 2010 s 188EG is equivalent to new CTA 2010 s 188DF and provides that where two or more claims for group relief for carried-forward losses are made at the same time, they are to be treated as made in such order as the company making them elects or companies making them jointly elect, failing which the order will be directed by HMRC.

New CTA 2010 s 188EH is equivalent to new CTA 2010 s 188DG and defines the overlapping period referred to in new CTA 2010 ss 188EC and 188EE. It closely matches CTA 2010 s 142, which is the equivalent provision for current-period group relief. The overlapping period is the period that is common to the claim period and the surrender period. However, if for any part of the overlapping period the relief condition (i.e. the group condition or any of the consortium conditions) is not met, that part is to be treated neither as part of the surrender period included in the overlapping period nor as part of the claim period included in the overlapping period.

New CTA 2010 ss 188EI–188EK impose further limitations on the amount of relief in relation to consortium claims. They are the equivalent provisions to those of CTA 2010 ss 143–149 for current-period group relief inasmuch as they relate to the corresponding consortium conditions and apply solely to claims conditional on consortium conditions 3 or 4 (or both).

New CTA 2010 s 188EI is the equivalent of new CTA 2010 s 188DJ but relates to consortium condition 4 rather than to consortium condition 2. It applies where the claimant company makes a claim under new CTA 2010 s 188CC reliant on consortium condition 4. It matches CTA 2010 s 146(1)–(3). Here, a limit is to be placed on the total amount of group relief for carried-forward losses that may be given on "relevant consortium claims" made by the link company and other companies in the group to which the link company belongs ("group companies").

That limit is the maximum amount of group relief for carried-forward losses that could be given to the link company on "relevant consortium claims", assuming that the link company was UK-related (which it need not be), and that no relevant consortium claims were made by group companies based on consortium condition 4, and ignoring any insufficiency of profits of the link company from which the deductions could be made. "Relevant consortium claims" are consortium claims in relation to which the surrendering company, the surrender period and the specified loss-making period are the same as for the claim made by the claimant company on which this section is premised.

New CTA 2010 s 188EJ is the equivalent anti-avoidance provision to new CTA 2010 s 188DK, but in this case aimed at countering arrangements to prevent the claimant company from controlling the surrendering company. It applies under both consortium conditions 3 and 4 and mirrors CTA 2010 s 146A. It applies where:

(1) the claimant company makes a claim under new CTA 2010 s 188CC that relies on consortium condition 3 and there are arrangements in place during any part of the overlapping period which enable a person to prevent the claimant company, either alone or together with one or more other consortium-member companies, from controlling the surrendering company; or

(2) the claimant company makes a claim under new CTA 2010 s 188CC that relies on consortium condition 4 and there are arrangements in place during any part of the overlapping period which enable a person to prevent the link company, either alone or together with one or more other consortium-member companies, from controlling the surrendering company,

and the arrangements are part of a scheme the main purpose or one of the main purposes of which is to enable the claimant company to obtain a tax advantage relating to group relief for carried-forward losses.

Where new CTA 2010 s 188EJ applies, the relief to be given under the claim is to be calculated as if the surrenderable amount for the overlapping period were 50% of what it would otherwise be.

New CTA 2010 s 188EK is the equivalent of new CTA 2010 s 188DL and also applies in relation to consortium conditions 3 and 4, limiting the relief where the claimant company is a member of a group of companies. It is the equivalent under this Part of CTA 2010 s 149. Where it applies, the surrendering company's surrenderable amounts for the surrender period which are attributable to the specified loss-making period are to be treated as reduced, but not below zero, by the "relevant amount". The "relevant amount" is the "group's potential relief", multiplied by the fraction A/B, where A is the sum of the surrendering company's surrenderable amounts for the surrender period which are attributable to the specified loss-making period and B is the sum of all the surrendering company's surrenderable amounts for the surrender period.

The "group's potential relief" is the maximum amount of group relief for carried-forward losses (i.e. relief under this Part, new CTA 2010 Part 5A) that could be given if every claim that could be based on the group condition in respect of the surrenderable amounts for the surrender period were in fact made, assuming that in every case the maximum possible claim was made, while ensuring that any claims made under new Part 5A before the current claim based on the group condition in relation to losses etc surrendered by another member of the same group of companies as the surrendering company are taken into account.

New CTA 2010 Part 5A Chapter 6 consists of four sections (new CTA 2010 ss 188FA-188FD) and contains miscellaneous and interpretative provisions.

New CTA 2010 s 188FA is the equivalent of CTA 2010 s 183 and provides that where an agreement exists between the claimant company and the surrendering company under which the claimant company makes a payment to the surrendering company in respect of group relief for carried-forward losses, that payment is to be ignored in determining the profits or losses of either company for the purposes of corporation tax and is not to be treated as a distribution.

New CTA 2010 s 188FB provides that questions as to whether a company is a member of a group or is owned by a consortium and other key concepts are to be interpreted as they are for the purposes of current-period group relief, by reference to CTA 2010 Part 5 Chapter 5. New CTA 2010 s 188FC defines "trading company" and "holding company", in terms identical for all practical purposes to the equivalent definitions in CTA 2010 s 185 (NB: the Queen's printer's copy of the Lords Bill erroneously omits the words "of companies" that should precede the word "that" in line 8 of page 231 from new CTA 2010 s 188FC(2)). New CTA 2010 s 188FD contains other definitions.

Schedule 4 Part 4 comprises paras 24–26 and amends the provisions for the carry-forward of BLAGAB trade losses by insurance companies, to align them with the new rules of Sch 4 Parts 1 and 2.

Schedule 4 para 24 introduces the amendments to be made to FA 2012 Part 2 Chapter 9. Schedule 4 para 25 amends FA 2012 s 124 (relief for BLAGAB trade losses against total profits) to restrict its application to pre-1 April 2017 losses.

Schedule 4 para 26 inserts new FA 2012 ss 124A–124E, which apply to post-1 April BLAGAB trade losses.

New FA 2012 s 124A provides that where an insurance company carrying on BLAGAB (basic life assurance and general annuity business) makes a post-1 April 2017 BLAGAB trade loss which it chooses not to set off in full against current-period total profits under CTA 2010 s 37 or surrender as group relief under CTA 2010 Part 5, it may carry the unrelieved amount forward to the next period, provided that it continues to carry on the BLAGAB in that period, for relief against BLAGAB trade profits. New FA 2012 s 124B provides that where the unrelieved amount of a post-1 April 2017 BLAGAB trade loss is carried forward to the next period but any part of it is not deducted from the BLAGAB trade profit of that period, a claim may be made for it to be set off against the company's total profits of that period, except and to the extent that it is not a shock loss of a Solvency 2 insurance company. New FA 2012 s 124C provides for a continuation of carry-forward relief. If not all of the unrelieved amount is set off in the next period, or surrendered as group relief for carried-forward losses under CTA 2010 Part 5A, what remains unrelieved may be carried forward to subsequent periods for set-off against BLAGAB trade profits of the subsequent period. In each case, set-off takes place by deduction from the relevant profits.

New FA 2012 s 124D restricts the total amount of deductions an insurance company may make in any later period under FA 2012 ss 124 and new ss 124A and 124C to the "relevant maximum". This is the sum of (a) the company's BLAGAB trade-profits deductions allowance for the accounting period and (b) 50% of what remains of the BLAGAB trade profit after deducting the BLAGAB trade-profits deductions allowance. The BLAGAB trade-profits deductions allowance is so much of the company's deductions allowance as it designates as such, subject to not exceeding the overall limit. New FA 2012 s 124E excludes the shock loss of a Solvency 2 insurance company from the restriction under new FA 2012 s 124D.

Schedule 4 Part 5 comprises paras 27–46 and imports the new loss carry-forward rules and loss restriction into the various reliefs for creative industries.

Schedule 4 paras 27–30 apply to film tax relief under CTA 2009 Part 15. Schedule 4 para 27 is introductory. Schedule 4 para 28 amends CTA 2009 s 1209, which restricts the relief for a pre-completion loss in the separate film trade to carry-forward relief under CTA 2010 s 45, to include also relief under new CTA 2010 s 45B, and to provide that losses carried forward under either CTA 2010 s 45 or new CTA 2010 s 45B are to be ignored when calculating the restriction on deductions from trade profits under new CTA 2010 s 269ZB. Schedule 4 para 29 amends CTA 2009 s 1210, which prescribes how losses in the separate film trade may be used in later periods. Where a loss from a pre-completion period is carried forward to the completion period and beyond, under new CTA 2010 s 45B, as well as under CTA 2010 s 45, so much of the loss as is not attributable to film tax relief is to be treated for the purposes of CTA 2010 s 37 and group relief under CTA 2010 Part 5 as if it were a loss made in the later period. These are "relevant deductions" for the purposes of new CTA 2010 s 269ZD and hence subject to restriction. As regards a loss made in a relevant later period, so much of that loss as is not attributable to film tax relief may be (a) deducted from total profits of the same or an earlier period under CTA 2010 s 37; (b) carried forward to be deducted from total profits of a later period under new CTA 2010 s 45A; or (c) surrendered as group relief under CTA 2010 Part 5. Losses used under new CTA 2010 s 45A are also "relevant deductions" under new CTA 2010 s 269ZD and thus subject to restriction. However, losses applied as deductions under CTA 2010 s 45 or new CTA 2010 s 45B from profits of the separate film trade are not subject to the restriction, to the extent they are attributable to film tax relief. Schedule 4 para 30 amends CTA 2009 s 1211, which provides for terminal loss relief when a company ceases to carry on a separate film trade ("trade X") that the company would otherwise have been able to carry forward under CTA 2010 s 45 by treating the terminal loss as if it were a loss of a different separate film trade ("trade Y" or "trade Z") that the company carries on. The section is amended to include the possibility of carry-forward under either new CTA 2010 ss 45A or 45B. Where deductions are made in trade Y or trade Z under CTA 2010 s 45 or new CTA 2010 s 45B, these deductions are ignored for the purpose of the restriction under new CTA 2010 s 269ZB, whereas deductions under new CTA 2010 s 45A are subject to the restriction under new CTA 2010 s 269ZD.

Schedule 4 paras 31–34 make the identical amendments, mutatis mutandis, to the treatment of the losses of a separate television-programme trade under CTA 2009 Part 15A, amending CTA 2009 ss 1216DA, 1216DB and 1216DC.

Schedule 4 paras 35–38 make the identical amendments, mutatis mutandis, to the treatment of the losses of a separate video-game trade under CTA 2009 Part 15B, amending CTA 2009 ss 1217DA, 1217DB and 1217DC.

Schedule 4 paras 39–42 make the identical amendments, mutatis mutandis, to the treatment of the losses of a separate theatrical trade under CTA 2009 Part 15C, amending CTA 2009 ss 1217MA, 1217MB and 1217MC.

Finally, **Sch 4 paras 43–46** make the identical amendments, mutatis mutandis, to the treatment of the losses of a separate orchestral trade under CTA 2009 Part 15D, amending CTA 2009 ss 1217SA, 1217SB and 1217SC.

Schedule 4 Part 6, comprising paras 47–55, imports the loss carry-forward rules and loss restriction into the provisions relating to oil and gas ring-fence trades. Schedule 4 para 47 is introductory. Schedule 4 para 48 inserts new CTA 2010 ss 303A-303D.

New CTA 2010 s 303A defines a "non-decommissioning loss" as a loss made by a company in a ring-fence trade to the extent that it is not attributable to relevant expenditure in relation to an agreement for decommissioning relief under FA 2013 s 80. The amount that is attributable to such expenditure is the smaller of the total expenditure brought into account in calculating the loss and the amount of the loss itself.

New CTA 2010 s 303B provides that where a company makes a non-decommissioning loss in an accounting period beginning after 31 March 2017 (a "post-1 April non-decommissioning loss") and does not obtain relief for all of that loss under CTA 2010 ss 37 or 42 (further extension of relief period for ring-fence losses) or as group relief under CTA 2010 Part 5, it may carry the unrelieved amount forward to the next accounting period (provided it continues to carry on the ring-fence trade in that period) and obtain relief in the next period by deduction from the profits of the trade in that period. No claim is necessary.

New CTA 2010 s 303C provides that where an amount of the non-decommissioning loss is carried forward to a later period under new CTA 2010 ss 303B or 303D, and any part of that amount is not then deducted in that period from profits of the ring-fence trade of that period, the company may make a claim for relief for the unrelieved amount by deduction from the company's total profits of the later period, provided that the ring-fence trade has not become small or negligible in the meantime and no other non-commerciality reasons prevail.

New CTA 2010 s 303D provides for further carry-forward of losses from the immediately following accounting period. Where a company, having made a post-1 April non-decommissioning loss, has carried it forward to the later accounting period under new CTA 2010 s 303B or this section itself, and any amount still remains unrelieved so far as not (a) deducted under new CTA 2010 s 303B from the company's profit of the later period; (b) deducted from the company's total profits of the later period under new CTA 2010 s 303C; or (c) surrendered as group relief for carried-forward losses under new CTA 2010 Part 5A, it may be carried forward to a subsequent period for deduction against the profits of that subsequent period.

Schedule 4 para 49 amends CTA 2010 s 304 in three respects. The restriction on relief for non-ring-fence losses (except to the extent arising from oil-extraction activities or oil rights) is extended from relief against ring-fence profits under CTA 2010 s 37 to relief under any of CTA 2009 s 753 (non-trading losses on intangible fixed assets), new CTA 2010 s 45A (carry-forward of post-1 April 2017 trade losses for deduction from total profits) and CTA 2010 s 62(3) (relief for losses of a UK property business). The conditional relief allowed under CTA 2010 s 45 by CTA 2010 s 304(5) is extended to relief under new CTA 2010 ss 45B, 303B(4) and 303D(5). Finally, new CTA 2010 s 304(7) provides that deductions in respect of ring-fence losses made under CTA 2010 s 45 (pre-1 April 2017 trade losses) or new CTA 2010 s 45B (restricted post-1 April trade losses) are to be ignored for the purposes of new CTA 2010 s 269ZB, and therefore not subject to the loss restriction.

Schedule 4 para 50 amends CTA 2010 s 305 to provide that group relief for carried-forward losses under new CTA 2010 Part 5A is not to be allowed against the claimant company's ring-fence profits.

Schedule 4 para 51 amends CTA 2010 s 307 to include relief given under new CTA 2010 ss 45B, 303B, 303C and 303D among the deductions in respect of which reductions must be made in determining the amount of ring-fence expenditure supplement to which a company may be entitled. Schedule 4 para 52 amends CTA 2010 s 321, which provides for post-commencement supplement, so that post-commencement supplement allowed in respect of a post-commencement period beginning after 31 March 2017 may also be treated as if it were a loss incurred in the carrying-on of the ring-fence trade and falling wholly to be used under new CTA 2010 s 45B. Schedule 4 para 53 amends CTA 2010 s 323 to include losses used under new CTA 2010 ss 45B or 303B in the definition of ring-fence losses.

Schedule 4 para 54 substitutes a new CTA 2010 s 327. Hitherto, that section has provided how reductions are to be made to the profits of a post-commencement period when one or more ring-fence losses are used under CTA 2010 s 45, principally by reducing the company's non-qualifying pool by the amount so used. The new section is similarly worded but directs that the non-qualifying pool is to be reduced by a sum equal to the relevant amount for the post-commencement period, as defined. The relevant amount includes relief given under new CTA 2010 ss 45B, 303B, 303C and 303D also. Schedule 4 para 55 amends CTA 2010 s 328A so that the adjustments it specifies are to be made to the ring-fence pool also take account of reductions under new CTA 2010 ss 45B, 303B, 303C and 303D.

Schedule 4 Part 7 comprises paras 56–59 and amends CTA 2010 Part 8ZA, which provides for the treatment of oil-contractor activities. Schedule 4 para 56 is introductory.

Schedule 4 para 57 amends CTA 2010 s 356NE to provide that relief in respect of a loss incurred by the contractor may also not be given against the contractor's ring-fence profits under new CTA 2010 s 45A as well as under CTA 2010 s 37 (except so far as the loss arises from oil-contractor activities) nor under CTA 2009 s 753 (non-trading losses on intangible fixed assets), new CTA 2010 s 303C (carry-forward of excess non-decommissioning losses for deduction from total profits) or CTA 2010 s 62(3) (relief for losses of a UK property business). Schedule 4 para 58 amends CTA 2010 s 356NF to provide that group relief for carried-forward losses under new CTA 2010 Part 5A is not to be allowed against the claimant company's contractor's ring-fence profits, except to the extent that the claim relates to losses arising from oil-contractor activities incurred by the surrendering company.

Schedule 4 para 59 inserts new CTA 2010 ss 356NH-356NI. New CTA 2010 s 356NH caps the "relevant deductions" from total profits that an oil contractor may make in any accounting period to the "relevant Part 8ZA maximum", which is the amount of the contractor's ring-fence profits-deductions allowance for the accounting period plus 50% of the contractor's ring-fence profits deductions for that period. The "relevant deductions" in question are:

(1) deductions under CTA 2010 s 45 from subsequent profits of pre-1 April 2017 trade losses carried forward, so far as the loss arises from oil-contractor activities;

(2) deductions under new CTA 2010 s 45A from total profits of post-1 April 2017 trade losses, so far as the deduction is set against the contractor's ring-fence profits; and

(3) any deduction of a loss etc as group relief for carried-forward losses under new CTA 2010 Part 5A, so far as the deduction is set against the contractor's ring-fence profits.

New CTA 2010 s 356NI prescribes how a company's contractor's ring-fence profits-deductions allowance and the company's deductions allowance for the purposes of the loss restriction are to be calculated.

The first step is to determine what the company's deductions allowance ("amount A") for the period would be in the absence of new CTA 2010 s 356NI. The second step is to determine the amount of the contractor's ring-fence profits-deductions allowance. This is so much of amount A as the company designates as its contractor's ring-fence profits-deductions allowance. The company's deductions allowance for the period is then equal to amount A less the amount of the company's ring-fence profits-deductions allowance for the period. In the event that the company receives a "relevant reversal credit" within the meaning of new CTA 2010 s 269ZY in the accounting period, its contractor's ring-fence profits-deductions allowance for the period is to be increased by the smaller of the relevant reversal credit and the amount of the contractor's ring-fence profits for the period.

New CTA 2010 s 356NJ provides that neither (a) the deduction of a post-1 April 2017 trade loss carried forward under new CTA 2010 s 45A nor (b) the deduction a loss etc by way of group relief for carried-forward losses under new CTA 2010 Part 5A, so far as either deduction is set against the company's ring-fence profits for the accounting period are to be treated as "relevant deductions" under new CTA 2010 s 269ZD, i.e. they are not to be subject to the loss restriction relating to deductions from total profits. Similarly, a deduction under CTA 2010 s 45(4) (pre-1 April trade loss carried forward against subsequent trade profits) of a loss arising from oil-contractor activities is to be ignored for the purposes of new CTA 2010 s 269ZB, meaning that it is not to be subject to the loss restriction relating to deductions from trading profits.

NB: the Queen's printer's copy of the Lords Bill appears to omit a paragraph 60.

Schedule 4 Part 8, comprising paras 61–68, adapts the new loss rules for the provisions relating to the transfer of a trade without a change of ownership. Schedule 4 para 61 is introductory and Sch 4 para 62 makes a minor consequential amendment. Schedule 4 para 63 inserts new CTA 2010 s 943A. This provides that the predecessor many not avail himself of the extended period over which relief may be given under CTA 2010 s 39 in respect of a terminal loss when making a claim under CTA 2010 s 37 for relief for a loss made in the transferred trade.

Schedule 4 para 64 amends CTA 2010 s 944 (modifying the relief for trade losses) so that it is now to apply solely to pre-1 April 2017 losses carried forward under CTA 2010 s 45. Schedule 4 para 65 inserts new CTA 2010 ss 944A–944E, which apply to post-1 April 2017 trade losses.

New CTA 2010 s 944A applies to transfers of a trade other than a ring-fence trade where:

(a) the predecessor made a loss in the transferred trade in the accounting period in which it ceased to carry on the trade and that period began after 31 March 2017;

(b) relief for the loss was not given under either CTA 2010 s 37 (relief against total profits of the loss-making period) or by way of group relief under CTA 2010 Part 5;

(c) but relief under CTA 2010 s 37 was not barred for non-commerciality or any of the other reasons numbered (3) and (4) in this Introduction in the note for new CTA 2010 s 45A; nor

(d) barred under CTA 2010 s 37 on the grounds that the successor made a non-commercial loss within the meaning of CTA 2010 s 44 in the accounting period in which the successor began to carry on the transferred trade.

Where these circumstances apply, the successor is able, broadly speaking, to claim relief under new CTA 2010 s 45A for losses made by the predecessor as if made by the successor.

New CTA 2010 s 944B is the equivalent provision modifying relief under new CTA 2010 s 45B. It applies to transfers of a trade where:

(a) the predecessor made a loss in the transferred trade in the accounting period in which it ceased to carry on the trade and that period began after 31 March 2017;

(b) relief for the loss was not given under either CTA 2010 ss 37 (relief against total profits of the loss-making period) or 42 (extended period of relief for ring-fence trades) or by way of group relief under CTA 2010 Part 5;

(c) relief under CTA 2010 s 37 was barred for non-commerciality or any of the other reasons numbered (3) and (4) in this Introduction in the note for new CTA 2010 s 45A; or

(d) relief under CTA 2010 s 37 was barred under CTA 2010 s 37 on the grounds that the successor made a non-commercial loss within the meaning of CTA 2010 s 44 in the accounting period in which the successor began to carry on the transferred trade; or

(e) relief under CTA 2010 s 37 was barred under CTA 2010 s 37 on the grounds that the trade is a ring-fence trade.

Where these circumstances apply, the successor is able, broadly speaking, to claim relief under new CTA 2010 s 45B for losses made by the predecessor as if made by the successor.

New CTA 2010 s 944C modifies the operation of new CTA 2010 s 45F (terminal-loss relief for post-1 April 2017 trade losses). It provides that the predecessor may not make a claim for terminal-loss relief under new CTA 2010 s 45F for a loss made in the transferred trade. However, this restriction is not to apply where the loss is a pre-1 April 2017 loss carried forward under CTA 2010 s 45 and the trade was transferred before 13 July 2017. It also provides that where a loss made by the predecessor is carried forward under any of CTA 2010 s 45 or new ss 45A or 45B to the accounting period in which the successor ceases to carry on the transferred trade, relief is not to be given to the successor in that period under any of those sections. Instead, new CTA 2010 s 45F is to have effect as if the successor had incurred the loss in the transferred trade in the period in which the successor began to carry it on.

New CTA 2010 s 944D modifies new CTA 2010 s 303B (non-decommissioning losses of a ring-fence trade carried forward) in much the same way as new CTA 2010 s 944A modifies new CTA 2010 s 45A. Thus, it applies to transfers of a ring-fence trade where the predecessor made a non-decommissioning loss in the transferred trade in the accounting period in which it ceased to carry on the trade, that period began after 31 March 2017, and relief for the loss was not given under either CTA 2010 s 37 (relief against total profits of the loss-making period) or 42 (extended period of relief for ring-fence trades) or by way of group relief under CTA 2010 Part 5.

Where these circumstances apply, the successor is able, broadly speaking, to claim relief under new CTA 2010 s 303B for non-decommissioning losses made by the predecessor as if made by the successor.

New CTA 2010 s 944E modifies new CTA 2010 s 303D (further carry-forward of non-decommissioning losses of a ring-fence trade) in much the same way as new CTA 2010 s 944A modifies new CTA 2010 s 45A. Thus, it applies to transfers of a ring-fence trade where

(a) the predecessor made a non-decommissioning loss in the transferred trade which was carried forward under new CTA 2010s 303B or 303D to the accounting period in which it ceased to carry on the trade;

(b) relief for the loss was not given by deduction under either new CTA 2010 s 303B or 303D from the predecessor's profit of the cessation period or from the predecessor's total profits of the cessation period on a claim under new CTA 2010 s 303C or by way of group relief for carried-forward losses under CTA 2010 Part 5A.

Where these circumstances apply, the successor is able, broadly speaking, to claim relief under new CTA 2010 s 303D for non-decommissioning losses made by the predecessor as if made by the successor.

Schedule 4 para 66 amends CTA 2010 s 945, which applies where the predecessor retains more liabilities than assets, to include its scope to include new CTA 2010 ss 944A–944E. Schedule 4 para 67 amends CTA 2010 s 951, which applies to transfers of a trade in which the transferee begins to carry on the transferred trade as part of its existing trade, so that in these circumstances when a loss made in the transferred trade is carried forward under any of new CTA 2010 ss 45A, 45B, 303B or 303D to an accounting period of the transferee, the provisions of new CTA 2010 ss 45A–45F and ss 303A–303D apply to the amount carried forward as if the part-trade were a separate trade. Schedule 4 para 68 makes a minor consequential amendment.

Schedule 4 Part 9 comprises paras 69–92 and makes new, or strengthens existing, anti-avoidance provisions so as to counter abuse of the new rules.

Schedule 4 para 69 amends CTA 2010 s 730F, which forms part of CTA 2010 Part 14B, which is intended to counter schemes known as "loss refresh", aimed at converting losses carried forward to current-period losses. The definition of "relevant carried-forward loss", to which the provisions of CTA 2010 Part 14B apply, is extended to include:

(1) the losses of a UK property business carried forward under CTA 2010 s 62;

(2) non-trading losses on intangible fixed assets carried forward under CTA 2009 s 753;

(3) post-1 April 2017 trade losses carried forward under new CTA 2010 ss 45A or 45B;

(4) non-trading deficits from a loan relationship carried forward under new CTA 2009 ss 463G or 463H.

Schedule 4 paras 70–91 amend the provisions of CTA 2010 Part 14, which restrict reliefs in certain cases where there is a change of ownership of a company accompanied by a change in the nature of the trade or business and/or certain other material changes. Schedule 4 para 71 amends the introductory section, CTA 2010 s 672, to introduce references to the four new Chapters (2A–2E) that are about to be inserted.

Schedule 4 para 72 amends CTA 2010 s 673, which defines the scope of the disallowance of losses when there is a change in ownership and within the same three-year period there is either a major change in the nature or conduct of the trade (condition A) or the trade had become small or negligible before the transfer (condition B). The effective period for condition A is now extended so that the disallowance is triggered if the major change in the nature or conduct of the trade occurs within a period of five (as opposed to three, hitherto) years beginning no more than three years before the change in ownership. However, for the new rule to apply, both the change in ownership and the major change in the nature or conduct of the trade must occur after 31 March 2017.

Schedule 4 para 73 amends CTA 2010 s 674, which specifies the types of loss relief disallowed, to include relief under new CTA 2010 ss 45B, 303B and 303D, and to provide that no relief may be given under new CTA 2010 ss 45A or 303C for a loss made by the company in an accounting period beginning before the change in ownership by carrying the loss forward and deducting it from the company's total profits of an accounting period ending after the change in ownership.

Schedule 4 para 74 inserts new CTA 2010 s 674A, which excepts certain ring-fence losses from being disallowed under CTA 2010 s 674. The exception extends to losses of a ring-fence trade that are not non-decommissioning losses in a situation when condition A applies but the major change in the nature or conduct of the trade does not occur within a period of three years in which the change in ownership occurs.

Schedule 4 para 75 inserts new CTA 2010 Part 14 Chapter 2A, which consists of 12 sections (new CTA 2010 ss 676AA–676AL), which impose restrictions on the use of post-1 April 2017 losses where there is a change in the company's activities.

New CTA 2010 s 676AA is introductory, and provides that new CTA 2010 Part 14 Chapter 2A is to apply where two conditions, A and B, are met. Condition A is that a change in the ownership of a company ("the transferred company") takes place after 31 March 2017. Condition B is that a major change in the business of the transferred company (NB: the change in wording over condition A in CTA 2010 s 673, which specifies a "major change in the nature or conduct of the trade carried on by the company") or of a "co-transferred company" (a defined in new CTA 2010 s 676AL) occurs after 31 March 2017 and within the "required period". The extent of the "required period" varies. For the purposes of new CTA 2010 s 676AF, it is the period of five years within the change in ownership occurs, beginning no more than three years before the change occurs. For the purposes of new CTA 2010 ss 676AG–676AK, on the other hand, it is a period of eight years, beginning no more than three years before the change in ownership.

New CTA 2010 s 676AB provides that the provisions of CTA 2010 Part 14 Chapters 2 and 3 are to have priority over the provisions of the new CTA 2010 Part 14 Chapter 2A where they would otherwise both apply in relation to the same loss etc.

New CTA 2010 s 676AC provides a non-exhaustive definition of a "major change in the business", which is one of the triggering events for the application of these provisions. Such a major change is to include:

(a) a major change in the nature or conduct of any trade or business carried on by the company, which includes, but is not limited to

  (i) a major change in the type of property dealt in, or services or facilities provided in, the trade or business concerned;

  (ii) a major change in customers, outlets or markets of the trade or business concerned; and

  (iii) a major change in the nature of the investments held by the company for the purposes of an investment business;

(b) a major change in the scale of any trade or business carried on by the company; and

(c) the commencement or cessation of the carrying-on of a particular trade or business.

These definitions are to apply even if the change is the result of a gradual process that began in the period of five (or eight, as the case may be) years referred to in new CTA 2010 s 676AA.

These non-exhaustive definitions are largely a restatement of the existing definitions in CTA 2010 ss 673(4) and 677(5), but for these purposes it is sufficient that there be a major change in the scale of the trade or business; the scale does not have to become small or negligible – it may indeed have become significantly larger.

Where a trade, business or property is transferred from a company to a related company (the relationship must exist immediately before the change in ownership and at the time of the transfer), the transfer is to be disregarded in determining whether there has been a major change in the business of either company.

New CTA 2010 s 676AD provides that for the purposes of new CTA 2010 Part 14 Chapter 2A, the accounting period ("the actual accounting period") in which the change in ownership occurs is to be treated as two separate, "notional" accounting periods, one ending with the change and the other consisting of the remainder of the period. This section is the equivalent of CTA 2010 s 678, which performs the same function for CTA 2010 Part 14 Chapter 3, which has effect for companies with investment business.

New CTA 2010 s 676AE defines "affected profits". These are profits of an accounting period ending after the change in ownership which arise in the five years following the end of the accounting period of the transferred company in which the change of ownership occurs, and which can fairly and reasonably be attributed to activities or other sources of income as a result wholly or partly of which the major change has occurred.

For these purposes, an accounting period straddling the end of the five-year period is to be treated as two separate accounting periods, the first ending on the fifth anniversary (the end date of the five-year period), and profits and losses are to be apportioned on a time basis.

New CTA 2010 ss 676AF–676AK contain the restrictions imposed by new CTA 2010 Part 14 Chapter 2A.

New CTA 2010 s 676AF imposes restrictions on the use of carried-forward post-1 April 2017 losses. It provides that a loss made by the transferred company in an accounting period beginning before the change in ownership may not be carried forward and deducted from the affected profits of an accounting period ending after the change in ownership under any of:

(1) new CTA 2010 s 45A (post-1 April 2017 trade losses carried forward);

(2) new CTA 2010 s 45F (terminal-loss relief for post-1 April trade losses carried forward);

(3) new CTA 2010 s 303C (excess non-decommissioning losses of a ring-fence trade carried forward); or

(4) new FA 2012 s 124B (excess carried-forward BLAGAB trade losses of an insurance company).

This section has its more limited equivalent in CTA 2010 s 674(2).

New CTA 2010 s 676AG imposes restrictions on loan-relationship debits in respect of the transferred company's loan relationships. It provides that the debits to be brought into account for the accounting period of the transferred company beginning immediately after the change in ownership and in any subsequent accounting period are not to include "relevant non-trading debits" (as defined in CTA 2010 s 730) to the extent that the amount A exceeds the amount of the company's taxable total profits of the accounting period ending with the change in ownership.

Amount A is the sum of those relevant non-trading debits and the amount of any such debits that have been brought into account in any previous accounting period ending after the change in ownership.

This section has its more limited equivalent in CTA 2010 s 679, which applies solely to companies with investment business.

New CTA 2010 s 676AH imposes restrictions on the carry-forward of post-1 April non-trading deficits from loan relationships of the transferred company, where those non-trading deficits ("pre-acquisition non-trading deficits") arise in an accounting period beginning before the change in ownership. No amount of such a deficit may be set off under new CTA 2010 s 463G against affected profits of the accounting period beginning immediately after the change in ownership or any subsequent accounting period. This prohibition only applies, however, where the whole of the pre-acquisition non-trading deficit carried forward is apportioned wholly to the first notional accounting period, as provided in the Table in CTA 2010 s 685(2).

This section has its more limited equivalent in CTA 2010 s 680, which applies solely to companies with investment business.

New CTA 2010 s 676AI imposes restrictions on relief for post-1 April 2017 non-trading losses on intangible fixed assets. It provides that a "relevant non-trading loss on intangible fixed assets" is to be available for relief under CTA 2009 s 753 only in relation to each of the notional accounting periods considered separately, and may not be deducted as a carried-forward loss from affected profits of an accounting period ending after the change in ownership. A "relevant non-trading loss on intangible fixed assets" is (or is to that extent) a loss of an accounting period beginning before the change in ownership and after 31 March 2017 or such a loss that has been carried forward under CTA 2009 s 753.

This section has its more limited equivalent in CTA 2010 s 681, which applies solely to companies with investment business.

New CTA 2010 s 676AJ imposes restrictions on the deduction of post-1 April excess expenses of management of a company with investment business. It provides that in calculating the taxable total profits of an accounting period of the transferred company ending after the change in ownership, there is to be no deduction in respect of either:

(a) expenses of management first deductible under CTA 2009 s 1219 for an accounting period beginning before the change in ownership but after 31 March 2017; or

(b) excess capital allowances falling to be made for an accounting period beginning before the change in ownership but after 31 March 2017.

This section has its equivalent in CTA 2010 s 682.

New CTA 2010 s 676AK imposes restrictions on the use of post-1 April 2017 losses of a UK property business. It provides that a loss from a UK property business made in an accounting period beginning before the change in ownership but after 31 March 2017 may not be deducted from affected profits of an accounting period ending after the change in ownership.

This section has its equivalent in CTA 2010 s 682.

New CTA 2010 s 676AL defines "co-transferred company" and "related company". A co-transferred company is one that is related to the transferred company both immediately before and immediately after the change in ownership. Two companies are related to one another at any time when the group condition or any of consortium conditions 1 to 4 are met in relation to both.

Schedule 4 para 76 inserts new CTA 2010 Part 14 Chapter 2B, which consists of five sections (new CTA 2010 ss 676BA–676BE), which impose restrictions on relief for post-1 April 2017 trade losses when there is a change in ownership and assets are transferred within a group.

New CTA 2010 s 676BA is introductory, and applies (presumably meaning the Chapter applies) if there is a change in ownership of a company after 31 March 2017 and either conditions 1 and 2 are met or condition 3 is met.

Condition 1 is that, following the change in ownership, the company acquires an asset from another member of its group on a no-gain, no-loss basis under TCGA 1992 s 171 or in a tax-neutral transfer under CTA 2009 s 775 (intra-group transfer of an intangible fixed asset).

Condition 2 is that within five years of the change in ownership, a chargeable gain accrues to the company on a disposal of that asset or, as regards an intangible fixed asset, a non-trading chargeable realisation gain accrues to the company on the realisation of the asset within the same period.

The alternative set of circumstances in which new CTA 2010 Part 14 Chapter 2B applies (condition 3) is where within five years of the change in ownership, a chargeable gain is treated as accruing to the company by virtue of an election under TCGA 1992 s 171A on a notional transfer within a group.

The gain to which conditions 2 and 3 refer is known as the "relevant gain".

Assets owned at a later time and deriving their value wholly or partly from an asset acquired as above may be assimilated to the acquired asset, as, for example, a freehold deriving its value from a leasehold to which the lessee has acquired the reversion.

This section has its more limited equivalent in CTA 2010 s 692, which applies solely to companies with investment business.

New CTA 2010 s 676BB provides that the accounting period in which the change of ownership occurs ("the actual accounting period") is to be treated as two separate, "notional" accounting periods, one ending with the change and the other consisting of the remainder of the period.

This section has its more limited equivalent in CTA 2010 s 695, which applies solely to companies with investment business.

New CTA 2010 s 676BC restricts relief under new CTA 2010 ss 45A, 45F and 303C and new FA 2012 s 124B for trade losses made by the company in the trade before the change in ownership. In the circumstances defined in the section, a loss made in an accounting period beginning before the change in ownership may not be deducted under any of the sections mentioned above from so much of the company's total profits of an accounting period ending after the change in ownership as represents the relevant gain. New CTA 2010 s 676BD defines the relevant provisions in accordance with which the requirements for new CTA 2010 s 676BC are to apply. Those provisions are TCGA 1992 s 8(1) and Sch 7A (company's total profits to include chargeable gains and restriction of set-off of pre-entry losses), and CTA 2009 Part 8 Chapter 6 (intangible fixed assets: how debits and credits are given effect).

This section has its limited equivalent in CTA 2010 s 694, which applies solely to companies with investment business.

New CTA 2010 s 676BE defines what is meant by the amount of profits that represents a relevant gain. That amount is to be found by comparing the amount ("Y") of the relevant gain with the amount ("Z") included in respect of chargeable gains or non-trading chargeable realisation gains for the accounting period concerned. If Y does not exceed Z, the amount of profits that represents the relevant gain is Y. If Y does exceed Z, that amount is Z. This section has its limited equivalent in CTA 2010 s 693, which applies solely to companies with investment business.

Schedule 4 para 77 inserts new CTA 2010 Part 14 Chapter 2C, which consists of nine sections (new CTA 2010 ss 676CA–676CI), which impose restrictions on group relief for carried-forward losses when there is a change in ownership.

New CTA 2010 s 676CA is introductory, and provides that new CTA 2010 Part 14 Chapter 2C is to apply where there is a change in ownership of a company ("the transferred company") after 31 March 2017.

New CTA 2010 s 676CB provides for the general rule restricting the surrender of losses carried forward. It applies where a claimant company would otherwise be eligible to make a claim under new CTA 2010 Part 5A for group relief for carried-forward losses for an accounting period ending after the change in ownership and in respect of an amount surrendered by the transferred company or a "co-transferred company" (as defined in new CTA 2010 s 676CI) which is a "relevant pre-acquisition loss" (as defined in new CTA 2010 s 676CH). Where it applies, the relief is not to be available at all.

For these purposes, an accounting period of the transferred company in which the change of ownership occurs is to be treated as two separate accounting periods, the first of which ends with the change.

A relevant pre-acquisition loss is any of the following:

(1) a non-trading deficit from loan relationships for an accounting period beginning before the change in ownership and carried forward to the surrender period under new CTA 2009 s 463G(6);

(2) a loss on intangible fixed assets so far as consisting of amounts carried forward to the surrender period under CTA 2009 s 753(3) from one or more accounting periods beginning before the change in ownership;

(3) excess expenses of management carried forward to the surrender period under CTA 2009 s 1223 and first deductible in an accounting period beginning before the change in ownership;

(4) a post-1 April trade loss made in an accounting period beginning before the change in ownership and carried forward to the surrender period under new CTA 2010 s 45A(3);

(5) a loss made in a UK property business in an accounting period beginning before the change in ownership and carried forward to the surrender period under CTA 2010 s 62(5)(b) or 63(3)(a);

(6) a post-1 April non-decommissioning loss of a ring-fence trade made in an accounting period beginning before the change in ownership and carried forward to the surrender period under new CTA 2010 ss 303B(2) or 303D(3); or

(7) a BLAGAB trade loss trade made in an accounting period beginning before the change in ownership and carried forward to the surrender period under new CTA 2010 ss 124A(2) or 124C(3).

This rule is time-limited in its effect by new CTA 2010 s 676CE(1).

New CTA 2010 s 676CC applies to restrict claims for group relief for carried-forward losses by the transferred company where consortium condition 1 or 2 was previously met. It applies to claims for an accounting period ending after the change in ownership in respect of a "relevant pre-acquisition loss" where either consortium condition 1 or consortium condition 2 was met immediately before the change in ownership in relation to the transferred company as the company owned by the consortium and the surrendering company.

For these purposes, an accounting period of the surrendering company in which the change of ownership occurs is to be treated as two separate accounting periods, the first of which ends with the change.

The "relevant pre-acquisition loss" is as defined in new CTA 2010 s 676CH and is as set out in this Introduction in the note to new CTA 2010 s 676CB.

In either case, the relief to be given in respect of the transferred company's total profits of the claim period may not exceed the relief that would be available based on the ownership proportion for the purposes of consortium condition 1 or 2, as the case may be. That proportion is the lowest of the proportions in relation to the transferred company as listed in this Introduction in the note for new CTA 2010 s 188DH, reading references to the claimant company there as references to the transferred company here.

This rule is time-limited in its effect by new CTA 2010 s 676CE(1).

New CTA 2010 s 676CD provides an exception to the general restriction on group relief for pre-acquisition losses carried forward. It applies to claims for group relief under new CTA 2010 s 188CC for an accounting period ending after the change of ownership in relation to a relevant pre-acquisition loss surrendered by the transferred company, where the loss is attributable to a specified loss-making period.

In these circumstances and where either consortium condition 3 or 4 was met throughout a period beginning before or during the specified loss-making period and ending with or after the change in ownership, the general rule in new CTA 2010 s 676CB(3) denying relief is not to prevent a claimant company making a claim for relief under new CTA 2010 s 188CC.

New CTA 2010 s 676CE provides two further exceptions to the general rule in new CTA 2010 s 676CB(3) denying relief altogether and to the restrictions imposed by new CTA 2010 s 676CC.

The first exception imposes a time limit of five years on the operation of those sections. They are to cease to have effect to deny or restrict the making of a deduction under new CTA 2010 s 188CK for group relief for carried-forward losses from the total profits of the claimant company which arise after the fifth anniversary of the end of the accounting period of the transferred company in which the change in ownership occurs.

The second exception applies if the group condition was met in relation to the transferred company and the claimant company immediately before the change in ownership. This may be the case where, for example, both companies were transferred into new ownership at the same time.

For these purposes, an accounting period of the transferred company or a "co-transferred company" in which the change of ownership occurs is to be treated as two separate accounting periods, the first of which ends with the change.

New CTA 2010 s 676CF, on the other hand, imposes further restrictions. It applies where both these provisions (new CTA 2010 Part 14 Chapter 2C) and either CTA 2010 Part 14 Chapter 2, new Chapter 2A or Chapter 3 also applies in relation to the change in ownership in the circumstances specified.

The circumstances are as follows.

(1) CTA 2010 Part 14 Chapter 2 (the existing provisions on the disallowance of trading losses on a change in company ownership) must apply to the change in ownership by virtue of the condition (condition A in CTA 2010 s 673) that there has been a major change in the nature or conduct of a trade carried on by the company within any period of three years in which the change of ownership occurs.

(2) CTA 2010 Part 14 Chapter 3 (the existing provisions restricting relief on a change in ownership of a company with investment business) must apply to the change in ownership by virtue of the condition (condition B in CTA 2010 s 677) that there is a major change in the nature or conduct of the business carried on by the company within the period of six years beginning three years before the change in ownership.

(3) New CTA 2010 Part 14 Chapter 2A (new CTA 2010 ss 676AA–676AL) applies to the change in ownership.

Where this Chapter (new CTA 2010 Part 14 Chapter 2C) and any of the other Chapters both apply to a given situation, the company to which the major change has occurred is not to be entitled to a deduction from its affected profits in respect of a claim for group relief for carried-forward losses for an accounting period ending after the change in ownership if the claim relates to a pre-acquisition loss, if it would otherwise be so entitled.

For these purposes, an accounting period of the transferred company or a "co-transferred company" in which the change of ownership occurs is to be treated as two separate accounting periods, the first of which ends with the change.

New CTA 2010 s 676CG defines "affected profits". The definition is identical to that in new CTA 2010 s 676AE (which applies for new CTA 2010 Part 14 Chapter 2A), but for additional cross-references to the mention in other provisions of the major change.

New CTA 2010 s 676CH defines "relevant pre-acquisition loss", for which see the note for new CTA 2010 s 676CB in this Introduction. New CTA 2010 s 676CI defines "co-transferred company" in identical terms to those in new CTA 2010 s 676AL.

Schedule 4 para 78 inserts new CTA 2010 Part 14 Chapter 2D, which consists of five sections (new CTA 2010 ss 676DA–676DE) imposing restrictions on group relief for carried-forward losses when there is a change in ownership and assets are transferred within a group. The sections in this Chapter mirror those of new CTA 2010 Part 14 Chapter 2B.

New CTA 2010 s 676DA is introductory, and applies (presumably meaning the Chapter applies) if there is a change in ownership of a company after 31 March 2017 and either conditions 1 and 2 are met or condition 3 is met. Its wording is identical to that of new CTA 2010 s 676BA, to the note on which in this Introduction reference should be made.

New CTA 2010 s 676DB provides that the accounting period in which the change of ownership occurs ("the actual accounting period") is to be treated as two separate, "notional" accounting periods, one ending with the change and the other consisting of the remainder of the period.

Its wording is identical to that of new CTA 2010 s 676BB, to the note on which in this Introduction further reference should be made.

New CTA 2010 s 676DC is the equivalent of new CTA 2010 s 676BC. It restricts relief under new CTA 2010 Part 5A Chapter 3 for carried-forward losses claimed against gains arising from the transferred assets where the losses arose before the change in ownership. In the circumstances defined in the section, a "relevant pre-acquisition loss" may not be deducted under new CTA 2010 s 188CK in respect of group relief for carried-forward losses from so much of the company's total profits of an accounting period ending after the change in ownership as represents the relevant gain. New CTA 2010 s 676DD defines the relevant provisions in accordance with which the requirements for new CTA 2010 s 676DC are to apply. Those provisions (TCGA 1992 s 8(1) and Sch 7A, and CTA 2009 Part 8 Chapter 6) are identical to those mentioned in new CTA 2010 s 676BD.

New CTA 2010 s 676DE defines what is meant by the "amount of profits which represents a relevant gain". That definition is identical to that in new CTA 2010 s 676BE, to the note on which in this Introduction reference should be made.

Schedule 4 para 79 inserts new CTA 2010 Part 14 Chapter 2E, which consists of five sections (new CTA 2010 ss 676EA–676EE), which impose restrictions on the use of post-1 April trade losses in cases involving the transfer of a trade after a change in ownership. New CTA 2010 s 676EA is introductory and provides that new CTA 2010 Part 14 Chapter 2E applies where there has been a change in ownership of a company ("the transferred company") after 31 March 2017.

New CTA 2010 s 676EB imposes a restriction on the use of trade losses carried forward following the transfer of a trade. It applies where within a period of eight years beginning three years before the change in ownership (therefore ending five years after that change):

(1) the transferred company transfers a trade to a successor company;

(2) the two companies are not related to one another either immediately before the transfer or at the time of the transfer; and

(3) the transfer is one to which CTA 2010 Part 22 Chapter 1 applies. Broadly speaking, this requires:

(i) that the same persons have a 75% interest in the transferred trade both at some time in the year immediately preceding the transfer and when the trade is transferred or at some time in the immediately following two years; and

(ii) the transferred trade is carried on solely by companies within the charge to UK corporation tax or income tax in respect of that trade.

In these circumstances, the successor company may not deduct a loss made by the transferred company in the transferred trade in an accounting period beginning before the change in ownership under either new CTA 2010 s 45A or new CTA 2010 s 303C from its "relevant profits" of an accounting period ending after the change in ownership.

"Relevant profits" are profits that arise before the fifth anniversary of the end of the accounting period in which the change in ownership occurs and which cannot fairly reasonably be attributed to the carrying-on of the transferred trade by the successor company.

For these purposes, an accounting period of the transferred company in which the change of ownership occurs is to be treated as two separate accounting periods, the first of which ends with the change. Similarly, an accounting period of the successor company in which the fifth anniversary occurs is to be treated as two separate accounting periods, the first of which ends with the anniversary.

New CTA 2010 s 676EC imposes a restriction on the surrender of trade losses carried forward by way of group relief following the transfer of a trade. It applies where, within a period of eight years beginning three years before the change in ownership (therefore ending five years after that change)

(1) the transferred company or a co-transferred company transfers a trade to a successor company;

(2) the transfer is one to which CTA 2010 Part 22 Chapter 1 applies (for which see the note in this Introduction on new CTA 2010 s 676EB); and

(3) a claimant company would otherwise be eligible under new CTA 2010 Part 5A to make a "relevant claim" for group relief for carried-forward losses.

A "relevant claim" is one that is made for an accounting period ending after the change in ownership and in relation to an amount of a loss surrendered by the successor company, made in the trade by the transferred company or the co-transferred company in an accounting period beginning before the change in ownership, and carried forward under one of new CTA 2010 ss 45A(3), 303B(2) or 303D(3) to the successor company's surrender period.

In these circumstances, the general rule is that the relief is not to be available.

The rule is time-limited, so that it no longer affects the giving of group relief for carried-forward losses by way of deduction from the total profits of the claimant company which arise after the fifth anniversary of the end of the accounting period of the transferred company in which the change in ownership occurs.

In addition, the general rule is not to apply where the group condition was met in relation to the transferred company and the claimant company immediately before the change in ownership.

For these purposes, an accounting period of the transferred company or co-transferred company in which the change of ownership occurs is to be treated as two separate accounting periods, the first of which ends with the change. Similarly, an accounting period of the claimant company in which the fifth anniversary occurs is to be treated as two separate accounting periods, the first of which ends with the anniversary.

New CTA 2010 s 676ED extends the restrictions to indirect transfers of a trade. Two situations are envisaged. The first is where a trade transferred by the transferred company or a co-transferred company is transferred further on a subsequent occasion to another company. Where this is the case, the transferred company or the co-transferred company is to be treated as having transferred the trade to that other company at the time that it was actually transferred to that other company. The second situation is where a trade ("the original trade") is transferred by the transferred company or a co-transferred company, the activities of that original trade are then subsumed into the activities of another trade ("the composite trade") and the composite trade is then transferred to another company. In these circumstances, the transferred company or the co-transferred company is to be treated as having transferred the original trade to that other company at the time that the composite trade was actually transferred to that other company. In this second case, the deemed transfer is to be treated as one to which CTA 2010 Part 22 Chapter 1 applies (one of the conditions for new CTA 2010 Part 14 Chapter 2E to apply) if the transfer of the composite trade to the other company is one to which the former Chapter applies.

New CTA 2010 s 676EE defines "co-transferred company" exactly as does new CTA 2010 s 676AL, to the note on which in this Introduction reference should be made.

Schedule 4 para 80 amends CTA 2010 s 677 to extend its period of application to a period of eight years (previously six) beginning three years before the change in ownership, but this amendment is to have effect only where both the change in ownership and the major change in the nature and conduct of the trade take place after 31 March 2017. CTA 2010 s 677 introduces CTA 2010 Part 14 Chapter 3, which applies to companies with investment business. Schedule 4 paras 81–83 make consequential amendments to CTA 2010 ss 681, 685 and 690, all of which also fall within CTA 2010 Part 14 Chapter 3.

Schedule 4 para 84 amends CTA 2010 s 692, which introduces CTA 2010 Part 14 Chapter 4. This imposes restrictions on the loan-relationship debits that a company with investment business may bring into account where there is a change in ownership and a transfer of an asset. A further condition is added so as to include gains arising by the operation of TCGA 1992 s 171B, but only where the change in ownership takes place after 31 March 2017. Schedule 4 paras 85 and 86 make consequential amendments to other provisions in that Chapter, namely CTA 2010 ss 696 and 702.

CTA 2010 Part 14 Chapter 5 imposes restrictions on the use of losses of a property business by companies with respect to which there has been both a change in ownership and a major change in the nature or conduct of a trade or property business or where the change in ownership occurs after the scale of the trade or property business has become irreversibly small or negligible. Schedule 4 paras 87 and 88 amend CTA 2010 ss 704 (UK property business) and 705 (overseas property business) to extend their period of application to a period of five years encompassing the change in ownership. Schedule 4 paras 89–92 make consequential or minor amendments to CTA 2010 ss 719 (amending the definition of a change in ownership), 721, 727 and 730C.

Schedule 4 Part 10 comprises paras 93–105, which amend the provisions on the Northern Ireland rate of corporation tax (CTA 2010 Part 8B) to align them with the new loss rules.

Schedule 4 para 93 is introductory and Sch 4 para 94 makes a minor consequential amendment. Schedule 4 para 95 substitutes new CTA 2010 ss 357JB and 357JC for the existing CTA 2010 ss 357JB–357JE.

New CTA 2010 s 357JB provides how relief under CTA 2010 ss 37 and new ss 45A–45F is to operate where a company has both Northern Ireland losses and mainstream losses. New CTA 2010 s 357JC restricts deductions under CTA 2010 ss 37 and new ss 45A, 45B and 45F in respect of Northern Ireland losses when the Northern Ireland rate of corporation tax is lower than the main (rest of UK) rate.

Schedule 4 para 96 inserts new CTA 2010 ss 357JHA–357JHD. New CTA 2010 s 357JHA provides how group relief for carried-forward losses under new CTA 2010 Part 5A is to operate when a company claims the relief in respect of a surrenderable Northern Ireland loss or a mainstream loss against profits some of which are Northern Ireland profits and some of which are not. New CTA 2010 s 357JHB restricts the relief for carried-forward Northern Ireland losses claimed against mainstream profits where the Northern Ireland rate of corporation tax is lower than the main (rest of UK) rate. New CTA 2010 s 357JHC modifies the application of new CTA 2010 Part 5A Chapter 4 (which limits the amount of relief that may be given on a claim under new CTA 188CB for group relief for carried-forward losses) where a claim is made in relation to surrenderable amounts that include a Northern Ireland loss, and new CTA 2010 s 357JHD does likewise for the application of new CTA 2010 Part 5A Chapter 5 (which limits the amount of relief that may be given on a claim under new CTA 188CC for group relief for carried-forward losses) where a claim is made in relation to surrenderable amounts that include a Northern Ireland loss.

Schedule 4 paras 97–105 make consequential amendments to the special Northern Ireland reliefs for the creative industries.

Schedule 4 Part 11, comprising paras 106–189, makes minor and consequential amendments to TA 1988 (para 106); FA 1998 (paras 107–122); CAA 2001 (paras 123–126); Energy Act 2004 (para 127); CTA 2009 (paras 128–144); CTA 2010 (paras 145–174); TIOPA 2010 (paras 175–181); F(No 3)A 2010 (para 182); and FA 2012 (paras 183–189).

Schedule 4 Part 12 (paras 190–194) provides for commencement and makes transitional provisions. Sch 4 para 190 provides that the amendments made by Sch 4 Parts 1–9 and Part 11 are to have effect in relation to accounting periods beginning after 31 March 2017. Where a company has an accounting period straddling 1 April 2017, the period is to be divided into two, the first ending on 31 March 2017 and the other beginning on 1 April. If amounts need to be apportioned between the two periods, a time basis is to be used, unless that would produce a result that was unjust or unreasonable. However, Sch 4 paras 191 and 192 contain special apportionment rules where the amount chargeable to corporation tax would have been smaller or an amount in respect of which corporation tax relief would have been greater but for the operation of new TIOPA 2010 Part 10 (the corporate interest restriction). Schedule 4 para 193 makes a minor amendment to the Corporation Tax (Northern Ireland) Act 2015. Schedule 4 para 194 makes a transitional provision in the operation of new CTA 2009 s 463H, which provides for the carry-forward of post-1 April 2017 non-trading deficits from loan relationships.

Section 19 constitutes a separate and new general anti-avoidance rule intended to counteract arrangements to obtain a "loss-related tax advantage". It provides that just and reasonable adjustments are to be made to counteract any loss-related tax advantage arising from a "relevant tax arrangement".

A loss-related tax advantage is a tax advantage resulting from a deduction or increased deduction under any of the following:

(1) CTA 2009 ss 457, 459, 461 and 462 and new CTA 2009 ss 463B, 463G and 463H (non-trading deficits from loan relationships);
(2) CTA 2009 s 753 (non-trading losses from intangible fixed assets);
(3) CTA 2009 s 1219 (excess management expenses of a company with investment business);
(4) CTA 2010 ss 37 and 45 and new CTA 2010 ss 45A, 45B and 45F (trade losses);
(5) CTA 2010 s 62(3) (losses of a UK property business);
(6) CTA 2010 Part 5 (group relief) and new CTA 2010 Part 5A (group relief for carried-forward losses);
(7) new CTA 2010 ss 303B, 303C and 303D (non-decommissioning losses of a ring-fence trade); and
(8) new FA 2012 ss 124A, 124B and 124C (BLAGAB trade losses carried forward).

A "relevant tax advantage" is one the main purpose, or one of the main purposes, of which is to obtain a loss-related tax advantage and in relation to which it is reasonable to regard the arrangements as circumventing the intended limits of relief under the provisions listed above or otherwise exploiting shortcomings in those provisions. In determining whether or not it is so reasonable, HMRC must have regard to all the relevant circumstances, including whether the arrangements include any steps that are contrived or abnormal or lack a genuine commercial purpose.

It is to be noted that this provision is of wider scope than the GAAR, albeit limited to loss-related tax advantages, and does not require application to an advisory panel.

Section 19 has effect in relation to tax advantages that relate (or would otherwise relate) to accounting periods beginning after 31 March 2017, regardless of when the arrangements were made. However, in relation to the following provisions: new CTA 2009 s 463H, CTA 2010 s 62(3), new CTA 2010 ss 303B, 303C and 303D, and new FA 2012 ss 124A and 124C, it has effect in relation to accounting periods beginning after 12 July 2017.

For these purposes, an accounting period straddling 1 April 2017 is to be split in two.

Section 20 introduces Sch 5, which imposes the corporate interest restriction.

Schedule 5 has its genesis in the OECD's BEPS (base erosion and profit shifting) project aimed at curbing tax avoidance by international groups of companies. As one of the action plans under the BEPS project, Action Plan 4 called for action to prevent base erosion through the use of interest payments (interest expense). The recommended approach is to restrict allowable deductions for interest expense to a fixed ratio of a company's taxable earnings before interest, taxes, depreciation and amortisation ("EBITDA"). Recognising that some multinational groups are highly indebted ("leveraged") with third-party debt, the OECD's recommended approach is to apply a group-ratio rule alongside the fixed ratio, allowing a company with net interest expense above the fixed ratio to deduct interest up to the level of the worldwide group's ratio of net interest to EBITDA. Schedule 5 represents the United Kingdom's interpretation of the recommendations.

Schedule 5 is even longer than Sch 4, extending to 156 pages (23.15%, or almost a quarter of the entire Act). It comprises 36 paragraphs, divided into 4 Parts. Part 1 (para 1) inserts the substantive provisions as new TIOPA 2010 Part 10 (requiring the existing TIOPA 2010 to be renumbered). Part 2 (para 2) provides for the responsibility for, and form and content of, the interest-restriction report that a worldwide group's reporting company must make in respect of each accounting period. These provisions take the form of new TIOPA 2010 Sch 7A. Part 3 (paras 3–24) makes consequential amendments, and Part 4 (paras 25–36) provides for commencement and makes transitional provisions.

Schedule 5 para 1 inserts a new Part 10, entitled "Corporate interest restriction', into TIOPA 2010, after Part 9A. New TIOPA 2010 Part 10 extends to no less than 126 sections, divided into 11 Chapters.

New TIOPA 2010 Part 10 Chapter 1 (new TIOPA 2010 ss 372–374) is introductory.

New TIOPA 2010 s 372 gives an overview of new TIOPA 2010 Part 10 and provides that it contains provisions disallowing certain deductions in respect of interest and other financing costs that a company would otherwise be entitled to make when computing its profits chargeable to corporation tax and allowing certain disallowed amounts from previous accounting periods to be brought forward and taken into account in later accounting periods.

New TIOPA 2010 s 373 defines key concepts such as "subject to interest restrictions" and "total disallowed amount". A "worldwide group" (defined in new TIOPA 2010 ss 473 and 474) is said to be "subject to interest restrictions" in a period of account of the group if the aggregate "net tax-interest expense" of the group (defined in new TIOPA 2010 s 390) for the period exceeds the "interest capacity" of the group (defined in new TIOPA 2010 s 392) for the period. A "period of account" of a worldwide group is the period in respect of which financial statements of the group are drawn up by or on behalf of the ultimate parent or a period in respect of which financial statements of the group are treated as drawn up for the purposes of new TIOPA 2010 s 480. The "total disallowed amount" of a worldwide group in a period of account of the group is that excess, if it is subject to interest restrictions in the period; otherwise, it is nil.

New TIOPA 2010 s 374 introduces new TIOPA 2010 Sch 7A, which requires worldwide groups to make interest-restriction returns via their reporting companies for every period of account.

New TIOPA 2010 Part 10 Chapter 2 (new TIOPA 2010 ss 375–381) provides for the disallowance and reactivation of "tax-interest expense amounts". "Tax-interest expense amount" is defined in new TIOPA 2010 s 382, and is, essentially, an amount that a company would bring into account as a loan-relationship debit, a derivative-contract debit or the financing cost of a finance lease, debt-factoring arrangement or a service-concession arrangement.

New TIOPA 2010 s 375 provides that a company that is listed in a full interest-restriction return made under new TIOPA 2010 Sch 7A para 20 including a statement that the worldwide group is subject to interest restrictions in the period of account for which the return is made must leave out of account tax-interest expense amounts equalling in total the interest disallowance that has been allocated to it in any accounting period of the company for which the disallowance is allocated. A "non-consenting company" (as defined in new TIOPA 2010 Sch 7A para 10 – essentially, a company that has not consented to accept an allocation of interest disallowance, except for the mandatory pro rata share of the disallowed amount, from its worldwide group) may elect not to take heed of the interest disallowance or to revoke a previous election. However, if a non-zero pro rata share of the disallowed amount has nevertheless been allocated to the company under new TIOPA 2010 Sch 7A para 24, it must leave out of account tax-interest expense amounts equal to its pro rata share.

New TIOPA 2010 s 376 provides that where no interest-restriction return has been made on behalf of a worldwide group that is subject to interest restrictions for a particular period of account, either because no reporting company has been appointed or the return is overdue, or a return has been submitted but is non-compliant, a company that was a member of the worldwide group at any time in the period of account must in any affected accounting period disallow deductions of an amount equal to the pro rata share allocated to it under new TIOPA 2010 Sch 7A para 24.

New TIOPA 2010 s 377 prescribes the order in which tax-interest expense amounts are to be left out of account in any accounting period of a company in which those amounts exceed the amounts that it must disallow. The order is:

(1) non-trading debits from loan relationships;
(2) non-trading debits from derivative contracts;
(3) trading debits from loan relationships;
(4) trading debits from derivative contracts; and
(5) interest expense on finance leases etc.

However, a company may elect to replace the statutory order with its own allocation.

New TIOPA 2010 s 378 permits disallowed tax-interest expense amounts to be carried forward to subsequent accounting periods. However, disallowed interest may not be carried forward beyond any period in which the company has ceased to carry on the trade to which the interest relates or the scale of activities has become negligible or in which the trade is uncommercial and non-statutory. Amounts that have been carried forward may be subject to "reactivation" under new TIOPA 2010 s 379.

New TIOPA 2010 s 379 provides for "reactivation", which is the equivalent in the interest-restriction regime to deducting losses carried forward from a subsequent period's profits. Reactivation is conditional on the making of a full interest-restriction return for a particular period of account of a worldwide group containing a statement that the group is "subject to interest reactivations" in the return period. A group is so subject, as defined in new TIOPA 2010 s 373(5), if the group's "interest-reactivation cap" is not nil and at least one member of the group is within the charge to UK corporation tax at any time during the period and has an amount available for reactivation (as defined in new TIOPA 2010 Sch 7A para 26) that is not nil. The reactivation statement must specify companies to which interest reactivations have been allocated. Such a company must then bring into account tax-interest expense amounts that have been brought forward from an earlier accounting period which in total equal the allocated reactivation for that period. A tax-interest expense amount that has been brought forward is brought into account by being treated as a tax-interest expense amount of the specified period.

New TIOPA 2010 s 380 prescribes the order in which tax-interest expense amounts brought forward are to be brought into account in any accounting period of a company in which those amounts exceed the amounts that it is permitted to bring into account. The order is:

(1) non-trading debits from loan relationships;
(2) non-trading debits from derivative contracts;
(3) trading debits from loan relationships;
(4) trading debits from derivative contracts; and
(5) interest expense on finance leases etc.

However, a company may elect to replace the statutory order with its own allocation.

New TIOPA 2010 s 381 caters for the unlikely but possible situation where a company is both required to disallow an amount of tax-interest expense and bring an amount of tax-interest expense brought forward into account in the same accounting period. The company is essentially required to net one amount against the other and either disallow or bring into account the excess, as the case may be.

New TIOPA 2010 Part 10 Chapter 3 (new TIOPA 2010 ss 382–391) defines various tax-interest amounts.

New TIOPA 2010 s 382 defines a "tax-interest expense amount" of a company for a period of account of a worldwide group as an amount that the company would normally expect to bring into account for corporation tax purposes in a "relevant accounting period" and is either a "relevant loan-relationship debit", a "relevant derivative-contract debit" or an amount in respect of the financing cost implicit in amounts under a finance lease, debt-factoring transaction or a service-concession arrangement.

An accounting period may include one or more "disregarded periods". These are periods that do not fall within the worldwide group's periods of account (these may not necessarily be coterminous – the worldwide group's period of account may be the calendar year, whereas the UK company's accounting period may be the year to 31 March, for example) – or periods when the company was not a member of the group. Where this is the case, the tax-interest expense amount must be reduced by an amount justly and reasonably attributable to the disregarded periods; this may include reducing the amount to nil.

New TIOPA 2010 s 383 defines a "relevant loan-relationship debit" as a debit that is, or otherwise would be, brought into account in respect of a loan relationship under CTA 2009 Part 3 (trading loan relationships) or CTA 2009 Part 5 (non-trading loan relationships) and is not a debit in respect of an exchange loss or an impairment loss.

New TIOPA 2010 s 384 defines a "relevant derivative-contract debit" as a debit that is, or otherwise would be, brought into account in respect of a derivative contract under CTA 2009 Part 3 and s 573 (trading derivative contract) or CTA 2009 Part 5 and s 574 (non-trading derivative contract) and is not a debit in respect of an exchange loss, an impairment loss or a hedging contract wholly for reasons unconnected with the capital structure of the worldwide group or any member of the group. An additional condition is that the underlying subject-matter of the contract must consist only of a prescribed number of assets.

New TIOPA 2010 s 385 defines a "tax-interest income amount" of a company for a period of account of a worldwide group as the converse of a tax-interest expense amount, namely an amount that the company would normally expect to bring into account for corporation tax purposes in a relevant accounting period and is either a "relevant loan-relationship credit", a "relevant derivative-contract credit" or an amount in respect of the financing income implicit in amounts under a finance lease, debt-factoring transaction or a service-concession arrangement.

A further condition is that the amount must be in respect of income that is receivable from another company in consideration of a guarantee of any borrowing of the other company.

The same provision is made in respect of any disregarded periods.

New TIOPA 2010 s 386 defines a "relevant loan-relationship credit" as a credit that is or otherwise would be brought into account in respect of a loan relationship under CTA 2009 Part 3 (trading loan relationships) or CTA 2009 Part 5 (non-trading loan relationships) and is not a credit in respect of an exchange gain or the reversal of an impairment loss.

New TIOPA 2010 s 387 defines a "relevant derivative-contract credit" as a credit that is, or otherwise would be, brought into account in respect of a derivative contract under CTA 2009 Part 3 and s 573 (trading derivative contract) or CTA 2009 Part 5 and s 574 (non-trading derivative contract) and is not a credit in respect of an exchange gain, the reversal of an impairment loss or a hedging contract wholly for reasons unconnected with the capital structure of the worldwide group or any member of the group. An additional condition is that the underlying subject-matter of the contract must consist only of a prescribed number of assets.

New TIOPA 2010 s 388 provides for double taxation relief by excluding from the amount of tax-interest income amount in respect of which the corporation tax payable has been reduced by a foreign tax credit by the amount of "notional untaxed income", which is the amount of the credit divided by the rate of corporation tax.

New TIOPA 2010 s 389 defines "net tax-interest expense" and "net tax-interest income". A company has net tax-interest expense for a period of account of the worldwide group when the total of its tax-interest expense amounts exceeds the total of its tax-interest income amounts for the period equal to the amount of the excess. Conversely, it has net tax-interest income for a period of account of the worldwide group when the total of its tax-interest income amounts exceeds the total of its tax-interest expense amounts for the period equal to the amount of the excess.

New TIOPA 2010 s 390 defines a worldwide group's aggregate net tax-interest expense or aggregate net tax-interest income as the sum of each "relevant company's net tax-interest expense and net tax-interest income amounts. A "relevant company" is a company that was a member of the group at any time during the period of account.

New TIOPA 2010 s 391 defines "impairment loss".

New TIOPA 2010 Part 10 Chapter 4 (new TIOPA 2010 ss 392–399) defines a worldwide group's interest capacity.

New TIOPA 2010 s 392 defines the interest capacity of a worldwide group for a period of account as A + B, where A is the group's "interest allowance" (defined in new TIOPA 2010 s 396) for the current period and B is the aggregate of the group's interest allowances for periods before the current period so far as they are available for that period. Notwithstanding, a worldwide group will have a default minimum interest capacity of £2 million for a period of account, reduced or increased pro rata for periods shorter or longer than one year.

New TIOPA 2010 s 393 defines a worldwide group's amount of interest allowance that is available for a later period. A worldwide group's amount of interest allowance for a period of account ("the originating period") available in a later period of account ("the receiving period") is the smaller of two amounts, A and B, but is nil if a full interest-restriction return has not been submitted for the originating period.

A is the amount of the interest allowance less the total of amounts comprised in that interest allowance that were "used" in the originating period or any subsequent period before the receiving period. B is the amount of the interest allowance for the originating period that is unexpired in the receiving period (defined in new TIOPA 2010 s 395).

New TIOPA 2010 s 394 defines the amount of the interest allowance that is "used" in any period of account of the group. The amount used in the originating period is the lower of (a) the interest allowance for the originating period and (b) the sum of the group's aggregate net tax-interest expense for the originating period and the total amount of tax-interest expense amounts brought forward that have had to be brought into account by way of reactivation under new TIOPA 2010 s 379. The amount used in a subsequent period ("the receiving period") is the lower of (a) the interest allowance, so far as it is available in the receiving period and the "relevant part" of the aggregate net tax-interest expense of the group for the receiving period. The relevant part is given by the expression $A - B - C$, where A is the aggregate net tax-interest expense of the group for the receiving period, B is the interest allowance of the group for the receiving period and C is the amount of the interest allowance of the group for any period before the originating period and used in the receiving period.

New TIOPA 2010 s 395 prescribes how to determine the amount of the interest allowance for a period of account ("the originating period") that is unexpired in a later period ("the receiving period"). If the receiving period begins five years or less after the originating period begins and ends five years or less after the originating period ends, all of the interest allowance is unexpired. At the other extreme, if the receiving period begins five years or more after the originating period ends, none of the interest allowance is unexpired.

If, on the other hand, the receiving period begins more than five years after the originating period begins and ends no more than five years after the originating period ends, the interest allowance for the originating period that remains unexpired in the receiving period is given by the formula:

$$(A - B) \times \frac{X}{Y}$$

where A is the interest allowance for the originating period; B is the lower of the aggregate net tax-interest expense of the group for the originating period and the interest allowance for the originating period; X is the number of days in the period beginning with the day on which the receiving period begins and ending with the day five years after the day on which the originating period ends; and Y is the number of days in the originating period. Call the result Γ.

If the receiving period begins no more than five years after the originating period begins and ends more than five years after the originating period ends, the interest allowance for the originating period that remains unexpired in the receiving period is given by the formula:

$$(C - D) \times \frac{X}{Z}$$

where C is the aggregate net tax-interest expense of the group for the receiving period; D is the lower of the aggregate net tax-interest expense of the group for the receiving period and the interest allowance of the group for the receiving period; X is as before and Z is the number of days in the receiving period. Call the result Δ.

Finally, if the receiving period begins more than five years after the originating period begins but not more than five years before the originating period ends, and ends more than five years after the originating period ends, the amount of the interest allowance that remains unexpired in the receiving period is the lower of amounts Γ and Δ.

Essentially, therefore, disallowed interest expense amounts of one period may be carried forward for a maximum of five years.

New TIOPA 2010 Part 10 Chapter 5 (new TIOPA 2010 ss 396–404) deals with the calculation of the interest allowance.

New TIOPA 2010 s 396 defines the interest allowance of a worldwide group for a period of account of the group as $A + B$, where A is the "basic interest allowance" of the group for the period and B is the amount (if any) of the aggregate net tax-interest income of the group for the period. Where no "group-ratio election" (see under new TIOPA 2010 Sch 7A para 13) is in force for the period, the basic interest allowance is to be calculated using the fixed-ratio method of new TIOPA 2010 s 397. When such an election is in force, the calculation is to be carried out by the group-ratio method of new TIOPA 2010 s 398.

New TIOPA 2010 s 397 provides that the fixed-ratio method of calculation is to take the lower of two amounts – 30% of the aggregate tax-EBITDA of the group for the period and the "fixed-ratio debt cap" of the group for the period – as the basic interest allowance.

New TIOPA 2010 s 398 provides that the group-ratio method of calculation is to take the lower of two other amounts – the "group-ratio percentage" of the group's aggregate tax-EBITDA for the period and the "group-ratio debt cap" of the group for the period.

New TIOPA 2010 s 399 defines the group-ratio percentage as A/B, where A is the "qualifying net group-interest expense" (defined in new TIOPA 2010 s 414) of the group for the period and B is the group-EBITDA (defined in new TIOPA 2010 s 416) of the group for the period (but see new TIOPA 2010 s 401). The result is set at 100 where the fraction would be negative or B is zero.

New TIOPA 2010 s 400 defines the two group debt caps – the fixed-ratio debt cap and the group-ratio debt cap – already referred to – and the "excess debt cap" introduced in this section.

The fixed-ratio debt cap of a worldwide group for a period of account is the sum of two amounts: (1) the "adjusted net group-interest expense" for the period (defined in new TIOPA 2010 s 413) and (2) the "excess debt cap" of the group generated in the immediately preceding period of account of the group.

The group-ratio debt cap of a worldwide group for a period of account is itself the sum of two amounts: (1) the qualifying net group-interest expense of the group for the period and (2) the "excess debt cap" of the group generated in the immediately preceding period of account of the group.

If no group-ratio election is in force for a period of account ("the generating period"), the excess debt cap of the group generated in the period is A – B, where A is the fixed-ratio debt cap of the group for the generating period and B is 30% of the aggregate tax-EBITDA of the group for the generating period.

If a group-ratio election is in force for the generating period, the excess debt cap of the group generated in the period is again A – B, where this time A is the group-ratio debt cap of the group for the generating period and B is the group-ratio percentage (see new TIOPA 2010 s 399) of the aggregate tax-EBITDA of the group for the generating period.

If either of the two A – B subtractions is negative, the excess debt cap is taken to be nil. If, on the other hand, the result exceeds the group's "carry-forward limit", the excess debt cap is itself capped at the carry-forward limit.

The carry-forward limit is the sum of (1) the excess debt cap generated in the period of account immediately preceding the generating period and (2) the total disallowed amount of the group in the generating period (see new TIOPA 2010 s 373).

New TIOPA 2010 s 401 provides for the effect of a "group-ratio (blended) election" on the group-ratio percentage. This election (made under new TIOPA 2010 Sch 7A para 14) allows a group to calculate its group-ratio percentage with reference to the group-ratio percentage of one or more related-party investors.

Where the election is in force, the group-ratio percentage is not calculated under new TIOPA 2010 s 399 but by multiplying, for each investor in the group, "the investor's applicable percentage" by the investor's share in the group and adding together those results. "The investor's applicable percentage" is the highest of the following percentages:

(1) 30;
(2) the s 399 percentage; and
(3) if the investor is a member of a different worldwide group, the group-ratio percentage of that group.

If the financial statements of the investor's worldwide group are not coterminous with those of the worldwide group in question, the group-ratio percentage of the investor's worldwide group is differently calculated.

New TIOPA 2010 s 402 provides for the effect of a group-ratio (blended) election on the group-ratio debt cap.

If such an election is in force for a period of account, the place of the "adjusted net group-interest expense" in the calculation of the group-ratio debt cap is taken by the "blended net group-interest expense", i.e. the group-ratio debt cap is given as the sum of (1) the blended net group-interest expense of the group for the period and (2) the "excess debt cap" of the group generated in the immediately preceding period of account of the group.

The blended net group-interest expense of the group for the period of account is determined by a four-step process. Step 1 applies to investors in the group whose applicable percentage is 30 and consists of multiplying for each investor the adjusted net group-interest expense of the group for the period by the investor share in the group. Step 2 applies to investors in the group whose applicable percentage is the s 399 percentage and consists of multiplying for each investor the qualifying net group-interest expense of the group for the period by the investor share in the group. Step 3 applies to investors in the group whose applicable percentage is the group-ratio percentage of the investor's worldwide group and consists of finding for each investor the applicable net group-interest expense of the investor's worldwide group, and adding the amounts found under each step. The procedure for finding the applicable net group-interest expense of the investor's worldwide group is set out in new TIOPA 2010 s 402(4). Adjustments are made to the calculations where the investor's worldwide group's periods of account do not coincide with those of the worldwide group in question or where there are cross-funding loan arrangements between the two groups.

New TIOPA 2010 s 403 allows the reporting company of the worldwide group that has made a group-ratio (blended) election to specify under that election which particular elections under new TIOPA 2010 Sch 7A are to be treated as being made or as not being made in respect of the investor's worldwide group.

New TIOPA 2010 s 404 contains the definitions of "investor", "related-party investor" and "investor's share".

New TIOPA 2010 Part 10 Chapter 6 (new TIOPA 2010 ss 405–409) defines the key concept of tax-EBITDA

New TIOPA 2010 s 405 defines the "aggregate tax-EBITDA" of a worldwide group for a period of account as the total of the tax-EBITDAs for the period of each company that was a member of the group at any time during the group or nil, if that total is negative.

New TIOPA 2010 s 406 prescribes how the tax-EBITDA of a company that is a member of a worldwide group is to be calculated.

Where the company has only one relevant accounting period in relation to the worldwide group's period of account, its tax-EBITDA is its "adjusted corporation tax earnings" for that accounting period. Where it has two or more relevant accounting periods, its tax-EBITDA is found by adding together the adjusted corporation tax earnings for each accounting period.

Adjusted corporation tax earnings are determined by adding together amounts brought into account by the company in determining its taxable total profits of the period and amounts that it would have so brought into account if it had made profits or more profits, disregarding in both cases amounts that are "excluded amounts".

An accounting period may include one or more disregarded periods. These are periods that do not fall within the worldwide group's periods of account or periods when the company was not a member of the group. Where this is the case, reductions must be made on a just and reasonable basis to account for amounts attributable to the disregarded periods.

New TIOPA 2010 s 407 defines what amounts are to be excluded in arriving at tax-EBITDA. Given the nature of EBITDA, these amounts are:

(1) tax-interest expense amounts and tax-interest income amounts;
(2) capital allowances and charges under CAA 2001;
(3) "excluded relevant intangibles debits and credits" (defined in new TIOPA 2010 s 408);
(4) losses made by the company in any other accounting period;
(5) losses that are not allowable losses under TCGA 1992;
(6) expenses of management of any other accounting period of a company with investment business;
(7) deficits of any other accounting period from the company's loan relationships;
(8) deductions in respect of group relief and group relief for carried-forward losses to the extent that they are surrenderable referable to times at which the surrendering company was a member of the worldwide group;
(9) "qualifying tax reliefs".

Qualifying tax reliefs are:

(1) R&D expenditure credits;
(2) additional relief for expenditure on R&D;
(3) deemed trading losses of an SME in respect of pre-trading expenditure;
(4) deductions in respect of the relief for expenditure on contaminated or derelict land;
(5) film tax relief, video-games tax relief, relief for theatrical productions, orchestra tax relief, museums and galleries exhibition tax relief;
(6) qualifying charitable donations; and
(7) patent-box deductions.

New TIOPA 2010 s 408 defines what intangibles debits and credits are to be excluded.

New TIOPA 2010 s 409 provides for double taxation relief by excluding from the amount of income otherwise includible in calculating tax-EBITDA amounts in respect of which the corporation tax payable is reduced by a foreign tax credit by the amount of "notional untaxed income", which is the amount of the credit divided by the rate of corporation tax.

New TIOPA 2010 Part 10 Chapter 7 (new TIOPA 2010 ss 410–431) defines the various types of group-interest expense and group EBITDA.

New TIOPA 2010 s 410 defines the net group-interest expense of a worldwide group for a period of account ("the relevant period of account") as A – B, where A is the sum of "relevant expense amounts" (payments of interest etc) recognised in the group's financial statements as items of profit or loss and B is the sum of "relevant income amounts" (receipts of interest etc) recognised in the group's financial statements as items of profit or loss. A is to include capitalised expenses in relation to an asset other than a "relevant asset" (defined in new TIOPA 2010 s 417) where part or all of the asset's carrying value is written down, and B is to include capitalised income in the same circumstances.

New TIOPA 2010 s 411 defines "relevant expense amounts" and "relevant income amounts". Relevant expense amounts are:

(1) interest payable under, and expenses ancillary to, a loan relationship;
(2) losses, other than exchange losses and impairment losses, from a loan relationship or a related transaction;
(3) dividends payable in respect of preference shares accounted for as a financial liability;
(4) losses arising from a relevant derivative contract or a related transaction, excluding exchange losses, impairment losses and losses from a hedging contract wholly for reasons unconnected with the capital structure of the worldwide group or any member of the group;
(5) expenses ancillary to a relevant derivative contract or related transaction;
(6) financing charges implicit in payments made under a finance lease;
(7) financing charges related to debt factoring;
(8) financing charges implicit in payments made under a service-concession arrangement to the extent accounted for as a financial liability;
(9) interest payable under a relevant non-lending relationship;
(10) alternative-finance return payable under alternative-finance arrangements;
(11) manufactured interest payable;
(12) financing charges in respect of the advance under a debtor repo or debtor quasi-repo;
(13) financing charges under income-factoring finance arrangements within CTA 2010 Part 16 Chapter 2.

Relevant income amounts are:

(1) interest receivable under a loan relationship;
(2) profits, other than exchange gains and reversals of impairment losses, from a loan relationship or a related transaction;
(3) dividends receivable in respect of preference shares accounted for as a financial asset;
(4) gains arising from a relevant derivative contract or a related transaction, excluding exchange gains, reversals of impairment losses and gains from a hedging contract wholly for reasons unconnected with the capital structure of the worldwide group or any member of the group;
(5) financing income implicit in amounts received under a finance lease;
(6) financing income related to debt factoring;
(7) financing income implicit in receipts under a service-concession arrangement to the extent accounted for as a financial asset;
(8) interest receivable under a relevant non-lending relationship;
(9) alternative-finance return receivable under alternative-finance arrangements;
(10) manufactured interest receivable;
(11) financing income in respect of the advance under a creditor repo or creditor quasi-repo;
(12) financing income under income-factoring finance arrangements within CTA 2010 Part 16 Chapter 2.

Amounts payable and amounts receivable under a pension scheme are to be disregarded.

New TIOPA 2010 s 412 defines what expenses are "ancillary" to a loan relationship or relevant derivative contract and what is a "relevant derivative contract", inter alia.

New TIOPA 2010 s 413 defines "adjusted net group-interest expense" of a worldwide group, used in the calculation under new TIOPA 2010 s 400 of the fixed-ratio debt cap, for a period of account as A + B − C, where A is the net group-interest expense, B the sum of "upward adjustments" and C the sum of "downward adjustments". Upward adjustments and downward adjustments largely adjust for capitalised interest and other items included in the carrying value of assets. The intention is that capitalised interest is included in adjusted net group-interest expense when capitalised and excluded when written down.

New TIOPA 2010 s 414 defines "qualifying net group-interest expense", used in the calculation under new TIOPA 2010 s 399 of the group-ratio percentage, as A − B, where A is the adjusted net group-interest expense for the group (see new TIOPA 2010 s 413) and B is the sum of any downward adjustments. These are relevant expense amounts arising on financial liabilities owed to related parties, amounts arising from results-dependent securities, or equity notes. New TIOPA 2010 s 415 excludes from the definition of "related party" persons who are considered under new TIOPA 2010 s 466 as related, solely by reason of their financial relationship, where the finance involved is a guarantee, indemnity etc provided before 1 April 2017, or by a member of the group, in the form of a share or loan pledge or as a performance guarantee. It also provides further definitions for the purposes of new TIOPA 2010 s 414.

New TIOPA 2010 s 416 defines group EBITDA of a worldwide group for a period of account as:

$$PBT + I + DA$$

where PBT is the group's profit before tax, I is the net group-interest expense for the period and DA is the group's depreciation and amortisation adjustment. The group's profit before tax is the sum of amounts recognised in the group's financial statements as items of profit or loss in respect of income of any description other than tax income *less* the sum of amounts recognised in the group's financial statements as items of profit or loss in respect of expenses of any description other than tax income.

New TIOPA 2010 s 417 defines the "capital (expenditure) adjustment", which is the first of the elements making up the group's depreciation and amortisation adjustment, as A − B − C, where A is the relevant capital expenditure brought into account in determining the group's profit before tax; B is the relevant capital expenditure reversals brought into account in determining the group's profit before tax; and C is the relevant capital income brought into account in determining the group's profit before tax. This adjustment is largely intended to remove amounts of capital expenditure on "relevant assets" recognised by way of depreciation and amortisation, incurred and recognised in the period of account, and recognised by way of provision for future capital expenditure.

"Relevant assets" are

(1) plant and machinery;
(2) investment property;
(3) intangible assets;
(4) goodwill;
(5) shares in a company; and
(6) interest in an entity that entitles the holder to a share of the entity's profits.

New TIOPA 2010 s 418 defines the "capital (fair-value movement) adjustment, which is the second of the elements making up the group's depreciation and amortisation adjustment, as the sum of any relevant fair-value movements. This adjustment is intended to remove revaluations and other movements in the carrying value of relevant assets valued under fair-value accounting from group EBITDA.

New TIOPA 2020 s 419 defines the "capital (disposals) adjustment", which is the third element making up the group's depreciation and amortisation adjustment, as A − B + C, where A is the sum of amounts brought into account in determining the group's profits before tax and which represent losses on disposals of relevant assets; B is the sum of amounts brought into account in determining the group's profits before tax and which represent profits on disposals of relevant assets; and C is the sum of any recalculated profit amounts.

New TIOPA 2010 ss 420 and 421 deal with the treatment of derivative contracts subject to fair-value accounting. The intention is to remove fair-value movements arising from derivative contracts in particular circumstances where they form part of an intended hedge, by application of the Disregard Regulations (SI 2004/3256).

New TIOPA 2010 s 422 provides for the effect of a group EBITDA (chargeable gains) election. When this election, made under new TIOPA 2010 Sch 7A para 15, is in force, the capital (disposals) adjustment in new TIOPA 2010 s 419 is effected replacing "C" (the sum of any recalculated profit amounts) by the sum of any "relevant gains" less the sum of any "relevant losses". Relevant gains and relevant losses occur on the disposal of a relevant asset or when a company leaves the group. The gains or losses are calculated under CGT rules, acting on the assumptions that all members of the group are within the charge to UK corporation tax and neither the substantial-shareholdings exemption nor double tax relief have effect.

New TIOPA 2010 s 423 provides for the effect of an interest-allowance (alternative calculation) election on the calculation of adjusted net group-interest expense. When this election, made under new TIOPA 2010 Sch 7A para 16, is in force, the calculation of adjusted net group-interest expense under new TIOPA 2010 s 413 is modified, by deleting the provisions concerning capitalised interest.

New TIOPA 2010 s 424 provides for the effect of an interest-allowance (alternative calculation) election on the calculation of the group's profit before tax with respect to employer's pension contributions. When this election is in force, the amounts recognised in the financial statements in respect of employer pension contributions are to be replaced by the amounts that would be deductible under the fiscal rules of FA 2004.

New TIOPA 2010 s 425 provides for the effect of an interest-allowance (alternative calculation) election on the calculation of the group's profit before tax with respect to employee share-acquisition arrangements. When this election is in force, the amounts recognised in the financial statements in respect of employee share-acquisition arrangements are to be replaced by the amounts that would be deductible under the fiscal rules of CTA 2009 Part 11.

New TIOPA 2010 s 426 provides for the effect of an interest-allowance (alternative calculation) election on the calculation of the group's profit before tax with respect to changes in accounting policy. When this election is in force, the financial statements of the group are to be subject to the adjustments that would be made to them under the existing UK provisions on change of accounting policy if the group were a company within the charge to corporation tax.

New TIOPA 2010 s 427 provides for the adjustments that need to be made when an interest allowance (non-consolidated investment) election, made under new TIOPA 2010 Sch 7A para 17, is in effect. The adjusted net group-interest expense of the worldwide group is to be treated as increased by the appropriate proportion of the adjusted net group-interest expense of each associated worldwide group. The qualifying net group-interest expense of the worldwide group is to be treated as increased by the appropriate proportion of the qualifying net group-interest expense of each associated worldwide group. The group EBITDA of the worldwide group is to be treated as increased by the appropriate proportion of the group EBITDA of each associated worldwide group. The "appropriate proportion" is the proportion of the profits or losses of the associated worldwide group to which the worldwide group is entitled.

New TIOPA 2010 s 428 defines an "associated worldwide group" as the worldwide group of which a specified "non-consolidated associate" is the ultimate parent and new TIOPA 2010 s 429 defines a "non-consolidated associate" of a worldwide group.

New TIOPA 2010 s 430 provides for the effect of an interest-allowance (consolidated partnerships) election, made under new TIOPA 2010 Sch 7A para 18. When this election is in force, the worldwide group's financial statements are to be treated as if no amounts were recognised in them as items of profit or loss in respect of any income or expenses of a specified consolidated partnership and instead each specified consolidated partnership were accounted for under the equity method. New TIOPA 2010 s 431 provides for interpretation.

New TIOPA 2010 Part 10 Chapter 8 (new TIOPA 2010 ss 432–449) adapts the workings of the corporate-interest restriction to certain public-infrastructure companies.

New TIOPA 2010 s 432 is introductory and provides that new TIOPA 2010 Part 10 is to have a modified effect in relation to "qualifying infrastructure companies". These must (a) be fully taxed in the United Kingdom; (b) operate by reference to the provision of public-infrastructure assets or the carrying-on of certain other related activities; and (c) the company's income and assets must be referable to activities in relation to public-infrastructure assets. The company must also make an election. Public-infrastructure assets are either tangible assets forming part of the infrastructure of the United Kingdom or the UK sector of the continental shelf meeting a public-benefit test or buildings or parts of buildings that are a part of a UK property business and are let or sublet on a short-term basis to unrelated parties. In either case, an asset is a public-infrastructure asset only if it has had, has or is likely to have an expected economic life of at least 10 years and it is shown in a balance-sheet of a member of the group that is fully taxed in the United Kingdom.

New TIOPA 2010 s 433 sets out the requirements for a company to be a "qualifying infrastructure company. These are:

(1) meeting the public-infrastructure income test;
(2) meeting the public-infrastructure assets test;
(3) that the company is fully taxed in the United Kingdom; and
(4) that the company makes an election.

Test (1) is met if all or all but an insignificant proportion of the company's income for the accounting period derives from (a) qualifying infrastructure activities carried on by it; or (b) shares in a qualifying infrastructure company; or (c) loan relationships or other financing arrangements to which the only other party is a qualifying infrastructure company.

Test (2) is met if all or all but an insignificant proportion of the total value of the company's assets derives from (a) tangible assets related to qualifying infrastructure activities; (b) service-concession arrangements in respect of assets related to qualifying infrastructure activities; (c) financial assets to which the company is a party in order for it or another qualifying infrastructure company to carry out qualifying infrastructure activities; (d) shares in a qualifying infrastructure company; or (e) loan relationships or other financing arrangements to which the only other party is a qualifying infrastructure company.

New TIOPA 2010 s 434 provides that in order to qualify as a qualifying infrastructure company, a company must make the election under new TIOPA 2010 s 434 before the beginning of the first accounting period for which it is to have effect. It then has effect until revoked, but the revocation cannot have effect for an accounting period that begins less than five years after the beginning of the first period for which it has effect

New TIOPA 2010 s 435 provides that two or more companies in the same worldwide group may make an election to modify the operation of new TIOPA 2010 ss 433 and 434. The effect of the election is (1) to modify the insignificance criterion in the tests; or (2) to cause all the elected companies to fail the relevant tests if one of their number fails a test.

New TIOPA 2010 s 436 defines a "qualifying infrastructure activity". A company carries on a qualifying infrastructure activity" if it provides an asset that is a public-infrastructure asset in relation to that company or carries on any other activity that is ancillary to or facilitates the provision of an asset that is a public-infrastructure asset in relation to that company.

New TIOPA 2010 s 437 provides a non-exhaustive list of items of infrastructure and lists the bodies qualifying as infrastructure authorities.

New TIOPA 2010 s 438 provides that certain amounts arising to a qualifying infrastructure company in an accounting period are not to be regarded as tax-interest amounts. These are amounts in relation to a financial liability due to an unrelated party or to another qualifying infrastructure company or is in respect of a "qualifying old loan relationship". In all cases, amounts cannot be excluded unless the recourse of each creditor is limited to income or assets of a qualifying infrastructure company or shares in or debt issued by a qualifying infrastructure company. New TIOPA 2010 s 439 defines a qualifying old loan relationship as one the company entered into before 13 May 2016, at which time at least 80% of the total value of the company's future qualifying infrastructure receipts for the qualifying period was highly predictable by reference to qualifying public contracts. The terms "qualifying period", qualifying infrastructure receipt" and "qualifying public contract" are defined.

New TIOPA 2010 s 440 provides that where a qualifying infrastructure company would otherwise have had tax-interest income amounts in any accounting period, it is to be treated as not having such amounts. New TIOPA 2010 s 441 provides that the tax EBITDA of a qualifying infrastructure company for any accounting period is nil.

New TIOPA 2010 s 442 provides that in calculating the adjusted and qualifying net group-interest income of a qualifying infrastructure company, amounts that are exempt amounts under new TIOPA 2010 s 438 or treated as mentioned in new TIOPA 2010 s 440 are to be left out of account.

New TIOPA 2010 s 443 defines the interest capacity of a group with a qualifying infrastructure company. The general rule is to be that the interest capacity is to be calculated under new TIOPA 2010 s 392 as if that section did not refer to a de minimis limit. There is an exception, where the total interest restrictions calculated including the rules of new TIOPA 2010 Part 10 Chapter 8 would exceed those that would result if this Chapter did not apply and new TIOPA 2010 s 392 contained only the de minimis limit. In that case, the interest capacity of the worldwide group is set at the limit, and no other provision in new TIOPA 2010 Part 10 Chapter 8 applies.

New TIOPA 2010 s 444 modifies the rules where there is a joint-venture company that is itself a qualifying infrastructure company and has at least one investor that is another qualifying infrastructure company and others who are not, and the joint-venture company makes an election. New TIOPA 2010 s 445 posits the situation where the joint-venture company is the ultimate parent company of a multi-company worldwide group. In such a case, the election made under new TIOPA 2010 s 444 by the joint-venture company is not to have effect unless all the other members of the group are qualifying infrastructure companies, are wholly owned subsidiaries of the joint-venture company and have the same accounting periods as the joint-venture company. New TIOPA 2010 s 446 makes further modifications of the rules when applied to joint-venture companies. New TIOPA 2010 s 447 provides how the public infrastructure test is to be applied where a qualifying infrastructure company is a member of a partnership or other transparent entity.

New TIOPA 2010 s 448 provides that the rules of new TIOPA 2010 Part 10 Chapter 8 may apply equally to the decommissioning of a public infrastructure asset. In determining whether a company is a qualifying infrastructure company, any shares in a decommissioning fund and any loan relationships or other financing arrangements to which a decommissioning fund is a party, as well as any income arising from those assets, are to be left out of account. New TIOPA 2010 s 449 contains minor definitions.

New TIOPA 2010 Part 10 Chapter 9 (new TIOPA 2010 ss 450–460) alters the rules of Part 10 in the case of particular types of company or business.

New TIOPA 2010 s 450 applies new TIOPA 2010 Part 10 to banking companies carrying on a trade consisting of or including dealing in financial instruments. Provisions modified are new TIOPA 2010 ss 382 (determination of tax-interest expense amounts), 385 (tax-interest income amounts) and 411 (relevant expense amounts and relevant income amounts).

New TIOPA 2010 s 451 applies to oil and gas companies, and provides that any amounts taken into account in calculating a company's ring-fence income or its aggregate gain or loss are to be ignored for the purposes of these rules.

New TIOPA 2010 s 452 applies to REITs. It provides that the exempt property-rental business and the residual business of the REIT are to be treated as separate members of the worldwide group. In addition, the assumption is made that the profits of the property-rental business are not exempt from corporation tax for the purposes of calculating tax-interest and tax EBITDA. It prescribes how the restricted interest is to be allocated between these companies and facilitates the carry-forward of excess amounts.

New TIOPA 2010 s 453 applies to insurance companies and other insurance entities that have a subsidiary held as a portfolio investment where the subsidiary would otherwise be a member of the group. For the purposes of new TIOPA 2010 Part 10, the subsidiary and any subsidiaries of its own are not to be included in the group and so none of them is to be regarded as a consolidated subsidiary of any member of the group.

New TIOPA 2010 s 454 applies to corporate members of Lloyd's. It provides that any interest of a company in respect of its underwriting business is included within the definition of tax-interest where brought into account under CTA 2009 Part 3. It also overrides FA 1994 s 226(3), which would otherwise exclude relevant contracts forming part of a premium trust fund from being derivative contracts.

New TIOPA 2010 s 455 applies to shipping companies under the tonnage tax rules. In any accounting period of a tonnage-tax company, the company's tonnage-tax profits for that period are to be taken as nil for the purpose of calculating the company's adjusted corporation tax earnings under new TIOPA 2010 s 406.

New TIOPA 2010 ss 456 and 457 apply to companies whose creditor relationships are determined on the basis of fair-value accounting. If they so elect under this section, they may disapply the fair-value rule and instead determine their creditor relationships under the amortised-cost basis of accounting for the purpose of calculating their tax-interest expense amounts and tax-interest income amounts. The election must be made no later than 12 months after the end of the first accounting period to which it is to apply and once made, it is irrevocable. Where, as a result of the election, the company's tax-interest expense amounts include notional debits, the worldwide group of which the company is a part is subject to interest restrictions for a period of account, and the total disallowed amount consists of or includes the notional debits, the company must bring a debit equal to the amount of the notional debits into account in the accounting period and bring a credit of an equal amount into account in the accounting period.

New TIOPA 2010 s 458 applies to cooperative and community-benefit societies. Where they would otherwise have a tax-interest expense amount or tax-interest income amount under new TIOPA 2010 ss 382 or 385 as a result of having a loan-relationship debit or credit, and that amount arises solely because CTA 2009 s 499 requires certain sums payable by them to be treated as debits of a loan relationship, those amounts are not to be treated as a tax-interest expense amount or a tax-interest income amount.

New TIOPA 2010 s 459 applies to charities. Where a company that is a wholly owned subsidiary of a charity and has a tax-interest expense amount in respect of a loan-relationship debit under which the creditor is the charity, the amount is not to be treated as a tax-interest expense amount of the company provided that the company would at all times be able to claim relief on any donation it were to make to the charity.

New TIOPA 2010 s 460 applies to companies having long funding operating leases and finance leases. In computing the company's adjusted corporation tax earnings, all the following are to be ignored: the lessor's deduction under a long funding operating lease; the reduction of the lessee's deduction in respect of a long funding operating lease; the capital component of the company's rental earnings under a finance lease that is not a long funding finance lease and depreciation in respect of any asset leased to the company under a finance lease that is not a long funding finance lease. An equivalent adjustment is made for the purposes of new TIOPA 2010 s 417 when using the group-ratio method.

New TIOPA 2010 Part 10 Chapter 10 (new TIOPA 2010 s 461) is an anti-avoidance provision. It provides that any tax advantage that would otherwise arise from "relevant" avoidance arrangements is to be counteracted by making just and reasonable adjustments.

Avoidance arrangements are "relevant" if their main purpose, or one of their main purposes, is to obtain a tax advantage wholly or partly attributable to the rules of new TIOPA 2010 Part 10.

New TIOPA 2010 Part 10 Chapter 11 (new TIOPA 2010 ss 462–498) contains supplementary, interpretative and commencement provisions.

New TIOPA 2010 ss 462–472 address the definition of "related parties". New TIOPA 2010 s 462 is introductory.

New TIOPA 2010 s 463 defines whether a person is generally a related party of another. The rule is that two parties are related if (a) throughout any period in which they are consolidated for accounting purposes; (b) on any day on which the participation condition is met; and (c) on any day on which the 25% investment condition is met. New TIOPA 2010 s 464 defines the 25% investment condition. New TIOPA 2010 s 465 attributes rights and interests when considering the relationship test in new TIOPA 2010 s 464. New TIOPA 2010 s 466 provides that certain loan relationships and other transactions are to be treated as made between related parties. New TIOPA 2010 s 467 prescribes how holdings of debt and equity in the same proportions are to be dealt with.

New TIOPA 2010 s 468 provides that, in a case where two related parties are debtor and creditor in a loan relationship, but there are unrelated parties holding more than 50% of the debt, the two related parties are to be treated for the purposes of new TIOPA 2010 Part 10 as if they were not related parties in relation to the loan. New TIOPA 2010 s 469 provides that where two parties to the same loan relationship as debtor and creditor become related as a result of a debt restructuring exercise in respect of distressed debt, the two parties are not to be treated as related in respect of the loan relationship for the purposes of new TIOPA 2010 Part 10.

New TIOPA 2010 s 470 applies where a debtor under a loan relationship has become related to the creditor as a result of certain circumstances but the loan relationship is not one to which the creditor is a party directly or indirectly as a result of those circumstances, the debtor and creditor are not to be treated as related in relation to the loan relationship for the purposes of new TIOPA 2010 Part 10.

New TIOPA 2010 s 471 provides that when a person receives a loan of money from a public body to which he is related, borrower and lender are not to be treated for the purposes of new TIOPA 2010 Part 10 as related parties in relation to the loan, provided that realising a profit is merely incidental to the making of the loan. New TIOPA 2010 s 472 provides that where an asset is leased under a lease granted before 20 March 2017 to a lessee for whom the lease is a finance lease, the lessor and lessee are not to be treated for the purposes of new TIOPA 2010 Part 10 as related parties in relation to the lease.

New TIOPA 2010 s 473 defines the terms "worldwide group" and "ultimate parent". A worldwide group consists of the ultimate parent and its consolidated subsidiaries. Note that this definition of a group differs from the definitions that apply for group relief or for VAT. To be an ultimate parent, an entity must be a "relevant entity" (as defined in new TIOPA 2010 s 474) and either not be a member of an IAS group or, if it is a member of an IAS group, not be a consolidated subsidiary of an entity that is itself a "relevant entity". New TIOPA 2010 s 474 defines a "relevant entity" as a company or other entity in which the shares or other interests are sufficiently widely held, that is to say, no participator in the entity may hold more than 10% by value of all the shares or other interests in the entity. New TIOPA 2010 s 475 defines "non-consolidated subsidiary" and "consolidated subsidiary".

New TIOPA 2010 s 476 provides for continuity of a worldwide group. A group that is a worldwide group at one point in time will be the same worldwide group that existed at an earlier time only if the ultimate parent of the group is the same on both occasions and was the ultimate parent of a worldwide group throughout the intervening period. New TIOPA 2010 s 477 provides that where two entities are stapled to each other and both would in the absence of the other be the ultimate parent of a worldwide group, they are to be regarded as consolidated subsidiaries of a deemed parent, which is then the ultimate parent of the group. The same rule applies under new TIOPA 2010 s 478 in the case of two entities which, although not stapled, are treated under international accounting standards as a single economic entity by virtue of being a business combination achieved by contract.

New TIOPA 2010 ss 479–489 make provisions for financial statements. Under new TIOPA 2010 s 479, references throughout new TIOPA 2010 Part 10 to "financial statements" are to be taken as references to the consolidated financial statements of the worldwide group's ultimate parent and its subsidiaries. However, where the worldwide group is at all times in the relevant period of account a single-company worldwide group, the references are to be taken as references to the financial statements of the ultimate parent.

New TIOPA 2010 s 480 provides that references to a period of account of a worldwide group are to a period in respect of which the group's financial statements have been drawn up by or on behalf of the ultimate parent, or a period in respect of which group financial statements are treated as drawn up under any of new TIOPA 2010 ss 481–485.

New TIOPA 2010 s 481 applies when the financial statements of a worldwide group have been drawn up, but not on acceptable principles. In such a case, the faulty financial statements are to be ignored and IAS financial statements are deemed to have been drawn up. Financial statements are considered to have been drawn up on acceptable principles only if:

(1) they are IAS financial statements; or

(2) the amounts recognised in the faulty statements are not materially different from those that would be recognised in IAS financial statements of the worldwide group; or

(3) the financial statements are drawn up in accordance with UK GAAP; or

(4) they are drawn up in accordance with generally accepted accounting principles and practice in one of the following: Canada, China, India, Japan, South Korea or the United States.

New TIOPA 2010 s 482 applies where financial statements have been prepared on acceptable principles but they fail to consolidate all the relevant subsidiaries. In such a case, the faulty financial statements are to be ignored, and consolidated financial statements of the ultimate parent and its IAS subsidiaries are to be treated as having been drawn up. Under new TIOPA 2010 s 483, if the ultimate parent draws up consolidated financial statements for a period but it was not the ultimate parent of that worldwide group for the entire length of that period, those financial statements are to be ignored, and consolidated financial statements of the ultimate parent and its IAS subsidiaries are to be treated as having been drawn up for the period during which the entity was the ultimate parent of the group. New TIOPA 2010 s 484 applies where financial statements have been prepared for the ultimate parent for a period but consolidated financial statements for the worldwide group have not been drawn up for the same period or any part of it. In that case, provided that the worldwide group was at any time in the relevant period a multi-company worldwide group, IAS financial statements for the worldwide group are deemed to have been drawn up, but the ultimate parent may elect that this deeming rule not apply in relation to financial statements for itself.

New TIOPA 2010 s 485 applies where no financial statements have been drawn up for any part of any period of account beginning after 31 March 2017, and none of new TIOPA 2010 ss 481–484 applies. In that case, IAS financial statements are deemed to have been drawn up for the accounts-free period. If the accounts-free period is longer than 12 months, the deemed financial statements are treated as having been drawn up for each 12-month period or part thereof. However, the ultimate parent of the group may elect under new TIOPA 2010 s 486 to deem the IAS statements to have been drawn up for a different period or periods, within certain limits. Under new TIOPA 2010 s 487, actual financial statements may be ignored for the purposes of new TIOPA 2010 Part 10 if they have been drawn up for a period longer than 18 months or were not drawn up within 30 months from the beginning of the period of account. New TIOPA 2010 s 488 defines "IAS financial statements", and new TIOPA 2010 s 489 defines what is meant by references to amounts "recognised" in financial statements.

New TIOPA 2010 s 490 defines "relevant accounting period" as an accounting period of a company which falls wholly or partly within a particular period of account of the worldwide group. New TIOPA 2010 s 491 defines "relevant public body". Other definitions follow: of "UK group company" (in new TIOPA 2010 s 492) and "embedded derivatives" (in new TIOPA 2010 s 493). New TIOPA 2010 s 494 contains other interpretations.

New TIOPA 2010 s 495 enables HMRC to make regulations for altering calculations prescribed in new TIOPA 2010 Part 10 Chapter 7 in order to address differences between the way amounts are recognised in the group's financial statements on the one hand and by subsidiaries in their own financial statements on the other. Under new TIOPA 2010 s 496, HMRC may make regulations entitling a UK group company that is a party to a capital-market arrangement elect to transfer the liability to another UK group company, provided the latter agrees. New TIOPA 2010 s 497 enables HM Treasury to amend new TIOPA 2010 Part 10 to take account of a change in accounting standards. Finally, new TIOPA 2010 s 498 confers general regulation-making powers.

Schedule 5 para 2 inserts new TIOPA 2010 Sch 7A. This Schedule has 76 paragraphs, divided into nine Parts. Part 1 (paras 1–11) deals with the appointment of a reporting company and that company's obligation to submit an interest-restriction return. Part 2 (paras 12–37) prescribes the contents of an interest-restriction return. Part 3 (paras 38–39) deals with the duty to keep and preserve records. Part 4 (paras 40–55) deals with enquiries into an interest-restriction return. Part 5 (paras 56–59) deals with determinations by HMRC. Part 6 (paras 60–61) deals with information powers exercisable by group members. Part 7 (paras 62–67) deals with information powers exercisable by HMRC. Part 8 (paras 68–73) deals with company tax returns, and Part 9 (paras 74–76) is supplementary.

New TIOPA 2010 Sch 7A para 1 provides that a worldwide group, acting through one of its members, may appoint an eligible group company to be the group's reporting company. The appointment continues in force unless revoked or until a replacement reporting company is appointed. The notice of appointment must be given within six months of the end of the first period of account of the worldwide group for which it is to have effect, must be authorised by at least 50% of eligible companies and contain a list of those companies. The notice may be accompanied by a statement that, although they may consent to the appointment of the reporting company, certain of those companies may not wish to be consenting companies with respect to the allocation of allowances and disallowances. A company is an eligible company only if it is a "UK group company" at the time of the specified period of account and not dormant.

New TIOPA 2010 Sch 7A para 2 provides that a member of a worldwide group may revoke a previous appointment, by notice in writing, specifying the first period of account in respect of which the revocation is to have effect. Like the original notice of appointment, the revocation is only effective if made no later than six months after the end of that first period of account and authorised by at least 50% of eligible companies.

Under new TIOPA 2010 Sch 7A para 3, HMRC may make regulations supplementing the first two paragraphs.

New TIOPA 2010 Sch 7A para 4 provides that if the worldwide group has made no appointment of a reporting company for a particular period of account and it is now too late for it to do so, HMRC will appoint an eligible company to be the reporting company, and may do so at any time no later than 36 months after the end of the period of account for which the appointment is to have effect, or even later if it is still possible for amounts in a UK group company's company tax return to be altered.

Under new TIOPA 2010 Sch 7A para 5, HMRC may appoint a replacement for the reporting company (whether it was appointed by the worldwide group or HMRC) if either they consider that the current reporting company has not complied with or will not comply with its statutory obligations under new TIOPA 2010 Sch 7A or the current reporting company has agreed to their doing so.

New TIOPA 2010 Sch 7A para 6 provides that a reporting company must within six months of its appointment notify each company that was a UK group company at any time in the period of account and the ultimate parent of its appointment.

New TIOPA 2010 Sch 7A para 7 provides that it is the duty of the reporting company to make an "interest-restriction return" for each period of account for which it is the reporting company and submit it before the filing date, which is the later of 12 months after the end of the period of account and three months after the day of its appointment. Under new TIOPA 2010 Sch 7A para 8, the reporting company may submit a revised return no later than the later of 36 months after the end of the relevant period of account and three months after its appointment. Where a member of the group amends its company tax return so as to affect any figures in the interest-restriction return, the reporting company must submit a revised return within three months. Under new TIOPA 2010 Sch 7A para 9, the 36-month time limit for submitting a "voluntary" revised return is extended to 60 months if the revised return is a replacement for an abbreviated return (see new TIOPA 2010 Sch 7A para 19) and the worldwide group is not subject to interest restrictions in the return period. New TIOPA 2010 Sch 7A para 10 defines "consenting company" and "non-consenting company". A consenting company is a group company that has consented to accept the allocation to it of disallowed amounts as shown on the interest-restriction return. All other companies in the group are "non-consenting". Under new TIOPA 2010 Sch 7A para 11, a company that consented to the appointment of the reporting company but did not indicate it was not consenting to interest allocations is regarded as consenting in that respect, unless and until it gives notice to the contrary.

New TIOPA 2010 Sch 7A Part 2 (paras 12–37) concerns itself with the interest-restriction return. New TIOPA 2010 Sch 7A para 12 specifies no less than seven elections that a reporting company may make on behalf of the worldwide group on the face of the return. These elections are:

(1) a group-ratio election;
(2) a group-ratio (blended) election;
(3) a group-EBITDA (chargeable gains) election;
(4) an interest-allowance (alternative calculation) election;
(5) an interest allowance (non-consolidated investment) election;
(6) an interest allowance (consolidated partnership) election; and
(7) an abbreviated-return election.

New TIOPA 2010 Sch 7A para 13 describes a group-ratio election as an election under which the reporting company may elect that the group's interest allowance be calculated using the group-ratio method or revoke an earlier election.

New TIOPA 2010 Sch 7A para 14 provides that, in connection with a group-ratio election, the reporting company may make a group-ratio (blended) election, under which the group's interest disallowance is calculated by reference also to the group ratio of an investor's worldwide group. In order for this to have effect, the worldwide group must have at least one related-party investor that is a member of a different worldwide group. The election may specify more than one investor worldwide group.

New TIOPA 2010 Sch 7A para 15 provides that a reporting company may make an election (the group-EBITDA (chargeable gains) election), under which group interest and group EBITDA is calculated using, essentially, TCGA rules, as specified in new TIOPA 2010 s 422. Unlike the previous elections, this election is irrevocable.

New TIOPA 2010 Sch 7A para 16 permits the reporting company to make an interest-allowance (alternative calculation) election. With this election, the worldwide group's group-interest and group EBITDA are calculated using the group-ratio method and the alternative-calculation provisions in new TIOPA 2010 ss 423–426. This election is also irrevocable.

New TIOPA 2010 Sch 7A para 17 provides for the reporting company to make an interest-allowance (non-consolidated investment) election. This election requires that the worldwide group's group-interest and group EBITDA are calculated using the group-ratio method and the non-consolidated investment provisions in new TIOPA 2010 ss 427 and 428. This election is revocable.

New TIOPA 2010 Sch 7A para 18 allows for the interest-allowance (consolidated partnership) election. Under this election, the worldwide group's group-interest and group EBITDA are calculated using the group-ratio method and the consolidated partnership provisions in new TIOPA 2010 s 430. This election is irrevocable.

New TIOPA 2010 Sch 7A para 19 provides for the reporting company to elect to submit an abbreviated interest-restriction return for a period of account.

New TIOPA 2010 Sch 7A para 20 prescribes the contents of a full interest-restriction return and an abbreviated interest-restriction return. A full return must be made for any period of account in which the worldwide group is subject to interest restrictions and in any period in which it is not subject to interest restrictions but there is no abbreviated-return election in force.

A full return must contain the following information:

(1) the name and UTR (if applicable) of the ultimate parent;
(2) the return period in question;
(3) the names and UTRs of all UK companies that were members of the worldwide group at any time in the return period, and whether they are consenting or non-consenting;
(4) a statement of calculations;
(5) where applicable, a statement that the group is subject to interest restrictions, the total disallowed amount and a statement of allocated interest restrictions;
(6) where applicable, a statement that the group is subject to interest reactivations, the interest-reactivation cap and a statement of allocated interest reactivations;
(7) the declaration as to correctness and completeness.

For a period in which the group is not subject to interest restrictions, and an abbreviated-return election is in force, the return need include only the items numbered (1)–(3) and (7), together with a statement that the group is not subject to interest restrictions for the return period.

New TIOPA 2010 Sch 7A para 21 specifies what the statement of calculations must contain for each company that was a UK group company at any time in the return period.

New TIOPA 2010 Sch 7A para 22 specifies what the statement of allocated interest restrictions must contain. It must list one or more companies that were UK group companies at any time in the return period and had net tax-interest expense for the period and allocate to them their share of the interest restriction (the allocated disallowance). The allocated disallowance for each consenting company must not exceed its net tax-interest expense and for non-consenting companies, must not exceed their pro rata share of the total disallowed amount.

New TIOPA 2010 Sch 7A para 23 specifies what is meant by a company's pro rata share of the total disallowed amount for the return period.

New TIOPA 2010 Sch 7A para 24 prescribes how a company's pro rata share for the return period is to be apportioned between the relevant accounting periods of the company, where the company's accounting period does not coincide exactly with the worldwide group's period of account.

New TIOPA 2010 Sch 7A para 25 prescribes the contents of a statement of allocated interest reactivations, when the group's tax EBITDA is sufficient to absorb excess interest disallowed in previous periods and brought forward to the current return period.

New TIOPA 2010 Sch 7A para 26 prescribes how to calculate the amount available for reactivation for a company in a period of account of the worldwide group. This is the lower of the company's interest-reactivation cap and the amount represented by:

$$A + B - C + D - E$$

where A is the total of the disallowed tax-interest expense amounts brought forward to the specified accounting period from earlier accounting periods; B is the total of the tax-interest expense amounts that the company is required to leave out of account in the specified accounting period but derive from previous periods of account; C is the total of the disallowed tax-interest expense amounts from previous periods of account that the company must now bring into account in the specified accounting period as a result of reactivation; and D and E are the equivalent amounts to B and C but derive from periods of account of another worldwide group of which the company was a member. The interest-reactivation cap for the company is A x B, where A is the interest-reactivation cap of the worldwide group in the period of account and B is the proportion of the period of account in which the company was a UK group company.

New TIOPA 2010 Sch 7A para 27 permits the use of estimated amounts in the statement of calculations, the statement of allocated interest restrictions and the statement of allocated interest reactivations. Estimates must be clearly indicated as such. If estimates have still not become final once 36months have elapsed since the end of the period of account, the company must inform HMRC, failing which it may incur a penalty of £500.

New TIOPA 2010 Sch 7A para 28 permits HMRC to correct an interest-restriction return within a period of nine months following its date of submission.

New TIOPA 2010 Sch 7A para 29 provides that a company that fails to submit an interest-restriction return by the filing date becomes liable to a fixed penalty of £500 if the return is no more than three months late, and £1,000 otherwise. Penalties are charged by assessment, and HMRC must make the assessment within 12 months of the filing date. There is a right of appeal.

New TIOPA 2010 Sch 7A para 30 provides that a company that submits a return containing an understatement of the total disallowed amount or an overstatement of the interest-reactivation cap is to be liable to a penalty if the mistake was either a careless inaccuracy or a deliberate inaccuracy. The penalty amount ranges from 100% of the notional tax in the case of a deliberate and concealed inaccuracy to 30% of the notional tax in the case of a careless inaccuracy.

New TIOPA 2010 Sch 7A para 31 defines what is meant by a deliberate inaccuracy that is concealed. Discovering an inaccuracy after a return is submitted and then failing to inform HMRC renders an inaccuracy careless or deliberate.

New TIOPA 2010 Sch 7A para 32 imposes a penalty of 100% of the notional tax on a company that deliberately provides inaccurate information to, or withholds information from, another company, causing that company to submit an inaccurate return.

New TIOPA 2010 Sch 7A para 33 permits HMRC to reduce the amount of a penalty under new TIOPA 2010 Sch 7A paras 30 or 32 for disclosure of an inaccuracy or where special circumstances exist.

New TIOPA 2010 Sch 7A para 34 provides that penalties under new TIOPA 2010 Sch 7A paras 30 or 32 are to be charged by assessment, and HMRC must make the assessment within 12 months of the day when the inaccuracy was corrected. There is a right of appeal. New TIOPA 2010 Sch 7A para 35 confers a right of appeal against the decision to impose a penalty and against the amount. New TIOPA 2010 Sch 7A para 36 provides that on the question whether a penalty is payable at all, the tribunal may confirm or cancel HMRC's decision. As regards the amount, the tribunal may confirm HMRC's decision or vary it to the extent that HMRC had power to do so. However, if the tribunal considers that HMRC's decision on mitigation was flawed, it may go beyond those mitigation limits. New TIOPA 2010 Sch 7A para 37 provides that payments made between companies in respect of penalties are not to be brought into account for tax purposes by either payer or payee, provided they do not exceed the amount of the penalty.

New TIOPA 2010 Sch 7A Part 3 (paras 38 and 39) concern record-keeping. New TIOPA 2010 Sch 7A para 38 requires a reporting company to keep records sufficient for it to submit a correct and complete interest-restriction return for any period and to preserve those records until at least six years after the end of the period of account, unless HMRC agree to an earlier date. Failure to comply with the duty under new TIOPA 2010 Sch 7A para 38 incurs a penalty of up to £3,000 under new TIOPA 2010 Sch 7A para 39.

New TIOPA 2010 Sch 7A Part 4 (paras 40–55) provide the procedure for HMRC enquiries into an interest-restriction return. The provisions are similar to those in FA 1998 Sch 18 Part 4, governing enquiries into company tax returns. New TIOPA 2010 Sch 7A para 40 provides that an officer of HMRC may open an enquiry into an interest-restriction return by giving notice to the company. The general rule is that an interest-restriction return may be the subject of one enquiry only, but a revised return is a new return for this purpose. The power to enquire into an interest-restriction return of a worldwide group does not affect the power to enquire into a company tax return of a member of the group.

New TIOPA 2010 Sch 7A para 41 provides that the normal time limit for opening an enquiry into a return is to be the latest of:

(1) 39 months after the end of the period of account;

(2) six months from the day the reporting company was appointed; and

(3) the 31 January, 30 April, 31 July or 31 October immediately following the first anniversary of the day on which HMRC receive the revised return.

New TIOPA 2010 Sch 7A para 42 allows the time limits to be extended, or a closed enquiry to be reopened, if an officer of HMRC discovers that an interest-restriction return is or may not be compliant with all the requirements imposed by new TIOPA 2010 Sch 7A para 20(3) (contents of return), there would or might be an increase in tax payable as a result, the discovery is made after the normal time limits have expired or after an enquiry has been closed, and the officer could not have been reasonably expected to be aware of the non-compliance at the time. In these circumstances, the time limits are to be extended to six years in a case of careless non-compliance and 20 years in the case of deliberate non-compliance, or to four years in any other case.

New TIOPA 2010 Sch 7A para 43 sets out the scope of the enquiry. It extends into anything that the return contains or should have contained but does not extend into an amount that is or should be included in a company tax return. However, HMRC may enquire into how such an amount ought to be treated under new TIOPA 2010 Part 10. Under new TIOPA 2010 Sch 7A para 44, HMRC may also enquire into the correct identification of the worldwide group and its members and into whether the return covered the correct period.

New TIOPA 2010 Sch 7A para 45 provides that HMRC may amend a company's tax return during an enquiry into an interest-restriction return, where they consider that the amount of tax stated as payable is insufficient. The company concerned must have been a member of the group at any time in the period of account for which the return was submitted.

New TIOPA 2010 Sch 7A para 46 applies when the reporting company submits a revised return while the enquiry into the original return is still in progress. The revision does not restrict the scope of the enquiry but HMRC may take it into account. So far as the revised return affects the tax payable by a company, it is not given effect until the enquiry is completed.

New TIOPA 2010 Sch 7A para 47 provides that an enquiry into an interest-restriction return is completed when HMRC issue a closure notice (no mention here of a partial closure notice) and what such a closure notice should contain. New TIOPA 2010 Sch 7A para 48 provides that a company may apply to the tribunal at any time for a direction to HMRC to complete an enquiry.

New TIOPA 2010 Sch 7A para 49 specifies the contents of a closure notice. Where the enquiry concludes the return was made for the wrong period of account, the closure notice must require the company to take steps to submit returns for the correct period(s). Similarly, if a closure notice requires a company to submit an interest-restriction for a period of account of a worldwide group, the company is to be treated as if it had been appointed as the reporting company for the group, notwithstanding that the original return may have been for a different worldwide group. New TIOPA 2010 Sch 7A para 50 provides that a return made in compliance with a closure notice must be submitted to an officer of HMRC and to be effective, must be made within three months of the date of the closure notice.

New TIOPA 2010 Sch 7A para 51 applies where HMRC came to the conclusion that the original return should have been submitted in respect of a different group and that one or more entities were incorrectly excluded. Where the ultimate parent is already the ultimate parent of an existing group, which has appointed a reporting company, HMRC must appoint that company as the reporting company for the new group. Any interest-restriction returns, notices of enquiry and appeals in relation to the original group are to the treated as withdrawn.

New TIOPA 2010 Sch 7A para 52 confers a right of appeal against a closure notice requiring the company to take the action specified and against a notice under new TIOPA 2010 Sch 7A para 51.

New TIOPA 2010 Sch 7A para 53 covers the situation in which a new worldwide group is designated after an enquiry, new TIOPA 2010 Sch 7A para 51 does not apply and the reporting company is not a member of the new group. HMRC must appoint a new reporting company. New TIOPA 2010 Sch 7A para 54 provides that where anything needs to be done under new TIOPA 2010 Part 10 on a just and reasonable basis, HMRC are not bound to follow the same just and reasonable basis. The basis they choose may be challenged as not being just and reasonable but on no other grounds. New TIOPA 2010 Sch 7A para 55 ensures that there is full continuity under new TIOPA 2010 Part 10 if there is a change in reporting company.

New TIOPA 2010 Sch 7A Part 5 (paras 56–59) provides for HMRC to make determinations in the absence of a return. New TIOPA 2010 Sch 7A para 56 applies where HMRC consider that a worldwide group was subject to interest restrictions in a particular period of account and the filing date has passed but either (a) the worldwide group has not appointed a reporting company; or (b) the reporting company that was appointed has failed to submit a return; or (c) a non-compliant return has been submitted. In these circumstances, HMRC may make a determination of the total interest disallowance and allocate it among the relevant UK group companies on a pro rata basis. New TIOPA 2010 Sch 7A para 57 provides that, following a determination, an interest-restriction return will be valid even if the normal time limit has expired provided that it is submitted no later than 12 months after the date of the determination.

New TIOPA 2010 Sch 7A para 58 applies where a company has been required to submit an interest-restriction return after the issue of a closure notice but has failed to do so or has submitted a non-compliant return. HMRC may again make a determination of a company's pro rata share of the total disallowed amount in relation to each relevant accounting period of the company. HMRC must, however, do this no later than three months after the end of the time limit for action by the company in response to the closure notice, which was itself three months from the date of the closure notice. New TIOPA 2010 Sch 7A para 59 confers the right of appeal against a determination under new TIOPA 2010 Sch 7A para 58.

New TIOPA 2010 Sch 7A Part 6 (paras 60 and 61) provides for information powers to be exercised by members of the group. New TIOPA 2010 Sch 7A para 60 provides that a reporting company is entitled to require a company that was a UK group company at any time during the relevant period of account of the worldwide group to provide it with the information that it needs to fulfil its obligations (notably, to complete the interest-restriction return). The reporting company is itself obliged as soon as reasonably practical after it has submitted an interest-restriction return to send a copy of it to each affected UK group company. Similarly, it is required to send each UK group company a copy of a closure notice that the company has received if they were members of the group at any time in the relevant period of account. New TIOPA 2010 Sch 7A para 61 prescribes what information group companies may require from each other in the absence of a reporting company.

New TIOPA 2010 Sch 7A Part 7 (paras 62–67) provides HMRC with information powers relevant to an enquiry into an interest-restriction return. Under new TIOPA 2010 Sch 7A para 62, HMRC may require a "group member" to provide information or produce a document that they reasonably require in order to check an interest-restriction return. A group member is any person HMRC believe is or may be a member of the worldwide group at any time in the relevant period of account. The person concerned need not be within the charge to UK income tax or corporation tax.

New TIOPA 2010 Sch 7A para 63 provides HMRC with the power to obtain information or documents from third parties (i.e. persons who are not members of the group). The issue of a third-party notice requires either the consent of a company that was a UK group company at any time during the period of account concerned or the approval of a tribunal. The third party contemplated should normally have been informed, given a reasonable opportunity to make representations etc, but the tribunal may agree to dispense with this if there is a danger to the revenue. The decision of the tribunal is final.

New TIOPA 2010 Sch 7A para 64 provides that the general rule is that a notice under new TIOPA 2010 Sch 7A paras 62 or 63 may not be given once an interest-restriction return has been submitted, but the rule is not to apply while an enquiry is in progress. Under new TIOPA 2010 Sch 7A para 65, a group member may appeal against a notice under new TIOPA 2010 Sch 7A para 61. A third party may appeal against a notice under new TIOPA 2010 Sch 7A para 63 if the tribunal has not approved the giving of a notice, but only on the grounds that it would be too onerous to comply. New TIOPA 2010 Sch 7A para 66 lists those provisions of FA 2008 Sch 36 (information and inspection powers) that are also to apply here. New TIOPA 2010 Sch 7A para 67 defines what is meant by references to "checking a return".

New TIOPA 2010 Sch 7A Part 8 (paras 68–73) provide for amendments to be made to a company tax return to reflect obligations or elections under new TIOPA 2010 Part 10. New TIOPA 2010 Sch 7A para 68 provides that a company must either make or revoke an election under new TIOPA 2010 ss 375 (non-consenting company leaving a pro rata share of the total disallowed amount out of account), 377 (company specifying tax-interest expense amounts to be left out of account) and 380 (company specifying tax-interest expense amounts to be brought into account) in its company tax return.

New TIOPA 2010 Sch 7A para 69 provides that a company may amend its company tax return in order to make or revoke an election under new TIOPA 2010 ss 375, 377 or 380 within the specified time limits. New TIOPA 2010 Sch 7A para 70 provides that where a company has delivered its company tax return and as a result of the submission of an interest-restriction return, information in that return becomes inaccurate, is taken to have amended its company tax return so as to correct the information, without actually needing to do so. New TIOPA 2010 Sch 7A para 71 gives HMRC the power to make regulations concerning matters in new TIOPA 2010 Sch 7A para 70. New TIOPA 2010 Sch 7A para 72 permits a company to amend, vary or revoke a "qualifying claim" following amendments or deemed amendments to its company tax return in compliance with a closure notice under new TIOPA 2010 Sch 7A para 47 or a notice of determination under new TIOPA 2010 Sch 7A paras 56 or 58 which have the effect of increasing the amount of corporation tax payable by the company. A "qualifying claim" is a claim the making, revocation or variation of which will have the effect of reducing its liability to corporation tax in the relevant accounting period. New TIOPA 2010 Sch 7A para 73 defines "company tax return".

New TIOPA 2010 Sch 7A Part 9 (paras 74–76) is supplementary. New TIOPA 2010 Sch 7A para 74 prevents double jeopardy. New TIOPA 2010 Sch 7A para 75 provides that notices of appeal under new TIOPA 2010 Part 10 must specify the grounds of appeal. New TIOPA 2010 Sch 7A para 76 specifies when amounts included in an interest-restriction return become conclusive.

Schedule 5 Part 3 (paras 3–24) makes consequential amendments. Noteworthy are the following. Schedule 5 para 10 provides that the existing TIOPA 2010 Part 10 becomes TIOPA 2010 Part 11, repeals the existing TIOPA 2010 ss 375 and 376, and renumbers the existing TIOPA 2010 ss 372–374 and 378–382 as TIOPA 2010 ss 499–501 and 502–507, respectively. Schedule 5 para 11 repeals the entire TIOPA 2010 Part 7 (TIOPA 2010 ss 260–353B) (worldwide debt cap etc) as superfluous.

Schedule 5 Part 4 (paras 25–36) provides for commencement and makes transitional provisions. The general rule is that the corporate interest restrictions have effect in relation to periods of account of worldwide groups beginning after 31 March 2017. Any regulations made under new TIOPA 2010 Part 10 before 1 April 2018 may have effect in relation to periods of account beginning after 31 March 2017.

Similarly, the repeal of TIOPA 2010 Part 7 has effect in relation to periods of account of the worldwide group beginning after 31 March 2018.

There are numerous transitional provisions.

Section 21 introduces Sch 6, which provides relief in connection with the production of museum and gallery exhibitions. The relief takes the same approach as the other creative-industry reliefs but is time-limited to expire on 31 March 2022.

Schedule 6 comprises three Parts. Part 1 (para 1) provides the provisions for the relief itself. Part 2 (paras 2–19) makes consequential amendments. Part 3 (paras 20–22) provides for commencement.

Schedule 6 para 1 inserts new CTA 2009 Part 15E, entitled "Relief for production of museum and gallery exhibitions". New CTA 2009 Part 15E itself consists of 34 sections, divided into six Chapters.

New CTA 2010 Part 15E Chapter 1 comprises five sections (new CTA 2009 ss 1218ZA–1218ZAD), and serves as an introduction. New CTA 2009 s 1218ZA gives an overview and provides that new CTA 2010 Part 15E Chapter 1 provides corporation tax relief for production companies in relation to museum and gallery exhibitions.

New CTA 2009 s 1218ZAA defines what is meant by an "exhibition" for these purposes. It is a curated public display of objects or works (or of a single object or work) considered to be of scientific, historic, artistic or cultural interest. However, a display is not an exhibition if:

(1) it is organised in connection with a competition of any kind;
(2) its main purpose or one of its main purposes is to sell anything displayed or to advertise or promote any goods or services;
(3) it includes a live performance by any person or anything displayed is alive;
(4) anything displayed is for sale – this would appear to rule out art exhibitions where the works of art are for sale.

The display must be open to the general public, whether or not they are charged admission, but this does not rule out a small number of private views etc.

New CTA 2009 s 1218ZAB defines a "touring exhibition" as an exhibition that meets five conditions (A to E). Condition A is that there is a "primary production company" for the exhibition and the company is within the charge to UK corporation tax. Condition B is that the primary production company (from now on, "PPC") intends when planning the exhibition that it will meet conditions C to E. Condition C is that the exhibition should be held at more than one venue. Condition D is that at least 25% of the objects displayed at the first venue are also displayed at every subsequent venue. Condition E is that the period between dismantling the exhibition at one venue and installing it at the next venue is no more than six months.

New CTA 2009 s 1218ZAC defines a primary production company (PPC) for an exhibition as a company meeting both conditions A and B. Condition A is that the company makes an effective creative, technical or artistic contribution to the exhibition and directly negotiates for, contracts for and pays for rights, goods and services, in relation to the exhibition. Condition B is that, if the exhibition is held at one venue only, the company be responsible for the production of the exhibition at that venue. If it is held at more than one venue, the company be responsible for the production of the exhibition at the first of those venues at least. For a single exhibition, there can be one PPC only.

New CTA 2009 s 1218ZAD defines a secondary production company ("SPC"). Such a company exists only for exhibitions with at least two venues. It is a company that (acting otherwise than in partnership) is responsible for the production of the exhibition at a venue (condition C) and is not the PPC (condition D). There can be more than one SPC for an exhibition held at two or more venues, but there can only be one SPC per venue.

New CTA 2009 Part 15E Chapter 2 comprises seven sections (new CTA 2010 ss 1218ZB–1281ZBF) and provides how the activities of a production company are to be taxed.

New CTA 2009 s 1218ZB provides that where a production company qualifies for museums and galleries exhibition tax relief in relation to the production of an exhibition, its activities in producing that exhibition are to be treated as a trade (the "separate exhibition trade") separate from any other activities it may carry on.

Where the company is the PPC for the exhibition, it is treated as beginning to carry on the separate exhibition trade at the earlier of (a) beginning of the production stage of the exhibition at the first venue at which it is held and (b) the time of the first receipt by the company of any income from the production of the exhibition. It is treated as ceasing to carry on the separate trade when the exhibition closes at the last venue at which it is held.

Where the company is an SPC for the exhibition, it is treated as beginning to carry on the separate exhibition trade at the earlier of (a) beginning of the production stage of the exhibition at the first venue for which the company is the SPC and (b) the time of the first receipt by the company of any income from the production of the exhibition. It is treated as ceasing to carry on the separate trade when the exhibition closes at the last venue for which the company is the SPC.

New CTA 2009 s 1218ZBA provides for the calculation of the profits or losses of the separate exhibition trade. For the first period of account, the costs of production incurred to date are to be brought into account as debits and the proportion of the estimated total income treated as earned at the end of that period is to be brought into account as a credit. That proportion for any period is given by $(C/T) \times I$, where C is the total to date of production costs incurred, T is the estimated total production cost and I is the estimated total income from the production of the exhibition. For subsequent periods, debits are the difference between the costs of production to date and the corresponding amount for the previous period; the credit is the difference between the proportion of estimated total income treated as earned at the end of that period and the corresponding amount for the previous period.

New CTA 2009 s 1218ZBB provides that income from the production is any receipts by the company in connection with the production or exploitation of the exhibition. These may include ticket sales or sales of rights; royalties or other payments for the exploitation of the exhibition or aspects of it; payments for rights to produce merchandise; a grant designated for the purposes of the exhibition; and the company's receipts by way of a profit-share agreement.

New CTA 2009 s 1218ZBC defines production costs. These are expenditure incurred by the company on activities involved in developing, producing, running, deinstalling (striking) and closing the exhibition or on activities with a view to exploiting the exhibition.

New CTA 2009 s 1218ZBD provides for when costs are taken to be incurred. The costs that have been incurred on the production of an exhibition at a given time are not to include any amount that has not been paid, unless it is the subject of an unconditional obligation to pay. When an obligation to pay an amount is linked to the earning of income from the production, the obligation is not treated as unconditional unless an appropriate amount of income is or has been brought into account.

New CTA 2009 s 1218ZBE provides for pre-trading expenditure. Production costs that are incurred before the start of the separate exhibition trade may be treated as incurred immediately after the company begins to carry on that trade.

New CTA 2009 s 1218ZBF provides that estimates must be made as at the balance-sheet date for each period of account on a just and reasonable basis, taking into consideration all relevant circumstances.

New CTA 2009 Part 15E Chapter 3 comprises 15 sections (new CTA 2010 ss 1218ZC–1218ZCN) and provides for the relief.

New CTA 2009 s 1218ZC is introductory and provides that relief is to be given by way of additional deductions (new CTA 2009 ss 1218ZCE–1218ZCG) and by way of tax credits (new CTA 2009 ss 1218ZCH–1218ZCK).

New CTA 2009 s 1218ZCA provides that for a company to qualify for museums and galleries exhibition tax relief in respect of the production of an exhibition: (a) it must be the PPC or an SPC for the exhibition; (b) the company is a charitable company maintaining a museum or gallery; be wholly owned by a charity maintaining a museum or gallery; or be wholly owned by a local authority maintaining a museum or gallery; (c) at the beginning of the planning stage, the company must intend that the exhibition should be public; and (d) the "EEA-expenditure condition" must be met. A "museum or gallery" includes a library or archive and a site where a collection of objects or works (or a single object or work) considered to be of scientific, historic, artistic or cultural interest is exhibited outdoors or partly outdoors. New CTA 2009 s 1218ZCB defines what it means for a company to be wholly owned by a charity or local authority.

New CTA 2009 s 121ZCC contains the EEA-expenditure condition, which is that at least 25% of the "core expenditure" incurred on the production of the exhibition by the company is EEA expenditure, i.e. expenditure on goods or services provided from within the European Economic Area. New CTA 2009 s 1218ZCD defines "core expenditure".

New CTA 2009 s 1218ZCE provides that the relief is to take the form of an additional deduction that the company may claim in respect of any accounting period. Upon the making of the claim, the company becomes entitled to make the additional deduction in calculating its profit or loss from the separate exhibition trade. New CTA 2009 s 1218ZCF sets the amount of the additional deduction. For the first period of account, the amount of the additional deduction, E, is the smaller of (a) so much of the "qualifying expenditure" incurred to date as is EEA expenditure and (b) 80% of the total amount of qualifying expenditure incurred to date. In subsequent periods of account, the additional expenditure is given by $E - P$, where P is the total amount of additional deductions given to date. New CTA 2009 s 1218ZCG defines "qualifying expenditure" as core expenditure that falls to be taken into account in calculating the profit or loss from the separate exhibition trade, is not otherwise relievable, and is incurred before 1 April 2022.

Under new CTA 2009 s 1218ZCH, a company may claim a "museums and galleries exhibition tax credit" instead of an additional deduction in an accounting period in which it has a "surrenderable loss". A company making such a claim may surrender the whole or part of that loss in return for the payment of a museums and galleries exhibition tax credit of 25% of the amount surrendered. New CTA 2009 s 1218ZCI provides that a company's surrenderable loss in any accounting period is the smaller of its "available loss" for that period in the separate exhibition trade and its "available qualifying expenditure" for that period. The available loss is given by $L + RUL$, where L is the company's loss for that period in the separate exhibition trade and RUL is the amount of any "relevant unused loss". The relevant unused loss is so much of the available loss for the previous accounting period as has neither been surrendered under new CTA 2009 s 1218ZCH nor brought forward under CTA 2010 s 45 or new s 45B and set off against profits of the separate exhibition trade. As for the available qualifying expenditure, in the first period of account this is simply E, as defined in new CTA 2009 s 1218ZCF; in any subsequent period, it is $E - S$, where S is the total amount previously surrendered under new CTA 2009 s 1218ZCH. The mechanism for payment of the museums and galleries exhibition tax credit is contained in new CTA 2009 s 1218ZCJ. Where a company claims payment of the credit, HMRC must make the payment, but the credit together with any interest on tax overpaid under TA 1988 s 826 may be used to discharge all or part of the company's liability to corporation tax. If there is an ongoing enquiry into the company's tax return for the accounting period in question, no payment of the credit need be made until the enquiry is completed; nor do HMRC need to make any payment of the credit where the company has any outstanding liabilities under PAYE or in respect of NICs. A payment of museums and galleries exhibition tax credit is not to be income of the company for any tax purpose.

New CTA 2009 s 1218ZCK imposes maxima on the amounts of museums and galleries exhibition tax credit that may be paid to any company. Where the separate exhibition trade relates to the production of a touring exhibition, the maximum amount that may be paid to the company is £100,000; if the exhibition is not a touring exhibition, the maximum is £80,000. In accordance with the EU General Block Exemption Regulation, No 651/2014/EU, the State Aid limit – the maximum that any undertaking (as defined in) may receive in museums and galleries exhibition tax credits in any year is €75 million. New CTA 2009 s 1218ZCL provides that production costs that remain unpaid four months after the end of a period of account are to be disregarded when determining the amount of costs incurred in that period.

New CTA 2009 s 1218ZCM is the standard anti-avoidance override. It provides that a company shall not qualify for museums and galleries exhibition tax relief in relation to the production of an exhibition if there any tax-avoidance arrangements in place relating to the production. Furthermore, new CTA 2009 s 1218ZCN provides that transactions are to be ignored insofar as they are attributable to arrangements, other than tax-avoidance arrangements, that are not entered into for genuine commercial reasons.

New CTA 2009 Part 15E Chapter 4 comprises 4 sections (new CTA 2009 ss 1218ZDA–1218ZDC) and provides for the treatment of losses in the separate exhibition trade.

New CTA 2009 s 1218ZD defines the term "completion period" as the accounting period in which the company ceases to carry on the separate exhibition trade. New CTA 2009 s 1218ZDA provides that the only form of relief for a loss in the separate exhibition trade in any accounting period other than the completion period is to carry it forward under CTA 2010 s 45 or new CTA 2010 s 45B to be deducted from profits of the separate exhibition trade in subsequent periods. New CTA 2009 s 1218ZDB deals with losses in the completion period, both losses brought forward and losses actually incurred in the completion period. As regards losses brought forward, the element of those losses not attributable to museums and galleries exhibition tax relief (i.e. what the losses would have been if there had been no additional deduction) may be treated as if incurred in the completion period. As for losses made in the separate exhibition trade in the completion period, actual or deemed, the amount of the loss that may be deducted under CTA 2010 s 37 from total profits of the same accounting period or an earlier period or that may be surrendered as group relief under CTA 2010 Pt 5 is also restricted to that element not attributable to museums and galleries exhibition tax relief. Terminal loss relief is provided under new CTA 2010 s 1218ZDC. A terminal loss for these purposes is a loss at the end of the completion period which the company would have been able to carry forward had it not ceased to carry on the separate exhibition trade. Two avenues for obtaining relief are available for this terminal loss. The first avenue is open where the company is carrying on another separate exhibition trade when it ceases to carry on the one in question. The company may then claim to transfer all or part of the terminal loss to the other separate exhibition trade, in which it is treated as brought forward under CTA 2010 s 45 or new CTA 2010 s 45B (as the case may be) to the first accounting period beginning after the cessation. The second avenue is open where the company is part of a group and there are one or more other companies carrying on a separate exhibition trade at the time of the cessation. In such a case, the company with the terminal loss may elect to surrender all or part of that loss to the other group company. When it does so, the loss is treated by the transferee company as a loss brought forward under CTA 2010 s 45 or new CTA 2010 s 45B (as the case may be) to the first accounting period beginning after the cessation. A deduction under either CTA 2010 s 45 or new CTA 2010 s 45B is to be disregarded for the purposes of calculating the carried-forward loss restriction under new CTA 2010 s 269ZB.

It will be seen that losses from a separate exhibition trade are strictly ring-fenced, and at no time are they available for set off against profits from a non-exhibition trade.

New CTA 2009 Part 15E Chapter 5 comprises two sections (new CTA 2009 ss 1218ZE and 1218ZEA) and provides for claims for, and clawback of, provisional relief.

New CTA 2009 s 1218ZE provides that a company is not entitled to museums and galleries exhibition tax relief in any interim accounting period (a period in which the company carries on the separate exhibition trade and precedes the accounting period in which it ceases to do so) unless in its company tax return for that period it has stated the amount of planned core expenditure on the production of the exhibition which is EEA expenditure and that amount is sufficient to indicate that the EEA expenditure condition (at least 25% EEA expenditure) will be met. If these requirements are met, the company is provisionally treated as if the EEA expenditure condition had been met. Under new CTA 2007 s 1218ZEA, if at any subsequent time, it appears that the EEA expenditure condition will not after all be met when the company ceases the separate exhibition trade, the company ceases to be entitled to museums and galleries exhibition tax relief for any accounting period for which its entitlement relief is lost, and the company must amend its company tax returns accordingly. Once a company has ceased the separate exhibition trade, a final statement of the core expenditure that is EEA expenditure must accompany the company tax return for the period of cessation. Where the final statement shows that the EEA expenditure condition has not been met, the company also loses entitlement to terminal loss relief under new CTA 2007 s 1218ZDC and the necessary adjustments must be made to the company's tax returns for the periods in question.

New CTA 2009 Part 15E Chapter 6 comprises two sections (new CTA 2010 ss 1218ZF and 1218ZFA) and provides regulatory powers and interpretation. New CTA 2010 s 1218ZF confers regulation-making powers on HM Treasury and new CTA 2010 s 1218ZFA contains definitions and cross-references to definitions.

Schedule 6 Part 2 contains paras 2–19 and makes consequential amendments. One such amendment is the insertion by Sch 6 para 11 of new CTA 2009 s 808E. This provides that an intangible fixed asset held by a museums and galleries exhibition production company may not be included in the CTA 2009 Pt 8 regime so far as it represents expenditure on an exhibition which is treated as expenditure of a separate exhibition trade. Also noteworthy is the insertion by Sch 6 para 17 in CTA 2010 Part 8B of new CTA 2010 Part 8B Chapter 14B, consisting of new CTA 2010 ss 357UR–357UY. These provide for the operation of museums and galleries exhibition tax relief for a company that is a Northern Ireland company. CTA 2010 Pt 8B will have effect from an appointed day, when the Northern Ireland Assembly may set a special Northern Ireland rate of corporation tax.

Schedule 6 Part 3 (paras 20–22) provides for commencement. The power to make regulations under Sch 6 is to come into force on 16 November 2017. The remainder of the amendments, except those made by Sch 6 paras 16–18, are to have effect for accounting periods beginning after 31 March 2017, with provision for straddling periods. Schedule 6 paras 16–18, which relate to the Northern Ireland rate of corporation tax, are to have effect from the appointed day(s) for CTA 2010 Part 8B, again with provision for straddling periods.

Section 22 introduces a new corporation tax relief for contributions to grassroots sport and makes consequential amendments. Section 22(5) inserts new CTA 2010 Part 6A, which provides for the relief.

New CTA 2010 Part 6A comprises four sections (new CTA 2010 ss 217A–217D). New CTA 2010 s 217A is the main relieving section. It provides that a payment made by a company which constitutes "qualifying expenditure on grassroots sport" and is not returned is to be allowed as a deduction from the company's total profits in computing the corporation tax chargeable for the accounting period in which the payment is made.

The amount of relief varies depending on whether the paying company is a "qualifying sport body" or not. If it is a qualifying sport body at the time of the payment, the allowable deduction is the full amount of the payment. If the paying company is not a qualifying sport body, it will still receive relief for the whole of the amount paid if it makes the payment to a qualifying sport body. If the payment is made directly to the grassroots organisation, the maximum deduction allowed in any accounting period is £2,500 (reduced proportionately for accounting periods of less than 12 months). In both cases, the deduction may not reduce the company's total taxable profits below zero.

Where a company receives income to be used for the charitable purpose of facilitating participation in amateur eligible sport, the deduction it may make under this provision is limited to the excess if any of the payment over the amount of the income that it does not have to bring into account for corporation tax and that has not previously been used to disallow a deduction under this provision.

The deduction is to be made from the company's total profits after all other relief, except relief under CTA 2010 Part 6 (charitable donations), group relief and group relief for carried-forward losses.

New CTA 2010 s 217B defines what is meant by "qualifying expenditure on grassroots sport". This is expenditure incurred for the charitable purposes of facilitating participation in amateur eligible sport, and for which no deduction would otherwise be allowed. New CTA 2010 s 217C defines "qualifying sport body". These are recognised sport governing bodies, such as the United Kingdom Sports Council, or bodies wholly owned by them. New CTA 2010 s 217D provides that if an amount would be deductible under this provision and under CTA 2010 Part 6 as a charitable donation or would be so except for the anti-abuse provisions for payments to community amateur sports clubs (CTA 2010 Part 6 Chapter 2A), the other rules will have priority.

Section 22 has effect for the purpose of allowing deductions for payments made after 31 March 2017.

Section 23 makes amendments to the Patent Box regime in CTA 2010 Part 8A in respect of cost-sharing agreements. The amendments have effect in relation to accounting periods beginning after 31 March 2017.

Section 23(2) inserts new CTA 2010 s 357BLEA in the set of sections (CTA 2010 ss 357BL–357BLH) dealing with the calculation of the R&D fraction. New CTA 2010 s 357BLEA applies where during the relevant period the company is a party to a cost-sharing agreement (as defined in new CTA 2010 s 357GC), incurs expenditure in making payments that new CTA 2010 s 357GCZC (inserted by s 23(3)) treats as having been subcontracted to an unconnected person in the cost-sharing agreement, and payments under the agreement are made to the company by unconnected persons in respect of relevant R&D that the company undertakes or has contracted out.

In these circumstances, an amount of the expenditure equal to the amount of payments received is to be disregarded in determining the R&D fraction for the sub-stream.

New CTA 2010 s 357BLEA also applies where during the relevant period the company is a party to a cost-sharing arrangement (as defined in new CTA 2010 s 357GC), incurs expenditure in making payments that new CTA 2010 s 357GCZC (inserted by s 23(3)) treats as having been subcontracted to a connected person in the cost-sharing arrangement, and payments under the arrangement are made to the company by connected persons in respect of relevant R&D that the company undertakes or has contracted out or are made in respect of assignments to it of a relevant qualifying IP right or a grant or transfer to it of an exclusive licence in respect of such a right.

In these circumstances also, an amount of the expenditure equal to the amount of payments received is to be disregarded in determining the R&D fraction for the sub-stream.

Section 23(3) substitutes for the existing CTA 2010 s 357GC (which defines a cost-sharing arrangement) new CTA 2010 ss 357GC–357GCZF.

New CTA 2010 s 357GC still contains the definition of a cost-sharing arrangement. The new definition is similar to the old but excludes the requirement that one of the parties hold a qualifying IP right or an exclusive licence in respect of such a right.

New CTA 2010 s 357GCZA allows a company that is a party to a cost-sharing arrangement under which another party holds a qualifying right in respect of the invention that is the subject of the cost-sharing arrangement and in respect of which right the company does not hold an exclusive licence to nevertheless be treated as if it held the right. In certain circumstances, where the company or the other party joined the arrangement after 31 March 2017 or if the right was already a new qualifying right for its holder, the right is to be treated as a new qualifying IP right for the company. The section is disapplied if the arrangement produces finance income for the company.

New CTA 2010 s 357GCZB is a similar provision. It allows a company that is a party to a cost-sharing arrangement under which another party holds an exclusive licence in respect of a qualifying IP right in respect of the invention that is the subject of the cost-sharing arrangement and in respect of which right the company does not hold the right or another exclusive licence to nevertheless be treated as if it held such an exclusive licence. In certain circumstances, where the company or the other party joined the arrangement after 31 March 2017 or if the right was already a new qualifying right for its holder, the right is to be treated as a new qualifying IP right for the company. The section is disapplied if the arrangement produces finance income for the company.

New CTA 2010 s 357GCZC provides that where a company is a party to a cost-sharing arrangement and another party undertakes R&D for the purpose of creating or developing the invention, the R&D is to be treated for the purposes of calculating the R&D fraction as having been contracted out by the company to the other party. Furthermore, where it is another party that subcontracts out R&D for the purpose of creating or developing the invention to a third party, and the company makes a payment under the arrangement to the other party or to the third party, the company is also to be treated for these purposes as having contracted out the R&D in fact contracted out to the third party to the other party to the arrangement, and the payments the company makes are to be treated as payments to the other party whether or not this is the case.

New CTA 2010 s 357GCZD is similar in intent and provides that where:

(1)   a company is a party to a cost-sharing arrangement;
(2)   a person assigns a qualifying IP right to another party to the arrangement;
(3)   the qualifying IP right is a right in respect of the invention; and
(4)   the company makes a payment under the arrangement in respect of the assignment, whether to the assignor or to the other party;

the payment is to be treated for the purposes of calculating the R&D fraction as a payment to the assignor in respect of the assignment of the right to the company.

Similarly, where:

(1)   a company is a party to a cost-sharing arrangement;
(2)   a person grants or transfers an exclusive licence in respect of a qualifying IP right to another party to the arrangement
(3)   the qualifying IP right is a right in respect of the invention; and
(4)   the company makes a payment under the arrangement in respect of the grant or transfer, whether to the grantor or transferor or to the other party,

the payment is to be treated for the purposes of calculating the R&D fraction as a payment to the grantor or transferor in respect of the grant or transfer of the licence to the company.

New CTA 2010 s 357GCZE provides that in any one of three different cases, where a company makes a payment in connection with a cost-sharing arrangement, a just and reasonable part of the payment is to be treated for the purposes of calculating the R&D fraction in return for becoming entitled to the IP right or licence in question.

The three cases are these.

(1)   The company makes a payment to a person in consideration of that person's entering into a cost-sharing arrangement with the company, and any party to the arrangement holds a qualifying IP right or an exclusive licence in respect of that right.
(2)   The company makes a payment to a party to a cost-sharing arrangement in consideration of that party's agreeing that the company should become a party to that arrangement, and any party to the arrangement holds a qualifying IP right or an exclusive licence in respect of that right.
(3)   A company that is a party to a cost-sharing arrangement makes a payment to another party to the arrangement in consideration for the latter's agreement that the company receive a greater share of the income or acquire additional rights, and any party to the arrangement holds a qualifying IP right or an exclusive licence in respect of that right.

New CTA 2010 s 357GCZF deals with a converse situation. It provides that in any one of three different cases, where a company receives a payment in connection with a cost-sharing arrangement, a just and reasonable part of the payment is to be treated as relevant IP income of the company.

The three cases are these.

(1)   The company receives in consideration of its entering into a cost-sharing arrangement, and the company holds a qualifying IP right or an exclusive licence in respect of that right.
(2)   The company, which is a party to a cost-sharing arrangement, receives a payment from a person in consideration of the company's agreeing that that person should become a party to that arrangement, and any party to the arrangement holds a qualifying IP right or an exclusive licence in respect of that right.
(3)   A company that is a party to a cost-sharing arrangement receives a payment from another party to the arrangement in consideration for the its agreement that the other party should receive a greater share of the income or acquire additional rights, and any party to the arrangement holds a qualifying IP right or an exclusive licence in respect of that right.

The amendments made by s 23 have effect in relation to accounting periods beginning after 31 March 2017.

Section 24 makes three relatively minor technical amendments to the hybrid mismatches regime in TIOPA 2010 Part 6A, which was introduced by FA 2016.

The first amendment (made by s 24(2)) reverses the effect of TIOPA 2010 s 259B(3), so that local taxes are now to be outside, and not potentially inside, the scope of the provisions.

The second set of amendments (made by s 24(3) and (4)) make the identical substitution of TIOPA 2010 s 259CC(2)(b) and 259DD(2)(b), with the effect that there is no longer to be a requirement to make a claim for a period to be a permitted period in relation to an amount of ordinary income where the period begins more than 12 months after the end of the payment period.

The third set of amendments (made by s 24(5)–(9)) have effect to disregard deductions for amortisation when considering whether there has been a mismatch under TIOPA 2010 ss 259EB (hybrid-payer deduction/non-inclusion mismatches and their extent), 259FA (deduction/non-inclusion mismatches relating to transfers by a permanent establishment), 259GB (hybrid-payee deduction/non-inclusion mismatches and their extent), 259HB (multinational payee deduction/non-inclusion mismatches: meaning of excessive PE deduction) and 259KB (imported mismatches: meaning of excessive PE deduction). In every case, the deduction for amortisation is defined as either a debit in respect of amortisation brought into account under CTA 2009 ss 729 or 731 (write-down of the capitalised cost of an intangible fixed asset) or an amount deductible in respect of amortisation under an equivalent foreign tax law.

The amendment excluding local taxes has effect in relation to accounting periods or relevant PE periods beginning after 12 July 2017; periods straddling 13 July 2017 are to be split for this purpose. The other amendments are deemed always to have had effect.

Section 25 introduces Sch 7, which makes amendments to the provisions relating to the Northern Ireland rate of corporation tax in CTA 2010 Part 8B.

Schedule 7 comprises two Parts. Part 1 (paras 1–25) contains the main amendments while Part 2 makes minor consequential amendments.

Schedule 7 para 1 is introductory. Schedule 7 para 2 amends CTA 2010 s 357H, which is the introductory section to CTA 2010 Part 8B, to the effect that the large-company rules in CTA 2010 Part 8B Chapter 7 are to apply not only to companies that are not SMEs but also to SMEs that are not a Northern Ireland employer but have made the election in new CTA 2010 s 357KA(2A), inserted by Sch 7 para 3.

Schedule 7 para 3 amends CTA 2010 s 357KA, which provides the definition of "Northern Ireland company", to which the NI rate of corporation tax is to apply. Hitherto, a Northern Ireland company has been defined as a company meeting either the "SME condition" or the "large company" condition. The amendments rename the SME condition the "SME (Northern Ireland employer) condition" and inserts a new alternative condition – the "SME (election) condition".

The "SME (election) condition" is met where:

(1) the company is an SME in relation to the period;
(2) it is not a Northern Ireland employer in relation to the period;
(3) the company has an "NIRE" in the period;
(4) the company is not a "disqualified close company" (as defined in new CTA 2010 s 357KEA, inserted by Sch 7 para 5); and
(5) the company has made the appropriate election, which is in force in relation to the period, to be treated as if it were a large company.

An "NIRE" is a Northern Ireland regional establishment, as defined in CTA 2010 Part 8B Chapter 5.

An election under new CTA 2010 s 357KA(2A) must specify the accounting period for which it is to apply and be made no more than 12 months after the end of that accounting period.

Schedule 7 para 4 amends CTA 2010 s 357KE, which contains the "Northern Ireland workforce conditions", which a company must meet to be a Northern Ireland employer, to include individuals who are participators in the company if that company is a close company or a company that would be close if UK-resident as members of the company's workforce for the purposes of the condition. Another amendment extends the definition of working time spent in a particular place to include the time spent by participators in providing services to a person other than the company in specified circumstances.

Schedule 7 para 5 inserts new CTA 2010 s 357KEA, which defines "disqualified close company". This is a company that is a close company or a company that would be close if UK-resident and in relation to which two conditions, A and B, are satisfied.

Condition A is that the company has an NIRE in the period as a result of tax-avoidance arrangements. Condition B is that:

(a) 50% or more of the working time spent in the United Kingdom during the period by members of the company's workforce is spent by participators in the company elsewhere than in Northern Ireland; or

(b) 50% or more of the company's workforce expenses attributable to working time spent in the United Kingdom by members of the company's workforce are attributable to working time spent by participators in the company elsewhere than in Northern Ireland.

Schedule 7 paras 6–13 make consequential amendments. Schedule 7 para 14 amends CTA 2010 s 357WA, which defines what is meant by a "Northern Ireland firm". It renames the "SME partnership condition" the "SME (Northern Ireland employer) partnership condition" and adds a further alternative condition that a partnership may meet to qualify as a Northern Ireland firm. This condition is the "SME (election) partnership condition", which operates in parallel terms to the SME (election) condition. A firm that is an SME but not a Northern Ireland employer, has an NIRE and is not a disqualified firm may elect to be treated as if it were a large partnership.

Schedule 7 para 15 inserts new CTA 2010 ss 357WBA–357WBC, which add and supplement new conditions, the Northern Ireland workforce partnership conditions. Hitherto, to qualify as a Northern Ireland workforce employer, a partnership has had to comply with the Northern Ireland workforce conditions for a company in CTA 2010 s 357KE, suitably modified. Those conditions are now replaced for a partnership by the conditions in new CTA 2010 s 357WBA.

New CTA 2010 s 357WBA provides that the Northern Ireland workforce partnership conditions are met if at least 75% of the working time spent in the United Kingdom by members of the firm's workforce is spent in Northern Ireland and at least 75% of the firm's workforce expenses that are attributable to working time spent in the United Kingdom by members of the firm's workforce are attributable to time spent in Northern Ireland. Definitions are provided of "members of the firm's workforce" and "the firm's workforce expenses". New CTA 2010 s 357WB contains further definitions and instructions, including how to calculate the amount of working time spent in any place by a partner in the firm. New CTA 2010 s 357WBC defines "disqualified firm", closely matching the equivalent definition in new CTA 2010 s 357KEA of a disqualified company. Thus, a disqualified firm is a firm in relation to which two conditions, A and B, are satisfied.

Condition A is that the company has an NIRE in the period as a result of tax-avoidance arrangements. Condition B is that (a) 50% or more of the working time spent in the United Kingdom during the period by members of the firm's workforce is working time spent by partners in the firm elsewhere than in Northern Ireland or (b) 50% or more of the firm's workforce expenses attributable to working time spent by members of the firm's workforce in the United Kingdom are attributable to working time spent by partners elsewhere than in Northern Ireland.

Schedule 7 paras 16–21 make consequential amendments to other provisions in CTA 2010 Part 8B. Schedule 7 paras 22–25 make amendments to CAA 2001 to accommodate the new conditions relating to Northern Ireland companies and firms. Schedule 7 paras 26–29 make minor consequential amendments. Schedule 7 para 30 provides for commencement, which will be on a day or days to be appointed under the Corporation Tax (Northern Ireland) Act 2015.

The Northern Ireland rate of corporation tax and the whole of CTA 2010 Part 8B are yet to come into effect.

Chargeable gains

Section 26 amends the treatment for capital gains tax of assets appropriated to trading stock. Hitherto, when an asset acquired by a person otherwise than as trading stock is appropriated for the purposes of the trade as trading stock, the person is treated for capital gains purposes as having sold the asset at its market value. However, the person may elect under TCGA 1992 s 161(3) to disapply the capital gains treatment and, instead, when computing the profits of the trade for corporation tax or income tax to reduce the market value (the amount of the proceeds and the cost price for the trade) by the amount of the chargeable gain that would otherwise have accrued or, where applicable, to increase the proceeds by the amount of the allowable loss that would otherwise have accrued. Concern that the election was being abused to convert the capital loss to a more flexible trading deduction has resulted in an amendment to the rule by limiting the election to instances of a chargeable gain. The amendment also eliminates the possibility of making an election under TCGA 1992 s 161(3A) in relation to an ATED-related loss.

Section 26 applies to appropriations made after 7 March 2017.

Sections 27 and 28 make amendments to the substantial-shareholdings legislation in TCGA 1992 Sch 7AC.

Section 27 has effect principally to remove the requirement that the investing company be a sole trading company or a member of a qualifying group.

Section 27(2) omits TCGA 1992 Sch 7AC para 18 and makes consequential amendments. The function of TCGA 1992 Sch 7AC para 18 was to make it a condition of the exemption for disposals of a substantial shareholding that the investing company (the company making the disposal) be a sole trading company or a member of a "qualifying group" throughout a qualifying period ending with the disposal. This requirement is now removed with effect for disposals made after 31 March 2017.

TCGA 1992 Sch 7AC para 7 has hitherto stipulated that the investing company must have held a substantial shareholding in the investee company at least throughout a 12-month period beginning no more than *two* years before the day of the disposal. With effect for disposals made after 31 March 2017, the amendment made by s 27(3) provides that the 12-month period may now occur at any time in the *six* years before the day of the disposal.

The effect of the amendment made by s 27(4) is to allow the period during which the investing company is considered as having held the shares to include the period during which the shares were held by a non-resident fellow group member before they were transferred to the investing company. For disposals made after 31 March 2017, it is no longer necessary for the shares to have been held by a resident fellow group member for the inclusion of the previous period to apply.

TCGA 1992 Sch 7AC para 19 has hitherto required the investee company (the company in which the investment is made) itself to be a trading company or the holding company of a trading group or trading sub-group immediately after the disposal as well as during the latest 12-month period to which reference is made in the substantial-shareholding requirement as expressed in TCGA 1992 Sch 7AC para 7. The amendments made by s 27(5) remove this requirement (in respect of a time after the disposal) generally for disposals made after 31 March 2017, but retain it in two instances – where the disposal is made to a person connected with the investing company or where the substantial-shareholding requirement of TCGA 1992 Sch 7AC para 7 is met only by virtue of an extension granted to the holding period by reference to the investee company's use of a trading asset transferred to it by another member of the group.

Section 28 introduces a simplified form of the substantial-shareholdings exemption for an investing company that is substantially owned by qualifying institutional investors immediately before the disposal.

Section 28(3) inserts new TCGA 1992 Sch 7AC paras 3A and 3B. New TCGA 1992 Sch 7AC para 3A provides that a "subsidiary exemption" shall be available to an investing company on a disposal of shares or an interest in shares in another company (called here "the investee company") where:

(1) the investing company meets the substantial-shareholding requirement and is not a "disqualified listed company"; but

(2) the investee company fails the requirement under TCGA 1992 Sch 7AC para 19 to itself be a trading company or the holding company of a trading group or trading sub-group immediately before the disposal and for the requisite period preceding the disposal; and

(3) the investing company is not a "disqualified listed company".

In these circumstances, where, immediately before the disposal, "qualifying institutional investors" own 80% or more of the ordinary share capital of the investing company, there shall nevertheless be no chargeable gain or allowable loss accruing to the investing company on the disposal.

Where, on the other hand, "qualifying institutional investors" own at least 25% but less than 80% of the ordinary share capital of the investing company immediately before the disposal, the amount of the chargeable gain or allowable loss accruing to the investing company on the disposal is to be reduced by the percentage of the ordinary share capital of the investing company owned by qualifying institutional investors.

A "disqualified listed company" is a company (a) any of whose ordinary shares are listed on a recognised stock exchange"; (b) which is not itself a qualifying institutional investor and (c) which is not a qualifying UK REIT.

A qualifying UK REIT, which is not barred from being an investing company to which the subsidiary exemption may apply, is a UK REIT meeting the condition that it is not a close company by virtue of having an institutional investor as a participant or is a company controlled by or on behalf of the Crown and for that reason not treated as a close company.

New TCGA 1992 Sch 7AC para 3B interprets terms in new TCGA 1992 Sch 7AC para 3A.

Section 28(3) inserts new TCGA 1992 Sch 7AC para 8A, which modifies the definition of a substantial shareholding where qualifying institutional investors own at least 25% of the ordinary share capital of the investing company. Where this is the case, the investing company is also regarded as holding a substantial shareholding if the cost of acquisition of its holding in the ordinary share capital of the investee company was at least £20 million, provided that the investing company is beneficially entitled to no less a proportion of the profits of the investee company available for distribution to equity holders and to no less a proportion of the investee company's assets available for distribution to equity holders on a winding-up than the proportion it holds of the investee company's share capital. Minor differences in the relative proportions are to be overlooked.

Section 28(5) inserts new TCGA 1992 Sch 7AC para 30A, which defines the class of qualifying institutional investors. These are persons who are either pension schemes (as defined), life-assurance businesses (as defined), sovereign wealth funds, charities, investment trusts, authorised investment funds or exempt unauthorised unit trusts.

The amendments made by s 28 have effect in relation to disposals made after 31 March 2017.

Domicile, overseas property etc

Sections 29–32 introduce new deemed-domicile provisions and amend the tax treatment of non-resident settlements and assets.

Section 29 inserts new ITA 2007 s 835BA and introduces Sch 8, which together introduce new deemed-domicile rules for income tax and capital gains tax.

New ITA 2007 s 835BA ("the deemed-domicile rule") provides that, for the purposes specified, an individual who is not under general law domiciled in the United Kingdom at any time in a tax year ("the current tax year") is nevertheless to be regarded as domiciled in the United Kingdom (abbreviated from now on to "UK-domiciled") if:

(1) the individual was born, and had a domicile of origin, in the United Kingdom and is resident in the United Kingdom (abbreviated from now on to "UK-resident") for the current tax year;

     (this is the case of the so-called returners); or

(2) the individual has been UK-resident for at least 15 of the 20 tax years immediately preceding the current tax year.

However, in respect of situation (2), the deemed-domicile rule is not to apply if there is no tax year beginning after 5 April 2017, including the current tax year, for which the individual was or is UK-resident.

This rule is to apply for the purposes of the provisions of the Income Tax Acts and TCGA 1992 listed and appropriately amended in Sch 8.

Schedule 8 comprises four Parts. Part 1 (paras 1–17) applies the deemed-domicile rule by making the appropriate amendments to TA 1988, TCGA 1992, ITEPA 2003 and ITA 2007. Part 2 (paras 18–40) provides protection for overseas trusts. Part 3 (paras 41–43) provides for CGT rebasing. Part 4 (paras 44–46) provides for the "cleansing" of mixed funds.

Schedule 8 para 1 amends TA 1988 s 266A (life-assurance premiums paid by employer), with effect from the tax year 2017/18.

Schedule 8 paras 2–9 amend TCGA 1992. Schedule 8 para 3 amends TCGA 1992 s 16ZA, which deals with the losses of individuals who are not domiciled in the United Kingdom (from now on, "non-domiciliaries") under the remittance basis. Unless they make an election under TCGA 1992 s 16ZA(2), their foreign losses in any tax year in which they are non-domiciled are not allowable losses for the purposes of CGT. TCGA 1992 s 16ZA as amended now provides that an individual may make an election in respect of the first tax year in which the remittance basis applies to the individual or the individual's first tax year back on the remittance basis after a period in which he has been UK-domiciled. If the individual does not make the election, foreign losses will as before not be allowable losses. However, the election loses force with effect from the tax year in which the individual again becomes UK-domiciled. The deemed-domicile rule applies. The amendments apply as from the tax year 2017/18. Consequential amendments are made to TCGA 1992 ss 16ZB and 16ZC.

The deemed-domicile rule is applied to TCGA 1992 s 69, which concerns the residence status of trustees. It has effect in cases where the settlement arises on the settlor's death for deaths after 5 April 2017, and in any other case, where the settlement was made or treated as made after 5 April 2017 (Sch 8 para 6); to TCGA 1992 s 86,which provides for the attribution of gains to settlors with an interest in non-resident or dual-resident trusts, with effect from the tax year 2017/18 (Sch 8 para 7); to TCGA 1992 s 275, which defines the location of assets, with effect from 6 April 2017, regardless of when the asset was acquired (Sch 8 para 8); and to TCGA 1992 Sch 5A, which provides for information powers relating to settlements with a foreign element, with effect in relation to settlements created after 5 April 2017 (Sch 8 para 9).

Schedule 8 para 10 applies the deemed-domicile rule to ITEPA 2003 s 355, which provides for deductions for corresponding payments by non-domiciled employees with foreign employers; to ITEPA 2003 s 373, which concerns a non-domiciled employee's travel costs and expenses for UK duties; to ITEPA 2003 s 374, which concerns the travel costs and expenses of a non-domiciled employee's spouse; and to ITEPA 2003 s 376, which concerns foreign-accommodation costs and subsistence expenses of overseas employment, all with effect from the tax year 2017/18.

Schedule 8 paras 11–17 apply the deemed-domicile rule to ITA 2007 s 476, which concerns the residence status of trustees, with effect for settlor deaths or settlements made (as the case may be) after 5 April 2017 (Sch 8 para 12) and to ITA 2007 s 718, which defines the meaning of "person abroad" for the purposes of the transfer of assets abroad rules, with effect from the tax year 2017/18 (Sch 8 para 13).

Schedule 8 para 14 adds the deemed-domicile rule to the remittance-basis provisions of ITA 2007 Part 14 Chapter A1, all with effect from the tax year 2017/18. It adds the rule to ITA 2007 s 809B, which provides for claims for the remittance basis; removes references to the previous 17-year residence test from ITA 2007 s 809C; adds the deemed-domicile rule to ITA 2007 s 809E, which concerns the application of the remittance basis in the absence of a claim; and removes references to the previous 17-year residence test from ITA 2007 s 809H.

Schedule 8 paras 15 and 16 provide that the deemed-domicile rule is not to apply to temporary non-residents who have made an election under TCGA 1992 s 10A as originally enacted or as substituted by FA 2013 Sch 45 para 119 and whose year of return is 2017/18 so as to make their foreign chargeable gains during an intervening year chargeable to tax in the year of return or such gains during a period of temporary non-residence beginning before 8 July 2015 chargeable to tax in a tax year including the period of return. Schedule 8 para 17 adds the deemed-domicile rule to ITA 2007 s 834, which concerns the residence of personal representatives, with effect from the tax year 2017/18.

Schedule 8 Part 2 provides protection for certain overseas trusts from the effect of the deemed-domicile rule. Schedule 8 para 18 inserts TCGA 1992 Sch 5 paras 5A and 5B.

New TCGA 1992 Sch 5 para 5A provides that TCGA 1992 s 86, which attributes gains to settlors with an interest in non-resident or dual-resident settlements, is not to apply in relation to a particular tax year if four conditions (A to D) are met. Condition A is that the particular year is 2017/18 or a later year. Condition B is that when the settlor created the settlement, the settlor was non-domiciled and, if the settlement was created after 5 April 2017, not deemed to be domiciled either. Condition C is that at no time in the particular year was the settlor actually UK-domiciled or deemed to be UK-domiciled. Condition D is that no property or income is provided, whether directly or indirectly, by the settlor or by the trustees of another settlement of which the settlor is the settlor or a beneficiary for the purposes of the settlement at any time in the "relevant period" when the settlor is either actually UK-domiciled or deemed to be UK-domiciled. The "relevant period" is the period beginning on the later of 6 April 2017 and the creation of the settlement and ending with the end of the particular year.

New TCGA 1992 Sch 5 para 5B provides that for the purposes of condition D, several items or events should be disregarded. These are:

(1) property or income provided under an arm's length transaction, excluding a loan;
(2) property or income (except under a loan) provided without any intention of conferring a gratuitous benefit;
(3) property or income provided under a liability incurred by any person before 6 April 2017;
(4) the principal of a loan made to the trustees of the settlement on arm's length terms;
(5) repayment to the trustees of the settlement of the principal of a loan made by them;
(6) the payment of interest to the trustees of the settlement on a loan made by them on arm's length terms;
(7) where the settlement's expenses on taxation and administration exceed its income for a tax year, property or income provided to them towards meeting the deficit, provided the value of what is provided does not exceed the greater of the excess and the amount by which the expenses exceed those expenses that may be paid out of income.

These disregards are themselves ignored in connection with loans, if either of two events occurs. These events are:

(A) in the case of an arm's length loan to the trustees by another settlement connected with the settlor, capitalisation of interest, any other failure to pay interest under the loan terms, or variation of the terms to a non-arm's length basis;
(B) in the case of a non-arm's length loan to the trustees by the settlor or trustees of another settlement connected with the settlor, the settlor's subsequently becoming deemed to be domiciled after 5 April 2017.

In the case of event A, the principal of the loan is regarded to have been provided to the trustees at the time of the event. In the case of B, any amount outstanding under the loan on the deemed-domicile date is regarded as property directly provided for the purposes of the settlement by the lender on the deemed-domicile date. There is a transitional saving for event B, provided that the principal and all interest is repaid before 6 April 2018, or, broadly, the loan is converted to an arm's length loan and interest is paid and remains payable under arm's length terms, beginning from 6 April 2017.

Schedule 8 para 19 makes a consequential amendment to FA 2004 Sch 15 para 8.

Schedule 8 paras 20–26 amend ITTOIA 2005. Schedule 8 para 20 is introductory. Schedule 8 para 21 makes a consequential amendment. Schedule 8 para 22 inserts new ITTOIA 2005 ss 628A-628C. The amendments introduce a limited protection from the provisions attributing income to the settlor of a settlor-interested settlement for "protected foreign-source income".

New ITTOIA 2005 s 628A provides that the rule (in ITTOIA 2005 s 624(1)) that the income of a settlement in which the settlor retains an interest is regarded for income tax purposes as the settlor's alone is not to apply to income arising under a settlement if the income is "protected foreign-source income" for a tax year. Income is protected foreign-source income if six conditions (A to F) are met.

Condition A is that the income would be "relevant foreign income" if it arose to a UK-resident individual. Relevant foreign income is, broadly, income of a non-domiciliary that is not taxed in the United Kingdom under the remittance basis unless remitted.

Condition B is that the income arises from property originating from the settlor.

Condition C is that when the settlor created the settlement, the settlor was non-domiciled and (if the settlement was created after 5 April 2017) and not deemed domiciled.

Condition D is that there is no time in the tax year concerned when the settlor is UK-domiciled or deemed domiciled.

Condition E is that the trustees of the settlement are not UK-resident for the tax year.

Condition F is that no property or income is provided, whether directly or indirectly, by the settlor or by the trustees of another settlement of which the settlor is the settlor or a beneficiary for the purposes of the settlement at any time in the "relevant period" when the settlor is either actually UK-domiciled or deemed to be UK-domiciled. The "relevant period" is the period beginning on the later of 6 April 2017 and the creation of the settlement and ending with the end of the particular year.

It will be seen that conditions C, D and F are identical to conditions B, C and D for the purposes of new TCGA 1992 Sch 5 para 5A, as one might expect.

For the purposes of new ITTOIA 2005 s 628A, the rule in ITTOIA 2005 s 648 that relevant foreign income is treated as arising under a settlement only if remitted to the United Kingdom is disapplied.

New ITTOIA 2005 s 628B provides a list of disregards when considering what property is regarded as provided for the purposes of condition F in new ITTOIA 2005 s 628A, identical to the disregards in new TCGA 1992 Sch 5 para 5B (inserted by Sch 8 para 18 and numbered (1) to (7) in this Introduction in the note on that paragraph). The identical conditions attaching to the disregards and the overrules of the disregards apply also to this section.

New ITTOIA 2005 s 628C provides transitional protection to foreign income arising under a settlement before 6 April 2017 but not remitted until on or after that date. It provides that such "transitional trust income" is not to be regarded under ITA 2007 s 809L as remitted to the United Kingdom for the purposes of the remittance basis. The income must have arisen in the tax years from 2008–09 to 2016–17 and have been protected foreign-source income if new ITTOIA 2005 s 628A had been in effect at that time.

New ITTOIA 2005 s 630A, inserted by Sch 8 para 23, disapplies the rule in ITTOIA 2005 s 629(1) that income paid to the relevant children of the settlor is income of the settlor where the income is protected foreign-source income.

Sch 8 paras 24 and 25 amend ITTOIA 2005 ss 635 and 636 to exclude protected foreign-source income from the ambit of those provisions. Schedule 8 para 26 makes a consequential amendment.

Schedule 8 paras 27–38 amend the legislation in ITA 2007 Part 13 Chapter 2 on the transfer of assets abroad to introduce the concept of protected foreign-source income into those provisions also.

Schedule 8 para 27 is introductory. Schedule 8 para 28 amends ITA 2007 s 721 to introduce two new rules (Rules 1 and 2) to determine the amount of income treated as arising to an individual who has the power to enjoy the income of a person abroad after a relevant transfer of assets. Rule 1 is that the income arising is to be the whole of the income of the person abroad if the individual is UK-domiciled at any time in the tax year or is deemed to be domiciled by virtue of being a "returner" (see the note in this Introduction to s 29). Rule 2 provides that, in any other case, the income arising is to exclude protected foreign-source income, which is to count as "protected income" under new ITA 2007 s 733A (inserted by Sch 8 para 36).

Schedule 8 para 29 inserts new ITA 2007 s 721A, which defines protected foreign-source income for the purposes of ITA 2007 s 721 as amended. The definition closely matches the definition of the same term in new ITTOIA 2005 s 628A, as indeed it must, but differentiates slightly between foreign income of a settlement and foreign income of a company.

If the income is that of a settlement, the definition is as follows:

(1) the income would be "relevant foreign income" if it were the individual's;
(2) the person abroad is the trustees of a settlement and the trustees are not UK-resident for the tax year;
(3) when the settlement was created, the individual was non-domiciled and (if the settlement was created after 5 April 2017) not deemed domiciled;
(4) no property or income is provided, whether directly or indirectly, by the individual or by the trustees of another settlement of which the individual is the settlor or a beneficiary for the purposes of the settlement at any time in the period beginning on the later of 6 April 2017 and the creation of the settlement and ending with the end of the particular year, when the individual is actually UK-domiciled or deemed domiciled.

If the income is that of a company, the definition is as follows:

(1) the income would be "relevant foreign income" if it were the individual's;
(2) the person abroad is a company;
(3) the trustees of a settlement are participators in the person abroad or participators in the first in a chain of companies in which the last company is the person abroad and each company except the last is a participator in the next company in the chain;
(4) the individual's power to enjoy the income results from the fact that the trustees are participators of the kind mentioned in (3);
(5) the trustees are not UK-resident for the tax year;

(6) when the settlement was created, the individual was non-domiciled and (if the settlement was created after 5 April 2017) not deemed domiciled;

(7) no property or income is provided, whether directly or indirectly, by the individual or by the trustees of another settlement of which the individual is the settlor or a beneficiary for the purposes of the settlement at any time in the period beginning on the later of 6 April 2017 and the creation of the settlement and ending with the end of the particular year, when the individual is actually UK-domiciled or deemed domiciled.

New ITA 2007 s 721B provides a list of disregards when considering what property is regarded as provided for the purposes of condition (4) (where the person abroad is trustees) or condition (7) (where the person abroad is a company) in new ITA 2005 s 721A, identical to the disregards in new TCGA 1992 Sch 5 para 5B (inserted by Sch 8 para 18 and numbered (1) to (7) in this Introduction in the note on that paragraph). The identical conditions attaching to the disregards and the overrules of the disregards apply also to this section as they apply to that paragraph.

Schedule 8 para 30 amends ITA 2007 s 726, with the effect that where foreign deemed income within that section arises earlier than 2017/18, but is remitted to the United Kingdom in 2017/18 or later, it is not to be treated as relevant foreign income of the individual to the extent that it is "transitionally protected income". The concept of "transitionally protected income" harks back to new ITTOIA 2005 s 628C (inserted by Sch 8 para 22), and is accordingly defined thus:

Transitionally protected income is foreign deemed income that the individual has power to enjoy which (a) arises before 2017/18; (b) would be protected foreign-source income as defined in new ITA 2007 s 721A if that section had had effect in tax years earlier than 2017/18 (omitting the conditions relating to the provision of property or income to the settlement); and (c) had not been distributed by the trustees of the settlement before 6 April 2017.

Schedule 8 para 31 amends ITA 2007 s 728. This defines when income is treated as arising to an individual who receives capital sums consequent upon a transfer of assets abroad. The amendment adds the same Rules 1 and 2 as are added to ITA 2007 s 721 by Sch 8 para 28 (for which see the note for that paragraph in this Introduction).

Schedule 8 para 32 inserts new ITA 2007 s 729A, which defines "protected foreign-source income" for the purposes of ITA 2007 s 728. The definition is identical to that in new ITA 2007 s 721A (inserted by Sch 8 para 29), which defines protected foreign-source income" for the purposes of ITA 2007 s 721. The definition refers back specifically to new ITA 2007 s 721B (also inserted by Sch 8 para 29), to apply the disregards for tainting there also to new ITA 2007 s 721A.

Schedule 8 para 33 amends ITA 2007 s 730 to exactly the same effect as Sch 8 para 30 amends ITA 2007 s 726, to define and exclude "transitionally protected income".

Schedule 8 paras 34–38 make important amendments to ITA 2007 ss 731–735A, which impose a charge to tax under the transfers of assets abroad legislation on non-transferors who receive certain benefits.

Schedule 8 para 34 amends ITA 2007 s 731. Since the charge is now to be extended beyond "non-transferors" as defined for these purposes, the reference in ITA 2007 s 731(1) to "non-transferors" is changed to a reference to "individuals" and a new matching rule is introduced. This provides that if the individual (whom ITA 2007 s 731 now charges to tax in place of the non-transferor) is non-resident for the tax year in which the benefit is received, there is to be a charge to tax on any "matched deemed income" (a) only to the extent that "matched deemed income" would be matched under ITA 2007 s 735A with an amount of relevant income (as defined in ITA 2007 s 733) that is protected income for the purposes of new ITA 2007 s 733A (inserted by Sch 8 para 36) and (b) only if the individual is the settlor of the settlement referred to in new ITA 2007 s 733A or the benefit is received by the individual at a time when the individual is a close family member of the settlor's family. "Matched deemed income" is income that is treated as arising to the individual under ITA 2007 s 732 and would be matched under ITA 2007 s 735A with the benefit, if that section applied for this purpose also.

Schedule 8 para 35 amends ITA 2007 s 732. This has hitherto imposed the charge to income tax under ITA 2007 s 731 to individuals who are UK-resident for a tax year in which they receive a benefit and are not liable to tax under either ITA 2007 s 720 or 727 by reference to a relevant transfer. The residence requirement is now removed and the condition of non-liability under either ITA 2007 s 720 or 727 restricted to individuals who are "relevantly domiciled" at any time in the tax year. An individual is relevantly domiciled if the individual is actually UK-domiciled or is deemed domiciled as a "returner" (see the note in this Introduction to s 29 under the deemed-domicile rule). Schedule 8 para 36 inserts new ITA 2007 s 733A, which imposes a charge to tax on a settlor in respect of a benefit received by a non-resident closely related beneficiary.

New ITA 2007 s 733A provides that where all of five conditions are met, and the individual who receives a benefit is (a) either non-resident at any time in the tax year or (b) is a non-domiciliary to whom the remittance basis applies and none of the income treated as arising under ITA 2007 s 732 is remitted to the United Kingdom in that year, the settlor of the settlement in question is liable for the tax charged under ITA 2007 s 731 as if the income had arisen to him, and there is to be no later charge on the individual in respect of the same income. Where part of the income is remitted, the settlor is charged to tax on the remainder.

The five conditions necessary for the charge to fall on the settlor are these:

(1) an amount of income is treated as arising to the individual under ITA 2007 s 732;
(2) if ITA 2007 s 735A applied, the income would be matched with an amount of relevant protected income and with a benefit received by the individual when the individual was a close member of the settlor's family;
(3) the trustees of the settlement are not UK-resident at any time in the tax year;
(4) the settlor *is* UK-resident at some time in the tax year but there is no time in the tax year when the settlor is UK-domiciled; and
(5) there is no time in the tax year when the settlor is deemed domiciled as a "returner" (see the note in this Introduction to s 29 under the deemed-domicile rule).

Where the settlor pays any tax as a result of these rules, the settlor is entitled to recover the amount from the individual.

Schedule 8 para 37 makes a consequential amendment to ITA 2007 s 735 and Sch 8 para 38 inserts new ITA 2007 s 735B, which amends the operation of ITA 2007 s 735.

New ITA 2007 s 735B concerns what is rather inelegantly called "transferred-liability deemed income". This is income treated under ITA 2007 s 732 as income arising to an individual ("the beneficiary") in respect of which the settlor is liable to tax under new ITA 2007 s 733A, and the remittance basis applies to that settlor for that year. This income is to be treated as "relevant foreign income" of the settlor for the purposes of ITA 2007 s 735, and is therefore regarded as remitted to the United Kingdom in that year for the purposes of the remittance basis.

Schedule 8 para 39 provides that the amendments made by Sch 8 paras 19–38 have effect from the tax year 2017/18.

Schedule 8 para 40 inserts FA 2008 Sch 8 para 172 into the transitional provisions for the remittance basis so as to include the deemed domicile rule for "returners" in those provisions.

Schedule 8 Part 3 (paras 41–43) allows for an amount of CGT rebasing of foreign assets held by long-term individuals on the remittance basis who are deemed to be domiciled under the "15/20 rule" (for which see the note in this Introduction to s 29, under the deemed-domicile rule).

Schedule 8 para 41 provides that the chargeable gain or loss on the disposal of a foreign-situs asset after 5 April 2017 may be computed on the assumption that it was acquired on 5 April 2017 for its market value at that time, if the disposal is made by an individual and certain conditions are satisfied in respect of the asset and of the individual. Those conditions are that:

(1) The asset must have been held by the individual on 5 April 2017, not have been situated in the United Kingdom at any time in the period beginning on the later of the date of acquisition and 16 March 2016 and ending on 5 April 2017; and
(2) The individual was taxed under the remittance basis for long-term residents (ITA 2007 s 809H) for any tax year before 2017/18, is not a "returner", and is deemed domiciled under the 15/20 rule in every tax year beginning from 2017/18 up to an including the tax year in which the disposal is made.

Schedule 8 para 42 relaxes the rule in Sch 8 para 41 that the asset must have remained abroad at all times before disposal if it was brought into the United Kingdom for reasons of public access, repair, intention to sell, or (in the case of clothing, footwear, jewellery or a watch) for personal use by the individual, the individual's spouse or civil partner, or the individual's minor child or grandchild, or its presence in the United Kingdom is overlooked for remittance-basis purposes because the notional remitted amount is less than £1,000.

Schedule 8 para 43 provides that an individual may make an irrevocable election to opt out of rebasing under Sch 8 para 41.

Schedule 8 Part 4 (paras 44–46) provides another measure of relief for remittance-basis users, allowing them to change the order in which transfers from mixed funds are regarded as made.

Schedule 8 para 44 allows a "qualifying individual" to "switch off" the statutory ordering of remittances to the United Kingdom from a "mixed fund" as specified in ITA 2007 s 809Q(3). A qualifying individual is an individual who has been taxed under the remittance basis (other than as a long-term resident under ITA 2007 s 809H) for any tax year before 2017/18 and is not deemed domiciled as a "returner" (for which see the note in this Introduction to s 29, under the deemed-domicile rule). A "mixed fund" (as defined in ITA 2007 s 809Q(4)) is a fund containing a mixture of income, gains and capital, or income gains and capital from two or more years. The statutory order under ITA 2007 s 809Q(3) is, broadly, last-in, first-out, with what might be called "worst-in, first-out" within each year – taking more highly taxed income before less highly taxed income and so on).

Where, however, the transfer is made in 2017/18 or 2018/19, and is a transfer of money from the mixed fund to another account and is the first transfer to have been made between those accounts in that direction, the individual may nominate the transfer as one to which Sch 8 para 44 is to apply. If the individual does so, the individual may specify what elements of the fund are contained in the transfer as the individual chooses, provided that each element specified does not exceed the amount of that element included in the fund before the transfer.

New Sch 8 para 45 applies to transfers out of mixed funds from one foreign account to another, when different rules (ITA 2007 s 809R(4)) usually apply. These decree that the amounts transferred are in proportion to their presence in the fund before the transfer. Provided that the same conditions as in Sch 8 para 44 apply, the individual may again specify the composition of the transferred funds, but only where the mixed fund from which the transfer is made is one containing pre-6 April 2008 income or chargeable gains.

However, the composition of the mixed fund out of which the transfer referred to in new Sch 8 para 45 is made is to be determined by the two-step process prescribed in Sch 8 para 46. Broadly, if the amount transferred does not exceed the total income and gains in the fund before the transfer, the transfer is taken to consist of income and gains in their relative proportions. If the transfer also included other capital, the transfer is to be taken as consisting of all the income and gains, the remainder being other capital.

Section 30 amends the existing deemed-domicile rule for inheritance tax to align it with the new rule for income tax and capital gains tax.

Deemed domicile rule

IHTA 1984 s 267 has hitherto provided that an individual who is not domiciled in the United Kingdom at any time ("the relevant time") is nevertheless regarded for the purposes of IHTA to be domiciled in the United Kingdom (abbreviated from now on to "UK-domiciled") if either (condition A) the individual was UK-domiciled in the three years immediately preceding that time or (condition B) the individual was UK-resident in at least 17 of the 20 tax years ending with the tax year in which the relevant time falls.

Under the new rule, condition A remains unchanged but condition B is reworded and a new condition is added. The new condition is that the individual is a "formerly domiciled resident" for the tax year in which the relevant time falls (this is "the relevant tax year"). Condition B is now that the individual was UK-resident for at least 15 of the 20 tax years immediately preceding the relevant tax year and for at least one of the four tax years ending with the relevant tax year ("the 15/20 rule").

Furthermore, the saving for individuals not UK-domiciled at any time since 9 December 1974 is repealed, but is retained for determining whether property added to a settlement on or before that date is excluded property.

A "formerly domiciled resident" in relation to a tax year is a person who was born, and had a domicile of origin, in the United Kingdom, is UK-resident for that tax year and was UK-resident for at least one of the two immediately preceding tax years. It should be noted that this definition differs slightly from the equivalent definition of "returners" for the purposes of income tax and CGT (see the note under s 29).

The new rules have effect in relation to times after 5 April 2017, but the 15/20 rule will not apply to individuals who are not UK-resident for any tax year beginning after

5 April 2017, or for determining whether settled property is excluded property if it was added to the settlement before 6 April 2017.

Excluded property

IHTA 1984 s 48 is amended so that it now provides that settlement property situated abroad is no longer excluded property at any time in the tax year even if the settlor was not UK-domiciled when the settlement was made if the settlor is a formerly domiciled resident for that tax year.

The amendment has effect in relation to times after 5 April 2017.

Ten-year anniversary charge

The rule in IHTA 1984 s 64(1B) excluding property situated abroad and comprised in a settlement made by a settlor who was not UK-domiciled settlor at the time from being regarded as relevant property for the purposes of the ten-year anniversary charge is disapplied if the settlor is a formerly domiciled resident for the tax year in which the ten-year anniversary falls.

The amendment has effect in relation to times after 5 April 2017.

Charge at other times on discretionary etc settlements

There is to be no charge to IHT where foreign property comprised in a settlement which ceased to be excluded property when the settlor became a formerly domiciled resident again becomes excluded property when the settlor becomes non-resident and loses formerly domiciled resident status.

The amendment has effect in relation to times after 5 April 2017.

Definition of excluded property

IHTA 1984 s 82 defines "excluded property" for the purposes of the charge to IHT on settlements without an interest in possession. It has hitherto provided that, as regards settlements in which the settlor or the settlor's spouse or civil partner had an initial interest (IHTA 1984 s 80) or property passing between settlements (IHTA 1984 s 81), property situated outside the United Kingdom could be excluded property only if the settlor (or in the case of IHTA 1984 s 81, the settlor of the second settlement), was not UK-domiciled when the settlement was made. It is now to be an additional condition that the property will be excluded property at any time only if the settlor in question is also not a formerly domiciled resident for the tax year in which that time falls.

The amendment has effect in relation to times after 5 April 2017.

Interest on overdue tax and return delivery-dates

Where the amount of IHT payable is greater as a result of these amendments than it would otherwise have been, the date from which interest begins to run under either IHTA 1984 s 233 or s 234 and the date for delivery of trustee returns relating to settlements without an interest in possession under IHTA 1984 s 216(6)(ad) is deferred to the later of the normal due date and 31 December 2017.

The amendment has effect in relation to times after 5 April 2017.

Interpretation

The definition of "formerly domiciled resident" is added to IHTA 1984 s 272, and the definition of "foreign-owned" is amended to exclude at any time property comprised in a settlement of which the settlor is a formerly domiciled resident for the tax year in which the time in question falls.

The amendment has effect in relation to times after 5 April 2017.

Section 31 introduces Sch 9, which amends provisions for valuing benefits received from non-resident or dual-resident settlements or from assets transferred abroad either by way of loan or the use of land or chattels.

Schedule 9 comprises three paragraphs.

Schedule 9 para 1 inserts new TCGA 1992 ss 97A–97C and makes a consequential amendment. Schedule 9 para 2 inserts new ITA 2007 ss 742B–742E. Schedule 9 para 3 provides for commencement. All the new sections apply with respect to non-resident and dual-resident settlements.

New TCGA 1992 s 97A quantifies the value of a benefit conferred on a beneficiary by a capital payment in the form of a loan. It provides that where a capital payment is made by way of a loan, the value of the benefit conferred on the person receiving it is, for each tax year in which the loan is outstanding, the amount by which interest at the official rate that would have been payable on the loan in the tax year exceeds the interest actually paid. The official rate is the rate applicable from time to time under FA 1989 s 178 for the purposes of valuing the benefit of beneficial loans under ITEPA 2003 Part 3 Chapter 7 (currently 3.0%).

New TCGA 1992 s 97B quantifies the value of a benefit conferred on a recipient by a capital payment that takes the form of making movable property (excluding money) available for use without transferring ownership. The value is given by the formula:

$$\left(\frac{CC \times R \times D}{Y}\right) - T$$

where CC is the capital cost of the movable property on the date it is first made available to the recipient in the tax year; R is the official rate of interest during the period in the tax year during which the property is available to the recipient; D is the number of days in that period; Y is the number of days in the tax year; and T is the amounts paid in the tax year by the recipient to the provider as consideration (including for repair, insurance, maintenance or storage of the property). Provision is made for any change in the official rate of interest during the period concerned.

Capital cost is taken to be the sum of:

(a) the greater of:
(i) the consideration given for the acquisition of the movable property by or on behalf of the provider; and
(ii) its market value at the time of the acquisition; and
(b) expenditure wholly and exclusively incurred on enhancing its value.

New TCGA 1992 s 97C quantifies the value of a benefit conferred on a recipient by a capital payment that takes the form of making land available for use without transferring ownership. The value for each tax year in which the benefit is conferred is given by the excess (if any) of the rental value of the land for the period of its availability and the total of payments made in the tax year by the recipient to the provider as consideration (including for repair, insurance or maintenance of the land). The rental value for these purposes is the rent that would have been payable if the land had been let to the recipient at an annual rent equal to the annual value (as defined).

Schedule 9 para 2 inserts new ITA 2007 ss 742B–742E. All the new sections apply in respect of the rules for the transfer of assets abroad in ITA 2007 Part 13 Chapter 2. New ITA 2007 s 742B is introductory.

New ITA 2007 s 742C quantifies the value of a benefit provided to the recipient in the form of a loan. It provides that where a payment is made by way of a loan, the value of the benefit conferred on the person receiving it is, for each tax year in which the loan is outstanding, the amount by which interest at the official rate that would have been payable on the loan in the tax year exceeds the interest actually paid. The official rate is the rate applicable from time to time under FA 1989 s 178 for the purposes of valuing the benefit of beneficial loans under ITEPA 2003 Part 3 Chapter 7 (currently 3.0%).

New ITA 2007 s 742D quantifies the value of a benefit provided to a recipient which takes the form of making movable property (excluding money) available for use without transferring ownership. The value is given by a formula identical to that in new TCGA 1992 s 97B, with the same terms and the same provisions.

New ITA 2007 s 742E quantifies the value of a benefit conferred on a recipient which takes the form of making land available for use without transferring ownership. The wording is identical to that of new TCGA 1992 s 97D.

Schedule 9 para 3 provides that the amendments made by Sch 9 have effect in relation to capital payments or benefits received in the tax year 2017/18 and subsequent years.

Section 32 makes amendments to the CGT rules for carried interest in TCGA 1992 Part III Chapter 5 to exclude gains from carried interest from the charge to CGT in relation to non-resident companies and non-resident settlements.

Attribution of gains to members of non-resident companies

TCGA 1992 s 13(1A) is amended to add chargeable gains from carried interest treated as accruing under TCGA 1992 s 103KA(2) or (3) ("carried-interest gains") to the classes of gain made by a non-resident closely held company which are excluded from those that may potentially be attributed to UK-resident participators.

Attribution of gains to settlors with an interest in non-resident or
dual-resident settlements

New TCGA 1992 s 86(4ZB) is inserted to exclude carried-interest gains from those gains on the disposal of settled property originating from the settlor which are attributable to the settlor.

Attribution of gains to beneficiaries of non-UK-resident settlements

New TCGA 1992 s 87(5B) is inserted to exclude carried-interest gains from those gains attributable to beneficiaries of non-resident settlements who have received capital payments.

All these amendments have effect in relation to carried-interest gains treated as accruing at any time.

Section 33 introduces **Sch 10**, which limits the extent to which overseas property the value of which is attributable to UK residential property may be excluded property.

Schedule 10 comprises 11 paragraphs. Sch 10 para 1 inserts new IHTA 1984 Sch A1, entitled "Non-excluded overseas property". New IHTA 1984 Sch A1 is itself comprised of three Parts. New IHTA 1984 Sch A1 Part 1 (paras 1–4) contains the main provisions; new IHTA 1984 Sch A1 Part 2 (paras 5–7) contains supplementary provisions; and new IHTA 1984 Sch A1 Part 3 (paras 8–10) provides for interpretation.

New IHTA 1984 Sch A1 para 1 is introductory and provides that property situated outside the United Kingdom is not excluded property if and to the extent that new IHTA 1984 Sch A1 paras 2 or 3 applies to it even where the person beneficially entitled to is domiciled outside the United Kingdom (IHTA 1984 s 6(1)) or the property is comprised in a settlement made when the settlor was domiciled outside the United Kingdom (IHTA 1984 s 48(3)(a)).

New IHTA 1984 Sch A1 para 2 applies to interests in a close company or partnership to the extent that the value of the interest is directly attributable to a "UK residential-property interest" (defined in new IHTA 1984 Sch A1 para 8) or indirectly so attributable by reason solely of an interest in a close company, an interest in a partnership or a loan etc to which new IHTA 1984 Sch A1 para 3 applies. Interests in a close company or partnership are to be disregarded if the value is less than 5% of the total value of all interests in the company or partnership. Interests held by a connected person are to be taken into account in applying the 5% test.

New IHTA 1984 Sch A1 para 3 applies to the rights of a creditor in respect of a "relevant loan" and to money or money's worth held or made available as security, collateral or guarantee for a "relevant loan" to the extent that it does not exceed the value of the "relevant loan". New IHTA 1984 Sch A1 para 4 defines a "relevant loan" as a loan the money or money's worth made available under which is used directly or indirectly to finance the acquisition by an individual, a partnership or trustees of (a) a "UK residential-property interest" or property to which new IHTA 1984 Sch A1 para 2 applies to any extent or (b) an interest in an intermediary close company or partnership and the acquisition by the intermediary of property described under (a). Indirect financing of an acquisition is also to include use of the money or money's worth to purchase property that is sold in order to use the sale proceeds to make the acquisition and the making or repayment of a loan to finance the acquisition of such property. References to the acquisition of a UK residential-property interest are to be taken as references also to its maintenance or enhancement. A loan ceases to be a relevant loan when the property interest is disposed of. References to a loan are to include an acknowledgement of a debt.

New IHTA 1984 Sch A1 para 5 provides for disposals and repayments. It applies to:

(1) consideration in money or money's worth for the disposal of an interest in a close company or partnership ("Para 2 property") or the disposal of a creditor's rights in respect of a relevant loan ("Para 3 property");

(2) money or money's worth paid in respect of a creditor's rights in respect of a relevant loan; and

(3) any property directly or indirectly representing property comprised in (1) or (2).

This property is also not to be regarded as excluded property for a two-year period and, if held in a qualifying foreign-currency account, is not to be excluded from the value of an estate at death by virtue of IHTA 1984 s 157 for that two-year period. The two-year period runs from the disposal referred to in (1) or the payment referred to in (2), as the case may be.

The value of any property in (3) is not to exceed the "relevant amount". Where the property in (3) directly or indirectly represents the property in (1), the relevant amount is the value of the consideration at the time of the disposal. Where the property in (3) directly or indirectly represents the property in (2), the relevant amount is the amount of the money or money's worth paid.

New IHTA 1984 Sch A1 para 6 provides that in determining whether and to what extent property is situated outside the United Kingdom, no account is to be taken of tax-avoidance arrangements intended to minimise the effect of new IHTA 1984 Sch A1.

New IHTA 1984 Sch A1 para 7 provides that nothing in a double tax treaty is to prevent liability to IHT under new IHTA 1984 Sch A1 in relation to any chargeable transfer if no tax similar to inheritance tax or tax at an effective rate of 0% is charged on the transfer in the treaty-partner country.

New IHTA 1984 Sch A1 para 8 defines a "UK residential-property interest" in line with TCGA 1992 Sch B1. New IHTA 1984 Sch A1 para 9 defines "close company" and "participator" by reference to the Corporation Tax Acts and CTA 2010 s 454, respectively. New IHTA 1984 Sch A1 para 10 defines a partnership as a partnership within the Partnership Act 1890, a limited partnership registered under the Limited Partnerships Act 1907; a limited-liability partnership under the Limited-Liability Partnerships Act 2000 or the equivalent NI legislation, and a firm or entity of a similar character formed under foreign law.

Schedule 10 paras 2–8 make consequential amendments to IHTA 1984. Schedule 10 para 5 amends IHTA 1984 s 65 to the effect that a charge to tax under that section on property comprised in a settlement without an interest in possession is not to be made solely by virtue of the fact that any part of that property ceases to be covered by new IHTA 1984 Sch A1 para 2 or 3 or new IHTA 1984 Sch A1 para 5 and thereby becomes excluded property.

Schedule 10 para 9 provides that amendments made by Sch 10 are to have effect in relation to times after 5 April 2017; however, new IHTA 1984 Sch A1 para 5 is not to apply to disposals of property taking place, or payments made, before 6 April 2017.

Schedule 10 paras 10 and 11 adjust the date from which interest on overdue IHT starts to run where by virtue of new IHTA 1984 Sch A1 an amount of tax is greater than it would otherwise have been to the later of the normal due date of payment or delivery and the last day of December 2017.

Disguised remuneration

Section 34 and **Sch 11**, which it introduces, make amendments to the provisions in ITEPA 2003 Part 7A on employment income provided through third parties ("disguised remuneration"), in relation to loans and quasi-loans still outstanding on 5 April 2019.

Section 34(1) amends ITEPA 2003 s 554XA (inserted by FA 2017 Sch 6 para 9), which excludes certain payments in respect of a tax liability from the charge to tax under ITEPA 2003 Part 7A, to the effect that payments to HMRC in respect of a relevant liability for income tax and national insurance contributions are no longer excluded from the charge, in relation to relevant steps taken after 20 July 2017.

Schedule 11 comprises five Parts. Part 1 (paras 1–19) provides for the application of ITEPA 2003 Part 7A to loans and quasi-loans still outstanding on 5 April 2019; Part 2 (paras 20–24) covers the approval process for qualifying loans; Part 3 (paras 25–35) provides for exclusions; Part 4 (paras 36–45) contains supplementary provisions; and Part 5 (paras 46 and 47) makes consequential amendments.

Schedule 11 para 1 provides that a person is to be treated as having taken a relevant step for the purposes of ITEPA 2003 Part 7A if he has made a loan or quasi-loan to a "relevant person" after 5 April 1999, an amount of which is outstanding immediately before the end of 5 April 2019. The person is to be treated as taking the step immediately before the end of the approved repayment date if he has made a loan that is an "approved fixed-term loan" (as defined in Sch 11 para 19) on 5 April 2019 or the end of 5 April 2019 in any other case. For the purposes of valuing the relevant step under ITEPA 2003 s 554Z3(1), the step is to be treated as involving a sum of money equal to the outstanding amount of the loan or quasi-loan at the time the step is treated as taken. "Relevant person" is as defined in ITEPA 2003 s 554C, i.e. broadly, the employee or the other person receiving the payments, assets or other benefits on the employee's behalf.

Schedule 11 para 2 defines a loan as any form of credit or a payment purported to be made by way of loan. A "quasi-loan" is made where the "lender" acquires a right to a payment or a transfer of assets, and there is a direct or indirect connection between the acquisition of the right and a payment made by way of loan or otherwise to the "borrower" (the relevant person) or a transfer of assets to the relevant person. The "approved repayment date" is the date by which under the terms of a fixed-term loan the whole of the loan must be repaid, as measured at the time an application is made to HMRC for approval of a qualifying loan.

Schedule 11 paras 3 and 4 define that an amount of a loan is outstanding if the "relevant principal amount" exceeds the "repayment amount". The "relevant principal amount" is the sum of the initial principal amount lent and any later sums that have become principal, excluding capitalised interest. The "repayment amount" is the sum of (a) the amount of principal repaid before 17 March 2016; and (b) payments in money made by the relevant person on or after that date by way of repayment of principal. A payment is to be disregarded if (a) the payment was made as part of a tax-avoidance arrangement or (b) the payment or a sum or asset directly or indirectly representing it is the subject of a relevant step taken after the payment was made or asset transferred but before the end of the relevant date. A payment under (b) is not to be disregarded if each relevant tax liability is paid in full before the end of the "relevant date". The "relevant date" is the approved repayment date if the loan is an approved fixed-term loan on 5 April 2019, or 5 April 2019 in any other case. Schedule 11 para 5 provides that where a loan was made to a relevant person after 5 April 1999 and, before the end of 5 April 2019, the employee or the employer acquires a right to payment of part or all of the loan, the amount of the loan in respect of which the employee or the employer has acquired a right to payment is to be treated as an amount of the loan outstanding immediately before the end of 5 April 2019.

Schedule 11 paras 6–10 define how loans and repayments made in a currency other than sterling, loans made in a depreciating currency, and repayments in a currency other than the loan currency are to be treated.

Schedule 11 paras 11 and 12 define that an amount of a quasi-loan is outstanding if the "initial debt amount" exceeds the "repayment amount". The "initial debt amount" is the sum of an amount equal to the value of the acquired debt and (where the "lender" acquires a further right) the value of the additional debt. The "repayment amount" is the sum of (a) the amount (if any) by which the initial debt amount has been reduced by repayment before 17 March 2016; (b) payments in money made by the relevant person after 16 March 2016 by way of repayment of the initial debt amount; and (c) if the acquired debt or additional debt is a right to a transfer of assets, which has taken place, an amount equal to the market value of the assets at the time of transfer. A payments or transfer is to be disregarded if (a) the payment is made as part of a tax-avoidance arrangement or (b) the payment or a sum or asset directly or indirectly representing it is the subject of a relevant step taken after the payment was made or asset transferred but before the end of the relevant date. A payment under (b) is not to be disregarded if each relevant tax liability is paid in full by the end of 5 April 2019. Schedule 11 para 13 provides that where a quasi-loan was made to a relevant person after 5 April 1999 and, before the end of 5 April 2019, the employee or the employer acquires a right to payment or transfer of assets under the quasi-loan, the value of the right the employee or the employer has acquired is to be treated as an amount of the quasi-loan made to the relevant person and outstanding immediately before the end of 5 April 2019, but for the purpose of valuing the relevant step under ITEPA 2003 s 554Z3(1), as the amount of the quasi-loan outstanding at the time the person is treated as having taken the relevant step.

Schedule 11 paras 14–18 define how quasi-loans and repayments made in a currency other than sterling, quasi-loans made in a depreciating currency, and repayments in a currency other than the quasi-loan currency are to be treated.

Schedule 11 para 19 provides that a loan is an "approved fixed-term loan" on 5 April 2019 if at any time on that day it is a "qualifying loan" approved by HMRC in accordance with Sch 11 para 20. A loan is a "qualifying loan" if it was made before 9 December 2010, its term cannot exceed 10 years and it is not an excluded loan. A loan is excluded if it has been directly or indirectly replaced by another loan or its terms have been altered in specified ways. Schedule 11 para 20 describes how applications for approval of a qualifying loan are to be made and treated. Loans may only be approved if they meet the "qualifying-payments condition" in Sch 11 para 21 and the "commercial-terms condition" in Sch 11 para 22.

Schedule 11 paras 23 and 24 prescribe how these provisions are to interact with the accelerated-payments regime of FA 2014 Part 4 Chapter 3. Broadly speaking, if the relevant person makes an accelerated payment under an accelerated-payment notice or partner-payment notice before the relevant date, and the payment relates to a charge to tax arising from a step taken under the arrangement for the making of the loan or quasi-loan, at a time when the amount of the loan or quasi-loan outstanding at the relevant date is no greater than the amount of the accelerated payment, the relevant person may apply to HMRC to defer the time at which the relevant benefit is deemed to arise to a date 30 days after any part of the accelerated payment is repaid. References to tax include references to NICs.

Schedule 11 paras 25–35 provide exclusions from the charge. These apply in the case of commercial transactions, where the exclusion closely follows that in ITEPA 2003 s 554F (Sch 11 paras 25 and 26); the transfer of employment-related loans, where the exclusion closely follows that in ITEPA 2003 s 554OA (Sch 11 paras 27 and 28); transactions under employee-benefit packages, where the exclusion closely follows that in ITEPA 2003 s 554G (Sch 11 paras 29 and 30); the purchase of employment-related securities, where the exclusion closely matches that in ITEPA 2003 s 554N(13)–(16) (Sch 11 paras 31 and 32); employee car-ownership schemes, where the exclusion closely follows that in ITEPA 2003 s 554O (Sch 11 paras 33 and 34); and the acquisition of unlisted employer shares, which is an exclusion not found in ITEPA 2003 Part 7A. It applies to loans and quasi-loans made before 9 December 2010 and applied to acquire ordinary unlisted shares in the employer company or a member of the employer company's group. The exclusion operates if the loan or quasi-loan is wholly repaid no later than 12 months after the shares have been sold or otherwise alienated (Sch 11 para 35).

Schedule 11 para 36 creates an obligation on the parties to the arrangement (normally the employee and the provider of the benefit) to provide the employer with the information necessary for the latter to comply with PAYE regulations. Schedule 11 para 37 prevents double taxation by disapplying the beneficial-loan charge under ITEPA 2003 Part 3 Chapter 7 if it would otherwise also apply to a loan subject to a charge under Sch 11. Schedule 11 paras 39–43 amend the remittance-basis to include references to the loan charge under Sch 11 and amend ITEPA 2003 ss 554Z11 and 554Z11A to ensure that the Sch 11 charge is included in taxable specific income in the tax year in which the relevant step is taken, so far as it is remitted to the United Kingdom. Schedule 11 paras 44 and 45 provide for interpretation. Schedule 11 paras 46 and 47 make consequential amendments to ITEPA 2003 and FA 2011.

Section 35 (and **Sch 12**, introduced by new ITTOIA 2005 s 23A) introduce a new charge on persons receiving income from a trade or business parallel to the disguised remuneration charge on employment income under ITEPA 2003 Part 7A, to counter avoidance of income tax and national insurance contributions. The charge relates to trading income provided through third parties.

Section 35(2) inserts new ITTOIA 2005 ss 23A–23H. New ITTOIA 2005 s 23A provides that a charge to tax under new ITTOIA 2005 s 23E on "relevant benefits" is to arise where all of five conditions, A to E, are met.

Condition A is that there is a person ("T") who is or has been carrying on a trade, profession or vocation ("the relevant trade") alone or in partnership.

Condition B is that there is an arrangement to which T is a party or otherwise relate to T, of which it is reasonable to suppose that it is essentially intended to provide, or be concerned with, "relevant benefits".

Condition C is that a "relevant benefit" arises to T or a person who is or was connected with T as a result of the arrangement or to any other person in circumstances in which the enjoyment conditions of new ITTOIA 2005 s 23F are met.

Condition D is that it is reasonable to suppose that the relevant benefit represents, or is otherwise connected with a "qualifying third-party payment".

Condition E is that it is reasonable to suppose that T or a person who is or was connected with T would obtain a tax advantage as a result of the arrangement.

New ITTOIA 2005 s 23B defines "relevant benefit" as any payment, including by way of a loan, transfer of money's worth or any other benefit. It includes the assumption by another person of a liability of T (treated as the provision of a relevant benefit to T). Where a person other than T assumes a liability of a person ("C") who is or has been connected with T, this is treated as the provision of a relevant benefit to C. "Loan" includes any form of credit and any payment that purports to be made by way of loan.

New ITTOIA 2005 s 23C defines "qualifying third-party payment". A "third-party payment" is defined as a payment made by T or some other person to another person or to T as trustee. Such a payment is a "qualifying third-party payment" if either "the deduction condition" or "the trade-connection condition" is met in relation to it.

The deduction condition is met if a deduction for the payment is made in calculating the profits of the relevant trade or in calculating the amount on which T is liable to income tax on T's share of partnership profits from the relevant trade.

The trade-connection condition is met where, broadly speaking, the payment is essentially consideration for goods or services provided in the course of the relevant trade or there is some other connection between the payment and the provision of those goods or services.

New ITTOIA 2005 s 23D contains definitions of "arrangement" and "tax avoidance" and refers to ITA 2007 s 993 (omitting s 993(4)) for the meaning of "connected".

New ITTOIA 2005 s 23E is the charging section. It provides that "the relevant benefit amount" is to be treated as profits of the relevant trade for the purposes of income tax in the tax year in which the relevant benefit arises. If T has ceased to carry on the relevant trade, the relevant benefit amount (RBA) is deemed to arise in the tax year of cessation.

Where the relevant benefit is a payment, the RBA is the amount of the payment. Where the relevant benefit is a payment by way of loan, the RBA is the principal. In any other case, the RBA is the greater of the market value of the relevant benefit at the time it arises and the cost of providing it.

New ITTOIA 2005 s 23F defines the "enjoyment conditions" where a person other than T receives the relevant benefit. These are that:

(1) the relevant benefit can be treated as accruing to T at some point in time;
(2) the relevant benefit operates to increase the value to T of any assets that T holds or are held for T's benefit;
(3) T receives or becomes entitled to receive at any time any benefit provided or deriving, now or in the future, from the relevant benefit;
(4) where the relevant benefit is a payment of a sum of money, that T may become entitled to the beneficial enjoyment of some or all of the sum through the exercise of powers by any person or that T is able to control the application of all or part of that sum.

An enjoyment condition is treated as met by T if it is met in relation to a person who is or has been connected with T.

New ITTOIA 2005 s 23G is an anti-avoidance provision. It provides that any arrangements designed to avoid the charge under new ITTOIA 2005 s 23 are to be disregarded, including any purported retiming of the relevant benefit to a date before 6 April 2017.

Section 35(5) provides that Sch 12 is to have effect to apply these provisions to loans and quasi-loans outstanding on 5 April 2019.

The amendments made by s 35 have effect in relation to relevant benefit arising after 5 April 2017.

Schedule 12 comprises 20 paragraphs.

Schedule 12 para 1 provides that a loan or quasi-loan made after 5 April 1999 and before 6 April 2017, an amount of which is outstanding immediately before the end of 5 April 2019, is to be treated as a "relevant benefit" for the purposes of new ITTOIA 2005 ss 23A–23H. For the purposes of the charge to tax under new ITTOIA 2005 s 23H, "the relevant benefit amount" is to be taken to be the outstanding amount of the loan or quasi-loan immediately before the end of the approved repayment date if the relevant benefit is an "approved fixed-term loan" (as defined in Sch 12 para 15) on 5 April 2019 or the end of 5 April 2019 in any other case. The year of charge is to be 2018/19, unless there is a later approved repayment date.

Schedule 12 para 2 defines a loan as any form of credit or a payment purported to be made by way of loan. A "quasi-loan" is made where the "lender" acquires a right to a payment or a transfer of assets, and there is a direct or indirect connection between the acquisition of the right and a payment made by way of loan or otherwise to the "borrower" (T, as in new ITTOIA 2005 s 23A) or a transfer of assets to T. References to T are to be read as references also to a person connected with T. The "approved repayment date" is the date by which the terms of a fixed-term loan the whole of the loan must be repaid, as measured at the time an application is made to HMRC for approval of a qualifying loan.

Schedule 12 para 3 defines that an amount of a loan is outstanding if the "relevant principal amount" exceeds the "repayment amount". The "relevant principal amount" is the sum of the initial principal amount lent and any later sums that have become principal, excluding capitalised interest. The "repayment amount" is the sum of the amount of principal repaid before 5 December 2016 and payments in money made by T on or after that date by way of repayment of principal, unless the payment was made as part of a tax-avoidance arrangement. Schedule 12 paras 4–8 define how loans and repayments made in a currency other than sterling, loans made in a depreciating currency, and repayments in a currency other than the loan currency are to be treated.

Schedule 12 para 9 defines that an amount of a quasi-loan is outstanding if the "initial debt amount" exceeds the "repayment amount". The "initial debt amount" is the sum of an amount equal to the value of the acquired debt and (where the "lender" acquires a further right) the value of the additional debt. The "repayment amount" is the sum of (a) the amount (if any) by which the initial debt amount has been reduced by repayment before 5 December 2016; (b) payments in money made by T after 4 December 2016 by way of repayment of the initial debt amount; and (c) if the acquired debt or additional debt is a right to a transfer of assets, which has taken place, an amount equal to the market value of the assets at the time of transfer. A payment or transfer is to be disregarded if made as part of a tax-avoidance arrangement. Schedule 12 paras 10–14 define how quasi-loans and repayments made in a currency other than sterling, quasi-loans made in a depreciating currency, and repayments in a currency other than the quasi-loan currency are to be treated.

Schedule 12 para 15 provides that a loan is an "approved fixed-term loan" on 5 April 2019 if at any time on that day it is a "qualifying loan" approved by HMRC in accordance with Sch 12 para 16. A loan is a "qualifying loan" if it was made before 9 December 2010, its term cannot exceed 10 years and it is not an excluded loan. A loan is excluded if it has been directly or indirectly replaced by another loan or its terms have been altered in specified ways. Schedule 12 para 16 describes how applications for approval of a qualifying loan are to be made and treated. Loans may only be approved if they meet the "qualifying-payments condition" in Sch 12 para 17 and the "commercial-terms condition" in Sch 12 para 18.

Schedule 12 paras 19 and 20 prescribe how these provisions are to interact with the accelerated-payments regime of FA 2014 Part 4 Chapter 3. Broadly speaking, if T makes an accelerated payment under an accelerated-payment notice or partner-payment notice before the relevant date, and the payment relates to a charge to tax under new ITTOIA 2005 s 23E, at a time when the amount of the loan or quasi-loan outstanding at the relevant date is no greater than the amount of the accelerated payment, T may apply to HMRC to defer the time at which the relevant benefit is deemed to arise to a date 30 days after any part of the accelerated payment is repaid.

Section 36 tightens the existing restrictions on the deduction in computing the profits of a person carrying on a trade, business or vocation in respect of contributions that person makes to disguised-remuneration schemes for the benefit of his employees ("employee-benefit schemes") unless an associated charge to PAYE income tax and national insurance contributions (NICs) is paid within a defined period of time.

ITTOIA 2005 s 38 already disallows a deduction for "employee-benefit contributions" (as defined in ITTOIA 2005 s 39) in a period except to the extent that "qualifying benefits" are provided or "qualifying expenses" paid within nine months of the end of the period ("in-period deduction"). However, the deduction is allowed in a later period if qualifying benefits are provided in that later period, without any time limitation. Broadly speaking, qualifying benefits are a payment of money or a transfer of assets that give rise or would give rise to an employment income tax charge and NIC charge.

Section 36(2) inserts ITTOIA 2005 s 38(1A) to add an extra condition to obtain a deduction under that section. It provides that no deduction is to be allowed under that section for an employee-benefit contribution for a period of account beginning more than five years after the end of the period of account in which the contribution is made.

Section 36(3) adds an extra condition for an in-period deduction, namely that the amount for which an in-period deduction is allowed must be a "qualifying amount". This is defined in new ITTOIA 2005 s 38(3D), inserted by s 36(4), as an amount the "relevant tax charges" in relation to which are paid before the end of the period of 12 months immediately following the end of the period of account for which the deduction would otherwise be allowable. "Relevant tax charges" are defined in new ITTOIA 2005 s 38(3E), inserted by s 36(4), as the employment income tax charge and NIC charge arising in respect of benefits provided in association with the amount of the contribution.

Section 36(4) inserts new ITTOIA 2005 s 38(3A)–(3F). These impose conditions on the amount of the deduction allowed in a later period on the provision of qualifying benefits in relation to a deduction that was disallowed in the period in which it was made. The amount must also be a "qualifying amount" for the later-period deduction to be allowed.

A further restriction is introduced by virtue of new ITTOIA 2005 s 38(3G) and (3H), inserted by s 38(5). These provide that where a deduction that may be characterised as an amount of employee remuneration also gives rise to an employee-benefit contribution, the question as to its allowability is to be determined solely by reference to the provisions of ITTOIA 2005 s 38.

Section 38(6)–(10) insert parallel provisions into ITTOIA 2005 s 866, which contains the equivalent restrictions on employee-benefit contributions made by an employer who is not carrying on a trade or a property business.

The amendments made by s 36 have effect in relation to employee-benefit contributions made or remuneration paid, as the case may be, after 5 April 2017.

Section 37 introduces similar restrictions on employers subject to corporation tax as those imposed by s 36 on employers subject to income tax.

CTA 2009 s 1290, which is the corporation tax equivalent of ITTOIA 2005 s 38, is amended to incorporate both the absolute five-year limit and the qualifying-amount condition, necessitating the payment of the related tax charges within 12 months of the end of the period of account following that for which the contributions would be allowable.

In this case, the amendments have effect in relation to contributions made or remuneration paid, as the case may be, after 31 March 2017.

Capital allowances

Section 38 introduces a new 100% first-year allowance for expenditure on plant or machinery for electric-vehicle charging points, the time window for which is relatively narrow.

New CAA 2001 s 45EA, inserted by s 38(3), provides that expenditure incurred between 23 November 2016 and no later than 31 March 2019 (or 5 April 2019, for the purposes of income tax) on plant or machinery for a charging point for electric vehicles which is unused and not second-hand is to be first-year qualifying expenditure for the purpose of plant and machinery capital allowances under CAA 2001 Part 2, unless it is excluded under CAA 2001 s 46. The plant or machinery must be installed solely for the purpose of charging electric vehicles, which are defined as road vehicles that can be propelled by electrical power, thereby allowing also for hybrid vehicles.

HM Treasury may extend the date for qualifying expenditure by statutory instrument.

Transactions in UK land

Section 39 alters the commencement rules for the new tax treatment of profits and gains realised from disposals concerned with land in the United Kingdom. With respect to income tax, the new rules were contained in FA 2016 ss 78 and 79, and with respect to corporation tax, in FA 2016 ss 76, 77 and 80. Under FA 2016 s 82, the income tax rules have had effect, subject to transitional provisions, in relation to disposals after 4 July 2016. Under FA 2016, s 81, the corporation tax rules have also had effect, subject to similar transitional provisions, in relation to disposals after 4 July 2016. However, for both income tax and corporation tax, the time of disposal for property disposed of under a contract is the time the contract is made (not the time at which the property is conveyed or transferred). This rule is now amended to give effect to all the amendments (FA 2016 ss 78–80) in relation to amounts recognised in GAAP accounts drawn up for any period of account beginning after 7 March 2017, or, in the case of a straddling period, amounts that would be recognised in GAAP accounts drawn up for a period of account beginning on 8 March 2017 and ending when the straddling period ends.

Co-ownership authorised contractual schemes

Sections 40–42 concern co-ownership authorised contractual schemes (CoACSs), which are schemes authorised for the purposes of FSMA 2000 by an authorisation order in force under FSMA 2000 s 261D(1). They are a type of collective investment scheme that is transparent for tax purposes.

Section 40 inserts CAA 2001 ss 262AA–262AF, which enable the operator of a CoACS to elect for an administrative simplification when complying with the capital allowances legislation.

New CAA 2001 s 262AA provides that participators in a CoACS are in general considered as together carrying on a qualifying activity, and each participant is regarded for the purposes of CAA 2001 as carrying on that qualifying activity, but only to the extent that profits or gains arising to the participant from the qualifying activity are or would be chargeable to tax.

New CAA 2001 s 262AB provides that the operator may make an election under that section. The effect of the election is to simplify the calculation of capital allowances, as provided in new CAA 2001 s 262AC. The election must be made by notice to an officer of HMRC and must specify an accounting period of the scheme as the first accounting period in relation to which the election is to have effect. That first accounting period must not be longer than 12 months and may not begin before 1 April 2017. Once made, the election is irrevocable.

New CAA 2001 s 262AC specifies how capital allowances are to be calculated and allocated to the participants once an election is in force. The assumptions that the operator must make to do so are essentially these:

(1) the scheme is a person and the qualifying activity carried on by the participants together is carried on by the scheme;

(2) property already in the scheme at the beginning of the first accounting period under the election is disposed of by the participants and acquired by the scheme at its tax written-down value (i.e. so as to give rise to neither a balancing allowance nor a balancing charge);

(3) property subsequently leaving the scheme has a disposal value equal to its tax written-down value;

(4) the scheme is not entitled to a first-year allowance or to an investment allowance;

(5) property for which a disposal value needs to be taken into account is assumed to be in its own pool;

(6) the operator allocates the allowances calculated under these assumptions to the participants in proportions that are just and reasonable, with regard to the relative size of each participant's holding of units in the scheme.

New CAA 2001 s 262AD provides for the effect of the election on the participants. A participant is deemed to have ceased to own his interest in the scheme property at the beginning of the first accounting period under the election, for a disposal value equal to its tax written-down value.

New CAA 2001 s 262AE provides that where a third-party purchaser purchases a fixture from the scheme, the purchaser's qualifying expenditure on the fixture is to be treated as nil, unless the operator makes a written statement of the fixture's "assumed disposal value" within two years of its leaving the scheme and the purchaser is able to obtain a copy of that statement. The assumed disposal value is the tax written-down value of the fixture when it leaves the scheme (the disposal value taken into account in the operator's calculation). Where this condition is satisfied, the purchaser's qualifying expenditure is capped at the assumed disposal value.

New CAA 2001 s 262AF contains definitions.

Section 41 provides that HM Treasury may impose information requirements on the operator of a CoACS by statutory instrument. Section 42 confers on HM Treasury the power to provide, again by statutory instrument, how participants in a CoACS are to be treated for the purposes of income tax or corporation tax in relation to investments the CoACS makes in an offshore fund.

Part 2 Indirect taxes

Section 43 increases the long-haul (Band B) rates of air passenger duty under FA 1994 s 30(4A) with effect from 1 April 2018, from £75 to £78 for the reduced rates and from £150 to £156 for the standard rates. As a result of these increases, the higher rates are automatically increased from £450 to £468. In Scotland, air passenger duty is to be replaced by air departure tax with effect from 1 April 2018.

Section 44 relates to petroleum revenue tax (PRT) and removes the conditions that need to be satisfied for the responsible person for a taxable field to make an election for the field to be non-taxable. These conditions are set out in FA 1993 Sch 20B.

The amendments made by s 44(1) replace FA 1993 Sch 20B paras 2–12 by new FA 1993 Sch 20B paras 2–7.

New FA 1993 Sch 20B paras 2–4 provide simply that the election must be made in writing, must be notified to HMRC, and is deemed to have been made on the day the notification was sent to HMRC. New FA 1993 Sch 20B para 5 provides that when the election is made, the field ceases to be taxable with effect from the start of the first chargeable period beginning after the election is made. New FA 1993 Sch 20B para 6 provides that from the start of the first taxable period after the election is made, no allowable loss accruing from that field is to qualify as an allowable unrelievable field loss for PRT purposes. New FA 1993 Sch 20B para 7 provides for interpretation.

Section 44(2) and (3) make minor consequential amendments.

The rate of PRT is 0%.

The amendments made by s 44 are to be treated as having come into force on 23 November 2016.

Section 45 increases the bands of gross gaming yield demarking the graduated rates of gaming duty under FA 1997 s 11(2) in line with the increase in RPI in the year ended 31 December 2016. The rates of duty are unchanged. The amendments to the charging bands have effect in relation to accounting periods beginning after 31 March 2017.

Section 46 imposes a charge to remote gaming duty under FA 2014 Part 3 on certain "freeplays". "Freeplays" are various incentives and promotions gambling operators offer customers, including free bets, freeplays and similar discounts and offers.

FA 2014 s 159 provides that where a chargeable person participates in remote gaming, the gaming payment (which constitutes the gross taxable income of the gaming provider) is the aggregate of the amount that entitles the person to participate in the gaming and any other amount payable in connection with the person's participation. "Chargeable persons" are any UK persons who participate in remote gaming and any body corporate not constituted in the United Kingdom that, broadly speaking, facilitates that person's participation. Duty is charged at 15% on the gaming provider's profits from remote gaming.

The amendments made to FA 2014 s 159 by s 46(2) provide that where a chargeable person participates in remote gaming in reliance of an offer waiving all of a gaming payment, that person is to be treated as nevertheless having made a gaming payment of the amount that he would have had to pay in the absence of the offer. Where only part of the gaming payment is waived, the chargeable person is treated as having made an additional gaming payment equal to the difference between the full amount and the payment actually made.

Such a deemed payment is to be treated as having been made to the gaming provider at the time when the chargeable person begins to participate in the remote gaming in question and as not having been returned or assigned to a gaming prize fund (and hence deductible from the gaming provider's dutiable profits).

However, new FA 2014 s 159A, inserted by s 46(3), provides an exception where an amount of the gaming payment is made out of "excluded winnings". Two conditions must be met before that amount is not to be taken into account in determining the gaming payment under FA 2014 s 159.

The first condition is that the money paid for the participation has itself been won by participation in the gaming, either in reliance on an offer waiving all or part of a gaming payment or out of money that has been recycled from excluded winnings from earlier participation involving a freeplay. The second condition is that the chargeable person is not entitled to use the money otherwise than for participation in the gaming.

In addition, where a chargeable participates in remote gaming in reliance on an offer wholly or partly waiving a gaming payment and has won the offer by earlier participation in the gaming without having been given the option of claiming a different benefit, the amount that would otherwise be treated as a gaming payment is not to be so treated.

FA 2014 s 160 defines what constitutes a prize for the purposes of remote gaming duty. The gaming provider may deduct expenditure on prizes when calculating his dutiable profits. Amendments made by s 46(4) provide that where a prize consisting of crediting an amount of money to an account, it may only be deducted if the person is entitled to withdraw the money on demand.

New FA 2014 s 160A, inserted by s 46(5), places a value on prizes consisting of freeplay offers. Where a prize consists of a freeplay offer, whether or not in the form of a voucher, the expenditure on the prize is taken to be nil, unless obtained from an unconnected person.

New FA 2014 s 188(3) amends the definition of a "game of chance" for the purposes of remote gaming duty, so that a game that can only be played by more than one person and no payment needs to be paid for participating in the game, is not a game of chance.

The amendments made by s 46 have effect in relation to duty accounting periods beginning after 31 July 2017.

Section 47 introduces a new mandatory licensing scheme for the acquisition, use or possession of "tobacco-products manufacturing machinery", which is defined as machinery designed primarily for manufacturing tobacco products. Details of the licensing scheme are to be provided in regulations to be made by HMRC.

Part 3 Fulfilment businesses

Part 3, consisting of ss 48–59, introduces new legislation requiring third-country "goods-fulfilment businesses" to be registered to trade in the United Kingdom by HMRC.

Section 48 defines a third-country goods-fulfilment business as a business carried on by a person which consists of storing third-country goods owned by a person who is not established in a Member State of the European Union or storing third-country goods on behalf of a person who is not established in a Member State in circumstances where there has been no supply of goods in the United Kingdom for the purposes of VATA 1994 and the goods are being offered for sale in the United Kingdom or elsewhere, except where these activities are incidental to the carriage of the goods. Goods are "third-country goods" if they have been imported from a place outside the Member States.

Section 49 provides that a person may carry on a third-country goods-fulfilment business only with the approval of HMRC, which will be given only if they are satisfied that the person is a fit and proper person to carry on such a business. Approval may be given for such periods and subject to such conditions or restrictions as HMRC may see fit, and may be revoked at any time for reasonable cause.

Under s 50, HMRC must maintain a register of approved persons and may make such information contained in the register publicly available as they consider necessary. Section 51 empowers HMRC to make provisions relating to approval, registration and other matters by statutory instrument.

Section 52 permits HMRC to disclose information held by them to approved persons to enable those persons to comply with obligations imposed on them by virtue of s 51. Section 53 provides that a person who carries on a third-country goods-fulfilment business without having obtained approval commits an offence. Persons found guilty of such an offence on summary conviction are liable to imprisonment or a fine or both. In England and Wales and in Scotland, the term of imprisonment may not exceed 12 months. The fine in Scotland and Northern Ireland may not exceed the statutory maximum, and in Northern Ireland, the term of imprisonment may not exceed six months. In the case of conviction on indictment, persons will be liable to imprisonment for a period not exceeding seven years or to fine or to both.

Section 54 provides for forfeiture of goods where a person who has not been approved to do so carries on a third-country goods-fulfilment business. The goods so liable are goods stored by the person, the storage of which constitutes or has constituted the carrying-on of such a business.

Section 55 imposes penalties. It introduces Sch 13, which provides for penalties payable by a person who carries on a third-country goods-fulfilment business without approval. Additional penalties for contravening conditions, restrictions or regulations may be imposed in regulations to be made by HMRC. The maximum penalty under regulations is to be £3,000.

Schedule 13 comprises 13 paragraphs.

Schedule 13 para 1 provides that a penalty is to be payable by a person who carries on a third-country goods-fulfilment business while not being an approved person. Schedule 13 para 2 provides that the amount of the penalty is to be the maximum amount (defined in Sch 13 para 10) if the contravention is deliberate and concealed. If the contravention is deliberate but not concealed, the penalty is to be 70% of the maximum amount; in any other case, it is to be 30% of the maximum amount. The contravention is concealed if the person makes arrangements to conceal it.

Schedule 13 para 3 provides for a reduction in the penalty when the person discloses a contravention. Disclosure is unprompted if the person makes it when he has no reason to believe that HMRC have discovered or are about to discover it; otherwise, it is prompted. Under Sch 13 para 4, the penalty for a prompted disclosure of a contravention that is deliberate but not concealed may not be reduced below 35% of the maximum amount. If the contravention is deliberate and concealed there may be no reduction; otherwise, the penalty may be reduced to no less than 20% of the maximum amount. The penalty for an unprompted disclosure of a contravention that is deliberate but not concealed may not be reduced below 20% of the maximum amount. If the contravention is deliberate and concealed the penalty may not be reduced below 30% of the maximum amount; otherwise, the penalty may be reduced to no less than 10% of the maximum amount.

Schedule 13 para 5 allows HMRC to reduce a penalty if special circumstances exist.

Schedule 13 para 6 provides that penalties are to be charged by assessment, and must be paid no later than 30 days after the assessment is issued. Assessments may be made no later than one year after sufficient evidence of the relevant facts has become known to HMRC.

Schedule 13 para 7 provides for a reasonable-excuse defence.

Schedule 13 para 8 provides for HMRC to allocate all or a proportion of the liability for a penalty under Sch 13 which falls on a company to officers of that company, if the actions of the company which gave rise to the penalty are attributable to an officer or officers. A "company" for these purposes includes a limited-liability partnership and an unincorporated association but excludes partnerships. For bodies corporate, except limited-liability partnerships, the term "officer" means a director, shadow director, a manager or a secretary. Any member of a limited-liability partnership is considered to be an officer of the partnership. Schedule 13 para 9 prevents double jeopardy.

Schedule 13 para 10 sets the maximum amount of the penalty at £10,000, which may be varied by regulations. Schedule 13 para 11 provides that the appropriate appeal tribunal is that specified in FA 1994 Part 1 Chapter 2.

Section 56 provides for the right of appeal under FA 1994 s 13A(2) against any decision by HMRC that a person is liable to a penalty or as to the amount of that penalty, and any decision regarding approval and conditions or restrictions relating to approval may be subject to review and appeal under FA 1994 Sch 5.

Section 57 confers further regulation-making powers and s 58 provides for interpretation. Section 59 provides that these provisions are to come into force on a day or days to be appointed, except that the power to make regulations comes into force on the 16 November 2017.

Part 4 Administration, avoidance and enforcement

Reporting and record-keeping

Sections 60–62 pave the way for Making Tax Digital, the mandatory system of digital record-keeping and quarterly reporting to which businesses within the charge to income tax are to be subject.

Section 60 inserts new TMA 1970 s 12C, which introduces new TMA 1970 Sch A1, providing for digital reporting and record-keeping.

New TMA 1970 Sch A1 comprises four Parts. Part 1 (paras 1–5) provides for application; Part 2 (paras 6–13) provides for digital reporting and record-keeping; Part 3 (paras 14–15) provides for exemptions and Part 4 (paras 16–18) makes supplementary provisions.

New TMA 1970 Sch A1 para 1 provides that new TMA 1970 Sch A1 ("the Schedule") is to apply to a person within the charge to income tax who carries on, otherwise than in partnership:

(1) a trade, profession or vocation the profits of which are chargeable to income tax under ITTOIA 2005 Part 2;

(2) a property business the profits of which are chargeable to income tax under ITTOIA 2005 Part 3; or

(3) any other activity that may give rise to profits or other income chargeable to income tax under ITTOIA 2005 Part 2 or 3.

However, new TMA 1970 Sch A1 para 2 provides that the Schedule is not to apply to the trustees of a charitable trust or to the trustees of an exempt unauthorised unit trust within the meaning of SI 2013/2819 unless the trustees elect for it to apply. Nor is the Schedule to apply to a person in respect of an "excluded activity" unless the person elects for it to apply to him in respect of that activity. Excluded activities are:

(1) the underwriting business of a member of Lloyd's;

(2) holding shares in respect of which a distribution may be made which is chargeable to income tax under ITTOIA 2005 Part 3 as a distribution to shareholders in an REIT;

(3) participation in an open-ended investment company that may make property-income distributions chargeable to income tax under ITTOIA 2005 Part 3.

New TMA 1970 Sch A1 para 3 provides that the Schedule is also to apply to a partnership if at least one partner is within the charge to income tax, but new

TMA 1970 Sch A1 para 4 excludes partnerships of all whose activities that give rise to profits or income are excluded activities, unless the partnership elects for the Schedule to apply.

New TMA 1970 Sch A1 para 5 provides that requirements imposed on a partnership are to be met by a nominated partner.

New TMA 1970 Sch A1 Part 2 (paras 6–13) prepares the ground for imposing specific reporting and record-keeping requirements. New TMA 1970 Sch A1 para 6 defines "business" for the purposes of new TMA 1970 Sch A1 Part 2 as an activity by virtue of which the Schedule applies to a person or persons and in relation to a partnership means any activity of the partnership.

Under new TMA 1970 Sch A1 para 7, regulations may require a person or partnership to provide HMRC with specified information, including financial information by electronic means on a regular basis. Regulations under new TMA 1970 Sch A1 para 8 may require statements about a person's business and information relevant to calculating the profits, losses or income of the business, including an end-of-period statement, to be provided along with a return under TMA 1970 ss 8 or 8A or, if earlier, by 31 January following the tax year. Regulations under new TMA 1970 Sch A1 para 9 may provide for the establishment and use of a facility enabling a person to comply with a notice to file under TMA 1970 ss 8 or 8A. Regulations under new TMA 1970 Sch A1 para 10 may require partnerships to provide electronic returns of information, including information that a partnership return under TMA 1970 s 12AA must include.

New TMA 1970 Sch A1 para 11 provides for the making of regulations requiring a person or partnership to keep specified records relating to the business in electronic form and preserve those records electronically for a specified period of time. New TMA 1970 Sch A1 para 12 provides for a penalty not exceeding £3,000 to be imposed on a person or partners in a partnership for failing to comply with record-keeping regulations. New TMA 1970 Sch A1 para 13 contains further details concerning what provision regulations under any of new TMA 1970 Sch A1 paras 7–11 may make.

New TMA 1970 Sch A1 Part 3 (paras 14 and 15) provides for exemptions. New TMA 1970 Sch A1 para 14 requires HMRC to make regulations allowing for exemption of persons or partnerships who are "digitally excluded" from requirements imposed by regulations under new TMA 1970 Sch A1 paras 7, 8 and 11. Regulations providing for further exemptions on grounds of income or other financial criteria may be made under new TMA 1970 Sch A1 para 15.

New TMA 1970 Sch A1 Part 4 (paras 16–18) make supplementary provisions. New TMA 1970 Sch A1 para 16 provides a right of appeal against any decision made by HMRC under regulations made under the Schedule. New TMA 1970 Sch A1 para 17 provides that the power to provide information conferred by the Schedule includes the power to require the provision of associated accounts, statements and documents. New TMA 1970 Sch A1 para 18 provides for general regulation-making powers under the Schedule.

The amendments made by s 60 are to come into force on an appointed day or days.

Section 61 introduces Sch 14, which makes further amendments to TMA 1970 and other Acts facilitating and consequential on the introduction of the digital reporting and record-keeping requirements of Making Tax Digital.

Schedule 14 comprises 49 paragraphs. Part 1 (paras. 1–30) amends TMA 1970. Part 2 (paras 31–49) makes amendments to other statutes.

Schedule 14 para 1 is introductory. Schedule 14 para 2 amends TMA 1970 s 7 so as to provide that all persons who have received a notice to file under TMA 1970 s 8 (as amended by Sch 14 para 3) are not also to be required to give notice of chargeability under TMA 1970 s 7.

Schedule 14 para 3 amends and renames TMA 1970 s 8. That section is now to be entitled "Notices to file: persons other than trustees". Under new TMA 1970 s 8(1), HMRC are to have the power to give persons to whom the section applies a notice to file for the tax year (strictly, for the "year of assessment" in line with the language of TMA 1970). Under that notice, as provided in new TMA 1970 s 8(1AA), (1AB), persons are now to be required to file not a return but "such information as may reasonably be required in pursuance of the notice", a "self-assessment" and a "final declaration", and to deliver to HMRC "such accounts, statements, or other documents … as may reasonably be required". New TMA 1970 s 8(1AC) provides that where a person is not required to provide an "end-of-period statement" for the year, the duty to file is fulfilled by making and delivering a return. Such persons will be those who are not subject to the requirement for digital reporting and digital record-keeping. TMA 1970 s 8(1C) is amended to provide that a person carrying on a trade, profession or vocation in partnership must include his share of partnership income as detailed in the partnership statement.

New TMA 1970 s 8(1D) preserves existing filing dates (31 October for non-electronic returns and 31 January for electronic returns) where the duty to file is fulfilled by making a return.

New (substituted) TMA 1970 s 8(2) defines the "final declaration" as a declaration by a person to the effect that to the best of that person's knowledge, the information and self-assessment filed in response to the notice under TMA 1970 s 8(1) is correct and complete.

New TMA 1970 s 8(7) provides that, unless there is provision to the contrary, a reference in the Taxes Acts to:

(1) a return under TMA 1970 s 8 for a year of assessment is to be taken as a reference to the information, self-assessment and final declaration filed for that year under TMA 1970 s 8;
(2) anything that must be included in a return under TMA 1970 s 8 for a year of assessment is to be taken as a reference to the information, self-assessment and final declaration filed for that year under TMA 1970 s 8 and to any "end-of-period statement" for the year required by HMRC; and
(3) to making or delivering a return under TMA 1970 s 8 is to be taken also as a reference to making the final declaration required by the notice to file.

Schedule 14 para 4 makes broadly similar amendments to TMA 1970 s 8A (trustees' returns). Schedule 14 para 5 makes consequential amendments to TMA 1970 s 8B. Schedule 14 para 6 makes consequential amendments to TMA 1970 s 9, to reflect the fact that the duty to make a self-assessment is now to be imposed in TMA 1970 ss 8 and 8A (as amended). Schedule 14 paras 7–13 make consequential amendments to TMA 1970 ss 12ZH, 12ZI, 12AA, 12AB, 12ABA, 12ABB and 12AC.

Schedule 14 para 14 amends TMA 1970 s 12B, which deals with the records to be kept for the purposes of returns, to ensure that the requirements apply also to the records necessary for making partnership returns under new TMA 1970 Sch A1 (inserted by s 60). Schedule 14 paras 15–21 make consequential amendments to TMA 1970 ss 28ZA, 28B, 28C, 28H, 28I, 29 and 30B.

Schedule 14 para 22 amends TMA 1970 s 42 to ensure that the procedure for making claims under that section is also to apply to claims made in a partnership return under TMA 1970 Sch A1. Schedule 14 paras 23–28 make consequential amendments to TMA 1970 ss 59A, 59B, 106C, 106D, 106E and 107A. Schedule 14 para 29 amends TMA 1970 s 118(1) to include the apposite new definitions. Schedule 14 para 30 amends TMA 1970 Sch 1AB para 3.

Schedule 14 Part 2 contains paras 31–49 and makes consequential amendments to TCGA 1992, FA 1998, CAA 2001, ITTOIA 2005, ITA 2007, Crossrail Act 2008, FA 2008, TIOPA 2010, FA 2014 and FA 2016.

As with the other MTD provisions, the amendments made by s 61 and Sch 14 are to take effect from a day or days to be appointed.

Section 62 amends VATA 1994 Sch 11 to prepare the ground for introducing digital record-keeping and reporting for the purposes of VAT. In particular new VATA 1994 Sch 11 para 6(5)–(11) provide for regulations:

(1) about the format and means of keeping and preserving records;
(2) exempting certain taxable persons from those requirements in any month by reference to the person's taxable supplies in the 12 months preceding the current month;
(3) modifying the exemption when a business is transferred as a going concern.

Section 62(5) amends VATA 1994 s 83(1) to allow a right of appeal against a decision by HMRC under regulations requiring returns to be made or information to be submitted by electronic communications or requiring records to be kept or preserves in electronic form.

Enquiries

Section 63 introduces Sch 15, which provides for the making of partial closure notices for HMRC enquiries under TMA 1970 ss 9A, 12ZM and 12AC and FA 1998 Sch 18. A partial closure notice is nowhere defined, however, except indirectly in Sch 15 para 12.

Schedule 15 comprises 44 paragraphs.

Schedule 15 paras 1–21 amend TMA 1970. Most of the amendments are consequential, but attention should be drawn to the following.

Schedule 15 para 2 amends TMA 1970 s 9A(5) to include the issue of final closure notices and partial closure notices as events causing the subject-matter of an enquiry into a taxpayer-amended return under TMA 1970 s 9ZA to matters to which the amendment relates. The same effect is achieved by Sch 15 para 5, which amends TMA 1970 s 12ZM, in relation to enquiries into NRCGT returns amended by the taxpayer under TMA 1970 s 12ZK, and by Sch 15 para 7, which amends TMA 1970 s 12AC, in relation to enquiries into partnership returns amended by the taxpayer under TMA 1970 s 12ABA.

Schedule 15 para 6 amends TMA 1970 s 12ZN, in relation to NRCGT returns amended by the taxpayer during an enquiry. The amendment has the effect that, to the extent the taxpayer's amendment affects the amount notionally chargeable, it is not to take effect until a partial closure notice is issued in relation to the matters to which the taxpayer amendment relates or, if there is no partial closure notice, until a final closure notice is issued. The same amendment, with the same effect, is made by Sch 15 para 8, which amends TMA 1970 s 12AD, in relation to partnership returns amended by the taxpayer during an enquiry.

Schedule 15 para 12 amends TMA 1970 s 28A, which deals with the completion of an enquiry into a personal, trustee or NRCGT return. As amended, TMA 1970 s 28A now provides that any matter to which the enquiry relates is to be completed when HMRC inform the taxpayer by means of a partial closure notice that they have completed their enquiries into that matter and that the enquiry as a whole is completed by the issue of a final closure notice. New TMA 1970 s 28A(8), inserted by Sch 17 para 12(6), now provides that references in the Taxes Acts to a closure notice under TMA 1970 s 28A are to be references to a partial or final closure notice. The same amendments are made, with the same effect, to TMA 1970 s 28B, which deals with the completion of an enquiry into a partnership return, by Sch 15 para 13.

Schedule 15 para 14 amends TMA 1970 s 29, which provides for discovery assessments. The amendments concern the second arm of the second of the two alternative conditions (condition B, as contained in TMA 1970 s 29(5)(b)) enabling a discovery assessment to be made if a return has been delivered in respect of the relevant tax year. The amendments have the effect that, where a notice of enquiry has been given, the second arm of condition B is now to refer to matters of which an officer of HMRC could reasonably been expected to be aware when a partial closure notice relating to the matter in question was issued (or, if there was no partial closure notice, when the final closure notice was issued). The same amendments are made, with the same effect, to TMA 1970 s 29A, which provides for "discovery determinations" with regard to NRCGT disposals, by Sch 15 para 14, and by Sch 15 para 15 to TMA 1970 s 30B, which provides for HMRC to amend a partnership return when a loss of tax is discovered.

Schedule 15 para 22 amends TCGA 1992 s 184I, which provides for when HMRC may give a company a "relevant notice" to counteract an avoidance scheme once an enquiry into a return has been completed, to allow for a partial closure notice to be issued on a matter unconnected with the relevant notice.

Schedule 15 paras 23–34 amend the provisions on company tax returns in FA 1998 Sch 18, to accommodate the giving of partial closure notices. They broadly match the amendments made to equivalent provisions in TMA 1970.

Schedule 15 paras 35 and 36 make minor amendments to Tax Credits Act 2002 and FA 2008.

Schedule 15 paras 37–43 make amendments to TIOPA 2010. They relate to the restrictions on giving counteraction notices after completion of an enquiry (Sch 15 paras 38 and 39), closure notices after a transfer-pricing notice has been given following an enquiry (Sch 15 para 40), giving a deduction notice or a receipt notice after completion of an enquiry (Sch 15 para 41, as regards the former TIOPA 2010 s 256), giving closure notices when a deduction notice or a receipt notice has been given after an enquiry has been opened (Sch 15 para 42, as regards the former TIOPA 2010 s 257) and the deadline under TIOPA 2010 s 371IJ for making, amending or withdrawing a CFC profits-exemption claim.

Schedule 15 para 44 provides for commencement. The amendments made by Sch 17 are to have effect in relation to an enquiry under TMA 1970 ss 9A, 12ZM or 12AC or FA 1998 Sch 18 notice of which is given after 15 November 2017 or which is in progress immediately before 16 November 2017.

Avoidance etc

Section 64 amends the penalty provisions in FA 2007 Sch 24 for errors in taxpayers' documents. The amendments are intended to ensure that taxpayers who have received advice in relation to certain tax-avoidance schemes may not in certain circumstances rely on that advice to show they have taken reasonable to avoid an inaccuracy in their documents.

Section 64(2) inserts new FA 2007 Sch 24 paras 3A and 3B. New FA 2007 Sch 24 para 3A applies where a person (P) gives HMRC a document of the kind listed in the Table in FA 2007 Sch 24 para 1 and containing an inaccuracy that arises because the document is submitted on the basis that particular avoidance arrangements had an effect that they in fact did not have. In such circumstances, the presumption is to be that the inaccuracy was careless, unless the inaccuracy was deliberate on P's part or P satisfies HMRC or the tribunal that he took reasonable care to avoid inaccuracy.

In coming to a decision whether P took reasonable care, neither HMRC nor the tribunal are to have any regard to evidence showing that P relied on advice that is "disqualified". Advice is "disqualified" if:

(1) it was given to P by an "interested person";
(2) it was given to P in connection with arrangements made between an "interested person" and the person who gave the advice;
(3) the person who gave the advice did not have the appropriate expertise;
(4) it took no account of P's individual circumstances (was generic); or
(5) it was addressed or given to a person other than P.

An "interested person" is one who participated in the arrangements or any associated transaction or who, for any consideration, facilitated P's entering into the avoidance arrangements.

Advice under (1) to (3) will nevertheless not be "disqualified" if P has taken reasonable steps to find out whether the advice fell within any of those three instances and reasonably believes that it does not. Advice given by an interested person is not to be disqualified for that reason if the person who gave the advice had the requisite expertise, the advice took account of P's individual circumstances and, broadly speaking, the tax advantage asserted by the arrangements had already been counteracted by a targeted anti-avoidance rule.

New FA 2007 Sch 24 para 3B defines "avoidance arrangements" and lists five characteristics or "conditions" that mark an avoidance arrangement for this purpose. These include DOTAS arrangements and disclosable VAT or indirect-tax arrangements, arrangements within the GAAR and arrangements that have elicited a follower notice.

The amendments made by s 64 are to have effect in relation to any document of a kind listed in the Table in FA 2007 Sch 24 para 1 and given to HMRC after 15 November 2017 and relating to a tax period beginning after 5 April 2017 and ending after 15 November 2017.

Section 65 introduces Sch 16, which legislates for penalties for persons who enable tax avoidance that is defeated. Enablers are defined as persons who design, market or otherwise facilitate abusive tax-avoidance arrangements that are defeated either in the courts or the tribunal, or are otherwise counteracted.

Schedule 16 comprises no less than 12 Parts. Part 1 (paras 1–2) establishes liability for the penalty; Part 2 (para 3) identifies abusive tax arrangements; Part 3 (paras 4–6) defines "defeat" in the context of abusive tax arrangements); and Part 4 (paras 7–14) defines enablers. Part 5 (paras 15–18) sets the amount of the penalty; Part 6 (paras 19–22) provides for assessment of the penalty; Part 7 (paras 23–36) provides the mechanism for obtaining the opinion of the GAAR Advisory Panel; and Part 8 (paras 37–39) provides for appeals. Part 9 (paras 40–45) provides for information powers; Part 10 (paras 46–51) provides for publication of details of penalised persons; Part 11 (paras 52–53) contains miscellaneous provisions; and Part 12 (paras 54–62) provides interpretations, confers regulatory powers, makes consequential amendments and provides for commencement. Certain basic definitions are copied from the GAAR provisions, as is the need to involve the GAAR Advisory Panel.

Schedule 16 para 1 provides that where a person has entered into "abusive tax arrangements" (defined in Sch 16 Part 2) and incurred a "defeat in respect of the arrangements" (defined in Sch 16 part 3), a penalty ("the enabler penalty") is to be payable by each "person who enabled the arrangements" (defined in Sch 16 Part 4). Schedule 16 para 2 is a signpost to the other Parts of the Schedule.

Schedule 16 para 3 defines what constitutes "abusive tax arrangements". "Tax arrangements" are first defined in identical words to the definition in FA 2013 s 207(1), namely that, "having regard to all the circumstances, it would be *reasonable* to conclude that the obtaining of a tax advantage was the main purpose or one of the main purposes of the arrangement". What makes a tax arrangement "abusive" is also defined identically to the first paragraph of FA 2013 s 207(2), namely that they are "arrangements the entering-into or carrying-out of which cannot *reasonably* be regarded as a *reasonable* course of action in relation to the relevant tax provisions, having regard to all the circumstances". Note the repetitive use of the adjective "reasonable" and its adverb. A non-exhaustive list of the circumstances to which regard must be had and a non-exhaustive list of factors indicating that tax arrangements are abusive (practically identical to FA 2013 s 207(2)(a), (b); s 207(4)) is provided. It is clarified that references to "income" in the list of factors pointing to abusive arrangements are to be taken to include "earnings" for the purposes of SSCBA 1992.

Schedule 16 paras 4–6 define that a person incurs a defeat in respect of abusive tax arrangements into which he enters when either of two conditions (A and B) is met. Condition A is that a person (or another person acting on the first person's behalf) has given HMRC a document of the type listed in FA 2007 Sch 24 para 1 (or communicated information to HMRC in any other way); that document or information was submitted on the basis that a tax advantage arose from the arrangements concerned; the relevant advantage has been counteracted; and the counteraction is final. Condition B is that HMRC have made an assessment to tax; the assessment counteracts a tax advantage that it is *reasonable* to assume the person concerned expected to obtain from the arrangements concerned; and the counteraction is final.

Schedule 16 para 7 defines the person who "enabled" the arrangements as their "designer" or "manager" or "marketer"; an "enabling participant" in the arrangements or a "financial enabler" in relation to them (cf the abbreviated definition in FA 2016 Sch 20 para 1 (enablers of offshore tax avoidance) – "encouraged, assisted or otherwise facilitated"). This core definition is then amplified. Schedule 16 para 8 defines a "designer" as a person who was, in the course of a business carried on by that person, to any extent responsible for the design of the arrangements or of a proposal that was implemented by the arrangements. Schedule 16 para 9 defines a "manager" of the arrangements as a person who, in the course of a business carried on by that person, was to any extent responsible for the organisation or management of the arrangements, or a person who, when carrying out any functions in relation to the organisation or management of the arrangements, knew or could reasonably be expected to know that the arrangements were abusive tax arrangements. This core definition is then amplified. Schedule 16 para 10 defines a "marketer" of the arrangements as a person who, in the course of a business carried on by that person, made available a proposal to the person who entered into the arrangements ("T") which was subsequently implemented by the arrangements or a person who communicated information to T or another person about a proposal that was subsequently implemented in relation to T by the arrangements and did so with a view to T's entering into the arrangements or transactions forming part of the arrangements.

Schedule 16 para 11 provides that a person is an "enabling participant" in the arrangements if he is a person (other than T) who enters into the arrangements or a transaction forming part of the arrangements in circumstances such that, without his participation in the arrangements (or that of another person acting in the same capacity), the arrangements could not have been expected to result in a tax advantage for Y, and when that person entered into the arrangements or transaction, he knew or could reasonably be expected to know that what was being entered into was abusive tax arrangements or a transaction forming part of such arrangements. Schedule 16 para 12 defines a "financial enabler" in relation to the arrangements as a person who, in the course of a business carried on by that person, provided a financial product directly or indirectly to a "relevant party", of whom it is reasonable to assume that the or a purpose of his obtaining the financial product was to participate in the arrangements and when the financial product was provided, knew or could reasonably be expected to know that the or a purpose of obtaining the product was to participate in abusive tax arrangements. This core definition is then amplified. Schedule 16 para 13 excludes T and, if T is a company, any companies in T's group from being enablers, even if they would otherwise fall within one of the definitions, while Sch 16 para 14 allows HM Treasury to add or subtract persons or categories of persons from the status of enablers.

Schedule 16 paras 15 and 16 set the amount of the penalty. The basic rule is that the amount of the penalty is the entire amount or value of the "relevant consideration" received or receivable by the enabler (excluding VAT) for anything done by the enabler which enabled the abusive tax arrangements in question, but disregarding any amount that has already been taken into consideration in calculating an earlier enabler penalty. Consideration paid to another person under arrangements with the enabler is to be regarded as paid to the enabler. Schedule 16 para 17 provides that the penalty will be reduced by the amount of any other penalty incurred by the enabler in respect of the same conduct. Schedule 16 para 18 provides that HMRC may, at its discretion, mitigate the penalty, entirely remit it or stay or agree a compromise in relation to proceedings.

Schedule 16 para 19 provides that an enabler penalty is to be collected by assessment. If HMRC do not yet have all the information required to determine the amount of the enabler's consideration, they may base the assessment on a reasonable estimate if they have taken all reasonable steps to obtain the information. Once assessed, the penalty must be paid within 30 days of the date of the assessment (Sch 16 para 20). However, before an assessment may be issued at all, HMRC must obtain the opinion of the GAAR Advisory Panel (see under Sch 16 paras 23–36). Schedule 16 para 21 provides that where more than one person has implemented a proposal for arrangements by entering into abusive tax arrangements that are substantially the same as each other, HMRC must not assess any enabler penalty until they reasonably believe that at least 50% of those arrangements have been defeated, unless an enabler requests an earlier assessment.

Schedule 16 para 22 places time limits on the ability to assess a penalty. The limits are as follows:

(1) Where a Panel opinion has already been obtained in relation to equivalent arrangements and notice has been given to the enabler under Sch 16 para 25: 12 months from the end of the period for making representations;
(2) Where a GAAR final-decision notice has been given under Sch 16 para 24: 12 months from the date on which the arrangements were defeated;
(3) Where the Panel has given its opinion on certain arrangements and HMRC believe that another person who has not yet been given notice of the referral is liable to the penalty in respect of those arrangements (and is therefore given a notice under Sch 16 para 35): 12 months from the end of the period for making representations.

The time limit may be extended if HMRC have had to wait for the 50% defeat threshold (under Sch 16 para 21) to be reached, an enabler has asked for an earlier pre-threshold assessment, or a materially inaccurate declaration as to legal privilege has been made (Sch 16 para 44).

Schedule 16 para 23 contains the general rule that HMRC may not assess an enabler penalty unless and until:

(1) an opinion has been obtained from the GAAR Advisory Panel in respect of the arrangements following a referral under Sch 16 para 26, the time limit for representations in relation to a notice under Sch 16 para 35 has expired, and the designated HMRC officer has considered both the Panel opinion and the representations (if any); or
(2) a GAAR final decision-notice has been given in relation to the arrangements or related arrangements, the time limit for making any representations in relation to a notice given to the enabler under Sch 16 para 25 has expired, and the designated HMRC officer has considered both the Panel opinion informing the final decision notice and the representations (if any).

When HMRC give notice of a penalty to the enabler, they must also produce an accompanying report on the Panel opinion informing the issue of the final decision notice or on the opinion obtained in procedure (1) above.

Schedule 16 para 24 clarifies that a GAAR final decision notice is the notice given by HMRC on whether or not to proceed with counteraction under any of FA 2013 Sch 43 para 12, Sch 43A paras 8 or 9, or Sch 43B para 8. When the Panel gives its opinion on any arrangements, that opinion also applies to equivalent arrangements.

Schedule 16 para 25 provides that where the designated HMRC officer is of the opinion that a person is liable to the enabler penalty in relation to particular arrangements and no GAAR final decision notice has yet been given in respect of those arrangements, but such a notice has been given in respect of equivalent arrangements, the officer must give the enabler written notice with details of the arrangements and a report on the Panel opinion concerned. The enabler then has 30 days within which to make representations as to why the arrangements that he has enabled are not equivalent to the arrangements contemplated in the final decision notice.

Schedule 16 para 26 provides that a designated HMRC officer may make a referral to the Advisory Panel if the officer considers that a person is liable to the enabler penalty in relation to particular arrangements and the requisite notice under Sch 16 para 28 has been given and the time for making representations has expired. The question to be put to the Panel is whether entering into and carrying out of the tax arrangements concerned is a reasonable course of action in relation to the relevant tax provisions. However, a referral may not be made under this paragraph if a GAAR final decision notice has already been given in relation to those arrangements or equivalent arrangements. Schedule 16 para 27 prescribes what information HMRC must give to the Panel when making the referral.

Schedule 16 para 28 provides that HMRC may not make a referral to the Advisory Panel under Sch 16 para 26 before HMRC have given each person they consider is liable to the enabler penalty a notice under this paragraph and the period for making representation in relation to the notice has expired. The notice must specify the arrangements, explain why HMRC consider them to be abusive and explain that HMRC are considering making a referral to the Advisory Panel in relation to those arrangements. The person to whom the notice is given then has 45 days (or longer, if HMRC agree) within which to make representations in response. Under Sch 16 para 29, HMRC must make the decision whether or not to refer as soon as reasonably practical and inform each person to whom they gave the notice of that decision.

Schedule 16 para 30 prescribes what additional information and documents HMRC must send to the Advisory Panel together with the referral statement. These include a copy of the representations (if any) made by the persons concerned. Schedule 16 para 31 provides that when making a referral under Sch 16 para 26, HMRC must notify the enabler of the referral and prescribes what information and documents must be provided to the enabler on or with the notice. Schedule 16 para 32 provides that a person who has received the notice under Sch 16 para 31 has 21 days (or longer, if the Panel agrees) within which to make written representations to the Advisory Panel, with a copy to HMRC.

Schedule 16 paras 33 and 34 prescribe what the Advisory Panel must do when it has received a referral under Sch 16 para 26. The Chair must convene a sub-panel consisting of three members (one of whom may be the Chair) to consider the referred question, and the sub-panel is entitled to invite the enablers and HMRC to provide further information. Under Sch 16 para 34, the sub-panel must produce either one opinion notice stating the joint opinion of all the members or two (or, indeed, three) opinion notices giving differing opinions. This requirement will be familiar from the GAAR referral procedure for arrangements themselves (see FA 2013 Sch 43 para 11). The opinion(s) must state whether entering into and carrying out the tax arrangements concerned was or was not a reasonable course of action in relation to the relevant tax provisions or whether there was insufficient evidence for reaching a view on the matter.

Schedule 16 para 35 provides that once the Advisory Panel has given its opinion on a referral, and HMRC consider that there is a person liable to the enabler penalty in respect of particular arrangements, but a notice under Sch 16 para 28 has not been given to that person (presumably because there are equivalent arrangements with different enablers), they must now give a notice with prescribed contents under this paragraph to such a person. That person then has 30 days (or longer, if HMRC agree) to make representations as to why the Panel opinion does not apply to the particular arrangements he is said to have enabled.

Schedule 16 para 36 provides that should proceedings ensue before a court or tribunal in connection with the enabler penalty, the judicial body concerned must take into account (but is not bound by) the relevant Panel opinion in deciding whether the arrangements were abusive.

Schedule 16 paras 37–39 concern appeals. Schedule 16 para 37 provides that a person (the enabler) may appeal against a decision by HMRC that an enabler penalty is payable by that person or a decision by HMRC as to the amount of that penalty. Schedule 16 para 38 provides that the appeal is to be treated as if it were an appeal against an assessment to the tax to which the arrangements relate, but the enabler is not required to pay the penalty assessed until the appeal is determined. Schedule 16 para 39 provides that on the question whether a penalty is payable at all, the tribunal may affirm or cancel HMRC's decision. As regards the amount, the tribunal may confirm HMRC's decision or vary it to the extent that HMRC had power to do so. However, if the tribunal considers that HMRC's decision on mitigation was flawed, it may go beyond those mitigation limits.

Schedule 16 para 40 provides that HMRC's powers of information and inspection under FA 2008 Sch 36 shall apply equally for the purpose of checking a person's position as regards liability to an enabler penalty, with the modifications described in Sch 16 paras 41–43.

Schedule 16 paras 44 and 45 deal with legal privilege (or in Scotland, protection from disclosure in legal proceedings on the grounds of confidentiality of communication). If there are communications that a person could rely on to establish that he is not liable to an enabler penalty, but those communications may not be disclosed on the grounds that they are privileged, Sch 16 para 44 provides that a "relevant lawyer" may give a declaration to that effect, which is to be regarded as conclusive of the matter. A "relevant lawyer" is a barrister, advocate, solicitor or other legal representative with whom those communications have been had. However, if a person carelessly or deliberately gives any incorrect information in a privilege declaration, that person is liable under Sch 16 para 45 to a penalty of up to £5,000.

Schedule 16 paras 46–51 provide for persons who have been assessed to an enabler penalty to be named and have other details concerning them to be published within prescribed circumstances. Schedule 16 para 46 provides that HMRC may publish prescribed information concerning a person who has incurred an enabler penalty that has become final if either the same enabler has already previously incurred 50 or more other "reckonable" enabler penalties or the total amount charged under that penalty and previous "reckonable" enabler penalties is more than £25,000. Schedule 16 para 47 provides that a penalty is "reckonable" if it becomes final at the same time as, or before, the penalty in question and the arrangements to which the penalties relate were entered into within no more than 12 months of each other. Schedule 16 para 48 places restrictions on the power to publish in the prescribed circumstances, and Sch 16 para 49 provides that publication may not take place more than 12 months after the last date on which the penalties on which it is based became final. Schedule 16 para 50 requires HMRC to inform the person concerned before publication and allow the person to make representations. Under Sch 16 para 51, HM Treasury may amend the sums and amounts specified in Sch 16 para 46 and time limits in Sch 16 para 47 by statutory instrument.

Schedule 16 para 52 prevents double jeopardy and Sch 16 para 53 applies TMA 1970 ss 108, 114 and 115 for the purposes of Sch 16. Schedule 16 para 54 defines the taxes that arrangements falling within Sch 16 are intended to avoid as:

(1) income tax;
(2) corporation tax and amounts chargeable as if they were corporation tax;
(3) capital gains tax;
(4) inheritance tax;
(5) stamp duty land tax;
(6) diverted profits tax;
(7) ATED;
(8) petroleum revenue tax; and
(9) national insurance contributions.

Schedule 16 para 55 defines "tax advantage" and Sch 16 para 56 contains other definitions. Schedule 16 para 57 provides that regulations under Sch 16 must be made by statutory instrument. Schedule 16 paras 58–61 make consequential amendments. Schedule 16 para 62 provides that Sch 16 is to have effect in relation to arrangements entered into after 15 November 2017, subject to transitional provisions.

Section 66 introduces Sch 17, which transfers the burden of disclosure from the user to the promoter and extends the scope of the disclosure regime for tax-avoidance schemes involving VAT, but also extends the disclosure regime to other indirect taxes. As a consequence, VATA 1994 s 58A and Sch 11A are to cease to have effect concerning disclosure of any scheme that was first entered into after 31 December 2017, constitutes arrangements notifiable under Sch 17 and implements proposals that are notifiable proposals under that Schedule. No voluntary notification under VATA 1994 Sch 11A para 9 may be made after 31 December 2017.

Section 66 and Sch 17 are to come into force on 1 January 2018, but the regulation-making powers are to have effect from 16 November 2017.

Schedule 17 comprises four Parts. Part 1 (paras 1–38) sets out the duty to disclose; Part 2 (paras 39–50) provides for penalties for failure to comply; Part 3 (paras 51–55) makes consequential amendments; and Part 4 (paras 56–57) is supplementary.

Schedule 17 para 1 is preliminary. Schedule 17 para 2 provides that Sch 17 applies to all of the following taxes, collectively referred to as "indirect tax":

Aggregates levy

Air passenger duty
Bingo duty
Climate change levy
Customs duties
[Excise] duties on spirits, beer, wine, made-wine and cider
Gaming duty
General betting duty
Hydrocarbon oils duty
Insurance premium tax
Landfill tax
Lottery duty
Machine games duty
Pool betting duty
Remote gaming duty
Soft drinks industry levy
Tobacco products duty and
VAT

Schedule 17 para 3 defines "notifiable arrangements" and "notifiable proposal". Both the definition of "notifiable arrangements" and the definition of "notifiable proposal" are taken directly from the direct-tax DOTAS definition in FA 2004 s 306. An arrangement is not notifiable until it is prescribed as such by regulations. Exceptions are provided, however. Arrangements are not to be notifiable if they implement a proposal that is excluded from being a notifiable proposal. A proposal is not to be a notifiable proposal if any of the following events occurs before 1 January 2018:

(1) a promoter first makes a firm approach to another person in relation to the proposal;
(2) a promoter makes the proposal available for implementation by any other person; or
(3) a promoter first becomes aware of any transaction forming part of arrangements implementing the proposal.

Schedule 17 paras 4 and 5 provide that HMRC must apply to a tribunal for an order that proposals or arrangements are notifiable, or, where HMRC have reasonable grounds for suspecting that a proposal or arrangements may be notifiable, they may apply to the tribunal to have the proposals or arrangements treated as notifiable.

Schedule 17 para 6 defines the "tax advantage", which notifiable proposals or arrangements are intended to enable, in relation to VAT. The definition is taken directly from the existing definition in VATA 1994 Sch 11A para 2, except that it adds avoiding an obligation to account for tax to the definition. Also imported directly from VATA 1994 Sch 11A para 2 and 2A are the definitions of "non-deductible tax", "incurred" (in relation to VAT incurred by a taxable person, and "non-refundable tax".

A "tax advantage" in relation to other indirect taxes is defined in Sch 17 para 7 as:

(1) relief or increased relief from tax;
(2) repayment or increased repayment of tax;
(3) avoidance or reduction of a charge to tax, an assessment of tax or a liability to pay tax;
(4) avoidance of a possible assessment to tax or liability to pay tax;
(5) deferral of a payment of tax or advancement of a repayment of tax; or
(6) avoidance of an obligation to deduct or account for tax.

The remainder of Sch 17 Part 1 contains definitions and provisions also lifted directly, practically word for word, from the DOTAS regime, as shown in the following Table.

Schedule 17 provision	Subject matter	FA 2004 (DOTAS) provision
Paragraph 8	Promoter	Section 307(1), (2), (3), (4), (5), (6)
Paragraph 9	Introducer	Section 307(1A), (5), (6)
Paragraph 10	Making a firm approach; marketing contact	Section 307(4A)–(4C)
Paragraphs 11–15	Duties of promoter	Section 308
Paragraph 16[1]	Duty of promoter: supplemental information	Section 308A

Paragraph 17	Duty of person dealing with promoter outside the UK	Section 309
Paragraph 18	Duty of parties to notifiable arrangements not involving promoter	Section 310
Paragraphs 19, 20	Duty to provide further information requested by HMRC	Sections 310A, 310B
Paragraph 21	Duty of promoters to produce updated information	Section 310C
Paragraph 22	Arrangements to be given reference number	Section 311
Paragraph 23	Duty of promoter to notify client of number	Section 312
Paragraph 24	Duty of client to notify parties of number	Section 312A, omitting s 312A(2A), (3)(b)–(d)
Paragraph 25[1]	Duty of client to provide information to promoter	Section 312B
Paragraph 26	Duty of parties to notifiable arrangements to notify HMRC of number etc	Section 313, omitting s 313(4)
Paragraph 27	Duty of promoter to provide details of clients	Section 313ZA
Paragraph 28[1]	Enquiry following disclosure of client details	Section 313ZB
Paragraph 29[1]	Pre-disclosure enquiry	Section313A
Paragraph 30[1]	Reasons for non-disclosure: supporting information	Section 313B
Paragraph 31[1]	Provision of information to HMRC by introducers	Section 313C
Paragraph 32	Legal professional privilege	Section 314
Paragraphs 33, 34	Information	Sections 316, 316A
Paragraph 35	Confidentiality	Section 316B
Paragraph 36	Publication by HMRC	Section 316C
Paragraph 37	Subsequent judicial rulings	Section 316D

Note:

[1] These paragraphs specify the length of a prescribed or relevant period, which in the DOTAS regime is left to regulations.

Schedule 17 para 38 enables HMRC to vary the definition of the relevant period in the paragraphs mentioned.

Schedule 17 Part 2 prescribes penalties for non-compliance.

Schedule 17 para 39 provides that a person who fails to comply with any of the provisions of Sch 17 Part 1 is to be liable to a penalty not exceeding £5,000, but failure to meet a requirement under any of Sch 17 paras 11(1), 12(1), 17(2), 18(2) or 19, to a daily penalty not exceeding £600 per day during the "initial period" (the period beginning with the relevant day and ending with the earlier of the day on which the penalty is determined and the last day before the failure ceases). If the failure continues after the initial penalty is imposed, a further penalty not exceeding £600 per day is to be imposed for each day on which the failure continues thereafter. The "relevant day" is given by the Table in Sch 17 para 39(4), but is normally the first day after the end of the "relevant period" referred to in the provision concerned.

Schedule 17 para 40 provides that in the case of a penalty under any of Sch 17 paras 11(1), 12(1), 17(2), 18(2) or 19, the amount of the penalty must take all relevant considerations into account, including, where applicable, the fees that the promoter has received or is likely to receive. If the maximum penalty (£600 per day) appears inappropriately low, it may be increased to no more than £1 million. Schedule 17 para 41 provides that where an order has been made by a tribunal under Sch 17 paras 4 and 5, but failure to notify persists, the maximum daily penalty may be increased to £5,000 for every day after the end of the period of 11 days counting from the date of the order.

Schedule 17 para 44 provides that a person who fails to comply with the duty under Sch 17 para 26 to notify HMRC of the number etc of any notifiable arrangements to which he is a party is to be liable to a penalty of no more than £5,000 in respect of each arrangement. One previous failure to comply under this heading within the previous 36 months increases the maximum penalty to £7,500 per arrangement, whereas two or more previous failures cause the maximum penalty to increase to £10,000 per arrangement.

Penalties under Sch 17 in respect of the initial period require an application to the First-tier Tribunal by an authorised officer of HMRC. Schedule 17 para 45 further provides that proceedings may not commence until 12 months have elapsed since sufficient evidence of the facts came to the knowledge of HMRC. If the First-tier Tribunal decides that the penalty is payable, the penalty is to be treated as if it were tax charged in an assessment and due and payable. The appellant may appeal to the Upper Tribunal against a decision that the penalty is payable and as regards the amount.

Schedule 17 para 46 provides that penalties for continuing failure and penalties under Sch 17 para 44 may be charged by assessment, to be made no more than 12 months since sufficient evidence of the facts came to the knowledge of HMRC. Under Sch 17 para 47, the person assessed may appeal against the decision that a penalty is payable and against the decision on amount. The person may not be required to pay the penalty until any appeal is determined.

Schedule 17 paras 48–50 provide a reasonable-excuse defence, but the making of an order as to notifiability under Sch 17 para 4 or 5 is not of itself to mean that the person did or did not have a reasonable excuse for failure to comply before the order was made.

Schedule 17 Part 3 makes consequential amendments to VATA 1994 and FA 2014. NB: the Queen's printer's copy of the Lords Bill incorrectly refers throughout Sch 17 Part 3 to penalties under "Schedule 17 to FA 2017 [sic]" when referring to penalties under this Schedule.

Schedule 17 para 51 makes a consequential amendment to VATA 1994 s 77(4A) (20-year time limit for assessments). Schedule 17 paras 52–54 amend FA 2014 Part 5 (Promoters of tax avoidance schemes) to include arrangements notifiable under Sch 17 to the provisions relating to defeated arrangements.

Schedule 17 para 55 amends FA 2016 Sch 18, which contains the serial tax-avoidance provisions, to include arrangements notifiable under Sch 17

In Sch 17 Part 4, Sch 17 para 56 provides for regulation-making powers, and Sch 17 para 57 for interpretation.

Section 67 introduces Sch 18, requiring persons who have undeclared past liabilities to UK income tax, capital gains tax or inheritance tax to notify HMRC and take other "corrective action".

Schedule 18 comprises four Parts. Part 1 (paras 1–13) establishes liability for the penalty; Part 2 (paras 14–25) sets the amount of the penalty and provides for assessment and appeal procedures; Part 3 (paras 26–31) makes further provisions relating to the requirement to correct; and Part 4 (para 32) provides interpretation.

Schedule 18 para 1 establishes that a penalty is to be payable by a person who has any "relevant offshore tax non-compliance" to correct at the end of 2016/17 and fails to do so within the period beginning on 6 April 2017 and ending on 30 September 2018. This period is referred to as "the RTC period". Taxpayers thus have a grace period of just under a year in which to take action to avoid incurring the penalty. Schedule 18 para 2 is introductory.

Schedule 18 paras 3–12 contain the key definitions. "Tax non-compliance" encompasses all of the following:

(1) failure to comply on or before the filing date to give notice of chargeability under TMA 1970 s 7;

(2) failure to comply on or before the filing date to deliver a return or other document;

(3) delivery of a return or other document containing an inaccuracy involving an understatement of liability to tax, a false or inflated statement of a loss or a false or inflated claim to a repayment of tax.

The documents referred to are listed in Sch 18 para 8(3), (4).

"Offshore tax non-compliance" is defined in Sch 18 para 7 as tax non-compliance that "involves an offshore matter or an "offshore transfer" (whether or not it also involves an onshore matter). The phrases "involves an offshore matter" and "involves an offshore transfer" are defined in Sch 18 para 9.

As regards failure to give notice of chargeability, tax non-compliance involves an offshore matter if the potential loss of revenue arises in connection with income with a foreign source, assets situated or held abroad, activities carried on wholly or mainly abroad and anything else having the same effect as the above. Tax non-compliance involves an offshore transfer if it does not involve an offshore matter but where the income or disposal proceeds (or assets derived from or representing the income or proceeds) involved was or were received abroad or transferred abroad before 6 April 2017.

As regards failure to deliver a return or document or delivery of an inaccurate return or document, tax non-compliance involves an offshore matter if the liability to tax that would have been disclosed or the information that should have been given includes a liability involving income with a foreign source, assets situated or held abroad, activities carried on wholly or mainly abroad and anything else having the same effect as the above. Tax non-compliance involves an offshore transfer if it does not involve an offshore matter but where the income or disposal proceeds (or assets derived from or representing the income or proceeds) involved was or were received abroad or transferred abroad before 6 April 2017. A slightly different definition applies to a liability to inheritance tax.

A person has relevant offshore tax non-compliance to correct at the end of the tax year 2016/17 where two conditions (A and B) are satisfied in respect of any offshore tax non-compliance committed by the person before 6 April 2017 ("the original offshore tax non-compliance"), and a third condition, condition C, is satisfied at the "relevant date", which is 6 April 2017 where the tax at stake is income tax or CGT and 17 November 2017 where the tax at stake is inheritance tax. Condition A is that the original offshore tax non-compliance has not been fully corrected before 6 April 2017. Condition B is that the original offshore tax non-compliance or the remaining uncorrected part of it involved a potential loss of revenue when the original non-compliance was committed. Condition C is that, broadly speaking, HMRC would, on the relevant date, have lawfully been able to assess the person concerned to the tax liability that should have been disclosed and corrected.

Schedule 18 para 13 specifies how offshore tax non-compliance may be corrected. This consists, essentially, of giving the requisite notice of chargeability to HMRC, delivering the requisite return or document, or amending the inaccurate document or delivering a new, accurate document.

Schedule 18 Part 2 (paras 14–25) deals with the amount of the penalty and the mechanism of assessment and appeal. Schedule 18 para 14 sets the penalty at 200% of the potential loss of revenue ("the offshore PLR") attributable to the uncorrected offshore tax non-compliance, but may be open to reduction. Schedule 18 para 15 provides for the offshore PLR to be determined by reference to FA 2008 Sch 41 para 7 (or TMA 1970 s 7(8) if the original non-compliance dates from before 1 April 2010) for failure to notify chargeability, to FA 2009 Sch 55 para 24 (or TMA 1970 s 93(9) if the original non-compliance dates from before 1 April 2011) for failure to deliver a return or document, and to FA 2007 Sch 24 paras 5–8 (or TMA 1970 s 95(2) if the original non-compliance dates from before 1 April 2008) for delivery of an incorrect return or document.

Schedule 18 para 16 provides for the penalty to be reduced if the person concerned makes a relevant disclosure or gives relevant assistance. The degree of the reduction is to depend on the quality of the disclosure or assistance, but the penalty may not be reduced below 100% of the offshore PLR. Schedule 18 para 17 provides for a reduction of the penalty if there are special circumstances. Reducing the penalty may involve staying it or agreeing a compromise in relation to proceedings.

Schedule 18 para 18 sets out the assessment procedure for the penalty, and requires payment of the penalty within 30 days of the date of the assessment and notice. Schedule 18 para 19 provides time limits for the making of a penalty assessment. Schedule 18 para 20 provides that a person may appeal against HMRC's decision that a penalty is payable or as to the amount of the penalty. Schedule 18 para 21 provides that a person is not required to pay a penalty under appeal until the appeal is determined. On appeal to the tribunal, Sch 18 para 22 provides that the tribunal may affirm or cancel HMRC's decision to impose the penalty and may vary the amount within the parameters allowed to HMRC. Schedule 18 para 23 establishes a reasonable-excuse defence.

Schedule 18 para 24 protects against double jeopardy and Sch 18 para 25 applies TMA 1970 ss 108, 114 and 115.

Schedule 18 Part 3 (paras 26–31) provides for an extension of the time limit for assessment and for further penalties. Schedule 18 para 26 provides that where the last day on which it would be lawful for HMRC to assess a person who has relevant offshore tax non-compliance at the end of the tax year 2016/17 would fall within a period beginning on 6 April 2017 and ending with 4 April 2021, the last lawful date for assessment is to be moved to 5 April 2021.

NB: the Queen's printer's copy of the Bill incorrectly refers throughout to penalties under "Schedule 18 to FA 2017" [sic] when referring in Sch 18 Part 3 to penalties under this Schedule.

Schedule 18 para 27 amends FA 2015 Sch 21, which imposes penalties in connection with offshore asset moves, so as to add a penalty under Sch 18 to the classes of original penalty in FA 2015 Sch 21 para 2 that may give rise to a penalty under that Schedule, to define the necessary deliberate failure (FA 2015 Sch 21 para 3) and define the relevant time (FA 2015 Sch 21 para 5).

Schedule 18 para 28 amends FA 2016 Sch 22, which imposes asset-based penalties for offshore inaccuracies and failures. It adds the penalty under Sch 18 to the "standard offshore penalties" listed in FA 2016 Sch 22 para 2 that may give rise to a penalty under that Schedule. Under new FA 2016 Sch 22 para 6A, inserted by Sch 18 para 28(6), only one asset-based penalty is to be payable by a person in relation to any given asset where a penalty has been imposed on that person by Sch 18.

Schedule 18 para 29 amends TMA 1970 ss 103ZA and 107A to add references to a penalty under this Schedule. Schedule 18 para 30 allows for HMRC to publish details of persons who have incurred a penalty or penalties under Sch 18 involving offshore PLR of more than £25,000 in aggregate or persons who have incurred more than four penalties under Sch 18. The £25,000 limit may be varied under regulations made under Sch 18 para 31.

Schedule 18 Part 4 (para 32) provides for interpretation.

Section 68 introduces a new penalty for transactions connected with VAT fraud. It inserts new VATA 1994 ss 69C-69E and makes consequential amendments.

New VATA 1994 s 69C provides that a person is to be liable to a penalty where the person has entered into a transaction involving the making of a supply to or by the person and three further conditions (A to C) are satisfied.

Condition A is that the transaction was connected with the fraudulent evasion of VAT by another person.

Condition B is that the person knew or should have known that the transaction was connected with the fraudulent evasion of VAT by another person.

Condition C is that HMRC have issued a "denial decision" in relation to the supply, preventing the person from exercising or relying on a VAT right in relation to the supply, based on the facts satisfying conditions A and B and applying a relevant principle of EU law.

The amount of the penalty is 30% of the potential lost VAT revenue, and an assessment of the penalty may not be made more than two years after the denial decision is issued

New VATA 1994 s 69D provides for HMRC to allocate all or a proportion of the liability for a penalty under new VATA 1994 s 69C which falls on a company to officers of that company, if the actions of the company which gave rise to the penalty are attributable to an officer or officers. Before doing so, HMRC must inform the officer(s) concerned that they are considering doing so and afford the officer(s) opportunity to make representations. A "company" for these purposes includes a limited-liability partnership and an unincorporated association but excludes partnerships, local authorities and local-authority associations. For bodies corporate, except limited-liability partnerships, the term "officer" means a director, shadow director, manager or secretary. Any member of a limited-liability partnership is considered to be an officer of the partnership.

New VATA 1994 s 69E allows HMRC to publish details of persons found to be liable to the penalty under new VATA 1994 s 69C, where the potential lost VAT revenue exceeds £50,000 and, in the case of officers to whom the liability has been allocated under new VATA 1994 s 69D, of those officers where the amount payable by the officer exceeds £25,000.

Appeals may be made under VATA 1994 s 83(1) as to liability to the penalty under new VATA 1994 s 69C, assessments of the penalty and the amounts of such assessments and against the giving of an allocation decision under new VATA 1994 s 69D or the portion of the penalty allocated.

New VATA 1994 s 69C is to apply in relation to transactions entered into after 15 November 2017.

Information

Section 69 extends HMRC's bulk data-gathering powers exercisable in relation to relevant data-holders under FA 2011 Sch 23 Part 2 to money-service businesses. It inserts new FA 2011 Sch 23 para 13D. This provides that a person who carries on the activities of operating a currency-exchange office, transmitting money or any representation of monetary value by any means, or cashing cheques made payable to customers, is a "relevant person" under the Money Laundering, Terrorist Financing and Transfer of Funds (Information on the Payer) Regulations 2017, and is not an excluded credit institution, is to be a "relevant data-holder" for these purposes. Section 69 is to have effect in relation to relevant data with a bearing on any period.

Part 5 Final

Section 70 updates a reference in FA 2016 s 44(2) to supplementary welfare payments in Northern Ireland.

Section 71 provides a key to interpretation of abbreviations of enactments used in the Act and **s 72** gives the short title.

Zigurds Kronbergs
November 2017

FINANCE (NO 2) ACT 2017

ARRANGEMENT OF SECTIONS

PART 1

DIRECT TAXES

An Act to grant certain duties, to alter other duties, and to amend the law relating to the national debt and the public revenue, and to make further provision in connection with finance.

[16 November 2017]

PART 1

DIRECT TAXES

Income tax: employment and pensions

1 Taxable benefits: time limit for making good

(1) Part 3 of ITEPA 2003 (employment income: earnings and benefits etc treated as earnings) is amended as follows.

(2) In section 87 (cash equivalent of benefit of non-cash voucher)—

(a) in subsection (2)(b), for "to the person incurring it" substitute ", to the person incurring it, on or before 6 July following the relevant tax year", and

(b) after subsection (2) insert—

"(2A) If the voucher is a non-cash voucher other than a cheque voucher, the relevant tax year is—

(a) the tax year in which the cost of provision is incurred, or

(b) if later, the tax year in which the employee receives the voucher.

(2B) If the voucher is a cheque voucher, the relevant tax year is the tax year in which the voucher is handed over in exchange for money, goods or services."

(3) In section 88(3) (time at which cheque voucher treated as handed over), at the beginning insert "For the purposes of subsection (2) and sections 87(2B) and 87A(6),".

(4) In section 94(2) (cash equivalent of benefit of credit-token), in paragraph (b), for the words from "employee" to the end substitute "employee—

(i) to the person incurring it, and

(ii) on or before 6 July following the tax year which contains the occasion in question."

(5) In section 105(2) (cash equivalent of benefit of living accommodation costing £75,000 or less), in paragraph (b), after "made good" insert ", on or before 6 July following the tax year which contains the taxable period,".

(6) In section 106(3) (cash equivalent of benefit of living accommodation costing over £75,000), in paragraph (a), for the words from "paid" to "exceeds" substitute "paid—

(i) by the employee,

(ii) in respect of the accommodation,

(iii) to the person providing it, and

(iv) on or before 6 July following the tax year which contains the taxable period, exceeds".

(7) In section 144 (deduction for payments for private use of car)—

(a) in subsection (1)(b), for "in" substitute "on or before 6 July following",

(b) in subsection (2), after "paid" insert "as mentioned in subsection (1)(b)", and

(c) in subsection (3), after "paid" insert "as mentioned in subsection (1)(b)".

(8) In section 151(2) (when cash equivalent of benefit of car fuel is nil)—

(a) in the words before paragraph (a) omit "in the tax year in question",

(b) in paragraph (a), at the beginning insert "in the tax year in question,", and

(c) in paragraph (b), at the end insert "on or before 6 July following that tax year".

(9) In section 152(2) (car fuel: proportionate reduction of cash equivalent)—

(a) in the words before paragraph (a) omit "for any part of the tax year in question",

(b) in paragraph (a), at the beginning insert "for any part of the tax year in question,",

(c) in paragraph (b), at the beginning insert "for any part of the tax year in question,", and

(d) in paragraph (c)—

   (i) after "employee", in the first place it occurs, insert "—
      (i) for any part of the tax year in question,", and

   (ii) for "and the employee does make good that expense" substitute ", and
      (ii) the employee does make good that expense on or before 6 July following that tax year".

(10) In section 158 (reduction for payments for private use of van)—

(a) in subsection (1)(b), for "in" substitute "on or before 6 July following",

(b) in subsection (2), after "paid" insert "as mentioned in subsection (1)(b)", and

(c) in subsection (3), after "paid" insert "as mentioned in subsection (1)(b)".

(11) In section 162(2) (when cash equivalent of benefit of van fuel is nil)—

(a) in the words before paragraph (a) omit "in the tax year in question",

(b) in paragraph (a), at the beginning insert "in the tax year in question,", and

(c) in paragraph (b), at the end insert "on or before 6 July following that tax year".

(12) In section 163(3) (van fuel: proportionate reduction of cash equivalent)—

(a) in the words before paragraph (a) omit "for any part of the tax year in question",

(b) in paragraph (a), at the beginning insert "for any part of the tax year in question,",

(c) in paragraph (b), at the beginning insert "for any part of the tax year in question,", and

(d) in paragraph (c)—

   (i) after "employee", in the first place it occurs, insert "—
      (i) for any part of the tax year in question,", and

   (ii) for "and the employee does make good that expense" substitute ", and
      (ii) the employee does make good that expense on or before 6 July following that tax year".

(13) In section 203(2) (cash equivalent of benefit treated as earnings), for "to the persons providing the benefit" substitute ", to the persons providing the benefit, on or before 6 July following the tax year in which it is provided".

(14) The amendments made by this section have effect for the purpose of calculating income tax charged for the tax year 2017–18 or any subsequent tax year.

GENERAL NOTE

Making good all or part of the cost of providing a benefit in kind reduces the amount of income tax and class 1A NICs payable on the benefit. HMRC's Employment Income Manual at EIM21120 considers the meaning of "making good".

HMRC consulted in 2016 on aligning the time limits for making good after the Office of Tax Simplification, employers and representative bodies reported confusion and practical difficulties in complying with the existing rules. F(No 2)A 2017 s 1 amends the benefits code (other than the rules for beneficial loans) to set a time limit of 6 July following the tax year.

ITEPA 2003 Pt 3 (employment income: earnings and benefits etc treated as earnings) is amended with effect for benefits (other than loans) taxable in 2017/18 and subsequent years.

The changes do not alter the time limits for making good in relation to benefits that are payrolled, i.e. accounted for in real time via PAYE. (See Income Tax (Pay As You Earn) Regulations, SI 2003/2682, regs 61A–61M as amended.)

HMRC published draft guidance on the changes on 20 March 2017 (see www.gov.uk/government/publications/changes-to-the-alignment-of-dates-for-making-good-on-benefits-in-kind).

Vouchers and credit tokens (ITEPA 2003 Pt 3 Ch 4)

Section 1(2) amends ITEPA 2003 s 87(2)(b) (benefit of non-cash voucher treated as earnings) so that the cash equivalent of the benefit is reduced by the amount made good on or before 6 July following the relevant tax year.

The relevant tax year for a cheque voucher is the year in which the voucher is handed over in exchange for money, goods or services. For other non-cash vouchers, the relevant tax year is that in which the cost of provision is incurred or, if later, that in which the employee receives the voucher.

There is a consequential amendment to ITEPA 2003 s 88(3) in relation to cheque vouchers.

Section 1(4) amends ITEPA 2003 s 94(2) (benefit of credit token treated as earnings) so that the cash equivalent of the benefit is reduced by the amount made good on or before 6 July following the tax year which contains the occasion on which the credit token is used to obtain money, goods or services.

Living accommodation (ITEPA 2003 Pt 3 Ch 5)

Section 1(5) amends ITEPA 2003 s 105(2) (cash equivalent: cost of accommodation not over £75,000) so that the cash equivalent of the benefit is reduced by the amount made good on or before 6 July following the tax year which contains the "taxable period" (defined in ITEPA 2003 s 102(2)).

Section 1(6) amends ITEPA 2003 s 106(3) (cash equivalent: cost of accommodation over £75,000) so that, to be counted towards any "excess rent" deductible in the step 4 of the calculation in ITEPA 2003 s 105(2), the rent paid by the employee must be paid on or before 6 July following the tax year which contains the taxable period.

Cars and vans (ITEPA 2003 Pt 3 Ch 6)

Cars

ITEPA 2003 s 144(1) (deduction for payments for private use) provides for a deduction to be made at step 8 in ITEPA 2003 s 121(1) (method of calculating the cash equivalent of the benefit of a car for a tax year) if the employee (a) is required in the tax year to pay an amount for private use of the car and (b) pays that amount in that year. Section 1(7) relaxes this rule so that the deduction is made if the employee pays the amount on or before 6 July following that year. There are consequential amendments to ITEPA 2003 s 144(2), (3).

ITEPA 2003 s 151 (car fuel: nil cash equivalent) provides that the cash equivalent of the benefit of car fuel treated as earnings is nil if condition A or B in that section is met. Condition A is met if, in the tax year in question, the employee (a) is required to make good the whole of the expense incurred in the provision of fuel for private use and (b) does make good that expense. Section 1(8) relaxes this rule so that condition A is met if (a) in the tax year in question the employee is required to make good the whole of the expense and (b) the employee makes good that expense on or before 6 July following that tax year.

ITEPA 2003 s 152(2) (car fuel: proportionate reduction of cash equivalent) provides for proportionate reduction where the condition in s 152(2)(a), (b) or (c) is met. Section 1(9) relaxes this rule so that the condition in s 152(2)(c) is met if: (a) for any part of the tax year in question the employee is required to make good the whole of the expense, and (b) the employee makes good that expense on or before 6 July following that tax year.

Vans

ITEPA 2003 s 158(1) (reduction for payments for private use) provides that the cash equivalent of the benefit of a van for a tax year under ITEPA 2003 s 155 – after any reduction for periods when the van is either unavailable or shared – is reduced if the employee: (a) is required in that year to pay an amount of money for that use, and (b) pays that amount in that year. Section 1(10) relaxes this rule so that the deduction is made if the employee pays the amount on or before 6 July following that year. There are consequential amendments to ITEPA 2003 s 158(2), (3).

ITEPA 2003 s 162 (van fuel: nil cash equivalent) provides that the cash equivalent of the benefit of the fuel is nil if condition A or B in that section is met. Condition A is met if, in the tax year in question, the employee (a) is required to make good the whole of the expense incurred in the provision of fuel for private use and (b) does make good that expense. Section 1(11) relaxes this rule so that condition A is met if: (a) in the tax year in question the employee is required to make good the whole of the expense, and (b) the employee makes good that expense on or before 6 July following that tax year.

ITEPA 2003 s 163(3) (van fuel: proportionate reduction of cash equivalent) provides for proportionate reduction where the condition in s 163(3)(a), (b) or (c) is met. Section 1(12) relaxes this rule so that the condition in s 163(3)(c) is met if: (a) for any part of the tax year in question the employee is required to make good the whole of the expense, and (b) the employee makes good that expense on or before 6 July following that tax year.

Residual liability

ITEPA 2003 Pt 3 Ch 10 sets out the "residual liability to charge" for an employment-related benefit that is not caught by the provisions of Chapters 3 to 9. ITEPA 2003 s 203(2) provides that the cash equivalent of such a benefit is the cost of the benefit less any part of that cost made good by the employee.

HMRC guidance at EIM21121 notes that the existing legislation sets no time limit on making good, but indicates that HMRC will not object to a "belated" making good if it is done within a reasonable time of the employee becoming aware that the tax charge can be reduced in this way. What constitutes a "reasonable time" will depend on the facts of the case, according to the guidance.

Section 1(13) amends ITEPA 2003 s 203(2) so that the cash equivalent is reduced by the amount made good on or before 6 July following the tax year in which the benefit is provided.

2 Taxable benefits: ultra-low emission vehicles

(1) ITEPA 2003 is amended as follows.

(2) In section 139 (car with a CO_2 emissions figure: the appropriate percentage), for subsections (1) to (6) substitute—

"(1) The appropriate percentage for a year for a car with a CO_2 emissions figure of less than 75 is determined in accordance with the following table.

Car	Appropriate percentage
Car with CO2 emissions figure of 0	2%
Car with CO2 emissions figure of 1 – 50	
Car with electric range figure of 130 or more	2%
Car with electric range figure of 70 – 129	5%
Car with electric range figure of 40 – 69	8%
Car with electric range figure of 30 – 39	12%
Car with electric range figure of less than 30	14%
Car with CO2 emissions figure of 51 – 54	15%
Car with CO2 emissions figure of 55 – 59	16%
Car with CO2 emissions figure of 60 – 64	17%
Car with CO2 emissions figure of 65 – 69	18%
Car with CO2 emissions figure of 70 – 74	19%

(2) For the purposes of subsection (1) and the table, if a CO_2 emissions figure or an electric range figure is not a whole number, round it down to the nearest whole number.

(3) The appropriate percentage for a year for a car with a CO_2 emissions figure of 75 or more is whichever is the lesser of—

(a) 20% plus one percentage point for each 5 grams per kilometre driven by which the CO_2 emissions figure exceeds 75, and

(b) 37%.

(4) For the purposes of subsection (3), if a CO_2 emissions figure is not a multiple of 5, round it down to the nearest multiple of 5.

(5) In this section, an "electric range figure" is the number of miles which is the equivalent of the number of kilometres specified in an EC certificate of conformity, an EC type-approval certificate or a UK approval certificate on the basis of which a car is registered, as being the maximum distance for which the car can be driven in electric mode without recharging the battery."

(3) In section 140 (car without a CO_2 emissions figure: the appropriate percentage)—

    (a) in subsection (2), in the table —

        (i) for "23%" substitute "24%", and

        (ii) for "34%" substitute "35%";

    (b) in subsection (3)(a), for "16%" substitute "2%".

(4) In section 142(2) (car first registered before 1 January 1998: the appropriate percentage), in the table—

    (a) for "23%" substitute "24%", and

    (b) for "34%" substitute "35%".

(5) Omit subsection 170(3).

(6) The amendments made by this section have effect for the tax year 2020–21 and subsequent tax years.

GENERAL NOTE

ITEPA 2003 s 139 (car with a CO_2 emissions figure: the appropriate percentage) sets out the percentage of the car's list price to be used as the basis of the income tax charge in ITEPA 2003 s 120 (benefit of car treated as earnings).

Autumn Statement 2016 announced, following consultation, that with effect from 2020/21 new, lower company car tax bands would be introduced to provide stronger incentives for the purchase of ultra-low emission vehicles.

Section 2 sets out a new, graduated scale of tax bands to be used in calculating the taxable benefit of a company car from 2020/21. Some of the lower bands will be based on the maximum distance the car can travel in pure electric mode without recharging the battery or using the combustion engine of the plug-in vehicle, as well as the CO_2 emissions figure.

The percentage depends on the car's CO_2 emissions figure. The appropriate percentages for cars for the tax years 2017/18 to 2020/21, incorporating the changes made by FA 2015 s 8, FA 2016 s 8 and F(No 2)A 2017 s 2, are set out in the tables below. (See further below regarding diesel cars.)

Appropriate percentages: 2017/18 to 2019/20

$CO2$ emissions (g/km)	Appropriate percentage		
	2017/18	*2018/19*	*2019/20*
up to 50	9%	13%	16%
51–75	13%	16%	19%
76–94	17%	19%	22%
95–99	18%	20%	23%
100–104	19%	21%	24%
105–109	20%	22%	25%
110–114	21%	23%	26%
115–119	22%	24%	27%
120–124	23%	25%	28%
125–129	24%	26%	29%

CO2 emissions (g/km)	Appropriate percentage		
	2017/18	*2018/19*	*2019/20*
130–134	25%	27%	30%
135–139	26%	28%	31%
140–144	27%	29%	32%
145–149	28%	30%	33%
150–154	29%	31%	34%
155–159	30%	32%	35%
160–164	31%	33%	36%
165–169	32%	34%	37%
170–174	33%	35%	37%
175–179	34%	36%	37%
180–184	35%	37%	37%
185–189	36%	37%	37%
190 or more	37%	37%	37%

Appropriate percentages: 2020/21

CO2 emissions (g/km)	Electric range (miles)	Appropriate percentage
		2020/21
Zero		2%
1–50	130 or more	2%
1–50	70–129	5%
1–50	40–69	8%
1–50	30–39	12%
1–50	less than 30	14%
51–54		15%
55–59		16%
60–64		17%
65–69		18%
70–74		19%
75–79		20%
80–84		21%
85–89		22%
90–94		23%
95–99		24%
100–104		25%
105–109		26%
110–114		27%

CO2 emissions (g/km)	Electric range (miles)	Appropriate percentage
115–119		28%
120–124		29%
125–129		30%
130–134		31%
135–139		32%
140–144		33%
145–149		34%
150–154		35%
155–159		36%
160 or more		37%

The electric range is the number of miles equivalent to the number of kilometres specified, as set out in section 1(5), as being the maximum distance for which the car can be driven in electric mode without recharging the battery.

As a result of the changes taking effect from 2020/21 there will no longer be a "relevant threshold", and the enabling power in ITEPA 2003 s 170(3) allowing HM Treasury to vary that threshold will be repealed.

The provisions of ITEPA 2003 s 139 remain subject to ITEPA 2003 s 141, which applies a supplement of three percentage points (subject to the maximum percentage of 37%) for diesel cars.

Section 1(3) amends ITEPA 2003 s 140 (car without a CO emissions figure: the appropriate percentage), and section 1(4) amends ITEPA 2003 s 140 (car first registered before 1 January 1998: the appropriate percentage), specifying the percentages applicable for 2020/21 onwards.

3 Pensions advice

(1) In Chapter 9 of Part 4 of ITEPA 2003, after section 308B insert—

"308C Provision of pensions advice: limited exemption

(1) No liability to income tax arises in respect of—

(a) the provision of relevant pensions advice to an employee or former or prospective employee, or

(b) the payment or reimbursement of costs incurred, by or in respect of an employee or former or prospective employee, in obtaining relevant pensions advice, if Condition A or B is met.

(2) But subsection (1) does not apply in relation to a person in a tax year so far as the value of the exemption in the person's case in that year exceeds £500.

(3) The "value of the exemption", in relation to a person and a tax year, is the amount exempted by subsection (1) from income tax in the person's case in that year, disregarding subsection (2) for this purpose.

(4) If in a tax year there is in relation to an individual more than one person who is an employer or former employer, subsections (1) to (3) apply in relation to the individual as employee or former or prospective employee of any one of those persons separately from their application in relation to the individual as employee or former or prospective employee of any other of those persons.

(5) "Relevant pensions advice", in relation to a person, means information, or advice, in connection with—

(a) the person's pension arrangements, or

(b) the use of the person's pension funds.

(6) Condition A is that the relevant pensions advice, or payment or reimbursement, is provided under a scheme that is open—

(a) to the employer's employees generally, or

(b) generally to the employer's employees at a particular location.

(7) Condition B is that the relevant pensions advice, or payment or reimbursement, is provided under a scheme that is open generally to the employer's employees, or generally to those of the employer's employees at a particular location, who—

(a) have reached the minimum qualifying age, or

(b) meet the ill-health condition.

(8) The "minimum qualifying age", in relation to an employee, means the employee's relevant pension age less 5 years.

(9) "Relevant pension age", in relation to an employee, means—

(a) where paragraph 22 or 23 of Schedule 36 to FA 2004 applies in relation to the employee and a registered pension scheme of which the employee is a member, the employee's protected pension age (see paragraph 22(8) and 23(8) of Schedule 36 to FA 2004), or

(b) in any other case, the employee's normal minimum pension age, as defined by section 279(1) of FA 2004.

(10) The "ill-health condition" is met by an employee if the employer is satisfied, on the basis of evidence provided by a registered medical practitioner, that the employee is (and will continue to be) incapable of carrying on his or her occupation because of physical or mental impairment."

(2) In section 228 of ITEPA 2003 (effect of exemptions on liability under provisions outside Part 2 of ITEPA 2003), in subsection (2), after paragraph (da) insert—

"(db) section 308C (provision of pensions advice),".

(3) Regulation 5 of the Income Tax (Exemption of Minor Benefits) Regulations 2002 (S.I. 2002/205) (exemption in respect of the provision of pensions advice) is revoked.

(4) In regulation 2 of the Income Tax (Exemption of Minor Benefits) (Amendment) Regulations 2004 (S.I. 2004/3087) omit the inserted regulation 5.

(5) The amendments made by this section have effect for the tax year 2017–18 and subsequent tax years.

GENERAL NOTE

Section 3 introduces for 2017/18 onwards a new exemption from income tax on employment income for "relevant pensions advice". This is a broader and more generous exemption than the previous exemption for pensions advice. It was announced at Budget 2016, and at Autumn Statement 2016 the government said it would allow advice "not only on pensions, but also on the general financial and tax issues relating to pensions".

Section 3(1) inserts new ITEPA 2003 s 308C, which provides that where condition A or condition B is met (see below) no liability arises in respect of: (a) the provision of relevant pensions advice to an employee, or (b) the payment or reimbursement of costs incurred, by or in respect of an employee, in obtaining relevant pensions advice. The exemption extends to provision for a former or prospective employee.

The value of the exemption is limited to £500 in the relevant tax year. If the individual has two employments, the exemption applies separately to each.

"Relevant pensions advice" is information or advice in connection with the employee's pension arrangements or the use of the employee's pension funds.

Condition A is that the relevant pensions advice (or payment or reimbursement) is provided under a scheme open to the employer's employees generally, or generally to the employer's employees at a particular location.

Condition B is that the relevant pensions advice (or payment or reimbursement) is provided under a scheme open generally to the employer's employees, or generally to those of the employer's employees at a particular location, who: (a) have reached a minimum qualifying age – the employee's relevant pension age less five years, or (b) meet an ill-health condition.

New ITEPA 2003 s 308(9), (10) define "relevant pension age" and "ill-health condition" for this purpose.

Regulation 5 of the Income Tax (Exemption of Minor Benefits) Regulations, SI 2002/205 is revoked. This provided an exemption of up to £150 a year in relation to pension information and advice.

4 Legal expenses etc

(1) ITEPA 2003 is amended as follows.

(2) In section 346 (deduction for employee liabilities)—

(a) in the heading, at the end insert "and expenses",
(b) after paragraph B (in subsection (1)) insert—

"**BA** Payment of any costs or expenses not falling within paragraph B which are incurred in connection with the employee giving evidence about matters related to the employment in, or for the purposes of—

(a) a proceeding or other process (whether or not involving the employee), or
(b) an investigation (whether or not likely to lead to any proceeding or other process involving the employee).

BB Payment of any costs or expenses not falling within paragraph B or BA which are incurred in connection with a proceeding or other process, or an investigation, in which—

(a) acts of the employee related to the employment, or
(b) any other matters related to the employment,

are being or are likely to be considered.",

(c) in paragraph C(b) (in subsection (1)), after "B" insert ", BA or BB",
(d) in subsection (2) for "or B" substitute "B, BA or BB",
(e) in subsection (2A), for "paragraph A, B or C" substitute "any of paragraphs A to C", and
(f) after subsection (3) insert—

"(4) In this section and section 349—

(a) "acts" includes failures to act and acts are "related to the employment" if the employee was acting—

(i) in the employee's capacity as holder of the employment, or
(ii) in any other capacity in which the employee was acting in the performance of the duties of the employment,

(b) "giving evidence" includes making a formal or informal statement or answering questions,
(c) "proceeding or other process" includes any civil, criminal or arbitration proceedings, any disciplinary or regulatory proceedings of any kind and any process operated for resolving disputes or adjudicating on complaints, and
(d) references to a proceeding or other process or an investigation include a reference to a proceeding or other process or an investigation that is likely to take place."

(3) In section 349 (section 346: meaning of "qualifying insurance contract"), in subsection (2)—

(a) after paragraph (c) insert—

"(ca) the payment of costs or expenses incurred in connection with an employee giving evidence about matters related to the employee's employment in, or for the purposes of—

(i) a proceeding or other process (whether or not involving the employee), or
(ii) an investigation (whether or not likely to lead to any proceeding or other process involving the employee),

(cb) the payment of any costs or expenses incurred in connection with a proceeding or other process, or an investigation, in which—

(i) acts of an employee related to the employment, or
(ii) any other matters related to the employment of an employee,

are being or are likely to be considered,", and

(b) in subsection (2)(d), after "(c)" insert ", (ca) or (cb)".

(4) In section 409 (payments and benefits on termination of employment etc: exception for payments and benefits in respect of employee liabilities and indemnity insurance)—

(a) in the heading, for "employee liabilities" substitute "certain legal expenses etc", and
(b) in subsection (3), at the end insert "or by the employer or former employer on behalf of the individual".

(5) In section 410 (payments and benefits on termination of employment etc: exception for certain payments and benefits received by personal representatives of deceased individual)—

(a) in the heading for "employee liabilities" substitute "certain legal expenses etc", and

(b) in subsection (3), at the end insert "or by the former employer on behalf of the individual's personal representatives".

(6) In section 558 (deductions for liabilities of former employees: meaning of "deductible payment")—

(a) after paragraph B (in subsection (1)) insert—

"BA Payment of any costs or expenses not falling within paragraph B which are incurred in connection with the former employee giving evidence about matters related to the former employment in, or for the purposes of—

(a) a proceeding or other process (whether or not involving the former employee), or

(b) an investigation (whether or not likely to lead to any proceeding or other process involving the former employee).

BB Payment of any costs or expenses not falling within paragraph B or BA which are incurred in connection with a proceeding or other process, or an investigation, in which—

(a) acts of the former employee related to the former employment, or

(b) any other matters related to the former employment,

are being or are likely to be considered.", and

(b) in paragraph C(b) (in subsection (1)), after "B" insert ", BA or BB",

(c) in subsection (2), for "or B" substitute "B, BA or BB",

(d) after subsection (3) insert—

"(4) In this section and section 560—

(a) "acts" includes failures to act and acts are "related to the former employment" if the former employee was acting—

(i) in the employee's capacity as holder of the former employment, or

(ii) in any other capacity in which the former employee was acting in the performance of the duties of that employment,

(b) "giving evidence" includes making a formal or informal statement or answering questions,

(c) "proceeding or other process" includes any civil, criminal or arbitration proceedings, any disciplinary or regulatory proceedings of any kind and any process operated for resolving disputes or adjudicating on complaints, and

(d) references to a proceeding or other process or an investigation include a reference to a proceeding or other process or an investigation that is likely to take place."

(7) In section 560 (section 558: meaning of "qualifying insurance contract"), in subsection (2)—

(a) after paragraph (c) insert—

"(ca) the payment of costs or expenses incurred in connection with a former employee giving evidence about matters related to the former employment in, or for the purposes of—

(i) a proceeding or other process (whether or not involving the former employee), or

(ii) an investigation (whether or not likely to lead to any proceeding or other process involving the former employee).

(cb) the payment of any costs or expenses incurred in connection with a proceeding or other process, or an investigation, in which—

(i) acts of a former employee related to the employment, or

(ii) any other matters related to the former employment of a former employee,

are being or are likely to be considered,", and

(b) in paragraph (d), after "(c)" insert ", (ca) or (cb)".

(8) The amendments made by this section have effect in relation to the tax year 2017–18 and subsequent tax years.

GENERAL NOTE

Section 4 amends ITEPA 2003 to extend from 2017/18 the scope of existing income tax exemptions that apply where an employer funds an employee's legal costs or indemnity insurance (see ITEPA 2003 ss 346–350, 409–410 and 555–564).

While the existing rules cover only legal support provided to employees who have had allegations made against them, the new rules apply in cases where no allegation has been made.

In ITEPA 2003 s 346 (deduction for employee liabilities), the heading is extended and new paragraphs BA and BB are inserted in subsection (1) so that a deduction from earnings from an employment is allowed for payment of:

– any costs or expenses not falling within the existing paragraph B that are incurred in connection with the employee giving evidence about matters related to the employment in, or for the purposes of: (a) a proceeding or other process (whether or not involving the employee), or (b) an investigation (whether or not likely to lead to any proceeding or other process involving the employee) (ITEPA 2003 s 246(1), para BA);

– payment of any costs or expenses not falling within the existing paragraph B or new paragraph BA that are incurred in connection with a proceeding or other process, or an investigation, in which either: (a) acts of the employee related to the employment, or (b) any other matters related to the employment are being, or are likely to be, considered (ITEPA 2003 s 246(1), para BB).

A new subsection (4) in ITEPA 2003 s 346 defines a number of expressions for this purpose.

Corresponding changes are made in ITEPA 2003 s 349 (meaning of "qualifying insurance contract"), ITEPA 2003 s 558 (deductions for liabilities of former employees: meaning of "deductible payment") and ITEPA s 560 (meaning of "qualifying insurance contract").

In ITEPA 2003 s 409 (termination payments, exception for payments and benefits in respect of employee liabilities and indemnity insurance), the heading is modified and condition A is amended so that relief is available where the amount is paid by the employer or former employer on behalf of the individual.

In ITEPA 2003 s 410 (termination payments, exception for payments and benefits in respect of employee liabilities and indemnity insurance: individual deceased) the heading is modified and condition A is amended so that relief is available where the amount is paid by the former employer on behalf of the individual's personal representatives.

5 Termination payments etc: amounts chargeable on employment income

(1) ITEPA 2003 is amended in accordance with subsections (2) to (9).

(2) In section 7(5) (list of provisions under which amounts are treated as earnings), before the "or" at the end of paragraph (c) insert—

"(ca) section 402B (termination payments, and other benefits, that cannot benefit from section 403 threshold),".

(3) Before section 403 (charge on payments and benefits in excess of £30,000 threshold) insert—

"402A Split of payments and other benefits between sections 402B and 403

(1) In this Chapter "termination award" means a payment or other benefit to which this Chapter applies because of section 401(1)(a).

(2) Section 402B (termination awards not benefiting from threshold treated as earnings) applies to termination awards to the extent determined under section 402C.

(3) Section 403 (charge on payment or benefit where threshold applies) applies to termination awards so far as they are not ones to which section 402B applies.

(4) Section 403 also applies to payments and other benefits to which this Chapter applies because of section 401(1)(b) or (c) (change in duties or earnings).

402B Termination awards not benefiting from threshold to be treated as earnings

(1) The amount of a termination award to which this section applies is treated as an amount of earnings of the employee, or former employee, from the employment.

(2) See also section 7(3)(b) and (5)(ca) (which cause amounts treated as earnings under this section to be included in general earnings).

(3) Section 403(3) (when benefits are received) does not apply in relation to payments or other benefits to which this section applies.

402C The termination awards to which section 402B applies

(1) This section has effect for the purpose of identifying the extent to which section 402B applies to termination awards in respect of the termination of the employment of the employee.

(2) In this section "relevant termination award" means a termination award that is neither—

    (a) a redundancy payment, nor

    (b) so much of an approved contractual payment as is equal to or less than the amount which would have been due if a redundancy payment had been payable.

(3) If the post-employment notice pay (see section 402D) in respect of the termination is greater than, or equal to, the total amount of the relevant termination awards in respect of the termination, section 402B applies to all of those relevant termination awards.

(4) If the post-employment notice pay in respect of the termination is less than the total amount of the relevant termination awards in respect of the termination but is not nil—

    (a) section 402B applies to a part of those relevant termination awards, and

    (b) the amount of that part is equal to the post-employment notice pay.

(5) Section 309(4) to (6) (meaning of "redundancy payment" and "approved contractual payment" etc) apply for the purposes of subsection (2) as they apply for the purposes of section 309.

402D "Post-employment notice pay"

(1) "The post-employment notice pay" in respect of a termination is (subject to subsection (11)) given by—

$$((BP \times D) / P) - T$$

where—

    BP, D and P are given by subsections (3) to (7), and

    T is the total of the amounts of any payment or benefit received in connection with the termination which—

        (a) would fall within section 401(1)(a) but for section 401(3),

        (b) is taxable as earnings under Chapter 1 of Part 3,

        (c) is not pay in respect of holiday entitlement for a period before the employment ends, and

        (d) is not a bonus payable for termination of the employment.

(2) If the amount given by the formula in subsection (1) is a negative amount, the post-employment notice pay is nil.

(3) Subject to subsections (5) and (6)—

    BP is the employee's basic pay (see subsection (7)) from the employment in respect of the last pay period of the employee to end before the trigger date,

    P is the number of days in that pay period, and

    D is the number of days in the post-employment notice period.

(4) See section 402E for the meaning of "trigger date" and "post-employment notice period".

(5) If there is no pay period of the employee which ends before the trigger date then—

    BP is the employee's basic pay from the employment in respect of the period starting with the first day of the employment and ending with the trigger date,

    P is the number of days in that period, and

    D is the number of days in the post-employment notice period.

(6) If the last pay period of the employee to end before the trigger date is a month, the minimum notice (see section 402E) is given by contractual terms and is expressed to be a whole number of months, and the post-employment notice period is equal in length to the minimum notice or is otherwise a whole number of months, then—

    BP is the employee's basic pay from the employment in respect of the last pay period of the employee to end before the trigger date,

    P is 1, and

    D is the length of the post-employment notice period expressed in months.

(7) In this section "basic pay" means—

    (a) employment income of the employee from the employment but disregarding—

        (i) any amount received by way of overtime, bonus, commission, gratuity or allowance,

        (ii) any amount received in connection with the termination of the employment,

        (iii) any amount treated as earnings under Chapters 2 to 10 of Part 3 (the benefits code) or which would be so treated apart from section 64,

(iv) any amount which is treated as earnings under Chapter 12 of Part 3 (amounts treated as earnings),

  (v) any amount which counts as employment income by virtue of Part 7 (income relating to securities and securities options), and

(vi) any employment-related securities that constitute earnings under Chapter 1 of Part 3 (earnings), and

(b) any amount which the employee has given up the right to receive but which would have fallen within paragraph (a) had the employee not done so.

(8) In subsection (7) "employment-related securities" has the same meaning as it has in Chapter 1 of Part 7 (see section 421B).

(9) The Treasury may by regulations amend this section for the purpose of altering the meaning of "basic pay".

(10) A statutory instrument containing regulations under subsection (9) may not be made unless a draft of it has been laid before, and approved by a resolution of, the House of Commons.

(11) Where the purpose, or one of the purposes, of any arrangements is the avoidance of tax by causing the post-employment notice pay calculated under subsection (1) to be less than it would otherwise be, the post-employment notice pay is to be treated as the amount which the post-employment notice pay would have been but for the arrangements.

(12) In subsection (11) "arrangements" includes any scheme, arrangement or understanding of any kind, whether or not legally enforceable, involving a single transaction or two or more transactions.

402E Meaning of "trigger date" and "post-employment notice period" in section 402D

(1) Subsections (2) and (4) to (6) have effect for the purposes of section 402D (and subsection (4) has effect also for the purposes of this section).

(2) The "trigger date" is—

(a) if the termination is not a notice case, the last day of the employment, and

(b) if the termination is a notice case, the day the notice is given.

(3) For the purposes of this section, the termination is a "notice case" if the employer or employee gives notice to the other to terminate the employment, and here it does not matter—

(a) whether the notice is more or less than, or the same as, the minimum notice, or

(b) if the employment ends before the notice expires.

(4) The "minimum notice" is the minimum notice required to be given by the employer to terminate the employee's employment by notice in accordance with the law and contractual terms effective—

(a) where the termination is not a notice case—

  (i) immediately before the employment ends, or

  (ii) where the employment ends by agreement entered into after the start of the employment, immediately before the agreement is entered into, and

(b) where the termination is a notice case, immediately before the notice is given.

(5) The "post-employment notice period" is the period—

(a) beginning at the end of the last day of the employment, and

(b) ending with the earliest lawful termination date.

(But see subsection (8) for provision about limited-term contracts.)

(6) If the earliest lawful termination date is, or precedes, the last day of the employment, the number of days in the post-employment period is nil.

(7) "The earliest lawful termination date" is the last day of the period which—

(a) is equal in length to the minimum notice, and

(b) begins at the end of the trigger date.

(8) In the case of a contract of employment which is a limited-term contract and which does not include provision for termination by notice by the employer, the post-employment notice period is the period—

(a) beginning at the end of the last day of the employment, and

(b) ending with the day of the occurrence of the limiting event.

(9) If, in a case to which subsection (8) applies, on the last day of the employment the day of the occurrence of the limiting event is not ascertained or ascertainable (because, for example, the limiting event is the performance of a task), then subsection (8) has effect as if for paragraph (b) there were substituted—

"(b) ending with the day on which notice would have expired if the employer had, on the last day of the employment, given to the employee the minimum notice required to terminate the contract under section 86 of the Employment Rights Act 1996 (assuming that that section applies to the employment)."

(10) In this section "limited-term contract" and "limiting event" have the same meaning as in the Employment Rights Act 1996 (see section 235(2A) and (2B))."

(4) In section 403 (charges on payments and benefits which can benefit from threshold)—

(a) in subsection (1), for "Chapter" substitute "section",
(b) in subsection (3), after "Chapter" insert "(but see section 402B(3))",
(c) in subsection (4), for the words from "when" to "exceeds" substitute
"when aggregated with—

(a) other payments or benefits in respect of the employee or former employee that are payments or benefits to which this section applies, and
(b) other payments or benefits in respect of the employee or former employee that are payments or benefits—

(i) received in the tax year 2017–18 or an earlier tax year, and
(ii) to which this Chapter applied in the tax year of receipt,
it exceeds",

(d) in subsection (5)(a), for "Chapter" substitute "section",
(e) in subsection (6), after "employment income" insert "or, as the case may be, in relation to whom section 402B(1) provides for an amount to be treated as an amount of earnings", and
(f) in the heading, at the end insert "where threshold applies".

(5) In section 404 (how the threshold applies)—

(a) in subsection (3)(b) (meaning of "termination or change date"), for "this Chapter" substitute "section 403", and
(b) after subsection (5) insert—

"(6) In subsection (3)(b), the reference to a payment or other benefit to which section 403 applies includes a reference to a payment or other benefit—

(a) received in the tax year 2017–18 or an earlier tax year, and
(b) to which this Chapter applied in the tax year of receipt."

(6) After section 404A insert—

"404B   Power to vary threshold

(1) The Treasury may by regulations amend the listed provisions by substituting, for the amount for the time being mentioned in those provisions, a different amount.

(2) The listed provisions are—

subsections (1), (4) and (5) of section 403, and
subsections (1), (4) and (5) of section 404 and its heading.

(3) Regulations under this section may include transitional provision.

(4) A statutory instrument containing regulations under this section which reduce the mentioned amount may not be made unless a draft of it has been laid before, and approved by a resolution of, the House of Commons."

(7) In section 406 (exception in cases of death, injury or disability)—

(a) the existing text becomes subsection (1), and
(b) after that subsection insert—

"(2) Although "injury" in subsection (1) includes psychiatric injury, it does not include injured feelings."

(8) In section 414(2) (proportionate reduction for foreign service in certain cases), for "otherwise count as employment income under this Chapter" substitute "otherwise—

(a) be treated as earnings by section 402B(1), or
(b) count as employment income as a result of section 403".

(9) In section 717(4) (regulations etc not subject to negative procedure), before "or section 681F(3)" insert ", section 402D(10) (meaning of basic pay for purpose of calculating charge on termination award), section 404B(4) (reduction of tax-free threshold for employment-termination etc payments)".

(10) The amendments made by this section have effect for the tax year 2018–19 and subsequent tax years.

GENERAL NOTE

Before delving into the legislative provisions, it is worth summarising the key changes that will be most relevant to most employers day to day. A full explanation is provided in the comments on the specific provisions, and a number of worked examples are also provided. In short:

Tax

(1) Non-contractual payments in lieu of notice (PILON) will cease to benefit from the £30,000 threshold and will be taxable as earnings. A statutory formula is to be applied to determine the "post-employment notice period" and the amount of "post employment notice pay" (PENP).
(2) Many payments made on the termiation of fixed term contracts are likely to be significantly impacted by the new treatment of PENP.
(3) The treatment of contractual PILON remains unchanged (already earnings subject to ITEPA 2003 s 62).
(4) Injury to feelings payments will no longer qualify for relief under ITEPA 2003 s 406 as payments on account of injury or disability.
(5) A subsequent Finance Act (FA 2018) rather than this Finance Act, will significantly curtail foreign service relief (this will be considered separately at that time).

NIC

The comments on NIC below are made in advance of the NIC Bill which has been delayed and so could be subject to change. At the time of writing, my current understanding is that one or both of the following provisions may now come into effect from 6 April 2019 (rather than 2018 as originally intended):

(1) Non contractual PILON will be liable to primary and secondary class 1 NIC.
(2) Qualifying termination payments will be liable to employer-only NIC (probably within Class 1A) to the extent they exceed £30,000.

ITEPA 2003 s 402A

New ITEPA 2003 s 402A splits termination awards between those which benefit from the exempt threshold (for the time being this is unchanged at £30,000) and those which do not. The latter will be subject to new s 402B and this is primarily intended to cause non-contractual payments in lieu of notice to become taxable as earnings without offset of the exempt threshold.

ITEPA 2003 s 402A(3), (4) simply signpost that s 403 continues to apply to other payments and benefits on termination of employment and supposedly also on a change in duties or earnings assuming, as always, they are not taxable elsewhere in ITEPA.

Relationship between "earnings" and "specific employment income"

ITEPA 2003 s 7(4), (6) deems any payment which counts as employment income under Part 6 (including termination payments) and Parts 7 and 7A, to be specific employment income, and consequently employment income under s 7(2).

The insertion of new para (ca) in ITEPA 2003 s 7(5) now treats payments which fall under s 402B (those which cannot benefit from the s 403 threshold) as "amounts treated as earnings", which are therefore now treated as general earnings under s 7(3)(b), as well as specific employment income.

It will need to be considered whether this has any unforeseen ramifications in legislation elsewhere. For example, although the following point may well be a "minority sport", in the formulae in FA 2004 Sch 34 involving TE and TSI, Part 6 payments could now be included in both TE and TSI, whereas previously they would only have been included in TSI. Ideally, these formulae should be amended to clarify that where a payment is included in both TE and TSI, it should only be counted once. Presumably HMRC would be agreeable to this in the meantime?

ITEPA 2003 s 402B

An amount of a termination award which is subject to new s 402B, is treated as earnings under this provision. The extent to which s 402B applies is determined by s 402C. Please also see the comments on the amendment to s 7(5) above.

Curiously, ITEPA 2003 s 402B(3) disapplies s 403(3) in relation to cash and non-cash benefits which are subject to s 402B. Section 403(3) would otherwise determine the time when such benefits are treated as received, which now seems less clear.

ITEPA 2003 s 402C

As noted above, new ITEPA 2003 s 402C determines the extent to which amounts within a termination award are treated as earnings under 402B, also referencing new s 402(D) and in turn s 402(E). The new sections also introduce a number of new terms with which it will be important to become very familiar when considering the tax treatment of termination payments going forward.

ITEPA 2003 s 402C(2) identifies a "relevant termination award" (RTA) as a termination award which is neither a redundancy payment nor an equivalent or lesser approved contractual payment. Note that these terms are defined in ITEPA 2003 s 309(4) to (6), the latter being more relevant in the public sector.

ITEPA 2003 s 402(C)(3) cross-references the "post-employment notice pay" (PENP), which is determined in accordance with new s 402D.

ITEPA 2003 s 402E defines the "date", "notice case", the "post-employment notice period" and the "earliest lawful termination date", all of which are relevant to determining PENP.

Then, crucially:

Where PENP >= total RTAs, the total RTAs will be earnings under s 402B; but

Where PENP < total RTAs, PENP will be treated as earnings under s 402B.

In essence, ITEPA 2003 s 402C is seeking to ensure that payments relating to periods of notice as determined under these new rules, are taxable as earnings. It is necessary to work through the further definitions in s 402D to fully understand how this is achieved.

ITEPA 2003 s 402D

ITEPA 2003 s 402D defines the "post-employment notice pay" (PENP) in respect of a termination as given by the formula:

$$PENP = \left(\frac{BP \times D}{P}\right) - T$$

In very simple terms, the formula calculates PENP as a simple fraction/multiple of BP (and then deducts T).

As this formula has changed since the first draft legislation, the following table is provided solely as an aide to understanding the key changes, particularly for those who have already familiarised themselves with the previous definitions. The definitions in the left-hand column are now the only ones relevant. The key change is that the basic pay reference period used to calculate PENP is now just one pay period, rather than a full year. Helpfully there is also a narrower definition of T, the taxable payments which can be deducted when calculating PENP. Please note that this table is not intended as a substitute for the full definitions which are set out clearly in the text of the legislation.

Term	Finance Act final version *(definitions to be adopted in legislation going forward)*	Previous draft legislation *(this column provided for comparison only and now superseded)*
BP	The employee's "basic pay" in respect of the last pay period* ending before the "trigger date".	the employee's "basic pay" from the employment for the year ending with the "trigger date".
D	the number of days in the "post-employment notice period".	No change.
P	The number of days in the last pay period.	Previously this was "Y" and was equal to 365.

T	In short, the total of the payments/benefits made in connection with the termination of employment which are taxable as earnings under Chapter 1 of Part 3, not being accrued holiday pay or a bonus.	Previously this included all other payments/benefits made in connection with the termination of employment, however they were taxable, and could therefore have included payments for restrictive covenants for example, which are treated as earnings under Chapter 12 of Part 3, rather than Chapter 1.

* In circumstances where there is no pay period between commencing employment and the trigger date, BP and P are both measured between the start of employment and the trigger date.

For simplicity, where the minimum contractual notice period, the last pay period and the post-employment notice period are all a whole number of months, then the formula should be solved using whole numbers of months, taking P as 1 and D as the number of whole months in the post-employment notice period.

Note that the definition of "basic pay" in ITEPA 2003 s 402D(7) appears to reflect the everyday meaning of this term, but it also includes any amount the employee has given up and would have fallen within the definition had they not done so, and that the meaning of "basic pay" can be amended by Regulations. This does not mean that termination payments cannot be sacrificed/waived in exchange for pension contributions which has long been accepted by HMRC. However, it does mean that if amounts are sacrificed from basic pay (rather than from any termination payment) the calculation of basic pay for the purposes of PENP will be based on pay prior to any amounts foregone.

Finally, note that s 402D(11) will counteract any arrangement which attempts to reduce PENP in order to avoid tax, by treating the value of PENP in such circumstances as the amount it would otherwise be, absent the arrangement.

Before considering a few examples to clarify the operation of the formula, it is first necessary to understand the meaning of "trigger date" and "post-employment notice period" as defined in ITEPA 2003 s 402E.

ITEPA 2003 s 402E

New ITEPA 2003 s 402E completes the plethora of new definitions needed to turn the cogs in the tax machinery of termination payments going forward. They are clearly explained in the legislation summarised in short as:

"**Trigger date**" – is used in s 402D when identifying pay in periods ending prior to (s 402D(3)) or on (s 403D(5)) the trigger date as the case may be. It is also used when determining the "earliest lawful termination date" in s 402E(7).

ITEPA 2003 s 402E(2) defines the trigger date as:

(a) if the termination is not a "notice case", the last day of the employment,
(b) if the termination is a "notice case", the day the notice is given."

A termination is a "notice case" if one party has given the other notice to terminate the employment.

"**Post-employment notice period**" – this period is used in the numerator (as a number of days or whole months if possible), when determining the fraction/multiple of BP that constitutes PENP. ITEPA 2003 s 402E(5) defines this as the period beginning at the end of the last day of the employment, and ending with the "earliest lawful termination date" in cases other than fixed term employments.

In the case of fixed term employments which do not provide for notice by the employer, the post-employment notice period ends with the "limiting event" (rather than the earliest lawful termination date) as defined in the Employment Rights Act 1996. Broadly speaking this is (a) the natural end of the contract, (b) the completion of the specific task for which the contract was entered into, or (c) the occurrence of an event specified in the contract which brings it to an end. Note that where (a) applies, this can result in a significant proportion, if not all of any termination payment in relation to a fixed term contract being taxable as PENP (see example 4 below).

"**Earliest lawful termination date**" – ITEPA 2003 s 402E(7) defines this as the last day of the period which is equal in length to the "minimum notice", and begins at the end of the trigger date.

"Minimum notice" – ITEPA 2003 s 402E(4) defines this as the minimum notice required to be given by the employer to terminate the employee's employment in accordance with the law and contractual terms effective:

(a) where the termination is not a notice case, immediately before the employment ends or immediately before an agreement is made to end the employment if applicable, and

(b) where the termination is a notice case, immediately before the notice is given.

The minimum notice definition could be interpreted in two ways: either (i) as the lower of the two notice requirements (comparing contract terms with statute); or (ii) as the amount of notice required by contract terms, unless statute provides for a longer period.

Further guidance will be required from HMRC to clarify the intention here, but for the purpose of the examples which follow, it is assumed that the latter interpretation at (ii) is intended to apply.

Examples

NB References to NIC liability in all the following examples are subject to the NIC Bill which has been delayed, unless the proposed NIC provisions can be introduced through alternative legislation.

Example 1: Contractual PILON

Say an employee's termination package consists of £10,000 compensation for loss of office and a contractual PILON of £15,000 in respect of a contractual notice period of three months. The employee's base pay is £5,000 per month up to when the employer terminates the employment without notice. The statutory notice period is four weeks based on service to date. So, in this example:

Minimum Notice	= 3 months (the contract prevails as statutory notice is shorter)
BP	= £5,000 (basic pay in the last pay period ending prior to the trigger date)
T	= £15,000 (already taxable under s 62 as contractual)
RTA	= £25,000 (the total relevant termination award)
D	= 3 (whole months are relevant here, so use months rather than days)
P	= 1 (since D is stated in months)
PENP	= (($£5,000 \times £$))/1 – £15,000 = Nil

RTA is greater than PENP, so the amount chargeable under ITEPA 2003 s 402B (and so s 62) is limited to PENP which is NIL.

Therefore, the £10,000 compensation payment will be taxable under s 403 and can benefit from the £30,000 theshhold. So, in this example £10,000 will be exempt from tax and NIC. (Had this amount exceeded £30,000, the excess would be subject to tax and employer-only NIC.)

Example 2: Actual termination package exceeds PENP(a)

Now, say, an employee's package includes:

-£750 statutory redundancy payment,

-£3,000 "compensation payment".

The employee has been in this employment for just over three years and the employment contract does not mention notice at all. In the last year, he was paid £150 for 20 weeks followed by £250 for 32 weeks (excluding overtime, commission etc). The employment is terminated with immediate effect.

Minimum Notice	= three weeks (the contract is silent and this is the statutory minimum notice corresponding to one week for each year of service).

BP	= £250 (basic pay in the last pay period ending prior to the trigger date)
T	= NIL (no parts of the package are taxable elsewhere in ITEPA)
RTA	= £3,000 (this is the only relevant taxable award excluding the redundancy payment)
D	= 21 (the number of days in the post-employment notice period)
P	= 7 (days in the payment period of one week)
PENP	= (£250 × 21)/7 − 0 = £750

RTA = £3,000 which is greater than PENP, so the amount chargeable under ITEPA 2003 s 402B is limited to PENP, which is £750. This will be taxable under s 402B (and so s 62) subject to PAYE and primary and secondary class 1 NIC.

So, in this example, the remaining £2,250 of the £3,000 compensation payment will fall within s 403 along with the £750 statutory redundancy payment, and thus a total of £3,000 (£2,250 + £750) can benefit from the £30,000 threshold and will be exempt from tax and NIC. (Had this amount exceeded £30,000, the excess would be subject to tax and employer-only NIC.)

Example 3: Actual termination package exceeds PENP(b)

Now, say, an employee's package comprises a single compensation payment of £45,000 payable under a compromise agreement, no amount of which is taxable elsewhere under ITEPA.

The employee has been in this employment for just over two years and the employment contract provides for six months' notice with no PILON clause. His basic pay was £75,000 p.a. The employment is terminated with immediate effect.

BP	= £6,250 (basic pay in the last pay period ending prior to the trigger date)
T	= NIL (no parts of the package are taxable elsewhere in ITEPA)
RTA	= £45,000
D	= 6 (whole months are relevant here, so use months rather than days)
P	= 1 (since D is stated in months)
PENP	= (£6,250 ×6)/1 − 0 = £37,500

RTA = £45,000, which is greater than PENP, so the amount chargeable under ITEPA 2003 s 402B is limited to PENP, which is £37,500. This will be taxable under s 402B (and so s 62) subject to PAYE and primary and secondary class 1 NIC.

The remaining £7,500 will fall within s 403. In this example, £7,500 can benefit from the £30,000 theshhold, so will be exempt from tax and NIC. (Had this amount exceeded £30,000, the excess would be subject to tax and employer only NIC.)

Example 4: Fixed Term Contracts

Assume a fixed term contract has been entered into for 4 years with salary £120,000 per annum, and that the contract does not contain a clause which would bring it to an end before that time e.g. on completion of a particular task.

Things don't work out and the contract is terminated after 26 months, leaving 22 months unworked, A compensation payment is made, say, £100,000.

The trigger date is the date of termination after 26 months.

The "limiting event" under ss 402E(8), (10) (rather than the earliest lawful termination date) as defined in the Employment Rights Act 1996 will be the natural end of the contract in these circumstances.

Then:

BP	= £10,000 (basic pay in the last pay period ending prior to the trigger date)
T	= NIL (no parts of the package are taxable elsewhere in ITEPA)
RTA	= £100,000
D	= 22 (whole months are relevant here, so use months rather than days)
P	= 1 (since D is stated in months)
PENP	= (£10,000 ×22)/1 – 0 = £220,000

RTA = £100,000, which is less than PENP, so £100,000 will be taxable in full under ITEPA 2003 s 402B (and so s 62) subject to PAYE and primary and secondary class 1 NIC. No amount of the payment can benefit from the £30,000 threshold.

Example 5: Sacrificing an element of the termination package

Say, an employee is on a six month notice period, earning £84,000 basic pay per annum. There is no PILON clause in his contract. The employer wishes to terminate the contract with immediate effect and is prepared to make a termination payment of £70,000, consisting of £40,000 PILON and £30,000 compensation.

The employee waives £50,000 of the termination payment and the employer agrees to make a contribution into the employee's pension plan instead. Since only small contributions to the plan were made in the last few years, there is no problem with the Annual Allowance.

BP	= £7,000 (basic pay in the last pay period ending prior to the trigger date)
T	= NIL
RTA	= £20,000 (£70,000 less £50,000 sacrificed)
D	= 6 (whole months are relevant here, so use months rather than days)
P	= 1 (since D is stated in months)
PENP	= (£7,000 ×6)/1 – 0 = £42,000

RTA is lower than PENP so the full amount of RTA i.e. £20,000 is treated as earnings under s 402B subject to PAYE and primary and secondary class 1 NIC.

Example 6: Salary sacrifice from basic pay

An employee has a pre-sacrifice gross (notional) salary of £120,000. Of this, she sacrifices £5,000 in respect of extra holiday and £5,000 in respect of private medical insurance (PMI), leaving post-sacrifice gross salary of £110,000. She has a contractual notice period of six months but the employment is terminated with immediate effect (no PILON clause). She receives a "compromise payment" of £70,000 and the employer will keep providing PMI for the six months after the termination date.

BP	= £10,000 (the two sacrifices are ignored when calculating BP)
T	= Nil
RTA	= £72,500 (£70,000 + 6 months of PMI worth £2,500)
D	= 6 (whole months are relevant here, so use months rather than days)
P	= 1 (since D is stated in months)
PENP	= (£10,000 ×6)/1 – 0 = £60,000

RTA = £72,500 which is greater than PENP, so the amount chargeable under ITEPA 2003 s 402B is limited to PENP, which is £60,000. This will be taxable under s 402B (and so s 62) subject to PAYE and primary and secondary class 1 NIC.

In this example, the remaining £12,500 will fall within s 403 and can benefit from the £30,000 theshhold, so will be exempt from tax and NIC. (Had this amount exceeded £30,000, the excess would be subject to tax and employer-only NIC.)

The examples above are intended to illustrate the basic mechanics for now, subject to any further changes in legislation that might be announced. Obviously there are numerous other permutations and it will be necessary to reflect on the relevant definitions and formulae to determine the correct outcome for any specific case.

ITEPA 2003 s 403 amendments

The amendments to ITEPA 2003 s 403 do not appear to change the time when cash benefits within Chapter 3 of Part 6 are treated as received. This implies that a termination made before 6 April 2018 could be subject to two sets of taxing rules if payments are made in instalments rather than a single lump sum i.e. the old rules applying to payments made prior to 6 April 2018, and the new rules applying to payments made on or after that date.

However, my previous understanding was that it was intended that payments should be grandfathered according to the date of the termination, which would certainly be easier to administer at the individual level. The same applies at a corporate level where a large redundancy programme may take several months to complete; the terms of payments to be made may have been agreed with employees/Unions with the tax consequences well understood under current rules. For employees subject to a redundancy programme commencing prior to 6 April (which may well be evidenced by the requisite disclosure to the Secretary of State made before that date), it would be helpful if termination payments could be treated consistently by grandfathering under the old rules.

We will need to await further guidance and possibly clarifications in the legislation as to whether grandfathering will apply at the individual and/or corporate levels.

ITEPA 2003 s 404B

Provision is made in ITEPA 2003 s 404B to vary the £30,000 exempt threshold through regulations. There is no known intention to amend the threshold at the present time.

ITEPA 2003 s 406 amendment

ITEPA 2003 s 406 is amended by the insertion of new s 406(2) which removes injury to feelings from the total exemption from Chapter 3 of Part 6, which normally applies to termination of employment by death, injury or disability. However, this provision ensures that psychiatric injury still benefits from this exemption.

ITEPA 2003 s 414 amendment

The insertion of the words "section 404B(4) (reduction in the tax-free threshold …)" is noted. Presumably a reduction is not intended for the time being. This measure seems to say that if a reduction in the threshold is made by Regulations, then s 717(3) does not apply. ITEPA 2003 s 717(3) permitted annulment in pursuance of a resolution of the House of Commons.

Commencement

See the comments in relation to grandfathering in s 403 above. Although the amendments take effect from 6 April 2018, it is not currently clear if they apply to payments in respect of terminations which have already been made before that date. Whether grandfathering will be afforded to such terminations will need to be clarified.

In addition, as noted above, the delay of the NIC Bill may result in some or all of the NIC changes being delayed until April 2019, unless the changes can be introduced in April 2018 as originally intended, perhaps through Regulations. This is not yet clear and further announcements may be made in due course.

6 PAYE settlement agreements

(1) In Chapter 5 of Part 11 of ITEPA 2003 (PAYE settlement agreements), in sections 703(a) and 704(1)(a), for "an officer of Revenue and Customs" substitute "Her Majesty's Revenue and Customs".

(2) The amendment made by this section has effect in relation to the tax year 2018–19 and subsequent tax years.

GENERAL NOTE

Section 6 amends ITEPA 2003 ss 703(*a*) and 704(1)(*a*), replacing "an officer of Revenue and Customs" with "Her Majesty's Revenue and Customs" with effect from 2018/19.

The stated intention is to reduce the administrative burden on employers of operating PAYE settlement agreements (PSAs, see ITEPA 2003 Pt 11 Ch 5) and to allow for "automated agreements" with HMRC.

A proposed new, digital process will allow employers to submit a PSA request at the year end. HMRC guidance will be strengthened with the aim of providing certainty for employers.

The changes follow a consultation held in 2016. The Office of Tax Simplification had recommended that the PSA process be streamlined, and suggested that in an era of self-assessment there should be no need to seek HMRC approval for what can be included in a PSA.

7 Money purchase annual allowance

(1) Part 4 of FA 2004 is amended as follows.

(2) In section 227ZA (chargeable amount), in subsection (1)(b), for "£10,000" substitute "£4,000".

(3) In section 227B (alternative chargeable amount), in subsections (1)(b) and (2), for "£10,000" substitute "£4,000".

(4) In section 227D (pension input amounts in respect of certain hybrid arrangements), in Steps 4 and 5 of subsection (4), for "£10,000" substitute "£4,000".

(5) The amendments made by this section have effect for the tax year 2017–18 and subsequent tax years.

GENERAL NOTE

In the Autumn Statement 2016 the Government announced its intention to reduce the money purchase annual allowance from £10,000 to £4,000 from 6 April 2017. It consulted until 15 February 2017 on the impact of this reduction. The aim of the change would be to limit the extent to which pension savings can be recycled to take advantage of an unintended double pension tax relief. The Government did not consider that earners over age 55 should be able to enjoy double pension tax relief on recycled pension savings, but still wished to continue offering scope for those who have needed to access their savings to rebuild them later. Subsequently the Government stated that the consultation had not produced any evidence that a reduction in the annual allowance to £4,000 would impact on the successful rollout of automatic enrolment, or have a disproportionate effect on different groups. So, section 16 introducing the reduction to the money purchase annual allowance from £10,000 to £4,000 for 2017/18 and subsequent years as initially proposed, appeared in the Finance Bill 2017 in March 2017 only to be dropped out when the General Election for 8 June 2017 was called and now re-appears as section 7 in the Finance (No 2) Act 2017.

Section 7 introduces the reduced money purchase annual allowance of £4,000 (previously £10,000) from 6 April 2017. It applies to individuals who, prior to that date, have accessed pension income flexibility. Where it applies, any contributions to a money purchase pension scheme in excess of £4,000 attract an income tax charge at the individual's marginal rate. Sub-sections (2) to (4) amend FA 2004 ss 227ZA, 227B and 227D respectively regarding the amount of the reduction and sub-section (5) brings the amendments into effect for 2017/18 and subsequent years.

Income tax: investments

8 Dividend nil rate for tax year 2018–19 etc

(1) In section 13A of ITA 2007 (income charged at the dividend nil rate), for "£5000", in each place, substitute "£2000".

(2) The amendments made by this section have effect for the tax year 2018–19 and subsequent tax years.

GENERAL NOTE

Section 8 amends ITA 2007 s 13A to reduce the maximum amount of income to be charged at the dividend nil rate with effect from 2018/19.

Spring Budget 2017 announced that the "dividend allowance" introduced in 2016 would be reduced from £5,000 to £2,000 in April 2018, in order "to reduce the tax differential between the self-employed and employed, and those working through a company, to raise revenue to invest in public services, and to ensure that support for investors is more effectively targeted". The Government estimated that a £2,000 dividend allowance would "continue to mean that 80% of general investors pay no dividend tax, including those with sizeable investments (typically, up to £50,000)".

The reference to a "dividend allowance" is misleading because income charged at the new dividend nil rate band may use up part of the basic rate band, increasing the rate of tax payable on dividend income in excess of £2,000.

9 Life insurance policies: recalculating gains on part surrenders etc

(1) ITTOIA 2005 is amended as follows.

(2) After section 507 (method for making periodic calculations in part surrender or assignment cases) insert—

"507A Recalculating gains under section 507

(1) An interested person may apply to an officer of Revenue and Customs for a review of a calculation under section 507 on the ground that the gain arising from it is wholly disproportionate.

(2) For the purposes of this section an interested person in relation to a calculation under section 507 is a person who would be liable for all or any part of the amount of tax that would be chargeable under this Chapter if the gain were not recalculated.

(3) Applications under subsection (1) must be—

    (a) made in writing, and
    (b) received by an officer of Revenue and Customs within—

        (i) the four tax years following the tax year in which the gain arose, or
        (ii) such longer period as the officer may agree.

(4) In considering whether the gain is wholly disproportionate, the officer may take into account (as well as the amount of the gain) any factor which the officer considers appropriate including, so far as the officer considers it appropriate to do so—

    (a) the economic gain on the rights surrendered or assigned,
    (b) the amount of the premiums paid under the policy or contract,
    (c) the amount of tax that would be chargeable under this Chapter if the gain were not recalculated.

(5) If, following an application under subsection (1), an officer considers that the gain arising from the calculation under section 507 is wholly disproportionate, the officer must recalculate the gain on a just and reasonable basis.

(6) Following a recalculation under subsection (5), references in this Chapter (but excluding this section) to a calculation under section 507 are to be regarded as references to a recalculation under this section.

(7) Following a recalculation under subsection (5), an officer of Revenue and Customs must notify the interested person of the result of the recalculation.

(8) If two or more persons are interested persons in relation to a calculation under section 507—

    (a) an application under subsection (1) may be made only by all the interested persons jointly, and
    (b) subsection (7) applies as if the reference to the interested person were a reference to each of the interested persons.

(9) Following a recalculation under subsection (5), all necessary adjustments and repayments of income tax are to be made.

(10) No recalculation is to be made under this section if the gain mentioned in subsection (1) arises as a result of one or more transactions which form part of arrangements, the main purpose, or one of the main purposes, of which is to obtain a tax advantage for any person.

(11) In this section—

"arrangements" includes any agreement, understanding, scheme, transaction or series of transactions (whether or not legally enforceable), and

"tax advantage" has the meaning given by section 1139 of CTA 2010."

(3) After section 512 (available premium left for relevant transaction in certain part surrender or assignment cases) insert—

"512A Recalculating gains under section 511

(1) An interested person may apply to an officer of Revenue and Customs for a review of a calculation under section 511 on the ground that the gain arising from it is wholly disproportionate.

(2) For the purposes of this section an interested person in relation to a calculation under section 511 is a person who would be liable for all or any part of the amount of tax that would be chargeable under this Chapter—

(a) if the gain were not recalculated, or

(b) if all rights under the policy or contract had been surrendered immediately after the surrender or assignment of rights which gave rise to the calculation.

(3) Applications under subsection (1) must be—

(a) made in writing, and

(b) received by an officer of Revenue and Customs within—

(i) the four tax years following the tax year in which the gain arose, or

(ii) such longer period as the officer may agree.

(4) In considering whether the gain is wholly disproportionate, the officer may take into account (as well as the amount of the gain) any factor which the officer considers appropriate including, so far as the officer considers it appropriate to do so—

(a) the economic gain on the rights surrendered or assigned,

(b) the amount of the premiums paid under the policy or contract,

(c) the amount of tax that would be chargeable under this Chapter if the gain were not recalculated.

(5) If, following an application under subsection (1), an officer considers that the gain arising from the calculation under section 511 is wholly disproportionate, the officer must recalculate the gain on a just and reasonable basis.

(6) Following a recalculation under subsection (5), references in this Chapter (but excluding this section) to a calculation under section 511 are to be regarded as references to a recalculation under this section.

(7) Following a recalculation under subsection (5), an officer of Revenue and Customs must notify the interested person of the result of the recalculation.

(8) If two or more persons are interested persons in relation to a calculation under section 511—

(a) an application under subsection (1) may be made only by all the interested persons jointly, and

(b) subsection (7) applies as if the reference to the interested person were a reference to each of the interested persons.

(9) Following a recalculation under subsection (5), all necessary adjustments and repayments of income tax are to be made.

(10) No recalculation is to be made under this section if the gain mentioned in subsection (1) arises as a result of one or more transactions which form part of arrangements, the main purpose, or one of the main purposes, of which is to obtain a tax advantage for any person.

(11) In this section—

"arrangements" includes any agreement, understanding, scheme, transaction or series of transactions (whether or not legally enforceable), and

"tax advantage" has the meaning given by section 1139 of CTA 2010."

(4) In section 538 (recovery of tax from trustees), after subsection (6) insert—

"(7) Subsection (8) applies where—

(a) an individual has recovered an amount from trustees under this section, and

(b) subsequently the individual's liability to tax under this Chapter has been reduced (or removed) as a result of a recalculation under section 507A or 512A.

(8) The individual must repay to the trustees the amount (if any) by which the recovered amount exceeds the individual's revised entitlement.

(9) In subsection (8) the individual's revised entitlement is the amount to which the individual is entitled under this section calculated by reference to the individual's liability to tax under this Chapter as reduced (or removed) as a result of the recalculation under section 507A or 512A."

(5) The amendments made by subsection (4) have effect in relation to amounts recovered before, as well as after, the day on which this Act is passed.

GENERAL NOTE

Over the last few years a number of cases have come before the Tax Tribunal about the rules for calculating gains on life insurance policies in ITTOIA 2005 Pt 4 Ch 9 following a part surrender or assignment by the policyholder. The rules operate in a mechanistic manner and it is possible for policyholders to incur a wholly disproportionate taxable gain unrelated to the economic gain on their policy simply through the way in which they choose to redeem their investment. The case of *Joost Lobler v HMRC Commissioners* ([2015] UKUT 152 (TCC), [2015] STC 1893) is a recent and particularly egregious example of how the rules can work against the taxpayer.

In response to the emerging issue the Association of British Insurers had already issued a good practice guide for insurers ("Cluster Policies – Good Practice for Providers") which, coupled with increased early intervention by providers themselves, had led to a significant decline in the number of cases.

Nevertheless as a result of these high profile cases and consequent lobbying by the insurance industry, financial advisers and tax bodies, the Government held a consultation on possible legislative remedies in the spring of 2016. The consultation document offered three potential solutions and invited ideas for other ways of addressing the problem beyond those identified by the Government.

In practice none of the three options met with universal approval so the Government has settled on a solution that retains the current rules unchanged but allows policyholders who have triggered a wholly disproportionate gain on the part surrender or part assignment of life insurance policies (including capital redemption policies and contracts for life annuities) to apply to an officer of HMRC to have their gain recalculated on a just and reasonable basis.

The expectation of both the Government and the insurance industry is that there will be very few cases to which the legislation will apply, not only because it is limited in its scope by the drafting but also as a result of preventative interventions already being taken by insurers.

Subsection 1 provides that ITTOIA 2005 Pt 4 Ch 9 is to be amended.

Subsection 2 introduces new ITTOIA 2005 s 507A which allows an interested person (broadly any person who would be liable to the whole or some of the tax arising on the gain absent this new provision) to apply in writing to an officer of HMRC to review the calculation of the gain. Any such application must be made by the end of the fourth tax year following that in which the gain arose or such longer period as HMRC may agree, the four year period mirroring the general time limit for making income tax claims in TMA 1970 s 43.

Given the specialist nature of the legislation in ITTOIA 2005 Pt 4 Ch 9 it is understood that responsibility for handling these applications will sit solely with insurance policyholder tax specialists at HMRC.

The legislation lists a number of factors which HMRC may consider in assessing whether the gain is wholly disproportionate: the actual economic gain, the amount of premiums paid and the tax charged in the absence of the new provisions. There may be other factors as well, although the three listed in the legislation appear, singly or in combination, to cover the circumstances of those cases that have come before the Tax Tribunal. In practice the key determinant is not likely to be the circumstances that gave rise to the gain but HMRC's assessment as to whether it is wholly disproportionate, a phrase that is not defined in the legislation. The Explanatory Notes to the legislation state that the phrase sets a high threshold but does not offer any indication of where it might be set.

Assuming that the HMRC officer agrees that the gain arising is wholly disproportionate, the gain is to be recalculated by the officer on a just and reasonable basis although the legislation is silent on what factors should be taken into account in arriving at such a basis. Having recalculated the gain the officer must notify the interested person of the result. It is not clear what action the interested person can take if dissatisfied with the outcome of the recalculation.

It is not unusual for more than one person to have an interest in a life insurance policy and in such circumstances an application for a recalculation may be made only by all of them jointly and, assuming their application is accepted, each must be notified separately.

Having made a recalculation, the legislation provides that all necessary adjustments and repayments of income tax are to be made.

In order to maintain a consistent approach, after any recalculation it is the recalculated gain that is used for all purposes in ITTOIA 2005 Ch 9. This means for example that when the policy is surrendered, the recalculated gain is deductible in arriving at the final gain on the policy. This has implications for the subsequent issue of chargeable event certificates which will show the gain as calculated from the provider's records, not the recalculated amount, which may lead to confusion especially if a long time has passed between the two events.

Finally as is increasingly normal the legislation contains its own targeted anti-avoidance provision which denies a recalculation in circumstances in which the gain arose as a result of one or more transactions forming part of arrangements the main purpose, or one of the main purposes, of which is to obtain a tax advantage for any person.

Subsection 3 introduces new ITTOIA 2005 s 512A which makes similar changes if a calculation under ITTIOA 2005 s 511 produces a wholly disproportionate gain. The difference between sub-ss 2 and 3 is in the definition of an interested person which for the latter is defined as a person who would be liable to tax on the gain arising under ITTOIA 2005 s 511 and any other person who would be liable if the policy were surrendered immediately afterwards and a gain arose. So if A assigned part of their policy to B then A is an interested person if they would be liable to tax on the gain. B is also an interested person if they would be liable to tax if the policy was fully surrendered immediately after and a gain arose. Otherwise there is no difference between the requirements and outcomes of the two sub-ss so the comments made above for sub-s 2 apply equally to sub-s 3.

Subsection 4 amends ITTOIA 2005 s 538 which in certain circumstances permits a policyholder to recover tax from the trustees of policy held in trust. Clearly it would not be appropriate for a policyholder to recover tax from trustees, apply for a recalculation of the tax which reduced the tax payable and keep the difference between the two amounts. The amendments introduced by sub-s 4 therefore require the policyholder to repay the trustees any difference between what was recovered from them and the revised amount calculated under new ITTOIA 2005 ss 507A or 512A.

Subsection 5 ensures that the changes made by sub-s 4 have effect regardless of whether the recovery of tax from the trustees occurred before or after the day on which F(No 2)A 2017 received Royal Assent in order to prevent retrospective advantage accruing to the policyholder given the four year period for making a claim that a gain is disproportionate.

Given the requirement on HMRC to determine whether any gain is wholly disproportionate and if so to recalculate the gain on a just and reasonable basis, it will be important that there is clear guidance on how HMRC will exercise the power vested in it. HMRC have shared a draft of the guidance on the legislation, which will be incorporated into the Insurance Policyholder Taxation Manual, with industry bodies for comment.

As noted above, the phrase wholly disproportionate is not defined in the legislation so the taxpayer is wholly in the hands of the HMRC officer. Beyond the bland statement in the Explanatory Notes that the phrase sets a high threshold there is currently no indication as to how HMRC will interpret the words. HMRC have indicated however that the guidance will allow associated impacts, for example on entitlement to Child and Working Tax Credits and the amount of student loan repayments, to be taken into account in assessing whether a gain is wholly disproportionate.

The legislation contains no sign posts as to how the gain should be recalculated. An obvious mechanism for recalculating the gain would be to compute it on an A/(A+B) basis (which was one of the options in the government consultation) although this would likely require information about the value of the policy from the provider.

Separately it is not clear how a taxpayer would exercise a right of appeal if HMRC decided that the gain was not wholly disproportionate or, HMRC having concluded that it was, that the recalculation was not just and reasonable. It may be that a taxpayer's only recourse would be through judicial review which itself seems a disproportionate response to the rejection of a legislative claim for relief from tax.

Finally the policy provider would not be given details of any recalculation so any chargeable event certificates issued following a successful claim for relief by the policyholder would show incorrect information which, as mentioned above, may cause practical compliance difficulties at a later date. To address this HMRC have stated that applicants will be supported throughout the process and advised how to get matters right when their policy ends.

10 Personal portfolio bonds

In section 520 of ITTOIA 2005 (property categories), after subsection (4) insert—

"(5) The Treasury may by regulations—

(a) amend the table in subsection (2) by adding, removing or amending a category of property;

(b) add, remove or amend a definition relating to any category of property in that table; and

(c) make consequential amendments.

(6) A statutory instrument containing regulations under this section which have the effect of removing a category of property from the table in subsection (2)—

(a) must be laid before the House of Commons; and

(b) ceases to have effect at the end of the period of 28 days beginning with the day on which it was made, unless it is approved during that period by a resolution of the House of Commons.

(7) In reckoning the period of 28 days, no account is to be taken of any time during which Parliament is dissolved or prorogued, or during which the House of Commons is adjourned for more than four days."

GENERAL NOTE

Section 10 concerns the property categories that can be selected for inclusion in a life insurance policy without bringing the tax treatment of the policy within the personal portfolio bonds (PPB) regime (ITTOIA 2005 ss 515–526). The PPB legislation provides for a special tax regime for individuals who seek to place personally selected assets in a life insurance policy in order to defer an income or capital gains tax charge on those assets. ITTOIA 2005 s 520(2) specifies categories of assets that can be selected for inclusion in a life insurance policy without triggering the PPB rules.

Section 10 introduces new subsections (ITTOIA 2005 s 520(5)–(7)) that permit the Treasury to amend through statutory instrument the permitted property table, contained in ITTOIA 2005 s 520(2), by "adding, removing or amending a category of property". These changes come into effect from the date of Royal Assent to Finance (No 2) Act 2017, with the regulations pertaining to the inclusion of new permitted property categories following shortly thereafter.

In a consultation running from 9 August 2016 to 3 October 2016, the Government sought views on the current permitted property categories and the potential inclusion of additional property types. The summary of responses to the consultation, published on 5 December 2016, stated that respondents requested the inclusion of various instruments including, but not restricted to, exchange traded funds, structured notes, and fixed interest products.

The Government response section of this document clarified that "equities, fixed interest (including UK government gilts), market place lending and cash in other currencies" will not be included within the PPB permitted property categories. The reason furnished for this exclusion revolves around the fact that the "nature of the assets" cannot effectively preclude the possibility of policyholders selecting personal assets for inclusion.

This, then, is an exemplar of the fundamental criterion that the Government will use to determine the assets that fall within the ambit of the legislation – those assets will be caught whose terms and conditions permit underlying asset selection at the policyholder's discretion (subject to at least one such asset falling outside the listed permitted property categories).

In light of the changing retail investment market landscape and the creation of new instruments and asset types, it is significant to note that the Government will regularly review the list of specified permitted property and retains the power to update the categories via regulations.

11 EIS and SEIS: the no pre-arranged exits requirement

(1) ITA 2007 is amended as follows.

(2) In section 177 (EIS: the no pre-arranged exits requirement), for subsection (2) substitute—

"(2) The arrangements referred to in subsection (1)(a) do not include—

(a) any arrangements with a view to such an exchange of shares, or shares and securities, as is mentioned in section 247(1), or

(b) any arrangements with a view to any shares in the issuing company being exchanged for, or converted into, shares in that company of a different class."

(3) In section 257CD (SEIS: the no pre-arranged exits requirement), for subsection (2) substitute—

"(2) The arrangements referred to in subsection (1)(a) do not include—

(a) any arrangements with a view to such an exchange of shares, or shares and securities, as is mentioned in section 257HB(1), or

(b) any arrangements with a view to any shares in the issuing company being exchanged for, or converted into, shares in that company of a different class."

(4) The amendments made by this section have effect in relation to shares issued on or after 5 December 2016.

GENERAL NOTE

For the last few years, HMRC have treated the conversion of shares as a disposal for the purposes of SEIS and EIS income tax reliefs. It followed that where shares were issued with the rights of conversion, HMRC considered that the "no pre-arranged exits requirement" of ITA 2007 ss 177 and 257CD applied to prevent EIS or SEIS relief being available for these shares.

Section 11 is designed to allow shares with conversion rights to be eligible for SEIS and EIS tax reliefs, provided all other SEIS and EIS conditions are met.

Section 11(2) amends ITA 2007 s 177(2) to state explicitly that conversion rights are not regarded as an arrangement for a disposal of the shares for EIS purposes. Section 11(3) similarly amends the SEIS legislation in ITA 2007 s 257CD(2).

Section 11(4) provides this relaxation for shares issued on or after 5 December 2016. This will be of assistance to companies who wish to make provision in their Articles for a reorganisation of share capital:

– prior to a flotation; or
– where share capital needs to be reorganised for a fund raising round or an exit.

HMRC's position continues to be that a conversion of shares is itself a disposal of shares, and so a conversion of shares within the restricted periods for SEIS and EIS can lead to a loss of the tax reliefs claimed.

12 VCTs: follow-on funding

(1) ITA 2007 is amended as follows.

(2) In section 326 (restructuring to which sections 326A and 327 apply)—

(a) in the heading to section 326, for "section 327 applies" substitute "sections 326A, 327 and 327A apply";

(b) in subsection (1), for "Sections 326A and 327 apply" substitute "Sections 326A, 327 and 327A apply".

(3) After section 327 insert—

"327A Follow-on funding

(1) Subsections (2) and (3) apply where—

(a) this section applies (see section 326(1)),

(b) the acquisition by the new company of all the old shares, which is provided for by the arrangements mentioned in section 326(1), takes place, and

(c) the acquisition falls within section 326(2).

(2) If, after the acquisition, another company makes an investment in the new company, section 280C (the permitted maximum age condition) has effect in relation to that investment as if—

(a) in subsection (4)(a) the reference to a relevant investment having been made in the relevant company before the end of the initial investing period included a reference to a relevant investment having been made in the old company before the acquisition and before the end of the initial investing period, and

(b) in subsection (6)(a) the reference to relevant investments made in the relevant company included a reference to relevant investments made in the old company before the acquisition.

(3) In relation to any relevant holding issued by the new company after the acquisition, section 294A (the permitted company age requirement) has effect as if—

(a) in subsection (3)(a) the reference to a relevant investment having been made in the relevant company before the end of the initial investing period included a reference to a relevant investment having been made in the old company before the acquisition and before the end of the initial investing period, and

(b) in subsection (5)(a) the reference to relevant investments made in the relevant company included a reference to relevant investments made in the old company before the acquisition.

(4) In subsection (3) "relevant holding" has the same meaning as in Chapter 4."

(4) The amendments made by this section have effect—

(a) for the purposes of section 280C of ITA 2007, in relation to investments made on or after 6 April 2017;

(b) for the purposes of section 294A of ITA 2007, in relation to relevant holdings issued on or after 6 April 2017.

GENERAL NOTE

Finance (No 2) Act 2015 introduced the permitted maximum age requirement for investments made by VCTs and under the Enterprise Investment Scheme. The requirement considers the date of the first commercial sale, and the investment must be made within the initial investing period (usually seven years after the first sale). Further investments can be made in the same company for the same business activities after the expiry of the initial investing period. Where a new "mirror image" holding company is superimposed in certain circumstances, further EIS investment is possible, but the ability for a VCT to invest after the initial investing period was lost.

Section 12 brings consistency between the EIS and VCT rules where a new "mirror image" holding company is superimposed over a company which has EIS or VCT investors. Under the EIS rules, HMRC have treated a new holding company as inheriting the funding history of the old company, and this can allow it to receive further follow-on funding after the initial investing period (usually seven years but ten years if the company is "knowledge intensive") following its first commercial sale.

Section 12(2) amends ITA 2007 s 326 for the insertion by section 12(3) of new ITA 2007 s 327A.

Section 12(4) confirms the provisions apply for investments made by VCTs after 5 April 2017.

13 VCTs: exchange of non-qualifying shares and securities

(1) Section 330 of ITA 2007 (power to facilitate company reorganisations etc involving exchange of shares) is amended as follows.

(2) After subsection (1) insert—

"(1A) The Treasury may by regulations make provision for the purposes of this Part for cases where—

(a) a holding of shares or securities that does not meet the requirements of Chapter 4 is exchanged for other shares or securities not meeting those requirements, and

(b) the exchange is made for genuine commercial reasons and does not form part of a scheme or arrangement the main purpose or one of the main purposes of which is the avoidance of tax."

(3) In subsection (2), for "subsection (1)" substitute "subsections (1) and (1A)".

(4) In subsection (3), for "The regulations" substitute "Regulations under subsection (1)".

(5) After subsection (3) insert—

"(3A) Regulations under subsection (1A) may, among other things, make provision—

(a) for the new shares or securities to be treated in any respect in the same way as the original shares and securities for any period;

(b) as to when the new shares or securities are to be regarded as having been acquired;

(c) as to the valuation of the original or the new shares or securities."

(6) In subsection (4), for "The regulations" substitute "Regulations under this section".

(7) In subsection (6). in paragraph (c), at the beginning insert "in the case of regulations under subsection (1)".

GENERAL NOTE

The VCT (Exchange of Shares and Securities) Regulations, SI 2002/2661, apply where there is a reorganisation of a VCT's qualifying investment. The aim of the Regulations is to treat the new holding as a qualifying investment, at least for a period. It is intended that the Regulations will be amended so that reorganisations of non-qualifying holdings will not cause a VCT to forfeit its status as a VCT.

Section 13 gives power for the VCT (Exchange of Shares and Securities) Regulations to be amended so that non-qualifying holdings are brought within the scope of the Regulations.

It should be noted that the Regulations have not been updated to reflect the introduction of ITA 2007, nor to reflect the wide reaching changes to the VCT legislation made in 2015 and 2016. Updating the Regulations and bringing non-qualifying holdings within the scope of the Regulations should provide more certainty to VCTs where investments are restructured or acquired.

14 Social investment tax relief

Schedule 1 makes provision about income tax relief for social investments.

GENERAL NOTE

Social investment tax relief (SITR) was introduced with effect from 1 April 2014.

Individuals who make eligible investments in social enterprises can claim the relief.

Section 14 introduces Schedule 1, which details the changes to the existing rules for SITR. The amendments will have effect for qualifying investments incurred on or after 6 April 2017.

Social enterprises have reported that they have difficulty raising investment. The objective of the changes is to make the relief attractive to a wider range of investors and so allow social enterprises to raise more funds through SITR.

15 Business investment relief

(1) Chapter A1 of Part 14 of ITA 2007 (remittance basis) is amended as follows.

(2) In section 809VC (qualifying investments), in subsection (1)(a), after "issued to" insert "or acquired by".

(3) In section 809VD (condition relating to qualifying investments)—

(a) in subsection (1), omit the "or" at the end of paragraph (b) and after that paragraph insert—

"(ba) an eligible hybrid company, or";

(b) in subsection (2)(b), for "2" substitute "5";

(c) in subsection (3)(c), for "2" substitute "5";

(d) after subsection (3) insert—

"(3A) A company is an "eligible hybrid company" if—

(a) it is a private limited company,

(b) it is not an eligible trading company or an eligible stakeholder company,

(c) it carries on one or more commercial trades or is preparing to do so within the next 5 years,

(d) it holds one or more investments in eligible trading companies or is preparing to do so within the next 5 years, and

(e) carrying on commercial trades and making investments in eligible trading companies are all or substantially all of what it does (or of what it is reasonably expected to do once it begins operating).";

(e) in subsection (4), for "reference in subsection (3)" substitute "references in subsections (3) and (3A)";

(f) in subsection (5)(a), for "2" substitute "5".

(4) In section 809VE (commercial trades), after subsection (5) insert—

"(6) A company which is a partner in a partnership is not to be regarded as carrying on a trade carried on by the partnership."

(5) In section 809VH (meaning of "potentially chargeable event")—

(a) in subsection (1)(a), after "eligible stakeholder company" insert "nor an eligible hybrid company";

(b) in subsection (1)(d), for "2-year" substitute "5-year";

(c) in subsection (2), for paragraph (b) substitute—

"(b) the value is received from any person in circumstances that are directly or indirectly attributable to the investment, and";

(d) omit subsection (4);

(e) in subsection (5)—

(i) for "2-year" substitute "5-year";

(ii) in paragraph (a), for "2" substitute "5";

(f) in subsection (6), omit the "or" at the end of paragraph (b) and after that paragraph insert—

"(ba) it is an eligible hybrid company but is not trading and—

(i) it holds no investments in eligible trading companies, or

(ii) none of the eligible trading companies in which it holds investments is trading, or";

(g) in subsection (10)(b), after "eligible stakeholder company" insert "or an eligible hybrid company".

(6) In section 809VJ (grace period), after subsection (2) insert—

"(2A) But subsection (2B) applies instead of subsections (1) and (2) where the potentially chargeable event is a breach of the 5-year start-up rule by virtue of section 809VH(5)(b).

(2B) The grace period allowed for the steps mentioned in section 809VI(2)(a) and (2)(b) is the period of 2 years beginning with the day on which a relevant person first became aware or ought reasonably to have become aware of the potentially chargeable event referred to in subsection (2A)."

(7) In section 809VN (order of disposals etc), in subsections (1)(c) and (5)(a) and (b), after "eligible stakeholder company" insert "or eligible hybrid company".

(8) The amendments made by this section have effect where the relevant event as defined in section 809VA of ITA 2007 occurs on or after 6 April 2017.

GENERAL NOTE

F(No 2)A 2017 sees the first major changes to the business investment relief (BIR) rules since they were introduced in 2012, although they are not as wide-ranging as initially thought in the consultation groups on the subject.

The Conservative Government seem very keen to widen the scope of the BIR rules, to encourage inward investment into the UK. However, as the September 2017 Finance Bill moved through Parliament, it was clear that the Labour Party has misgivings over the impact of BIR and sees it as just another way for non-doms to pay even less tax.

The main changes to ITA 2007 Pt 14 Ch A1 (inserted by section 15) can be summarised as follows:

– Investors can now (from 6 April 2017) purchase shares in existing companies rather than just subscribing for shares. This opens up the range of eligible investment much more widely, as AIM listed companies can qualify for BIR provided that the other qualifying conditions are met. Investors can therefore potentially purchase existing shares on the AIM.

– The qualifying start-up period is increased from two to five years for each of the categories of qualifying companies under the relief, meaning that some types of business that were difficult to move to trading status within the old two-year window could now qualify.

– An additional type of qualifying company, an "eligible hybrid company", has been added for investments on or after 6 April 2017. An eligible hybrid company is a company that is both a trading company (or is preparing to trade in the next five years) and also holds investments in trading companies (or is preparing to do so in the next five years). This opens up the possibility of investors owning a company that invests in trading companies and also trades in its own name (note that a property rental business qualifies under the BIR rules).

- There is a clarification that a company which is a partner in a partnership is not to be regarded as carrying on the trade of the partnership, meaning that unless the target company is carrying on a commercial trade in its own right, it will not qualify for BIR.
- There is a softening of the provisions of ITA 2007 s 809VH, dealing with the potential tax charge incurred if a benefit is received as a result of an investment, such that "involved companies" will no longer cause a benefits problem from 6 April 2017. In essence, the legislation now treats the extraction of value rule as having been breached where a benefit is received from anyone in circumstances directly or indirectly attributable to the investment. Previously the rule was breached if an investor received any benefits directly or indirectly from the investee company or any associated company, whether or not the benefit was actually connected to the investment.

Income tax: trading and property businesses

16 Calculation of profits of trades and property businesses

Schedule 2 contains provision about the calculation of the profits of a trade, profession or vocation or a property business, in particular the calculation of profits on the cash basis.

GENERAL NOTE

Section 16 introduces Schedule 2, which details the extension of the cash basis for property income, taking effect from 6 April 2017.

In an attempt to remove administrative burdens on business, the treatment of capital expenditure under the cash basis has been amended to provide a statutory rule.

Existing rules require taxable profits from a property business to be calculated in accordance with GAAP. The amendments introduced by Schedule 2 allow for the cash basis to be used by landlords (who are individuals or a partnership made up of individuals) where the cash basis receipts do not exceed £150,000.

As part of the Government's drive to simplify the tax system, the changes are expected to make it easier and cheaper for eligible businesses to calculate their tax liabilities.

17 Trading and property allowances

Schedule 3 contains provision about a trading allowance and a property allowance giving relief from income tax.

GENERAL NOTE

Section 17 introduces Schedule 3, which details the new trading and property allowances (£1,000 each), taking effect from 6 April 2017.

Individuals who make £1,000 or less (before expenses) for trading or property income will no longer have to declare or pay tax on this income.

Those with income over the £1,000 allowance can either claim the allowance or actual expenses.

As part of the Government's drive to simplify the tax system, the new allowances provide simplicity for individuals with small amounts of trading and property income.

Corporation tax

18 Carried-forward losses

(1) Schedule 4 makes provision about corporation tax relief for losses and other amounts that are carried forward.

(2) The Commissioners for Her Majesty's Revenue and Customs may by regulations made by statutory instrument make provision consequential on any provision made by Schedule 4.

(3) Regulations under subsection (2)—

(a) may make provision amending or modifying any provision of the Taxes Acts (including any provision inserted by Schedule 4),
(b) may make incidental, supplemental, transitional, transitory or saving provision, and
(c) may make different provision for different purposes.

(4) A statutory instrument containing regulations under subsection (2) is subject to annulment in pursuance of a resolution of the House of Commons.

(5) In this section "the Taxes Acts" has the same meaning as in the Taxes Management Act 1970 (see section 118(1) of that Act).

GENERAL NOTE

Section 18 introduces Schedule 4 which has a large number of provisions relating to corporation tax relief for losses and other amounts carried forward. Section 18 permits HMRC to make provisions consequential on any part of Schedule 4 by statutory instrument, which can amend or modify any part of the Taxes Acts.

19 Losses: counteraction of avoidance arrangements

(1) Any loss-related tax advantage that would (in the absence of this section) arise from relevant tax arrangements is to be counteracted by the making of such adjustments as are just and reasonable.

(2) Any adjustments required to be made under this section (whether or not by an officer of Revenue and Customs) may be made by way of—

(a) an assessment,
(b) the modification of an assessment,
(c) amendment or disallowance of a claim,

or otherwise.

(3) For the purposes of this section arrangements are "relevant tax arrangements" if conditions A and B are met.

(4) Condition A is that the purpose, or one of the main purposes, of the arrangements is to obtain a loss-related tax advantage.

(5) Condition B is that it is reasonable to regard the arrangements as circumventing the intended limits of relief under the relevant provisions or otherwise exploiting shortcomings in the relevant provisions.

(6) In determining whether or not condition B is met all the relevant circumstances are to be taken into account, including whether the arrangements include any steps that—

(a) are contrived or abnormal, or
(b) lack a genuine commercial purpose.

(7) In this section "loss-related tax advantage" means a tax advantage as a result of a deduction (or increased deduction) under a provision mentioned in subsection (8).

(8) The provisions are—

(a) sections 457, 459, 461, 462, 463B, 463G and 463H of CTA 2009 (non-trading deficits from loan relationships);
(b) section 753 of CTA 2009 (non-trading losses on intangible fixed assets);
(c) section 1219 of CTA 2009 (management expenses etc);
(d) sections 37, 45, 45A, 45B and 45F of CTA 2010 (deductions in respect of trade losses);
(e) section 62(3) of CTA 2010 (losses of a UK property business);
(f) Part 5 of CTA 2010 (group relief);
(g) Part 5A of CTA 2010 (group relief for carried-forward losses);
(h) sections 303B, 303C and 303D of CTA 2010 (non-decommissioning losses of ring-fence trades);
(i) sections 124A, 124B and 124C of FA 2012 (carried-forward BLAGAB trade losses).

(9) In this section—

"arrangements" includes any agreement, understanding, scheme transaction or series of transactions (whether or not legally enforceable);
"tax advantage" has the meaning given by section 1139 of CTA 2010.

(10) This section has effect in relation to a tax advantage that relates (or would apart from this section relate) to an accounting period beginning on or after 1 April 2017 (regardless of when the arrangements in question were made).

(11) Where a tax advantage would (apart from this subsection) relate to an accounting period beginning before 1 April 2017 and ending on or after that date ("the straddling period")—

(a) so much of the straddling period as falls before 1 April 2017, and so much of that period as falls on or after that date, are treated as separate accounting periods, and
(b) the extent (if any) to which the tax advantage relates to the second of those accounting periods is to be determined by apportioning amounts—

    (i) in accordance with section 1172 of CTA 2010 (time basis), or
    (ii) if that method would produce a result that is unjust or unreasonable, on a just and reasonable basis.

(12) In the case of a tax advantage as a result of a deduction (or increased deduction) under—

(a) section 463H of CTA 2009,
(b) section 62(3) of CTA 2010,
(c) section 303B, 303C or 303D of CTA 2010, or
(d) section 124A or 124C of FA 2012,

subsections (10) and (11) have effect as if the references to 1 April 2017 were to 13 July 2017.

GENERAL NOTE

Section 19 is a general anti-avoidance rule targeted at corporate loss reliefs. It permits the counteraction of any "loss-related tax advantage" that arises from "relevant tax arrangements". Adjustments can be made by way of assessment, modification of assessment, amendment or disallowance of a claim or otherwise.

Scope

Relevant tax arrangements must satisfy conditions A and B. Condition A is that the main purpose of arrangements must be to obtain a loss related tax advantage. Condition B is that it must be reasonable to view the arrangements as either circumventing the intended limits of the relief or as exploiting shortcomings in the legislation. All relevant circumstances must be taken into account including whether the arrangements include contrived or abnormal steps or steps lacking a genuine commercial purpose.

As is normal in these forms of provisions, arrangements will include any agreement, understanding, scheme, transaction or series of transactions, whether or not they are legally enforceable.

A loss-related tax advantage is defined as a tax advantage resulting from a deduction or increased deduction in respect of the following:

– Non-trading deficits from loan relationships.
– Non-trading losses on intangible fixed assets.
– Management expenses, etc.
– Deductions in respect of trade losses.
– Losses of a UK property business.
– Group relief, including the new group relief for carried forward losses.
– Non-decommissioning losses of ring fence trades.
– Carried-forward BLAGAB trade losses.

Commencement

The new rules apply to tax advantages relating to accounting periods beginning on or after 1 April 2017, without regard to when the original arrangements were actually made. Where a company's accounting period straddles the commencement date, the accounting period is deemed, for the purposes of this legislation to amount to two separate accounting periods, one ending 31 March 2017 and the other starting on 1 April 2017, with the new anti-avoidance rule applying to the latter.

Under certain circumstances, for some losses on non-trading deficits from loan relationships, UK property business losses, non-decommissioning losses of ring-fence trades and carried forward BLAGAB losses, the commencement date is based on 13 July 2017, not 1 April 2017.

20 Corporate interest restriction

Schedule 5 makes provision about the amounts that may be brought into account for the purposes of corporation tax in respect of interest and other financing costs.

GENERAL NOTE

Overview

Section 20 and Schedule 5 introduce a new corporate interest restriction legislation, which is being enacted to implement the best practice recommendations in the OECD Base Erosion and Profit Shifting Project: Action 4 (limiting base erosion involving interest deductions and financing payments). The corporate interest restriction legislation takes effect from 1 April 2017 and is being introduced as a new TIOPA 2010 Part 10. The existing Part 10 is being renumbered as Part 11 and the sections contained therein are also being renumbered with some repeals.

Groups (and companies that are not members of groups) will be able to deduct up to £2 million of net interest expense and similar financing costs, which are referred to in the legislation as net tax-interest expense (see TIOPA 2010 s 392(2), (3)) in computing their taxable profits for corporation tax purposes. Where a group's (or in the case of a company that is not a member of a group (see TIOPA 2010 473(1)(a), (3)), the company's) net tax-interest expense exceeds £2 million a restriction will apply to the amount of the excess for which the group (or company) may claim tax relief in computing its profits for corporation tax purposes. The restriction is calculated by reference to the fixed ratio method, or where a group so elects (under new TIOPA 2010 Sch 7A, para 13), the group ratio method. This election may be made on a period of account by period of account basis.

Under the fixed ratio method (see TIOPA 2010 s 397) the amount of net tax-interest expense (see TIOPA 2010 ss 382–391) in excess of £2 million for which the group may claim tax relief for corporation tax purposes is the lower of:

– 30% of the aggregate UK tax-EBITDA of group companies that are within the charge to corporation tax (see TIOPA 2010 s 405); and
– the fixed ratio debt cap.

The aggregate tax-EBITDA is, broadly, the UK taxable profits of members of the group that are within the charge to UK corporation tax, adding back certain finance related income and expense amounts, capital allowances and most debits and credits arising in respect of intangible fixed assets (see TIOPA 2010 ss 405–408).

The fixed ratio debt cap is the adjusted net group-interest expense of the group (ANGIE) for the period (see TIOPA 2010 s 413), as increased by any excess of the debt cap over the net tax-interest expense for which UK tax relief was permitted in the immediately preceding period of account of the group (see TIOPA 2010 s 400).

ANGIE is broadly the net interest and other financing costs as shown in the consolidated accounts of the worldwide group for the relevant period of account, adjusted for:

– certain amounts of capitalised interest income and expense;
– interest and other financing costs recognised in equity or shareholder's funds;
– amounts that are brought into account under regular 3A of the Taxation of Regulatory Capital Securities Regulations 2013 (or which would be so brought into account were the relevant company within the charge to corporation tax);
– debt releases that are exempt from tax under CTA 2009 s 322 (or which would be so exempt were the relevant company within the charge to corporation tax);
– certain credits and reversals of credits arising in respect of the substantial modification of a debtor relationship to which CTA 2009 s 323A applies (or to which it would apply were the relevant company within the charge to corporation tax); and
– dividends payable in respect of preference shares that are treated as a liability in the consolidated accounts of the worldwide group.

It is broadly intended to track the amounts that are taken into account in determining a group's net tax-interest expense. As ANGIE is determined by reference to the consolidated accounts it will only comprise interest and other financing costs payable or receivable otherwise than from members of the group (as intra-group payments will be eliminated on consolidation).

The group ratio method is defined in TIOPA 2010 s 398 as the lower of:

– the group ratio percentage of the aggregate tax-EBITDA of group companies

within the charge to corporation tax for the period of account of the worldwide group (see TIOPA 2010 ss 405–409); and
– the group ratio debt cap of the group for the period (TIOPA 2010 s 400(2)).

The group ratio percentage is defined in TIOPA 2010 s 399 as:

$$\frac{\text{The qualifying net group-interest expense of the group for the period}}{\text{The group-EBITDA of the group for the period (see section 416)}} \times 100\%$$

The QNGIE (see TIOPA 2010 s 414) of a worldwide group for a period of account is its ANGIE adjusted to remove expenses arising in respect of:
– transactions with and financial liabilities owed to persons who were related parties of the group at any time during the period (see Chapter 11);
– results-dependent securities. Securities are treated as being results dependent where the consideration given by the entity for the use of the principal secured depends (to any extent) on the results of all or part of the entity's business, or the results of all or part of the business of any other entity that was a member of the group at any time during the period of account, excluding certain amounts (see TIOPA 2010 s 415(5)–(8)), being:
    – amounts that are treated as an alternative finance return (within the meaning of CTA 2010 s 1019(2),
    – securities to which the Taxation of Regulatory Capital Securities 2013 (SI 2013/3209) applies, and
    – securities where the interest payable is adjusted inversely by reference to the entity's results, reducing if the results improve and increase as the results deteriorate; and
    – equity notes, being securities that have a term of 50 years or more (see TIOPA 2010 s 415(7)).

The group-EBITDA (see TIOPA 2010 s 416) is broadly the group's profit before tax as shown in the consolidated worldwide accounts adding back the net group-interest expense of the group for the period and the group's depreciation and amortisation adjustment. Either or both of those adjustments can be negative dependent on the fact pattern. It is broadly intended to track the way in which the tax-EBITDA of UK group companies is determined.

The group ratio debt cap of the group for the period of account of the worldwide group is defined in TIOPA 2010 s 400(2) as is the sum of:
– the QNGIE of the group for that period (see TIOPA 2010 s 414); and
– the excess of the debt cap of the group that was generated in the immediately preceding period of account over the group's net tax-interest expense for that period (if any) (see TIOPA 2010 s 400(3)–(8)).

A group is required to appoint a group company that is within the charge to corporation tax to apportion the disallowance amongst group companies that are within the charge to corporation tax (UK group companies) (TIOPA 2010 Sch 7A paras 1–7). The disallowance that is apportioned to a UK group company cannot exceed its net tax-interest expense for the relevant period of account of the worldwide group (TIOPA 2010 Sch 7A para 22(3)(a)). It is open to a UK group company to which a disallowance is allocated to object to the allocation, in which case the disallowance that is allocated to that company will be determined on a pro rata basis by reference to its net tax-interest expense for the period as compared to the aggregate net tax-interest expense of group companies within the charge to corporation tax for the period (TIOPA 2010 Sch 7A paras 22(3)(b), 23, 24).

21 Museum and gallery exhibitions

Schedule 6 makes provision about relief in respect of the production of museum and gallery exhibitions.

GENERAL NOTE

The Government announced at Budget 2016 a new tax relief for the production of new exhibitions by qualifying museums and galleries, following the introduction of "highly successful" reliefs to support investment and innovation in the creative industries.

At Autumn Statement 2016 the Government confirmed, following consultation, that the new relief to take effect in April 2017 would be based on the existing creative sector tax relief model set out in CTA 2009 Pt 15. It would be broader than originally proposed, in that it would extend to permanent exhibitions.

Relief is set at a rate of 25% for touring exhibitions and 20% for non-touring exhibitions, with a cap of £500,000 of qualifying expenditure per exhibition. The relief will expire in April 2022 if not renewed – the Government has undertaken to review the relief in 2020.

The measure is intended to "encourage museums and galleries to develop creative new exhibitions and to display their collections to a wider audience, supporting British culture". HMRC estimated that more than 1,500 institutions would be within the scope of the new relief.

Section 21 and Sch 6 introduce corporation tax relief for museums, galleries and other qualifying heritage institutions from 1 April 2017.

F(No 2)A 2017 Sch 6 Pt 1 amends CTA 2009 with effect for accounting periods beginning on or after 1 April 2017.

In F(No 2)A 2017 Sch 6 Pt 2 (consequential amendments), paragraphs 2–15 and 19 also have effect for accounting periods beginning on or after 1 April 2017. Provision is made for the apportionment of profits where a company's accounting period straddles that date.

22 Grassroots sport

(1) CTA 2010 is amended as follows.

(2) In section 1(2) (overview of Act)—

    (a) omit the "and" at the end of paragraph (g), and

    (b) after that paragraph insert—

      "(ga) relief for expenditure on grassroots sport (see Part 6A), and".

(3) In section 99(1) (group relief: losses and other amounts which may be surrendered), after paragraph (d) insert—

    "(da) amounts allowable as qualifying expenditure on grassroots sport (see Part 6A),".

(4) In section 105(4) (group relief: order in which amounts are treated as surrendered)—

    (a) after paragraph (a) insert—

    "(aa) second, expenditure within section 99(1)(da),",

    (b) in paragraph (b), for "second" substitute "third",

    (c) in paragraph (c), for "third" substitute "fourth", and

    (d) in paragraph (d), for "fourth" substitute "fifth".

(5) After Part 6 insert—

"PART 6A

RELIEF FOR EXPENDITURE ON GRASSROOTS SPORT

217A Relief for expenditure on grassroots sport

(1) A payment made by a company which is qualifying expenditure on grassroots sport (and which is not refunded) is allowed as a deduction in accordance with this section from the company's total profits in calculating the corporation tax chargeable for the accounting period in which the payment is made.

(2) The deduction is from the company's total profits for the accounting period after any other relief from corporation tax other than—

    (a) relief under Part 6,

    (b) group relief, and

    (c) group relief for carried-forward losses.

(3) If the company is a qualifying sport body at the time of the payment, a deduction is allowed for the amount of the payment.

See section 217C for the meaning of "qualifying sport body".

(4) If the company is not a qualifying sport body at the time of the payment, a deduction is allowed—

    (a) if the payment is to a qualifying sport body, for the amount of the payment, and

    (b) if the payment does not fall within paragraph (a) (a "direct payment"), in accordance with subsections (7) and (8).

(5) If at any time on or after 1 April 2017 the company receives income for use for charitable purposes which are purposes for facilitating participation in amateur eligible sport, a deduction is allowed only if, and in so far as, the payment exceeds an amount which is equal to the amount of that income which—

    (a) the company does not have to bring into account for corporation tax purposes, and

    (b) has not previously been taken into account under this subsection to disallow a deduction under this Part of all or any part of a payment.

See section 217B(3) for the meaning of terms used in this subsection.

(6) But in any case, the amount of the deduction is limited to the amount that reduces the company's taxable total profits for the accounting period to nil.

(7) If the total of all the direct payments made by the company in the accounting period is equal to or less than the maximum deduction for direct payments, a deduction is allowed under subsection (4)(b) in respect of that total.

(8) If the total of all the direct payments made by the company in the accounting period is more than the maximum deduction for direct payments, a deduction is allowed under subsection (4)(b) in respect of so much of that total as does not exceed the maximum deduction for direct payments.

(9) The maximum deduction for direct payments is £2,500 or, if the accounting period is shorter than 12 months, a proportionately reduced amount.

(10) The Treasury may by regulations amend subsection (9) by substituting a higher amount for the amount for the time being specified there.

217B Meaning of qualifying expenditure on grassroots sport

(1) For the purposes of this Part, a payment is qualifying expenditure on grassroots sport if—

    (a) it is expenditure incurred for charitable purposes which are purposes for facilitating participation in amateur eligible sport, and

    (b) apart from this Part, no deduction from total profits, or in calculating any component of total profits, would be allowed in respect of the payment.

For the meaning of charitable purposes, see sections 2, 7 and 8 of the Charities Act 2011.

(2) Where expenditure is incurred for both—

    (a) charitable purposes which are purposes for facilitating participation in amateur eligible sport, and

    (b) other purposes,

then, for the purposes of subsection (1), it is to be apportioned between the purposes in paragraph (a) and the purposes in paragraph (b) on a just and reasonable basis.

(3) For the purposes of section 217A(5) and subsection (1)(a)—

    (a) paying a person to play or take part in a sport does not facilitate participation in amateur sport, but paying coaches or officials for their services may do so, and

    (b) "eligible sport" means a sport that for the time being is an eligible sport for the purposes of Chapter 9 of Part 13 (see section 661).

217C Meaning of qualifying sport body

(1) For the purposes of this Part, a "qualifying sport body" is—

    (a) a recognised sport governing body;

    (b) a body which is wholly owned by a recognised sport governing body.

(2) A "recognised sport governing body" is a body which is included from time to time in a list, maintained by the National Sports Councils, of governing bodies of sport recognised by them.

(3) The Treasury may by regulations—

    (a) amend this section for the purpose of altering the meaning of "qualifying sport body";

    (b) designate bodies to be treated as qualifying sport bodies for the purposes of this Part.

(4) Regulations under section (3)(b) may designate a body by reference to its inclusion in a class or description of bodies.

(5) In this section "the National Sports Councils" means—

    (a) the United Kingdom Sports Council,

    (b) the English Sports Council,

    (c) the Scottish Sports Council,

(d) the Sports Council for Wales, and
(e) the Sports Council for Northern Ireland.

(6) Regulations under subsection (3)(b) made before 1 April 2018 may include provision having effect in relation to times before the regulations are made (but not times earlier than 1 April 2017).

217D Relationship between this Part and Part 6

If, but for section 217A, an amount—

(a) would be deductible under Part 6, or
(b) would be deductible under Part 6 but for Chapter 2A of Part 6,

the amount is not deductible under this Part, and nothing in this Part affects the amount's deductibility (or non-deductibility) under Part 6."

(6) The amendments made by this section have effect for the purpose of allowing deductions for payments made on or after 1 April 2017.

(7) Where a company has an accounting period beginning before 1 April 2017 and ending on or after that date, the accounting period for the purposes of the new section 217A(9) is so much of the accounting period as falls on or after 1 April 2017.

GENERAL NOTE

Section 22 inserts a new CTA 2010 Pt 6A, introducing a new corporation tax deduction for contributions made on or after or 1 April 2017 to "grassroots sports". The stated aim is to encourage participation in grassroots sports and reduce administrative burdens for some organisations making contributions to grassroots sports.

Following consultation in 2016 the government announced that the new rules would allow companies to deduct all contributions to grassroots sports through recognised sport governing bodies, and allow deductions of up to £2,500 in total annually for direct contributions. Sport governing bodies would be able to deduct all their contributions to grassroots sports.

Existing reliefs under CTA 2010 allow deductions for qualifying charitable donations, including payments to community amateur sports clubs (CASCs). In the absence of those reliefs the "wholly and exclusively" rule in CTA 2009 s 54(1)(a) could deny a deduction.

Relief for expenditure on grassroots sport

A payment made (and not refunded) by a company which is qualifying expenditure on grassroots sport is allowed as a deduction in calculating the corporation tax chargeable for the accounting period in which the payment is made. The deduction is from the company's total profits after any other relief from corporation tax other than charitable donations relief, group relief, and group relief for carried-forward losses. The amount of the deduction is limited to the amount that reduces the company's taxable profits to nil.

If the company is a "qualifying sport body" (see below) at the time of the payment, a deduction is allowed for the amount of the payment. For other companies a deduction is allowed: (a) if the payment is to a qualifying sport body, for the amount of the payment, and (b) for direct payments grassroots sport, as set out below.

New CTA 2010 s 217A(5) provides that a company cannot claim a deduction for a payment that is made out of an amount received for grassroots sport purposes which has not been brought into account in computing the company's taxable profits. For example, a company which makes a payment to a qualifying sport body deducts that amount from its taxable profits, but the receipt may not be taxable in the hands of the qualifying sport body. Broadly, if a company receives income for use for charitable purposes which are purposes for facilitating participation in amateur "eligible sport" (see below), a deduction is allowed only if and in so far as the payment exceeds an amount of that income which the company does not have to bring into account for corporation tax. New CTA 2010 s 217B(3) defines certain terms for this purpose.

The maximum deduction for direct payments made in the accounting period is £2,500 (or a proportion of that amount if the accounting period is shorter than 12 months). This limit may be increased by regulations.

There are consequential amendments to CTA 2010 ss 1(2) (overview), 99 and 105 (group relief).

Meaning of qualifying expenditure on grassroots sport

New CTA 2010 s 217B provides that a payment is qualifying expenditure on grassroots sport if: (a) it is expenditure incurred for charitable purposes which are purposes for facilitating participation in amateur eligible sport, and (b) apart from Part 6A no deduction from total profits, or in calculating any component of total profits, would be allowed in respect of the payment. Charitable purposes are defined in Charities Act 2011 ss 2, 7 and 8. Provision is made for apportioning expenditure where necessary.

Paying a person to play or take part in a sport does not facilitate participation in amateur sport, but paying coaches or officials for their services may do so. "Eligible sport" is a sport that for the time being is an eligible sport for the purposes of CTA 2010 Pt 13 Ch 9 (community amateur sports clubs, see CTA 2010 s 661).

Meaning of qualifying sport body

A "qualifying sport body" is a recognised sport governing body (see below) or a body that is wholly owned by a recognised sport governing body. A "recognised sport governing body" is a body included from time to time in a list of governing bodies of sport recognised by the national sports councils. These provisions may be amended by regulations and the Treasury may designate bodies as qualifying sport bodies.

Relationship between Part 6A and Part 6

New CTA 2010 s 217D provides that a deduction under Part 6A will be available only if deductions under Part 6 for charitable donations, including payments to CASCs, are not available.

Commencement

The new relief is available for payments made on or after 1 April 2017. If a company's accounting period straddles that date, the accounting period for the purposes of the £2,500 limit is so much of the period as falls on or after that date.

23 Profits from the exploitation of patents: cost-sharing arrangements

(1) Part 8A of CTA 2010 (profits from the exploitation of patents) is amended as follows.

(2) After section 357BLE insert—

"357BLEA Cases where the company is a party to a CSA

(1) Subsection (2) applies if during the relevant period—

    (a) the company is a party to a cost-sharing arrangement (see section 357GC),

    (b) the company incurs expenditure in making payments under the arrangement that are within section 357BLC(2) by reason of section 357GCZC, and

    (c) persons who are not connected with the company make payments under the arrangement to the company in respect of relevant research and development undertaken or contracted out by the company.

(2) So much of the expenditure referred to in paragraph (b) of subsection (1) as is equal to the amount of the payments referred to in paragraph (c) of that subsection is to be disregarded in determining the R&D fraction for the sub-stream.

(3) Subsection (4) applies if during the relevant period—

    (a) the company is a party to a cost-sharing arrangement,

    (b) the company incurs expenditure in making payments under the arrangement that are within subsection (5), and

    (c) the company receives payments under the arrangement that are within subsection (6).

(4) So much of the expenditure referred to in paragraph (b) of subsection (3) as is equal to the amount of the payments referred to in paragraph (c) of that subsection is to be disregarded in determining the R&D fraction for the sub-stream.

(5) A payment is within this subsection if—

    (a) it is within section 357BLD(2) by reason of section 357GCZC, or

    (b) it is within section 357BLE(2) or (3) by reason of section 357GCZD.

(6) A payment is within this subsection if—

(a) it is made by persons connected with the company in respect of relevant research and development undertaken or contracted out by the company, or

(b) it is made in respect of an assignment to the company of a relevant qualifying IP right or a grant or transfer to the company of an exclusive licence in respect of such a right."

(3) For section 357GC substitute—

"357GC Meaning of "cost-sharing arrangement" etc

(1) This section applies for the purposes of this Part.

(2) A "cost-sharing arrangement" is an arrangement under which—

(a) each of the parties to the arrangement is required to contribute to the cost of, or undertake activities for the purpose of, creating or developing an item or process,

(b) each of those parties—

    (i) is entitled to a share of any income attributable to the item or process, or

    (ii) has one or more rights in respect of the item or process, and

(c) the amount of any income received by each of those parties is proportionate to its participation in the arrangement as described in paragraph (a).

(3) "Invention", in relation to a cost-sharing arrangement, means the item or process that is the subject of the arrangement (or any item or process incorporated within it).

357GCZA Qualifying IP right held by another party to CSA

(1) This section applies if—

(a) a company is a party to a cost-sharing arrangement,

(b) another party to the arrangement ("P") holds a qualifying IP right granted in respect of the invention, and

(c) the company does not hold an exclusive licence in respect of the right.

(2) But this section does not apply if the arrangement produces for the company a return within section 357BG(1)(c).

(3) The company is to be treated for the purposes of this Part as if it held the right.

(4) The right is to be treated for the purposes of this Part as a new qualifying IP right in relation to the company if—

(a) the company or P (or both) became a party to the arrangement on or after 1 April 2017, or

(b) the right is a new qualifying IP right in relation to P (or would be if P was a company).

(5) Subsection (4) does not apply if—

(a) the company held an exclusive licence in respect of the right immediately before it became a party to the arrangement, and

(b) that licence was granted to the company before the relevant date.

(6) The right is to be treated for the purposes of this Part as an old qualifying IP right in relation to the company if it is not to be treated as a new qualifying IP right by reason of subsection (4).

(7) Subsections (7) and (8) of section 357BP (meaning of "relevant date") apply for the purposes of subsection (5) of this section as they apply for the purposes of subsection (6) of that section.

357GCZB Exclusive licence held by another party to CSA

(1) This section applies if—

(a) a company is a party to a cost-sharing arrangement,

(b) another party to the arrangement ("P") holds an exclusive licence in respect of a qualifying IP right granted in respect of the invention, and

(c) the company does not hold the right or another exclusive licence in respect of it.

(2) But this section does not apply if the arrangement produces for the company a return within section 357BG(1)(c).

(3) The company is to be treated for the purposes of this Part as if it held an exclusive licence in respect of the right.

(4) The right is to be treated for the purposes of this Part as a new qualifying IP right in relation to the company if—

(a) the company or P (or both) became a party to the arrangement on or after 1 April 2017, or

(b) the right is a new qualifying IP right in relation to P (or would be if P was a company).

(5) Subsection (4) does not apply if—

(a) the company held the right immediately before it became a party to the arrangement, and

(b) either—

(i) the right had been granted or issued to the company in response to an application filed before 1 July 2016, or

(ii) the right had been assigned to the company before the relevant date.

(6) Subsection (4) also does not apply if—

(a) the company held an exclusive licence in respect of the right immediately before it became a party to the arrangement, and

(b) that licence was granted to the company before the relevant date.

(7) The right is to be treated for the purposes of this Part as an old qualifying IP right in relation to the company if it is not to be treated as a new qualifying IP right by reason of subsection (4).

(8) Subsections (7) and (8) of section 357BP (meaning of "relevant date") apply for the purposes of subsections (5) and (6) of this section as they apply for the purposes of subsections (5) and (6) of that section.

357GCZC   R&D undertaken or contracted out by another party to CSA

(1) Subsection (2) applies if—

(a) a company is a party to a cost-sharing arrangement, and

(b) another party to the arrangement ("P") undertakes research and development for the purpose of creating or developing the invention.

(2) The research and development is to be treated for the purposes of sections 357BLC and 357BLD as having been contracted out by the company to P.

(3) Subsection (4) applies if—

(a) a company is a party to a cost-sharing arrangement,

(b) another party to the arrangement ("P") contracts out to another person ("A") research and development for the purpose of creating or developing the invention, and

(c) the company makes a payment under the arrangement in respect of that research and development (whether to P or to A).

(4) For the purposes of sections 357BLC and 357BLD—

(a) the company is to be treated as having contracted out to P research and development which is the same as that contracted out by P to A, and

(b) the payment mentioned in subsection (3)(c) is to be treated as if it were a payment made to P in respect of the research and development the company is treated as having contracted out to P.

(5) In this section "research and development" has the meaning given by section 1138.

357GCZD   Acquisition of qualifying IP rights etc by another party to CSA

(1) Subsection (2) applies if—

(a) a company is a party to a cost-sharing arrangement,

(b) a person ("A") assigns to another party to the arrangement ("P") a qualifying IP right,

(c) the qualifying IP right is a right in respect of the invention, and

(d) the company makes under the arrangement a payment in respect of the assignment (whether to A or to P).

(2) The payment is to be treated for the purposes of section 357BLE as if it were a payment to A in respect of the assignment by A to the company of the right.

(3) Subsection (4) applies if—

(a) a company is a party to a cost-sharing arrangement,

(b) a person ("A") grants or transfers to another party to the arrangement ("P") an exclusive licence in respect of qualifying IP right,

(c) the qualifying IP right is a right granted in respect of the invention, and

(d) the company makes a payment under the arrangement in respect of the grant or transfer (whether to A or to P).

(4) The payment is to be treated for the purposes of section 357BLE as if it were a payment to A in respect of the grant or transfer by A to the company of the licence.

357GCZE Treatment of expenditure in connection with formation of CSA etc

(1) Where—

(a) a company makes a payment to a person ("P") in consideration of that person entering into a cost-sharing arrangement with the company, and

(b) P holds a qualifying IP right granted in respect of the invention or holds an exclusive licence in respect of such a right,

a just and reasonable amount of the payment is to be treated for the purposes of section 357BLE as if it was an amount paid in respect of the assignment to the company of the right or (as the case may be) the transfer to the company of the licence.

(2) Where—

(a) a company makes a payment to a party to a cost-sharing arrangement ("P") in consideration of P agreeing to the company becoming a party to the arrangement (whether in place of P or in addition to P), and

(b) any party to the arrangement holds a qualifying IP right in respect of the invention or holds an exclusive licence in respect of such a right,

a just and reasonable amount of the payment is to be treated for the purposes of section 357BLE as if it was an amount paid in respect of the assignment to the company of the right or (as the case may be) the transfer to the company of the licence.

(3) Where—

(a) a company that is a party to a cost-sharing arrangement makes a payment to another party to the arrangement in consideration of that party agreeing to the company becoming entitled to a greater share of the income attributable to the invention or acquiring additional rights in relation to the invention, and

(b) any party to the arrangement holds a qualifying IP right in respect of the invention or holds an exclusive licence in respect of such a right,

a just and reasonable amount of the payment is to be treated for the purposes of section 357BLE as if it was an amount paid in respect of the assignment to the company of the right or (as the case may be) the transfer to the company of the licence.

357GCZF Treatment of income in connection with formation of CSA etc

(1) Where—

(a) a company receives a payment in consideration of its entering into a cost-sharing arrangement, and

(b) the company holds a qualifying IP right granted in respect of the invention or holds an exclusive licence in respect of such a right,

a just and reasonable amount of the payment is to be treated as relevant IP income of the company.

(2) Where—

(a) a company that is a party to a cost-sharing arrangement receives a payment from a person in consideration of its agreeing to that person becoming a party to the arrangement (whether in place of the company or in addition to it), and

(b) any party to the arrangement holds a qualifying IP right in respect of the invention or holds an exclusive licence in respect of such a right,

a just and reasonable amount of the payment is to be treated as relevant IP income of the company.

(3) Where—

(a) a company that is a party to a cost-sharing arrangement receives a payment from another party to the arrangement in consideration of its agreeing to that party becoming entitled to a greater share of the income attributable to the invention or acquiring additional rights in relation to the invention, and

(b) any party to the arrangement holds a qualifying IP right in respect of the invention or holds an exclusive licence in respect of such a right,

a just and reasonable amount of the payment is to be treated as relevant IP income of the company."

(4) In section 357BP (meaning of "new qualifying IP right") after subsection (12) insert—

"(13) This section has effect subject to section 357GCZA (qualifying IP right held by another party to a cost-sharing arrangement) and section 357GCZB (exclusive licence held by another party to a cost-sharing arrangement)."

(5) The amendments made by this section have effect in relation to accounting periods beginning on or after 1 April 2017.

GENERAL NOTE

The patent box legislation was amended by FA 2016 s 64 in order to make it compliant with the requirements of Action 5 of the OECD Base Erosion and Profit Shifting Project. The changes introduced by section 23 take effect for accounting periods beginning on or after 1 April 2017 and address cases where IP is developed under a cost-sharing arrangement between two or more persons. These changes have been the subject of a consultation exercise. The overall aim of the amendments is to ensure that companies that undertake R&D collaboratively through cost-sharing arrangements are neither advantaged or disadvantaged.

New CTA 2010 s 357BLEA applies where a company is a party to a cost-sharing arrangement with persons who are unrelated to the company and such persons make payments to the company in respect of the cost-sharing arrangement. Such payments are set against the expenditure that the company itself has incurred in respect of the arrangement and only the net expenditure incurred by the company is taken into account in determining the R&D fraction for the sub-stream.

This section also covers cases where a company is a party to a cost-sharing arrangement and the company makes payments to, or receives payments from, persons in connection with subcontracting of R&D under the terms of the cost-sharing arrangement. In such cases payments made by the company under the cost-sharing arrangement are disregarded in determining the R&D fraction for the sub-stream to the extent that they are offset by amounts received by the company under the cost-sharing arrangement.

New CTA 2010 s 357GC defines the meaning of cost-sharing arrangement and replaces the former definition. Unlike the former definition it does not require that one of the parties to the cost-sharing arrangement owns IP or has an exclusive licence to it. This is in recognition of the fact that companies may enter into cost-sharing arrangements to develop IP.

New CTA 2010 s 357GCZA provides for a company that is a party to a cost-sharing arrangement to be treated as holding a qualifying IP right in cases where another party (P) to the cost-sharing arrangement holds such right in respect of an invention and also specifies when such right is treated as a new qualifying IP right. This is where the company or P (or both) joined the cost-sharing arrangement on or after 1 April 2017, or where the right was already a new qualifying IP right for P at the date that it joined the cost-sharing arrangement (or would be if P was a company).

The IP in question is treated as an old qualifying IP right where the company held an exclusive licence to the IP in question immediately before it became a party to the cost-sharing arrangement, and the IP was treated as old qualifying IP. In such cases as regards the company joining the cost-sharing arrangement the IP in question is treated as old qualifying IP. This is designed to prevent old qualifying IP from being converted into new qualifying IP by virtue of the company that owns the exclusive licence joining a cost-sharing arrangement with the company that owns the IP. For example, where the company gives up its right to the exclusive licence upon joining the cost-sharing arrangement.

Section 357GCZA does not apply where the arrangement produces a return for the company that is economically equivalent to interest.

New section CTA 2010 s 357GCZB provides for a company that is a party to a cost-sharing arrangement to be treated as holding an exclusive licence to a qualifying IP right if another person (P) that is a party to the cost-sharing arrangement holds such a licence. It also specifies the circumstances in which such right is treated as new qualifying IP of the company. This is where P joined the cost-sharing arrangement on or after 1 April 2017, or where the right was already new qualifying IP right for P at the date that it joined the cost-sharing arrangement (or would have been were P a company).

The IP in question is not treated as new qualifying IP for the company where it held the right or an exclusive licence to the IP in question, which was treated as old qualifying IP, immediately before it became a party to the cost-sharing arrangement. In such cases as regards the company joining the cost-sharing arrangement the IP in question is treated as old qualifying IP. This is designed to prevent old qualifying IP held by a company from being converted into new qualifying IP by virtue of the company joining a cost-sharing arrangement.

CTA 2010 s 357GCZB does not apply where the arrangement produces a return for the company that is economically equivalent to interest.

New section CTA 2010 s 357GCZC treats R&D undertaken by another member of the cost-sharing arrangement as having been subcontracted to that member by the company. It also provides that where another member of the cost-sharing arrangement (P) subcontracts research and development to another party (A) and the company makes a payment in respect of such research and development (whether to P or A), the company is treated as having contracted to P research and development that P contracted out to A for the purposes of calculating the R&D fraction.

New section CTA 2010 s 357GCZD applies where a company is a party to a cost-sharing arrangement. It treats acquisition and licensing costs incurred in relation to the acquisition of qualifying IP by another member of the cost-sharing arrangement (P) as having been acquired by the company itself for the purposes of calculating the R&D fraction, to the extent that the company makes a payment in respect of such costs, whether to P or to the person from whom P acquired such right.

New section CTA 2010 s 357GCZE addresses various situations in which a company becomes, or is a, party to a cost-sharing arrangement and makes payments and becomes entitled to benefit from IP held within the cost-sharing arrangement as part of changes to the structure of the cost-sharing arrangement. In such cases the company is treated for the purposes of calculating the R&D fraction as having acquired the IP. Inter alia, this is to prevent the patent box rules on acquisitions being circumvented by companies entering into cost-sharing arrangements and getting the use of IP but not actually owning or licensing the IP. It applies in three cases:

- The first is where the company makes a payment to another person who holds qualifying IP and the two parties enter into a cost-sharing arrangement.
- The second is where a company joins an existing cost-sharing arrangement and makes a payment to a person who is a party to the cost-sharing arrangement and who holds qualifying IP.
- The final is where within an existing cost-sharing arrangement the company makes a payment to another party to the cost-sharing arrangement, who holds rights and as a result the company becomes entitled to some additional benefit, for example a greater income share under the cost-sharing arrangement or an entitlement to exploit further rights.

In each of the above cases a just and reasonable amount of the payment is treated as acquisition expenditure in the R&D fraction.

New section CTA 2010 s 357GCZF is the converse of new section 357GCZE. It also applies in three cases:

- The first is where a company holds qualifying IP and receives a payment from another person in return for the company entering into a cost-sharing arrangement with that other person.
- The second is where a company is a party to a cost-sharing arrangement and it receives a payment from another person in return for agreeing to that person becoming a party to the cost-sharing arrangement.
- The third is where a company that is a party to the cost-sharing arrangement receives a payment from another party to the arrangement in return for that party becoming entitled to a greater share of the invention or acquiring additional rights in relation to the invention.

In all such cases a just and reasonable amount of the payment that the company receives is treated as being relevant IP income of the company.

Section 23(4) amends the definition of new qualifying IP right to accommodate the introduction of the new CTA 2010 ss 357GCZA and 357GCZB.

Section 23(5) provides that the amendments introduced by the section will have effect for accounting periods beginning on or after 1 April 2017. There is no provision for an accounting period to be split into two where an accounting period straddles this date.

24 Hybrid and other mismatches

(1) Part 6A of TIOPA 2010 (hybrid and other mismatches) is amended as follows.

(2) In section 259B(3) (local taxes), for "is not outside the scope of subsection (2) by reason only that" substitute "is outside the scope of subsection (2) if".

(3) In section 259CC(2) (hybrid and other mismatches from financial instruments: meaning of "permitted" taxable period of a payee), for paragraph (b) substitute—

"(b) the period begins at a later time and it is just and reasonable for the amount of ordinary income to arise for the period (rather than an earlier one)."

(4) In section 259DD(2) (hybrid transfer deduction/non-inclusion mismatches: meaning of "permitted" taxable period of a payee), for paragraph (b) substitute—

"(b) the period begins at a later time and it is just and reasonable for the amount of ordinary income to arise for the period (rather than an earlier one)."

(5) In section 259EB (hybrid payer deduction/non-inclusion mismatches and their extent), after subsection (1) insert—

"(1A) But there is no hybrid payer deduction/non-inclusion mismatch so far as the relevant deduction is—

(a) a debit in respect of amortisation that is brought into account under section 729 or 731 of CTA 2009 (writing down the capitalised cost of an intangible fixed asset), or

(b) an amount that is deductible in respect of amortisation under a provision of the law of a territory outside the United Kingdom that is equivalent to either of those sections."

(6) In section 259FA (deduction/non-inclusion mismatches relating to transfers by permanent establishments), after subsection (4) insert—

"(4A) For the purposes of this section "the PE deduction" does not include—

(a) a debit in respect of amortisation that is brought into account under section 729 or 731 of CTA 2009 (writing down the capitalised cost of an intangible fixed asset), or

(b) an amount that is deductible in respect of amortisation under a provision of the law of a territory outside the United Kingdom that is equivalent to either of those sections."

(7) In section 259GB (hybrid payee deduction/non-inclusion mismatches and their extent), after subsection (1) insert—

"(1A) But there is no hybrid payee deduction/non-inclusion mismatch so far as the relevant deduction is—

(a) a debit in respect of amortisation that is brought into account under section 729 or 731 of CTA 2009 (writing down the capitalised cost of an intangible fixed asset), or

(b) an amount that is deductible in respect of amortisation under a provision of the law of a territory outside the United Kingdom that is equivalent to either of those sections."

(8) In section 259HB (multinational payee deduction/non-inclusion mismatches and their extent), after subsection (1) insert—

"(1A) But there is no multinational payee deduction/non-inclusion mismatch so far as the relevant deduction is—

(a) a debit in respect of amortisation that is brought into account under section 729 or 731 of CTA 2009 (writing down the capitalised cost of an intangible fixed asset), or

(b) an amount that is deductible in respect of amortisation under a provision of the law of a territory outside the United Kingdom that is equivalent to either of those sections."

(9) In section 259KB (imported mismatches: meaning of "excessive PE deduction" etc), after subsection (3) insert—

"(3A) For the purposes of this section a "PE deduction" does not include—

(a) a debit in respect of amortisation that is brought into account under section 729 or 731 of CTA 2009 (writing down the capitalised cost of an intangible fixed asset), or

(b) an amount that is deductible in respect of amortisation under a provision of the law of a territory outside the United Kingdom that is equivalent to either of those sections."

(10) The amendment made by subsection (2)—

(a) has effect, in the case of its application to Chapter 6 of Part 6A of TIOPA 2010, in relation to excessive PE deductions in relation to which the relevant PE period begins on or after 13 July 2017,

(b) has effect, in the case of its application to Chapter 9 or 10 of that Part, in relation to accounting periods beginning on or after that date, and

(c) has effect, in the case of its application to any other Chapter of that Part, in relation to—

(i) payments made on or after date, or

(ii) quasi-payments in relation to which the payment period begins on or after that date.

(11) For the purposes of subsection (10)(a), (b) and (c)(ii), where there is a straddling period—

(a) so much of the straddling period as falls before 13 July 2017, and so much of it as falls on or after that date, are to be treated as separate accounting periods or separate taxable periods (as the case may be), and

(b) if it is necessary to apportion an amount for the straddling period to the two separate periods, it is to be apportioned—

(i) on a time basis according to the respective length of the separate periods, or

(ii) if that would produce a result that is unjust or unreasonable, on a just and reasonable basis.

(12) A "straddling period" means an accounting period or payment period (as the case may be) beginning before 13 July 2017 and ending on or after that date.

(13) Part 6A of TIOPA 2010 has effect, and is to be deemed always to have had effect, with the amendments set out in subsections (3) to (9).

GENERAL NOTE

Part 6A of TIOPA 2010 ("Hybrid and other mismatches") was inserted by Finance Act 2016. Section 24 makes three changes to TIOPA 2010 Pt 6A, two of which were proposed in December 2016 and were originally included in Finance Bill 2017, before being excluded pending the snap General Election in June 2017. The changes are as follows:

– Section 259B defines the meaning of "tax" for the purposes of Pt 6A. Originally, s 259B(3) confirmed that taxes "chargeable under the law of a province, state or other part of a country, or ... levied by or on behalf of a municipality or other local body" were not excluded from the definition of "tax" simply because such taxes are chargeable/levied by those "parts" of a country. Section 259B(3) is amended to confirm that such taxes **are** excluded from the definition of "tax" (without exception). This change was announced on 13 July 2017 and therefore applies from this date onwards. Where a period straddles this date, there is a transitional provision to split it into two notional periods, and time apportion relevant amounts to these, with a "just and reasonable" override if relevant.

– Each chapter dealing with the various types of mismatch contemplated by Pt 6A defines the concept of a "permitted taxable period" – broadly, the period within which taxable income must arise in order to establish that no mismatch arises in relation to the deduction to which it corresponds. Generally this is any period that begins no later than 12 months after the end of the period in which the deduction arises – although this potentially can be later if it is "just and reasonable" for the taxable income to have arisen so late, and subject to a claim being made. The change here is to remove the requirement for a claim to be made, specifically in relation to Chs 3 and 4 only (dealing respectively with hybrid financial instruments and hybrid transfers). The rationale for this relaxation is that a claim requirement for these types of mismatch could lead to a very high number of individual claims, with an onerous compliance burden. It applies from 1 January 2017 (i.e. the introduction of Pt 6A); as noted above, it was originally proposed in December 2016. The claim requirement for late "just and reasonable" permitted taxable periods for the other chapters remains.

– Chapters 3 to 8 cover "deduction/non-inclusion" mismatches, generally arising from payments (or deemed payments) that give rise to "relevant deductions", for which there is no corresponding taxable income. Chapters 5, 6, 7 and 8 are changed to explicitly provide that deductions arising from intangible asset amortisation (whether under CTA 2009 Pt 8 or an equivalent overseas rule) cannot give rise to deduction/non-inclusion mismatches for the purposes of those chapters. This change also applies from 1 January 2017 (and was also originally proposed in December 2016). No similar change is made in respect of tangible fixed assets.

25 Trading profits taxable at the Northern Ireland rate

Schedule 7 contains—

(a) amendments of Part 8B of CTA 2010 (trading profits taxable at the Northern Ireland rate), and

(b) amendments consequential on or related to those amendments.

GENERAL NOTE

Schedule 7 amends CTA 2010 Pt 8B (ss 357H–357XI, trading profits taxable at the Northern Ireland rate), which is to be inserted by the Corporation Tax (Northern Ireland) Act 2015 (CTNIA 2015) s 1 with effect for accounting periods beginning on or after the first day of the financial year appointed by HM Treasury, and amends certain provisions of CAA 2001.

CTNIA 2015 devolves to the Northern Ireland Assembly the power to set, by means of a resolution, the rate of corporation tax to be charged on profits of certain trades and activities in Northern Ireland (the "Northern Ireland rate").

The UK government has committed to implementing the CTNIA 2015 reform once the Northern Ireland Executive (NIE) has demonstrated that its finances are on a sustainable footing. The NIE has committed to setting a Northern Ireland rate of 12.5% from April 2018. However, the Northern Ireland Assembly collapsed in January 2017, and following an election in March 2017 the major parties failed to agree on a power-sharing arrangement. At the time of writing, talks have failed to achieve a restoration of devolved government.

Chargeable gains

26 Elections in relation to assets appropriated to trading stock

(1) Section 161 of TCGA 1992 (appropriations to and from trading stock) is amended as follows.

(2) In subsection (3)—

(a) for "a person's appropriation of an asset for the purposes of a trade" substitute "a case where a chargeable gain would have accrued to a person on the appropriation of an asset for the purposes of a trade as mentioned in that subsection", and

(b) for "the chargeable gain or increased by the amount of the allowable loss referred to in subsection (1), and where that subsection" substitute "that chargeable gain, and where subsection (1)".

(3) In subsection (3ZB)—

(a) in paragraph (a)—

(i) omit "or loss", and

(ii) omit "or an allowable loss",

(b) in paragraph (b)—

(i) omit ", or increased by the amount of any loss," and

(ii) omit "or allowable loss", and

(c) in paragraph (c), at the end insert "and a loss which accrues on that disposal which is not ATED-related is also unaffected by the election".

(4) The amendments made by this section have effect in relation to appropriations of assets made on or after 8 March 2017.

GENERAL NOTE

The section looks to amend the existing rules for businesses that transfer a capital asset to trading stock. The existing rules are in TCGA 1992 s 161.

Under the existing rules, the appropriation of a capital asset to trading stock is treated as taking place at market value and can give a capital gain or allowable loss.

An election can be made to reduce the capital gain or allowable loss to zero, by rebasing the transfer value of the asset.

The changes introduced by section 26 will allow the election to be made only if there is a capital gain on the appropriation of the asset to trading stock. If there is an allowable loss, no election can be made and the loss will remain under the chargeable gains rules.

Section 26 also looks at disposals of assets that give rise to an ATED-related gain or loss (ATED = Annual Tax on Enveloped Dwellings). A similar election under existing rules could be made. Section 26 amends the rules to allow the election only for non-ATED related gains on disposals (i.e. the gain or loss that accrued whilst the asset was not within the charge to ATED) and not for non-ATED related losses. ATED-related gains and losses were already ineligible for the election, and this remains the case.

The amendments made by this section have effect for appropriations of assets made on or after 8 March 2017.

27 Substantial shareholding exemption

(1) Schedule 7AC to TCGA 1992 (exemptions for disposals by companies with substantial shareholding) is amended as follows.

(2) Omit the following (which relate to requirements to be met by investing company)—

  (a) in paragraph 1(2), "the investing company and";
  (b) in paragraph 3—
    (i) in sub-paragraph (2)(b), "(but see sub-paragraph (3) below)";
    (ii) sub-paragraph (3);
    (iii) in sub-paragraph (4), "of paragraph 18(1)(b) and";
  (c) in the heading to Part 3, "investing company and";
  (d) paragraph 18 and the preceding italic heading;
  (e) in paragraph 23(3), "a member of a trading group or".

(3) In paragraph 7 (substantial shareholding requirement), for "two" substitute "six".

(4) In paragraph 10 (effect of earlier no-gain/no-loss transfer), in sub-paragraph (2)(b), after "but for" insert "subsection (1A) or".

(5) In paragraph 19 (requirements relating to company invested in)—

  (a) in sub-paragraph (1)(b), at the beginning insert "in a case where sub-paragraph 1A) applies,";
  (b) after sub-paragraph (1) insert—

  "(1A) This sub-paragraph applies where—

    (a) the disposal is a disposal to a person connected with the investing company, or
    (b) the requirement in paragraph 7 is met by virtue of paragraph 15A.";

  (c) at the end insert—

  "(4) Section 1122 of CTA 2010 (meaning of "connected" persons) applies for the purposes of sub-paragraph (1A)(a)."

(6) The amendments made by this section have effect in relation to disposals made on or after 1 April 2017.

GENERAL NOTE

Section 27 is a relatively short provision but which has a major impact by virtue of the way in which it amends the substantial shareholdings exemption in TCGA 1992 Sch 7AC.

Scope

The substantial shareholding requirement

The substantial shareholding requirement remains at 10% of the ordinary share capital, profits available for distribution to equity holders and assets available for distribution to equity holders on a winding up. However, the qualifying period is amended from a continuous 12-month period starting not more than two years before the date of disposal to a continuous twelve-month period starting not more than six years before the date of the disposal.

The original provision effectively meant that, if a sub-10% shareholding was disposed of within 12 months of a disposal from a shareholding of 10% or more, the later disposal could qualify for the substantial shareholdings exemption, so long as the other conditions for exemption were satisfied. That 12-month run-off period is now effectively extended to five years, which gives companies a great deal more flexibility in cases where shareholdings are being disposed of over a period of time.

Non-UK shareholders

Paragraph 10 of the Schedule currently provides that the period of ownership for the purposes of the substantial shareholding includes all periods during which the relevant shares were held by UK resident companies in a group, so that transfers of shares between UK companies in the group did not start the clock running again.

This rule is now extended to include any companies in the group, so that a period of ownership by a non-UK company in a group, followed by a transfer to a UK company and the disposal by that company, can qualify for the substantial shareholdings exemption, so long as the aggregate period of ownership by the group as a whole is at least 12 months.

Requirements for investing company

The requirement for the vendor company to be either a sole trading company or a member of a qualifying group (which broadly means a trading group) is removed completely. Disposals by non-trading companies will now qualify for the exemption.

Requirements for company invested in

The current requirement in respect of the company whose shares are being sold is that it be a trading company itself or the holding company of a trading group or subgroup. It was necessary for this condition to be satisfied for at least 12 months (longer for run-off disposals) prior to the disposal, as well as immediately afterwards.

The requirement that the company be trading immediately afterward is now removed except for two situations: the first is where the shares are disposed of to a person connected with the vendor (within the meaning of CTA 2010 s 1122). The second situation is where the disposal is one to which TCGA 1992 Sch 7AC para 15A applies, whereby a trade is hived down into a new subsidiary prior to sale and the disposal is treated as qualifying for the exemption, so long as the assets that were transferred in the hove-down were used in trade carried on by the transferor company or a member of its group.

Commencement

All of these amendments apply to disposals on or after 1 April 2017.

28　Substantial shareholding exemption: institutional investors

(1) Schedule 7AC to TCGA 1992 (exemptions for disposals by companies with substantial shareholding) is amended as follows.

(2) After paragraph 3 insert—

"Subsidiary exemption: qualifying institutional investors

3A (1) This paragraph applies in relation to a gain or loss accruing to a company ("the investing company") on a disposal of shares or an interest in shares in another company ("the company invested in").

(2) This paragraph applies if—

  (a) the requirement in paragraph 7 is met (substantial shareholder requirement),

  (b) the requirement in paragraph 19 is not met (requirement relating to company invested in), and

  (c) the investing company is not a disqualified listed company.

(3) If, immediately before the disposal, 80% or more of the ordinary share capital of the investing company is owned by qualifying institutional investors, no chargeable gain or loss accrues on the disposal.

(4) If, immediately before the disposal, at least 25% but less than 80% of the ordinary share capital of the investing company is owned by qualifying institutional investors, the amount of the chargeable gain or loss accruing on the disposal is reduced by the percentage of the ordinary share capital of the investing company which is owned by the qualifying institutional investors.

(5) A company is a "disqualified listed company" for the purposes of this Part of this Schedule if—

  (a) any of the shares forming part of the ordinary share capital of the company are listed on a recognised stock exchange,

  (b) the company is not a qualifying institutional investor, and

  (c) the company is not a qualifying UK REIT

(6) In sub-paragraph (5)(c) "qualifying UK REIT" means a UK REIT within the meaning of Part 12 of CTA 2010 which—

  (a) meets the condition in section 528(4)(b) of that Act (company not a close company by virtue of having an institutional investor as a participant), or

(b) by virtue of section 443 of that Act (companies controlled by or on behalf of Crown) is not treated as a close company.

3B (1) This paragraph applies for the purposes of paragraph 3A.

(2) A person "owns" ordinary share capital if the person owns it—

(a) directly,

(b) indirectly, or

(c) partly directly and partly indirectly.

(3) Sections 1155 to 1157 of CTA 2010 (meaning of "indirect ownership" and calculation of amounts owned indirectly) apply for the purposes of sub-paragraph (2).

(4) For the purposes of sections 1155 to 1157 of CTA 2010 as applied by sub-paragraph (3)—

(a) ordinary share capital may not be owned through a disqualified listed company;

(b) treat references to a body corporate as including an exempt unauthorised unit trust (and references to ordinary share capital, in the case of such a trust, as references to units in the trust).

(5) A person is also to be regarded as owning ordinary share capital in a company in circumstances where a person would, under paragraphs 12 and 13 of this Schedule, be regarded as holding shares in a company.

(6) Where the assets of a partnership include ordinary share capital of a company, each partner is to be regarded as owning a proportion of that share capital equal to the partner's proportionate interest in that ordinary share capital.

(7) In this Schedule "exempt unauthorised unit trust" has the same meaning as in the Unauthorised Unit Trusts (Tax) Regulations 2013 (SI 2013/2819)."

(3) After paragraph 8 insert—

"8A (1) This paragraph applies in a case where at least 25% of the ordinary share capital of the investing company is owned by qualifying institutional investors.

(2) The investing company also holds a "substantial shareholding" in the company invested in for the purposes of this Schedule if—

(a) the investing company holds ordinary shares, or interests in ordinary shares, in the company invested in the cost of which on acquisition was at least £20,000,000, and

(b) by virtue of those shares or interests or any other shares or interests in shares in the company invested in, the investing company—

(i) is beneficially entitled to not less than a proportionate percentage of the profits available for distribution to equity holders of the company invested in, and

(ii) would be beneficially entitled on a winding up to not less than a proportionate percentage of the assets of the company invested in available for distribution to equity holders.

(3) In sub-paragraph (2)—

"cost" means the amount or value of the consideration, in money or money's worth, given by the investing company or on its behalf wholly and exclusively for the acquisition of the ordinary shares or interests in ordinary shares, together with the incidental costs to it of the acquisition;

"proportionate percentage" means a percentage equal to the percentage of the ordinary share capital held by the investing company by virtue of the ordinary shares and interests in ordinary shares referred to in sub-paragraph (2)(a).

(4) For the purposes of sub-paragraph (2)(a) it does not matter whether there was a single acquisition or a series of acquisitions.

(5) If—

(a) the percentage ("the actual percentage") of the profits or assets to which the investing company is, or would be, beneficially entitled as mentioned in sub-paragraph (2)(b)(i) or (ii) is less than the proportionate percentage, but

(b) having regard to the proportion that the actual percentage bears to the proportionate percentage, the difference can reasonably be regarded as insignificant,

the investing company is treated as meeting the condition in sub-paragraph (2)(b)(i) or (ii) (as the case may be).

(6) Paragraph 3B (owning ordinary share capital) applies for the purposes of sub-paragraph (1).

(7) Paragraph 8(2) applies for the purposes of sub-paragraph (2).

(8) In this paragraph "ordinary shares" means shares in the ordinary share capital of the company invested in."

(4) In paragraph 9 (aggregation), in sub-paragraph (1), for "paragraph 7" substitute "paragraphs 7 and 8A(2)".

(5) After paragraph 30 insert—

"Meaning of "qualifying institutional investor"

30A (1) In this Schedule "qualifying institutional investor" means a person falling within any of A to G below.

Pension schemes

A

The trustee or manager of—

(a) a registered pension scheme, other than an investment-regulated pension scheme, or

(b) an overseas pension scheme, other than one which would be an investment-regulated pension scheme if it were a registered pension scheme.

"Investment-regulated pension scheme" has the same meaning as in Part 1 of Schedule 29A to the Finance Act 2004.

"Overseas pension scheme" has the same meaning as in Part 4 of that Act.

Life assurance businesses

B

A company carrying on life assurance business, if immediately before the disposal its interest in the investing company is held as part of its long-term business fixed capital.

"Life assurance business" has the meaning given in section 56 of the Finance Act 2012.

Section 137 of that Act applies for the purposes of determining whether an interest forms part of the long-term business fixed capital of a company.

Sovereign wealth funds etc

C

A person who cannot be liable for corporation tax or income tax (as relevant) on the ground of sovereign immunity.

Charities

D

A charity.

Investment trusts

E

An investment trust.

Authorised investment funds

F

An authorised investment fund which meets the genuine diversity of ownership condition throughout the accounting period of the fund in which the disposal is made.

"Authorised investment fund" has the same meaning as in the Authorised Investment Funds (Tax) Regulations 2006 (SI 2006/964).

Regulation 9A of the Authorised Investment Funds (Tax) Regulations 2006 (genuine diversity of ownership) applies for this purpose.

Exempt unauthorised unit trusts

G

The trustees of an exempt unauthorised unit trust, where the trust meets the genuine diversity of ownership condition throughout the accounting period of the trust in which the disposal is made.

Regulation 9A of the Authorised Investment Funds (Tax) Regulations 2006 (genuine diversity of ownership) applies for this purpose (treating references to an authorised investment fund as including an exempt unauthorised unit trust).

(2) The Treasury may by regulations amend this Schedule so as to add or remove a person as a "qualifying institutional investor" (and may in particular do so by changing the conditions subject to which a person is a qualifying institutional investor)."

(6) In paragraph 31 (index), at the appropriate places insert—

"Exempt unauthorised unit trust | paragraph 3B(7)"
"Qualifying institutional investor | paragraph 30A".

(7) The amendments made by this section have effect in relation to disposals made on or after 1 April 2017.

GENERAL NOTE

Section 28 introduces an entirely new exemption which "piggybacks" on the substantial shareholdings exemption for some of its conditions. The new relief broadly applies to disposals of shares in non-trading companies where the company whose shares are being sold is partly owned by qualifying institutional investors.

Scope

Like the substantial shareholding exemption, this new relief has a number of detailed conditions.

Substantial shareholding requirement

For the purposes of this new relief, the main provisions requiring a substantial shareholding are the same as for the main relief. That is, a shareholding of at least 10% of the ordinary share capital, including rights to 10% of the profits available for distribution to equity holders and 10% of the rights of equity holders to assets on the winding up of a company, must have been held for a continuous period of at least 12 months starting not more than six years before the date of the disposal.

There is an extension to the substantial shareholding requirement, however, so that a vendor company can qualify even if it holds less than 10% of the shares of a company, so long as, when acquired, that shareholding cost at least £20 million. This means the amount of consideration given wholly and exclusively for the ordinary shares, together with incidental costs of acquisition.

To qualify under this provision, the proportion of the ordinary share capital held by the investor must be reflected in the investor's beneficial entitlement to profits available for distribution to equity holders and to their entitlement to assets of the company available for distribution to equity holders. If those rights are smaller than the proportion of ordinary share capital that is held, and the difference can reasonably be regarded as insignificant, then the difference can effectively be ignored.

Non-trading requirement

The second requirement for this new exemption is that the company invested in must fail the test at TCGA 1992 Sch 7AC para 19, which broadly means that it cannot be a trading company. This is, of course, in marked contrast to the main exemptions, which require the company to be a trading company.

Technically, the new exemption can also apply where the company invested in is a trading company, if the disposal is to a connected person or falls within TCGA 1992 Sch 7AC para 15A, but the company does not trade immediately after the disposal. This scenario will also fail the test at TCGA 1992 Sch 7AC para 19.

Disqualified listed companies

The exemption is not available if the investing company is a disqualified listed company, meaning a company any of whose ordinary share capital is listed on a recognised stock exchange unless the company itself is a qualifying institutional investor or a qualifying UK region.

Mechanism for relief

If an investor qualifies for relief, and at least 80% of the ordinary share capital of the company invested in is held by qualifying institutional investors, then any gains on disposals by the investing company are exempt under this new provision.

If the amount of ordinary share capital held by qualifying institutional investors is at least 25% but does not reach 80%, then the gain on a disposal is reduced by the same percentage as the shareholdings by qualifying institutional investors. For example, if qualifying institutional investors hold 60% of the company invested in, then 60% of any gain on disposal of shares by the investor will be exempt.

Qualifying institutional investors

For the purposes of this legislation, qualifying institutional investors fall into one of the following seven categories:
- Trustees or managers of certain pension schemes.
- A company carrying on life assurance business, so long as the interest in the investing company is part of the long-term business fixed capital.
- Sovereign wealth funds, i.e. persons who cannot be liable for corporation tax or income tax because of their sovereign immunity.
- Charities.
- Investment trusts.
- Authorised investment funds which meet the genuine diversity of ownership condition throughout the accounting period of the fund in which the disposal is made.
- Exempt unauthorised unit trusts where the trust meets the genuine diversity of ownership condition throughout the accounting period of the trust in which the disposal is made.

Commencement

This relief applies for disposals on or after 1 April 2017.

Domicile, overseas property etc

29 Deemed domicile: income tax and capital gains tax

(1) In Chapter 2A of Part 14 of ITA 2007 (income tax liability: domicile), after section 835B insert—

"835BA Deemed domicile

(1) This section has effect for the purposes of the provisions of the Income Tax Acts or TCGA 1992 which apply this section.

(2) An individual not domiciled in the United Kingdom at a time in a tax year ("the relevant tax year") is to be regarded as domiciled in the United Kingdom at that time if—

(a) condition A is met, or
(b) condition B is met.

(3) Condition A is that—

(a) the individual was born in the United Kingdom,
(b) the individual's domicile of origin was in the United Kingdom, and
(c) the individual is UK resident for the relevant tax year.

(4) Condition B is that the individual has been UK resident for at least 15 of the 20 tax years immediately preceding the relevant tax year.

(5) But Condition B is not met if—

(a) the individual is not UK resident for the relevant tax year, and
(b) there is no tax year beginning after 5 April 2017 and preceding the relevant tax year in which the individual was UK resident."

(2) Schedule 8 contains—

(a) provision applying section 835BA of ITA 2007, and
(b) further provision relating to this section.

GENERAL NOTE

F(No 2)A 2017 introduces a definition for deemed domiciled for income and capital gains tax purposes to apply from 6 April 2017, and also amends the IHT definition.

For income tax and capital gains tax purposes, ITA 2007 s 835BA is inserted by section 29 to define deemed domicile. There are two types of deemed domiciles, as follows:

"Condition A non-doms"

The first type of deemed domiciles are individuals who meet all three of the criteria below:
- the individual was born in the UK;
- the individual's domicile of origin was in the UK; and

– the individual is UK resident for the relevant tax year.

"Condition B non-doms"

The second type of non-dom is someone who has been resident in the UK for at least 15 out of the 20 tax years immediately preceding the relevant tax year, unless:
– the individual is not UK resident for the relevant tax year; and
– there is no tax year beginning after 5 April 2017 and preceding the relevant tax year in which the individual was UK resident.

The effect of the above wording is that someone who would become potentially deemed domicile on the 5 April 2017 by virtue of the 15/20 year rule, but who was non-resident on 5 April 2017 and subsequently, won't actually become deemed domicile under this new rule unless they become UK resident subsequently. This is an important transitional provision.

Schedule 8 deals with the income tax and capital gains provisions impacted by the new deemed domicile rule.

30 Deemed domicile: inheritance tax

(1) In section 267 of IHTA 1984 (persons treated as domiciled in the United Kingdom), in subsection (1)—

(a) in paragraph (a), omit the final "or";
(b) after that paragraph insert—
    "(aa) he is a formerly domiciled resident for the tax year in which the relevant time falls ("the relevant tax year"), or";
(c) for paragraph (b) substitute—
    "(b) he was resident in the United Kingdom—
        (i) for at least fifteen of the twenty tax years immediately preceding the relevant tax year, and
        (ii) for at least one of the four tax years ending with the relevant tax year."

(2) In that section, omit subsection (3).

(3) In that section, in subsection (4), for "in any year of assessment" substitute "for any tax year".

(4) In section 48 of that Act (settlements: excluded property)—

(a) in subsection (3)(b), for "and (3D)" substitute "to (3E)";
(b) in subsection (3A)(b), for "subsection (3B)" substitute "subsections (3B) and (3E)";
(c) after subsection (3D) insert—

"(3E) In a case where the settlor of property comprised in a settlement is not domiciled in the United Kingdom at the time the settlement is made, the property is not excluded property by virtue of subsection (3) or (3A) above at any time in a tax year if the settlor was a formerly domiciled resident for that tax year."

(5) In section 64 of that Act (charge at ten-year anniversary), in subsection (1B), after "was made" insert "and is not a formerly domiciled resident for the tax year in which the ten-year anniversary falls".

(6) In section 65 of that Act (charge at other times), after subsection (7A) insert—

"(7B) Tax shall not be charged under this section by reason only that property comprised in a settlement becomes excluded property by virtue of section 48(3E) ceasing to apply in relation to it."

(7) In section 82 of that Act (excluded property)—

(a) for subsection (1) substitute—

"(1) In a case where, apart from this section, property to which section 80 or 81 applies would be excluded property by virtue of section 48(3)(a) above, that property shall not be taken to be excluded property at any time ("the relevant time") for the purposes of this Chapter (except sections 78 and 79) unless Conditions A and B are satisfied.";

(b) in subsection (2), for "the condition in subsection (3) below" substitute "Condition A";
(c) in subsection (3), for "The condition" substitute "Condition A";
(d) after subsection (3) insert—

"(4) Condition B referred to in subsection (1) above is—

(a) in the case of property to which section 80 above applies, that the person who is the settlor in relation to the settlement first mentioned in that section, and

(b) in the case of property to which subsection (1) or (2) of section 81 above applies, that the person who is the settlor in relation to the first or second of the settlements mentioned in that subsection,

was not a formerly domiciled resident for the tax year in which the relevant time falls."

(8) In section 272 of that Act (interpretation)—

(a) for the definition of "foreign-owned" substitute—

""foreign-owned", in relation to property at any time, means property—

(a) in the case of which the person beneficially entitled to it is at that time domiciled outside the United Kingdom, or

(b) if the property is comprised in a settlement, in the case of which the settlor—

(i) is not a formerly domiciled resident for the tax year in which that time falls, and

(ii) was domiciled outside the United Kingdom when the property became comprised in the settlement;";

(b) at the appropriate place insert—

""formerly domiciled resident", in relation to a tax year, means a person—

(a) who was born in the United Kingdom,

(b) whose domicile of origin was in the United Kingdom,

(c) who was resident in the United Kingdom for that tax year, and

(d) who was resident in the United Kingdom for at least one of the two tax years immediately preceding that tax year;".

(9) The amendments made by this section have effect in relation to times after 5 April 2017, subject to subsections (10) to (12).

(10) The amendment to section 267(1) of IHTA 1984 made by subsection (1)(c) does not have effect in relation to a person if—

(a) the person is not resident in the United Kingdom for the relevant tax year, and

(b) there is no tax year beginning after 5 April 2017 and preceding the relevant tax year in which the person was resident in the United Kingdom.

In this subsection "relevant tax year" is to be construed in accordance with section 267(1) of IHTA 1984 as amended by subsection (1).

(11) The amendment to section 267(1) of IHTA 1984 made by subsection (1)(c) also does not have effect in determining—

(a) whether settled property which became comprised in the settlement on or before that date is excluded property for the purposes of IHTA 1984;

(b) the settlor's domicile for the purposes of section 65(8) of that Act in relation to settled property which became comprised in the settlement on or before that date;

(c) whether, for the purpose of section 65(8) of that Act, the condition in section 82(3) of that Act is satisfied in relation to such settled property.

(12) Despite subsection (2), section 267(1) of IHTA 1984, as originally enacted, shall continue to be disregarded in determining—

(a) whether settled property which became comprised in the settlement on or before 9 December 1974 is excluded property for the purposes of IHTA 1984;

(b) the settlor's domicile for the purposes of section 65(8) of that Act in relation to settled property which became comprised in the settlement on or before that date;

(c) whether, for the purpose of section 65(8) of that Act, the condition in section 82(3) of that Act is satisfied in relation to such settled property.

(13) Subsections (14) and (15) apply if an amount of inheritance tax—

(a) would not be charged but for the amendments made by this section, or

(b) is, because of those amendments, greater than it would otherwise have been.

(14) Section 233 of IHTA 1984 (interest on unpaid inheritance tax) applies in relation to the amount of inheritance tax as if the reference, in the closing words of subsection (1) of that section, to the end of the period mentioned in paragraph (a), (aa), (b) or (c) of that subsection were a reference to—

(a) the end of that period, or

(b) if later, the end of the month immediately following the month in which this Act is passed.

(15) Subsection (1) of section 234 of IHTA 1984 (cases where inheritance tax payable by instalments carries interest only from instalment dates) applies in relation to the amount of inheritance tax as if the reference, in the closing words of that subsection, to the date at which an instalment is payable were a reference to—

(a) the date at which the instalment is payable, or

(b) if later, the end of the month immediately following the month in which this Act is passed.

(16) Subsection (17) applies if—

(a) a person is liable as mentioned in section 216(1)(c) of IHTA 1984 (trustee liable on 10-year anniversary, and other trust cases) for an amount of inheritance tax charged on an occasion, and

(b) but for the amendments made by this section—

(i) no inheritance tax would be charged on that occasion, or

(ii) a lesser amount of inheritance tax would be charged on that occasion.

(17) Section 216(6)(ad) of IHTA 1984 (delivery date for accounts required by section 216(1)(c)) applies in relation to the account to be delivered in connection with the occasion as if the reference to the expiration of the period of 6 months from the end of the month in which the occasion occurs were a reference to—

(a) the expiration of that period, or

(b) if later, the end of the month immediately following the month in which this Act is passed.

GENERAL NOTE

Deemed domicile for IHT

The change introduced by section 30 amends the rules defining domicile for IHT purposes. There is already a concept of deemed domicile within the IHT rules and therefore these new provisions supplement the existing test for determining a person's domicile status.

The provision under which a person who was domiciled in the UK under the general law within the preceding three years remains deemed domiciled is retained.

The existing provision under which an individual becomes deemed domiciled for IHT purposes after 17 out of 20 years of UK tax residence is amended to match the new provision in section 29 for income tax and capital gains tax. The applicable period of UK residence is now shortened to 15 out of 20 tax years. There is a change in the way in which the test is carried out. The existing test requires somebody to be resident in the UK in not less than 17 of the 20 years ending in the year for which domicile is being tested. The new test requires a person to be resident in 15 out of the 20 years ending in the year immediately preceding the year in which the test is carried out.

The 15/20 year rule is qualified such that for an individual to be deemed domiciled for IHT purposes, as well as meeting the 15/20 year rule, the individual must also have been resident in the UK for at least one of the four tax years ending with the relevant tax year. Note the difference between the IHT test and the income tax test, in that for income tax purposes, there is a requirement to be tax resident in the tax year, whereas for IHT purposes there is only a requirement to be resident in one of the last four tax years.

Transitional rules apply for individuals who ceased to be UK tax resident before 6 April 2017 and have not resumed UK tax residence after that point. Say, for example, an individual was about to become deemed domiciled under the old 17/20 year test and therefore left the UK on 5 April 2017. In the absence of any transitional provisions, such an individual would become deemed domiciled on 6 April 2017 because he had been resident in the UK for 15 out of the previous 20 tax years and at least one of the last four. He would not however, because of the different test, be deemed domiciled for income tax purposes. This transitional rule therefore stops such individuals who have just left the UK to avoid breaching the old deemed domicile test from being treated as deemed domiciled immediately after leaving.

In addition a new category of deemed domiciled individual is introduced termed a "formerly domiciled resident".

Formerly domiciled residents are those who:

(a) were born in the UK,

(b) whose domicile of origin is in the UK,

(c) are resident in the UK for the tax year, and

(d) were resident in the UK for at least one of the two preceding tax years.

For income tax and capital gains tax, returning UK domiciliaries become deemed domiciled immediately but there is, in effect, a year's grace given for IHT purposes to those who resume UK residency.

Excluded property settlements

The concept of a "formerly domiciled resident" is also then brought forward into amendments concerning excluded property settlements. Such settlements will lose their excluded property status for any period in which the settlor becomes a "formerly domiciled resident". This means that periodic and proportionate charges will apply to the trust property whilst the settlor is UK resident.

31 Settlements and transfer of assets abroad: value of benefits

Schedule 9 makes provision about the value of benefits received in relation to settlements and the transfer of assets abroad.

GENERAL NOTE

Section 31 introduces Schedule 9, which contains statutory valuation rules for certain non-monetary capital payments/benefits. The new rules apply to:
- The capital gains tax (CGT) non-UK resident settlements: anti-avoidance legislation (TCGA 1992 s 86A to s 96 and TCGA 1992 Sch 4C).
- The Income Tax Transfer of Assets Abroad legislation (ITA 2007 Pt 13, Ch 2).

Schedule 9 contains legislative provisions setting out how to value the following capital payments/benefits:
- a payment to the individual by way of a loan;
- making movable property available to an individual; and
- making land available to an individual.

Schedule 9 starts with the CGT capital payment valuation rules, which are inserted after TCGA 1992 s 97 and then progresses to the transfer of assets abroad benefits valuation rules, which are inserted into ITA 2007 Pt 13, Ch 2.

Whilst the wording used is not completely identical the valuation rules are aligned. The actual tax payable will differ given the divergence between income tax and CGT rates and the possibility of the CGT supplementary charge applying.

The legislation is effective for 2017/18 and subsequent tax years.

In the Finance Act contents section 31 is shown under the "Domicile, overseas property etc" heading. The changes came about as a result of the discussions on the introduction of the deemed domicile provisions and the trust protections. However, the statutory valuation rules apply regardless of the affected individual's domicile status.

32 Exemption from attribution of carried interest gains

(1) TCGA 1992 is amended as follows.

(2) In section 13(1A) (attribution of gains to members of non-resident companies)—
    (a) omit the "or" at the end of paragraph (a), and
    (b) at the end of paragraph (b), insert ", or
        (c) a chargeable gain treated as accruing under section 103KA(2) or (3) (carried interest gains)."

(3) In section 86 (attribution of gains to settlors with interest in non-resident or dual resident settlements), after subsection (4ZA) insert—

"(4ZB) Where (apart from this subsection) the amount mentioned in subsection (1)(e) would include an amount of chargeable gains treated as accruing under section 103KA(2) or (3) (carried interest gains), the amount of the gains is to be disregarded for the purposes of subsection (1)(e)."

(4) In section 87 (non-UK resident settlements: attribution of gains to beneficiaries), after subsection (5A) insert—

"(5B) Where (apart from this subsection) the amount mentioned in subsection (4)(a) would include an amount of chargeable gains treated as accruing under section 103KA(2) or (3) (carried interest gains), the amount of the gains is to be disregarded for the purposes of determining the section 2(2) amount."

(5) The amendments made by this section have effect in relation to chargeable gains treated as accruing under section 103KA(2) or (3) of TCGA 1992 at any time before, as well as after, the passing of this Act.

GENERAL NOTE

Section 32 of the Finance Act makes amendments to the Taxation of Chargeable Gains Act 1992 ("TCGA") to ensure that chargeable gains treated as accruing to an individual under TCGA 1992 s 103KA(2) or (3) ("carried interest gains") are excluded from the scope of certain other provisions that also treat chargeable gains as accruing to a person. This exclusion is intended to operate in a similar way as the exclusion for gains within the non-resident capital gains tax regime for UK residential property. The amendments have effect in relation to carried interest gains treated as accruing at any time before, as well as after, the passing of the Finance Act. Section 32 is in the part of the Act headed "Domicile, overseas property etc" which also includes the new deemed domicile rules, and HMRC's explanatory notes on the clause say that it is related to a series of reforms announced at the summer 2015 Budget to the tax rules for individuals who are not domiciled in the UK under the general law.

The amendments are as follows:

–   Section 32(2) amends TCGA 1992 s 13(1A) to provide that section 13 (which attributes certain gains to UK resident participators in a non-UK resident closely held company) will not apply to carried interest gains.
–   Section 32(3) inserts TCGA 1992 s 86(4ZB) to provide that section 86 (which attributes certain gains to certain UK resident and domiciled settlors with an interest in non-UK resident or dual resident settlements following a disposal of settled property) will not apply to carried interest gains.
–   Section 32(4) inserts TCGA 1992 s 87(5B) to provide that section 87 (which attributes certain gains to UK resident beneficiaries of non-UK resident settlements) will not apply to carried interest gains.

By way of background, TCGA 1992 s 103KA was introduced with effect from 8 July 2015 and operates by treating a chargeable gain as accruing to an individual who performs investment management services in respect of an investment scheme under arrangements involving at least one partnership, where "carried interest" (as defined) arises to the individual pursuant to ITA 2007 Pt 13 Ch 5E. This ensures that carried interest amounts are subject to a minimum capital gains tax rate where this is less than the tax that would be charged based on the underlying nature of the investment scheme profits allocated. Section 103KA(2) operates in the case of a disposal of assets held by the partnership(s), and section 103KA(3) operates in any other circumstances.

"Carried interest" means, broadly, a profit related return from an investment scheme where there is significant risk that the individual will not receive a payment, as well as arrangements in a classically structured private equity type carry model (ITA 2007 ss 809EZC and 809EZD).

From 22 October 2015, carried interest "arises" to an individual not only if it arises to them directly, but also if it arises to other persons where the individual could potentially benefit from the payment (originally the legislation taxed amounts arising "directly or indirectly" to the individual). The carried interest legislation also treats carried interest as a UK source capital gain for remittance basis users (even if the underlying fund profit was non-UK source) to the extent they have performed services for the fund in the UK (TCGA 1992 s 103KC).

Prior to the amendments made by section 32 there may have been, in theory, the potential for some overlap between amounts that actually arise to another person but are treated as arising to an individual under the carried interest provisions, and amounts that actually arise to another person but are treated as arising to an individual under the other provisions mentioned above. It is understood that the new provisions are intended to ensure that the carried interest capital gains tax charge takes priority, which applies a higher minimum rate (currently 28%) under TCGA 1992 s 4 and has strict rules on permitted deductions.

33 Inheritance tax on overseas property representing UK residential property

Schedule 10 makes provision about the extent to which overseas property is excluded property for the purposes of inheritance tax, in cases where the value of the overseas property is attributable to residential property in the United Kingdom.

GENERAL NOTE

Section 33 introduces Schedule 10, which extends the scope of Inheritance Tax (IHT), so that IHT will apply to:

- UK residential property owned by foreign domiciliaries (or trusts settled by foreign domiciliaries) through a foreign company or partnership;
- relevant loans (broadly a loan where the funds are used for the acquisition, maintenance or enhancement of an interest in UK residential property); and
- security, collateral or a guarantee given in connection with a relevant loan.

Disguised remuneration

34 Employment income provided through third parties

(1) In section 554XA of ITEPA 2003 (employment income provided through third parties: exclusion for payments in respect of a tax liability), in subsection (2), omit paragraphs (a) and (b).

(2) The amendment made by subsection (1) has effect in relation to relevant steps taken on or after 21 July 2017.

(3) Schedule 11 makes provision about the application of Part 7A of ITEPA 2003 in relation to loans and quasi-loans that are outstanding on 5 April 2019.

GENERAL NOTE

Section 34 and Sch 11 represent another attempt by the Government to stop Employee Benefit Trust (EBT) and similar structures being used to provide what is in effect employment income without a PAYE and NIC liability arising. The Schedule is mainly concerned with existing EBT structures and imposes a PAYE liability on most loans to individuals from EBTs if they are outstanding on 5 April 2019. Parallel NIC will also be introduced. The provisions are retroactive, in that the charge can arise on loans taken out as far as back as 1999. The legislation operates by deeming the amount of the outstanding loan to be a relevant step under the disguised remuneration legislation in ITEPA 2003 Part 7A.

Employment income provided through third parties

Subsection (1) amends ITEPA 2003 s 554XA by omitting paragraphs (2)(a) and (b). The intention of those paragraphs, which were introduced in the first Finance Act of 2017, was that a relevant step would not be triggered if trustees made payments directly to HMRC in relation to tax liabilities. As originally drafted those payments included income tax, national insurance, inheritance tax and corporation tax. The effect of this new amendment is that payments of income tax and national insurance by trustees will be a relevant step (as they were prior to FA 2017). This is, according to the 6 September 2017 Finance Bill resolutions, to correct an unintended consequence of the relief in the FA 2017 provisions. Relief will still be available for inheritance tax and corporation tax payments: in other words, the trustees can make payments of those taxes to HMRC without the payment triggering a relevant step.

Under subsection (2), the amendment in (1) above has effect for relevant steps taken on or after 21 July 2017.

Subsection (3) introduces Schedule 11, which introduces a charge on loans etc. outstanding on 5 April 2019.

35 Trading income provided through third parties

(1) ITTOIA 2005 is amended as follows.

(2) After section 23 insert—

"Trading income provided through third parties

23A Application of section 23E: conditions

(1) Section 23E (tax treatment of relevant benefits) applies if Conditions A to E are met.

(2) Condition A is that a person ("T") is or has been carrying on a trade (the "relevant trade") alone or in partnership.

(3) Condition B is that—

(a) there is an arrangement ("the arrangement") in connection with the relevant trade to which T is a party or which otherwise (wholly or partly) covers or relates to T, and

(b) it is reasonable to suppose that, in essence—

    (i) the arrangement, or

    (ii) the arrangement so far as it covers or relates to T,

is (wholly or partly) a means of providing, or is otherwise concerned with the provision of, relevant benefits.

(4) Condition C is that—

    (a) a relevant benefit arises to T, or a person who is or has been connected with T, in pursuance of the arrangement, or

    (b) a relevant benefit arises to any other person in pursuance of the arrangement and any of the enjoyment conditions (see section 23F) is met in relation to the relevant benefit.

(5) Condition D is that it is reasonable to suppose that the relevant benefit (directly or indirectly) represents, or has arisen or derives from, or is otherwise connected with, the whole or part of a qualifying third party payment.

(6) Condition E is that it is reasonable to suppose that a tax advantage would be obtained by T, or a person who is or has been connected with T, as a result of the arrangement.

(7) For the purposes of subsection (3) in particular, all relevant circumstances are to be taken into account in order to get to the essence of the matter.

(8) In this section and sections 23B to 23H, "this group of sections" means this section and those sections.

(9) The provisions of this group of sections apply to professions and vocations as they apply to trades.

(10) See Schedule 12 to F(No.2)A 2017 for provision about the application of this group of sections in relation to loans and quasi-loans that are outstanding on 5 April 2019.

23B Meaning of "relevant benefit"

(1) The following provisions apply for the purposes of this group of sections.

(2) "Relevant benefit" means any payment (including a payment by way of a loan), a transfer of money's worth, or any other benefit.

(3) The assumption of a liability of T by another person is to be treated as the provision of a relevant benefit to T.

(4) The assumption, by a person other than T, of a liability of a person ("C") who is or has been connected with T, is to be treated as the provision of a relevant benefit to C.

(5) "Loan" includes—

    (a) any form of credit;

    (b) a payment that is purported to be made by way of a loan.

23C Meaning of "qualifying third party payment"

(1) The following provisions apply for the purposes of this group of sections.

(2) A payment is a "third party payment" if it is made (by T or another person) to—

    (a) T acting as trustee, or

    (b) any person other than T.

(3) A third party payment is a "qualifying third party payment" if the deduction condition or the trade connection condition is met in relation to the payment.

(4) The "deduction condition" is met in relation to a payment if—

    (a) a deduction for the payment is made in calculating the profits of the relevant trade, or

    (b) where the relevant trade is or has been carried on in partnership, a deduction for the payment is made in calculating the amount on which T is liable to income tax in respect of the profits of the trade.

(5) The "trade connection condition" is met in relation to a payment if it is reasonable to suppose that in essence—

    (a) the payment is by way of consideration for goods or services provided in the course of the relevant trade, or

    (b) there is some other connection (direct or indirect) between the payment and the provision of goods or services in the course of the relevant trade.

(6) For the purposes of subsection (5) in particular, all relevant circumstances are to be taken into account in order to get to the essence of the matter.

23D Other definitions

(1) The following provisions apply for the purposes of this group of sections.

(2) "Arrangement" includes any agreement, understanding, scheme, settlement, trust, transaction or series of transactions (whether or not legally enforceable).

(3) A "tax advantage" includes—

    (a) relief or increased relief from tax,
    (b) repayment or increased repayment of tax,
    (c) avoidance or reduction of a charge to tax or an assessment to tax,
    (d) avoidance of a possible assessment to tax,
    (e) deferral of a payment of tax or advancement of a repayment of tax, and
    (f) avoidance of an obligation to deduct or account for tax.

(4) Section 993 of ITA 2007 (meaning of "connected" persons) applies for the purposes of this group of sections as if subsection (4) of that section 993 were omitted.

23E Tax treatment of relevant benefits

(1) Where this section applies (see section 23A), the relevant benefit amount is to be treated for income tax purposes as profits of the relevant trade for—

    (a) the tax year in which the relevant benefit arises, or
    (b) if T has ceased to carry on the relevant trade in a tax year (the "earlier tax year") before the tax year referred to in paragraph (a), the earlier tax year.

(2) For the purposes of this section, "the relevant benefit amount" means—

    (a) if the relevant benefit is a payment otherwise than by way of a loan, an amount equal to the amount of the payment,
    (b) if the relevant benefit is a payment by way of loan, an amount equal to the principal amount lent, or
    (c) in any other case, an amount equal to the value of the relevant benefit.

(3) For the purposes of subsection (2)(c), the value of a relevant benefit is—

    (a) its market value at the time it arises, or
    (b) if higher, the cost of providing it.

(4) In subsection (3) "market value" has the same meaning as it has for the purposes of TCGA 1992 by virtue of Part 8 of that Act.

23F Relevant benefits: persons other than T

(1) For the purposes of section 23A(4), the enjoyment conditions are—

    (a) that the relevant benefit, or part of it, is in fact so dealt with by any person as to be calculated at some time to enure for the benefit of T;
    (b) that the arising of the relevant benefit operates to increase the value to T of any assets—
        (i) which T holds, or
        (ii) which are held for the benefit of T;
    (c) that T receives, or is entitled to receive, at any time any benefit provided or to be provided out of, or deriving or to be derived from, the relevant benefit (or part of it);
    (d) where the relevant benefit is the payment of a sum of money (including a payment by way of loan), that T may become entitled to the beneficial enjoyment of the sum or part of the sum if one or more powers are exercised or successively exercised (and for these purposes it does not matter who may exercise the powers or whether they are exercisable with or without the consent of another person);
    (e) where the relevant benefit is the payment of a sum of money (including a payment by way of loan), that T is able in any manner to control directly or indirectly the application of the sum or part of the sum.

(2) Where an enjoyment condition is met in relation to part only of a relevant benefit, that part is to be treated as a separate benefit for the purposes of section 23A(4).

(3) In subsection (1) references to T include references to a person who is or has been connected with T.

(4) In determining whether any of the enjoyment conditions is met in relation to a relevant benefit, regard must be had to the substantial result and effect of all the relevant circumstances.

23G Anti-avoidance

(1) In determining whether section 23E applies in relation to a relevant benefit, no regard is to be had to any arrangements the main purpose, or one of the main purposes, of which is to secure that section 23E does not apply in relation to the whole, or any part, of—

(a) the relevant benefit, or

(b) the relevant benefit and one or more other relevant benefits (whether or not all arising to the same person).

(2) Where arrangements are disregarded under subsection (1), and a relevant benefit (or part of it)—

(a) would, if the arrangements were not disregarded, arise before 6 April 2017, but

(b) would, when the arrangements are disregarded, arise on or after that date,

the relevant benefit (or part) is to be regarded for the purposes of this group of sections as arising on the date on which it would arise apart from the arrangements.

23H Double taxation

(1) This section applies where—

(a) income tax is charged on an individual by virtue of the application of section 23E in relation to a relevant benefit amount, and

(b) at any time, a tax (whether income tax or another tax) is charged on the individual or another person otherwise than by virtue of the application of section 23E in relation to the relevant benefit concerned.

(2) In order to avoid a double charge to tax, the individual may make a claim for one or more consequential adjustments to be made in respect of the tax charged as mentioned in subsection (1)(b).

(3) On a claim under this section an officer of Revenue and Customs must make such of the consequential adjustments claimed (if any) as are just and reasonable.

(4) The value of any consequential adjustments must not exceed the lesser of—

(a) the income tax charged on the individual as mentioned in subsection (1)(a), and

(b) the tax charged as mentioned in subsection (1)(b).

(5) Consequential adjustments may be made—

(a) in respect of any period,

(b) by way of an assessment, the modification of an assessment, the amendment of a claim, or otherwise, and

(c) despite any time limit imposed by or under any enactment."

(3) In section 7(2) (income charged: profits of a tax year) at the end insert "(including amounts treated as profits of the tax year under section 23E(1))."

(4) The amendments made by this section have effect in relation to relevant benefits arising on or after 6 April 2017.

(5) Schedule 12 contains provision about the application of new sections 23A to 23H of ITTOIA 2005 in relation to loans and quasi-loans that are outstanding on 5 April 2019.

GENERAL NOTE

Section 35 and Schedule 12 introduce new anti-avoidance measures designed to prevent the use of loans and other non-taxable amounts to avoid liability to income tax by sole traders and partnerships. They build on the general framework of ITEPA 2003 Pt 7A Disguised remuneration – but are tailored to fit with the framework of taxing businesses. They are astonishingly widely drawn and in effect create a general anti-avoidance framework for income tax on businesses without any of the safeguards built into the GAAR.

Section 35(1) introduces amendments to ITTOIA 2005. Subsection (2) introduces new ITTOIA 2005 ss 23A to 23H.

ITTOIA 2005 ss 23A–23H

ITTOIA 2005 s 23A(1) introduces the concept of relevant benefits and explains that conditions A to E (sub-ss (2)–(6)) must be met:

– Condition A is that a person (referred to as T) is or has been carrying on a trade either alone or in partnership.

– Condition B is that there is an arrangement in connection with the relevant trade to which T is either a party or which covers (wholly or partly) or relates to T, and it is reasonable to suppose that the arrangement, either as a whole or to the extent that it covers T is wholly or mainly concerned with the provision of relevant benefits as defined in s 23B below.

- Condition C is that a relevant benefit arises to T or a person connected with T, or a relevant benefit arises to another person. In the latter case the condition is only satisfied where the enjoyment condition (s 23F) is met.
- Condition D is that it is reasonable to suppose that the relevant benefit represents or arises from or is otherwise connected with a qualifying third party payment (s 23C).
- Condition E is that it is reasonable to suppose that a tax advantage would be obtained by T or a person connected with him/her as a result of the arrangement.

ITTOIA 2005 s 23A(7) explains that all relevant circumstances are to be taken into account in order to get to, what the legislation rather oddly describes as, "the essence of the matter". This is particularly the case in relation to condition B but applies to all of the conditions.

ITTOIA 2005 s 23A(8) is a minor drafting amendment.

ITTOIA 2005 s 23A(9) states that the provisions of ss 23A to 23H apply to professions and vocations as well as trades.

ITTOIA 2005 s 23A(10) refers to Schedule 12 of this act which has further provisions relating to loans etc. outstanding on 5 April 2019.

Meaning of relevant benefit

ITTOIA 2005 s 23B(1) introduces the section, which deals with relevant benefits.

ITTOIA 2005 s 23B(2) states that relevant benefit means any payment, including a payment by way of loan, a transfer of money's worth or any other benefit. In essence therefore virtually anything can be a relevant benefit.

ITTOIA 2005 s 23B(3) deals with indirect benefits. If another person takes over a liability from T that is treated as a relevant benefit to T.

ITTOIA 2005 s 23B(4) further extends the s 23B(3) definition: the assumption by a person of a liability of a person (C) who is or was connected to T, is the provision of a relevant benefit to C. This does not apply if T takes on a liability of C.

ITTOIA 2005 s 23B(5) specifies that loan includes any form of credit or a payment purported to be made by way of loan.

Meaning of qualifying third party payment

ITTOIA 2005 s 23C introduces the section, which deals with qualifying third party payments.

ITTOIA 2005 s 23C(2) explains that a payment is a third-party payment if it is made to T acting as a trustee or to any other person. The payment can be made by T or another person. This is an enormously wide definition which would apply to any payment anywhere in the world from one person to another. There is no requirement that the payer and payee have any connection. The reference to T acting as a trustee is to catch situations where a person makes a payment to himself in a trustee capacity. Without this provision, it would be relatively easy to circumvent the rules by arranging transactions where a person acts as trustee for what is essentially his own money and claims that there is no third-party payment.

As observed above virtually every payment is a third-party payment. ITTOIA 2005 s 23C(3) then narrows the scope of the test by defining a qualifying third party payment. That is one which meets either the deduction condition or the trade connection condition.

ITTOIA 2005 s 23C(4) states that the deduction condition is met if a deduction is made for the payment in computing the profits of the trade or of the partnership.

ITTOIA 2005 s 23C(5) provides that the trade connection is met if it reasonable to suppose that in essence the payment is consideration for goods or services provided in the course of the trade or there is some other connection (direct or indirect) between the payment and the provision of goods or services.

ITTOIA 2005 s 23C(6) explains that all relevant circumstances, particularly in considering the trade connection test, are to be taken into account in order to get to the essence of the matter.

ITTOIA 2005 s 23D(1) introduces definitions for this new charge.

ITTOIA 2005 s 23D(2) states that arrangement takes its usual wide definition.

ITTOIA 2005 s 23D(3) defines tax advantage. This is similar to definitions used elsewhere, but note that included at (d) is "avoidance of a possible assessment to tax", which is not something which is generally included in the definition of tax advantage.

ITTOIA 2005 s 23D(4) states that the definition of connected persons in ITA 2007 s 993 applies for these provisions except that members of a partnership (and their spouses/civil partners and relatives) are not connected to each other.

Tax treatment of relevant benefits

ITTOIA 2005 s 23E(1) explains that where these new provisions apply, the amount of the relevant benefit is to be treated as profits of the relevant trade for the year in which the benefit arises. Where the trade has ceased at the point that the relevant benefit arises it is treated as a profit of the year of cessation. Note that the amount is treated as profits and not income.

ITTOIA 2005 s 23E(2) states that where the relevant benefit is a payment (other than a loan payment) the benefit is equal to the amount of the payment. Where the relevant benefit is a loan the benefit is the amount of the principal lent (i.e. with no revaluation for potential recoverability). In any other case the relevant benefit amount is the value of the relevant benefit.

ITTOIA 2005 s 23E(3) states that the value of a relevant benefit is the higher of its market value at the time it arises and the cost of providing it.

ITTOIA 2005 s 23E(4) stipulates that market value takes the same meaning as in TCGA 1992 Pt 8.

Relevant benefits: persons other than T

ITTOIA 2005 s 23F(1)(a)–(e) set out the enjoyment conditions. These are independent tests. Only one of them has to be met – it is not necessary to meet all of them.

(a) This is oddly phrased: "the relevant benefit, or part of it, is in fact so dealt with by any person as to be calculated at some time to enure for the benefit of T". This appears to mean that although the benefit might be provided to another person, if it does in fact operate to provide T with a benefit then it will be a relevant benefit.

(b) The second condition is that the benefit increases the value of an asset held by T or which is held for his benefit.

(c) The third condition is that T receives or is entitled to receive any benefit provided out of or derived from all or part of the relevant benefit. So, for example, the relevant benefit provided to a third party might be a freehold property and T is provided with a leasehold interest in that property.

(d) The fourth condition is widely drawn. Where the benefit is a sum of money (including a loan) the test is met if T is beneficially entitled to all or part of it by the exercise of powers by any person in any order and with or without consent. So, for example if a loan is made to T it does not matter whether T applies for, or consents to receive, the money.

(e) The fifth condition also concerns sums of money (including loans). The test is that T is able to control directly the application of the money. The condition would be satisfied, for example, if a third party has a sum of money and T directs that it is to be paid to a person of his choosing.

ITTOIA 2005 s 23F(2) allows for apportionment where the enjoyment condition is met in relation to only part of the relevant benefit.

ITTOIA 2005 s 23F(3) stipulates that references to T include persons who are or have been connected with T.

ITTOIA 2005 s 23F(4) provides that the substantial result and effect of all of the relevant circumstances must be taken into account in determining whether any of the enjoyment conditions are met.

Anti-avoidance

ITTOIA 2005 s 23G(1) states that arrangements which have as their main purpose, or one of their main purposes, to secure that a charge does not arise under these provisions are to be ignored.

ITTOIA 2005 s 23G(2) is an anti-forestalling provision. If the effect of the arrangements would give rise to a relevant benefit before 6 April 2017 but the effect of disregarding them would be that the relevant benefit would arise on or after that date, the relevant benefit is treated as arising on or after 6 April 2017.

Double taxation

Because of the wide-ranging nature of these provisions it is possible that income tax charges will also arise on the arrangements under other provisions of the taxes acts. ITTOIA 2005 s 23H allows for relief against this possible double taxation.

ITTOIA 2005 s 23H(1) applies where an individual is charged under new s 23E and at any time tax – which can be income tax or any other tax – is charged in relation to the relevant benefit on the individual or another person.

ITTOIA 2005 s 23H(2) explains that the individual may make a claim for consequential adjustments to be made in respect of the other tax charge. Note it is not the charge under s 23E which is adjusted – that takes priority and remains in place.

ITTOIA 2005 s 23H(3) states that an officer of HMRC must give effect to the consequential adjustments which were claimed to the extent that they are just and reasonable.

ITTOIA 2005 s 23H(4) explains that the value of consequential adjustments is restricted to the lower of the income tax charged under s 23E and the tax charged under the other provision. Note that the adjustment is given in terms of tax and not in respect of the amount which is charged.

ITTOIA 2005 s 23H(5) provides that consequential adjustments can be made in respect of any period and by any mechanism. Time limits which would otherwise apply are overridden.

Section 35(3)–(5)

Subsection (3) is a minor drafting amendment.

Subsection (4) stipulates that the provisions in ITTOIA 2005 ss 23A–23H take effect for relevant benefits arising on or after 6 April 2017.

Subsection (5) introduces Sch 12 which makes provisions for extending the charge under ITTOIA 2005 ss 23A to 23H to loans etc. which are outstanding on 5 April 2019.

36 Disguised remuneration schemes: restriction of income tax relief

(1) Section 38 of ITTOIA 2005 (restriction of deductions: employee benefit contributions) is amended in accordance with subsections (2) to (5).

(2) After subsection (1) insert—

"(1A) No deduction is allowed under this section in respect of employee benefit contributions for a period of account which starts more than 5 years after the end of the period of account in which the contributions are made."

(3) After subsection (2) insert—

"(2AA) Subsection (2) is subject to subsections (1A) and (2AB).

(2AB) Where subsection (3C) applies, no deduction is allowed for an amount in respect of the contributions for the period except so far as the amount is a qualifying amount (see subsection (3D))."

(4) After subsection (3) insert—

"(3A) Subsection (3) is subject to subsections (1A) and (3B).

(3B) Where subsection (3C) applies, an amount disallowed under subsection (2) is allowed as a deduction for a subsequent period only so far as it is a qualifying amount.

(3C) This subsection applies where the provision of qualifying benefits out of, or by way of, the contributions gives rise both to an employment income tax charge and to an NIC charge.

(3D) An amount in respect of employee benefit contributions is a "qualifying amount" if the relevant tax charges are paid before the end of the relevant period (and are not repaid).

(3E) For the purposes of subsection (3D)—

(a) the "relevant tax charges", in relation to an amount, are the employment income tax charge and the NIC charge arising in respect of benefits which are provided out of, or by way of, that amount, and

(b) the "relevant period" is the period of 12 months immediately following the end of the period of account for which the deduction for the employee benefit contributions would (apart from this section) be allowable.

(3F) For the purposes of subsections (3C) and (3E), "employment income tax charge" and "NIC charge" have the meaning given by section 40(7)."

(5) After subsection (3F) (inserted by subsection (4)) insert—

"(3G) Subsection (3H) applies where—

(a) a deduction would, apart from this section, be allowable for an amount (the "remuneration amount") in respect of employees' remuneration, and

(b) in consequence of the payment of the employees' remuneration, employee benefit contributions are made, or are to be made, in respect of the remuneration amount.

(3H) In calculating for income tax purposes the profits of a trade, the deduction referred to in subsection (3G)(a) is to be treated as a deduction in respect of employee benefit contributions made or to be made (and is to be treated as not being a deduction in respect of employees' remuneration)."

(6) Section 866 of ITTOIA 2005 (employee benefit contributions: non-trades and non-property businesses) is amended in accordance with subsections (7) to (10).

(7) After subsection (2) insert—

"(2A) No deduction is allowed under this section in respect of employee benefit contributions for a period of account which starts more than 5 years after the end of the period of account in which the contributions are made."

(8) After subsection (3) insert—

"(3A) Subsection (3) is subject to subsections (2A) and (3B).

(3B) Where subsection (4C) applies, no deduction is allowed for an amount in respect of the contributions for the period except so far as the amount is a qualifying amount (see subsection (4D))."

(9) After subsection (4) insert—

"(4A) Subsection (4) is subject to subsections (2A) and (4B).

(4B) Where subsection (4C) applies, an amount disallowed under subsection (3) is allowed as a deduction for a subsequent period only so far as it is a qualifying amount.

(4C) This subsection applies where the provision of qualifying benefits out of, or by way of, the contributions gives rise both to an employment income tax charge and to an NIC charge.

(4D) An amount in respect of employee benefit contributions is a "qualifying amount" if the relevant tax charges are paid before the end of the relevant period (and are not repaid).

(4E) For the purposes of subsection (4D)—

(a) the "relevant tax charges", in relation to an amount, are the employment income tax charge and the NIC charge arising in respect of benefits which are provided out of, or by way of, that amount, and

(b) the "relevant period" is the period of 12 months immediately following the end of the period of account for which the deduction for the employee benefit contributions would (apart from this section) be allowable.

(4F) For the purposes of subsections (4C) and (4E), "employment income tax charge" and "NIC charge" have the meaning given by section 40(7)."

(10) After subsection (4F) (inserted by subsection (9)) insert—

"(4G) Subsection (4H) applies where—

(a) a deduction would, apart from this section, be allowable for an amount (the "remuneration amount") in respect of employees' remuneration, and

(b) in consequence of the payment of the employees' remuneration, employee benefit contributions are made, or are to be made, in respect of the remuneration amount.

(4H) In calculating for income tax purposes a person's profits or other income, the deduction referred to in subsection (4G)(a) is to be treated as a deduction in respect of employee benefit contributions made or to be made (and is to be treated as not being a deduction in respect of employees' remuneration)."

(11) The amendments made by subsections (2) to (4) and (7) to (9) have effect in relation to employee benefit contributions made, or to be made, on or after 6 April 2017.

(12) The amendments made by subsections (5) and (10) have effect in relation to remuneration paid on or after 6 April 2017.

GENERAL NOTE

Section 36 (and s 37 which sets out essentially the same rules for corporation tax) tighten the rules governing the deductibility of tax relief for contributions to a disguised remuneration scheme. The existing rules in ITTOA 2005 s 38/CTA 2009 s 1290 are intended to create symmetry between the deductibility of contributions and the PAYE and NIC charge on the recipient but they have been found not to be effective in all situations.

Section 36(1) introduces amendments to ITTOIA 2005 s 38, which currently sets out the rules relating to the deductibility of employee benefit contributions for income tax.

Section 36(2) introduces a new subsection (1A), which denies relief for any contributions made for a period of account which starts more than five years after the end of the period of account in which the contribution is made. At the moment there is no temporal restriction, so that an EBT contribution made in 2008 (and disallowed at the time) which created a Part 7A charge in 2015 would qualify for relief in the relevant period of account in 2015. Under the new rules the contribution would never qualify for relief.

Section 36(3) introduces new ITTOIA 2005 s 38(2AA) and (2AB). Currently employee benefit contributions are disallowed when they are made unless qualifying benefits are provided during the period of account in which they are made or within nine months of the end of the period. This mirrors the normal rule for employee remuneration. Section 36(3) imposes a further test. The amounts also have to be a qualifying amount as defined in ITTOIA 2005 s 38(3D).

Section 36(4) introduces ITTOIA 2005 s 38(3A)–(3F). Under current rules a deduction which is disallowed when it is made becomes deductible in the period in which qualifying benefits are provided, or when qualifying benefits are provided within nine months of the period end. Subsections (3A) to (3F) introduce a further restriction as follows:

(3A): This provides that sub-s (3) is subject to sub-ss (1A) and (3B).

(3B): This provides that when sub-s (3) applies the amount previously disallowed is only deductible if it is a qualifying amount.

(3C): Sub-s (3) applies when the provision of qualifying benefits out of the contributions gives rise to an employment income charge and an NIC charge.

(3D): An amount is a qualifying amount only if the relevant tax charges are paid before the end of the relevant period (as defined below) and are not repaid. At the moment there is no requirement for any tax charges to be paid – only that a qualifying benefit is provided. This has led to timing mismatches and also avoidance opportunities.

(3E): The relevant tax charges are the employment income charge and the NIC charge arising in respect of benefits provided out of the employee benefit contribution. The relevant period is 12 months from the end of the period for which the contributions would otherwise be deductible.

Example

In the period to 31 December 2017 Sam makes employee benefit contributions of £1m to benefit employees of his sole trader business. The contributions are retained by the trustees and invested. No deduction is due for the period to 31/12/2017. In July 2020 the trustee trigger a relevant step in respect of the £1m by earmarking it for specific employees. Under the existing rules Sam's business would be entitled to a deduction in the period to 31/12/2020 regardless of when PAYE and NIC was paid in respect of the relevant step. Under the new rules the PAYE and NIC must be paid over by 31 December 2021 – i.e. 12 months from the end of the period in which the relevant step was triggered.

However, the position is different if there was a dispute over whether a relevant step was actually triggered in July 2020 and PAYE and NIC was not accounted for at the time. What happens if the company did not accept until December 2024 that there was a PAYE and NIC obligation and paid it over in January 2025? This is more than five years from the end of the period of account in which the contribution was actually made. The overriding 5-year rule in sub-s (1A) would apply and hence no relief would ever be due. A business which attempts to circumvent the Part 7A rules and enters into a protracted dispute over whether a PAYE and NIC charge has been triggered risks permanently losing the benefit of the tax relief on the contribution. This is clearly the aim of the new provision.

(3F): This defines employment income tax charge and NIC charge by reference to ITTOIA 2005 s 40(7).

Section 36(5) inserts new sub-ss (3G) and (3H):

(3G): This introduces ITTOIA 2005 s 38(3H), which applies where a deduction would otherwise be allowable in respect of employees' remuneration, and employee benefit contributions are, or are to be, made in respect of the remuneration amount.

(3H): The deduction is only allowable under ITTOIA 2005 s 38 (employee benefit contributions) and not under any other provisions. This is to prevent businesses running the argument that a deduction is due under general principles and thus sidestepping the anti-avoidance provisions introduced into s 38.

Section 36(6)–(10) replicate (with only minor drafting changes) the provisions in sub-ss (1) to (5) above and, by amending ITTOIA 2005 s 866, apply them to non-trades and non-property businesses.

Commencement

All of the amendments other than those in sub-ss (5) and (10) apply in relation to employee benefit contributions made, or to be made, on or after 6 April 2017.

The amendments in sub-ss (5) and (10) have effect in relation to remuneration paid on or after 6 April 2017.

37 Disguised remuneration schemes: restriction of corporation tax relief

(1) Section 1290 of CTA 2009 (restriction of deductions: employee benefit contributions) is amended in accordance with subsections (2) to (5).

(2) After subsection (1) insert—

"(1A) No deduction is allowed under this section in respect of employee benefit contributions for a period of account which starts more than 5 years after the end of the period of account in which the contributions are made."

(3) After subsection (2) insert—

"(2A) Subsection (2) is subject to subsections (1A) and (2B).

(2B) Where subsection (3C) applies, no deduction is allowed for an amount in respect of the contributions for the period except so far as the amount is a qualifying amount (see subsection (3D))."

(4) After subsection (3) insert—

"(3A) Subsection (3) is subject to subsections (1A) and (3B).

(3B) Where subsection (3C) applies, an amount disallowed under subsection (2) is allowed as a deduction for a subsequent period only so far as it is a qualifying amount.

(3C) This subsection applies where the provision of qualifying benefits out of, or by way of, the contributions gives rise both to an employment income tax charge and to an NIC charge.

(3D) An amount in respect of employee benefit contributions is a "qualifying amount" if the relevant tax charges are paid before the end of the relevant period (and are not repaid).

(3E) For the purposes of subsection (3D)—

(a) the "relevant tax charges", in relation to an amount, are the employment income tax charge and the NIC charge arising in respect of benefits which are provided out of, or by way of, that amount, and

(b) the "relevant period" is the period of 12 months immediately following the end of the period of account for which the deduction for the employee benefit contributions would (apart from this section) be allowable.

(3F) For the purposes of subsections (3C) and (3E), "employment income tax charge" and "NIC charge" have the meaning given by section 1292(7)."

(5) After subsection (3F) (inserted by subsection (4)) insert—

"(3G) Subsection (3H) applies where—

(a) a deduction would, apart from this section, be allowable for an amount (the "remuneration amount") in respect of employees' remuneration, and

(b) in consequence of the payment of the employees' remuneration, employee benefit contributions are made, or are to be made, in respect of the remuneration amount.

(3H) In calculating for corporation tax purposes the profits of a company, the deduction referred to in subsection (3G)(a) is to be treated as a deduction in respect of employee benefit contributions made or to be made (and is to be treated as not being a deduction in respect of employees' remuneration)."

(6) The amendments made by subsections (2) to (4) have effect in relation to employee benefit contributions made, or to be made, on or after 1 April 2017.

(7) The amendment made by subsection (5) has effect in relation to remuneration paid on or after 1 April 2017.

GENERAL NOTE

These replicate the provisions in section 36, which apply to income tax, for corporation tax purposes. They do so by amending CTA 2009 s 1290. The commentary on section 36 is not repeated in full here. Instead cross references are made to the appropriate subsections of section 36.

Section 37(1) mirrors s 36(1).

Section 37(2) mirrors s 36(2).

Section 37(3) mirrors s 36(3).

Section 37(4) mirrors s 36(4).

Section 37(5) mirrors s 36(5).

Section 37(6) states that amendments in sub-ss (2) to (4) take effect for employee benefit contributions made on or after 1 April 2017.

Section 37(7) states that the amendment in sub-s (5) has effect for remuneration paid on or after 1 April 2017.

Capital allowances

38 First-year allowance for expenditure on electric vehicle charging points

(1) CAA 2001 is amended as follows.

(2) In section 39 (first-year qualifying expenditure) after the entry for section 45E insert—

"section 45EA   expenditure on plant or machinery for electric vehicle charging point".

(3) After section 45E insert—

"45EA Expenditure on plant or machinery for electric vehicle charging point

(1) Expenditure is first-year qualifying expenditure if—

    (a) it is incurred in the relevant period,

    (b) it is expenditure on plant or machinery for an electric vehicle charging point where the plant or machinery is unused and not second-hand, and

    (c) it is not excluded by section 46 (general exclusions).

(2) For the purposes of this section expenditure on plant or machinery for an electric vehicle charging point is expenditure on plant or machinery installed solely for the purpose of charging electric vehicles.

(3) The "relevant period" is the period beginning with 23 November 2016 and ending with—

    (a) in the case of expenditure incurred by a person within the charge to corporation tax, 31 March 2019, and

    (b) in the case of expenditure incurred by a person within the charge to income tax, 5 April 2019.

(4) The Treasury may by regulations amend subsection (3) so as to extend the relevant period.

(5) In this section—

    "electric vehicle" means a road vehicle that can be propelled by electrical power (whether or not it can also be propelled by another kind of power);

    "electric vehicle charging point" means a facility for charging an electric vehicle."

(4) In section 46 (general exclusions), in subsection (1) after the entry for section 45E insert—

    "section 45EA (expenditure on plant or machinery for electric vehicle charging point)".

(5) In section 52 (amount of first-year allowances)—

(a) in the table in subsection (3), after the entry for expenditure qualifying under section 45E insert—

"Expenditure qualifying under section 45EA (expenditure on plant or | 100%" machinery for electric vehicle charging point) |

   (b) after subsection (3) insert—

   "(3A) Subsection (3B) applies where the Treasury make regulations under section 45EA(4) (power to extend relevant period).

   (3B) The regulations may amend the amount specified in column 2 of the Table in subsection (3) for expenditure qualifying under section 45EA, but only in relation to expenditure incurred after the date on which the relevant period would have ended but for the regulations."

GENERAL NOTE

This section inserts a new section into the Capital Allowances Act 2001, CAA 2001 s 45EA, relating to first-year allowances (FYAs) for expenditure incurred by a company on electric vehicle charging points, and makes consequent amendments to other sections in that Act.

FYAs are made available at the rate of 100% for expenditure incurred within a defined period, called the "relevant period".

The relevant period begins on 23 November 2016 (the date of the Chancellor's Autumn Statement) and ends on 31 March 2019 for corporation tax purposes, or 5 April 2019 for income tax purposes (new CAA 2001 s 45EA(3)).

The plant or machinery acquired must be installed solely for the purpose of charging electric vehicles (new CAA 2001 s 45EA(2)). Plant installed for dual use, i e charging electric vehicles plus another use, would not qualify for FYAs. As an electric vehicle is defined as "a road vehicle that can be propelled by electrical power", it is conceivable that a charging point could be intended to be used by both road vehicles and, say, lawn mowers. As the latter are not road vehicles, and the charging point would not therefore be solely used by "electric vehicles" as defined, no FYAs would be available.

The plant and machinery must be new and not second-hand. Also, it must not fall within the general exclusions of CAA 2001 s 46, which include the provision of plant or machinery for leasing.

Transactions in UK land

39 Disposals concerned with land in United Kingdom

(1) The FA 2016 amendments have effect (so far as they would not otherwise have effect) in relation to—

   (a) amounts that are recognised in GAAP accounts drawn up for any period of account beginning on or after 8 March 2017, or

   (b) in the case of a straddling period, amounts that would be recognised in GAAP accounts drawn up for a period of account beginning on 8 March 2017 and ending when the straddling period ends.

(2) In subsection (1)—

"the FA 2016 amendments" means—

   (a) the amendments made by sections 76, 77 and 80 of FA 2016 (corporation tax treatment of certain profits and gains realised from disposals concerned with land in the United Kingdom), or

   (b) the amendments made by sections 78 and 79 of that Act (corresponding rules for income tax purposes),

"GAAP accounts" means accounts drawn up in accordance with generally accepted accounting practice,

"recognised" means recognised as an item of profit or loss, and

"straddling period" means a period of account beginning before 8 March 2017 and ending on or after that date.

(3) In section 161 of TCGA 1992 (appropriations to and from stock), in subsection (5)(a), for "CTA 2010" substitute "ITA 2007".

(4) Section 79(10) of FA 2016 (which substitutes paragraph (a) of section 161(5) of TCGA 1992) is to be regarded as always having had effect with the amendment made by subsection (3).

GENERAL NOTE

Transactions in UK land

Section 39 makes certain changes to the legislation introduced by FA 2016 in relation to "Transactions in UK Land".

The amendments originally made by FA 2016 ss 76, 77 and 80 and FA 2016 ss 78 and 79 were intended to ensure that all profits (and losses) from dealing in or developing land in the UK, including deemed disposals arising under TCGA 1992 s 161(2) would be within the scope of UK corporation tax or UK income tax. The rules applied irrespective of the place of residence of the person making the disposal and took effect in relation to disposals of UK land on or after 5 July 2016.

The subsequent amendments introduced by F(No 2)A 2017 s 39 are intended to ensure those profits from dealing in or developing land in the UK which are recognised in the accounts for any period of account beginning on or after 8 March 2017 will be taxed. The F(No 2)A 2017 changes should therefore bring into charge arrangements under which a contract was entered into before 5 July 2016 but where profits are recognised in accounts prepared under Generally Accepted Accounting Practice, after 8 March 2017. HMRC have clarified that it was not their intention to exclude from the FA 2016 changes, profits arising months or even years after a contract was agreed.

Co-ownership authorised contractual schemes

40 Co-ownership authorised contractual schemes: capital allowances

In Part 2 of CAA 2001 (plant and machinery), in Chapter 20 (supplementary provisions), after the Chapter heading insert—

"Co-ownership authorised contractual schemes

262AA Co-ownership schemes: carrying on qualifying activity

(1) This section applies where the participants in a co-ownership authorised contractual scheme together carry on a qualifying activity.

(2) Each participant in the scheme is for the purposes of this Part to be regarded as carrying on the qualifying activity.

(3) Subsection (2) applies in relation to a participant only to the extent that the profits or gains arising to the participant from the qualifying activity are, or (if there were any) would be, chargeable to tax.

(4) But in determining for the purposes of subsection (1) whether or to what extent the participants in a co-ownership authorised contractual scheme together carry on a qualifying activity, assume that profits or gains arising to all participants from the qualifying activity are, or (if there were any) would be, chargeable to tax.

262AB Co-ownership schemes: election

(1) The operator of a co-ownership authorised contractual scheme may make an election under this section.

(2) The election must specify an accounting period of the scheme as the first accounting period in relation to which the election has effect.

(3) That first accounting period must not—

    (a) be longer than 12 months, or

    (b) begin before 1 April 2017.

(4) The election has effect for that first accounting period and all subsequent accounting periods of the scheme.

(5) The election is irrevocable.

(6) The election is made by notice to an officer of Revenue and Customs.

262AC Co-ownership schemes: calculation of allowance after election

(1) This section applies where an election under section 262AB has effect for an accounting period of a co-ownership authorised contractual scheme ("the relevant period").

(2) The operator of the scheme is to calculate the allowances that would be available to the scheme under this Part in relation to the relevant period on the basis of the assumptions in subsection (3).

(3) The assumptions are—

(a) the scheme is a person;

(b) the relevant period is a chargeable period for the purposes of this Act;

(c) any qualifying activity carried on by the participants in the scheme together is carried on by the scheme;

(d) property which was subject to the scheme at the beginning of the first accounting period for which the election has effect—

    (i) ceased to be owned by the participants at that time, and

    (ii) was acquired by the scheme at that time;

(e) the disposal value to be brought into account in relation to the cessation of ownership and the acquisition referred to in paragraph (d) is the tax written-down value;

(f) any property which became subject to the scheme at a time during an accounting period for which the election has effect was acquired by the scheme at that time;

(g) property which ceased to be subject to the scheme at any such time ceased to be owned by the scheme at that time;

(h) the disposal value to be brought into account in relation to the cessation of ownership referred to in paragraph (g) is the tax written-down value;

(i) the scheme is not entitled to a first-year allowance or an annual investment allowance in respect of any expenditure.

(4) The operator of the co-ownership authorised contractual scheme must allocate to each participant in the scheme a proportion (which may be zero) of the allowances calculated under this section.

(5) The allocation is to be on the basis of what is just and reasonable.

(6) In determining what is just and reasonable—

(a) regard is to be had in particular to the relative size of each participant's holding of units in the scheme;

(b) no regard is to be had to—

    (i) whether or to what extent a participant is liable to income tax or corporation tax, or

    (ii) any other circumstances relating to a participant's liability to tax.

(7) If the participants in the scheme together carry on more than one qualifying activity, the calculation and allocation under this section are to be made separately for each activity.

(8) The proportion of an allowance allocated by the operator to a participant under this section for a qualifying activity is the total amount of the allowance available to the participant under this Part in relation to the relevant period by virtue of carrying on that activity as a participant in the scheme.

(9) In this section "tax written-down value", in relation to any cessation of ownership or acquisition, means such amount as would give rise to neither a balancing allowance nor a balancing charge.

(10) For the purposes of subsection (9) assume that expenditure to which the disposal value relates is in its own pool.

(11) For the purposes of subsections (3)(c) and (9), assume that profits or gains arising to all participants from the qualifying activity are, or (if there were any) would be, chargeable to tax.

262AD Co-ownership schemes: effect of election for participants

(1) This section has effect where an election under section 262AB is made by the operator of a co-ownership authorised contractual scheme.

(2) For the purposes of sections 61(1) and 196(1) (disposal events and values)—

(a) a participant in the scheme is to be regarded as ceasing to own the participant's interest in the property subject to the scheme at the beginning of the first accounting period of the scheme for which the election has effect, and

(b) the disposal value to be brought into account in relation to that cessation of ownership is the tax written-down value.

(3) In subsection (2)(b) "tax written-down value" means such amount as would give rise to neither a balancing allowance nor a balancing charge.

(4) For the purposes of subsection (3) assume that—

(a) expenditure to which the disposal value relates is in its own pool;

(b) profits or gains arising to all participants from the qualifying activity are, or (if there were any) would be, chargeable to tax.

262AE Co-ownership schemes: effect of election for purchasers

(1) This section has effect where—

(a) an election under section 262AB is made by the operator of a co-ownership authorised contractual scheme,

(b) property consisting of a fixture ceased to be subject to the scheme at any time in an accounting period for which the election has effect,

(c) in a calculation made by the operator of the scheme under section 262AC(2) the assumption in section 262AC(3)(g) was made in relation to that fixture, and

(d) a person ("the current owner") is treated as the owner of the fixture as a result of incurring capital expenditure on its provision ("the new expenditure").

(2) In determining the current owner's qualifying expenditure—

(a) if the disposal value statement requirement is not satisfied, the new expenditure is to be treated as nil, and

(b) in any other case, any amount of the new expenditure which exceeds the assumed disposal value is to be left out of account (or, if such an amount has already been taken into account, is to be treated as an amount that should never have been taken into account).

(3) The disposal value statement requirement is that—

(a) the operator of the scheme has, no later than 2 years after the date when the fixture ceased to be property subject to the scheme, made a written statement of the assumed disposal value, and

(b) the current owner has obtained that statement or a copy of it (directly or indirectly) from the operator of the scheme.

(4) Sections 185 (fixture on which a plant and machinery allowance has been claimed) and 187A (effect of changes in ownership of fixture) do not apply in relation to the new expenditure.

(5) In this section "assumed disposal value" means the disposal value that, in making the calculation referred to in subsection (1)(c), was assumed to be brought into account pursuant to section 262AC(3)(h).

262AF Co-ownership schemes: definitions relating to schemes

In sections 262AA to 262AE and this section—

"co-ownership authorised contractual scheme" means a co-ownership scheme which is authorised for the purposes of the Financial Services and Markets Act 2000 by an authorisation order in force under section 261D(1) of that Act;

"co-ownership scheme" has the same meaning as in Part 17 of that Act (see section 235A(2) of that Act);

"operator" and "units", in relation to a co-ownership authorised contractual scheme, have the meanings given by section 237(2) of that Act;

"participant", in relation to such a scheme, is to be read in accordance with section 235 of that Act."

GENERAL NOTE

The Act contains three sections (40 to 42) relating to Co-ownership Authorised Contractual Schemes (CoACSs). These are concerned with capital allowances, information reporting requirements and investments in offshore funds. Much of the detail is left to secondary legislation and, at time of writing, the relevant regulations remain in draft. A separate set of draft regulations (to be made under existing regulation making powers rather than a new power in the Act) makes changes to the taxation of gains and losses arising on the disposal of CoACS units. The following commentary includes comment on these sets of draft regulations.

Authorised Contractual Schemes (ACS) are a form of collective investment scheme introduced in the UK in 2013 in order to provide a UK alternative to tax-transparent fund structures available in Luxembourg and Ireland. The CoACS structure has proved successful as, since the regime was introduced, tens of billions of investment assets have been transferred into CoACSs by UK insurance companies and pension schemes.

An ACS can take one of two legal forms: partnerships or co-ownership. The UK tax code generally applies to partnership ACS in the same way as it applies to partnerships generally and so special rules are not required. In contrast, special tax rules are applied to CoACSs and participants in CoACSs in order to create a fund vehicle which is tax transparent as regards income but not capital.

The Act and accompanying draft regulations introduce a number of refinements and clarifications to the taxation of participants in CoACSs and create new duties for operators of CoACSs to report information to CoACS participants and HMRC. The provisions of the Act will have very limited effect on those CoACSs whose participants are all tax-exempt bodies.

Capital allowances

Section 40 modifies CAA 2001 to accommodate CoACSs which invest in real estate. Previously, the strict position had been that every transaction in CoACS units was treated as a part disposal of each and every asset in the portfolio for capital allowances purposes. In order to ease the considerable compliance burden which this created, the Act introduces a new elective regime.

New sections 262AA to 262AF are inserted into CAA 2001. These provide that, where an election is made, capital allowances pooling is done in aggregate for the whole CoACS and that participants are allocated their share of allowances on a just and reasonable basis. The relative sizes of unit holdings must be taken into account and so some form of pro rata apportionment is implied. The precise mechanics of the allocation is not prescribed (for example, the legislation does not specify whether the relative sizes of holding should be considered at the time capital expenditure is incurred or at the time the allowances become deductible so this potentially allows some commercial flexibility). However, it is not permitted to bias the allocation of allowances towards those participants who are in the charge to UK tax.

The election in irrevocable and can be made for CoACS accounting periods beginning on or after 1 April 2017.

A consequence of the election is that some of the flexibility associated with the capital allowances regime is removed. Specifically, disposals of property by a CoACS must be at a notional tax written down value (TWDV) rather than at a value determined by the parties to the transaction. Similarly, all assets are treated as being transferred from the participants to the CoACS at TWDV at the point the election first takes effect.

In many (but not necessarily all) cases, the elective regime should be seen as a favourable and pragmatic way to allow CoACS participants to benefit from capital allowances.

41 Co-ownership authorised contractual schemes: information requirements

(1) The Treasury may by regulations impose requirements on the operator of a co-ownership authorised contractual scheme in relation to—

    (a) the provision of information to participants in the scheme;
    (b) the provision of information to Her Majesty's Revenue and Customs.

(2) Regulations under subsection (1)(a) may be made only for the purpose of enabling participants in a co-ownership authorised contractual scheme to meet their tax obligations in the United Kingdom with respect to their interests in the scheme.

(3) Regulations under subsection (1)(b) may in particular require the provision of information about—

    (a) who the participants in the scheme were in any accounting period of the scheme;
    (b) the number and classes of units in the scheme in any such period;
    (c) the amount of income per unit of any class in any such period;
    (d) what information has been provided to participants.

(4) Regulations under this section may specify—

    (a) the time when information is to be provided;
    (b) the form and manner in which information is to be provided.

(5) Regulations under this section may make provision for the imposition of penalties in respect of contravention of, or non-compliance with, the regulations, including provision—

    (a) for Her Majesty's Revenue and Customs to exercise a discretion as to the amount of a penalty, and
    (b) about appeals in relation to the imposition of a penalty.

(6) Regulations under this section may in particular be framed by reference to an accounting period of a co-ownership authorised contractual scheme beginning on or after 1 April 2017.

(7) Regulations under this section may contain consequential, supplementary and transitional provision.

(8) Regulations under this section must be made by statutory instrument.

(9) A statutory instrument containing regulations under this section is subject to annulment in pursuance of a resolution of the House of Commons.

(10) In this section—

"co-ownership authorised contractual scheme" means a co-ownership scheme which is authorised for the purposes of the Financial Services and Markets Act 2000 by an authorisation order in force under section 261D(1) of that Act;

"co-ownership scheme" has the same meaning as in Part 17 of that Act (see section 235A(2) of that Act);

"operator" and "units", in relation to a co-ownership authorised contractual scheme, have the meanings given by section 237(2) of that Act;

"participant", in relation to such a scheme, is to be read in accordance with section 235 of that Act.

GENERAL NOTE

Section 41 grants HMT the power to make regulations to impose requirements on the operator of a CoACS to provide information to the scheme participants and to HMRC. This power can be used in respect of CoACS accounting periods beginning on or after 1 April 2017.

This power is intended to ensure that participants in a CoACS are provided with sufficient information about their share of taxable income, amounts taxable as income (such as market value movements on loan relationships), expenses and other amounts to allow them to compute their UK tax liabilities.

Draft regulations were published on 20 March 2017. The draft regulations set the information reporting date as six months after the end of the CoACS accounting period and makes clear that the information needs to be "sufficient". The information which is required to be provided will vary depending on the tax status of the participant. Thus, if the participant in question is a tax-exempt body, such as a pension scheme, little or no information should be required.

The power is also intended to give HMRC the means to monitor compliance though the CoACS operator providing the names and addresses of participants and the amount of income per unit for each class of unit in the scheme. In addition, HMRC can give notice that they require details of the information provided to participants in the scheme in respect of accounting periods ending in the previous five years. These provisions are considered necessary as a CoACS is not in the charge to tax and (unlike a partnership) is not required to submit a tax return.

42 Co-ownership authorised contractual schemes: offshore funds

(1) The Treasury may by regulations make provision about how participants in a co-ownership authorised contractual scheme are to be treated for income tax purposes or corporation tax purposes in relation to investments made for the purposes of the scheme in an offshore fund.

(2) Regulations under subsection (1) may, among other things, make provision—

(a) for the operator of a co-ownership authorised contractual scheme to allocate to participants in the scheme amounts relating to investments made for the purposes of the scheme in an offshore fund;

(b) for those amounts to be regarded as income of the participants to whom they are allocated;

(c) as to when that income is to be brought into account for income tax purposes or corporation tax purposes.

(3) Regulations under this section may—

(a) modify an enactment (whenever passed or made);

(b) contain consequential, supplementary and transitional provision.

(4) Regulations under this section must be made by statutory instrument.

(5) A statutory instrument containing regulations under this section is subject to annulment in pursuance of a resolution of the House of Commons.

(6) References in this section to investments made for the purposes of a co-ownership authorised contractual scheme in an offshore fund include investments so made through one or more other co-ownership authorised contractual schemes.

(7) In this section—

"co-ownership authorised contractual scheme" means a co-ownership scheme which is authorised for the purposes of the Financial Services and Markets Act 2000 by an authorisation order in force under section 261D(1) of that Act;

"co-ownership scheme" has the same meaning as in Part 17 of that Act (see section 235A(2) of that Act);

"offshore fund" has the meaning given by section 355 of TIOPA 2010;

"operator", in relation to a co-ownership authorised contractual scheme, has the meaning given by section 237(2) of the Financial Services and Markets Act 2000;

"participant", in relation to such a scheme, is to be read in accordance with section 235 of that Act.

GENERAL NOTE

Section 42 grants HMT the power to make regulations about how participants in CoACS are to be treated when the CoACS invests in offshore funds (as defined by TIOPA 2015).

The intention is for relevant amounts relating to the offshore fund to be regarded as income of the CoACS participants for UK tax purposes. This puts beyond doubt that the CoACS is regarded as tax-transparent for this purpose and that the position of CoACS participants should be similar to the position that they would have been in had they invested in the offshore fund directly.

Again, draft regulations were published on 20 March 2017. These new reporting obligations for CoACS are modelled on the obligations that reporting funds have when they invest in other offshore funds (as set out in the Offshore Funds (Tax) Regulations SI 2009/3001). The regulations relating to offshore funds will have effect for CoACS accounting periods beginning on or after the date the regulations comes into force (and at time of writing that date is not known).

Chargeable gains

A further set of regulations was published in draft on 20 March 2017. These are made under the existing powers at TCGA 1992 s 103C and TIOPA 2005 s 354 rather than the Act. They generally apply to disposals of CoACS units made on or after the date on which they come into force.

These regulations introduce a new section 103D in to TCGA to clarify how participants in tax transparent funds are to compute chargeable gains. This new section applies to investments in both CoACS and tax transparent offshore funds (within the meaning of regulation 11 of the Offshore Funds (Tax) Regulations 2009).

The intention of the new section 103D is to put beyond doubt that amounts taken into account by participants in calculating taxable income, such as debits and credits on loan relationships (in the case of participants who are in the charge to corporation tax) are directly taxable or relievable in the hands of fund participants and that compensating adjustments are made to base cost for chargeable gains purposes to prevent double taxation or double relief. Similarly, adjustments are made to base cost where anything is paid or transferred to a fund participant (when such adjustments are considered alongside the base cost adjustments in respect of income the effect is to prevent double taxation or double relief). At time of writing, the content of these regulations was not final and changes to the detail of these provisions remained possible.

The draft regulations also make a number of other refinements to the calculation of chargeable gains for participants in CoACS. These include an amendment to section 210C of TCGA. This provides that a disposal of CoACS units by an insurance company to a connected CoACS operator does not give rise to a connected party loss. This is a welcome change and aligns the treatment of CoACS with the existing position for other forms of authorised collective investment scheme.

PART 2

INDIRECT TAXES

43 Air passenger duty: rates of duty from 1 April 2018

(1) In section 30 of FA 1994 (air passenger duty: rates of duty), in subsection (4A) (long haul rates of duty)—

   (a) in paragraph (a), for "£75" substitute "£78";

(b) in paragraph (b), for "£150" substitute "£156".

(2) The amendments made by this section have effect in relation to the carriage of passengers beginning on or after 1 April 2018.

GENERAL NOTE

The reduced and standard rates of Air Passenger Duty (APD) on flights in Band B will increase from £75 to £78 and from £150 to £156 respectively with effect from 1 April 2018. The new rates apply to the carriage of passengers beginning on or after 1 April 2018.

The rates of Band A journeys remain unchanged.

Note

Band B journeys are where the destination is in a country or territory, the capital city of which is more than 2,000 miles away from London.

44 Petroleum revenue tax: elections for oil fields to become non-taxable

(1) In Schedule 20B to FA 1993, for paragraphs 2 to 12 substitute—

"Method of election

2 An election must be made in writing.

3 An election must be notified to the Commissioners.

4 An election is deemed to have been made on the date on which notification of the election was sent to the Commissioners.

Effect of election

5 If an election is made, the field ceases to be taxable with effect from the start of the first chargeable period to begin after the election is made.

No unrelievable field losses from field

6 From the start of the first chargeable period to begin after an election is made, no allowable loss that accrues from the oil field is an allowable unrelievable field loss for the purposes of petroleum revenue tax.

Interpretation

7 (1) In this Schedule—

"Commissioners" means the Commissioners for Her Majesty's Revenue and Customs;

"participator", in relation to a particular time, means a person who is a participator in the chargeable period which includes that time.

(2) Expressions used in this Schedule and in Part 1 of the Oil Taxation Act 1975 have the same meaning in this Schedule as in Part 1 of that Act."

(2) In OTA 1975, in section 6(1A), for "paragraph 5" substitute "paragraph 6".

(3) In FA 1980, in paragraph 15(9A) of Schedule 17, for "paragraph 5" substitute "paragraph 6".

(4) The amendment made by this section is to be treated as having come into force on 23 November 2016.

GENERAL NOTE

Section 44 changes the basis on which field owners are able to "opt out" of the PRT rules. Previously it was necessary to be able to demonstrate that the field would not pay any PRT in the future. Following the reduction in the rate of PRT to zero with effect from 1 January 2016, this is no longer a requirement and any field group can now elect for the field to become a non-taxable field.

Unless the owners expect to be able to recover PRT previously paid, or expect there to be an unrelievable field loss (UFL) on the field, there will no longer be any need to continue to file PRT returns for any fields. There has however to be agreement between all of the partners who may not always be in the same position.

Subsection (4)

The change is deemed to have come into effect on 23 November 2016 which enables the provision to apply to chargeable periods beginning on or after 1 January 2017, but only if the opt out election had been made by the responsible person before the start of the chargeable period. HMRC have previously stated that they would accept elections in 2016 even though the new legislation had not been enacted at that time.

45 Gaming duty: rates

(1) In section 11(2) of FA 1997 (rates of gaming duty), for the table substitute—
"Table

Part of gross gaming yield	Rate
The first £2,423,500	15%
The next £1,670,500	20%
The next £2,925,500	30%
The next £6,175,500	40%
The remainder	50%".

(2) The amendment made by this section has effect in relation to accounting periods beginning on or after 1 April 2017.

GENERAL NOTE

Section 45 amends the gross gaming yield bands for gaming duty with effect for accounting periods beginning on or after 1 April 2017. The bands have been increased in line with inflation (the Retail Price Index).

Gaming duty is paid on profits from gaming in land based casinos that takes place in the UK. It is calculated on the gross gaming yield of the premises, which is the total value of stakes and charges made for gaming less winnings paid out. The rate of gaming duty depends upon the premise's gross gaming yield. Gaming duty is payable in accounting periods of six months, generally beginning 1 April and 1 October.

The amendment increases the bands, not the rates; as noted in the Explanatory Notes to the Bill, this "ensures that casino operators' profits are not subject to the higher gaming duty bands simply as a result of inflation".

46 Remote gaming duty: freeplay

(1) Part 3 of FA 2014 (general betting duty, pool betting duty and remote gaming duty) is amended in accordance with subsections (2) to (8).

(2) In section 159 (remote gaming duty: gaming payments), for subsection (4) substitute—

"(4) For the purposes of this Chapter—

(a) where the chargeable person participates in the remote gaming in reliance on an offer which waives all of a gaming payment, the person is to be treated as having made a gaming payment of the amount which would have been required to be paid without the offer ("the full amount"), and

(b) where the chargeable person participates in the remote gaming in reliance on an offer which waives part of a gaming payment, the person is to be treated as having made an additional gaming payment of the difference between the gaming payment actually made and the full amount.

(5) Where a person is treated by subsection (4) as having made a gaming payment, the payment is to be treated for the purposes of this Chapter—

(a) as having been made to the gaming provider at the time when the chargeable person begins to participate in the remote gaming to which it relates, and

(b) as not having been—

(i) returned, or

(ii) assigned to a gaming prize fund.

(6) The Commissioners may by regulations make further provision about how a gaming payment which a person is treated as having made under subsection (4) is to be treated for the purposes of this Chapter.

(7) This section has effect subject to section 159A."

(3) After section 159 insert—

"159A Play using the results of successful freeplay

(1) Where a chargeable person participates in remote gaming, an amount is not to be taken into account in determining the "gaming payment" (if any) under section 159 so far as the amount is paid out of money in relation to which the first and second conditions are met ("excluded winnings").

(2) The first condition is that the money has been won by participation in the gaming either—

(a) in reliance on an offer which waives all or part of a gaming payment, or
(b) in a case where the gaming payment was paid out of money in relation to which this condition and the second condition were met.

(3) The second condition is that the chargeable person is not entitled to use the money otherwise than for the purpose of participation in the gaming.

(4) Subsection (5) applies where—

(a) a chargeable person participates in remote gaming in reliance on an offer which waives all or part of a gaming payment, and
(b) that offer has been won in the course of the person's participation in the gaming (and the person was not given the choice of receiving a different benefit instead of the offer).

(5) The amount which would, apart from this subsection, be treated by section 159(4)(a) or (b) as a gaming payment (or additional gaming payment) is not to be so treated.

(6) For the purposes of this section, where a payment is made out of moneys which include both excluded winnings and money which is not excluded winnings (the "other funds"), the payment is not taken to be made out of excluded winnings except so far as the amount of the payment exceeds the amount of those other funds.

(7) In this section "money" includes any amount credited and any other money's worth."

(4) In section 160 (remote gaming duty: prizes)—

(a) in subsection (1), in the opening words, after "account" insert "only",
(b) omit subsection (2),
(c) in subsection (3), at the end insert "(but where a gaming payment is returned by being credited to an account this subsection has effect subject to subsection (1))", and
(d) at the end insert—

"(9) This section has effect subject to section 160A."

(5) After section 160 insert—

"160A Prizes: freeplay

(1) Where a prize is a freeplay offer (whether or not in the form of a voucher) which does not fall within section 160(4)—

(a) for the purposes of sections 156 and 157, the expenditure on the prize is nil, and
(b) subsections (5) to (7) of section 160 do not apply in relation to the prize.

(2) Where a prize is a voucher which gives the recipient a choice of using it in place of money for freeplay or as whole or partial payment for another benefit, section 160(5)(b) has effect as if after "used" there were inserted "if it is used as payment for a benefit other than freeplay".

(3) In this section—

"freeplay" means participation, in reliance on a freeplay offer, in—

(a) remote gaming, or
(b) an activity in respect of which a gambling tax listed in section 161(4) is charged;

"freeplay offer" means an offer which waives all or part of—

(a) a gaming payment, or
(b) a payment in connection with participation in an activity in respect of which a gambling tax listed in section 161(4) is charged."

(6) In section 188 (gaming), after subsection (2) insert—

"(3) But a game is not a "game of chance" for the purposes of this Part if—

(a) it can only be played with the participation of two or more persons, and

(b) no amounts are paid or required to be paid—

(i) in respect of entitlement to participate in the game, or

(ii) otherwise for, on account of or in connection with participation in the game."

(7) In section 190 (index), in the Table, in the entry for "game of chance", for "188(1)(b)" substitute "188(1)(b) and (3)".

(8) In section 194(4) (regulations under Part 3 to which the procedure in section 194(5) is to apply), before paragraph (a), insert—

"(za) regulations under section 159(6);".

(9) The amendments made by this section have effect with respect to accounting periods beginning on or after 1 August 2017.

GENERAL NOTE

Section 46 amends the remote gaming duty (RGD) provisions to charge duty on certain freeplays, with effect for RGD accounting periods starting on or after 1 August 2017.

Freeplays are incentives offered by gambling operators to gamble at a reduced or no cost. Under the amendment, remote gaming freeplays will have a value in terms of determining an operator's profit for the purpose of calculating RGD. This amendment intends to bring the RGD treatment of freeplays into line with the treatment of freeplays under general betting duty. The amendment was originally announced in Budget 2016, and has been subject to consultation.

47 Tobacco products manufacturing machinery: licensing scheme

(1) After section 8U of TPDA 1979 insert—

"8V Tobacco products manufacturing machinery: licensing scheme

(1) In this section "tobacco products manufacturing machinery" means machinery that is designed primarily for use for the purpose of (or for purposes including) manufacturing tobacco products.

(2) The Commissioners may by regulations—

(a) prohibit a person from purchasing, acquiring, owning or being in possession of, or carrying out other specified activities in respect of, an item of tobacco products manufacturing machinery, except in accordance with a licence granted under the regulations;

(b) provide that if a person contravenes the prohibition in relation to an item of tobacco products manufacturing machinery, the machinery is liable to forfeiture.

(3) The regulations may provide that the prohibition does not apply—

(a) in relation to persons, or items of tobacco products manufacturing machinery, of a specified description;

(b) in specified circumstances.

(4) Regulations under this section may include provision—

(a) imposing obligations on licensed persons;

(b) for a licensed person who fails to comply with a condition or restriction of a licence, or with an obligation imposed by the regulations, to be liable to a penalty of the amount for the time being specified in section 9(2)(b) of the Finance Act 1994;

(c) for exceptions from liability to a penalty under the regulations;

(d) for the assessment and recovery of a penalty, including provision for two or more contraventions to be treated as a single contravention for the purposes of assessment;

(e) for the Commissioners, if they think it right because of special circumstances, to remit, reduce (including reduce to nil) or stay a penalty, or agree a compromise in relation to proceedings for a penalty;

(f) about reviews by the Commissioners, or by an officer of Revenue and Customs, of decisions in connection with licensing and the imposition of penalties under the regulations and about appeals against those decisions (which may include provision for specified decisions of the Commissioners to be treated as if they were listed in section 13A(2) of, or Schedule 5 to, the Finance Act 1994);

(g) for the Customs and Excise Management Act 1979 to have effect in relation to licensed persons as it has effect in relation to revenue traders, subject to such modifications as may be specified in the regulations.

(5) The Commissioners may, by or under regulations under this section, make provision—

(a) regulating the grant of licences, including provision about the circumstances in which a licence may be granted and the requirements to be met by or in relation to the applicant (which may include a requirement that the applicant is a fit and proper person to hold a licence);

(b) about the form, manner and content of an application for or in respect of a licence;

(c) for licences to be subject to specified conditions or restrictions;

(d) regulating the variation or revocation of a licence, or of any condition or restriction to which a licence is subject;

(e) about the renewal, surrender or transfer of a licence;

(f) for communications by or with the Commissioners in connection with a licence to be made electronically;

(g) as to the arrangements for licensing bodies corporate which are members of the same group (as defined in the regulations);

(h) for members of a group to be jointly and severally liable for any penalties imposed under the regulations."

(2) In section 9 of TPDA 1979 (regulations), in subsection (1A), for "or 8U" substitute ", 8U or 8V".

GENERAL NOTE

Section 47 amends the Tobacco Products Duty Act 1979 (TPDA) to require owners and leasers of tobacco manufacturing machinery to obtain a licence for each machine.

Section 47 defines the machinery to be covered by the new rules, and provides for regulations to be made for the granting of licences and the operation of the scheme, including the imposition of penalties.

In the 2015 Autumn Statement, the Government announced that it would consult on a licensing scheme as part of its obligations under the World Health Organisation's Framework Convention on Tobacco Control Illicit Trade Protocol. The consultation took place in early 2016. This measure has now been introduced (as per the Explanatory Notes), "to give HMRC additional powers to tackle the evasion of excise duty on tobacco products through the control and ownership of tobacco products manufacturing machinery and to help prevent the illicit manufacture of tobacco products".

Applications for licences will be accepted from 1 April 2018 and the scheme will come into force on 1 August 2018.

PART 3
FULFILMENT BUSINESSES

48 Carrying on a third country goods fulfilment business

(1) For the purposes of this Part a person carries on a third country goods fulfilment business if the person, by way of business—

(a) stores third country goods which are owned by a person who is not established in a Member State, or

(b) stores third country goods on behalf of a person who is not established in a Member State,

at a time when the conditions in subsection (2) are met in relation to the goods.

(2) The conditions are that—

(a) there has been no supply of the goods in the United Kingdom for the purposes of VATA 1994, and

(b) the goods are being offered for sale in the United Kingdom or elsewhere.

(3) But a person does not carry on a third country goods fulfilment business if the person's activities within subsection (1) are incidental to the carriage of the goods.

(4) Goods are "third country" goods if they have been imported from a place outside the Member States within the meaning of section 15 of VATA 1994.

(5) Whether a person is established in a Member State is to be determined in accordance with Article 10 of Council Implementing Regulation (EU) No 282/2011 of 15 March 2011 laying down implementing measures for Directive 2006/112/EC on the common system of value added tax.

BACKGROUND NOTE

Section 7 of the VAT Act 1994 provides "place-of-supply" rules for determining where, for UK VAT purposes, a supply of goods takes place. In brief, where goods are physically located in the UK at the time of supply, VATA 1994 s 7(2) determines that the place of supply is the UK. If there is a supply of goods in the UK by a taxable person acting as such then the supply is within the scope of UK VAT. This rule applies even if the taxable person in question is not established in the UK.

As an example, if an Australian business owns goods that are physically located in Sheffield, and it supplies those goods to another UK business (without the goods being moved), the supply takes place in the UK. Since 2012, any non-UK established business making supplies of goods or services in the UK (as in the above example) has been required to register for VAT in the UK irrespective of the turnover derived from such supplies.

With the advent of the internet, it is not uncommon for non-UK businesses to ship goods to a location in the UK (so as to meet demand for the goods in a timely way). Often, these goods are stored at a third party warehouse and, when an order is received from a customer, the order is fulfilled (usually by the third party holding the goods – i.e. a fulfilment business) from the UK stock.

Under the place-of-supply rule, such supplies clearly take place in the UK and the non-UK established supplier is required to register for UK VAT and account for UK VAT in relation to such supplies.

Whilst many businesses comply with these rules, in practice, many businesses do not. A business that does not comply with the VAT rules is at a clear competitive advantage if it supplies goods in the UK without either registering or accounting for UK VAT and it is with this in mind that HMRC have introduced these new provisions. In essence, where third country goods are sold through a UK fulfilment business, the new law requires the fulfilment business to be approved by HMRC before it can legitimately carry on such a business.

General Note

Section 48(1) defines who is regarded as carrying on a third country goods fulfilment business. A person is so regarded if in the course of business he:

(a) stores third country goods that are owned by a person not established in a Member State of the EU; or

(b) stores third country goods on behalf of a person not established in a Member State of the EU

if the conditions in section 48(2) are met.

Section 48(2) states that the conditions are that:

(a) there has been no supply of the goods in the UK (as defined in VAT Act 1994), and

(b) the goods are being offered for sale in the UK.

Section 48(3) provides that a person is not to be regarded as carrying on a third country goods fulfilment business if the storage of those goods is incidental to the carriage of the goods. For example, where a freight forwarder is transporting the goods from place A to place B and the goods are held in a temporary location before being transported by him to B.

Section 48(4) defines "third country goods" as being those goods that have been imported from a place outside the Member States within the meaning of VATA 1994 s 15 (i.e. the goods arrive in the UK from a place outside the EU where such arrival triggers a customs debt on entry).

For the purposes of determining whether or not a business is established in the EU, section 48(5) stipulates that the "establishment" rules contained in Article 10 of Council Implementing Regulation (EU) No 282/2011 of 15 March 2011 laying down implementing measures for Directive 2006/112/EC on the common system of value added tax are to be used.

49 Requirement for approval

(1) A person may not carry on a third country goods fulfilment business otherwise than in accordance with an approval given by the Commissioners under this section.

(2) The Commissioners may approve a person to carry on a third country goods fulfilment business only if they are satisfied that the person is a fit and proper person to carry on the business.

(3) The Commissioners may approve a person to carry on a third country goods fulfilment business for such periods and subject to such conditions or restrictions as they may think fit or as they may by regulations made by them prescribe.

(4) The Commissioners may at any time for reasonable cause vary the terms of, or revoke, an approval under this section.

(5) In this Part "approved person" means a person approved under this section to carry on a third country goods fulfilment business.

GENERAL NOTE

Section 49(1) stipulates that but for an approval granted by HMRC, a business may not carry on a third country goods fulfilment business.

Section 49(2) states that HMRC will grant an approval if and only if they are satisfied that the person in question is a fit and proper person to carry on such a business.

Section 49(3) gives HMRC powers to grant approvals for such periods and subject to such conditions or restrictions as they think necessary or as they prescribe in regulations.

Section 49(4) allows HMRC to vary the terms of the approval or to revoke it in its entirety.

Section 49(5) defines an "approved person" as any person approved by HMRC to carry on a third country goods fulfilment business.

50 Register of approved persons

(1) The Commissioners must maintain a register of approved persons.

(2) The register is to contain such information relating to approved persons as the Commissioners consider appropriate.

(3) The Commissioners may make publicly available such information contained in the register as they consider necessary to enable those who deal with a person who carries on a third country goods fulfilment business to determine whether the person in question is an approved person in relation to that activity.

(4) The information may be made available by such means (including the internet) as the Commissioners consider appropriate.

GENERAL NOTE

Section 50(1) requires HMRC to maintain a register of approved persons.

Section 50(2) specifies that the details to be kept in the register of approved persons is such information relating to approved persons as the Commissioners consider appropriate.

Section 50(3) states that the register may be made available to the public so that any person dealing with a third country goods fulfilment business will be able to tell whether or not that fulfilment business is approved by HMRC.

Section 50(4) provides that the information may be made available by such means (including through the use of the internet) as HMRC consider appropriate.

51 Regulations relating to approval, registration etc.

(1) The Commissioners may by regulations make provision—

    (a) regulating the approval and registration of persons under this Part,

    (b) regulating the variation or revocation of any such approval or registration, or of any condition or restriction to which such an approval or registration is subject,

    (c) about the register maintained under section 50,

    (d) regulating the carrying on of a third country goods fulfilment business, and

    (e) imposing obligations on approved persons.

(2) The regulations may, in particular, make provision—

(a) requiring applications, and other communications with the Commissioners, to be made electronically;

(b) as to the procedure for the approval and registration of bodies corporate which are members of the same group;

(c) requiring approved persons to keep and make available for inspection such records as may be prescribed by or under the regulations.

GENERAL NOTE

Section 51(1) states that secondary legislation (i.e. regulations) will govern the approval process and the registration of third country goods fulfilment businesses. In particular, regulations will cover:

(a) the approval and registration of persons

(b) the variation or revocation of any such approval or registration, or of any condition or restriction to which such an approval or registration is subject,

(c) the register of approved persons

(d) regulating the carrying on of a third country goods fulfilment business, and

(e) the imposition of obligations on an approved person.

Section 51(2) gives HMRC power when making regulations to:

(a) require the application process and other communications with HMRC to be by electronic means;

(b) establish procedures for dealing with the approval and registration of businesses within the same corporate group;

(c) require approved persons to keep and make available for inspection such records as may be prescribed by or under the regulations.

52 Disclosure of information by HMRC

(1) The Commissioners may disclose to an approved person information held by Her Majesty's Revenue and Customs in connection with a function of Her Majesty's Revenue and Customs, but only for the purpose mentioned in subsection (2).

(2) The purpose is to assist the approved person in complying with obligations imposed on that person by virtue of section 51.

(3) An approved person to whom information is disclosed under subsection (1)—

(a) may use the information only for the purpose of complying with obligations imposed on that person by virtue of section 51, and

(b) may not further disclose the information except with the consent of the Commissioners.

(4) Section 19 of the Commissioners for Revenue and Customs Act 2005 (offence) applies to a disclosure in contravention of subsection (3)(b) as it applies to a disclosure, in contravention of section 20(9) of that Act, of revenue and customs information relating to a person whose identity is specified in the disclosure or can be deduced from it.

GENERAL NOTE

Section 52(1) provides that the Commissioners may disclose information to an approved person for the purpose of meeting its obligations vis-à-vis third country goods suppliers (but only for the purpose set out in section 52(2))

Section 52(2) states that the purpose is to assist the approved person to comply with the obligations imposed on him by virtue of this new law.

Section 52(3) stipulates that the use to which a person can put the disclosed information is that which is necessary for it to comply with its section 51 obligations. A person cannot disclose information obtained from HMRC for any other purpose unless approved by HMRC to do so.

Section 52(4) treats a "wrongful disclosure" as an offence under the Commissioners of Revenue and Customs Act 2005 s 19.

53 Offence

(1) A person who—

    (a) carries on a third country goods fulfilment business, and

    (b) is not an approved person,

commits an offence.

(2) In proceedings for an offence under subsection (1) it is a defence to show that the person did not know, and had no reasonable grounds to suspect, that the person—

    (a) was carrying on a third country goods fulfilment business, or

    (b) was not an approved person.

(3) A person is taken to have shown the fact mentioned in subsection (2) if—

    (a) sufficient evidence of that fact is adduced to raise an issue with respect to it, and

    (b) the contrary is not proved beyond reasonable doubt.

(4) A person guilty of an offence under this section is liable on summary conviction—

    (a) in England and Wales, to imprisonment for a term not exceeding 12 months, or a fine, or both;

    (b) in Scotland, to imprisonment for a term not exceeding 12 months, or a fine not exceeding the statutory maximum, or both;

    (c) in Northern Ireland, to imprisonment for a term not exceeding 6 months, or a fine not exceeding the statutory maximum, or both.

(5) A person guilty of an offence under this section is liable on conviction on indictment to—

    (a) imprisonment for a period not exceeding 7 years,

    (b) a fine, or

    (c) both.

(6) In relation to an offence committed before the commencement of section 154(1) of the Criminal Justice Act 2003 the reference in subsection (4)(a) to 12 months is to be read as a reference to 6 months.

GENERAL NOTE

Section 53(1) stipulates that where a person carries on a third country goods fulfilment business and is not an approved person, he commits an offence.

Section 53(2) provides a statutory defence to the offence if the person in question can show that he did not know nor had reasonable grounds to suspect that he was:

(a) carrying on a third country goods fulfilment business, or

(b) not an approved person.

Section 53(3) stipulates that the defence provided by section 53(2) is to be taken as having been shown if there is sufficient evidence to support it and the contrary is not proven beyond reasonable doubt.

Section 53(4) sets out the relevant penalty for a person who is found to be guilty of an offence under section 53(1). On summary conviction, a person will be liable as follows:

(a) in England and Wales, to imprisonment for a term not exceeding 12 months, or a fine, or both;

(b) in Scotland, to imprisonment for a term not exceeding 12 months, or a fine not exceeding the statutory maximum, or both;

(c) in Northern Ireland, to imprisonment for a term not exceeding 6 months, or a fine not exceeding the statutory maximum, or both.

Section 53(5) states that on indictment, a person found guilty of an offence under section 53(1) will be liable to:

(a) imprisonment for a period not exceeding 7 years

(b) a fine,

(c) or both.

Section 53(6) provides that as far as section 53(4)(a) is concerned, this section adjusts the maximum sentence to 6 months (from 12 months) where the offence was committed before section 154(1) of the Criminal Justice Act 2003 came into force.

54 Forfeiture

(1) If a person—

    (a) carries on a third country goods fulfilment business, and

(b) is not an approved person,

any goods within subsection (2) are liable to forfeiture under CEMA 1979.

(2) Goods are within this subsection if—

(a) they are stored by the person, and

(b) their storage by the person constitutes, or has constituted, the carrying on of a third country goods fulfilment business by the person.

GENERAL NOTE

Section 54(1) stipulates that if a person carries on a third country goods fulfilment business and he is not an approved person, any goods stored by him may be liable to forfeiture under the provisions of Customs and Excise Management Act 1979 s 139.

Section 54(2) states that the goods liable to forfeiture under section 54(1) are those goods stored by that person where the person is storing the goods in question in the course of the carrying on of a third country goods fulfilment business (pursuant to section 48(1)).

55 Penalties

(1) Schedule 13 provides for a penalty to be payable by a person who carries on a third country goods fulfilment business and is not an approved person.

(2) The Commissioners may make regulations ("penalty regulations") imposing a penalty for the contravention of—

(a) any condition or restriction imposed under this Part;

(b) regulations under this Part.

(3) The amount of a penalty imposed by the penalty regulations is to be specified in the regulations, but must not exceed £3,000.

(4) The penalty regulations may make provision for the assessment and recovery of a penalty imposed by the regulations.

(5) The Commissioners may by regulations make provision for corporate bodies which are members of the same group to be jointly and severally liable for any penalties imposed under—

(a) Schedule 13;

(b) penalty regulations.

GENERAL NOTE

Section 55(1) states that where a person carries on a third country fulfilment business and is not an approved person then, notwithstanding the offence provisions of section 53 and the forfeiture provisions of section 54, that person may be liable to a penalty (maximum £10,000) pursuant to F(No 2)A 2017 Schedule 13.

Section 55(2) provides that the Commissioners are also given powers to impose a civil penalty where a person is either in breach of conditions imposed under this Part or is in breach of regulations made under this Part.

Section 55(3) states that the amount of any such penalty is to be specified in the penalty regulations but must not exceed £3,000.

Section 55(4) stipulates that the particular penalty regulations should make provision for assessment and recovery of the amount assessed as penalty

Section 55(5) provides that as far as groups of companies are concerned, this section allows HMRC to make regulations with the intention of making groups of companies jointly and severally liable for any penalties imposed under Schedule 13 or regulations.

56 Appeals

(1) FA 1994 is amended as follows.

(2) In section 13A(2) (customs and excise reviews and appeals: relevant decisions) after paragraph (gb) insert—

"(gc) any decision by HMRC that a person is liable to a penalty, or as to the amount of a person's liability, under—

(i) regulations under section 55 of the Finance (No 2) Act 2017, or

(ii) Schedule 13 to that Act;".

(3) In Schedule 5 to that Act (decisions subject to review and appeal) after paragraph 9A insert—

"The Finance (No 2) Act 2017

9B Any decision for the purposes of Part 3 of the Finance (No 2) Act 2017 (third country goods fulfilment businesses) as to—

(a) whether or not, and in which respects, any person is to be, or to continue to be, approved and registered, or

(b) the conditions or restrictions subject to which any person is approved and registered."

GENERAL NOTE

Section 56(1) provides for an amendment to the Finance Act 1994.

Section 56(2) amends FA 1994 s 13A(2) by including a right of appeal against a decision by HMRC that a person is liable:

(a) to a penalty, or as to the amount of a person's liability, under regulations under F(No 2)A 2017 s 55, or

(b) Schedule 13 to that Act;

Section 56(3) amends FA 1994 Sch 5 (decision subject to review and appeal) to include a right of appeal against any decision for the purposes of F(No 2)A 2017 Pt 3 (third country goods fulfilment businesses) as to:

(a) whether or not, and in which respects, any person is to be, or to continue to be, approved and registered, or

(b) the conditions or restrictions subject to which any person is approved and registered.

57 Regulations

(1) Regulations under this Part may—

(a) make provision which applies generally or only for specified cases or purposes;

(b) make different provision for different cases or purposes;

(c) include incidental, consequential, transitional or transitory provision;

(d) confer a discretion on the Commissioners;

(e) make provision by reference to a notice to be published by the Commissioners.

(2) Regulations under this Part are to be made by statutory instrument.

(3) A statutory instrument containing regulations under this Part is subject to annulment in pursuance of a resolution of the House of Commons.

(4) This section does not apply to regulations under section 59 (commencement).

GENERAL NOTE

Section 57(1) stipulates that as far as this Part is concerned regulations may:

(a) make provision which applies generally or only for specified cases or purposes;

(b) make different provision for different cases or purposes;

(c) include incidental, consequential, transitional or transitory provision;

(d) confer a discretion on the Commissioners;

(e) make provision by reference to a notice to be published by the Commissioners.

Section 57(2) to section 57(4) deal with the mechanics of the making of regulations (i.e. by statutory instrument).

58 Interpretation

(1) In this Part—

"approved person" has the meaning given by section 49(5);

"the Commissioners" means the Commissioners for Her Majesty's Revenue and Customs.

(2) For the purposes of this Part two or more bodies corporate are members of a group if—

(a) one of them controls each of the others,

(b) one person (whether a body corporate or an individual) controls all of them, or

(c) two or more individuals carrying on a business in partnership control all of them.

(3) A body corporate is to be taken to control another body corporate if—

(a) it is empowered by or under legislation to control that body's activities, or

(b) it is that body's holding company within the meaning of section 1159 of, and Schedule 6 to, the Companies Act 2006.

(4) An individual or individuals are to be taken to control a body corporate if the individual or individuals (were the individual or individuals a company) would be that body's holding company within the meaning of section 1159 of, and Schedule 6 to, the Companies Act 2006.

GENERAL NOTE

Section 58(1) provides definitions of the terms "approved person" and "the Commissioners".

Section 58(2) stipulates that for the purposes of this Part two or more bodies corporate are members of a group if:

(a) one of them controls the others;

(b) one person (whether a body corporate or an individual) controls all of them; or

(c) two or more individuals carrying on a business in partnership control all of them.

Section 58(3) defines what is meant by control in relation to a body corporate. A body is regarded as controlling another if:

(a) it is empowered by or under legislation to control that body's activities, or

(b) it is that body's holding company within the meaning of section 1159 of, and Schedule 6 to, the Companies Act 2006.

Section 58(4) explains when an individual might be regarded as having control of a body corporate.

59 Commencement

(1) This Part comes into force—

(a) so far as it confers powers to make regulations, on the day on which this Act is passed, and

(b) for all other purposes, on such day as the Commissioners may by regulations made by statutory instrument appoint.

(2) Regulations under subsection (1)(b) may appoint different days for different purposes.

GENERAL NOTE

Section 59(1) states that Part 3 of the Act comes into force:

(a) so far as it confers powers to make regulations, on the day on which this Act is passed, and

(b) for all other purposes, on such day as the Commissioners may by regulations made by statutory instrument appoint.

Section 59(2) provides that regulations under section 59(1)(b) may appoint different days for different purposes.

PART 4

ADMINISTRATION, AVOIDANCE AND ENFORCEMENT

Reporting and record-keeping

60 Digital reporting and record-keeping for income tax etc

(1) TMA 1970 is amended as set out in subsections (2) and (3).

(2) After section 12B insert—

"Digital reporting and record-keeping

12C Digital reporting and record-keeping

Schedule A1 (digital reporting and record-keeping) has effect."

(3) Before Schedule 1AA insert—

"SCHEDULE A1

Section 12C

DIGITAL REPORTING AND RECORD-KEEPING

PART 1

APPLICATION

Application: persons

1 (1) This Schedule applies to a person within the charge to income tax who, otherwise than in partnership, carries on (or has carried on)—

(a) a trade, profession or vocation the profits of which are chargeable to income tax under Part 2 of ITTOIA 2005,

(b) a property business the profits of which are chargeable to income tax under Part 3 of ITTOIA 2005, or

(c) any other activity which may give rise to profits or other income chargeable to income tax under Part 2 or 3 of ITTOIA 2005.

(2) This is subject to paragraph 2.

2 (1) This Schedule does not apply to—

(a) the trustees of a charitable trust, or

(b) the trustees of an exempt unauthorised unit trust (within the meaning of the Unauthorised Unit Trusts (Tax) Regulations 2013 (S.I. 2013/2819)),

unless the trustees elect for this Schedule to apply to them.

(2) This Schedule does not apply to a person in respect of an excluded activity unless the person elects for this Schedule to apply to the person in respect of the excluded activity.

(3) The following are excluded activities—

(a) the underwriting business of a member of Lloyd's (within the meaning of section 184 of the Finance Act 1993),

(b) holding shares in respect of which a distribution may be made which is chargeable to income tax under Part 3 of ITTOIA 2005 by virtue of section 548(6) of CTA 2010 (distributions to shareholders in real estate investment trusts), and

(c) participating in an open-ended investment company which may make distributions chargeable to income tax under Part 3 of ITTOIA 2005 by virtue of regulation 69Z18 of the Authorised Investment Funds (Tax) Regulations 2006 (S.I. 2006/964) (property income distributions).

(4) The Commissioners may by regulations make provision about elections under this paragraph and the withdrawal of such elections, including provision—

(a) about how an election may be made or withdrawn, and

(b) about the period for which an election or withdrawal has effect.

Application: partnerships

3 (1) This Schedule applies to a partnership if one or more of the partners is within the charge to income tax.

(2) This is subject to paragraph 4.

4 (1) If all the activities of a partnership which may give rise to profits or income are excluded activities, this Schedule does not apply to the partnership unless the partnership elects for this Schedule to apply to it.

(2) The following are excluded activities—

(a) the underwriting business of a Lloyd's partnership (as defined in section 184(1) of the Finance Act 1993),

(b) holding shares in respect of which a distribution may be made which is chargeable to income tax under Part 3 of ITTOIA 2005 by virtue of section 548(6) of CTA 2010 (distributions to shareholders in real estate investment trusts), and

(c) participating in an open-ended investment company which may make distributions chargeable to income tax under Part 3 of ITTOIA 2005 by virtue of regulation 69Z18 of the Authorised Investment Funds (Tax) Regulations 2006 (S.I. 2006/964) (property income distributions).

(3) The Commissioners may by regulations make provision about elections under this paragraph and the withdrawal of such elections, including provision—

(a) about how an election may be made or withdrawn, and

(b) about the period for which an election or withdrawal has effect.

Nominated partners

5 (1) Requirements imposed by regulations under this Schedule on a partnership are to be met by a nominated partner.

(2) A "nominated partner" is a partner nominated for the purposes of this Schedule—

(a) by the partners, or

(b) by the Commissioners.

(3) A nomination, or a revocation of a nomination, by the partners does not have effect until notice of the revocation or nomination is given to HMRC.

(4) The Commissioners may by regulations make provision about nominations and the revocation of nominations, including provision about the circumstances in which the Commissioners may nominate a partner.

(5) In this Act references to a nominated partner are to a partner nominated for the purposes of this Schedule.

PART 2

DIGITAL REPORTING AND RECORD-KEEPING

Interpretation

6 In this Part of this Schedule "business"—

(a) in relation to a person to whom this Schedule applies (see paragraphs 1 and 2), means the activity by virtue of which this Schedule applies to the person (and if more than one, means each of them), and

(b) in relation to a partnership to which this Schedule applies (see paragraphs 3 and 4), means any activity of the partnership.

Periodic updates

7 (1) The Commissioners may by regulations require a person or partnership to whom this Schedule applies to provide to HMRC, by electronic communications, specified information about the business of the person or partnership.

(2) The information which may be specified includes any information ("financial information") relevant to calculating profits, losses or income of the business, including information about receipts and expenses.

(3) The regulations may require information to be provided at or for specified intervals, times or periods.

(4) The regulations may not require financial information about the business to be provided more often than once every 3 months.

End of period statement

8 (1) The Commissioners may by regulations require a person to whom this Schedule applies to provide to HMRC, by electronic communications, a statement containing specified information about the person's business in relation to each relevant period.

(2) "Relevant period" means—

(a) in relation to a business the profits or income of which are chargeable to income tax under Chapter 2 of Part 2 of ITTOIA 2005, a basis period (see Chapter 15 of that Part), and

(b) otherwise, a tax year.

(3) The information which may be specified includes any information relevant to calculating profits, losses or income of the business for the relevant period, including information about receipts and expenses.

(4) Regulations under this paragraph may require the statement to include a declaration to the effect that the information included in it is correct and complete.

(5) An end of period statement for a tax year must be provided to HMRC at or before—

(a) the time at which the person delivers a return under section 8 or 8A for the tax year (see section 8(7)(c) and 8A(7)(c)), or

(b) if earlier, the end of 31 January following the tax year.

(6) In this Act—

(a) references to an end of period statement are to a statement required by regulations under this paragraph;

(b) references to an end of period statement for a tax year are to an end of period statement for that tax year or, where the relevant period is a basis period, for the basis period for that tax year.

Facility for complying with notice to file under section 8 or 8A

9 The Commissioners may by regulations make provision for the establishment and use of a facility enabling a person to whom this Schedule applies to file or deliver, by electronic communications—

(a) anything which under section 8(1AB) may be required to be filed or delivered by a notice to file under section 8;

(b) anything which under section 8A(1AB) may be required to be filed or delivered by a notice to file under section 8A.

Partnership return

10 (1) The Commissioners may by regulations require a partnership to which this Schedule applies to provide to HMRC, by electronic communications, a return containing specified information about the partnership's business in relation to each tax year.

(2) The information which may be specified includes any information which is or may be required to be included in a section 12AA partnership return, including information in respect of any partners within the charge to corporation tax.

(3) In particular, the information which may be specified includes the information required to be included in a section 12AA partnership return by section 12AB (partnership statements).

(4) Regulations under this paragraph may require the return to include a declaration to the effect that the information included in it is correct and complete.

(5) A Schedule A1 partnership return for a tax year must be provided to HMRC on or before 31 January following the tax year.

(6) In this Act—

(a) references to a Schedule A1 partnership return are to a return required by regulations under this paragraph, and

(b) references to a partnership statement, in relation to a Schedule A1 partnership return, are to information required to be included in the return by virtue of sub-paragraph (3).

(7) In the Taxes Acts, unless the contrary intention appears, a reference (whether general or specific) to a return under, or a return required under, this Act includes a reference to a Schedule A1 partnership return.

Record-keeping

11 (1) The Commissioners may by regulations require a person or partnership to whom this Schedule applies to—

(a) keep specified records relating to the business in electronic form, and

(b) preserve those records in electronic form for a specified period.

(2) The records which may be specified are any records the Commissioners consider relevant to ascertaining information required to be provided by regulations under this Part of this Schedule.

(3) A requirement imposed by regulations under this paragraph is in addition to, and not in place of, any other requirement that the person or partnership keep and preserve records (or keep and preserve records in a particular form).

(4) Paragraph 5(1) (requirements imposed on partnership to be met by nominated partner) does not apply to requirements imposed by regulations under this paragraph.

12 (1) This paragraph applies where requirements imposed by regulations under paragraph 11 for any period are not complied with.

(2) The person, or in the case of a partnership each relevant partner, is liable for a penalty.

(3) "Relevant partner" means any person who was a partner in the partnership at any time during the period in question.

(4) The amount of the penalty must not exceed £3,000.

(5) A person or relevant partner is not liable to a penalty under this paragraph in relation to a period if the person or relevant partner is liable to a penalty under section 12B(5) in relation to that period.

Electronic communications and records: supplementary powers

13 (1) This paragraph applies to regulations under paragraphs 7, 8, 9, 10 and 11.

(2) The regulations may (amongst other things) make provision—

    (a) as to the electronic form to be taken by information provided and records kept or preserved,

    (b) requiring persons to prepare and keep records of information provided by means of electronic communications,

    (c) for the production of the contents of records kept or preserved in accordance with regulations under this Part of this Schedule,

    (d) as to conditions that must be complied with in connection with the use of electronic communications or the keeping or preservation of electronic records,

    (e) for treating information as not having been provided or records as not having been kept or preserved unless conditions are complied with,

    (f) for determining the time at which and person by whom information is taken to have been delivered, and

    (g) for authenticating information or records.

(3) The regulations may also make provision (which may include provision for the application of conclusive or other presumptions) about the manner of proving for any purpose—

    (a) whether any use of electronic communications is to be taken as having resulted in the provision of information,

    (b) the time at which information was provided,

    (c) the person by whom information was provided,

    (d) the contents of any information provided,

    (e) the contents of any records, and

    (f) any other matter for which provision may be made by the regulations.

(4) The regulations may allow or require use to be made of intermediaries in connection with—

    (a) the provision of information by means of electronic communications, and

    (b) the authentication or security of anything transmitted by any such means.

(5) The regulations may—

    (a) allow any authorisation or requirement for which the regulations may provide to be given by means of a specific or general direction given by the Commissioners, and

    (b) provide that the conditions of an authorisation or requirement are to be taken to be satisfied only where the Commissioners are satisfied as to specified matters.

(6) The regulations may provide—

    (a) that information provided must meet standards of accuracy and completeness set by specific or general directions given by the Commissioners, and

    (b) that failure to meet those standards may be treated as a failure to provide the information, or as a failure to comply with the requirements of the regulations.

PART 3

EXEMPTIONS

Exemption for the digitally excluded

14 (1) The Commissioners must by regulations make provision—

    (a) for a person to be exempt from requirements imposed by regulations under paragraphs 7, 8 and 11 if the Commissioners are satisfied that the person is digitally excluded, and

    (b) for a partnership to be exempt from requirements imposed by regulations under paragraphs 7, 10 and 11 if the Commissioners are satisfied that the partnership is digitally excluded.

(2) A person is digitally excluded if the digital exclusion condition is met in relation to the person.

(3) A partnership is digitally excluded if the digital exclusion condition is met in relation to each partner.

(4) The digital exclusion condition is met in relation to a person or partner if—

(a) the person or partner is a practising member of a religious society or order whose beliefs are incompatible with using electronic communications or keeping electronic records, or

(b) for any reason (including age, disability or location) it is not reasonably practicable for the person or partner to use electronic communications or to keep electronic records.

Further exemptions

15 (1) The Commissioners may by regulations make provision for further exemptions.

(2) The exemptions for which provision may be made include exemptions based on income or other financial criteria.

PART 4
SUPPLEMENTARY PROVISION

Appeals

16 (1) An appeal may be brought against any decision made by the Commissioners, or by an officer of Revenue and Customs, under regulations under this Schedule.

(2) Notice of an appeal under this paragraph must be given to HMRC within 30 days after the day on which notice of the decision is given.

(3) The notice of appeal must—

(a) be in writing, and

(b) specify the grounds of appeal.

Interpretation

17 Any power in this Schedule to require the provision of information includes power to require the provision of accounts, statements and documents relating to that information.

Regulations

18 (1) Regulations under this Schedule may—

(a) make provision which applies generally or only for specified cases or purposes;

(b) make different provision for different cases or purposes;

(c) include incidental, supplemental, consequential, saving, transitional or transitory provision;

(d) make provision for matters to be specified by the Commissioners in accordance with the regulations.

(2) Sub-paragraph (1)(d) does not apply to any interval, time or period specified by virtue of paragraph 7(3) (which may be specified only by the regulations).

(3) Regulations under this Schedule may make provision for a person or partnership to whom this Schedule applies, but who would not otherwise be subject to a requirement imposed by the regulations, to elect to be subject to that requirement.

(4) Regulations under this Schedule may provide that, for the purposes of any provision of this Schedule or of the regulations, a change in the accounting date of a business is to be disregarded (and its period of account determined accordingly).

(5) The power to make regulations under this Schedule is exercisable by statutory instrument.

(6) A statutory instrument containing regulations under this Schedule is subject to annulment in pursuance of a resolution of the House of Commons."

(4) Subsections (1) to (3) come into force on such day as the Treasury may by regulations made by statutory instrument appoint.

(5) Regulations under subsection (4) may appoint different days for different purposes.

GENERAL NOTE

Section 60 amends TMA 1970 by introducing new Schedule A1, which sets out the requirements of digital record keeping and reporting for income tax. Although recent announcements have indicated that the mandation for income tax will not commence until 2020 at the earliest, HMRC are keen to get the legislation set down so that those affected have time to understand what will be needed once the regime comes into force.

Who is affected?

The obligation to comply is placed on persons within the charge to tax who carry on (alone and not in partnership) either a trade or a property business, or any other activity which is liable to tax under parts 2 (trading income) or 3 (property income).

The principal exclusions are set out as excluded persons – the trustees of a charitable trust and the trustees of an exempt unauthorised unit trust. There are also excluded activities and persons carrying on those activities are also not liable to comply. These are:

– Lloyds underwriting;
– holding shares in a real estate investment trust; and
– participating in an open-ended investment company whose distributions are taxed as property income.

Separately, a partnership is also required to comply if one or more partners is liable to income tax unless the only activities the partnership carries on are excluded activities. Compliance will be met by the nominated partner of a partnership.

What must they do?

Regulations will provide the detail of what is needed, but persons liable must supply to HMRC periodic updates by electronic communication of information relevant to the calculation of the profit or loss of the business, including receipts and payments. The intervals for provision of the periodic updates are restricted to no more often than every three months, but all remaining detail is to be provided by secondary legislation.

In addition to the periodic updates, a person will also be required to supply an end of period statement, again by electronic communication. The period referred to in the case of trading is a basis period, and in other cases is a tax year. The statement will include a declaration that the information in it is correct and complete. The content of this statement will again be set in regulations, but the due dates are shown as:

– when the self-assessment return is filed, or
– if earlier, 31 January following the tax year.

For partnerships the requirement also includes an end of period statement to include the information shown on the current partnership statement within the partnership tax return, i.e. partners and their share of the profits or losses of the partnership for the period, and this is referred to as a return. The partnership end of period statement must be submitted by 31 January after the end of the tax year. The new style partnership return is known as a Schedule A1 return.

Electronic record keeping

There are also enabling powers to permit regulations to specify the content of accounting records. The Act sets out that records will be kept in electronic form and preserved in electronic form for a specified period – as yet undetermined. In this case, the nominated partner is excused direct responsibility for compliance with this obligation – so the responsibility falls on all partners in a firm equally. The Act also sets down a penalty for non-compliance of up to £3,000, which in the case of a partnership may be imposed on each member of the partnership during the period in question.

There are wide powers for additional regulations to specify the form of electronic records and various powers in relation to the production of electronic records, and conditions associated with the keeping or production of electronic records. Regulations may also specify a standard of accuracy and hold that unless that is met, the obligations have not been complied with.

Digital exclusion

As indicated during the consultation on Making Tax Digital, the existing definition in place and used for VAT is also applied in precisely the same terms to obligations under income tax. The obligations to keep digital records, make periodic updates and a period end statement are all removed when the person (or the partnership) is digitally excluded. For a partnership to be digitally excluded, all partners must be digitally excluded.

For clarity, the definition of digital exclusion is repeated in this legislation:

- the person or partner is a practising member of a religious society or order whose beliefs are incompatible with using electronic communications or keeping electronic records, or
- for any reason (including age, disability or location) it is not reasonably practicable for the person or partner to use electronic communications or to keep electronic records.

There is also the option for additional exemptions to be introduced, by reference to income or other financial criteria.

Final points

A right of appeal, with the usual conditions, is set down; appeal is permitted against any decision of Revenue and Customs about matters in the new Schedule. The most obvious candidate for appeal is a decision regarding digital exclusion.

Various powers to make regulations follow, one notable inclusion is the power given in regulations to ignore a change of accounting date and determine the accounting periods accordingly. This is clearly intended to deal with businesses seeking to change their accounting date to 31 March from 5 April to delay the start of digital record keeping and reporting.

Finally, the commencement date will be set by Treasury, and different dates can apply for different purposes.

61 Digital reporting and record-keeping for income tax etc: further amendments

(1) Schedule 14 contains provision amending TMA 1970 and other Acts.

(2) The Commissioners for Her Majesty's Revenue and Customs may by regulations amend or modify any provision of the Taxes Acts in consequence of the provision made by section 60 or Schedule 14.

(3) Regulations under subsection (2) may make transitional, transitory or saving provision.

(4) Regulations under subsection (2) must be made by statutory instrument.

(5) A statutory instrument containing regulations under subsection (2) may not be made unless a draft of the instrument has been laid before, and approved by a resolution of, the House of Commons.

(6) Subsections (1) to (5) and Schedule 14 come into force on such day as the Treasury may by regulations made by statutory instrument appoint.

(7) Regulations under subsection (6) may appoint different days for different purposes.

GENERAL NOTE

Section 61 and Schedule 14 largely set out consequential amendments arising from the content of Section 60.

62 Digital reporting and record-keeping for VAT

(1) Schedule 11 to VATA 1994 (administration, collection and enforcement) is amended as set out in subsections (2) to (4).

(2) In paragraph 2 (accounting and payment)—

(a) in sub-paragraph (1) for "and the making of returns" substitute ", the making of returns and the submission of information";

(b) after sub-paragraph (11) insert—

"(11A) Regulations under this paragraph may include incidental, supplemental, consequential, saving, transitional or transitory provision."

(3) In paragraph 6 (duty of taxable person to keep records)—

(a) omit sub-paragraph (4);

(b) at the end insert—

"(5) The Commissioners may by regulations make provision about the form in which, and means by which, records are to be kept and preserved.

(6) Regulations under sub-paragraph (5) may—

(a) make different provision for different cases;

(b) provide for any provision of the regulations to be subject to conditions or exceptions specified in writing by the Commissioners;

(c) include incidental, supplemental, consequential, saving, transitional or transitory provision.

(7) If regulations under sub-paragraph (5) make provision requiring records to be kept or preserved in electronic form they must make provision for a taxable person to be exempt from those requirements for any month ("the current month") if—

(a) the value of the person's taxable supplies, in the period of one year ending with the month before the current month, was less than the VAT threshold, and

(b) the person was not subject to those requirements in the month before the current month.

(8) The regulations may modify the exemption for cases where a business or part of a business carried on by a taxable person is transferred to another person as a going concern.

(9) The "VAT threshold" means the amount specified in paragraph 1(1)(a) of Schedule 1 on the first day of the current month.

(10) Regulations under sub-paragraph (5) requiring records to be kept or preserved in electronic form may (among other things) make provision—

(a) as to the electronic form in which records are to be kept or preserved,

(b) for the production of the contents of records kept or preserved in accordance with the regulations,

(c) as to conditions that must be complied with in connection with the keeping or preservation of electronic records,

(d) for treating records as not having been kept or preserved unless conditions are complied with,

(e) for authenticating records,

(f) about the manner of proving for any purpose the contents of any records (including provision for the application of conclusive or other presumptions).

(11) Regulations under sub-paragraph (5) requiring records to be kept or preserved in electronic form may—

(a) allow any authorisation or requirement for which the regulations may provide to be given by means of a specific or general direction given by the Commissioners,

(b) provide that the conditions of an authorisation or requirement are to be taken to be satisfied only where the Commissioners are satisfied as to specified matters."

(4) In paragraph 6A (power to direct keeping of records), for sub-paragraph (7) substitute—

"(7) Regulations under paragraph 6(5) apply for the purposes of this paragraph as they apply for the purposes of paragraph 6."

(5) In section 83(1) of VATA 1994 (appealable decisions), for paragraph (zc) substitute—

"(zc) a decision of the Commissioners about the application of any provision of regulations under paragraph 2 or 6 of Schedule 11, or of regulations under section 135 or 136 of the Finance Act 2002 relating to VAT, which—

(i) requires returns to be made or information to be submitted by electronic communications, or

(ii) requires records to be kept or preserved in electronic form,

(including in particular a decision as to whether such a requirement applies and a decision to impose a penalty)."

(6) Subsections (3)(a) and (4) of this section come into force when the first regulations under paragraph 6(5) of Schedule 11 to VATA 1994 come into force.

(7) Regulations under paragraph 6(5) of Schedule 11 to VATA 1994 may not make provision requiring records to be kept or preserved in electronic form which has effect before 1 April 2019.

GENERAL NOTE

Section 62 sets out the primary legislation in relation to Making Tax Digital (MTD) for VAT. Following the announcements in July 2017, VAT will be the first tax to be mandated into MTD. Regulations will again follow, but much of the detail will simply be referenced across to existing VAT obligations, so the new regulations are not expected to be too lengthy.

The approach taken by the new legislation is to amend existing VAT requirements. As for income tax, the existing term "making a return" is amplified to include "making a return and submission of information".

Power to make regulations about record keeping is set down, with a limitation where the records are required to be in electronic form. This requires a person to be exempt from the requirements when their taxable turnover in the 12 months to the previous month end is less than the VAT registration threshold, and they were not subject to the requirement in the previous month. This, in effect, disapplies any new requirements for those with taxable turnover of less than the VAT threshold, but once a person has exceeded the VAT limit they will be required to comply with the electronic requirements, even when the value of their taxable supplies falls, unless they de-register for VAT.

Rights of appeal are extended to include decisions about electronic record keeping and electronic submission of information, and penalties related to those obligations.

Finally the commencement date for any changes made by regulations may not be before 1 April 2019.

Note that in implementing MTD for VAT, there are no changes to the filing cycle for businesses, so those using the annual accounting period will still be permitted to file annually. There are also no changes to any of the existing schemes such as the cash accounting scheme or the flat rate scheme. The existing obligation to file returns electronically will essentially continue, but with modifications regarding digital record keeping and possibly some wording designed to meet HMRC's ambition of an "end to end" digital process. It is clear that in policy terms, HMRC accept that some businesses have such complex VAT affairs that a single accounting system may not be sufficient to calculate and submit VAT returns electronically, and that often additional electronic resources (possibly in the form of spreadsheets) may be required.

Enquiries

63 Partial closure notices

Schedule 15 makes provision for partial closure notices in respect of enquiries under sections 9A, 12ZM and 12AC of TMA 1970 and Schedule 18 to FA 1998.

GENERAL NOTE

Section 63 introduces Schedule 15, which makes amendments to the Taxes Management Act 1970 and Schedule 18 of the Finance Act 1998. The amendments provide HMRC and taxpayers with an ability to resolve specific matters during an enquiry through the issue of Partial Closure Notices, ahead of a Final Closure Notice.

The legislation was first announced in the Autumn Statement 2014 and subject to consultation, which identified a desire for there to be a reciprocal power. Taxpayers will be able to apply to the First-tier Tax Tribunal for a direction requiring HMRC to issue a Partial Closure Notice in relation to a matter or matters in an open enquiry.

Should HMRC issue a Partial Closure Notice and amend a tax return, taxpayers may appeal against, and apply for postponement of, any tax arising from the amendment to the tribunal.

HMRC will issue Partial Closure Notices only in enquiries where the tax affairs are complex, there is avoidance or where the quantum of tax at risk is significant. At the request of a taxpayer, HMRC may agree to issue a Partial Closure Notice by mutual agreement.

The provisions come into effect on Royal Assent, and apply to any enquiries under TMA 1970 ss 9A, 12ZM or 12AC, or under FA 1998 Sch 18, which have not been concluded by means of a closure notice before that date, and to notices of enquiry given on or after that date.

Avoidance etc

64 Errors in taxpayers' documents

(1) Schedule 24 to FA 2007 (penalties for errors) is amended as set out in subsections (2) and (3).

(2) After paragraph 3 insert—

"Errors related to avoidance arrangements

3A (1) This paragraph applies where a document of a kind listed in the Table in paragraph 1 is given to HMRC by a person ("P") and the document contains an inaccuracy which—

(a) falls within paragraph 1(2), and

(b) arises because the document is submitted on the basis that particular avoidance arrangements (within the meaning of paragraph 3B) had an effect which in fact they did not have.

(2) It is to be presumed that the inaccuracy was careless, within the meaning of paragraph 3, unless—

(a) the inaccuracy was deliberate on P's part, or

(b) P satisfies HMRC or (on an appeal notified to the tribunal) the tribunal that P took reasonable care to avoid inaccuracy.

(3) In considering whether P took reasonable care to avoid inaccuracy, HMRC and (on an appeal notified to the tribunal) the tribunal must take no account of any evidence of any reliance by P on advice where the advice is disqualified.

(4) Advice is "disqualified" if any of the following applies—

(a) the advice was given to P by an interested person;

(b) the advice was given to P as a result of arrangements made between an interested person and the person who gave the advice;

(c) the person who gave the advice did not have appropriate expertise for giving the advice;

(d) the advice took no account of P's individual circumstances;

(e) the advice was addressed to, or given to, a person other than P;

but this is subject to sub-paragraphs (5) and (7).

(5) Where (but for this sub-paragraph) advice would be disqualified under any of paragraphs (a) to (c) of sub-paragraph (4), the advice is not disqualified under that paragraph if at the relevant time P—

(a) has taken reasonable steps to find out whether the advice falls within that paragraph, and

(b) reasonably believes that it does not.

(6) In sub-paragraph (4) "an interested person" means—

(a) a person, other than P, who participated in the avoidance arrangements or any transaction forming part of them, or

(b) a person who for any consideration (whether or not in money) facilitated P's entering into the avoidance arrangements.

(7) Where (but for this sub-paragraph) advice would be disqualified under paragraph (a) of sub-paragraph (4) because it was given by a person within sub-paragraph (6)(b), the advice is not disqualified under that paragraph if—

(a) the person giving the advice had appropriate expertise for giving it,

(b) the advice took account of P's individual circumstances, and

(c) at the time when the question whether the advice is disqualified arises—

(i) Condition E in paragraph 3B(5) is met in relation to the avoidance arrangements, but

(ii) none of Conditions A to D in paragraph 3B(5) is or has at any time been met in relation to them.

(8) If the document mentioned in sub-paragraph (1) is given to HMRC by P as a personal representative of a deceased person ("D")—

(a) sub-paragraph (4) is to be read as if—

(i) the references in paragraphs (a) and (b) to P were to P or D;

(ii) the reference in paragraph (d) to P were to D, and

(iii) the reference in paragraph (e) to a person other than P were to a person who is neither P nor D,

(b) sub-paragraph (6) is to be read as if—

(i) the reference in paragraph (a) to P were a reference to the person to whom the advice was given, and

(ii) the reference in paragraph (b) to P were to D (or, where P also participated in the avoidance arrangements, P or D), and

(c) sub-paragraph (7) is to be read as if the reference in paragraph (b) to P were to D.

(9) In this paragraph—

"arrangements" includes any agreement, understanding, scheme, transaction or series of transactions (whether or not legally enforceable);

"the relevant time" means the time when the document mentioned in sub-paragraph (1) is given to HMRC;

"the tribunal" has the same meaning as in paragraph 17 (see paragraph 17(5A)).

3B (1) In paragraph 3A "avoidance arrangements" means, subject to sub-paragraph (3), arrangements which fall within sub-paragraph (2).

(2) Arrangements fall within this sub-paragraph if, having regard to all the circumstances, it would be reasonable to conclude that the obtaining of a tax advantage was the main purpose, or one of the main purposes, of the arrangements.

(3) Arrangements are not avoidance arrangements for the purposes of paragraph 3A if (although they fall within sub-paragraph (2))—

(a) they are arrangements which accord with established practice, and

(b) HMRC had, at the time the arrangements were entered into, indicated its acceptance of that practice.

(4) If, at any time, any of Conditions A to E is met in relation to particular arrangements—

(a) for the purposes of this Schedule the arrangements are to be taken to fall within (and always to have fallen within) sub-paragraph (2), and

(b) in relation to the arrangements, sub-paragraph (3) (and the reference to it in sub-paragraph (1)) are to be treated as omitted.

This does not prevent arrangements from falling within sub-paragraph (2) other than by reason of one or more of Conditions A to E being met.

(5) Conditions A to E are as follows—

(a) Condition A is that the arrangements are DOTAS arrangements within the meaning given by section 219(5) and (6) of FA 2014;

(b) Condition B is that the arrangements are disclosable VAT arrangements or disclosable indirect tax arrangements for the purposes of Schedule 18 to FA 2016 (see paragraphs 8A to 9A of that Schedule);

(c) Condition C is that both of the following apply—

(i) P has been given a notice under a provision mentioned in sub-paragraph (6) stating that a tax advantage arising from the arrangements is to be counteracted, and

(ii) that tax advantage has been counteracted under section 209 of FA 2013;

(d) Condition D is that a follower notice under section 204 of FA 2014 has been given to P by reference to the arrangements (and not withdrawn) and—

(i) the necessary corrective action for the purposes of section 208 of FA 2014 has been taken in respect of the denied advantage, or

(ii) the denied advantage has been counteracted otherwise than as mentioned in sub-paragraph (i);

(e) Condition E is that a tax advantage asserted by reference to the arrangements has been counteracted (by an assessment, an amendment of a return or claim, or otherwise) on the basis that an avoidance-related rule applies in relation to P's affairs.

(6) The provisions referred to in sub-paragraph (5)(c)(i) are—

(a) paragraph 12 of Schedule 43 to FA 2013 (general anti-abuse rule: notice of final decision);

(b) paragraph 8 or 9 of Schedule 43A to that Act (pooled or bound arrangements: notice of final decision);

(c) paragraph 8 of Schedule 43B to that Act (generic referrals: notice of final decision).

(7) In sub-paragraph (5)(d) the reference to giving a follower notice to P includes giving a partnership follower notice in respect of a partnership return in relation to which P is a relevant partner; and for the purposes of this sub-paragraph—

(a) "relevant partner" has the meaning given by paragraph 2(5) of Schedule 31 to FA 2014;

(b) a partnership follower notice is given "in respect of" the partnership return mentioned in paragraph 2(2)(a) or (b) of that Schedule.

(8) For the purposes of sub-paragraph (5)(d) it does not matter whether the denied advantage has been dealt with—

(a) wholly as mentioned in one or other of sub-paragraphs (i) and (ii) of sub-paragraph (5)(d), or

(b) partly as mentioned in one of those sub-paragraphs and partly as mentioned in the other;

and "the denied advantage" has the same meaning as in Chapter 2 of Part 4 of FA 2014 (see section 208(3) of and paragraph 4(3) of Schedule 31 to that Act).

(9) For the purposes of sub-paragraph (5)(e) a tax advantage has been "asserted by reference to" the arrangements if a return, claim or appeal has been made by P on the basis that the tax advantage results from the arrangements.

(10) In this paragraph—

"arrangements" has the same meaning as in paragraph 3A;

"avoidance-related rule" has the same meaning as in Part 4 of Schedule 18 to FA 2016 (see paragraph 25 of that Schedule);

a "tax advantage" includes—

(a) relief or increased relief from tax,

(b) repayment or increased repayment of tax,

(c) avoidance or reduction of a charge to tax or an assessment to tax,

(d) avoidance of a possible assessment to tax,

(e) deferral of a payment of tax or advancement of a repayment of tax,

(f) avoidance of an obligation to deduct or account for tax, and

(g) in relation to VAT, anything which is a tax advantage for the purposes of Schedule 18 to FA 2016 under paragraph 5 of that Schedule."

(3) In paragraph 18, after sub-paragraph (5) insert—

"(6) Paragraph 3A applies where a document is given to HMRC on behalf of P as it applies where a document is given to HMRC by P (and in paragraph 3B(9) the reference to P includes a person acting on behalf of P)."

(4) In FA 2014, omit section 276 (which is superseded by the provision inserted by subsections (2) and (3)).

(5) The amendments made by this section have effect in relation to any document of a kind listed in the Table in paragraph 1 of Schedule 24 to FA 2007 which—

(a) is given to HMRC on or after the day on which this Act is passed, and

(b) relates to a tax period that—

(i) begins on or after 6 April 2017, and

(ii) ends on or after the day on which this Act is passed.

(6) In subsection (5) "tax period", and the reference to giving a document to HMRC, have the same meaning as in Schedule 24 to FA 2007 (see paragraph 28 of that Schedule).

GENERAL NOTE

HMRC guidance states that the aim of the amendments to FA 2007 Sch 24 is to act as a disincentive to entering into tax avoidance by amending penalties for errors and preventing reasonable excuse in certain situations. A taxpayer who enters into tax avoidance arrangements and claims they took reasonable care based on advice will be denied a claim for reasonable excuse where that advice is supplied by those not qualified to give it or who are connected to the avoidance in question. The measure will apply to inaccuracies in documents given to HMRC on or after the day the Act is passed and relating to tax periods which begin on or after 6 April 2017 or end on or after the day the Act is passed.

The new FA 2007 Sch 24 para 3A(1) provides that paragraph 3A applies when a person gives HMRC a document containing an inaccuracy which leads to an understatement of tax, a false or inflated loss or a false or inflated claim for repayment of tax and the inaccuracy relates to certain tax avoidance arrangements. Paragraphs 3B(1) and (2) define tax arrangements for these purposes and include arrangements where having regard to all the circumstances, it would be reasonable to conclude that the obtaining of a tax advantage was the main purpose, or one of the main purposes, of the arrangements. Paragraph 3B(3) provides that arrangements are not avoidance arrangements where they accord with established practice and where HMRC have indicated their acceptance of them. DOTAS, disclosable VAT arrangements and those subject to follower notices and counteraction notices are arrangements for these purposes.

Where there is an arrangement para 3A(2) presumes careless behaviour unless it was deliberate or reasonable care can be demonstrated. Paragraph 3A(3) provides that reliance on disqualified advice is not taken into account when considering reasonable excuse. Disqualified advice includes that provided by an interested person, where an interested person is connected to the person providing the advice, the adviser did not have appropriate expertise, and where advice is not tailored to the circumstances. Paragraphs 3A(6) and (7) expand on "interested person" to be one broadly involved (who participated in) with and receiving consideration (money's worth or otherwise) from the arrangements or part of the arrangements, or who facilitated the involvement of the taxpayer for any consideration (whether or not in money).

Para 3B(5) provides that certain arrangements will always be deemed to be within the scope of the new restriction, e.g. DOTAS arrangements or arrangements that have been counteracted. The term "appropriate expertise" is open to interpretation and could include a professional holding a relevant qualification, or someone who specialises and practices in that area or Queen's Counsel. Similarly, the terms "consideration" and "facilitated" are likely to be tested.

65 Penalties for enablers of defeated tax avoidance

Schedule 16 makes provision for penalties for persons who enable tax avoidance which is defeated.

GENERAL NOTE

Section 65 and Schedule 16 introduce a new penalty on enablers of defeated tax avoidance.

The penalty is the latest in a succession of government measures that have been introduced over the last few years to tackle, in particular, marketed tax avoidance.

The penalty applies to anyone who enables the use of tax avoidance arrangements that HMRC later defeat, and focuses on abusive schemes that, according to HMRC, "no-one could mistake for a reasonable commercial arrangement". It targets those individuals and entities that make a profit from enabling abusive tax arrangements by imposing a fixed 100% fee-based penalty on everyone in the supply chain.

It is closely based on the wording of the General Anti-Abuse Rule (GAAR) which was introduced in FA 2013. External scrutiny will be provided by the GAAR Advisory Panel.

The Government's stated policy objective behind the measure is to "influence and promote behavioural change in the minority of tax agents, intermediaries and others who design, market or facilitate the use of abusive avoidance, and benefit financially from their use. It is to ensure that these enablers can be held accountable for their activities should the tax avoidance they have enabled later be defeated".

The measure follows a period of consultation in autumn 2016 during which HMRC consulted widely with the tax, accountancy and legal profession. The profession was concerned that the original proposals, which were widely drafted, would have inhibited their members' ability to provide clients with advice on bona fide commercial transactions which could in no sense be regarded as "tax avoidance".

In their response to the consultation paper on 5 December 2016, HMRC announced that the measure would use the GAAR definition of "abusive tax arrangements" in order to focus the measure more narrowly on enablers of tax avoidance schemes, while the vast majority of professionals providing advice to their clients on genuine commercial arrangements would have "nothing to fear" (paragraph 1.11).

At paragraph 1.4 of their response, they stated that:

> "The government recognises that the vast majority of professionals providing advice on genuine commercial arrangements help their clients to comply with their tax obligations. The government wants to ensure they can continue to do so without being concerned that they might be caught by these new penalties".

Later in paragraph 4.9, HMRC refer to the revised Professional Conduct in Relation to Taxation (PCRT) which was published by the seven leading tax and accountancy bodies, including CIOT, on 1 November 2016 and which took effect from 1 March 2017. This sets out, for the first time, that members:

> "must not create, encourage or promote tax planning arrangements or structures that:
> (i) set out to achieve results that are contrary to the clear intention of parliament in enacting relevant legislation and/or
> (ii) are highly artificial or highly contrived and seek to exploit shortcomings within the relevant legislation".

HMRC have said that provided members act wholly within the spirit of the new PCRT standard for tax planning, the government would not expect that they would normally be affected by the new penalty for enablers of defeated tax avoidance. The legislation itself does not specifically protect an adviser who acts within PCRT, but HMRC's guidance is expected to state that such a person is unlikely to come within the scope of the enablers' penalty.

The CIOT welcomed the increased focus of the measure on the "small minority of advisers who profit from devising, marketing and facilitating aggressive tax avoidance schemes". In a press release dated 5 December 2016, John Cullinane, CIOT's Tax Policy Director, said: "It is pleasing to see that after a wide ranging consultation with the CIOT and other stakeholders, the government has taken on board our concerns and recognises that the vast majority of tax professionals providing advice on commercial arrangements are in no sense "enabling tax avoidance" but are simply helping their clients to understand as well as comply with their tax obligations. It is crucial that they can continue to do so without being exposed to this new penalty".

The Solicitors Regulation Authority (SRA) is not one of the bodies signed up to PCRT. On 21 September 2017 the SRA published its own guidance for its members providing tax planning services in a "Warning Notice" on tax avoidance, and noted that its members who work in tax should "be familiar with PCRT and adhere to its standards".

It is expected that HMRC's guidance will indicate that a bank that is fully complying with its commitments under the Code of Practice on Taxation of Banks is unlikely to be affected by the enablers' penalty, although the legislation itself does not provide specific protection.

It is advisable that tax practitioners familiarise themselves with the definition of "enabler" before providing advice to clients on a tax arrangement, including one designed by others, that is potentially within the GAAR, in order to minimise any risk of exposing themselves to an enabling penalty.

The new penalty comes into effect from Royal Assent to the Finance (No 2) Act 2017 in relation to enabling actions carried out on or after that date and tax arrangements entered into on or after that date.

It is expected that HMRC will publish guidance and examples shortly after Royal Assent is given. Because of the overlap with the GAAR legislation, the guidance on the enabling penalty should be read in conjunction with the existing GAAR Guidance. The GAAR Guidance will be updated following the enactment of the enabling penalty legislation.

66 Disclosure of tax avoidance schemes: VAT and other indirect taxes

(1) Schedule 17 contains provision about the disclosure of tax avoidance schemes involving VAT or other indirect taxes.

(2) In consequence of the provision made by Schedule 17, section 58A of, and Schedule 11A to, VATA 1994 (disclosure of VAT avoidance schemes) cease to have effect to require a person to disclose any scheme which—

    (a) is first entered into by that person on or after 1 January 2018,
    (b) constitutes notifiable arrangements under Schedule 17,
    (c) implements proposals which are notifiable proposals under Schedule 17.

(3) No scheme or proposed scheme may be notified to the Commissioners under paragraph 9 of Schedule 11A to VATA 1994 (voluntary notification of schemes) on or after 1 January 2018.

(4) This section and Schedule 17 come into force—

    (a) so far as is necessary for enabling the making of regulations under that Schedule, on the passing of this Act, and
    (b) for all other purposes, on 1 January 2018.

GENERAL NOTE

Section 66 introduces Schedule 17 which changes the way indirect tax avoidance is notified to HMRC, moving the primary responsibility for disclosing details of a scheme to the promoter (rather than the user).

The legislation applies to VAT and most other indirect taxes (which are set out in para 2 of the Schedule) and takes effect on 1 January 2018.

This is the first time that excise taxes, customs duties and insurance premium tax have been encompassed by the legislation (plus other indirect taxes) highlighting the Government's determination to reduce avoidance from all areas of the tax system. The change means that existing legislation in VATA 1994 Sch 11A will cease to apply from 1 January 2018.

67 Requirement to correct certain offshore tax non-compliance
Schedule 18 makes provision for and in connection with requiring persons to correct any offshore tax non-compliance subsisting on 6 April 2017.

GENERAL NOTE
The objective of the legislation is to enable and incentivise taxpayers with UK tax irregularities relating to offshore interests to regularise their tax affairs. The legislation offers a Requirement to Correct ("RTC") period that ends on 30 September 2018. After this date, it is intended there will be tougher sanctions for offshore tax non-compliance. The legislation introduces an obligation for taxpayers to bring their tax affairs up to date and imposes significant penalties for those who do not.

68 Penalty for transactions connected with VAT fraud etc
(1) VATA 1994 is amended as follows.

(2) After section 69B (penalty for breach of record-keeping requirements imposed by directions) insert—

"69C Transactions connected with VAT fraud

(1) A person (T) is liable to a penalty where—
    (a) T has entered into a transaction involving the making of a supply by or to T ("the transaction"), and
    (b) conditions A to C are satisfied.

(2) Condition A is that the transaction was connected with the fraudulent evasion of VAT by another person (whether occurring before or after T entered into the transaction).

(3) Condition B is that T knew or should have known that the transaction was connected with the fraudulent evasion of VAT by another person.

(4) Condition C is that HMRC have issued a decision ("the denial decision") in relation to the supply which—
    (a) prevents T from exercising or relying on a VAT right in relation to the supply,
    (b) is based on the facts which satisfy conditions A and B in relation to the transaction, and
    (c) applies a relevant principle of EU case law (whether or not in circumstances that are the same as the circumstances in which any relevant case was decided by the European Court of Justice).

(5) In this section "VAT right" includes the right to deduct input tax, the right to apply a zero rate to international supplies and any other right connected with VAT in relation to a supply.

(6) The relevant principles of EU case law for the purposes of this section are the principles established by the European Court of Justice in the following cases—
    (a) joined Cases C-439/04 and C-440/04 *Axel Kittel v. Belgian State*; *Belgium v. Recolta Recycling* (denial of right to deduct input tax), and
    (b) Case C-273/11 Mecsek-Gabona Kft v Nemzeti Adó- és Vámhivatal Dél-dunántúli Regionális Adó Fo"igazgatósága (denial of right to zero rate),

as developed or extended by that Court (whether before or after the coming into force of this section) in other cases relating to the denial or refusal of a VAT right in order to prevent abuses of the VAT system.

(7) The penalty payable under this section is 30% of the potential lost VAT.

(8) The potential lost VAT is—
    (a) the additional VAT which becomes payable by T as a result of the denial decision,
    (b) the VAT which is not repaid to T as a result of that decision, or

(c) in a case where as a result of that decision VAT is not repaid to T and additional VAT becomes payable by T, the aggregate of the VAT that is not repaid and the additional VAT.

(9) Where T is liable to a penalty under this section the Commissioners may assess the amount of the penalty and notify it to T accordingly.

(10) No assessment of a penalty under this section may be made more than two years after the denial decision is issued.

(11) The assessment of a penalty under this section may be made immediately after the denial decision is made (and notice of the assessment may be given to T in the same document as the notice of the decision).

(12) Where by reason of actions involved in making a claim to exercise or rely on a VAT right in relation to a supply T—

(a) is liable to a penalty for an inaccuracy under paragraph 1 of Schedule 24 to the Finance Act 2007 for which T has been assessed (and the assessment has not been successfully appealed against by T or withdrawn), or
(b) is convicted of an offence (whether under this Act or otherwise),

those actions do not give rise to liability to a penalty under this section.

69D Penalties under section 69C: officers' liability

(1) Where—

(a) a company is liable to a penalty under section 69C, and
(b) the actions of the company which give rise to that liability were attributable to an officer of the company ("the officer"),

the officer is liable to pay such portion of the penalty (which may be equal to or less than 100%) as HMRC may specify in a notice given to the officer (a "decision notice").

(2) Before giving the officer a decision notice HMRC must—

(a) inform the officer that they are considering doing so, and
(b) afford the officer the opportunity to make representations about whether a decision notice should be given or the portion that should be specified.

(3) A decision notice—

(a) may not be given before the amount of the penalty due from the company has been assessed (but it may be given immediately after that has happened), and
(b) may not be given more than two years after the denial decision relevant to that penalty was issued.

(4) Where the Commissioners have specified a portion of the penalty in a decision notice given to the officer—

(a) section 70 applies to the specified portion as to a penalty under section 69C,
(b) the officer must pay the specified portion before the end of the period of 30 days beginning with the day on which the notice is given,
(c) section 76(9) applies as if the decision notice were an assessment notified under section 76, and
(d) a further decision notice may be given in respect of a portion of any additional amount assessed in an additional assessment.

(5) HMRC may not recover more than 100% of the penalty through issuing decision notices in relation to two or more persons.

(6) A person is not liable to pay an amount by virtue of this section if the actions of the company concerned are attributable to the person by reference to conduct for which the person has been convicted of an offence.

In this subsection "conduct" includes omissions.

(7) In this section "company" means a body corporate or unincorporated association but does not include a partnership, a local authority or a local authority association.

(8) In its application to a body corporate other than a limited liability partnership "officer" means—

(a) a director (including a shadow director within the meaning of section 251 of the Companies Act 2006),
(b) a manager, or
(c) a secretary.

(9) In in its application to a limited liability partnership "officer" means a member.

(10) In its application in any other case, "officer" means—

(a) a director,
(b) a manager,

(c) a secretary, or

(d) any other person managing or purporting to manage any of the company's affairs.

69E Publication of details of persons liable to penalties under section 69C

(1) The Commissioners may publish information about a person if—

(a) in consequence of an investigation the person has been found liable to one or more penalties under section 69C (the amount of which has been assessed), and

(b) the potential lost VAT in relation to the penalty (or the aggregate of the potential lost VAT in relation to each of the penalties) exceeds £50,000.

(2) The information that may be published under subsection (1) is—

(a) the person's name (including any trading name, previous name or pseudonym),

(b) the person's address (or registered office),

(c) the nature of any business carried on by the person,

(d) the amount of the penalty or penalties in question,

(e) the periods or times to which the actions giving rise to the penalty or penalties relate,

(f) any other information that the Commissioners consider it appropriate to publish in order to make clear the person's identity.

(3) In a case where—

(a) the requirements in subsection (1)(a) and (b) are met in relation to a penalty or penalties for which a company is liable,

(b) information about the company is published by virtue of this section,

(c) a person ("the officer") has been given a decision notice under section 69D specifying a portion of the penalty (or, if there is more than one penalty, of any of the penalties) payable by the company as a portion which the officer is liable to pay, and

(d) the amount (or, if the decision notice specifies portions of more than one penalty, the aggregate amount) which the officer is liable to pay under the decision notice exceeds £25, 000,

the Commissioners may publish information about the officer.

(4) The information that may be published under subsection (3) is—

(a) the officer's name,

(b) the officer's address,

(c) the officer's position (or former position) in the company,

(d) the amount of any penalty imposed on the company of which a portion is payable by the officer under the decision notice and the portion so payable,

(e) the periods or times to which the actions giving rise to any such penalty relate,

(f) any other information that the Commissioners consider it appropriate to publish in order to make clear the officer's identity.

(5) Information published under this section may be published in any manner that the Commissioners consider appropriate.

(6) Before publishing any information under this section the Commissioners must—

(a) inform the person or officer to which it relates that they are considering doing so (in the case of an officer, on the assumption that they publish information about the company), and

(b) afford the person or officer the opportunity to make representations about whether it should be published.

(7) No information may be published under subsection (1) before the day on which the penalty becomes final or, where more than one penalty is involved, the latest day on which any of the penalties becomes final.

(8) No information may be published under subsection (1) for the first time after the end of the period of one year beginning with that day.

(9) No information may be published under subsection (3) before whichever is the later of—

(a) the day mentioned in subsection (7), and

(b) the day on which the decision notice given to the officer becomes final.

(10) No information may be published under subsection (3) for the first time after the end of the period of one year beginning with the later of the two days mentioned in subsection (9).

(11) No information may be published (or continue to be published) under subsection (1) or (3) after the end of the period of three years beginning with the day mentioned in subsection (7).

(12) For the purposes of this section a penalty or a decision notice becomes final when the time for any appeal or further appeal relating to it expires or, if later, any appeal or final appeal relating to it is finally determined.

(13) The Treasury may by regulations made by statutory instrument—

(a) amend subsection (1) to vary the amount for the time being specified in paragraph (b), or
(b) amend subsection (3) to vary the amount for the time being specified in paragraph (d).

(14) A statutory instrument containing regulations under subsection (13) is subject to annulment in pursuance of a resolution of the House of Commons."

(3) In section 70 (mitigation of penalties)—

(a) in the heading, for "and 67" substitute "67, 69A and 69C",
(b) in subsection (1) for "or 69A" substitute "69A or 69C", and
(c) after subsection (4) insert—

"(5) In the application of subsections (3) and (4) in relation to a penalty under section 69C, subsection (4) has effect with the omission of paragraphs (b) and (c)."

(4) In section 76 (assessment of amounts due by way of penalty etc), in subsection (1)(b) for "to 69B" (in both places) substitute "to 69C".

(5) In section 83(1) (appeals), after paragraph (n) insert—

"(na) any liability to a penalty under section 69C, any assessment of a penalty under that section or the amount of such an assessment;
(nb) the giving of a decision notice under section 69D or the portion of a penalty assessed under section 69C which is specified in such a notice;".

(6) After paragraph 21 of Schedule 24 to FA 2007 (penalties for errors: double jeopardy) insert—

"21ZA (1) A person is not liable to a penalty under paragraph 1 in respect of an inaccuracy if—

(a) the inaccuracy involves a claim by the person to exercise or rely on a VAT right (in relation to a supply) that has been denied or refused by HMRC as mentioned in subsection (4) of section 69C of VATA 1994, and
(b) the person has been assessed to a penalty under that section (and the assessment has not been successfully appealed against or withdrawn).

(2) In sub-paragraph (1)(a) "VAT right" has the same meaning as in section 69C of VATA 1994."

(7) Section 69C does not apply in relation to transactions entered into before this section comes into force.

GENERAL NOTE

Advisers need to be aware of the new paras 69C to 69E that have been inserted into VATA 1994. A VAT registered business or person involved in a deal could be liable to a penalty if it "should have known" that a transaction was fraudulent (VATA 1994 s 69C). This is a different test to HMRC being required to prove that a business or person "knew" it was involved in a fraudulent transaction before a penalty could be triggered. The new legislation works on the "knowledge principle" but there is a concern that naïve or inexperienced people will be captured with the "should have known" clause ie innocent parties that had no intention of defrauding or underpaying VAT. It is important that directors and owners in high risk trades where there has been past links to carousel fraud are particularly aware of the new legislation e.g. mobile phone and computer chip entities.

The penalty charged will be 30% of the potential lost VAT and there is scope in VATA1994 s 69D for the penalty or part of the penalty to be attributed to an officer in the case of limited companies and LLPs. This could be a director, manager or secretary in the case of companies and a member of an LLP. However, in no case may HMRC recover more than 100% of the penalty.

The main outcome of VATA1994 s 69E is that a business or an individual deemed guilty of being connected with a fraudulent transaction could be "named and shamed" by HMRC. There is no differentiation in this clause between offenders who "knew" rather than "should have known" about a VAT fraud. Naming and shaming will not apply unless the potential lost VAT exceeds £50,000 (in the case of an individual, unless the amount which the individual is liable to pay exceeds £25,000).

The denial of input tax for a business where there has been a fraudulent transaction in a supply chain was confirmed in the European case of Axel Kittel v Belgian State (C-430/04). This is known as the "Kittel principle".

Information

69 Data-gathering from money service businesses

(1) In Part 2 of Schedule 23 to FA 2011 (data-gathering powers: relevant data-holders), after paragraph 13C insert—

"Money service businesses

13D (1) A person is a relevant data-holder if the person—

(a) carries on any of the activities in sub-paragraph (2) by way of business,
(b) is a relevant person within the meaning of regulation 8(1) of the Money Laundering, Terrorist Financing and Transfer of Funds (Information on the Payer) Regulations 2017 (S.I. 2017/692), and
(c) is not an excluded credit institution.

(2) The activities referred to in sub-paragraph (1)(a) are—

(a) operating a currency exchange office;
(b) transmitting money (or any representation of monetary value) by any means;
(c) cashing cheques which are made payable to customers.

(3) An excluded credit institution is a credit institution which has permission to carry on the regulated activity of accepting deposits—

(a) under Part 4A of the Financial Services and Markets Act 2000 (permission to carry on regulated activities), or
(b) resulting from Part 2 of Schedule 3 to that Act (exercise of passport rights by EEA firms).

(4) Sub-paragraph (3) is to be read with section 22 of and Schedule 2 to the Financial Services and Markets Act 2000, and any order under that section (classes of regulated activities).

(5) In this paragraph "credit institution" has the meaning given by Article 4.1(1) of Regulation (EU) No 575/2013 of the European Parliament and of the Council of 26 June 2013 on prudential requirements for credit institutions and investment firms."

(2) This section applies in relation to relevant data with a bearing on any period (whether before, on or after the day on which this Act is passed).

GENERAL NOTE

Section 69 introduces a targeted extension to HMRC's bulk data-gathering powers and a new category of dataholder, money service businesses. The explanatory notes to the Finance Bill set out that the purpose of such data is "to assist with the efficient and effective discharge of HMRC's tax functions, including for example for risk analysis, enabling HMRC to target its compliance work more accurately". Specific reference is made to improving the ability to identify those in the hidden economy although it will also enable the checking and risk assessment of many taxpaying businesses.

Subsection 1 inserts paragraph 13D into FA 2011 Sch 23 Pt 2 and introduces a new category of relevant data-holder: "money service businesses".

FA 2011 Sch 23 para 13D(1)(a)–(c) define the new category of relevant data-holder, which are: those carrying on activities specified in paragraph 13D(2); a person within regulation 8(1) of the Money Laundering, Terrorist Financing and Transfer of Funds (Information on the Payer) Regulations 2017; and a person who is not an excluded credit institution.

Persons caught within the scope of FA 2011 Sch 23 para 13D(1)(b) include: credit institutions; financial institutions; auditors; insolvency practitioners; external accountants and tax advisers; independent legal professionals; trust or company service providers; estate agents; high value dealers; casinos. The new power therefore has significant implications for professionals and gives rise to concerns about how HMRC will use this information power.

FA 2011 Sch 23 para 13D(3) defines "excluded credit institutions", which will fall outside the scope of para 13D. This includes banks and building societies operating in the UK that are either regulated in the UK or regulated in another EEA country with "passporting" rights in the UK. It should be noted that data gathering powers already exist for such entities.

Subsection 2 provides that data can be required for periods before the law comes into effect although subject to the time limits in FA 2011 Sch 23.

Treasury regulations are needed to specify the relevant data that HMRC may require from money service businesses. Draft regulations were published on 5 December 2016 and the Government intends to introduce them to Parliament by the end of 2017.

PART 5

FINAL

70 Northern Ireland welfare payments: updating statutory reference

In section 44(2) of FA 2016 (tax treatment of supplementary welfare payments: Northern Ireland) for "the Housing Benefit (Amendment) Regulations (Northern Ireland) 2016 (S.R. (N.I.) 2016 No. 258)" substitute "the Housing Benefit (Amendment No 2) Regulations (Northern Ireland) 2016 (S.R. (N.I.) 2016 No. 326)".

GENERAL NOTE

Section 70 updates a statutory reference in FA 2016 s 44 (tax treatment of supplementary welfare payments: Northern Ireland), which enables the Treasury to make regulations providing that supplementary welfare payments funded by the Northern Ireland Executive under transitional protection arrangements are chargeable to income tax if they supplement a taxable benefit and exempt from income tax if they supplement a tax-exempt benefit. FA 2016 s 44(2) is amended to refer to the currently relevant Housing Benefit regulations.

71 Interpretation

In this Act the following abbreviations are references to the following Acts.

CAA 2001	Capital Allowances Act 2001
CEMA 1979	Customs and Excise Management Act 1979
CTA 2009	Corporation Tax Act 2009
CTA 2010	Corporation Tax Act 2010
CT(NI)A 2015	Corporation Tax (Northern Ireland) Act 2015
FA, followed by a year	Finance Act of that year
F(No 2)A, followed by a year	Finance (No 2) Act of that year
F(No 3)A, followed by a year	Finance (No 3) Act of that year
ICTA	Income and Corporation Taxes Act 1988
IHTA 1984	Inheritance Tax Act 1984
ITA 2007	Income Tax Act 2007
ITEPA 2003	Income Tax (Earnings and Pensions) Act 2003
ITTOIA 2005	Income Tax (Trading and Other Income) Act 2005
OTA 1975	Oil Taxation Act 1975
TCGA 1992	Taxation of Chargeable Gains Act 1992
TIOPA 2010	Taxation (International and Other Provisions) Act 2010
TMA 1970	Taxes Management Act 1970
TPDA 1979	Tobacco Products Duty Act 1979
VATA 1994	Value Added Tax Act 1994

72 Short title

This Act may be cited as the Finance (No 2) Act 2017.

SCHEDULE 1
SOCIAL INVESTMENT TAX RELIEF

Section 14

PART 1
AMENDMENTS OF PART 5B OF ITA 2007

Introductory

1 ITA 2007 is amended as follows.

Date by which investment must be made to qualify for SI relief

2 In section 257K(1)(a)(iii) (date by which investment must be made to qualify for SI relief) for "6 April 2019" substitute "6 April 2021".

The existing investments requirement

3 After section 257LD insert—

"257LDA   The existing investments requirement

(1) If at the time immediately before the investment is made the investor holds any shares in or debentures of—

(a) the social enterprise, or

(b) a company which at that time is a qualifying subsidiary of the social enterprise,

those shares or debentures must be risk finance investments or (in the case of shares) permitted subscriber shares.

(2) A share or debenture is a "risk finance investment" for the purposes of this section if—

(a) it is a share that was issued to the investor, or a debenture of which the investor is the holder in return for advancing an amount, and

(b) at any time, a compliance statement under section 205, 257ED or 257PB is provided in respect of it or of shares or investments including it.

(3) Subscriber shares are "permitted subscriber shares" for the purposes of this section if—

(a) they were issued to the investor and have been continuously held by the investor since they were issued, or

(b) they were acquired by the investor at a time when the company which issued them—

(i) had issued no shares other than subscriber shares, and

(ii) had not begun to carry on or make preparations for carrying on any trade or business.

(4) In this section "debenture" is to be read in accordance with section 257L(6)."

The no disqualifying arrangements requirement

4 After section 257LE insert—

"257LEA   The no disqualifying arrangements requirement

(1) The investment must not be made, and money raised by the social enterprise from the making of the investment must not be employed,—

(a) in consequence or anticipation of disqualifying arrangements, or

(b) otherwise in connection with disqualifying arrangements.

(2) Arrangements are "disqualifying arrangements" if—

(a) the main purpose, or one of the main purposes, of the arrangements is to secure both that an activity is or will be carried on by the social enterprise or a 90% social subsidiary of the social enterprise and that—

(i) one or more persons (whether or not including any party to the arrangements) may obtain relevant tax relief in respect of a qualifying investment which raises money for the purposes of that activity, or

(ii) shares issued by the social enterprise which raise money for the purposes of that activity may comprise part of the qualifying holdings of a VCT,

(b) that activity is the relevant qualifying activity, and

(c) one or both of conditions A and B are met.

(3) Condition A is that, as a (direct or indirect) result of the money raised by the investment being employed as required by section 257MM, an amount representing the whole or the majority of the amount raised is, in the course of the arrangements, paid to or for the benefit of a relevant person or relevant persons.

(4) Condition B is that, in the absence of the arrangements, it would have been reasonable to expect that the whole or greater part of the component activities of the relevant qualifying activity would have been carried on as part of another business by a relevant person or relevant persons.

(5) For the purposes of this section it is immaterial whether the social enterprise is a party to the arrangements.

(6) In this section—

"90% social subsidiary" is to be read in accordance with section 257MV;

"component activities" means the carrying on of a qualifying trade or preparing to carry on such a trade, which constitutes the relevant qualifying activity;

a "qualifying investment" means—

(a) shares in the social enterprise, or

(b) a qualifying debt investment in the social enterprise (see section 257L);

"qualifying holdings", in relation to the social enterprise, is to be construed in accordance with section 286 (VCTs: qualifying holdings);

"relevant person" means a person who is a party to the arrangements or a person connected with such a party;

"relevant qualifying activity" means the qualifying trade or activity mentioned in section 257ML(1) for the purposes of which the investment raised money;

"relevant tax relief" has the meaning given by subsection (7).

(7) "Relevant tax relief"—

(a) in relation to a qualifying debt investment, means SI relief in respect of that investment;

(b) in relation to shares, means one or more of the following—

(i) SI relief in respect of the shares;

(ii) EIS relief (within the meaning of Part 5) in respect of the shares;

(iii) SEIS relief (within the meaning of Part 5A) in respect of the shares;

(iv) relief under Chapter 6 of Part 4 (losses on disposal of shares) in respect of the shares;

(v) relief under section 150A or 150E of TCGA 1992 (EIS and SEIS) in respect of the shares;

(vi) relief under Schedule 5B to that Act (EIS: reinvestment) in consequence of which deferral relief is attributable to the shares (see paragraph 19(2) of that Schedule);

(vii) relief under Schedule 5BB to that Act (SEIS: re-investment) in consequence of which SEIS re-investment relief is attributable to the shares (see paragraph 4 of that Schedule)."

5 (1) Section 257SH (power to require information where reason to believe SI relief may not be due because of certain kinds of arrangements, etc) is amended as follows.

(2) In subsection (1) after "257LE," insert "257LEA,".

(3) In subsection (4) at the appropriate place insert—

"Section 257LEA	The investor, the social enterprise, any person controlling the social enterprise and any person whom an officer of Revenue and Customs has reason to believe may be a party to the arrangements in question"

Limits on amounts that may be invested

6 (1) In the italic heading before section 257M, after "enterprise" insert ": general".

(2) Omit sections 257MA and 257MB (which are superseded by the provision inserted by sub-paragraph (3) below).

(3) After section 257MN insert—

"Limits on amounts that may be invested

257MNA Maximum amount where investment made in first 7 years

(1) This section applies where—

(a) the investment is made before the end of the period of 7 years beginning with the relevant first commercial sale, or

(b) the investment is made after that period but—

(i) a relevant investment was made in the social enterprise before the end of that period, and

(ii) some or all of the money raised by that relevant investment was employed for the purposes of (or of part of) the qualifying activity for which the money raised by the investment is employed.

(2) Where this section applies, the total amount of relevant investments made in the social enterprise on or before the date when the investment is made must not exceed £1.5 million.

(3) The reference in subsection (2) to relevant investments "made in the social enterprise" is to be read with section 257MNB.

(4) In this section—

"qualifying activity" means—

(a) a qualifying trade within paragraph (a) of section 257ML(1) carried on by the social enterprise or a 90% social subsidiary of the social enterprise, or

(b) an activity within paragraph (b) of section 257ML(1) so carried on;

"the relevant first commercial sale" has the meaning given by section 175A(6), reading—

(a) references to the issuing company as references to the social enterprise,

(b) references to the issue date as references to the investment date, and

(c) references to money raised by the issue of the relevant shares as references to money raised by the investment;

"relevant investment" has the meaning given by section 173A(3) (reading references in section 173A(3) to a company as including any social enterprise).

(5) Section 173A(4) and (5) apply to determine for the purposes of this section when a relevant investment is made.

(6) Where the social enterprise is an accredited social impact contractor—

(a) the reference in subsection (1)(a) to the relevant first commercial sale is to be read as a reference to the date on which the social enterprise first entered into a social impact contract;

(b) the reference in subsection (1)(b) to the qualifying activity mentioned there is to be read as a reference to the carrying out of the social impact contract for which the money raised by the investment is employed.

(7) For provision about maximum amounts where this section does not apply, see section 257MNC.

257MNB Section 257MNA: supplementary

(1) In section 257MNA(2) the reference to relevant investments "made in the social enterprise" includes—

(a) relevant investments made in a company which, at the material date, is or has been a 51% subsidiary of the social enterprise,

(b) any other relevant investment made in a company to the extent that the money raised by that relevant investment has been employed for the purposes of a trade carried on by another company ("company X") which, at the material date, is or has been a 51% subsidiary of the social enterprise, and

(c) any other relevant investment made in a company if—

(i) the money raised by that relevant investment has been employed for the purposes of a trade carried on by that company or another person, and

(ii) after that relevant investment was made, but on or before the material date, that trade became a transferred trade (see subsection (5)).

(2) The investments within paragraph (a) of subsection (1)—

(a) include investments made in a company mentioned in that paragraph before it became a 51% subsidiary of the social enterprise, but

(b) where a company mentioned in that paragraph is not a 51% subsidiary of the social enterprise at the material date, do not include any investments made in that company after it last ceased to be such a subsidiary.

(3) For the purposes of subsection (1)(b), where company X is not a 51% subsidiary of the social enterprise at the material date, any money employed after company X last ceased to be such a subsidiary is to be ignored.

(4) Where only a proportion of the money raised by a relevant investment is employed for the purposes of a trade which becomes a transferred trade, only the corresponding proportion of that relevant investment is to be treated as falling within subsection (1)(c).

(5) For the purposes of this section, if—

(a) on or before the material date a trade is transferred—

(i) to the social enterprise,

(ii) to a company which, at the material date, is or has been a 51% subsidiary of the social enterprise, or

(iii) to a partnership of which the social enterprise, or a company within sub-paragraph (ii), is a member, and

(b) the trade or part of it was at any time before the transfer carried on by another person,

the trade or part mentioned in paragraph (b) becomes a "transferred trade" when it is transferred as mentioned in paragraph (a).

(6) The cases within subsection (5)(a)—

(a) include the case where the trade is transferred to a company within subsection (5)(a)(ii), or a partnership of which such a company is a member, before the company became a 51% subsidiary of the social enterprise, but

(b) where a company within subsection (5)(a)(ii) is not a 51% subsidiary of the social enterprise at the material date, do not include the case where the trade is transferred to that company, or a partnership of which that company is a member, after that company last ceased to be such a subsidiary.

(7) In this section—

"the material date" means the date on which the investment is made;

"relevant investment" has the meaning given by section 173A(3) (reading references in section 173A(3) to a company as including any social enterprise).

(8) Section 173A(4) and (5) apply to determine for the purposes of this section when a relevant investment is made.

(9) Section 173A(6) and (7) (meaning of "trade" etc) apply also for the purposes of this section.

257MNC Maximum amount for cases outside section 257MNA

(1) This section applies where—

(a) the investment is made at any time after the period mentioned in section 257MNA(1)(a), and

(b) it is not the case that the conditions in section 257MNA(1)(b)(i) and (ii) are met.

(2) Where this section applies—

(a) the total amount of relevant investments made in the social enterprise on or before the date when the investment is made must not exceed £1.5 million, and

(b) the amount invested must not be more than the amount mentioned in subsection (3).

(3) That amount is the amount given by the formula—

$$((€200{,}000 - M) / (RCG + RSI)) - T$$

where—

T is the total of any relevant investments made in the social enterprise in the aid period,

M is the total of any de minimis aid, other than relevant investments, that is granted during the aid period—

(a) to the social enterprise, or

(b) to a qualifying subsidiary of the social enterprise at a time when it is such a subsidiary,

RCG is the highest rate at which capital gains tax is charged in the aid period, and

RSI is the highest SI rate in the aid period.

(4) In subsection (3) "the aid period" means the 3 years—

(a) ending with the day on which the investment is made, but

(b) in the case of that day, including only the part of the day before the investment is made.

(5) In this section "de minimis aid" means de minimis aid which fulfils the conditions laid down—

(a) in Commission Regulation (EU) No. 1407/2013 (de minimis aid) as amended from time to time, or

(b) in any EU instrument from time to time replacing the whole or any part of that Regulation.

(6) For the purposes of subsection (3), the amount of any de minimis aid is the amount of the grant or, if the aid is not in the form of a grant, the gross grant equivalent amount within the meaning of that Regulation as amended from time to time.

(7) For the purposes of subsection (3), if—

(a) the investment or any relevant investment is made, or

(b) any aid is granted,

in sterling or any other currency that is not the euro, its amount is to be converted into euros at an appropriate spot rate of exchange for the date on which the investment is made or the aid is paid.

(8) In this section "relevant investment" has the meaning given by section 173A(3) (reading references in section 173A(3) to a company as including any social enterprise).

(9) Section 173A(4) and (5) apply to determine for the purposes of this section when a relevant investment is made.

(10) Section 257MNB (which expands the meaning of "relevant investments made in the social enterprise") applies for the purposes of each of subsections (2) and (3) above as it applies for the purposes of section 257MNA(2).

257MND Limit on investment in shorter applicable period

(1) This section applies where condition A or condition B is met.

(2) Condition A is that—

(a) a company becomes a 51% subsidiary of the social enterprise at any time during the shorter applicable period,

(b) all or part of the money raised by the investment is employed for the purposes of a qualifying activity which consists wholly or partly of a trade carried on by that company, and

(c) that trade (or part of it) was carried on by that company before it became a 51% subsidiary as mentioned in paragraph (a).

(3) Condition B is that all or part of the money raised by the investment is employed for the purposes of a qualifying activity which consists wholly or partly of a trade which, during the shorter applicable period, becomes a transferred trade (see subsection (9)).

(4) Where this section applies, at each time in the shorter applicable period ("the relevant time") the total of the relevant investments made in the social enterprise before that time must not exceed £1.5 million.

(5) In subsection (4) the reference to relevant investments "made in the social enterprise" includes—

(a) relevant investments made in a company which at any time before the relevant time has been a 51% subsidiary of the social enterprise,

(b) any other relevant investment made in a company to the extent that the money raised by that relevant investment has been employed for the purposes of a trade carried on by another company ("company X") which at any time before the relevant time has been a 51% subsidiary of the social enterprise, and

(c) any other relevant investment made in a company if—

(i) the money raised by that relevant investment has been employed for the purposes of a trade carried on by that company or another person, and

(ii) after that relevant investment was made, but before the relevant time, that trade (or part of it) became a transferred trade.

(6) The investments within paragraph (a) of subsection (5)—

(a) include investments made in a company mentioned in that paragraph before it became a 51% subsidiary of the social enterprise, but

(b) where a company mentioned in that paragraph is not a 51% subsidiary of the social enterprise at the relevant time, do not include any investments made in that company after it last ceased to be such a subsidiary.

(7) For the purposes of subsection (5)(b), where company X is not a 51% subsidiary of the social enterprise at the relevant time, any money employed after company X last ceased to be such a subsidiary is to be ignored.

(8) Where only a proportion of the money raised by a relevant investment is employed for the purposes of a trade which becomes a transferred trade, only the corresponding proportion of that relevant investment is to be treated as falling within subsection (5)(c).

(9) For the purposes of this section, if—

(a) before the relevant time, a trade is transferred—

    (i) to the social enterprise,

    (ii) to a company which, at the relevant time, is or has been a 51% subsidiary of the social enterprise, or

    (iii) to a partnership of which the social enterprise, or a company within sub-paragraph (ii), is a member, and

(b) the trade or part of it was at any time before the transfer carried on by another person,

the trade or part mentioned in paragraph (b) becomes a "transferred trade" when it is transferred as mentioned in paragraph (a).

(10) The cases within subsection (9)(a)—

(a) include the case where the trade is transferred to a company within subsection (9)(a)(ii), or a partnership of which such a company is a member, before the company became a 51% subsidiary of the social enterprise, but

(b) where a company within subsection (9)(a)(ii) is not a 51% subsidiary of the social enterprise at the relevant time, do not include the case where the trade is transferred to that company, or a partnership of which that company is a member, after that company last ceased to be such a subsidiary.

(11) In this section—

"qualifying activity" has the same meaning as in section 257MNA (see subsection (4) of that section);

"relevant investment" has the meaning given by section 173A(3) (reading references in section 173A(3) to a company as including any social enterprise).

(12) Section 173A(4) and (5) apply to determine for the purposes of this section when a relevant investment is made.

(13) Section 173A(6) and (7) (meaning of "trade" etc) apply also for the purposes of this section.

257MNE   Power to amend limits on amounts that may be invested

(1) The Treasury may by regulations substitute a different figure for the figure for the time being specified in section 257MNA(2), 257MNC(2) or (3) or 257MND(4).

(2) Regulations under this section may make incidental, supplemental, consequential, transitional or saving provision.

(3) Regulations under this section may not be made unless a draft of the instrument containing them has been laid before, and approved by a resolution of, the House of Commons."

(4) In section 1014 (orders and regulations), in subsection (5)(b) (orders and regulations excluded from subsection (4)) for sub-paragraph (iiia) substitute—

    "(iiia) section 257MNE (social investment relief: amendment of limits on investments),".

Number of employees limit

7 In section 257MH (the number of employees requirement), in each of subsections (1) and (2) for "500" substitute "250".

Financial health requirement

8 After section 257MI insert—

"257MIA   The financial health requirement

(1) The social enterprise must meet the financial health requirement at the beginning of the shorter applicable period.

(2) The financial health requirement is that the social enterprise is not in difficulty.

(3) The social enterprise is "in difficulty" if it is reasonable to assume that it would be regarded as a firm in difficulty for the purposes of the Community Guidelines on State Aid for Rescuing and Restructuring Firms in Difficulty (2004/C 244/02)."

Purposes for which money raised can be used

9 (1) Section 257MM (requirement to use money raised and to trade for minimum period) is amended as follows.

(2) After subsection (3) insert—

    "(3A) Employing money on the repayment of a loan does not amount to employing the money for the funded purpose."

(3) In subsection (7)(c) after "(3)," insert "(3A),".

Excluded activities

10 (1) Section 257MQ (meaning of "excluded activity") is amended as set out in sub-paragraphs (2) to (4).

(2) In subsection (1)—

  (a) in paragraph (b) omit "(but see subsection (2))";

  (b) after paragraph (b) insert—

    "(ba) leasing (including letting ships on charter or other assets on hire),

    (bb) receiving royalties or licence fees,

    (bc) operating or managing nursing homes or residential care homes or managing property used as a nursing home or residential care home (see section 257MQA),

    (bd) generating electricity, exporting electricity (see subsection (3)) or making electricity generating capacity available,

    (be) generating heat,

    (bf) generating any form of energy not within paragraph (bd) or (be),

    (bg) producing gas or fuel,";

  (c) omit paragraph (f) (subsidised generation or export of electricity).

(3) Omit subsection (2).

(4) After subsection (2) insert—

  "(3) For the purposes of subsection (1)(bd) electricity is exported if it is exported onto a distribution system or transmission system (within the meaning of section 4 of the Electricity Act 1989)."

(5) After section 257MQ insert—

"257MQA Excluded activities: nursing homes and residential care homes

  (1) This section supplements section 257MQ(1)(bc).

  (2) "Nursing home" means any establishment which exists wholly or mainly for the provision of nursing care—

    (a) for persons suffering from sickness, injury or infirmity, or

    (b) for women who are pregnant or have given birth.

  (3) "Residential care home" means any establishment which exists wholly or mainly for the provision of residential accommodation, together with board and personal care, for persons in need of personal care because of—

    (a) old age,

    (b) mental or physical disability,

    (c) past or present dependence on alcohol or drugs,

    (d) any past illnesses, or

    (e) past or present mental disorder.

  (4) The activities of a person are not to be taken to fall within section 257MQ(1)(bc) unless that person has an estate or interest in, or is in occupation of, the nursing home or residential care home in question."

(6) Omit section 257MS (subsidised generation or export of electricity).

PART 2

CONSEQUENTIAL AMENDMENTS

11 (1) ITA 2007 is amended as follows.

(2) In section 178A (EIS: the no disqualifying arrangements requirement), in subsection (6), in the definition of "relevant tax relief" after paragraph (b) insert—

  "(ba) SI relief under Part 5B in respect of the shares;".

(3) In section 257CF (SEIS: the no disqualifying arrangements requirement), in subsection (6), in the definition of "relevant tax relief" after paragraph (b) insert—

  "(ba) SI relief under Part 5B in respect of the shares;".

(4) In section 299A (VCTs: the no disqualifying arrangements requirement), in subsection (6), in the definition of "relevant tax relief" after paragraph (c) insert—

  "(ca) SI relief (within the meaning of Part 5B) in respect of the shares;".

12 In Schedule 6 to FA 2015 (investment reliefs: excluded activities) omit paragraph 13 (which is superseded by paragraph 10 of this Schedule).

13 In Part 2 of Schedule 24 to FA 2016 (tax advantages about which information may be obtained from certain persons), after the entry relating to relief granted to investors in a company under the enterprise investment scheme insert—

| "Relief granted to investors in a social enterprise | Part 5B of ITA 2007 | The social enterprise" |

PART 3
COMMENCEMENT

14 (1) The amendments made by paragraphs 3 and 6 to 9 have effect in relation to investments made on or after 6 April 2017.

(2) Nothing in sub-paragraph (1) prevents investments made before 6 April 2017 from constituting "relevant investments" for any purpose of section 257MNA, 257MNB, 257MNC or 257MND of ITA 2007.

(3) Subject to sub-paragraph (4), the amendments made by paragraphs 4 and 5 have effect in relation to investments made on or after 6 April 2017.

(4) Arrangements which include any transaction entered into before 6 April 2017 are not "disqualifying arrangements" for the purposes of section 257LEA of ITA 2007.

15 The amendments made by paragraph 10—

(a) so far as they apply for the purposes of section 257JD of ITA 2007, come into force on 6 April 2017;
(b) so far as they apply for the purposes of sections 257MJ and 257MP of ITA 2007, have effect in relation to investments made on or after 6 April 2017.

16 (1) Subject to sub-paragraph (3), the amendments made by paragraph 11(2) and (3) have effect in relation to shares issued on or after 6 April 2017.

(2) Subject to sub-paragraph (3), the amendment made by paragraph 11(4) has effect for the purpose of determining whether shares or securities issued on or after 6 April 2017 are to be regarded as comprised in a company's qualifying holdings.

(3) The amendments made by paragraph 11 do not have effect for the purposes of determining any question whether particular arrangements which include any transaction entered into before 6 April 2017 are "disqualifying arrangements" for the purposes of section 178A, 257CF or 299A of ITA 2007.

GENERAL NOTE

Part 1 – Amendment of Part 5B of ITA 2007

The date the investment must be made to qualify for SITR is extended to 6 April 2021.

Existing investments requirement

If at the time immediately before the investment is made the investor holds any shares in or debentures of:

(a) the social enterprise, or
(b) a company which at that time is a qualifying subsidiary of the social enterprise,

those shares or debentures must be risk finance investments or permitted subscriber shares.

Risk finance investments are defined as:

– a share that was issued to the investor, or a debenture of which the investor is the holder in return for advancing an amount, and
– at any time, a compliance statement under ITA 2007 s 205, 257ED or 257PB is provided in respect of it or of shares or investments including it.

Permitted subscriber shares are defined as:

– issued to the investor and have been continuously held by the investor since they were issued, or
– acquired by the investor at a time when the company which issued them (i) had no shares other than subscriber shares, and (ii) had not begun to carry on, or make preparations for carrying on, any trade or business.

No disqualifying arrangements requirement

The investment must not be made, and money raised by the social enterprise from the investment cannot be used:

(a) in consequence or anticipation of disqualifying arrangements, or
(b) otherwise in connection with disqualifying arrangements.

Disqualifying arrangements are defined as:

− the main purpose, or one of the main purposes, of the arrangements is that the social enterprise, or a 90% social subsidiary of the social enterprise, will carry on an activity and:

  (i) one or more persons will obtain relevant tax relief for a qualifying investment (shares or qualifying debt investment in the social enterprise) that provides funds for that activity, or
  (ii) shares issued by the social enterprise to raise funds for that activity are part of the qualifying holdings of a VCT;

− that the activity is the relevant qualifying activity;
− that one or both of conditions A and B are met:

  Condition A − as a direct or indirect result of the funds from the investment being used, as part of the arrangements, either the whole or majority of those funds are paid to a relevant person or relevant persons (person who is party to the arrangements or a person connected with such a party);

  Condition B − if the arrangements were not in place, it would be reasonable to expect a relevant person or relevant persons would have carried on the whole or greater part of the component activities of the relevant qualifying activity as part of another business.

It does not matter if the social enterprise is a party to the arrangements.

Relevant tax relief under (i) above includes:

− SITR for a qualifying debt investment;
− SITR for shares;
− EIS relief for shares;
− SEIS relief for shares;
− ITA 2007 Pt 4 Ch 6 − losses on disposal of shares;
− Relief under TCGA 1992 s 150A or s 150E (EIS and SEIS);
− Relief under Schedule 5B (EIS reinvestment) or 5BB (SEIS reinvestment) of TCGA 1992.

Limits on amounts that may be invested

The amount of investment a social enterprise may receive using SITR over its lifetime is increased to £1.5 million.

The investment is to be made within seven years from the first relevant commercial sale (ITA 2007 s 175A(6)) − or after seven years if a relevant investment was made within the seven year period and some or all of the investment funds have been used for the qualifying activity. For investments made outside this time limit so that the post-5 April rules do not apply, limits similar to the pre-6 April 2017 rules apply with the addition of the £1.5 million ceiling.

Relevant investments include investments made in 51% subsidiaries of the social enterprise.

Number of employees limit

The maximum number of full time employees of the social enterprise is reduced from 500 to 250.

Volunteers do not count towards this limit.

Financial health requirement

The financial health requirement is that the social enterprise is not in difficulty.

Purposes for which money raised

Included now is that employing money on the repayment of a loan does not amount to employing money for the funded purpose.

Excluded activities

The list of excluded activities is amended to include:

- leasing (including letting ships on charter or other assets on hire);
- receiving royalties or licence fees;
- operating or managing nursing homes or residential care homes or managing property used as a nursing home or residential care home;
- generating electricity, exporting electricity or making electricity generating capacity available;
- generating heat;
- generating any form of energy not already mentioned;
- producing gas or fuel.

Commencement

The amendments made by this schedule have effect in relation to investments made on or after 6 April 2017.

SCHEDULE 2
TRADES AND PROPERTY BUSINESSES: CALCULATION OF PROFITS

Section 16

PART 1
TRADES ETC: AMENDMENTS OF ITTOIA 2005

1 ITTOIA 2005 is amended as follows.

2 For section 33A (cash basis: capital expenditure) substitute—

"33A Cash basis: capital expenditure

(1) This section applies in relation to the calculation of the profits of a trade on the cash basis.

(2) No deduction is allowed for an item of a capital nature incurred on, or in connection with, the acquisition or disposal of a business or part of a business.

(3) No deduction is allowed for an item of a capital nature incurred on, or in connection with, education or training.

(4) No deduction is allowed for an item of a capital nature incurred on, or in connection with, the provision, alteration or disposal of—

    (a) any asset that is not a depreciating asset (see subsections (6) and (7)),

    (b) any asset not acquired or created for use on a continuing basis in the trade,

    (c) a car (see subsection (14)),

    (d) land,

    (e) a non-qualifying intangible asset (see subsections (8) to (11)), or

    (f) a financial asset (see subsection (12)).

(5) But subsection (4)(d) does not prevent a deduction being made for expenditure that—

    (a) is incurred on the provision of a depreciating asset which, in being provided, is installed or otherwise fixed to land so as to become, in law, part of the land, but

    (b) is not incurred on, or in connection with, the provision of—

        (i) a building,

        (ii) a wall, floor, ceiling, door, gate, shutter or window or stairs,

        (iii) a waste disposal system,

        (iv) a sewerage or drainage system, or

        (v) a shaft or other structure in which a lift, hoist, escalator or moving walkway may be installed.

(6) An asset is a "depreciating" asset if, on the date the item of a capital nature is incurred, it is reasonable to expect that before the end of 20 years beginning with that date—

    (a) the useful life of the asset will end, or

    (b) the asset will decline in value by 90% or more.

(7) The useful life of an asset ends when it could no longer be of use to any person for any purpose as an asset of a business.

(8) "Intangible asset" means anything that is capable of being an intangible asset within the meaning of FRS 105 and, in particular, includes—

(a) an internally-generated intangible asset, and

(b) intellectual property.

(9) An intangible asset is "non-qualifying" unless, by virtue of having a fixed maximum duration, it must cease to exist before the end of 20 years beginning with the date on which the item of a capital nature is incurred.

(10) An intangible asset is "non-qualifying" if it consists of a right, whether conditional or not, to obtain an intangible asset without a fixed maximum duration by virtue of which that asset must, assuming the right is exercised at the last possible time, cease to exist before the end of 20 years beginning with the date on which the item of a capital nature is incurred.

(11) Where—

(a) the trader has an intangible asset, and

(b) the trader grants a licence or any other right in respect of that asset to another person,

any intangible asset that consists of a licence or other right granted to the trader in respect of the intangible asset mentioned in paragraph (a) is "non-qualifying".

(12) A "financial asset" means any right under or in connection with—

(a) a financial instrument, or

(b) an arrangement that is capable of producing a return that is economically equivalent to a return produced under any financial instrument.

(13) A reference to acquisition, provision, alteration or disposal includes potential acquisition, provision, alteration or (as the case may be) disposal.

(14) In this section—

"arrangement" includes any agreement, understanding, scheme, transaction or series of transactions (whether or not legally enforceable);

"building" includes any fixed structure;

"car" has the same meaning as in Part 2 of CAA 2001 (see section 268A of that Act);

"financial instrument" has the same meaning as in FRS 105;

"FRS 105" means Financial Reporting Standard 105 (the Financial Reporting Standard applicable to the Micro-entities Regime), issued by the Financial Reporting Council in July 2015;

"intellectual property" means—

(a) any patent, trade mark, registered design, copyright or design right, plant breeders' rights or rights under section 7 of the Plant Varieties Act 1997,

(b) any right under the law of a country or territory outside the United Kingdom corresponding or similar to a right within paragraph (a),

(c) any information or technique not protected by a right within paragraph (a) or (b) but having industrial, commercial or other economic value, or

(d) any licence or other right in respect of anything within paragraph (a), (b) or (c);

"provision" includes creation, construction or acquisition;

"the trader" means the person carrying on the trade."

3 In section 95A (application of Chapter 6 of Part 2 (trade profits: receipts) to the cash basis)—

(a) the existing text becomes subsection (1),

(b) in that subsection, omit the entry relating to section 96A, and

(c) after that subsection insert—

"(2) Section 96A makes provision about capital receipts in certain cases where the profits of a trade are calculated on the cash basis or have previously been calculated on the cash basis (and see also section 96B)."

4 (1) Section 96A (cash basis: capital receipts) is amended as follows.

(2) For the heading substitute "Capital receipts under, or after leaving, cash basis".

(3) For subsections (1) to (3) substitute—

"(1) This section applies in relation to a trade carried on by a person in two cases—

(a) Case 1 (see subsections (2) to (3A)), and

(b) Case 2 (see subsections (3B) to (3E)).

(2) Case 1 is a case in which conditions A and B are met.

(3) Condition A is that the person receives disposal proceeds or a capital refund in relation to an asset at a time when an election under section 25A (cash basis for trades) has effect in relation to the trade.

For the meaning of "disposal proceeds" and "capital refund" see subsections (3F) and (3G).

(3A) Condition B is that—

    (a) an amount of capital expenditure (see subsection (3H)) relating to the asset has been brought into account in calculating the profits of the trade on the cash basis, or

    (b) an amount of capital expenditure relating to the asset which—

        (i) has been incurred (or treated as incurred) by the person before the tax year for which the person last entered the cash basis, and

        (ii) is cash basis deductible in relation to that tax year (see section 96B(4)),

has been brought into account in calculating the profits of the trade for a tax year for which no election under section 25A had effect in relation to the trade.

The reference in this paragraph to expenditure brought into account includes a reference to expenditure brought into account under CAA 2001 (see section 96B(5)).

(3B) Case 2 is a case in which—

    (a) condition C is met, and

    (b) condition D or E is met.

(3C) Condition C is that disposal proceeds or a capital refund arise to the person in relation to an asset at a time—

    (a) when no election under section 25A has effect in relation to the trade, and

    (b) which is after a time when such an election had had effect in relation to the trade.

(3D) Condition D is that an amount of capital expenditure relating to the asset—

    (a) has been paid at a time when an election under section 25A had effect in relation to the trade,

    (b) has been brought into account in calculating the profits of the trade on the cash basis, and

    (c) on the assumption that an election under section 25A had not had effect at the time the expenditure was paid, would not have been qualifying expenditure.

(3E) Condition E is that an amount of capital expenditure relating to the asset has been brought into account in calculating the profits of the trade for a tax year—

    (a) for which no election under section 25A had effect in relation to the trade, and

    (b) which is before the tax year for which the person last entered the cash basis.

The reference in this subsection to expenditure brought into account does not include a reference to expenditure brought into account under CAA 2001 (see section 96B(5)).

(3F) "Disposal proceeds" means—

    (a) any proceeds arising from the disposal of an asset or any part of it,

    (b) any proceeds arising from the grant of any right in respect of, or any interest in, the asset, or

    (c) any amount of damages, proceeds of insurance or other compensation received in respect of the asset.

See also subsections (4) and (5) for circumstances in which a person is to be regarded as disposing of an asset.

(3G) "Capital refund" means an amount that is (in substance) a refund of capital expenditure relating to an asset.

(3H) "Capital expenditure" means expenditure of a capital nature incurred, or treated as incurred, on or in connection with—

    (a) the provision, alteration or disposal of an asset, or

    (b) the potential provision, alteration or disposal of an asset.

(3I) The disposal proceeds or capital refund mentioned in condition A or (as the case may be) condition C are to be brought into account as a receipt in calculating the profits of the trade.

(3J) In a case where only part of the total capital expenditure incurred, or treated as incurred, by the person in relation to the asset has been brought into account in calculating the profits of the trade (whether or not on the cash basis), the amount brought into account under subsection (3I) is proportionately reduced.

The reference in this subsection to expenditure brought into account includes a reference to expenditure brought into account under CAA 2001 (see section 96B(5)).

(3K) Subsection (3I) does not apply if the whole of the amount which would otherwise be brought into account under that subsection—

(a) has already been brought into account as a receipt in calculating the profits of the trade under this section,

(b) is brought into account as a receipt in calculating the profits of the trade under any other provision of this Part (except section 240D(3) (assets not fully paid for)), or

(c) is brought into account under any Part of CAA 2001 as a disposal value.

(3L) If part of the amount which would otherwise be brought into account under subsection (3I) has already been or is brought into account as mentioned in subsection (3K), subsection (3I) applies in relation to the remainder of that amount."

(4) Omit subsection (7).

5 After section 96A insert—

"96B Section 96A: supplementary provision

(1) This section has effect for the purposes of section 96A.

(2) Any question as to whether or to what extent expenditure is brought into account in calculating the profits of a trade is to be determined on such basis as is just and reasonable in all the circumstances.

(3) A person carrying on a trade "enters the cash basis" for a tax year if—

(a) an election under section 25A has effect in relation to the trade for the tax year, and

(b) no such election had effect in relation to the trade for the previous tax year.

(4) Expenditure is "cash basis deductible" in relation to a tax year if, on the assumption that the expenditure was paid in that tax year, a deduction would be allowed in respect of the expenditure in calculating the profits of the trade on the cash basis for that tax year.

(5) Expenditure is "brought into account under CAA 2001" in calculating the profits of a trade if and to the extent that—

(a) a capital allowance made under Part 2, 5, 6, 7 or 8 of that Act in respect of the expenditure is treated as an expense in calculating those profits (see, for example, section 247 of that Act), or

(b) qualifying expenditure (within the meaning of Part 2, 7 or 8 of CAA 2001) is allocated to a pool for the trade and is set-off against different disposal receipts.

(6) An amount of qualifying expenditure is "set-off against different disposal receipts" if—

(a) the amount would have been unrelieved qualifying expenditure carried forward in the pool for the trade, but

(b) the amount is not so carried forward because (and only because) one or more disposal values in respect of one or more assets, other than the asset in respect of which the qualifying expenditure was incurred (or treated as incurred), have at any time been brought into account in that pool.

(7) For the purposes of subsection (6), an amount of qualifying expenditure incurred (or treated as incurred) by a person is not to be regarded as not carried forward because the person enters the cash basis.

(8) In this section and in section 96A—

"disposal value" means—

(a) in section 96A(3K)(c)—

(i) a disposal value for the purposes of Part 2, 4A, 5, 6, 7 8 or 10 of CAA 2001 (for example, in relation to Part 2 of that Act, see (in particular) section 61 of that Act), or

(ii) proceeds from a balancing event for the purposes of Part 3 or 3A of that Act (see sections 316 and 360O of that Act), and

(b) in subsection (6), a disposal value for the purposes of—

(i) Part 2 of that Act (see, in particular, section 61 of that Act),

(ii) Part 7 of that Act (see section 462 of that Act), or

(iii) Part 8 of that Act (see sections 476 and 477 of that Act);

"market value amount" means the amount that would be regarded as normal and reasonable—

(a) in the market conditions then prevailing, and

(b) between persons dealing with each other at arm's length in the open market;

"pool" means—

(a) the main pool or a class pool to which qualifying expenditure is allocated under Part 2 of CAA 2001 (see section 54 of that Act),

    (b) a pool to which qualifying expenditure is allocated under Part 7 of that Act (see section 456 of that Act), or

    (c) a pool to which qualifying expenditure is allocated under Part 8 of that Act (see section 470 of that Act);

"provision" includes creation, construction or acquisition;

"qualifying expenditure" means—

    (a) qualifying expenditure within the meaning of Part 2 of CAA 2001 (see section 11(4) of that Act for the general rule),

    (b) qualifying expenditure within the meaning of Part 5 of that Act (see section 395 of that Act),

    (c) qualifying expenditure within the meaning of Part 6 of that Act (see section 439 of that Act),

    (d) qualifying expenditure within the meaning of Part 7 of that Act (see section 454 of that Act), or

    (e) qualifying trade expenditure within the meaning of Part 8 of that Act (see section 468 of that Act);

"unrelieved qualifying expenditure" means unrelieved qualifying expenditure for the purposes of—

    (a) Part 2 of CAA 2001 (see section 59(1) and (2) of that Act),

    (b) Part 7 of that Act (see section 461 of that Act), or

    (c) Part 8 of that Act (see section 475 of that Act)."

6 In section 106D (capital receipts), for "(cash basis: capital receipts)" substitute "(capital receipts under, or after leaving, cash basis)".

7 (1) Section 240C (unrelieved qualifying expenditure) is amended as follows.

(2) For the heading substitute "Unrelieved qualifying expenditure: Parts 2, 7 and 8 of CAA 2001".

(3) In subsection (1)(b), after "unrelieved qualifying expenditure" insert "relating to the trade".

(4) In subsection (3), for "the relevant portion of the expenditure" substitute "any cash basis deductible amount of the expenditure".

(5) For subsection (4) substitute—

    "(4) A "cash basis deductible amount" of the expenditure means any amount of the expenditure for which a deduction would be allowed in calculating the profits of the trade on the cash basis on the assumption that the expenditure was paid in the current tax year."

(6) In subsection (5), for "The relevant portion" substitute "Any cash basis deductible amount".

(7) After subsection (5) insert—

    "(5A) For the purposes of subsection (1)(b), in determining the unrelieved qualifying expenditure the person has to carry forward, disregard sections 59(4), 461A(1) and 475A(1) of CAA 2001 (which provide that an amount is not to be carried forward as unrelieved qualifying expenditure when a person enters the cash basis)."

(8) For subsection (6) substitute—

    "(6) In this section "unrelieved qualifying expenditure" means unrelieved qualifying expenditure for the purposes of—

    (a) Part 2 of CAA 2001 (see section 59(1) and (2) of that Act),

    (b) Part 7 of that Act (see section 461 of that Act), or

    (c) Part 8 of that Act (see section 475 of that Act)."

8 After section 240C insert—

"240CA Unrelieved qualifying expenditure: Part 5 of CAA 2001

(1) This section applies if a person carrying on a mineral extraction trade enters the cash basis for a tax year ("the current tax year").

(2) But this section does not apply if section 240D applies.

(3) In calculating the profits of the trade for the current tax year, a deduction is allowed for any amount of expenditure—

    (a) which would, apart from section 419A(1) of CAA 2001, have been unrelieved qualifying expenditure for the current tax year, and

    (b) for which a deduction would be allowed in calculating the profits of the trade on the cash basis on the assumption that the expenditure was paid in the current tax year.

(4) In this section—

"mineral extraction trade" has the meaning given in section 394 of CAA 2001;
"unrelieved qualifying expenditure" means unrelieved qualifying expenditure for
the purposes of Part 5 of CAA 2001 (see section 419 of that Act)."

9 (1) Section 240D (assets not fully paid for) is amended as follows.

(2) In subsection (1)(b), for "obtained" to the end substitute "incurred relevant expenditure, and".

(3) After subsection (1) insert—

"(1A) "Relevant expenditure" means expenditure—

(a) for which a deduction would be allowed in calculating the profits of the trade
on the cash basis on the assumption that the expenditure was paid in the tax year,
and

(b) in respect of which the person has obtained capital allowances under Part 2, 5,
6, 7 or 8 of CAA 2001."

(4) In subsection (4), for "The amount of any capital allowance obtained in respect of
expenditure on the provision of any plant or machinery" substitute "Any question as to
whether or to what extent expenditure is relevant expenditure, or as to whether or to
what extent any capital allowance obtained is in respect of relevant expenditure,".

(5) In subsection (5), after "given" insert "under Part 2 of CAA 2001".

(6) Omit subsection (6).

10 In section 786(6) (meaning of "rent-a-room receipts"), for "(capital receipts)"
substitute "(capital receipts under, or after leaving, cash basis)".

11 In section 805(5) (meaning of "qualifying care receipts"), for "(capital receipts)"
substitute "(capital receipts under, or after leaving, cash basis)".

PART 2

PROPERTY BUSINESSES: AMENDMENTS OF ITTOIA 2005

12 ITTOIA 2005 is amended as follows.

13 In Chapter 3 of Part 3 (profits of property businesses: basic rules), after section 271
insert—

"Basis of calculation of profits

271A Basis of calculation of profits: GAAP required

(1) The profits of a property business for a tax year must be calculated in accordance
with GAAP if condition A, B, C, D or E is met.

(2) Condition A is that the business is carried on at any time in the tax year by—

(a) a company,

(b) a limited liability partnership,

(c) a corporate firm, or

(d) the trustees of a trust.

(3) For the purposes of subsection (2) a firm is a "corporate firm" if a partner in the
firm is not an individual.

(4) Condition B is that the cash basis receipts for the tax year exceed £150,000.

(5) In subsection (4) "the cash basis receipts for the tax year" means the total of the
amounts that would be brought into account as receipts in calculating the profits of
the property business for the tax year on the cash basis (see section 271D).

(6) If the property business is carried on for only part of the tax year, the sum given
in subsection (4) is proportionately reduced.

(7) Condition C is that—

(a) the property business is carried on by an individual ("P"),

(b) a share of joint property income is brought into account in calculating the
profits of the business for the tax year,

(c) a share of that joint property income is brought into account in calculating the
profits for the tax year of a property business carried on by another individual
("Q's property business"), and

(d) the profits of Q's property business for the tax year are calculated in accordance with GAAP.

(8) In subsection (7) "joint property income" means income to which P and Q are
treated for income tax purposes as beneficially entitled in equal shares by virtue of
section 836 of ITA 2007.

(9) Condition D is that—

(a) an allowance under Part 3A of CAA 2001 (business premises renovation allowances) is made at any time in calculating the profits of the property business, and

(b) if the profits of the business were to be calculated in accordance with GAAP for the tax year, there would be a day in the tax year on which the occurrence of a balancing event (within the meaning of that Part) would give rise to a balancing adjustment for the tax year (see section 360M of that Act).

(10) Condition E is that an election under this subsection made by the person who is or has been carrying on the property business has effect in relation to the business for the tax year.

(11) An election under subsection (10) must be made on or before the first anniversary of the normal self-assessment filing date for the tax year for which the election is made.

(12) The Treasury may by regulations—

(a) amend subsection (2);

(b) amend subsection (4) so as to substitute another sum for the sum for the time being specified in that subsection.

(13) A statutory instrument containing regulations under subsection (12) may not be made unless a draft of the instrument has been laid before, and approved by a resolution of, the House of Commons.

(14) Subsection (13) does not apply if the regulations omit one or more paragraphs of subsection (2) and make no other provision.

271B Calculation of profits in accordance with GAAP

(1) In this Part, references to calculating the profits of a property business in accordance with GAAP are to calculating the profits in accordance with generally accepted accounting practice, subject to any adjustment required or authorised by law in calculating profits for income tax purposes.

(2) A requirement under this Part to calculate profits in accordance with GAAP does not—

(a) require a person to comply with the requirements of the Companies Act 2006 or subordinate legislation made under that Act except as to the basis of calculation, or

(b) impose any requirements as to audit or disclosure.

(3) See section 272 (application of trading income rules: GAAP) which applies only where profits are calculated in accordance with GAAP.

271C Basis of calculation of profits: cash basis required

The profits of a property business for a tax year must be calculated on the cash basis if none of conditions A, B, C, D or E in section 271A is met.

271D Calculation of profits on the cash basis

(1) In this Part, references to calculating the profits of a property business on the cash basis are to calculating the profits in accordance with subsections (2) and (3).

(2) In calculating the profits, receipts of the business are brought into account at the time they are received, and expenses of the business are brought into account at the time they are paid.

(3) Subsection (2) is subject to any adjustment required or authorised by law in calculating profits for income tax purposes.

(4) For provision about the application of Chapter 4 (profits of property businesses: lease premiums etc) in relation to profits calculated on the cash basis, see section 276A.

(5) For provision about the application of Chapter 5 (rules about deductions and receipts) in relation to profits calculated on the cash basis, see section 307A.

(6) The following provisions apply only where profits are calculated on the cash basis—

(a) section 272ZA (application of trading income rules: cash basis), and

(b) Chapter 7A (cash basis: adjustments for capital allowances)."

14 In the italic heading before section 272, at the end insert "*: application of trading income rules*".

15 After that italic heading insert—

"271E Profits of a property business: application of trading income rules

(1) The profits of a property business are calculated in the same way as the profits of a trade.

(2) But this is subject to—

(a) section 272, which limits the rule in subsection (1) in relation to a property business whose profits are calculated in accordance with GAAP, and

(b) section 272ZA, which limits that rule in relation to a property business whose profits are calculated on the cash basis."

16 (1) Section 272 (profits of a property business: application of trading income rules) is amended as follows.

(2) For the heading substitute "Application of trading income rules: GAAP".

(3) Omit subsection (1).

(4) In subsection (2), for the words before the table substitute "In relation to a property business whose profits are calculated in accordance with GAAP, the provisions of Part 2 (trading income) which apply as a result of section 271E(1) are limited to the following—".

(5) In the table in subsection (2), omit the entry relating to section 25 (generally accepted accounting practice).

17 After section 272 insert—

"272ZA Application of trading income rules: cash basis

(1) In relation to a property business whose profits are calculated on the cash basis, the provisions of Part 2 (trading income) which apply as a result of section 271E(1) are limited to the following—

In Chapter 3 (basic rules)—	
section 26	losses calculated on same basis as profits
section 28A	money's worth
section 29	interest
In Chapter 4 (rules restricting deductions)—	
section 34	expenses not wholly and exclusively for trade and unconnected losses
sections 38 to 42 and 44	employee benefit contributions
sections 45 to 47	business entertainment and gifts
section 52	exclusion of double relief for interest
section 53	social security contributions
section 54	penalties, interest and VAT surcharges
section 55	crime-related payments
section 55A	expenditure on integral features
In Chapter 5 (rules allowing deductions)—	
section 57	pre-trading expenses
sections 58 and 59	incidental costs of obtaining finance
section 69	payments for restrictive undertakings
sections 70 and 71	seconded employees
section 72	payroll deduction schemes: contributions to agents' expenses
sections 73 to 75	counselling and retraining expenses
sections 76 to 80	redundancy payments etc
section 81	personal security expenses
sections 82 to 86	contributions to local enterprise organisations or urban regeneration companies
sections 86A and 86B	contributions to flood and coastal erosion risk management projects

sections 87 and 88	scientific research
sections 89 and 90	expenses connected with patents, designs and trade marks
section 91	payments to Export Credits Guarantee Department
In Chapter 6 (receipts)—	
section 96	capital receipts
section 97	debts incurred and later released
section 104	distribution of assets of mutual concerns
section 105(1) and (2)(b) and (c)	industrial development grants
section 106	sums recovered under insurance policies etc
In Chapter 6A (amounts not reflecting commercial transactions)—	
section 106C	amounts not reflecting commercial transactions
section 106D	capital receipts
section 106E	gifts to charities etc
In Chapter 7 (gifts to charities etc)—	
section 109	receipt by donor or connected person of benefit attributable to certain gifts

(2) In those provisions, the expression "this Part" is to be read as a reference to those provisions as applied by subsection (1) and to the other provisions of Part 3.

(3) In section 106D, the reference to subsection (4) or (5) of section 96A is to be read as a reference to subsection (2), (3) or (5) of section 307F (deemed capital receipts under, or after leaving, cash basis)."

18 After section 272ZA insert—

"Calculation of profits: other general rules".

19 In section 272A (restricting deductions for finance costs related to residential property), after subsection (6) insert—

"(7) See also section 307D (cash basis: modification of deduction for costs of loans)."

20 (1) Section 274 (relationship between rules prohibiting and allowing deductions) is amended as follows.

(2) For subsection (1)(b) substitute—

"(b) is subject to—

(i) section 36 (unpaid remuneration), as applied by section 272,

(ii) section 38 (employee benefit contributions), as applied by sections 272 and 272ZA,

(iii) section 48 (car hire), as applied by section 272,

(iv) section 55 (crime-related payments), as applied by sections 272 and 272ZA,

(v) section 272A (finance costs), and

(vi) section 307D (cash basis: modification of deduction for costs of loans)."

(3) In subsection (3)—

(a) after "section 272" insert ", or sections 38 and 55 as applied by section 272ZA", and

(b) for "section 272A" insert "sections 272A and 307D".

(4) In subsection (4), after "section 272" insert "or 272ZA".

21 In section 276(5) (introduction: profits of property businesses: lease premiums etc), after "292" insert "; but see also section 276A".

22 After section 276 insert—

"276A Application of Chapter to property businesses using cash basis

The following provisions of this Chapter do not apply in calculating the profits of a property business on the cash basis—

(a) sections 291 to 294 (tenants under taxed leases: deductions), and

(b) sections 296 and 298 (ICTA modifications)."

23 In Chapter 5 of Part 3 (profits of property businesses: other rules about receipts and deductions), after the Chapter heading insert—

"Cash basis: application of Chapter

307A Cash basis: application of Chapter

(1) The following provisions of this Chapter apply only where the profits of a property business are calculated on the cash basis—

    (a) section 307B (cash basis: capital expenditure),

    (b) section 307C (cash basis: deduction for costs of loans), and

    (c) section 307D (cash basis: modification of deduction for costs of loans).

(2) Sections 307E and 307F make provision about capital receipts in certain cases where the profits of a property business are calculated on the cash basis or have previously been calculated on the cash basis.

Property businesses using cash basis

307B Cash basis: capital expenditure

(1) This section applies in relation to the calculation of the profits of a property business on the cash basis.

(2) No deduction is allowed for an item of a capital nature incurred on, or in connection with, the acquisition or disposal of a business or part of a business.

(3) No deduction is allowed for an item of a capital nature incurred on, or in connection with, education or training.

(4) No deduction is allowed for an item of a capital nature incurred on, or in connection with, the provision, alteration or disposal of land.

(5) But subsection (4) does not prevent a deduction being made for expenditure that—

    (a) is incurred on the provision of a depreciating asset which, in being provided, is installed or otherwise fixed to qualifying land (see subsection (8)) so as to become, in law, part of the land, but

    (b) is not incurred on, or in connection with, the provision of—

        (i) a building,

        (ii) a wall, floor, ceiling, door, gate, shutter or window or stairs,

        (iii) a waste disposal system,

        (iv) a sewerage or drainage system, or

        (v) a shaft or other structure in which a lift, hoist, escalator or moving walkway may be installed.

(6) No deduction is allowed for an item of a capital nature incurred on, or in connection with, the provision, alteration or disposal of an asset for use in ordinary residential property (see subsection (8)).

But see section 311A (replacement domestic items relief).

(7) If an asset is provided partly for use in ordinary residential property and partly for other purposes, such apportionment of the expenditure incurred on, or in connection with, the provision, alteration or disposal of the asset is to be made for the purposes of subsection (6) as is just and reasonable.

(8) In relation to the calculation of profits for a tax year—

    (a) "ordinary residential property" means a dwelling-house or part of a dwelling-house in relation to which an ordinary property business (see subsection (9)) is carried on in the tax year, and

    (b) "qualifying land" means land not falling within paragraph (a).

(9) "Ordinary property business" means—

    (a) so much of a UK property business as does not consist of the commercial letting of furnished holiday accommodation (within the meaning of Chapter 6) in the UK, or

    (b) so much of an overseas property business as does not consist of the commercial letting of furnished holiday accommodation in one or more EEA states.

(10) No deduction is allowed for an item of a capital nature incurred on, or in connection with, the provision, alteration or disposal of—

    (a) any asset that is not a depreciating asset (see subsections (11) and (12)),

    (b) any asset not acquired or created for use on a continuing basis in the property business,

    (c) a car (see subsection (20)),

    (d) a non-qualifying intangible asset (see subsections (13) to (16)), or

(e) a financial asset (see subsection (17)).

(11) An asset is a "depreciating" asset if, on the date the item of a capital nature is incurred, it is reasonable to expect that before the end of 20 years beginning with that date—

(a) the useful life of the asset will end, or
(b) the asset will decline in value by 90% or more.

(12) The useful life of an asset ends when it could no longer be of use to any person for any purpose as an asset of a business.

(13) "Intangible asset" means anything that is capable of being an intangible asset within the meaning of FRS 105 and, in particular, includes—

(a) an internally-generated intangible asset, and
(b) intellectual property.

(14) An intangible asset is "non-qualifying" unless, by virtue of having a fixed maximum duration, it must cease to exist before the end of 20 years beginning with the date on which the item of a capital nature is incurred.

(15) An intangible asset is "non-qualifying" if it consists of a right, whether conditional or not, to obtain an intangible asset without a fixed maximum duration by virtue of which that asset must, assuming the right is exercised at the last possible time, cease to exist before the end of 20 years beginning with the date on which the item of a capital nature is incurred.

(16) Where—

(a) the person carrying on the property business ("P") has an intangible asset, and
(b) P grants a licence or any other right in respect of that asset to another person,

any intangible asset that consists of a licence or other right granted to P in respect of the intangible asset mentioned in paragraph (a) is "non-qualifying".

(17) A "financial asset" means any right under or in connection with—

(a) a financial instrument, or
(b) an arrangement that is capable of producing a return that is economically equivalent to a return produced under any financial instrument.

(18) A reference to acquisition, provision, alteration or disposal includes potential acquisition, provision, alteration or (as the case may be) disposal.

(19) If there is a letting of accommodation only part of which is furnished holiday accommodation, such apportionments as are just and reasonable in all the circumstances are to be made for the purposes of this section.

(20) In this section—

"arrangement" includes any agreement, understanding, scheme, transaction or series of transactions (whether or not legally enforceable);
"building" includes any fixed structure;
"car" has the same meaning as in Part 2 of CAA 2001 (see section 268A of that Act);
"financial instrument" has the same meaning as in FRS 105;
"FRS 105" means Financial Reporting Standard 105 (the Financial Reporting Standard applicable to the Micro-entities Regime), issued by the Financial Reporting Council in July 2015;
"intellectual property" means—

(a) any patent, trade mark, registered design, copyright or design right, plant breeders' rights or rights under section 7 of the Plant Varieties Act 1997,
(b) any right under the law of a country or territory outside the United Kingdom corresponding or similar to a right within paragraph (a),
(c) any information or technique not protected by a right within paragraph (a) or (b) but having industrial, commercial or other economic value, or
(d) any licence or other right in respect of anything within paragraph (a), (b) or (c);

"provision" includes creation, construction or acquisition.

307C Cash basis: deduction for costs of loans

(1) Section 307D applies in calculating the profits of a property business for a tax year if conditions A to D are met.

(2) Condition A is that the profits of the business are calculated on the cash basis for the tax year.

(3) Condition B is that a deduction for costs of a loan is allowed in calculating the profits of the business for the tax year or, ignoring section 272A (restricting

deductions for finance costs related to residential property) and section 307D (cash basis: modification of deduction for costs of loans), would be so allowed.

In this section such a loan is referred to as a "relevant loan".

(4) Condition C is that an amount of the principal of one or more relevant loans is outstanding at the end time (and a relevant loan in respect of which such an amount is outstanding at the end time is referred to in this section as an "outstanding relevant loan").

(5) Condition D is that—

$$L > V$$

where—

L is the total outstanding amount of relevant loans (see subsections (6) and (7)), and

V is the sum of the values of all relevant properties (see subsections (8) to (10)).

(6) The "total outstanding amount of relevant loans"—

(a) if there is only one outstanding relevant loan, is the outstanding business amount of that loan, and

(b) if there are two or more outstanding relevant loans, is found by calculating the outstanding business amount of each such loan and adding those amounts together.

(7) The "outstanding business amount" of a relevant loan is given by—

$$(X/Y) \times A$$

where—

A is the amount of the principal of the loan which is outstanding at the end time, X is the amount of the deduction for costs of the loan that would be allowed, apart from sections 272A and 307D, in calculating the profits of the business for the tax year, and

Y is the amount of the deduction for costs of the loan that would be allowed, apart from the wholly and exclusively rule and sections 272A and 307D, in calculating the profits of the business for the tax year.

(8) A property is a "relevant property" if—

(a) it is involved in the property business at the end time, or

(b) although it is not involved in the business at the end time—

(i) it was last involved in the business at an earlier time in the tax year, and

(ii) the person carrying on the business holds the property throughout the period beginning with that earlier time and ending with the end time.

(9) The "value" of a relevant property is the total of—

(a) the market value of the property at the time that it is first involved in the property business, and

(b) such amount of any expenditure of a capital nature incurred by the person carrying on the business in respect of the property as is not brought into account in calculating the profits of the business for the tax year or any previous tax year.

(10) A property is "involved in the property business" if it is a property whose exploitation forms the whole or part of the business.

(11) The "end time" is—

(a) the time immediately before the end of the tax year, or

(b) if in the tax year the person carrying on the business permanently ceases to carry it on, the time immediately before the person permanently ceases to carry on the business.

(12) "Costs", in relation to a loan, means—

(a) interest on the loan,

(b) an amount in connection with the loan that, for the person receiving or entitled to the amount, is a return in relation to the loan which is economically equivalent to interest, or

(c) incidental costs of obtaining finance by means of the loan.

(13) Section 58(2) to (4) (meaning of "incidental costs of obtaining finance") apply for the purposes of subsection (12)(c).

(14) In this section—

"market value", in relation to a property, means the price which the property might reasonably be expected to fetch—

(a) in the market conditions then prevailing, and

(b) between persons dealing with each other at arm's length in the open market;

"property" means an estate, interest or right in or over land;
"the wholly and exclusively rule" means the rule in section 34 (expenses not wholly and exclusively for trade and unconnected losses), as applied by section 272ZA (application of trading income rules: cash basis).

307D Cash basis: modification of deduction for costs of loans

(1) Where section 307C provides that this section applies in calculating the profits of a property business for a tax year, the amount which is allowed as a deduction for costs of a loan in calculating the profits for the tax year is the non-adjusted deduction multiplied by the relevant fraction.

This is subject to section 272A (restricting deductions for finance costs related to residential property).

(2) "The non-adjusted deduction" means the deduction for costs of the loan that would be allowed, apart from section 272A and this section, in calculating the profits of the business for the tax year.

(3) "The relevant fraction" means—

V / L

where V and L have the same meaning as in section 307C.

(4) For the meaning of "costs of a loan" see section 307C.

Property businesses that use, or have used, cash basis

307E Capital receipts under, or after leaving, cash basis

(1) This section applies in relation to a property business carried on by a person in two cases—

(a) Case 1 (see subsections (2) to (4)), and
(b) Case 2 (see subsections (5) to (8)).

(2) Case 1 is a case in which conditions A and B are met.

(3) Condition A is that the person receives disposal proceeds or a capital refund in relation to an asset in a tax year for which the profits of the property business are calculated on the cash basis (see section 271D).

For the meaning of "disposal proceeds" and "capital refund" see subsections (9) and (10).

(4) Condition B is that—

(a) an amount of capital expenditure (see subsection (11)) relating to the asset has been brought into account in calculating the profits of the property business on the cash basis, or
(b) an amount of relevant capital expenditure (see subsection (17)) relating to the asset has been brought into account in calculating the profits of the property business in accordance with GAAP (see section 271B)—

(i) by means of a deduction allowed under section 58 or 59 (incidental costs of obtaining finance) (as applied by section 272) or section 311A (replacement domestic items relief), or
(ii) under CAA 2001 (see subsection (20)).

(5) Case 2 is a case in which—

(a) condition C is met, and
(b) condition D or E is met.

(6) Condition C is that disposal proceeds or a capital refund arise to the person in relation to an asset in a tax year—

(a) for which the profits of the property business are calculated in accordance with GAAP, and
(b) which is after a tax year for which the profits of the business had been calculated on the cash basis.

(7) Condition D is that an amount of capital expenditure relating to the asset—

(a) has been paid in a tax year for which the profits of the property business were calculated on the cash basis,
(b) has been brought into account in calculating the profits of the business on the cash basis, and
(c) on the assumption that the profits had not been calculated on the cash basis at the time the expenditure was paid, would not have been qualifying expenditure.

(8) Condition E is that—

(a) an amount of capital expenditure relating to the asset has been brought into account in calculating the profits of the property business for a tax year in accordance with GAAP by means of a deduction allowed under section 58 or 59 (as applied by section 272) or section 311A, and

(b) that tax year is before the tax year for which the person last entered the cash basis.

(9) "Disposal proceeds" means—

(a) any proceeds arising from the disposal of an asset or any part of it,

(b) any proceeds arising from the grant of any right in respect of, or any interest in, the asset, or

(c) any amount of damages, proceeds of insurance or other compensation received in respect of the asset.

See also section 307F for circumstances in which a person is to be regarded as disposing of an asset.

(10) "Capital refund" means an amount that is (in substance) a refund of capital expenditure relating to an asset.

(11) "Capital expenditure" means expenditure of a capital nature incurred, or treated as incurred, on or in connection with—

(a) the provision, alteration or disposal of an asset, or

(b) the potential provision, alteration or disposal of an asset.

(12) The disposal proceeds or capital refund mentioned in condition A or (as the case may be) condition C are to be brought into account as a receipt in calculating the profits of the property business.

(13) In a case where only part of the total capital expenditure incurred, or treated as incurred, by the person in relation to the asset has been brought into account in calculating the profits of the property business (whether or not on the cash basis), the amount brought into account under subsection (12) is proportionately reduced.

The reference in this subsection to expenditure brought into account includes a reference to expenditure brought into account under CAA 2001 (see subsection (20)).

(14) Subsection (12) does not apply if the whole of the amount which would otherwise be brought into account under that subsection—

(a) has already been brought into account as a receipt in calculating the profits of the property business under this section,

(b) is brought into account as a receipt in calculating the profits of the business under any other provision of this Part (except section 334D(4) (assets not fully paid for)), or

(c) is brought into account under Part 2 or 3A of CAA 2001 as a disposal value.

The reference to any other provision of this Part in paragraph (b) includes a reference to any provision applied by section 272 or 272ZA.

(15) If part of the amount which would otherwise be brought into account under subsection (12) has already been or is brought into account as mentioned in subsection (14), subsection (12) applies in relation to the remainder of that amount.

(16) For the purposes of this section, any question as to whether or to what extent expenditure is brought into account in calculating the profits of a property business is to be determined on such basis as is just and reasonable in all the circumstances.

(17) In subsection (4)(b) "relevant capital expenditure" means capital expenditure which—

(a) has been incurred (or treated as incurred) by the person before the tax year for which the person last entered the cash basis, and

(b) is cash basis deductible in relation to that tax year.

(18) For the purposes of this section, a person carrying on a property business "enters the cash basis" for a tax year if the profits of the business are calculated—

(a) on the cash basis for the tax year, and

(b) in accordance with GAAP for the previous tax year.

(19) Expenditure is "cash basis deductible" in relation to a tax year if, on the assumption that the expenditure was paid in that tax year, a deduction would be allowed in respect of the expenditure in calculating the profits of the property business on the cash basis for that tax year.

(20) For the purposes of this section, expenditure is "brought into account under CAA 2001" in calculating the profits of a property business if and to the extent that—

(a) a capital allowance made under Part 2 of that Act in respect of the expenditure is treated as an expense in calculating those profits (see sections 248 to 250A of that Act), or

(b) qualifying expenditure (within the meaning of Part 2 of CAA 2001) is allocated to a pool for a relevant qualifying activity and is set-off against different disposal receipts.

(21) An amount of qualifying expenditure is "set-off against different disposal receipts" if—

(a) the amount would have been unrelieved qualifying expenditure carried forward in the pool for the relevant qualifying activity, but

(b) the amount is not so carried forward because (and only because) one or more disposal values in respect of one or more assets, other than the asset in respect of which the qualifying expenditure was incurred (or treated as incurred), have at any time been brought into account in that pool.

(22) For the purposes of subsections (20) and (21), an activity is a "relevant qualifying activity" if—

(a) it is a qualifying activity mentioned in section 15(1)(b) to (da) of CAA 2001 (property business activities), and

(b) the property business consists of or includes that qualifying activity.

(23) For the purposes of subsection (21), an amount of qualifying expenditure incurred (or treated as incurred) by a person is not to be regarded as not carried forward because the person enters the cash basis.

(24) In this section—

"disposal value" means—

(a) in subsection (14)(c)—

(i) a disposal value for the purposes of Part 2 of CAA 2001 (see, in particular, section 61 of that Act), or

(ii) proceeds from a balancing event for the purposes of Part 3A of that Act (see section 360O of that Act), and

(b) in subsection (21), a disposal value for the purposes of Part 2 of that Act;

"pool" means the main pool or a class pool to which qualifying expenditure is allocated under Part 2 of CAA 2001 (see section 54 of that Act);

"provision" includes creation, construction or acquisition;

"qualifying expenditure" means qualifying expenditure within the meaning of Part 2 of CAA 2001 (see section 11(4) of that Act for the general rule);

"unrelieved qualifying expenditure" means unrelieved qualifying expenditure for the purposes of Part 2 of CAA 2001 (see section 59(1) and (2) of that Act).

307F Deemed capital receipts under, or after leaving, cash basis

(1) This section makes provision supplementary to section 307E.

(2) If—

(a) at any time a person ceases to use an asset or any part of it for the purposes of a property business (other than in the circumstances mentioned in subsection (5)), but

(b) the person does not dispose of the asset (or that part) at that time,

the person is to be regarded for the purposes of section 307E as disposing of the asset (or that part) at that time for an amount equal to the market value amount.

(3) If at any time there is a material increase in the person's non-business use of an asset or any part of it, the person is to be regarded for the purposes of section 307E as disposing of the asset (or that part) at that time for an amount equal to the relevant proportion of the market value amount.

(4) For the purposes of subsection (3)—

(a) there is an increase in a person's non-business use of an asset (or part of an asset) if—

(i) the proportion of the person's use of the asset (or that part) that is for the purposes of the property business decreases, and

(ii) the proportion of the person's use of the asset (or that part) that is for other purposes (the "non-business use") increases;

(b) "the relevant proportion" is the difference between—

(i) the proportion of the person's use of the asset (or part of the asset) that is non-business use, and

(ii) the proportion of the person's use of the asset (or that part) that was non-business use before the increase mentioned in subsection (3).

(5) If—

(a) the property business in respect of which capital expenditure relating to an asset has been brought into account as mentioned in section 307E is an overseas property business, and

(b) there is a move overseas,

the person is to be regarded for the purposes of section 307E as disposing of the asset at the time of the move overseas for an amount equal to the market value amount.

(6) For the purposes of subsection (5) there is a "move overseas" if—

(a) the person ceases to be UK resident, or

(b) the tax year is, as respects the person, a split year, and the overseas part of the tax year is the later part.

(7) The move overseas occurs—

(a) in a case falling within subsection (6)(a), on the last day of the tax year for which the person is UK resident, or

(b) in a case falling within subsection (6)(b), on the last day of the UK part of the tax year.

(8) In this section—

"capital expenditure" has the same meaning as in section 307E,

"market value amount" means the amount that would be regarded as normal and reasonable—

(a) in the market conditions then prevailing, and

(b) between persons dealing with each other at arm's length in the open market."

24 In section 311A (replacement domestic items relief), in subsection (15)—

(a) for the definition of "the capital expenditure rule" substitute—

""the capital expenditure rule" means—

(a) in relation to a property business whose profits are calculated in accordance with GAAP, section 33 (capital expenditure), as applied by section 272, and

(b) in relation to a property business whose profits are calculated on the cash basis, section 307B (cash basis: capital expenditure);";

(b) in the definition of "the wholly and exclusively rule"—

(i) omit "the rule in", and

(ii) after "section 272" insert "or 272ZA".

25 In section 315 (deduction for expenditure on sea walls), after subsection (6) insert—

"(7) In calculating the profits of a property business on the cash basis, any reference in this section to the incurring of expenditure is to the paying of expenditure."

26 In section 322 (commercial letting of furnished holiday accommodation), after paragraph (za) in subsections (2) and (2A) insert—

"(zaa) section 307B (cash basis: capital expenditure),".

27 After section 329 insert—

"329A Application of Chapter where cash basis used

This Chapter applies if—

(a) the profits of a property business are calculated—

(i) on the cash basis for a tax year (see section 271D), and

(ii) in accordance with GAAP (see section 271B) for the following tax year, or

(b) the profits of a property business are calculated—

(i) in accordance with GAAP for a tax year, and

(ii) on the cash basis for the following tax year."

28 In section 331 (income charged)—

(a) the existing text becomes subsection (1), and

(b) after that subsection insert—

"(2) This is subject to section 334A (spreading on leaving cash basis and related election)."

29 After section 334 insert—

"Spreading of adjustment income on leaving cash basis

334A Spreading on leaving cash basis and related election

Sections 239A (spreading on leaving cash basis) and 239B (election to accelerate charge under section 239A) apply for the purposes of this Chapter as they apply for the purposes of Chapter 17 of Part 2, but as if—

(a) for section 239A(1) there were substituted—

"(1) This section applies if the profits of a property business are calculated—

    (a) on the cash basis for a tax year (see section 271D), and

    (b) in accordance with GAAP (see section 271B) for the following tax year.",
and

(b) any reference to section 239A or 239B were to the section concerned as applied by this section.

CHAPTER 7A
CASH BASIS: ADJUSTMENTS FOR CAPITAL ALLOWANCES

334B "Entering the cash basis"

For the purposes of this Chapter, a person carrying on a property business enters the cash basis for a tax year if the profits of the business are calculated—

    (a) on the cash basis for the tax year (see section 271D), and

    (b) in accordance with GAAP (see section 271B) for the previous tax year.

334C Unrelieved qualifying expenditure

(1) This section applies if—

    (a) a person carrying on a property business enters the cash basis for a tax year ("the current tax year"), and

    (b) the person would, apart from section 59(4A) of CAA 2001, have unrelieved qualifying expenditure relating to a relevant property business activity to carry forward from the chargeable period which is the previous tax year.

(2) But this section does not apply if section 334D applies.

(3) In calculating the profits of the property business for the current tax year, a deduction is allowed for any cash basis deductible amount of the expenditure relating to each relevant property business activity.

(4) A "cash basis deductible amount" of the expenditure means any amount of the expenditure for which a deduction would be allowed in calculating the profits of the property business on the cash basis on the assumption that the expenditure was paid in the current tax year.

(5) Any cash basis deductible amount of the expenditure is to be determined on such basis as is just and reasonable in all the circumstances.

(6) In this section—

"relevant property business activity" means—

    (a) in relation to a UK property business, an ordinary UK property business and a UK furnished holiday lettings business (within the meaning of Part 2 of CAA 2001 (see sections 16 and 17 of that Act)), and

    (b) in relation to an overseas property business, an ordinary overseas property business and an EEA furnished holiday lettings business (within the meaning of Part 2 of that Act (see sections 17A and 17B of that Act));

"unrelieved qualifying expenditure" means unrelieved qualifying expenditure for the purposes of Part 2 of CAA 2001 (see section 59(1) and (2) of that Act).

334D Assets not fully paid for

(1) This section applies if—

    (a) a person carrying on a property business enters the cash basis for a tax year ("the current tax year"),

    (b) at any time before the end of the chargeable period which is the previous tax year the person has incurred relevant expenditure, and

    (c) not all of the relevant expenditure has actually been paid by the person.

(2) "Relevant expenditure" means expenditure on plant or machinery—

    (a) for which a deduction would be allowed in calculating the profits of the property business on the cash basis on the assumption that the expenditure was paid in the current tax year, and

    (b) in respect of which the person has obtained capital allowances.

(3) If the amount of the relevant expenditure that the person has actually paid exceeds the amount of capital allowances given in respect of the relevant expenditure, the difference is to be deducted in calculating the profits of the property business for the current tax year.

(4) If the amount of the relevant expenditure that the person has actually paid is less than the amount of capital allowances given in respect of the relevant expenditure, the difference is to be treated as a receipt in calculating the profits of the property business for the current tax year.

(5) Any question as to whether or to what extent expenditure is relevant expenditure, or as to whether or to what extent any capital allowance obtained is in respect of relevant expenditure, is to be determined on such basis as is just and reasonable in all the circumstances.

(6) If the amount of capital allowances given in respect of the relevant expenditure has been reduced under section 205 or 207 of CAA 2001 (reduction where asset provided or used only partly for qualifying activity), the amount of the relevant expenditure that the person has actually paid is to be proportionately reduced for the purposes of this section.

334E Effect of election where predecessor and successor are connected persons

(1) This section applies if—

    (a) a person carrying on a property business enters the cash basis for a tax year,

    (b) the person is the successor for the purposes of section 266 of CAA 2001, and

    (c) as a result of an election under that section, relevant plant or machinery is treated as sold by the predecessor to the successor at any time during the tax year.

(2) The provisions of this Chapter have effect in relation to the successor as if everything done to or by the predecessor had been done to or by the successor.

(3) Any expenditure actually incurred by the successor on acquiring the relevant plant or machinery is to be ignored for the purposes of calculating the profits of the property business for the tax year.

(4) In this section—

    "the predecessor" has the same meaning as in section 266 of CAA 2001, and

    "relevant plant or machinery" has the same meaning as in section 267 of that Act."

30 In section 351 (income charged), after subsection (2) insert—

"(3) Further to subsection (2), section 254 applies for the purposes of this Chapter as if for subsection (2A) of that section there were substituted—

"(2A) If the time immediately before the person permanently ceases to carry on the UK property business falls in a cash basis tax year, assume for the purposes of subsection (2) that the profits of the business are calculated on the cash basis."

(4) For the purposes of sections 254 (as so applied) and 353, a tax year is "a cash basis tax year" in relation to a property business if the profits of the business for the tax year are calculated on the cash basis (see section 271D)."

31 In section 353 (basic meaning of "post-cessation receipt"), after subsection (1) insert—

"(1A) If the time immediately before a person permanently ceases to carry on a UK property business falls in a cash basis tax year (see section 351(4)), a sum is to be treated as a post-cessation receipt only if it would have been brought into account in calculating the profits of the business on the cash basis had it been received at that time."

32 In section 356 (application to businesses within the charge to corporation tax), in subsection (1), for "section 355" substitute "sections 353(1A) and 355, and in the modification of section 254 in section 351(3)".

33 In section 786 (meaning of "rent-a-room receipts"), after subsection (6) insert—

"(6A) Subsections (6B) and (7) apply if—

    (a) the receipts would otherwise be brought into account in calculating the profits of a UK property business, and

    (b) the profits are calculated on the cash basis (see section 271D).

(6B) Any amounts brought into account under section 307E (capital receipts under, or after leaving, cash basis) as a receipt in calculating the profits of the property business are to be treated as receipts within paragraph (a) of subsection (1) above."

34 In section 860 (adjustment income), in subsection (5), after "Chapter 17 of Part 2" insert ", or under section 239B as applied to property businesses by section 334A,".

35 In section 866 (employee benefit contributions: non-trades and non-property businesses), in subsection (7)(b), for "section 272" substitute "sections 272 and 272ZA".

36 In section 867 (business entertainment and gifts: non-trades and non-property businesses), in subsection (7)(b), for "section 272" substitute "sections 272 and 272ZA".

37 In section 868 (social security contributions: non-trades etc), in subsection (6)(b), for "section 272" insert "sections 272 and 272ZA".

38 In section 869 (penalties, interest and VAT surcharges: non-trades etc), in subsection (6)(b), for "section 272" substitute "sections 272 and 272ZA".

39 In section 870 (crime-related payments: non-trades and non-property businesses), in subsection (4)(b), for "section 272" substitute "sections 272 and 272ZA".

40 In section 872 (losses calculated on same basis as miscellaneous income), in subsection (4)(b), for "section 272" substitute "sections 272 and 272ZA".

41 In Part 2 of Schedule 4 (index of defined expressions), at the appropriate place insert—

"the cash basis (in Part 3)	section 271D
in accordance with GAAP (in Part 3)	section 271B".

PART 3
TRADES ETC: AMENDMENTS OF OTHER ACTS

TMA 1970

42 In section 42 of TMA 1970 (procedure for making claims etc), in subsection (7)(e), after "194" insert ", 271A(10)".

TCGA 1992

43 TCGA 1992 is amended as follows.

44 In section 37 (consideration chargeable to tax on income), after subsection (1) insert—

"(1A) There is to be excluded from the consideration for a disposal of an asset taken into account in the computation of the gain a sum equal to any amount that is taken into account by the person making the disposal as a receipt under section 96A or 307E of ITTOIA 2005 (capital receipts under, or after leaving, cash basis) as a result of the operation of any deemed disposal provision in relation to the asset.

(1B) But subsection (1A) applies only to the extent that the sum has not been excluded from the consideration for an earlier disposal of the asset.

(1C) The following are "deemed disposal provisions"—

(a) in relation to trades, professions and vocations, subsections (4) and (5) of section 96A of ITTOIA 2005 (which provide for circumstances in which a person is to be regarded as disposing of an asset for the purposes of that section), and
(b) in relation to property businesses, section 307F of ITTOIA 2005 (which provides for circumstances in which a person is to be regarded as disposing of an asset for the purposes of section 307E of that Act)."

45 (1) Section 41 (restriction of losses by reference to capital allowances etc) is amended as follows.

(2) In subsection (4), after paragraph (a) insert—

"(zaa) any deduction allowable in respect of capital expenditure in calculating profits on the cash basis (see sections 33A and 307B of ITTOIA 2005),".

(3) After subsection (6) insert—

"(6A) Where—

(a) capital allowances have been made or may be made in respect of expenditure, and
(b) the capital allowances include a deduction mentioned in subsection (4)(zaa),

the capital allowances to be taken into account under this section are to be regarded as equal to the total amount of expenditure which has qualified for capital allowances less any balancing charge to which the person making the disposal is liable under the Capital Allowances Act."

(4) In subsection (7), after "Capital Allowances Act," insert "and subsection (6A) does not apply,"

(5) After subsection (8) insert—

"(9) In this section—

(a) in relation to a trade, profession or vocation, references to calculating profits on the cash basis are to calculating the profits of a trade, profession or vocation in relation to which an election under section 25A of ITTOIA 2005 (cash basis for trades) has effect, and

(b) in relation to a property business, references to calculating profits on the cash basis are to be construed in accordance with section 271D of that Act (calculation of profits of property businesses on the cash basis).

(10) In this section—

"capital expenditure" means expenditure of a capital nature incurred on, or in connection with, the creation, construction, acquisition, alteration or disposal of an asset, and

"property business" means a UK property business or an overseas property business within the meaning of Part 3 of ITTOIA 2005 (see sections 264 and 265 of that Act)."

46 (1) Section 47A (exemption for disposals by persons using cash basis) is amended as follows.

(2) For the heading substitute "Exemption for certain disposals under, or after leaving, cash basis".

(3) In subsection (1), for "A to D" substitute "A, B and D".

(4) For subsection (2) substitute—

"(2) Condition A is that the asset is not land."

(5) In subsection (3), for "or vocation" substitute ", vocation or property business".

(6) Omit subsection (4).

(7) For subsection (5) substitute—

"(5) Condition D is that relevant disposal proceeds—

(a) are brought into account as a receipt (whether or not on the cash basis) under section 96A(3I) of ITTOIA 2005 in calculating the profits of a trade, profession or vocation (capital receipts under, or after leaving, cash basis: trades, professions and vocations), or

(b) are brought into account as a receipt (whether or not on the cash basis) under section 307E(12) of that Act in calculating the profits of a property business (capital receipts under, or after leaving, cash basis: property businesses).

(5A) "Relevant disposal proceeds" means disposal proceeds as mentioned in section 96A(3F) of ITTOIA 2005 or (as the case may be) section 307E(9) of that Act which arise from the disposal mentioned in subsection (1)."

(8) For subsection (6) substitute—

"(6) Subsection (7) applies in the case of the disposal of, or of an interest in, an asset—

(a) which, in the period of ownership of the person making the disposal—

(i) has been used partly for the purposes of the trade, profession or vocation and partly for other purposes, or

(ii) has been used for the purposes of the trade, profession or vocation for part of that period, or

(b) expenditure on which by the person has qualified in part only for capital allowances."

(9) In subsection (7)—

(a) in paragraph (a), for "was, or (as the case may be)" to the end substitute "qualified for capital allowances", and

(b) in paragraph (c), at the end insert ", or to the expenditure qualifying for capital allowances."

(10) After subsection (7) insert—

"(8) In this section "property business" means a UK property business or an overseas property business within the meaning of Part 3 of ITTOIA 2005 (see sections 264 and 265 of that Act)."

47 Section 47B (disposals made by persons after leaving cash basis) is omitted.

CAA 2001

48 CAA 2001 is amended as follows.

49 In section 1 (capital allowances), omit subsections (4) and (5).

50 After section 1 insert—

"1A Capital allowances and charges: cash basis

(1) This section applies in relation to a chargeable period for which the profits of a trade, profession, vocation or property business ("the relevant activity") carried on by a person are calculated on the cash basis.

(2) The person is not entitled to any allowance or liable to any charge under this Act except as provided by subsections (4) and (7).

(3) No disposal value is to be brought into account except as provided by subsections (5) and (8).

(4) If, apart from subsection (2), the person would be entitled to an allowance in respect of expenditure incurred on the provision of a car or liable to a charge in connection with such an allowance, the person is so entitled or (as the case may be) so liable.

(5) If, apart from subsection (3), a disposal value would be brought into account in respect of a car, the disposal value is brought into account in respect of the car.

(6) Subsections (7) and (8) apply if—

(a) a person carrying on a relevant activity incurs qualifying expenditure relating to an asset at a time when the profits of that activity are not calculated on the cash basis,

(b) after incurring the expenditure, the person enters the cash basis for a tax year, and

(c) no deduction would be allowed in respect of the expenditure in calculating the profits of the relevant activity on the cash basis for that tax year, on the assumption that the expenditure was paid in that tax year.

(7) If, apart from subsection (2), the person would be liable to a charge in connection with allowances in respect of the qualifying expenditure mentioned in subsection (6), the person is so liable.

(8) If, apart from subsection (3), a disposal value would be brought into account in respect of the asset mentioned in subsection (6), the disposal value is brought into account in respect of the asset.

(9) For the purposes of this section a person carrying on a trade, profession or vocation "enters the cash basis" for a tax year if—

(a) an election under section 25A of ITTOIA 2005 (cash basis for trades) has effect in relation to the trade, profession or vocation for the tax year, and

(b) no such election has effect in relation to the trade, profession or vocation for the previous tax year.

(10) For the purposes of this section a person carrying on a property business "enters the cash basis" for a tax year if the profits of the business are calculated—

(a) on the cash basis for the tax year (see section 271D of ITTOIA 2005), and

(b) in accordance with GAAP (see section 271B of that Act) for the previous tax year.

(11) In this section—

(a) references to calculating the profits of a trade, profession or vocation on the cash basis are to calculating the profits of a trade, profession or vocation in relation to which an election under section 25A of ITTOIA 2005 has effect, and

(b) references to calculating the profits of a property business on the cash basis are to be construed in accordance with section 271D of that Act (calculation of profits of property businesses on the cash basis).

(12) In this section—

"car" has the same meaning as in Part 2 (see section 268A);

"disposal value" means—

(a) a disposal value for the purposes of Part 2, 4A, 5, 6, 7, 8 or 10, or

(b) proceeds from a balancing event for the purposes of Part 3 or 3A;

"qualifying expenditure" means qualifying expenditure within the meaning of any Part of this Act."

51 (1) Section 4 (capital expenditure) is amended as follows.

(2) In subsection (2)—

(a) omit "or" at the end of paragraph (a), and

(b) after paragraph (a) insert—

"(aa) any cash basis expenditure, other than expenditure incurred on the provision of a car, or".

(3) After subsection (2) insert—

"(2ZA) In subsection (2)(aa)—

"cash basis expenditure" means any expenditure incurred—

(a) in the case of a trade, profession or vocation, at a time when an election under section 25A of ITTOIA 2005 has effect in relation to the trade, profession or vocation, or

(b) in the case of a property business, in a tax year for which the profits of the business are calculated on the cash basis (see section 271D of that Act); and

"car" has the same meaning as in Part 2 (see section 268A)."

52 (1) Section 59 (unrelieved qualifying expenditure) is amended as follows.

(2) In subsection (4), for "no amount may be carried forward as unrelieved qualifying expenditure" substitute "any cash basis deductible amount may not be carried forward as unrelieved qualifying expenditure in a pool for the trade, profession or vocation".

(3) After subsection (4) insert—

"(4A) If a person carrying on a property business enters the cash basis for a tax year, any cash basis deductible amount may not be carried forward as unrelieved qualifying expenditure in a pool for a relevant qualifying activity from the chargeable period which is the previous tax year."

(4) Omit subsection (5).

(5) After subsection (5) insert—

"(5A) A "cash basis deductible amount" means any amount of unrelieved qualifying expenditure for which a deduction would be allowed in calculating the profits of the trade, profession, vocation or property business (as the case may be) on the cash basis on the assumption that the expenditure was paid in the tax year for which the person enters the cash basis."

(6) In subsection (6), for "the amount of unrelieved qualifying expenditure incurred on the provision of a car" substitute "any cash basis deductible amount".

(7) For subsection (7) substitute—

"(7) Subsections (9), (10) and (11) of section 1A (capital allowances and charges: cash basis) apply for the purposes of this section as they apply for the purposes of that section.

(7A) In subsection (4A) "relevant qualifying activity" means—

(a) in relation to a UK property business, an ordinary UK property business and a UK furnished holiday lettings business, and

(b) in relation to an overseas property business, an ordinary overseas property business and an EEA furnished holiday lettings business."

53 (1) Section 66A (persons leaving cash basis) is amended as follows.

(2) For subsection (1) substitute—

"(1) This section applies if—

(a) a person carrying on a trade, profession, vocation or property business ("the business") leaves the cash basis in a chargeable period,

(b) the person has incurred expenditure at a time when the profits of the business are calculated on the cash basis,

(c) some or all of the expenditure was brought into account in calculating the profits of the business on the cash basis, and

(d) the expenditure would have been qualifying expenditure if the profits of the business had not been calculated on the cash basis at the time the expenditure was incurred."

(3) In subsection (2)(a)—

(a) for "amount of that expenditure for which" substitute "higher of the following",

(b) in sub-paragraphs (i) and (ii), at the beginning insert "the amount of that expenditure for which", and

(c) in both places, for "or vocation" substitute ", vocation or property business".

(4) After subsection (6) insert—

"(7) For the purposes of this section a person carrying on a property business leaves the cash basis in a chargeable period ("tax year X") if the profits of the business are calculated—

(a) in accordance with GAAP (see section 271B of ITTOIA 2005) for tax year X, and

(b) on the cash basis (see section 271D of that Act) for the previous tax year.

(8) Subsection (11) of section 1A (capital allowances and charges: cash basis) applies for the purposes of this section as it applies for the purposes of that section."

54 After section 419 insert—

"419A Unrelieved qualifying expenditure: entry to cash basis

(1) If a person carrying on a mineral extraction trade enters the cash basis for a tax year, for the purpose of determining the person's unrelieved qualifying expenditure

for the chargeable period ending with the basis period for the tax year and subsequent chargeable periods (see section 419), only the non-cash basis deductible portion of qualifying expenditure incurred before the chargeable period ending with the basis period for the tax year is to be taken into account.

(2) The "non-cash basis deductible portion" of qualifying expenditure means the amount of qualifying expenditure for which no deduction would be allowed in calculating the profits of the trade on the cash basis on the assumption that the expenditure was paid in the tax year for which the person enters the cash basis.

(3) Subsections (9) and (11) of section 1A (capital allowances and charges: cash basis) apply for the purposes of this section as they apply for the purposes of that section."

55 After section 431C insert—

"431D Persons leaving cash basis

(1) This section applies if—

(a) a person carrying on a mineral extraction trade leaves the cash basis in a chargeable period,

(b) the person has incurred expenditure at a time when an election under section 25A of ITTOIA 2005 (cash basis for trades) has effect in relation to the trade,

(c) some or all of the expenditure was brought into account in calculating the profits of the trade on the cash basis, and

(d) the expenditure would have been qualifying expenditure if an election under section 25A of that Act had not had effect at the time the expenditure was incurred.

(2) In this section—

(a) the "relieved portion" of the expenditure is the higher of the following—

(i) the amount of that expenditure for which a deduction was allowed in calculating the profits of the trade, or

(ii) the amount of that expenditure for which a deduction would have been so allowed if the expenditure had been incurred wholly and exclusively for the purposes of the trade;

(b) the "unrelieved portion" of the expenditure is any remaining amount of the expenditure.

(3) An amount of the expenditure equal to the amount (if any) by which the unrelieved portion of the expenditure exceeds the relieved portion of the expenditure is to be regarded as qualifying expenditure incurred by the person in the chargeable period.

(4) For the purposes of this section a person carrying on a trade leaves the cash basis in a chargeable period if—

(a) immediately before the beginning of the chargeable period an election under section 25A of ITTOIA 2005 had effect in relation to the trade, and

(b) such an election does not have effect in relation to the trade for the chargeable period."

56 After section 461 insert—

"461A Unrelieved qualifying expenditure: entry to cash basis

(1) If a person carrying on a trade enters the cash basis for a tax year, any cash basis deductible amount may not be carried forward as unrelieved qualifying expenditure in the pool for the trade from the chargeable period ending with the basis period for the previous tax year.

(2) A "cash basis deductible amount" means any amount of unrelieved qualifying expenditure for which a deduction would be allowed in calculating the profits of the trade on the cash basis on the assumption that the expenditure was paid in the tax year for which the person enters the cash basis.

(3) Any cash basis deductible amount is to be determined on such basis as is just and reasonable in all the circumstances.

(4) Subsections (9) and (11) of section 1A (capital allowances and charges: cash basis) apply for the purposes of this section as they apply for the purposes of that section."

57 After section 462 insert—

"462A Persons leaving cash basis

(1) This section applies if—

(a) a person carrying on a trade leaves the cash basis in a chargeable period,

(b) the person has incurred expenditure at a time when an election under section 25A of ITTOIA 2005 (cash basis for trades) has effect in relation to the trade,

(c) some or all of the expenditure was brought into account in calculating the profits of the trade on the cash basis, and

(d) the expenditure would have been qualifying expenditure if an election under section 25A of that Act had not had effect at the time the expenditure was incurred.

(2) In this section the "relieved portion" of the expenditure is the higher of the following—

(a) the amount of that expenditure for which a deduction was allowed in calculating the profits of the trade, or

(b) the amount of that expenditure for which a deduction would have been so allowed if the expenditure had been incurred wholly and exclusively for the purposes of the trade.

(3) For the purposes of determining the person's available qualifying expenditure in the pool for the trade for the chargeable period (see section 456)—

(a) the whole of the expenditure must be allocated to the pool for the trade in that chargeable period, and

(b) the available qualifying expenditure in that pool is reduced by the relieved portion of that expenditure.

(4) For the purposes of determining any disposal values (see section 462), the expenditure incurred by the person is to be regarded as qualifying expenditure.

(5) For the purposes of this section a person carrying on a trade leaves the cash basis in a chargeable period if—

(a) immediately before the beginning of the chargeable period an election under section 25A of ITTOIA 2005 had effect in relation to the trade, and

(b) such an election does not have effect in relation to the trade for the chargeable period."

58 After section 475 insert—

"475A Unrelieved qualifying expenditure: entry to cash basis

(1) If a person carrying on a trade enters the cash basis for a tax year, any cash basis deductible amount may not be carried forward as unrelieved qualifying expenditure in the pool for the trade from the chargeable period ending with the basis period for the previous tax year.

(2) A "cash basis deductible amount" means any amount of unrelieved qualifying expenditure for which a deduction would be allowed in calculating the profits of the trade on the cash basis on the assumption that the expenditure was paid in the tax year for which the person enters the cash basis.

(3) Any cash basis deductible amount is to be determined on such basis as is just and reasonable in all the circumstances.

(4) Subsections (9) and (11) of section 1A (capital allowances and charges: cash basis) apply for the purposes of this section as they apply for the purposes of that section."

59 After section 477 insert—

"477A Persons leaving cash basis

(1) This section applies if—

(a) a person carrying on a trade leaves the cash basis in a chargeable period,

(b) the person has incurred expenditure at a time when an election under section 25A of ITTOIA 2005 (cash basis for trades) has effect in relation to the trade,

(c) some or all of the expenditure was brought into account in calculating the profits of the trade on the cash basis, and

(d) the expenditure would have been qualifying trade expenditure if an election under section 25A of that Act had not had effect at the time the expenditure was incurred.

(2) In this section the "relieved portion" of the expenditure is the amount of that expenditure for which a deduction was allowed in calculating the profits of the trade.

(3) For the purposes of determining the person's available qualifying expenditure in the pool for the trade for the chargeable period (see section 470)—

(a) the whole of the expenditure must be allocated to the pool for the trade in that chargeable period, and

(b) the available qualifying expenditure in that pool is reduced by the relieved portion of that expenditure.

(4) For the purposes of determining any disposal receipts (see section 476), the expenditure incurred by the person is to be regarded as qualifying trade expenditure.

(5) For the purposes of this section a person carrying on a trade leaves the cash basis in a chargeable period if—

(a) immediately before the beginning of the chargeable period an election under section 25A of ITTOIA 2005 had effect in relation to the trade, and

(b) such an election does not have effect in relation to the trade for the chargeable period."

ITA 2007

60 ITA 2007 is amended as follows.

61 In Part 4 (loss relief), in section 59 (overview of Part), in subsection (3)(b)—

(a) for "section 272" substitute "sections 272 and 272ZA", and

(b) for "applies" substitute "apply".

62 (1) Chapter 4 of Part 4 (losses from property businesses) is amended as follows.

(2) In section 120 (deduction of property losses from general income), in subsection (7), at the end insert "and section 127BA (restriction of relief: cash basis)".

(3) After section 127B insert—

"127BA   Restriction of relief: cash basis

(1) This section applies if—

(a) in a tax year a person makes a loss in a UK property business or overseas property business (whether carried on alone or in partnership), and

(b) the profits of the business are calculated on the cash basis for the tax year (see section 271D of ITTOIA 2005).

(2) No property loss relief against general income may be given to the person for the loss."

63 In Chapter 1 of Part 8 (relief for interest payments), in section 384B(1) (restriction on relief for interest payments where cash basis applies), after "for the tax year" insert "or if the profits of a UK property business or overseas property business carried on by the partnership are calculated on the cash basis for the tax year (see section 271D of ITTOIA 2005)."

PART 4

COMMENCEMENT AND TRANSITIONAL PROVISION

64 (1) The amendments made by this Schedule have effect for the tax year 2017–18 and subsequent tax years.

(2) If—

(a) disregarding this sub-paragraph, under section 33A of ITTOIA 2005, as inserted by paragraph 2 of Part 1, a deduction would not be allowed in calculating the profits of a trade, profession or vocation on the cash basis for the tax year 2017–18, but

(b) if the amendment made by paragraph 2 were not to have effect for that tax year, that deduction would be allowed in calculating the profits of that trade, profession or vocation on that basis for that tax year,

that deduction is to be allowed in calculating the profits of that trade, profession or vocation on that basis for that tax year.

(3) Sub-paragraph (2) is to be disregarded in determining any question as to whether or to what extent an amount of expenditure would, on the assumption that it was paid in the tax year 2017–18, be brought into account in calculating the profits of a trade, profession or vocation for the tax year 2017–18 for the purposes of—

(a) the following provisions of CAA 2001—

(i) section 1A (capital allowances and charges: cash basis),

(ii) section 59 (unrelieved qualifying expenditure),

(iii) section 419A (unrelieved qualifying expenditure: entry to cash basis),

(iv) section 461A (unrelieved qualifying expenditure: entry to cash basis), and

(v) section 475A (unrelieved qualifying expenditure: entry to cash basis); and

(b) the following provisions of ITTOIA 2005—

(i) section 96A (capital receipts under, or after leaving, cash basis),

(ii) section 240C (unrelieved qualifying expenditure: Parts 2, 7 and 8 of CAA 2001),

(iii) section 240CA (unrelieved qualifying expenditure: Part 5 of CAA 2001), and

(iv) section 240D (assets not fully paid for).

(4) But sub-paragraph (2) is not to be disregarded in determining any question as to whether or to what extent an amount of expenditure is actually brought into account in calculating the profits of a trade, profession or vocation for the tax year 2017–18 for the purposes of the provisions mentioned in paragraphs (a) and (b) of sub-paragraph (3).

GENERAL NOTE

Part 1 – amendments to ITTOIA 2005

ITTOIA 2005 s 33A Cash basis: capital expenditure

When calculating the profits of a trade on the cash business, no deduction is allowed for an item of a capital nature incurred on, or in connection with:
– the acquisition or disposal of a business or part of a business;
– education or training;
– the provision, alteration or disposal of:
  (a) any asset that is not a depreciating asset (will have a useful life of 20 years or less, or the asset will decline in value by 90% in that 20 year period);
  (b) any asset not acquired or created for use on a continuing basis in the trade;
  (c) a car (meaning in Part 2 of CAA 2001);
  (d) land (there are exemptions for depreciating assets attached to the land);
  (e) a non-qualifying intangible asset (intangible asset has the meaning of FRS 105 – non-qualifying if it exists for more than 20 years);
  (f) a financial asset (any right under or in connection with a financial instrument or an arrangement capable of producing a return equivalent to a financial instrument).

ITTOIA 2005 s 96A (cash basis: capital receipts) includes subsections (1) to (3), which bring capital amounts into account as receipts under the cash basis in two cases:

Case 1 – where conditions A and B are met:
  – Condition A – the person receives disposal proceeds or a capital refund in relation to an asset at a time when using the cash basis for the trade;
  – Condition B – an amount of capital expenditure relating to the asset has been brought into account in calculating the profits of the trade on the cash basis or in the tax year before the cash basis and is cash basis deductible.

Case 2 – where conditions C and D or C and E are met:
  – Condition C – disposal proceeds or a capital refund arise to a person in relation to an asset at a time when the business is not using the cash basis, but it has used the cash basis before;
  – Condition D – an amount of capital expenditure relating to the asset has been paid at a time when the business is using the cash basis, has been brought into account in calculating the profits and if the business was not using the cash basis when the expenditure was paid, it would not have been qualifying expenditure;
  – Condition E – an amount of capital expenditure relating to an asset has been brought into account in calculating the profits of the trade for a tax year where the business is not using the cash basis and is before the year where the person last entered the cash basis.

ITTOIA 2005 s 96B states that the amount of expenditure brought into account by section 96A is to be calculated on a just and reasonable basis.

Part 2 – property businesses: amendments to ITTOIA 2005

ITTOIA 2005 s 271A Basis of calculation of profits: GAAP required

The profits of a business must be calculated in accordance with GAAP (and so not the cash basis) if condition A, B, C, D or E is met.
– Condition A – the business is carried on at any time in the tax year by:
  – a company;
  – a limited liability partnership;
  – a corporate firm (if the partner in the firm is not an individual);
  – the trustees of a trust.

- Condition B – the cash basis receipts for the tax year exceed £150,000 (proportionally reduced if only carried on for part of the tax year).
- Condition C – a property within the business is treated as beneficially owned in equal shares with a spouse or civil partner by virtue of ITA 2007 s 836, and the spouse or civil partner calculates their property business's profits in accordance with GAAP.
- Condition D – an allowance under Part 3A of CAA 2001 (business premises renovation allowances) is made at any time in calculating the profits of the property business and if GAAP was used there would be a balancing event giving rise to a balancing adjustment for the tax year.
- Condition E – an election under this subsection by a person who is or has been carrying on a property business has effect in relation to the business for the tax year.

ITTOIA 2005 s 271B Calculation of profits in accordance with GAAP

A requirement under ITTOIA 2005 Pt 3 to calculate profits in accordance with GAAP does not require a person to comply with Companies Act 2006 or subordinate legislation except as to the basis of the legislation or impose any requirement as to audit or disclosure.

ITTOIA 2005 s 271C Basis of calculation of profits: cash basis required

The profits of a property business for a tax year must be calculated on the cash basis if none of conditions A, B, C, D or E in section 271A is met.

ITTOIA 2005 s 271D Calculation of profits on the cash basis

Using the cash basis, receipts and expenses of the business are brought into account at the time they are received or paid.

ITTOIA 2005 s 271E Profits of a property business: application of trading income rules

The profits of a property business are calculated in the same way as the profits of a trade (limited by sections 272 and 272ZA).

ITTOIA 2005 s 272 is amended to limit the general rule under s 271E only where the profits are calculated using GAAP.

ITTOIA 2005 s 272ZA is introduced to limit the general rule under s 271E only where the profits are calculated using the cash basis. It provides a list of provisions of the trading income rules that are applicable to property businesses using the cash basis.

ITTOIA 2005 s 276A prevents any deductions for a premium paid by a property business using the cash basis. It disapplies sections 291 to 294, 296 and 298 for the cash basis.

ITTOIA 2005 s 307A Cash basis: application of chapter

This section outlines the new provisions that are only applicable to a property business that calculates its profits using the cash basis.

ITTOIA 2005 s 307B Cash basis: capital expenditure

When calculating the profits of a property business on the cash business, no deduction is allowed for an item of a capital nature incurred on, or in connection with:

- the acquisition or disposal of a business or part of a business;
- education or training;
- the provision, alteration or disposal of land (though deductions are allowed for depreciating assets attached to the land);
- the provision, alteration or disposal of an asset for use in ordinary residential property (a dwelling-house, or part of, used in a property business other than the commercial letting of furnished holiday accommodation).
- the provision, alteration or disposal of:
  (a) any asset that is not a depreciating asset (will have a useful life of 20 years or less, or the asset will decline in value by 90% in that 20 year period);
  (b) any asset not acquired or created for use on a continuing basis in the property business;
  (c) a car (meaning in Part 2 of CAA 2001);
  (d) a non-qualifying intangible asset (intangible asset has the meaning of FRS 105 – non-qualifying if it exists for more than 20 years);

(e) a financial asset (any right under or in connection with a financial instrument or an arrangement capable of producing a return equivalent to a financial instrument).

ITTOIA 2005 s 307C Cash basis: deduction for costs of loans

This section applies in calculating the profits of a property business for a tax year if conditions A to D are met.
– Condition A – the profits of the business are calculated using the cash basis for the year.
– Condition B – deduction for costs of a loan is allowed or would be allowed if ITTOIA 2005 s 272A and s 307D were ignored.
– Condition C – the amount of principal of one or more loans that meet condition B is outstanding on the last day of the tax year.
– Condition D – is L > V, where L is the total outstanding loans and V is the value of the properties.

The value of the property is the market value of the property at the time it is first involved in the property business and any capital expenditure, which has not been brought into account in calculating the profits of the business.

ITTOIA 2005 s 307E Capital receipts under, or after leaving, cash basis

Applies for a property business in two cases.
Case 1 – conditions A and B are met:
– Condition A – the person receives disposal proceeds or a capital refund in relation to an asset at a time when using the cash basis for the property business.
– Condition B – an amount of capital expenditure relating to the asset has been brought into account in calculating the profits of the property business on the cash basis or in accordance with GAAP by means of a deduction for the incidental costs of obtaining finance or replacement domestic items relief or under CAA 2001.
Case 2 – where conditions C and D or C and E are met:
– Condition C – disposal proceeds or a capital refund arise to a person in relation to an asset at a time when the business is not using the cash basis, but it has used the cash basis before.
– Condition D – an amount of capital expenditure relating to the asset has been paid at a time when the business is using the cash basis, has been brought into account in calculating the profits and if the business was not using the cash basis when the expenditure was paid, it would not have been qualifying expenditure.
– Condition E – an amount of capital expenditure relating to an asset has been brought into account in calculating the profits of the property business on the GAAP basis by means of a deduction for the incidental costs of obtaining finance or replacement domestic items relief and is before the year where the person last entered the cash basis.

ITTOIA 2005 s 307F Deemed capital receipts under, or after leaving, cash basis

This section provides that an asset is deemed to be disposed of, and subject to the rules under section 307E, if the landlord ceases to use the asset in the property business or materially increases its non-business use. The disposal proceeds are the market value of the property or a proportion equivalent to the increase in the non-business use. Where a person who has an overseas property business ceases to be UK resident, they are treated as disposing of assets at market value at the date they cease to be UK resident.

ITTOIA 2005 s 329A Application of Chapter 7 where cash basis used

This section provides that the rules on adjustment income in ITTOIA 2005 Pt 3, Ch 7 apply to a property business moving between cash basis and GAAP. This is subject to the new section 334A that spreads any adjustment over six years when a business leaves the cash basis. This is done in accordance with the spreading rules for the trade cash basis at ITTOIA 2005 s 239A. A landlord can similarly elect under ITTOIA 2005 s 239B to accelerate the income adjustment. They can choose any amount of the adjustment income to be brought into account in the current year, with the remainder being spread over the remainder of the original six years.

ITTOIA 2005 Ch 7A Cash basis: adjustments for capital allowances

For the property cash basis, similar rules are adopted to those which govern the interaction of capital allowances and the cash basis for traders, which are at ITTOIA 2005 Pt 2 Ch 7A.

Where capital allowances have been claimed previously, and a landlord now enters the cash basis, there may be unrelieved qualifying expenditure for capital allowances purposes. A deduction is allowed on a just and reasonable basis for expenditure which would have been allowed if it had been paid during that period. This is intended to permit a cash basis deduction of the unrelieved capital expenditure on plant and machinery, so long as the amounts have actually been paid, which would be a potentially valuable acceleration of allowances.

Part 3 – Trades etc: amendments of other Acts

TCGA 1992 s 37 consideration chargeable to tax on income

Subsections (1A) to (1C) have been added to prevent capital proceeds brought into account as receipts under the cash basis being included as consideration on disposal of an asset for capital gains purposes.

Entering and leaving the cash basis – mineral extraction allowances, know-how allowances and patent allowances

With a fundamental change to what types of capital expenditure can be relieved under the trade cash basis, further amendments have been made to ensure that the rules for mineral extraction allowances, know-how allowances and patent allowances follow those already established for plant and machinery allowances. Where there is unrelieved qualifying expenditure for mineral extraction allowances and know-how allowances, a cash basis deduction is allowed for such expenditure, so long as the amounts have actually been paid. Likewise, on leaving the cash basis, a trader will bring back any unrelieved capital expenditure into the relevant capital allowance pool. The provisions for mineral extraction allowances are introduced by CAA 2001 ss 419A and 431D. The provisions for know-how allowances are introduced by CAA 2001 ss 461A and 462A. The provisions for patent allowances are introduced by CAA 2001 ss 475A and 477A

Note that despite the introduction of these provisions, mineral extraction trades are currently excluded trades for cash basis purposes.

ITA 2007 s 127BA Restriction of relief: cash basis

If a person makes a loss from a property business using the cash basis, the loss cannot be relieved against general income.

Part 4 – Commencement and transitional provision

The amendments made by Schedule 2 have effect for the tax year 2017/18 and subsequent years.

SCHEDULE 3

TRADING AND PROPERTY ALLOWANCES

Section 17

PART 1

MAIN PROVISIONS

1 In ITTOIA 2005, after section 783 insert—

"PART 6A

INCOME CHARGED UNDER THIS ACT: TRADING AND PROPERTY ALLOWANCES

CHAPTER 1

TRADING ALLOWANCE

Introduction

783A Relief under this Chapter

  (1) This Chapter gives relief to an individual on—

    (a) the income of a relevant trade (see section 783AA), and

(b) miscellaneous income (see section 783AB).

(2) If the individual qualifies for full relief (see section 783AE), the individual's relevant income (see section 783AC) is not charged to income tax (see sections 783AF and 783AG).

(3) If the individual qualifies for partial relief (see section 783AH), the individual's relevant income is calculated by alternative methods (see sections 783AI to 783AK).

(4) Any provision of this Chapter which gives relief is subject to sections 783AN to 783AQ, which specify circumstances in which relief under this Chapter is not given.

Basic definitions

783AA "Relevant trade" of an individual

(1) For the purposes of this Chapter, a trade carried on by an individual is a "relevant trade" of the individual for a tax year if—

(a) the individual carries on the trade otherwise than in partnership, and

(b) the trade is not a rent-a-room trade in relation to the individual for the tax year.

(2) For the purposes of subsection (1)(b) a trade is a "rent-a-room trade" in relation to an individual for a tax year if—

(a) the individual qualifies for rent-a-room relief for the tax year, and

(b) the individual has rent-a-room receipts for the tax year which would, apart from Chapter 1 of Part 7 (rent-a-room relief), be brought into account in calculating the profits of the trade.

See section 783AR for definitions relevant to this subsection.

(3) In this Chapter references to a trade include references to a profession or vocation.

783AB "Miscellaneous income"

(1) For the purposes of this Chapter, an individual's "miscellaneous income" for a tax year is all the income arising to the individual in the tax year which would be chargeable to income tax under Chapter 8 of Part 5 (income not otherwise charged) for the tax year.

(2) But if—

(a) the individual qualifies for rent-a-room relief for the tax year, and

(b) the individual has rent-a-room receipts for the tax year which would, apart from Chapter 1 of Part 7, be chargeable to income tax under Chapter 8 of Part 5,

the rent-a-room receiptsare not miscellaneous income.

(3) The reference in subsection (1) to the amount which would be chargeable to income tax under Chapter 8 of Part 5 is to the amount which would be so chargeable—

(a) apart from this Chapter, and

(b) if no deduction were made for expenses or any other matter.

783AC The individual's "relevant income"

(1) For the purposes of this Chapter, an individual's "relevant income" for a tax year is the sum of the following—

(a) the receipts for the tax year of the individual's relevant trades for the tax year, and

(b) the individual's miscellaneous income for the tax year.

(2) In subsection (1)(a) the reference to the receipts of a trade for a tax year is to all the amounts which would, apart from this Chapter, be brought into account as a receipt in calculating the profits of the trade for the tax year.

783AD The individual's trading allowance

(1) For the purposes of this Chapter, an individual's trading allowance for a tax year is £1,000.

(2) The Treasury may by regulations amend subsection (1) so as to substitute a higher sum for the sum for the time being specified in that subsection.

Full relief

783AE Full relief: introduction

(1) An individual qualifies for full relief for a tax year if—

(a) the individual has relevant income for the tax year,

(b) the relevant income does not exceed the individual's trading allowance for the tax year, and

(c) no election by the individual under section 783AL has effect for the tax year (election for full relief not to be given).

(2) An individual also qualifies for full relief for a tax year if—

(a) the individual has relevant income for the tax year which consists of or includes receipts of one or more relevant trades,

(b) the relevant income exceeds the individual's trading allowance for the tax year,

(c) the conditions mentioned in subsection (3) are met,

(d) no election by the individual under section 783AL has effect for the tax year, and

(e) no election by the individual under section 783AM has effect for the tax year (election for partial relief).

(3) The conditions are that—

(a) no election by the individual under section 25A (cash basis for trades) has effect for the tax year,

(b) the individual's relevant income would not exceed the individual's trading allowance for the tax year if it were to be assumed that an election by the individual under section 25A had effect for the tax year,

(c) the individual is eligible to make an election under section 25A (see section 31A) for the tax year, and

(d) if any trade carried on by the individual in the tax year was carried on in the immediately preceding tax year—

   (i) an election by the individual under section 25A had effect for that preceding tax year, or

   (ii) the individual was eligible to make such an election for that preceding tax year.

783AF Full relief: trade profits

(1) This section applies if—

(a) an individual qualifies for full relief for a tax year, and

(b) the individual's relevant income for the tax year consists of or includes receipts of one or more relevant trades.

(2) The profits or losses of each such trade for the tax year are treated as nil.

783AG Full relief: miscellaneous income

(1) This section applies if—

(a) an individual qualifies for full relief for a tax year, and

(b) the individual's relevant income for the tax year consists of or includes miscellaneous income.

(2) The amount of—

(a) the miscellaneous income arising in the tax year, less

(b) any expenses associated with that income,

is treated as nil.

Partial relief

783AH Partial relief: alternative calculation of profits: introduction

An individual qualifies for partial relief for a tax year if—

(a) the individual has relevant income for the tax year,

(b) the relevant income exceeds the individual's trading allowance for the tax year, and

(c) an election by the individual under section 783AM has effect for the tax year (election for partial relief).

783AI Partial relief: alternative calculation of trade profits

(1) This section applies if—

(a) an individual qualifies for partial relief for a tax year, and

(b) the individual's relevant income for the tax year consists of or includes receipts of one or more relevant trades.

(2) The profits or losses for the tax year of each of the individual's relevant trades are given by taking the following steps—

Step 1

Calculate the total of all the amounts which would, apart from this Chapter, be brought into account as a receipt in calculating the profits of the trade for the tax year.

Step 2

Subtract the deductible amount.

Step 3

Subtract from the amount given by step 2 any deduction for overlap profit allowed in calculating the profits of the trade for the tax year under section 205 (deduction for overlap profit in final tax year) or section 220 (deduction for overlap profit on change of accounting date).

(3) Subject to section 783AK, the deductible amount is equal to the individual's trading allowance for the tax year.

(4) "Overlap profit" has the same meaning in this section as it has in Chapter 15 of Part 2 (see sections 204 and 204A).

783AJ Partial relief: alternative calculation of chargeable miscellaneous income

(1) This section applies if—

    (a) an individual qualifies for partial relief for a tax year, and
    (b) the individual's relevant income for the tax year consists of or includes miscellaneous income.

(2) The amount of miscellaneous income chargeable to income tax for the tax year is—

    (a) the miscellaneous income for the tax year, less
    (b) the deductible amount.

(3) Subject to section 783AK, the deductible amount is equal to the individual's trading allowance for the tax year.

783AK Deductible amount: splitting of trading allowance

(1) This section applies where the individual's relevant income for the tax year includes—

    (a) receipts of a relevant trade, and
    (b) receipts of any other relevant trade or miscellaneous income (or both).

(2) The references in section 783AI and (where it applies) section 783AJ to the deductible amount are to amounts which, in total, equal the individual's trading allowance for the tax year.

(3) The question of how to allocate the individual's trading allowance for the tax year for the purposes of subsection (2) is to be decided by the individual, subject to subsections (4) and (5).

(4) The deductible amount in respect of a relevant trade must not be such that the amount given by step 2 of section 783AI(2) is negative.

(5) The deductible amount in respect of miscellaneous income must not be such as to result in the individual making a loss in the transactions giving rise to the miscellaneous income.

Elections

783AL Election for full relief not to be given

(1) An individual may elect not to be given full relief for a tax year (see sections 783AF and 783AG).

(2) An election must be made on or before the first anniversary of the normal self-assessment filing date for the tax year for which the election is made.

783AM Election for partial relief

(1) An individual may elect for partial relief to be given for a tax year if the individual's relevant income for the tax year exceeds the individual's trading allowance for the tax year (see sections 783AI and 783AJ).

(2) An election must be made on or before the first anniversary of the normal self-assessment filing date for the tax year for which the election is made.

Exclusions from relief

783AN Exclusion from relief: expenses deducted against rent-a-room receipts

(1) No relief under this Chapter is given to an individual for a tax year if—

(a) the individual qualifies for rent-a-room relief for the tax year,

(b) the individual has rent-a-room receipts mentioned in subsection (2) for the tax year, and

(c) condition A or B is met.

(2) The rent-a-room receipts mentioned in subsection (1) are—

(a) rent-a-room receipts which would, apart from Chapter 1 of Part 7 (rent-a-room relief), be brought into account in calculating the profits of a trade, or

(b) rent-a-room receipts which would, apart from Chapter 1 of Part 7, be chargeable to income tax under Chapter 8 of Part 5 (income not otherwise charged).

(3) Condition A is that—

(a) the individual's total rent-a-room amount for the tax year does not exceed the individual's limit for the tax year (see section 783AR), and

(b) an election by the individual under section 799 has effect to disapply full rent-a-room relief for the tax year.

(4) Condition B is that—

(a) the individual's total rent-a-room amount for the tax year exceeds the individual's limit for the tax year, and

(b) no election by the individual under section 800 has effect to apply the alternative method of calculating profits for the tax year.

783AO Exclusion from relief: payments by employer

No relief under this Chapter is given to an individual for a tax year if—

(a) the individual has relevant income for the tax year, and

(b) the income includes a payment made by, or on behalf of, a person at a time when the individual is—

(i) an employee of the person, or

(ii) the spouse or civil partner of an employee of the person.

783AP Exclusion from relief: payments by firm

No relief under this Chapter is given to an individual for a tax year if—

(a) the individual has relevant income for the tax year, and

(b) the income includes a payment made by, or on behalf of, a firm at a time when the individual is—

(i) a partner in the firm, or

(ii) connected with a partner in the firm.

783AQ Exclusion from relief: payments by close company

(1) No relief under this Chapter is given to an individual for a tax year if—

(a) the individual has relevant income for the tax year, and

(b) the income includes a payment made by, or on behalf of, a close company at a time when the individual is—

(i) a participator in the close company, or

(ii) an associate of a participator in the close company.

(2) In this section "associate" and "participator" have the same meanings as in Part 10 of CTA 2010 (see sections 448 and 454).

Interpretation

783AR Interpretation of this Chapter

In this Chapter—

(a) "rent-a-room relief", "rent-a-room receipts" and "total rent-a-room amount" have the same meanings as in Chapter 1 of Part 7 (rent-a-room relief: see sections 784, 786 and 788), and

(b) references to "the individual's limit" are to be construed in accordance with section 789 (the individual's limit for the purposes of rent-a-room relief).

CHAPTER 2
PROPERTY ALLOWANCE

Introduction

783B Relief under this Chapter

(1) This Chapter gives relief to an individual on certain income of a relevant property business (see sections 783BA and 783BB).

(2) The form of relief depends on whether the individual's relevant property income exceeds the individual's property allowance (see sections 783BC and 783BD).

(3) If the individual's relevant property income does not exceed the individual's property allowance, the income is not charged to income tax (unless the individual elects otherwise) (see sections 783BE and 783BF).

(4) If the individual's relevant property income does exceed the individual's property allowance, the individual may elect for an alternative method of calculating the income (see sections 783BG to 783BI).

(5) Any provision of this Chapter which gives relief is subject to sections 783BL to 783BP, which specify circumstances in which relief under this Chapter is not given.

Basic definitions

783BA "Relevant property business" of an individual

(1) Subject to subsection (3), for the purposes of this Chapter an individual's property business is a "relevant property business" for a tax year if the business is not a rent-a-room property business in relation to the individual for the tax year.

(2) For the purposes of subsection (1) a property business is a "rent-a-room property business" in relation to an individual for a tax year if—

(a) the individual qualifies for rent-a-room relief for the tax year, and

(b) all the receipts which would, apart from Chapter 1 of Part 7 (rent-a-room relief), be brought into account in calculating the profits of the business, are rent-a-room receipts.

See section 783BQ for definitions relevant to this subsection.

(3) If an individual receives—

(a) property income distributions which are treated as profits of a UK property business by virtue of regulation 69Z18(1) or (2) of the AIF Regulations (property AIF distributions: liability to tax), or

(b) distributions which are treated as profits of a UK property business by virtue of section 548(6) of CTA 2010 (REIT distributions: liability to tax),

that separate property business (see regulation 69Z18(6) of the AIF Regulations and section 549(5) of CTA 2010) is not a relevant property business of the individual.

(4) In subsection (3) "the AIF Regulations" means the Authorised Investment Funds (Tax) Regulations 2006 (S.I. 2006/964).

783BB "Relievable receipts" of a property business

(1) For the purposes of this Chapter, the "relievable receipts" of an individual's relevant property business for a tax year are all the amounts which would, apart from this Chapter, be brought into account as a receipt in calculating the profits of the business for the tax year.

This is subject to subsections (2) and (3).

(2) If—

(a) the individual qualifies for rent-a-room relief for the tax year, and

(b) the individual has rent-a-room receipts for the tax year which would, apart from Chapter 1 of Part 7, be brought into account in calculating the profits of the property business,

the rent-a-room receipts are not relievable receipts of the business.

(3) Non-relievable balancing charges in respect of the property business for the tax year are not relievable receipts of the business.

(4) In subsection (3) "non-relievable balancing charges", in respect of a property business for a tax year, means balancing charges falling to be made for the tax year under Part 2 of CAA 2001 which do not relate to a business or transaction which is carried on, or entered into, for the purpose of generating receipts which are relievable receipts of the property business.

783BC The individual's "relevant property income"

For the purposes of this Chapter, an individual's "relevant property income" for a tax year is the relievable receipts for the tax year of the individual's relevant property businesses for the tax year.

783BD The individual's property allowance

(1) For the purposes of this Chapter, an individual's property allowance for a tax year is £1,000.

(2) The Treasury may by regulations amend subsection (1) so as to substitute a higher sum for the sum for the time being specified in that subsection.

Relief if relevant property income does not exceed property allowance

783BE Full relief: introduction

An individual qualifies for full relief for a tax year if—

(a) the individual has relevant property income for the tax year,

(b) the relevant property income does not exceed the individual's property allowance for the tax year, and

(c) no election by the individual under section 783BJ has effect for the tax year (election for full relief not to be given).

783BF Full relief: property profits

(1) If an individual qualifies for full relief for a tax year, this section applies in relation to the calculation of the profits of the individual's relevant property business for the tax year or, where the individual's relevant property income for the tax year consists of the relievable receipts of two relevant property businesses, the profits of each property business for the tax year.

(2) The following are not brought into account—

(a) the relievable receipts of the property business for the tax year, and

(b) any expenses associated with those receipts.

Relief if relevant property income exceeds property allowance

783BG Partial relief: alternative calculation of property profits: introduction

An individual qualifies for partial relief for a tax year if—

(a) the individual has relevant property income for the tax year,

(b) the relevant property income exceeds the individual's property allowance for the tax year, and

(c) an election by the individual under section 783BK has effect for the tax year (election for partial relief).

783BH Partial relief: alternative calculation of property profits

(1) If an individual qualifies for partial relief for a tax year, this section applies in relation to the calculation of the profits of the individual's relevant property business for the tax year or, where the individual's relevant property income for the tax year consists of the relievable receipts of two relevant property businesses, the profits of each property business for the tax year.

(2) The relievable receipts of the property business for the tax year are brought into account.

(3) No relevant expenses are brought into account.

(4) The deductible amount is brought into account.

(5) Subject to section 783BI, the deductible amount is equal to the individual's property allowance for the tax year.

(6) In subsection (3) "relevant expenses" means all the amounts—

(a) which would, apart from this section, be brought into account as a deduction in calculating the profits of the business for the tax year, and

(b) which are associated with the relievable receipts.

783BI Deductible amount: splitting of property allowance

(1) This section applies where the individual's relevant property income for the tax year consists of the relievable receipts of two relevant property businesses.

(2) The references in section 783BH to the deductible amount are to amounts which, in total, equal the individual's property allowance for the tax year.

(3) The question of how to allocate the individual's property allowance for the tax year for the purposes of subsection (2) is to be decided by the individual, subject to subsection (4).

(4) The deductible amount in respect of a relevant property business must not be such as to result in a loss of the business.

Elections

783BJ Election for full relief not to be given

(1) An individual may elect not to be given full relief for a tax year (see section 783BF).

(2) An election must be made on or before the first anniversary of the normal self-assessment filing date for the tax year for which the election is made.

783BK Election for partial relief

(1) An individual may elect for partial relief to be given for a tax year if the individual's relevant property income for the tax year exceeds the individual's property allowance for the tax year (see section 783BH).

(2) An election must be made on or before the first anniversary of the normal self-assessment filing date for the tax year for which the election is made.

Exclusions from relief

783BL Exclusion from relief: tax reduction under section 274A

No relief under this Chapter is given to an individual for a tax year if, in calculating the individual's liability to income tax for the tax year, a tax reduction under section 274A (property business: relief for non-deductible costs of a dwelling-related loan) is applied at Step 6 of the calculation in section 23 of ITA 2007.

783BM Exclusion from relief: expenses deducted against rent-a-room receipts

(1) No relief under this Chapter is given to an individual for a tax year if—

(a) the individual qualifies for rent-a-room relief for the tax year,

(b) the individual has rent-a-room receipts for the tax year which would, apart from Chapter 1 of Part 7 (rent-a-room relief), be brought into account in calculating the profits of a property business, and

(c) condition A or B is met.

(2) Condition A is that—

(a) the individual's total rent-a-room amount for the tax year does not exceed the individual's limit for the tax year (see section 783BQ), and

(b) an election by the individual under section 799 has effect to disapply full rent-a-room relief for the tax year.

(3) Condition B is that—

(a) the individual's total rent-a-room amount for the tax year exceeds the individual's limit for the tax year, and

(b) no election by the individual under section 800 has effect to apply the alternative method of calculating profits for the tax year.

783BN Exclusion from relief: payments by employer

No relief under this Chapter is given to an individual for a tax year if—

(a) the individual has relevant property income for the tax year, and

(b) the income includes a payment made by, or on behalf of, a person at a time when the individual is—

(i) an employee of the person, or

(ii) the spouse or civil partner of an employee of the person.

783BO Exclusion from relief: payments by firm

No relief under this Chapter is given to an individual for a tax year if—

(a) the individual has relevant property income for the tax year, and

(b) the income includes a payment made by, or on behalf of, a firm at a time when the individual is—

(i) a partner in the firm, or

(ii) connected with a partner in the firm.

783BP Exclusion from relief: payments by close company

(1) No relief under this Chapter is given to an individual for a tax year if—

   (a) the individual has relevant property income for the tax year, and
   (b) the income includes a payment made by, or on behalf of, a close company at a time when the individual is—

      (i) a participator in the close company, or
      (ii) an associate of a participator in the close company.

(2) In this section "associate" and "participator" have the same meanings as in Part 10 of CTA 2010 (see sections 448 and 454).

Interpretation

783BQ Interpretation of this Chapter

In this Chapter—

   (a) "rent-a-room relief", "rent-a-room receipts" and "total rent-a-room amount" have the same meanings as in Chapter 1 of Part 7 (rent-a-room relief: see sections 784, 786 and 788), and
   (b) references to "the individual's limit" are to be construed in accordance with section 789 (the individual's limit for the purposes of rent-a-room relief)."

PART 2

CONSEQUENTIAL AMENDMENTS

ITTOIA 2005

2 ITTOIA 2005 is amended in accordance with paragraphs 3 to 11.

3 In section 1 (overview of Act), before paragraph (a) of subsection (5) insert—

   "(za) provision about a trading allowance and property allowance (see Part 6A),".

4 In Chapter 2 of Part 2 (trading income: income taxed as trade profits), after section 22 insert—

"Trading allowance

22A Trading allowance

(1) The rules for calculating the profits of a trade, profession or vocation carried on by an individual are subject to Chapter 1 of Part 6A (trading allowance).

(2) That Chapter gives relief on relevant income and, where relief is given, disallows most deductions under this Part (see, in particular, sections 783AC, 783AF and 783AI)."

5 In Chapter 15 of Part 2 (basis periods), after section 204 insert—

"204A Overlap profit and trading allowance under Chapter 1 of Part 6A

(1) This section makes provision about the amount of profit treated as arising in an overlap period which falls within the basis period of a trade for two tax years ("tax year A" and "tax year B") where relief is given under Chapter 1 of Part 6A (trading allowance) in respect of the trade for at least one of those tax years.

(2) The profit which arises in the overlap period is treated as nil if—

   (a) the profits or losses of the trade for tax year A or tax year B (or both) are treated as nil under section 783AF (full relief: trade profits), or
   (b) in relation to tax year A or tax year B (or both)—

      (i) section 783AI applies in calculating the profits or losses of the trade (partial relief: alternative calculation of trade profits), and
      (ii) the deductible amount subtracted at step 2 of section 783AI(2) in relation to the trade is greater than or equal to the non-adjusted overlap profit.

(3) Subsection (6) applies if conditions 1 and 2 are met.

(4) Condition 1 is that, in relation to either tax year A or tax year B—

   (a) section 783AI applies in calculating the profits or losses of the trade, and
   (b) the deductible amount subtracted at step 2 of section 783AI(2) in relation to the trade is less than the non-adjusted overlap profit.

(5) Condition 2 is that neither section 783AF nor section 783AI applies in relation to the trade—

   (a) where condition 1 is met in relation to tax year A, for tax year B, or
   (b) where condition 1 is met in relation to tax year B, for tax year A.

(6) The profit which arises in the overlap period is treated as equal to the non-adjusted overlap profit less the deductible amount mentioned in subsection (4)(b).

(7) Subsection (8) applies if, in relation to each of tax year A and tax year B—

(a) section 783AI applies in calculating the profits or losses of the trade, and
(b) the deductible amount subtracted at step 2 of section 783AI(2) in relation to the trade is less than the non-adjusted overlap profit.

(8) The profit which arises in the overlap period is treated as equal to the non-adjusted overlap profit less the higher of the following—

(a) the deductible amount subtracted at step 2 of section 783AI(2) in calculating the profits or losses of the trade for tax year A, and
(b) the deductible amount subtracted at step 2 of section 783AI(2) in calculating the profits or losses of the trade for tax year B.

(9) In this section "non-adjusted overlap profit" means the amount of profit that would arise in the overlap period apart from—

(a) Chapter 1 of Part 6A, and
(b) this section."

6 In section 227A (application of Chapter where cash basis used), after subsection (2) insert—

"(3) This section is subject to section 227C (application of Chapter where section 227B applies)."

7 After section 227A insert—

"227B Cash basis treatment: full relief under Chapter 1 of Part 6A (trading allowance)

(1) Subsection (2) applies if—

(a) an individual carries on a trade in a tax year, and
(b) the profits or losses of the trade for the tax year are treated as nil under section 783AF (trade profits: full relief under Chapter 1 of Part 6A) by virtue of the fact that the conditions in section 783AE(2) are met.

(2) For the purposes of determining if this Chapter applies, an election under section 25A is to be treated as having effect in relation to the trade for the tax year.

227C Application of Chapter where section 227B applies

(1) This section applies if, as a result of the operation of section 227B, the basis on which profits of a trade are calculated is treated as changed as mentioned in section 227A(1).

(2) This Chapter applies as if—

(a) in sections 232(1) and 233(1), for "the first period of account for which the new basis is adopted" there were substituted "the first tax year for which the profits or losses of the trade are not treated as nil under section 783AF", and
(b) sections 235, 236, 237, 239A and 239B were omitted.

(3) If there is no tax year after the change of basis for which the profits or losses of the trade are not treated as nil under section 783AF, this Chapter does not apply."

8 After section 307F (inserted by Schedule 2 to this Act) insert—

"Property allowance

307G Property allowance

(1) The rules for calculating the profits of an individual's property business are subject to Chapter 2 of Part 6A (property allowance).

(2) That Chapter gives relief on relevant property income and, where relief is given, disallows all deductions under this Part which relate to that income (see, in particular, sections 783BC, 783BF and 783BH)."

9 In section 688 (income charged under Chapter 8 of Part 5), before paragraph (a) of subsection (2) insert—

"(za) Chapter 1 of Part 6A (which gives relief on relevant income which may consist of or include income chargeable under this Chapter: see, in particular, sections 783AB, 783AC, 783AG and 783AJ),".

10 In section 828 (overlap profit), in subsection (3), for "section 204" substitute "sections 204 and 204A".

11 In Part 2 of Schedule 4 (defined expressions)—

(a) at the appropriate places insert—

"individual's property allowance (in Chapter 2 of Part 6A) | section 783BD

individual's trading allowance (in Chapter 1 of Part 6A)	section 783AD
miscellaneous income (in Chapter 1 of Part 6A)	section 783AB
relevant income (in Chapter 1 of Part 6A)	section 783AC
relevant property business (in Chapter 2 of Part 6A)	section 783BA
relevant property income (in Chapter 2 of Part 6A)	section 783BC
relevant trade (in Chapter 1 of Part 6A)	section 783AA
relievable receipts (in Chapter 2 of Part 6A)	section 783BB",

  (b) in the entry for "overlap profit", for "section 204" substitute "sections 204 and 204A".

TIOPA 2010

12 In TIOPA 2010—

  (a) in section 22(8) (credit for foreign tax on overlap profit if credit for that tax already allowed), in the definition of "overlap profit", for "section 204" substitute "sections 204 and 204A", and

  (b) in section 24(8) (claw-back of relief under section 22(2)), in the definition of "overlap profit", for "section 204" substitute "sections 204 and 204A".

PART 3

COMMENCEMENT

13 The amendments made by this Schedule have effect for the tax year 2017–18 and subsequent tax years.

GENERAL NOTE

Part 1 – Main provisions

ITTOIA 2005 Pt 6A, Ch 1 – Trading allowance

This chapter looks at the relief for individuals who have:

– Income from a relevant trade;
– Miscellaneous income.

Relevant trade is defined as:

– An individual carrying on a trade – excluding partnerships and if claiming rent a room relief.

Miscellaneous income is defined as:

– Income not otherwise chargeable (ITTOIA 2005 Pt 5 Ch 8).

The trading allowance is £1,000 per year.

The trading allowance can be claimed if an individual has income from a relevant trade or miscellaneous income. The trading allowance can be claimed even if there are multiple relevant trades, or an individual has both relevant trade income and miscellaneous income.

The maximum trading allowance per person, per year, is £1,000 – irrespective of the number of relevant trades or if there is relevant trade income and miscellaneous income.

If the relevant trading income or miscellaneous income is £1,000 or less, that income receives full relief and is not charged to income tax.

If the relevant trading income or miscellaneous income exceeds £1,000 for the year, an election can be made and the trading allowance can still be claimed. The expenses associated to that income cannot be claimed though (you either claim the actual expenses or the £1,000 trading allowance).

If an individual has relevant trade income or miscellaneous income (of £1,000 or less) and the expenses would create a loss, by using the trading allowance that loss will be treated as nil. Before the introduction of the trading allowance, that loss could be carried forward against future profits, offset against other income in the current year or carried back.

An individual can elect not to use the trading allowance.

Exclusions from the relief:

– receiving payments from an employer, or your spouse or civil partner receiving payments from an employer;

- receiving income from a firm where you are a partner or connected with a partner of the firm;
- payments from a close company where you are a participator or associate of a participator.

ITTOIA 2005 Pt 6A, Ch 2 – Property allowance

This chapter gives relief to an individual on certain property business income. If the individual's property income does not exceed the property allowance, the income is not charged to income tax (unless the individual elects otherwise).

If the individual's income does exceed the property allowance, the individual can elect for an alternative method to calculate the taxable income.

An individual's property business is a relevant property business if the business is not a rent-a-room property business for the tax year.

The individual's property allowance is £1,000 for the tax year.

An individual qualifies for full relief for a tax year if the individual has relevant property income for the year, does not exceed £1,000 and the individual has not elected out of full relief.

If the individual qualifies for full relief, the income and expenses of the property business are not brought into account for income tax.

Previously, if an individual made a property loss, then the loss would be carried forward against future property profits. By claiming the property allowance, if the expenses do exceed the income, that property loss will not be available for future relief.

Partial relief can be claimed if the relevant property income exceeds the property allowance and an election is made for partial relief. No expenses are brought into account for the tax year if partial relief is claimed.

If the individual has more than one property businesses, the property allowance can be split amongst the businesses, but a property loss cannot be created.

An individual can elect not to use the property allowance.

Exclusions from the relief:

- receiving payments from an employer, or your spouse or civil partner receiving payments from an employer;
- receiving income from a firm where you are a partner or connected with a partner of the firm;
- payments from a close company where you are a participator or associate of a participator.

Commencement

The amendments made by this schedule have effect for the tax year 2017/18 and subsequent tax years.

SCHEDULE 4

RELIEF FOR CARRIED-FORWARD LOSSES

Section 18

PART 1

AMENDMENT OF GENERAL RULES ABOUT CARRYING FORWARD LOSSES

Non-trading deficits from loan relationships

1 Part 5 of CTA 2009 (loan relationships) is amended as follows.

2 In the heading of Chapter 16 (non-trading deficits) at the end insert ": pre-1 April 2017 deficits and charities".

3 In section 456 (introduction to Chapter 16) in subsection (1)—

    (a) after "if" insert "—

        (a) ", and

    (b) at the end insert ", and

        (b) either—

            (i) that accounting period begins before 1 April 2017, or

(ii) at the end of that accounting period the company is a charity".

4 After section 463 insert—

"CHAPTER 16A

NON-TRADING DEFICITS: POST 1 APRIL 2017 DEFICITS

463A Introduction to Chapter

(1) This Chapter applies if—

(a) for any accounting period beginning on or after 1 April 2017 a company has a non-trading deficit from its loan relationships under section 301(6), and

(b) at the end of that accounting period the company is not a charity.

(2) In this Chapter "the deficit" and "the deficit period" mean that deficit and that period respectively.

(3) Sections 463B and 463C deal with claims to set off the deficit against profits of the deficit period or earlier periods.

(4) Sections 463D to 463F deal with the consequences of such claims.

(5) Sections 463G to 463I provide for so much of the deficit as is not—

(a) set off against profits under section 463B, or

(b) surrendered as group relief under Part 5 of CTA 2010,

to be carried forward to later accounting periods.

463B Claim to set off deficit against profits of deficit period or earlier periods

(1) The company may make a claim for the whole or part of the deficit—

(a) to be set off against any profits of the company (of whatever description) for the deficit period, or

(b) to be carried back to be set off against profits for earlier accounting periods.

(2) No claim may be made under subsection (1) in respect of so much of the deficit as is surrendered as group relief under Part 5 of CTA 2010.

(3) For time limits and other provisions applicable to claims under subsection (1), see section 463C.

(4) For what happens when a claim is made under subsection (1)(a), see section 463D.

(5) For what happens when a claim is made under subsection (1)(b), and the profits available for relief when such a claim is made, see sections 463E and 463F.

463C Time limits for claims under section 463B(1)

(1) A claim under section 463B(1) must be made within—

(a) the period of 2 years after the deficit period ends, or

(b) such further period as an officer of Revenue and Customs allows.

(2) Different claims may be made in respect of different parts of a non-trading deficit for any deficit period.

(3) But no claim may be made in respect of any part of a deficit to which another such claim relates.

463D Claim to set off deficit against profits for the deficit period

(1) This section applies if a claim is made under section 463B(1)(a) for the whole or part of the deficit to be set off against profits for the deficit period.

(2) The amount of the deficit to which the claim relates must be set off against the profits of the company for the deficit period which are identified in the claim.

(3) Those profits are reduced accordingly.

(4) Relief under this section must be given before relief is given against profits for the deficit period—

(a) under section 37 or 62(1) to (3) of CTA 2010 (deduction of losses from total profits for the same or earlier accounting periods), or

(b) as a result of a claim under section 463B(1)(b) (carry-back) in respect of a deficit for a later period.

(5) No relief may be given under this section against ring fence profits of the company within the meaning of Part 8 of CTA 2010 (oil activities) or contractor's ring fence profits of the company within the meaning of Part 8ZA of that Act (oil contractors).

463E Claim to carry back deficit to earlier periods

(1) This section applies if a claim is made under section 463B(1)(b) for the whole or part of the deficit to be carried back to be set off against profits for accounting periods before the deficit period.

(2) The claim has effect only if it relates to an amount no greater than the lesser of—

(a) so much of the deficit as is not an amount in relation to which a claim is made under section 463B(1)(a), and

(b) the total amount of the profits available for relief under this section.

(3) Section 463F explains which profits are so available.

(4) The amount to which the claim relates is set off against those profits by treating them as reduced accordingly.

(5) If those profits are profits for more than one accounting period, the relief is applied by setting off the amount to which the claim relates against profits for a later period before setting off any remainder of that amount against profits for an earlier period.

463F Profits available for relief under section 463E

(1) The profits available for relief under section 463E are the amounts which (apart from the relief) would be charged under this Part as profits for accounting periods ending within the permitted period after giving every prior relief.

(2) In this section—

"the permitted period" means the period of 12 months immediately before the deficit period, and

"prior relief" means a relief which subsection (5) provides must be given before relief under section 463E.

(3) If an accounting period ending within the permitted period begins before it, only a part of the amount which (apart from the relief) would be chargeable under this Part for the period, after giving every prior relief, is available for relief under section 463E.

(4) That part is so much as is proportionate to the part of the accounting period in the permitted period.

(5) The reliefs which must be given before relief under section 463E are—

(a) relief as a result of a claim under section 459(1)(a) or section 463B(1)(a) (claim for deficit to be set off against total profits for the deficit period),

(b) relief in respect of a loss or deficit incurred or treated as incurred in an accounting period before the deficit period,

(c) relief under Part 6 of CTA 2010 (charitable donations relief in respect of payments made wholly and exclusively for the purposes of a trade),

(d) relief under section 37 of CTA 2010 (losses deducted from total profits of the same or an earlier accounting period), and

(e) if the company is a company with investment business for the purposes of Part 16 (companies with investment business)—

(i) any deduction in respect of management expenses under section 1219 (expenses of management of a company's investment business),

(ii) relief under Part 6 of CTA 2010 in respect of payments made wholly and exclusively for the purposes of its business, and

(iii) any allowance under Part 2 of CAA 2001 (plant and machinery allowances).

463G Carry forward of unrelieved deficit against total profits

(1) This section applies if conditions A to D are met.

(2) Condition A is that—

(a) any amount of the deficit ("the unrelieved amount") is not—

(i) set off against profits on a claim under section 463B(1), or

(ii) surrendered as group relief under Part 5 of CTA 2010.

(3) Condition B is that it is not the case—

(a) that the company ceased to be a company with investment business in the deficit period, or

(b) (if the company was a company with investment business immediately before the beginning of the deficit period) that its investment business became small or negligible in the deficit period.

(4) Condition C is that (if the company is a Solvency 2 insurance company) it is not the case that the whole of the deficit is a shock loss.

(5) Condition D is that (if the company is a general insurance company) the first accounting period after the deficit period is not an excluded accounting period.

(6) The unrelieved amount is carried forward to the first accounting period after the deficit period.

(7) The company may make a claim for the whole or part of the unrelieved amount to be set off against the company's total profits for the first accounting period after the deficit period.

(8) If a claim is made under subsection (7)—

(a) the unrelieved amount, or the part of it to which the claim relates, must be set off against the company's total profits for the first accounting period after the deficit period, and

(b) those profits are reduced accordingly.

(9) No claim may be made under subsection (7) in respect of so much of the unrelieved amount as is surrendered under Part 5A of CTA 2010 (group relief for carried-forward losses).

(10) A claim under subsection (7) must be made within—

(a) the period of two years after the end of the first accounting period after the deficit period, or

(b) such further period as an officer of Revenue and Customs allows.

(11) No relief may be given under this section against ring fence profits of the company within the meaning of Part 8 of CTA 2010 (oil activities) or contractor's ring fence profits of the company within the meaning of Part 8ZA of that Act (oil contractors).

(12) If —

(a) the company is a Solvency 2 insurance company, and

(b) the deficit is partly (but not wholly) a shock loss,

subsections (6) to (9) have effect as if references to the unrelieved amount were to the eligible amount (see subsection (13)).

(13) In this section "the eligible amount" means so much of the unrelieved amount as is not a shock loss; and for the purpose of determining how much of the unrelieved amount is, or is not, a shock loss, it is to be assumed that in setting off or surrendering amounts as mentioned in subsection (2)(a)(i) and (ii) the company uses shock losses before other amounts.

(14) In this Chapter—

"company with investment business" has the same meaning as in Part 16 (see section 1218B);

"excluded accounting period" has the meaning given by section 269ZG of CTA 2010;

"general insurance company" is to be interpreted in accordance with section 269ZG of CTA 2010;

"shock loss" has the meaning given by section 269ZK of CTA 2010;

"Solvency 2 insurance company" means an insurance company as defined in section 269ZP(2) of CTA 2010.

(15) In this Chapter references to a company's investment business are to be construed in accordance with section 1219(2).

463H   Carry forward of unrelieved deficit against non-trading profits

(1) Subsections (4) to (8) apply if—

(a) section 463G would apply but for the fact that the company's investment business became small or negligible in the accounting period mentioned in subsection (3)(b) of that section,

(b) section 463G would apply but for condition D in that section (no carry-forward to an excluded accounting period of a general insurance company), or

(c) the company is a Solvency 2 insurance company and any amount of the deficit would be eligible to be carried forward under section 463G(6) were that amount not a shock loss (see section 463G(4), (12) and (13)).

(2) Subsections (4) to (8) also apply if—

(a) subsections (6) to (10) of section 463G would apply but for the fact that the company's investment business became small or negligible in the accounting period mentioned in section 463I(1)(c)(ii), or

(b) subsections (6) to (10) of section 463G would apply but for section 463I(1)(d) (no carry-forward under those subsections to an excluded accounting period of a general insurance company).

(3) In this section the "unrelieved amount"—

(a) in a case within paragraph (a) or (b) of subsection (1), is to be interpreted in accordance with section 463G(2);

(b) in a case within paragraph (c) of subsection (1), means the amount mentioned in that paragraph;

(c) in a case within subsection (2), means so much of the deficit mentioned in section 463I(1)(a) as is not set off as mentioned in section 463I(1)(b)(i) or surrendered as mentioned in section 463I(1)(b)(ii).

(4) The unrelieved amount is carried forward to the first accounting period ("period 2") after—

(a) (in a case within subsection (1)) the deficit period, or

(b) (in a case within subsection (2)) the period mentioned in section 463I(1)(a).

(5) So much of the unrelieved amount as is not the subject of a claim under subsection (7) must be set off against the non-trading profits of the company for period 2.

(6) Those profits are reduced accordingly.

(7) The company may make a claim for relief under subsection (5) not to be given in period 2 for the unrelieved amount or so much of it as is specified in the claim.

(8) A claim under subsection (7) is effective if, and only if, it is made—

(a) within the period of two years after the end of period 2, or

(b) within such further period as an officer of Revenue and Customs may allow.

(9) Subsection (10) applies if any amount is carried forward under subsection (4) to an accounting period ("the carry forward period") and—

(a) cannot be set off under subsection (5) against non-trading profits of that period, or

(b) is the subject of a claim under subsection (7).

(10) If the company continues to be a company with investment business throughout the carry forward period, subsections (4) to (8) have effect as if—

(a) references to the unrelieved amount were to the amount mentioned in subsection (9), and

(b) references to—

(i) the deficit period, or

(ii) the period mentioned in section 463I(1)(a),

were to the carry forward period.

(11) In this section "non-trading profits", in relation to a company, means so much of the company's profits as does not consist of trading income for the purposes of section 37 of CTA 2010 (deduction of trading losses from total profits of the same or an earlier period).

463I Re-application of section 463G if any deficit remains after previous application

(1) This section applies if—

(a) any amount of the deficit is carried forward to an accounting period ("the later period") of the company under section 463G(6),

(b) any of that amount is not—

(i) set off against the company's total profits for the later period on a claim under section 463G(7), or

(ii) surrendered as group relief for carried-forward losses under Part 5A of CTA 2010,

(c) it is not the case—

(i) that the company ceased to be a company with investment business in the later period, or

(ii) (if the company was a company with investment business immediately before the beginning of the later period) that its investment business became small or negligible in the later period, and

(d) it is not the case that the first accounting period after the later period is an excluded accounting period of a general insurance company.

(2) Subsections (6) to (10) of section 463G apply as if—

(a) references to the unrelieved amount were to so much of the amount of the deficit carried forward to the later period as is not set off or surrendered as mentioned in subsection (1)(b), and

(b) references to the deficit period were to the later period."

Non-trading losses on intangible fixed assets

5 (1) Section 753 of CTA 2009 (treatment of non-trading loss) is amended as follows.

(2) In subsection (3) (carry forward of non-trading loss)—

(a) in the words before paragraph (a), after "not" insert ", in any period ("the reference period")";

(b) in the words after paragraph (b) for "debit of" substitute "loss on intangible fixed assets for".

(3) After subsection (3) insert—

"(4) But subsection (3) does not apply if the company ceased to be a company with investment business in the reference period.

(5) In the application of subsection (3) to an amount of a loss previously carried forward under that subsection, the reference in paragraph (b) to group relief under Part 5 of CTA 2010 is to be read as a reference to group relief for carried-forward losses under Part 5A of that Act.

(6) In this section "company with investment business" has the same meaning as in Part 16 (see section 1218B)."

Expenses of management of investment business etc

6 (1) Section 1223 of CTA 2009 (carrying forward expenses of management and other amounts) is amended as follows.

(2) In subsection (1)(b)—

(a) for "amounts" substitute "an amount", and

(b) after "(2)(c)," insert "—

(i) a claim relating to the whole of the amount has not been made under subsection (3B), or".

(3) After subsection (3) insert—

"(3A) But subsection (3) does not apply in relation to so much of the excess as is surrendered as group relief under Part 5 of CTA 2010 or as group relief for carried-forward losses under Part 5A of that Act.

(3B) A deduction in respect of the excess may be made under section 1219 for the next accounting period only on the making by the company of a claim.

(3C) A claim may relate to the whole of the excess or to part of it only.

(3D) A claim must be made—

(a) within the period of two years after the end of the next accounting period, or

(b) within such further period as an officer of Revenue and Customs may allow.

(3E) Subsection (1A) of section 1219 does not apply in relation to a deduction in respect of the excess made for the next accounting period."

Trading losses

7 Chapter 2 of Part 4 of CTA 2010 (trade losses) is amended as follows.

8 In section 36 (introduction to Chapter) for subsection (1) substitute—

"(1) This Chapter provides relief for a loss made by a company in a trade (see sections 37 to 47)".

9 For the italic heading before section 37 substitute—

"Relief in loss-making period and carry back relief".

10 (1) Section 45 (carry forward of trade loss against subsequent trade profits) is amended as follows.

(2) In the heading, after "of" insert "pre-1 April 2017".

(3) In subsection (1) after "accounting period" insert "beginning before 1 April 2017".

(4) In subsection (4)(b) for "cannot be" substitute "is not".

(5) After subsection (4) insert—

"(4A) But the company may make a claim that the profits of the trade of an accounting period specified in the claim are not to be reduced by the unrelieved loss, or are not to be reduced by the unrelieved loss by more than an amount specified in the claim.

(4B) A claim under subsection (4A) may specify an accounting period only if it begins on or after 1 April 2017.

(4C) A claim under subsection (4A) is effective if, and only if, it is made—

(a) within the period of two years after the end of the accounting period specified in the claim, or

(b) within such further period as an officer of Revenue and Customs may allow."

(6) In subsection (5) for "section" (in the second place it occurs) substitute ", sections 45B, 45F and".

11 After section 45 insert—

"45A Carry forward of post-1 April 2017 trade loss against total profits

(1) This section applies if—

(a) in an accounting period ("the loss-making period") beginning on or after 1 April 2017 a company carrying on a trade makes a loss in the trade,

(b) relief under section 37 or Part 5 (group relief) is not given for an amount of the loss ("the unrelieved amount"),

(c) the company continues to carry on the trade in the next accounting period ("the later period"), and

(d) the conditions in subsection (3) are met.

(2) But this section does not apply if the trade is a ring fence trade.

(3) The conditions are that—

(a) the trade did not become small or negligible in the loss-making period,

(b) relief under section 37 was not unavailable for the loss by reason of —

(i) section 37(5), 44, 48 or 52, or

(ii) section 1209, 1216DA, 1217DA, 1217MA, 1217SA or 1218ZDA of CTA 2009,

(c) relief under section 37 would not be unavailable by reason of section 44 for a loss (assuming there was one) made in the trade in the later period,

(d) if the company is a Solvency 2 insurance company the loss is not a shock loss (see subsections (9) and (10)), and

(e) the later period is not an excluded accounting period of a general insurance company.

(4) The unrelieved amount is carried forward to the later period.

(5) The company may make a claim for relief to be given in the later period for the unrelieved amount or for any part of it specified in the claim.

(6) If the company makes a claim, the relief is given by deducting the unrelieved amount, or the specified part of it, from the company's total profits of the later period.

(7) A claim under this section must be made—

(a) within the period of two years after the end of the later period, or

(b) within such further period as an officer of Revenue and Customs may allow.

(8) Relief under this section is subject to restriction or modification in accordance with provisions of the Corporation Tax Acts.

(9) For the purposes of this section and section 45B, a loss which is partly, but not wholly, a shock loss is to be treated as if—

(a) the amount that is a shock loss, and

(b) the amount that is not,

were separate losses.

(10) In this section—

"excluded accounting period" has the meaning given by section 269ZG;

"general insurance company" is to be interpreted in accordance with section 269ZG(6);

"ring fence trade" has the same meaning as in Part 8 (see section 277);

"Solvency 2 insurance company" means an insurance company as defined in section 269ZP(2);

"shock loss" has the meaning given by section 269ZK.

45B Carry forward of post-1 April 2017 trade loss against trade profits

(1) This section applies if—

(a) in an accounting period ("the loss-making period") beginning on or after 1 April 2017 a company carrying on a trade makes a loss in the trade,

(b) relief under section 37 or 42 or Part 5 (group relief) is not given for an amount of the loss ("the unrelieved amount"),

(c) the company continues to carry on the trade in the next accounting period ("the later period"), and

(d) case 1, 2 or 3 applies.

Case 1 is that any of the conditions in section 45A(3) are not met.

Case 2 is that relief for the unrelieved amount was not available under section 45A by reason of section 1210(5), 1216DB(5) or 1217DB(5) of CTA 2009.

Case 3 is that the trade is a ring fence trade.

(2) The unrelieved amount is carried forward to the later period.

(3) Relief for the unrelieved amount is given to the company in the later period if the company makes a profit in the trade in the later period.

(4) The relief is given by reducing the profits of the trade of the later period by the unrelieved amount.

(5) But the company may make a claim for relief not to be given in the later period for the unrelieved amount or for any part of it specified in the claim.

(6) A claim under subsection (5) is effective if, and only if, it is made—

(a) within the period of two years after the end of the later period, or
(b) within such further period as an officer of Revenue and Customs may allow.

(7) If the trade is a ring fence trade, this section has effect only in relation to so much of the loss mentioned in subsection (1)(a) as is not a non-decommissioning loss.

(8) Relief under this section is subject to restriction or modification in accordance with provisions of the Corporation Tax Acts.

(9) In this section—

"non-decommissioning loss" is to be interpreted in accordance with section 303A;
"ring fence trade" has the same meaning as in Part 8 (see section 277).

(10) See also section 45A(9) (splitting for the purposes of that section and this section of losses that are partly, but not wholly, shock losses of insurance companies).

45C Re-application of section 45A if loss remains after previous application

(1) This section applies if—

(a) an amount of a loss made in a trade is carried forward to an accounting period ("the later period") of a company under section 45A(4),
(b) any of that amount is not deducted from the company's total profits of the later period on a claim under section 45A(5) or surrendered by way of group relief for carried forward-losses under Part 5A,
(c) the company continues to carry on the trade in the accounting period ("the further period") after the later period, and
(d) the conditions in subsection (2) are met.

(2) The conditions are that—

(a) the trade did not become small or negligible in the later period,
(b) relief under section 37 would not be unavailable by reason of section 44 for a loss (assuming there was one) made in the trade in the further period, and
(c) the further period is not an excluded accounting period of a general insurance company.

(3) Subsections (4) to (8) of section 45A apply as if—

(a) references to the unrelieved amount were to so much of the amount carried forward to the later period as is not deducted or surrendered as mentioned in subsection (1)(b), and
(b) references to the later period were to the further period.

(4) In this section "excluded accounting period" and "general insurance company" have the same meaning as in section 45A.

45D Application of section 45B if loss remains after application of section 45A

(1) This section applies if—

(a) an amount of a loss made in a trade is carried forward to an accounting period ("the later period") of a company under section 45A(4),
(b) any of that amount is not deducted from the company's total profits of the later period on a claim under section 45A(5) or surrendered by way of group relief for carried forward-losses under Part 5A,
(c) the company continues to carry on the trade in the accounting period ("the further period") after the later period, and
(d) any of the conditions in section 45C(2) is not met.

(2) Subsections (2) to (8) of section 45B apply as if—

(a) references to the unrelieved amount were to so much of the amount carried forward to the later period as is not deducted or surrendered as mentioned in subsection (1)(b), and

(b) references to the later period were to the further period.

45E Re-application of section 45B if loss remains after previous application

(1) This section applies if—

(a) an amount of a loss made in a trade is carried forward to an accounting period ("the later period") of a company under section 45B(2),

(b) any of that amount is not used under section 45B(4) to reduce profits of the trade for the later period, and

(c) the company continues to carry on the trade in the accounting period ("the further period") after the later period.

(2) Subsections (2) to (8) of section 45B apply as if—

(a) references to the unrelieved amount were to so much of the amount carried forward to the later period as was not used as mentioned in subsection (1)(b), and

(b) references to the later period were to the further period.

45F Terminal losses: relief unrestricted by Part 7ZA and 7A

(1) This section applies if—

(a) a company makes a loss in a trade in an accounting period (the "loss-making period"),

(b) an amount of that loss is carried forward to an accounting period of the company ("the terminal period") under section 45, 45A or 45B,

(c) relief in the terminal period is not given under section 45, 45A or (as the case may be) 45B for that amount or for any part of it, and

(d) the company ceases to carry on the trade in the terminal period.

(2) The company may make a claim for relief to be given for the unrelieved amount under this section.

(3) If the company makes a claim the relief is given by deducting the unrelieved amount from the relevant profits of the company of—

(a) the terminal period, and

(b) previous accounting periods so far as they fall (wholly or partly) within the period of 3 years ending with the end of the terminal period.

(4) But no deduction is to be made under subsection (3) for any accounting period which is—

(a) the loss-making period,

(b) a period before the loss-making period, or

(c) a period beginning before 1 April 2017.

(5) The amount of a deduction to be made under subsection (3) for any accounting period is the amount of the unrelieved amount so far as it cannot be deducted under that subsection for a subsequent accounting period.

(6) The company's claim must be made—

(a) within the period of two years after the end of the terminal period, or

(b) within such further period as an officer of Revenue and Customs may allow.

(7) In this section—

"the unrelieved amount" means so much of the amount mentioned in subsection (1)(b) for which relief is not given in the terminal period under section 45, 45A or (as the case may be) 45B, and

"relevant profits", in relation to the terminal period or any previous accounting period, means—

(a) the total profits of the company of the period, in a case where the unrelieved amount was carried forward to the terminal period under section 45A,

(b) the profits of the trade of the period, in a case where the unrelieved amount was carried forward to the terminal period under section 45 or 45B.

(8) Relief under this section is subject to restriction or modification in accordance with provisions of the Corporation Tax Acts.

45G Section 45F: accounting period falling partly within 3 year period

(1) This section applies if an accounting period falls partly within the period of 3 years mentioned in section 45F(3)(b).

(2) The amount of the deduction for the unrelieved amount for the accounting period is not to exceed an amount equal to the overlapping proportion of the company's relevant profits of that period.

(3) The overlapping proportion is the same as the proportion that the part of the accounting period falling within the period of 3 years bears to the whole of the accounting period.

(4) In this section "the unrelieved amount" and "relevant profits" have the meaning given by section 45F(7).

45H Section 45F: transfers of trade to obtain relief

Section 45F does not apply by reason of a company ceasing to carry on a trade if—

(a) on the company ceasing to carry on the trade, any of the activities of the trade begin to be carried on by a person who is not (or by persons any or all of whom are not) within the charge to corporation tax, and
(b) the company's ceasing to carry on the trade is part of a scheme or arrangement the main purpose, or one of the main purposes, of which is to secure that that section applies by reason of the cessation."

UK property business losses

12 Chapter 4 of Part 4 of CTA 2010 (property losses) is amended as follows.

13 (1) Section 62 (relief for losses made in UK property business) is amended as follows.

(2) In subsection (4)—

(a) in the words before paragraph (a), for "Subsection (5) applies" substitute "Subsections (5) to (5C) apply", and
(b) for paragraph (a) substitute—
"(a) an amount of the loss is not deducted as mentioned in subsection (3) or surrendered by way of group relief under Part 5,".

(3) In subsection (5), for the words before paragraph (a) substitute "The amount".

(4) After subsection (5) insert—

"(5A) But relief under subsection (2) for the amount is given to the company in the next accounting period only on the making by the company of a claim.

(5B) A claim may relate to the whole of the amount or to part of it only.

(5C) A claim must be made—
(a) within the period of two years after the end of the next accounting period, or
(b) within such further period as an officer of Revenue and Customs may allow.

(5D) In the application of this section to an amount of a loss previously carried forward under subsection (5), the reference in subsection (4)(a) to group relief under Part 5 is to be read as a reference to group relief for carried-forward losses under Part 5A."

14 (1) Section 63 (company with investment business ceasing to carry on UK property business) is amended as follows.

(2) For subsection (2) substitute—

"(2) Subsections (3) to (7) apply if an amount of loss made in carrying on the UK property business would be carried forward to the next accounting period under section 62(5) but for the company ceasing to carry on the business or to be within the charge to corporation tax in respect of it."

(3) In subsection (3)(b) for "that" substitute "the next accounting".

(4) After subsection (3) insert—

"(4) But a deduction in respect of the amount of loss may be made under section 1219 of CTA 2009 for the next accounting period only on the making by the company of a claim.

(5) A claim may relate to the whole of the amount of the loss or to part of it only.

(6) A claim must be made—
(a) within the period of two years after the end of the next accounting period, or
(b) within such further period as an officer of Revenue and Customs may allow.

(7) Subsection (1A) of section 1219 of CTA 2009 does not apply in relation to a deduction in respect of the amount of loss made for the next accounting period."

PART 2

RESTRICTION ON DEDUCTIONS IN RESPECT OF CARRIED-FORWARD LOSSES

15 CTA 2010 is amended as follows.

16 After section 269 insert—

"PART 7ZA

RESTRICTIONS ON OBTAINING CERTAIN DEDUCTIONS

Introduction

269ZA Overview of Part

This Part contains provision restricting the amount of certain deductions which a company may make in calculating its taxable total profits for an accounting period.

Restrictions on obtaining certain deductions

269ZB Restriction on deductions from trading profits

(1) This section has effect for determining the taxable total profits of a company for an accounting period.

(2) The sum of any deductions made by the company for the accounting period which fall within subsection (3) may not exceed the relevant maximum.

But this is subject to subsection (10).

(3) The following deductions fall within this subsection—

(a) any deductions under section 45(4)(b) or 45B;
(b) any deduction under section 303B(4) or 303D(5), so far as it is a restricted deduction.

(4) For the purposes of this section a deduction under section 303B(4) or 303D(5) is a "restricted deduction" so far as it would not be available but for section 304(5) (reduction of income derived from related activities).

(5) In this section the "relevant maximum" means the sum of—

(a) 50% of the company's relevant trading profits for the accounting period, and
(b) the company's trading profits deductions allowance for the accounting period.

(6) Section 269ZF contains provision for determining a company's relevant trading profits for an accounting period.

(7) A company's "trading profits deductions allowance" for an accounting period—

(a) is so much of the company's deductions allowance for the period as is specified in the company's tax return as its trading profits deductions allowance for the period, and
(b) accordingly, is nil if no amount of the company's deductions allowance for the period is so specified.

(8) An amount specified under subsection (7)(a) as a company's trading profits deductions allowance for an accounting period may not exceed the difference between—

(a) the amount of the company's deductions allowance for the period, and
(b) the total of any amounts specified for the period under section 269ZC(5)(a) (non-trading profits deductions allowance) and section 124D(4) of FA 2012 (BLAGAB trade profits deductions allowance).

(9) A company's "deductions allowance" for an accounting period is to be determined in accordance with section 269ZR where, at any time in that period—

(a) the company is a member of a group (see section 269ZZB), and
(b) one or more other companies within the charge to corporation tax are members of that group.

Otherwise, a company's "deductions allowance" for an accounting period is to be determined in accordance with section 269ZW.

(10) Subsection (2) does not apply in relation to a company for an accounting period where, in determining the company's relevant trading profits, the amount given by step 1 in section 269ZF(3) is not greater than nil.

269ZC Restriction on deductions from non-trading profits

(1) This section has effect for determining the taxable total profits of a company for an accounting period.

(2) The sum of any deductions made by the company for the accounting period under section 457(3) and 463H(5) of CTA 2009 (carry forward of non-trading deficits from loan relationships against subsequent non-trading profits) may not exceed the relevant maximum.

But this is subject to subsection (8).

(3) In this section the "relevant maximum" means the sum of—

    (a) 50% of the company's relevant non-trading profits for the accounting period, and

    (b) the amount of the company's non-trading profits deductions allowance for the accounting period.

(4) Section 269ZF contains provisions for determining a company's relevant non-trading profits for an accounting period.

(5) A company's "non-trading profits deductions allowance" for an accounting period—

    (a) is so much of the company's deductions allowance for the period as is specified in the company's tax return as its non-trading profits deductions allowance for the period, and

    (b) accordingly, is nil if no amount of the company's deductions allowance for the period is so specified.

(6) An amount specified under subsection (5)(a) as a company's non-trading profits deductions allowance for an accounting period may not exceed the difference between—

    (a) the amount of the company's deductions allowance for the period, and

    (b) the total of any amounts specified for the period under section 269ZB(7)(a) (trading profits deductions allowance) and section 124D(4) of FA 2012 (BLAGAB trade profits deductions allowance).

(7) A company's "deductions allowance" for an accounting period is to be determined in accordance with section 269ZR where, at any time in that period—

    (a) the company is a member of a group (see section 269ZZB), and

    (b) one or more other companies within the charge to corporation tax are members of that group.

Otherwise, a company's "deductions allowance" for an accounting period is to be determined in accordance with section 269ZW.

(8) Subsection (2) does not apply in relation to a company for an accounting period where, in determining the company's relevant non-trading profits for the period, the amount given by step 1 in section 269ZF(3) is not greater than nil.

269ZD Restriction on deductions from total profits

(1) This section has effect for determining the taxable total profits of a company for an accounting period.

(2) The sum of any relevant deductions made by the company for the accounting period may not exceed the difference between—

    (a) the relevant maximum, and

    (b) the sum of—

        (i) any deductions falling within section 269ZB(3) (carry forward of trade loss against subsequent trade profits) made by the company for the accounting period,

        (ii) any deductions made by the company for the accounting period under sections 457(3) and 463H(5) of CTA 2009 (carry forward of non-trading deficits from loan relationships against subsequent non-trading profits), and

        (iii) any deductions made by the company for the accounting period under sections 124(5), 124A(5) and 124C(6) of FA 2012 (carry forward of BLAGAB trade losses against BLAGAB trade profits).

But this is subject to subsection (7) and section 269ZE.

(3) The following deductions made for an accounting period are "relevant deductions" for the purposes of this section—

    (a) a deduction under section 463G of CTA 2009 (carry forward of non-trading deficit against total profits);

(b) a deduction under section 753 of CTA 2009 (non-trading losses on intangible fixed assets) in respect of a loss treated by subsection (3) of that section (carry forward of losses) as if it were a loss of the accounting period;

(c) a deduction under section 1219 of CTA 2009 (expenses of management of a company's investment business) in respect of an amount treated by section 1223(3) of that Act (carrying forward of expenses of management and other amounts) as expenses of management deductible for the accounting period;

(d) a deduction under section 1219 of CTA 2009 (expenses of management of a company's investment business) in respect of a loss treated by section 63(3) (carrying forward of certain losses made by company with investment business which ceases to carry on UK property business) as an expense of management deductible for the accounting period;

(e) a deduction under section 37 (relief for trade losses against total profits) made in reliance on section 1210(3), 1216DB(3), 1217DB(3), 1217MB(2), 1217SB(2) or 1218ZDB(2) of CTA 2009;

(f) a deduction under section 45A (carry forward of trade loss against total profits);

(g) a deduction under section 62(3) (relief for losses made in UK property business) in respect of a loss treated by subsection (5)(b) of that section (carry forward of losses) as a loss made by the company in the accounting period;

(h) a deduction under section 303C (excess carried forward non-decommissioning losses of ring fence trade: relief against total profits);

(i) a deduction under Part 5 (group relief) made in respect of a loss surrendered under that Part in reliance on section 1210(3), 1216DB(3), 1217DB(3), 1217MB(2), 1217SB(2) or 1218ZDB(2) of CTA 2009;

(j) a deduction under Part 5A (group relief for carried-forward losses);

(k) a deduction under section 124B of FA 2012 (deduction from total profits of excess carried-forward BLAGAB trade losses),

(but see section 269ZJ (insurance companies: shock losses)).

(4) In this section the "relevant maximum" means the sum of—

(a) 50% of the company's relevant profits for the accounting period, and

(b) the amount of the company's deductions allowance for the accounting period.

(5) A company's "relevant profits" for an accounting period are the sum of—

(a) the company's relevant trading profits for the accounting period (see section 269ZF(1)),

(b) the company's relevant non-trading profits for the accounting period (see section 269ZF(2), and

(c) the company's relevant BLAGAB trade profits for the accounting period.

In this subsection "relevant BLAGAB trade profits" has the same meaning as in section 124D of FA 2012.

(6) A company's "deductions allowance" for an accounting period is to be determined in accordance with section 269ZR where, at any time in that period—

(a) the company is a member of a group (see section 269ZZB), and

(b) one or more other companies within the charge to corporation tax are members of that group.

Otherwise, the company's "deductions allowance" for the accounting period is to be determined in accordance with section 269ZW.

(7) Subsection (2) does not apply in relation to a company for an accounting period where the sum of—

(a) the amount given by paragraph (1) of step 1 in section 269ZF(3), and

(b) the company's BLAGAB trade profit for the accounting period,

is not greater than nil.

269ZE Restriction on deductions from total profits: insurance companies

(1) Where the conditions in subsection (2) are met, section 269ZD has effect as if, for subsection (2) of that section there were substituted—

"(2) The sum of any relevant deductions made by the company for the accounting period may not exceed the modified loss cap (as defined in section 269ZE).

But this is subject to subsection (7)."

(2) The conditions are that—

(a) the company referred to in section 269ZD(1) carries on business to which the charge to corporation tax under section 68 of FA 2012 (charge to tax on I-E profit) applies and has an I-E profit for the accounting period,

(b) the policyholders' share (if any) of the I-E profit is not the whole of that profit, and

(c) the adjusted shareholders' I-E profit for the accounting period is less than the BLAGAB-related loss capacity.

(3) The "adjusted shareholders' I-E profit" is equal to—

(a) the shareholders' share of the I-E profit, less

(b) any excess capacity.

(4) The "BLAGAB-related loss capacity" is equal to $A + B - C$ where—

A is 50% of the company's relevant BLAGAB trade profits for the accounting period (as defined in section 124D of FA 2012);

B is the company's BLAGAB trade profits deductions allowance for the period (if any) (as defined in section 124D of FA 2012);

C is the total of any deductions made by the company for the accounting period under sections 124(5), 124A(5) and 124C(6) of FA 2012.

(5) To determine the modified loss cap, take the following steps—

Step 1: find the basic loss cap.

Step 2: reduce that amount by the BLAGAB-related loss capacity.

Step 3: add to the result of step 2 the adjusted shareholders' I-E profit.

The result is the modified loss cap.

(6) In this section "the basic loss cap" means the difference referred to in the opening words of section 269ZD(2) (assuming that that section has effect without the modification set out in subsection (1) of this section) (but, if applicable, taking account of section 269ZJ).

(7) In this section "excess capacity" means the amount (if any) by which—

(a) the section 269ZF step 2 amount, is less than

(b) what the section 269ZF step 2 amount would be if in paragraph (d) of section 269ZF(4) the reference to any I-E profit were to the policyholders' share of any I-E profit.

(8) In subsection (7) the reference to the "section 269ZF step 2 amount" is to the sum given by paragraph (1) of step 2 of section 269ZF(3) in calculating the company's relevant trading profits and relevant non-trading profits for the accounting period: but for this purpose disregard paragraph (4) of step 1 of section 269ZF(3).

(9) For the purposes of this section the "shareholders' share" of an insurance company's I-E profit for an accounting period is equal to—

(a) the amount of the I-E profit, less

(b) the policyholders' share (if any) of that profit.

(10) In this section references to the policyholders' share of I-E profit are to that share as determined in accordance with section 103 of FA 2012.

Relevant profits

269ZF "Relevant trading profits" and "relevant non-trading profits"

(1) A company's "relevant trading profits" for an accounting period are—

(a) the company's qualifying trading profits for the accounting period (see subsection (3)), less

(b) the company's trading profits deductions allowance for the accounting period (see section 269ZB(7)).

But if the allowance mentioned in paragraph (b) exceeds the profits mentioned in paragraph (a), the company's "relevant trading profits" for the accounting period are nil.

(2) A company's "relevant non-trading profits" for an accounting period are—

(a) the company's qualifying non-trading profits for the accounting period (see subsection (3)), less

(b) the company's non-trading profits deductions allowance for the accounting period (see section 269ZC(5)).

But if the allowance mentioned in paragraph (b) exceeds the profits mentioned in paragraph (a), the company's "relevant non-trading profits" for the accounting period are nil.

(3) To determine a company's qualifying trading profits and qualifying non-trading profits for an accounting period—

Step 1 – modified total profits

(1) Calculate the company's total profits for the accounting period.

(2) For the purposes of this subsection assume that the company's total profits for the accounting period are to be calculated with the modifications set out in subsection (4).

(3) If the company's total profits for the accounting period (as modified under paragraph (2)) are not greater than nil, the company's qualifying trading profits and relevant non-trading profits for the accounting period are both nil.

(4) Otherwise, proceed with steps 2 to 5.

Step 2 – negative amount for apportioning under step 4

(1) Calculate the sum ("the step 2 amount") of any amounts which (on the assumption set out in paragraph (2) of step 1), could be relieved against the company's total profits of the accounting period.

(2) But in calculating that sum, ignore the amount of any excluded deductions for the accounting period (see subsection (5)).

(3) If the company's total profits for the accounting period (as modified under step 1(2)) do not exceed the amount given by this step, the qualifying trading profits and the qualifying non-trading profits are both nil.

(4) Otherwise, proceed with steps 3 to 5.

Step 3 – trade profits and non-trade profits

Divide the company's total profits for the accounting period (as modified under step 1(2)) into—

(a) profits of a trade of the company (the company's "trade profits"), and
(b) profits that are not profits of a trade of the company (the company's "non-trade profits").

Step 4 – apportioning the step 2 amount

Take the step 2 amount and do one of the following—

(a) reduce the company's trade profits by the whole of that amount,
(b) reduce the company's non-trade profits by the whole of that amount, or
(c) reduce the company's trade profits by part of that amount and reduce the company's non-trade profits by the remaining part of that amount.

Apply this step in a way which ensures that neither the company's trade profits nor the company's non-trade profits are reduced below nil.

Step 5 – amount of qualifying trading or non-trading profits (if not determined under step 1 or 2)

The amounts resulting from step 3, after any reduction under step 4, are—

(a) in the case of the amount in step 3(a), the company's qualifying trading profits, and
(b) in the case of the amount in step 3(b), the company's qualifying non-trading profits.

(4) For the purposes of subsection (3) the company's total profits for an accounting period are to be calculated with the following modifications—

(a) ignore any income so far as it falls within, and is dealt with under, Part 9A of CTA 2009 (company distributions);
(b) ignore any ring fence profits (as defined in section 276);
(c) ignore any contractor's ring fence profits (as defined in section 356LD);
(d) if the company is an insurance company, ignore any I-E profit (see section 141(2) of FA 2012);
(e) make no deductions under sections 45(4)(b) and 45B (carry forward of trade loss against subsequent trade profits) other than deductions that would be ignored for the purposes of section 269ZB by reason of—

(i) section 1209(3), 1210(5A) or 1211(7A) of CTA 2009 (losses of film trade),
(ii) section 1216DA(3), 1216DB(5A) or 1216DC(7A) of that Act (losses of television programme trade),
(iii) section 1217DA(3), 1217DB(5A) or 1217DC(7A) of that Act (losses of video game trade),
(iv) section 1217MA(3) or 1217MC(9) of that Act (losses of theatrical trade),
(v) section 1217SA(3) or 1217SC(9) of that Act (losses of orchestral trade),
(vi) section 1218ZDA(3) or 1218ZDC(9) of that Act (losses of museum or gallery exhibition trade),
(vii) section 65(4B) or 67A(5A) (losses of UK or EEA furnished holiday lettings business),
(viii) section 269ZJ(1) (insurance companies: shock losses),
(ix) section 304(7) (certain losses of ring fence trades), or
(x) section 356NJ(2) (pre-1 April 2017 loss arising from oil contractor activities);

(f) make no restricted deductions (as defined in section 269ZB(4)) under section 303B(4) or 303D(5)); and

(g) make no deductions under section 457(3) or 463H(5) of CTA 2009 (carry forward of non-trading deficits from loan relationships against subsequent non-trading profits), other than deductions that would be ignored for the purposes of section 269ZC by reason of section 269ZJ(2) (insurance companies: shock losses).

(5) The following are "excluded deductions" for an accounting period ("the current accounting period")—

(a) a deduction for the current accounting period which is a relevant deduction for the purposes of section 269ZD (see subsection (3) of that section);

(b) a deduction under section 37 (relief for trade losses against total profits) in relation to a loss made in an accounting period after the current accounting period;

(c) a deduction under section 45F (terminal losses);

(d) a deduction under section 260(3) of CAA 2001 (special leasing of plant or machinery: carry back of excess allowances) in relation to capital allowances for an accounting period after the current accounting period; and

(e) a deduction under section 463E of CTA 2009 (non-trading deficit from loan relationships) in relation to a deficit for a period after the current accounting period.

Exclusion for certain general insurance companies

269ZG General insurance companies: excluded accounting periods

(1) Nothing in sections 269ZB to 269ZE has effect for determining the taxable total profits of a general insurance company for an excluded accounting period.

(2) An accounting period of a general insurance company is an "excluded accounting period" if conditions A and B are met.

(3) Condition A is that—

(a) the company is subject to insolvency procedures (see section 269ZH) at the end of the accounting period,

(b) immediately before it became subject to insolvency procedures the company—

(i) was unable to pay its debts as they fell due, and

(ii) met the non-viability condition, and

(c) the company's liabilities in respect of qualifying latent claims (see section 269ZI) were the main factor contributing to the company's meeting the non-viability condition at that time.

(4) Condition B is that—

(a) at the end of the accounting period the company meets the non-viability condition, and

(b) the company's liabilities in respect of qualifying latent claims are the main factor contributing to the company's meeting that condition at that time.

(5) At any time, a general insurance company meets the non-viability condition if there is no realistic prospect that it will subsequently write any new insurance business.

(6) For the purposes of this section a person who carries on the activity of effecting or carrying out contracts of general insurance is a "general insurance company" if—

(a) the person has permission under Part 4A of the Financial Services and Markets Act 2000 to carry on that activity,

(b) the person is of the kind mentioned in paragraph 5(d) or (da) of Schedule 3 to the Financial Services and Markets Act 2000 (EEA passport rights) and carries on that activity in the United Kingdom through a permanent establishment there, or

(c) the person qualifies for authorisation under Schedule 4 to the Financial Services and Markets Act 2000 (Treaty rights) and carries on that activity in the United Kingdom through a permanent establishment there.

(7) The definition in subsection (6) is subject to the following qualifications—

(a) a friendly society within the meaning of Part 3 of FA 2012 is not a general insurance company, and

(b) an insurance special purpose vehicle (as defined in section 139 of FA 2012) is not a general insurance company.

(8) In this section—

"contract of general insurance" means a contract of a type described in Part 1 of Schedule 1 to the Financial Services and Markets Act 2000 (Regulated Activities) Order 2001 (S.I. 2001/544);

"liability" includes a contingent or prospective liability.

269ZH "Insolvency procedures"

(1) For the purposes of section 269ZG a company is subject to insolvency procedures if—

    (a) it is in liquidation,
    (b) it is in administration,
    (c) it is in receivership, or
    (d) a relevant scheme has effect in relation to it.

(2) A company is "in liquidation" for the purposes of this section if—

    (a) it is in liquidation within the meaning of section 247 of the Insolvency Act 1986 or Part 3 of the Insolvency (Northern Ireland) Order 1989 (S.I. 1989/2405 (N.I. 19), or
    (b) a corresponding situation under the law of a country or territory outside the United Kingdom exists in relation to the company.

(3) A company is "in administration" for the purposes of this section if—

    (a) it is in administration within the meaning of Schedule B1 to the Insolvency Act 1986 or Schedule B1 to the Insolvency (Northern Ireland) Order 1989, or
    (b) there is in force in relation to it under the law of a country or territory outside the United Kingdom any appointment corresponding to the appointment of an administrator under either of those Schedules.

(4) A company is "in receivership" for the purposes of this section if there is in force in relation to it—

    (a) an order for the appointment of an administrative receiver, a receiver and manager or a receiver under Chapter 1 or 2 of Part 3 of the Insolvency Act 1986 or Part 4 of the Insolvency (Northern Ireland Order) 1989, or
    (b) any corresponding order under the law of a country or territory outside the United Kingdom.

(5) In this section "relevant scheme" means a compromise or arrangement—

    (a) under section 425 of the Companies Act 1985, Article 418 of the Companies (Northern Ireland) Order 1986 (S.I. 1986/1032 (N.I. 6)) or Part 26 of the Companies Act 2006, or
    (b) under any corresponding provision of the law of a country or territory outside the United Kingdom.

269ZI "Qualifying latent claims"

(1) This section applies for the purposes of section 269ZG.

(2) Where a general insurance company has a liability in respect of a claim, the claim is a "qualifying latent claim" if conditions A to C are met.

(3) In this section "claim" means a claim (whether actual or potential) under an insurance policy.

(4) Condition A is that—

    (a) the claim is of a type that was not reasonably foreseeable at the time when the insurance policy concerned was entered into, and
    (b) it is likely that, had the company foreseen that type of claim, the price or other terms of the policy would have been significantly different.

(5) Condition B is that the latency period associated with that type of claim (see subsection (7)) is more than 10 years.

(6) Condition C is that the insurance policy, or the part of the insurance policy under which the claim is or would be made, is—

    (a) an employer's liability policy, or
    (b) a public or products liability policy.

(7) The "latency period" associated with a type of claim is the mean period for claims of the type between—

    (a) the insured event giving rise to the claim, and
    (b) notification of the claim.

(8) The mean period mentioned in subsection (7) is to be determined as at the end of the accounting period mentioned in section 269ZG(2).

(9) In this section—

"employer's liability policy" means an insurance policy against the risks of the person insured incurring liabilities to the insured's employees for injury, illness or death arising out of their employment during the course of business;
"general insurance company" is to be interpreted in accordance with section 269ZG;

"insurance policy" includes any contract of insurance;
"liability" includes a contingent or prospective liability;
"public or products liability policy" means an insurance policy against the risks of the person insured incurring liabilities to third parties for damage to property, injury, illness or death, arising in the course of the insured's business.

269ZJ Exclusion of shock losses from restrictions

(1) If a shock loss is—

(a) carried forward to an accounting period of an insurance company (see section 269ZP(2)), and
(b) deducted under section 45B (post-1 April 2017 trade losses carried forward against trade profits),

the deduction is to be treated as not falling within section 269ZB(3).

(2) If a shock loss is—

(a) carried forward to an accounting period of an insurance company, and
(b) deducted under section 463H of CTA 2009 (carry forward of unrelieved non-trading deficit from loan relationships against non-trading profits),

the company is to be treated for the purposes of sections 269ZC and 269ZD(2)(b)(ii) as not having made that deduction.

(3) If an insurance company makes a deduction of (or in respect of) a shock loss, that deduction is not a "relevant deduction" for the purposes of section 269ZD (restriction on deductions from total profits).

(4) See also section 124E of FA 2012 (exclusion from the restriction on deductions from BLAGAB trade profits).

269ZK Meaning of "shock loss": requirement to make a claim

(1) If the conditions in subsection (3) are met, an insurance company may make a claim in respect of—

(a) a loss or other amount (the "specified loss"), and
(b) a period of 12 months ("the specified period") which is a solvency shock period (see section 269ZM).

(2) A claim may specify more than one 12 month period under subsection (1)(b) (but periods specified by an insurance company under this section may not overlap with one another).

(3) The conditions are that—

(a) the accounting period (for corporation tax purposes) in which the specified loss arises ("the loss-making period") begins on or after 1 April 2017,
(b) the specified loss is, or is capable of being, carried forward to a subsequent accounting period, and
(c) the loss-making period and the specified period have one or more days in common.

(4) A claim under this section must be made within—

(a) the period of two years after the end of the loss-making period, or
(b) such further period as an officer of Revenue and Customs allows.

(5) If—

(a) a claim is made under this section, and
(b) the whole of the loss-making period is, or falls within, the specified period,

the specified loss is a "shock loss".

(6) If—

(a) a claim is made under this section, and
(b) the loss-making period falls partly, but not wholly, in the specified period,

the specified loss is a "shock loss" so far as it is attributable to the specified period.

(7) For the purposes of subsection (6) the specified loss is "attributable to" the specified period in the proportion—

P / N

Where P is the number of days of the loss-making period that fall within the specified period and N is the number of days in the loss-making period.

(8) If the method in subsection (7) would produce a result that is unjust or unreasonable, the apportionment of the specified loss for the purposes of subsection (6) is to be made on a just and reasonable basis.

269ZL Further provision about claims under section 269ZK

(1) A claim under section 269ZK is not effective unless—

(a) the claim—

(i) states the company's solvency capital requirement at the beginning of the specified period,

(ii) states the company's shock loss threshold for that period, and sets out the calculation of that amount (as described in steps 2 to 5 of 269ZN(1)), and

(iii) states the amount of the company's solvency loss for that period (see section 269ZO), and

(b) the company submits with the claim—

(i) information ("the submitted information") corresponding to the information specified in the template mentioned in point (i), (j) or (k) (as the case requires) of Article 4 of the technical standards implementing Regulation, and

(ii) a report provided by the appropriate person which meets the condition in subsection (2).

(2) The condition is that the report includes an opinion confirming that—

(a) the submitted information is prepared in all material respects in accordance with any relevant requirements which would apply if the submitted information were disclosed as part of the company's report on solvency and financial condition,

(b) the calculation of the company's shock loss threshold (not including step 1(a) of section 269ZN(1)) complies in all material respects with section 269ZN, and

(c) the company's solvency loss is calculated in all material respects in accordance with section 269ZO.

(3) In this section "relevant requirements" means—

(a) requirements under rules made by the Prudential Regulation Authority, and

(b) requirements under any directly applicable EU regulation made under the Solvency 2 Directive.

(4) In this section "the appropriate person" means—

(a) the company's chief actuary, or

(b) (if the company is not a PRA-authorised person) a person with equivalent functions.

(5) Subsections (1)(b)(i), (2)(a) and (3) have effect in relation to a third-country insurance undertaking as if it were an insurance undertaking.

269ZM Meaning of "solvency shock period"

A period of 12 months is a "solvency shock period" in relation to an insurance company if the company has a solvency loss for that period (see section 269ZO) which exceeds the company's shock loss threshold for that period (see section 269ZN).

269ZN Determination of shock loss threshold

(1) A company's shock loss threshold for a 12 month period is determined as follows.

Step 1

(a) Calculate the company's solvency capital requirement at the beginning of that period.

(b) But any adjustment for the loss-absorbing capacity of deferred taxes is to be calculated, and applied, on the assumption that that period is a solvency shock period in relation to the company.

(c) The resulting amount is the company's "adjusted SCR".

Step 2

Calculate the deductible amount (see subsection (2)) for each relevant ring-fenced fund of the company.

Step 3

Deduct the total of the amounts found under step 2 from the company's adjusted SCR.

Step 4

Multiply the amount found under step 3 by 90%.

Step 5

The result is the company's shock loss threshold for the period.

(2) The deductible amount for a relevant ring-fenced fund is the lesser of A and B, where—

(a) A is the amount of basic own funds within that fund at the beginning of the period (or zero, if greater);

(b) B is the notional solvency capital requirement for that fund at the beginning of that period.

(3) But in calculating amount A for the purposes of subsection (2)—

(a) no account is to be taken of the value of future transfers attributable to shareholders;

(b) a restricted own-fund item within the fund is to be disregarded if the company's with-profits actuary provides a written opinion confirming that the condition in subsection (4) is met.

(4) The condition is that—

(a) the item is available as a restricted own-fund item pursuant to conditional support arrangements, and

(b) if at the time mentioned in subsection (2)(a) or any subsequent time (when the conditional support arrangements are in place) the value of the company's interest in the item were to be (or is in fact) greater than zero, that value would be recognised for the purposes of a balance sheet drawn up at the time in question by the company in accordance with generally accepted accounting practice.

(5) In this section "conditional support arrangements" means arrangements under which the relevant restrictions would cease to apply if specified conditions relating to the financial strength of the fund were met.

(6) In subsection (5) "the relevant restrictions" means the restrictions on transferability as a result of which the item is a restricted own-fund item.

(7) In this section "adjustment for the loss-absorbing capacity of deferred taxes" means—

(a) an adjustment pursuant to Article 103(c) of the Solvency 2 Directive, or

(b) any corresponding adjustment made pursuant to Subsection 3 of Section 4 of Chapter 6 of Title 1 of the Solvency 2 Directive (solvency capital requirement full and partial internal models).

(8) Where the company is a third-country insurance undertaking—

(a) steps 1(b) and 2 to 5 of subsection (1), and

(b) subsections (2) to (7),

have effect with any modifications that are appropriate as a result of the reference in step 1(a) of subsection (1) to the "solvency capital requirement" having effect in accordance with section 269ZP(1)(b).

269ZO Calculation of solvency loss

(1) An insurance company's solvency loss (if any) for a 12 month period is determined as follows.

(2) Calculate, in the manner set out in subsections (5) to (11)—

(a) whether the total amount of the company's basic own funds at the beginning of the period ("opening BOF") exceeds the total amount of the company's basic own funds at the end of the period ("closing BOF"), and

(b) if so, the amount by which opening BOF exceeds closing BOF.

(3) The company has a solvency loss for the 12 month period only if an excess of opening BOF over closing BOF is found under subsection (2)(a).

(4) The amount found under subsection (2)(b) is the amount of the solvency loss.

(5) The method of calculation under subsection (2) must fairly represent the method by which the company calculates its solvency capital requirement.

But this is subject to subsections (6) to (10).

(6) Closing BOF is to be calculated on the assumption that the 12 month period mentioned in subsection (1) is a solvency shock period in relation to the company.

(7) The following adjustments are to be made in calculating the company's basic own funds at the beginning and end of the period—

1. Find (with respect to each of those times) what that amount would be in the absence of this subsection.

2. Find the surplus in respect of each relevant ring-fenced fund of the company (at the time in question).

3. Deduct the total of the amounts found under paragraph 2 from the amount found under paragraph 1.

The result is to be taken to be the amount of the company's basic own funds at the beginning, or (as the case may be) the end, of the period.

(8) The surplus in respect of a relevant ring-fenced fund (at any time) is equal to—

    (a) the amount of basic own funds attributable to policyholders, or

    (b) zero, if greater.

(9) For any relevant ring-fenced fund, the amount of basic own funds attributable to policyholders (at any time) is equal to—

$A - B$

where—

A is the amount of basic own funds within the relevant ring-fenced fund;

B is the total of any items in the fund that fall within subsection (10).

(10) The items are—

    (a) the value of future transfers attributable to shareholders;

    (b) any restricted own-fund item in relation to which the company's with-profits actuary provides a written opinion confirming that the condition in subsection (4) of section 269ZN is met.

(11) In subsection (5) the reference to the "method" of a calculation is to the—

    (a) taking into account, and

    (b) leaving out of account,

of variations in items of basic own funds for the purposes of the calculation.

(12) If the company is a third-country insurance undertaking, subsections (1) to (11) have effect in relation to it as if it were an insurance undertaking.

269ZP Interpretation of sections 269ZJ to 269ZO

(1) In sections 269ZJ to 269ZO "solvency capital requirement"—

    (a) in relation to an insurance undertaking or a reinsurance undertaking, means the solvency capital requirement pursuant to Section 4 of Chapter 6 of Title 1 of the Solvency 2 Directive;

    (b) in relation to a third-country insurance undertaking, means the amount that would be the undertaking's solvency capital requirement pursuant to Section 4 of Chapter 6 of Title 1 of the Solvency 2 Directive if that undertaking were an insurance undertaking.

(2) In sections 269ZJ to 269ZO and this section—

"actuarial function", in relation to a PRA-authorised person, has the meaning given by the PRA Rulebook;

"basic own funds" is to be interpreted in accordance with Article 88 of the Solvency 2 Directive;

"chief actuary", in relation to a PRA-authorised person, means a person who has the function of having responsibility for the actuarial function;

"insurance company" means a company which is an insurance undertaking, a reinsurance undertaking or a third-country insurance undertaking;

"insurance undertaking" has the meaning given in Article 13(1) of the Solvency 2 Directive;

"notional solvency capital requirement", in relation to a ring-fenced fund, has the same meaning as in Commission Delegated Regulation (EU) 2015/35 supplementing the Solvency 2 Directive;

"PRA-authorised person" has the same meaning as in the Financial Services and Markets Act 2000 (see section 2B(5) of that Act);

"the PRA Rulebook" means the Rulebook made by the Prudential Regulation Authority under the Financial Services and Markets Act 2000 (as that Rulebook has effect from time to time);

"reinsurance undertaking" has the meaning given in Article 13(4) of the Solvency 2 Directive;

"relevant ring-fenced fund" means a ring-fenced fund that is a with-profits fund;

"report on solvency and financial condition" means a report on solvency and financial condition pursuant to Article 51 of the Solvency 2 Directive;

"restricted own-fund item" is to be interpreted in accordance with Article 80(2) of Commission Delegated Regulation (EU) 2015/35 supplementing the Solvency 2 Directive;

"ring-fenced fund" has the same meaning as in Commission Delegated Regulation (EU) 2015/35 supplementing the Solvency 2 Directive;

"Solvency 2 Directive" means Directive 2009/138/EC of the European Parliament and the Council of 25 November 2009 on the taking-up and pursuit of the business of Insurance and Reinsurance (Solvency II);

"technical standards implementing Regulation" means Commission Implementing Regulation (EU) 2015/2452 of 2 December 2015 laying down implementing technical standards with regard to the procedures, formats and templates of the solvency and financial condition report in accordance with the Solvency 2 Directive;

"third-country insurance undertaking" means an undertaking that has received authorisation under Article 162 of the Solvency 2 Directive from the Prudential Regulation Authority or the Financial Conduct Authority;

"value of future transfers attributable to shareholders" has the same meaning as in Article 80 of Commission Delegated Regulation (EU) 2015/35 supplementing the Solvency 2 Directive;

"with-profits fund" has the meaning given by the Glossary forming part of the PRA Rulebook;

"with-profits actuary" has the meaning given by the Glossary forming part of the Handbook made by the Financial Conduct Authority under the Financial Services and Markets Act 2000 (as that Handbook has effect from time to time).

269ZQ   Power to amend

(1) The Treasury may by regulations make such amendments of the provisions mentioned in subsection (2) as they consider appropriate in consequence of—

(a) any change made to, or replacement of, the PRA Rulebook or the FCA Handbook;

(b) any regulatory requirement, or change to a regulatory requirement, imposed by EU legislation, or by or under any Act (whenever adopted, enacted or made).

(2) The provisions are—

(a) sections 269ZJ to 269ZP,

(b) sections 124A to 124E of FA 2012.

(3) Regulations under this section may include transitional provision.

(4) In this section—

"the PRA Rulebook" means the Rulebook made by the Prudential Regulation Authority under the Financial Services and Markets Act 2000 (as that Rulebook has effect from time to time);

"the FCA Handbook means the Handbook made by the Financial Conduct Authority under the Financial Services and Markets Act 2000 (as that Handbook has effect from time to time).

Deductions allowance

269ZR   Deductions allowance for company in a group

(1) This section makes provision as to the deductions allowance of a company for an accounting period where, at any time in the period—

(a) the company is a member of a group, and

(b) one or more other companies within the charge to corporation tax are members of that group.

(2) The company's deductions allowance for the accounting period is the sum of—

(a) any amounts of group deductions allowance allocated to the company for the period in accordance with sections 269ZS to 269ZV, and

(b) the appropriate amount of non-group deductions allowance of the company for the period,

up to a limit of £5,000,000.

(3) The "appropriate amount of non-group deductions allowance" of the company, for the accounting period, is—

$(DNG / DAC) \times £5,000,000$

where—

"DNG" is the number of days in the period on which the company is not a member of a group that has another member that is a company within the charge to corporation tax, and

"DAC" is the total number of days in the period.

(4) If the accounting period is less than 12 months—

(a) the appropriate amount of non-group deductions allowance, and

(b) the limit in subsection (2),

are proportionally reduced.

269ZS   Group deductions allowance and the nominated company

(1) This section applies where—

(a) two or more members of a group are companies within the charge to corporation tax, and

(b) all the companies within the charge to corporation tax that are members of the group together nominate ("the group allowance nomination") one of their number ("the nominated company") for the purposes of this Part.

(2) The "group deductions allowance" for the group is £5,000,000 for each accounting period of the nominated company throughout which the group allowance nomination has effect.

(3) If the group allowance nomination takes effect, or ceases to have effect, part of the way through an accounting period of the nominated company, the "group deductions allowance" for the group for that period is—

(DN / DAC) × £5,000,000

where—

"DN" is the number of days in the accounting period on which a group allowance nomination that nominates the nominated company in relation to the group has effect, and

"DAC" is the total number of days in the accounting period.

(4) If an accounting period of the nominated company is less than 12 months, the group deductions allowance for that period is proportionally reduced.

(5) A group allowance nomination must state the date on which it is to take effect (which may be earlier than the date the nomination is made).

(6) A group allowance nomination is of no effect unless it is signed by the appropriate person on behalf of each company that is, when the nomination is made, a member of the group and within the charge to corporation tax.

(7) A group allowance nomination ceases to have effect—

(a) immediately before the date on which a new group allowance nomination in respect of the group takes effect,

(b) upon the appropriate person in relation to a company within the charge to corporation tax that is a member of the group notifying an officer of Revenue and Customs, in writing, that the group allowance nomination is revoked, or

(c) upon the nominated company ceasing to be a company within the charge to corporation tax or ceasing to be a member of the group.

(8) The Commissioners for Her Majesty's Revenue and Customs may by regulations make further provision about a group allowance nomination or any notification under this section including, in particular, provision—

(a) about the form and manner in which a nomination or notification may be made,

(b) about how a nomination may be revoked and the form and manner of such revocation,

(c) requiring a person to notify HMRC of the making or revocation of a nomination,

(d) requiring a person to give information to HMRC in connection with the making or revocation of a nomination or the giving of a notification,

(e) imposing time limits in relation to making or revoking a nomination or giving a notification, and

(f) providing that a nomination or its revocation, or a notification, is of no effect, or ceases to have effect, if time limits or other requirements under the regulations are not met.

(9) In this Part "the appropriate person", in relation to a company, means—

(a) the proper officer of the company, or

(b) such other person as may for the time being have the express, implied or apparent authority of the company to act on its behalf for the purposes of this Part.

(10) Subsections (3) and (4) of section 108 of TMA 1970 (responsibility of company officers: meaning of "proper officer") apply for the purposes of subsection (9) as they apply for the purposes of that section.

269ZT Group allowance allocation statement: submission

(1) A company must submit a group allowance allocation statement to HMRC for each of its accounting periods in which it is the nominated company in relation to a group.

This is subject to subsections (2) and (3).

(2) If a company ceases to be the nominated company in relation to a group before it submits a group allowance allocation statement to HMRC for an accounting period—

    (a) that company may not submit the statement, and

    (b) the company that is for the time being the nominated company in relation to the group must do so.

(3) But if a new group allowance nomination in respect of the group takes effect on a date before it is made, that does not affect the validity of the submission of any group allowance allocation statement submitted before the date the new nomination is made.

(4) A group allowance allocation statement under this section must be received by HMRC before the first anniversary of the filing date for the company tax return for the accounting period to which the statement relates.

(5) A group allowance allocation statement under this section may be submitted at a later time if an officer of Revenue and Customs allows it.

(6) A group allowance allocation statement under this section must comply with the requirements of section 269ZV.

269ZU Group allowance allocation statement: submission of revised statement

(1) This section applies if a group allowance allocation statement has been submitted under section 269ZT, or this section, in respect of an accounting period of a company that is, or was, a nominated company ("the nominee's accounting period").

(2) A revised group allowance allocation statement in respect of the nominee's accounting period may be submitted to HMRC by the company that is for the time being the nominated company in relation to the group.

(3) But if a new group allowance nomination in respect of the group takes effect on a date before it is made, that does not affect the validity of the submission of any revised group allowance allocation statement submitted before the date the new nomination is made.

(4) A revised group allowance allocation statement may be submitted on or before whichever is the latest of the following dates—

    (a) the first anniversary of the filing date for the company tax return for the nominee's accounting period,

    (b) if notice of enquiry (within the meaning of Schedule 18 to FA 1998) is given into a relevant company tax return, 30 days after the enquiry is completed,

    (c) if, after such an enquiry, an officer of Revenue and Customs amends the return under paragraph 34(2) of that Schedule, 30 days after the notice of amendment is issued,

    (d) if an appeal is brought against such an amendment, 30 days after the date on which the appeal is finally determined.

(5) A revised group allowance allocation statement may be submitted at a later time if an officer of Revenue and Customs allows it.

(6) In this section "relevant company tax return" means a company tax return of a company for an accounting period for which an amount of group deductions allowance was, or could have been, allocated by a previous group allowance allocation statement in respect of the nominee's accounting period.

(7) The references in subsection (4) to an enquiry into a relevant company tax return do not include an enquiry resulting from an amendment of such a return where—

    (a) the scope of the enquiry is limited as mentioned in paragraph 25(2) of Schedule 18 to FA 1998 (enquiry into amendments when time limit for enquiry into return as originally submitted is passed), and

    (b) the amendment relates only to the allocation of group deductions allowance for the nominee's accounting period.

(8) A group allowance allocation statement under this section must comply with the requirements of section 269ZV.

269ZV Group allowance allocation statement: requirements and effects

(1) This section applies in relation to a group allowance allocation statement submitted under section 269ZT or 269ZU.

(2) The statement must be signed by the appropriate person in relation to the company giving the statement.

(3) The statement must—

    (a) identify the group to which it relates,

(b) specify the accounting period, of the company that is or was the nominated company, to which the statement relates ("the nominee's accounting period"),

(c) specify the days in the nominee's accounting period on which that company was the nominated company in relation to the group or state that that company was the nominated company throughout the period,

(d) state the group deductions allowance the group has for the nominee's accounting period,

(e) list one or more of the companies that were members of the group and within the charge to corporation tax in the nominee's accounting period ("listed companies"),

(f) allocate amounts of the group deductions allowance to the listed companies, and

(g) for each amount of group deductions allowance allocated to a listed company, specify the accounting period of the listed company for which it is allocated.

(4) An amount of group deductions allowance allocated to a listed company must be allocated to that company for an accounting period that falls wholly or partly in the nominee's accounting period.

(5) The maximum amount of group deductions allowance that may be allocated, by the group allowance allocation statement, to a listed company for an accounting period of that company is—

(DAP/ DNAP) × GSA

where—

"DAP" is the number of days in the accounting period of the listed company that are—

(a) days in the nominee's accounting period, and

(b) days on which the company was a member of the group,

"DNAP" is the number of days in the nominee's accounting period, and

"GSA" is the group deductions allowance of the group for the nominee's accounting period.

(6) The sum of the amounts allocated to listed companies by the group allowance allocation statement may not exceed the group deductions allowance for the nominee's accounting period.

(7) If a group allowance allocation statement is submitted that does not comply with subsection (5) or (6), the company that is, for the time being, the nominated company in relation to the group must submit a revised group allowance allocation statement that does comply with those subsections within 30 days of the date on which the group allowance allocation statement that did not comply was submitted or within such further period as an officer of Revenue and Customs allows.

(8) If a group allowance allocation statement—

(a) complies with those subsections when it is submitted, but

(b) subsequently ceases to comply with either of them,

the company that is, for the time being, the nominated company in relation to the group must submit a revised group allowance allocation statement that does comply with those subsections within 30 days of the date on which the group allowance allocation statement ceased to comply with one of those subsections or within such further period as an officer of Revenue and Customs allows.

(9) If a company fails to comply with subsection (7) or (8), an officer of Revenue and Customs may by written notice to the company amend the group allowance allocation statement as the officer thinks fit for the purpose of making it comply with subsections (5) and (6).

(10) An officer of Revenue and Customs who issues a notice under subsection (9) to a company must, at the same time, send a copy of the notice to each of the listed companies.

(11) The time limits otherwise applicable to the amendment of a company tax return do not apply to any such amendment to the extent that it is made in consequence of a group allowance allocation statement being submitted in accordance with section 269ZT or 269ZU.

(12) The Commissioners for Her Majesty's Revenue and Customs may by regulations make further provision about a group allowance allocation statement including, in particular, provision—

(a) about the form of a statement and the manner in which it is to be submitted,

(b) requiring a person to give information to HMRC in connection with a statement,

(c) as to the circumstances in which a statement that is not received by the time specified in section 269ZU(4) is to be treated as if it were so received, and

(d) as to the circumstances in which a statement that does not comply with the requirements of this section is to be treated as if it did comply.

269ZW Deductions allowance for company not in a group

(1) This section makes provision as to the deductions allowance of a company for an accounting period where section 269ZR (deductions allowance for company in a group) does not apply.

(2) The company's deductions allowance for the accounting period is £5,000,000.

(3) If the accounting period is less than 12 months, the company's deductions allowance for the period is proportionally reduced.

269ZX Increase of deductions allowance where provision for onerous lease reversed

(1) This section applies if—

(a) a relevant reversal credit (see section 269ZY) is brought into account in calculating a company's specified profits for an accounting period, and

(b) the amount of the company's specified profits for the accounting period is greater than nil.

(2) For the purposes of this section a company's "specified profits" for an accounting period are the sum of—

(a) the company's total profits for the accounting period, calculated with the modifications set out in section 269ZF(4), and

(b) any I-E profit of the company for the accounting period.

(3) The company's deductions allowance for the accounting period (as determined in accordance with section 269ZR or 269ZW) is to be treated (for all purposes) as increased by—

(a) the amount of the relevant reversal credit, or

(b) if lower, the amount of the specified profits.

269ZY Meaning of "relevant reversal credit"

(1) For the purposes of section 269ZX a "relevant reversal credit" is a credit, or other income, brought into account in respect of the relevant reversal (see subsections (3) and (5)) of a relevant onerous lease provision.

(2) A provision in the accounts of a company ("C") is a "relevant onerous lease provision" if—

(a) the provision relates to a lease of land under which C is the tenant (and "L" is the landlord),

(b) the provision is required, for accountancy purposes, as a provision for an onerous lease, and

(c) the lease was entered into at arm's length.

(3) The reversal (in whole or in part) of a relevant onerous lease provision is a "relevant reversal" if—

(a) the reversal is required for accountancy purposes as a result of an arrangement ("C's arrangement") made at arm's length under which C's obligations under the lease are varied or cancelled,

(b) subsection (4) does not apply, and

(c) at least one of conditions X, Y and Z in subsection (7) is met.

(4) This subsection applies if—

(a) C and L are connected at the time when C's arrangement is made, or

(b) the landlord who granted the lease (whether that was L or another person) and the tenant to whom it was granted (whether that was C or another person) were connected at the time when the lease was granted.

(5) The reversal (in whole or in part) of a relevant onerous lease provision is a "relevant reversal" if—

(a) the lease has been granted out of a lease ("the superior lease"),

(b) L and C are members of the same group of companies,

(c) the reversal would be a relevant reversal by virtue of subsection (3) if the condition in subsection (3)(b) (lack of connection between C and L) were met,

(d) the terms of C's arrangement substantially reflect those of an arrangement ("L's arrangement") made at arm's length under which L's obligations under the superior lease are varied or cancelled, and

(e) subsection (6) does not apply.

(6) This subsection applies if—

(a) at the time when L's arrangement is made, the landlord under the superior lease ("S") is connected with L or C, or

(b) the landlord who granted the superior lease (whether that is S or another person) and the tenant to whom it was granted (whether that was L or another person) were connected at the time when that lease was granted.

(7) The conditions mentioned in subsection (3)(c) are as follows.

Condition X is that—

(a) it is reasonable to suppose that immediately before C's arrangement was made there was a material risk that at some time within the next 12 months C would be unable to pay its debts as they fell due, and

(b) the sole or main purpose of C's arrangement was to avert that risk (whether directly or indirectly).

Debts due to a person connected with C are to be regarded as not being debts for the purposes of paragraph (a).

Condition Y is that C is in insolvent administration.

Condition Z is that C's arrangement is, or is part of, a statutory insolvency arrangement.

(8) In this section "statutory insolvency arrangement" means—

(a) a voluntary arrangement that has taken effect under, or as a result of, the Insolvency Act 1986 or the Insolvency (Northern Ireland) Order 1989 (S.I. 1989/ 2405 (N.I. 19)),

(b) a compromise or arrangement that has taken effect under Part 26 of the Companies Act 2006, or

(c) an arrangement or compromise of a kind corresponding to any of those mentioned in paragraph (a) or (b) that has taken effect under, or as a result of, the law of a country or territory outside the United Kingdom,

(and for the purposes of this section an arrangement which is, or is part of, a statutory insolvency arrangement is taken to be "made" when the statutory insolvency arrangement takes effect).

(9) For the purposes of this section a company in administration is in insolvent administration if—

(a) it entered administration under Schedule B1 to the Insolvency Act 1986, or Schedule B1 to the Insolvency (Northern Ireland) Order 1989, at a time when its assets were insufficient for the payment of its debts and other liabilities and the expenses of the administration, or

(a) under the law of a country or territory outside the United Kingdom circumstances corresponding to those mentioned in paragraph (a) exist.

(10) In the application of subsection (5) to Scotland, the reference to the lease having been granted out of the superior lease is to the lease being a sublease of land subject to the superior lease.

(11) Section 152 (groups of companies) applies for the purposes of this section as it applies for the purposes of Part 5.

(12) For the purposes of this section any question whether a person is connected with another is to be determined in accordance with section 1122.

269ZZ Company tax return to specify amount of deductions allowance

(1) A company's tax return for an accounting period must specify—

(a) the amount of the company's deductions allowance for the period, and

(b) if section 269ZX (increase of deductions allowance where provision for onerous lease reversed) applies, what that amount would be without the increase provided for by subsection (3) of that section.

(2) But subsection (1) applies only if the company makes for the accounting period a deduction to which section 269ZB(2), 269ZC(2) or 269ZD(2) or section 124D(1) of FA 2012 applies.

269ZZA Excessive specifications of deductions allowance

(1) This section applies if a company's tax return for an accounting period specifies an excessive amount as—

(a) the company's deductions allowance for the period,

(b) the company's trading profits deductions allowance for the period,

(c) the company's non-trading profits deductions allowance for the period,

(d) the company's contractor's ring fence profits deductions allowance for the period, or

(e) the company's BLAGAB trade profits deductions allowance for the period.

(2) The company must, so far as it may do so, amend the company tax return so that the amount specified is not excessive.

(3) If an officer of Revenue and Customs considers that an undue amount of relief has been given as a consequence of the amount specified being excessive, the officer may make an assessment to tax in the amount which in the officer's opinion ought to be charged.

(4) If—

(a) the amount specified became excessive in consequence of an alteration being made to the amount of group deductions allowance allocated to the company for the accounting period concerned, and

(b) the company has failed, or is unable, to amend its company tax return in accordance with subsection (2),

an assessment under subsection (3) is not out of time if it is made within 12 months of the date on which the alteration took place.

(5) The power in subsection (3) is without prejudice to the power to make a discovery assessment under paragraph 41(1) of Schedule 18 to FA 1998.

269ZZB Meaning of "group"

(1) In this Part "group" means two or more companies which together meet the following condition.

(2) The condition is that one of the companies is—

(a) the ultimate parent of each of the other companies, and

(b) is not the ultimate parent of any other company.

(3) A company ("A") is the "ultimate parent" of another company ("B") if—

(a) A is the parent of B, and

(b) no company is the parent of both A and B.

(4) A company ("A") is the "parent" of another company ("B") if—

(a) B is a 75% subsidiary of A,

(b) A is beneficially entitled to at least 75% of any profits available for distribution to equity holders of B, or

(c) A would be beneficially entitled to at least 75% of any assets of B available for distribution to its equity holders on a winding up.

(5) The following apply for the purposes of subsection (4)—

(a) Chapter 6 of Part 5 (equity holders and profits or assets available for distribution) other than sections 169 to 182, and

(b) Chapter 3 of Part 24 (subsidiaries).

This is subject to subsections (6) and (7).

(6) In applying Chapter 3 of Part 24 for the purposes of subsection (4)—

(a) share capital of a registered society is to be treated as if it were ordinary share capital, and

(b) a company ("the shareholder") that directly owns shares in another company is to be treated as not owning those shares if a profit on their sale would be a trading receipt of the shareholder.

(7) In applying Chapter 6 of Part 5 (other than sections 169 to 182) and Chapter 3 of Part 24 for the purposes of subsection (4), they are to be read with all modifications necessary to ensure that—

(a) they apply to a company which does not have share capital, and to holders of corresponding ordinary holdings in such a company, in a way which corresponds to the way they apply to companies with ordinary share capital and holders of ordinary shares in such companies,

(b) they apply to a company which is an unincorporated association in a way which corresponds to the way they apply to companies which are bodies corporate,

(c) they apply in relation to ownership through an entity (other than a company), or any trust or other arrangement, in a way which corresponds to the way they apply to ownership through a company, and

(d) for the purposes of achieving paragraphs (a) to (c), profits or assets are attributed to holders of corresponding ordinary holdings in unincorporated associations, entities, trusts or other arrangements in a manner which corresponds to the way profits or assets are attributed to holders of ordinary shares in a company which is a body corporate.

(8) In this section "corresponding ordinary holding" in an unincorporated association, entity, trust or other arrangement means a holding or interest which provides the holder with economic rights corresponding to those provided by a holding of ordinary shares in a body corporate".

17 (1) Section 269C (overview of Chapter 3 of Part 7A: restriction on banking company obtaining certain deductions) is amended as follows.

(2) After subsection (1) insert—

"(1A) This Chapter applies in relation to a banking company in addition to Part 7ZA (which contains provision restricting the amount of certain deductions which any kind of company may make in calculating its taxable total profits for an accounting period)."

(3) In subsection (2) for "269CD" substitute "269CC"

18 (1) Section 269CA (restriction on deductions for pre-1 April 2015 trading losses) is amended as follows.

(2) In subsection (2), in the second sentence—

(a) for "269CD" substitute "269ZF", and

(b) omit "step 5 in".

(3) In subsection (3), for the words from "where" to the end substitute "in relation to a banking company for an accounting period where, in determining the company's relevant trading profits for the period, the amount given by step 1 in section 269ZF(3) is not greater than nil".

19 (1) Section 269CB (restriction on deductions for pre-1 April 2015 non-trading deficits from loan relationships) is amended as follows.

(2) In subsection (2), in the second sentence—

(a) for "269CD" substitute "269ZF", and

(b) for "step 6 in subsection (1)" substitute "subsection (2)".

(3) In subsection (3), for the words from "where" to the end substitute "in relation to a banking company for an accounting period where, in determining the company's relevant non-trading profits for the period, the amount given by step 1 in section 269ZF(3) is not greater than nil"

20 (1) Section 269CC (restriction on deductions for pre-1 April 2015 management expenses etc) is amended as follows.

(2) In subsection (3) for the words from "does not apply" to the end substitute "is subject to subsection (8)".

(3) In subsection (7)—

(a) in the second sentence of step 1, for "269CD" substitute "269ZD(5)",

(b) in step 2 for the words from "which are" to the end substitute "under—

(a) section 45 (carry forward of pre-1 April 2017 trade loss against subsequent trade profits),

(b) section 45B (carry forward of post-1 April 2017 trade loss against subsequent trade profits), or

(c) section 457 of CTA 2009 (carry forward of pre-1 April 2017 non-trading deficits from loan relationships)."

(4) After subsection (7) insert—

"(8) Subsection (2) does not apply in relation to a banking company for an accounting period where, in determining the company's relevant profits for the period, the amount given by step 1 in section 269ZF(3) is not greater than nil."

21 Section 269CD (relevant profits) is omitted.

22 (1) Section 269CN (definitions for the purposes of Part 7A) is amended as follows.

(2) In the definition of "relevant non-trading profits" for the words from "means" to the end substitute "has the meaning given by section 269ZF(2)".

(3) In the definition of "relevant profits" for the words from "means" to the end substitute "has the meaning given by section 269ZD(5)".

(4) In the definition of "relevant trading profits" for the words from "means" to the end substitute "has the meaning given by section 269ZF(1)".

PART 3

GROUP RELIEF FOR CARRIED-FORWARD LOSSES

23 After section 188 of CTA 2010 insert—

"PART 5A

GROUP RELIEF FOR CARRIED-FORWARD LOSSES

CHAPTER 1

INTRODUCTION

188AA Introduction to Part

(1) This Part—

(a) allows a company to surrender losses and other amounts that have been carried forward to an accounting period of the company (see Chapter 2), and

(b) enables, in certain cases involving groups or consortiums of companies, other companies to claim corporation tax relief for the losses and other amounts that are surrendered (see Chapter 3).

(2) Chapters 4 and 5 contain limitations on the amount of corporation tax relief which may be given on a claim under Chapter 3.

(3) See Chapter 5 for definitions that apply for the purposes of this Part and miscellaneous provisions.

(4) The corporation tax relief mentioned in this section is called "group relief for carried-forward losses."

CHAPTER 2

SURRENDER OF COMPANY'S CARRIED-FORWARD LOSSES ETC

188BA Overview of Chapter

(1) This Chapter allows a company to surrender losses and other amounts that have been carried forward to an accounting period of the company.

(2) Section 188BB sets out the basic provisions about the surrendering of losses and other amounts.

(3) Sections 188BC to 188BJ place restrictions on the surrendering of losses and other amounts.

188BB Surrender of carried-forward losses and other amounts

(1) Subsection (2) applies if—

(a) a loss or other amount is carried forward to an accounting period of a company under any of the following provisions—

(i) section 463G(6) of CTA 2009 (carry forward of post-1 April 2017 non-trading deficit from loan relationships);

(ii) section 753(3) of that Act (carry forward of non-trading loss on intangible fixed assets);

(iii) section 1223 of that Act (carry forward of expenses of management of investment business);

(iv) section 45A(4) of this Act (carry forward of post-1 April 2017 trade loss);

(v) sections 62(5)(a) and 63(3)(a) of this Act (carry forward of loss made in UK property business); or

(b) section 303C of this Act (excess carried forward non-decommissioning losses of ring fence trade: relief against total profits) applies in relation to an amount.

(2) The company may surrender the loss or other amount under this Chapter so far as the loss or other amount is eligible for corporation tax relief (apart from this Part).

(3) Subsection (4) applies if any of a BLAGAB trade loss made by an insurance company for an accounting period is carried forward to an accounting period of the company ("the later period") under section 124A(2) or 124C(3) of FA 2012.

(4) The company may surrender the remaining carried forward amount under this Chapter so far as that amount is eligible for corporation tax relief (apart from this Part).

(5) In subsection (4) "the remaining carried forward amount" means so much of the amount carried forward (as mentioned in subsection (3)) as cannot be deducted under section 124A(5) or 124C(6) of FA 2012 from the company's BLAGAB trade profit (if any) of the later period.

(6) Under paragraph 70(1) of Schedule 18 to FA 1998, the company surrenders losses or other amounts, so far as eligible for surrender under this Chapter, by consenting to

one or more claims for group relief for carried-forward losses in relation to the amounts (see requirement 1 in section 188CB(3) and requirement 1 in section 188CC(3)).

(7) In this Part, in relation to losses or other amounts within subsection (1) or (4) that a company has carried forward to an accounting period—

"the surrenderable amounts" means those losses and other amounts so far as eligible for surrender under this Chapter,

"surrendering company" means the company that has the losses or other amounts,

"the surrender period" means the accounting period to which the losses and other amounts have been carried forward.

(8) See sections 188BC to 188BJ for provisions restricting what the surrendering company may surrender under this section.

188BC Restriction on surrendering pre-1 April 2017 losses etc

(1) The surrendering company may not surrender under this Chapter—

(a) a loss carried forward to the surrender period under section 753(3) of CTA 2009 in so far as the loss is made up of an amount previously carried forward under that section from an accounting period beginning before 1 April 2017,

(b) expenses carried forward to the surrender period under section 1223 of CTA 2009 if the expenses were first deductible under section 1219 of that Act for an accounting period beginning before that date, or

(c) a loss carried forward to the surrender period under section 62(5)(a) or 63(3)(a) of this Act if the loss was made in an accounting period beginning before that date.

(2) The surrendering company may not surrender under this Chapter a qualifying charitable donation carried forward to the surrender period under section 1223 of CTA 2009.

188BD Restriction where investment business has become small or negligible

(1) The surrendering company may not surrender under this Chapter—

(a) a loss carried forward to the surrender period under section 753(3) of CTA 2009 if an investment business carried on by the surrendering company became small or negligible before the beginning of that period,

(b) expenses carried forward to the surrender period under section 1223 of CTA 2009 if the surrendering company's investment business became small or negligible before the beginning of that period, or

(c) a loss carried forward to the surrender period under section 62(5)(a) or 63(3)(a) if the surrendering company's investment business became small or negligible before the beginning of that period.

(2) In this section—

(a) "company with investment business" has the same meaning as in Part 16 of CTA 2009 (see section 1218B of that Act);

(b) references to a company's investment business are to be construed in accordance with section 1219(2) of CTA 2009.

188BE Restriction where surrendering company could use losses etc itself

The surrendering company may not surrender any losses or other amounts under this Chapter if—

(a) section 269ZD(2) applies in determining the taxable total profits of the surrendering company for the surrender period, and

(b) the sum of the relevant deductions (within the meaning of section 269ZD(3)) made for the surrender period is less than the maximum permitted by section 269ZD(2).

188BF Restriction where surrendering company has no income-generating assets

The surrendering company may not surrender any losses or other amounts under this Chapter if at the end of the surrender period the surrendering company has no assets capable of producing income.

188BG Restrictions for certain insurance companies

(1) If the surrendering company is a general insurance company and the surrender period is an excluded accounting period, the company may not surrender under this Chapter—

(a) a loss carried forward to the surrender period under section 753(3) of CTA 2009;

(b) expenses carried forward to the surrender period under section 1223 of CTA 2009;

(c) a loss carried forward to the surrender period under section 62(5)(a) or 63(3)(a).

(2) In subsection (1) "excluded accounting period" and "general insurance company" are to be interpreted in accordance with section 269ZG.

(3) If the surrendering company is a Solvency 2 insurance company it may not surrender under this Chapter—

(a) a loss carried forward to the surrender period under section 753(3) of CTA 2009,

(b) expenses carried forward to the surrender period under section 1223 of CTA 2009, or

(c) a loss carried forward to the surrender period under section 62(5)(a) or 63(3)(a),

so far as the loss is, or (as the case may be) the expenses are, a shock loss.

188BH   Restriction on surrender of losses etc made when UK resident

(1) This section applies in relation to a loss or other amount carried forward to the surrender period if the surrendering company was UK resident during the loss-making period.

(2) The surrendering company may not surrender the loss or other amount under this Chapter so far as the loss or other amount—

(a) is attributable to a permanent establishment through which the company carried on a trade outside the United Kingdom during the loss-making period (see subsection (3)), and

(b) is, or represents, an amount within subsection (5).

(3) A loss or other amount is attributable to a permanent establishment of the surrendering company if (ignoring this section) the amount could be included in the company's surrenderable amounts for the surrender period if those amounts were determined—

(a) by reference to that establishment alone, and

(b) by applying, in relation to that establishment, principles corresponding in all material respects to those mentioned in subsection (4).

(4) The principles are those that would be applied for corporation tax purposes in determining an equivalent loss or other amount in the case of a permanent establishment through which a non-UK resident company carried on a trade in the United Kingdom.

(5) An amount is within this subsection if, for the purposes of non-UK tax chargeable under the law of the territory in which the permanent establishment was situated, the amount is or at any time has been (in any period) deductible from or otherwise allowable against non-UK profits of a person other than the surrendering company.

(6) Subsection (7) applies for the purposes of subsection (5) if, in order to determine if an amount is or at any time has been deductible or otherwise allowable for the purposes of non-UK tax chargeable under the law of a territory, it is necessary under that law to know if the amount (or a corresponding amount) is or has been deductible or otherwise allowable for tax purposes in the United Kingdom.

(7) The amount is to be treated as deductible or otherwise allowable for the purposes of the non-UK tax chargeable under the law of the territory concerned if (and only if) the surrendering company is treated as resident in that territory for the purposes of the non-UK tax.

(8) In this section and section 188BI—

"the loss-making period", in relation to a loss or other amount, means the accounting period in which the loss was made or the amount arose,

"non-UK tax" has the meaning it has in Part 5 (see section 187), and

"non-UK profits" has the meaning given by section 108.

188BI   Restriction on surrender of losses made when non-UK resident

(1) This section applies in relation to a loss or other amount carried forward to the surrender period if during the loss-making period the surrendering company was a non-UK resident company—

(a) carrying on a trade of dealing in or developing UK land, or

(b) carrying on a trade in the United Kingdom through a permanent establishment.

(2) If the surrendering company was established in the EEA during the loss-making period, it may surrender the loss or other amount under this Chapter only so far as conditions A and B are met.

Subsection (8) imposes restrictions on a surrender under this subsection.

(3) In any other case, the surrendering company may surrender the loss or other amount under this Chapter only so far as conditions A, B and C are met in relation to the loss or amount.

(4) Condition A is that the loss or other amount is attributable to activities of the surrendering company in respect of which it is within the charge to corporation tax for the loss-making period.

(5) Condition B is that the loss or other amount is not attributable to activities of the surrendering company that are double taxation exempt for the loss-making period (within the meaning given by section 186).

(6) Condition C is that—

  (a) the loss or other amount does not correspond to, and is not represented in, an amount with subsection (7), and
  (b) no amount brought into account in calculating the loss or other amount corresponds to, or is represented in, an amount within subsection (7).

(7) An amount is within this subsection if, for the purposes of non-UK tax chargeable under the law of a territory, the amount is or at any time has been (in any period) deductible from or otherwise allowable against non-UK profits of any person.

(8) A loss or other amount may not be surrendered by virtue of subsection (2) if and to the extent that it, or any amount brought into account in calculating it, corresponds to, or is represented in, amounts within subsection (9).

(9) An amount is within this subsection if, for the purposes of non-UK tax chargeable under the law of a territory, the amount has (in any period) been deducted from or otherwise allowed against non-UK profits of any person.

(10) But an amount is not to be taken to be within subsection (7) or (9) by reason only that it is—

  (a) an amount of profits brought into account for the purpose of being excluded from non-UK profits of the person, or
  (b) an amount brought into account in calculating an amount of profits brought into account as mentioned in paragraph (a).

(11) Subsection (12) applies for the purposes of subsection (7) if, in order to determine if an amount is or at any time has been deductible or otherwise allowable for the purposes of non-UK tax chargeable under the law of a territory, it is necessary under that law to know if the amount (or a corresponding amount) is or at any time has been deductible or otherwise allowable for tax purposes in the United Kingdom.

(12) The amount is to be treated as deductible or otherwise allowable for the purposes of the non-UK tax chargeable under the law of the territory concerned.

(13) For the purposes of this section a company is established in the EEA if—

  (a) it is constituted under the law of the United Kingdom or an EEA territory, and
  (b) it has its registered office, central administration or principal place of business within the European Economic Area.

(14) In subsection (13) "EEA territory", in relation to any time, means a territory outside the United Kingdom that is within the European Economic Area at that time.

188BJ Restriction on surrender losses etc made when dual resident

The surrendering company may not surrender a loss or other amount under this Chapter if the company was not eligible to surrender the loss or other amount under Chapter 2 of Part 5 by reason of section 109 (restriction on losses etc surrenderable by dual resident).

CHAPTER 3

CLAIMS FOR GROUP RELIEF FOR CARRIED-FORWARD LOSSES

Introduction

188CA Overview of Chapter

This Chapter sets out how a company may claim group relief for carried-forward losses and how the relief is given.

Claiming group relief for carried-forward losses

188CB Claims in relation to all the surrenderable amounts

(1) This section applies in relation to the surrendering company's surrenderable amounts for the surrender period under Chapter 2.

(2) If the requirements in subsection (3) are met, a company ("the claimant company") may make a claim for group relief for carried-forward losses for an accounting period ("the claim period") in relation to the surrenderable amounts.

(3) The requirements are as follows—

Requirement 1
The surrendering company consents to the claim.
Requirement 2
There is a period ("the overlapping period") that is common to the claim period and the surrender period.
Requirement 3
At a time during the overlapping period—
    (a) the group condition is met (see section 188CE)
    (b) consortium condition 1 is met (see section 188CF), or
    (c) consortium condition 2 is met (see section 188CG).

(4) A claim under this section may relate to the whole of the surrenderable amounts or to part of them only.

(5) This section is subject to section 188CD (claim not allowed by company with unused carried-forward losses of its own).

188CC Claims in relation to the surrenderable amounts that are attributable to a specified accounting period

(1) This section applies in relation to the surrendering company's surrenderable amounts for the surrender period under Chapter 2.

(2) If the requirements in subsection (3) are met, a company ("the claimant company") may make a claim for group relief for carried-forward losses for an accounting period ("the claim period") in relation to the surrenderable amounts that are attributable to an accounting period of the surrendering company specified in the claim ("the specified loss-making period").

(3) The requirements are as follows—

Requirement 1
The surrendering company consents to the claim.
Requirement 2
There is a period ("the overlapping period") that is common to the claim period and the surrender period.
Requirement 3
Consortium condition 3 (see section 188CH) or consortium condition 4 (see section 188CI) is met throughout a period which—
    (a) begins before or during the specified loss-making period, and
    (b) ends during or after the overlapping period.

(4) A claim under this section may relate to the whole of the surrenderable amounts attributable to the specified loss-making period or to part of them only.

(5) This section is subject to section 188CD (claim not allowed by company with unused carried-forward losses of its own)

188CD Claim not allowed by company with unused carried-forward losses of its own

A company may not make a claim for group relief for carried-forward losses for an accounting period if—

    (a) any amount carried forward to that period under any provision mentioned in section 188BB(1), or any amount which is carried forward to that period and falls within section 124B(1)(b) of FA 2012, is not deducted in full from the total profits of the company for that period at Step 2 of section 4(2),
    (b) the company makes a claim under section 458(1) of CTA 2009 for any amount of a deficit to be excepted from being set off against profits of that period,
    (c) the company makes a claim under section 45(4A) that the profits of a trade of that period are not to be reduced or are not to be reduced by more than a specified amount, or
    (d) the company makes a claim under section 45B(5) for relief not to be given in that period for an amount of a loss or for a specified part of an amount of a loss.

188CE   The group condition

(1) The group condition is met if the surrendering company and the claimant company—

    (a) are members of the same group of companies, and

    (b) are both UK related.

(2) For the meaning of "UK related" in subsection (1)(b) and in sections 188CF to 188CI, see section 188CJ.

188CF   Consortium condition 1

(1) Consortium condition 1 is met if—

    (a) the claimant company is a trading company or a holding company,

    (b) the claimant company is owned by a consortium,

    (c) the surrendering company is a member of the consortium, and

    (d) both companies are UK related.

(2) But consortium condition 1 is not met if a profit on a sale within subsection (3) by the surrendering company would be a trading receipt of the surrendering company.

(3) A sale is within this subsection if it is a sale of—

    (a) the share capital the surrendering company owns in the claimant company, or

    (b) if the claimant company is owned by the consortium as a result of section 153(3) (consortiums involving holding companies), the share capital the surrendering company owns in the holding company in question.

188CG   Consortium condition 2

(1) Consortium condition 2 is met if—

    (a) the claimant company is a trading company or a holding company,

    (b) the claimant company is owned by a consortium,

    (c) the surrendering company is not a member of the consortium,

    (d) the surrendering company is a member of the same group of companies as a third company ("the link company"),

    (e) the link company is a member of the consortium,

    (f) the surrendering company and the claimant company are both UK related.

(2) But consortium condition 2 is not met if a profit on a sale within subsection (3) by the link company would be a trading receipt of that company.

(3) A sale is within this subsection if it is a sale of—

    (a) the share capital the link company owns in the claimant company, or

    (b) if the claimant company is owned by the consortium as a result of section 153(3) (consortiums involving holding companies), the share capital the link company owns in the holding company in question.

188CH   Consortium condition 3

(1) Consortium condition 3 is met if—

    (a) the surrendering company is a trading company or a holding company,

    (b) the surrendering company is owned by a consortium,

    (c) the claimant company is a member of the consortium, and

    (d) both companies are UK related.

(2) But consortium condition 3 is not met if a profit on a sale within subsection (3) by the claimant company would be a trading receipt of the claimant company.

(3) A sale is within this subsection if it is a sale of—

    (a) the share capital the claimant company owns in the surrendering company, or

    (b) if the surrendering company is owned by the consortium as a result of section 153(3) (consortiums involving holding companies), the share capital the claimant company owns in the holding company in question.

188CI   Consortium condition 4

(1) Consortium condition 4 is met if—

    (a) the surrendering company is a trading company or a holding company,

    (b) the surrendering company is owned by a consortium,

    (c) the claimant company is not a member of the consortium,

    (d) the claimant company is a member of the same group of companies as a third company ("the link company"),

    (e) the link company is a member of the consortium, and

    (f) the claimant company and the surrendering company are both UK related.

(2) But consortium condition 4 is not met if a profit on a sale within subsection (3) by the link company would be a trading receipt of that company.

(3) A sale is within this subsection if it is a sale of—

(a) the share capital the link company owns in the surrendering company, or

(b) if the surrendering company is owned by the consortium as a result of section 153(3) (consortiums involving holding companies), the share capital the link company owns in the holding company in question.

188CJ Meaning of "UK related" company

For the purpose of sections 188CE to 188CI a company is UK related if—

(a) it is a UK resident company, or

(b) it is a non-UK resident company carrying on a trade in the United Kingdom through a permanent establishment.

Giving group relief for carried-forward losses

188CK Deductions from total profits

(1) If a claimant company makes a claim under section 188CB or 188CC, the group relief for carried-forward losses is given by the making of a deduction from the claimant company's total profits of the claim period.

(2) In the case of a claim under section 188CB, the amount of the deduction under subsection (1) is—

(a) an amount equal to the surrendering company's surrenderable amounts for the surrender period, or

(b) if the claim is in relation to only part of those amounts, an amount equal to that part.

(3) Subsection (2) is subject to—

(a) subsections (6) to (9),

(b) the limitations set out in Chapter 4, and

(c) section 269ZD (restriction on deductions from total profits).

(4) In the case of a claim under section 188CC, the amount of the deduction under subsection (1) is—

(a) an amount equal to the surrendering company's surrenderable amounts for the surrender period that are attributable to the specified loss-making period, or

(b) if the claim is in relation to only part of those amounts, an amount equal to that part.

(5) Subsection (4) is subject to—

(a) subsections (6) to (9),

(b) the limitations set out in Chapter 5, and

(c) section 269ZD (restriction on deductions from total profits).

(6) A deduction under subsection (1) is to be made—

(a) before deductions for relief within subsection (7), but

(b) after all other deductions to be made at Step 2 in section 4(2) (apart from deductions for group relief for carried-forward losses on other claims).

(7) The deductions within this subsection are deductions for relief—

(a) under section 37 in relation to a loss made in an accounting period after the claim period,

(b) under section 260(3) of CAA 2001 in relation to capital allowances for an accounting period after the claim period, and

(c) under section 389 or 463B of CTA 2009 in relation to a deficit of a deficit period after the claim period.

(8) For the purposes of subsection (6)(b) it is to be assumed that the claimant company has claimed all relief available to it for the claim period under section 37 of this Act or section 260(3) of CAA 2001.

(9) Corporation tax relief is not to be given more than once for the same amount, whether—

(a) by giving group relief for carried-forward losses and by giving some other relief (for any accounting period) to the surrendering company, or

(b) by giving group relief for carried-forward losses more than once.

CHAPTER 4

LIMITATIONS ON RELIEF: CLAIMS UNDER SECTION 188CB

Introduction

188DA Overview

This Chapter sets out limitations on the amount of relief which may be given on a claim under section 188CB.

General limitation on amount of relief

188DB Limitation on amount of relief applying to all claims under section 188CB

(1) The amount of group relief for carried-forward losses to be given on a claim under section 188CB ("the current claim") is limited to whichever is the lesser of—

(a) the amount mentioned in subsection (2), and
(b) the amount mentioned in subsection (3).

(2) The amount referred to in subsection (1)(a) is the unused part of the surrenderable amounts (see section 188DC).

(3) The amount referred to in subsection (1)(b) is the difference between—

(a) the claimant company's relevant maximum for the overlapping period (see section 188DD), and
(b) the amount of previously claimed group relief for carried-forward losses for the overlapping period (see section 188DE).

188DC Unused part of the surrenderable amounts

(1) The unused part of the surrenderable amounts is the amount equal to—

(a) the surrenderable amount for the overlapping period (see subsection (2)), less
(b) the amount of prior surrenders for that period (see subsections (3) to (5)).

(2) To determine the surrenderable amount for the overlapping period—

(a) take the proportion of the surrender period included in the overlapping period, and
(b) apply that proportion to the surrenderable amounts for the surrender period.

The surrenderable amount for the overlapping period is the amount given as a result of paragraph (b).

(3) To determine the amount of prior surrenders for the overlapping period—

(a) identify any prior claims for the purposes of this section (see subsection (4)), and
(b) take the steps set out in subsection (5) in relation to each such claim.

The amount of prior surrenders for the overlapping period is the total of the previously used amounts given at step 3 in subsection (5) for all the prior claims.

(4) A claim is a prior claim for the purposes of this section if—

(a) it is either—

(i) a claim under section 188CB by any company which relates to the same amounts as the current claim, or
(ii) a claim under section 188CC by any company which relates to amounts included in the amounts to which the current claim relates,

(b) it is made before the current claim, and
(c) it has not been withdrawn.

(5) These are the steps referred to in subsection (3)(b) to be taken in relation to each prior claim.

Step 1
Identify the overlapping period for the prior claim.
Step 2
Identify any period that is common to the overlapping period for the current claim and the overlapping period for the prior claim.
If there is a common period, go to step 3.
If there is no common period, there is no previously used amount in relation to the prior claim (and ignore step 3).
Step 3
Determine the previously used amount of group relief for carried-forward losses in relation to the prior claim (see subsection (6)).

(6) To determine the previously used amount of group relief for carried-forward losses in relation to a prior claim—

(a) take the proportion of the overlapping period for the prior claim that is included in the common period identified at step 2 in relation to that claim, and
(b) apply that proportion to the amount of group relief for carried-forward losses given on the prior claim.

The previously used amount of group relief for carried-forward losses in relation to the prior claim is the amount given as a result of paragraph (b).

(7) For the meaning of the "overlapping period" see section 188DG.

188DD   Claimant company's relevant maximum for overlapping period

(1) The claimant company's relevant maximum for the overlapping period is determined as follows—

Step 1
Calculate the claimant company's relevant maximum for the claim period in accordance with section 269ZD(4).

Step 2
Deduct from that amount the sum of—

(a) any deductions made by the company for the claim period
  (i) under section 45(4)(b) or 45B(4), or
  (ii) under section 303B or 303D by virtue of section 304(5),

(b) any deductions made by the company for the claim period under section 457(3) or 463H(5) of CTA 2009,
(c) any deductions made by the company for the claim period under section 124(5), 124A(5) or 124C(6) of FA 2012, and
(d) any deductions made by the company for the claim period which are deductions within any of paragraphs (a) to (i) and (k) of section 269ZD(3).

Step 3
Take the proportion of the claim period included in the overlapping period and apply that proportion to the amount arrived at under step 2.

(2) In step 2 of subsection (1)—

(a) in paragraph (a)(i), the references to deductions under section 45(4)(b) or 45B(4) do not include deductions that would be ignored for the purposes of section 269ZB by reason of—
  (i) section 1209(3), 1210(5A) or 1211(7A) of CTA 2009 (losses of film trade),
  (ii) section 1216DA(3), 1216DB(5A) or 1216DC(7A) of that Act (losses of television programme trade),
  (iii) section 1217DA(3), 1217DB(5A) or 1217DC(7A) of that Act (losses of video game trade),
  (iv) section 1217MA(3) or 1217MC(9) of that Act (losses of theatrical trade),
  (v) section 1217SA(3) or 1217SC(9) of that Act (losses of orchestral trade),
  (vi) section 1218ZDA(3) or 1218ZDC(9) of that Act (losses of museum or gallery exhibition trade),
  (vii) section 65(4B) or 67A(5A) (losses of UK or EEA furnished holiday lettings business),
  (viii) section 269ZJ(1) (insurance companies: shock losses),
  (ix) section 304(7) (certain losses of ring fence trades), or
  (x) section 356NJ(2) (pre-1 April 2017 loss arising from oil contractor activities);

(b) in paragraph (b) the reference to a deduction under section 463H(5) does not include the deduction of a shock loss.

(3) If the amount of the claimant company's relevant profits for the claim period (calculated in accordance with section 269ZD(5)) is less than the amount of the claimant company's deductions allowance for the claim period (determined in accordance with section 269ZD(6)), subsection (1) has effect as if step 1 was modified as follows—

Step 1
Calculate the claimant company's relevant profits for the claim period in accordance with section 269ZD(5).

(4) If section 269ZD has effect in relation to the claimant company for the claim period with the modifications set out in section 269ZE(1) (special loss cap for insurance companies in certain cases), subsection (1) has effect as if steps 1 and 2 were modified as follows—

Step 1

Determine, in accordance with section 269ZE(5), the modified loss cap for the claimant company and the claim period.

Step 2

Reduce that amount by the total of any deductions made by the claimant company for the claim period which are deductions within any of paragraphs (a) to (i) and (k) of section 269ZD(3).

(5) Subsection (2) is to be ignored if subsection (3) applies.

188DE Previously claimed group relief for carried-forward losses

(1) To determine the amount of previously claimed group relief for carried-forward losses for the overlapping period—

(a) identify any prior claims for the purposes of this section (see subsection (2)), and

(b) take the steps set out in subsection (3) in relation to each such claim.

The amount of previously claimed group relief for carried-forward losses for the overlapping period is the total of the previously claimed amounts given at step 3 in subsection (3) for all the prior claims.

(2) A claim is a prior claim for the purposes of this section if—

(a) it is a claim under section 188CB or 188CC by the claimant company for group relief for carried-forward losses which would be given by way of a deduction from the company's total profits of the claim period,

(b) it is made before the current claim, and

(c) it has not been withdrawn.

(3) These are the steps referred to in subsection (1)(b) to be taken in relation to each prior claim.

Step 1

Identify the overlapping period for the prior claim.

Step 2

Identify any period that is common to the overlapping period for the current claim and the overlapping period for the prior claim.

If there is a common period, go to step 3.

If there is no common period, there is no previously claimed amount in relation to the prior claim (and ignore step 3).

Step 3

Determine the previously claimed amount of group relief for carried forward losses in relation to the prior claim (see subsection (4)).

(4) To determine the previously claimed amount of group relief for carried-forward losses in relation to a prior claim—

(a) take the proportion of the overlapping period for the prior claim that is included in the common period identified at step 2 in relation to that claim, and

(b) apply that proportion to the amount of group relief for carried-forward losses given on the prior claim.

The previously claimed amount of group relief for carried-forward losses in relation to the prior claim is the amount given as a result of paragraph (b).

188DF Sections 188DC to 188DE: supplementary

(1) If two or more claims for group relief for carried-forward losses are made at the same time, for the purpose of section 188DC and 188DE treat the claims as made—

(a) in such order as the company making them may elect or the companies making them may jointly elect, or

(b) if no such election is made, in such order as an officer of Revenue and Customs may direct.

(2) For the purpose of step 3 in each of section 188DC(5) and 188DE(3) the amount of group relief for carried-forward losses given on a prior claim is determined on the basis that relief is given on the claim before it is given on any later claim.

(3) If the use of any proportion mentioned in subsection (4), would, in the circumstances of a particular case, produce a result that is unjust or unreasonable, the proportion is to be modified so far as necessary to produce a result that is just and reasonable.

(4) The proportions are those found in—

(a) section 188DC(2),

(b) section 188DC(6),

(c) step 3 in section 188DD(1), and

(d) section 188DE(4)

188DG Sections 188DC and 188DE: meaning of "the overlapping period"

(1) In sections 188DC and 188DE "the overlapping period", in relation to a claim for group relief for carried-forward losses, means the period that is common to the claim period and the surrender period (see Requirement 2 in section 188CB(3) and Requirement 2 in section 188CC(3)).

(2) But if during any part of the overlapping period the relief condition is not met, that part is treated as not forming part of the overlapping period but instead as forming—

(a) a part of the surrender period that is not included in the overlapping period, and

(b) a part of the claim period that is not included in the overlapping period.

(3) The relief condition is the condition on which the claim for group relief for carried forward losses is based, that is—

the group condition,
consortium condition 1,
consortium condition 2,
consortium condition 3, or
consortium condition 4.

Further limitations on amount of relief if claim based on consortium conditions 1 or 2

188DH Condition 1: ownership proportion

(1) This section applies if—

(a) the claimant company makes a claim under section 188CB for group relief for carried-forward losses, and

(b) the claim is based on consortium condition 1.

(2) The relief to be given on the claim is limited to the ownership proportion of the claimant company's relevant maximum for the overlapping period (see section 188DD to determine the claimant company's relevant maximum for the overlapping period).

(3) The ownership proportion is the same as the lowest of the following proportions prevailing during the overlapping period—

(a) the proportion of the ordinary share capital of the claimant company that is beneficially owned by the surrendering company,

(b) the proportion of any profits available for distribution to equity holders of the claimant company to which the surrendering company is beneficially entitled,

(c) the proportion of any assets of the claimant company available for distribution to such equity holders on a winding up to which the surrendering company would be beneficially entitled, and

(d) the proportion of the voting power in the claimant company that is directly possessed by the surrendering company.

(4) If any of the proportions in subsection (3) changes during the overlapping period, use the average of that proportion during that period.

(5) If the claimant company is owned by the consortium company as a result of section 153(3) (consortium company involving holding companies), references in subsection (3) to the claimant company are to be read as references to the holding company in question.

(6) In this section "the overlapping period" is to be read in accordance with section 188DG.

(7) Chapter 6 of Part 5 (equity holders and profits or assets available for distribution) applies for the purposes of subsection (3)(b) and (c).

188DI Condition 2: ownership proportion

(1) This section applies if—

(a) the claimant company makes a claim under section 188CB for group relief for carried-forward losses, and

(b) the claim is based on consortium condition 2.

(2) The limitation on relief in section 188DH applies in relation to the claim, but for this purpose references in section 188DH(3) to the surrendering company are to be read as reference to the link company.

188DJ Condition 2: companies in link company's group

(1) Where—

(a) the claimant company makes a claim under section 188CB, and

(b) the claim is based on consortium condition 2,

the amount of relief to be given on the claim is limited by subsections (2) and (3).

(2) There is a limit on the amount of group relief for carried-forward losses that can be given, in total, to the claimant company for the claim period on consortium claims made in relation to losses and other amounts surrendered by the link company and group companies.

(3) That limit is the same as the limit that, as a result of section 188DH(2), would apply for the purposes of a consortium claim made by the claimant company for the claim period in relation to losses or other amounts surrendered by the link company, assuming that the link company was UK related.

(4) In determining the limit that would apply as a result of section 188DH(2) it is to be assumed that the accounting period of the link company is the same as the accounting period of the claimant company.

(5) In this section—

"consortium claim" means a claim for group relief for carried-forward losses under section 188CB,

"group company" means a company that is a member of the same group of companies as the link company (other than the link company itself), and

"UK related", in relation to a company, has the meaning given by section 188CJ.

188DK Conditions 1 and 2: claimant company not controlled by surrendering company etc

(1) This section applies if—

(a) the claimant company makes a claim under section 188CB for group relief for carried-forward losses,

(b) the claim is based on consortium condition 1, and

(c) during any part of the overlapping period, arrangements within subsection (3) are in place which enable a person to prevent the surrendering company, either alone or together with one or more other companies that are members of the consortium, from controlling the claimant company.

(2) This section also applies if—

(a) the claimant company makes a claim under section 188CB for group relief for carried-forward losses,

(b) the claim is based on consortium condition 2, and

(c) during any part of the overlapping period, arrangements within subsection (3) are in place which enable a person to prevent the link company, either alone or together with one or more other companies that are members of the consortium, from controlling the claimant company.

(3) Arrangements are within this subsection if—

(a) the company, either alone or together with one or more other companies that are members of the consortium, would control the claimant company, but for the existence of the arrangements, and

(b) the arrangements form part of a scheme the main purpose, or one of the main purposes, of which is to enable the claimant company to obtain a tax advantage under this Chapter.

(4) The relief to be given on the claim is to be determined as if the claimant company's relevant maximum for the overlapping period was 50% of what it would be but for this section (see section 188DD to determine the claimant company's relevant maximum for the overlapping period).

(5) In this section "the overlapping period" is to be read in accordance with section 188DG

(6) Section 1139 ("tax advantage") applies for the purposes of this section.

188DL Conditions 1 and 2: claimant company in group of companies

(1) This section applies if—

(a) the claimant company makes a claim under section 188CB based on consortium condition 1 or 2, and

(b) the claimant company is a member of a group of companies.

(2) In determining the claimant company's relevant maximum for the overlapping period under section 188DD, the amount calculated at step 1 of that section is to be treated as reduced (but not below nil) by the group's potential relief.

(3) The group's potential relief is the sum of—

(a) the maximum amount of group relief for carried-forward losses that could be claimed by the claimant company for the claim period on claims under section 188CB based on the group condition, and

(b) the maximum amount of group relief under Part 5 that could be claimed by the claimant company for the claim period on claims under section 130 based on the group condition.

(4) Before determining the maximum amount of potential group relief for carried-forward losses or potential group relief under subsection (3) take account of any claim made before the claim mentioned in subsection (1) that—

(a) is a claim for group relief or group relief for carried-forward losses based on the group condition made by another member of the same group of companies as the claimant company, and

(b) is in relation to losses or other amounts surrendered.

CHAPTER 5
LIMITATIONS ON RELIEF: CLAIMS UNDER SECTION 188CC

Introduction

188EA Overview of Chapter

This Chapter sets out limitations on the amount of relief which may be given on a claim under section 188CC.

General limitation on amount of relief

188EB Limitation on amount of relief applying to all claims under section 188CC

(1) The amount of group relief for carried-forward losses to be given on a claim under section 188CC ("the current claim") is limited to whichever is the lesser of—

(a) the amount mentioned in subsection (2),

(b) the amount mentioned in subsection (3), and

(c) the amount mentioned in subsection (4).

(2) The amount referred to in subsection (1)(a) is the unused part of the surrenderable amounts that are attributable to the specified loss-making period (see section 188EC).

(3) The amount referred to in subsection (1)(b) is the difference between—

(a) the claimant company's relevant maximum for the overlapping period (see section 188ED), and

(b) the amount of previously claimed group relief for carried-forward losses for the overlapping period (see section 188EE).

(4) The amount referred to in subsection (1)(c) is the potential Part 5 group relief amount (see section 188EF).

188EC Unused part of surrenderable amounts attributable to specified loss-making period

(1) The unused part of the surrenderable amounts that are attributable to the specified loss-making period is the amount equal to—

(a) the surrenderable amount for the overlapping period (see subsection (2)), less

(b) the amount of prior surrenders for that period (see subsections (3) to (5)).

(2) To determine the surrenderable amount for the overlapping period—

(a) take the proportion of the surrender period included in the overlapping period, and

(b) apply that proportion to the surrenderable amounts for the surrender period that are attributable to the specified loss-making period.

The surrenderable amount for the overlapping period is the amount given as a result of paragraph (b).

(3) To determine the amount of prior surrenders for the overlapping period—

(a) identify any prior claims for the purposes of this section (see subsection (4)), and

(b) take the steps set out in subsection (5) in relation to each such claim.

The amount of prior surrenders for the overlapping period is the total of the previously used amounts given at step 3 in subsection (5) for all the prior claims.

(4) A claim is a prior claim for the purposes of this section if—

    (a) it is either—

        (i) a claim under section 188CB by any company which relates to the amounts to which the current claim relates (as well as any other amounts), or

        (ii) a claim under section 188CC by any company which relates to the same amounts to which the current claim relates,

    (b) it is made before the current claim, and

    (c) it has not been withdrawn.

(5) These are the steps referred to in subsection (3)(b) to be taken in relation to each prior claim.

Step 1
Identify the overlapping period for the prior claim.

Step 2
Identify any period that is common to the overlapping period for the current claim and the overlapping period for the prior claim.
If there is a common period, go to step 3.
If there is no common period, there is no previously used amount in relation to the prior claim (and ignore step 3).

Step 3
Determine the previously used amount of group relief for carried-forward losses in relation to the prior claim (see subsections (6) to (8)).

(6) To determine the previously used amount of group relief for carried-forward losses in relation to a prior claim made under section 188CB—

Step 1
Take the proportion of the overlapping period for the prior claim that is included in the common period identified at step 2 in subsection (5) in relation to that claim.

Step 2
Apply that proportion to the amount of group relief for carried-forward losses given on the claim.

Step 3
Multiply the amount arrived at under step 2 by the fraction set out in subsection (7).

(7) The fraction is—

A / B

where—

    A is the sum of the surrenderable amounts that are attributable to the specified loss-making period, and

    B is the sum of all the surrenderable amounts.

(8) To determine the previously used amount of group relief for carried-forward losses in relation to a prior claim made under section 188CC—

    (a) take the proportion of the overlapping period for the prior claim that is included in the common period identified at step 2 in subsection (5) in relation to that claim, and

    (b) apply that proportion to the amount of group relief for carried-forward losses given on the prior claim.

The previously used amount of group relief for carried-forward losses in relation to the prior claim is the amount given as a result of paragraph (b).

188ED Claimant company's relevant maximum for the overlapping period

(1) The claimant company's relevant maximum for the overlapping period is determined as follows—

Step 1
Calculate the claimant company's relevant maximum for the claim period in accordance with section 269ZD(4).

Step 2
Deduct from that amount the sum of—

    (a) any deductions made by the company for the claim period

        (i) under section 45(4)(b) or 45B(4), or

        (ii) under section 303B or 303D by virtue of section 304(5),

    (b) any deduction made by the company for the claim period under section 457(3) or 463H(5) of CTA 2009,

(c) any deductions made by the company for the claim period under section 124(5), 124A(5) or 124C(6) of FA 2012, and

(d) any deductions made by the company for the claim period which are deductions within any of paragraphs (a) to (i) and (k) of section 269ZD(3).

Step 3

Take the proportion of the claim period included in the overlapping period and apply that proportion to the amount arrived at under step 2.

(2) In step 2 of subsection (1)—

(a) in paragraph (a)(i), the references to deductions under section 45(4)(b) or 45B(4) do not include deductions that would be ignored for the purposes of section 269ZB by reason of—

(i) section 1209(3), 1210(5A) or 1211(7A) of CTA 2009 (losses of film trade),

(ii) section 1216DA(3), 1216DB(5A) or 1216DC(7A) of that Act (losses of television programme trade),

(iii) section 1217DA(3), 1217DB(5A) or 1217DC(7A) of that Act (losses of video game trade),

(iv) section 1217MA(3) or 1217MC(9) of that Act (losses of theatrical trade),

(v) section 1217SA(3) or 1217SC(9) of that Act (losses of orchestral trade),

(vi) section 1218ZDA(3) or 1218ZDC(9) of that Act (losses of museum or gallery exhibition trade),

(vii) section 65(4B) or 67A(5A) (losses of UK or EEA furnished holiday lettings business),

(viii) section 269ZJ(1) (insurance companies: shock losses),

(ix) section 304(7) (certain losses of ring fence trades), or

(x) section 356NJ(2) (pre-1 April 2017 loss arising from oil contractor activities);

(b) in paragraph (b) the reference to a deduction under section 463H(5) does not include the deduction of a shock loss.

(3) If the amount of the claimant company's relevant profits for the claim period (calculated in accordance with section 269ZD(5)) is less than the amount of the claimant company's deductions allowance for the claim period (determined in accordance with section 269ZD(6)), subsection (1) has effect as if step 1 was modified as follows—

Step 1

Calculate the claimant company's relevant profits for the claim period in accordance with section 269ZD(5).

(4) If section 269ZD has effect in relation to the claimant company for the claim period with the modifications set out in section 269ZE(1) (special loss cap for insurance companies in certain cases), subsection (1) has effect as if steps 1 and 2 were modified as follows—

Step 1

Determine, in accordance with section 269ZE(5), the modified loss cap for the claimant company and the claim period.

Step 2

Reduce that amount by the total of any deductions made by the claimant company for the claim period which are deductions within any of paragraphs (a) to (i) and (k) of section 269ZD(3).

(5) Subsection (2) is to be ignored if subsection (4) applies.

188EE Previously claimed group relief for carried-forward losses

(1) To determine the amount of previously claimed group relief for carried-forward losses for the overlapping period—

(a) identify any prior claims for the purposes of this section (see subsection (2)), and

(b) take the steps set out in subsection (3) in relation to each such claim.

The amount of previously claimed group relief for carried-forward losses for the overlapping period is the total of the previously claimed amounts given at step 3 in subsection (3) for all the prior claims.

(2) A claim is a prior claim for the purposes of this section if—

(a) it is a claim under section 188CB or 188CC by the claimant company for group relief for carried-forward losses which would be given by way of a deduction from the company's total profits of the claim period,

(b) it is made before the current claim, and

(c) it has not been withdrawn.

(3) These are the steps referred to in subsection (1)(b) to be taken in relation to each prior claim.

Step 1
Identify the overlapping period for the prior claim.

Step 2
Identify any period that is common to the overlapping period for the current claim and the overlapping period for the prior claim.
If there is a common period, go to Step 3.
If there is no common period, there is no previously claimed amount in relation to the prior claim (and ignore step 3).

Step 3
Determine the previously claimed amount of group relief for carried forward losses in relation to the prior claim (see subsection (4)).

(4) To determine the previously claimed amount of group relief for carried-forward losses in relation to a prior claim—

(a) take the proportion of the overlapping period for the prior claim that is included in the common period identified at step 2 in subsection (3) in relation to that claim, and

(b) apply that proportion to the amount of group relief for carried-forward losses given on the prior claim.

The previously claimed amount of group relief for carried-forward losses in relation to the prior claim is the amount given as a result of paragraph (b).

188EF The potential Part 5 group relief amount

(1) The potential Part 5 group relief amount is determined as follows—

Step 1
Calculate the maximum amount of group relief that could have been given to the claimant company under Part 5 in relation to losses or other amounts within section 99(1) which the surrendering company had for the specified loss-making period.
In applying this step, ignore any lack of profits of the claimant company from which deductions could have been made as mentioned in section 137(1).

Step 2
Deduct from the amount arrived at under step 1 the amount of any group relief actually given to the claimant company under Part 5 in relation to losses or other amounts within section 99(1) which the surrendering company had for the specified loss-making period.

Step 3
Multiply the amount arrived at following step 2 by the fraction in subsection (2).

Step 4
Deduct from the amount arrived at following step 3 any group relief for carried-forward losses previously given to the claimant company on claims under section 188CC which are related to the current claim.

(2)
The fraction referred to in step 3 is—
A / B
where—

A is the sum of the losses or other amounts within section 99(1)(a), (c), (e), (f) and (g) which the surrendering company had for the specified loss-making period, and

B is the sum of the losses or other amounts within section 99(1) (a) to (g) which the surrendering company had for the specified loss-making period.

(3) References in subsection (2) to losses or other amounts are references to losses or other amounts only in so far as they were eligible for surrender under Chapter 2 of Part 5.

(4) A claim under section 188CC is related to the current claim if the surrendering company and the specified loss-making period are the same in relation to both claims.

188EG Sections 188EC to 188EE: supplementary

(1) If two or more claims for group relief for carried-forward losses are made at the same time, for the purpose of section 188EC and 188EE treat the claims as made—

(a) in such order as the company making them may elect or the companies making them may jointly elect, or

(b) if no such election is made, in such order as an officer of Revenue and Customs may direct.

(2) For the purpose of step 3 in each of sections 188EC(5) and 188EE(3) the amount of group relief for carried-forward losses given on a prior claim is determined on the basis that relief is given on the claim before it is given on any later claim.

(3) If the use of any proportion mentioned in subsection (4), would, in the circumstances of a particular case, produce a result that is unjust or unreasonable, the proportion is to be modified so far as necessary to produce a result that is just and reasonable.

(4) The proportions are those found in—

(a) section 188EC(2)(a),
(b) step 1 in section 188EC(6),
(c) section 188EC(8)(a),
(d) step 3 in section 188ED(1), and
(e) section 188EE(4)(a).

188EH Sections 188EC and 188EE: meaning of "the overlapping period"

(1) In sections 188EC and 188EE "the overlapping period", in relation to a claim for group relief for carried-forward losses, means the period that is common to the claim period and the surrender period (see Requirement 2 in section 188CB(3) and Requirement 2 in section 188CC(3)).

(2) But if during any part of the overlapping period the relief condition is not met, that part is treated as not forming part of the overlapping period but instead as forming—

(a) a part of the surrender period that is not included in the overlapping period, and
(b) a part of the claim period that is not included in the overlapping period.

(3) The relief condition is the condition on which the claim for group relief for carried forward losses is based, that is—

the group condition,
consortium condition 1,
consortium condition 2,
consortium condition 3, or
consortium condition 4.

Further limitations on amount of relief that apply in particular cases

188EI Condition 4: companies in link company's group

(1) Where—

(a) the claimant company makes a claim under section 188CC, and
(b) the claim is based on consortium condition 4

the amount of relief to be given on the claim is limited by subsections (2) and (3).

(2) There is a limit on the amount of group relief for carried-forward losses that can be given, in total, on relevant consortium claims made by the link company and group companies.

(3) That limit is the maximum amount of group relief for carried-forward losses that could be given to the link company on relevant consortium claims—

(a) assuming that no relevant consortium claims were made by group companies based on consortium condition 4,
(b) assuming that the link company was UK related, and
(c) ignoring any lack of profits of the link company from which deductions could be made as mentioned in section 188CK(1).

(4) In this section—

"consortium claim" means a claim made under section 188CC for group relief for carried-forward losses,
"group company" means a company that is a member of the same group of companies as the link company (other than the link company),
"relevant consortium claim" means a consortium claim in relation to which the surrendering company, the surrender period and the specified loss-making period are the same as is the case for the claim mentioned in subsection (1), and
"UK related", in relation to a company, has the meaning given by section 188CJ.

188EJ Condition 3 or 4: surrendering company not controlled by claimant company etc

(1) This section applies if—

(a) the claimant company makes a claim under section 188CC for group relief for carried-forward losses,

(b) the claim is based on consortium condition 3, and

(c) during any part of the overlapping period, arrangements within subsection (3) are in place which enable a person to prevent the claimant company, either alone or together with one or more other companies that are members of the consortium, from controlling the surrendering company.

(2) This section also applies if—

(a) the claimant company makes a claim under section 188CC for group relief for carried-forward losses,

(b) the claim is based on consortium condition 4, and

(c) during any part of the overlapping period, arrangements within subsection (3) are in place which enable a person to prevent the link company, either alone or together with one or more other companies that are members of the consortium, from controlling the surrendering company.

(3) Arrangements are within this subsection if—

(a) the company, either alone or together with one or more other companies that are members of the consortium, would control the surrendering company, but for the existence of the arrangements, and

(b) the arrangements form part of a scheme the main purpose, or one of the main purposes, of which is to enable the claimant company to obtain a tax advantage under this Chapter.

(4) The relief to be given on the claim is to be determined as if the surrenderable amount for the overlapping period were 50% of what it would be but for this section (see section 188EC(2) to determine the surrenderable amount for the overlapping period).

(5) In this section "the overlapping period" is to be read in accordance with section 188EH.

(6) Section 1139 ("tax advantage") applies for the purposes of this section.

188EK Condition 3 or 4: surrendering company in group of companies

(1) This section applies if—

(a) the claimant company makes a claim under section 188CC for group relief for carried-forward losses, and

(b) the surrendering company is a member of a group of companies.

(2) The surrendering company's surrenderable amounts for the surrender period that are attributable to the specified loss-making period are to be treated as reduced (but not below nil) by the relevant amount.

(3) To determine the relevant amount—

Step 1

Calculate the group's potential relief.

Step 2

Multiply the amount arrived at under step 1 by the fraction set out in subsection (6).

(4) The group's potential relief is the maximum amount of group relief for carried-forward losses that could be given if every claim that could be made based on the group condition in respect of the surrenderable amounts for the surrender period was in fact made (and for this purpose it is to be assumed that the maximum possible claim is made in each case).

(5) Before determining the maximum amount of potential group relief for carried-forward losses under subsection (4), take account of any claim made before the current claim that—

(a) is a claim for group relief for carried-forward losses based on the group condition, and

(b) is in relation to losses or other amounts surrendered by a member of the same group of companies as the surrendering company (other than the surrendering company itself).

(6) The fraction mentioned in step 2 in subsection (3) is—

A / B

where—

A is the sum of the surrendering company's surrenderable amounts for the surrender period that are attributable to the specified loss-making period, and

B is the sum of all the surrendering company's surrenderable amounts for the surrender period.

CHAPTER 6
MISCELLANEOUS PROVISIONS AND INTERPRETATION OF PART

Miscellaneous

188FA Payments for group relief for carried-forward losses

(1) This section applies if—

(a) the surrendering company and the claimant company have an agreement between them in relation to losses and other amounts of the surrendering company ("the agreed loss amounts"),

(b) group relief for carried-forward losses is given to the claimant company in relation to the agreed loss amounts, and

(c) as a result of the agreement the claimant company makes a payment to the surrendering company that does not exceed the total amount of the agreed loss amounts.

(2) The payment—

(a) is not to be taken into account in determining the profits or losses of either company for corporation tax purposes, and

(b) for corporation tax purposes is not to be regarded as a distribution.

Interpretation

188FB Subsidiaries, groups and consortiums

Chapter 5 of Part 5 (which explains certain key concepts for the purposes of Part 5, including (in particular) how to determine if a company is a member of a group of companies or is a member of, or is owned by a consortium) applies for the purposes of this Part as it applies for the purposes of Part 5.

188FC "Trading company" and "holding company"

(1) In this Part "trading company" means a company the business of which consists wholly or mainly in the carrying on of a trade.

(2) In this Part "holding company" means a company the business of which consists wholly or mainly in the holding of shares or securities that—

(a) are its 90% subsidiaries, and

(b) are trading companies.

188FD Other definitions

(1) In this Part—

"the claimant company" has the meaning given by section 188CB(2) or 188CC(2),

"the claim period" has the meaning given by section 188CB(2) or 188CC(2),

"company" means any body corporate,

"group relief for carried-forward losses" has the meaning given by section 188AA(4),

"profits" means income and chargeable gains, except in so far as the context otherwise requires,

"shock loss" has the meaning given by section 269ZK,

"Solvency 2 insurance company" means an insurance company as defined in section 269ZP(2),

"the specified loss-making period", in relation to a claim for group relief for carried forward losses made under section 188CC, has the meaning given by subsection (2) of that section,

"the surrenderable amounts" has the meaning given by section 188BB(7),

"surrendering company" has the meaning given by 188BB(7), and

"the surrender period" has the meaning given by section 188BB(7).

(2) In this Part, except in so far as the context otherwise requires—

(a) references to a trade include an office, and

(b) reference to carrying on a trade include holding an office."

PART 4
INSURANCE COMPANIES: CARRYING FORWARD BLAGAB TRADE LOSSES

24 Chapter 9 of Part 2 of FA 2012 (relief for BLAGAB trade losses) is amended as follows.

25 (1) Section 124 (carry forward of BLAGAB trade losses against subsequent profits) is amended as follows.

(2) In the heading, after "of" insert "pre-1 April 2017".

(3) In subsection (1), after "accounting period" insert "beginning before 1 April 2017".

(4) In subsection (5), at the end insert "(but see also section 124D)".

26 After section 124 insert—

"124A Carry forward of post-1 April 2017 BLAGAB trade losses against subsequent profits

(1) This section applies if—

(a) an insurance company carrying on basic life assurance and general annuity business makes a BLAGAB trade loss for an accounting period beginning on or after 1 April 2017 ("the loss-making period"),

(b) relief under—

section 37 of CTA 2010 (as applied by section 123), or
Part 5 of CTA 2010 (group relief) (as applied by section 125),

is not given for an amount of the loss ("the unrelieved amount"), and

(c) the company continues to carry on basic life assurance and general annuity business in the next accounting period ("the later period").

(2) The unrelieved amount is carried forward to the later period.

(3) Relief for the unrelieved amount is given to the company in the later period if the company has a BLAGAB trade profit for the later period.

(4) The relief is given as set out in subsection (5).

(5) For the purposes of—

(a) section 93 (minimum profits charge), and
(b) section 104 (policyholders' rate of tax),

the BLAGAB trade profit of the later period is reduced by the unrelieved amount (but see also section 124D).

(6) Relief under this section is subject to restriction or modification in accordance with section 137(7) of CTA 2010 and other applicable provisions of the Corporation Tax Acts.

124B Excess carried forward post-1 April 2017 losses: relief against total profits

(1) This section applies if—

(a) an amount of an insurance company's BLAGAB trade loss for an accounting period is carried forward to an accounting period of the company ("the later period") under section 124A(2) or 124C(3), and

(b) any of that amount ("the unrelieved amount") is not deducted under section 124A(5) or 124C(6) (as the case may be) from the company's BLAGAB trade profit (if any) of the later period.

(2) The company may make a claim for relief to be given for the unrelieved amount under this section.

(3) If the company makes a claim, the relief is given by deducting the unrelieved amount, or any part of it specified in the claim, from the company's total profits of the later period.

(4) But (if the company is a Solvency 2 insurance company)—

(a) the company may not make a claim under this section if the unrelieved amount is wholly a shock loss, and

(b) the company may not make a claim specifying a part of the unrelieved amount if that part is (to any extent) a shock loss.

(5) For the purposes of subsection (4) assume that in any use by the company of the BLAGAB trade loss for relief under—

(a) section 37 of CTA 2010 (as applied by section 123),
(b) Part 5 of CTA 2010 (as applied by section 125), or
(c) section 124A(5) or 124C(6),

any part of it that is a shock loss is used before any part of it that is not a shock loss.

(6) A claim under this section must be made—

    (a) within the period of two years after the end of the later period, or

    (b) within such further period as an officer of Revenue and Customs may allow.

(7) Relief under this section is subject to restriction or modification in accordance with section 137(7) of CTA 2010 and other applicable provisions of the Corporation Tax Acts.

(8) In this section—

    "Solvency 2 insurance company" means an insurance undertaking, a reinsurance undertaking or a third-country insurance undertaking;

    "insurance undertaking" has the meaning given in Article 13(1) of the Solvency 2 Directive;

    "reinsurance undertaking" has the meaning given in Article 13(4) of the Solvency 2 Directive;

    "Solvency 2 Directive" means Directive 2009/138/EC of the European Parliament and the Council of 25 November 2009 on the taking-up and pursuit of the business of Insurance and Reinsurance (Solvency II);

    "shock loss" has the meaning given by section 269ZK of CTA 2010;

    "third-country insurance undertaking" means an undertaking that has received authorisation under Article 162 of the Solvency 2 Directive from the Prudential Regulation Authority or the Financial Conduct Authority.

124C Further carry forward against subsequent profits of post-1 April 2017 loss not fully used

(1) This section applies if—

    (a) an amount of an insurance company's BLAGAB trade loss for an accounting period is carried forward to an accounting period ("the later period") of the company under section 124A(2) or subsection (3) of this section,

    (b) any of that amount is unrelieved in the later period, and

    (c) the company continues to carry on basic life assurance and general annuity business in the accounting period ("the further period") after the later period.

(2) An amount carried forward as mentioned in subsection (1)(a) is "unrelieved in the later period" so far as it is not—

    (a) deducted under section 124A(5) or subsection (6) of this section from the company's BLAGAB trade profit (if any) of the later period,

    (b) deducted from the company's total profits of the later period on a claim under 124B, or

    (c) surrendered by way of group relief for carried-forward losses under Part 5A of CTA 2010.

(3) So much of the amount mentioned in subsection (1)(a) as is unrelieved in the later period is carried forward to the further period.

(4) Relief for the amount carried forward under subsection (3) ("the remaining carried forward amount") is given to the company in the further period if the company has a BLAGAB trade profit for that period.

(5) The relief is given as set out in subsection (6).

(6) For the purposes of—

    (a) section 93 (minimum profits charge), and

    (b) section 104 (policyholders' rate of tax),

the BLAGAB trade profit of the further period is reduced by the remaining carried forward amount (but see also section 124D).

(7) Relief under this section is subject to restriction or modification in accordance with section 137(7) of CTA 2010 and other applicable provisions of the Corporation Tax Acts.

124D Restriction on deductions from BLAGAB trade profits

(1) The sum of any deductions made by a company for an accounting period under sections 124(5), 124A(5) and 124C(6) may not exceed the relevant maximum.

But this is subject to subsection (6).

(2) In this section the "relevant maximum" means the sum of—

    (a) 50% of the company's relevant BLAGAB trade profits for the accounting period, and

    (b) the company's BLAGAB trade profits deductions allowance for the accounting period.

(3) A company's "relevant BLAGAB trade profits" for an accounting period are—

    (a) the company's BLAGAB trade profit for the accounting period, less

    (b) the company's BLAGAB trade profits deductions allowance for the accounting period.

But if the allowance mentioned in paragraph (b) exceeds the profit mentioned in paragraph (a), the company's "relevant BLAGAB trade profits" for the accounting period are nil.

(4) A company's "BLAGAB trade profits deductions allowance" for an accounting period—

    (a) is so much of the company's deductions allowance for the period as is specified in the company's tax return as its BLAGAB trade profits deductions allowance for the period, and

    (b) accordingly, is nil if no amount of the company's deductions allowance for the period is so specified.

(5) An amount specified under subsection (4)(a) as a company's BLAGAB trade profits deductions allowance for an accounting period may not exceed the difference between—

    (a) the amount of the company's deductions allowance for the period, and

    (b) the total of any amounts specified for the period under sections 269ZB(7)(a) of CTA 2010 (trading profits deduction allowance) and 269ZC(5)(a) of CTA 2010 (non-trading profits deduction allowance).

(6) Subsection (1) does not apply to a company for an accounting period if the company's BLAGAB trade profit for the accounting period is not greater than nil.

(7) Section 269ZB(9) of CTA 2010 gives the meaning of "deductions allowance" in relation to a company and an accounting period.

124E Section 124D: shock losses excluded from the restriction

(1) Subsection (2) applies where the company making a deduction under section 124A(5) or 124C(6) is a Solvency 2 insurance company.

(2) The deduction is to be ignored for the purposes of section 124D(1) and section 269ZD(2)(b)(iii) of CTA 2010 so far as it is a deduction of a shock loss.

(3) Where, by virtue of subsection (2), any deductions made by a Solvency 2 insurance company for an accounting period would be ignored for the purposes of section 124D(1), the references in section 124D(3)(a) and (6) to the company's BLAGAB trade profit have effect as references to that profit as reduced by those deductions.

(4) In this section "Solvency 2 insurance company" and "shock loss" have the same meaning as in section 124B."

PART 5

CARRYING FORWARD TRADE LOSSES IN CERTAIN
CREATIVE INDUSTRIES

Losses of film trade

27 Chapter 4 of Part 15 of CTA 2009 (losses of separate film trade) is amended as follows.

28 (1) Section 1209 (restriction on use of losses while film in production) is amended as follows.

(2) In subsection (2)—

    (a) after "45" insert "or 45B", and

    (b) for "set against" substitute "deducted from".

(3) After subsection (2) insert—

    "(3) If the loss is carried forward under section 45 or 45B of CTA 2010 and deducted from profits of the separate film trade in a subsequent period, the deduction is to be ignored for the purposes of section 269ZB of CTA 2010 (restriction on deductions from trading profits)."

29 (1) Section 1210 (use of losses in later periods) is amended as follows.

(2) In subsection (2) after "45" insert "or 45B".

(3) In subsection (3) for "loss relief" substitute "section 37 and Part 5 of CTA 2010".

(4) In subsection (4) for "Subsection (5) applies" substitute "Subsections (5) and (5A) apply".

(5) In subsection (5) after paragraph (a) insert—

"(ab) carried forward under section 45A of that Act to be deducted from the total profits of a later period,"

(6) After subsection (5) insert—

"(5A) A deduction under section 45 or 45B of CTA 2010 which is made in respect of so much of the loss as is attributable to film tax relief is to be ignored for the purposes of section 269ZB of that Act (restriction on deductions from trading profits)."

30 (1) Section 1211 (terminal losses) is amended as follows.

(2) In subsection (1)(c)—

(a) after "45" insert ", 45A or 45B", and
(b) omit "trade X in".

(3) In subsection (3) for the words after "treated" to the end substitute "—

(a) in a case where the loss could have been carried forward under section 45 of CTA 2010 had trade X not ceased, as if it were a loss carried forward under that section to be set against the profits of trade Y of the first accounting period beginning after the cessation and so on, and
(b) in a case where the loss could have been carried forward under section 45A or 45B of CTA 2010 had trade X not ceased, as if it were a loss made in trade Y which has been carried forward under section 45B of that Act to the first accounting period beginning after the cessation."

(4) In subsection (6) for the words after "treated" to the end substitute "—

(a) in a case where the amount could have been carried forward under section 45 of CTA 2010 had trade X not ceased, as if it were a loss carried forward under that section to be set against the profits of trade Z of the first accounting period beginning after the cessation and so on, and
(b) in a case where the amount could have been carried forward under section 45A or 45B of CTA 2010 had trade X not ceased, as if it were a loss made in trade Z which has been carried forward under section 45B of that Act to the first accounting period beginning after the cessation."

(5) After subsection (7) insert—

"(7A) A deduction under section 45 or 45B of CTA 2010 which is made in reliance on this section is to be ignored for the purposes of section 269ZB of that Act (restriction on deductions from trading profits)."

Losses of television programme trade

31 Chapter 4 of Part 15A of CTA 2009 (losses of separate television programme trade) is amended as follows.

32 (1) Section 1216DA (restriction on use of losses while programme in production) is amended as follows.

(2) In subsection (2)—

(a) after "45" insert "or 45B", and
(b) for "set against" substitute "deducted from".

(3) After subsection (2) insert—

"(3) If the loss is carried forward under section 45 or 45B of CTA 2010 and deducted from profits of the separate programme trade in a subsequent period, the deduction is to be ignored for the purposes of section 269ZB of CTA 2010 (restriction on deductions from trading profits)."

33 (1) Section 1216DB (use of losses in later periods) is amended as follows.

(2) In subsection (2) after "45" insert "or 45B".

(3) In subsection (3) for "loss relief" substitute "section 37 and Part 5 of CTA 2010".

(4) In subsection (4) for "Subsection (5) applies" substitute "Subsections (5) and (5A) apply".

(5) In subsection (5) after paragraph (a) insert—

"(ab) carried forward under section 45A of that Act to be deducted from the total profits of a later period,"

(6) After subsection (5) insert—

"(5A) A deduction under section 45 or 45B of CTA 2010 which is made in respect of so much of the loss as is attributable to television tax relief is to be ignored for the purposes of section 269ZB of that Act (restriction on deductions from trading profits)."

34 (1) Section 1216DC (terminal losses) is amended as follows.

(2) In subsection (1)(c)—

    (a) after "45" insert ", 45A or 45B", and

    (b) omit "trade X in".

(3) In subsection (3) for the words after "treated" to the end substitute "—

    (a) in a case where the loss could have been carried forward under section 45 of CTA 2010 had trade X not ceased, as if it were a loss carried forward under that section to be set against the profits of trade Y of the first accounting period beginning after the cessation and so on, and

    (b) in a case where the loss could have been carried forward under section 45A or 45B of CTA 2010 had trade X not ceased, as if it were a loss made in trade Y which has been carried forward under section 45B of that Act to the first accounting period beginning after the cessation."

(4) In subsection (6) for the words after "treated" to the end substitute "—

    (a) in a case where the amount could have been carried forward under section 45 of CTA 2010 had trade X not ceased, as if it were a loss carried forward under that section to be set against the profits of trade Z of the first accounting period beginning after the cessation and so on, and

    (b) in a case where the amount could have been carried forward under section 45A or 45B of CTA 2010 had trade X not ceased, as if it were a loss made in trade Z which has been carried forward under section 45B of that Act to the first accounting period beginning after the cessation."

(5) After subsection (7) insert—

"(7A) A deduction under section 45 or 45B of CTA 2010 which is made in reliance on this section is to be ignored for the purposes of section 269ZB of that Act (restriction on deductions from trading profits)."

Losses of video game trade

35 Chapter 4 of Part 15B of CTA 2009 (losses of separate video game trade) is amended as follows.

36 (1) Section 1217DA (restriction on use of losses while video game in development) is amended as follows.

(2) In subsection (2)—

    (a) after "45" insert "or 45B", and

    (b) for "set against" substitute "deducted from".

(3) After subsection (2) insert—

"(3) If the loss is carried forward under section 45 or 45B of CTA 2010 and deducted from profits of the separate video game trade in a subsequent period, the deduction is to be ignored for the purposes of section 269ZB of CTA 2010 (restriction on deductions from trading profits)."

37 (1) Section 1217DB (use of losses in later periods) is amended as follows.

(2) In subsection (2) after "45" insert "or 45B".

(3) In subsection (3) for "loss relief" substitute "section 37 and Part 5 of CTA 2010".

(4) In subsection (4) for "Subsection (5) applies" substitute "Subsections (5) and (5A) apply".

(5) In subsection (5) after paragraph (a) insert—

    "(ab) carried forward under section 45A of that Act to be deducted from the total profits of a later period,"

(6) After subsection (5) insert—

"(5A) A deduction under section 45 or 45B of CTA 2010 which is made in respect of so much of the loss as is attributable to video games tax relief is to be ignored for the purposes of section 269ZB of that Act (restriction on deductions from trading profits)."

38 (1) Section 1217DC (terminal losses) is amended as follows.

(2) In subsection (1)(c)—

    (a) after "45" insert ", 45A or 45B", and

    (b) omit "trade X in".

(3) In subsection (3) for the words after "treated" to the end substitute "—

    (a) in a case where the loss could have been carried forward under section 45 of CTA 2010 had trade X not ceased, as if it were a loss carried forward under that section to be set against the profits of trade Y of the first accounting period beginning after the cessation and so on, and

    (b) in a case where the loss could have been carried forward under section 45A or 45B of CTA 2010 had trade X not ceased, as if it were a loss made in trade Y which has been carried forward under section 45B of that Act to the first accounting period beginning after the cessation."

(4) In subsection (6) for the words after "treated" to the end substitute "—

    (a) in a case where the amount could have been carried forward under section 45 of CTA 2010 had trade X not ceased, as if it were a loss carried forward under that section to be set against the profits of trade Z of the first accounting period beginning after the cessation and so on, and

    (b) in a case where the amount could have been carried forward under section 45A or 45B of CTA 2010 had trade X not ceased, as if it were a loss made in trade Z which has been carried forward under section 45B of that Act to the first accounting period beginning after the cessation."

(5) After subsection (7) insert—

    "(7A) A deduction under section 45 or 45B of CTA 2010 which is made in reliance on this section is to be ignored for the purposes of section 269ZB of that Act (restriction on deductions from trading profits)."

Losses of theatrical trade

39 Part 15C of CTA 2009 (theatrical productions) is amended as follows.

40 (1) Section 1217MA (restriction on use of losses before completion period) is amended as follows.

(2) In subsection (1) for "Subsection (2)" substitute "This section".

(3) In subsection (2)—

    (a) after "45" insert "or 45B", and

    (b) for "set against" substitute "deducted from".

(4) After subsection (2) insert—

    "(3) If the loss is carried forward under section 45 or 45B of CTA 2010 and deducted from profits of the separate theatrical trade in a subsequent period, the deduction is to be ignored for the purposes of section 269ZB of CTA 2010 (restriction on deductions from trading profits)."

41 (1) Section 1217MB (use of losses in the completion period) is amended as follows.

(2) In subsection (1) after "45" insert "or 45B".

(3) In subsection (2) for "loss relief" substitute "section 37 and Part 5 of CTA 2010".

42 (1) Section 1217MC (terminal losses) is amended as follows.

(2) In subsection (1)(b) after "45" insert "or 45B".

(3) In subsection (3) for the words after "treated" to the end substitute "—

    (a) in a case where the loss could have been carried forward under section 45 of CTA 2010 had trade 1 not ceased, as if it were a loss carried forward under that section to be set against the profits of trade 2 of the first accounting period beginning after the cessation and so on, and

    (b) in a case where the loss could have been carried forward under section 45B of CTA 2010 had trade 1 not ceased, as if it were a loss made in trade 2 which has been carried forward under that section to the first accounting period beginning after the cessation."

(4) In subsection (6) for the words after "treated" to the end substitute "—

    (a) in a case where the amount could have been carried forward under section 45 of CTA 2010 had trade 1 not ceased, as if it were a loss carried forward by company B under that section to be set against the profits of company B's trade of the first accounting period beginning after the cessation and so on, and

    (b) in a case where the amount could have been carried forward under section 45B of CTA 2010 had trade 1 not ceased, as if it were a loss made in company B's trade which has been carried forward under that section to the first accounting period beginning after the cessation."

(5) After subsection (8) insert—

"(9) A deduction under section 45 or 45B of CTA 2010 which is made in reliance on this section is to be ignored for the purposes of section 269ZB of that Act (restriction on deductions from trading profits)."

Losses of orchestral trade

43 Chapter 4 of Part 15D of CTA 2009 (losses of separate orchestral trade) is amended as follows.

44 (1) Section 1217SA (restriction on use of losses before completion period) is amended as follows.

(2) In subsection (1) for "Subsection (2)" substitute "This section".

(3) In subsection (2)—

(a) after "45" insert "or 45B", and

(b) for "set against" substitute "deducted from".

(4) After subsection (2) insert—

"(3) If the loss is carried forward under section 45 or 45B of CTA 2010 and deducted from profits of the separate orchestral trade in a subsequent period, the deduction is to be ignored for the purposes of section 269ZB of CTA 2010 (restriction on deductions from trading profits)."

45 (1) Section 1217SB (use of losses in the completion period) is amended as follows.

(2) In subsection (1) after "45" insert "or 45B".

(3) In subsection (2) for "loss relief" substitute "section 37 and Part 5 of CTA 2010".

46 (1) Section 1217SC (terminal losses) is amended as follows.

(2) In subsection (1)(b) after "45" insert "or 45B".

(3) In subsection (3) for the words after "treated" to the end substitute "—

(a) in a case where the loss could have been carried forward under section 45 of CTA 2010 had trade 1 not ceased, as if it were a loss carried forward under that section to be set against the profits of trade 2 of the first accounting period beginning after the cessation and so on, and

(b) in a case where the loss could have been carried forward under section 45B of CTA 2010 had trade 1 not ceased, as if it were a loss made in trade 2 which has been carried forward under that section to the first accounting period beginning after the cessation."

(4) In subsection (6) for the words after "treated" to the end substitute "—

(a) in a case where the amount could have been carried forward under section 45 of CTA 2010 had trade 1 not ceased, as if it were a loss carried forward by company B under that section to be set against the profits of company B's trade of the first accounting period beginning after the cessation and so on, and

(b) in a case where the amount could have been carried forward under section 45B of CTA 2010 had trade 1 not ceased, as if it were a loss made in company B's trade which has been carried forward under that section to the first accounting period beginning after the cessation."

(5) After subsection (8) insert—

"(9) A deduction under section 45 or 45B of CTA 2010 which is made in reliance on this section is to be ignored for the purposes of section 269ZB of that Act (restriction on deductions from trading profits)."

PART 6

OIL ACTIVITIES

47 Part 8 of CTA 2010 (oil activities) is amended as follows.

48 After section 303 insert—

"303A Introduction to sections 303B to 303D: post-1 April 2017 non-decommissioning losses of ring fence trades

(1) This section has effect for the purposes of sections 303B to 303D.

(2) A loss made by a company in a ring fence trade is a "non-decommissioning loss" so far as it is not attributable to expenditure which is relevant expenditure in relation to a decommissioning relief agreement.

(3) Where a company makes a loss for an accounting period in a ring fence trade, the amount (if any) of that loss that is "attributable to" expenditure which is relevant expenditure in relation to a decommissioning relief agreement is equal to—

(a) the total amount of such expenditure brought into account in calculating that loss, or

(b) if lower, the amount of the loss.

(4) Expenditure is "relevant expenditure" in relation to a decommissioning relief agreement if it is decommissioning expenditure (as defined in section 81 of FA 2013) to which the provision of the agreement described in section 80(2)(b) of that Act relates.

In this subsection the reference to section 81 of FA 2013 is to that section as it has effect when the agreement in question is made.

(5) In this section "decommissioning relief agreement" has the meaning given by section 80 of FA 2013.

303B Carry forward of losses against subsequent profits

(1) This section applies if—

(a) in an accounting period beginning on or after 1 April 2017 ("the loss-making period") a company makes a non-decommissioning loss in a ring fence trade,

(b) relief under—

section 37 or 42, or

Part 5 (group relief),

is not given for an amount of the loss ("the unrelieved amount"), and

(c) the company continues to carry on the ring fence trade in the next accounting period ("the later period").

(2) The unrelieved amount is carried forward to the later period.

(3) Relief for the unrelieved amount is given to the company in the later period if the company makes a profit in the trade for the later period.

(4) The relief is given by reducing the profits of the trade in the later period by the unrelieved amount.

(5) Relief under this section is subject to restriction or modification in accordance with the provisions of the Corporation Tax Acts.

303C Excess carried forward losses: relief against total profits

(1) This section applies if—

(a) an amount of a non-decommissioning loss made in a ring fence trade is carried forward to an accounting period of a company ("the later period") under section 303B(2) or 303D(3), and

(b) any of that amount ("the unrelieved amount") is not deducted under section 303B(4) or 303D(5) (as the case may be) from the company's profits of the trade (if any) of the later period.

(2) The company may make a claim for relief to be given for the unrelieved amount under this section (but see subsection (4)).

(3) If the company makes a claim, the relief is given by deducting the unrelieved amount, or any part of it specified in the claim, from the company's total profits of the later period.

(4) The company may not make a claim if—

(a) the ring fence trade became small or negligible in the loss-making period or any intervening period,

(b) relief under section 37 was unavailable for the non-decommissioning loss by reason of section 37(5) or 44, or

(c) relief under section 37 would be unavailable by reason of section 44 for a loss (assuming there was one) made in the ring fence trade in the later period or any intervening period.

(5) In subsection (4)—

"intervening period" means an accounting period of the company which begins after the loss-making period and before the later period, and

"the loss-making period" means the accounting period of the company in which the non-decommissioning loss was made.

(6) A claim under this section must be made—

(a) within the period of two years after the end of the later period, or

(b) within such further period as an officer of Revenue and Customs may allow.

(7) Relief under this section is subject to restriction or modification in accordance with the provisions of the Corporation Tax Acts.

303D Further carry forward against subsequent profits of loss not fully used

(1) This section applies if—

(a) an amount of a loss made in a ring fence trade is carried forward to an accounting period ("the later period") of a company under section 303B(2) or subsection (3) of this section,

(b) any of that amount is unrelieved in the later period, and

(c) the company continues to carry on the ring fence trade in the accounting period ("the further period") after the later period.

(2) An amount carried forward as mentioned in subsection (1)(a) is "unrelieved in the later period" so far as it is not—

(a) deducted under section 303B(4) or subsection (5) of this section from the company's profit (if any) of the later period,

(b) deducted from the company's total profits of the later period on a claim under section 303C, or

(c) surrendered by way of group relief for carried-forward losses under Part 5A of CTA 2010.

(3) So much of the amount mentioned in subsection (1)(a) as is unrelieved in the later period is carried forward to the further period.

(4) Relief for the amount carried forward under subsection (3) ("the remaining carried forward amount") is given to the company in the further period if the company has a profit in the trade for that period.

(5) The relief is given by reducing the profits of the trade of the further period by the remaining carried forward amount.

(6) Relief under this section is subject to restriction or modification in accordance with the provisions of the Corporation Tax Acts."

49 (1) Section 304 (losses) is amended as follows.

(2) After subsection (1) insert—

"(1A) Relief in respect of a loss incurred by a company may not be given against that company's ring fence profits under any provision listed in subsection (1B).

(1B) The provisions are—

(a) section 753 of CTA 2009 (non-trading losses on intangible fixed assets);

(b) section 45A (carry forward of trade loss against total profits);

(c) section 62(3) (relief for losses made in UK property business)."

(3) In subsection (5), after "45" insert "45B, 303B(4) or 303D(5)".

(4) After subsection (6) insert—

"(7) A deduction in respect of a loss made in a ring fence trade is to be ignored for the purposes of section 269ZB (restriction on deductions from trading profits) if the deduction is under—

(a) section 45 (carry forward of pre-1 April 2017 trade loss against subsequent profits), or

(b) section 45B (carry forward of post-1 April 2017 trade loss against total profits)."

50 (1) Section 305 (group relief) is amended as follows.

(2) In the heading, at the end insert "and group relief for carried-forward losses".

(3) After subsection (1) insert—

"(1A) On a claim under Chapter 3 of Part 5A, group relief for carried-forward losses may not be allowed against the claimant company's ring fence profits."

(4) For subsection (4) substitute—

"(4) In this section—

"claimant company" is to be read in accordance with Part 5 (see section 188) or Part 5A (see sections 188CB(2) and 188CC(2)), as the case requires;

"surrendering company" is to be read in accordance with Part 5 (see section 188)."

51 In section 307 (overview of Chapter 5 of Part 8: ring fence expenditure supplement) in subsection (6) for paragraph (c) substitute—

"(c) relief given under sections 45, 45B, 303B, 303C and 303D for ring fence losses carried forward from earlier periods,".

52 (1) Section 321 (supplement in respect of a post-commencement period) is amended as follows.

(2) In subsection (2) (treatment of supplement as loss etc)—

(a) in the words before paragraph (a) after "period" insert "beginning before 1 April 2017", and

(b) in paragraph (b) after "forward of" insert "pre-1 April 2017".

(3) After subsection (2) insert—

"(2A) Any post-commencement supplement allowed on a claim in respect of a post-commencement period beginning on or after 1 April 2017 is to be treated for the purposes of the Corporation Tax Acts (other than the post-commencement supplement provisions or Part 4 of Schedule 19B to ICTA) as if it were a loss—

(a) which is incurred in carrying on the ring fence trade in that period, and

(b) which falls in whole to be used under section 45B (carry forward of post-1 April 2017 trade loss against subsequent trade profits) to reduce trading income from the ring fence trade in succeeding accounting periods."

53 (1) Section 323 (meaning of "ring fence losses") is amended as follows.

(2) In subsection (1)—

(a) for paragraph (b) substitute—

"(b) some or all of the loss falls to be carried forward to the following accounting period under section 45, 45B or 303B (carry forward of trade losses against subsequent profits)", and

(b) in the words after paragraph (b) for "used" substitute "carried forward".

(3) In subsection (2) for "used" substitute "carried forward".

54 For section 327 substitute—

"327 Reductions in respect of relief for carried-forward ring fence losses

(1) Reductions are to be made in accordance with this section in a post-commencement period if the relevant amount for the period (see subsection (4)) is not nil.

(2) If the company has a non-qualifying pool, the amount in the non-qualifying pool is to be reduced (but not below nil) by setting against it a sum equal to the relevant amount for the post-commencement period.

(3) If—

(a) any of that sum remains after being so set against the amount in the non-qualifying pool, or

(b) the company does not have a non-qualifying pool,

the amount in the ring fence pool is to be reduced (but not below nil) by setting against it so much of that sum as so remains or (as the case may be) a sum equal to the relevant amount for the post-commencement period.

(4) For the purposes of this section, the relevant amount for a post-commencement period is the sum of—

(a) the amount of any relief given in respect of ring fence losses in the post-commencement period under sections 45, 45B, 303B, 303C and 303D, and

(b) the amount of any relief prevented from being given in respect of ring fence losses in the post-commencement period by claims made under sections 45(4A) and 45B(5)."

55 In section 328A (adjustment of pool to remove pre-2013 losses after the initial 6 periods) in subsection (11)—

(a) in paragraph (a) for the words from the beginning to "a loss" substitute "no account is to be taken of a loss in determining under section 327(4) the relevant amount for a post-commencement period", and

(b) in paragraph (b) for the words from "ring fence losses" to the end substitute "any such profits are reduced by the use under section 45, 45B, 303B, 303C and 303D of ring fence losses that are not represented by the reduction".

PART 7

OIL CONTRACTORS

56 Part 8ZA of CTA 2010 (oil contractors) is amended as follows.

57 (1) Section 356NE (losses) is amended as follows.

(2) The existing text becomes subsection (1) of that section.

(3) In subsection (1)—

(a) after "the contractor" insert "(or an amount of such a loss)";

(b) after "profits)" insert "or section 45A (carry forward of post-1 April 2017 trade loss against total profits)";

(c) after "the loss" insert "(or amount)".

(4) After subsection (1) insert—

"(2) Relief in respect of a loss incurred by the contractor may not be given against the contractor's ring fence profits under any provision listed in subsection (3).

(3) The provisions are—

(a) section 753 of CTA 2009 (non-trading losses on intangible fixed assets);

(b) section 62(3) (relief for losses made in UK property business);

(c) section 303C(3) (excess carried forward non-decommissioning losses of ring fence trade: relief against total profits)."

58 (1) Section 356NF (group relief) is amended as follows.

(2) In the heading, at the end insert "and group relief for carried-forward losses".

(3) After subsection (3) insert—

"(3A) On a claim under Chapter 3 of Part 5A, group relief for carried-forward losses may not be allowed against the claimant company's contractor's ring fence profits, except so far as the claim relates to losses incurred by the surrendering company that arose from oil contractor activities."

(4) For subsection (4) substitute—

"(4) In this section—

"claimant company" is to be read in accordance with Part 5 (see section 188) or Part 5A (see sections 188CB(2) and 188CC(2)), as the case requires;

"surrendering company" is to be read in accordance with Part 5 (see section 188) or Part 5A (see section 188BB(7)), as the case requires."

59 After section 356NG insert—

"Restriction on obtaining certain deductions

356NH Restriction on deductions from contractor's ring fence profits

(1) For the purpose of determining the contractor's taxable total profits for an accounting period, the sum of any relevant deductions from total profits made by the contractor for the accounting period may not exceed the relevant Part 8ZA maximum.

(2) In this section "relevant deduction from total profits" means—

(a) any deduction of a loss (or an amount of a loss) under section 45(4)(b) (carry forward of pre-1 April 2017 loss against subsequent profits), so far as the loss arises from oil contractor activities,

(b) any deduction of a loss (or an amount of a loss) under section 45A (carry forward of post-1 April 2017 trade loss against total profits), so far as the amount is set against the contractor's ring fence profits, and

(c) any deduction of a loss or other amount under Part 5A (group relief for carried-forward losses), so far as the amount in question is set against the contractor's ring fence profits.

(3) In this section "the relevant Part 8ZA maximum" means the sum of—

(a) 50% of the contractor's ring fence profits for the accounting period, and

(b) the amount of the contractor's ring fence profits deductions allowance for the period.

356NI Deductions allowances where company has contractor's ring fence profits

(1) This section applies if a company ("C") has contractor's ring fence profits for an accounting period.

(2) Subsections (3) to (6) set out how to determine, for the accounting period—

(a) C's deductions allowance for the purposes of Part 7ZA (restrictions on obtaining certain deductions), and

(b) C's contractor's ring fence profits deductions allowance.

(3) Determine in accordance with Part 7ZA what C's deductions allowance for the period would be in the absence of this section (and call this "amount A").

(4) Determine C's contractor's ring fence profits deductions allowance for the period in accordance with subsection (5).

(5) C's "contractor's ring fence profits deductions allowance" for an accounting period—

(a) is so much of amount A as is specified in C's company tax return as its contractor's ring fence profits deductions allowance for the period, and

(b) accordingly, is nil if no amount is so specified.

(6) Subsection (7) applies if a relevant reversal credit is brought into account in calculating C's contractor's ring fence profits for the accounting period.

In this subsection the reference to bringing into account a relevant reversal credit is to be interpreted in accordance with section 269ZY.

(7) C's contractor's ring fence profits deductions allowance for the accounting period (as determined in accordance with subsection (5)) is to be treated for all purposes as increased by—

(a) the amount of the relevant reversal credit, or

(b) if lower, the amount of the contractor's ring fence profits for the accounting period.

(8) C's deductions allowance for the period for the purposes of Part 7ZA is to be taken to be an amount equal to amount A less the amount of C's ring fence profits deductions allowance for the period.

356NJ Modification of provisions restricting the use of losses

(1) The following deductions are to be treated as not being relevant deductions for the purposes of section 269ZD (restrictions on deductions from total profits)—

(a) the deduction of a loss (or an amount of a loss) under section 45A (carry forward of post- 1 April 2017 trade loss against total profits), so far as the amount is set against the company's contractor's ring fence profits for the accounting period;

(b) the deduction under Part 5A (group relief for carried-forward losses) of a loss or other amount, so far as the amount is set against the company's contractor's ring fence profits for the accounting period.

(2) A deduction under section 45(4)(b) (carry forward of pre-1 April 2017 trade loss against subsequent profits) of a loss arising from oil contractor activities is to be ignored for the purposes of section 269ZB of CTA 2010 (restriction on deductions from trading profits)."

PART 8

TRANSFERRED TRADES

61 Chapter 1 of Part 22 of CTA 2010 (transfers of trade without a change of ownership) is amended as follows.

62 In section 940A (overview of Chapter) in subsection (4) for "944" substitute "943A".

63 Before section 944 (but after the italic heading preceding that section) insert—

"943A Disapplication of section 39

If this Chapter applies to a transfer of a trade, section 39 (terminal losses: extension of periods for which relief may be given) does not apply in relation to a claim under section 37 by the predecessor for relief for a loss made in the transferred trade."

64 (1) Section 944 (modified application of Chapter 2 of Part 4) is amended as follows.

(2) In the heading for "Chapter 2 of Part 4" substitute "section 45".

(3) Omit subsections (1) and (2).

(4) In subsection (3)—

(a) for "Relief" substitute "If this Chapter applies to a transfer of a trade, relief", and

(b) after "carry forward of" insert "pre-1 April 2017".

(5) In subsection (4) after paragraph (a) insert—

"(ab) any claim made by the predecessor under section 45F in reliance on subsection (2) of section 944C,".

65 After section 944 insert—

"944A Modified application of section 45A

(1) Subsection (2) applies if—

(a) this Chapter applies to a transfer of a trade,

(b) the transferred trade is not a ring fence trade,

(c) the predecessor made a loss in the transferred trade in the accounting period in which it ceased to carry it on,

(d) that accounting period began on or after 1 April 2017,

(e) relief for an amount of that loss is not given under section 37 or Part 5,

(f) relief under section 37 was not unavailable for that loss by reason of a provision mentioned in section 45A(3)(b)(i) or (ii), and

(g) relief under section 37 would not be unavailable by reason of section 44 for a loss (assuming there was one) made by the successor in the transferred trade in the accounting period in which the successor begins to carry on the transferred trade ("the successor's start-up accounting period").

(2) Subsections (4) to (8) of section 45A (carry-forward of post-1 April 2017 trade loss against total profits) apply as if—

(a) references to the unrelieved amount were to the amount referred to in subsection (1)(e),

(b) references to the later period were to the successor's start-up accounting period, and

(c) references to the company were to the successor.

(3) Subsection (4) applies if—

(a) this Chapter applies to a transfer of a trade,

(b) an amount of a loss made in the transferred trade was carried forward under section 45A(4) to the accounting period of the predecessor in which the predecessor ceased to carry on the trade,

(c) any of that amount was not deducted from the predecessor's total profits on a claim under section 45A(5) or surrendered by the predecessor by way of group relief for carried-forward losses under Part 5A, and

(d) relief under section 37 would not be unavailable by reason of section 44 for a loss (assuming there was one) made by the successor in the transferred trade in the accounting period in which the successor begins to carry on the transferred trade ("the successor's start-up accounting period").

(4) Subsections (4) to (8) of section 45A apply as if—

(a) references to the unrelieved amount were to so much of the amount referred to in subsection (3)(b) as was not deducted or surrendered as mentioned in subsection (3)(c),

(b) references to the later period were to the successor's start-up accounting period, and

(c) references to the company were to the successor.

(5) In this section "ring fence trade" has the same meaning as in Part 8 (see section 277).

944B Modified application of section 45B

(1) Subsection (2) applies if—

(a) this Chapter applies to a transfer of a trade,

(b) the predecessor made a loss in the transferred trade in the accounting period in which it ceased to carry it on,

(c) that accounting period began on or after 1 April 2017,

(d) relief under section 37 or 42 or Part 5 is not given for an amount of the loss, and

(e) it is the case that—

(i) relief under section 37 was unavailable for the loss by reason of any provision mentioned in section 45A(3)(b)(i) or (ii),

(ii) relief under section 37 would be unavailable by reason of section 44 for a loss (assuming there was one) made by the successor in the transferred trade in the accounting period in which the successor begins to carry on the transferred trade ("the successor's start-up accounting period"), or

(iii) the transferred trade is a ring fence trade.

(2) Subsections (2) to (8) of section 45B (carry forward of post-1 April 2017 trade loss against trade profits) apply as if—

(a) references to the unrelieved amount were to the amount mentioned in subsection (1)(d),

(b) references to the later period were to the successor's start-up accounting period,

(c) references to the company were to the successor, and

(d) references to the trade were to the transferred trade.

(3) Subsection (4) applies if—

(a) this Chapter applies to a transfer of a trade,

(b) an amount of a loss made in the transferred trade was carried forward under section 45B(2) to the accounting period in which the predecessor ceased to carry on the trade, and

(c) any of that amount is not used under section 45B(4) to reduce profits of the transferred trade of the accounting period in which the predecessor ceases to carry on the trade.

(4) Subsections (2) to (8) of section 45B apply as if—

(a) references to the unrelieved amount were to so much of the amount referred to in subsection (3)(b) as is not used as mentioned in subsection (3)(c),

(b) references to the later period were to the accounting period of the successor in which the successor begins to carry on the transferred trade,

(c) references to the company were to the successor, and

(d) references to the trade were to the transferred trade.

944C Modified application of section 45F

(1) If this Chapter applies to a transfer of a trade, the predecessor may not make a claim under section 45F for relief to be given for an amount of a loss made in the transferred trade.

(2) But subsection (1) does not apply if—

(a) the trade is transferred before 13 July 2017, and

(b) the amount of the loss is carried forward to the accounting period in which the predecessor ceases to carry on the trade under section 45 (carry forward of pre-1 April 2017 trade losses).

(3) Subsection (4) applies if—

(a) this Chapter applies to a transfer of a trade,

(b) an amount of a loss made by the predecessor in the transferred trade is carried forward under section 45, 45A or 45B to the accounting period of the successor in which the successor ceases to carry on the transferred trade, and

(c) relief in that accounting period is not given to the successor under section 45, 45A or (as the case may be) 45B for that amount or for any part of it.

(4) Section 45F has effect as if the loss was made by the successor in the transferred trade in the accounting period in which it began carrying on the transferred trade.

944D Modified application of section 303B

(1) Subsection (2) applies if—

(a) this Chapter applies to a transfer of a trade,

(b) the transferred trade is a ring-fence trade,

(c) the predecessor made a non-decommissioning loss in the transferred trade in the accounting period in which it ceased to carry it on,

(d) that accounting period began on or after 1 April 2017, and

(e) relief under section 37 or 42 or Part 5 is not given for an amount of the loss.

(2) Subsections (2) to (5) of section 303B (carry forward of non-decommissioning losses against subsequent profits) have effect as if—

(a) references to the unrelieved amount were to the amount mentioned in subsection (1)(e),

(b) references to the later period were to the accounting period of the successor in which the successor begins to carry on the transferred trade,

(c) references to the company were to the successor, and

(d) references to the trade were to the transferred trade.

(3) Section 303A (meaning of non-decommissioning loss) applies for the purposes of this section.

(4) In this section "ring fence trade" has the same meaning as in Part 8 (see section 277).

944E Modified application of section 303D

(1) Subsection (2) applies if—

(a) this Chapter applies to a transfer of a trade,

(b) the trade is a ring-fence trade,

(c) an amount of a loss made in the trade was carried forward under section 303B(2) or 303D(3) to the accounting period in which the predecessor ceased to carry on the trade ("the cessation period"), and

(d) any of that amount was not—

(i) deducted under section 303B(4) or 303D(5) from the predecessor's profit (if any) of the cessation period,

(ii) deducted from the predecessor's total profits of the cessation period on a claim under section 303C(2), or

(iii) surrendered by the predecessor by way of group relief for carried-forward losses under Part 5A.

(2) Subsections (3) to (6) of section 303D have effect as if—

(a) the reference to so much of the amount mentioned in section 303D(1)(a) as is unrelieved in the later period were to so much of the amount mentioned in subsection (1)(c) of this section as was not deducted or surrendered as mentioned in subsection (1)(d),

(b) references to the further period were to the accounting period of the successor in which the successor begins to carry on the transferred trade,

(c) references to the company were to the successor, and

(d) references to the trade were to the transferred trade.

(3) In this section "ring fence trade" has the same meaning as in Part 8 (see section 277)."

66 In section 945 (cases in which predecessor retains more liabilities than assets) in subsection (4), for "section 944(3)" (in both places where those words occur) substitute "sections 944 to 944E".

67 (1) Section 951 (part of trade treated as separate trade) is amended as follows.

(2) After subsection (6) insert—

"(7) Subsection (8) applies if—

(a) a company ("the transferor") ceases to carry on a trade ("trade Z"),

(b) another company ("the transferee") begins to carry on the activities of trade Z as part of its trade ("part Z") and

(c) by reason of this Chapter an amount of a loss made in trade Z is carried forward under section 45A(4), 45B(2), 303B(2) or 303D(3) to an accounting period of the transferee.

(8) The provisions of sections 45A to 45F and 303B to 303D have effect, in so far as they apply (or re-apply) in relation to the amount carried forward (or any part of it), as if the transferee carries or carried on part Z as a separate trade."

68 In section 952 (apportionment if part of trade treated as separate trade) in subsection (1) for "or (4)" substitute ", (4) or (8)"."

PART 9

TAX AVOIDANCE

Restriction on refreshing losses

69 (1) Section 730F of CTA 2010 (meaning of "relevant carried-forward loss") is amended as follows.

(2) In subsection (1)—

(a) after paragraph (a) insert—

"(aa) a carried-forward UK property business loss (see subsection (2A)),";

(b) after paragraph (b) insert—

"(ba) a carried-forward non-trading loss on intangible fixed assets (see subsection (3A)),".

(3) In subsection (2)—

(a) after "45" insert ", 45A or 45B";

(b) omit "against subsequent trade profits".

(4) In subsection (3), after "457" insert ", 463G or 463H".

(5) After subsection (2) insert—

"(2A) "Carried-forward UK property business loss", in relation to a company and an accounting period, means a loss in a UK property business carried on by the company which is carried forward from a previous accounting period under section 62(5)."

(6) After subsection (3) insert—

"(3A) "Carried-forward non-trading loss on intangible fixed assets", in relation to a company and an accounting period, means a non-trading loss on intangible fixed assets which is carried forward from a previous accounting period under section 753 of CTA 2009 (treatment of non-trading losses)."

(7) At the end insert—

"(5) In this section "non-trading loss on intangible fixed assets" is to be   read in accordance with Part 8 of CTA 2009."

Change in company ownership

70 Part 14 of CTA 2010 (change in company ownership) is amended as follows.

71 In section 672 (overview of Part) after subsection (1) insert—

"(1A) Chapter 2A restricts relief in some further cases involving a change in the company's activities.

(1B) Chapter 2B restricts relief for trading losses in some cases involving the transfer of an asset.

(1C) Chapters 2C and 2D restrict group relief for carried-forward losses in some cases.

(1D) Chapter 2E restricts relief for trading losses in some cases involving the transfer of a trade."

72 (1) Section 673 (introduction to Chapter 2: disallowance of trading losses) is amended as follows.

(2) In subsection (2), for "of 3 years in which the change in ownership" substitute "beginning no more than 3 years before the change in ownership occurs which is a period of 5 years in which that change".

(3) In subsection (4), in the words after paragraph (b), for "3" substitute "5".

(4) The amendments made by this paragraph do not have effect unless both the change in ownership referred to in section 673(1) and the major change in the nature or conduct of a trade referred to in section 673(2) occur on or after 1 April 2017.

73 (1) Section 674 (disallowance of trading losses) is amended as follows.

(2) In subsection (2), after "45" insert ", 45B, 303B or 303D".

(3) After subsection (2) insert—

"(2A) No relief may be given under section 45A or 303C for a loss made by the company in an accounting period beginning before the change in ownership by carrying forward the loss and deducting it from a company's total profits of an accounting period ending after the change in ownership."

74 After section 674 insert—

"674A   Section 674: exception for certain losses of ring fence trade

(1) Section 674 does not prevent relief being given for a loss if—

(a) the loss is made in a ring fence trade,
(b) the loss is not a non-decommissioning loss,
(c) it is condition A in section 673 that is met, and
(d) the major change by reference to which that condition is met did not occur within a period of 3 years in which the change in ownership occurred.

(2) In this section—

"non-decommissioning loss" is to be interpreted in accordance with section 303A; "ring fence trade" has the same meaning as in Part 8 (see section 277)."

75 After Chapter 2 insert—

"CHAPTER 2A

POST-1 APRIL 2017 LOSSES: FURTHER CASES INVOLVING A CHANGE IN THE COMPANY'S ACTIVITIES

676AA   Introduction to Chapter

(1) This Chapter applies if conditions 1 and 2 are met.

(2) Condition 1 is that on or after 1 April 2017 there is a change in the ownership of a company ("the transferred company").

(3) Condition 2 is that a major change in the business of the transferred company or a co-transferred company occurs within the required period but not before 1 April 2017.

(4) The required period is—

(a) for the purposes of section 676AF, any period beginning no more than 3 years before the change in ownership occurs which is a period of 5 years in which that change occurs,

(b) for the purposes of sections 676AG to 676AK, the period of 8 years beginning 3 years before the change in ownership.

(5) In this Chapter—

"the change in ownership" means the change in ownership mentioned in subsection (2);

"the transferred company" has the meaning given by subsection (2);

"trade" includes an office.

676AB Priority of provisions of Chapters 2 and 3 over this Chapter

(1) If and so far as —

(a) a relevant provision of this Chapter, and

(b) a relevant provision of Chapter 2 or 3,

would each (if the other provision were ignored) apply in relation to the same loss or other amount, the relevant provision of this Chapter does not apply in relation to that amount.

(2) In this section "relevant provision"—

(a) in relation to this Chapter means any of the provisions of sections 676AF to 676AK;

(b) in relation to Chapters 2 and 3 means any of the provisions of sections 674 and 679 to 683.

676AC "Major change in the business" of a company

(1) In this Chapter references to a "major change in the business" of a company include—

(a) a major change in the nature or conduct of any trade or business carried on by the company,

(b) a major change in the scale of any trade or business carried on by the company, and

(c) beginning or ceasing to carry on a particular trade or business.

(2) In subsection (1) the reference to a major change in the "nature or conduct" of a trade or business includes—

(a) a major change in the type of property dealt in, or services or facilities provided in, the trade or business concerned,

(b) a major change in customers, outlets or markets of the trade or business concerned,

(c) a major change in the nature of the investments held by the company for the purposes of an investment business.

(3) The definitions in subsections (1) and (2) apply even if the change is the result of a gradual process which began before the period of 5 years mentioned in section 676AA(4)(a) or (as the case may be) the period of 8 years mentioned in section 676AA(4)(b).

(4) Where the condition in subsection (5) is met in the case of any two companies, the transfer of a trade or business, or any property, from one of them to the other is to be disregarded in determining for the purposes of section 676AA(3) whether or not there is a major change in the business of either of those companies.

(5) The condition is that the companies are related to one another both—

(a) immediately before the change in ownership, and

(b) at the time of the transfer mentioned in subsection (4).

676AD Notional split of accounting period in which change in ownership occurs

(1) This section applies for the purposes of this Chapter.

(2) The accounting period in which the change in ownership occurs ("the actual accounting period") is treated as two separate accounting periods ("notional accounting periods"), the first ending with the change and the second consisting of the remainder of the period.

(3) Section 685 (apportionment of amounts) applies for the purposes of this Chapter as it applies for the purposes of Chapter 3.

(4) The amounts for the actual accounting period in column 1 of the table in section 685(2) are apportioned to the two notional accounting periods in accordance with section 685.

(5) In this Chapter, and in sections 685 and 686 as they apply by virtue of subsection (3), "the actual accounting period" and "notional accounting periods" have the same meaning as in this section.

676AE   "Affected profits"

(1) This section has effect for the purposes of this Chapter.

(2) Profits of an accounting period ending after the change in ownership are "affected profits" if and so far as—

   (a) they arise before the 5th anniversary of the end of the accounting period of the transferred company in which the change in ownership occurs, and

   (b) they can fairly and reasonably be attributed to activities, or other sources of income, as a result of which, or partly as a result of which, the major change referred to in section 676AA(3) has occurred.

(3) If an accounting period of the company begins before, and ends after, the anniversary mentioned in subsection (2), then for the purposes of that subsection—

   (a) the accounting period is treated as two separate accounting periods, the first ending with that date and the second consisting of the remainder of the period, and

   (b) the profits or losses of the accounting period are apportioned to the two periods.

(4) Any apportionment under subsection (3)(b) is to be made on a time basis according to the respective lengths of the two deemed accounting periods.

(5) But if that method of apportionment would work unjustly or unreasonably in any case, such other method is to be used as is just and reasonable.

676AF   Restriction on use of carried-forward post-1 April 2017 trade losses

A loss made by the transferred company in an accounting period beginning before the change in ownership may not be deducted from affected profits of an accounting period ending after the change in ownership under any of the following provisions—

   (a) section 45A(5) (carry-forward of post-1 April 2017 trade losses),

   (b) section 45F(3) (carried-forward losses: terminal relief),

   (c) section 303C(3) (excess carried-forward non-decommissioning losses of ring fence trade), and

   (d) section 124B(3) of FA 2012 (excess carried-forward BLAGAB trade losses).

676AG   Restriction on debits to be brought into account

(1) This section has effect for the purpose of restricting the debits to be brought into account for the purposes of Part 5 of CTA 2009 (loan relationships) in respect of the transferred company's loan relationships.

(2) The debits to be brought into account for the purposes of Part 5 of CTA 2009 for—

   (a) the accounting period beginning immediately after the change in ownership, or

   (b) any subsequent accounting period,

do not include relevant non-trading debits so far as amount A exceeds amount B.

(3) Amount A is the sum of—

   (a) the amount of those relevant non-trading debits, and

   (b) the amount of any relevant non-trading debits which have been brought into account for the purposes of that Part for any previous accounting period ending after the change in ownership.

(4) Amount B is the amount of the taxable total profits of the accounting period ending with the change in ownership.

(5) For the meaning of "relevant non-trading debit", see section 730.

676AH   Restriction on the carry forward of post-1 April 2017 non-trading deficit from loan relationships

(1) This section has effect for the purpose of restricting the carry forward under Chapter 16A of Part 5 of CTA 2009 (non-trading deficits: post 1 April 2017 deficits) of a pre-acquisition non-trading deficit from the transferred company's loan relationships.

(2) For the purposes of this section an amount is a "pre-acquisition" non-trading deficit from a company's loan relationships if it is a non-trading deficit from the company's loan relationships for an accounting period beginning before the change in ownership.

(3) Subsection (4) applies if, in the case of a pre-acquisition non-trading deficit from the transferred company's loan relationships, the non-trading deficit in column 1 of row 4 of the table in section 685(2) is apportioned in accordance with section 685(2) to the first notional accounting period.

(4) None of that deficit may, by virtue of section 463G (carry forward of unrelieved deficit), be set off against affected profits of—

    (a) the accounting period beginning immediately after the change in ownership, or

    (b) any subsequent accounting period.

676AI Restriction on relief for post-1 April 2017 non-trading loss on intangible fixed assets

(1) This section has effect for the purpose of restricting relief under section 753 of CTA 2009 (treatment of non-trading losses) in respect of a relevant non-trading loss on intangible fixed assets.

(2) An amount is a "relevant non-trading loss on intangible fixed assets" if and so far as—

    (a) it is by virtue of section 751 of CTA 2009 a non-trading loss on intangible fixed assets for a relevant pre-acquisition accounting period, or

    (b) it is made up of an amount falling within paragraph (a) which has been carried forward under section 753(3) of CTA 2009.

(3) "Relevant pre-acquisition accounting period" means an accounting period beginning—

    (a) before the change in ownership, and

    (b) on or after 1 April 2017.

(4) In the case of a relevant non-trading loss on intangible fixed assets, relief under section 753 of CTA 2009 against the total profits of the actual accounting period is available only in relation to each of the notional accounting periods considered separately.

(5) A relevant non-trading loss on intangible fixed assets may not be deducted as a result of section 753(3) of CTA 2009 (losses carried forward) from affected profits of an accounting period ending after the change in ownership.

676AJ Restriction on deduction of post-1 April 2017 expenses of management

(1) This section has effect for the purpose of restricting deductions for post-1 April 2017 relevant expenses of management of the transferred company.

(2) Any amounts which—

    (a) are, or are treated as, expenses of management referable to the actual accounting period, and

    (b) are apportioned to either of the two notional accounting periods in accordance with section 685,

are treated for the purposes of Chapter 2 of Part 16 of CTA 2009 (companies with investment business) as expenses of management referable to that notional accounting period.

(3) Any allowances which are apportioned to either of the notional accounting periods in accordance with section 685 are treated for the purposes of section 253 of CAA 2001 and section 1233 of CTA 2009 (companies with investment business: excess capital allowances) as falling to be made in that notional accounting period.

(4) In calculating the taxable total profits of an accounting period of the transferred company ending after the change in ownership—

    (a) relevant expenses of management, and

    (b) relevant allowances,

may not be deducted from affected profits of the accounting period.

(5) In this section "relevant expenses of management" means expenses of management which are first deductible under section 1219 of CTA 2009 for an accounting period beginning—

    (a) on or after 1 April 2017, and

    (b) before the change in ownership.

(6) In this section "relevant allowances" means allowances falling to be made for an accounting period beginning—

    (a) on or after 1 April 2017, and

    (b) before the change in ownership.

676AK   Restriction on use of post-1 April 2017 UK property business losses

(1) This section has effect for the purpose of restricting relief under sections 62 and 63 for a relevant UK property business loss made by the transferred company.

(2) In this section "relevant UK property business loss" means a loss made in a UK property business in an accounting period beginning—

    (a) on or after 1 April 2017, and

    (b) before the change in ownership.

(3) In relation to a relevant UK property business loss, relief under section 62(3) is available only in relation to each of the notional accounting periods considered separately.

(4) A relevant UK property business loss may not be deducted as a result of section 62(5) or 63(3) from affected profits of an accounting period ending after the change in ownership.

676AL   "Co-transferred company" and "related company"

(1) In this Chapter "co-transferred company" means any company which is related to the transferred company both immediately before and immediately after the change in ownership.

(2) For the purposes of this Chapter any two companies ("T") and ("C") are "related" to one another at any time when—

    (a) the group condition is met in relation to T and C, or

    (b) any of consortium conditions 1 to 4 is met in relation to T and C,

(whether on the assumption that T is the claimant company and C is the surrendering company or vice versa).

(3) In this Chapter—

    "consortium condition 1" is to be interpreted in accordance with section 188CF,

    "consortium condition 2" is to be interpreted in accordance with section 188CG,

    "consortium condition 3" is to be interpreted in accordance with section 188CH,

    "consortium condition 4" is to be interpreted in accordance with section 188CI,

    "the group condition" is to be interpreted in accordance with section 188CE."

76 After Chapter 2A insert—

"CHAPTER 2B

ASSET TRANSFERRED WITHIN GROUP: RESTRICTION OF RELIEF FOR POST-1 APRIL TRADE LOSSES

676BA   Introduction to Chapter

(1) This section applies if there is a change in the ownership of a company ("the company") on or after 1 April 2017 and—

    (a) conditions 1 and 2 are met, or

    (b) condition 3 is met.

(2) Condition 1 is that after the change in ownership the company acquires an asset from another company in circumstances such that—

    (a) section 171 of TCGA 1992 (no gain/no loss transfer within group), or

    (b) section 775 of CTA 2009 (tax-neutral transfer within group),

applies to the acquisition.

(3) Condition 2 is that—

    (a) in a case within subsection (2)(a), a chargeable gain accrues to the company on a disposal of the asset within the period of 5 years beginning with the change in ownership, or

    (b) in a case within subsection (2)(b), there is a non-trading chargeable realisation gain on the realisation of the asset within that period.

(4) Condition 3 is that a chargeable gain on a disposal of an asset within the period of 5 years beginning immediately after the change in ownership (or an amount of such a gain) is treated as accruing to the company by virtue of an election under section 171A of TCGA 1992 (notional transfers within a group).

(Accordingly, references in this Chapter to the accrual of a relevant gain are to be read in the light of section 171B(2) and (3) of TCGA 1992.)

(5) For the purposes of subsection (3), an asset (P) acquired by the company as mentioned in subsection (2) is treated as the same as an asset (Q) owned at a later time by the company if the value of Q is derived in whole or in part from P.

(6) In particular, P is treated as the same as Q for those purposes if—

(a) Q is a freehold,
(b) P was a leasehold, and
(c) the lessee has acquired the reversion.

(7) In this Chapter—

"the change in ownership" means the change in ownership mentioned in subsection (1),

"the company" has the same meaning as in this section,

"non-trading chargeable realisation gain" means a chargeable realisation gain (within the meaning of Part 8 of CTA 2009 (intangible fixed assets)) which is a non-trading credit for the purposes of that Part (see section 746 of that Act),

"realisation" has the meaning given by section 734 of CTA 2009, and

"the relevant gain" means the gain (or amount of a gain) within subsection (3)(a) or (b) or (4).

676BB Notional split of accounting period in which change in ownership occurs

(1) This section applies for the purposes of this Chapter.

(2) The accounting period in which the change in ownership occurs ("the actual accounting period") is treated as two separate accounting periods ("notional accounting periods"), the first ending with the change and the second consisting of the remainder of the period.

(3) Section 702 (apportionment of amounts) applies for the purposes of this Chapter as it applies for the purposes of Chapter 4.

(4) The amounts for the actual accounting period in column 1 of the table in section 702(2) are apportioned to the two notional accounting periods in accordance with section 702.

(5) In this Chapter, and in sections 702 and 703 as they apply by virtue of subsection (3), "the actual accounting period" and "notional accounting periods" have the same meaning as in this section.

676BC Disallowance of relief for trade losses

(1) This section has effect for the purposes of restricting relief under sections 45A, 45F and 303C of this Act and section 124B of FA 2012 for a loss made by the company in a trade before the change in ownership.

(2) But this section applies only if, in accordance with the relevant provisions and section 702, an amount is included in respect of chargeable gains or, as the case may be, non-trading chargeable realisation gains in the total profits of the accounting period in which the relevant gain accrues or arises.

(3) Relief under section 45A or 303C of this Act or section 124B of FA 2012 is available only in relation to each of the notional accounting periods considered separately.

(4) A loss made in an accounting period beginning before the change in ownership—

(a) may not be deducted as a result of section 45A or 303C of this Act or section 124B of FA 2012 from so much of the total profits of an accounting period ending after the change in ownership as represents the relevant gain;

(b) may not be deducted by virtue of paragraph (a) of the definition of "relevant profits" in section 45F(7) from so much of the total profits of an accounting period ending after the change in ownership as represents the relevant gain.

676BD Meaning of "the relevant provisions"

In this Chapter "the relevant provisions" means—

(a) section 8(1) of, and Schedule 7A to, TCGA 1992 (amounts included in respect of chargeable gains in total profits), or

(b) Chapter 6 of Part 8 of CTA 2009 (intangible fixed assets: how credits and debits are given effect).

676BE Meaning of "amount of profits which represents a relevant gain"

(1) In this Chapter, the amount of any profits which represents a relevant gain is found by comparing—

(a) the amount ("Y") of the relevant gain, with

(b) the amount ("Z") which is included in respect of chargeable gains or, as the case may be, non-trading chargeable realisation gains for the accounting period concerned.

(2) If Y does not exceed Z, the amount of the profits which represents the relevant gain equals Y.

(3) If Y exceeds Z, the amount of those profits equals Z."

77 After Chapter 2B insert—

"CHAPTER 2C
DISALLOWANCE OF GROUP RELIEF FOR CARRIED-FORWARD LOSSES: GENERAL PROVISION

676CA Introduction to Chapter

(1) This Chapter applies if on or after 1 April 2017 there is a change in the ownership of a company ("the transferred company").

(2) In this Chapter—

"the change in ownership" means the change in ownership mentioned in subsection (1);

"the transferred company" has the meaning given by subsection (1).

676CB Restriction on surrender of carried-forward losses

(1) Subsection (3) applies if a company ("the claimant company") would, (apart from this section), be eligible under Part 5A to make a relevant claim for group relief for carried-forward losses.

(2) For the purposes of this section a claim for group relief for carried-forward losses is a "relevant claim" if it is—

(a) for an accounting period ending after the change in ownership, and

(b) in respect of an amount surrendered by the transferred company or a co-transferred company which is a relevant pre-acquisition loss.

(3) The general rule is that the relief is not available.

(4) The general rule is subject to the exceptions in sections 676CD and 676CE.

(5) For the purposes of this section—

(a) the accounting period of the company mentioned in subsection (2)(b) in which the change in ownership occurs is treated as two separate accounting periods, the first ending with the change and the second consisting of the remainder of the period, and

(b) the profits or losses of the accounting period are apportioned to the two periods.

(6) Any apportionment under subsection (5)(b) is to be made on a time basis according to the respective lengths of the two periods.

(7) But if that method of apportionment would work unjustly or unreasonably in any case, such other method is to be used as is just and reasonable.

676CC Cases where consortium condition 1 or 2 was previously met

(1) Subsection (4) applies in relation to a claim for group relief for carried-forward losses by the transferred company if conditions A and B are met.

(2) Condition A is that the claim is—

(a) for an accounting period ending after the change in ownership, and

(b) in respect of a relevant pre-acquisition loss.

(3) Condition B is that consortium condition 1 was met in relation to—

(a) the transferred company (as the company owned by a consortium as mentioned in section 188CF(1)(b)), and

(b) the surrendering company (as the company mentioned in section 188CF(1)(c)),

immediately before the change in ownership ("time T").

(4) The relief given under section 188CK in respect of the transferred company's total profits of the claim period may not exceed the relief that would be available on the assumption that the claim is based on consortium condition 1 and the ownership proportion for the purposes of that condition is equal to the lowest of the following proportions—

(a) the proportion of the ordinary share capital of the transferred company that was beneficially owned by the surrendering company at time T,

(b) the proportion of any profits available for distribution to equity holders of the transferred company to which the surrendering company was beneficially entitled at that time,

(c) the proportion of any assets of the transferred company available for distribution to such equity holders on a winding up to which the surrendering company would be beneficially entitled (as determined at that time), and

(d) the proportion of the voting power in the transferred company that was directly possessed by the surrendering company at that time.

(5) Subsection (8) applies in relation to a claim for group relief for carried-forward losses by the transferred company if conditions A and B are met.

(6) Condition A is that the claim is—

(a) for an accounting period ending after the change in ownership, and

(b) in respect of a a relevant pre-acquisition loss.

(7) Condition B is that consortium condition 2 was met in relation to—

(a) the transferred company (as the company owned by a consortium as mentioned in section 188CG(1)(b)), and

(b) the surrendering company (as the company mentioned in section 188CG(1)(c)),

immediately before the change in ownership ("time T").

(8) The relief given under section 188CK in respect of the transferred company's total profits of the claim period may not exceed the relief that would be available on the assumption that the claim is based on consortium condition 2 and the ownership proportion for the purposes of that condition is equal to the lowest of the following proportions—

(a) the proportion of the ordinary share capital of the transferred company that was beneficially owned by the link company at time T,

(b) the proportion of any profits available for distribution to equity holders of the transferred company to which the link company was beneficially entitled at that time,

(c) the proportion of any assets of the transferred company available for distribution to such equity holders on a winding up to which the link company would be beneficially entitled (as determined at that time), and

(d) the proportion of the voting power in the transferred company that was directly possessed by the link company at that time.

(9) For the purposes of this section—

(a) the accounting period of the surrendering company mentioned in subsection (3)(b) or (7)(b) (as the case may be) in which the change in ownership occurs is treated as two separate accounting periods, the first ending with the change and the second consisting of the remainder of the period, and

(b) the profits or losses of the accounting period are apportioned to the two periods.

(10) Any apportionment under subsection (9)(b) is to be made on a time basis according to the respective lengths of the two periods.

(11) In this section—

"the link company" means the company which is the link company (see section 188CG(1)(d)) for the purposes of the meeting of consortium condition 2 as mentioned in subsection (7),

"the claim period" and "the surrendering company" has the same meaning as in Part 5A (see section 188FD(1)).

(12) Chapter 6 of Part 5 (equity holders and profits or assets available for distribution) applies for the purposes of subsections (4)(b) and (c) and (8)(b) and (c).

676CD Cases where consortium condition 3 or 4 was previously met

(1) If the requirement in subsection (3) is met, section 676CB(3) does not prevent a company from making under section 188CC a claim for group relief for carried-forward losses falling within subsection (2).

(2) A claim falls within this subsection if it is—

(a) for an accounting period ("the claim period") ending after the change in ownership, and

(b) in relation to an amount surrendered by the transferred company which is a relevant pre-acquisition loss and is attributable to an accounting period of that company specified in the claim ("the specified loss-making period").

(3) The requirement is that consortium condition 3 or consortium condition 4 is met throughout a period which—

(a) begins before or during the specified loss-making period, and

(b) ends with or after the time when the change in ownership occurs.

(4) For the purposes of a claim by virtue of this section, section 188CC(3) has effect as if requirement 3 were omitted.

676CE　Exceptions to restrictions

(1) Nothing in section 676CB(3) or 676CC affects the giving of group relief for carried-forward losses by the making of a deduction under section 188CK(1) from total profits of the claimant company which arise after the 5th anniversary of the end of the accounting period of the transferred company in which the change in ownership occurs.

(2) Nothing in section 676CB(3) or 676CC affects the availability of relief under Part 5A if immediately before the change in ownership the group condition was met in relation to the transferred company and the claimant company.

But see also section 676CF.

(3) If an accounting period of the claimant company begins before, and ends after, the anniversary mentioned in subsection (1), then for the purposes of that subsection—

(a) the accounting period is treated as two separate accounting periods, the first ending with that date and the second consisting of the remainder of the period, and
(b) the profits or losses of the accounting period are apportioned to the two periods.

(4) Any apportionment under subsection (3)(b) is to be made on a time basis according to the respective lengths of the two periods.

(5) But if that method of apportionment would work unjustly or unreasonably in any case, such other method is to be used as is just and reasonable.

(6) In this section "the claimant company" has the same meaning as in Part 5A (see section 188FD(1)).

676CF　Cases where Chapter 2, 2A or 3 also applies

(1) This section applies if—

(a) Chapter 2 applies in relation to the change in ownership by virtue of condition A in section 673 being met,
(b) Chapter 2A applies in relation to the change in ownership, or
(c) Chapter 3 applies in relation to the change in ownership by virtue of condition B in section 677 being met.

(2) This section also applies if—

(a) the condition in subsection (1)(a) would be met if in subsection (4A) of section 719 (meaning of "change in the ownership of a company") the reference to Chapter 2C included a reference to Chapter 2, or
(b) the condition in subsection (1)(c) would be met if in subsection (4A) of section 719 the reference to Chapter 2C included a reference to Chapter 3.

(3) Where the company in relation to which the major change mentioned in section 673(4), 676AA(3) or 677(3) has occurred would (apart from this section) be eligible under Part 5A to claim in respect of a relevant pre-acquisition loss group relief for carried-forward losses for an accounting period ending after the change in ownership, no deduction in respect of that loss may be made from affected profits under section 188CK.

See section 676CG for the meaning of "affected profits".

(4) For the purposes of this section—

(a) the accounting period in which the change in ownership occurs is treated as two separate accounting periods, the first ending with the change and the second consisting of the remainder of the period, and
(b) the profits or losses of the accounting period are apportioned to the two periods.

(5) Any apportionment under subsection (4)(b) is to be made on a time basis according to the respective lengths of the two deemed accounting periods.

(6) But if that method of apportionment would work unjustly or unreasonably in any case, such other method is to be used as is just and reasonable.

676CG　"Affected profits"

(1) This section has effect for the purposes of section 676CF.

(2) Profits of an accounting period ending after the change in ownership are "affected profits" if and so far as—

(a) they arise before the 5th anniversary of the end of the accounting period of the transferred company in which the change in ownership occurs, and

(b) they can fairly and reasonably be attributed to activities, or other sources of income, as a result of which, or partly as a result of which, the major change mentioned in section 673(4), 676AA(3) or 677(3) (as the case may be) has occurred.

(3) If an accounting period of the company in relation to which the major change mentioned in section 673(4), 676AA(3) or 677(3) has occurred begins before, and ends after, the anniversary mentioned in subsection (2), then for the purposes of that subsection—

(a) the accounting period is treated as two separate accounting periods, the first ending with that date and the second consisting of the remainder of the period, and

(b) the profits or losses of the accounting period are apportioned to the two periods.

(4) Any apportionment under subsection (3)(b) is to be made on a time basis according to the respective lengths of the two deemed accounting periods.

(5) But if that method of apportionment would work unjustly or unreasonably in any case, such other method is to be used as is just and reasonable.

676CH "Relevant pre-acquisition loss"

(1) In this Chapter "relevant pre-acquisition loss" means—

(a) a non-trading deficit from loan relationships for an accounting period beginning before the change in ownership carried forward to the surrender period under section 463G(6) of CTA 2009,

(b) a loss on intangible fixed assets so far as it is made up of amounts carried forward to the surrender period under section 753(3) of CTA 2009 from one or more accounting periods beginning before the change in ownership,

(c) expenses carried forward to the surrender period under section 1223 of CTA 2009 (carry forward of expenses of management of investment business) which were first deductible in an accounting period beginning before the change in ownership,

(d) a loss made in an accounting period beginning before the change in ownership and carried forward to the surrender period under section 45A(3) (post- 1 April 2017 trade loss),

(e) a loss made in an accounting period beginning before the change in ownership and carried forward to the surrender period under section 62(5)(b) or 63(3)(a) (loss made in UK property business),

(f) a loss made in an accounting period beginning before the change in ownership and carried forward to the surrender period under section 303B(2) or 303D(3) (post-1 April non-decommissioning losses of ring fence trade),

(g) a BLAGAB trade loss made in an accounting period beginning before the change in ownership and carried forward to the surrender period under section 124A(2) or 124C(3) of FA 2012.

(2) In this section "the surrender period" is to be interpreted in accordance with section 188BB(7).

676CI Interpretation of Chapter

(1) In this Chapter "co-transferred company" means any company which is related to the transferred company both immediately before and immediately after the change in ownership.

(2) For the purposes of this Chapter any two companies ("T") and ("C") are "related" to one another at any time when—

(a) the group condition is met in relation to T and C, or

(b) any of consortium conditions 1 to 4 is met in relation to T and C,

(whether on the assumption that T is the claimant company and C is the surrendering company or vice versa).

(3) In this Chapter—

"consortium condition 1" is to be interpreted in accordance with section 188CF,
"consortium condition 2" is to be interpreted in accordance with section 188CG,
"consortium condition 3" is to be interpreted in accordance with section 188CH,
"consortium condition 4" is to be interpreted in accordance with section 188CI,
"the group condition" is to be interpreted in accordance with section 188CE."

78 After Chapter 2C insert—

"CHAPTER 2D

ASSET TRANSFERRED WITHIN GROUP: RESTRICTION OF GROUP RELIEF FOR CARRIED-FORWARD LOSSES

676DA Introduction to Chapter

(1) This section applies if—

(a) there is a change in the ownership of a company ("the company") on or after 1 April 2017, and

(b) the following are met—

conditions 1 and 2, or

condition 3.

(2) Condition 1 is that after the change in ownership the company acquires an asset from another company in circumstances such that—

(a) section 171 of TCGA 1992 (no gain/no loss transfer within a group), or

(b) section 775 of CTA 2009 (tax-neutral transfer within a group),

applies to the acquisition.

(3) Condition 2 is that—

(a) in a case within subsection (2)(a), a chargeable gain accrues to the company on a disposal of the asset within the period of 5 years beginning with the change in ownership, or

(b) in a case within subsection (2)(b), there is a non-trading chargeable realisation gain on the realisation of the asset within that period.

(4) Condition 3 is that a chargeable gain on a disposal of an asset within the period of 5 years beginning immediately after the change in ownership (or an amount of such a gain) is treated as accruing to the company by virtue of an election under section 171A of TCGA 1992 (notional transfers within a group).

(Accordingly, references in this Chapter to the accrual of a relevant gain are to be read in the light of section 171B(2) and (3) of TCGA 1992.)

(5) For the purposes of subsection (3), an asset (P) acquired by the company as mentioned in subsection (2) is treated as the same as an asset (Q) owned at a later time by the company if the value of Q is derived in whole or in part from P.

(6) In particular, P is treated as the same as Q for those purposes if—

(a) Q is a freehold,

(b) P was a leasehold, and

(c) the lessee has acquired the reversion.

(7) In this Chapter

"the change in ownership" means the change in ownership mentioned in subsection (1),

"the company" has the same meaning as in this section,

"non-trading chargeable realisation gain" means a chargeable realisation gain (within the meaning of Part 8 of CTA 2009 (intangible fixed assets)) which is a non-trading credit for the purposes of that Part (see section 746 of that Act),

"realisation" has the meaning given by section 734 of CTA 2009, and

"the relevant gain" means the gain (or amount of a gain) within subsection (3)(a) or (b) or (4).

676DB Notional split of accounting period in which change in ownership occurs

(1) This section applies for the purposes of this Chapter.

(2) The accounting period in which the change in ownership occurs ("the actual accounting period") is treated as two separate accounting periods ("notional accounting periods"), the first ending with the change and the second consisting of the remainder of the period.

(3) Section 702 (apportionment of amounts) applies for the purposes of this Chapter as it applies for the purposes of Chapter 4.

(4) The amounts for the actual accounting period in column 1 of the table in section 702(2) are apportioned to the two notional accounting periods in accordance with section 702.

(5) In this Chapter, and in sections 702 and 703 as they apply by virtue of subsection (3), "the actual accounting period" and "notional accounting periods" have the same meaning as in this section.

676DC Disallowance of group relief for carried-forward losses

(1) This section has effect for the purposes of restricting relief under Chapter 3 of Part 5A (group relief for carried-forward losses).

(2) But this section applies only if, in accordance with the relevant provisions and section 702, an amount is included in respect of chargeable gains or, as the case may be, non-trading chargeable realisation gains in the total profits of the accounting period in which the relevant gain accrues or arises.

(3) In calculating the company's taxable total profits of the accounting period in which the relevant gain accrues or arises, a relevant pre-acquisition loss may not be deducted, as a result of section 188CK (group relief for carried-forward losses: deductions from total profits) from so much of the total profits of the accounting period as represents the relevant gain.

(4) "Relevant pre-acquisition loss" means—

(a) a non-trading deficit from loan relationships for an accounting period beginning before the change in ownership carried forward to the surrender period under section 463G(6) of CTA 2009,

(b) a loss on intangible fixed assets so far as it is made up of amounts carried forward to the surrender period under section 753(3) of CTA 2009 from one or more accounting periods beginning before the change in ownership,

(c) expenses carried forward to the surrender period under section 1223 of CTA 2009 (carrying forward expenses of management and other amounts) which were first deductible in an accounting period beginning before the change in ownership,

(d) a loss made in an accounting period beginning before the change in ownership and carried forward to the surrender period under section 45A(3) (post- 1 April 2017 trade loss);

(e) a loss made in an accounting period beginning before the change in ownership and carried forward to the surrender period under section 62(5)(b) or 63(3)(a) (loss made in UK property business),

(f) a loss made in an accounting period beginning before the change in ownership and carried forward to the surrender period under section 303B(2) or 303D(3) (post-1 April non-decommissioning losses of ring fence trade),

(g) a BLAGAB trade loss made in an accounting period beginning before the change in ownership and carried forward to the surrender period under section 124A(2) or 124C(3) of FA 2012.

(5) In this section "the surrender period" is to be interpreted in accordance with section 188BB(7).

676DD Meaning of "the relevant provisions"

In this Chapter "the relevant provisions" means—

(a) section 8(1) of, and Schedule 7A to, TCGA 1992 (amounts included in respect of chargeable gains in total profits), or

(b) Chapter 6 of Part 8 of CTA 2009 (intangible fixed assets: how credits and debits are given effect).

676DE Meaning of "amount of profits which represents a relevant gain"

(1) In this Chapter, the amount of any profits which represents a relevant gain is found by comparing—

(a) the amount ("Y") of the relevant gain, with

(b) the amount ("Z") which is included in respect of chargeable gains or, as the case may be, non-trading chargeable realisation gains for the accounting period concerned.

(2) If Y does not exceed Z, the amount of the profits which represents the relevant gain equals Y.

(3) If Y exceeds Z, the amount of those profits equals Z."

79 After Chapter 2D insert—

"CHAPTER 2E

POST-1 APRIL 2017 TRADE LOSSES: CASES INVOLVING THE TRANSFER OF A TRADE

676EA Introduction to Chapter

(1) This Chapter applies if on or after 1 April 2017 there is a change in the ownership of a company ("the transferred company").

(2) In this Chapter—

"the change in ownership" means the change in ownership mentioned in subsection (1);

"the transferred company" has the meaning given by subsection (1).

676EB Restriction on use of trade losses carried-forward on transfer of trade

(1) Subsection (2) applies if—

(a) the transferred company transfers a trade to another company ("the successor company") within the period of 8 years beginning 3 years before the change in ownership,

(b) the transfer is a transfer to which Chapter 1 of Part 22 applies, and

(c) the transferred company and the successor company are not related to one another both immediately before the change in ownership and at the time of the transfer.

(2) A loss made by the transferred company in the transferred trade in an accounting period beginning before the change in ownership may not be deducted under section 45A or 303C from the relevant profits of an accounting period of the successor company ending after the change in ownership.

(3) Profits of an accounting period of the successor company ending after the change in ownership are "relevant profits" if and so far as—

(a) they arise before the 5th anniversary of the end of the accounting period of the transferred company in which the change in ownership occurs, and

(b) they cannot fairly and reasonably be attributed to the carrying on by the successor company of the transferred trade.

(4) If an accounting period of the transferred company begins before, and ends after the change in ownership, then for the purposes of subsection (2)—

(a) the accounting period is treated as two separate accounting period, the first ending with the change and the second consisting on the remainder of the period, and

(b) a loss made in the trade in the accounting period is apportioned to the two periods.

(5) If an accounting period of the successor company begins before, and ends after, the anniversary mentioned in subsection (3), then for the purposes of that subsection—

(a) the accounting period is treated as two separate accounting periods, the first ending with that date and the second consisting of the remainder of the period, and

(b) the profits of the accounting period are apportioned to the two periods.

(6) Any apportionment under subsection (4)(b) or (5)(b) is to be made on a time basis according to the respective lengths of the two deemed accounting periods.

(7) But if that method of apportionment would work unjustly or unreasonably in any case, such other method is to be used as is just and reasonable.

676EC Restriction on surrender of trade losses carried forward on transfer of trade

(1) This section applies if—

(a) the transferred company or a co-transferred company transfers a trade to another company ("the successor company") within the period of 8 years beginning 3 years before the change in ownership,

(b) the transfer is a transfer to which Chapter 1 of Part 22 applies, and

(c) another company ("the claimant company") would, apart from this section, be eligible under Part 5A to make a relevant claim for group relief for carried-forward losses.

(2) For the purposes of this section a claim for group relief for carried forward-losses is a relevant claim if it is—

(a) for an accounting period ending after the change in ownership, and

(b) in respect of an amount surrendered by the successor company which is an amount of a loss—

(i) made in the trade by the transferred company or the co-transferred company in an accounting period beginning before the change in ownership, and

(ii) carried forward to the surrender period of the successor company under section 45A(3), 303B(2) or 303D(3).

(3) The general rule is that the relief is not available.

(4) Subsection (3) does not affect the giving of group relief for carried-forward losses by the making of a deduction under section 188CK(1) from the total profits of the

claimant company which arise after the 5th anniversary of the end of the accounting period of the transferred company in which the change in ownership occurs.

(5) Subsection (3) does not affect the availability of relief under Part 5A if immediately before the change in ownership the group condition was met in relation to the claimant company and the transferred company.

(6) If an accounting period of the transferred company or co-transferred company begins before, and ends after the change in ownership, then for the purposes of subsection (2)(b)—

(a) the accounting period is treated as two separate accounting period, the first ending with the change and the second consisting on the remainder of the period, and

(b) a loss made in the trade in the accounting period is apportioned to the two periods.

(7) If an accounting period of the claimant company begins before, and ends after, the anniversary mentioned in subsection (4), then for the purposes of that subsection—

(a) the accounting period is treated as two separate accounting period, the first ending with that date and the second consisting of the remainder of the period, and

(b) the profits of the accounting period are apportioned to the two periods.

(8) Any apportionment under subsection (6)(b) or (7)(b) is to be made on a time basis according to the respective lengths of the two deemed accounting periods.

(9) But if that method of apportionment would work unjustly or unreasonably in any case, such other method is to be used as is just and reasonable.

676ED Indirect transfers of a trade

(1) Subsections (2) and (3) apply if a trade transferred by the transferred company or a co-transferred company is transferred on a subsequent occasion to another company.

(2) The transferred company or (as the case may be) the co-transferred company is to be treated for the purposes of this Chapter—

(a) as having transferred the trade to that other company, and

(b) as having done so at the time it was actually transferred to that other company.

(3) The deemed transfer is to be treated for the purposes of this Chapter as a transfer to which Chapter 1 of Part 22 applies if the actual transfer to the other company was a transfer to which that Chapter applies.

(4) Subsections (5) and (6) apply if—

(a) a trade ("the original trade") is transferred by the transferred company or a co-transferred company,

(b) the activities of the original trade are included in the activities of another trade ("the composite trade"), and

(c) the composite trade is transferred to another company.

(5) The transferred company or (as the case may be) the co-transferred company is to be treated for the purposes of this Chapter—

(a) as having transferred the original trade to that other company, and

(b) as having done so at the time the composite trade was actually transferred to that other company.

(6) The deemed transfer is to be treated for the purposes of this Chapter as a transfer to which Chapter 1 of Part 22 applies if the transfer of the composite trade to the other company was a transfer to which that Chapter applies.

676EE Interpretation of Chapter

(1) Section 940B (meaning of "transfer of trade" and related expressions) applies for the purposes of this Chapter as it applies for the purposes of Chapter 1 of Part 22.

(2) In this Chapter "co-transferred company" means any company which is related to the transferred company both immediately before and immediately after the change in ownership.

(3) For the purposes of this Chapter any two companies ("T") and ("C") are "related" to one another at any time when—

(a) the group condition is met in relation to T and C, or

(b) any of consortium conditions 1 to 4 is met in relation to T and C,

(whether on the assumption that T is the claimant company and C is the surrendering company or vice versa).

(4) In this Chapter—

"consortium condition 1" is to be interpreted in accordance with section 188CF,
"consortium condition 2" is to be interpreted in accordance with section 188CG,
"consortium condition 3" is to be interpreted in accordance with section 188CH,
"consortium condition 4" is to be interpreted in accordance with section 188CI,
"the group condition" is to be interpreted in accordance with section 188CE.""

80 (1) Section 677 (introduction to Chapter 3) is amended as follows.

(2) In subsection (3), for "6" substitute "8".

(3) In subsection (5), for "6" substitute "8".

(4) The amendments made by this paragraph do not have effect unless both the change in ownership referred in section 677(1) and the major change in the nature or conduct of a business referred to in section 677(3) occur on or after 1 April 2017.

81 (1) Section 681 (restriction on relief for non-trading loss on intangible fixed assets) is amended as follows.

(2) In subsection (3)(b), for "debit of" substitute "loss on intangible fixed assets for".

82 (1) Section 685 (apportionment of amounts) is amended as follows.

(2) In subsection (2), in column 1 of row 4 in the table, for the words from "of CTA 2009" to the end substitute ", 463G(6) or 463H(4) of CTA 2009."

(3) In subsection (2), in column 1 of row 6 of the table, for "debit of" substitute "loss on intangible fixed assets for".

(4) Where the change in ownership referred to in section 677(1) occurs before 13 July 2017 this paragraph has effect as if sub-paragraph (2) provided as follows—

"(2) In subsection (2), in column 1 of row 4 in the table, for the words from "of CTA 2009" to the end substitute "or 463G(6) of CTA 2009."

83 (1) In section 690 (meaning of "significant increase in the amount of a company's capital: amount B), in subsection (3) for "3" substitute "5".

(2) The amendment made by this paragraph does not have effect unless the change in ownership referred in section 677(1) occurs on or after 1 April 2017.

84 (1) Section 692 (introduction to Chapter 4) is amended as follows.

(2) In subsection (1), for paragraph (b) substitute—

"(b) the following are met—

condition 1, and

conditions 2 and 3 or condition 4.

(3) In subsection (4)(a), for "3" substitute "5".

(4) After subsection (4) insert—

"(4A) Condition 4 is that a chargeable gain on a disposal of an asset within the period of 5 years beginning immediately after the change in ownership (or an amount of such a gain) is treated as accruing to the company by virtue of an election under section 171A of TCGA 1992 (election to reallocate gain or loss to another member of the group).

(Accordingly, references in this Chapter to the accrual of a relevant gain are to be read in the light of section 171B(2) and (3) of TCGA 1992.)"

(5) In subsection (7), in the definition of "the relevant gain", for "within subsection (4)(a) or (b)" substitute "(or amount of a gain) within subsection (4)(a) or (b) or (4A)".

(6) The amendments made by this paragraph do not have effect unless the change in ownership referred to in section 692(1) occurs on or after 1 April 2017.

85 In section 696 (restriction of debits to be brought into account), in subsection (4)(b), after "461" insert "or 463B(1)(a)".

86 (1) Section 702 (apportionment of amounts) is amended as follows.

(2) In subsection (2), in column 1 of row 5 of the table, for the words from "of CTA 2009" to the end substitute ", 463G(6) or 463H(4) of CTA 2009."

(3) In subsection (2), in column 1 of row 7 of the table, for "debit of" substitute "loss on intangible fixed assets for".

(4) Where the change in ownership referred to in section 692(1) occurs before 13 July 2017 this paragraph has effect as if sub-paragraph (2) provided as follows—

"(2) In subsection (2), in column 1 of row 5 in the table, for the words from "of CTA 2009" to the end substitute "or 463G(6) of CTA 2009."

87 (1) Section 704 (company carrying on UK property business) is amended as follows.

(2) In subsection (2), for "3" substitute "5".

(3) In subsection (10), in the words after paragraph (b), for "3" substitute "5".

(4) The amendments made this paragraph do not have effect unless both the change in ownership referred in section 704(1) and the major change in the nature or conduct of a trade or business referred to in section 704(2) occur on or after 1 April 2017.

88 (1) Section 705 (company carrying on overseas property business) is amended as follows.

(2) In subsection (2), for "3" substitute "5".

(3) In subsection (9), in the words after paragraph (b), for "3" substitute "5".

(4) The amendments made by this paragraph do not have effect unless both the change in ownership referred in section 705(1) and the major change in the nature or conduct of a trade or business referred to in section 705(2) occur on or after 1 April 2017.

89 In section 719 (meaning of "change of ownership of a company"), after subsection (4) insert—

"(4A) For the purposes of Chapters 2A to 2D there is also a change in the ownership of a company ("C") if, as a result of the acquisition by a person of a holding of the ordinary share capital of the company, the group condition (as defined in section 188CE) is met in relation to C and another company ("A") (which was not a member of the same group of companies as C before the acquisition).

In this subsection the reference to membership of a group of companies is to be interpreted in accordance with section 188FB."

90 In section 721 (when things other than ordinary share capital may be taken into account), in subsection (4), in the words before paragraph (a), after "2," insert "2A, 2B, 2C, 2D,".

91 In section 727 (extended time limit for assessment) for "3" substitute "5".

Deduction buying

92 (1) Section 730C of CTA 2010 is amended as follows.

(2) In subsection (2)—

    (a) omit "or" at the end of paragraph (a),

    (b) after paragraph (b) insert ", or

        (c) Chapter 3 of Part 5A (group relief for carried-forward losses)."

(3) In subsection (3), for "A deductible amount that meets conditions A and B" substitute "In the case of a relevant claim within subsection (2)(a) or (b), a deductible amount that meets conditions A and B (a "restricted deductible amount")".

(4) After subsection (3) insert—

"(3A) A relevant claim within subsection (2)(c) may not be made in respect of a loss or other amount which has been carried forward under any provision mentioned in paragraphs (a) to (e) of section 188BB(1), so far as that amount is made up of an amount which was (in a previous accounting period) a restricted deductible amount."

(5) In subsection (4)—

    (a) for "subsection (3) does" substitute "subsections (3) and (3A) do", and

    (b) for "the claim" substitute "or as a result of, the claim concerned".

(6) After subsection (7) insert—

"(7A) For the purposes of determining how much of an amount carried forward as mentioned in subsection (3A) is made up of an amount which was (in a previous accounting period) a restricted deductible amount, assume that in previous accounting periods amounts have been brought into account as deductions (see section 730B(2)) in the order that results in the greatest amount being excluded by subsection (3A)."

(7) The amendments made by this paragraph do not have effect if the relevant day (as defined in section 730B(1) of CTA 2010) is before 1 April 2017.

PART 10

NORTHERN IRELAND TRADING LOSSES ETC

93 Part 8B of CTA 2010 (trading profits taxable at the Northern Ireland rate) is amended as follows.

94 In the italic heading before section 357JB for "section 37" substitute "Chapter 2 of Part 4".

95 For sections 357JB to 357JE substitute—

"357JB   Availability of relief

(1) The references in section 37 and sections 45A to 45F (relief for trade losses) to a loss are, where a company carrying on a trade in an accounting period has Northern Ireland losses of the trade or mainstream losses of the trade, references to those Northern Ireland losses or mainstream losses.

(2) If a company has a Northern Ireland loss and a mainstream loss in the same accounting period, sections 37 and 45A to 45F have effect in relation to each of those losses separately.

(3) If by reason of this section a company is entitled under section 37(2), 45A(5), 45B(5) or 45F(2) to make a claim in relation to a Northern Ireland loss (or an amount of such a loss) and a claim in relation to a mainstream loss (or an amount of such a loss), the company may make—

    (a) one of those claims only, or

    (b) both of those claims in either order.

(4) Where—

    (a) relief is given under section 37, 45A, 45B or 45F for a Northern Ireland loss (or an amount of such a loss), and

    (b) the profits against which the relief is given includes some profits of the trade that are Northern Ireland profits and some that are not,

the relief is given first, so far as possible, against the Northern Ireland profits.

(5) Where—

    (a) relief is given under section 37, 45, 45A, 45B or 45F for a loss (or an amount of a loss) that is not a Northern Ireland loss, and

    (b) the profits against which the relief is given include some profits of the trade that are Northern Ireland profits and some that are not,

the relief is given first, so far as possible, against the profits that are not Northern Ireland profits.

357JC   Restriction on deductions

(1) Subsection (2) applies where—

    (a) relief is given under section 37 for a Northern Ireland loss ("the loss"),

    (b) the profits against which the relief is given include profits that are not Northern Ireland profits, and

    (c) at any time during the accounting period for which the relief is given ("the profit period") the Northern Ireland rate is lower than the main rate.

(2) The reference in section 37(4) to "the amount of the loss" is to the restricted deduction for the loss, as determined under section 357JJ (restricted deduction where Northern Ireland rate lower than main rate).

(3) Subsection (4) applies where—

    (a) relief is given under section 45A, 45B or 45F for an amount of a Northern Ireland loss ("the loss"),

    (b) the profits against which the relief is given include profits that are not Northern Ireland profits, and

    (c) at any time during the accounting period for which the relief is given ("the profit period"), the Northern Ireland rate is lower than the main rate.

(4) The reference in section 45A(6), 45B(4) or (as the case may be) 45F(5) to "the unrelieved amount" is to so much of that amount as is equal to the restricted deduction for the loss, as determined under section 357JJ."

96 After section 357JH insert—

"Loss relief in relation to Northern Ireland profits and losses: Part 5A

357JHA   Availability of relief

(1) The reference in section 188BB(1)(a) (group relief for carried-forward losses: surrendering of carried-forward losses and other amounts) to a loss carried forward to an accounting period of a company under section 45A(4) is, where a company has Northern Ireland losses or mainstream losses carried forward to an accounting period under that section, a reference to those Northern Ireland losses or mainstream losses.

(2) Where—

    (a) a company makes a claim for group relief for carried-forward losses under Part 5A in relation to a surrenderable amount that is a Northern Ireland loss, and

    (b) the profits against which the relief is claimed include some profits that are Northern Ireland profits and some that are not, the relief in relation to that surrenderable amount is given first, so far as possible, against the Northern Ireland profits.

(3) Where—

(a) a company makes a claim for group relief for carried-forward losses under Part 5A in relation to a surrenderable amount that is not a Northern Ireland loss, and

(b) the profits against which the relief is claimed include some profits that are Northern Ireland profits and some that are not,

the relief in relation to that surrenderable amount is given first, so far as possible, against the profits that are not Northern Ireland profits.

357JHB Restriction on deductions

(1) Subsection (2) applies where—

(a) a company makes a claim for group relief for carried-forward losses under Part 5A in relation to a surrenderable amount that is a Northern Ireland loss ("the loss"),

(b) the profits against which the relief is claimed include profits that are not Northern Ireland profits, and

(c) at any time during the accounting period for which the relief is claimed ("the profit period"), the Northern Ireland rate is lower than the main rate.

(2) In section 188CK(2) and (4) (amount of deduction)—

(a) the reference in paragraph (a) to "an amount equal to" the surrendering company's surrenderable amounts is, so far as those surrenderable amounts comprise the loss, to the restricted deduction for the loss, as determined under section 357JJ (restricted deduction where Northern Ireland rate lower than main rate);

(b) the reference in paragraph (b) to "an amount equal to" part of the surrendering company's surrenderable amounts is, so far as that part comprises the loss, to the restricted deduction for the loss, as determined under section 357JJ.

357JHC Modifications of Chapter 4 of Part 5A

(1) Chapter 4 of Part 5A (limitations on group relief for carried-forward losses: claims under section 188CB) has effect, in relation to a claim under section 188CB in relation to surrenderable amounts that include a Northern Ireland loss, subject to the following provisions of this section.

(2) In section 188DB(1) (limitation on amount of group relief for carried-forward losses applying to all claims under section 188CB)—

(a) paragraphs (a) and (b) are treated as imposing separate limits;

(b) the limit in paragraph (a) on the amount of group relief for carried-forward losses to be given on a claim under section 188CB has effect as a limit on the amount of losses and other surrenderable amounts in relation to which relief is to be given on the claim;

(c) the limit in paragraph (b) on the amount of group relief for carried-forward losses to be given on a claim under section 188CB has effect as a limit on the amount of the deduction to be made as a result of the claim.

(3) In section 188DC(6)(b) (unused part of the surrenderable amounts), and in section 188DF(2) so far as it applies in relation to section 188DC, references to the amount of group relief for carried-forward losses given on a claim are to the amount of losses and other surrenderable amounts in relation to which relief is given on the claim.

(4) In section 188DE(4)(b) (previously claimed group relief for carried-forward losses), and in section 188DF(2) so far as it applies in relation to section 188DE, references to the amount of group relief for carried-forward losses given on a claim are to the amount of the deduction made as a result of the claim.

(5) In section 188DH (limitation on group relief for carried-forward losses where claim under section 188CB is based on consortium condition 1), the limit in subsection (2) on the amount of group relief for carried-forward losses to be given on a claim has effect as a limit on the amount of the deduction to be made as a result of the claim.

(6) In section 188DL (limitation on group relief for carried-forward losses where claim under section 188CB is made by member of a group of companies)—

(a) the reference in subsection (3)(a) to the maximum amount of group relief for carried-forward losses that could be claimed by the claimant company has effect as a reference to the maximum amount of the deduction that could be made as a result of claims by the claimant company, and

(b) the reference in subsection (3)(b) to the maximum amount of group relief under Part 5 that could be claimed by the claimant company has effect as a reference to the maximum amount of the deduction that could be made as a result of claims by the claimant company.

357JHD Modifications of Chapter 5 of Part 5A

(1) Chapter 5 of Part 5A (limitations on group relief for carried-forward losses: claims under section 188CC) has effect, in relation to a claim under section 188CC in relation to surrenderable amounts that include a Northern Ireland loss, subject to the following provisions of this section.

(2) In section 188EB(1) (limitation on amount of group relief for carried-forward losses applying to all claims under section 188CC)—

(a) paragraphs (a), (b) and (c) are treated as imposing separate limits;

(b) the limit in paragraph (a) on the amount of group relief for carried-forward losses to be given on a claim under section 188CC has effect as a limit on the amount of losses and other surrenderable amounts in relation to which relief is to be given on the claim;

(c) the limits in paragraphs (b) and (c) on the amount of group relief for carried-forward losses to be given on a claim under section 188CC have effect as limits on the amount of the deduction to be made as a result of the claim.

(3) In section 188EC(6) and (8)(b) (unused part of the surrenderable amounts attributable to the specified-loss making period), and in section 188EG(2) so far as it applies in relation to section 188EC, references to the amount of group relief for carried-forward losses given on a claim are to the amount of losses and other surrenderable amounts in relation to which relief is given on the claim.

(4) In section 188EE(4)(b) (previously claimed group relief for carried-forward losses), and in section 188EG(2) so far as it applies in relation to section 188EE, references to the amount of group relief for carried-forward losses given on a claim are to the amount of the deduction made as a result of the claim.

(5) In section 188EI (condition 4: companies in link company's group), the limit in subsections (2) and (3) on the amount of group relief for carried-forward losses to be given on a claim has effect as a limit on the amount of the deduction to be made as a result on the claim.

(6) In section 188EK (condition 3 or 4: surrendering company in group of companies), the reference in subsection (4) to the maximum amount of group relief for carried-forward losses that could be given has effect as a reference to the maximum amount of losses and other surrenderable amounts in relation to which relief could be given."

97 In section 357JJ (restricted deduction: Northern Ireland rate lower than main rate)—

(a) in subsection (1) for "357JC(2), 357JE(2) or 357JG(2)" substitute "357JC(2) or (4), 357JG(2) or 357JHB(2)", and

(b) in subsection (6) for "section 357JC(1), 357JE(1) or 357JG(1)" substitute "357JC(1) or (3), 357JG(1) or 357JHB(1)".

98 In section 357RF (losses of film trade: restriction on use of losses while film is in production) in subsection (2) for "subsection (2)" substitute "subsections (2) and (3)".

99 In section 357RG (losses of film trade: use of losses in later periods) in subsection (3) after "subsections (5)" insert ", (5A)".

100 In section 357SF (losses of television programme trade: restriction on use of losses while programme in production) in subsection (2) for "subsection (2)" substitute "subsections (2) and (3)".

101 In section 357SG (losses of television programme trade: use of losses in later periods) in subsection (3) after "subsections (5)" insert ", (5A)".

102 In section 357TF (losses of video game trade: restriction on use of losses while video game in development) in subsection (2) for "subsection (2)" substitute "subsections (2) and (3)".

103 In section 357TG (losses of video game trade: use of losses in later periods) in subsection (3) after "subsections (5)" insert ", (5A)".

104 In section 357UF (losses of theatrical trade: restriction on use of losses before completion period) in subsection (2) for "subsection (2)" substitute "subsections (2) and (3)".

105 In section 357UO (losses of orchestral trade: restriction on use of losses before completion period) in subsection (2) for "subsection (2)" substitute "subsections (2) and (3)".

PART 11
MINOR AND CONSEQUENTIAL AMENDMENTS

ICTA

106 (1) Section 826 of ICTA (interest on tax overpaid) is amended as follows.

(2) After subsection (7A) insert—

"(7AA) In any case where—

(a) a company ceases to carry on a trade in an accounting period ("the terminal period"),

(b) as a result of a claim under section 45F of CTA 2010, the whole or any part of a loss made in the trade is relieved for the purposes of corporation tax against profits (of whatever description) of an earlier accounting period ("the earlier period") which does not fall wholly within the period of 12 months immediately preceding the terminal period, and

(c) a repayment falls to be made of corporation tax paid for the earlier period or of income tax in respect of a payment received by the company in that accounting period,

then, in determining the amount of interest (if any) payable under this section on the repayment referred to in paragraph (c) above, no account shall be taken of so much of the amount of that repayment as falls to be made as a result of the claim under section 45F, except so far as concerns interest for any time after the date on which any corporation tax for the terminal period became (or, as the case may be, would have become) due and payable, as mentioned in subsection (7D) below."

(3) In subsection (7D) (meaning of references to the date on which corporation tax became payable) after "(7A)," insert "(7AA),".

(4) In subsection (7E) (power conferred by section 59E of TMA 1970 not to include power to change the meaning of references to the date on which corporation tax became payable) after "(7A)," insert "(7AA)".

FA 1998

107 Schedule 18 to FA 1998 (company tax returns, assessments and related matters) is amended in accordance with paragraphs 108 to 122.

108 In paragraph 61(1)(c) (consequential claims etc arising out of certain Revenue amendments or assessments), in the words in brackets, after "relief" insert "or group relief for carried-forward losses".

109 In the heading of Part 8 (claims for group relief) at the end insert "and group relief for carried-forward losses".

110 For paragraph 66 (introduction to Part 8) substitute—

"**66** (1) This Part of this Schedule applies to—

(a) claims for group relief under Part 5 of the Corporation Tax Act 2010, and

(b) claims for group relief for carried-forward losses under Part 5A of that Act.

(2) In this Part of this Schedule (except where otherwise indicated)—

(a) references to "relief" are to either of those forms of relief, and

(b) references to "a claim" are to a claim for either of those forms of relief."

111 In paragraph 67 (claim to be included in company tax return) omit "for group relief".

112 (1) Paragraph 68 (content of claims) is amended as follows.

(2) In sub-paragraph (1), in the words before paragraph (a), omit "for group relief".

(3) After sub-paragraph (4) insert—

"(5) A claim for group relief for carried-forward losses made under section 188CB of the Corporation Tax Act 2010 must also state whether or not there is a company mentioned in sub-paragraph (6) that was not resident in the United Kingdom in either or both of the following periods—

(a) the accounting period of the surrendering company to which the claim relates,

(b) the corresponding accounting period of the claimant company.

(6) Those companies are the claimant company, the surrendering company and any other company by reference to which—

(a) the claimant company and the surrendering company are members of the same group,

(b) consortium condition 1 in section 188CF or consortium condition 2 in section 188CG of the Corporation Tax Act 2010 is satisfied in the case of the claimant company and the surrendering company.

(7) A claim for group relief for carried forward-losses made under section 188CC of the Corporation Tax Act 2010 must also state whether or not there is a company mentioned in sub-paragraph (8) that was not resident in the United Kingdom in any or all of the following periods—

(a) the specified loss-making period of the surrendering company,

(b) the accounting period of the surrendering company to which the surrender relates,

(c) the accounting period of the claimant company that corresponds with the period mentioned in paragraph (b).

(8) Those companies are the claimant company, the surrendering company and any other company by reference to which consortium condition 3 in section 188CH or consortium condition 4 in section 188CI is satisfied in the case of the claimant company and the surrendering company."

113 (1) Paragraph 69 (claims for more or less than the amount available for surrender) is amended as follows.

(2) In subsection (1) omit "for group relief".

(3) In subsection (3), in the first step, after "Part 5" insert "or (as the case may be) Part 5A".

114 (1) Paragraph 70 (consent to surrender) is amended as follows.

(2) For sub-paragraph (1) substitute—

"(1) In accordance with Requirement 1 in section 130(2), 135(2), 188CB(3) or (as the case may be) 188CC(3) of the Corporation Tax Act 2010, a claim requires the consent of the surrendering company."

(3) In sub-paragraph (4) omit "for group relief".

(4) In sub-paragraph (6)—

(a) after "means" insert "—
    (a) ",

(b) at the end insert— ",
    (b) a claim for group relief for carried-forward losses under section 188CB of that Act based on consortium condition 1 or 2 (see Requirement 3 in that section), and
    (c) a claim for group relief for carried-forward losses under section 188CC of that Act based on consortium condition 3 or 4 (see Requirement 3 in that section).

115 In Paragraph 71 (notice of consent) after sub-paragraph (1) insert—

"(1A) Notice of consent given in respect of a claim for carried-forward losses made under section 188CC of the Corporation Tax Act 2010 must also state which accounting period of the surrendering company is the specified loss-making period.

Otherwise the notice is ineffective.

116 After paragraph 71 insert—

"Notice of consent: additional requirements where claim is for group relief for carried-forward losses

71A (1) Where notice of consent by the surrendering company is given in respect of a claim for carried-forward losses, the notice must comply with the additional requirements in this paragraph.

Otherwise the notice is ineffective.

(2) The notice must identify the particular losses and other amounts carried forward to the surrender period that are to be treated as surrendered in satisfaction of the claim.

(3) The notice must identify a loss or other amount by specifying—

(a) the provision of the Corporation Tax Act 2009 or the Corporation Tax Act 2010 under which it was carried forward to the surrender period, and

(b) in a case where the surrendering company is owned by a consortium, the accounting period of the surrendering company to which the loss or other amount is attributable.

(4) Section 153 of the Corporation Tax Act 2010 (companies owned by consortiums) applies for the purposes of this paragraph."

117 (1) Paragraph 72 (notice of consent requiring amendment of return) is amended as follows.

(2) For sub-paragraph (1) substitute—

"(1) Where notice of consent by the surrendering company relates to a loss or other amount in respect of which corporation tax relief has been given to the company for any accounting period, the company must at the same time amend its company tax return for that accounting period so as to reflect the notice of consent."

(3) Omit sub-paragraph (2).

(4) In sub-paragraph (3) omit "or (2)".

(5) In sub-paragraph (4) omit "or (2)".

118 (1) Paragraph 73 (withdrawal or amendment of claim) is amended as follows.

(2) In sub-paragraph (1) omit "for group relief".

(3) In sub-paragraph (2) omit "for group relief".

119 (1) Paragraph 74 (time limit for claims) is amended as follows.

(2) In sub-paragraph (1), in the words before paragraph (a), omit "for group relief".

(3) In sub-paragraph (2) omit "for group relief".

(4) In sub-paragraph (3) omit "for group relief".

(5) In sub-paragraph (4) omit "for group relief" in both places those words occur.

120 (1) Paragraph 75A (assessment on other claimant companies) is amended as follows.

(2) In sub-paragraph (2) omit "group".

(3) In sub-paragraph (6) omit "for group relief".

121 (1) Paragraph 76 (assessment to recover excessive relief) is amended as follows.

(2) In the italic heading omit "group".

(3) In sub-paragraph (1) omit "group".

122 (1) Paragraph 77 (joint amended returns) is amended as follows.

(2) In sub-paragraph (1)—

(a) in paragraph (a) omit "for group relief", and
(b) in paragraph (b) omit "group" in the second and third places that word occurs.

(3) In sub-paragraph (3), in paragraph (a), omit "for group relief".

CAA 2001

123 CAA 2001 is amended as follows.

124 (1) Section 212Q (restrictions on capital allowance buying when there are postponed allowances) is amended as follows.

(2) In subsection (4) after "37," insert "45A,".

(3) In subsection (6)—

(a) after "may not be set off" insert "by a company ("the claimant company")",
(b) after "CTA 2010" insert "or group relief for carried forward losses in accordance with Part 5A of CTA 2010", and
(c) omit "by a company ("the claimant company")".

125 In section 138 (deferment of balancing charge arising when there is a disposal event in respect of a ship: limit on amount of deferral) in subsection (2)(b) after "45" insert ", 45A or 45B".

126 In Schedule A1 (first-year tax credits) in paragraph 20 (list of provisions to which restriction on carrying forward losses applies) in paragraph (a) for "section 45" substitute "sections 45, 45A and 45B".

Energy Act 2004

127 In section 27 of the Energy Act 2004 (tax exemption for NDA activities) in subsection (1)(b) for the words from "relieved" to the end substitute "—

(i) relieved under section 37, 45, 45A, 45B or 45F of the Corporation Tax Act 2010 (relief for trading losses),
(ii) surrendered under Part 5 of that Act (group relief), or
(iii) surrendered under Part 5A of that Act (group relief for carried-forward losses)."

CTA 2009

128 CTA 2009 is amended as follows.

129 In section 39(3) (losses of mines, quarries and other concerns)—

(a) omit "and", and

(b) after "(group relief)" insert "and Part 5A of that Act (group relief for carried forward losses)".

130 (1) Section 364 (group relief claims involving impaired or released consortium debts) is amended as follows.

(2) In subsection (4) at the end insert ", and

"group relief" means—

(a) group relief under Part 5 of CTA 2010 (see section 97(2) of that Act), and

(b) group relief for carried-forward losses under Part 5A of CTA 2010 (see section 188AA(4) of that Act)."

(3) In subsection (5) for "or 144" substitute ", 144 or 188DH".

131 In section 371 (group relief claims involving impaired or released consortium debts: interpretation) for the definition of "group relief" substitute—

"group relief" has the meaning given by section 364(4),".

132 In section 387 (treatment of deficit on basic life assurance and general annuity business: introduction) in subsection (1) for "Chapter 16" substitute "Chapters 16 and 16A".

133 (1) Section 1048 (treatment of deemed trading loss under section 1045) is amended as follows.

(2) In subsection (1) at the end insert "("the deemed loss-making period")".

(3) In subsection (3)—

(a) before paragraph (a) insert—

"(za) the deemed loss-making period begins before 1 April 2017",

(b) in paragraph (a) for "the accounting period" substitute "the deemed loss-making period".

(4) After subsection (4) insert—

"(4A) Subsection (4B) applies if—

(a) the deemed loss-making period begins on or after 1 April 2017,

(b) the company—

(i) begins to carry on a trade in the deemed loss-making period which it continues to carry on in the following accounting period, or

(ii) begins to carry on a trade in an accounting period after the deemed-loss making period, and

(c) the trade is derived from the research and development in relation to which the relief mentioned in subsection (1) was obtained.

(4B) In that case, so far as—

(a) the company has not obtained relief in respect of the trading loss under any other provision, and

(b) the loss has not been surrendered under Part 5 of CTA 2010 (group relief) (surrender of relief to group or consortium members),

the trading loss is to be treated as if it were a loss of that trade brought forward under the relevant provision (see subsection (4C)) to the relevant period (see subsection (4D).

(4C) In subsection (4B) "the relevant provision" is—

(a) section 45A(4) of CTA 2010 if—

(i) the trade is not a ring fence trade within the meaning of Part 8 of CTA 2010 (see section 277 of that Act), and

(ii) relief under section 37 of CTA 2010 would not be unavailable by reason of section 44 of that Act for a loss (assuming there was one) made in the trade in the relevant period (see subsection (4D), and

(b) section 45B(2) of CTA 2010 if either of the conditions in paragraph (a) is not met.

(4D) In subsection (4B) and (4C) "the relevant period" means—

(a) in a case where the company began the trade in the deemed loss-making period and continued to carry on the trade in the following accounting period, that following accounting period, and

(b) in a case where the company began the trade in an accounting period after the deemed loss-making period, the accounting period in which the company began the trade."

(5) In subsection (5) for "Subsection (4) is" substitute "Subsections (4) and (4B) are".

134 In section 1056 (amount of trading loss which is "unrelieved")—

    (a) in subsection (2)(c) after "Part 5" insert "or Part 5A", and

    (b) in subsection (3)(a) after "45" insert ", 45A or 45B".

135 In section 1062(2) (restriction on losses carried forward where R&D tax credit claimed)—

    (a) for "section 45" substitute "sections 45, 45A and 45B", and

    (b) omit "trading" in the second place that word occurs.

136 In section 1116 (meaning of "the actual reduction in tax liability") in subsection (4) after "Part 5" insert "or Part 5A".

137 In section 1153 (amount of loss which is "unrelieved")—

    (a) in subsection (1)(c) after "Part 5" insert "or Part 5A", and

    (b) in subsection (2)(a) after "45" insert ", 45A, 45B".

138 In section 1158(2) (restriction on losses carried forward where land remediation tax credit claimed)—

    (a) for "section 45" substitute "sections 45, 45A and 45B", and

    (b) omit "trading" in the second place that word occurs.

139 In section 1201 (film tax credit claimable if company has surrenderable loss) in subsection (2B)(b) after "45" insert "or 45B".

140 In section 1216CH (television tax credit claimable if company has surrenderable loss) in subsection (4)(b) after "45" insert "or 45B".

141 In section 1217CH (video game tax credit claimable if company has surrenderable loss) in subsection (4)(b) after "45" insert "or 45B".

142 In section 1217KA (theatre tax credits: amount of surrenderable loss) in subsection (3)(b) after "45" insert "or 45B".

143 In section 1217RH (orchestra tax credits: amount of surrenderable loss) in subsection (3)(b) after "45" insert "or 45B".

144 In section 1223 (carry forward expenses of management and other amounts), in subsection (1)(b), after sub-paragraph (i) (as inserted by paragraph 6(2)(b)) insert—

    "(ii) section 269ZD of CTA 2010 (restrictions on deductions from total profits) has effect for the accounting period, or

    (iii) ".

CTA 2010

145 CTA 2010 is amended as follows.

146 (1) Section 1 (overview of Act) is amended as follows.

(2) In subsection (2) (list of reliefs provided by Parts 4 to 7) after paragraph (f) insert—

    "(fa) group relief for carried-forward losses (see Part 5A),"

(3) After subsection (2) insert—

    "(2A) Part 7ZA contains provision restricting the amount of certain deductions which may be made in calculating the profits of a company on which corporation tax is chargeable."

147 (1) Section 17 (interpretation of Chapter 4 of Part 2) is amended as follows.

(2) In subsection (2) (meaning of "carried-back amount")—

    (a) after paragraph (a) insert—

    "(aa) an amount carried back under section 45F (relief for terminal trade losses),", and

    (b) in paragraph (c) after "459(1)(b)" insert "or 463B(1)(b)".

(3) In subsection (3) (meaning of "carried-forward amount")—

    (a) in paragraph (a) after "forward of" insert "pre-1 April 2017",

    (b) after paragraph (a) insert—

    "(aa) an amount carried forward under section 45A (carry forward of post 1-April 2017 trade loss against total profits),

    (ab) an amount carried forward under section 45B (carry forward of post-1 April 2017 trade loss against subsequent trade profits),", and

    (c) in paragraph (i) after "457(3)" insert ", 463G(6) or 463H(4)".

148 (1) Section 46 (use of trade-related interest and dividends if insufficient trade profits) is amended as follows.

(2) For subsection (1) substitute—

    "(1) This section applies if in an accounting period a company carrying on a trade makes a loss in the trade and either—

(a) relief for the loss could be given in a later accounting period under section 45(4)(b) or 45B(4) but for the fact that there are no profits of the trade of the later accounting period, or

(b) the amount of relief for the loss that could be given in a later accounting period under section 45(4)(b) or 45B(4) is limited by reason of the amount of profits of the trade of the later accounting period."

(3) In subsection (2) at the beginning insert "For the purposes of section 45 and 45B,".

149 In section 47 (registered societies), in subsection (1), for "section 45" substitute "sections 45 and 45B".

150 In section 53 (leasing contracts and company reconstructions), in subsection (1)(e), for "or 45" substitute ", 45, 45A or 45B".

151 In section 54 (non-UK resident company: receipts of interest, dividends or royalties), in subsection (2), for "or 45" substitute ", 45, 45A or 45B".

152 (1) Section 56 (restriction on reliefs for limited partners) is amended as follows.

(2) In subsection (2)—

  (a) in paragraph (a) after "37" insert "or 45A",

  (b) omit "or" at the end of paragraph (a), and

  (c) after paragraph (b) insert ", or

    (c) under Part 5A (group relief for carried-forward losses)".

(3) In subsection (4)—

  (a) after "37" insert "or 45A", and

  (b) after "5" insert "or 5A".

153 (1) Section 59 (restriction on relief for members of LLPs) is amended as follows.

(2) In subsection (2)—

  (a) in paragraph (a) after "37" insert "or 45A",

  (b) omit "or" at the end of paragraph (a), and

  (c) after paragraph (b) insert ", or

    (c) under Part 5A (group relief for carried-forward losses)".

(3) In subsection (4)—

  (a) after "37" insert "or 45A", and

  (b) after "5" insert "or 5A".

154 (1) Section 61 (unrelieved losses of member of LLP brought forward) is amended as follows.

(2) In subsection (1), in the words before paragraph (a), for "This section" substitute "Subsection (2)".

(3) After subsection (2) insert—

"(2A) Subsection (2B) applies if—

  (a) a company ("the member company") carries on a trade as a member of an LLP at a time during an accounting period ("the current period"), and

  (b) as a result of section 59, relief under section 45A or Part 5A (group relief for carried forward losses) has not been given for an amount of loss made in the trade by the member company as a member of the LLP in a previous accounting period.

(2B) For the purposes of determining the relief under section 45A or Part 5A to be given to any company, the amount of loss is treated as having been made by the member company in the current period so far as it is not excluded by subsection (3) or (4)."

(4) In subsection (3)—

  (a) after "37" insert "or 45A", and

  (b) after "Part 5" insert "or Part 5A".

155 (1) Chapter 4 of Part 4 (property losses) is amended as follows.

(2) In section 65 (UK furnished holiday lettings business treated as trade) for subsection (4A) substitute—

"(4A) Chapter 2 applies as if the following were omitted—

  (a) sections 37 to 44,

  (b) the words "beginning before 1 April 2017" in section 45(1),

  (c) sections 45A to 45H, and

  (d) sections 48 to 54.

(4B) Any deduction made under section 45(4)(b) from the profits of the trade treated as carried on under this section is to be ignored for the purposes of section 269ZB (restriction on deductions from trading profits)."

(3) In section 67A (EEA furnished holiday lettings business treated as trade) for subsection (5) substitute—

"(5) Chapter 2 applies as if the following were omitted—
  (a) sections 37 to 44,
  (b) the words "beginning before 1 April 2017" in section 45(1),
  (c) sections 45A to 45H, and
  (d) sections 48 to 54.

(5A) Any deduction made under section 45(4)(b) from the profits of the trade treated as carried on under this section is to be ignored for the purposes of section 269ZB (restriction on deductions from trading profits)."

156 (1) Section 95 (write-off of government investment: meaning of "carry forward losses") is amended as follows.

(2) In subsection (1), in Type 1, after "45," insert "45A, 45B,".

(3) In subsection (2) after "(group relief)" insert "or Part 5A (group relief for carried forward losses)".

157 In section 99 (surrendering of losses and other amounts) in subsection (1)(c) after "16" insert "or 16A".

158 In section 104 (meaning of "non-trading loss on intangible fixed assets" for purposes of section 99(1)(g)), for subsection (2) substitute—

"(2) But it does not include a loss treated as a non-trading loss on intangible fixed assets for the surrender period as a result of section 753(3) of CTA 2009."

159 In section 137 (giving of group relief: deduction from total profits) in subsection (5) (list of deductions to be made after group relief is given)—

  (a) omit "and" at the end of paragraph (b),
  (b) in paragraph (c) for "or 459" substitute ", 459 or 463B", and
  (c) after paragraph (c) insert ", and
    (d) under section 188CK (giving of group relief for carried-forward losses: deductions from total profits)".

160 In section 189(2) (relief for qualifying charitable donations) at the end insert "and group relief for carried-forward losses".

161 In section 269DA (surcharge on banking companies) in subsection (2) (calculation of "surcharge profits")—

  (a) in the formula, after "NBGR+" insert "NBGRCF+", and
  (b) after the definition of "NBGR" insert—
    ""NBGRCF" is the amount (if any) of non-banking group relief for carried-forward losses that is given in determining those taxable total profits (see section 269DBA);".

162 After section 269DB insert—

"269DBA Meaning of "non-banking group relief for carried-forward losses"

  (1) In section 269DA(2) "non-banking group relief for carried-forward losses" means group relief for carried-forward losses that relates to losses or other amounts that the surrendering company has for a surrender period in relation to which it is not a banking company.

  (2) In this section "surrendering company" and "surrender period" have the same meaning as in Part 5A (see section 188FD)."

163 (1) Section 269DC (surcharge on banking companies: meaning of "non-banking or pre-2016 loss relief) is amended as follows.

(2) In subsection (3)(b)—

  (a) after "45" insert ", 45A or 45B", and
  (b) omit "trade" in the second place that word occurs.

(3) In subsection (4)(b)—

  (a) after "457" insert ", 463G or 463H", and
  (b) omit "non-trading".

(4) Omit subsection (5).

164 In section 385 (sales of lessors: no carry back of loss against the income) in subsection (2) after "periods)" insert "or section 45F (relief for terminal trade losses)".

165 In section 398D (sales of lessors: restrictions on use of losses etc) after subsection (2) insert—

"(2A) Group relief for carried-forward losses is not to be given under Part 5A against so much of the total profits of A as are attributable to the carrying on of the relevant activity."

166 In section 427 (sales of lessors: no carry back of loss against the income) in subsection (2) after "periods)" insert "or section 45F (relief for terminal trade losses)".

167 (1) Chapter 5 of Part 9 (sales of lessors: anti-avoidance provisions) is amended as follows.

(2) In section 432 (introduction to section 433)—

(a) in subsection (1), in the words before paragraph (a), for "Section 433 applies" substitute "Sections 433 and 433A apply", and
(b) in subsection (2) after "that section" insert "and section 433A".

(3) In section 433 (restrictions on relief for expenses treated as incurred under Chapter 3 or 4)—

(a) in subsection (3)—
  (i) in paragraph (a) after "of" insert "pre-1 April 2017",
  (ii) after that paragraph insert—
  "(ab) section 45B (carry forward of post-1 April 2017 trade loss against subsequent trade profits),
(b) in subsection (5) after "profits)" insert "or section 45A (carry forward of trade loss against total profits)", and
(c) in subsection (6)—
  (i) after "set off" insert "—
  (a) ", and
  (ii) at the end insert ", or
  "(b) by way of group relief for carried-forward losses in accordance with Chapter 2 of Part 5A (surrender of company's carried forward losses)".

(4) After section 433 insert—

"433A Restrictions not applying to the restricted loss amount

(1) Any deduction made under section 45 or 45B in respect of the restricted loss amount is to be ignored for the purposes of the restriction in section 269ZB (restriction on sum of deductions from trading profits).

(2) Any deduction made under section 62 or 63 in respect of the restricted loss amount is to be ignored for the purposes of the restriction in section 269ZD (restriction on sum of deductions from total profits)."

168 In section 599 (real estate investment trusts: calculation of profits) after subsection (8) insert—

"(9) No account is to be taken of Part 7ZA of this Act (restrictions on obtaining certain deductions in respect of carried-forward losses)."

169 In section 601 (availability of group reliefs to a group UK REIT) in subsection (2)—

(a) omit "and" at the end of paragraph (f), and
(b) after paragraph (g) insert ", and
  "(h) Part 5A of this Act (group relief for carried-forward losses)".

170 In section 705E (shell companies: restriction on relief for non-trading loss on intangible fixed assets), in subsection (3)(b), for "debit of" substitute "loss on intangible fixed assets for".

171 In section 705F(2) (shell companies: apportionment of amounts), in column 1 of the table—

(a) in row 4, after "457(1)" insert ", 463G or 463H",
(b) in row 4, omit "basic rule for deficits:",
(c) in row 5, omit from ", but excluding" to the end, and
(d) in row 6, omit from "and treated" to the end.

172 In section 730C (disallowance of deductible amounts: relevant claims) in subsection (2) (meaning of "relevant claim")—

(a) omit "or" at the end of paragraph (a),
(b) after paragraph (a) insert—
  "(aa) section 45A (carry forward of post-1 April 2017 trade loss against total profits)," and
(c) after paragraph (b) insert ", or
  (c) Chapter 3 of Part 5A (group relief for carried-forward losses)".

173 (1) Section 888 (restrictions on leasing partnership losses) is amended as follows.

(2) In subsection (3) after "37" insert "or 45A".

(3) In subsection (4)—

  (a) after "set off" insert "—
    (a) ", and

  (b) at the end insert ", or
    (b) by way of group relief for carried-forward losses in accordance with Chapter 2 of Part 5A (surrender of company's carried-forward losses etc)".

(4) In subsection (6) in the definition of "relevant loss relief provision"—

  (a) in paragraph (a) after "of" insert "pre-1 April 2017", and

  (b) after that paragraph insert—
    "(ab) section 45B (carry forward of post-1 April 2017 trade loss against subsequent trade profits),".

174 (1) Schedule 4 (index of defined expressions) is amended as follows.

(2) At the appropriate places insert—

"the claimant company (in Part 5A)	section 188FD"
"the claim period (in Part 5A)	section 188FD"
"company (in Part 5A)	section 188FD"
"group relief for carried-forward losses"	section 188AA(4)"
"holding company (in Part 5A)	section 188FC(2)"
"member of a consortium (in Part 5A)	section 153(2) (applied by section 188FB)"
"member of the same group of companies (in Part 5A)	section 152 (applied by section 188FB)"
"owned by a consortium (in Part 5A)	section 153(1) and (3) (applied by section 188FB)"
"profits (in Part 5A)	section 188FD"
"the specified loss-making period" (in Part 5A)	section 188FD"
"75% subsidiary (in Part 5A)	section 151 (applied by section 188FB)"
"the surrenderable amounts (in Part 5A)	section 188FD"
"the surrendering company (in Part 5A)	section 188FD
"the surrender period (in Part 5A)	section 188FD"
"trade (in Part 5A)	section 188FD"
"trading company (in Part 5A)	section 188FC(1)"

(3) In the entry for "75% subsidiary (except in Part 5)" after "Part 5" insert "and Part 5A".

TIOPA 2010

175 TIOPA 2010 is amended as follows.

176 In section 54 (double taxation relief by way of credit: non-trading debits on loan relationships) in subsection (7)—

  (a) in paragraph (b) of the definition of "carry-back claim", after "459(1)(b)" insert "or 463B(1)(b)",

  (b) in paragraph (b) of the definition of "carry-forward provision", after "457(1)" insert ", 463G(5) or 463H(4)", and

  (c) in paragraph (b) of the definition of "current-year provision or claim", after "459(1)(a)" insert "or 463B(1)(a)".

177 In section 55 (double taxation relief by way of credit: current year's non-trading deficits on loan relationships)—

  (a) in subsection (4)(b), after "459(1)(a)" insert "or 463B(1)(a)", and

  (b) in subsection (5), for "or 459(1)(a)" substitute ", 459(1)(a) or 463B(1)(a)".

178 In section 156(1) (meaning of "losses" in Part 4)—

  (a) in paragraph (e) after "Chapter 16" insert "or Chapter 16A",

  (b) omit "or" at the end of paragraph (f), and

  (c) after paragraph (g) insert ", or
    (h) Part 5A of CTA 2010 (group relief for carried-forward losses)."

179 In section 371IF (determining the profits of a CFC's qualifying loan relationship), in paragraph (b) of step 5, after "16" insert "or Chapter 16A".

180 After section 371SK insert—

"371SKA Restrictions on certain deductions: deductions allowances

(1) This section applies for the purposes of—

(a) applying Part 7ZA of CTA 2010 (restrictions on obtaining certain deductions), and

(b) applying any provision of Part 7ZA of CTA 2010 for the purposes of Part 7A of that Act (restrictions on obtaining certain deductions: banking companies).

(2) Assume that each of the following is nil—

(a) the CFC's deductions allowance for the relevant accounting period,

(b) the CFC's trading profits deductions allowance for the relevant accounting period, and

(c) the CFC's non-trading profits deductions allowance for the relevant accounting period.

(3) But if section 269ZX of CTA 2010 (increase of deductions allowance where provision for onerous lease reversed) applies in relation to the relevant accounting period, the reference in subsection (2) to "nil" is to be read as a reference to an amount equal to the increase provided for by subsection (3) of that section."

181 In subsection (2)(a) of section 371SL (group relief etc)—

(a) after "(group relief)" insert "or Part 5A of that Act (group relief for carried-forward losses)", and

(b) after "by way of group relief" insert "or group relief for carried-forward losses".

F (No. 3) A 2010

182 (1) In paragraph 10 of Schedule 9 to F(No.3)A 2010 (interest), the new Part A1 to be inserted into Schedule 54 to FA 2009 is amended as follows.

(2) In paragraph A1 (interest on tax repaid as a result of carrying back a non-trading deficit on company's loan relationships)—

(a) in sub-paragraph (1)(c) for "or 459(1)(b)" substitute ", 459(1)(b) or 463B(1)(b)", and

(b) in sub-paragraph (2) for "or 459(1)(b)" substitute ", 459(1)(b) or 463B(1)(b)".

(3) After paragraph A2 insert—

"A2A (1) This paragraph applies where—

(a) a company has profits arising in an accounting period ("the earlier period"),

(b) the company ceases to carry on a trade in a later accounting period ("the later period"),

(c) on a claim under section 45F of CTA 2010 (terminal losses), the whole or any part of a loss incurred in the trade has been set off for the purposes of corporation tax against the profits of the earlier period,

(d) the earlier period does not fall wholly within the period of 12 months immediately preceding the later period, and

(e) a repayment falls to be made of corporation tax paid for the earlier period or of income tax in respect of a payment received by the company in that period.

(2) So much of the repayment mentioned in sub-paragraph (1)(e) as falls to be made as a result of the claim under section 45F does not carry repayment interest.

(3) But sub-paragraph (2) does not apply (and, accordingly, the amount mentioned in that sub-paragraph carries repayment interest) after the expiry of 9 months from the end of the later period."

(4) In paragraph A3 (interest on tax repaid as a result of a claim under section 77 of TIOPA 2010) in sub-paragraph (4) after "A4" insert "or A5".

(5) After paragraph A4 insert—

"A5 (1) This paragraph applies where—

(a) a company has profits arising in an accounting period ("the middle period"),

(b) the company ceases to carry on a trade in a later accounting period ("the later period"),

(c) on a claim under section 45F of CTA 2010 (terminal losses), the whole or any part of a loss incurred in the trade has been set off for the purposes of corporation tax against the profits of the middle period,

(d) the middle period does not fall wholly within the period of 12 months immediately preceding the later period,

(e) as a result of the claim under section 45F, an excess or increased excess arises in the middle period as described in section 72 of TIOPA 2010 (amounts of unrelieved foreign tax),

(f) on a claim under section 77 of that Act, credit for the whole or any part of the excess is allowed against corporation tax in respect of an accounting period before the middle period ("the earlier period") and,

(g) a repayment falls to be made of corporation tax paid for the earlier period or of income tax in respect of a payment received by the company in that period.

(2) So much of the repayment mentioned in sub-paragraph (1)(g) as falls to be made as a result of the claim under section 77 does not carry repayment interest.

(3) But sub-paragraph (2) does not apply (and, accordingly, the amount mentioned in that sub-paragraph carries repayment interest) after the expiry of 9 months from the end of the later period."

FA 2012

183 FA 2012 is amended as follows.

184 In section 78 (meaning of expressions used in section 76), in subsection (5), for the words from "means" to the end substitute "means any of the following—

(a) a BLAGAB trade loss of the company for the accounting period in question, so far as relief is given for the loss under—

(i) section 37 of CTA 2010 (relief for trade losses against total income), as applied by section 123, or

(ii) Chapter 4 of Part 5 of that Act (group relief), as applied by section 125;

(b) an amount deducted under section 124B (relief for excess carried forward post-1 April BLAGAB trade losses) from the company's total profits of the accounting period in question;

(c) an amount of a BLAGAB trade loss of the company relieved under Chapter 3 of Part 5A of CTA 2010 (group relief for carried-forward losses) if the surrender period (see section 188BB(7)) to which the claim relates is the accounting period in question."

185 In section 93 (minimum profits test), in subsection (2), in the words after paragraph (b), for "and 124" substitute ", 124, 124A and 124C".

186 In section 104 (meaning of "the adjusted amount")—

(a) in subsection (3), after "124" insert ", 124A or 124C";

(b) in subsection (4), for "that section" substitute "any of those sections";

(c) in subsection (5)(a), for "or no relief is available under that section," substitute ", 124A or 124C or no relief is available under those sections,".

187 In section 125 (group relief), at the end insert—

"(4) For provision about the application of Part 5A of CTA 2010 (group relief for carried-forward losses) in relation to BLAGAB trade losses see subsections (3) to (5) of section 188BB of that Act."

188 (1) Section 126 (restrictions in respect of non-trading deficit) is amended as follows.

(2) After subsection (1) insert—

"(1A) A loss falls within subsection (1B) so far as it—

(a) would (apart from that subsection) be available for relief under section 124B (excess carried forward post-1 April 2017 losses: relief against total profits), and

(b) arose in an accounting period for which the insurance company has a relevant non-trading deficit.

(1B) A loss (or amount of a loss) falling within this subsection is available for relief under section 124B only so far as it exceeds the amount of that relevant non-trading deficit.

(1C) A loss falls within subsection (1D) so far as it—

(a) is an amount which a company ("the surrendering company") may surrender by virtue of section 188BB(4) (surrender of carried-forward BLAGAB trade losses), and

(b) arose in an accounting period for which the surrendering company has a relevant non-trading deficit.

(1D) A loss (or amount of a loss) falling within this subsection is available for relief under Chapter 3 of Part 5A of CTA 2010 (claims for group relief) only so far as it exceeds the amount of that relevant non-trading deficit.

(1E) For the purposes of subsections (1A) and (1C) it is to be assumed (where relevant) that in previous accounting periods losses which arose earlier have been utilised before losses which arose later."

(3) In subsection (2)—

(a) for "The reference" substitute "In this section references";

(b) for "is a reference" substitute "are".

189 In section 127 (no relief against policyholders' share of I-E profit), in subsection (3)—

(a) before paragraph (a) insert—

"(za) relief under section 124B (relief of excess carried-forward BLAGAB trade losses against total profits),";

(b) after paragraph (c) insert—

"(ca) relief under Chapter 3 of Part 5A of CTA 2010 (group relief for carried-forward losses),".

PART 12

COMMENCEMENT ETC

Parts 1 to 9 and 11

190 (1) The amendments made by Parts 1 to 9 and 11 of this Schedule have effect in relation to accounting periods beginning on or after 1 April 2017.

(2) For the purposes of those amendments, where a company has an accounting period beginning before 1 April 2017 and ending on or after that date ("the straddling period")—

(a) so much of the straddling period as falls before 1 April 2017, and so much of that period as falls on or after that date, are treated as separate accounting periods, and

(b) where it is necessary to apportion an amount for the straddling period to the two separate accounting periods, it is to be apportioned—

(i) in accordance with section 1172 of CTA 2010 (time basis), or

(ii) if that method would produce a result that is unjust or unreasonable, on a just and reasonable basis.

(3) But sub-paragraph (2)(b) is to be ignored if paragraph 191 or 192 applies.

191 (1) This paragraph applies if—

(a) an accounting period of a company ("the straddling period") is treated as two separate accounting periods under paragraph 190(2)(a),

(b) it is necessary to apportion an amount ("the amount concerned") for the straddling period to the two separate accounting periods, and

(c) the amount concerned is either—

(i) an amount chargeable to corporation tax which would have been less but for Part 10 of TIOPA 2010 (corporate interest restriction), or

(ii) an amount in respect of which corporation tax relief is available which would have been greater but for Part 10 of TIOPA 2010.

(2) The amount concerned is to be apportioned as follows—

Step 1

Determine what the amount concerned would have been but for Part 10 of TIOPA 2010 ("the notional amount").

Step 2

Determine what amount of the notional amount would have been apportioned to the first separate accounting period had paragraph 190(2)(b) applied ("the notional apportioned amount").

If the notional apportioned amount is less than the amount concerned, proceed with steps 3 and 4.

If the notional apportioned amount is equal to or greater than the amount concerned, the whole of the amount concerned is to be apportioned to the first separate accounting period.

Step 3

Take so much of the amount concerned as is equal to the notional apportioned amount and apportion it to the first accounting period.

Step 4

Take the remainder of the amount concerned and apportion it to the second separate accounting period.

192 (1) This paragraph applies if—

(a) an accounting period of a company ("the straddling period") is treated as two separate accounting periods under paragraph 190(2)(a),

(b) it is necessary to apportion an amount ("the amount concerned") for the straddling period to the two separate accounting period,

(c) the amount concerned is an amount chargeable to corporation tax, and

(d) the amount concerned would not have arisen but for Part 10 of TIOPA 2010 (whether or not an amount in respect of which corporation tax relief would have been available would have arisen instead).

(2) The whole of the amount concerned is apportioned to the second separate accounting period.

Part 10

193 Section 5(4) to (6) of CT(NI)A 2015 (commencement) has effect as if references to Part 8B of CTA 2010 were to that Part as amended by Part 10 of this Schedule.

Transitional provision

194 (1) An amount of a non-trading deficit from a company's loan relationships which is carried forward under section 463H of CTA 2009 is to be disregarded for the purposes of section 730F of CTA 2010 (as amended by paragraph 69(4)), unless it is a post-13 July 2017 amount.

(2) An amount of a non-trading deficit from a company's loan relationships which is deducted under section 463H(5) of CTA 2009 is to be disregarded for the purposes sections 188DD and 188ED of CTA 2010, unless it is a post-13 July 2017 amount.

(3) For the purposes of this paragraph an amount of a non-trading deficit from a company's loan relationships ("the deficit amount") is a post-13 July 2017 amount—

(a) if the deficit period begins on or after 13 July 2017 or,

(b) (where the deficit period is one that begins before, and ends on or after 13 July 2017 (a "straddling deficit period")), so far as the deficit is apportioned under sub-paragraphs (4) and (5) to the part of the deficit period that begins with 13 July 2017.

(4) For the purposes of sub-paragraph (3)(b)—

(a) a straddling deficit period is to be treated as consisting of two parts, namely the part that precedes, and the part that begins with, 13 July 2017,

(b) the deficit amount is to be apportioned to those parts (see sub-paragraph (5)).

(5) The apportionment is to be made—

(a) in accordance with section 1172 of CTA 2010 (time basis), or

(b) if that method would produce a result that is unjust or unreasonable, on a just and reasonable basis.

(6) In this paragraph "deficit period" is to be interpreted in accordance with section 463A(2) of CTA 2009.

GENERAL NOTE

Schedule 4 covers the following:

- Flexible use of carried forward losses.
- Group relied for carried forward losses.
- Restriction of use of carried forward losses for companies with large profits.

Flexible use of carried forward losses

The broad thrust of Part 1 of Schedule 4 is to allow the more flexible use of various types of corporate loss that are carried forward, in contrast to the old regime which generally restricts the use of losses to being used against sources of income similar to that in which they arose. A general theme throughout the Schedule is therefore that losses crystallised as at 31 March 2017 have to be identified, as these will be subject to the previous loss regime, albeit with minor changes in some cases to fit in with the new regime. Losses arising on or after 1 April 2017 will, therefore, be subject to the new regime.

This means that it may be necessary for companies to effectively prepare corporation tax computations as at 31 March 2017 in order to appropriately apportion losses arising in straddling accounting periods.

Non-trading loan relationship deficits

The new provisions apply to non-trading deficits from a company's loan relationships in an accounting period beginning on or after 1 April 2017, so long as the company is not a charity at the end of the accounting period. The new legislation introduces a new chapter 16A into the loan relationships rules in CTA 2009.

Use in deficit period or earlier

The first part of the new rules largely mirrors the existing rules. A company may claim to have the whole or part of the deficit set against the total profits of the company in the deficit period itself, or to be carried back to set against total profits of the company for the period of 12 months immediately prior to the deficit period.

Claims must be made within two years after the end of the period unless HMRC allow a longer period. And claims cannot be made in respect of any of the deficit that has been surrendered as group relief. It is implicit that the claim must specify the amount of relief claimed for the deficit period itself or the previous 12-month period.

Relief for the deficit period must be given before relief for trading profits of the deficit period, UK property business losses for the period and relief for non-trading deficits carried back from a later period. Relief cannot be given against ring fence profits of the company.

Relief to carry back the deficit to earlier periods can only apply to any part of the deficit that has not been used to cover profits of the deficit period itself. Where there is more than one accounting period, or deemed accounting period, within the previous 12-month period, the deficit must be used to reduce the profits of the later period. Only once the profits of the later period are eliminated can profits be used against the earlier period. Where necessary, for an accounting period starting before the prior 12-month period and ending within it, the losses of that period must be apportioned appropriately.

Relief for the carry back of non-trading deficits is given after the following reliefs:

- Reliefs for non-trading deficits of that earlier period.
- Relief in respect of any loss or deficit incurred or treated as incurred in an accounting period before the deficit period, which would include losses or deficits brought forward from earlier periods.
- Relief for charitable donations in respect of payments made for the purposes of the trade.
- Trading losses of that period or carried back from a later period.
- Where the company has an investment business, deductions in respect of expenses of management, plant and machinery allowances and charitable donations.

Use in later periods

Unrelieved deficits are carried forward and set against total profits of the following accounting period of the company "(the later period"), subject to satisfying four conditions and to making a claim.

The conditions are that:

- The deficit has not previously been set off against total profits of the deficit period or an earlier period or group relieved (Condition A).
- The company did not cease to be a company with investment business during the deficit period or, if it had an investment period immediately before the beginning of the deficit period, that investment business has not become small or negligible during the deficit period (Condition B).

  This might be seen as imposing a condition that the carry forward of a deficit requires the company to have an investment business. However, our interpretation is that if a company does not have an investment business, there is no investment business that can become small or negligible, or cease.

- The loss is not a shock loss of a Solvency 2 insurance company (Condition C). If only part of the deficit is such a shock loss, the remaining part of the loss can be relieved under this provision.
- The first accounting period after the deficit period must not be an excluded period of a general insurance company (Condition D).

Claims to relief must specify the amount to be set off against the company's total profits for the subsequent period and must be made within two years of the end of the deficit period or such longer time as HMRC might allow.

Claims cannot be made in respect of deficits that are surrendered as group relief in the subsequent period under the new CTA 2010 Pt 5A and relief for carried forward deficits cannot be given against the company's ring fence profits.

Subject to a claim and satisfying various conditions, deficits not used in the later period (i.e. the first period after the deficit period) can be carried forward to later accounting periods ("the subsequent period").

The conditions are:

– The company must not have ceased to be a company with investment business in the later period nor must its investment business have become small or negligible in the later period.

– The first accounting period after the later period must not be an excluded accounting period of a general insurance company.

Once again, the claim must specify the amount to be set off in the subsequent accounting period and must be made within two years of the end of that period or such longer time as HMRC might allow.

In certain circumstances, if a company is not permitted to carry forward a deficit to set against total profits of the later period or of a subsequent period, the deficit may still be set against non-trading profits of the later period or of a subsequent period.

In terms of the later period, this will apply if:

– A company's investment business became small or negligible in the year of deficit.

– The carry forward is to an excluded accounting period of general insurance company.

– The deficit is a shock loss of a Solvency 2 insurance company.

The first two of these conditions also apply to carry forward to any subsequent accounting periods. Shock losses of Solvency 2 insurance companies are not included which, prima facie, suggests that a shock loss can only be carried forward to the later period and not to subsequent periods.

Once again, the relief must be claimed, specifying the amount of relief and must be made within two years of the end of the accounting period or such longer period as HMRC might allow.

In very broad terms, the overall impact is that generally non-trading loan relationship deficits can be carried forward indefinitely and set off against total profits of the company in future accounting periods in such amounts as may be claimed. If, however, the company no longer qualifies, which is most likely to be because an investment business has become small or negligible, then the deficit can only be carried forward and set against non-trading profits of the later or subsequent periods.

Non-trading losses on intangible fixed assets

The existing legislation permits a non-trading loss to be set against a company's total profits for a period, subject to a claim within two years of the end of the period or such longer period as an HMRC might allow. Otherwise, the loss is carried forward and treated as a non-trading loss of the subsequent period, with its use being subject to a claim in respect of that later period.

The new rules introduce a condition that, if a company ceases to be a company with investment business in an accounting period, no non-trading losses on intangible fixed assets can be carried forward to later periods. Once again, we believe that this only applies where the company had an investment business in the first place.

Secondly, a loss can only be carried forward to the extent that it has not previously been set off against total profits of the company for an earlier accounting period, or surrendered as group relief in the loss period. The restriction is now extended to take into account the possibility of surrender as group relief in a later period.

Expenses of management of investment business, etc

Currently, if the expenses of management of a company's investment business are not deducted in full against investment income, they are carried forward and treated as expenses of management deductible in the subsequent accounting period. Similarly, qualifying charitable donations made in the accounting period are carried forward as management expenses of the later accounting period.

The new provision firstly ensures that amounts carried forward from an accounting period are reduced by any amounts surrendered as group relief under CTA 2010 Pt 5 or 5A (in respect of the former, this appears to be the correction of an omission).

The new rules also require that a claim is made for relief to be given for all or part of the management expenses in the later period. The claim must be made within two years of the end of the accounting period or such longer period as HMRC might allow. This introduces flexibility as to how much of the excess management expenses is used in the later years.

Trading losses

Changes to relief for old losses

The current rules for trading losses allow losses to be used against total profits of the loss period or to be carried back for a period of up to 12 months. Losses can also be surrendered as group relief for the loss period. Losses that are not relieved by any of these methods are carried forward and set against the profits of the same trade in a later period, taking an earlier period before later, until the losses are completely used up.

The new provisions introduce a claim process, so that the quantum of old losses that are set against the profits of an accounting period that begins on or after 1 April 2017 can be determined by the company, to maximise flexibility in the context of the new regime.

A claim must be made within two years of the end of the specified accounting period or such later time as HMRC might permit.

Use of new losses

Losses arising on or after 1 April 2017, to the extent that they have not been used in the loss-making period or a previous period, or surrendered as group relief, are still automatically carried forward to a subsequent accounting period and can now be set against total profits of the company for that later period. The company must still be carrying on the trade in the later period and this does not apply to ring fence trades.

There are a number of specific conditions that must apply before this flexible use of losses is available, as follows (new section CTA 2010 s 45A(3)):

- The trade must not have become small or negligible in the loss-making period.
- Relief under CTA 2010 s 37 (against total income of the loss period or of a previous period) must not be unavailable by virtue of the following provisions:
  - CTA 2010 s 37(5), that the trade was carried on wholly outside the UK
  - CTA 2010 s 44 which states that the trade must be carried on commercially and with a view to profit;
  - CTA 2010 s 48, which restricts the use of certain losses arising from farming or market gardening trades;
  - CTA 2010 s 52, which restricts the use of losses arising from trading in commodity futures;
  - the provisions relating to creative industries (film production, TV production, video games, theatrical productions, orchestras and museums and galleries), whereby losses cannot be used under CTA 2010 s 37 if they arise during certain periods relating to the production, etc.
- The trade in the later period must also be carried on commercially and with a view of profit.
- Relief is denied so far as the company is a Solvency 2 insurance company and the loss is a shock loss.
- The later period must not be an excluded accounting period of the general insurance company.

The claim to relief must state the amount of relief to be given in the later period, and the claim must be made within two years of the end of the later period or such later time as HMRC might permit.

Losses can be carried forward from the later period (the period immediately following the loss period) to subsequent periods, to the extent that they have not been relieved under the previous provisions or as group relief under CTA 2010 Pt 5A (the new rules on group relief for carried-forward losses), so long as the company continues to carry on the trade in the subsequent period. Further conditions are that the trade did not become small or negligible in the later period, the trade in the subsequent period must be carried on commercially and with a view of profit and the further period must not be an excluded accounting period of a general insurance company.

Under certain circumstances, losses will not be relievable against total profits of the later or subsequent periods but might, instead, be relievable against the profits of the trade in those future periods, so long as the company continues to carry on the trade. This rule applies in three cases:

- Case 1 is where losses cannot be used against total profits of the trade by virtue of any of the reasons in CTA 2010 s 45A(3), listed above.
- Case 2 is where the loss is attributable to the creative sector reliefs for film

production, TV production or video game. It is noted that Case 2 does not refer to theatrical productions, orchestras or museums and galleries, which may simply be an omission.
– Case 3 is that the trade is a ring fence trade.
A claim is required, specifying the amount of loss to be used. The claim must be made within two years of the end of the claim period or such longer time as HMRC might allow.

Terminal losses

The current rule is that a company can use terminal losses (losses arising in the final 12 months of trading) by setting them against total profits of the trade in earlier periods starting up to three years before cessation.

This is extended by the new rules so that a terminal loss relief claim can include losses carried forward under any of the relevant provisions of CTA 2010 that have not been used by the time the trade has ceased. However, these extended terminal losses cannot be carried back beyond 1 April 2017, they cannot be carried back beyond the period in which they arose and nor can they be used to relieve unrelieved profits of the loss-making period, itself.

Relief under this provision must be claimed within two years after the end of the terminal period or within such further period as HMRC might permit.

In many cases, the use of terminal losses will mean carrying back the losses to an accounting period that falls partly within and partly without the relevant three-year period. Where this happens, the amount of relief available for that overlapping period is to be determined by time apportionment of the overlapping period.

The extended terminal loss relief rule does not apply if the trade is subsequently continued by somebody who is not within the charge to corporation tax and the company's cessation is part of a scheme or arrangements to obtain the benefit of these new terminal loss relief rules by virtue of the company's cessation. This is, obviously, an anti-avoidance provision to prevent a company transferring trading activities to another person while taking the benefit of the terminal loss relief in the company, itself.

Restriction on use of carried forward losses

Part 2 of Schedule 4 provides new rules on restricting deductions for carried forward losses.

Very broadly, where a company or group has profits in excess of £5 million in any period, the maximum amount of loss relief that can be used in that period in respect of carried forward losses is £5 million plus half the difference between £5 million and the total profits of the company. For example, a company with a profit of £10 million in a period, and, say £9 million of carry forward losses, will only be able to set off the first £5 million and half the difference, i.e. another £2.5 million leaving £1.5 million to be carried forward.

The rules are in new CTA 2010 Pt 7ZA.

Computing the restriction

Various types of deductions are looked at separately in computing the restriction.

The restriction

Firstly, we look at deductions which are only allowed from trading profits, i.e. trading losses brought forward under CTA 2010 s 45 from before 1 April 2017, and losses carried forward under CTA 2010 s 45B (losses not qualified to use against total profits). The same restriction also applies to deductions under sections 303B(4) and 303D(5), which relate to non-decommissioning losses of ring fenced trades (see Part 6).

We must compute the relevant maximum of deductions allowed, which is the sum of the company's "trading profits deductions allowance" for the period and 50% of the company's "relevant trading profits" for the period.

The trading profits deductions allowance is the £5 million, or such smaller number as might be required due to the company having a short accounting period or being a member of a group. In a simple case, like that suggested above, the trading profits deductions allowance is simply the deductions allowance of £5 million, and the 50% of the relevant trading profits is the £2.5 million.

Although the provision refers to the trading profits deductions allowance, there is nothing in the legislation that explicitly requires the general deductions allowance to be split between trading, non-trading and other activities of the company. However, the trading profits deductions allowance for an accounting period is stated to be the amount specified in a company's tax return as the trading profits deductions allowance for the period, so it appears that the company can simply choose how much of its overall deductions allowance is to be treated as a trading profits deductions allowance. If no trading profit deductions allowances shown in the tax return, however, then the trading profits deductions allowance is nil.

There is a virtually identical provision to restrict the deductions from non-trading profits by reference to a company's "relevant non-trading profits" and its "non-trading profits deductions allowance". This provision applies specifically to deductions for carried forward non-trading loan relationship deficits that can only be set against non-trading profits, i.e. under CTA 2009 ss 457(3) and 463H(5). Once again it appears that the company can choose how much of its deductions allowance is to be its non-trading profits deductions allowance in its tax return, but if no amount is specified then the allowance is nil.

The third provision sweeps up all other types of losses and states that the maximum deductions allowable are the difference between the relevant maximum and the sum of deductions under the provisions referred to above (trading losses, non-trading loan relationships deficits and certain deduction under the BLAGAB rules for insurance companies). The relevant maximum is the sum of the company's deductions allowance for the accounting period and 50% of the relevant profits.

This provision gives a comprehensive list of all the deductions to which it applies, which appears to be all normal deductions that a company can make against its profits. However, noticeably, the restrictions do not appear to apply to losses that can be carried back. So, prima facie, the restriction applies to the use of carried forward losses but any shortfall might be made up by being able to carry back losses from a future accounting period.

The basic rule is modified for insurance companies whose profits are calculated by reference to I − E where policyholders' share in the profits is less than the whole amount and is also less than the BLAGAB-related loss capacity. In that case, the maximum use of losses, the "modified loss", is found by reducing the normal restrictions by the BLAGAB-related loss capacity and adding the shareholders' I − E profit.

Determining relevant profits

The next step is to determine the company's relevant trading profits and relevant non-trading profits. The relevant trading profits of the company are its qualifying trading profits less the company's trading profits deductions allowance for the period. If the result is nil or less, the relevant trading profits for the accounting period are nil. Similarly, the relevant non-trading profits for an accounting period are the qualifying non-trading profits less the non-trading profits deductions, and the outcome will be treated as nil if it does not exceed zero.

The mechanism for determining a company's qualifying trading profits and qualifying non-trading profits for an accounting period is given by a five-step process.

In step 1, we must determine the company's total profits for the accounting period. This must be done by ignoring any of the following:

− Company distributions received
− Ring fence profits
− Contractors ring fence profits
− I − E profits of an insurance company
− Deductions for carried forward trade losses that can only be set against subsequent trade profits (CTA 2010 ss 45 and 45B), in most cases
− Restricted deductions under sections 303B and 303D for non-decommissioning losses of ring fenced trade
− Deductions for carried forward non-trading deficits from loan relationships which are restricted to use against non-trading profits under CTA 2009 ss 457(3) or 463H(5).

If as a result of step 1 the company's total profits of the accounting period do not exceed zero, both the qualifying trading profits and the relevant non-trading profits of the accounting period are nil.

Step 2 requires the calculation of the amounts that can be relieved against the company's total profits. In computing this figure we are required to effectively exclude any reliefs arising for losses and other deficits from other accounting periods. Specifically, we are told to ignore all deductions for brought forward reliefs, as listed in section 269ZD, as well as trading losses carried back from later accounting periods under CTA 2010 s 37 or under the new terminal loss rules of s 45F (but not the old terminal loss provisions), the carry back of excess capital allowances under the special leasing rules of CAA 2001 s 260(3) and the carry back of non-trading loan relationship deficits under CTA 2009 s 463E.

If the result of the step 2 calculation is that the relievable amounts exceed the total profits of the accounting period, both qualifying trading profits and qualifying non-trading profits are nil.

Step 3 requires the company's total profits to be apportioned into trade and non-trade profits.

Step 4 requires the allocation of the allowable deductions, computed under step 2, between the trade and non-trade profits. The rules explicitly state that it is permissible to set all the deductions against the trading profits or against the non-trading profits or to split them between the two in order to obtain a result whereby they are both either nil or positive. In other words, this allocation cannot be used to create, for example, a trading loss and a non-trading profit or vice versa.

In step 5 the amounts obtained by the allocation in step 4 are stated to be the company's qualifying trading profits and qualifying non-trading profits for the accounting period.

There is an exclusion from these normal rules for general insurance companies with excluded accounting periods. These are generally accounting periods where the company is subject to insolvency procedures because it is unable to pay its debts, largely as a result of qualifying latent claims.

Calculation of deductions allowance

Where a company is not a member of a group for the whole of an accounting period, the deductions allowance for a 12-month accounting period is £5 million, proportionally reduced for a shorter accounting period.

A non-group deductions allowance arises where a company is not a member of a group for part of the accounting period, or is part of a group but is the only company in that group that is subject to UK corporation tax. The amount is found by apportioning £5 million on a time basis between the number of days in the accounting period that the company was not a member of a group for these purposes, and the total length of the accounting period.

The allocation rules for group companies apply where one or more companies within the charge to corporation tax are members of a group. The maximum deductions allowance for an accounting period for a group company is £5 million, made up of the aggregate of any group deductions allowance allocated to the company for the period and any non-group deductions allowance available. The limits are reduced for short accounting periods.

The group deductions allowance is always calculated by reference to the accounting period of the nominated company. If the nominated company is not the nominated company for the whole of its accounting period, the allowance is reduced proportionally.

The allocation to a group company must take into account the extent to which it was a member of the group in the nominated company's accounting period, as well as of non-contiguous accounting periods. This is achieved by restricting the allocation by reference to the number of days in the nominated company's accounting period during which the other company was a member of the nominated company's group, divided by the length of the nominated company's accounting period.

A company's total deductions allowance will be the aggregate of its non-group deductions allowance and any amounts allocated to it as part of a group deductions allowance.

There are special provisions to increase deductions allowances where a provision for an onerous lease over land has been reversed.

Definition of a group

A group is defined as being two or more companies where one is the ultimate parent of all of the others and is not the ultimate parent of any other company. The company is an ultimate parent if it is the parent of another company but no company is the parent of both. A company is a parent of another company if the other company is a

75% subsidiary of the first, if the parent company has the right to at least 75% of profits available for distribution to equity holders, or it would be beneficially entitled to at least 75% of the assets available for distribution to equity holders of the subsidiary on a winding up. These are alternative tests, so a company could be a member of the group even if the parent company does not own 75% of its ordinary share capital.

This is subject to the normal rules about equity holders in CTA 2010 Pt 5 Ch 6 and also the rules about subsidiaries in CTA 2010 Pt 24 Ch 3.

The rules for equity holders are modified to apply equally to companies which do not have share capital, to unincorporated associations, to ownership through a non-corporate entity such as a trust or other arrangement. These modifications are to be applied by treating holders of the appropriate interest in these other entities as if they were holders of shares in a body corporate.

Administration

In groups, all members of the group that are companies within the charge to corporation tax must nominate a "nominated company", which is the company responsible for allocating the group deductions allowance throughout the relevant companies in the group and for informing HMRC of that allocation. This "group allowance nomination" must be signed by the appropriate person on behalf of each company that is a member of the group within the charge to corporation tax when the nomination is made. The nomination must state the date on which it is to take effect, which may be earlier than the date that the nomination is made.

A nomination ceases to have effect immediately before the date on which a new nomination is made, where the nomination is revoked – which can be done by any company in the group that is within the charge to UK corporation tax at the time – or where the nominated company ceases to be either a member of the group or within the charge to corporation tax.

HMRC may make further administrative provisions in respect to these nominations by regulation.

The nominated company must submit a group allowance allocation statement to HMRC for each accounting period, which must be received by HMRC before the first anniversary of the filing date for the nominated company's tax return for that accounting period, or such later time as HMRC might permit.

The group allowance allocation statement must give the following information:

– It must identify the group to which it relates.
– It must specify the accounting period of the nominated company to which the statement relates.
– It must specify how many days of the nominated company's accounting period for which it was the nominated company of the group.
– It must state the groups deductions allowance for the nominee's accounting period.
– It must list the companies which were within the group and within the charge to corporation tax during that accounting period.
– It must allocate the amounts of the group deductions allowance to the listed company.
– It must specify the accounting period for each company for which that allocation is made.

There are also detailed provisions relating to changes in the nominated company for a group, submissions of amended allowance allocation statements, correction of incorrect statements, etc.

Each company's tax return must specify the company's deductions allowance for a period. However, this only applies where the company is within the scope of these restrictions, in the first place. We assume, although it is not clear, that the requirement to state the trading and non-trading profits deductions allowances in the company's return is, similarly, not required if the company is not within the scope of these restrictions.

Group relief using carried forward losses

Part 3 of Schedule 4 provides new rules for surrendering carried forward losses as group relief, by inserting a new Part 5A to CTA 2010.

Surrenderable losses

Firstly, the new provisions explain which losses can be surrendered. They are exhaustively listed in the legislation but the main theme is that the only losses which can be surrendered as group relief in a subsequent year are those which are carried forward and can be used against total profits of the company for that year. Only losses, etc., arising on or after 1 April 2017 are available for group relief of carried forward losses.

The full list refers to:

- Non-trading deficits from loan relationships.
- Non-trading losses on intangible fixed assets.
- Expenses of management of any investment business.
- Carried forward trading losses.
- Carry forward losses in a UK property business.
- Certain excess non-decommissioning losses of ring fenced trades.

Finally, there are special rules for BLAGAB trade losses of insurance companies.

Exclusions and restrictions applicable to surrendering company

There are a large number of exclusions and restrictions. Firstly, as noted above, no losses can be surrendered in so far as they arose before 1 April 2017 and the company may also not surrender a qualifying charitable donation carried forward to the surrender period under the management expenses rules.

A surrendering company cannot surrender losses arising from intangible fixed assets if an investment business carried on by the company became small or negligible before the beginning of the period. We assume, as highlighted previously, that this provision only applies if the company had an investment business that has become small or negligible and not if the company did not have an investment business in the first place.

Management expenses or losses on UK property businesses brought forward also cannot be surrendered if the relevant investment business has become small negligible for the beginning of the period.

A company cannot surrender losses if it still has profits that it, itself, could use those losses against.

A surrendering company may not surrender losses if it has no assets capable of producing income at the end of the surrender period. This is apparently designed to prevent groups maintaining otherwise dormant companies to access their losses.

There are restrictions on surrendering of losses by a general insurance company if the surrender period is an excluded accounting period. And Solvency 2 insurance companies cannot surrender certain shock losses.

A UK resident company cannot surrender losses that arise from a non-UK permanent establishment of the surrendering company, if those losses could have been deducted against the profits of the permanent establishment in its home jurisdiction. The principles to be used in establishing the quantum of such losses are the same principles as would be applied to a trading permanent establishment of a non-UK resident company.

There are also rules for restricting the amounts that can be surrendered by a non-UK resident company which is either carrying on a trade in the UK through a permanent establishment or is carrying on a trade of dealing in or developing UK land. For EEA companies, losses can be surrendered so long as they are attributable to the activities of the surrendering company that are subject to UK corporation tax for the loss-making period and those losses are not double taxation exempt. A further provision restricts the losses surrenderable by an EEA company if the amounts have in any period been deducted from or otherwise allowed against the non-UK profits of any person.

For non-EEA countries a further restriction requires that the loss is not one which is deductible or allowable at any time against non-UK profits of any person.

If a dual resident company was not eligible to surrender the losses under the group relief rules in Part 5, relating to the year in which the losses arise, then that company will not be allowed to surrender those losses as carried forward losses under Part 5A.

General restrictions applicable to claimant company

A company cannot make a claim in cases where it has losses of its own brought forward from earlier periods which have not been relieved. So, all available losses must be used to reduce the claimant company's profits for the period before group relief under Part 5A can be claimed.

There are also detailed rules for restricting relief for non-contiguous periods, etc, which are set out in more detail below.

Giving effect to claims

Once valid claims have been established, the group relief is given effect by deduction from the claimant company's total profits of the claim period. The amount so deducted is equal either to the surrendering company's surrenderable amounts for the surrender period or any part of those amounts specified in the claim.

Deductions under Part 5A are given before deductions for relief under CTA 2010 s 37 (carried back trading losses), losses under CAA 2001 s 260(3), in relation to capital allowances for a later period, and under CTA 2009 ss 389 or 463B in respect of loan relationship deficits for later periods. Otherwise, all other deductions from total profits rank ahead of group relief under Part 5A.

Claims are however restricted in respect of non-contiguous accounting periods and also the general restriction on deductions from total profits (for companies with profits in excess of £5 million, etc).

Conditions where claimant company in a group or owned by a consortium

Where the claimant company is a member of a group or is owned by a consortium, a number of conditions apply for a valid claim:

- The surrendering company must consent to the claim.
- There must be an overlapping period common to the claim period and the surrender period.
- At any time during the overlapping period either the group condition or one of consortium conditions 1 and 2 must be met.

A claim can be made in respect of either the whole or just part of the surrenderable amounts.

The group condition

The group condition is met if the surrendering company and the claimant company are members of the same group of companies and both are UK related. To be UK related a company must be a UK resident company or a non-UK resident company carrying on a trade in the UK through a permanent establishment.

The consortium conditions

Consortium condition 1 is met if the claimant company is trading or a holding company and is owned by a consortium of which the surrendering company is a member. Both companies must be UK related. Shareholdings that are trading stock are ignored for these purposes.

Consortium condition 2 applies if the claimant company is trading or a holding company that is owned by a consortium and the surrendering company is not a member of the consortium but is a member of the same group as a link company that is a member of the consortium. Once again, the surrendering and claimant companies must both be UK related and shareholdings that are trading stock are ignored for these purposes.

General limits to relief

The maximum relief that can be claimed is the smaller of two amounts:

- the unused surrenderable amount of the surrendering company; and
- the difference between the claimant company's relevant maximum for the period and previously claimed group relief for that period (effectively, the claimant company's unused capacity for group relief).

The unused surrenderable amount for an overlapping period is found by taking the proportion of the surrender period included in the overlapping period and applying that proportion to the surrenderable amounts for the period. That gives the surrenderable amount for the overlapping period. If this apportionment gives an unjust or unreasonable result, a just and reasonable figure can be used, instead.

This sum is then restricted in respect of any prior surrenders in respect of those losses.

The relevant maximum of the claimant company is determined by first of all finding the larger of the claimant company's relevant maximum for the claim period in accordance with CTA 2010 s 269ZD(4) or its relevant profits for the claim period according to section 269ZD(5). This amount is then reduced by various losses for which deductions have been claimed by the claimant company for the claim period. The losses referred to constitute a comprehensive list of losses that can be brought forward and set against the claimant's profits for the claim period.

The resultant figure is effectively the claimant company's unused capacity for loss relief. This is then apportioned by reference to the proportion of the claim period included in the overlapping period.

The final restriction is by reference to prior claims for group relief for the relevant overlapping period. These are claims under Part 5A that were made before the current claim and have not been withdrawn.

In determining priority of claims, where two or more claims are made at the same time effect shall be given to those claims in the order chosen by the company or companies making the claims. In the absence of an election, HMRC can make a direction.

Limits to relief for consortium claims

For consortium claims there is a further restriction based on the ownership proportions of the relevant companies.

For claims based on consortium condition 1, the restriction for the ownership proportion is based on the lowest of the following:

- The proportion of ordinary share capital of the claimant company beneficially owned by the surrendering company.
- The proportion of profits available to distribution to equity holders of the claimant company to which the surrendering company is beneficially entitled.
- The proportion of assets of the claimant company available to distribution to equity holders on a winding up to which the surrendering company would be beneficially entitled.
- The proportion of the voting power of the claimant company directly possessed by the surrendering company.

To the extent that any of these change during the relevant period, an average is to be used.

Where claims are made under consortium condition 2, for losses surrendered by a member of a link company's group, the maximum claim that can be made by a claimant company is restricted to the proportionate ownership of the claimant company by the link company, using the same tests as above, i.e. beneficial ownership of share capital, rights to distributions to equity holders, rights to assets on a winding up to equity holders and voting rights.

Where a claimant company is both a member of a group of companies and a member of a consortium, the claimant company's maximum claim is reduced by the aggregate of the maximum amounts it could claim from other group companies in the group under CTA 2010 Pts 5 and 5A, i.e. amounts it could claim as group relief, rather than as consortium relief.

Anti-avoidance

There is an anti-avoidance provision which applies if there are arrangements in place whereby somebody other than the consortium company or companies control the claimant company. If the arrangements have a main purpose of enabling the claimant company to obtain a tax advantage in respect of the surrendered losses, then the proportion of losses which the claimant company can claim is reduced by 50% from the otherwise computed amount.

Conditions where surrendering company owned by a consortium

Where the surrendering company is a member of a group or is owned by a consortium, slightly different conditions apply for a valid claim:

- The surrendering company must consent to the claim.
- There must be an overlapping period common to the claim period and the surrender period.
- One of consortium conditions 3 or 4 are met throughout the period beginning before or during the specified loss-making period and ending during or after the overlapping period.

A claim under these provisions can relate to the whole or just part of the surrender of all amounts.

General limits to relief

The maximum relief that can be claimed is the smaller of three amounts:
- the unused surrenderable amount of the surrendering company; and
- the difference between the claimant company's relevant maximum for the period and previously claimed group relief for that period (effectively, the claimant company's unused capacity for group relief);
- the potential Part 5 group relief amount.

The unused surrenderable amount for an overlapping period is found by taking the proportion of the surrender period included in the overlapping period and applying that proportion to the surrenderable amounts for the period. That gives the surrenderable amount for the overlapping period. If this apportionment gives an unjust or unreasonable result, a just and reasonable figure can be used, instead.

This sum is then restricted in respect of any prior surrenders in respect of those losses.

The relevant maximum of the claimant company is determined by first of all finding the larger of the claimant company's relevant maximum for the claim period in accordance with CTA 2010 s 269ZD(4) or its relevant profits for the claim period according to section 269ZD(5). This amount is then reduced by various losses for which deductions have been claimed by the claimant company for the claim period. The losses referred to constitute a comprehensive list of losses that can be brought forward and set against the claimants profits for the claim period.

The resultant figure is effectively the claimant company's unused capacity for loss relief. This is then apportioned by reference to the proportion of the claim period included in the overlapping period.

The final restriction is by reference to prior claims for group relief for the relevant overlapping period. These are claims under Part 5A that were made before the current claim and have not been withdrawn.

In determining priority of claims, where two or more claims are made at the same time effect shall be given to those claims in the order chosen by the company or companies making the claims. In the absence of an election, HMRC can make a direction.

The potential group relief amount is designed to measure the maximum amount of group relief that a claimant could receive, less any relief already given under Part 5 or 5A by the same company for the same period. The legislation requires us to calculate the maximum amount of relief that could have been surrendered to the claimant company under Part 5 in respect of losses or other amounts within CTA 2010 s 99 which the surrendering company had for the specified loss-making period. We then deduct from that the amounts in respect of those losses which the surrendering company had actually surrendered to the claimant company under Part 5.

This amount is then adjusted by a fraction whereby the numerator is the sum of surrenderable trading losses, non-trading loan relationship deficits, losses from UK property businesses, excess management expenses and non-trading losses on intangible fixed assets and the denominator is the sum of all losses listed within CTA 2010 s 99, i.e. all of the above as well as excess capital allowances and charitable donations. The reason for this adjustment is not clear.

Finally, we deduct any group relief for carried forward losses which have been given by the same surrendering company in the same specified loss-making period.

Restriction on claims through link company

Where a claim is made through a link company, and is based on consortium condition 4, there is a further restriction on the amounts that can be claimed. The limitation is effectively the amount of group relief for carried forward losses under Part 5A that could be given to the link company by the surrendering company, assuming that the link company was UK related and also able to claim those losses.

Restriction where surrendering company in a group

Where a claimant company makes a claim and the surrendering company is a member of a group of companies, the surrenderable amount is to be reduced by the maximum amount of losses surrenderable under Part 5A that can be given by the surrendering company to other members of its group, assuming that all claims that could be made by other group companies are made to the maximum possible extent. However, this deduction can be reduced by reference to losses or other amounts surrendered by other members of the same group of companies.

The resultant figure is then reduced by the proportion of the surrendering companies surrenderable amounts for the surrender period that are attributable to the specific loss-making period divided by the sum of the surrendering company's surrenderable amounts for the surrender period. In effect, therefore, the surrendering company is to be treated as if it had surrendered the maximum amount of group relief to fellow group companies before it can surrender losses or other amounts under Part 5A to a consortium company directly or through a link company.

Anti-avoidance

There is an anti-avoidance provision which applies if there are arrangements in place whereby somebody other than the consortium companies control the surrendering company. If the arrangements have a main purpose of enabling the claimant company to obtain a tax advantage in respect of the surrendered losses, then the proportion of losses which the claimant company can claim is reduced by 50% from the otherwise computed amount.

Payments for group relief

Where a claimant company makes a payment to a surrendering company for the surrender of group relief, the payment is not to be taken into account as a profit or loss of either company, or as a distribution. The payment must be made under an agreement between the companies in relation to the losses and other amounts of the surrendering company.

Carrying forward BLAGAB trade losses

Part 4 of Schedule 4 provides new rules for carried forward BLAGAB trade losses of insurance companies, by amending FA 2012 Pt 2 Ch 9.

Where there is an insurance company carrying on basic life assurance and general annuity businesses, and that company makes a BLAGAB trade loss on or after 1 April 2017, any surplus after relief under CTA 2010 s 37 or Pt 5 is carried forward to the subsequent period, so long as the company carries on the basic life assurance and general annuity business in that later period. Relief is firstly given against the BLAGAB trade profits for the later period, subject to restrictions or modifications in accordance with the general provisions relating to the use of carried forward losses.

After set off against the company's BLAGAB trade profit of the later period, the company may claim for the unrelieved amount, or any specified part of it, to be deducted from the company's total profits of that later period. A claim must be made within two years of the end of the later period, or such longer period as HMRC might allow.

No claim can be made in respect of shock losses if the company is a Solvency 2 insurance company. Shock losses can, however, be used for the purposes of BLAGAB trade loss relief under CTA 2010 s 37 or Pt 5, or their applications by virtue of these specific rules for insurance companies, before any losses that are not shock losses.

If the company continues to carry on basic life insurance and general annuity business in a further accounting period after the later period, and has BLAGAB trading losses that are unrelieved, relief is given against the BLAGAB profits of the company for the further period.

It appears that unused BLAGAB losses can be carried forward indefinitely and set against future BLAGAB trade profits of the company, so long as it continues to carry on basic life assurance and general annuity business in the further periods. However, it appears that relief against total profits is not available beyond the first later period.

Deductions under these provisions cannot exceed the relevant maximum, being the sum of 50% of the company's relevant BLAGAB trade profits from the accounting period and its BLAGAB trade profits deductions allowance for the accounting period (see Part 2 of Schedule 4, above). This restriction excludes shock losses of solvency to insurance companies.

Carrying forward trade losses in certain creative industries

Part 5 of Schedule 4 provides new rules for carried forward trade losses of companies subject to the special rules for trades of film production, television production, video games, theatrical productions and orchestral trades. The new relief for museums and galleries is not dealt with in Schedule 4.

The current rule for film loss relief is that a pre-completion loss can only be carried forward under CTA 2010 s 45 to be set against profits of the separate film trade in a subsequent period. The minor change is to add a new CTA 2010 s 45B and to replace the phrase "set against" with "deducted from".

Such a loss is ignored for the purposes of the restriction on deductions from trading profits in CTA 2010 s 269ZB.

Where losses were made in a pre-completion period and carried forward to a relevant later period, the original rule was that they were to be treated as a loss of that later period. In this context, a relevant later period is either the completion period or any subsequent accounting period during which the separate film trade continues.

This provision is now amended to refer to losses carried forward under CTA 2010 ss 45 or 45B and the phrase "loss relief" is replaced by references to CTA 2010 s 37 or Pt 5, to ensure that any such losses carried forward in a film company are relevant deductions for the purposes of the loss restriction under Part 7ZA.

If the trade continues and there are losses in a relevant later period, those losses may be deducted from total profits of later periods under CTA 2010 s 45A, so long as they are not amounts attributable to film tax relief.

To the extent that such carried forward losses cannot be deducted under section 45A from total profits, they can be deducted from profits of the same trade under sections 45 or 45B.

The rules for terminal losses of a film production company are also amended. Currently, if the company ceases to carry on its separate trade in relation to the film where the losses arose, but is carrying on a separate trade in relation to another qualifying film, it can elect to set the carried forward loss against the profits arising from the new film. Alternatively, if there is another group company carrying on a film production trade in relation to a qualifying film, the original company may surrender the terminal loss, or part of it, to that other group company.

This provision is now amended to refer to losses carried forward under any of CTA 2010 ss 45, 45A and 45B, had the trade not ceased. The restriction still remains, however, in that the loss can only be set against profits of the new trade of the company for accounting periods after cessation, or surrendered to another group company to use against the profits of its film production trade, not total profits.

Part 5 of the Schedule then makes similar provisions in respect of the losses of a television programme trade, a video game trade, a theatrical trade and an orchestral trade.

In the case of theatrical and orchestral trades, the terminal loss provisions are amended so that they only relate to the losses so far as they are not attributable to the additional deduction that the company has claimed under the theatrical or orchestral productions regimes.

Oil activities

Part 6 of Schedule 4 introduces new rules into CTA 2010 Pt 8 (oil activities) relating to losses that are non-decommissioning losses of ring-fence rates. A company with a ring-fence trade has a non-decommissioning loss if the loss exceeds the total amount of relevant expenditure in relation to a decommissioning relief agreement in the period.

To the extent that such a loss is not relieved against current year profits under CTA 2010 ss 37 or 42, or group relieved under Part 5, the losses are carried forward to the next period and relief is given by reducing the trading profits in that later period, so long as the company continues to carry on the ring-fence trade in that later period.

To the extent that the losses are not relieved in the later period, they can be carried forward to further periods and relieved against the profits of the ring-fence trade in those subsequent periods, so long as the company continues to carry on the ring-fence trade.

In any period after the period of loss, once all the ring-fence trade profits have been relieved by the use of carried forward losses, the company can claim to have all or part of the unrelieved losses used to reduce its total profits for the period, as well. However, this does not apply if:

- The ring-fenced trade has become small or negligible during the loss-making period or any intervening period before the period in which the claim is made.
- The non-decommissioning loss was not available for relief under section 37 by virtue of the ring-fence trade having been carried on wholly outside the UK or not having been carried on commercially and with a view of profit.

— Relief under CTA 2010 s 37 would not be available for any hypothetical loss arising after the year of loss but before the year of claim, due to the trade not been carried on commercially and with a view of profit.

Claims for relief against total profits must be made within two years of the end of the later or subsequent period, or within such longer period as HMRC may allow.

Part 6 also contains various amendments to the loss relief rules for ring-fence trades to implement the rules restricting the use of losses for companies with large profits, the ability to group relieve carried forward losses, etc.

Oil contractors

Part 7 of Schedule 4 amends CTA 2010 Pt 8ZA, in respect of oil activities. There are various amendments designed to restrict or stream losses arising from oil contractor activities.

Firstly, only losses carried forward under CTA 2010 s 45A that arise from the oil contractor activities can be used to reduce the profits of oil contractor activities.

Profits arising from oil contractor activities cannot be reduced by non-trading losses on intangible fixed assets, UK property business losses or non-decommissioning losses of ring-fence trades.

A company's oil contractor profits can only be reduced by claiming group relief in respect of carried forward losses if the surrendered loss arose from oil contractor activities of the surrendering company.

For losses carried forward from 31 March 2017, or carried forward under CTA 2010 s 45A from 1 April 2017, and losses surrendered under Part 5A, the allowable deduction against total profits is restricted to the aggregate of the deductions allowance allocated to the contractor's ring-fence profits plus 50% of the ring-fence profits for the accounting period.

There are detailed rules to determine the contractor's ring-fence profits deductions allowance. This must be specified in the return, otherwise the deductions allowance for the contractor's ring-fence profits is nil (similar to the requirements for trading deductions allowances and non-trading deductions allowances for non-ring fence companies).

Transferred trades

Part 8 of Schedule 4 amends the provisions relating to the transfers of trades in line with the new rules for carried forward losses.

Firstly, the current rules are modified so that it is clear that they only apply to losses carried forward under CTA 2010 s 45 and that the predecessor company cannot claim terminal loss relief following the trade transfer.

New CTA 2010 ss 944A and 944B then provide that, where there is a transfer of trade to which this legislation applies, CTA 2010 ss 45A and 45B apply to the transferred losses, which will generally be treated as losses of the successor company.

Similar rules also apply to non-decommissioning losses of ring-fence trades on a transfer of trade.

A new rule is introduced to ensure that terminal losses under CTA 2010 s 45F also cannot be claimed by the predecessor company after a trade transfer. If the losses were brought forward under section 45, i.e. they are pre-1 April 2017 trade losses, this restriction only applies if the trade was transferred on or after 13 July 2017.

The new rules on transfers of trade are all made subject to the limitation in CTA 2010 s 945 where some or all of the predecessor company's liabilities are not transferred to the successor company.

Finally, CTA 2010 s 951, which applies where the successor company carries on the transferred trading activities as part of its own trade, is also amended to take account of the new rules for carried forward losses.

Anti-avoidance

Part 9 of Schedule 4 introduces a series of anti-avoidance provisions relating to the use of losses following a change of ownership of a company.

Loss refresh rules

The loss refresh rules in CTA 2010 Pt 14B are extended to carried forward UK property business losses and carried forward non-trading losses on intangible fixed assets.

The rules are also extended to trading losses brought forward under CTA 2010 ss 45A and 45B arising on or after 1 April 2017, and to non-trading loan relationship deficits arising or after that date and carried forward under the new rules.

Changes of ownership and major changes of trade

The rules in Part 14 CTA 2010 relating to changes of ownership of companies and major changes in the nature or conduct of the trade currently only apply where the change in the trade occurs within three years of the change in ownership of the company. This is now extended to encompass a period of five years beginning no more than three years before the change of ownership and will apply where both the major change in the trade and the change of ownership occur on or after 1 April 2017.

The main restricting provision is then extended so that it applies to trading losses arising on after 1 April 2017 that are carried forward under CTA 2010 ss 45A, 45B or 45F (terminal losses), as well as to non-decommissioning losses of ring-fence traders.

Where these provisions apply, these losses are eliminated completely, if they arose before the change of ownership.

Ring-fence trade losses

Losses of a ring-fence trade that are not non-decommissioning losses will remain subject to the previous timing rule, whereby the major change must occur within three years of the change of ownership, rather than the new extended time period.

Restriction on use of losses where Chapters 2 and 3 do not apply

A new Chapter 2A is introduced to restrict the use of carried forward losses where there is a change in the ownership of the company and a major change in the nature or conduct of its business or of the business of a co-transferred company on or after 1 April 2017. This set of provisions only applies if Chapter 2 (trading losses) or Chapter 3 (investment companies) do not apply to eliminate the carry forward losses, in any case.

The major change in the trade or business must take place within five years of the change in ownership, beginning not more than three years before the change in ownership. However, where there is a major change in an investment business this can be within a period of eight years beginning three years before the change of ownership.

If there is such a major change within the relevant period, we have to compute the "affected profits". These are the profits that arise as a result of the major change in the company's business activities.

A company is not allowed to deduct carried forward trading losses from total profits of the company, so far as they are affected profits. This applies to trading losses arising before the change of ownership and carried forward under CTA 2010 ss 45A or 45F, or ring-fence losses under CTA 2010 s 303C (non-decommissioning losses) or FA 2012 s 124B. This restriction does not prevent those losses being carried forward to deduct against total profits of the company that are not affected profits.

Similar rules apply to:

- non-trading loan relationship deficits that arose before the change in ownership;
- non-trading loan relationship losses on intangible fixed assets that arose before the change in ownership;
- expenses of management that arose before the change in ownership;
- losses of UK property businesses that arose before the change in ownership.

There is also a restriction as to the amount of certain non-trading loan relationship debits that may be set against total profits in accounting periods following the change of ownership, where those debits exceeded the profits of the period ending with the change of ownership.

Restriction on use of losses against certain gains

A new Chapter 2B prevents the use of trading losses to shelter certain gains arising within five years following the change of ownership. The rules apply where, following the change of ownership, the company acquires an asset from another company whereby the no gain/no loss provisions of TCGA 1992 s 171 apply, the tax neutral provisions for intangible assets apply (CTA 2009 s 775) or a gain is deemed to arise on the company within five years of the change of ownership of the company by virtue of an election under TCGA 1992 s 171A.

In these circumstances a trading loss made in an accounting period or notional accounting period beginning before the change of ownership effectively cannot be used to set off against the relevant gain, in so far as that gain is reflected in the company's taxable profits.

Restriction on surrenders of group relief

New Chapter 2C will apply to the group relief for carried forward losses. Losses arising to a company before it joins a group are not available for members of that group to claim from such a surrendering company for five years after the company joined the group.

Similar rules apply to the surrender and claim of group relief for consortium companies.

The restriction does not apply where the claimant and surrendering companies were able to claim and surrender losses due to their group relationship prior to their joining the new group, as would occur if the new group has acquired a group of companies together.

Where this restriction applies, but there has also been both a change of ownership and a major change in the company's activities, triggering some of the other restrictions, there is a further restriction to ensure that carried forward losses cannot be surrendered under Part 5A to set against the affected profits of a claimant company.

Restriction on group relief following transfers of assets

New Chapter 2D prevents group relief for carried forward losses under Part 5A being used to shelter a gain where there has been a change of ownership of the company, following the change of ownership either a tangible or an intangible asset was transferred within the group under the no gain/no loss or tax neutral provisions, or there was a deemed gain as a result of an election under TCGA 1992 s 171A, and a gain (or deemed gain) on disposal of the assets occurs within five years of the change of ownership.

The restriction applies to prevent relevant pre-acquisition losses – very broadly, losses arising before the change of ownership – being surrendered to set against the gains.

Restriction on use of losses after transfer of trade

Where there has been a transfer of trade without a change of ownership, following a change of ownership of the company, and the change of ownership occurs on or after 1 April 2017, the use of trade losses will be restricted by new Chapter 2E.

The restriction applies where the company which has joined a group transfers a trade to another member of the group within the eight-year period beginning three years before the change of ownership of the company, and the companies were not related to one another immediately before the change of ownership and at the time of the transfer.

Where the restriction applies, trading losses carried forward in the trade that was transferred, including non-decommissioning losses of a ring-fence trade, cannot be deducted from the "relevant profits" of the successor company ending after the change of ownership.

Relevant profits are those that arise before the fifth anniversary of the change of ownership and which cannot be fairly and reasonably attributed to the successor company carrying on the trade that was transferred to it.

Restriction on group relief after transfer of trade

Similarly, where the company that has joined the group transfers a trade without a change of ownership to a successor company within the eight-year period beginning three years before the change of ownership, and another company could make a claim under Part 5A (group relief for carried forward losses of the trade), relief is not generally available where the losses arose before the change of ownership of the transferor company.

The main exception to this rule is when companies would have been able to claim and surrender group relief before the change of ownership, i.e. they were effectively in the same group or consortium beforehand.

Profits of the claimant company arising more than five years after the change of ownership of the transfer or company can be reduced by a claim under Part 5A.

There are also rules to apply the restrictions where there is an indirect transfer of a trade or a transfer of the trade into another trading company followed by a further transfer of the composite trade.

Change of ownership and change of investment business

The rule relating to a change of ownership of an investment company, together with a major change in its investment business, hitherto applied if a major change in the nature or conduct of the company's business occurred within a six-year period beginning three years before the change of ownership. This is now extended to a period of eight years beginning three years before the change of ownership, so long as both the change of ownership and the major change of business both occur or after 1 April 2017.

Northern Ireland trading losses

Part 10 of Schedule 4 introduces amendments relating to the use of losses under the special regime for Northern Ireland. The main change is to ensure that deductions arising from Northern Ireland losses are restricted to the extent that they are to be set against mainstream profits, if the Northern Ireland corporation tax rate is lower than the main UK rate in the year in which the relief is claimed.

There are also consequential amendments to the provisions relating to losses of film trades, of television programme trades, of video game trades and of theatrical trades.

Minor and consequential amendments

Part 11 of Schedule 4 contains minor and consequential amendments.

Commencement

The new rules effectively apply to losses arising on or after 1 April 2017. For these purposes, where a company's accounting period straddles that date, the accounting period is deemed for the purposes of this legislation to amount to two separate accounting periods, one ending 31 March 2017 and the other starting on first of April 2017.

SCHEDULE 5

CORPORATE INTEREST RESTRICTION

Section 20

PART 1

NEW PART 10 OF TIOPA 2010

1 In TIOPA 2010, after Part 9A insert—

"PART 10

CORPORATE INTEREST RESTRICTION

CHAPTER 1

INTRODUCTION

372 Overview

(1) This Part contains provision that—

(a) disallows certain amounts that a company would (apart from this Part) be entitled to bring into account for the purposes of corporation tax in respect of interest and other financing costs, and

(b) allows certain amounts disallowed under this Part in previous accounting periods to be brought into account in later accounting periods.

(2) In this Chapter—

(a) section 373 defines some key concepts including, in particular, "the total disallowed amount" in relation to a period of account of a worldwide group, and

(b) section 374 provides for Schedule 7A to have effect.

(3) Chapter 2 provides for—

(a) the disallowance in certain circumstances of tax-interest expense amounts of companies that are members of a worldwide group, and

(b) the carrying forward of disallowed tax-interest expense amounts, and for bringing those amounts into account in certain circumstances in relation to a later period of account of the worldwide group.

(4) Chapter 3—

(a) defines "a tax-interest expense amount" and "a tax-interest income amount" of a company for a period of account of a worldwide group, which are amounts that are (or apart from this Part would be) brought into account for the purposes of corporation tax,

(b) defines "the net tax-interest expense" of a company for a period of account of a worldwide group, which is any excess of the company's tax-interest expense amounts for the period over its tax-interest income amounts for the period,

(c) defines "the net tax-interest income" of a company for a period of account of a worldwide group, which is any excess of the company's tax-interest income amounts for the period over its tax-interest expense amounts for the period, and

(d) defines "aggregate net tax-interest expense" and "aggregate net tax-interest income" of a worldwide group for a period of account of the worldwide group, which are made up of each member of the group's net tax-interest expense or net tax-interest income for the period.

(5) Chapter 4 contains provision about the calculation of "the interest capacity" of a worldwide group for a period of account of the group, which is the aggregate of the interest allowance for the period and any unused interest allowance of the group from the previous 5 years (or, if that aggregate is less than the de minimis amount, the de minimis amount).

(6) Chapter 5 makes provision about the calculation of "the interest allowance" of a worldwide group for a period of account of the group.

The interest allowance for a period of account is calculated using the fixed ratio method unless the group elects for the group ratio method to be used for the period.

(7) Chapter 6 defines concepts used in Chapter 5 including—

the "tax-EBITDA" of a company for a period of account of a worldwide group (which is an amount derived from amounts brought into account for the purposes of corporation tax);

the "aggregate tax-EBITDA" of a worldwide group for a period of account of the group (which is an amount derived from the tax-EBITDA of members of the group).

(8) Chapter 7 defines additional concepts used in Chapter 5 including—

"the net group-interest expense", "the adjusted net group-interest expense" and "the qualifying net group-interest expense" of a worldwide group for a period of account of the group (which are amounts derived from the financial statements of the worldwide group);

the "group-EBITDA" of the worldwide group for a period of account of the group (which is an amount derived from the financial statements of the worldwide group).

(9) Chapter 8 contains provision altering the way in which this Part has effect in relation to the provision of public infrastructure assets or the carrying on of certain other related activities.

(10) Chapter 9 contains special provision altering the operation of certain provisions of this Part in relation to—

(a) particular types of company (for example, banking companies, companies carrying on oil-related activities, REITs or insurance companies), or

(b) particular types of transaction or accounting (for example, long funding operating leases or fair value accounting).

(11) Chapter 10 contains rules connected with tax avoidance.

(12) Chapter 11 contains the remaining interpretative and supplementary provision, including definitions of—

"related party";
"a worldwide group";
"ultimate parent";
"period of account" of a worldwide group.

373 Meaning of "subject to interest restrictions", "the total disallowed amount" etc

(1) A worldwide group is "subject to interest restrictions" in a period of account of the group if—

(a) the aggregate net tax-interest expense of the group for the period (see section 390), exceeds

(b) the interest capacity of the group for the period (see section 392).

(2) "The total disallowed amount" of a worldwide group in a period of account of the group is—

(a) if the group is subject to interest restrictions in the period, the amount of the excess mentioned in subsection (1);

(b) otherwise, nil.

(3) "The interest reactivation cap" of a worldwide group in a period of account of the group is (subject to subsection (4))—

(a) the interest allowance of the group for the period (see section 396), less

(b) the aggregate net tax-interest expense of the group for the period.

(4) If the amount determined under subsection (3) is a negative amount, the interest reactivation cap of the worldwide group in the period is nil.

(5) A worldwide group is "subject to interest reactivations" in a period of account of the group if—

(a) the interest reactivation cap of the group in the period is not nil, and

(b) at least one member of the group is within the charge to corporation tax at any time during the period, and has an amount available for reactivation in the return period that is not nil (see paragraph 26 of Schedule 7A).

(6) This section has effect for the purposes of this Part.

374 Interest restriction returns

(1) Schedule 7A makes provision about—

(a) the preparation and submission of interest restriction returns by reporting companies of worldwide groups, and

(b) other related matters such as enquiries and information powers.

(2) Part 1 of that Schedule includes provision—

(a) for the appointment of a reporting company of a worldwide group for a period of account, but

(b) for companies ("non-consenting companies") to elect to be unaffected by allocations of interest restrictions made by the company.

(3) Part 2 of that Schedule includes provision—

(a) for various elections to be made in an interest restriction return that are relevant to the operation of this Part (for example, the group ratio election),

(b) entitling the reporting company of a worldwide group to allocate interest restrictions among its members but with a rule that allocates a pro-rata share to a non-consenting company, and

(c) entitling the reporting company of a worldwide group to allocate interest reactivations among its members.

(4) The remaining Parts of that Schedule contain provision about—

(a) the keeping and preservation of records (see Part 3),

(b) enquiries into interest restriction returns (see Part 4),

(c) determinations made by officers of Revenue and Customs in the event of the breach of filing or other obligations (see Part 5),

(d) information powers exercisable by members of the group (see Part 6),

(e) information powers exercisable by officers of Revenue and Customs (see Part 7), and

(f) the amendment of company tax returns to reflect the effect of this Part of this Act and supplementary matters (see Parts 8 and 9).

CHAPTER 2

DISALLOWANCE AND REACTIVATION OF TAX-INTEREST
EXPENSE AMOUNTS

375 Disallowance of deductions: full interest restriction return submitted

(1) This section applies where—

(a) an interest restriction return is submitted for a period of account of a worldwide group ("the relevant period of account"),

(b) the return complies with the requirements of paragraph 20(3) of Schedule 7A (requirements for full interest restriction return), and

(c) the return includes a statement that the group is subject to interest restrictions in the return period.

(2) A company that is listed on the statement under paragraph 22 of Schedule 7A (statement of allocated interest restrictions) must, in any accounting period for which the statement specifies an allocated disallowance, leave out of account tax-interest expense amounts that, in total, equal that allocated disallowance.

(3) A non-consenting company in relation to the return may—

(a) elect that subsection (2) is not to apply in relation to such relevant accounting period of the company as is specified in the election, or

(b) revoke an election previously made.

(4) If—

(a) an election under this section has effect in relation to an accounting period of a company, and

(b) paragraph 24 of Schedule 7A allocates to that period a pro-rata share of the total disallowed amount that is not nil,

the company must leave out of account in that period tax-interest expense amounts that, in total, equal that pro-rata share.

(5) See section 377 for provision as to which tax-interest expense amounts are to be left out of account as a result of this section.

376 Disallowance of deductions: no return, or non-compliant return, submitted

(1) This section applies where—

(a) a worldwide group is subject to interest restrictions in a period of account of the group ("the relevant period of account"),

(b) the relevant date has passed, and

(c) condition A, B or C is met.

(2) In this section "the relevant date" means—

(a) where the appointment of a reporting company has effect in relation to the relevant period of account, the filing date in relation to the period (see paragraph 7(5) of Schedule 7A);

(b) otherwise, the last day of the period of 12 months beginning with the end of the relevant period of account.

(3) Condition A is that no appointment of a reporting company has effect in relation to the relevant period of account.

(4) Condition B is that—

(a) the appointment of a reporting company has effect in relation to the relevant period of account, and

(b) no interest restriction return has been submitted for the period.

(5) Condition C is that—

(a) the appointment of a reporting company has effect in relation to the relevant period of account,

(b) an interest restriction return has been submitted for the period, and

(c) the return does not comply with the requirements of paragraph 20(3) of Schedule 7A (for example by including inaccurate figures).

(6) A relevant company must, in any accounting period to which paragraph 24 of Schedule 7A allocates a pro-rata share of the total disallowed amount that is not nil, leave out of account tax-interest expense amounts that, in total, equal that pro-rata share.

(7) See section 377 for provision as to which tax-interest expense amounts are to be left out of account as a result of this section.

(8) In this section "relevant company" means a company that was a member of the worldwide group at any time during the relevant period of account.

377 Disallowance of deductions: identification of the tax-interest amounts to be left out of account

(1) This section applies where—

(a) a company is required to leave tax-interest expense amounts out of account in an accounting period under section 375 or 376, and

(b) the total of the tax-interest expense amounts that, apart from that provision, would be brought into account in the accounting period exceeds the total of the tax-interest expense amounts that are required by that provision to be left out of account in that period.

(2) Tax-interest expense amounts must (subject to the following provisions of this section) be left out of account in the following order.

First, leave out of account tax-interest expense amounts that meet condition A in section 382 and would (if brought into account) be brought into account under Part 5 of CTA 2009 (non-trading debits in respect of loan relationships).

Second, leave out of account tax-interest expense amounts that meet condition B in section 382 and would (if brought into account) be brought into account under Part 5 of CTA 2009 as a result of section 574 of that Act (non-trading debits in respect of derivative contracts).

Third, leave out of account tax-interest expense amounts that meet condition A in section 382 and would (if brought into account) be brought into account under Part 3 of CTA 2009 as a result of section 297 of that Act (debits in respect of loan relationships treated as expenses of trade).

Fourth, leave out of account tax-interest expense amounts that meet condition B in section 382 and would (if brought into account) be brought into account under Part 3 of CTA 2009 as a result of section 573 of that Act (debits in respect of derivative contracts treated as expenses of trade).

Fifth, leave out of account tax-interest expense amounts that meet condition C in section 382 and do not also meet condition A or B in that section (finance leases, debt factoring and service concession arrangements).

(3) The company may—

    (a) elect that subsection (2) is not to apply to the accounting period, or

    (b) revoke an election previously made.

(4) An election under this section must specify the particular tax-interest expense amounts that are to be left out of account.

378 Disallowed tax-interest expense amounts carried forward

(1) For the purposes of this Part a tax-interest expense amount of a company is "disallowed" in an accounting period if the company is required to leave it out of account in that accounting period under section 375 or 376.

(2) A tax-interest expense amount of a company that is disallowed in an accounting period is (subject to the remaining provisions of this section) carried forward to subsequent accounting periods.

(3) Where—

    (a) a tax-interest expense amount of a company would (apart from this Part) be brought into account in calculating the profits or losses of a trade carried on by the company in an accounting period,

    (b) the tax-interest expense amount is disallowed in that accounting period, and

    (c) in a subsequent accounting period ("the later accounting period") the company ceases to carry on the trade, or the scale of the activities in the trade becomes small or negligible,

the tax-interest expense amount is not carried forward to the later accounting period or accounting periods after the later accounting period.

(4) Where—

    (a) a tax-interest expense amount of a company would (apart from this Part) be brought into account in calculating the profits or losses of a trade carried on by the company in an accounting period,

    (b) the tax-interest expense amount is disallowed in that accounting period, and

    (c) in a subsequent accounting period ("the later accounting period") the trade is uncommercial and non-statutory,

the tax-interest expense amount is not carried forward to the later accounting period or accounting periods after the later accounting period.

(5) For the purposes of subsection (4), a trade is "uncommercial and non-statutory" in an accounting period if, were the company to have made a loss in the trade in the period, relief for the loss under section 37 of CTA 2010 (relief for trade losses against total profits) would have been unavailable by virtue of section 44 of that Act (trade must be commercial or carried on for statutory functions).

(6) Where—

(a) a tax-interest expense amount of a company would (apart from this Part) be brought into account in calculating the profits or losses of an investment business carried on by the company in an accounting period,

(b) the tax-interest expense amount is disallowed in that accounting period, and

(c) in a subsequent accounting period ("the later accounting period") the company ceases to carry on the investment business, or the scale of the activities in the investment business becomes small or negligible,

the tax-interest expense amount is not carried forward to the later accounting period or accounting periods after the later accounting period.

(7) Where a tax-interest expense amount—

(a) is disallowed in an accounting period,

(b) is carried forward to a subsequent accounting period ("the later accounting period"), and

(c) is brought into account in the later accounting period in accordance with section 379,

it is not carried forward to accounting periods after the later accounting period.

379 Reactivation of interest

(1) This section applies where—

(a) an interest restriction return is submitted for a period of account of a worldwide group ("the relevant period of account"),

(b) the return complies with the requirements of paragraph 20(3) of Schedule 7A (requirements for full interest restriction return), and

(c) the return contains a statement that the group is subject to interest reactivations in the return period.

(2) A company that is listed on the statement under paragraph 25 of Schedule 7A (statement of allocated interest reactivations) must, in the specified accounting period, bring into account tax-interest expense amounts that—

(a) are brought forward to the specified accounting period from an earlier accounting period, and

(b) in total, equal the allocated reactivation for the return period.

(3) A tax-interest expense amount is brought into account in the specified accounting period under subsection (2) by being treated as a tax-interest expense amount of the specified accounting period (so that, for example, a tax-interest expense amount that is a relevant loan relationship debit falling within section 383(2)(a)(ii) is brought into account in the specified period as a non-trading debit under Part 5 of CTA 2009).

(4) See section 380 for provision as to which tax-interest expense amounts are to be brought into account under subsection (2).

(5) In this section "the specified accounting period" means—

(a) the earliest relevant accounting period of the company, or

(b) where the company became a member of the relevant worldwide group during the relevant period of account, the earliest relevant accounting period of the company in which it was a member of the group.

380 Reactivation of deductions: identification of the tax-interest amounts to be brought into account

(1) This section applies where—

(a) a company is required to bring tax-interest expense amounts into account in an accounting period under section 379, and

(b) the total of the tax-interest expense amounts that are brought forward to the accounting period from earlier accounting periods exceeds the total of the tax-interest expense amounts that are required by that provision to be brought into account in that accounting period.

(2) Tax-interest expense amounts must (subject to the following provisions of this section) be brought into account in the following order.

First, bring into account tax-interest expense amounts that meet condition A in section 382 and are brought into account under Part 5 of CTA 2009 (non-trading debits in respect of loan relationships).

Second, bring into account tax-interest expense amounts that meet condition B in section 382 and are brought into account under Part 5 of CTA 2009 as a result of section 574 of that Act (non-trading debits in respect of derivative contracts).

Third, bring into account tax-interest expense amounts that meet condition A in section 382 and are brought into account under Part 3 of CTA 2009 as a result of section 297 of that Act (debits in respect of loan relationships treated as expenses of trade).

Fourth, bring into account tax-interest expense amounts that meet condition B in section 382 and are brought into account under Part 3 of CTA 2009 as a result of section 573 of that Act (debits in respect of derivative contracts treated as expenses of trade).

Fifth, bring into account tax-interest expense amounts that meet condition C in section 382 and do not also meet condition A or B in that section (finance leases, debt factoring and service concession arrangements).

(3) The company may—

    (a) elect that subsection (2) is not to apply to the accounting period, or

    (b) revoke an election previously made.

(4) An election under this section must specify the particular tax-interest expense amounts that are to be brought into account.

381 Set-off of disallowances and reactivations in the same accounting period

(1) This section applies where, as a result of the operation of this Part in relation to different periods of account (whether of the same or a different worldwide group), a company would, apart from this section—

    (a) be required to leave out of account one or more tax-interest expense amounts in an accounting period under section 375 or 376, and

    (b) be required to bring one or more tax-interest expense amounts into account in that accounting period under section 379.

(2) In this section—

    (a) "the gross disallowed amount" means the amount, or total of the amounts, mentioned in subsection (1)(a);

    (b) "the gross reactivated amount" means the amount, or total of the amounts, mentioned in subsection (1)(b).

(3) Where the gross disallowed amount is equal to the gross reactivated amount, no tax-interest expense amounts are to be left out of account in the accounting period under this Part or brought into account in the accounting period under this Part.

(4) Where the gross disallowed amount is more than the gross reactivated amount—

    (a) the requirement in section 375 or 376 is to leave out of account tax-interest expense amounts that, in total, equal the gross disallowed amount less the gross reactivated amount, and

    (b) no amount is to be brought into account in the accounting period under section 379.

(5) Where the gross reactivated amount is more than the gross disallowed amount—

    (a) no amount to be left out of account in the accounting period under section 375 or 376, and

    (b) the requirement in section 379 is to bring into account the gross reactivated amount less the gross disallowed amount.

CHAPTER 3

TAX-INTEREST AMOUNTS

Tax-interest expense and income amounts: basic rules

382 The tax-interest expense amounts of a company

(1) References in this Part to a "tax-interest expense amount" of a company for a period of account of a worldwide group are to any amount that—

    (a) is (or apart from this Part would be) brought into account for the purposes of corporation tax in a relevant accounting period of the company, and

    (b) meets condition A, B or C.

(2) Condition A is that the amount is a relevant loan relationship debit (see section 383).

(3) Condition B is that the amount is a relevant derivative contract debit (see section 384).

(4) Condition C is that the amount is in respect of the financing cost implicit in amounts payable under a relevant arrangement or transaction.

(5) In subsection (4) "relevant arrangement or transaction" means—

(a) a finance lease,

(b) debt factoring, or any similar transaction, or

(c) a service concession arrangement if and to the extent that the arrangement is accounted for as a financial liability.

(6) Subsection (8) applies if an accounting period in which a tax-interest expense amount is (or apart from this Part would be) brought into account for the purposes of corporation tax contains one or more disregarded periods.

(7) A "disregarded period" is any period falling within the accounting period—

(a) which does not fall within the period of account of the worldwide group, or

(b) throughout which the company is not a member of the group.

(8) Where this subsection applies, the tax-interest expense amount mentioned in subsection (6) is reduced by such amount as is referable, on a just and reasonable basis, to the disregarded period or periods mentioned in that subsection.

(9) An amount may be reduced to nil under subsection (8).

(10) If—

(a) an amount would have met condition A, B or C but for the application of a rule preventing its deduction,

(b) some or all of it is deductible at a subsequent time as a result of the application of another rule, and

(c) none of conditions A to C are met at that time,

so much of the amount as is subsequently deductible is treated, at that time, as meeting whichever of condition A, B or C would have been met but for the application of the rule mentioned in paragraph (a).

(11) An example of a case to which subsection (10) applies is a case where—

(a) an amount is prevented from being deducted as a result of any provision made by Part 6A (hybrid and other mismatches), and

(b) another provision of that Part subsequently applies so as to permit some or all of it to be deducted from total profits.

383 Relevant loan relationship debits

(1) This section applies for the purposes of section 382.

(2) An amount is a "relevant loan relationship debit" if—

(a) it is a debit that is (or apart from this Part would be) brought into account for the purposes of corporation tax in respect of a loan relationship under—

(i) Part 3 of CTA 2009 as a result of section 297 of that Act (loan relationships for purposes of trade), or

(ii) Part 5 of that Act (other loan relationships), and

(b) is not an excluded debit.

(3) A debit is "excluded" for the purposes of subsection (2)(b) if—

(a) it is in respect of an exchange loss (within the meaning of Parts 5 and 6 of CTA 2009), or

(b) it is in respect of an impairment loss.

384 Relevant derivative contract debits

(1) This section applies for the purposes of section 382.

(2) An amount is a "relevant derivative contract debit" if—

(a) it is a debit that is (or apart from this Part would be) brought into account for the purposes of corporation tax in respect of a derivative contract under—

(i) Part 3 of CTA 2009 as a result of section 573 of that Act (derivative contracts for purposes of trade), or

(ii) Part 5 of that Act as a result of section 574 of that Act (other derivative contracts),

(b) it is not an excluded debit, and

(c) the condition in subsection (4) is met.

(3) A debit is "excluded" for the purposes of subsection (2)(b) if—

(a) it is in respect of an exchange loss (within the meaning of Part 7 of CTA 2009),

(b) it is in respect of an impairment loss, or

(c) it is in respect of a derivative contract which hedges risks arising in the ordinary course of a trade where the contract was entered into wholly for reasons unrelated to the capital structure of the worldwide group (or any member of the worldwide group).

(4) The condition referred to in subsection (2)(c) is that the underlying subject matter of the derivative contract consists only of one or more of the following—

(a) interest rates;

(b) any index determined by reference to income or retail prices;

(c) currency;

(d) an asset or liability representing a loan relationship;

(e) any other underlying subject matter which is—

(i) subordinate in relation to any of the matters mentioned in paragraphs (a) to (d), or

(ii) of small value in comparison with the value of the underlying subject matter as a whole.

(5) For the purposes of this section, whether part of the underlying subject matter of the derivative contract is subordinate or of small value is to be determined by reference to the time when the company enters into or acquires the contract.

(6) In this section "underlying subject matter" has the same meaning as in Part 7 of CTA 2009.

385 The tax-interest income amounts of a company

(1) References in this Part to a "tax-interest income amount" of a company for a period of account of a worldwide group are to any amount that—

(a) is (or apart from this Part would be) brought into account for the purposes of corporation tax in a relevant accounting period of the company, and

(b) meets condition A, B, C or D.

(2) Condition A is that the amount is a relevant loan relationship credit (see section 386).

(3) Condition B is that the amount is a relevant derivative contract credit (see section 387).

(4) Condition C is that the amount is in respect of the financing income implicit in amounts receivable under a relevant arrangement or transaction.

(5) In subsection (4) "relevant arrangement or transaction" means—

(a) a finance lease,

(b) debt factoring, or any similar transaction, or

(c) a service concession arrangement if and to the extent that the arrangement is accounted for as a financial asset.

(6) Condition D is that the amount is in respect of income that—

(a) is receivable from another company, and

(b) is in consideration of the provision of a guarantee of any borrowing of that other company.

(7) Subsection (9) applies if an accounting period in which a tax-interest income amount is (or apart from this Part would be) brought into account for the purposes of corporation tax contains one or more disregarded periods.

(8) A "disregarded period" is any period falling within the accounting period—

(a) which does not fall within the period of account of the worldwide group, or

(b) throughout which the company is not a member of the group.

(9) Where this subsection applies, the tax-interest income amount mentioned in subsection (7) is reduced by such amount as is referable, on a just and reasonable basis, to the disregarded period or periods mentioned in that subsection.

(10) An amount may be reduced to nil under subsection (9).

386 Relevant loan relationship credits

(1) This section applies for the purposes of section 385.

(2) An amount is a "relevant loan relationship credit" if—

(a) it is a credit that is (or apart from this Part would be) brought into account for the purposes of corporation tax in respect of a loan relationship under—

(i) Part 3 of CTA 2009 as a result of section 297 of that Act (loan relationships for purposes of trade), or

(ii) Part 5 of that Act (other loan relationships), and

(b) it is not an excluded credit.

(3) A credit is "excluded" for the purposes of subsection (2)(b) if—

(a) it is in respect of an exchange gain (within the meaning of Parts 5 and 6 of CTA 2009), or

(b) it is in respect of the reversal of an impairment loss.

387 Relevant derivative contract credits

(1) This section applies for the purposes of section 385.

(2) An amount is a "relevant derivative contract credit" if—

(a) it is a credit that is (or apart from this Part would be) brought into account for the purposes of corporation tax in respect of a derivative contract under—

(i) Part 3 of CTA 2009 as a result of section 573 of that Act (derivative contracts for purposes of trade), or

(ii) Part 5 of that Act as a result of section 574 of that Act (other derivative contracts),

(b) is not an excluded credit, and

(c) the condition in subsection (4) is met.

(3) A credit is "excluded" for the purposes of subsection (2)(b) if—

(a) it is in respect of an exchange gain (within the meaning of Part 7 of CTA 2009),

(b) it is in respect of the reversal of an impairment loss, or

(c) it is in respect of a derivative contract which hedges risks arising in the ordinary course of a trade where the contract was entered into wholly for reasons unrelated to the capital structure of the worldwide group (or any member of the worldwide group).

(4) The condition referred to in subsection (2)(c) is that the underlying subject matter of the derivative contract consists only of one or more of the following—

(a) interest rates;

(b) any index determined by reference to income or retail prices;

(c) currency;

(d) an asset or liability representing a loan relationship;

(e) any other underlying subject matter which is—

(i) subordinate in relation to any of the matters mentioned in paragraphs (a) to (d), or

(ii) of small value in comparison with the value of the underlying subject matter as a whole.

(5) For the purposes of this section, whether part of the underlying subject matter of the derivative contract is subordinate or of small value is to be determined by reference to the time when the company enters into or acquires the contract.

(6) In this section "underlying subject matter" has the same meaning as in Part 7 of CTA 2009.

Double taxation relief

388 Double taxation relief

(1) This section applies where—

(a) apart from this section, an amount ("the relevant amount") would be a tax-interest income amount brought into account for the purposes of corporation tax in a relevant accounting period ("the relevant accounting period") of a company, and

(b) the amount of corporation tax chargeable in respect of the relevant amount is reduced under section 18(2) (entitlement to credit for foreign tax reduces UK tax by amount of the credit).

(2) The relevant amount is not a tax-interest income amount to the extent that it consists of notional untaxed income.

(3) For this purpose, the amount of the relevant amount that consists of "notional untaxed income" is—

A / B

where—

A is the amount of the reduction mentioned in subsection (1)(b);

B is the rate of corporation tax payable by the company, before any credit under Part 2 (double taxation relief), on the company's profits for the relevant accounting period.

Net tax-interest expense

389 The "net tax-interest expense" or "net tax-interest income" of a company

(1) A company has "net tax-interest expense" for a period of account of a worldwide group if the total of its tax-interest expense amounts for the period exceeds the total of its tax-interest income amounts for the period.

(2) The amount of the net tax-interest expense of the company for the period is the amount of the excess.

(3) A company has "net tax-interest income" for a period of account of a worldwide group if the total of its tax-interest income amounts for the period exceeds the total of its tax-interest expense amounts for the period.

(4) The amount of the net tax-interest income of the company for the period is the amount of the excess.

(5) The net tax-interest expense or net tax-interest income of a company for a period of account of a worldwide group is "referable" to an accounting period of the company to the extent that it comprises tax-interest expense amounts or tax-interest income amounts that are (or apart from this Part would be) brought into account in the accounting period.

(6) This section applies for the purposes of this Part.

390 The worldwide group's aggregate net tax-interest expense and income

(1) The "aggregate net tax-interest expense" of a worldwide group for a period of account of the group is (subject to subsection (2))—

(a) the total of the net tax-interest expense for the period of each relevant company that has such an amount, less
(b) the total of the net tax-interest income for the period of each relevant company that has such an amount.

(2) Where the amount determined under subsection (1) is negative, the "aggregate net tax-interest expense" of the group for the period is nil.

(3) The "aggregate net tax-interest income" of a worldwide group for a period of account of the group is (subject to subsection (4))—

(a) the total of the net tax-interest income for the period of each relevant company that has such an amount, less
(b) the total of the net tax-interest expense for the period of each relevant company that has such an amount.

(4) Where the amount determined under subsection (3) is negative, the "aggregate net tax-interest income" of the group for the period is nil.

(5) In this section "relevant company" means a company that was a member of the group at any time during the period of account of the group.

(6) This section applies for the purposes of this Part.

Interpretation

391 Meaning of "impairment loss"

(1) In this Part "impairment loss" means a loss in respect of the impairment of a financial asset.

(2) A reference to a debit in respect of an impairment loss does not include a debit that is (or apart from this Part would be) brought into account in an accounting period in respect of an asset for which fair value accounting is used.

CHAPTER 4

INTEREST CAPACITY

392 The interest capacity of a worldwide group for a period of account

(1) For the purposes of this Part "the interest capacity" of a worldwide group for a period of account of the group ("the current period") is (subject to subsection (2)) —

$A + B$

where—

A is the interest allowance of the group for the current period (see Chapter 5);
B is the aggregate of the interest allowances of the group for periods before the current period so far as they are available in the current period (see section 393).

(2) Where the amount determined under subsection (1) is less than the de minimis amount for the current period, the interest capacity of the worldwide group for the period is the de minimis amount.

(3) For this purpose "the de minimis amount" for a period of account is—

(a) £2 million, or

(b) where the period is more than or less than a year, the amount mentioned in paragraph (a) proportionately increased or reduced.

393 Amount of interest allowance for a period that is "available" in a later period

(1) This section applies for the purposes of this Chapter.

(2) The amount of the interest allowance of a worldwide group for a period of account ("the originating period") that is "available" in a later period of account of the group ("the receiving period") is (subject to subsection (5)) the lower of amounts A and B.

(3) Amount A is—

(a) the amount of the interest allowance for the originating period, less

(b) the total of the amount or amounts (if any) of that interest allowance that were used in the originating period, or in any subsequent period of account of the group before the receiving period (see section 394).

(4) Amount B is the amount (if any) of the interest allowance for the originating period that is unexpired in the receiving period (see section 395).

(5) The amount of the interest allowance for the originating period that is "available" in the receiving period is nil if—

(a) an abbreviated return election is made in relation to the originating period, the receiving period or any intervening period of account of the group, or

(b) an interest restriction return is not submitted for any such period.

394 When interest allowance is "used"

(1) This section applies for the purposes of this Chapter.

(2) The amount of the interest allowance of a worldwide group for a period of account of the group ("the originating period") that is "used" in the originating period is the lower of—

(a) the interest allowance for the originating period, and

(b) the sum of—

(i) the aggregate net tax-interest expense of the group for the originating period;

(ii) the total amount of tax-interest expense amounts required to be brought into account in the originating period under section 379 (reactivation of interest) by members of the group.

(3) The amount of the interest allowance for the originating period that is "used" in a later period of account of the group ("the receiving period") is the lower of—

(a) the interest allowance so far as it is available in the receiving period (see section 393), and

(b) the relevant part of the aggregate net tax-interest expense of the group for the receiving period (see subsection (4)).

(4) In subsection (3)(b) "the relevant part of the aggregate net tax-interest expense of the group for the receiving period" is (subject to subsection (5))—

$$A - B - C$$

where—

A is the aggregate net tax-interest expense of the group for the receiving period;

B is the interest allowance of the group for the receiving period;

C is the amount of the interest allowance of the group for any period before the originating period that is used in the receiving period.

(5) Where the amount determined under subsection (4) is negative, "the relevant part of the aggregate net tax-interest expense of the group for the receiving period" is nil.

395 Amount of interest allowance for a period of account that is "unexpired" in later period

(1) This section contains provision for determining for the purposes of this Chapter the extent to which an interest allowance of a worldwide group for a period of account ("the originating period") is "unexpired" in a later period of account of the group ("the receiving period").

(2) If the receiving period—

    (a) begins 5 years or less after the originating period begins, and

    (b) ends 5 years or less after the originating period ends,

all of the interest allowance for the originating period is unexpired in the receiving period.

(3) If the receiving period begins 5 years or more after the originating period ends, none of the interest allowance for the originating period is unexpired in the receiving period.

(4) Subsection (5) applies if the receiving period—

    (a) begins more than 5 years after the originating period begins, and

    (b) ends 5 years or less after the originating period ends.

(5) The amount of the interest allowance for the originating period that is unexpired in the receiving period is—

$$(A - B) \times (X / Y)$$

where—

    A is the interest allowance for the originating period;

    B is—

        (a) the aggregate net tax-interest expense of the group for the originating period, or

        (b) if lower, the interest allowance for the originating period;

    X is the number of days in the period—

        (a) beginning with the day on which the receiving period begins, and

        (b) ending with the day 5 years after the day on which the originating period ends;

    Y is the number of days in the originating period.

(6) Subsection (7) applies if the receiving period—

    (a) begins 5 years or less after the originating period begins, and

    (b) ends more than 5 years after the originating period ends.

(7) The amount of the interest allowance for the originating period that is unexpired in the receiving period is—

$$(C - D) \times (X / Z)$$

where—

    C is the aggregate net tax-interest expense of the group for the receiving period;

    D is—

        (a) the interest allowance of the group for the receiving period, or

        (b) if lower, the aggregate net tax-interest expense of the group for the receiving period;

    X has the same meaning as in subsection (5);

    Z is the number of days in the receiving period.

(8) Subsection (9) applies if—

    (a) the receiving period—

        (i) begins more than 5 years after the originating period begins, and

        (ii) ends more than 5 years after the originating period ends, and

    (b) subsection (3) does not apply.

(9) The amount of the interest allowance for the originating period that is unexpired in the receiving period is the lower of the amounts determined under subsections (5) and (7).

CHAPTER 5

INTEREST ALLOWANCE

Interest allowance

396 The interest allowance of a worldwide group for a period of account

(1) For the purposes of this Part "the interest allowance" of a worldwide group for a period of account of the group is—

$$A + B$$

where—

    A is the basic interest allowance of the group for the period;

    B is the amount (if any) of the aggregate net tax-interest income of the group for the period (see section 390(3) and (4)).

(2) In subsection (1) "the basic interest allowance" means—

(a) where no group ratio election is in force in relation to the period, the basic interest allowance calculated using the fixed ratio method (see section 397);

(b) where such an election is in force in relation to the period, the basic interest allowance calculated using the group ratio method (see section 398).

397 Basic interest allowance calculated using fixed ratio method

(1) For the purposes of section 396, the basic interest allowance of a worldwide group for a period of account of the group, calculated using the fixed ratio method, is the lower of the following amounts—

(a) 30% of the aggregate tax-EBITDA of the group for the period;

(b) the fixed ratio debt cap of the group for the period.

(2) See—

section 400 for the meaning of "fixed ratio debt cap";

section 405 for the meaning of "aggregate tax-EBITDA".

398 Basic interest allowance calculated using group ratio method

(1) For the purposes of section 396, the basic interest allowance of a worldwide group for a period of account of the group, calculated using the group ratio method, is the lower of the following amounts—

(a) the group ratio percentage of the aggregate tax-EBITDA of the group for the period;

(b) the group ratio debt cap of the group for the period.

(2) See—

section 399 for the meaning of "group ratio percentage";

section 400 for the meaning of "group ratio debt cap";

section 405 for the meaning of "aggregate tax-EBITDA".

399 The group ratio percentage

(1) For the purposes of this Part "the group ratio percentage" of a worldwide group for a period of account of the group is (subject to subsection (2)) the following proportion expressed as a percentage—

A / B

where—

A is the qualifying net group-interest expense of the group for the period;

B is the group-EBITDA of the group for the period.

(2) "The group ratio percentage" is 100% where—

(a) the percentage determined under subsection (1) is negative or higher than 100%, or

(b) B in that subsection is zero.

(3) See—

section 414 for the meaning of "qualifying net group-interest expense";

section 416 for the meaning of "group-EBITDA".

400 The debt cap

(1) For the purposes of section 397 (and this section), "the fixed ratio debt cap" of a worldwide group for a period of account of the group is the sum of the following amounts—

(a) the adjusted net group-interest expense of the group for the period;

(b) the excess debt cap of the group that was generated in the immediately preceding period of account of the group (if any) (see subsections (3) to (7)).

(2) For the purposes of section 398 (and this section), "the group ratio debt cap" of a worldwide group for a period of account of the group is the sum of the following amounts—

(a) the qualifying net group-interest expense of the group for the period;

(b) the excess debt cap of the group that was generated in the immediately preceding period of account of the group (if any) (see subsections (3) to (7)).

(3) Where no group ratio election is in force in relation to a period of account of a worldwide group ("the generating period"), "the excess debt cap" of the group that is generated in the period is (subject to subsections (5) and (6))—

$A - B$

where—

A is the fixed ratio debt cap of the group for the generating period;

B is 30% of the aggregate tax-EBITDA of the group for the generating period.

(4) Where a group ratio election is in force in relation to a period of account of a worldwide group ("the generating period"), "the excess debt cap" of the group that is generated in the period is (subject to subsections (5) and (6))—

$A - B$

where—

A is the group ratio debt cap of the group for the generating period;

B is the group ratio percentage of the aggregate tax-EBITDA of the group for the generating period.

(5) Where the amount determined under subsection (3) or (4) is negative, "the excess debt cap" of the group that is generated in the period is nil.

(6) Where the amount determined under subsection (3) or (4) is greater than the carry-forward limit, "the excess debt cap" of the group that is generated in the period is the carry-forward limit.

(7) For this purpose the "carry-forward limit" is the sum of the following amounts—

(a) the excess debt cap generated in the period of account of the group immediately preceding the generating period (if any);

(b) the total disallowed amount of the group in the generating period.

(8) See—

section 373 for the meaning of "the total disallowed amount";

section 405 for the meaning of "aggregate tax-EBITDA";

section 413 for the meaning of "adjusted net group-interest expense";

section 414 for the meaning of "qualifying net group-interest expense".

Effect of group ratio (blended) election

401 Effect of group ratio (blended) election on group ratio percentage

(1) Where a group ratio (blended) election (see paragraph 14 of Schedule 7A) has effect in relation to a period of account of a worldwide group ("the relevant period of account"), this Chapter applies subject to this section.

(2) Section 399 (meaning of "group ratio percentage") does not apply for the purpose of determining the group ratio percentage of the group for the relevant period of account.

(3) Instead, the group ratio percentage of the group for the relevant period of account is determined by taking the following steps—

Step 1

For each investor in the group, multiply the investor's applicable percentage by the investor's share in the group.

Step 2

Add together the amounts found under Step 1.

(4) For the purposes of this section, an investor's "applicable percentage" is the highest of the following percentages—

(a) 30%;

(b) the percentage determined under section 399;

(c) in the case of a related party investor that, throughout the relevant period of account, is a member of a worldwide group ("the investor's worldwide group") other than that mentioned in subsection (1), the group ratio percentage of the investor's worldwide group for the relevant period of account.

(5) Subsection (6) applies where financial statements of the investor's worldwide group are drawn up in respect of one or more periods ("the investor's periods of account") that are comprised in or overlap with (but are not coterminous with) the relevant period of account.

(6) The group ratio percentage of the investor's worldwide group for the relevant period of account is to be determined for the purposes of subsection (4)(c) by taking the following steps—

Step 1

Find the group ratio percentage of the investor's worldwide group for each of the investor's periods of account.

Step 2

Find the proportion of the relevant period of account that coincides with each of the investor's periods of account.

Step 3

For each of the investor's periods of account, multiply the group ratio percentage found under Step 1 by the proportion found under Step 2.
Step 4
Add together the amounts found under Step 3.

402 Effect of group ratio (blended) election on group ratio debt cap

(1) Where a group ratio (blended) election (see paragraph 14 of Schedule 7A) has effect in relation to a period of account of a worldwide group ("the relevant period of account"), this Chapter applies subject to this section.

(2) In section 400 (the debt cap), subsection (2)(a) is treated as if—

(a) it did not refer to the qualifying net group-interest expense of the group for the period, and
(b) instead it referred to the blended net group-interest expense of the group for the period, as determined in accordance with this section.

(3) The blended net group-interest expense of the group for the relevant period of account is determined by taking the following steps—

Step 1
For each investor in the group whose applicable percentage for the purposes of section 401 is the percentage mentioned in subsection (4)(a) of that section, multiply the adjusted net group-interest expense of the group for the period by the investor's share in the group.
Step 2
For each investor in the group whose applicable percentage for the purposes of section 401 is the percentage mentioned in subsection (4)(b) of that section, multiply the qualifying net group-interest expense of the group for the period by the investor's share in the group.
Step 3
For each investor in the group whose applicable percentage for the purposes of section 401 is the percentage mentioned in subsection (4)(c) of that section, find the applicable net group-interest expense of the investor's worldwide group for the period (see subsections (4) to (8) of this section).
Step 4
Add together the amounts found under Steps 1, 2 and 3.

(4) For the purposes of this section, the "applicable net group-interest expense" of the investor's worldwide group for a period of account is so much of the qualifying net group-interest expense of the investor's worldwide group for the period as relates to loans to, or other financial arrangements with, members of the investor's worldwide group that are used to fund (directly or indirectly) loans to, or other financial arrangements with, members of the worldwide group mentioned in subsection (1).

(5) Subsection (6) applies where periods of account of the investor's worldwide group ("the investor's periods of account") are comprised in or overlap with (but are not coterminous with) the relevant period of account.

(6) The applicable net group-interest expense of the investor's worldwide group for the relevant period of account is the aggregate of so much of the applicable net group-interest expense of the investor's worldwide group for each of the investor's periods of account as is referable, on a just and reasonable basis, to the relevant period of account.

(7) Subsection (8) applies where—

(a) a loan is made to, or another financial arrangement is entered into with, a member of the investor's worldwide group, and
(b) the loan or other financial arrangement is—

(i) in part used to fund (directly or indirectly) loans to, or other financial arrangements with, members of the worldwide group mentioned in subsection (1), and
(ii) in part used for other purposes.

(8) In determining the applicable net group-interest expense of the investor's worldwide group for any period, the amount of the qualifying net group-interest expense of the investor's worldwide group for the period that is brought into account, in respect of the loan or other financial arrangement mentioned in subsection (7)(a), is confined to such amount as is referable, on a just and reasonable basis, to the use mentioned in subsection (7)(b)(i).

(9) In this section—

"financial arrangements" does not include the holding of shares;
"the investor's worldwide group" has the same meaning as in section 401.

403 Calculations under sections 401 and 402: investor worldwide groups

(1) This section applies—

(a) in determining, under section 401, the group ratio percentage of the investor's worldwide group for a period of account;

(b) in determining, under section 402, the qualifying net group-interest expense of the investor's worldwide group for a period of account.

(2) Where the group ratio (blended) election specifies that a particular election under Schedule 7A ("the investor's election") is to be treated as having effect, or as not having effect, in relation to periods of account of the investor's worldwide group, the investor's election is to be so treated in determining the amounts mentioned in subsection (1).

(3) Where the group ratio (blended) election does not specify that a particular election under Schedule 7A ("the investor's election") is to be treated as having effect, or as not having effect, in relation to periods of account of the investor's worldwide group, the investor's election is to be treated as having effect in determining the amounts mentioned in subsection (1) only if it was in fact made in relation to the period of account in question by a reporting company of the investor's worldwide group.

(4) In this section "the investor's worldwide group" has the same meaning as in section 401.

404 Meaning of "investor", "related party investor" and investor's "share"

(1) An entity is an "investor" in a worldwide group if it has an interest in the ultimate parent of the group that entitles it to a proportion of the profits or losses of the group.

(2) An investor in a worldwide group is a "related party investor" of the group in relation to a period of account of the group if, throughout the period, it is a related party of the ultimate parent of the group.

(3) The "share" of an investor in a worldwide group, in relation to a period of account of the group, is the proportion (expressed as a percentage) of the profits or losses of the group that arise in the period to which the investor is entitled by virtue of the investor's interest in the group's ultimate parent.

(4) This section has effect for the purposes of this Part.

CHAPTER 6

TAX-EBITDA

405 The aggregate tax-EBITDA of a worldwide group

For the purposes of this Part "the aggregate tax-EBITDA" of a worldwide group for a period of account of the group is—

(a) the total of the tax-EBITDAs for the period of each company that was a member of the group at any time during the period, or

(b) where the amount specified in paragraph (a) is negative, nil.

406 The tax-EBITDA of a company

(1) For the purposes of this Part the "tax-EBITDA" of a company for a period of account of the worldwide group is—

(a) where the company has only one relevant accounting period, the company's adjusted corporation tax earnings for that accounting period;

(b) where the company has more than one relevant accounting period, the total of the company's adjusted corporation tax earnings for each of those accounting periods.

(2) The company's "adjusted corporation tax earnings" for an accounting period is the total (which may be negative) of the amounts that meet condition A or B.

(3) Condition A is that the amount—

(a) is brought into account by the company in determining its taxable total profits of the period (within the meaning given by section 4(2) of CTA 2010), and

(b) is not an excluded amount for the purposes of this condition (see section 407).

(4) Condition B is that the amount—

(a) is not brought into account as mentioned in subsection (3)(a), but would have been so brought into account if the company had made profits, or more profits, of any description in the period, and

(b) is not an excluded amount for the purposes of this condition (see section 407).

(5) Subsection (7) applies if an amount—

(a) is brought into account as mentioned in subsection (3)(a), or

(b) is not brought into account as mentioned in subsection (4)(a),

in an accounting period which contains one or more disregarded periods.

(6) A "disregarded period" is any period falling within the accounting period—

(a) which does not fall within the period of account of the worldwide group, or

(b) throughout which the company is not a member of the group.

(7) Where this subsection applies, the amount mentioned in subsection (5) is reduced, for the purposes of subsection (2), by such amount (if any) as is referable, on a just and reasonable basis, to the disregarded period or periods mentioned in subsection (5).

(8) An amount may be reduced to nil under subsection (7).

407 Amounts not brought into account in determining a company's tax-EBITDA

(1) An amount is an excluded amount for the purposes of conditions A and B in section 406 if it is any of the following—

(a) a tax-interest expense amount or a tax-interest income amount;

(b) an allowance or charge under CAA 2001;

(c) an excluded relevant intangibles debit or an excluded relevant intangibles credit (see section 408);

(d) a loss that—

(i) is made by the company in an accounting period other than that mentioned in section 406(2), and

(ii) is not an allowable loss for the purposes of TCGA 1992;

(e) a deficit from the company's loan relationships for an accounting period other than that mentioned in section 406(2);

(f) expenses of management of the company that are referable to an accounting period other than that mentioned in section 406(2);

(g) a deduction under section 137 of CTA 2010 (group relief) or section 188CK of that Act (group relief for carried-forward losses) if and to the extent that it constitutes a loss of the worldwide group;

(h) a qualifying tax relief.

(2) For the purposes of subsection (1)(g) the deduction constitutes a "loss of the worldwide group" if and to the extent that it comprises surrenderable amounts that are referable to times at which the surrendering company was a member of the worldwide group.

(3) An amount is a qualifying tax relief for the purposes of subsection (1)(h) if it is any of the following—

(a) an R&D expenditure credit within the meaning of section 104A of CTA 2009;

(b) a deduction under section 1044, 1063, 1068 or 1087 of CTA 2009 (additional relief for expenditure on research and development);

(c) an amount which is treated as a trading loss as a result of section 1092 of CTA 2009 (SMEs: deemed trading loss for pre-trading expenditure);

(d) a deduction under section 1147 or 1149 of CTA 2009 (relief for expenditure on contaminated or derelict land);

(e) a deduction under section 1199 of CTA 2009 (film tax relief);

(f) a deduction under section 1216CF of CTA 2009 (television tax relief);

(g) a deduction under section 1217CF of CTA 2009 (video games tax relief);

(h) a deduction under section 1217H of CTA 2009 (relief in relation to theatrical productions);

(i) a deduction under section 1217RD of CTA 2009 (orchestra tax relief);

(j) a deduction under section 1218ZCE of CTA 2009 (museums and galleries exhibition tax relief);

(k) a qualifying charitable donation (whether made in the accounting period mentioned in section 406(2) or an earlier one);

(l) a deduction under section 357A of CTA 2010 (profits from patents etc chargeable at lower rate of corporation tax).

(4) An amount is an excluded amount for the purposes of condition B in section 406 if it is an allowable loss for the purposes of TCGA 1992.

408 Excluded relevant intangibles debits and excluded relevant intangibles credits

(1) For the purposes of section 407 (and this section)—

(a) a debit is a "relevant intangibles debit" if it is brought into account under a provision of Part 8 of CTA 2009 (intangible fixed assets) that is listed in column 1 of the following table;

(b) a relevant intangibles debit is "excluded" to the extent indicated in the corresponding entry in column 2 of the table.

Provision	Excluded debits
section 729	excluded in full
section 731	excluded in full
section 732	excluded if and to the extent that its amount is determined by reference to an excluded intangibles credit
section 735	excluded in full
section 736	excluded in full
section 872	excluded in full
section 874	excluded in full

(2) For the purposes of section 407 (and this section)—

(a) a credit is a "relevant intangibles credit" if it is brought into account under a provision of Part 8 of CTA 2009 (intangible fixed assets) that is listed in column 1 of the following table;

(b) a relevant intangibles credit is "excluded" to the extent indicated in the corresponding entry in column 2 of the table.

Provision	Excluded credits
section 723	excluded if and to the extent that its amount is determined by reference to excluded intangible debits and excluded intangible credits
section 725	excluded if and to the extent that its amount is determined by reference to an excluded intangibles debit
section 735	excluded if and to the extent that the cost of the asset in question exceeds its tax written-down value
section 872	excluded in full
section 874	excluded in full

(3) In the table in subsection (2)—

(a) "tax written-down value" has the same meaning as in Part 8 of CTA 2009 (see Chapter 5 of that Part);

(b) "the cost of the asset" has the same meaning as in section 736 of that Act.

409 Double taxation relief

(1) This section applies where—

(a) apart from this section, an amount of income ("the relevant amount") would meet condition A or B in section 406 in relation to a relevant accounting period of a company, and

(b) the amount of corporation tax chargeable in respect of the relevant amount is reduced under section 18(2) (entitlement to credit for foreign tax reduces UK tax by amount of the credit).

(2) The relevant amount is treated, for the purposes of section 406(2) (meaning of "adjusted corporation tax earnings") as not meeting the condition mentioned in subsection (1)(a) to the extent that it consists of notional untaxed income.

(3) For this purpose, the amount of the relevant amount that consists of "notional untaxed income" is—

A / B

where—

A is the amount of the reduction mentioned in subsection (1)(b);

B is the rate of corporation tax payable by the company, before any credit under Part 2 (double taxation relief), on the company's profits for the relevant accounting period.

CHAPTER 7

GROUP-INTEREST AND GROUP-EBITDA

Group-interest

410 Net group-interest expense

(1) For the purposes of this Part the "net group-interest expense" of a worldwide group for a period of account of the group ("the relevant period of account") is—

A – B

where—

A is the sum of the relevant expense amounts that are recognised in the financial statements of the group for the period as items of profit or loss;

B is the sum of the relevant income amounts that are recognised in the financial statements of the group for the period as items of profit or loss.

(2) Subsection (3) applies where—

(a) a relevant expense amount ("the capitalised expense") is brought into account in financial statements of the group (whether for the relevant period of account or any earlier period) in determining the carrying value of an asset,

(b) the asset is not a relevant asset, and

(c) in the financial statements of the group for the relevant period of account, any of the carrying value is written down.

(3) A in subsection (1) is treated as including so much of the amount written down as is attributable to the capitalised expense.

(4) Subsection (5) applies where—

(a) a relevant income amount ("the capitalised income") is brought into account in financial statements of the group (whether for the relevant period of account or any earlier period) in determining the carrying value of an asset,

(b) the asset is not a relevant asset, and

(c) in the financial statements of the group for the relevant period of account, any of the carrying value is written down.

(5) B in subsection (1) is treated as including the amount of the reduction in the amount written down that is attributable to the capitalised income.

(6) See—

section 411 for the definitions of "relevant expense amount" and "relevant income amount";

section 417(5) and (6) for the definition of "relevant asset";

section 420 for provision affecting amounts recognised in financial statements in respect of certain profits or losses arising from derivative contracts.

411 "Relevant expense amount" and "relevant income amount"

(1) In this Chapter "relevant expense amount" means (subject to subsection (3)) an amount in respect of any of the following—

(a) interest payable under a loan relationship;

(b) expenses ancillary to a loan relationship;

(c) losses arising from a loan relationship or a related transaction, other than—

(i) exchange losses, and

(ii) impairment losses;

(d) dividends payable in respect of preference shares accounted for as a financial liability;

(e) losses arising from a relevant derivative contract or a related transaction, other than—

(i) exchanges losses,

(ii) impairment losses, and

(iii) losses where the contract hedges risks arising in the ordinary course of a trade and the contract was entered into wholly for reasons unrelated to the capital structure of the worldwide group (or any member of the worldwide group);

(f) expenses ancillary to a relevant derivative contract or related transaction;

(g) financing charges implicit in payments made under a finance lease;

(h) financing charges relating to debt factoring;

(i) financing charges implicit in payments made under a service concession arrangement if and to the extent that the arrangement is accounted for as a financial liability;

(j) interest payable in respect of a relevant non-lending relationship;

(k) alternative finance return payable under alternative finance arrangements;

(l) manufactured interest payable;

(m) financing charges in respect of the advance under a debtor repo or debtor quasi-repo;

(n) financing charges so far as they are made up of amounts which—

(i) are treated as interest payable under a loan relationship under a relevant provision of Chapter 2 of Part 16 of CTA 2010 (finance arrangements), or

(ii) would be so treated if the company in question were within the charge to corporation tax.

(2) In this Chapter "relevant income amount" means (subject to subsection (3)) an amount in respect of any of the following—

(a) interest receivable under a loan relationship;
(b) profits arising from a loan relationship or a related transaction, other than—
  (i) exchange gains, and
  (ii) the reversal of impairment losses;
(c) dividends receivable in respect of preference shares accounted for as a financial asset;
(d) gains arising from a relevant derivative contract or a related transaction, other than—
  (i) exchange gains,
  (ii) the reversal of impairment losses, and
  (iii) gains where the contract hedges risks arising in the ordinary course of a trade and the contract was entered into wholly for reasons unrelated to the capital structure of the worldwide group (or any member of the worldwide group);
(e) financing income implicit in amounts received under a finance lease;
(f) financing income relating to debt factoring;
(g) financing income implicit in amounts received under a service concession arrangement if and to the extent that the arrangement is accounted for as a financial asset;
(h) interest receivable in respect of a relevant non-lending relationship;
(i) alternative finance return receivable under alternative finance arrangements;
(j) manufactured interest receivable;
(k) financing income in respect of the advance under a creditor repo or creditor quasi-repo;
(l) financing income so far as it is made up of amounts which—
  (i) are treated as interest receivable under a loan relationship under a relevant provision of Chapter 2 of Part 16 of CTA 2010 (finance arrangements), or
  (ii) would be so treated if the company in question were within the charge to corporation tax.

(3) In this Chapter—

(a) "relevant expense amount" does not include an amount payable under a pension scheme;
(b) "relevant income amount" does not include an amount receivable under a pension scheme.

(4) In subsection (3) "pension scheme" has the meaning given by section 150(1) of FA 2004.

412 Section 411: interpretation

(1) For the purposes of section 411(1)(b), expenses are "ancillary" to a loan relationship if and only if they are incurred directly—

(a) in bringing, or attempting to bring, the relationship into existence,
(b) in making payments under the loan relationship, or
(c) in taking steps to ensure the receipt of payments under the loan relationship.

(2) For the purposes of section 411(1)(e) and (2)(d) a derivative contract is "relevant" if its underlying subject matter consists only of one or more of the following—

(a) interest rates;
(b) any index determined by reference to income or retail prices;
(c) currency;
(d) an asset or liability representing a loan relationship;
(e) any other underlying subject matter which is—
  (i) subordinate in relation to any of the matters mentioned in paragraphs (a) to (d), or
  (ii) of small value in comparison with the value of the underlying subject matter as a whole.

(3) Whether part of the underlying subject matter of a derivative contract is subordinate or of small value is to be determined for the purposes of subsection (2)(e) by reference to the time when the company enters into or acquires the contract.

(4) For the purposes of section 411(1)(f) expenses are "ancillary" to a relevant derivative contract or related transaction if and only if they are incurred directly—

(a) in bringing, or attempting to bring, the derivative contract into existence,

(b) in entering into or giving effect to, or attempting to enter into or give effect to, the related transaction,

(c) in making payments under the derivative contract or as a result of the related transaction, or

(d) in taking steps to secure the receipt of payments under the derivative contract or in accordance with the related transaction.

(5) For the purposes of section 411(1)(n) and (2)(l), the following provisions of Chapter 2 of Part 16 of CTA 2010 are "relevant"—

(a) section 761(3) (type 1 finance arrangements: borrower a company);

(b) section 762(3) (type 1 finance arrangements: borrower a partnership);

(c) section 766(3) (type 2 finance arrangements);

(d) section 769(3) (type 3 finance arrangements).

(6) In section 411—

(a) in subsections (1)(c) and (2)(b), "related transaction", "exchange loss" and "exchange gain" have the same meaning as in Parts 5 and 6 of CTA 2009 (see sections 304 and 475 of that Act);

(b) in subsections (1)(e) and (2)(d), "related transaction", "exchange loss" and "exchange gain" have the same meaning as in Part 7 of that Act (see sections 596 and 705 of that Act).

(7) In section 411 and this section—

"alternative finance arrangements" has the same meaning as in Parts 5 and 6 of CTA 2009 (see section 501(2) of that Act);

"alternative finance return" has the same meaning as in Part 6 of CTA 2009 (see sections 511 to 513 of that Act);

"creditor quasi-repo" has the same meaning as in Chapter 10 of Part 6 of CTA 2009 (see section 544 of that Act);

"creditor repo" has the same meaning as in Chapter 10 of Part 6 of CTA 2009 (see section 543 of that Act);

"debtor quasi-repo" has the same meaning as in Chapter 10 of Part 6 of CTA 2009 (see section 549 of that Act);

"debtor repo" has the same meaning as in Chapter 10 of Part 6 of CTA 2009 (see section 548 of that Act);

"manufactured interest" has the same meaning as in Chapter 9 of Part 6 of CTA 2009 (see section 539(5) of that Act);

"relevant non-lending relationship" has the same meaning as in Chapter 2 of Part 6 of CTA 2009 (see sections 479 and 480 of that Act);

"underlying subject matter" has the same meaning as in Part 7 of CTA 2009 (see section 583 of that Act).

413 Adjusted net group-interest expense

(1) For the purposes of this Part the "adjusted net group-interest expense" of a worldwide group for a period of account of the group is (subject to subsection (2))—

$$A + B - C$$

where—

A is the net group-interest expense of the group for the period (see section 410);

B is the sum of any upward adjustments (see subsection (3));

C is the sum of any downward adjustments (see subsection (4)).

(2) Where the amount determined under subsection (1) is negative, the "adjusted net group-interest expense" of the group for the period is nil.

(3) In this section "upward adjustment" means any of the following amounts—

(a) a relevant expense amount that is brought into account in the financial statements of the group for the period in determining the carrying value of an asset or liability;

(b) an amount that is included in the net group-interest expense of the group for the period by virtue of section 410(5) (capitalised income written off);

(c) a relevant expense amount that—

(i) in the financial statements of the group for the period is recognised in equity or shareholders' funds, and is not recognised as an item of profit or loss or as an item of other comprehensive income, and

(ii) is brought into account for the purposes of corporation tax by a member of the group under a relevant enactment, or would be so brought into account if the member were within the charge to corporation tax;

(d) a relevant income amount that is recognised in the financial statements of the group for the period, as an item of profit or loss, so far as it—

(i) is prevented from being brought into account for the purposes of corporation tax by a member of the group by section 322(2) or 323A of CTA 2009 (cases where credits not required to be brought into account), or

(ii) would be so prevented if the member were within the charge to corporation tax.

(4) In this section "downward adjustment" means any of the following amounts—

(a) a relevant income amount that is brought into account in the financial statements of the group for the period in determining the carrying value of an asset or liability;

(b) an amount that is included in the net group-interest expense of the group for the period by virtue of section 410(3) (capitalised expense written off);

(c) a relevant income amount that—

(i) in the financial statements of the group for the period is recognised in equity or shareholders' funds, and is not recognised as an item of profit or loss or as an item of other comprehensive income, and

(ii) is brought into account for the purposes of corporation tax by a member of the group under a relevant enactment, or would be so brought into account if the member were within the charge to corporation tax;

(d) a relevant expense amount that is recognised in the financial statements of the group for the period, as an item of profit or loss, so far as it—

(i) is prevented from being brought into account for the purposes of corporation tax by a member of the group by section 323A of CTA 2009 (cases where credits not required to be brought into account), or

(ii) would so prevented if the member were within the charge to corporation tax;

(e) a relevant expense amount that is recognised in the financial statements of the group for the period, as an item of profit or loss, so far as—

(i) the amount represents a dividend payable in respect of preference shares, and

(ii) those shares are recognised as a liability in the financial statements of the group for the period.

(5) The references in subsections (3)(a) and (4)(a) to amounts brought into account in determining the carrying value of an asset or liability do not include amounts so brought into account as the result of writing off any part of an amount which was itself so brought into account.

(6) In subsections (3)(c)(ii) and (4)(c)(ii), "relevant enactment" means—

(a) section 321 or 605 of CTA 2009 (credits and debits recognised in equity), or

(b) regulation 3A of the Taxation of Regulatory Capital Securities Regulations 2013 (S.I. 2013/3209) (amounts recognised in equity).

414 Qualifying net group-interest expense

(1) For the purposes of this Part the "qualifying net group-interest expense" of a worldwide group for a period of account of the group is (subject to subsection (2))—

$A - B$

where

A is the adjusted net group-interest expense of the group for the period (see section 413);

B is the sum of any downward adjustments (see subsection (3)).

(2) Where the amount determined under subsection (1) is negative, "the qualifying net group-interest expense" of the group for the period is nil.

(3) In this section "downward adjustment" means a relevant expense amount that meets the condition in subsection (4), so far as it relates to—

(a) a transaction with, or a financial liability owed to, a person who, at any time during the period, is a related party of a member of the group,

(b) results-dependent securities, or

(c) equity notes.

(4) The condition mentioned in subsection (3) is that the amount—

(a) is recognised in the financial statements of the group for the period, as an item of profit and loss, and is not (and is not comprised in) a downward adjustment for the purposes of section 413 (adjusted net group-interest expense), or

(b) is (or is comprised in) an upward adjustment for the purposes of that section.

(5) In a case where—

    (a) the person mentioned in subsection (3)(a) is not a related party of a member of the group during any part of the period of account, or

    (b) during any part of the period of account, the financial liability mentioned in subsection (3)(a) is owed to a person who is not a related party of a member of the group,

the amount of the downward adjustment under subsection (3)(a) is to be reduced by such amount (if any) as is attributable, on a just and reasonable basis, to that part.

415 Section 414: interpretation

(1) For the purposes of section 414 a person is treated as not being a related party of a member of the group at any time ("the relevant time") if at the relevant time—

    (a) the person would (apart from this subsection) be a related party of the member by virtue only of section 466(2) (parties to loan relationship treated as related parties by virtue of financial assistance provided by a related party), and

    (b) any of the following conditions is met in relation to the guarantee, indemnity or other financial assistance in question.

(2) The conditions are—

    (a) that the financial assistance is provided before 1 April 2017;

    (b) that the financial assistance is provided by a member of the group;

    (c) that the financial assistance relates only to an undertaking in relation to—

        (i) shares in the ultimate parent of the group, or

        (ii) loans to a member of the group;

    (d) that the financial assistance is a non-financial guarantee.

(3) Financial assistance is "a non-financial guarantee" if—

    (a) it guarantees the performance by any person of contractual obligations to provide goods or services to a member of the group,

    (b) it is given by the person providing the goods or services or by a related party of that person, and

    (c) the maximum amount for which the guarantor is liable does not exceed the consideration given under the contract for the provision of the goods or services.

(4) The reference in section 414(3)(b) to "results-dependent securities" is (subject to subsection (8)) to securities issued by an entity where the consideration given by the entity for the use of the principal secured depends (to any extent) on—

    (a) the results of the entity's business, or

    (b) the results of the business of any other entity that was a member of the group at any time during the period of account of the group.

In this subsection references to a business include part of a business.

(5) For the purposes of subsection (4) the consideration given by the entity for the use of the principal secured does not fall within paragraph (a) or (b) of that subsection merely because the terms of the security provide—

    (a) for the consideration to be reduced if the results mentioned in that paragraph improve, or

    (b) for the consideration to be increased if the results mentioned in that paragraph deteriorate.

(6) An amount does not fall within section 414(3)(b) so far as it is relevant alternative finance return (within the meaning given by section 1019(2) of CTA 2010).

(7) The reference in section 414(3)(c) to "equity notes" is (subject to subsection (8)) to equity notes within the meaning given by section 1016 of CTA 2010.

(8) A regulatory capital security (within the meaning of Taxation of Regulatory Capital Securities Regulations 2013 (S.I. 2013/3209)) is not—

    (a) a results-dependent security for the purposes of section 414(3)(b), or

    (b) an equity note for the purposes of section 414(3)(c).

Group-EBITDA

416 Group-EBITDA

(1) For the purposes of this Part "the group-EBITDA" of a worldwide group for a period of account of the group ("the relevant period of account") is—

    PBT + I + DA

    where—

        PBT is the group's profit before tax (which may be a negative amount) (see subsection (2));

I is the net group-interest expense of the group for the period (which may be a negative amount) (see section 410);

DA is the group's depreciation and amortisation adjustment (which may be a negative amount) (see subsection (3)).

(2) For the purposes of this Chapter a worldwide group's "profit before tax" is—

(a) the sum of the amounts that are recognised in the financial statements of the group for the period, as items of profit or loss, in respect of income of any description other than tax income, less

(b) the sum of the amounts that are recognised in the financial statements of the group for the period, as items of profit or loss, in respect of expenses of any description other than tax expense.

In this subsection "tax income" and "tax expense" have the meaning they have for accounting purposes.

(3) In this section the group's "depreciation and amortisation adjustment" means the sum of the following amounts (any of which may be negative)—

(a) the capital (expenditure) adjustment (see section 417);

(b) the capital (fair value movement) adjustment (see section 418);

(c) the capital (disposals) adjustment (see section 419).

(4) The following expressions have the same meaning in sections 417 to 419 as they have in this section—

"the relevant period of account";

"the group's profit before tax".

(5) For provision affecting amounts recognised in financial statements in respect of certain profits or losses arising from derivative contracts, see section 420.

417 The capital (expenditure) adjustment

(1) For the purposes of section 416, "the capital (expenditure) adjustment" is—

$A - B - C$

where—

A is the sum of the amounts (if any) in respect of relevant capital expenditure which are brought into account in determining the group's profit before tax;

B is the sum of the amounts (if any) in respect of relevant capital expenditure reversals which are brought into account in determining the group's profit before tax;

C is the sum of the amounts (if any) in respect of relevant capital income which are brought into account in determining the group's profit before tax.

(2) In this section "relevant capital expenditure" means—

(a) expenditure of a capital nature that relates to relevant assets (including any relevant expense amounts previously included in the carrying value of relevant assets) that is recognised in the relevant period of account by way of depreciation or amortisation, or as the result of an impairment review,

(b) expenditure of a capital nature that relates to relevant assets that is incurred and recognised in the relevant period of account, and

(c) amounts recognised in the relevant period of account by way of provision in respect of future expenditure of a capital nature that relates to relevant assets.

(3) In this section "relevant capital expenditure reversals" means the reversal in the relevant period of account of any relevant capital expenditure recognised in an earlier period of account.

(4) In this section "relevant capital income" means income of a capital nature that relates to relevant assets.

(5) In this Chapter "relevant asset" means an asset that is—

(a) plant, property and equipment,

(b) an investment property,

(c) an intangible asset,

(d) goodwill,

(e) shares in a company, or

(f) an interest in an entity which entitles the holder to a share of the profits of the entity.

(6) In subsection (5)—

(a) "plant, property and equipment" has the meaning it has for accounting purposes;

(b) "investment property" has the meaning it has for accounting purposes;

(c) "intangible asset" has the meaning it has for accounting purposes (and includes an internally-generated intangible asset);

(d) "goodwill" has the meaning it has for accounting purposes (and includes internally-generated goodwill);

(e) "entity" includes anything which is treated as an entity in the financial statements of the group (regardless of whether it has a legal personality as a body corporate).

Section 712(2) and (3) of CTA 2009 ("intangible asset" includes intellectual property) applies for the purposes of paragraph (c).

(7) An amount does not fall within A in subsection (1) if it is brought into account in determining a profit or loss on the disposal of a relevant asset.

418 The capital (fair value movement) adjustment

(1) In section 416, "the capital (fair value movement) adjustment" means the sum of any relevant fair value movements.

(2) For the purposes of subsection (1) there is a "relevant fair value movement" where—

(a) the carrying value of a relevant asset is measured, for the purposes of the financial statements of the group, using fair value accounting, and

(b) an amount representing a change in the carrying value of the asset is brought into account in determining the group's profit before tax.

(3) The amount of the relevant fair value movement is the amount of the change mentioned in subsection (2)(b) and—

(a) is a positive amount where the change is a loss;

(b) is a negative amount where the change is a profit.

(4) References in this section to a change in the carrying value of a relevant asset do not include a change where the amount brought into account in respect of the change as mentioned in subsection (2)(b) is of a revenue nature.

419 The capital (disposals) adjustment

(1) For the purposes of section 416, "the capital (disposals) adjustment" is—

$A - B + C$

where—

A is the sum of the amounts (if any) that are brought into account in determining the group's profit before tax and that represent losses on disposals of relevant assets;

B is the sum of the amounts (if any) that are brought into account in determining the group's profit before tax and that represent profits on disposals of relevant assets;

C is the sum of any recalculated profit amounts (see subsections (2) to (8)).

(2) For the purposes of the definition of C in subsection (1) there is a "recalculated profit amount" where the following two conditions are met.

(3) The first condition is that an amount is brought into account in determining the group's profit before tax in respect of a profit or loss on the disposal of a relevant asset.

(4) The second condition is that—

(a) the relevant proceeds, exceeds

(b) the relevant cost.

(5) The amount of the recalculated profit amount is the amount of the excess mentioned in subsection (4).

(6) In this section "the relevant proceeds" means the amount of income of a capital nature that is brought into account in determining the profit or loss mentioned in subsection (3).

(7) In this section "the relevant cost" means (subject to subsection (8)) the amount of expenditure of a capital nature that is brought into account in determining the profit or loss mentioned in subsection (3).

(8) For the purposes of subsection (7), any adjustment made to the amount brought into account as mentioned in that subsection is to be disregarded where the adjustment is in respect of amounts that—

(a) are otherwise recognised, in the financial statements of the group for the relevant period of account, as items of profit or loss, or

(b) were so recognised in the financial statements of the group for an earlier period.

(9) References in this section to a relevant asset include part of a relevant asset.

(10) References in this section to the disposal of a relevant asset do not include a disposal where the profit or loss (if any) on the disposal is of a revenue nature.

(11) The condition in subsection (3) is met even if no amount is brought into account as mentioned in that subsection if that is because no gain or loss accrued on the disposal; and subsections (6) to (8) apply accordingly.

Treatment of derivative contracts in financial statements of worldwide group

420 Derivative contracts subject to fair value accounting

(1) This section makes provision about the amounts recognised in a worldwide group's financial statements for a period of account ("the relevant period of account") in respect of derivative contracts.

(2) Subsection (3) applies where one or more excluded derivative contract amounts are recognised in the group's financial statements for the relevant period of account as items of profit or loss.

(3) The financial statements are treated for the purposes of this Part (apart from this section) as if the excluded derivative contract amounts were not recognised in the group's financial statements for the relevant period of account.

(4) In subsections (2) and (3) "excluded derivative contract amount" means an amount which would, on the relevant assumptions, be excluded from section 597(1) of CTA 2009 (amounts recognised in determining a company's profit or loss) as a result of a relevant provision of the Disregard Regulations.

(5) Subsection (6) applies where, on the relevant assumptions, one or more amounts ("replacement derivative contract amounts") would be brought into account by members of the group for the purposes of corporation tax in relevant accounting periods as a result of regulation 9 or 10 of the Disregard Regulations.

(6) The financial statements are treated for the purposes of this Part (apart from this section) as if the replacement derivative contract amounts were recognised in the group's financial statements for the relevant period of account.

(7) Subsection (9) applies if an accounting period in which a replacement derivative contract amount would, on the relevant assumptions, be brought into account for the purposes of corporation tax contains one or more disregarded periods.

(8) A "disregarded period" is any period falling within the accounting period—

　(a) which does not fall within the relevant period of account, or
　(b) throughout which the company is not a member of the group.

(9) Where this subsection applies, the replacement derivative contract amount mentioned in subsection (7) is reduced by such amount as is referable, on a just and reasonable basis, to the disregarded period or periods mentioned in that subsection.

(10) An amount may be reduced to nil under subsection (9).

421 Derivative contracts subject to fair value accounting: interpretation

(1) In section 420 "the relevant assumptions" means the following assumptions—

　(a) that all members of the group are within the charge to corporation tax;
　(b) that elections under regulation 6A of the Disregard Regulations have effect in relation to each derivative contract of each member of the group;
　(c) that paragraph (5) of regulation 7 of the Disregard Regulations is of no effect;
　(d) that where—

　　(i) a member of the group ("member A") holds a derivative contract,
　　(ii) the group has a hedging relationship between that derivative contract (on the one hand), and an asset, liability, receipt or expense (on the other), and
　　(iii) the asset, liability, receipt or expense is held, or is expected to be received or incurred, by a member of the group other than member A,

the asset, liability, receipt or expense is held, or is expected to be received or incurred, by member A;

　(e) that the financial statements of members of the group deal with derivative contracts and hedged items in the same way as they are dealt with in the group's financial statements.

(2) For the purposes of subsection (1)(d) the group has a "hedging relationship" between a derivative contract (on the one hand) and an asset, liability, receipt or

expense (on the other) if, were those things held, received or incurred by a single company, the company would have a hedging relationship between them.

(3) Regulation 2(5) of the Disregard Regulations (hedging relationships of a company) applies for the purposes of this section.

(4) For the purposes of section 420 and this section—

(a) "the Disregard Regulations" means the Loan Relationship and Derivative Contracts (Disregard and Bringing into Account of Profits and Losses) Regulations 2004 (S.I. 2004/3256);

(b) the following are "relevant provisions" of the Disregard Regulations—

(i) regulation 7 (fair value profits or losses arising from derivative contracts which are currency contracts);

(ii) regulation 8 (profits or losses arising from derivative contracts which are commodity contracts or debt contracts);

(iii) regulation 9 (profits or losses arising from derivative contracts which are interest rate contracts).

Effect of group-EBITDA (chargeable gains) election

422 Group-EBITDA (chargeable gains) election

(1) Where a group-EBITDA (chargeable gains) election has effect in relation to a period of account of a worldwide group ("the relevant period of account"), this Chapter applies in relation to the period subject to this section.

(2) Section 419 (the capital (disposals) adjustment) has effect as if—

(a) the definition of C in subsection (1) of that section did not apply, and

(b) instead, C were defined for the purposes of that section as—

(i) the sum of any relevant gains, less

(ii) the sum of any relevant losses,

or, where that is a negative amount, nil.

(3) For the purposes of this section, there is a "relevant gain" or "relevant loss" where condition A or B is met.

(4) Condition A is that a member of the group disposes of a relevant asset during the relevant period of account.

(5) Condition B is that—

(a) a member of the group ceases to be a member of the group during the relevant period of account, and

(b) the member held a relevant asset immediately before ceasing to be a member of the group.

(6) Where condition A is met, the amount of the relevant gain or relevant loss is the amount of the chargeable gain or allowable loss that would, on the assumptions in subsection (8), accrue to the member on the disposal.

(7) Where condition B is met, the amount of the relevant gain or relevant loss is the amount of the chargeable gain or allowable loss that would, on the assumptions in subsection (8), accrue to the member if the member—

(a) disposed of the relevant asset immediately before ceasing to be a member of the group, and

(b) received such consideration for that disposal as it is just and reasonable to attribute to it, having regard to the consideration received by the group for its interests in the member.

(8) The assumptions mentioned in subsections (6) and (7) are that—

(a) all members of the group are within the charge to corporation tax;

(b) Schedule 7AC to TCGA 1992 (exemptions for disposals by companies with substantial shareholdings) is of no effect;

(c) Part 2 (double taxation relief) is of no effect.

(9) Where—

(a) the sum of any relevant losses, exceeds

(b) the sum of any relevant gains,

the amount of the excess is treated as a relevant loss in relation to the period of account of the group immediately after the relevant period of account.

(10) In this section "relevant asset" does not include shares in (or other interests giving an entitlement to share in the profits of) a member of the group.

Effect of interest allowance (alternative calculation) election

423 Capitalised interest brought into account for tax purposes in accordance with GAAP

(1) Where an interest allowance (alternative calculation) election (see paragraph 16 of Schedule 7A) has effect in relation to a period of account of a worldwide group ("the relevant period of account"), this Chapter applies in relation to the period subject to this section.

(2) Section 413 (adjusted net group-interest expense of a worldwide group) has effect as if—

(a) subsections (3)(a) and (4)(a) (which relate to capitalised interest) did not apply in relation to a GAAP-taxable asset or liability, and
(b) subsections (3)(b) and (4)(b) (which relate to capitalised interest written off) did not apply in relation to a GAAP-taxable asset or liability.

(3) But subsection (2)(b) of this section is of no effect where the adjusted net group-interest expense of the group for a period of account before the relevant period of account included any amount by virtue of section 413(3)(a) or (4)(a) in respect of the GAAP-taxable asset or liability.

(4) For the purposes of this section an asset or liability is "GAAP-taxable" if any profit or loss for corporation tax purposes in relation to the asset or liability falls to be calculated in accordance with generally accepted accounting practice.

(5) For the purposes of this section, all members of the group are treated as within the charge to corporation tax.

424 Employers' pension contributions

(1) Where an interest allowance (alternative calculation) election has effect in relation to a period of account of a worldwide group, this Chapter applies in relation to the period subject to this section.

(2) The definition of "the group's profit before tax" in subsection (2) of section 416 has effect as if references to amounts that are recognised in the financial statements of the group for the period, as items of profit or loss, did not include amounts so recognised in respect of employer pension contributions.

(3) The group's profit before tax, as defined in that section, is reduced by the total of the relief to which members of the group are entitled, by virtue of sections 196 to 200 of FA 2004, in respect of relevant employer pension contributions paid during the period.

(4) In this section—

(a) "employer pension contributions" means contributions paid by an employer under a registered pension scheme in respect of an individual;
(b) employer pension contributions are "relevant" if they are paid at a time at which the employer is a member of the group.

425 Employee share acquisitions

(1) Where an interest allowance (alternative calculation) election has effect in relation to a period of account of a worldwide group, this Chapter applies in relation to the period subject to this section.

(2) The definition of "the group's profit before tax" in subsection (2) of section 416 has effect as if references to amounts that are recognised in the financial statements of the group for the period, as items of profit or loss, did not include amounts so recognised in respect of employee share acquisition arrangements.

(3) The group's profit before tax, as defined in that section, is reduced by such amount as, on a just and reasonable basis, reflects the effect on the group in the period of—

(a) deductions allowed to members of the group under Part 11 of CTA 2009 (relief for particular employee share acquisition schemes) and amounts treated as received by members of the group under that Part, and
(b) relief given to members of the group under Part 12 of that Act (other relief for employee share acquisitions).

(4) In this section "employee share acquisition arrangements" means arrangements the corporation tax treatment of which is determined under Part 11 or 12 of CTA 2009.

(5) For the purposes of this section, all members of the group are treated as within the charge to corporation tax.

426 Changes in accounting policy

(1) Where an interest allowance (alternative calculation) election has effect in relation to a period of account of a worldwide group ("the relevant period of account"), this Chapter applies in relation to the period subject to this section.

(2) The financial statements of the group for the relevant period of account are to be treated as subject to such adjustments as would be made to them under the change of accounting policy provisions if the group were a company that—

(a) was within the charge to corporation tax,

(b) held the assets and owed the liabilities recognised in the financial statements, to the extent that they are so recognised, and

(c) carried on the trades and other activities giving rise to amounts recognised in the financial statements as items of profit and loss.

(3) In this section "the change of accounting policy provisions" means—

(a) Chapter 14 of Part 3 of CTA 2009 (trading profits);

(b) sections 315 to 319 of that Act (loan relationships);

(c) sections 613 to 615 of that Act (derivative contracts);

(d) Chapter 15 of Part 8 of that Act (intangible fixed assets);

(e) the Loan Relationships and Derivative Contracts (Change of Accounting Practice) Regulations 2004 (S.I. 2004/3271).

(4) For the purposes of subsection (2)—

(a) the change of accounting policy provisions are to be read subject to the necessary modifications, and

(b) it is to be assumed that any election under the change of accounting policy provisions (as applied) has been made.

Effect of interest allowance (non-consolidated investment) election

427 Group interest and group-EBITDA

(1) Where an interest allowance (non-consolidated investment) election (see paragraph 17 of Schedule 7A) has effect in relation to a period of account of a worldwide group, this Chapter applies in relation to the period subject to this section.

(2) In this section and section 428 (which contains further interpretative provision)—

(a) "the principal worldwide group" means the worldwide group mentioned in subsection (1);

(b) "the relevant period of account" means the period of account mentioned in subsection (1).

(3) The financial statements of the principal worldwide group for the relevant period of account are treated as if—

(a) no relevant income amounts were recognised in them, as items of profit or loss, so far as they relate to financial liabilities owed to any member of the principal worldwide group by any member of an associated worldwide group, and

(b) no amounts were recognised in them, as items of profits or loss, in respect of any profit or loss attributable to an interest held by any member of the principal worldwide group in any member of an associated worldwide group

(4) The adjusted net group-interest expense of the principal worldwide group for the relevant period of account is treated as increased by the appropriate proportion of the adjusted net group-interest expense for the period of each associated worldwide group.

(5) The qualifying net group-interest expense of the principal worldwide group for the relevant period of account is treated as increased by the appropriate proportion of the qualifying net group-interest expense for the period of each associated worldwide group.

(6) The group-EBITDA of the principal worldwide group for the relevant period of account is treated as increased by the appropriate proportion of the group-EBITDA of each associated worldwide group for the period.

(7) In this section "the appropriate proportion", in relation to an associated worldwide group means the proportion of the profits or losses of the associated worldwide group arising in the relevant period of account to which the principal worldwide group is entitled.

428 Section 427: associated worldwide groups

(1) This section has effect for the purposes of section 427 and this section.

(2) "Associated worldwide group" means the worldwide group of which a specified non-consolidated associate is the ultimate parent.

(3) Where (apart from this subsection) a specified non-consolidated associate does not fall within section 473(1)(a) (conditions for being the ultimate parent of a worldwide group), it is treated as if it did fall within that provision.

(4) Where (apart from this subsection) financial statements of an associated worldwide group are not drawn up in respect of the relevant period of account, IAS financial statements of the associated worldwide group are treated as having been drawn up in respect of that period.

(5) The associated worldwide group's financial statements for the relevant period of account are treated as if no relevant expense amounts were recognised in them, as items of profit or loss, so far as they relate to financial liabilities owed to any member of the principal worldwide group by any member of the associated worldwide group.

(6) The reference in section 427(6) to profits or losses of the associated worldwide group to which the principal worldwide group is entitled does not include any profits or losses that relate to times when the non-consolidated associate is a member of the principal worldwide group.

(7) Subsection (8) has effect in the application of this Part (for the purposes mentioned in subsection (1)) in relation to the financial statements of an associated worldwide group for the relevant period of account.

(8) The associated worldwide group is treated—

(a) as having made an interest allowance (alternative calculation) election if and only if such an election has effect in relation to the relevant period of account of the principal worldwide group, and

(b) as not having made any other election under this Part.

(9) In this section "specified" means specified in the interest allowance (non-consolidated investment) election.

429 Meaning of "non-consolidated associate"

(1) An entity is a "non-consolidated associate" of a worldwide group, in relation to a period of account of the group ("the relevant period of account") if condition A, B or C is met.

(2) Condition A is that the entity is accounted for in the financial statements of the group for the relevant period of account—

(a) as a joint venture or an associate, and

(b) using the gross equity method or the equity method.

(3) Condition B is that—

(a) the entity is a partnership, and

(b) an interest allowance (consolidated partnership) election has effect in relation to the relevant period of account.

(4) Condition C is the entity is a non-consolidated subsidiary of the ultimate parent at any time during the relevant period of account.

(5) In this section the following expressions have the meaning they have for accounting purposes—

"associate";

"equity method";

"gross equity method";

"joint venture".

(6) In this section "entity" includes anything which is treated as an entity in the financial statements of the worldwide group (regardless of whether it has a legal personality as a body corporate).

(7) This section has effect for the purposes of this Part.

Effect of interest allowance (consolidated partnerships) election

430 Interest allowance (consolidated partnerships) election

(1) Where an interest allowance (consolidated partnerships) election (see paragraph 18 of Schedule 7A) has effect in relation to a period of account of a worldwide group, this Chapter applies in relation to the period subject to this section.

(2) The financial statements of the group for the period are treated as if—

(a) no amounts were recognised in them, as items of profit or loss, in respect of any income or expenses of a specified consolidated partnership, and

(b) instead, each specified consolidated partnership were accounted for using the equity method.

(3) In subsection (2)(b) "the equity method" has the meaning it has for accounting purposes.

(4) In this Part "consolidated partnership", in relation to a period of account of a worldwide group, means a partnership in relation to which conditions A and B are met.

(5) Condition A is that, in the financial statements of the worldwide group for the period, the results of the partnership are consolidated with those of the ultimate parent as the results of a single economic entity.

(6) Condition B is that at no time during the period does the partnership have a subsidiary that is a company.

(7) In this section—

(a) "specified" means specified in the interest allowance (consolidated partnerships) election or elections;

(b) "subsidiary" has the meaning given by international accounting standards.

Interpretation

431 Interpretation of Chapter

In this Chapter the following expressions have the meaning they have for accounting purposes—

"item of profit or loss";

"item of other comprehensive income".

CHAPTER 8

PUBLIC INFRASTRUCTURE

Overview

432 Overview of Chapter

(1) This Chapter —

(a) alters the way in which this Part has effect in relation to companies (referred to as "qualifying infrastructure companies") that are fully taxed in the United Kingdom, and

(b) operates by reference to the provision of public infrastructure assets or the carrying on of certain other related activities.

(2) In addition to the requirement for the company to be fully taxed in the United Kingdom, the qualifying requirements are—

(a) a requirement designed to ensure that the company's income and assets are referable to activities in relation to public infrastructure assets, and

(b) a requirement for the company to make an election (which may be revoked, subject to a 5-year rule in relation to the revocation and the ability to make a fresh election).

(3) Two different types of asset meet the definition of a "public infrastructure asset", namely—

(a) tangible assets forming part of the infrastructure of the United Kingdom (or the UK sector of the continental shelf) that meet a public benefit test, and

(b) buildings (or parts of buildings) that are part of a UK property business and are let (or sub-let) on a short-term basis to unrelated parties.

(4) In either case an asset counts as a public infrastructure asset only if—

(a) it has had, has or is likely to have an expected economic life of at least 10 years, and

(b) it is shown in a balance sheet of a member of the group that is fully taxed in the United Kingdom.

(5) The detail of the above tests is set out in sections 433 to 437.

(6) The substantive rules provide that an amount does not count as a tax-interest expense amount if—

(a) the creditor in relation to the amount is an unrelated party or another qualifying infrastructure company or the amount is in respect of a loan relationship entered into on or before 12 May 2016 (see sections 438 and 439), and

(b) the recourse of the creditor in relation to the amount is limited to the income or assets of, or shares in or debt issued by, a qualifying infrastructure company (ignoring certain financial assistance and certain non-financial guarantees).

(7) In addition—

(a) provision is made for adjusting the operation of this Part to take into account the effect of the above rules (for example, the tax-EBITDA of a qualifying infrastructure company is treated as nil (see section 441)),

(b) provision is made modifying the operation of this Chapter in the case of joint venture companies or partnerships or other transparent entities (see sections 444 to 447), and

(c) provision is made in relation to the decommissioning of a public infrastructure asset (see section 448).

Key concepts

433 Meaning of "qualifying infrastructure company"

(1) For the purposes of this Chapter a company is a "qualifying infrastructure company" throughout an accounting period if—

(a) it meets the public infrastructure income test for the accounting period (see subsections (2) to (4)),

(b) it meets the public infrastructure assets test for the accounting period (see subsections (5) to (10)),

(c) it is fully taxed in the United Kingdom in the accounting period (see subsection (11)), and

(d) it has made an election for the purposes of this section that has effect for the accounting period (see section 434).

(2) A company meets the public infrastructure income test for an accounting period if all, or all but an insignificant proportion, of its income for the accounting period derives from—

(a) qualifying infrastructure activities carried on by the company (see sections 436 and 437),

(b) shares in a qualifying infrastructure company, or

(c) loan relationships or other financing arrangements to which the only other party is a qualifying infrastructure company.

(3) A company also meets the public infrastructure income test for an accounting period if it has no income for the period.

(4) In determining whether the public infrastructure income test for an accounting period is met, income which does not derive from any of the matters mentioned in subsection (2)(a) to (c) is ignored if, having regard to all the circumstances, it is reasonable to regard the amount of the income as insignificant.

(5) A company meets the public infrastructure assets test for an accounting period if all, or all but an insignificant proportion, of the total value of the company's assets recognised in an appropriate balance sheet on each day in that period derives from—

(a) tangible assets that are related to qualifying infrastructure activities,

(b) service concession arrangements in respect of assets that are related to qualifying infrastructure activities,

(c) financial assets to which the company is a party for the purpose of the carrying on of qualifying infrastructure activities by the company or another associated qualifying infrastructure company,

(d) shares in a qualifying infrastructure company, or

(e) loan relationships or other financing arrangements to which the only other party is a qualifying infrastructure company.

(6) If a company has no assets recognised in an appropriate balance sheet on any day in an accounting period, the company is to be taken as meeting the public infrastructure assets test in respect of that day.

(7) In determining whether the public infrastructure assets test for an accounting period is met in respect of any day, the value of an asset which does not derive from any of the matters mentioned in subsection (5)(a) to (e) is ignored if, having regard to all the circumstances, it is reasonable to regard the value of the asset as insignificant.

(8) For the purposes of subsection (5)(a) and (b) assets are "related to qualifying infrastructure activities" in the case of a company if the assets are—

(a) public infrastructure assets (see section 436(2) and (5)) in relation to the company that are provided by the company, or

(b) other assets used in the course of a qualifying infrastructure activity carried on by the company or by an associated qualifying infrastructure company.

(9) For the purposes of this section the reference to the value of an asset recognised in an appropriate balance sheet of a company on a day is to the value which is, or would be, recognised in a balance sheet of the company drawn up on that day.

(10) A company is not to be taken as failing to meet the public infrastructure assets test for an accounting period if, ignoring this subsection, that test would have been failed on a particular day or days merely as a result of particular circumstances—

(a) which existed, and

(b) which were always intended to exist,

for a temporary period of an insignificant duration.

(11) A company is fully taxed in the United Kingdom in an accounting period if—

(a) every activity that the company carries on at any time in the accounting period is within the charge to corporation tax,

(b) the company has not made an election under section 18A of CTA 2009 (exemption for profits or losses of foreign permanent establishments) that has effect for the accounting period, and

(c) the company has not made a claim for relief under Chapter 2 of Part 2 (double taxation relief) for the accounting period.

434 Elections under section 433

(1) An election under section 433—

(a) must be made before the beginning of the accounting period in relation to which it is to have effect, and

(b) has effect in relation to that accounting period and all subsequent accounting periods (subject to subsections (2) to (4)).

(2) An election under section 433 may be revoked.

(3) A revocation of an election under section 433—

(a) must be made before the beginning of the accounting period from which the revocation is to have effect, but

(b) cannot have effect in relation to any accounting period that begins before the end of the period of 5 years beginning with the first day of the first accounting period in relation to which the election had effect.

(4) Once revoked, a fresh election may be made under section 433 but cannot have effect in relation to any accounting period that begins before the end of the period of 5 years beginning with the first day of the accounting period from which the revocation had effect.

(5) If—

(a) a qualifying infrastructure company transfers to another company a business, or a part of a business, that consists of the carrying on of qualifying infrastructure activities, and

(b) the transferee has not made an election under section 433 that has effect for the accounting period in which the transfer takes place,

the transferee is to be treated as if it had made the election under that section that the transferor had made.

(6) If a company has made an election under section 433 that has effect in relation to an accounting period, the company—

(a) may not make an election under section 18A of CTA 2009 that has effect for the accounting period, and

(b) may not make a claim for relief under Chapter 2 of Part 2 for the accounting period.

435 Group elections modifying the operation of sections 433 and 434

(1) Two or more companies which are members of the same worldwide group may jointly make an election under this section modifying the operation of sections 433 and 434 in relation to them for the times during which they remain members of that group.

(2) An election under this section—

(a) has effect from a date specified in the election;

(b) may be revoked jointly by the members of the group in relation to which the election has effect from a date specified in the revocation;

(c) ceases to have effect in relation to a company which gives a notice to an officer of Revenue and Customs, and to the companies in relation to which the election has effect, notifying them of its withdrawal from the election from a date specified in the notice.

(3) A date specified in an election, revocation or notice may not be before the date on which it is made or given.

(4) An election under this section which has effect at particular times ("relevant times") in relation to particular companies ("elected companies") modifies the operation of sections 433 and 434 as follows.

(5) If an elected company ("C") has made an election under section 433 which has effect for an accounting period that includes relevant times, that section has effect as if, in determining whether anything is insignificant for the purposes of section 433(2), (4), (5) or (7), C also had the income and assets that the other elected companies had at those times.

(6) If—

(a) an elected company ("C") has made an election under section 433 which has effect for an accounting period including relevant times, and
(b) C fails to meet one or more of the tests in subsection (1)(a) to (c) of that section in relation to that accounting period otherwise than as a result of this subsection,

all the other elected companies are also treated as failing to meeting those tests for so much of their accounting periods as consists of the relevant times in the accounting period of C.

(7) If, in a case where subsection (6) applies, the deemed failed period does not coincide with an accounting period of another elected company ("E"), the accounting period of E is treated for the purposes of this Part as if it consisted of separate accounting periods beginning and ending at such times as secure that none of the separate accounting periods fall partly within the deemed failed period.

(8) For this purpose "the deemed failed period" means the period consisting of the relevant times in the accounting period of C mentioned in subsection (6).

(9) All such apportionments as are necessary for the purposes of, or in consequence of, subsections (5) to (7) are to be made on a just and reasonable basis.

(10) If—

(a) elected companies have made elections under section 433 which have effect for accounting periods including relevant times, and
(b) more than half of those elected companies have each made an election under that section that has had effect for a period of at least 5 years,

section 434(3)(b) does not apply in relation to any of the elected companies.

436 Meaning of "qualifying infrastructure activity"

(1) For the purposes of this Chapter a company carries on a "qualifying infrastructure activity" if the company—

(a) provides an asset that is a public infrastructure asset in relation to it (see subsections (2) and (5)), or
(b) carries on any other activity that is ancillary to, or facilitates, the provision of an asset that is a public infrastructure asset in relation to it.

(2) For the purposes of this Chapter an asset is a "public infrastructure asset" in relation to a company at any time if—

(a) the asset is, or is to be, a tangible asset forming part of the infrastructure of the United Kingdom or the UK sector of the continental shelf,
(b) the asset meets the public benefit test (see subsections (3) and (4)),
(c) the asset has had, has or is likely to have an expected economic life of at least 10 years, and
(d) the asset meets the group balance sheet test (see subsection (10)) in relation to the company.

(3) An asset meets the "public benefit test" if—

(a) the asset is, or is to be, procured by a relevant public body, or
(b) the asset is, or is to be, used in the course of a regulated activity.

(4) An asset is used in the course of a "regulated activity" if its use—

(a) is regulated by an infrastructure authority (see section 437(2)), or
(b) could be regulated by an infrastructure authority if the authority exercised any of its powers.

(5) For the purposes of this Chapter a building, or part of a building, is also a "public infrastructure asset" in relation to a company at any time if—

(a) the company, or another member of the worldwide group of which it is a member at that time, carries on a UK property business consisting of or including the building or part,

(b) the building or part is, or is to be, let on a short-term basis to persons who, at that time, are not related parties of the company or member,

(c) the building or part has had, has or is likely to have an expected economic life of at least 10 years, and

(d) the building or part meets the group balance sheet test in relation to the company.

(6) A building, or part of a building, is "let" to a person if the person is entitled to the use of the building or part under a lease or other arrangement.

(7) A building, or part of a building, is let on a "short-term basis" if the lease or other arrangement in question—

(a) has an effective duration which is 50 years or less, and

(b) is not an arrangement to which any provision of Chapter 2 of Part 16 of CTA 2010 applies (finance arrangements).

(8) Whether or not a lease or other arrangement has an effective duration which is 50 years or less is determined in accordance with Chapter 4 of Part 4 of CTA 2009 (reading any reference to a lease as a reference to a lease or other arrangement within subsection (6)).

(9) For the purposes of this section references to a building or part of a building being let include the building or part being sub-let, and, accordingly, references to a lease include a sub-lease.

(10) An asset meets the "group balance sheet test" in relation to a company at any time if—

(a) an entry in respect of the asset is, or would be, recognised (whether as a tangible asset or otherwise) in a balance sheet of the company, or an associated company, that is drawn up at that time, and

(b) the company or associated company is within the charge to corporation tax at that time in respect of all of its sources of income and no election or claim mentioned in section 433(11)(b) or (c) has effect for a period including that time.

(11) For the purposes of this Chapter references to provision, in relation to a public infrastructure asset, include its acquisition, design, construction, conversion, improvement, operation or repair.

437 Section 436: supplementary

(1) In section 436 "infrastructure" includes—

(a) water, electricity, gas, telecommunications or sewerage facilities,

(b) oil pipelines, oil terminals or oil refineries,

(c) railway facilities (including rolling stock), roads or other transport facilities,

(d) health or educational facilities,

(e) facilities or housing accommodation provided for use by members of any of the armed forces or of any police force,

(f) court or prison facilities,

(g) waste processing facilities, and

(h) buildings (or parts of buildings) occupied by any relevant public body.

(2) Each of the following is an "infrastructure authority" for the purposes of section 436(4)—

(a) the Civil Aviation Authority so far as exercising functions in relation to the provision of airports (within the meaning of the Airports Act 1986),

(b) each of the following so far as exercising functions in relation to waste processing—

    (i) the Environment Agency,

    (ii) the Scottish Environmental Protection Agency,

    (iii) the Northern Ireland Environment Agency, or

    (iv) Natural Resources Wales,

(c) the Gas and Electricity Markets Authority,

(d) each of the following so far as exercising functions in relation to the management of ports or harbours—

    (i) a harbour authority within the meaning of the Harbours Act 1964, or

(ii) a harbour authority within the meaning of the Harbours Act (Northern Ireland) 1970,

(e) the Northern Ireland Authority for Utility Regulation,

(f) the Office of Communications so far as exercising functions in relation to the provision of electronic communication services (within the meaning of the Communications Act 2003) or the management of the radio spectrum,

(g) the Office of Nuclear Regulation,

(h) the Office of Rail and Road,

(i) the Oil and Gas Authority,

(j) the Water Services Regulation Authority or the Water Industry Commission for Scotland, or

(k) any other public authority which has functions of a regulatory nature exercisable in relation to the use of tangible assets forming part of the infrastructure of the United Kingdom or the UK sector of the continental shelf.

(3) The Commissioners may by regulations amend the definition of "infrastructure authority".

Exemption and related provision

438 Exemption for interest payable to third parties etc

(1) Amounts that arise to a qualifying infrastructure company in a relevant accounting period are not to be regarded for the purposes of this Part as tax-interest expense amounts of the company so far as they qualify as exempt amounts in that period (see subsections (2) and (3)).

(2) An amount qualifies as an exempt amount so far as it is attributable, on a just and reasonable apportionment, to the times in the relevant accounting period when—

(a) each creditor in relation to the amount is within subsection (3) or the amount is in respect of a qualifying old loan relationship (see section 439), and

(b) the recourse of each creditor in relation to the amount is limited to relevant infrastructure matters (see subsections (4) to (6)).

(3) A creditor is within this subsection if—

(a) the creditor is not a related party of the company, or

(b) the creditor is a company which is a qualifying infrastructure company,

but section 466(2) does not apply for the purposes of paragraph (a).

(4) The recourse of a creditor is limited to relevant infrastructure matters if, in the event that the company fails to perform its obligations in question, the recourse of the creditor is limited to—

(a) income of a qualifying infrastructure company,

(b) assets of a qualifying infrastructure company, or

(c) shares in or debt issued by a qualifying infrastructure company,

whether the income, assets, shares or debt relate to the company concerned or another qualifying infrastructure company.

(5) For the purposes of subsection (4) a guarantee, indemnity or other financial assistance in favour of the creditor is ignored if—

(a) it is provided before 1 April 2017, or

(b) it is provided at any later time by a person who, at that time, is not a related party of the company or is a relevant public body.

(6) For the purposes of subsection (4) a non-financial guarantee in favour of the creditor is ignored if—

(a) it guarantees the performance by any person of contractual obligations to provide goods or services to a qualifying infrastructure company,

(b) it is given by the person providing the goods or services or by a person who is a related party of that person, and

(c) the maximum amount for which the guarantor is liable does not exceed the consideration given under the contract for the provision of the goods or services.

(7) In this section "creditor" means—

(a) if the amount meets condition A in section 382, the person who is party to the loan relationship as creditor,

(b) if the amount meets condition B in that section, the person other than the company who is party to the derivative contract, and

(c) if the amount meets condition C in that section, the person other than the company who is party to the relevant arrangement or transaction.

439 Exemption in respect of certain pre-13 May 2016 loan relationships

(1) A loan relationship is a "qualifying old loan relationship" of a qualifying infrastructure company if—

(a) the company entered into the loan relationship on or before 12 May 2016, and

(b) as at that date, at least 80% of the total value of the company's future qualifying infrastructure receipts for the qualifying period was highly predictable by reference to qualifying public contracts,

but see subsection (8) for cases where a loan relationship is not a qualifying old loan relationship of the company.

(2) For the purposes of this section "the qualifying period" means—

(a) in a case where the loan relationship would cease to subsist at any time before 12 May 2026 (if any amendments of the loan relationship made on or after 12 May 2016 are ignored), the period beginning with 12 May 2016 and ending with that time, and

(b) in any other case, the period of 10 years beginning with 12 May 2016.

(3) For the purposes of this section "qualifying infrastructure receipts", in relation to a company ("C"), means—

(a) receipts arising from qualifying infrastructure activities carried on by C, and

(b) such proportion of the receipts arising from qualifying infrastructure activities carried on by another company as, on a just and reasonable basis, is attributable to C's interests in the other company (whether direct or indirect) arising as a result of shares or loans.

(4) For the purposes of this section receipts are highly predictable by reference to qualifying public contracts so far as their value can be predicted with a high degree of certainty because—

(a) the amounts of the receipts are fixed by a qualifying public contract, and

(b) the factors affecting the volume of receipts are fixed by a qualifying public contract or are otherwise capable of being predicted with a high degree of certainty.

(5) For this purpose any provision of a qualifying public contract (however expressed) that adjusts the amount of a receipt for changes in the general level of prices or earnings is to be ignored.

(6) For the purposes of this section a contract is a "qualifying public contract" if—

(a) it was entered into at any time on or before 12 May 2016 and, as at that time, it was expected to have effect for at least 10 years, and

(b) it was entered into either with a relevant public body or following bids made in an auction conducted by a relevant public body.

(7) If a qualifying old loan relationship is amended after 12 May 2016 so as to increase the amount lent or extend the period for which the relationship is to subsist—

(a) section 438 is to have effect as if none of those amendments were made (and, accordingly, the exemption under that section has no effect in relation to the increase in the amount or the period of the extension), and

(b) such apportionments of amounts in respect of the relationship are to be made as are just and reasonable.

(8) A loan relationship to which a qualifying infrastructure company is a party at any time is not a qualifying old loan relationship of the company at that or any subsequent time if, on the relevant assumptions, the condition in subsection (1)(b) would not have been met.

(9) The relevant assumptions are that—

(a) the assets held by the company at that time were the only assets that the company held on 12 May 2016,

(b) the assets held at that time by any other company in which it has interests (whether direct or indirect) arising as a result of shares or loans were the only assets that the other company held on 12 May 2016, and

(c) a qualifying infrastructure receipt could not be regarded as highly predictable if, on 12 May 2016, the public infrastructure asset in question did not exist or was not in the course of being constructed or converted.

(10) For the purposes of this section the value of a receipt on 12 May 2016 is taken to be its present value on that date, discounted using a rate that can reasonably be regarded as one that, in accordance with normal commercial criteria, is appropriate for the purpose.

(11) In this section "receipts" means receipts of a revenue nature.

440 Loans etc made by qualifying infrastructure companies to be ignored

(1) This section applies where—

(a) a company is a qualifying infrastructure company throughout an accounting period, and

(b) the company would (but for this section) have had tax-interest income amounts in the accounting period.

(2) For the purposes of this Part, the company is treated as if it did not have any tax-interest income amounts in the accounting period.

441 Tax-EBITDA of qualifying infrastructure company to be nil

(1) This section applies where a company is a qualifying infrastructure company throughout an accounting period.

(2) For the purposes of this Part, the tax-EBITDA of the company for the accounting period is nil.

442 Amounts of qualifying infrastructure company left out of account for other purposes

(1) This section applies where a company is a qualifying infrastructure company throughout a relevant accounting period.

(2) In calculating—

(a) the adjusted net group-interest expense of the worldwide group for the period of account concerned, or

(b) the qualifying net group-interest expense of the worldwide group for the period of account concerned,

amounts that are exempt amounts of the company under section 438, or are treated as mentioned in section 440, are to be left out of account.

(3) For the purposes of this Part the group EBITDA of the worldwide group for the period of account concerned is to be calculated as if the group did not include the company in respect of the relevant accounting period.

443 Interest capacity for group with qualifying infrastructure company etc

(1) If a worldwide group for a period of account includes a qualifying infrastructure company at any time, the general rule is that the interest capacity of the group for the period is calculated as if section 392 did not contain the de minimis provisions.

(2) But this is subject to an exception that depends on the following comparison.

(3) The following amounts must be compared with each other—

(a) the total disallowed amount of the group in the period calculated as if this Chapter (including subsection (1) of this section but ignoring the remainder of it) were contained in this Part ("the Chapter 8 amount"), and

(b) the total disallowed amount of the group in the period calculated as if this Chapter were not contained in this Part and as if section 392 contained only the de minimis provisions ("the ordinary amount").

(4) If the Chapter 8 amount exceeds the ordinary amount, the interest capacity of the worldwide group for the period is taken to be the de minimis amount (as defined by 392(3)).

(5) If the interest capacity of the worldwide group for the period is given by subsection (4), nothing else in this Chapter has effect in relation to the worldwide group for the period.

(6) For the purposes of this section the reference to section 392 not containing the de minimis provisions is a reference to that section not containing subsections (2) and (3) of that section.

(7) For the purposes of this section the reference to section 392 containing only the de minimis provisions is a reference to that section having effect as if for subsections (1) and (2) of that section there were substituted—

"(1) For the purposes of this Part the "interest capacity" of a worldwide group for a period of account of the group is the de minimis amount."

Supplementary

444 Joint venture companies

(1) This section makes modifications of this Part in relation to an accounting period of a qualifying infrastructure company ("the joint venture company") where—

(a) one or more qualifying infrastructure companies ("the qualifying investor or investors") have shares in the joint venture company,

(b) other persons ("the other investors") who are not qualifying infrastructure companies have all the other shares in the joint venture company,

(c) each of the investors (that is to say, the qualifying investor or investors and the other investors) has lent money to the joint venture company,

(d) the amounts each of the investors has lent stand in the same, or substantially the same, proportion as the shares in the joint venture company that each of them has,

(e) at all times in the accounting period the investors have the same rights in relation to the shares in or assets of the joint venture company and the same rights in relation to the money debt or debts in question, and

(f) the joint venture company makes an election for the purposes of this section that has effect for the accounting period (but see section 445 for further provision about elections).

(2) Section 401 has effect as if the qualifying investor or investors were not investors in the group for times in the accounting period falling in the relevant period of account.

(3) Section 427 has effect as if, in determining the appropriate proportion in relation to an associated worldwide group, it is assumed that the qualifying investor or investors were not investors in the group for times in the accounting period falling in the relevant period of account.

(4) In consequence of subsection (2) or (3), the shares of the qualifying investor or investors in the group are treated as distributed for times in the accounting period falling in the relevant period of account among the other investors in proportion to the actual shares of the other investors in the group.

(5) For the purposes of section 438 there is a reduction in any amount that would otherwise qualify as an exempt amount in the accounting period where—

(a) the exemption operates by reference to creditors being within subsection (3) of that section, and

(b) the creditor in relation to the amount is not an investor.

(6) The amount qualifying as an exempt amount is to be reduced so that only the qualifying proportion of it qualifies.

(7) For the purposes of this section—

"the qualifying proportion" means the proportion of the shares that the qualifying investor or investors have in the joint venture company in the accounting period, and

"the non-qualifying proportion" means the proportion of the shares that the other investors have in the joint venture company in the accounting period.

(8) The treatment mentioned in section 440(2) is to extend only to the qualifying proportion of the tax-interest income amounts in the accounting period.

(9) Section 441(2) has effect as if the tax-EBITDA of the company for the accounting period were the amount determined as follows.

Step 1
Find the tax-EBIDTA of the company for the accounting period if section 441 were ignored.
Step 2
The tax-EBITDA of the company for the accounting period is equal to the non-qualifying proportion of that amount.

(10) Section 442(3) has effect as if for the words "the group did not include the company" there were substituted "amounts of the company were limited to the non-qualifying proportion of those amounts".

445 Joint venture groups

(1) This section applies if the joint venture company is the ultimate parent of a multi-company worldwide group at any time in the accounting period.

(2) An election made by the joint venture company under section 444 in relation to the accounting period is of no effect unless all the other members of the group—

(a) are qualifying infrastructure companies for the accounting period,

(b) are wholly-owned subsidiaries of the joint venture company throughout the accounting period, and

(c) have the same accounting periods as the joint venture company.

(3) In determining whether the conditions in section 444(1)(c) to (e) are met in relation to the accounting period of the joint venture company, any loans made to any of the other members of the group are treated as if they were made to the joint venture company.

(4) If the joint venture company makes an election under section 444 for the accounting period, the modifications made by subsections (5) to (10) of that section are also to apply in relation to each of the other members of the group.

446 Joint ventures: supplementary

(1) If—

(a) the joint venture company makes an election under section 444 in relation to an accounting period,

(b) that company, or any member of the worldwide group of which it is a member, is the creditor for the purposes of section 438 in any case, and

(c) the company mentioned in that section in that case is a not a member of that group at any time in the accounting period,

section 438 has effect in that case as if subsection (3)(b) were of no effect in relation to that time.

(2) Section 434(1) to (5) apply to an election under section 444 as they apply to an election under section 433.

(3) For the purposes of section 444 the investors are not to be regarded as having the same rights in relation to the shares in or assets of the joint venture company, or in relation to the money debt or debts in question, at any time if—

(a) provision is in force at that time in respect of any of the relevant matters that differs in relation to different persons or has, or is capable of having, a different effect in relation to different persons (whether at that or any subsequent time),

(b) arrangements are in place at that time the effect of which is that, at that or any subsequent time, the rights of some persons in relation to any of the relevant matters differ, or will or may differ, from the rights of others in relation to the matters in question, or

(c) any other circumstances exist at that time as a result of which the rights of some persons in relation to any of the relevant matters cannot reasonably be regarded as being, in substance, the same rights as others in relation to the matters in question at that or any subsequent time.

(4) In this section—

(a) "the relevant matters" means the shares in or assets of the joint venture company or the money debt or debts in question,

(b) "rights" includes powers,

(c) "different persons" includes persons of a different class or description, and

(d) "arrangements" include any agreement, understanding, scheme, transaction or series of transactions (whether or not legally enforceable).

447 Partnerships and other transparent entities

(1) Subsections (2) to (4) apply where a company is a member of a partnership.

(2) For the purposes of section 433 the cases in which assets recognised in a balance sheet of the company are regarded as deriving their value from the matters mentioned in subsection (5)(a) to (e) of that section include any case where—

(a) the company's interest in the partnership is recognised in the balance sheet of the company, and

(b) that partnership interest derives its value from those matters.

(3) For the purposes of section 436 the cases in which an entry in respect of an asset is (or would be) recognised in a balance sheet of the company include any case where—

(a) the asset is (or would be) recognised in a balance sheet of the partnership, and

(b) the company has a significant interest in the partnership.

(4) For the purposes of section 438(4)—

(a) the obligations mentioned there include any case where the obligations are those of the partnership, and

(b) references to a qualifying infrastructure company in that case include the partnership.

(5) Subsections (2) to (4) apply (with any necessary modifications) in relation to transparent entities that are not partnerships as they apply in relation to partnerships.

(6) For this purpose an entity is "transparent" if it is not chargeable to corporation tax or income tax as a person (ignoring any exemptions).

448 Decommissioning

(1) This Chapter applies in relation to an activity consisting of the decommissioning of a public infrastructure asset as it applies in relation to its provision.

(2) In determining whether a company is a qualifying infrastructure company the following assets of the company are ignored (and the income arising from them is, accordingly, also ignored)—

    (a) any shares in a decommissioning fund, and

    (b) any loan relationships or other financing arrangements to which a decommissioning fund is party.

(3) A decommissioning fund is to be regarded as a qualifying infrastructure company.

(4) For the purposes of this section "a decommissioning fund" means a fund which—

    (a) holds particular investments for the sole purpose of funding activities for, or in connection with, the decommissioning or other provision of public infrastructure assets, and

    (b) is prevented from using the proceeds of the investments, or the income arising from them, for any purpose other than the purpose mentioned in paragraph (a) or returning surplus funds.

(5) In this section "decommissioning" includes demolishing and putting out of use.

449 Minor definitions for purposes of this Chapter

(1) For the purposes of this Chapter—

"balance sheet" means a balance sheet that is drawn up in accordance with generally accepted accounting practice,

"financial asset" has the same meaning as it has for accounting purposes,

"loan relationships or other financing arrangements" means—

    (a) loan relationships,

    (b) derivative contracts in relation to which the condition in section 387(4) is met (underlying subject matter to be interest rates etc),

    (c) finance leases, or

    (d) debt factoring or similar transactions, and

"the UK sector of the continental shelf" means the areas designated by Order in Council under section 1(7) of the Continental Shelf Act 1964.

(2) For the purposes of this Chapter references to a company which is "associated" with another company at any time are references to companies that are members of the same worldwide group at that time.

CHAPTER 9

CASES INVOLVING PARTICULAR TYPES OF COMPANY OR BUSINESS

Banking companies

450 Banking companies

(1) This section applies in relation to a banking company carrying on a trade so far as the activities of the trade consist of or include dealing in financial instruments.

(2) For the purposes of section 382 an amount is treated as meeting condition A, B or C if it is a debit arising directly from dealing in financial instruments other than one in respect of an impairment loss.

(3) An amount—

    (a) which is treated as meeting condition A, B or C for the purposes of section 382 as a result of subsection (2) of this section, and

    (b) which, but for that subsection, would not be a tax-interest expense amount,

is to be left out of account, or brought into account, as a result of section 377(2) or 380(2) after the second but before the third kind of tax-interest expense amounts mentioned there.

(4) For the purposes of section 385 an amount is treated as meeting condition A, B, C or D if it is a credit arising directly from dealing in financial instruments other than one in respect of the reversal of an impairment loss.

(5) In determining a relevant expense amount under section 411 in the case of the company, that section has effect as if it also included a reference to losses arising directly from dealing in financial instruments other than impairment losses.

(6) In determining a relevant income amount under section 411 in the case of the company, that section has effect as if it also included gains arising directly from dealing in financial instruments other than the reversal of impairment losses.

(7) In this section—

"banking company" has the same meaning as in Part 7A of CTA 2010 (see sections 269B to 269BD), and

"financial instruments" includes—

(a) loan relationships,

(b) derivative contracts, and

(c) shares or other securities.

Oil and gas

451 Oil and gas

(1) For the purposes of this Part any amount which is, or is taken into account in calculating—

(a) the ring fence income of a company within the meaning of section 275 of CTA 2010, or

(b) a company's aggregate gain or loss under section 197(3) of TCGA 1992,

is to be ignored.

(2) For the purpose of applying subsection (1) in relation to the financial statements of a worldwide group of which the company is a member such adjustments are to be made to those statements as are just and reasonable.

REITs

452 Real Estate Investment Trusts

(1) This section applies if a company (a "property rental business company")—

(a) is a company which has profits for an accounting period which are not charged to corporation tax as a result of section 534(1) or (2) of CTA 2010, or

(b) is a company to which gains accrue in an accounting period that are not chargeable gains as a result of section 535(1) or (5) of CTA 2010.

(2) In this section "the residual business company" means the company which—

(a) so far as it carries on residual business, is treated, as a result of section 541 of CTA 2010, as a separate company distinct from the property rental business company, but

(b) ignoring that section, is in fact the same company as the property rental business company.

(3) In applying the provisions of this Part—

(a) the property rental business company and the residual business company are at all times to be regarded as separate members of the same worldwide group (despite the provisions of section 541(3) of CTA 2010), but

(b) in the case of the application of section 433 (qualifying infrastructure company), the property rental business company and the residual business company are to be regarded as being one company (and any election (or its revocation) is, therefore, regarded as made by each company).

(4) This Part has effect as if—

(a) section 534(1) and (2) of CTA 2010, and

(b) section 535(1) and (5) of CTA 2010,

do not apply in relation to the property rental business company for the accounting period.

(5) The allocated disallowance for the property rental business company (if any) for the accounting period must be limited to such amount as secures that section 530(3)(b) or (5) of CTA 2010 (distribution of profits not required if would result in unlawful distribution) do not apply.

(6) This subsection—

(a) sets out steps to be taken in order to facilitate the operation of Chapter 2 (disallowance and reactivation of tax-interest expense amounts), and

(b) has effect in relation to an accounting period of the residual business company whether or not it has net tax-interest expense referable to that period.

If the residual business company does not have net tax-interest expense referable to that period, it is treated for the purposes of steps 1 to 4 in the rest of this subsection as if it had instead a nil amount of tax-interest expense referable to that period.

Step 1

Determine the maximum amount that could be the allocated disallowance for the property rental business company for the accounting period if subsection (5) were ignored and the maximum amount that could be the allocated disallowance for the residual business company for the accounting period (ignoring step 5).

The sum of those maximum amounts is referred to in this subsection as "the total REIT expenses".

Step 2

Determine the amount (if any) that is the allocated disallowance for the property rental business for the accounting period, applying subsection (5) and all other rules in this Part.

This amount is referred to in this subsection as "the actual disallowed amount".

Step 3

Deduct from the total REIT expenses the actual disallowed amount.

Step 4

Determine whether so much of the total REIT expenses as remains after step 3 exceeds the net tax-interest expense of the residual business company referable to the accounting period (ignoring step 5).

Step 5

If the application of step 4 produces an excess, the residual business company is required to bring into account in the accounting period matching tax-interest expense and income amounts in accordance with the following provisions of this section.

(7) The residual business company—

(a) must bring a tax-interest expense amount equal to the excess into account in the accounting period, and

(b) must bring a tax-interest income amount equal to the excess into account in the accounting period,

but nothing in this subsection affects any calculation required under any other provision of this Part in relation to the accounting period of the residual business company.

(8) The bringing into account of a tax-interest expense amount under subsection (7) is subject to the operation of the other provisions of this Part (which may result in some or all of the amount not being brought into account).

(9) The tax-interest expense amount under subsection (7) must be matched in amount and nature to an amount comprised in the total REIT expenses.

Section 377(2) to (4) (which, subject to an election made by the company, set out the order in which amounts are left out of account) apply for the purposes of this subsection.

(10) The tax-interest expense or income amounts under subsection (7) are treated as being of the same nature as each other.

(11) An interest restriction return—

(a) must, in relation to any company carrying on residual business or property rental business, specify that fact, and

(b) must contain information about how the return has taken into account the effect of this section.

(12) Expressions which are used in this section and in Part 12 of CTA 2010 have the same meaning in this section as they have in that Part.

Insurance companies etc

453 Insurance entities

(1) This section applies where—

(a) an insurance entity is a member of a worldwide group,

(b) the entity has a subsidiary ("S") which it holds as a portfolio investment, and

(c) apart from this section, S would be a member of the group.

(2) For the purposes of this Part—

(a) the group does not include S (or its subsidiaries), and

(b) accordingly, none of those entities is regarded as a consolidated subsidiary of any member of the group.

(3) For the purposes of this section an insurance entity holds an interest in an entity as "a portfolio investment" if—

(a) the insurance entity holds the interest as an investment, and

(b) the insurance entity judges the value that the interest has to it wholly or mainly by reference to the market value of the interest.

(4) In this section—

"insurance entity" means—

(a) an insurance company,

(b) a friendly society within the meaning of Part 3 of FA 2012 (see section 172), or

(c) a body corporate which carries on underwriting business as a member of Lloyd's, and

"subsidiary" has the meaning given by international accounting standards.

454 Members of Lloyd's

In the case of a body corporate carrying on underwriting business as a member of Lloyd's—

(a) any reference in this Part to an amount being brought into account under Part 3 of CTA 2009 as a result of section 297 or 573 of that Act is to be read as a reference to its being brought into account under that Part as a result of section 219 of FA 1994, and

(b) any reference in this Part to a derivative contract is to be read as if subsection (3) of section 226 of FA 1994 (which provides that relevant contracts forming part of a premium trust fund are not derivative contracts) were omitted.

Shipping companies

455 Shipping companies subject to tonnage tax

(1) This section applies in relation to an accounting period of a tonnage tax company.

(2) The company's tonnage tax profits for the accounting period are treated as nil for the purpose of calculating the company's adjusted corporation tax earnings for the accounting period under section 406(2).

(3) In this section "tonnage tax company" and "tonnage tax profits" have the same meaning as in Schedule 22 to FA 2000 (see paragraphs 2 to 5).

Fair value accounting

456 Creditor relationships of companies determined on basis of fair value accounting

(1) A company may elect for all of its creditor relationships which are dealt with on the basis of fair value accounting ("fair-value creditor relationships") to be subject to the provision made by this section for all of its accounting periods.

(2) For the purpose of calculating under this Part—

(a) tax-interest expense amounts of the company, and

(b) tax-interest income amounts of the company,

the relevant loan relationship debits and relevant loan relationship credits in respect of the company's fair-value creditor relationships are instead to be determined for the accounting periods on an amortised cost basis of accounting.

(3) If—

(a) a company has a hedging relationship between a relevant contract ("the hedging instrument") and the asset representing a loan relationship subject to the election, and

(b) the loan relationship is dealt with in the company's accounts on the basis of fair value accounting,

it is to be assumed in applying the amortised cost basis of accounting that the hedging instrument has where possible been designated for accounting purposes as a fair value hedge of the loan relationship.

(4) An election under this section—

(a) must be made before the end of 12 months from the end of the relevant accounting period,

(b) has effect for that accounting period and all subsequent accounting periods, and

(c) is irrevocable.

(5) For this purpose "relevant accounting period" means—

(a) the first accounting period in which the company has a fair-value creditor relationship, or

(b) if that accounting period has ended before 1 April 2017, the first accounting period in relation to which any provision of this Part applies.

(6) In this section "amortised cost basis of accounting", in relation to an accounting period, has the same meaning as in Part 5 of CTA 2009 (see section 313), but, in the case of creditor relationships relating to insurance activities, as if that basis of accounting required recognition only of—

(a) interest accrued for the period in respect of the creditor relationships, or
(b) if the creditor relationships arise as a result of section 490 of CTA 2009 (OEICs, unit trusts and offshore funds), amounts that can reasonably be regarded as equating to interest accrued for the period in respect of those relationships.

(7) In subsection (6) "creditor relationships relating to insurance activities" means creditor relationships which—

(a) are held by an insurance company, a friendly society within the meaning of Part 3 of FA 2012 (see section 172) or a body corporate which carries on underwriting business as a member of Lloyd's, or
(b) are held in connection with the regulation of underwriting business carried on by members of Lloyd's.

(8) The Commissioners may by regulations amend the definition of "amortised cost basis of accounting" in this section.

(9) Other expressions which are used in this section and in Part 5 of CTA 2009 have the same meaning in this section as they have in that Part.

457 Elections under section 456: deemed debits and credits

(1) This section applies if—

(a) as a result of an election under section 456, the tax-interest expense amounts of a company include notional debits for an accounting period,
(b) the worldwide group of which the company is a member is subject to interest restrictions for a period of account, and
(c) the total disallowed amount for the period of account consists of or includes the notional debits.

(2) In order to facilitate the operation of Chapter 2 (disallowance and reactivation of tax-interest expense amounts)—

(a) the company must bring a debit equal to the amount of the notional debits into account in the accounting period, and
(b) the company must bring a credit equal to the amount of the notional debits into account in the accounting period,

but nothing in this subsection affects any calculation required under any other provision of this Part in relation to the accounting period of the company.

(3) The bringing into account of a debit under subsection (2)(a) is subject to the operation of the other provisions of this Part (which may result in some or all of the debit not being brought into account).

(4) The debits and credits under subsection (2) are of the same nature as the notional debits that give rise to them.

(5) For the purposes of this section a debit is a "notional debit" if the debit is created as a result of the determination required by the election or so far as the amount of the debit is increased as a result of that determination.

Exemption for tax-interest expense or income amounts

458 Co-operative and community benefit societies etc

(1) This section applies where—

(a) apart from this section, an amount would be a tax-interest expense amount or tax-interest income amount of a company as a result of meeting condition A in section 382 or 385 (loan relationships), and
(b) the amount meets that condition only because of section 499 of CTA 2009 (certain sums payable by co-operative and community benefit societies or UK agricultural or fishing co-operatives treated as interest under loan relationship).

(2) The amount is treated as not being a tax-interest expense amount or tax-interest income amount of the company.

459 Charities

(1) This section applies where—

(a) apart from this section, an amount would be a tax-interest expense amount of a company as a result of meeting condition A in section 382 (loan relationship debits),

(b) the creditor is a charity,

(c) the company is a wholly-owned subsidiary of the charity, and

(d) the charitable gift condition is met at all times during the accounting period in which the amount is (or apart from this Part would be) brought into account.

(2) The amount is treated as not being a tax-interest expense amount of the company.

(3) For the purposes of this section the "charitable gift condition" is met at any time at which, were the company to make a donation to the charity at that time, it would be a qualifying charitable donation (see section 190 of CTA 2010).

(4) In this section—

"charity" has the same meaning as in Chapter 2 of Part 6 of CTA 2010 (see section 202 of that Act as read with Schedule 6 to FA 2010), and

"the creditor" means the person who is party to the loan relationship in question as creditor.

Leases

460 Long funding operating leases and finance leases

(1) In calculating a company's adjusted corporation tax earnings for an accounting period under section 406(2), each of the following amounts is to be ignored—

(a) the amount of a deduction under section 363 of CTA 2010 (lessor under long funding operating lease);

(b) the amount by which a deduction is reduced under section 379 of CTA 2010 (lessee under long funding operating lease);

(c) the capital component of the company's rental earnings under a finance lease which is not a long funding finance lease;

(d) the amount of depreciation in respect of any asset leased to the company under a finance lease which is not a long funding finance lease.

(2) The definition of "relevant capital expenditure" in section 417(2) includes the amount of depreciation in respect of any relevant asset leased under a finance lease for some or all of the relevant period of account to a company that is a member of the worldwide group in question.

(3) For the purposes of this section the capital component of a company's rental earnings under a finance lease is so much of those earnings as do not constitute tax-interest income amounts of the company.

(4) For the purposes of this section the amount of depreciation in respect of any asset leased to a company under a finance lease is the amount which, in accordance with generally accepted accounting practice, falls (or would fall) to be shown as depreciation in respect of the asset in the applicable accounts.

(5) In this section "the applicable accounts" are—

(a) in a case within subsection (1)(d), the company's accounts for any period, and

(b) in a case within subsection (2), the financial statements of the worldwide group for the relevant period of account in question.

(6) In this section "long funding finance lease" means a finance lease which is a long funding lease (within the meaning of section 70G of CAA 2001).

CHAPTER 10

ANTI-AVOIDANCE

461 Counteracting effect of avoidance arrangements

(1) Any tax advantage that would (in the absence of this section) arise from relevant avoidance arrangements is to be counteracted by the making of such adjustments as are just and reasonable.

(2) Any adjustments required to be made under this section (whether or not by an officer of Revenue and Customs) may be made by way of an assessment, the modification of an assessment, amendment or disallowance of a claim or otherwise.

(3) For the purposes of this section arrangements are "relevant avoidance arrangements" if conditions A and B are met.

(4) Condition A is that the main purpose, or one of the main purposes, of the arrangements is to enable a company to obtain a tax advantage.

(5) Condition B is that the tax advantage is attributable (or partly attributable) to any company—

(a) not leaving tax-interest expense amounts out of account that it otherwise would have left out of account,

(b) leaving tax-interest expense amounts out of account that are lower than they otherwise would have been,

(c) leaving tax-interest expense amounts out of account in an accounting period other than that in which it otherwise would have left them out of account,

(d) bringing tax-interest expense amounts into account that it otherwise would not have brought into account,

(e) bringing tax-interest expense amounts into account that are higher than they otherwise would have been, or

(f) bringing tax-interest expense amounts into account in an accounting period other than that in which it otherwise would have brought them into account.

(6) In subsection (5)—

(a) references to leaving amounts out of account are to leaving them out of account under this Part;

(b) references to bringing amounts into account are to bringing them into account under this Part.

(7) In this section—

"arrangements" includes any agreement, understanding, scheme, transaction or series of transactions (whether or not legally enforceable), and

"tax advantage" includes—

(a) relief or increased relief from tax,

(b) repayment or increased repayment of tax,

(c) avoidance or reduction of a charge to tax or an assessment to tax,

(d) avoidance of a possible assessment to tax,

(e) deferral of a payment of tax or advancement of a repayment of tax, and

(f) avoidance of an obligation to deduct or account for tax.

(8) For the purposes of the definition of "tax advantage" any reference to tax includes—

(a) any amount chargeable as if it were corporation tax or treated as if it were corporation tax, and

(b) diverted profits tax.

CHAPTER 11

INTERPRETATION ETC

Related parties

462 Expressions relating to "related parties": introduction

(1) Section 463 sets out the circumstances in which a person is a related party of another person for the purposes of this Part.

(2) That section—

(a) applies generally in relation to any amount, and

(b) is supplemented by sections 464 and 465 (which contain provisions that have effect for the purposes of that section).

(3) Sections 466 and 467 make provision for treating persons as if they were related parties of each other but only in relation to certain matters.

(4) Sections 468 to 472—

(a) make provision for treating persons as if they were not related parties of each other but only in relation to certain matters, and

(b) take priority over sections 466 and 467.

463 Whether a person is generally a "related party" of another

(1) For the purposes of this Part a person ("A") is a "related party" of another person ("B")—

(a) throughout any period for which A and B are consolidated for accounting purposes,

(b) on any day on which the participation condition is met in relation to them, or

(c) on any day on which the 25% investment condition is met in relation to them.

(2) A and B are consolidated for accounting purposes for a period if—

(a) their financial results for a period are required to be comprised in group accounts,

(b) their financial results for the period would be required to be comprised in group accounts but for the application of an exemption, or

(c) their financial results for a period are in fact comprised in group accounts.

(3) In subsection (2) "group accounts" means accounts prepared under—

(a) section 399 of the Companies Act 2006, or

(b) any corresponding provision of the law of a territory outside the United Kingdom.

(4) The participation condition is met in relation to A and B ("the relevant parties") on a day if, within the period of 6 months beginning or ending with that day—

(a) one of the relevant parties directly or indirectly participates in the management, control or capital of the other, or

(b) the same person or persons directly or indirectly participate in the management, control or capital of each of the relevant parties.

(5) For the interpretation of subsection (4), see sections 157(1), 158(4), 159(1) and 160(1) (which have the effect that references in that subsection to direct or indirect participation are to be read in accordance with provisions of Chapter 2 of Part 4).

(6) If one of the relevant parties is a securitisation company within the meaning of Chapter 4 of Part 13 of CTA 2010, the relevant parties are not to be regarded as related parties of each other as a result of subsection (4) merely by reference to the fact that—

(a) the securitisation company is held by a trustee of a settlement, and

(b) the other relevant party is a settlor in relation to that settlement.

(7) The 25% investment condition is met in relation to A and B if—

(a) one of them has a 25% investment in the other, or

(b) a third person has a 25% investment in each of them.

(8) Sections 464 and 465 apply for the purpose of determining whether a person has a "25% investment" in another person.

464 Meaning of "25% investment"

(1) A person ("P") has a 25% investment in another person ("C") if—

(a) P possesses or is entitled to acquire 25% or more of the voting power in C,

(b) in the event of a disposal of the whole of the equity in C, P would receive 25% or more of the proceeds,

(c) in the event that the income in respect of the equity in C were distributed among the equity holders in C, P would receive 25% or more of the amount so distributed, or

(d) in the event of a winding-up of C or in any other circumstances, P would receive 25% or more of C's assets which would then be available for distribution among the equity holders in C in respect of the equity in C.

(2) In this section references to the equity in C are to—

(a) the shares in C other than restricted preference shares, or

(b) loans to C other than normal commercial loans.

(3) For this purpose "shares in C" includes—

(a) stock, and

(b) any other interests of members in C.

(4) For the purposes of this section a person is an equity holder in C if the person possesses any of the equity in C.

(5) For the purposes of this section—

"normal commercial loan" means a loan which is a normal commercial loan for the purposes of section 158(1)(b) or 159(4)(b) of CTA 2010, and

"restricted preference shares" means shares which are restricted preference shares for the purposes of section 160 of CTA 2010.

(6) In applying for the purposes of this section the definitions of "normal commercial loan" and "restricted preference shares" in a case where—

(a) C is not a company, or

(b) C is a company which does not have share capital,

sections 160(2) to (7) and 161 to 164 of CTA 2010 (and any other relevant provisions of that Act) have effect with the necessary modifications.

(7) In this section references to a person receiving any proceeds, amount or assets include—

(a) the direct or indirect receipt of the proceeds, amount or assets, and

(b) the direct or indirect application of the proceeds, amount or assets for the person's benefit,

and it does not matter whether the receipt or application is at the time of the disposal, distribution, winding-up or other circumstances or at a later time.

(8) If—

(a) there is a direct receipt or direct application of any proceeds, amount or assets by or for the benefit of a person ("A"), and

(b) another person ("B") directly or indirectly owns a percentage of the equity in A,

there is, for the purposes of subsection (7), an indirect receipt or indirect application of that percentage of the proceeds, amount or assets by or for the benefit of B.

(9) For this purpose the percentage of the equity in A directly or indirectly owned by B is to be determined by applying the rules in sections 1155 to 1157 of CTA 2010 with such modifications (if any) as may be necessary.

(10) Subsection (7) is not to result in a person being regarded as having a 25% investment in another person merely as a result of their being parties to a normal commercial loan.

(11) Any reference in this section, in the case of a person who is a member of a partnership, to the proceeds, amount or assets of the person includes the person's share of the proceeds, amount or assets of the partnership (apportioning those things between the partners on a just and reasonable basis).

465 Attribution of rights and interests

(1) In determining for the purposes of section 464 the investment that a person ("P") has in another person, P is to be taken to have all of the rights and interests of—

(a) any person connected with P,

(b) any person who is a member of a partnership, or is connected with a person who is member of a partnership, of which P is a member, or

(c) any person who is a member of a partnership, or is connected with a person who is a member of a partnership, of which a person connected with P is a member.

(2) For the purposes of subsection (1)—

(a) section 1122 of CTA 2010 ("connected" persons) applies but as if subsections (7) and (8) of that section were omitted, but

(b) a person is not to be regarded as connected with another person merely as a result of their being parties to a loan that is a normal commercial loan for the purposes of section 464.

(3) In determining for the purposes of section 464 the investment that a person ("P") has in another person ("U"), P is to be taken to have all of the rights and interests of a third person ("T") with whom P acts together in relation to U.

(4) For this purpose P "acts together" with T in relation to U if (and only if)—

(a) for the purpose of influencing the conduct of U's affairs—

(i) P is able to secure that T acts in accordance with P's wishes (or vice versa), or

(ii) T can reasonably be expected to act, or typically acts, in accordance with P's wishes (or vice versa),

(b) P and T are party to an arrangement that it is reasonable to conclude is designed to affect the value of any equity in U possessed by T, or

(c) the same person manages some or all of any equity in U possessed by P and T.

In paragraphs (b) and (c) references to equity in U are to be read in accordance with section 464.

(5) But P does not "act together" with T in relation to U under subsection (4)(c) if—

(a) the managing person does so as the operator of different collective investment schemes, and

(b) the management of the schemes is not coordinated for the purpose of influencing the conduct of U's affairs.

(6) For this purpose "collective investment scheme" and "operator" have the same meaning as in Part 17 of the Financial Services and Markets Act 2000 (see sections 235 and 237).

(7) In determining for the purposes of section 464 the investment that a person ("P") has in another person ("U"), P is to be taken to have all of the rights and interests of one or more third persons with whom P has entered into a qualifying arrangement in relation to U.

(8) For this purpose P has entered into a qualifying arrangement with one or more third persons in relation to U if they are parties to an arrangement concerning U as a result of which, by reference to shares held, or to be held, by any one or more of them in U, they can reasonably be expected to act together—

(a) so as to exert greater influence in relation to U than any one of them would be able to exert if acting alone, or

(b) otherwise so as to be able to achieve an outcome in relation to U that, if attempted by any one of them acting alone, would be significantly more difficult to achieve.

(9) For this purpose the reference to shares in U includes shares in U that may be held as a result of the exercise of any right or power and includes rights or interests in U that are of a similar character to shares.

(10) In this section "arrangement" includes any agreement, understanding, scheme, transaction or series of transactions (whether or not legally enforceable).

466 Certain loan relationships etc to be treated as made between related parties

(1) This section—

(a) makes provision for treating a person ("D") who is not a related party of another person ("C") as if they were related parties of each other but only in respect of particular liabilities or transactions, and

(b) is expressed to apply in relation to loan relationships but also applies (with any necessary modifications) in relation to any other financial liability owed to, or any transaction with, C.

(2) If at any time—

(a) D is party to a loan relationship as debtor and C is party to the relationship as creditor, and

(b) another person ("G") who is a related party of D provides a guarantee, indemnity or other financial assistance in respect of the liability of D that represents the loan relationship,

D and C are treated for the purposes of this Part as if, in relation to the loan relationship concerned (and anything done under or for the purposes of it), they were related parties of each other at that time.

(3) Subsection (2) is subject to—

(a) section 415 (qualifying net group-interest expense), and

(b) section 438(3) (infrastructure: interest payable to third parties etc).

(4) If at any time—

(a) D is party to a loan relationship as debtor and C is party to the relationship as creditor, and

(b) another person ("G") who is a related party of D indirectly stands in the position of a creditor as respects the debt in question by reference to a series of loan relationships or other arrangements,

D and C are treated for the purposes of this Part as if, in relation to the loan relationship concerned (and anything done under or for the purposes of it), they were related parties of each other at that time.

(5) For the purposes of this section "arrangements" include any agreement, understanding, scheme, transaction or series of transactions (whether or not legally enforceable).

467 Holdings of debt and equity in same proportions

(1) This section applies at any time where—

(a) persons have lent money to another person ("U"),

(b) the lenders also have shares or voting power in U,

(c) the amounts each of the lenders has lent stand in the same, or substantially the same, proportion as the shares or voting power in U that each of them has, and

(d) for the purposes of section 464 the lenders (taken together) have a 25% investment in U.

(2) The lenders are treated for the purposes of this Part as if, in relation to the loans (and anything done under or for the purposes of them), they were related parties of U at that time (so far as that would not otherwise be the case).

(3) If—

(a) some or all of the rights under the loan are transferred, and

(b) the transferred rights are held by, or for the benefit of, another person ("the transferee") at any time,

the transferee is treated for the purposes of this Part as if, in relation to the loan (and anything done under or for the purposes of it), the transferee were a related party of U at that time (so far as that would not otherwise be the case).

(4) This applies whether or not the transferee has any shares or voting power in U.

(5) For the purposes of this section references to shares in U include shares in U that may be held as a result of the exercise of any right or power and include rights or interests in U that are of a similar character to shares.

(6) This section applies (with any necessary modifications) in relation to any other financial liability owed to, or any transaction with, U as it applies to loans made to U.

468 Debts with same rights where unrelated parties hold more than 50%

(1) This section applies if—

(a) a person ("D") is party to a loan relationship as debtor in a period of account of a worldwide group of which it is a member,

(b) a person ("C") who is party to the loan relationship as creditor is a related party of D at any time in that period,

(c) there are persons ("the relevant creditors") other than C who are parties to the loan relationship, or are parties to other loan relationships entered into at the same time, as creditors but who are not related parties of D at any time in that period,

(d) at all times in that period the rights of the relevant creditors are rights in relation to at least 50% of the total amount of the money debt or debts in question, and

(e) at all times in that period C and the relevant creditors have the same rights in relation to the money debt or debts in question.

(2) D and C are treated for the purposes of this Part as if, in relation to the loan relationship concerned (and anything done under or for the purposes of it), they were not related parties of each other at any time in that period.

(3) Persons are not to be regarded as having the same rights in relation to a money debt or debts at any time if—

(a) the terms or conditions on which any of the money is lent and which are in force at that time make different provision in relation to different persons or have, or are capable of having, a different effect in relation to different persons (whether at that or any subsequent time),

(b) arrangements are in place at that time the effect of which is that, at that or any subsequent time, the rights of some persons in relation to any of the debts differ, or will or may differ, from the rights of others in relation to any of the debts, or

(c) any other circumstances exist at that time as a result of which the rights of some persons in relation to any of the debts cannot reasonably be regarded as being, in substance, the same rights as others in relation any of the debts at that or any subsequent time.

(4) For the purposes of this section—

"arrangements" include any agreement, understanding, scheme, transaction or series of transactions (whether or not legally enforceable),

"different persons" includes persons of a different class or description, and

"rights" includes powers.

469 Debt restructuring

(1) This section—

(a) makes provision for treating a person ("D") who is a related party of another person ("C") as if they were not related parties of each other but only in respect of particular liabilities or transactions, and

(b) is expressed to apply in relation to loan relationships but also applies (with any necessary modifications) in relation to any other financial liability owed to, or any transaction with, C.

(2) If—

(a) D is party to a loan relationship as debtor and C is party to the loan relationship as creditor,

(b) D subsequently becomes a related party of C in consequence of a relevant release of debt, and

(c) before D became a related party of C in consequence of the release none of the parties to the loan relationship had been related parties of each other,

D and C are treated for the purposes of this Part as if, in relation to the loan relationship (and anything done under or for the purposes of it), they were not related parties of each other at times on or after the release.

(3) There is a "relevant release of debt" at any time for the purposes of this section if—

(a) a liability to pay an amount under a person's debtor relationship is released under the arrangements,

(b) that person is D or a person who is a related party of D at that time, and

(c) immediately before the release, it is reasonable to conclude that, without the release and any arrangements of which the release forms part, there would be a material risk that, at some time within the next 12 months, D or the related party would be unable to pay its debts.

(4) For the purposes of this section "debtor relationship" has the meaning given by section 302(6) of CTA 2009 (reading the references in that subsection to a company as references to a person).

470 Ordinary independent financing arrangements by banks and others

(1) This section applies where—

(a) at any time, a person ("C") is party to a loan relationship as creditor and the party to the loan relationship as debtor ("D") is a related party of C as a result of any circumstances, and

(b) the loan relationship is not one to which C is a party at that time directly or indirectly in consequence of, or otherwise in connection with, the existence of any of those circumstances.

(2) C and D are treated for the purposes of this Part as if, in relation to the loan relationship (and anything done under or for the purposes of it), they were not related parties of each other at that time.

471 Loans made by relevant public bodies

(1) This section applies at any time where—

(a) a relevant public body ("B") lends money to a person ("P"),

(b) B is a related party of P, and

(c) the realising of a profit is merely incidental to the making of the loan.

(2) B and P are treated for the purposes of this Part as if, in relation to the loan (and anything done under or for the purposes of it), they were not related parties of each other at that time.

472 Finance leases granted before 20 March 2017

(1) This section applies at any time where an asset is leased by a person ("A") to another ("B") under a lease which is granted before 20 March 2017 and which, in the case of B, is a finance lease.

(2) A and B are treated for the purposes of this Part as if, in relation to the lease (and anything done under or for the purposes of it), they were not related parties of each other at that time.

Determining the worldwide group

473 Meaning of "a worldwide group", "ultimate parent" etc

(1) In this Part "a worldwide group" means—

(a) any entity which—

(i) is a relevant entity (see section 474), and

(ii) meets the first or second non-consolidation condition (see subsections (2) and (3)), and

(b) each consolidated subsidiary (if any) of the entity mentioned in paragraph (a).

(2) The first non-consolidation condition is that the entity—

(a) is a member of an IAS group, and

(b) is not a consolidated subsidiary of an entity that—

(i) is a relevant entity, and

(ii) itself meets the first non-consolidation condition.

(3) The second non-consolidation condition is that the entity is not a member of an IAS group.

(4) In this Part—

(a) references to "a member" of a worldwide group are to an entity mentioned in subsection (1)(a) or (b);

(b) references to "the ultimate parent" of a worldwide group are to the entity mentioned in subsection (1)(a);

(c) references to "a single-company worldwide group" are to a worldwide group whose only member is its ultimate parent;

(d) references to "a multi-company worldwide group" are to a worldwide group with two or more members.

(5) In this section "IAS group" means a group within the meaning given by international accounting standards.

474 Interpretation of section 473: "relevant entity"

(1) In section 473 "relevant entity" means—

(a) a company, or

(b) an entity the shares or other interests in which are listed on a recognised stock exchange and are sufficiently widely held.

(2) Shares or other interests in an entity are "sufficiently widely held" if no participator in the entity holds more than 10% by value of all the shares or other interests in the entity.

Section 454 of CTA 2010 (meaning of participator) applies for the purposes of this subsection.

(3) The following are not relevant entities—

(a) the Crown,

(b) a Minister of the Crown,

(c) a government department,

(d) a Northern Ireland department, or

(e) a foreign sovereign power.

475 Meaning of "non-consolidated subsidiary" and "consolidated subsidiary"

(1) An entity ("X") is a "non-consolidated subsidiary" of another entity ("Y") at any time ("the relevant time") if—

(a) X is a subsidiary of Y at the relevant time, and

(b) if Y were required at the relevant time to measure its investment in X, it would be required to do so using fair value accounting.

(2) An entity ("X") is a "consolidated subsidiary" of another entity ("Y") at any time if, at that time, X is a subsidiary, but not a non-consolidated subsidiary, of Y.

(3) In this section "subsidiary" has the meaning given by international accounting standards.

(4) For the purposes of this section, assume that all entities are subject to international accounting standards.

(5) This section has effect for the purposes of this Part.

476 Continuity of identity of a worldwide group through time

(1) This section applies for the purpose of determining whether a group of entities that constitutes a worldwide group at any time ("Time 2") is the same worldwide group as a group of entities that constitutes a worldwide group at an earlier time ("Time 1").

(2) The group at Time 2 is the same worldwide group as the group at Time 1 if and only if the entity that is the ultimate parent of the group at Time 2—

(a) was the ultimate parent of the group at Time 1, and

(b) was the ultimate parent of a worldwide group at all times between Time 1 and Time 2.

477 Treatment of stapled entities

(1) This section applies where two or more entities—

(a) would, apart from this section, each be the ultimate parent of a worldwide group, and

(b) are stapled to each other.

(2) This Part has effect as if—

(a) the entities were consolidated subsidiaries of another entity (the "deemed parent"), and

(b) the deemed parent fell within section 473(1)(a) (conditions for being the ultimate parent of a worldwide group).

(3) For the purpose of this section an entity ("entity A") is "stapled" to another entity ("entity B") if, in consequence of the nature of the rights attaching to the shares or other interests in entity A (including any terms or conditions attaching to the right to transfer the interests), it is necessary or advantageous for a person who has, disposes of or acquires shares or other interests in entity A also to have, dispose of or acquire shares or other interests in entity B.

478 Treatment of business combinations

(1) This section applies where two entities—

(a) would, apart from this section, each be the ultimate parent of a worldwide group, and

(b) are treated under international accounting standards as a single economic entity by reason of being a business combination achieved by contract.

(2) This Part has effect as if—

(a) the two entities were consolidated subsidiaries of another entity (the "deemed parent"), and

(b) the deemed parent fell within section 473(1)(a) (conditions for being the ultimate parent of a worldwide group).

(3) In this section "business combination" has the meaning given by international accounting standards.

Financial statements and periods of account

479 "Financial statements" of a worldwide group

(1) References in this Part to "financial statements" of a worldwide group for a period are (subject to subsection (2)) to consolidated financial statements of the worldwide group's ultimate parent and its subsidiaries in respect of the period.

(2) Where the worldwide group is at all times during the period a single-company worldwide group, the references are to financial statements of the ultimate parent in respect of the period.

(3) The basic rule is that the references mentioned in subsections (1) and (2) are to financial statements that are drawn up by or on behalf of the ultimate parent.

(4) But see—

(a) section 481 for provision under which, in specified circumstances, financial statements of a worldwide group are treated as having been drawn up in accordance with different accounting standards from those in accordance with which they are drawn up by or on behalf of the ultimate parent;

(b) section 482 for provision under which, in specified circumstances, financial statements of a worldwide group are treated as consolidating different subsidiaries from those consolidated in financial statements drawn up by or on behalf of the ultimate parent;

(c) section 483 for provision under which, in specified circumstances, financial statements of a worldwide group are treated as having been drawn up where the ultimate parent has drawn up consolidated financial statements covering more than one worldwide group;

(d) sections 484 to 486 for provision under which, where financial statements of a worldwide group are not drawn up by or on behalf of the ultimate parent, financial statements of the group are treated as having been drawn up.

(5) See also section 487 (under which financial statements drawn up by or on behalf of an entity, but for too long a period or too late, are ignored for the purposes of this Part).

480 "Period of account" of worldwide group

References in this Part to a "period of account" of a worldwide group are to—

(a) a period in respect of which financial statements of the group are drawn up by or on behalf of the ultimate parent, or

(b) a period in respect of which financial statements of the group are treated as drawn up for the purposes of this section (whether under any of sections 481 to 485 or under any other enactment).

481 Actual financial statements not drawn up on acceptable principles

(1) This section applies where financial statements of a worldwide group for a period drawn up by or on behalf of the ultimate parent are not drawn up on acceptable principles.

(2) For the purposes of this Part (apart from this section)—

(a) the financial statements mentioned in subsection (1) are to be ignored, and
(b) IAS financial statements of the worldwide group are treated as having been drawn up in respect of the period.

(3) For the purposes of this Chapter financial statements are "drawn up on acceptable principles" only if condition A, B, C or D is met.

(4) Condition A is that the financial statements are IAS financial statements.

(5) Condition B is that the amounts recognised in the financial statements are not materially different from those that would be recognised in IAS financial statements of the worldwide group, if such statements were drawn up.

(6) Condition C is that the financial statements are drawn up in accordance with UK generally accepted accounting practice.

(7) Condition D is that the financial statements are drawn up in accordance with generally accepted accounting principles and practice of one of the following territories—

(a) Canada;
(b) China;
(c) India;
(d) Japan;
(e) South Korea;
(f) the United States of America.

(8) The Commissioners may by regulations amend this section so as to alter the circumstances in which financial statements are "drawn up on acceptable principles" for the purposes of this Chapter.

482 Actual financial statements drawn up on acceptable principles but consolidating wrong subsidiaries

(1) This section applies where financial statements of a worldwide group for a period drawn up by or on behalf of the ultimate parent are drawn up on acceptable principles but—

(a) do not consolidate one or more entities that are IAS subsidiaries, or
(b) consolidate one or more entities that are not IAS subsidiaries.

(2) In this section "IAS subsidiary", in relation to a period, means an entity which would be required to be consolidated with those of the ultimate parent in IAS financial statements of the group for the period.

(3) For the purposes of this Part (apart from this section)—

(a) the financial statements mentioned in subsection (1) are to be ignored, and
(b) consolidated financial statements of the ultimate parent and its IAS subsidiaries are treated as having been drawn up in respect of the period.

(4) The financial statements treated by subsection (3)(b) as drawn up are treated as drawn up in accordance with the same accounting principles and practice as the financial statements mentioned in subsection (1).

(5) In this section a reference to financial statements consolidating the results of an entity is to consolidating its results with those of the ultimate parent as the results of a single economic entity.

483 Actual financial statements covering more than one worldwide group

(1) This section applies where—

(a) consolidated financial statements of an entity and its subsidiaries are drawn up by or on behalf of the entity in respect of a period ("the actual period of account"), and
(b) the entity was the ultimate parent of a worldwide group for a part (but not all) of that period.

(2) For the purposes of this Part (apart from this section)—

(a) the financial statements mentioned in subsection (1)(a) are to be ignored, and
(b) consolidated financial statements of the entity and its IAS subsidiaries are treated as having been drawn up in respect of the part of the actual period of account mentioned in subsection (1)(b).

(3) The financial statements treated by subsection (2)(b) as drawn up are treated as drawn up—

(a) where the financial statements mentioned in subsection (1)(a) are drawn up on acceptable principles, in accordance with the same accounting principles and practice as those financial statements;

(b) otherwise, in accordance with international accounting standards.

(4) In this section "IAS subsidiary" has the same meaning as in section 482.

484 No actual financial statements: ultimate parent draws up financial statements

(1) Subsection (2) applies where—

(a) financial statements of the ultimate parent of a worldwide group are drawn up by or on behalf of the ultimate parent in respect of a period ("the relevant period"),

(b) consolidated financial statements of the ultimate parent and its subsidiaries are not drawn up by or on behalf of the ultimate parent in respect of the relevant period or any part of it, and

(c) the group was, at any time during the relevant period, a multi-company worldwide group.

(2) For the purposes of this Part (apart from this section) IAS financial statements of the worldwide group are treated as drawn up in respect of the relevant period.

(3) The ultimate parent may elect that subsection (2) is not to apply in relation to financial statements of the ultimate parent.

(4) An election under subsection (3)—

(a) has effect in relation to financial statements in respect of periods ending on or after such date as is specified in the election, and

(b) is irrevocable.

(5) The date specified in the election may not be before the day on which the election is made.

485 No actual financial statements: other cases

(1) In this section "accounts-free period" means (subject to subsection (2)) any period—

(a) which begins on or after 1 April 2017,

(b) throughout which a worldwide group exists, and

(c) in respect of no part of which are financial statements of the group—

(i) drawn up by or on behalf of the ultimate parent, or

(ii) treated as drawn up for the purposes of this section (whether under section 481, 482, 483 or 484 or any other enactment).

(2) A period is not an "accounts-free period" if it forms part of an accounts-free period.

(3) If an accounts-free period in relation to a worldwide group is 12 months or less, IAS financial statements of the worldwide group are treated for the purposes of this Part (apart from this section) as having been drawn up for the accounts-free period.

(4) If an accounts-free period in relation to a worldwide group is more than 12 months, IAS financial statements of the worldwide group are treated for the purposes of this Part (apart from this section) as having been drawn up for each of the following periods—

(a) the first period of 12 months falling within the accounts-free period;

(b) any subsequent period of 12 months falling within the accounts-free period;

(c) any period of less than 12 months which—

(i) begins immediately after the end of a period mentioned in paragraph (a) or (b), and

(ii) ends at the end of the accounts-free period.

486 Election altering period of account deemed under section 485

(1) This section applies where, disregarding this section, IAS financial statements of a worldwide group would be treated under section 485(4)(a) or (b) as drawn up for a period ("the default period of account") during an accounts-free period.

(2) The ultimate parent of the group may make an election under this section in relation to the default period of account.

(3) Where an election under this section is made, section 485 has effect as if subsection (4)(a) or (b) of that section—

(a) did not treat IAS financial statements of the group as having been drawn up for the default period of account;

(b) instead, treated IAS financial statements of the group as having been drawn up for the period—

(i) beginning with the day on which the default period of account begins ("the start day"), and

(ii) ending with such day after the start day as is specified in the election ("the end day").

(4) The end day must—

(a) fall within the accounts-free period, and

(b) not be later than the final day of the period of 18 months beginning with the start day.

(5) An election under this section—

(a) must be made before the end day, and

(b) is irrevocable.

(6) The fact that the ultimate parent of a worldwide group makes an election under this section in relation to a default period of account ("the earlier elected period") does not prevent it from making an election in relation to a later default period of account ("the later elected period").

(7) But where it does so, the end day in relation to the later elected period must be 3 years or more after the end day in relation to the earlier elected period.

(8) Where this section modifies section 485(4)(a) or (b) so that it treats IAS financial statements of the group as having been drawn up for the period mentioned in subsection (3)(b) of this section ("the elected period"), section 485(4)(b) and (c) apply in relation to any part of the accounts-free period following the end of the elected period.

(9) In this section "accounts-free period" has the same meaning as in section 485.

487 Actual financial statements ignored if for too long a period or too late

Financial statements drawn up by or on behalf of any entity are to be ignored for the purposes of this Part (apart from this section) if—

(a) the period in respect of which they are drawn up is more than 18 months, or

(b) they are drawn up after the end of the period of 30 months beginning with the beginning of the period in respect of which they are drawn up.

488 Meaning of "IAS financial statements"

(1) References in this Part to "IAS financial statements" of a worldwide group for a period are (subject to subsection (2)) to consolidated financial statements of the worldwide group's ultimate parent and its subsidiaries, drawn up in respect of the period in accordance with international accounting standards.

(2) If the worldwide group is at all times during the period a single-company worldwide group, the references are instead to financial statements of the ultimate parent, drawn up in respect of the period in accordance with international accounting standards.

489 References to amounts recognised in financial statements

(1) References in this Part to an amount "recognised" in financial statements—

(a) include an amount comprised in an amount so recognised;

(b) are, where the amount is expressed in a currency other than sterling, to that amount translated into its sterling equivalent.

(2) The exchange rate by reference to which an amount is to be translated under subsection (1)(b) is the average rate of exchange for the period of account, calculated from daily spot rates.

(3) References in this Part to an amount recognised in financial statements "for a period" as an item of profit or loss include references to an amount that—

(a) was previously recognised as an item of other comprehensive income, and

(b) is transferred to become an item of profit or loss in determining the profit or loss for the period.

Other definitions

490 Meaning of "relevant accounting period"

For the purposes of this Part a "relevant accounting period" of a company, in relation to a period of account of a worldwide group, means any accounting period that falls wholly or partly within the period of account of the worldwide group.

491 Meaning of "relevant public body"

(1) In this Part "relevant public body" means—

(a) the Crown,

(b) a Minister of the Crown,

(c) a government department,

(d) a Northern Ireland department,

(e) a foreign sovereign power,

(f) a designated educational establishment (within the meaning given by section 106 of CTA 2009),

(g) a health service body (within the meaning given by section 986 of CTA 2010),

(h) a local authority or local authority association,

(i) any other body that acts under any enactment for public purposes and not for its own profit, or

(j) any wholly-owned subsidiary of any body falling within any of the above paragraphs of this subsection.

(2) In this section "enactment" includes—

(a) an enactment contained in subordinate legislation within the meaning of the Interpretation Act 1978,

(b) an enactment contained in, or in an instrument made under, an Act of the Scottish Parliament,

(c) an enactment contained in, or in an instrument made under, a Measure or Act of the National Assembly for Wales, and

(d) an enactment contained in, or in an instrument made under, Northern Ireland legislation.

(3) The Commissioners may by regulations amend this section so as to alter the meaning of "relevant public body".

(4) The provision that may be made by the regulations does not include provision altering the meaning of "relevant public body" so that it includes a person who has no functions of a public nature.

492 Meaning of "UK group company"

In this Part "UK group company", in relation to any time during a period of account of a worldwide group, means a company—

(a) which is within the charge to corporation tax at that time, and

(b) which is a member of the group at that time.

493 Embedded derivatives

Sections 415 and 585 of CTA 2009 (loan relationships with embedded derivatives) apply for the purposes of this Part of this Act.

494 Other interpretation

(1) In this Part—

"the Commissioners" means the Commissioners for Her Majesty's Revenue and Customs;

"fair value accounting" means a basis of accounting under which—

(a) assets and liabilities are measured in the company's balance sheet at their fair value, and

(b) changes in the fair value of assets and liabilities are recognised as items of profit or loss;

"fair value" has the meaning it has for accounting purposes;

"finance lease", in relation to a company or a worldwide group, means a lease that, in accordance with generally accepted accounting practice, falls (or would fall) to be treated as a finance lease or loan in the accounts of the company or the financial statements of the group;

"interest restriction return" means a return submitted under any provision of Schedule 7A;

"reporting company" means a company which is for the time being appointed under any provision of Schedule 7A;

"the return period", in relation to an interest restriction return of a worldwide group, means the period of account of the group to which the return relates;

"service concession arrangement" has the meaning given by international accounting standards;

"wholly-owned subsidiary" has the meaning given by section 1159(2) of the Companies Act 2006.

(2) For the purposes of this Part a person who is not a company is regarded as being a party to a loan relationship if the person would be so regarded for the purposes of Part 5 of CTA 2009 if the person were a company.

Regulations

495 Financial statements: different treatment by group or members

(1) The Commissioners may make regulations for the purpose of altering any calculation under Chapter 7 where—

(a) the financial statements of a worldwide group for a period include or omit an amount in respect of any matter, and

(b) any member of the group deals with that matter for tax or accounting purposes in a different way.

(2) The regulations—

(a) may make provision subject to an election or other specified circumstances, and

(b) may make provision having effect in relation to any period beginning before the regulations are made if the period begins at some time in the calendar year in which the regulations are made.

496 Parties to capital market arrangements

(1) The Commissioners may make regulations entitling—

(a) a UK group company which has a liability to corporation tax as a result of this Part and which is a party to a capital market arrangement, and

(b) another UK group company,

to make a joint election transferring the liability to the other UK group company.

(2) The regulations may include provision—

(a) specifying other conditions that must be met for an election to be made,

(b) requiring an election to be made on or before a particular time (for example, before the accounting period for which the liability arises),

(c) authorising or requiring an officer of Revenue and Customs (on the exercise of a discretion or otherwise) to accept or reject an election,

(d) authorising or requiring an officer of Revenue and Customs (on the exercise of a discretion or otherwise) to revoke an election previously in force and dealing with the effect of the revocation, and

(e) dealing with the effect of the transfer of the corporation tax liability on any other liabilities that relate to the transferred corporation tax liability.

(3) In this section "capital market arrangement" has the same meaning as in section 72B(1) of the Insolvency Act 1986 (see paragraph 1 of Schedule 2A to that Act).

497 Change in accounting standards

(1) The Treasury may by regulations amend this Part to take account of a change in the way in which amounts are, or may be, presented or disclosed in financial statements where the change results from the issue, revocation, amendment or recognition of, or withdrawal of recognition from, an accounting standard by an accounting body.

(2) For this purpose—

"accounting standard" includes any statement of practice, guidance or other similar document, and

"accounting body" means—

(a) the International Accounting Standards Board (or successor body), or

(b) the Accounting Standards Board (or successor body).

(3) The regulations—

(a) may make provision subject to an election or other specified circumstances, and

(b) may make provision having effect in relation to any period beginning before the regulations are made if the change mentioned in subsection (1) is relevant to that period.

(4) A statutory instrument containing regulations which are capable of increasing the liability of a company to corporation tax may not be made unless a draft of the instrument is laid before, and approved by a resolution of, the House of Commons.

498 Regulations

Regulations under this Part may—

(a) make different provision for different cases or circumstances,

(b) include supplementary, incidental and consequential provision, or

(c) make transitional provision and savings."

PART 2

NEW SCHEDULE 7A TO TIOPA 2010

2 In TIOPA 2010, after Schedule 7 insert—

"SCHEDULE 7A

INTEREST RESTRICTION RETURNS

Section 374

PART 1

THE REPORTING COMPANY

Appointment by a worldwide group of a reporting company

1 (1) A member of a worldwide group may, by notice to an officer of Revenue and Customs, appoint an eligible company to be the group's reporting company.

(2) The notice must specify the first period of account of the group ("the specified period of account") in relation to which the appointment is to have effect.

(3) An appointment under this paragraph has effect in relation to—

(a) the specified period of account, and

(b) subsequent periods of account of the group.

(4) The notice is of no effect unless—

(a) it is given during the period of six months beginning with the end of the specified period of account,

(b) it is authorised by at least 50% of eligible companies, and

(c) it is accompanied by a statement containing the required information.

(5) For this purpose "the required information" means—

(a) a list of the eligible companies that have authorised the notice, and

(b) a statement that the listed companies constitute at least 50% of eligible companies.

(6) The notice may be accompanied by a statement that such of the companies listed under sub-paragraph (5)(a) as are specified in the statement do not wish to be consenting companies in relation to returns submitted by the reporting company.

For provision as to the effect of a statement under this sub-paragraph, see paragraph 11.

(7) For the purposes of this paragraph a company is "eligible" if and only if the company —

(a) was a UK group company at a time during the specified period of account, and

(b) was not dormant throughout that period.

Revocation by worldwide group of appointment under paragraph 1

2 (1) A member of a worldwide group may, by notice to an officer of Revenue and Customs, revoke an appointment previously made under paragraph 1.

(2) The notice must specify the first period of account of the group ("the specified period of account") in relation to which the appointment is to be revoked.

(3) An appointment that is revoked under this paragraph ceases to have effect in relation to—

(a) the specified period of account, and

(b) subsequent periods of account of the group.

(4) The notice is of no effect unless—

(a) it is given during the period of six months beginning with the end of the specified period of account,

(b) it is authorised by at least 50% of eligible companies, and

(c) it is accompanied by a statement containing the required information.

(5) For this purpose "the required information" means—

(a) a list of the eligible companies that have authorised the notice, and

(b) a statement that the listed companies constitute at least 50% of eligible companies.

(6) The revocation of an appointment does not prevent the making of a further appointment under paragraph 1 (whether at the same time as the revocation, or later).

(7) For the purposes of this paragraph a company is "eligible" if and only if the company —

(a) was a UK group company at a time during the specified period of account, and

(b) was not dormant throughout that period.

Regulations supplementing paragraphs 1 and 2

3 The Commissioners may by regulations make further provision about an appointment under paragraph 1 or the revocation of such an appointment under paragraph 2, including in particular provision—

(a) about the form and manner in which an appointment or revocation may be made;

(b) requiring a person to give information to an officer of Revenue and Customs in connection with the making of an appointment or revocation;

(c) prohibiting a company from being appointed unless it meets conditions specified in the regulations;

(d) about the time from which an appointment or revocation has effect;

(e) providing that an appointment or revocation is of no effect, or (in the case of an appointment) ceases to have effect, if a requirement under the regulations is not met.

Appointment of reporting company by Revenue and Customs

4 (1) This paragraph applies where—

(a) no appointment of a reporting company under paragraph 1 has effect in relation to a period of account of a worldwide group ("the relevant period of account"), and

(b) as a result of sub-paragraph (4)(a) of that paragraph, an appointment of a reporting company under that paragraph that has effect in relation to the relevant period of account is no longer possible.

(2) An officer of Revenue and Customs may, by notice to an eligible company, appoint it to be the group's reporting company.

(3) The notice must specify the relevant period of account (whether by specifying the dates on which it begins and ends or, if the officer does not have that information, by reference to a date or dates).

(4) The appointment has effect in relation to the relevant period of account.

(5) The appointment may be made—

(a) at any time before the end of the period of 36 months beginning with the end of the relevant period of account, or

(b) at any time after the end of that period if, at that time, an amount stated in the company tax return of a UK group company for a relevant accounting period can be altered.

(6) Paragraph 88(3) to (5) of Schedule 18 to FA 1998 (meaning of "can no longer be altered") applies for the purposes of this paragraph.

(7) For the purposes of this paragraph a company is "eligible" if and only if the company —

(a) was a UK group company at a time during the relevant period of account, and

(b) was not dormant throughout that period.

Appointment by officer of Revenue and Customs of replacement reporting company

5 (1) This paragraph applies where—

(a) an appointment of a reporting company under paragraph 1 or 4 or this paragraph has effect in relation to a period of account of a worldwide group ("the relevant period of account"), and

(b) condition A or B is met.

(2) Condition A is that an officer of Revenue and Customs considers that the reporting company mentioned in sub-paragraph (1)(a) has not complied with, or will not comply with, a requirement under or by virtue of this Schedule.

(3) Condition B is that the reporting company mentioned in sub-paragraph (1)(a) has agreed that an officer of Revenue of Customs may exercise the power in this paragraph.

(4) An officer of Revenue and Customs may, by notice—

(a) revoke the appointment of the reporting company mentioned in sub-paragraph (1)(a), and

(b) appoint in its place an eligible company to be the reporting company of the group.

(5) The notice must—

(a) be given to each of the companies mentioned in sub-paragraph (4), and

(b) specify the relevant period of account (whether by specifying the dates on which it begins and ends or, if the officer does not have that information, by reference to a date or dates).

(6) Where the power in sub-paragraph (4) is exercised—

(a) the appointment that is revoked ceases to have effect in relation to—

(i) the relevant period of account, and

(ii) subsequent periods of account of the group;

(b) the appointment of the replacement has effect in relation to the relevant period of account.

(7) For the purposes of this paragraph a company is "eligible" if and only if the company —

(a) was a UK group company at a time during the relevant period of account, and

(b) was not dormant throughout that period.

Obligation of reporting company to notify group members of its status

6 (1) This paragraph applies where the appointment of a reporting company has effect in relation to a period of account of a worldwide group ("the relevant period of account").

(2) The reporting company must, as soon as reasonably practicable after the relevant time, notify each relevant company that it is the group's reporting company in relation to the relevant period of account.

(3) In sub-paragraph (2) "the relevant time" means—

(a) if the relevant period of account is the first period of account in relation to which the appointment has effect, the time of the appointment;

(b) otherwise, the end of the period of 6 months beginning with the end of the relevant period of account.

(4) Sub-paragraph (2) does not require the reporting company to notify a relevant company if the reporting company notified that company under that sub-paragraph in relation to an earlier period of account.

(5) The duty to comply with sub-paragraph (2) is enforceable by the company required to be notified under that sub-paragraph.

(6) For the purposes of this paragraph a company is "relevant" if and only if the company meets condition A or B.

(7) Condition A is that the company—

(a) was a UK group company at a time during the relevant period of account, and

(b) was not dormant throughout that period.

(8) Condition B is that the company is the ultimate parent of the worldwide group.

Obligation of reporting company to submit interest restriction return

7 (1) This paragraph applies where the appointment of a reporting company has effect in relation to a period of account of a worldwide group.

(2) If the reporting company was appointed under paragraph 1 or 4, it must submit a return for the period of account to an officer of Revenue and Customs.

(3) If the reporting company was appointed under paragraph 5, it must submit a return for the period of account to an officer of Revenue and Customs unless a return for the period has already been submitted under sub-paragraph (2) or this sub-paragraph.

(4) A return submitted under this paragraph must be received by an officer of Revenue and Customs before the filing date in relation to the period of account.

(5) In this Part of this Act "the filing date", in relation to a period of account of a worldwide group, means—

(a) the end of the period of 12 months beginning with the end of the period of account, or

(b) if later, the end of the period of 3 months beginning with the day on which the appointment of a reporting company that has effect in relation to the period was made.

(6) A return submitted under this paragraph is of no effect unless it is received by an officer of Revenue and Customs before—

(a) the end of the period of 36 months beginning with the end of the period of account, or

(b) if later, the end of the period of 3 months beginning with the day on which the reporting company was appointed.

This is subject to paragraph 57.

Revised interest restriction return

8 (1) This paragraph applies where—

(a) the appointment of a reporting company has effect in relation to a period of account of a worldwide group, and

(b) a return ("the previous interest restriction return") was submitted under paragraph 7, or this paragraph, for the period of account.

(2) The reporting company may submit a revised interest restriction return for the period of account to an officer of Revenue and Customs.

(3) A revised interest restriction return submitted under sub-paragraph (2) is of no effect unless it is received by an officer of Revenue and Customs before—

(a) the end of the period of 36 months beginning with the end of the period of account, or

(b) if later, the end of the period of 3 months beginning with the day on which the reporting company was appointed.

This is subject to paragraphs 9 and 57.

(4) Where—

(a) a member of the group amends, or is treated as amending, its company tax return, and

(b) as a result of the amendment any of the figures contained in the previous interest restriction return have become incorrect,

the reporting company must submit a revised interest restriction return to an officer of Revenue and Customs.

(5) A revised interest restriction return submitted under sub-paragraph (4) must be received by an officer of Revenue and Customs before the end of the period of 3 months beginning with—

(a) the day on which the amended company tax return was received by an officer of Revenue and Customs, or

(b) (as the case may be) the day as from which the company tax return was treated as amended.

(6) A return submitted under this paragraph—

(a) must indicate the respects in which it differs from the previous return, and

(b) supersedes the previous return.

Extended period for submission of full return in place of abbreviated return

9 (1) This paragraph applies where—

(a) a reporting company has submitted an abbreviated interest restriction return for a period of account of a worldwide group in accordance with this Schedule, and

(b) the worldwide group is not subject to interest restrictions in the return period.

(2) Despite the passing of the time limit in paragraph 8(3), a full interest restriction return for the period of account submitted under paragraph 8 has effect if it is received before the end of the period of 60 months beginning with the end of the period of account.

Meaning of "consenting company" and "non-consenting company"

10 (1) This paragraph makes provision for the purposes of this Part of this Act about whether a company is a "consenting company" in relation to an interest restriction return submitted by a reporting company.

(2) The company is a "consenting company" in relation to the return if, before the return is submitted—

(a) it has notified the appropriate persons that it wishes to be a consenting company in relation to interest restriction returns submitted by the reporting company, and

(b) it has not notified the appropriate persons that it no longer wishes to be a consenting company in relation to such returns.

(3) In sub-paragraph (2) "the appropriate persons" means—

(a) an officer of Revenue and Customs, and

(b) the reporting company in relation to the period of account.

(4) The company is a "non-consenting company", in relation to the return, if it is not a consenting company in relation to the return.

Company authorising reporting company appointment treated as consenting company

11 (1) This paragraph applies where a company—

(a) is listed in a statement under sub-paragraph (4)(c) of paragraph 1 (list of companies authorising appointment of reporting company), and

(b) is not included in a statement under sub-paragraph (6) of that paragraph (companies authorising appointment of reporting company but not wishing to be consenting companies).

(2) The company is treated as having given, at the time of the appointment, a notice under paragraph 10(2)(a) in relation to interest restriction returns submitted by the reporting company.

(3) Sub-paragraph (2) does not prevent the company, at any time after the appointment, from giving a notice under paragraph 10(2)(b) in relation to interest restriction returns submitted by the reporting company.

PART 2

CONTENTS OF INTEREST RESTRICTION RETURN

Elections

12 (1) An election to which this paragraph applies must be made in an interest restriction return for the period of account (or, as the case may be, the first period of account) to which the election relates.

(2) If an election to which this paragraph applies is capable of being revoked, the revocation must be made in an interest restriction return for the period of account (or, as the case may be, the first period of account) to which the revocation relates.

(3) This paragraph applies to the following elections—

(a) a group ratio election (see paragraph 13);

(b) a group ratio (blended) election (see paragraph 14);

(c) a group-EBITDA (chargeable gains) election (see paragraph 15);

(d) an interest allowance (alternative calculation) election (see paragraph 16);

(e) an interest allowance (non-consolidated investment) election (see paragraph 17);

(f) an interest allowance (consolidated partnerships) election (see paragraph 18);

(g) an abbreviated return election (see paragraph 19).

Group ratio election

13 (1) This paragraph applies where the appointment of a reporting company has effect in relation to a period of account of a worldwide group.

(2) The reporting company may—

(a) elect that the interest allowance of the group is to be calculated using the group ratio method, or

(b) revoke an election previously made.

(3) An election or revocation under this paragraph has effect in relation to the period of account.

(4) An election under this paragraph is referred to in this Part of this Act as a "group ratio election".

(5) For provision as to the effect of a group ratio election, see section 396.

Group ratio (blended) election

14 (1) This paragraph applies where—

(a) the appointment of a reporting company has effect in relation to a period of account of a worldwide group,

(b) the reporting company makes a group ratio election in respect of the period of account, and

(c) a related party investor in relation to the period of account is, throughout the period of account, a member of a worldwide group (an "investor worldwide group") other than that mentioned in paragraph (a).

(2) The reporting company may—

(a) elect that Chapter 5 of Part 10 (interest allowance) is to apply subject to the blended group ratio provisions, or

(b) revoke an election previously made.

(3) An election under this paragraph may—

(a) specify one or more investor worldwide groups,

(b) specify, in relation to any such group, one or more elections under this Schedule that are capable of being made in relation to a period of account by a reporting company of a worldwide group, and

(c) specify that the election is to be treated, for the purposes of the blended group ratio provisions, as having effect, or as not having effect, in relation to periods of account of the investor's worldwide group.

(4) Sub-paragraph (5) applies where—

(a) an election under this paragraph is made in relation to a period of account,

(b) an election under this paragraph was made in relation to any earlier period of account of the group,

(c) the election mentioned in paragraph (b) specified, under sub-paragraph (3)(c), that an election ("the investor's election") was to be treated as having effect in relation to periods of account of the investor's worldwide group, and

(d) the investor's election was an election which, if made by a reporting company of a worldwide group, would have been irrevocable.

(5) The election mentioned in sub-paragraph (4)(a) must specify, under sub-paragraph (3)(c), that the investor's election is to be treated as having effect in relation to periods of account of the investor's worldwide group.

(6) An election or revocation under this paragraph has effect in relation to the period of account.

(7) An election under this paragraph is referred to in this Part of this Act as a "group ratio (blended) election".

(8) In this paragraph "the blended group ratio provisions" means the provisions of sections 401 to 403.

Group-EBITDA (chargeable gains) election

15 (1) This paragraph applies where the appointment of a reporting company has effect in relation to a period of account of a worldwide group.

(2) The reporting company may elect that Chapter 7 of Part 10 (group-interest and group-EBITDA) is to apply subject to the chargeable gains provisions.

(3) An election under this paragraph—

(a) has effect in relation to the period of account and subsequent periods of account of the worldwide group, and

(b) is irrevocable.

(4) An election under this paragraph is referred to in this Part of this Act as a "group-EBITDA (chargeable gains) election".

(5) In this paragraph "the chargeable gains provisions" means the provisions of section 422.

Interest allowance (alternative calculation) election

16 (1) This paragraph applies where the appointment of a reporting company has effect in relation to a period of account of a worldwide group.

(2) The reporting company may elect that Chapter 7 of Part 10 (group-interest and group-EBITDA) is to apply subject to the alternative calculation provisions.

(3) An election under this paragraph—

(a) has effect in relation to the period of account and subsequent periods of account of the worldwide group, and

(b) is irrevocable.

(4) An election under this paragraph is referred to in this Part of this Act as an "interest allowance (alternative calculation) election".

(5) In this paragraph "the alternative calculation provisions" means sections 423 to 426.

Interest allowance (non-consolidated investment) election

17 (1) This paragraph applies where the appointment of a reporting company has effect in relation to a period of account of a worldwide group.

(2) The reporting company may—

(a) elect that Chapter 7 of Part 10 (group-interest and group-EBITDA) is to apply subject to the non-consolidated investment provisions, or

(b) revoke an election previously made.

(3) An election under this paragraph must specify, for the purposes of the non-consolidated investment provisions, one or more non-consolidated associates of the worldwide group.

(4) An election or revocation under this paragraph has effect in relation to the period of account.

(5) An election under this paragraph is referred to in this Part of this Act as an "interest allowance (non-consolidated investment) election".

(6) In this paragraph "the non-consolidated investment provisions" means sections 427 and 428.

Interest allowance (consolidated partnerships) election

18 (1) This paragraph applies where the appointment of a reporting company has effect in relation to a period of account of a worldwide group.

(2) The reporting company may elect that Chapter 7 of Part 10 (group-interest and group-EBITDA) is to apply subject to the consolidated partnership provisions.

(3) An election under this paragraph must specify, for the purposes of the consolidated partnership provisions, one or more consolidated partnerships of the worldwide group.

(4) Where an election under this paragraph has been made in relation to a worldwide group, a further election may be made specifying, for the purposes of the consolidated partnership provisions, one or more additional consolidated partnerships of the worldwide group.

(5) An election under this paragraph—

(a) has effect in relation to the period of account and subsequent periods of account of the worldwide group, and

(b) is irrevocable.

(6) An election under this paragraph is referred to in this Part of this Act as an "interest allowance (consolidated partnerships) election".

(7) In this paragraph "the consolidated partnership provisions" means the provisions of section 430.

Abbreviated return election

19 (1) This paragraph applies where the appointment of a reporting company has effect in relation to a period of account of a worldwide group.

(2) The reporting company may—

(a) elect to submit an abbreviated interest restriction return, or

(b) revoke an election previously made.

(3) An election or revocation under this paragraph has effect in relation to the period of account.

(4) An election under this paragraph is referred to in this Part of this Act as an "abbreviated return election".

(5) For provision as to the effect of an abbreviated return election, see—

paragraph 20 of this Schedule (which limits the required contents of the interest restriction return);

section 393 (which deprives the group of the use of the interest allowance for the return period, or any earlier period, in future periods of account).

Required contents of interest restriction return: full returns and abbreviated returns

20 (1) This paragraph makes provision about the contents of an interest restriction return submitted by the reporting company of a worldwide group.

(2) Sub-paragraph (3) applies if—

(a) the worldwide group is subject to interest restrictions in the return period, or

(b) the worldwide group is not subject to interest restrictions in the return period, and no abbreviated return election has effect in relation to the period.

(3) The interest restriction return must—

(a) state the name and (where it has one) the Unique Taxpayer Reference of the ultimate parent of the worldwide group;

(b) specify the return period;

(c) state the names and Unique Taxpayer References (where they have them) of the companies that were UK group companies at any time during the return period, specifying in relation to each whether it is a consenting or a non-consenting company in relation to the return;

(d) contain a statement of calculations (see paragraph 21);

(e) if the group is subject to interest restrictions in the return period—

(i) contain a statement of that fact,

(ii) specify the total disallowed amount, and

(iii) contain a statement of allocated interest restrictions (see paragraph 22);

(f) if the group is subject to interest reactivations in the return period—

(i) contain a statement of that fact,

(ii) specify the interest reactivation cap,

(iii) contain a statement of allocated interest reactivations (see paragraph 25);

(g) contain a declaration by the person making the return that the return is, to the best of that person's knowledge, correct and complete.

(4) Sub-paragraph (5) applies if—

(a) the worldwide group is not subject to interest restrictions in the return period, and

(b) an abbreviated return election has effect in relation to the period.

(5) The interest restriction return must—

(a) state that the group is not subject to interest restrictions in the return period, and

(b) comply with paragraphs (a) to (c) and (g) of sub-paragraph (3).

(6) If the ultimate parent of the worldwide group is a deemed parent by virtue of section 477 (stapled entities) or 478 (business combinations), the requirement in sub-paragraph (3)(a) is to state the name and (where it has one) Unique Taxpayer Reference of each of the entities mentioned in that paragraph.

(7) In this Part of this Act—

(a) a return prepared in accordance with sub-paragraph (3) is referred to as "a full interest restriction return";

(b) a return prepared in accordance with sub-paragraph (5) is referred to as "an abbreviated interest restriction return".

Statement of calculations

21 The statement of calculations required by paragraph 20(3)(d) to be included in a full interest restriction return must include the following information—

(a) for each company that was a UK group company at any time during the return period—

(i) the company's net tax-interest expense, or net tax-interest income, for the return period (see section 389);

(ii) the company's tax-EBITDA for the return period (see section 406);

(b) the aggregate net tax-interest expense, and aggregate net tax-interest income, of the group for the return period (see section 390);

(c) the interest capacity of the group for the return period (see section 392);

(d) the aggregate of interest allowances of the group for periods before the return period so far as they are available in the return period (see section 393);

(e) the interest allowance of the group for the return period (see section 396);

(f) the aggregate tax-EBITDA of the group for the return period (see section 405);

(g) where the interest allowance is calculated using the fixed ratio method and that allowance is given by section 397(1)(b), the adjusted net group-interest expense of the group for the return period (see section 413);

(h) where the interest allowance is calculated using the group ratio method—

   (i) the group ratio percentage (see section 399 or 401);

   (ii) the qualifying net group-interest expense of the group for the return period (see section 414);

   (iii) the group-EBITDA of the group for the return period (see section 416).

Statement of allocated interest restrictions

22 (1) The statement of allocated interest restrictions required by paragraph 20(3)(e) to be included in a full interest restriction return must—

(a) list one or more companies that—

   (i) were UK group companies at any time during the return period, and

   (ii) had net tax-interest expense for the period,

(b) in relation to each company listed under paragraph (a), specify an amount, and

(c) show the total of the amounts specified under paragraph (b).

(2) The amount specified under sub-paragraph (1)(b) in relation to a company is referred to in this Part of this Act as the "allocated disallowance" of the company for the return period.

(3) The allocated disallowance of a company for the return period—

(a) must not exceed the net tax-interest expense of the company for the return period,

(b) where the company is a non-consenting company in relation to the return, must not exceed the company's pro-rata share of the total disallowed amount (see paragraph 23), and

(c) must not be a negative amount.

(4) The sum of the allocated disallowances for the return period of the companies listed in the statement must equal the total disallowed amount.

(5) The statement must also specify an amount in relation to each relevant accounting period of each company listed in the statement.

(6) The amount specified under sub-paragraph (5) in relation to an accounting period of a company is referred to in this Part of this Act as the "allocated disallowance" of the company for the accounting period.

(7) In the case of a company that has only one relevant accounting period, the allocated disallowance of the company for that accounting period must be equal to the allocated disallowance of the company for the return period.

(8) In the case of a company that has more than one relevant accounting period, the allocated disallowance of the company for any of those accounting periods—

(a) must not exceed so much of the net tax-interest expense of the company for the return period as is referable to the accounting period,

(b) where the company is a non-consenting company in relation to the return, must not exceed the accounting period's pro-rata share of the total disallowed amount (see paragraph 24), and

(c) must not be a negative amount.

(9) The sum of the allocated disallowances of the company for its relevant accounting periods must be equal to the allocated disallowance of the company for the return period.

A company's pro-rata share of the total disallowed amount

23 (1) This paragraph—

(a) applies in relation to a worldwide group that is subject to interest restrictions in a period of account of the group, and

(b) allocates the total disallowed amount of the group in the period to companies that are UK group companies at any time during the period.

(2) The amount allocated to a company under this paragraph is referred to in this Part of this Act as the company's "pro-rata share" of the total disallowed amount.

(3) Sub-paragraph (4) applies in relation to a company that has net tax-interest expense for the period of account.

(4) The amount of the total disallowed amount that is allocated to the company is—

$A \times (B / C)$

where—

A is the total disallowed amount;
B is the net tax-interest expense of the company for the period of account;
C is the sum of the net tax-interest expense for the period of account of each company that has net tax-interest expense for the period.

(5) Where this paragraph does not allocate any of the total disallowed amount to a company, the company's "pro-rata share" of the total disallowed amount is nil.

Accounting period's pro-rata share of the total disallowed amount

24 (1) This paragraph—

(a) applies in relation to a worldwide group that is subject to interest restrictions in a period of account of the group ("the relevant period of account"), and
(b) allocates the total disallowed amount of the group in the period of account to relevant accounting periods of companies that are UK group companies at any time during that period.

(2) The amount allocated to an accounting period under this paragraph is referred to in this Part of this Act as the accounting period's "pro-rata share" of the total disallowed amount.

(3) Sub-paragraph (4) applies where—

(a) a company's pro-rata share of the total disallowed amount is not nil, and
(b) the company has only one relevant accounting period.

(4) The amount of the total disallowed amount that is allocated to the accounting period is the company's pro-rata share of the total disallowed amount.

(5) Sub-paragraph (6) applies where—

(a) a company's pro-rata share of the total disallowed amount is not nil, and
(b) the company has more than one relevant accounting period.

(6) The amount of the total disallowed amount that is allocated to a relevant accounting period of the company is—

$A \times (B / C)$

where—

A is the company's pro-rata share of the total disallowed amount;
B is the net tax-interest expense of the company for the accounting period;
C is the sum of the net tax-interest expenses of the company for each relevant accounting period.

(7) Where this paragraph does not allocate any of the total disallowed amount to an accounting period of a company, the accounting period's "pro-rata share" of the total disallowed amount is nil.

(8) For the purposes of this paragraph, the "net tax-interest expense" of a company for a relevant accounting period is—

(a) so much of the net tax-interest expense of the company for the relevant period of account as is referable to the accounting period, or
(b) if the amount determined under paragraph (a) is negative, nil.

Statement of allocated interest reactivations

25 (1) The statement of allocated interest reactivations required by paragraph 20(3)(f) to be included in a full interest restriction return must—

(a) list one or more companies that are UK group companies at any time during the return period,
(b) in relation to each company listed under paragraph (a), specify an amount, and
(c) show the total of the amounts specified under paragraph (b).

(2) The amount specified under sub-paragraph (1)(b) in relation to a company is referred to in this Part of this Act as the "allocated reactivation" of the company for the return period.

(3) The allocated reactivation of a company for the return period—

(a) must not exceed the amount available for reactivation of the company in the return period (see paragraph 26), and
(b) must not be a negative amount.

(4) The sum of the allocated reactivations for the return period of the companies listed in the statement must equal—

(a) the sum of the amounts available for reactivation of each company in the return period, or

(b) if lower, the interest reactivation cap of the worldwide group in the return period.

"Amount available for reactivation" of company in period of account of group

26 (1) This paragraph applies for the purposes of this Part of this Act.

(2) The "amount available for reactivation" of a company in a period of account of a worldwide group ("the relevant worldwide group") is—

(a) the amount determined under sub-paragraph (3), or

(b) if lower, the company's interest reactivation cap (see sub-paragraph (5)).

(3) The amount referred to in sub-paragraph (2)(a) is—

$$A + B - C + D - E$$

where—

A is the total of the disallowed tax-interest expense amounts (if any) that are brought forward to the specified accounting period from earlier accounting periods;

B is the total of the tax-interest expense amounts (if any) that the company is required to leave out of account in the specified accounting period as a result of the operation of this Part of this Act in relation to a period of account of the worldwide group before the period of account;

C is the total of the disallowed tax-interest expense amounts (if any) that the company is required to bring into account in the specified accounting period as a result of the operation of this Part of this Act in relation to a period of account of the worldwide group before the period of account;

D is the total of the tax-interest expense amounts (if any) that the company is required to leave out of account in the specified accounting period as a result of the operation of this Part of this Act in relation to a period of account of a worldwide group of which the company was a member before it became a member of the relevant worldwide group;

E is the total of the disallowed tax-interest expense amounts (if any) that the company is required to bring into account in the specified accounting period as a result of the operation of this Part of this Act in relation to a period of account of a worldwide group of which the company was a member before it became a member of the relevant worldwide group.

(4) In sub-paragraph (3) "the specified accounting period" means—

(a) the earliest relevant accounting period of the company, or

(b) where the company became a member of the relevant worldwide group during the period of account, the earliest relevant accounting period of the company in which it was a member of the group.

(5) For the purposes of sub-paragraph (2)(b) "the interest reactivation cap" of the company is—

$$A \times B$$

where—

A is the interest reactivation cap of the worldwide group in the period of account;

B is the proportion of the period of account in which the company is a UK group company.

Estimated information in statements

27 (1) This paragraph applies in relation to a statement under—

(a) paragraph 21 (statement of calculations),

(b) paragraph 22 (statement of allocated interest restrictions), or

(c) paragraph 25 (statement of allocated interest reactivations).

(2) Where any information is included in the statement that is (or is derived from) estimated information, the statement—

(a) must state that fact, and

(b) must identify the information in question.

(3) Where—

(a) estimated information (or information deriving from estimated information) is included in an interest restriction return for a period of account in reliance on this paragraph, and

(b) a period of 36 months beginning with the end of that period of account has passed without the information becoming final,

the reporting company must give a notice to an officer of Revenue and Customs within the period of 30 days beginning with the end of that 36-month period.

(4) The notice—

(a) must identify the information in question that is not final, and

(b) must indicate when the reporting company expects the information to become final.

(5) If a company fails to comply with the duty under sub-paragraph (3), it is liable to a penalty of £500.

(6) An officer of Revenue and Customs may, in a particular case, treat a revised interest restriction submitted after the end of the applicable period under paragraph 8(3)(a) or (b) as having effect if—

(a) the revisions to the return are limited to those necessary to take account of information that has become final,

(b) the officer considers that it was not possible to make those revisions before the end of that period, and

(c) the reporting company has complied with the duty under sub-paragraph (3).

Correction of return by officer of Revenue and Customs

28 (1) An officer of Revenue and Customs may amend an interest restriction return submitted by a company so as to correct—

(a) obvious errors or omissions in the return (whether errors of principle, arithmetical mistakes or otherwise), and

(b) anything else in the return that the officer has reason to believe is incorrect in the light of information available to the officer.

(2) A correction under this paragraph is made by notice to the company.

(3) A correction under this paragraph must not be made more than 9 months after the day on which the return was submitted.

(4) A correction under this paragraph is of no effect if the company—

(a) revises the return so as to reject the correction, or

(b) after the end of the period mentioned in paragraph 8(3)(a) or (b) but within 3 months from the date of the issue of the notice of correction, gives notice rejecting the correction.

(5) Notice under sub-paragraph (4)(b) must be given to the officer of Revenue and Customs by whom notice of the correction was given.

Penalty for failure to deliver return

29 (1) A company is liable to a penalty if the company—

(a) is required to submit an interest restriction return under paragraph 7 for a period of account of a worldwide group, and

(b) fails to do so by the filing date in relation to the period (see sub-paragraph (5) of that paragraph).

(2) The penalty is—

(a) £500 if the return is delivered within 3 months after the filing date, and

(b) £1,000 in any other case.

(3) If a company becomes liable to a penalty under this paragraph, an officer of Revenue and Customs must—

(a) assess the penalty, and

(b) notify the company.

(4) The assessment must be made within the period of 12 months beginning with the filing date mentioned in sub-paragraph (1)(b).

(5) A company may, by notice, appeal against a decision of an officer of Revenue and Customs that a penalty is payable under this paragraph.

(6) Notice of appeal under this paragraph must be given—

(a) within 30 days after the penalty was notified to the company,

(b) to the officer of Revenue and Customs who notified the company.

(7) A penalty under this paragraph must be paid before the end of the period of 30 days beginning with—

(a) the day on which the company was notified of the penalty, or

(b) if notice of appeal against the penalty is given, the day on which the appeal is finally determined or withdrawn.

Penalty for incorrect or uncorrected return

30 (1) A company is liable to a penalty if—

(a) the company (or a person acting on its behalf) submits an interest restriction return to an officer of Revenue and Customs for a period of account of a worldwide group,

(b) there is an inaccuracy in the return which meets condition A or B, and

(c) the inaccuracy is due to a failure by the company (or a person acting on its behalf) to take reasonable care (a "careless inaccuracy") or the company makes the inaccuracy deliberately (a "deliberate inaccuracy").

(2) An inaccuracy meets condition A if it consists of understating the total disallowed amount in the period of account of the group (including a case where no amount is specified in the return).

(3) An inaccuracy meets condition B if it consists of overstating the interest reactivation cap in the period of account of the group.

(4) A penalty payable under this paragraph is equal to the appropriate part of the notional tax.

(5) For the purposes of this Part of this Schedule—

"the appropriate part" means—

(a) in the case of a careless inaccuracy, 30%,

(b) in the case of a deliberate inaccuracy that is not concealed, 70%, and

(c) in the case of a deliberate inaccuracy that is concealed, 100%, and

"the notional tax" means the result produced by applying the average rate of the main corporation tax rate applicable in each of the days of the period of account to the total of the amount of the understatement referred to in condition A and the amount of the overstatement referred to in condition B.

(6) A company is not liable to a penalty under this paragraph in respect of anything done or omitted to be done by the company's agent if the company took reasonable care to avoid the inaccuracy.

Meaning of "deliberate inaccuracy that is concealed" and discovering inaccuracy after return submitted

31 (1) For the purposes of this Part of this Schedule a deliberate inaccuracy made by a company is concealed if the company makes arrangements to conceal it (for example, by submitting false evidence in support of an inaccurate figure).

(2) An inaccuracy in an interest restriction return which was not a careless or deliberate inaccuracy made by a company (or a person acting on its behalf) when the return was submitted is taken to be a careless inaccuracy made by the company for the purposes of this Part of this Schedule if the company (or a person acting on its behalf)—

(a) discovers the inaccuracy at some later time, and

(b) does not take reasonable steps to inform an officer of Revenue and Customs.

Inaccuracy in return attributable to another company

32 (1) A company ("C") is liable to a penalty if—

(a) another company submits an interest restriction return for a period of account of a worldwide group,

(b) there is an inaccuracy in the return which meets condition A or B in paragraph 30, and

(c) the inaccuracy was attributable to C deliberately supplying false information to the other company, or to C deliberately withholding information from the other company, with the intention of the return containing the inaccuracy.

(2) A penalty is payable under this paragraph in respect of an inaccuracy whether or not the other company is liable to a penalty under paragraph 30 in respect of the same inaccuracy.

(3) A penalty payable under this paragraph is equal to the notional tax.

Reductions in amount of penalty for disclosure or special circumstances

33 (1) If a company liable to a penalty under paragraph 30 or 32 in respect of an inaccuracy discloses the inaccuracy—

(a) the penalty must be reduced to one that reflects the quality of the disclosure (including its timing, nature and extent), but

(b) the penalty may not be reduced below the applicable minimum.

(2) In the case of a penalty under paragraph 30, the applicable minimum is—

(a) in the case of a careless inaccuracy, 0% of the notional tax if the disclosure is unprompted and 15% otherwise,

(b) in the case of a deliberate inaccuracy that is not concealed, 30% of the notional tax if the disclosure is unprompted and 45% otherwise, and

(c) in the case of a deliberate inaccuracy that is concealed, 40% of the notional tax if the disclosure is unprompted and 60% otherwise.

(3) In the case of a penalty under paragraph 32, the applicable minimum is 40% of the notional tax if the disclosure is unprompted and 60% otherwise.

(4) For the purposes of this paragraph—

(a) a person makes a disclosure of an inaccuracy by telling an officer of Revenue and Customs about it, giving an officer of Revenue and Customs reasonable help in quantifying it and allowing an officer of Revenue and Customs access to records to ensure that it is fully corrected, and

(b) a person makes an "unprompted" disclosure at any time if the person has no reason at that time to believe that an officer of Revenue and Customs have discovered, or are about to discover, the inaccuracy.

(5) If they think it right because of special circumstances, an officer of Revenue and Customs may—

(a) reduce a penalty under paragraph 30 or 32, or

(b) stay the penalty or agree a compromise in relation to proceedings for the penalty.

(6) The reference to special circumstances does not include an ability to pay but, subject to that, is taken to include, or exclude, such other circumstances as are prescribed by regulations made by the Commissioners.

(7) The power to prescribe circumstances includes power to prescribe circumstances by reference to the notional tax and the extent to which the notional tax exceeds, or is likely to exceed, any actual loss of tax to the Crown.

Assessment, payment and enforcement of penalty

34 (1) If a person becomes liable to a penalty under paragraph 30 or 32, an officer of Revenue and Customs must—

(a) assess the penalty, and

(b) notify the person.

(2) The assessment must be made within the period of 12 months beginning with the day on which the inaccuracy is corrected.

(3) The penalty must be paid before the end of the period of 30 days beginning with—

(a) the day on which the person was notified of the penalty, or

(b) if notice of appeal against the penalty is given, the day on which the appeal is finally determined or withdrawn.

(4) An assessment may be enforced—

(a) as if it were an assessment to corporation tax (which, among other things, secures the application of Chapters 6 and 7 of Part 22 of CTA 2010 (corporation tax payable by non-UK resident companies: recovery from others)), and

(b) as if that assessment were also an assessment to corporation tax of any company which was a UK group company of the group at any time in the period of account in relation to which the interest restriction return contained an inaccuracy.

Right to appeal against penalty or its amount

35 A person may, by notice, appeal against—

(a) a decision of an officer of Revenue and Customs that a penalty under paragraph 30 or 32 is payable, or

(b) a decision of an officer of Revenue and Customs as to the amount of a penalty under paragraph 30 or 32.

Procedure on appeal

36 (1) Notice of an appeal under paragraph 35 must be given—

(a) within 30 days after the penalty was notified to the person,

(b) to an officer of Revenue and Customs.

(2) On an appeal notified to the tribunal against a decision that a penalty is payable, the tribunal may confirm or cancel the decision.

(3) On an appeal notified to the tribunal against the amount of a penalty, the tribunal may—

(a) confirm the decision, or

(b) substitute for the decision another decision that an officer of Revenue and Customs had power to make.

(4) If the tribunal substitutes its decision for a decision of an officer of Revenue and Customs, the tribunal may rely on paragraph 33(5)—

(a) to the same extent as an officer of Revenue and Customs (which may mean applying the same percentage reduction as the officer to a different starting point), or

(b) to a different extent, but only if the tribunal thinks that the decision in respect of the application of paragraph 33(5) was flawed.

(5) For this purpose "flawed" means flawed when considered in the light of the principles applicable in proceedings for judicial review.

(6) Subject to this Part of this Schedule, the provisions of Part 5 of TMA 1970 relating to appeals have effect in relation to appeals under this Part of this Schedule as they have effect in relation to appeals against an assessment to corporation tax.

Payments between companies in respect of penalties

37 (1) This paragraph applies if—

(a) a company ("P") liable to a penalty under this Part of this Schedule has an agreement in relation to the penalty with one or more other companies within the charge to corporation tax, and

(b) as a result of the agreement, P receives a payment or payments in respect of the penalty that do not, in total, exceed the amount of the penalty.

(2) The payment—

(a) is not to be taken into account in calculating the profits for corporation tax purposes of either P or the company making the payment, and

(b) is not to be regarded as a distribution for corporation tax purposes.

PART 3

DUTY TO KEEP AND PRESERVE RECORDS

Duty to keep and preserve records

38 (1) A company which is a reporting company in relation to a period of account of a worldwide group must—

(a) keep such records as may be needed to enable it to submit a correct and complete interest restriction return for the period, and

(b) preserve those records in accordance with this paragraph.

(2) The records must be preserved until the end of the relevant day.

(3) In this paragraph "the relevant day" means—

(a) the sixth anniversary of the end of the period of account, or

(b) such earlier date as may be specified in writing by an officer of Revenue and Customs (and different days may be specified for different cases).

(4) If the company is required to submit an interest restriction return for the period before the end of the relevant day, the records must be preserved until any later date on which—

(a) any enquiry into the return is complete, or

(b) if there is no enquiry, an officer of Revenue and Customs no longer has the power to enquire into the return (but, for this purpose, paragraph 42 is to be ignored).

(5) If the company is required to submit an interest restriction return for the period after the end of the relevant day and has in its possession at that time any records that may be needed to enable it to submit a correct and complete return, it is under a duty to preserve those records until the date on which—

(a) any enquiry into the return is complete, or

(b) if there is no enquiry, an officer of Revenue and Customs no longer has the power to enquire into the return (but, for this purpose, paragraph 42 is to be ignored).

(6) The duty under this paragraph to preserve records may be discharged—

(a) by preserving them in any form and by any means, or

(b) by preserving the information contained in them in any form and by any means,

subject to any conditions or exceptions specified in writing by an officer of Revenue and Customs.

(7) The Commissioners may by regulations—

(a) provide that the records required to be kept and preserved under this paragraph include, or do not include, records specified in the regulations, and

(b) provide that those records include supporting documents so specified.

(8) The regulations may make provision by reference to things specified in a notice published by the Commissioners in accordance with the regulations (and not withdrawn by a subsequent notice).

Penalty for failure to keep and preserve records

39 (1) A company which fails to comply with paragraph 38 is liable to a penalty not exceeding £3,000.

(2) If a company becomes liable to a penalty under this paragraph, an officer of Revenue and Customs must—

(a) assess the penalty, and

(b) notify the company.

(3) The assessment must be made within the period of 12 months beginning with the day on which an officer of Revenue and Customs first becomes aware that the company has failed to comply with paragraph 38.

(4) A company may, by notice, appeal against a decision of an officer of Revenue and Customs that a penalty is payable under this paragraph.

(5) Notice of appeal under this paragraph must be given—

(a) within 30 days after the penalty was notified to the company,

(b) to the officer of Revenue and Customs who notified the company.

(6) A penalty under this paragraph must be paid before the end of the period of 30 days beginning with—

(a) the day on which the company was notified of the penalty, or

(b) if notice of appeal against the penalty is given, the day on which the appeal is finally determined or withdrawn.

PART 4

ENQUIRY INTO INTEREST RESTRICTION RETURN

Notice of enquiry

40 (1) An officer of Revenue and Customs may enquire into an interest restriction return submitted by a reporting company if the officer gives notice to the company of the officer's intention to do so ("notice of enquiry").

(2) The general rule is that an interest restriction return which has been the subject of one notice of enquiry may not be the subject of another.

(3) If a return ("the previous return") is superseded by an interest restriction return submitted under paragraph 8 ("the revised return"), notice of enquiry may be given in relation to the revised return even though notice of enquiry has been given in relation to the previous return.

(4) But see paragraph 43(5) for a limitation in certain circumstances on the scope of an enquiry into an interest restriction return submitted under paragraph 8.

(5) The power to give notice of enquiry into an interest restriction return for a period of account of a worldwide group does not restrict the power to give notice of enquiry into a company tax return of a company that is a member of the group at any time in that period.

(6) Accordingly, an amendment of the company's company tax return may be required as a result of an enquiry into the interest restriction return even though a closure notice has been given in respect of an enquiry into that company tax return.

(7) But see paragraph 43(2) for a limitation on the scope of an enquiry into an interest restriction return so far as affecting amounts in a company tax return.

Normal time limits for opening enquiry

41 (1) This paragraph applies where an interest restriction return is submitted by a reporting company for a period of account.

(2) Notice of enquiry may be given at any time before whichever is the latest of—

(a) the end of the period of 39 months beginning with the end of the period of account;

(b) the end of the period of 6 months beginning with the day on which the reporting company was appointed; and

(c) the end of 31 January, 30 April, 31 July or 31 October next following the first anniversary of the day on which an officer of Revenue and Customs receives the revised return.

(3) If—

(a) estimated information (or information deriving from estimated information) is included in an interest restriction return for a period of account in reliance on paragraph 27, and

(b) a period of 36 months beginning with the end of that period of account has passed without the information becoming final,

notice of enquiry may be given at any time up to and including the end of the period of 12 months beginning with the end of that 36-month period.

(4) This paragraph is subject to paragraph 42 (which allows notices of enquiry to be given after the time allowed by this paragraph or an enquiry previously closed to be re-opened).

Extended time limits for opening enquiries: discovery of errors

42 (1) Notice of enquiry may be given later than the time allowed under paragraph 41, or a closed enquiry may be re-opened, if—

(a) an officer of Revenue and Customs discovers that an interest restriction return submitted to an officer of Revenue and Customs does not, or might not, comply with the requirements of paragraph 20(3) in any respect,

(b) there would be, or might be, an increase in tax payable by any company for any accounting period if the return had complied with those requirements in that respect,

(c) the discovery is made after the time allowed under paragraph 41 or after an enquiry into the return has been closed, and

(d) the officer could not, at the relevant time and by reference to the relevant information, have been reasonably expected to be aware of the respects in which the return might not comply with those requirements.

(2) For this purpose "the relevant time" means—

(a) in a case where no notice of enquiry has been given within the time allowed under paragraph 41, when an officer of Revenue and Customs ceased to be entitled to give a notice, or

(b) in a case where an enquiry has been closed, when the officer gave the closure notice.

(3) For this purpose "the relevant information" means information which—

(a) is contained in the interest restriction return in question or either of the two returns for the immediately preceding periods of account of the group,

(b) is contained in any documents, financial statements or other accounts or information produced or provided to an officer of Revenue or Customs for the purposes of an enquiry into the interest restriction return in question or either of the two returns for the immediately preceding periods of account of the group,

(c) is information the existence of which, and the relevance of which as regards the situation mentioned in sub-paragraph (1)(b), could reasonably be expected to be inferred by an officer of Revenue and Customs from information falling with paragraph (a) or (b) of this sub-paragraph, or

(d) is information the existence of which, and the relevance of which as regards the situation mentioned in sub-paragraph (1)(b), are notified in writing to an officer of Revenue and Customs by the reporting company for the period of account or a person acting on its behalf.

(4) Notice of enquiry into an interest restriction return for a period of account may not be given, or a closed enquiry may not be re-opened, as a result of this paragraph more than the applicable number of years after the end of the period of account.

(5) The "applicable number of years" is—

(a) 20 years in a case involving deliberate non-compliance by the reporting company for the period of account or by a qualifying person,

(b) 6 years in a case involving careless non-compliance by the reporting company for the period of account or by a qualifying person, and

(c) 4 years in any other case.

(6) For this purpose "qualifying person" means—

(a) a person acting on behalf of the reporting company for the period of account, or

(b) a person who was a partner of the reporting company for the period of account at the relevant time.

(7) For the purposes of this paragraph an enquiry is "closed" when a closure notice is given in relation to the enquiry.

Scope of enquiry

43 (1) An enquiry into an interest restriction return extends to anything contained, or required to be contained, in the return (including any election included in the return).

(2) But the enquiry does not extend to an enquiry into an amount—

(a) which is contained, or required to be contained, in a company tax return of a UK group company, and

(b) which is taken into account in any calculation required for the purposes of the interest restriction return.

(3) Sub-paragraph (2) does not affect—

(a) any question as to whether or not, as a result of this Part of this Act, the amount falls to be left out of account, or to be brought into account, in any accounting period of the company, or

(b) the way in which, by reference to that amount and other matters, any provision of this Part of this Act has effect to determine whether or not the amount, or any other amount, is to be left out of, or brought into account, in any accounting period (whether of that company or another company).

(4) Nor does sub-paragraph (2) limit the operation of any provision of Part 4 of Schedule 18 to FA 1998 (determinations and assessments made by officers of Revenue and Customs).

(5) If—

(a) at any time an enquiry into an interest restriction return ("the previous return") has been closed, and

(b) the previous return is subsequently superseded by an interest restriction return submitted under paragraph 8 ("the revised return"),

the enquiry into the revised return extends only to matters arising as a result of information that was not included in the previous return.

(6) For this purpose an enquiry is "closed" when a closure notice is given in relation to the enquiry.

Enquiry into return for wrong period or wrong group

44 (1) If it appears to an officer of Revenue and Customs that the period of account for which an interest restriction return has been submitted is or may be the wrong period, the power to enquire into the return includes power to enquire into the period for which the return ought to have been made.

(2) If sub-paragraph (1) applies, paragraph 41 (normal time limits for opening enquiry) has effect as if the return were one that had been submitted for the correct period of account.

(3) If it appears to an officer of Revenue and Customs that the worldwide group ("the relevant group") in relation to which an interest restriction return has been submitted—

(a) consists of, or may consist of, two or more worldwide groups,

(b) includes, or may include, entities that are members of a different worldwide group or groups, or

(c) does not include, or may not include, entities that should be members of the relevant group,

the power to enquire into the return includes power to enquire into the returns for the periods of account of the worldwide groups which ought to have been made.

Amendment of self-assessment during enquiry to prevent loss of tax

45 (1) If after notice of enquiry has been given into an interest restriction return but before the enquiry is completed, an officer of Revenue and Customs forms the opinion that—

(a) the amount stated in the self-assessment of a company as the amount of tax payable is insufficient,

(b) the deficiency is attributable to matters in relation to which the enquiry extends, and

(c) unless the assessment is immediately amended there is likely to be a loss of tax to the Crown,

the officer may by notice to the company amend its self-assessment to make good the deficiency.

(2) In sub-paragraph (1) the reference to a company is to a company that was a member of the group at any time in the period of account for which the interest restriction return was submitted.

(3) An appeal may be brought, by notice, against an amendment of a company's self-assessment by an officer of Revenue and Customs under this paragraph.

(4) Notice of appeal must be given—

(a) within 30 days after the amendment was notified to the company,

(b) to the officer of Revenue and Customs by whom the notice of amendment was given.

(5) None of the steps mentioned in section 49A(2)(a) to (c) of TMA 1970 (reviews of the matter or notification of appeal to tribunal) may be taken in relation to the appeal before the completion of the enquiry.

(6) In this paragraph "self-assessment" has the meaning given by paragraph 7 of Schedule 18 to FA 1998.

Revision of interest restriction return during enquiry

46 (1) This paragraph applies if a reporting company submits a revised interest restriction return at a time when an enquiry is in progress into the previous return.

(2) The submission of the revised return does not restrict the scope of the enquiry but the revisions may be taken into account (together with any matter arising) in the enquiry.

(3) So far as the revised return affects the tax payable by a company, it does not take effect until the enquiry is completed (and, accordingly, paragraph 70 has effect subject to this sub-paragraph).

(4) But sub-paragraph (3) does not affect any claim by the company under section 59DA of TMA 1970 (claim for repayment in advance of liability being established).

(5) The submission of a revised return whose effect is deferred under sub-paragraph (3) takes effect as follows—

(a) if the conclusions in the closure notice state either—

(i) that the revisions were not taken into account in the enquiry, or

(ii) that no revision of the revised return is required arising from the enquiry,

the revision takes effect on the completion of the enquiry, and

(b) in any other case, the revisions take effect as part of the steps required to be taken in order to give effect to the conclusions stated in the closure notice.

(6) For the purposes of this paragraph the period during which an enquiry into an interest restriction return is in progress is the whole of the period—

(a) beginning with the day on which an officer of Revenue and Customs gives notice of enquiry into the return, and

(b) ending with the day on which the enquiry is completed.

Completion of enquiry

47 (1) An enquiry into an interest restriction return submitted by a reporting company is completed when an officer of Revenue and Customs by notice (a "closure notice")—

(a) informs the company that the officer has completed the enquiry, and

(b) states the officer's conclusions.

(2) The closure notice takes effect when it is given.

(3) If an officer of Revenue and Customs concludes that the return should have been made for one or more different periods of account of the group, the closure notice must designate the period of account (or periods of account) for which the return should have been made.

(4) If an officer of Revenue and Customs concludes that an interest restriction return in relation to a worldwide group should have been submitted—

(a) in relation to one or more different worldwide groups, or

(b) in relation to a different membership,

the closure notice must designate each period of account of a worldwide group for which an interest restriction return should have been made or for which an interest restriction return should have been submitted in relation to a different membership.

(5) If the officer concludes that the group in relation to which the return was submitted has a different membership, the designation under sub-paragraph (4) must also include details of the members of the group that the officer considers are UK group companies.

(6) If the officer concludes that the return should have been submitted in relation to one or more different worldwide groups, the designation under sub-paragraph (4) must also include—

(a) sufficient details to identify the different worldwide group or groups, and

(b) details of the members of the group that the officer considers are UK group companies.

(7) A designation by a closure notice of a period of account under this paragraph must specify the dates on which the period of account begins and ends.

(8) In this paragraph references to UK group companies, in relation to a period of account, do not include UK group companies that are dormant throughout the period.

Direction to complete enquiry

48 (1) An application may be made at any time to the tribunal for a direction that an officer of Revenue and Customs gives a closure notice in respect of an enquiry into an interest restriction return within a specified period.

(2) The application is to be made by the reporting company for the period of account of the group for which the return was submitted.

(3) The application is subject to the relevant provisions of Part 5 of TMA 1970 (see, in particular, section 48(2)(b) of that Act).

(4) The tribunal must give a direction unless satisfied that an officer of Revenue and Customs has reasonable grounds for not giving a closure notice within a specified period.

Conclusions of enquiry

49 (1) This paragraph applies where a closure notice is given under paragraph 47 to a company by an officer.

(2) The closure notice must—

(a) state that, in the officer's opinion, no steps are required to be taken by the company as a result of the enquiry, or

(b) state the steps that the company is required to take in order to give effect to the conclusions stated in the notice.

(3) The closure notice may (but need not) specify the allocated disallowance for particular companies specified in the notice.

(4) If—

(a) the return was made for the wrong period, and

(b) a period of account designated under paragraph 47(3) begins or ends at any time in that period,

the closure notice must require the company to take steps to make the return one appropriate to that designated period of account.

(5) If there is more than one designated period of account within sub-paragraph (4), the closure notice must require the company to submit an interest restriction return for each of those designated periods of account.

(6) If—

(a) a period of account of a worldwide group ("the relevant group") is designated under paragraph 47(4),

(b) the company is a member of the relevant group for that period of account, and

(c) condition A or B is met,

the closure notice must require the company to submit an interest restriction return for the designated period of account of the relevant group.

(7) Condition A is met if the UK group companies comprised in the relevant group were regarded as members of the worldwide group in relation to which the return was made.

(8) Condition B is met if—

(a) the relevant group includes UK group companies that were not regarded as members of the group in relation to which the return was made, and

(b) the ultimate parent of the relevant group is not the ultimate parent of a worldwide group in relation to which a reporting company has been appointed for a period of account that includes a time falling within the designated period of account of the relevant group.

(9) If sub-paragraph (6) applies in relation to two or more designated periods of account of a worldwide group (whether those periods are of the same or different groups), the closure notice must require the company to submit separate interest restriction returns for each of the designated periods of account.

(10) If, as a result of this paragraph, a closure notice requires a company to submit an interest restriction return for a period of account of a worldwide group, the company is treated for the purposes of this Part of this Act as if it had been appointed as the reporting company of the group in relation to the period.

(11) For this purpose it does not matter whether the return that was subject to the enquiry was submitted in relation to a different worldwide group.

(12) Sub-paragraph (10) is ignored in determining the period within which the return must be submitted (as to which, see instead paragraph 50(2)).

Interest restriction returns to be submitted to an officer of Revenue and Customs

50 (1) If, as a result of a closure notice given under paragraph 47 (closure notice in respect of a return subject to enquiry), a company is required to submit one or more interest restriction returns, the return or returns must—

(a) be submitted to an officer of Revenue and Customs,

(b) give effect to the conclusions stated in the notice, and

(c) contain such consequential provision as the company considers appropriate.

(2) A return submitted in compliance with the closure notice is of no effect unless it is received by an officer of Revenue and Customs before the end of the period of 3 months beginning with the day on which the closure notice is given to the company.

(3) A return submitted in compliance with the closure notice—

(a) must indicate the respects in which it differs from the return that was the subject of the enquiry, and

(b) supersedes that return.

(4) For provision dealing with cases where no return is submitted before the end of the period mentioned in sub-paragraph (2), see paragraph 58.

Return in relation to a worldwide group: other entities part of another group

51 (1) This paragraph applies if—

(a) an enquiry has been made into an interest restriction return ("the original return") for a period of account of a worldwide group ("the original group"),

(b) a closure notice has been given in respect of the enquiry that designates a period of account of a worldwide group under paragraph 47(4) ("the new group"),

(c) the new group consists of both UK group companies that were not regarded as members of the original group and other UK group companies, and

(d) the ultimate parent of the new group is the ultimate parent of a worldwide group ("the existing group") in relation to which a reporting company has been appointed for a period of account that includes a time falling within the designated period of account of the new group.

(2) An officer of Revenue and Customs must give a notice to that company appointing it as the reporting company in relation to each designated period of account of the new group.

(3) The notice of appointment must be given within the period of 30 days beginning with the day on which the closure notice was given.

(4) If—

(a) an interest restriction return has been submitted for a period of account of the existing group, and

(b) that period of account begins or ends at any time in a designated period of account of the new group,

the return is to be treated as withdrawn.

(5) Accordingly—

(a) any notice of enquiry or closure notice in relation to the return is also to be treated as withdrawn,

(b) any appeal in respect of any matter stated in a closure notice in relation to the return is treated as withdrawn, and

(c) any determination of any such appeal is treated as being of no effect.

(6) If—

(a) an interest restriction return for a period of account is treated as withdrawn as a result of sub-paragraph (4), and

(b) the period of account begins at any time before a designated period of account of the new group,

the notice under sub-paragraph (2) is also to be treated as if it constituted, on the day on which it is given, the appointment of the company in relation to a period of account of the existing group beginning with that time and ending immediately before the beginning of the designated period of account.

(7) If—

(a) enquiries are open at any time in relation to more than one interest restriction return, and

(b) this paragraph is capable of applying by reference to a closure notice to be given in respect of any one of those enquiries (so that a worldwide group could be either the original group or the existing group),

an officer of Revenue and Customs must select the company that, in the officer's opinion, ought to be the reporting company in relation to the new group.

(8) For this purpose an enquiry is "open" in relation to an interest restriction return if no closure notice has been given in relation to the enquiry.

Appeal against closure notice or notice under paragraph 51

52 (1) If a closure notice —

(a) is given to a company under paragraph 47, and

(b) contains a statement under paragraph 49(2)(b),

the company may appeal against the statement.

(2) If a notice is given to a company under paragraph 51, the company may appeal against the notice.

(3) Notice of appeal under this paragraph must be given—

(a) within 30 days after the notice was given to the company,

(b) to the officer of Revenue and Customs by whom the notice in question was given.

New groups without existing reporting company

53 (1) This paragraph applies if—

(a) a closure notice is given to a company under paragraph 47,

(b) a period of account of a worldwide group ("the new group") is designated under paragraph 47(4) in the closure notice,

(c) the company is not a member of the new group at any time in that period of account, and

(d) paragraph 51 does not apply.

(2) An officer of Revenue and Customs may appoint a company to be the reporting company of the new group in relation to that period.

(3) The appointment—

(a) must be of a company that was a UK group company at any time during that period and was not dormant throughout that period, and

(b) must be made before the end of the period of 3 months beginning with the day on which the closure notice is given to the company.

Matters required to be done on a "just and reasonable" basis

54 (1) This paragraph applies if—

(a) anything is required to be done under any provision of this Part of this Act on a "just and reasonable" basis,

(b) in preparing an interest restriction return the reporting company adopts a particular basis for dealing with that thing, and

(c) notice of enquiry is given into the return.

(2) An officer of Revenue and Customs may determine that, in preparing the return, a different just and reasonable basis should have been adopted for dealing with that thing.

(3) A closure notice given in respect of the return must require the reporting company to whom the notice is given to revise the return to give effect to that determination.

(4) The officer's determination may be questioned on an appeal under paragraph 52 on the ground that the basis to be adopted is not just and reasonable (but not on any other ground).

References to a reporting company where replaced

55 (1) This paragraph applies where—

(a) the appointment of a reporting company has effect in relation to a period of account of a worldwide group, and

(b) another reporting company is appointed in place of that company and the appointment has effect in relation to that period of account.

(2) Any reference in this Part of this Schedule (however expressed) to the reporting company in relation to that period of account at any time is to the company which is the reporting company at that time in relation to that period of account.

PART 5

DETERMINATIONS BY OFFICERS OF REVENUE AND CUSTOMS

Power of Revenue and Customs to make determinations where no return filed etc

56 (1) This paragraph applies where—

(a) an officer of Revenue and Customs considers that a worldwide group was subject to interest restrictions in a period of account of the group ("the relevant period of account"),

(b) the determination date has passed, and

(c) condition A, B or C is met.

(2) In this paragraph "the determination date", in relation to a period of account of a worldwide group, means—

(a) where the appointment of a reporting company has effect in relation to the period of account, the filing date in relation to the period (see paragraph 7(5));

(b) otherwise, the end of the period of 12 months beginning with the end of the period of account.

(3) Condition A is that no appointment of a reporting company has effect in relation to the relevant period of account.

(4) Condition B is that—

(a) the appointment of a reporting company has effect in relation to the relevant period of account, and

(b) no interest restriction return has been submitted for the period.

(5) Condition C is that—

(a) the appointment of a reporting company has effect in relation to the relevant period of account,

(b) an interest restriction return has been submitted for the period, and

(c) the return does not comply with the requirements of paragraph 20(3) (for example by including inaccurate figures).

(6) An officer of Revenue and Customs may determine, to the best of the officer's information and belief—

(a) a company's pro-rata share of the total disallowed amount of the group for the relevant period of account, and

(b) in relation to each relevant accounting period of the company, the accounting period's pro-rata share of the total disallowed amount.

(7) If, as a result of the determination, an accounting period's pro-rata share of the total disallowed amount is not nil, the company must leave out of account tax-interest expense amounts in that period that, in total, equal that pro-rata share.

(8) A notice of determination under this paragraph must be given to the company, and to the reporting company, stating the date on which the determination is made.

(9) No determination under this paragraph may be made after the end of the period of 3 years beginning with the determination date.

Time limit: interest restriction return following determination under paragraph 56

57 (1) Sub-paragraph (2) applies where—

    (a) a notice of determination under paragraph 56 is given to a company, and

    (b) at the time the notice is given, no interest restriction return for the relevant period of account has been submitted under paragraph 7.

(2) Despite the passing of the time limit in paragraph 7(6), an interest restriction return for the relevant period of account submitted under paragraph 7 has effect if it is received before the end of the period of 12 months beginning with the date on which the notice is given.

(3) Sub-paragraph (4) applies where—

    (a) a notice of determination under paragraph 56 is given to a company, and

    (b) at the time the notice is given, an interest restriction return for the relevant period of account has been submitted under paragraph 7.

(4) Despite the passing of the time limit in paragraph 8(3), an interest restriction return for the relevant period of account submitted under paragraph 8 has effect if it is received before the end of the period of 12 months beginning with the date on which the notice is given.

(5) In this paragraph "the relevant period of account" means the period of account to which the determination in question relates.

Power of Revenue and Customs to make determinations following enquiry

58 (1) This paragraph applies where—

    (a) as a result of a closure notice given under paragraph 47 (closure notice in respect of a return subject to enquiry), a company is required to submit an interest restriction return ("the return") in relation to a worldwide group,

    (b) the worldwide group is subject to interest restrictions in the return period, and

    (c) condition A or B is met.

(2) Condition A is that the time limit in paragraph 50(2) for submission of the return has passed without the return being received by an officer of Revenue and Customs.

(3) Condition B is that—

    (a) the return has been received by an officer of Revenue and Customs before the time limit in paragraph 50(2), and

    (b) the officer considers that the return does not comply with the requirements of the closure notice.

(4) An officer of Revenue and Customs may determine, to the best of the officer's information and belief—

    (a) a company's pro-rata share of the total disallowed amount of the group for the period of account in question, and

    (b) in relation to each relevant accounting period of the company, the accounting period's pro-rata share of the total disallowed amount.

(5) If, as a result of the determination, an accounting period's pro-rata share of the total disallowed amount is not nil, the company must leave out of account tax-interest expense amounts in that period that, in total, equal that pro-rata share.

(6) A notice of determination under this paragraph must be given to the company, and to the reporting company, stating the date on which the determination is made.

(7) No determination under this paragraph may be made after the end of the period of 3 months beginning with the end of the period mentioned in paragraph 50(2).

Appeal against determination under paragraph 58

59 (1) If a notice of determination under paragraph 58 is given to a company, the company may appeal against the notice.

(2) The only ground on which an appeal under this paragraph may brought is that the determination is inconsistent with the requirements of the closure notice to which it relates.

(3) Notice of appeal under this paragraph must be given—

    (a) within 30 days after the notice of determination was given to the company,

(b) to the officer of Revenue and Customs by whom the notice of determination was given.

PART 6

INFORMATION POWERS EXERCISABLE BY MEMBERS OF GROUP

Provision of information to and by the reporting company

60 (1) The reporting company in relation to a period of account of a worldwide group may, by notice, require a company that was a UK group company at any time during the period to provide it with information that it needs for the purpose of exercising functions under or by virtue of this Part of this Act.

(2) A notice under sub-paragraph (1) must specify the information to be provided.

(3) The duty to comply with a notice under sub-paragraph (1) is enforceable by the reporting company.

(4) As soon as reasonably practicable after submitting an interest restriction return to an officer of Revenue and Customs under any provision of this Schedule, the reporting company must send a copy of it to each company that was a UK group company at any time during the period of account.

(5) If a reporting company receives a closure notice under paragraph 47, the reporting company must, as soon as reasonably practicable, send a copy of the notice to every company that was a UK group company at any time during the period of account that was subject to the enquiry.

(6) The duty to comply with sub-paragraph (4) or (5) is enforceable by any person to whom the duty is owed.

Provision of information between members of group where no reporting company appointed

61 (1) This paragraph applies where condition A or B is met in relation to a period of account of a worldwide group.

(2) Condition A is that—

(a) no appointment of a reporting company has effect in relation to the period of account, and

(b) as a result of sub-paragraph (4)(a) of paragraph 1, an appointment of a reporting company under that paragraph that has effect in relation to the relevant period of account is no longer possible.

(3) Condition B is that—

(a) an appointment of a reporting company has effect in relation to the period of account,

(b) a full interest restriction return has not been submitted in accordance with this Part for the period, and

(c) the filing date in relation to the period has passed (see paragraph 7(5)).

(4) A company that was a UK group company at any time during the period of account may, by notice, require any other such company to provide it with information that it needs for the purpose of determining whether, or the extent to which, it is required to leave tax-interest expense amounts out of account, or bring them into account, under this Part of this Act.

(5) A notice under sub-paragraph (4) must specify the information to be provided.

(6) The duty to comply with a notice under sub-paragraph (4) is enforceable by the company that gives the notice.

PART 7

INFORMATION POWERS EXERCISABLE BY OFFICERS OF REVENUE AND CUSTOMS

Power to obtain information and documents from members of worldwide group

62 (1) An officer of Revenue and Customs may, by notice, require a group member—

(a) to provide information, or

(b) to produce a document,

if the information or document is reasonably required by the officer for the purpose of checking an interest restriction return for, or exercising any of the powers under this Part of this Act in relation to, a period of account of a worldwide group.

(2) For the purposes of this Part of this Schedule a person is a "group member" if, in the opinion of an officer of Revenue and Customs, the person is or might be a member of the worldwide group at any time in the period of account.

(3) A group member may (subject to the operation of any provision of Part 4 of Schedule 36 to FA 2008 as applied by paragraph 66(1) of this Schedule) be required to provide information, or produce a document, that relates to one or more other group companies.

(4) A notice under this paragraph may be given to a person even if the person is not within the charge to corporation tax or income tax.

(5) A notice under this paragraph may specify or describe the information or documents to be provided or produced.

Power to obtain information and documents from third parties

63 (1) An officer of Revenue and Customs may, by notice, require a third party—

(a) to provide information, or
(b) to produce a document,

if the information or document is reasonably required by the officer for the purpose of checking an interest restriction return for, or exercising any of the powers under this Part of this Act in relation to, a period of account of a worldwide group.

(2) A person is a "third party" if the person is not a group member at any time in the period of account.

(3) A notice may not be given under this paragraph unless—

(a) a company which is a UK group company of the group at any time in the period of account agrees to the giving of the notice, or
(b) on an application made by an officer of Revenue and Customs, the tribunal approves the giving of the notice.

(4) The tribunal may not approve the giving of a notice to a third party unless—

(a) the tribunal is satisfied that, in the circumstances, the officer giving the notice is justified in doing so, and
(b) either the requirements of sub-paragraph (5) are met or the tribunal is satisfied that it is appropriate to dispense with meeting those requirements because to meet them might prejudice the assessment or collection of tax.

(5) The requirements in this sub-paragraph are met if—

(a) the third party has been told that the information or documents referred to in the notice are required,
(b) the third party has been given a reasonable opportunity to make representations to an officer of Revenue and Customs,
(c) the tribunal has been given a summary of any representations made by the third party, and
(d) a company which is a UK group company of the group at any time in the period of account has been given a summary of the reasons why the information and documents are required.

(6) Sub-paragraph (5)(d) does not apply if an officer of Revenue and Customs has insufficient information to identify a company mentioned in that paragraph.

(7) No notice of the application for the approval of the tribunal needs to be given to the third party by an officer of Revenue and Customs.

(8) A notice under this paragraph to the third party must give details of the worldwide group unless—

(a) the notice is approved by the tribunal, and
(b) the tribunal is satisfied that no details should be given because to do so might seriously prejudice the assessment or collection of tax.

(9) An officer of Revenue and Customs must give a copy of a notice under this paragraph to a company which is a UK group company of the group at any time in the period of account unless—

(a) the tribunal has approved the notice and is satisfied that no copy should be given because to do so might prejudice the assessment or collection of tax, or
(b) an officer of Revenue and Customs has insufficient information to identify such a company.

(10) A decision of the tribunal under this paragraph is final (despite the provisions of sections 11 and 13 of the Tribunals, Courts and Enforcement Act 2007).

(11) A notice under this paragraph—

(a) may specify or describe the information or documents to be provided or produced, and

(b) if given with the approval of the tribunal, must state that fact.

Notices following submitted interest restriction returns

64 (1) The general rule is that, if an interest restriction return for a period of account of a worldwide group has been received by an officer of Revenue and Customs, a notice under paragraph 62 or 63 may not be given in relation to the period of the account of the group.

(2) But the general rule does not apply if—

(a) a notice of enquiry has been given in respect of the return, and

(b) the enquiry has not been completed.

Appeals

65 (1) A group member may appeal against a notice under paragraph 62.

(2) A person to whom a notice is given under paragraph 63 in a case where the tribunal has not approved the giving of the notice may appeal against the notice on the ground that it would be unduly onerous to comply with it.

(3) No appeal may be made under this paragraph in relation to a requirement to provide any information, or produce any documents, that forms part of the statutory records of any company which is a UK group company of the group at any time in the period of account.

(4) "Statutory records" has the same meaning given by paragraph 62 of Schedule 36 to FA 2008.

(5) In this Part of this Schedule references to an appeal against a notice include an appeal against a requirement of the notice.

Application of provisions of Schedule 36 to FA 2008

66 (1) The following provisions of Schedule 36 to FA 2008 (information and inspection powers) apply in relation to notices under paragraph 62 or 63—

(a) paragraph 7 (complying with notices),

(b) paragraph 8 (producing copies of documents),

(c) paragraph 15 (power to copy documents),

(d) paragraph 16 (power to remove documents),

(e) paragraph 18 (documents not in person's possession or power),

(f) paragraph 19 (types of information),

(g) paragraph 20 (old documents),

(h) paragraph 23 (privileged communications),

(i) paragraphs 24 to 27 (auditors and tax advisers),

(j) every paragraph contained in Part 7 (penalties),

(k) every paragraph contained in Part 8 (offence), and

(l) paragraph 56 (application of provisions of TMA 1970).

(2) Paragraph 32 of Schedule 36 to FA 2008 (procedure on appeals) applies in relation to an appeal under this Part of this Schedule against a notice under this Part of this Schedule.

References to checking an interest restriction return etc

67 (1) For the purposes of this Part of this Schedule references to checking an interest restriction return include—

(a) determining whether or not an interest restriction return should be submitted for a period of account of a worldwide group,

(b) determining whether or not a worldwide group is, or may be, subject to interest restrictions in a period of account, (and, if so, determining the total disallowed amount of the group),

(c) determining the membership of a worldwide group (or determining the members that are UK group companies), and

(d) determining any other question that is relevant to the operation of this Part of this Schedule in relation to an interest restriction return or anything required to be included in it.

(2) For the purposes of this Part of this Schedule references to a worldwide group include one that an officer of Revenue and Customs suspects may exist.

PART 8
COMPANY TAX RETURNS

Elections under section 375, 377 or 380

68 The following elections (or their revocation) must be made by a company in its company tax return (whether as originally made or by amendment) for the accounting period to which the election (or revocation) relates—

(a) an election under section 375 (a non-consenting company leaving pro-rata share of total disallowed amount out of account),

(b) an election under section 377 (a company specifying tax-interest expense amounts to be left out of account), and

(c) an election under section 380 (a company specifying tax-interest expense amounts to be brought into account).

Amendments to take account of operation of this Part of this Act (including elections)

69 (1) A company may amend its company tax return for an accounting period so as to make (or revoke) an election under section 375 at any time before—

(a) the filing date in relation to the period of account of the worldwide group to which the interest restriction return in question relates (see paragraph 7(5)), or

(b) if later, the end of the period of 3 months beginning with the day on which the interest restriction return in question is received by an officer of Revenue and Customs.

(2) A company that amends its company tax return for an accounting period as mentioned in sub-paragraph (1) must, before the time limit specified in that sub-paragraph, also amend the return to take account of the election (or revocation).

(3) If—

(a) a company is required by section 376 to leave an amount out of account in an accounting period, and

(b) the company has already delivered a company tax return for the period,

the company must amend its company tax return to take account of the requirement.

(4) The amendment must be made before the end of the period of 3 months beginning with the day after the relevant date (within the meaning of section 376).

(5) A company may amend its company tax return for an accounting period so as to make (or revoke) an election under section 377 or 380 at any time before—

(a) the end of the period of 36 months beginning with the day after the end of the accounting period, or

(b) if later, the end of the period of 3 months beginning with the day on which a relevant interest restriction return was received by an officer of Revenue and Customs.

(6) A company that amends its company tax return for an accounting period as mentioned in sub-paragraph (5) must, before the time limit specified in that sub-paragraph, also amend the return to take account of the election (or revocation).

(7) In sub-paragraph (5) "a relevant interest restriction return" means an interest restriction return for a period of account in relation to which the accounting period is a relevant accounting period."

(8) The time limit for amending a company tax return given by paragraph 15(4) of Schedule 18 to FA 1998 is subject to the time limits given by this paragraph.

Cases where company treated as amending return

70 (1) If—

(a) a company has delivered a company tax return for an accounting period, but

(b) as a result of the submission of an interest restriction return, information contained in the company tax return is incorrect (for example, there is a change in the amount of profits on which corporation tax is chargeable),

the company is treated as having amended its company tax return for the accounting period so as to correct the information.

(2) If—

(a) a notice of determination under paragraph 56 or 58 is given to a company in relation to an accounting period, and

(b) the company has already delivered a company tax return for the period,

the company is treated as having amended its company tax return to take account of the determination.

Regulations for purposes of paragraph 70 etc

71 (1) The Commissioners may by regulations—

(a) make provision generally for the purposes of paragraph 70, and
(b) make provision for other cases where a company is to be treated as having amended its company tax return.

(2) The provision that may be made by the regulations includes provision—

(a) permitting or requiring the company to deliver an amended company tax return for the accounting period;
(b) specifying amendments that may or must be made in the return;
(c) specifying a time limit for the delivery of the return that is later than that determined under paragraph 15(4) of Schedule 18 to FA 1998 (amendment of return by company).

Consequential claims to company tax returns

72 (1) This paragraph applies if—

(a) a company amends, or is treated as amending, its company tax return for an accounting period in consequence of a closure notice given in respect of an interest restriction return under paragraph 47 or a notice of determination given to the company under paragraph 56 or 58, and
(b) the amendment has the effect of increasing the amount of corporation tax payable by the company for the accounting period.

(2) Any qualifying claim may be made or given within the period of one year beginning with the day on which the company receives a copy of the closure notice under paragraph 60(5) or the notice of determination.

(3) Any qualifying claim previously made which is not irrevocable—

(a) may be revoked or varied within that one-year period, and
(b) if it is revoked or varied, must be done so in the same manner as it was made and by or with the consent of the same person or persons who made or consented to it (or, if a person has died, by or with the consent of the person's personal representatives).

(4) For the purposes of this paragraph a claim is a "qualifying" claim if its making, revocation or variation has the effect of reducing the liability of the company to corporation tax for the accounting period (whether or not it also reduces the liability to tax of the company for other periods).

(5) But a claim is not a "qualifying" claim if—

(a) the making, revocation or variation of the claim would alter the liability to tax of any person other than the company, or
(b) the making, revocation or variation of the claim is such that, if it were to be made, revoked or varied, the total of the reductions in liability to tax of the company would exceed the additional liability to corporation tax resulting from the amendment.

(6) If a qualifying claim is made, revoked or varied as a result of this paragraph, all such adjustments must be made as are required to take account of the effect of taking that action on the liability of the company to tax for any period.

(7) The adjustments may be made by way of discharge or repayment of tax or the making of amendments, assessments or otherwise.

(8) The provisions of TMA 1970 relating to appeals against decisions on claims apply with any necessary modifications to a decision on the revocation or variation of a claim as a result of this paragraph.

(9) In this paragraph (except in sub-paragraph (8)) "claim" includes an election, an application and a notice, and references to making a claim are to be read accordingly.

(10) In this paragraph "tax" (except in the expression "corporation tax") includes income tax and capital gains tax.

Meaning of "company tax return"

73 In this Schedule "company tax return" has the meaning given by paragraph 3 of Schedule 18 to FA 1998.

PART 9
SUPPLEMENTARY

Double jeopardy

74 A person is not liable to a penalty under any provision of this Schedule in respect of anything in respect of which the person has been convicted of an offence.

Notice of appeal

75 Notice of an appeal under this Schedule must specify the grounds of appeal.

Conclusiveness of amounts stated in interest restriction return

76 (1) This paragraph applies to an amount stated in an interest restriction return submitted under paragraph 7 or 8 ("the interest restriction return"), other than an amount that is also stated in a company tax return.

(2) If the amount can no longer be altered, it is taken to be conclusively determined for the purposes of the Corporation Tax Acts.

(3) An amount is regarded as one that can no longer be altered if—

(a) the interest restriction return has not been superseded by a subsequent interest restriction return;

(b) the applicable time limit has passed;

(c) any enquiry into the interest restriction return has been completed;

(d) if the closure notice in relation to an enquiry into the interest restriction return contained a statement under paragraph 49(2)(b), the period within which an appeal against the statement may be brought has ended; and

(e) if such an appeal is brought, the appeal has been finally determined.

(4) For the purposes of sub-paragraph (3) the "applicable time limit" means the time limit in paragraph 8(3) or, in a case where paragraph 57(2) or (4) applies and imposes a later time limit for submission of the interest restriction return, that later time limit.

(5) Nothing in this paragraph affects—

(a) the power under paragraph 42 (extended time limits for opening enquiries: discovery of errors), or

(b) any power to make a determination under paragraph 56 or 58 (determinations by officers of Revenue and Customs)."

PART 3
CONSEQUENTIAL AMENDMENTS

TMA 1970

3 (1) In section 98 of TMA 1970 (special returns, etc), in the table in subsection (5), in the first column, the entry relating to regulations under section 283, 284, 285, 295 or 297 of TIOPA 2010 is repealed.

(2) In consequence of sub-paragraph (1), paragraph 157(3) of Schedule 8 to TIOPA 2010 is repealed.

FA 1998

4 In paragraph 88 of Schedule 18 to FA 1998 (conclusiveness of amounts stated in company tax returns), at the end insert—

"(9) Nothing in this paragraph affects the operation of any provision of Part 10 of TIOPA 2010 (corporate interest restriction)."

CTA 2009

5 In section A1 of CTA 2009 (overview of the Corporation Tax Acts), in subsection (2)—

(a) omit paragraph (i), and

(b) after paragraph (ja) insert—

"(jb) Part 10 of that Act (corporate interest restriction),".

CTA 2010

6 CTA 2010 is amended as follows.

7 After section 937N (risk transfer schemes) insert—

"937NA Priority

For the purposes of this Part, the provisions of Part 10 of TIOPA 2010 (corporate interest restriction) are to be treated as of no effect."

8 In section 938N (group mismatch schemes: priority), for paragraph (e) substitute—

"(e) Part 10 of that Act (corporate interest restriction)."

9 In section 938V (tax mismatch schemes: priority), for paragraph (d) substitute—

"(d) Part 10 of that Act (corporate interest restriction)."

TIOPA 2010: consequential renumbering

10 (1) In consequence of the insertion of a new Part 10 of TIOPA 2010 by Part 1 of this Schedule, the existing Part 10 of that Act becomes a new Part 11.

(2) The following provisions of TIOPA 2010 are repealed—

(a) the existing sections 375 and 376 (which contain powers that are no longer exercisable), and

(b) the existing section 381(2)(e) and (f) (which refer to those sections);

but the repeals made by this sub-paragraph do not affect any orders made under section 375 or 376 before the passing of this Act.

(3) As a result of the provision made by sub-paragraphs (1) and (2), the following provisions of TIOPA 2010 are renumbered as follows—

(a) the existing section 372 becomes section 499;

(b) the existing section 373 becomes section 500;

(c) the existing section 374 becomes section 501;

(d) the existing section 377 becomes section 502;

(e) the existing section 378 becomes section 503;

(f) the existing section 379 becomes section 504;

(g) the existing section 380 becomes section 505;

(h) the existing section 381 becomes section 506;

(i) the existing section 382 becomes section 507.

(4) Consequently—

(a) in section 287(2A) of TCGA 1992, for "372" substitute "499";

(b) in section 1014(2)(fa) of ITA 2007, for "372" substitute "499";

(c) in section 1171(2)(f) of CTA 2010, for "372" substitute "499";

(d) in section 1 of TIOPA 2010—

(i) in subsection (4), for "10" substitute "11";

(ii) in subsection (5), for "373" substitute "500";

(e) in section 381(2) of TIOPA 2010—

(i) in paragraph (a), for "372" substitute "499";

(ii) in paragraph (b), for "373" substitute "500";

(iii) in paragraph (d), for "374" substitute "501";

(iv) in paragraph (g), for "377(2) and (3)" substitute "502(2) and (3)";

(v) in paragraph (h), for "380" substitute "505";

(vi) in paragraph (i), for "382" substitute "507".

(5) In section 379(1) and (2) of TIOPA 2010 (index of defined expressions), for "8" substitute "10".

TIOPA 2010: repeal of Part 7

11 (1) Part 7 of TIOPA 2010 (tax treatment of financing costs and income) is repealed; and accordingly the following provisions of that Act are also repealed—

(a) section 1(1)(d) (overview);

(b) in Schedule 9, Part 7 (transitional provision);

(c) in Schedule 11, Part 5 (index of defined expressions).

(2) In consequence of sub-paragraph (1), the following enactments (which amend provisions repealed by that sub-paragraph) are repealed—

(a) in F(No.3)A 2010, section 11 and Schedule 5;

(b) in FA 2011, in Schedule 13, paragraphs 29 and 30;

(c) in FA 2012—

(i) section 31 and Schedule 5;

(ii) in Schedule 16, paragraphs 242 and 243(a);

(iii) in Schedule 20, paragraphs 43 to 45;

(d) in FA 2013, section 44;

(e) in FA 2014, section 39.

(3) The following regulations were made under powers contained in Part 7 of TIOPA 2010 and are therefore revoked by virtue of sub-paragraph (1)—

(a) the Corporation Tax (Financing Costs and Income) Regulations 2009 (S.I. 2009/3173);

(b) the Corporation Tax (Tax Treatment of Financing Costs and Income) (Acceptable Financial Statements) Regulations 2009 (S.I. 2009/3217);

(c) the Corporation Tax (Exclusion from Short-Term Loan Relationships) Regulations 2009 (S.I. 2009/3313);

(d) the Tax Treatment of Financing Costs and Income (Available Amount) Regulations 2010 (S.I. 2010/2929);

(e) the Tax Treatment of Financing Costs and Income (Correction of Mismatches) Regulations 2010 (S.I. 2010/3025);

(f) the Taxation (International and Other Provisions) Act 2010 (Part 7) (Amendment) Regulations 2012 (S.I. 2012/3045);

(g) the Tax Treatment of Financing Costs and Income (Correction of Mismatches: Partnerships and Pensions) Regulations 2012 (S.I. 2012/3111);

(h) the Tax Treatment of Financing Costs and Income (Excluded Schemes) Regulations 2013 (S.I. 2013/2892);

(i) the Tax Treatment of Financing Costs and Income (Change of Accounting Standards: Investment Entities) Regulations 2015 (S.I. 2015/662).

TIOPA 2010: other amendments

12 TIOPA 2010 is amended as follows.

13 In section 1 (overview of Act), in subsection (1)—

(a) omit the "and" at the end of paragraph (d), and

(b) after paragraph (e) insert—

"(f) Part 9A (controlled foreign companies), and

(g) Part 10 (corporate interest restriction)."

14 In section 155 (transfer pricing: "potential advantage" in relation to United Kingdom taxation), in subsection (6), for paragraph (a) substitute—

"(a) Part 10 (corporate interest restriction),".

15 In section 157 (direct participation), in subsection (1)—

(a) omit the "and" at the end of paragraph (c), and

(b) after paragraph (d) insert ", and

(e) in Part 10, section 463(4)."

16 In section 159 (indirect participation: potential direct participant), in subsection (1)—

(a) omit the "and" at the end of paragraph (c), and

(b) after paragraph (d) insert ", and

(e) in Part 10, section 463(4)."

17 In section 160 (indirect participation: one of several major participants), in subsection (1)—

(a) omit the "and" at the end of paragraph (c), and

(b) after paragraph (d) insert ", and

(e) in Part 10, section 463(4)."

18 In section 259CB (financial instruments: hybrid or otherwise impermissible deduction/non-inclusion mismatches and their extent), in subsection (6), for paragraph (e) substitute—

"(e) Part 10 (corporate interest restriction)."

19 In section 259DC (hybrid transfer deduction/non-inclusion mismatches and their extent), in subsection (5), for paragraph (d) substitute—

"(d) Part 10 (corporate interest restriction)."

20 After section 259NE (treatment of a person who is a member of a partnership) insert—

"Priority

259NEA Priority

For the purposes of this Part, the provisions of Part 10 (corporate interest restriction) are to be treated as of no effect."

21 (1) Chapter 3 of Part 9A (CFCs: the CFC charge gateway) is amended as follows.

(2) In section 371CE (which makes provision for determining whether Chapter 6 of Part 9A applies)—

(a) in subsection (2)(a), after "period" insert "(see section 371CEA)", and

(b) omit subsections (4) and (5).

(3) After section 371CE insert—

"371CEA Section 371CE: meaning of "group treasury company"

(1) This section makes provision for determining whether the CFC is a group treasury company in the accounting period for the purposes of section 371CE.

(2) The CFC is a group treasury company in the accounting period if—

(a) it is a member of a worldwide group in relation to a period of account in which the accounting period wholly or partly falls,

(b) throughout the accounting period—

(i) all, or substantially all, of the activities undertaken by it consist of treasury activities undertaken for the group, and

(ii) all, or substantially all, of its assets and liabilities relate to such activities, and

(c) at least 90% of its relevant income for the accounting period is group treasury revenue.

(3) For the purposes of this section a company undertakes treasury activities for the group if it does one or more of the following in relation to, or on behalf of, the group or any of its members—

(a) managing surplus deposits of money or overdrafts,

(b) making or receiving deposits of money,

(c) lending money,

(d) subscribing for or holding shares in a company which is a UK group company undertaking treasury activities for the group at least 90% of whose relevant income is group treasury revenue for its relevant accounting period,

(e) investing in debt securities, and

(f) hedging assets, liabilities, income or expenses.

(4) For the purposes of this section "group treasury revenue", in relation to a company, means revenue—

(a) arising from the treasury activities that the company undertakes for the group, and

(b) accounted for as such under generally accepted accounting practice,

before any deduction (whether for expenses or otherwise).

(5) But revenue consisting of a dividend or other distribution is not group treasury revenue of the company unless it is from a company that meets the conditions in subsection (3)(d).

(6) In this section—

"debt security" has the same meaning as in the Handbook made by the Financial Conduct Authority or Prudential Regulation Authority under the Financial Services and Markets Act 2000 (as the Handbook in question has effect from time to time),

"period of account" has the same meaning as in Part 10,

"relevant accounting period" has the same meaning as in Part 10,

"relevant income", in relation to a company, means income—

(a) arising from the activities of the company, and

(b) accounted for as such under generally accepted accounting practice,

before any deduction (whether for expenses or otherwise),

"UK group company" has the same meaning as in Part 10, and

"worldwide group" has the same meaning as in Part 10."

(4) In consequence of the amendments made by this paragraph, in Schedule 47 to FA 2013, omit paragraph 17.

22 (1) Chapter 9 of Part 9A (CFCs: exemption for profits from qualifying loan relationships) is amended as follows.

(2) For section 371IE substitute—

"371IE The "matched interest profits" exemption

(1) This section applies if—

(a) there are profits of qualifying loan relationships which are not exempt after sections 371IB and 371ID have been applied to each qualifying loan relationship,

(b) the relevant corporation tax accounting period (as defined in section 371BC(3)) of company C is a relevant accounting period of it in relation to a period of account of a worldwide group,

(c) the CFC's accounting period ends in that period of account, and

(d) apart from this section, the profits mentioned in paragraph (a) would be included in the chargeable profits of the CFC.

(2) In this section "the matched interest profits" means so much of the profits mentioned in subsection (1)(a) as remain after excluded credits and excluded debits are left out of account.

(3) If the aggregate net tax-interest expense of the group for the period is nil, all of the matched interest profits are exempt.

(4) Otherwise, there is a more limited exemption if the relevant proportion of the matched interest profits apportioned to C or other relevant chargeable companies exceeds the aggregate net tax-interest expense of the group for the period.

(5) For the purposes of this section "the relevant proportion of the matched interest profits apportioned to C or other relevant chargeable companies" is determined as follows.

Step 1

For each relevant chargeable company (including C) determine the percentage (P%) of the CFC's chargeable profits that are apportioned to the company under step 5 of section 371BC(1).

Step 2

For each relevant chargeable company (including C) multiply P% by the matched interest profits.

Step 3

The sum of the amounts for each company found under step 2 is "the relevant proportion of the matched interest profits apportioned to C or other relevant chargeable companies".

(6) For the purposes of this section a company is a relevant chargeable company if the relevant corporation tax accounting period of the company is a relevant accounting period in relation to the period of account of the group.

(7) The limited exemption is given effect by treating the matched interest profits as equal to the amount found by multiplying the amount that they would otherwise be by—

$$E / RPMIP$$

where—

E is the amount of the excess mentioned in subsection (4), and

RPMIP is the relevant proportion of the matched interest profits apportioned to C or other relevant chargeable companies.

(8) For the purposes of this section the aggregate net tax-interest expense of a worldwide group for a period of account is determined in accordance with Part 10 (corporate interest restriction) but without regard to debits, credits or other amounts arising from—

(a) banking business carried on by a company within the charge to corporation tax, or

(b) insurance business carried on by a company within the charge to corporation tax.

(9) For the purposes of this section—

"excluded credit" has the meaning given by section 386(3),

"excluded debit" has the meaning given by section 383(3), and

"period of account", "relevant accounting period" and "worldwide group" have the same meanings as in Part 10."

(3) In section 371IJ (claims), in subsection (6), for "the tested income amount or the tested expense amount mentioned in section 371IE(2)" substitute "the aggregate net tax-interest expense that is mentioned in section 371IE".

23 (1) Chapter 19 of Part 9A (CFCs: assumed taxable total profits, assumed total profits and the corporation tax assumptions) is amended as follows.

(2) In section 371SL (group relief etc), at the end insert—

"(4) This section is subject to section 371SLA (corporate interest restriction)."

(3) After section 371SL insert—

"371SLA Corporate interest restriction

(1) This section applies for the purpose of applying Part 10 (corporate interest restriction).

(2) Assume—

(a) that the CFC is a member of a worldwide group for a period of account of which it would be a member if section 371SL were ignored, and

(b) that the CFC is the only UK group company in the period (within the meaning of that Part).

(3) Assume also that Part 10 applies as if subsections (2) and (3) of section 392 (interest capacity of the group: the de minimis amount) were omitted."

24 In Schedule 11, at the end insert—

"PART 7

CORPORATE INTEREST RESTRICTION: INDEX OF DEFINED
EXPRESSIONS USED IN PART 10

abbreviated interest restriction return (in Part 10)	paragraph 20 of Schedule 7A
abbreviated return election (in Part 10)	paragraph 19 of Schedule 7A
accounting period (in Part 10)	Chapter 2 of Part 2 of CTA 2009 (applied by section 1119 of CTA 2010)
adjusted net group-interest expense of a worldwide group (in Part 10)	section 413
aggregate net tax-interest expense of a worldwide group (in Part 10)	section 390
aggregate net tax-interest income of a worldwide group (in Part 10)	section 390
aggregate tax-EBITDA of a worldwide group (in Part 10)	section 405
allocated reactivation of company for period of account (in Part 10)	paragraph 25 of Schedule 7A
allowable loss (in Part 10)	TCGA 1992 (applied by section 1119 of CTA 2010)
associated (in Chapter 8 of Part 10)	section 449(2)
amount available for reactivation of company in period of account (in Part 10)	paragraph 26 of Schedule 7A
available, in relation to interest allowance (in Chapter 4 of Part 10)	section 393
balance sheet (in Chapter 8 of Part 10)	section 449(1)
chargeable gain (in Part 10)	TCGA 1992 (applied by section 1119 of CTA 2010)
the Commissioners (in Part 10)	section 494(1)
company (in Part 10)	section 1121 of CTA 2010

company tax return (in Schedule 7A)	paragraph 73 of Schedule 7A
consenting company (in Part 10)	paragraph 10 of Schedule 7A
consolidated partnership (in Part 10)	section 430
consolidated subsidiary of another entity (in Part 10)	section 475
derivative contract (in Part 10)	Part 7 of CTA 2009 (applied by section 1119 of CTA 2010)
disallowed, in relation to tax-interest expense amount (in Part 10)	section 378
drawn up on acceptable principles, in relation to financial statements (in Chapter 11 of Part 10)	section 481
fair value accounting (in Part 10)	section 494(1)
fair value (in Part 10)	section 494(1)
filing date, in relation to a period of account of a worldwide group (in Part 10)	paragraph 7(5) of Schedule 7A
finance lease (in Part 10)	section 494(1)
financial asset (in Chapter 8 of Part 10)	section 449(1)
financial statements of a worldwide group (in Part 10)	section 479
fixed ratio method (in Part 10)	section 397
for accounting purposes (in Part 10)	section 1127(4) of CTA 2010
full interest restriction return (in Part 10)	paragraph 20 of Schedule 7A
generally accepted accounting practice (in Part 10)	section 1127(1) and (3) of CTA 2010
group-EBITDA (chargeable gains) election (in Part 10)	paragraph 15 of Schedule 7A
group ratio election (in Part 10)	paragraph 13 of Schedule 7A
group ratio (blended) election (in Part 10)	paragraph 14 of Schedule 7A
group ratio method (in Part 10)	section 398
group ratio percentage (in Part 10)	section 399
IAS financial statements (in Part 10)	section 488
impairment loss (in Part 10)	section 391

income (in Part 10)	section 1119 of CTA 2010
insurance company (in Part 10)	section 141 of FA 2012
interest allowance of a worldwide group (in Part 10)	section 396
interest allowance (alternative calculation) election (in Part 10)	paragraph 16 of Schedule 7A
interest allowance (consolidated partnerships) election (in Part 10)	paragraph 18 of Schedule 7A
interest allowance (non-consolidated investment) election (in Part 10)	paragraph 17 of Schedule 7A
interest capacity of a worldwide group (in Part 10)	section 392
interest reactivation cap of a worldwide group (in Part 10)	section 373
interest restriction return (in Part 10)	section 494(1)
international accounting standards (in Part 10)	section 1127(5) of CTA 2010
investor in a worldwide group (in Part 10)	section 404
loan relationship (in Part 10)	Part 5 of CTA 2009 (applied by section 1119 of CTA 2010)
loan relationships or other financing arrangements (in Chapter 8 of Part 10)	section 449(1)
local authority (in Part 10)	section 1130 of CTA 2010
local authority association (in Part 10)	section 1131 of CTA 2010
member of a worldwide group (in Part 10)	section 473(4)(a)
multi-company worldwide group (in Part 10)	section 473(4)(d)
net group-interest expense of a worldwide group (in Part 10)	section 410
net tax-interest expense of a company (in Part 10)	section 389
net tax-interest income of a company (in Part 10)	section 389
non-consenting company (in Part 10)	paragraph 10 of Schedule 7A
non-consolidated associate of a worldwide group (in Part 10)	section 429
non-consolidated subsidiary of an entity (in Part 10)	section 475
notice (in Part 10)	section 1119 of CTA 2010

party to a loan relationship (in Part 10)	section 494(2)
period of account of a worldwide group (in Part 10)	section 480
profit before tax, of a worldwide group (in Chapter 7 of Part 10)	section 416
pro-rata share of company (of total disallowed amount) (in Part 10)	paragraph 23 of Schedule 7A
pro-rata share of accounting period (of total disallowed amount) (in Part 10)	paragraph 24 of Schedule 7A
provision (in relation to a public infrastructure asset) (in Chapter 8 of Part 10)	section 436
public infrastructure asset (in Chapter 8 of Part 10)	section 436
qualifying charitable donation (in Part 10)	Part 6 of CTA 2010 (applied by section 1119 of CTA 2010)
qualifying infrastructure company (in Chapter 8 of Part 10)	section 433
qualifying infrastructure activity (in Chapter 8 of Part 10)	section 436
qualifying net group-interest expense of a worldwide group (in Part 10)	section 414
recognised, in financial statements (in Part 10)	section 489
recognised stock exchange (in Part 10)	section 1137 of CTA 2010
registered pension scheme (in Part 10)	section 150(2) of FA 2004 (applied by section 1119 of CTA 2010)
related party (in Part 10)	sections 462 to 472
related party investor (in Part 10)	section 404
relevant asset (in Chapter 7 of Part 10)	section 417
relevant accounting period (in Part 10)	section 490
relevant expense amount (in Chapter 7 of Part 10)	section 411
relevant income amount (in Chapter 7 of Part 10)	section 411
relevant public body (in Part 10)	section 491
reporting company (in Part 10)	section 494(1)
the return period (in Part 10)	section 494(1)
service concession agreement (in Part 10)	section 494(1)
share, of an investor in a worldwide group (in Part 10)	section 404

single-company worldwide group (in Part 10)	section 473(4)(c)
subject to interest reactivations (in Part 10)	section 373
subject to interest restrictions (in Part 10)	section 373
tax (in Part 10)	section 1119 of CTA 2010
tax-EBITDA of a company (in Part 10)	section 406
tax-interest expense amount of a company (in Part 10)	section 382
tax-interest income amount of a company (in Part 10)	section 385
trade (in Part 10)	section 1119 of CTA 2010
total disallowed amount of a worldwide group (in Part 10)	section 373
UK generally accepted accounting practice (in Part 10)	section 1127(2) of CTA 2010
UK group company (in Part 10)	section 492
UK property business (in Part 10)	Chapter 2 of Part 4 of CTA 2009 (applied by section 1119 of CTA 2010)
the UK sector of the continental shelf (in Chapter 8 of Part 10)	section 449(1)
the ultimate parent, of a worldwide group (in Part 10)	section 473(4)(b)
unexpired (in Chapter 4 of Part 10)	section 395
United Kingdom (in Part 10)	section 1170 of CTA 2010
used (in Chapter 4 of Part 10)	section 394
within the charge to corporation tax (in Part 10)	section 1167 of CTA 2010
wholly-owned subsidiary (in Part 10)	section 494(1)
a worldwide group (in Part 10)	section 473"

PART 4

COMMENCEMENT AND TRANSITIONAL PROVISION

Commencement: new Part 10 of TIOPA

25 (1) The corporate interest restriction amendments have effect in relation to periods of account of worldwide groups that begin on or after 1 April 2017.

(2) In this paragraph "the corporate interest restriction amendments" means the amendments made by Parts 1 to 3 of this Schedule, apart from those made by paragraph 11 (repeal of Part 7 of TIOPA 2010).

(3) Any regulations made by the Treasury or Commissioners under Part 10 of TIOPA 2010 before 1 April 2018 may have effect in relation to periods of account of worldwide groups that begin on or after 1 April 2017.

(4) Sub-paragraphs (6) to (11) apply if—

(a) financial statements of a worldwide group are drawn up by or on behalf of the ultimate parent in respect of a period that begins before, and ends on or after, 1 April 2017,

(b) the period in respect of which the financial statements are drawn up is 18 months or less, and

(c) the financial statements are drawn up before the end of the period of 30 months beginning with the beginning of the period in respect of which they are drawn up.

(5) In sub-paragraphs (6) to (11)—

(a) "the group's actual financial statements" means the financial statements mentioned in sub-paragraph (4);

(b) "the straddling period of account" means the period in respect of which those financial statements are drawn up.

(6) For the purposes of Part 10 of TIOPA 2010, the group's actual financial statements are treated as not having been drawn up.

(7) Instead, financial statements of the worldwide group are treated for those purposes as having been drawn up in respect of each of the following periods—

(a) the period beginning at the time the straddling period of account begins and ending with 31 March 2017, and

(b) the period beginning with 1 April 2017 and ending at the time the straddling period of account ends.

(8) Where condition C or D in section 481 of TIOPA 2010 is met in relation to the group's actual financial statements, the financial statements treated as drawn up by sub-paragraph (7) are treated as drawn up in accordance with the generally accepted accounting principles and practice with which the group's actual financial statements were drawn up.

(9) Where neither of those conditions is met in relation to the group's actual financial statements, the financial statements treated as drawn up by sub-paragraph (7) are IAS financial statements.

(10) Where, for the purpose of determining amounts recognised in the financial statements treated as drawn up by sub-paragraph (7), it is expedient to apportion any amount that is recognised in the group's actual financial statements, the apportionment is to be made in accordance with section 1172 of CTA 2010 (apportionment on a time basis).

(11) But if it appears that apportionment in accordance with that section would work unjustly or unreasonably, the apportionment is to be made on a just and reasonable basis.

(12) Expressions used in this paragraph and in Part 10 of TIOPA 2010 have the same meaning in this paragraph as they have in that Part.

Commencement: repeal of Part 7 of TIOPA 2010

26 (1) The repeals and revocations made by paragraph 11 of this Schedule have effect in relation to periods of account of the worldwide group that begin on or after 1 April 2017.

(2) Sub-paragraphs (4) to (10) apply if financial statements of the worldwide group are drawn up in respect of a period that begins before, and ends on or after, 1 April 2017.

(3) In sub-paragraphs (4) to (10)—

(a) "the group's actual financial statements" means the financial statements mentioned in sub-paragraph (2);

(b) "the straddling period of account" means the period in respect of which those financial statements are drawn up.

(4) For the purposes of Part 7 of TIOPA 2010, the group's actual financial statements are treated as not having been drawn up.

(5) Instead, financial statements of the worldwide group are treated for those purposes as having been drawn up in respect of each of the following periods—

(a) the period beginning at the time the straddling period of account begins and ending with 31 March 2017, and

(b) the period beginning with 1 April 2017 and ending at the time the straddling period of account ends.

(6) Where condition B, C or D in regulation 2 of the Acceptable Financial Statements Regulations is met in relation to the group's actual financial statements, the financial statements treated as drawn up by sub-paragraph (5) are treated as drawn up in accordance with the generally accepted accounting principles and practice with which the group's actual financial statements were drawn up.

(7) Where none of those conditions is met in relation to the group's actual financial statements, the financial statements treated as drawn up by sub-paragraph (5) are IAS financial statements.

(8) Where, for the purpose of determining amounts recognised in the financial statements treated as drawn up by sub-paragraph (5), it is expedient to apportion any amount that is recognised in the group's actual financial statements, the apportionment is to be made in accordance with section 1172 of CTA 2010 (apportionment on a time basis).

(9) But if it appears that apportionment in accordance with that section would work unjustly or unreasonably, the apportionment is to be made on a just and reasonable basis.

(10) In sub-paragraph (6), "the Acceptable Financial Statements Regulations" means the Corporation Tax (Tax Treatment of Financing Costs and Income) (Acceptable Financial Statements) Regulations 2009 (S.I. 2009/3217).

(11) Expressions used in this paragraph and in Part 7 of TIOPA 2010 have the same meaning in this paragraph as they have in that Part.

Time limits for elections relating to financial statements of a worldwide group

27 (1) In section 484 of TIOPA 2010, subsection (5) (which requires the date specified in an election under subsection (3) of that section to be on or after the day on which the election is made) does not apply in relation to an election made on or before 31 March 2018.

(2) In section 486 of that Act, subsection (5)(a) (which requires an election under that section to be made before the end-day of the new period of account) does not apply in relation to an election made on or before 31 March 2018.

Time limit relating to appointment of reporting company or filing interest restriction return

28 (1) Paragraph 1(4)(a) of Schedule 7A to TIOPA 2010 (notice of the appointment of reporting company ineffective if given outside the period specified in that provision) does not apply to a notice that—

(a) is given on or before 31 March 2018, and

(b) would otherwise be of no effect by reason only of the expiry of the period specified in that provision.

(2) Paragraph 2(4)(a) of that Schedule (notice of the revocation of the appointment of reporting company ineffective if given outside the period specified in that provision) does not apply to a notice that—

(a) is given on or before 31 March 2018, and

(b) would otherwise be of no effect by reason only of the expiry of the period specified in that provision.

(3) Where the date determined under paragraph 7(5) of that Schedule as the filing date in relation to a period of account of a worldwide group would (apart from this sub-paragraph) be a date before 30 June 2018, that provision has effect as if it provided for the filing date in relation to the period to be 30 June 2018.

Change of accounting policy

29 (1) For the purposes of Part 10 of TIOPA 2010 a debit or credit to which this paragraph applies is to be ignored.

(2) This paragraph applies to a debit or credit if—

(a) it is brought into account under the Loan Relationships and Derivative Contracts (Change of Accounting Practice) Regulations 2004 (S.I. 2004/3271), and

(b) the later period, in relation to the change of accounting policy to which the debit or credit relates, begins before 1 April 2017.

(3) In sub-paragraph (2) "the later period" has the same meaning as in the regulations mentioned in that sub-paragraph.

Adjustments under Schedule 7 to F(No.2)A 2015

30 (1) For the purposes of Part 10 of TIOPA 2010 a debit or credit to which this paragraph applies is to be ignored.

(2) This paragraph applies to a debit or credit if—

(a) it is brought into account for the purposes of Part 5 of CTA 2009 by virtue of paragraphs 115 and 116 of Schedule 7 to F(No.2)A 2015 (transitional adjustments relating to loan relationships), or

(b) it is brought into account for the purposes of Part 7 of CTA 2009 by virtue of paragraphs 120 and 121 of that Schedule (transitional adjustments relating to derivative contracts).

Power to make elections under Disregard Regulations for pre-1 April 2020 derivative contracts

31 (1) A company which is a UK group company of a worldwide group on 1 April 2017 may elect for the Disregard Regulations to have effect as if—

(a) the company had made an election ("the disregard election") under regulation 6A of those Regulations for the purposes of regulation 6(1)(a) of those Regulations,

(b) the disregard election applied to regulations 7, 8 and 9 of those Regulations, and

(c) the disregard election had effect in relation to derivative contracts entered into by the company before 1 April 2020.

(2) The election has effect for the calculation under Part 10 of TIOPA 2010 of—

(a) the tax-interest expense amounts and tax-interest income amounts of the company and any relevant transferee company, and

(b) the adjusted corporation tax earnings under section 406 of that Act of the company and any relevant transferee company.

(3) A company is a "relevant transferee company" if regulation 6B or 6C of the Disregard Regulations applies in relation to the company as the transferee mentioned in the regulation (on the assumption that an election has been made before the transfer under this paragraph).

(4) An election under this paragraph has effect only if every company which was a UK group company of the worldwide group on 1 April 2017 (other than one which was dormant on that date or at the time the election is made) also makes an election under this paragraph.

(5) An election under this paragraph—

(a) must be made before 1 April 2018, and

(b) is irrevocable.

(6) Section 457 of TIOPA 2010 is to apply in relation to debits resulting from an election under this paragraph.

(7) In this paragraph "the Disregard Regulations" means the Loan Relationships and Derivative Contracts (Disregard and Bringing into Account of Profits and Losses) Regulations 2004 (S.I. 2004/3256).

(8) Expressions used in this paragraph and in Part 10 of TIOPA 2010 have the same meaning in this paragraph as they have in that Part.

Qualifying infrastructure companies

32 (1) In the case of an accounting period of a company beginning before 1 April 2018, the company may make an election under section 433 or 444 of TIOPA 2010 before that date.

(2) Companies making an election under section 435 of TIOPA 2010 before 1 April 2018 may specify a date in the election from which it has effect which is before the date on which the election is made.

33 (1) This paragraph applies in the case of an accounting period of a company beginning before 1 April 2018 ("the transitional accounting period") if—

(a) the company does not meet the public infrastructure assets test, or the public infrastructure income test, for the transitional accounting period, but

(b) in the case of each test that it does not meet as mentioned in paragraph (a), the company would meet the test for an accounting period that includes that date and is at least 3 months long.

(2) For the purposes of section 433 of TIOPA 2010 the company is treated as meeting the test (or tests) for the transitional accounting period.

(3) For the purposes of sections 438 and 440 to 442 of TIOPA 2010 such adjustments to the relevant amounts are to be made as are just and reasonable, having regard to the extent to which, but for this paragraph, the company would not have met the public infrastructure assets test, or the public infrastructure income test, for the transitional accounting period.

(4) For this purpose "the relevant amounts" means—

(a) amounts that would otherwise have qualified as exempt amounts under section 438,

(b) amounts that would otherwise have been treated as mentioned in section 440,

(c) the tax-EBITDA of the company, and

(d) the amounts that would otherwise have been left of account as a result of section 442.

(5) Expressions used in this paragraph and in section 433 of TIOPA 2010 have the same meaning in this paragraph as they have in that section.

Counteracting effect of avoidance arrangements

34 (1) This paragraph applies in relation to section 461 of TIOPA 2010.

(2) Section 461 applies in relation to arrangements whenever entered into.

(3) Arrangements are not "relevant avoidance arrangements" for the purposes of section 461 so far as—

(a) they secure that an amount paid before 1 April 2017 is brought into account in an accounting period ending before that date, and

(b) directly in consequence of the amount being brought into account as mentioned in paragraph (a), there is a reduction in the tax-interest expense amounts that could otherwise have been left out of account under Part 10 of TIOPA 2010.

(4) If an accounting period begins before 1 April 2017 and ends on or after that date, sub-paragraph (3) is to have effect as if so much of the accounting period as falls before that date, and so much of that period as falls on or after that date, were treated as separate accounting periods.

(5) Arrangements are not "relevant avoidance arrangements" for the purposes of section 461 if the obtaining of any tax advantages that would otherwise arise from them can reasonably be regarded as arising wholly from commercial restructuring arrangements entered into in connection with the commencement of Part 10 of TIOPA 2010.

(6) For this purpose "commercial restructuring arrangements" means—

(a) arrangements that, but for that Part, would have resulted in significantly more corporation tax becoming payable as a result of one or more loan relationships being brought within the charge to corporation tax, or

(b) arrangements that—

(i) are designed to secure, in a way that is wholly consistent with its policy objectives, the benefit of a relief expressly conferred by a provision of that Part, and

(ii) are effected by taking only ordinary commercial steps in accordance with a generally prevailing commercial practice.

(7) This paragraph is to be read as if it formed part of section 461.

Commencement of orders or regulations containing consequential provision

35 (1) This paragraph applies in relation to any order or regulations made before 1 April 2018 by the Treasury or Commissioners containing provision that is consequential on provision made by this Schedule.

(2) Any order or regulations to which this paragraph applies may contain provision (however expressed) for securing that the consequential provision made by the order or regulations has effect in accordance with paragraph 25 (commencement) as if the consequential provision were included in the corporate interest restriction amendments mentioned in that paragraph.

Interpretation

36 References in this Part of this Schedule to Part 10 of TIOPA 2010 are to Part 10 of that Act as inserted by Parts 1 and 2 of this Schedule.

GENERAL NOTE

TIOPA 2010 Part 10 is divided into 11 Chapters.

Chapter 1 provides an overview of the legislation.

Chapter 2 provides for the disallowance of tax-interest expense amounts and the carrying forward and reactivation of tax-interest expense amounts for which tax relief has been disallowed.

Chapter 3 sets out what is included in determining the tax-interest expense amounts and tax-interest income amounts of a group company that is within the charge to corporation tax.

Chapter 4 covers the calculation of the interest capacity of a worldwide group for a period of account of the group.

Chapter 5 covers the interest allowance of a worldwide group.

Chapter 6 sets out how the aggregate tax-EBITDA of a worldwide group is to be determined.

Chapter 7 sets out how a worldwide group's net group-interest expense and group-EBITDA are to be determined.

Chapter 8 modifies the provisions of TIOPA 2010 Pt 10 in relation to qualifying infrastructure companies.

Chapter 9 modifies the application of TIOPA 2010 Pt 10 in relation to certain types of company or businesses.

Chapter 10 contains section 461, a regime anti-avoidance rule, that is designed to counteract attempts to manipulate the provisions of TIOPA 2010 Pt 10.

Chapter 11, inter alia, contains several definitions that apply for the purposes of TIOPA 2010 Pt 10, including the definition of a worldwide group.

TIOPA 2010 Pt 10 Ch 1 – overview

This Chapter provides an overview of Chapters 2 to 11 and the new TIOPA 2010 Sch 7A, as well as introducing certain key definitions.

TIOPA 2010 s 372 provides an overview of Chapters 2 to 11.

TIOPA 2010 s 373 sets out the circumstances in which a restriction will arise under TIOPA 2010 Pt 10. It also sets out the circumstances in which interest and other financing costs for which a worldwide group has been denied tax relief may be brought into account in a later period of account of the worldwide group (broadly cases where the group's net tax-interest expense for that future period is less than the interest restriction limit that applies for that period).

It also defines the meaning of:

- subject to interest restrictions;
- the total disallowed amount;
- interest reactivation cap; and
- subject to interest reactivations.

TIOPA 2010 s 374 introduces a new TIOPA 2010 Sch 7A (submission of returns and compliance) and provides an overview of Sch 7A.

TIOPA 2010 Pt 10 Ch 2 – disallowance of net tax-interest expense and reactivation of disallowed tax interest-expense amounts

This Chapter provides for the disallowance of tax-interest expense amounts and the carrying forward and reactivation of tax-interest expense amounts for which tax relief has been disallowed.

TIOPA 2010 s 375 applies where a valid interest restriction return is submitted on behalf of a worldwide group by a reporting company that is appointed to act on behalf of the worldwide group. The normal rule is that the interest disallowance that arises to a UK group company (a company that is a member of the worldwide group and is within the charge to corporation tax – see TIOPA 2010 s 492) is that set out in the interest restriction return. This section provides that where an interest disallowance is allocated to a company in a statement of interest restriction submitted by the reporting company, the company is required to leave out of account tax-interest expense amounts that, in total, equal its allocated disallowance. It is possible, however, for a UK group company to elect that the interest disallowance arising to it for an accounting period should be determined on a pro-rata basis by reference to its net tax-interest expense for the relevant period of account of the worldwide group as compared to the aggregate net tax-interest expense of group companies within the charge to corporation for that period (see new TIOPA 2010 Sch 7A paras 22(3)(b), 23 and 24).

TIOPA 2010 s 376 covers cases where no reporting company has been appointed in relation to the preparation of an interest restriction return for a period of account of the worldwide group, no interest restriction return has been submitted for a period, or a return that has been submitted does not comply with the requirements of TIOPA 2010 Sch 7A. In such cases the interest restriction arising to UK group companies which have net tax-interest expense for that period is determined on a pro rata basis by reference to each company's net tax-interest expense for the period, as compared to the aggregate net tax-interest expense for the period of group companies that are within the charge to corporation tax.

TIOPA 2010 s 377 specifies the order of priority which is to be used to determine tax-interest amounts that are to be left out of account where an interest restriction applies to a UK group company that has net tax-interest expense for a period of account of the worldwide group. It is possible, however, for a company to elect for a different basis to be used to determine its tax-interest amounts that are to be left out of account for that period.

TIOPA 2010 s 378 provides that, subject to the following, where a tax-interest expense amount is disallowed it may be carried forward indefinitely for relief in a future period where a group's interest allowance for that future period (see Chapter 5) exceeds its net tax-interest expense for that period.

Under TIOPA 2010 s 378 a disallowed tax-interest expense amount may not be carried forward in the following cases:

1. where the tax-interest amount that is disallowed is an amount that would have been deductible in computing a company's trading profits and in a subsequent accounting period (later accounting period):

   (a) the company ceases to carry on the trade, or the scale of the activities of the trade become small or negligible; or

   (b) the trade is uncommercial and non-statutory (such that relief for the loss would be denied under CTA 2010 s 44); or

2. where the tax-interest expense amount is an amount that would be brought into account in calculating the profits or losses of an investment business carried on by the company and in the later accounting period the company ceases to carry on the investment business, or the scale of the activities in the investment business become small or negligible,

the company is not permitted to carry the disallowed tax-interest expense forward to accounting periods beginning on or after the later accounting period.

TIOPA 2010 s 379 provides that where an interest restriction return states that a disallowed tax-interest expense of a company is to be reactivated in an accounting period (reactivation period) such amount is to be brought into account as a tax-interest expense arising in the reactivation period in the same form (e.g. a disallowed non-trading loan relationship deficit that is reactivated is treated as a non-trading debit arising in the reactivation period).

TIOPA 2010 s 380 specifies the order in which disallowed tax-interest expense amounts are to be reactivated. It is open to a company to elect for the reactivation to be determined on a different basis.

TIOPA 2010 s 381 provides for an exceptional case where an interest disallowance and interest reactivation arise in the same accounting period. This might be relevant where an accounting period of a UK group company straddles two periods of account of the worldwide group, one in which it is allocated a disallowance and another in which it is allocated a reactivation amount.

TIOPA 2010 Pt 10 Ch 3 – tax interest expense amounts and tax-interest income amounts

This Chapter sets out what is included in determining the tax-interest expense amounts and tax-interest income amounts of a group company that is within the charge to corporation tax.

TIOPA 2010 s 382 defines tax-interest expense amounts being:

– relevant loan relationship debits (see TIOPA 2010 s 383);
– relevant derivative contract debits (see TIOPA 2010 s 384);
– the financing cost implicit in amounts payable under a finance lease, debt factoring or any similar transaction, or a service concession arrangement if and to the extent that it is accounted for as a financial liability.

Appropriate adjustments are made on a just and reasonable basis to a company's tax-interest expense amounts where for all or part of the company's accounting period it was not a member of the worldwide group, or where all or part of the company's accounting period does not fall within the relevant period of account of the worldwide group. Under TIOPA 2010 Sch 7A para 54 HMRC have the power to determine that a different just and reasonable basis should be used. In such cases the taxpayer has a right of appeal that the basis determined by HMRC is not just and reasonable.

TIOPA 2010 s 383 defines relevant loan relationship debits. These are debits that arise, or which are treated as arising from, loan relationships, whether they are taken into account for the purposes of CTA 2009 Pt 3 or Pt 5, other than exchange losses and impairment losses.

TIOPA 2010 s 384 defines relevant derivative contract debits. These are debits arising in respect of a derivative contract that would be brought into account in computing a company's profits for the purposes of CTA 2009 Pt 3 or 5, other than excluded debits, where the underlying subject matter of the derivative contract consists of one or more of the following:

- interest rates;
- any index determined by reference to income or retail prices;
- currency;
- an asset or liability representing a loan relationship; and
- any other underlying subject matter which is subordinate in relation to any of the foregoing or is of small value in comparison with the value of the underlying subject matter as a whole. These tests are to be determined at the time the company becomes a party to the derivative contract.

The definition of excluded debits covers:

- exchange losses;
- impairment losses; and
- debits arising in respect of a derivative contract which hedges risks arising in the ordinary course of a trade where the contract was entered into wholly for reasons unrelated to the capital structure of the worldwide group, or any member of it.

TIOPA 2010 s 385 defines the tax-interest income amounts of a company. These are:

- relevant loan relationship credits (see TIOPA 2010 s 386);
- relevant derivative contract credits (see TIOPA 2010 s 387);
- financing income implicit in amounts receivable under a finance lease, debt factoring or any similar transaction, or a service concession arrangement if and to the extent that the arrangement is accounted for as a financial asset; and
- amounts receivable from a borrower in respect of guarantees provided by the company in respect of a loan made to the borrower.

Appropriate adjustments are made on a just and reasonable basis where part of a company's accounting period does not fall within the period of account of the worldwide group, or where for part of an accounting period the company was not a member of the worldwide group. Under TIOPA 2010 Sch 7A para 54 HMRC can substitute their own adjustment if they do not consider that the adjustment made is just and reasonable. In such circumstances the taxpayer has a right of appeal that the apportionment made by HMRC is not just and reasonable.

TIOPA 2010 s 386 defines relevant loan relationship credits. These are credits that would be brought into account for corporation tax in respect of a loan relationship under either CTA 2009 Pt 3 or Pt 5, other than exchange gains or amounts representing the reversal of an impairment loss.

TIOPA 2010 s 387 defines relevant derivative contract credits. These are credits that would be brought into account for corporation tax purposes in respect of a derivative contract under CTA 2009 Pt 3 or 5, other than excluded credits, where the underlying subject matter of the derivative consists of one or more of the following:

- interest rates;
- any index determined by reference to income or retail prices;
- currency;
- an asset or liability representing a loan relationship;
- any other underlying subject matter which is subordinate in relation to any of the foregoing or is of small value in comparison with the value of the underlying subject matter as a whole. These tests are to be judged at the time that the company becomes a party to the derivative contract.

The definition of excluded credits covers:

- an exchange gain;
- the reversal of an impairment loss; and
- credits arising from a derivative contract which hedges risks arising in the ordinary course of a trade where the contract was entered into wholly for reasons unrelated to the capital structure of the worldwide group (or any member of it).

TIOPA 2010 s 388 provides that where a tax-interest income amount carries an entitlement to double tax credit relief the amount that is brought into account in determining the company's tax-interest income for the purposes of TIOPA 2010 Pt 10 is to be reduced to the extent income has been sheltered by double tax credit relief.

TIOPA 2010 s 389 provides that:

- a company will have a net tax-interest expense for a period of account of the worldwide group where the total of its tax-interest expense amounts for its accounting period that is referable to that period of account exceeds the total of its tax-interest income amounts for that accounting period; and
- a company will have net tax-interest income for a period of account of the

worldwide group where the total of its tax-interest income amounts for its accounting period that is referable to that period of account exceeds the total of its tax interest-expense amounts for that accounting period.

TIOPA 2010 s 390 defines the aggregate net tax-interest expense and aggregate net tax-interest income of a worldwide group for a period of account (being the sum of the net tax-interest expense and net tax-interest income of companies that were members of the worldwide group and within the charge to corporation tax for that period of account).

TIOPA 2010 s 391 defines an impairment loss as being a loss in respect of the impairment of a financial asset, other than a debit that is brought into account in respect of an asset for which fair value accounting is used.

TIOPA 2010 Pt 10 Ch 4 – calculation of interest capacity of a worldwide group

This Chapter covers the calculation of the interest capacity of a worldwide group for a period of account.

TIOPA 2010 s 392 defines the interest capacity of a worldwide group for a period of account of the group. This is the interest allowance of the group for the period (as defined in Chapter 5) as increased by the aggregate of the unused interest allowances of the group for previous periods to the extent that they are available in the current period. Where the interest allowance is less than the de minimis limit the de minimis limit applies. The de minimis limit is £2 million, proportionally reduced where the period of account is less than 12 months in length.

TIOPA 2010 ss 393–395 provide that where a group's interest allowance for a period of account (originating period) exceeds its net tax-interest expense for that period the excess may be carried forward for relief against net tax-interest expense arising in periods of account that begin before and end within five years of the end of the originating period. Where a future period begins within five years of the end of the originating period and ends after five years of the end of the originating period, the interest allowance which may be carried forward to that future period (the receiving period) is proportionately reduced by reference to the proportion of the receiving period falling within the five-year limit.

Where the group has net tax-interest income for a period of account the excess interest allowance that it can carry forward for that period is increased by the amount of its net tax-interest income for that period (TIOPA 2010 s 396(1), as applied by TIOPA 2010 s 392).

No carry forward of an excess interest allowance is possible where an abbreviated return election is made for the period of account in which the excess arises or in any intervening period or in the receiving period. Nor is a carry forward of an excess allowance possible where an interest restriction return has not been submitted for any such period (TIOPA 2010 s 393(5)). Where an abbreviated return has been filed for a period of account it is possible for a full return to be filed for that period within 60 months of the end of that period of account (TIOPA 2010 Sch 7A para 9) so that, inter alia, an excess interest allowance can be carried forward from that period.

TIOPA 2010 Pt 10 Ch 5 – calculation of interest allowance for a worldwide group

This Chapter covers the interest allowance of a worldwide group.

TIOPA 2010 s 396 sets out how the interest allowance of a worldwide group is to be determined. This is the basic interest allowance of the group for the period, as increased by the aggregate net tax-interest income of the group for the period.

Where no group ratio election is in force the basic interest allowance is calculated using the fixed ratio method and where such election is in force the allowance is calculated using the group ratio method.

TIOPA 2010 s 397 sets out the fixed ratio method. This is the lower of:
- 30% of the aggregate tax-EBITDA of the group for the period (see Chapter 6); and
- the fixed ratio debt cap of the group for the period (see TIOPA 2010 s 400(1))

TIOPA 2010 s 398 sets out how the interest allowance is to be calculated using the group ratio method. This is the lower of:
- the group ratio percentage of the aggregate tax-EBITDA of the group for the period; and
- the group ratio debt cap of the group for the period (see TIOPA 2010 s 400(2)).

TIOPA 2010 s 399 sets out how the group ratio percentage of a worldwide group is to be determined. This is:

$$\frac{\text{The qualifying net group-interest expense of the group for the period}}{\text{The group-EBITDA of the group for the period}} \times 100\%$$

Qualifying net group-interest expense is defined in TIOPA 2010 s 414 and group-EBITDA is defined in TIOPA 2010 s 416.

TIOPA 2010 s 400 defines the debt cap.

The fixed ratio debt cap of a worldwide group for a period of account of the group is the sum of

- the adjusted net group-interest expense of the group for the period (see TIOPA 2010 s 413); and
- the excess debt cap of the group that was generated in the immediately preceding period of account of the group (if any):

The group ratio debt cap of a worldwide group for a period of account of the group is the sum of:

- the qualifying net group-interest expense of the group for that period (see TIOPA 2010 s 414); and
- the excess debt cap of the group that was generated in the immediately preceding period of account of the group (if any).

The excess debt cap of the worldwide group for the immediately preceding period of account depends on whether a group ratio election was in force for that preceding period.

Where no group ratio election was in force for the preceding period of account (the generating period) the excess debt cap of the group that is generated in the generating period is:

- the fixed ratio debt cap of the group for the generating period less 30% of the aggregate tax-EBITDA of the group for the generating period.

Where a group ratio election was in force for the generating period the excess debt cap of the group is:

- the group ratio debt cap of the group for the generating period less the group ratio percentage of the aggregate tax-EBITDA of the group for that period.

In both the above cases where the calculation gives rise to a negative amount the excess debt cap is nil.

Further, where the amount determined under either calculation exceeds the carry-forward limit the amount that may be carried forward is restricted to the carry-forward limit. The carry-forward limit is:

- the excess debt cap generated in the period of account of the group immediately preceding the generating period (if any); and
- the total disallowed amount of the group in the generating period.

TIOPA 2010 s 401 sets out how the group ratio percentage is to be determined where a group blended election is in force for the relevant period of account. Very broadly, this permits a group ratio to be determined for a group (first group) by reference to not only the group ratio percentage of the first group for the period but also by reference to the group ratio percentage of one or more related party investors in the first group that are members of another worldwide group. In their draft guidance at CFM96860 HMRC state that this election is aimed, inter alia, at joint venture companies which might have significant amounts of related party debt and thus might have a low group ratio, whereas their investors might have high group ratios. The election enables such companies to access a higher group ratio than would otherwise be possible, thus enabling the amount of the interest restriction to be reduced or, possibly, eliminated.

TIOPA 2010 s 402 sets out how the group ratio debt cap is to be determined where a group ratio blended election is in force.

TIOPA 2010 s 403 applies in cases where a group ratio blended election is in force. It permits the worldwide group, when making a group ratio (blended) election to specify that an election under TIOPA 2010 Sch 7A is to be treated as having or as not having effect in relation to periods of account of the investor's worldwide group in calculating the group ratio percentage and/or group-EBITDA of the investor's worldwide group. Where the group ratio (blended) election does not specify that a particular election (the investor's election) under TIOPA 2010 Sch 7A is to be treated as having, or as not having, effect in relation to a period of account of the investor's worldwide group, the investor's election is only treated as having effect if it was made by the reporting company of the investor's worldwide group in relation to the period of account in question. TIOPA 2010 s 404 contains certain definitions that apply for TIOPA 2010 ss 401 to 403.

TIOPA 2010 Pt 10 Ch 6 – calculation of aggregate tax-EBITDA of a worldwide group

This Chapter sets out how the aggregate tax-EBITDA of a worldwide group is to be determined.

TIOPA 2010 s 405 provides that the aggregate tax-EBITDA for a period of account of the worldwide group is:

- the total of the tax-EBITDAs for the period of each company that was a member of the group at any time during that period; or
- where the total of the tax-EBITDAs is negative, nil.

TIOPA 2010 s 406 provides that a company's tax-EBITDA for a period of account of the worldwide group is its adjusted corporation tax earnings for that period. A company's adjusted corporation tax earnings for an accounting period are amounts brought into account in determining its total taxable profits (within the meaning of CTA 2010 s 4(2)) for that period, other than excluded amounts (see TIOPA 2010 s 407) or amounts that would have been so brought into account if the company had made profits or more profits of any description (and the amount is not an excluded amount). The section also covers cases where more than one accounting period of the company falls within the period of account of the worldwide group. In such cases appropriate adjustments are made on a just and reasonable basis so that only amounts that are referable to the part of the accounting period falling within the period of account of the worldwide group are brought into account.

TIOPA 2010 s 407 sets out the amounts that are not to be brought into account in determining a company's tax-EBITDA. These are:

- a tax-interest expense amount or a tax-interest income amount (see TIOPA 2010 ss 382 and 385);
- an allowance or a charge under CAA 2001;
- an excluded relevant intangibles debit or an excluded relevant intangibles credit (see TIOPA 2010 s 408);
- a loss made in a different accounting period other than an allowable loss for the purposes of TCGA 1992;
- a deficit from the company's loan relationships that is carried forward or is carried back to that accounting period;
- expenses of management that are referable to an accounting period other than the current accounting period;
- losses, including brought forward losses, that are claimed as group relief; and
- qualifying tax reliefs. These are certain sundry tax reliefs, including certain R&D expenditure reliefs and various reliefs for creative industries.

TIOPA 2010 s 408 defines the meaning of excluded relevant intangibles debits and credits. Broadly, these are amounts that are taken into account in determining a company's profits or losses for the purposes of the intangible fixed assets legislation.

TIOPA 2010 s 409 provides that where an amount of taxable income carries an entitlement to double tax credit relief, the amount of the income that is included in computing the company's tax-EBITDA is to be reduced to the extent income has been sheltered by double tax credit relief.

TIOPA 2010 Pt 10 Ch 7 – calculation of net group interest expense and group-EBITDA

This Chapter sets out how a group's net group-interest expense and group-EBITDA are to be determined.

TIOPA 2010 s 410 defines the net group-interest expense of a worldwide group for a period of account as being:

- the sum of amounts in respect of relevant expense amounts that are recognised in the financial statements of the group for the period as items of profit or loss; less
- the sum of the amounts in respect of relevant income amounts that are recognised in the financial statements of the group for the period as items of profit or loss.

The amounts in respect of relevant expense amounts are increased by any write-down during the period of account of any expenditure that has been capitalised in respect of an asset that is not a relevant asset. Relevant asset is defined in TIOPA 2010 s 417(5).

Similarly, the amounts in respect of relevant income amounts are increased by any income that has been capitalised as part of the carrying value of an asset, other than a relevant asset, that is written off in the relevant period of account.

TIOPA 2010 s 411 prescribes the amounts that are to be included in determining relevant expense amounts and relevant income amounts. Broadly, the amounts that are included are intended to track the amounts that are taken into account in determining the tax-interest expense amounts and tax-interest income amounts of a UK group company (see TIOPA 2010 ss 382 and 385).

TIOPA 2010 s 412 contains definitions of certain terms used in TIOPA 2010 s 411.

Adjusted net group-interest expense

TIOPA 2010 s 413 defines the meaning of adjusted net group-interest expense. This is:
- the net group-interest expense of the group for the period;
- increased by any upward adjustments; and
- reduced by any downward adjustments.

The definition of upwards adjustments covers:
- relevant expense amounts that have been capitalised during the period in determining the carrying value of an asset or liability;
- capitalised income that is written off which is included in the net group-interest expense of the group for the period by virtue of TIOPA 2010 s 410(5);
- amounts in respect of relevant expense amounts that are recognised in equity or shareholders' funds, which are not recognised as an item of profit or loss and which are brought into account in computing a company's taxable profits for the relevant period of account under CTA 2009 ss 321 or 605, or regulation 3A of the Taxation of Regulatory Capital Securities Regulations 2013 (SI 2013/3209), or which would be so brought into account were the relevant member of the group within the charge to corporation tax; and
- credits arising from the release or amendment to the terms of a loan that are prevented from being brought into charge to tax under CTA 2009 s 322(2) or 323A, or which would be so prevented were the relevant company within the charge to corporation tax.

The definition of a downwards adjustment covers:
- relevant income amounts that are capitalised during the period in determining the carrying value of an asset or liability;
- an amount that is included in group-interest expense of the group under TIOPA 2010 s 410(3) (capitalised interest written off);
- amounts in respect of relevant income amounts recognised in equity or shareholders' funds (and that are not recognised as an item of profit or loss), which are brought into account for corporation tax purposes by a member of the group under CTA 2009 s 321 or s 605 or regulation 3A of the Taxation of Regulatory Capital Securities Regulations 2013 (SI 2013/3209), or which would be so brought into account were the relevant member within the charge to corporation tax;
- the reversal of a credit which was exempt from tax under CTA 2009 s 323A, or which would have been so exempt had the debtor been within the charge to corporation tax; and
- amounts recognised as an item of profit or loss in the financial statements of the group for the relevant period of account in respect of dividends payable on preference shares that are recognised as a liability in those financial statements.

Qualifying net group-interest expense

This is defined in TIOPA 2010 s 414 as:
- the adjusted net group-interest expense of the group for the period; less
- the sum of any downward adjustments.

Where this calculation produces a negative amount the qualifying net group-interest expense of the group is nil.

The definition of downward adjustment covers:
- relevant expense amounts arising as a result of a transaction with or financial

liability owed to a related party (see TIOPA 2010 ss 462–465). Where a person was not a related party throughout the whole of the relevant period of account appropriate adjustments are made to exclude amounts referable to the part of the period for which the person was not a related party;
- results-dependent securities (see TIOPA 2010 s 415(4)–(6), (8)(a)); and
- equity notes within the meaning of CTA 2010 s 1016, other than a regulatory capital security within the meaning of the Taxation of Regulatory Capital Securities Regulations 2013 (SI 2013/3209) (see TIOPA 2010 s 415(7)).

A downward adjustment will only arise where the amount is recognised in the financial statements of the group period as an item of profit and loss and is not (and is not comprised in) a downward adjustment for the purposes of TIOPA 2010 s 413, or it is (or is comprised in) an upward adjustment for the purposes of that section.

For the purposes of calculating the qualifying net group-interest expense of the group for the relevant period of account a person will not be treated as being a related party where that person is a party to a loan relationship and has only been treated as a related party because the loan relationship has been guaranteed by a person that is a related party in relation to the borrower provided any of the following conditions are satisfied:
- the financial assistance was provided before 1 April 2017;
- the financial assistance is provided by a member of the group;
- the financial assistance relates only to an undertaking in relation to shares in the ultimate parent company group or loans to a member of the group; or
- the financial assistance is a performance guarantee in relation to the provision of goods or services (TIOPA 2010 s 415(1)–(3)).

Results-dependent securities are securities issued by an entity where the consideration given by the entity for the use of the principal secured depends (to any extent) on the results of all or part of the entity's business, or the results of all or part of the business of any other entity that was a member of the group at any time during the period of account of the group (TIOPA 2010 s 415(4)). The definition of results-dependent securities excludes amounts that are treated as an alternative finance return (within the meaning of CTA 2010 s 1019(2) (Islamic finance)), or a regulatory capital security within the meaning of the Taxation of Regulatory Capital Securities Regulations 2013 (SI 2013/3209)). It also excludes cases where interest is treated as results-dependent solely because the terms of the security provide for the consideration given for the use of the principal to be reduced if the results of the entity's business improve, or for the consideration to increase if the results of the business deteriorate (TIOPA 2010 s 415(5)).

Group-EBITDA

The group-EBITDA of a worldwide group for a period of account of the group (the relevant period) is defined in TIOPA 2010 s 416 as:
- the group's profit before tax;
- plus the net group-interest expense of the group for the period (see TIOPA 2010 s 410);
- plus the group's depreciation and amortisation adjustment.

Depreciation and amortisation adjustment

The group's depreciation and amortisation adjustment is defined in TIOPA 2010 s 416(3) as being the sum of:
- the capital (expenditure) adjustment;
- the capital (fair value movement) adjustment; and
- the capital (disposals) adjustment.

Capital (expenditure) adjustment

Broadly, this adjustment adds back amounts in respect of capital expenditure incurred by the group in respect of a relevant asset (including any relevant expense amounts previously included in the carrying value of relevant assets that are brought into account in determining the group's profit before tax for the period of account, including as a result of depreciation, amortisation, an impairment review, or the reversal of provisions made in previous periods) (see TIOPA 2010 s 417).

Relevant assets are defined as:
- plant, property and equipment;
- an investment property;
- an intangible asset;

- goodwill;
- shares in the company; or
- an interest in an entity which entitles the holder to a share of the profits of the entity (TIOPA 2010 s 417(5)).

The capital (fair value movement) adjustment

Broadly, this adjustment eliminates any profits or losses that are reflected in arriving at the group's profit before tax for the period of account in respect of relevant assets that are carried at fair value (see TIOPA 2010 s 418).

The capital (disposals) adjustment

Broadly, this adjustment eliminates profits or losses arising from the disposals of relevant assets that are brought into account for a period of account in determining the group's profit before tax and instead brings a gain (but not a loss) into account to the extent that the disposal proceeds of a relevant asset exceed its cost (see TIOPA 2010 s 419).

It is possible for a reporting company to make an irrevocable election for the gain arising on the disposal of a relevant asset to be determined in line with the provisions of the TCGA 1992, subject to the following modifications (see TIOPA 2010 s 422 and Sch 7A para 15):

- all members of the group are assumed to be within the charge to corporation tax;
- the substantial shareholding exemption is deemed not to apply;
- TIOPA 2010 Pt 2 (double tax relief) does not apply; and
- there is a deemed disposal of a relevant asset held by a member of the group if that member ceases to be a member of the group at any time during the relevant accounting period. In such cases where the company leaves the group as a result of the sale of its shares, the disposal proceeds of the relevant asset is such part of the disposal consideration received for the shares as it is just and reasonable to attribute to that asset. In the first instance the just and reasonable attribution is to be determined by the reporting company (TIOPA 2010 s 422(7)). HMRC, however, has the power to determine that a different just and reasonable basis should have been adopted. Such determination may be challenged on appeal on the grounds that the basis adopted by HMRC is not just and reasonable (TIOPA 2010 Sch 7A para 54).

The definition of a relevant asset does not include shares in (or other interests giving an entitlement to share in the profits of) a member of the group: TIOPA 2010 s 422(10).

Derivative contract subject to fair value accounting

In order to avoid any distortions arising on relevant derivative contracts that are used for hedging purposes and to which any of regulations 7 to 9 of the Loan Relationships and Derivative Contracts (Disregard and Bringing into Account of Profits and Losses) Regulations 2004 (SI 2004/3256) (Disregard Regulations) apply (or would apply if an election to apply these regulations had been made), the profit or loss that is recognised in respect of such contracts in the financial statements of the worldwide group is disregarded. Instead, the group is required to recognise the amounts which would have been recognised had regulations 7, 8 or 9 of the Disregard Regulations applied to such relevant contracts (see further TIOPA 2010 ss 420 and 421). This is to align the basis of recognition of profits and losses on such derivative contracts with the basis on which profits and losses are recognised for tax purposes in respect of UK group companies that have elected for the profits and losses arising on such contracts to be determined under regulations 7 to 9 of the Disregard Regulations.

This treatment could give rise to a mismatch where a company in the worldwide group that is within the charge to corporation tax (UK group company) has not elected to apply regulations 7, 8 and/or 9 of the Disregard Regulations to derivative contracts that it uses for hedging purposes. In such cases a UK group company can elect to compute its tax-interest expense or tax-interest income and its adjusted corporation tax earnings under TIOPA s 406 for the purposes of TIOPA 2010 Pt 10 as if such regulations applied to the derivative contracts in question. Such an election has effect for derivative contracts entered into before 1 April 2020, but only if a similar election is made by each UK group company (other than dormant companies) that was a UK group company on 1 April 2017. The election, which is irrevocable, must be made by 1 April 2018 (see F(No 2)A 2017 Sch 5 para 31).

Alternative calculation election

It is open for a reporting company to make an interest allowance (alternative calculation) election under TIOPA 2010 Sch 7A para 16. Where such an election is made the following provisions have effect for the purposes of determining the group-interest and group-EBITDA of the worldwide group.

Capitalised interest brought into account in accordance with GAAP

Normally capitalised interest is brought into account for the purposes of determining the adjusted net group-interest expense for the period in which it is capitalised. Where the interest is capitalised as part of the cost of an asset, the profits or losses on which fall to be calculated for corporation tax purposes on the basis in which they are recognised in a company's accounts in accordance with IFRS or UK GAAP, it is possible for a group to elect for such amounts to be brought into account in determining the adjusted net group-interest expense for the accounting period in which such amounts are recognised in profit or loss. Inter alia, this election is designed to assist property developers where interest is capitalised as part of work in progress and is recognised as part of the profit or loss arising on the disposal of the asset (see further TIOPA 2010 s 423).

Employers' pension contributions

Amounts in respect of employer pension contributions are excluded in arriving at the group's profit before tax. Instead the group profit before tax is reduced by the amount of the relief which members of the group are entitled by virtue of FA 2004 ss 196 to 200 in respect of pension contributions paid at a time when the relevant employer was a member of the worldwide group (see further TIOPA 2010 s 424).

Employee share acquisitions

Amounts recognised in arriving at the group's profit before tax in respect of employee share acquisition arrangements are disregarded. Instead a deduction is permitted for the deductions that would be allowed under CTA 2009 Pts 11 or 12. For these purposes all members of the group are deemed to be within the charge to corporation tax (see TIOPA 2010 s 425).

Changes in accounting policy

Where there is a change in accounting policy, under TIOPA 2010 s 426, the financial statements of the worldwide group are treated as being subject to the change of accounting policy adjustments that would apply for corporation tax purposes for the calculation of trading profits, loan relationships profits, derivative contracts profits and intangible fixed assets profits, as well under as the Loan Relationships and Derivative Contracts (Change of Accounting Practice) Regulations 2004 (SI 2004/3271) (COAP Regulations). This is to align the calculation of the profits of the worldwide group with the basis on which the taxable profits of UK group companies are calculated.

Debits or credits that are recognised under the COAP Regulations in respect of changes in accounting policy in an accounting period beginning before 1 April 2017 are disregarded (see F(No 2)A Sch 5 para 29).

Group interest and group-EBITDA

Under TIOPA 2010 ss 427–429 and Sch 7A para 17, it is possible for a reporting company of a worldwide group (first group) to elect for a period of account to include the group's portion of the adjusted net group-interest expense, qualifying net-group interest expense and group-EBITDA of:

- an associated worldwide group, whose results have not been consolidated on a line by line basis in the financial statements of the first group for the relevant period of account;
- a subsidiary which the parent company of the first group carries at fair value in its accounts (and thus whose results have not been consolidated on a line by line basis in the worldwide accounts of the first group); and/or
- a partnership for which an election under TIOPA 2010 s 430 and Sch 7A para 18 has been made by the first group.

Interest allowance (consolidated partnerships) election

Under TIOPA 2010 Sch 7A para 18 and s 430 it is possible for a reporting company to make an irrevocable election for income and expenses of a specified partnership, the results of which have been consolidated in the worldwide accounts of the group, not to be treated as items of profit or loss in the financial statements of the worldwide group and instead for the partnership to be accounted for using the equity method, under which the group would recognise its share of the overall profit or loss of the partnership for the relevant period (as opposed to separately recognising each of the items making up the partnership's profit or loss before tax in arriving at the group's profit before tax in the group's consolidated financial statements). Such an election cannot be made where a partnership has a subsidiary that is a company at any time during the relevant period of account.

TIOPA 2010 Pt 10 Ch 8 – public infrastructure

This Chapter modifies the provisions of TIOPA 2010 Pt 10 in relation to qualifying infrastructure companies. A qualifying infrastructure company is a company that is fully taxed in the UK, where all (or all but an insignificant portion) of the company's income and assets are referable to activities in relation to UK infrastructure assets. The definition of UK infrastructure assets covers:

– tangible assets forming part of the infrastructure of the UK; and
– buildings (or parts of buildings) that are let or sublet to unconnected persons as a part of a property business for a period of less than 50 years.

In either case the asset has to have (or is likely to have) an expected economic life of at least 10 years and it must be shown in a balance sheet of a member of the group that is fully taxed in the UK (see TIOPA 2010 s 433(1)(c), 434). A company is treated as being fully taxed in the UK if any activity that the company carries on at any time during the accounting period is within the charge to corporation tax, the company has not made an election under CTA 2009 s 18A to exempt the activities of its overseas permanent establishments from corporation tax and the company has not made a claim for double tax relief (TIOPA 2010 s 433(11)).

A company is required to elect for the modified treatment to apply and such election must be made before the start of the first accounting period for which it is to have effect and cannot be revoked until five years after the start of the first accounting period for which it has effect. If an election is revoked a new election cannot be made for five years beginning with the start of the accounting period in which the revocation takes effect (TIOPA 2010 s 434).

Where the modified treatment applies interest and other amounts payable to unrelated third parties, or to a qualifying infrastructure company, are not treated as tax-interest expense amounts provided the recourse of the creditor is limited to income or assets of a qualifying infrastructure company, or shares in or debt issued by a qualifying infrastructure company (TIOPA 2010 s 438). Interest and other expenses on certain loan relationships to which a qualifying infrastructure company was a party before 12 May 2016 are also not treated as tax-interest expense amounts of the company (TIOPA 2010 s 439). Any tax-interest income of a qualifying infrastructure company is also disregarded for the purposes of the corporate interest restriction legislation and any tax-interest expense of a company that is disregarded and its tax-interest income are left out of account in calculating the adjusted net group-interest expense of the worldwide group and further the group-EBITDA of the group is determined as if the group did not include the qualifying infrastructure company (TIOPA 2010 ss 440–442). Further, where the qualifying infrastructure company is a member of the worldwide group the de minimis £2 million allowance does not normally apply (TIOPA 2010 s 443).

In order for a company to be treated as a qualifying infrastructure company for an accounting period:

– it has to meet the public infrastructure income test for the accounting period (TIOPA 2010 s 433(2)–(4));
– it has to meet the public infrastructure assets test for that accounting period (TIOPA 2010 s 433(5)–(10));
– it must be fully taxed in the United Kingdom. This will be satisfied where any activities company carries on accounting period is within the charge to corporation tax, the company has not made an election under CTA 2009 s 18A to exempt the profits of an overseas branch from corporation tax and the company has not made a claim for double tax relief (TIOPA 2010 s 433(11)); and
– the company has made an election for such modified treatment apply (TIOPA 2010 ss 433(1)(d), 434).

The chapter also contains provisions to cover cases where a qualifying infrastructure company has an interest in a partnership or other tax transparent entity (TIOPA 2010 s 447) and where the qualifying infrastructure company is a joint venture company (TIOPA 2010 s 444–445).

TIOPA 2010 Pt 10 Ch 9 – application of corporate interest legislation to particular types of company etc

This Chapter modifies the application of TIOPA 2010 Pt 10 in relation to certain types of company or businesses.

Banking companies

TIOPA 2010 s 450 provides that all amounts arising to a banking company (as defined in CTA 2010 Pt 7A) from a trade of dealing in financial instruments (other than impairment losses and the reversal of impairment losses) are to be taken into account in the calculation of its net tax-interest income or net tax-interest expense for the purposes of Chapter 3. Financial instruments are defined as including:

– loan relationships
– derivative contracts; and
– shares or other securities.

Oil and gas

TIOPA 2010 s 451 provides that amounts which fall to be included in computing the ring fence income of a company (within the meaning of CTA 2010 s 275) or a company's aggregate gain or loss under TCGA 1992 s 197(3) (disposals of interests in oil fields: ring fence provisions) are to be ignored. Where the company is a member of a worldwide group appropriate adjustments are to be made to exclude such amounts from the financial statements of the worldwide group.

Real estate investment trusts

TIOPA 2010 s 452 provides that the excluded property rental business and the residual business of a REIT are deemed to be separate members of a worldwide group. Further, the profits of the property rental business are deemed not to be exempt from corporation tax for the purposes of allocating the disallowance. The section sets out how an interest disallowance is to be allocated between the two businesses.

Insurance entities

TIOPA 2010 s 453 provides that subsidiaries (and any subsidiaries of such subsidiaries) that are held by an insurance entity as a portfolio investment are not treated as being a member of the worldwide group. An insurance entity is regarded as holding a subsidiary as a portfolio investment if it judges the value that the interest has to it wholly or mainly by reference to the market value of the interest.

An insurance entity is defined as:

– an insurance company;
– a friendly society within the meaning of FA 2012 Pt 3; or
– a body corporate which carries on underwriting business as a member of Lloyds.

Subsidiary has the meaning given by International accounting standards.

Members of Lloyd's

TIOPA 2010 s 454 provides that the interest expense and interest income of a company that is a member of Lloyd's is to be included in its tax-interest expense and tax-interest-income for the purposes of TIOPA 2010 Pt 10 where such interest is brought into account under CTA 2009 Pt 3 (trade profits). Further, the exclusion that applies for derivative contracts forming part of a premium trust fund does not apply for the purposes of TIOPA 2010 Pt 10.

Shipping company subject to tonnage tax

Under TIOPA 2010 s 455 a tonnage tax company's tonnage tax profits are excluded from the calculation of its tax-EBITDA.

Creditor relationships of companies determined using a fair value basis of accounting

Under TIOPA 2010 s 456, company may make an irrevocable election to determine the tax-interest expense amounts and tax-interest income amounts arising on creditor loan relationships, which are accounted for on a fair value basis, on an amortised cost basis of accounting for the purposes of TIOPA 2010 Pt 10. Where such an election is made and a company has a hedging relationship between a loan relationship, which is accounted for on a fair value basis, and a derivative contract, for the purposes of TIOPA 2010 Pt 10 it is permissible for the company to revalue the loan relationship to the same extent that it would be permitted for accounting purposes if the derivative contract had been designated as a fair value hedge of the creditor relationship.

The deadline for making such an election is 12 months from the end of the first accounting period in which a company accounts for a creditor loan relationship on a fair value basis, or where this accounting period ended before 1 April 2017, the first accounting period to which any provision of the corporate interest restriction legislation applies.

TIOPA 2010 s 457 sets out how a disallowance is to arise to a company which has made such an election. As the debits are notional debits, the company is required to include an amount of notional credits in its tax computation equal to the amount of the notional debits, such that a disallowance of notional debits will give rise to a taxable profit as the corresponding notional credits will no longer be fully offset by notional debits.

Co-operative and community benefit societies

Under TIOPA 2010 s 458 amounts payable by co-operative and community benefit societies, or UK agricultural or fishing cooperatives, that are treated as being amounts payable in respect of a loan relationship under CTA 2009 s 499 are not treated as being tax-interest expense amounts or tax-interest income amounts.

Charities

Under TIOPA 2010 s 459, interest payable by a wholly owned subsidiary of a charity on borrowings from the charity is excluded from the calculation of tax-interest expense where any donation from the subsidiary to the charity would qualify for gift aid relief.

Long funding operating leases and finance leases

TIOPA 2010 s 460 makes provision for the calculation of tax-EBITDA in respect of long funding operating leases and finance leases that are not long funding leases. The intention is to ensure that the treatment of amounts excluded from tax-EBITDA in respect of such leases is aligned to the accounting classification of whether a lease is an operating lease or a finance lease and not on whether or not it is a long funding lease. It also aligns the treatment of a long funding lease with the definition of tax-interest which is based on whether or not a lease is a finance lease.

An equivalent adjustment is made for depreciation in respect of an asset held under a finance lease by including such amount in the capital (expenditure) adjustment (see TIOPA 2010 s 417).

TIOPA 2010 Pt 10 Ch 10 – Anti-avoidance

This Chapter contains TIOPA 2010 s 461, a regime anti-avoidance rule, that is designed to counteract attempts to manipulate the provisions of TIOPA 2010 Pt 10. It is modelled on the tax anti-avoidance rules that apply for the purposes of the loan relationships and derivative contracts legislation (see CTA 2009 ss 455B–455C (loan relationships) and CTA 2009 ss 698B–698C (derivative contracts)).

TIOPA 2010 Pt 10 Ch 11 – Interpretations etc

This Chapter, inter alia, contains a number of definitions that apply for the purposes of TIOPA 2010 Pt 10, including the definition of a worldwide group.

Related parties

The meaning of related parties is set out in TIOPA 2010 ss 462 to 465.

Loans treated as made between related parties

A loan made to a borrower from an unrelated lender will be treated as being a related party borrowing where a guarantee, indemnity or other financial assistance in respect of the liability is provided on or after 1 April 2017 (see TIOPA 2010 ss 415(2)(a), 438(5)(a)) by a person related to the borrower. Third-party loans which are guaranteed by a related party will not be treated as related party debt where the conditions in TIOPA 2010 s 415(2) are satisfied (see TIOPA 2010 s 466(1)–(3)).

Third party loans that are guaranteed by related parties will also not be treated as related party debt where TIOPA 2010 s 438(3) applies (loans to qualifying infrastructure companies from third parties) (see TIOPA 2010 s 466(1)–(3).

A loan from an unconnected party lender is treated as being a related party borrowing where a related party indirectly stands in the position as a creditor in respect of the debt in question. See further TIOPA 2010 s 466(3).

Holdings of debt and equity in the same proportion

TIOPA 2010 s 467 provides that where lenders to a company hold debt and equity (or voting power) in the company in the same (or substantially the same) proportions and together the lenders have a 25 per cent investment in the company (see TIOPA 2010 s 464), the lenders are treated as if they were related to the borrower in respect of the loans (and anything done under or for the purposes of them). In such cases where a lender transfers all or part of its loan to another person the loan continues to be treated as a related party loan in the hands of the transferee, whether or not equity is transferred and whether or not the transferee holds shares or voting rights in the borrower. The provision applies with appropriate modifications in the case of any other financial liability owed by the debtor company.

Loan relationships held more than 50% by unrelated parties

A loan relationship that is held by a related party will not be treated as a related party debt where more than 50% of the loan relationship is held by unrelated parties. In order for this exemption to apply all holders must have the same rights in respect of the loan relationship. See further TIOPA 2010 s 468.

Debt restructuring

Where a creditor becomes a related party of a company in return for treating part of a loan relationship or other financial liability owed by the company, or a person related to the company, as released the creditor will not be treated as connected with the company in respect of that loan relationship or the other financial liability where the release is a relevant release of debt. This will be the case where the company, or a person who is a related party of the company, is a party to the debtor relationship, or other financial liability, and immediately before the release it is reasonable to conclude that, without the release and any arrangements of which the release forms part, there would be a material risk that at some time within the next 12 months, the company or the related party would be unable to pay its debts. See further TIOPA 2010 s 469.

Loans made by banks and others

TIOPA 2010 s 470 provides that where a bank or other lender makes a loan to a related company, the loan will not be treated as a related party loan where the creditor is not a party to the loan as a result of any of the circumstances which make the two parties related. HMRC cite as an example in the Explanatory Notes on clause 20 and Schedule 5 at 128, a case where a creditor is attributed with rights of another person and the creditor had no knowledge that the other person held those rights. In their draft guidance at CFM96320, HMRC give a further example being where a company carrying on a lending business advances a loan to a borrower unaware that another group company has a 30% equity investment in the borrower.

Loans made by relevant public bodies

Loans made by relevant public bodies to a related party are treated as not being related party loans where the realising of a profit is merely incidental to the making of the loan (see further TIOPA 2010 s 471). A relevant public body is defined in TIOPA 2010 s 491 as:

– the Crown;
– a minister of the Crown;

- a government department;
- a Northern Ireland department;
- a foreign sovereign power;
- a designated educational establishment within the meaning of CTA 2009 s 106;
- a health service body within the meaning of CTA 2010 s 986;
- a local authority or local authority association;
- any other body that acts under any enactment for public purposes and not for its own profit; or
- any wholly owned subsidiary of any of the above.

The Commissioners of HMRC have the power, by regulation, to amend the meaning of the relevant public body but cannot, by regulation, include a person who has no functions of a public nature (TIOPA 2010 s 491(3), (4)).

Related parties-finance leases granted before 20 March 2017

The two parties to a finance lease are not treated as being related to each other in respect of the finance lease where the finance lease was granted before 20 March 2017 (see TIOPA 2010 s 472).

Determining the worldwide group

TIOPA 2010 ss 473 to 478 set out how the worldwide group is to be determined. Essentially a group consists of an ultimate parent company and all its subsidiaries.

The ultimate parent company is, itself, either

- a company; or
- an entity the shares or other interests in which are listed on a recognised stock exchange and are sufficiently widely held. This requirement will be satisfied if no participator (the CTA 2010 s 454 meaning applies) in the entity holds more than 10% by value of all the shares or other interests in the entity (TIOPA 2010 s 474).

In either case the entity has to be a member of a group within the meaning given by International accounting standards and not be a consolidated subsidiary of another entity (TIOPA 2010 s 473(2), (4)–(5)).

The following are not treated under TIOPA 2010 s 474(3) as being the parent of a worldwide group or an entity to which the corporate interest restriction legislation applies:

- the Crown;
- a minister of the Crown;
- government department;
- a Northern Ireland department; or
- a foreign sovereign power.

It is also possible for an entity to be treated as being the sole member of a worldwide group. This is so as to ensure that the corporate interest restriction legislation is capable of applying to a company that is not a member of a group (TIOPA 2010 s 473(3)).

Except in the case of single-member groups, the group consists of the ultimate parent company and all its subsidiaries (within the meaning of International accounting standards), other than subsidiaries which a parent company is required to carry at fair value (TIOPA 2010 s 473(1), 475(1)).

There are provisions to cover cases where a group takes over, or is taken over by, another group, (TIOPA 2010 s 476), stapled entities (TIOPA 2010 s 477) and business combinations that are treated under international accounting standards as a single economic entity (TIOPA 2010 s 478).

Financial statements and periods of account

The normal rule is that the financial statements of a worldwide group are the consolidated financial statements of the worldwide group's ultimate parent and its subsidiaries. In the case of a single-member group the financial statements are the financial statements of that company (TIOPA 2010 s 479).

Where the financial statements of the group are not acceptable, the group will be required to prepare consolidated accounts in accordance with international accounting standards (IAS) for the purposes of TIOPA 2010 Pt 10. The following financial statements are treated under TIOPA 2010 s 481(4)–(7) as acceptable:

- financial statements drawn up in accordance with IAS;
- the amounts recognised in the financial statements are not materially different

from those that would be recognised in IAS financial statements of the worldwide group if such statements were drawn up;
- the financial statements drawn up in accordance with UK GAAP; or
- the financial statements are drawn up in accordance with generally accepted accounting principles and practices of Canada, China, India, Japan, South Korea or the USA.

HMRC may, by regulations alter the circumstances in which financial statements are to be treated as being acceptable (TIOPA 2010 s 481(8)).

TIOPA 2010 s 482 covers cases where consolidated accounts are drawn up on acceptable principles but do not consolidate one or more entities that would have been consolidated had IAS accounts being prepared, or consolidate subsidiaries that would not have been consolidated had IAS accounts been prepared. In such cases the financial statements of the group are ignored and instead the group is required to prepare consolidated accounts in accordance with IAS for the purposes of the corporate interest restriction legislation using the same principles and practices as in the actual accounts, but consolidating the subsidiaries that would have been consolidated had the group's accounts been prepared in accordance with IAS.

Where the ultimate parent company of the group is taken over at any time during a period of account, for the purposes of TIOPA 2010 Pt 10 separate accounts are required to be drawn up for the part of the period for which the parent company was the ultimate parent company of the group (see TIOPA 2010 s 483).

Where a parent entity of the worldwide group prepares financial statements, but does not prepare consolidated financial statements, normally consolidated financial statements are required to be prepared for the purposes of TIOPA 2010 Pt 10 by reference to the period of account of the ultimate parent company (TIOPA 2010 s 484). It is possible, however, for the ultimate parent company to specify by election for consolidated financial statements to be drawn up for a different period. The maximum period for which financial statements may be drawn up is 18 months (see TIOPA 2010 s 487).

Where the ultimate parent company does not prepare any financial statements it is normally required to prepare IAS financial statements for each 12-month period and any stub period falling within the overall period for which it does not draw up financial statements. It is possible, however, for the ultimate parent company to elect for financial statements to be deemed to be drawn up for different periods, provided that the maximum period for which financial statements are deemed to be drawn up does not exceed 18 months (TIOPA 2010 ss 485, 486).

Actual financial statements that are drawn up will be ignored if they are drawn up for a period in excess of 18 months or if they are drawn up after the period of 30 months beginning with the start of the period for which they are drawn up (see TIOPA 2010 s 487.)

Where amounts included in financial statements are expressed in a currency other than sterling such amounts are required to be translated into sterling by reference to an average rate for the period calculated from daily spot rates (see TIOPA 2010 s 489(1), (2)).

Amounts recognised in financial statements for a period of account as an item of profit or loss include amounts that are recycled to profit or loss from other comprehensive income (see TIOPA 2010 s 489(3)).

TIOPA 2010 ss 490, 492 and 494 contain sundry definitions.

TIOPA 2010 s 493 provides that CTA 2009 ss 415 and 585 (loan relationships with embedded derivatives) also apply for the purposes of the corporate interest restriction legislation.

Power to amend the legislation by regulation

TIOPA 2010 s 495 permits HMRC to make regulations altering the calculation for the purposes of Chapter 7 (group interest and group-EBITDA) where the financial statements of a worldwide group for a period include or omit an amount in respect of any matter and any member of the group deals with that matter for tax or accounting purposes in a different way. At the time of writing it was proposed that regulations would be introduced under this provision in the following three situations:
- where on 1 April 2017 a company was party to a loan relationship which is dealt with in the company's accounts using an amortised cost basis of accounting, and in the financial statements of the worldwide group, of which the company is a member, the loan relationship is recognised using a fair value basis of accounting, or is the hedged item under a designated fair value hedge (and thus is

revalued in the company's accounts for movements in the risk that is being hedged). In such cases it was proposed that for the purposes of calculating the net group-interest expense, the adjusted net group-interest expense, the qualifying net group-interest expense and the group-EBITDA, it would be assumed that the loan relationship is accounted for in the financial statements of the worldwide group using an amortised cost basis of accounting;

– where at 1 April 2017 there was a loan relationship between two group members, which was previously recognised in the worldwide group financial statements, and which was derecognised in the financial statements of the worldwide group as a result of either: (i) the loan being acquired by group member; or (ii) the creditor becoming a group member; and neither CTA 2009 s 361 nor s 362 applied on the occasion of either of those events. In such cases it was proposed that for the purposes of calculating the net group-interest expense, the adjusted net group-interest expense, the qualifying net group-interest expense and the group-EBITDA, an amount equal to the gain or loss recognised in the group financial statements in respect of the derecognition of the loan would be treated as being brought into account on a just and reasonable basis over the remaining term of the loan; and

– where a company directly or indirectly transfers an asset or a right to income to a group pension scheme, recognises a finance charge in connection with the transfer that is treated as interest payable under a transaction or a loan relationship under CTA 2010 ss 761(3), 762(3), 766(3) or 769(3) and the arrangement is treated as an acceptable structured finance arrangement within the meaning of FA 2004 ss 196C, 196E, or 196G in connection with a contribution paid by an employer under a registered pension scheme for which the employer is entitled to relief under FA 2004 Pt 4 Ch 4. In such cases for the purposes of calculating the net group-interest expense, the adjusted net group-interest expense, the qualifying net-group interest expense and the group-EBITDA, it was proposed that an amount equal to the finance charge would be bought into account as if it were a relevant expense amount recognised in the financial statements of the worldwide group.

TIOPA 2010 s 496 allows HMRC to make provision by regulation enabling a group company that is a party to a capital market arrangement (within the meaning of IA 1986 Sch 2A para 1) to make an election with another group company transferring its liability to corporation tax as a result of an interest restriction arising under TIOPA 2010 Pt 10 to that other company. This provision tracks an equivalent provision that was included within the worldwide debt cap legislation but no regulations were introduced under that provision. It is intended to apply in the case of whole business securitisations. These are arrangements whereby a subgroup of a group of companies (securitisation subgroup) borrows on a secured basis against the income flows and assets of the subgroup. The intention is to enable a member of the securitisation subgroup to elect for any additional tax liability, which arises to it as a result of the allocation to it of an interest disallowance, to be borne by another member of the wider group. To date the market has been comfortable with the wider group undertaking to indemnify the subgroup against any additional tax liabilities that arise to the subgroup as a result of it being a member of the wider group and this is why no regulations have been introduced under the predecessor provision.

The Treasury has the power to amend the legislation by regulation to take account of changes in accounting standards. Such changes may take effect in relation to any period beginning before the regulations are made. See further TIOPA 2010 s 497.

New TIOPA 2010 Schedule 7A

TIOPA 2010 Sch 7A Pt 1 – the reporting company

TIOPA 2010 Sch 7A paras 1–11 cover the appointment and obligations of a reporting company. A reporting company is a company that is required to provide an interest restriction return to HMRC on behalf of each UK group company (a company that is a member of the worldwide group and is within the charge to UK corporation tax) see TIOPA 2010 s 492)).

The normal rule is that the reporting company has to be appointed by at least 50% of UK group companies (excluding dormant companies). The reporting company, itself, must be a UK group company that is not a dormant company for the relevant period of account. It is possible for an election appointing a reporting company to be revoked by 50% or more of UK group companies (excluding dormant companies) with effect from a stated period of account (paras 1, 2).

If no reporting company is appointed HMRC may appoint a UK group company as a reporting company for the relevant period of account. It is possible for HMRC to revoke the appointment of a reporting company that has been appointed by UK group companies, or by HMRC, if HMRC consider that the reporting company has not or will not comply with its obligations under TIOPA 2010 Sch 7A to submit an interest restriction return, or where the company itself has agreed that HMRC may exercise such power (paras 4, 5).

TIOPA 2010 Sch 7A Pt 2 – contents of interest restriction return

TIOPA 2010 Sch 7A paras 12–27 set out the contents of an interest restriction return as well as the option of a reporting company to make a:

- group ratio election;
- group ratio (blended) election;
- group-EBITDA (chargeable gains) election;
- interest allowance (alternative calculation) election;
- interest allowance (non-consolidated investment) election;
- interest allowance (consolidated partnerships) election; and
- abbreviated return election.

The return must set out the disallowance which is allocated to each UK group company which has a net tax-interest expense for the relevant period of account. The disallowance that is allocated to a UK group company may not exceed the company's net tax-interest expense for the relevant period of account (para 22(3)(a)).

It is open to a UK group company to object to the disallowance that is allocated to it for a period of account, in which case the disallowance that is allocated to that company must be determined on a pro rata basis by reference to its net tax-interest expense, as compared to the aggregate net tax-interest expense of all UK group companies for that period (see paras 10, 22(3)(b), 23).

The reporting company is also required to specify how any interest reactivation amounts are to be allocated amongst UK group companies (paras 25, 26).

TIOPA 2010 Sch 7A paras 28–37 cover inter alia:

- correction of returns by an officer of HMRC to amend anything in the return to correct any obvious errors or omissions, or anything that the officer has reason to believe is incorrect on the basis of information available to that officer;
- penalties for failure to deliver a return, incorrect or uncorrected return, assessment, payment, reduction and enforcement of penalties;
- right to appeal against a penalty or its amount and the procedure on appeal; and
- payments between companies in respect of penalties (the payment is disregarded for tax purposes and is not treated as a distribution).

TIOPA 2010 Sch 7A Pt 3 – Duty to keep and preserve records

TIOPA 2010 Sch 7A paras 38–39 set out the obligations of a reporting company to keep and preserve records and the penalty which applies if a company fails to comply with such obligations.

TIOPA 2010 Sch 7A Pt 4 – Enquiry into interest restriction return

TIOPA 2010 Sch 7A paras 40–54 set out HMRC's powers to enquire into an interest restriction return, its powers to require a company to amend its self-assessment return and its powers to amend a company self-assessment return.

TIOPA 2010 Sch 7A para 55 provides that references to a reporting company for a period of account also include a company that is appointed to replace the reporting company during that period of account.

TIOPA 2010 Sch 7A Pt 5 – Determinations by officers of HMRC

TIOPA 2010 Sch 7A paras 56–57 set out the powers of HMRC to make a determination in cases where no reporting company has been appointed, no interest restriction return has been submitted, or an interest restriction return has been submitted and this does not comply with the requirements of TIOPA 2010 Sch 7A para 20(3). In such cases HMRC may determine a company's pro-rata share of the total disallowed amount of UK group companies for the relevant period of account.

TIOPA 2010 Sch 7A para 58 covers the powers of HMRC to make a determination following an enquiry and a company fails to file a revised return within the required time period, or a revised return that has been filed does not comply with the requirements of the closure notice.

TIOPA 2010 Sch 7A para 59 sets out the limited circumstances in which a company can appeal against a determination notice issued under para 58, being that the determination is inconsistent with the closure notice.

TIOPA 2010 Sch 7A Pt 6 – Information powers exercisable by members of a group

TIOPA 2010 Sch 7A paras 60–61 cover the provision of information to and by a reporting company and the provision of information between members of the group where no reporting company has been appointed.

TIOPA 2010 Sch 7A Pt 7 – Information powers exercisable by officers of HMRC

TIOPA 2010 Sch 7A paras 62–67 cover the powers of HMRC to obtain information and documents from members of the worldwide group and from third parties, as well as the right of a group member or a third party to appeal against a notice from HMRC requiring the provision of information or documents.

TIOPA 2010 Sch 7A Pt 8 – Company tax returns

This part, inter alia, addresses:
- amendments to company tax returns to accommodate an election under TIOPA ss 375, 377 or 380; and
- cases where a company amends or is treated as amending a return to reflect the allocation of an interest disallowance.

TIOPA 2010 Sch 7A Part 9 – Supplementary

TIOPA 2010 Sch 7A para 74 provides that a person is not liable to a penalty under Sch 7A in respect of anything for which that person has been convicted of an offence.
TIOPA 2010 Sch 7A para 75 provides that any appeal under Sch 7A must set out the grounds of appeal.
TIOPA 2010 Sch 7A para 76 sets out the rules that apply to determine whether an amount stated in an interest restriction return can no longer be altered.

Consequential amendments

F(No 2)A 2017 Sch 5 makes consequential amendments to other provisions of the Corporation Tax Acts. Inter alia, the corporate interest restriction legislation is disregarded for the purposes of the hybrid and other mismatches legislation (see TIOPA 2010 s 259NEA, introduced by F(No 2)A 2017 Sch 5 para 20).
Paragraph 21(3) introduces a new definition of group treasury company for the purposes of the controlled foreign companies (CFC) legislation. This is because the previous definition cross-referred to that used for the purposes of the worldwide debt cap legislation, which is being repealed by F(No 2)A 2017 Sch 5 paras 11, 26.
Paragraph 22 inserts a new TIOPA 2010 s 371IE (matched interest profits exemption) for the purposes of the CFC legislation, which is intended to be equivalent to the former provision and is required because the former provision cross-referred to the worldwide debt cap legislation that is being repealed by F(No 2)A 2017 Sch 5 paras 11, 26.
Paragraph 23 introduces a new TIOPA 2010 s 371SLA, which sets out how the corporate interest restriction legislation is to apply to a CFC. It provides that the CFC is to be treated as a member of a worldwide group for the relevant period of account, that it is the only UK group company and that the £2 million de minimis limit does not apply.

Commencement and transitional provisions

F(No 2)A 2017 Sch 5 Pt 4 sets out the commencement and transitional provisions. Inter alia, it provides that the legislation takes effect for periods of account beginning on or after 1 April 2017. Where a period of account straddles this date it is split into two periods, with the second period beginning on 1 April 2017 and financial statements of the group are treated as having been drawn up for each of the two periods. Normally amounts are apportioned between the two deemed periods on a time basis unless such apportionment would work unreasonably or unjustly, in which case a just and reasonable basis is to be used (see F(No 2)A 2017 Sch 5 para 25).

Paragraphs 11 and 26 repeal the worldwide debt cap legislation with effect from 1 April 2017.

Paragraph 27 provides transitional provisions in respect of certain elections that can be made to where a worldwide group does not draw up consolidated accounts.

Paragraph 28 contains transitional provisions that apply in respect of the appointment of, or the revocation of the appointment of, a reporting company and for filing an interest restriction return.

Paragraph 29 provides that amounts that are brought into account under the Loan Relationships and Derivative Contracts (Change of Accounting Practice) Regulations 2004 (SI 2004/3256) are disregarded for the purposes of the corporate interest restriction legislation where the change of accounting practice took place in an accounting period beginning before 1 April 2017.

Paragraph 30 provides that a transitional adjustment arising in respect of a loan relationship contract under F(No 2)A 2015 Sch 7 paras 115–116 and in respect of a derivative contract under F(No 2)A 2015 Sch 7 paras 120–121 is to be disregarded for the purposes of the corporate interest restriction legislation.

Paragraph 31 permits a company to elect to apply regulations 7–9 of the Loan Relationships and Derivative Contracts (Disregard and Bringing into Account of Profits and Losses) Regulations 2004 (SI 2000/3256) (Disregard Regulations) to compute for the purposes of the corporate interest restriction legislation the profits arising on a derivative contract that is used for hedging. The election is intended to cover cases where a company has not elected to apply regulations 7–9 of the Disregard Regulations and is included because for the purposes of calculating the adjusted net group-interest expense and qualifying net group-interest expense of a worldwide group, it is assumed that the regulations 7, 8 of 9 of the Disregard Regulations applied to derivative contracts that are used for hedging purposes and that the profit or loss arising on such contracts is recognised on the basis in which it would be recognised in computing a computing a company's taxable profits under regulation 9 or 10 of the Disregard Regulations (see TIOPA 2010 ss 420–421). Such an election must be made by 1 April 2018 and is irrevocable. In order for the election to have effect it must be made by each company (other than dormant companies) that was a member of the worldwide group and within the charge to corporation tax at 1 April 2017.

Paragraphs 32 and 33 contains certain transitional provisions for qualifying infrastructure companies.

Paragraph 34 contains transitional provisions in respect of TIOPA 2010 s 461 (counteraction of avoidance arrangements).

Paragraph 35 permits HMRC to make consequential changes to secondary legislation and for such changes to take effect under the commencement rules that apply for the purposes of the corporate interest restriction legislation.

SCHEDULE 6

RELIEF FOR PRODUCTION OF MUSEUM AND
GALLERY EXHIBITIONS

Section 21

PART 1

AMENDMENT OF CTA 2009

1 After Part 15D of CTA 2009 insert—

"PART 15E

MUSEUMS AND GALLERIES EXHIBITION TAX RELIEF

CHAPTER 1

INTRODUCTION

Overview

1218ZA Overview

    (1) This Part is about the production of museum and gallery exhibitions, and applies for corporation tax purposes.

(2) This Chapter explains what is meant by "exhibition" and "touring exhibition" and how a company comes to be treated as the primary production company or a secondary production company for an exhibition.

(3) Chapter 2 is about the taxation of the activities of a production company and includes—

(a) provision for the company's activities in relation to its exhibition to be treated as a separate trade, and

(b) provision about the calculation of the profits and losses of that trade.

(4) Chapter 3 is about relief (called "museums and galleries exhibition tax relief") which may be given to a production company in relation to an exhibition—

(a) by way of additional deductions to be made in calculating the profits or losses of the company's separate trade, or

(b) by way of a payment (a "museums and galleries exhibition tax credit") to be made on the company's surrender of losses from that trade,

and describes the conditions a company must meet to qualify for museums and galleries exhibition tax relief.

(5) Chapter 4 contains provision about the use of losses of the separate trade (including provision about relief for terminal losses).

(6) Chapter 5 provides—

(a) for relief under Chapters 3 and 4 to be given on a provisional basis, and

(b) for such relief to be withdrawn if it turns out that conditions that must be met for such relief to be given are not actually met.

Interpretation

1218ZAA "Exhibition"

(1) In this Part "exhibition" means a curated public display of an organised collection of objects or works (or of a single object or work) considered to be of scientific, historic, artistic or cultural interest.

(2) But a display is not an exhibition if—

(a) it is organised in connection with a competition of any kind,

(b) its main purpose, or one of its main purposes, is to sell anything displayed or to advertise or promote any goods or services,

(c) it includes a live performance by any person,

(d) anything displayed is for sale, or

(e) anything displayed is alive.

(3) Subsection (2) does not prevent a display being an exhibition if it includes a live performance by a person which is merely incidental to, or forms a merely incidental part of, the collection displayed.

(4) A display is "public" if the general public is admitted to it, whether or not the public is charged for admission.

(5) A display does not fall outside subsection (4) just because visitors other than the general public are admitted to it for a single session or a small number of sessions.

1218ZAB "Touring exhibition"

(1) In this Part an exhibition is a "touring exhibition" if conditions A to E are met.

(2) Condition A is that—

(a) there is a primary production company for the exhibition (see section 1218ZAC), and

(b) the primary production company is within the charge to corporation tax.

(3) Condition B is that the primary production company intends, when planning the exhibition, that conditions C, D and E should be met in relation to it.

(4) Condition C is that the exhibition is held at two or more venues.

(5) Condition D is that at least 25% of the objects or works displayed at the first venue at which the exhibition is held are also displayed at every subsequent venue at which the exhibition is held.

(6) Condition E is that the period between the deinstalling of the exhibition at one venue and the installation of the exhibition at the next venue does not exceed 6 months.

1218ZAC Primary production company

(1) In this Part a company is the primary production company for an exhibition if the company (acting otherwise than in partnership) meets conditions A and B.

(2) Condition A is that the company—

(a) makes an effective creative, technical or artistic contribution to the exhibition, and

(b) directly negotiates for, contracts for and pays for rights, goods and services in relation to the exhibition.

(3) Condition B is that—

(a) where the exhibition is held at just one venue, the company is responsible for the production of the exhibition at that venue;

(b) where the exhibition is held at two or more venues, the company is responsible for the production of the exhibition at (at least) the first of those venues.

(4) For the purposes of this section and section 1218ZAD, a company is responsible for the production of the exhibition at a venue if—

(a) it is responsible for producing and running the exhibition at the venue,

(b) where the exhibition is at the venue for a limited time, it is responsible for deinstalling and closing the exhibition at the venue, and

(c) it is actively engaged in decision-making in relation to the exhibition at the venue.

(5) If more than one company meets conditions A and B in relation to the production of the exhibition, the company that most directly meets those conditions is the primary production company for the exhibition.

(6) If no company meets conditions A and B in relation to the production of the exhibition, there is no primary production company for the exhibition.

1218ZAD Secondary production company

(1) If an exhibition is held at two or more venues, there may be one or more secondary production companies for the exhibition.

(2) In this Part a company is the secondary production company for an exhibition at a venue if the company meets conditions C and D.

(3) Condition C is that the company (acting otherwise than in partnership) is responsible for the production of the exhibition at the venue.

(4) Condition D is that the company is not the primary production company.

(5) If more than one company meets conditions C and D in relation to the production of the exhibition at the venue, the company that is most directly responsible for the production of the exhibition at the venue is the secondary production company for the exhibition at the venue.

(6) If no company meets conditions C and D in relation to the production of the exhibition at the venue, there is no secondary production company for the exhibition at the venue.

CHAPTER 2
TAXATION OF ACTIVITIES OF PRODUCTION COMPANY

Separate exhibition trade

1218ZB Separate exhibition trade

(1) Subsection (2) applies to a company in relation to an exhibition if, and only for so long as, the company qualifies for museums and galleries exhibition tax relief in relation to the production of the exhibition (see section 1218ZCA).

(2) The company's activities in relation to the production of the exhibition are treated as a trade separate from any other activities of the company (including activities in relation to the production of any other exhibition).

(3) In this Part the separate trade mentioned in subsection (2) is called "the separate exhibition trade".

(4) Subsections (5) and (6) apply where the company is the primary production company for the exhibition.

(5) The company is treated as beginning to carry on the separate exhibition trade—

(a) at the beginning of the production stage of the exhibition at the first venue at which it is held, or

(b) if earlier, at the time of the first receipt by the company of any income from the production of the exhibition.

(6) The company is treated as ceasing to carry on the separate trade when the exhibition closes at the last venue at which it is held.

(7) Subsections (8) and (9) apply where the company is a secondary production company for the exhibition.

(8) The company is treated as beginning to carry on the separate exhibition trade—

(a) at the beginning of the production stage of the exhibition at the first venue for which the company is the secondary production company, or

(b) if earlier, at the time of the first receipt by the company of any income from the production of the exhibition.

(9) The company is treated as ceasing to carry on the separate trade when the exhibition closes at the last venue for which the company is the secondary production company.

Profits and losses of separate exhibition trade

1218ZBA Calculation of profits or losses of separate exhibition trade

(1) This section applies for the purpose of calculating the profits or losses of the separate exhibition trade.

(2) For the first period of account during which the separate exhibition trade is carried on, the following are brought into account—

(a) as a debit, the costs of the production of the exhibition incurred to date;

(b) as a credit, the proportion of the estimated total income from that production treated as earned at the end of that period.

(3) For subsequent periods of account the following are brought into account—

(a) as a debit, the difference between the amount ("C") of the costs of the production of the exhibition incurred to date and the amount corresponding to C for the previous period, and

(b) as a credit, the difference between the proportion ("PI") of the estimated total income from that production treated as earned at the end of that period and the amount corresponding to PI for the previous period.

(4) The proportion of the estimated total income treated as earned at the end of a period of account is—

$(C / T) \times I$

where—

C is the total to date of costs incurred;

T is the estimated total cost of the production of the exhibition;

I is the estimated total income from the production of the exhibition.

1218ZBB Income from the production

(1) References in this Chapter to income from a production of an exhibition are to any receipts by the company in connection with the production or exploitation of the exhibition.

(2) This includes—

(a) receipts from the sale of tickets or of rights in the exhibition;

(b) royalties or other payments in connection with the exploitation of the exhibition or aspects of it (such as a particular exhibit);

(c) payments for rights to produce merchandise;

(d) a grant designated as made for the purposes of the exhibition;

(e) receipts by the company by way of a profit share agreement.

1218ZBC Costs of the production

(1) References in this Chapter to the costs of a production of an exhibition are to expenditure incurred by the company on—

(a) activities involved in developing, producing, running, deinstalling and closing the exhibition, or

(b) activities with a view to exploiting the exhibition.

(2) This is subject to any provision of the Corporation Tax Acts prohibiting the making of a deduction, or restricting the extent to which a deduction is allowed, in calculating the profits of a trade.

1218ZBD When costs are taken to be incurred

(1) For the purposes of this Chapter, the costs that have been incurred on a production of an exhibition at a given time do not include any amount that has not been paid unless it is the subject of an unconditional obligation to pay.

(2) Where an obligation to pay an amount is linked to income being earned from the production of the exhibition, the obligation is not treated as having become unconditional unless an appropriate amount of income is or has been brought into account under section 1218ZBA.

1218ZBE Pre-trading expenditure

(1) This section applies if, before the company begins to carry on the separate exhibition trade, it incurs expenditure on activities falling within section 1218ZBC(1)(a).

(2) The expenditure may be treated as expenditure of the separate exhibition trade and as if incurred immediately after the company begins to carry on that trade.

(3) If expenditure so treated has previously been taken into account for other tax purposes, the company must amend any relevant company tax return accordingly.

(4) Any amendment or assessment necessary to give effect to subsection (3) may be made despite any limitation on the time within which an amendment or assessment may normally be made.

1218ZBF Estimates

Estimates for the purposes of section 1218ZBA must be made as at the balance sheet date for each period of account, on a just and reasonable basis taking into consideration all relevant circumstances.

CHAPTER 3

MUSEUMS AND GALLERIES EXHIBITION TAX RELIEF

Introduction

1218ZC Overview of museums and galleries exhibition tax relief

(1) Relief under this Chapter ("museums and galleries exhibition tax relief") is given by way of—

(a) additional deductions (see sections 1218ZCE to 1218ZCG), and
(b) museums and galleries exhibition tax credits (see sections 1218ZCH to 1218ZCK).

(2) See Schedule 18 to FA 1998 (in particular, Part 9D) for provision about the procedure for making claims for museums and galleries exhibition tax relief.

Companies qualifying for museums and galleries exhibition tax relief

1218ZCA Companies qualifying for museums and galleries exhibition tax relief

(1) A company qualifies for museums and galleries exhibition tax relief in relation to the production of an exhibition if conditions A to D are met.

(2) Condition A is that the company is—

(a) the primary production company for the exhibition, or
(b) a secondary production company for the exhibition.

(3) Condition B is that the company is—

(a) a charitable company which maintains a museum or gallery,
(b) wholly owned by a charity which maintains a museum or gallery, or
(c) wholly owned by a local authority which maintains a museum or gallery.

See section 1218ZCB for the interpretation of paragraphs (b) and (c).

(4) Condition C is that at the beginning of the planning stage, the company intends that the exhibition should be public (within the meaning given by section 1218ZAA).

(5) Condition D is that the EEA expenditure condition is met (see section 1218ZCC).

(6) For the purposes of subsection (3) "museum or gallery" includes—

(a) a library or archive, and
(b) a site where a collection of objects or works (or a single object or work) considered to be of scientific, historic, artistic or cultural interest is exhibited outdoors (or partly outdoors).

(7) There is further related provision in section 1218ZCM (tax avoidance arrangements).

1218ZCB Interpretation of section 1218ZCA(3)(b) and (c)

(1) For the purposes of section 1218ZCA(3)(b) a company is "wholly owned by a charity which maintains a museum or gallery" if condition A or B is met.

(2) Condition A is that—

  (a) the company has an ordinary share capital, and

  (b) every part of that share capital is owned by—

    (i) a charity which maintains a museum or gallery, or

    (ii) two charities, each of which maintains a museum or gallery.

(3) Condition B is that—

  (a) the company is limited by guarantee,

  (b) there are no more than two beneficiaries of the company, and

  (c) the beneficiary, or each beneficiary, is—

    (i) a charity which maintains a museum or gallery, or

    (ii) a company wholly owned by a charity which maintains a museum or gallery.

(4) For the purposes of section 1218ZCA(3)(c) a company is "wholly owned by a local authority" if—

  (a) where the company has an ordinary share capital, every part of that share capital is owned by the local authority, or

  (b) where the company is limited by guarantee, the local authority is the sole beneficiary of the company.

(5) Ordinary share capital of a company is treated as owned by a charity or a local authority if the charity or local authority (as the case may be)—

  (a) directly or indirectly owns that share capital within the meaning of Chapter 3 of Part 24 of CTA 2010, or

  (b) would be taken so to own it if references in that Chapter to a body corporate included references to a charity or local authority which is not a body corporate.

(6) A beneficiary of a company is a person who—

  (a) is beneficially entitled to participate in the company's divisible profits, or

  (b) will be beneficially entitled to share in any of the company's net assets available for distribution on its winding up.

(7) In this section "museum or gallery" has the same meaning it has for the purposes of section 1218ZCA.

1218ZCC The EEA expenditure condition

(1) The "EEA expenditure condition" is that at least 25% of the core expenditure on the production of the exhibition incurred by the company is EEA expenditure.

(2) In this Part "EEA expenditure" means expenditure on goods or services that are provided from within the European Economic Area.

(3) Any apportionment of expenditure as between EEA and non-EEA expenditure for the purposes of this Part is to be made on a just and reasonable basis.

(4) The Treasury may by regulations—

  (a) amend the percentage specified in subsection (1);

  (b) amend subsection (2).

(5) See also sections 1218ZE and 1218ZEA (which are about the giving of relief provisionally on the basis that the EEA expenditure condition will be met).

1218ZCD "Core expenditure"

(1) Subject to the following provisions of this section, in this Part "core expenditure", in relation to a company's production of an exhibition, means expenditure on the activities involved in producing, deinstalling and closing the exhibition at every relevant venue.

(2) For the purposes of subsection (1) a venue is a "relevant venue" in relation to a company if the company's activities in relation to the exhibition at the venue form part of the company's separate exhibition trade.

(3) Expenditure on the activities involved in deinstalling and closing the exhibition at a venue is core expenditure only if the period between the opening and closing of the exhibition at the venue is 12 months or less.

(4) Expenditure on the storage of exhibits for an exhibition which is held at just one venue is not core expenditure.

(5) Where a company incurs expenditure on the storage of exhibits for an exhibition which is held at two or more venues, the amount of such expenditure which is core expenditure is limited to the amount of relevant storage expenditure (if any) incurred by the company in respect of a period of 4 months or less.

(6) For the purposes of subsection (5) expenditure in relation to the exhibition is "relevant storage expenditure" if—

(a) the expenditure is incurred in respect of the storage of exhibits between the deinstallation of the exhibition at one venue and the opening of the exhibition at the next venue, and

(b) the exhibits are not stored at a venue at which the exhibition has been held or is to be held.

(7) Expenditure of the following kinds is not core expenditure—

(a) expenditure on any matters not directly involved with putting on the exhibition (for instance, financing, marketing, legal services and promotional events),

(b) speculative development expenditure on initial exhibition concepts and feasibility,

(c) expenditure on the ordinary running of the exhibition (for instance, invigilation and the maintenance of exhibits),

(d) expenditure in relation to any live performance,

(e) expenditure on further development of the exhibition during the running stage,

(f) expenditure on purchasing the exhibits, and

(g) expenditure on infrastructure, unless that expenditure is incurred solely for the purposes of the exhibition.

Additional deduction

1218ZCE Claim for additional deduction

(1) A company which qualifies for museums and galleries exhibition tax relief in relation to the production of an exhibition may claim an additional deduction in relation to the production.

(2) A claim under subsection (1) is made with respect to an accounting period.

(3) Where a company has made a claim, the company is entitled to make an additional deduction, in accordance with section 1218ZCF, in calculating the profit or loss of the separate exhibition trade for the accounting period concerned.

(4) Where the company tax return in which a claim is made is for an accounting period later than that in which the company begins to carry on the separate exhibition trade, the company must make any amendments of company tax returns for earlier periods that may be necessary.

(5) Any amendment or assessment necessary to give effect to subsection (4) may be made despite any limitation on the time within which an amendment or assessment may normally be made.

1218ZCF Amount of additional deduction

(1) The amount of an additional deduction to which a company is entitled as a result of a claim under section 1218ZCE is calculated as follows.

(2) For the first period of account during which the separate exhibition trade is carried on, the amount of the additional deduction is E, where E is—

(a) so much of the qualifying expenditure incurred to date as is EEA expenditure, or

(b) if less, 80% of the total amount of qualifying expenditure incurred to date.

(3) For any period of account after the first, the amount of the additional deduction is—

$$E - P$$

where E is—

(a) so much of the qualifying expenditure incurred to date as is EEA expenditure, or

(b) if less, 80% of the total amount of qualifying expenditure incurred to date, and

P is the total amount of the additional deductions given for previous periods.

(4) The Treasury may by regulations amend the percentage specified in subsection (2) or (3).

(5) If a period of account of the separate exhibition trade does not coincide with an accounting period, any necessary apportionments are to be made by reference to the number of days in the periods concerned.

1218ZCG "Qualifying expenditure"

(1) In this Chapter "qualifying expenditure", in relation to the production of an exhibition, means core expenditure (see section 1218ZCD) on the production that—

(a) falls to be taken into account under sections 1218ZBA to 1218ZBF in calculating the profit or loss of the separate exhibition trade for tax purposes,

(b) is not expenditure which is otherwise relievable, and

(c) is incurred on or before 31 March 2022.

(2) For the purposes of this section expenditure is "otherwise relievable" if it is expenditure in respect of which (assuming a claim were made) the company would be entitled to—

(a) an R&D expenditure credit under Chapter 6A of Part 3,

(b) relief under Part 13 (additional relief for expenditure on research and development),

(c) film tax relief under Chapter 3 of Part 15,

(d) television tax relief under Chapter 3 of Part 15A,

(e) video games tax relief under Chapter 3 of Part 15B,

(f) an additional deduction under Part 15C (theatrical productions),

(g) a theatre tax credit under Part 15C, or

(h) orchestra tax relief under Chapter 3 of Part 15D.

(3) The Treasury may by regulations amend paragraph (c) of subsection (1) so as to substitute a later date for the date for the time being specified in that paragraph.

Museums and galleries exhibition tax credits

1218ZCH Museums and galleries exhibition tax credit claimable if company has surrenderable loss

(1) A company which qualifies for museums and galleries exhibition tax relief in relation to the production of an exhibition may claim a museums and galleries exhibition tax credit in relation to the production for an accounting period in which the company has a surrenderable loss.

(2) Section 1218ZCI sets out how to calculate the amount of any surrenderable loss that the company has in the accounting period.

(3) A company making a claim may surrender the whole or part of its surrenderable loss in the accounting period.

(4) Subject to section 1218ZCK, the amount of the museums and galleries exhibition tax credit to which a company making a claim is entitled for the accounting period is—

(a) 25% of the amount of the loss surrendered if the exhibition is a touring exhibition (see section 1218ZAB), or

(b) 20% of the amount of the loss surrendered if the exhibition is not a touring exhibition.

(5) The company's available loss for the accounting period (see section 1218ZCI(2)) is reduced by the amount surrendered.

1218ZCI Amount of surrenderable loss

(1) The company's surrenderable loss in the accounting period is—

(a) the company's available loss for the period in the separate exhibition trade (see subsections (2) and (3)), or

(b) if less, the available qualifying expenditure for the period (see subsections (4) and (5)).

(2) The company's available loss for an accounting period is—

L + RUL

where—

L is the amount of the company's loss for the period in the separate exhibition trade, and

RUL is the amount of any relevant unused loss of the company (see subsection (3)).

(3) The "relevant unused loss" of a company is so much of any available loss of the company for the previous accounting period as has not been—

(a) surrendered under section 1218ZCH, or

(b) carried forward under section 45 or 45B of CTA 2010 and set against profits of the separate exhibition trade.

(4) For the first period of account during which the separate exhibition trade is carried on, the available qualifying expenditure is the amount that is E for that period for the purposes of section 1218ZCF(2).

(5) For any period of account after the first, the available qualifying expenditure is—

E – S

where—

E is the amount that is E for that period for the purposes of section 1218ZCF(3), and

S is the total amount previously surrendered under section 1218ZCH.

(6) If a period of account of the separate exhibition trade does not coincide with an accounting period, any necessary apportionments are to be made by reference to the number of days in the periods concerned.

1218ZCJ Payment in respect of museums and galleries exhibition tax credit

(1) If a company—

(a) is entitled to a museums and galleries exhibition tax credit for an accounting period, and

(b) makes a claim,

the Commissioners for Her Majesty's Revenue and Customs ("the Commissioners") must pay the amount of the credit to the company.

(2) An amount payable in respect of—

(a) a museums and galleries exhibition tax credit, or

(b) interest on a museums and galleries exhibition tax credit under section 826 of ICTA,

may be applied in discharging any liability of the company to pay corporation tax.

To the extent that it is so applied the Commissioners' liability under subsection (1) is discharged.

(3) If the company's company tax return for the accounting period is enquired into by the Commissioners, no payment in respect of a museums and galleries exhibition tax credit for that period need be made before the Commissioners' enquiries are completed (see paragraph 32 of Schedule 18 to FA 1998).

In those circumstances the Commissioners may make a payment on a provisional basis of such amount as they consider appropriate.

(4) No payment need be made in respect of a museums and galleries exhibition tax credit for an accounting period before the company has paid to the Commissioners any amount that it is required to pay for payment periods ending in that accounting period—

(a) under PAYE regulations, or

(b) in respect of Class 1 national insurance contributions under Part 1 of the Social Security Contributions and Benefits Act 1992 or Part 1 of the Social Security Contributions and Benefits (Northern Ireland) Act 1992.

(5) A payment in respect of a museums and galleries exhibition tax credit is not income of the company for any tax purpose.

1218ZCK Maximum museums and galleries exhibition tax credits payable

(1) Subsections (2) and (3) prescribe the maximum amount of museums and galleries exhibition tax credits which may be paid to a company under section 1218ZCJ in respect of the company's separate exhibition trade.

(2) Where the separate exhibition trade relates to the production of a touring exhibition, the maximum amount which may be paid to the company is £100,000.

(3) Where the separate exhibition trade relates to the production of an exhibition which is not a touring exhibition, the maximum amount which may be paid to the company is £80,000.

(4) In accordance with Commission Regulation (EU) No. 651/2014 of 17 June 2014 declaring certain categories of aid compatible with the internal market, the total amount of museums and galleries exhibition tax credits payable under section 1218ZCJ in the case of any undertaking is not to exceed 75 million euros per year.

1218ZCL No account to be taken of amount if unpaid

(1) In determining for the purposes of this Chapter the amount of costs incurred on a production of an exhibition at the end of a period of account, ignore any amount that has not been paid 4 months after the end of that period.

(2) This is without prejudice to the operation of section 1218ZBD (when costs are taken to be incurred).

Anti-avoidance etc

1218ZCM Tax avoidance arrangements

(1) A company does not qualify for museums and galleries exhibition tax relief in relation to the production of an exhibition if there are any tax avoidance arrangements relating to the production.

(2) Arrangements are "tax avoidance arrangements" if their main purpose, or one of their main purposes, is the obtaining of a tax advantage.

(3) In this section—

"arrangements" includes any scheme, agreement or understanding, whether or not legally enforceable;

"tax advantage" has the meaning given by section 1139 of CTA 2010.

1218ZCN Transactions not entered into for genuine commercial reasons

(1) A transaction is to be ignored for the purpose of determining museums and galleries exhibition tax relief so far as the transaction is attributable to arrangements (other than tax avoidance arrangements) entered into otherwise than for genuine commercial reasons.

(2) In this section "arrangements" and "tax avoidance arrangements" have the same meaning as in section 1218ZCM.

CHAPTER 4

LOSSES OF SEPARATE EXHIBITION TRADE

1218ZD Application of sections 1218ZDA to 1218ZDC

(1) Sections 1218ZDA to 1218ZDC apply to a company which is treated under section 1218ZB(2) as carrying on a separate trade in relation to the production of an exhibition.

(2) In those sections "the completion period" means the accounting period in which the company ceases to carry on the separate exhibition trade.

1218ZDA Restriction on use of losses before completion period

(1) This section applies if a loss is made by the company in the separate exhibition trade in an accounting period preceding the completion period.

(2) The loss is not available for loss relief, except to the extent that the loss may be carried forward under section 45 or 45B of CTA 2010 to be deducted from profits of the separate exhibition trade in a subsequent period.

(3) If the loss is carried forward under section 45 or 45B of CTA 2010 and deducted from profits of the separate exhibition trade in a subsequent period, the deduction is to be ignored for the purposes of section 269ZB of CTA 2010 (restriction on deductions from trading profits).

(4) In this section "loss relief" includes any means by which a loss might be used to reduce the amount in respect of which a company, or any other person, is chargeable to tax.

1218ZDB Use of losses in the completion period

(1) Subsection (2) applies if a loss made in the separate exhibition trade is carried forward under section 45 or 45B of CTA 2010 to the completion period.

(2) So much (if any) of the loss as is not attributable to museums and galleries exhibition tax relief (see subsection (4)) may be treated for the purposes of section 37 and Part 5 of CTA 2010 as if it were a loss made in the completion period.

(3) If a loss is made in the separate exhibition trade in the completion period, the amount of the loss that may be—

(a) deducted from total profits of the same or an earlier period under section 37 of CTA 2010, or

(b) surrendered as group relief under Part 5 of that Act,

is restricted to the amount (if any) that is not attributable to museums and galleries exhibition tax relief (see subsection (4)).

(4) The amount of a loss in any period that is attributable to museums and galleries exhibition tax relief is found by—

(a) calculating what the amount of the loss would have been if there had been no additional deduction under Chapter 3 in that or any earlier period, and

(b) deducting that amount from the total amount of the loss.

(5) This section does not apply to a loss surrendered, or treated as carried forward, under section 1218ZDC (terminal losses).

1218ZDC Terminal losses

(1) This section applies if—

(a) the company ceases to carry on the separate exhibition trade, and
(b) if the company had not ceased to carry on that trade, it could have carried forward an amount under section 45 or 45B of CTA 2010 to be set against profits of that trade in a later period ("the terminal loss").

Below in this section the company is referred to as "company A" and the separate exhibition trade is referred to as "trade 1".

(2) If company A—

(a) is treated under section 1218ZB(2) as carrying on a separate trade in relation to the production of another exhibition ("trade 2"), and
(b) is carrying on trade 2 when it ceases to carry on trade 1,

company A may (on making a claim) make an election under subsection (3).

(3) The election is to have the terminal loss (or a part of it) treated—

(a) in a case where the loss could have been carried forward under section 45 of CTA 2010 had trade 1 not ceased, as if it were a loss carried forward under that section to be set against the profits of trade 2 of the first accounting period beginning after the cessation and so on, and
(b) in a case where the loss could have been carried forward under section 45B of CTA 2010 had trade 1 not ceased, as if it were a loss made in trade 2 which has been carried forward under that section to the first accounting period beginning after the cessation.

(4) Subsection (5) applies if—

(a) another company ("company B") is treated under section 1218ZB(2) as carrying on a separate trade ("company B's trade") in relation to the production of—
  (i) the exhibition which is the subject of trade 1, or
  (ii) another exhibition,
(b) company B is carrying on company B's trade when company A ceases to carry on trade 1, and
(c) company B is in the same group as company A for the purposes of Part 5 of CTA 2010 (group relief).

(5) Company A may surrender the loss (or a part of it) to company B.

(6) On the making of a claim by company B the amount surrendered is treated—

(a) in a case where the amount could have been carried forward under section 45 of CTA 2010 had trade 1 not ceased, as if it were a loss carried forward by company B under that section to be set against the profits of company B's trade of the first accounting period beginning after the cessation and so on, and
(b) in a case where the amount could have been carried forward under section 45B of CTA 2010 had trade 1 not ceased, as if it were a loss made in company B's trade which has been carried forward under that section to the first accounting period beginning after the cessation.

(7) The Treasury may by regulations make administrative provision in relation to the surrender of a loss under subsection (5) and the resulting claim under subsection (6).

(8) "Administrative provision" means provision corresponding, subject to such adaptations or other modifications as appear to the Treasury to be appropriate, to that made by Part 8 of Schedule 18 to FA 1998 (company tax returns: claims for group relief).

(9) A deduction under section 45 or 45B of CTA 2010 which is made in reliance on this section is to be ignored for the purposes of section 269ZB of that Act (restriction on deductions from trading profits).

CHAPTER 5

PROVISIONAL ENTITLEMENT TO RELIEF

1218ZE Provisional entitlement to relief

(1) In relation to a company and the production of an exhibition, "interim accounting period" means any accounting period that—

(a) is one in which the company carries on the separate exhibition trade, and
(b) precedes the accounting period in which it ceases to do so.

(2) A company is not entitled to museums and galleries exhibition tax relief for an interim accounting period unless—

(a) its company tax return for the period states the amount of planned core expenditure on the production of the exhibition that is EEA expenditure (see section 1218ZCC(2)), and

(b) that amount is such as to indicate that the EEA expenditure condition (see section 1218ZCC) will be met.

If those requirements are met, the company is provisionally treated in relation to that period as if the EEA expenditure condition were met.

1218ZEA Clawback of provisional relief

(1) If a statement is made under section 1218ZE(2) but it subsequently appears that the EEA expenditure condition will not be met on the company's ceasing to carry on the separate exhibition trade, the company—

(a) is not entitled to museums and galleries exhibition tax relief for any period for which its entitlement depended on such a statement, and

(b) must amend accordingly its company tax return for any such period.

(2) When a company ceases to carry on the separate exhibition trade, the company's company tax return for the period in which that cessation occurs must—

(a) state that the company has ceased to carry on the separate exhibition trade, and

(b) be accompanied by a final statement of the amount of the core expenditure on the production of the exhibition that is EEA expenditure.

(3) If that statement shows that the EEA expenditure condition is not met—

(a) the company is not entitled to museums and galleries exhibition tax relief or to relief under section 1218ZDC (transfer of terminal losses) for any period, and

(b) must amend accordingly its company tax return for any period for which such relief was claimed.

(4) Any amendment or assessment necessary to give effect to this section may be made despite any limitation on the time within which an amendment or assessment may normally be made.

CHAPTER 6

INTERPRETATION

1218ZF Regulations about activities in relation to an exhibition

The Treasury may by regulations amend section 1218ZBC (costs of the production) or 1218ZCD ("core expenditure") for the purpose of providing that activities of a specified description are, or are not, to be regarded as activities involved in developing or (as the case may be) producing, running, deinstalling or closing—

(a) an exhibition, or

(b) an exhibition of a specified description.

1218ZFA Interpretation

In this Part—

"company tax return" has the same meaning as in Schedule 18 to FA 1998 (see paragraph 3(1) of that Schedule);

"core expenditure" has the meaning given by section 1218ZCD;

"costs", in relation to an exhibition, has the meaning given by section 1218ZBC;

"EEA expenditure" has the meaning given by section 1218ZCC(2);

"EEA expenditure condition" has the meaning given by section 1218ZCC;

"exhibition" has the meaning given by section 1218ZAA;

"income", in relation to an exhibition, has the meaning given by section 1218ZBB;

"museums and galleries exhibition tax relief" is to be read in accordance with Chapter 3 (see in particular section 1218ZC(1));

"primary production company" has the meaning given by section 1218ZAC;

"qualifying expenditure" has the meaning given by section 1218ZCG;

"secondary production company" has the meaning given by section 1218ZAD;

"the separate exhibition trade" is to be read in accordance with section 1218ZB;

"touring exhibition" has the meaning given by section 1218ZAB."

PART 2

CONSEQUENTIAL AMENDMENTS

ICTA

2 (1) Section 826 of ICTA (interest on tax overpaid) is amended as follows.

(2) In subsection (1), after paragraph (fd) insert—

"(fe) a payment of museums and galleries exhibition tax credit falls to be made to a company; or".

(3) In subsection (3C), for "or orchestra tax credit" substitute ", orchestra tax credit or museums and galleries exhibition tax credit".

(4) In subsection (8A)—

(a) in paragraph (a), for "or (fd)" substitute ", (fd) or (fe)", and
(b) in paragraph (b)(ii), after "orchestra tax credit" insert "or museums and galleries exhibition tax credit".

(5) In subsection (8BA), after "orchestra tax credit" (in both places) insert "or museums and galleries exhibition tax credit".

FA 1998

3 Schedule 18 to FA 1998 (company tax returns, assessments and related matters) is amended in accordance with paragraphs 4 to 6.

4 In paragraph 10 (other claims and elections to be included in return), in sub-paragraph (4), for "or 15D" substitute ", 15D or 15E".

5 (1) Paragraph 52 (recovery of excessive repayments etc) is amended as follows.

(2) In sub-paragraph (2), after paragraph (bh) insert—

"(bi) museums and galleries exhibition tax credit under Part 15E of that Act,".

(3) In sub-paragraph (5)—

(a) after paragraph (aj) insert—
"(ak) an amount of museums and galleries exhibition tax credit paid to a company for an accounting period,", and
(b) in the words after paragraph (b), after "(aj)" insert ", (ak)".

6 In Part 9D (certain claims for tax relief)—

(a) in the heading, for "or 15D" substitute ", 15D or 15E", and
(b) in paragraph 83S (introduction), after sub-paragraph (f) insert—
"(g) museums and galleries exhibition tax relief."

CAA 2001

7 In Schedule A1 to CAA 2001 (first-year tax credits), in paragraph 11(4), omit the "and" at the end of paragraph (f) and after paragraph (g) insert ", and

(h) Chapter 3 of Part 15E of that Act (museums and galleries exhibition tax credits)."

FA 2007

8 In Schedule 24 to FA 2007 (penalties for errors), in paragraph 28(fa) (meaning of "corporation tax credit"), omit the "or" at the end of paragraph (ivd) and after that paragraph insert—

"(ive) a museums and galleries exhibition tax credit under Chapter 3 of Part 15E of that Act, or".

CTA 2009

9 CTA 2009 is amended in accordance with paragraphs 10 to 14.

10 In section 104BA (restriction on claiming other tax reliefs), after subsection (4) insert—

"(5) For provision prohibiting an R&D expenditure credit being given under this Chapter and relief being given under Chapter 3 of Part 15E (museums and galleries exhibition tax relief), see section 1218ZCG(2)."

11 In Part 8 (intangible fixed assets), in Chapter 10 (excluded assets), after section 808D insert—

"808E Assets representing expenditure incurred in course of separate exhibition trade

(1) This Part does not apply to an intangible fixed asset held by a museums and galleries exhibition production company so far as the asset represents expenditure on an exhibition that is treated under Part 15E as expenditure of a separate trade (see particularly sections 1218ZB and 1218ZBE).

(2) In this section—

"exhibition" has the same meaning as in Part 15E (see section 1218ZAA);
"museums and galleries exhibition production company" means a company which, for the purposes of that Part, is the primary production company or a secondary production company for an exhibition (see sections 1218ZAC and 1218ZAD)."

12 In section 1040ZA (restriction on claiming other tax reliefs), after subsection (4) insert—

"(5) For provision prohibiting relief being given under this Part and under Chapter 3 of Part 15E (museums and galleries exhibition tax relief), see section 1218ZCG(2)."

13 In section 1310 (orders and regulations), in subsection (4), after paragraph (eo) insert—

"(ep) section 1218ZCC (EEA expenditure condition),
(eq) section 1218ZCF (amount of additional deduction),
(er) section 1218ZF (regulations about activities in relation to exhibition),".

14 In Schedule 4 (index of defined expressions), insert at the appropriate places—

"company tax return (in Part 15E)	section 1218ZFA"
"core expenditure (in Part 15E)	section 1218ZCD"
"costs, in relation to an exhibition (in Part 15E)	section 1218ZBC"
"EEA expenditure (in Part 15E)	section 1218ZCC(2)"
"EEA expenditure condition (in Part 15E)	section 1218ZCC"
"exhibition (in Part 15E)	section 1218ZAA"
"income, in relation to an exhibition (in Part 15E)	section 1218ZBB"
"museums and galleries exhibition tax relief (in Part 15E)	section 1218ZC(1)"
"primary production company (in Part 15E)	section 1218ZAC"
"qualifying expenditure (in Part 15E)	section 1218ZCG"
"secondary production company (in Part 15E)	section 1218ZAD"
"separate exhibition trade (in Part 15E)	section 1218ZB"
"touring exhibition (in Part 15E)	section 1218ZAB".

FA 2009

15 In Schedule 54A to FA 2009 (which is prospectively inserted by F(No. 3)A 2010 and contains provision about the recovery of certain amounts of interest paid by HMRC), in paragraph 2—

(a) in sub-paragraph (2), omit the "or" at the end of paragraph (h) and after paragraph (i) insert ", or
(j) a payment of museums and galleries exhibition tax credit under Chapter 3 of Part 15E of CTA 2009 for an accounting period.";
(b) in sub-paragraph (4), for "(i)" substitute "(j)".

CTA 2010

16 In Part 8B of CTA 2010 (trading profits taxable at Northern Ireland rate), in section 357H(7) (introduction), after "Chapter 14A for provision about orchestra tax relief;" insert "Chapter 14B for provision about museums and galleries exhibition tax relief;".

17 In Part 8B of CTA 2010, after section 357UQ insert—

"CHAPTER 14B

MUSEUMS AND GALLERIES EXHIBITION TAX RELIEF

Introductory

357UR Introduction and interpretation

(1) This Chapter makes provision about the operation of Part 15E of CTA 2009 (museums and galleries exhibition tax relief) in relation to expenditure incurred by a company in an accounting period in which it is a Northern Ireland company.

(2) In this Chapter—

(a) "Northern Ireland expenditure" means expenditure incurred in a trade to the extent that the expenditure forms part of the Northern Ireland profits or Northern Ireland losses of the trade;
(b) "the separate exhibition trade" has the same meaning as in Part 15E of CTA 2009 (see section 1218ZB(3) of that Act);
(c) "qualifying expenditure" has the same meaning as in Chapter 3 of that Part (see section 1218ZCG of that Act).

(3) References in Part 15E of CTA 2009 to "museums and galleries exhibition tax relief" include relief under this Chapter.

Museums and galleries exhibition tax relief

357US Northern Ireland additional deduction

(1) In this Chapter "a Northern Ireland additional deduction" means so much of a deduction under section 1218ZCE of CTA 2009 (claim for additional deduction) as is calculated by reference to qualifying expenditure that is Northern Ireland expenditure.

(2) A Northern Ireland additional deduction forms part of the Northern Ireland profits or Northern Ireland losses of the separate exhibition trade.

357UT Northern Ireland supplementary deduction

(1) This section applies where—

(a) a company is entitled under section 1218ZCE of CTA 2009 to an additional deduction in calculating the profit or loss of the separate exhibition trade in an accounting period,

(b) the company is a Northern Ireland company in the period,

(c) the additional deduction is wholly or partly a Northern Ireland additional deduction, and

(d) any of the following conditions is met—

(i) the company does not have a surrenderable loss in the accounting period;

(ii) the company has a surrenderable loss in the accounting period, but does not make a claim under section 1218ZCH of CTA 2009 (museums and galleries exhibition tax credit claimable if company has surrenderable loss) for the period;

(iii) the company has a surrenderable loss in the accounting period and makes a claim under that section for the period, but the amount of Northern Ireland losses surrendered on the claim is less than the Northern Ireland additional deduction.

(2) The company is entitled to make another deduction ("a Northern Ireland supplementary deduction") in respect of qualifying expenditure.

(3) See section 357UU for provision about the amount of the Northern Ireland supplementary deduction.

(4) The Northern Ireland supplementary deduction—

(a) is made in calculating the profit or loss of the separate exhibition trade, and

(b) forms part of the Northern Ireland profits or Northern Ireland losses of the separate exhibition trade.

(5) In this section "surrenderable loss" has the meaning given by section 1218ZCI of CTA 2009.

357UU Northern Ireland supplementary deduction: amount

(1) This section contains provision for the purposes of section 357UT(2) about the amount of the Northern Ireland supplementary deduction.

(2) If the accounting period falls within only one financial year, the amount of the Northern Ireland supplementary deduction is—

$$(A - B) \times ((MR - NIR) / NIR)$$

where—

A is the amount of the Northern Ireland additional deduction brought into account in the accounting period;

B is the amount of Northern Ireland losses surrendered in any claim under section 1218ZCH of CTA 2009 for the accounting period;

MR is the main rate for the financial year;

NIR is the Northern Ireland rate for the financial year.

(3) If the accounting period falls within more than one financial year, the amount of the Northern Ireland supplementary deduction is determined by taking the following steps.

Step 1

Calculate, for each financial year, the amount that would be the Northern Ireland supplementary deduction for the accounting period if it fell within only that financial year (see subsection (2)).

Step 2

Multiply each amount calculated under step 1 by the proportion of the accounting period that falls within the financial year for which it is calculated.

Step 3

Add together each amount found under step 2.

357UV Museums and galleries exhibition tax credit: Northern Ireland supplementary deduction ignored

For the purpose of determining the available loss of a company under section 1218ZCI of CTA 2009 (amount of surrenderable loss) for any accounting period, any Northern Ireland supplementary deduction made by the company in the period (and any Northern Ireland supplementary deduction made in any previous accounting period) is to be ignored.

Losses of separate exhibition trade

357UW Restriction on use of losses before completion period

(1) Section 1218ZDA of CTA 2009 (restriction on use of losses before completion period) has effect subject as follows.

(2) The reference in subsection (1) of that section to a loss made in the separate exhibition trade in an accounting period preceding the completion period is, if the company is a Northern Ireland company in that period, a reference to—

(a) any Northern Ireland losses of the trade of the period, or

(b) any mainstream losses of the trade of the period;

and references to losses in subsections (2) and (3) of that section are to be read accordingly.

(3) Subsection (4) applies if a Northern Ireland company has, in an accounting period preceding the completion period—

(a) both Northern Ireland losses of the trade and mainstream profits of the trade, or

(b) both mainstream losses of the trade and Northern Ireland profits of the trade.

(4) The company may make a claim under section 37 (relief for trade losses against total profits) for relief for the losses mentioned in subsection (3)(a) or (b).

(5) But relief on such a claim is available only—

(a) in the case of a claim for relief for Northern Ireland losses, against mainstream profits of the trade of the same period;

(b) in the case of a claim for relief for mainstream losses, against Northern Ireland profits of the trade of the same period.

(6) In this section "the completion period" has the same meaning as in section 1218ZDA of CTA 2009 (see section 1218ZD(2) of that Act).

357UX Use of losses in the completion period

(1) Section 1218ZDB of CTA 2009 (use of losses in the completion period) has effect subject as follows.

(2) The reference in subsection (1) of that section to a loss made in the separate exhibition trade is, in relation to a loss made in a period in which the company is a Northern Ireland company, a reference to—

(a) any Northern Ireland losses of the trade of the period, or

(b) any mainstream losses of the trade of the period;

and references to losses in subsections (2) and (4) of that section are to be read accordingly.

(3) The references in subsection (3) of that section to a loss made in the separate exhibition trade in the completion period are, where the company is a Northern Ireland company in the period, references to—

(a) any Northern Ireland losses of the trade of the period, or

(b) any mainstream losses of the trade of the period;

and references to losses in subsection (4) of that section are to be read accordingly.

(4) Subsection (4) of that section has effect, in relation to Northern Ireland losses, as if the reference to an additional deduction under Chapter 3 of Part 15E of CTA 2009 included a reference to a Northern Ireland supplementary deduction under this Chapter.

357UY Terminal losses

(1) Section 1218ZDC of CTA 2009 (terminal losses) has effect subject as follows.

(2) Where—

(a) a company makes an election under subsection (3) of that section (election to treat terminal loss as loss brought forward of different trade) in relation to all or part of a terminal loss, and

(b) the terminal loss is a Northern Ireland loss,

that subsection has effect as if the reference in it to a loss brought forward were to a Northern Ireland loss brought forward.

(3) Where—

(a) a company makes a claim under subsection (6) of that section (claim to treat terminal loss as loss brought forward by different company) in relation to part or all of a terminal loss, and

(b) the terminal loss is a Northern Ireland loss,

that subsection has effect as if the reference in it to a loss brought forward were to a Northern Ireland loss brought forward."

18 (1) Schedule 4 to CTA 2010 (index of defined expressions) is amended as follows.

(2) In the entry for "Northern Ireland expenditure"—

(a) for "14A" substitute "14B", and

(b) for "and 357UJ(2)" substitute ", 357UJ(2) and 357UR(2)".

(3) Insert at the appropriate places—

"qualifying expenditure (in Chapter 14B of Part 8B)	section 357UR(2)"
"the separate exhibition trade (in Chapter 14B of Part 8B)	section 357UR(2)"

FA 2016

19 In Schedule 24 to FA 2016 (tax advantages constituting the grant of state aid), in Part 1, in the table headed "*Creative tax reliefs*", after the entry for "Orchestra tax relief" insert—

"Museums and galleries exhibition tax relief	Part 15E of CTA 2009"

PART 3

COMMENCEMENT

20 Any power to make regulations conferred on the Treasury by virtue of this Schedule comes into force on the day on which this Act is passed.

21 (1) The amendments made by the following provisions of this Schedule have effect in relation to accounting periods beginning on or after 1 April 2017—

(a) Part 1, and

(b) in Part 2, paragraphs 2 to 15 and 19.

(2) Sub-paragraph (3) applies where a company has an accounting period beginning before 1 April 2017 and ending on or after that date ("the straddling period").

(3) For the purposes of Part 15E of CTA 2009—

(a) so much of the straddling period as falls before 1 April 2017, and so much of that period as falls on or after that date, are separate accounting periods, and

(b) any amounts brought into account for the purposes of calculating for corporation tax purposes the profits of a trade for the straddling period are apportioned to the two separate accounting periods on such basis as is just and reasonable.

22 (1) Section 4 of CT(NI)A 2015 (power to make consequential amendments) has effect as if paragraphs 16 to 18 of this Schedule were contained in that Act.

(2) Section 5(4) to (6) of CT(NI)A 2015 (commencement) has effect as if—

(a) references to Part 8B of CTA 2010 were to that Part as amended by paragraphs 16 and 17 of this Schedule, and

(b) references to the amendments made by Schedules 1 and 2 to CT(NI)A 2015 included the amendments made by paragraph 18 of this Schedule.

GENERAL NOTE

Schedule 6 Pt 1 inserts new CTA 2009 Pt 15E (ss 1218ZA to 1218ZFA, museum and gallery exhibition tax relief).

Introduction

CTA 2009 Pt 15E Ch 1 (ss 1218ZA to 1218ZAD) defines "exhibition", "touring exhibition", "primary production company" and "secondary production company". An exhibition is a curated public display of an organised collection of objects or works, or of a single object or work, considered to be of scientific, historic, artistic or cultural interest. There are a number of exceptions, including exhibitions in connection with a competition; those whose main purpose is to sell anything displayed; and those including live performances other than performances incidental to the exhibition.

Taxation of activities of production company

CTA 2009 Pt 15E Ch 2 (ss 1218ZB to 1218ZBF) provides for a qualifying company's activities in relation to an exhibition to be treated as an exhibition trade that is separate from the company's other activities (including the production of any other exhibition), and sets out the calculation of profits and losses of this "separate exhibition trade".

- The primary production company (see CTA 2009 s 1218ZAC) is treated as beginning to carry on this separate trade at the beginning of the production stage of the exhibition at its first venue or, if earlier, when the company first receives any income from the production. The company is treated as ceasing to carry on the separate trade when the exhibition closes at its final venue.
- A secondary production company (see CTA 2009 s 1218ZAD) is treated as beginning to carry on the separate trade at the beginning of the production stage of the exhibition at the first exhibition venue for which it is the secondary production company or, if earlier, when the company first receives any income from the production. The company is treated as ceasing to carry on the separate trade when the exhibition closes at the final venue for which the company is the secondary production company.
- CTA 2009 s 1218ZBA sets out the calculation of profits or losses for the separate exhibition trade. For the first period of account: (a) the costs of production incurred to date, and (b) the proportion of the estimated total income from that production treated as earned at the end of that period (see below), are taken into account as a debit and credit respectively. Estimates are to be made as at the balance sheet date, on a just and reasonable basis.

  For later periods: (a) the debit is the difference between the amount ("C") of the costs of the production incurred to date and the amount corresponding to C for the previous period, and (b) the credit is the difference between (i) the proportion ("PI") of the estimated total income from that production treated as earned at the end of that period, and (ii) the amount corresponding to PI for the previous period.
- The proportion of the estimated total income treated as earned at the end of a period of account is:

  $C/T \times 1$

  where C is the total to date of costs incurred, T is the estimated total cost of the production of the exhibition, and I is the estimated total income from the production of the exhibition.
- CTA 2009 s 1218ZBB provides that income from a production of an exhibition includes any receipts by the company in connection with the production or exploitation of the exhibition, and specifies certain types of receipt that are included in this definition.
- CTA 2009 ss 1218ZBC and 1218ZBD specify the costs of production that are deductible – including expenditure on developing, producing, running, de-installing and closing the exhibition – and when those costs are taken to be incurred. Expenditure incurred before commencement of the separate exhibition trade may be allowable pre-trading expenditure (CTA 2009 s 1218ZBE).

Museums and galleries exhibition tax relief

CTA 2009 Pt 15E Ch 3 (ss 1218ZC to 1218ZCN) sets out the conditions for relief and the operation of the relief, which is given by way of: (a) additional deductions made in calculating the separate exhibition trade's profits and losses, and (b) a payment – a museums and galleries exhibition tax credit – made on surrender of the losses from that trade.

- A company qualifies for relief if conditions A to D in s 1218ZCA are met. Condition A is that the company is either the primary production company or a secondary production company for the exhibition. Condition B is that the company is:
  - (a) a charitable company that maintains a "museum or gallery" (see the extended definition given by s 1218ZCA(6));
  - (b) wholly owned by a charity that maintains a museum or gallery; or
  - (c) wholly owned by a local authority that maintains a museum or gallery.

    These terms and expressions are defined in CTA 2009 s 1218ZCB. Condition C is that at the beginning of the planning stage the company intends that the exhibition should be public. Condition D is that the EEA condition in s 1218ZCC is met. This condition, which HM Treasury may vary by means of regulations, concerns expenditure on goods or services provided from within the European Economic Area. See also below regarding anti-avoidance measures.

- **Additional deduction** (CTA 2009 ss 1218ZCE to 1218ZCG). A company that qualifies for museums and galleries exhibition tax relief in relation to the production of an exhibition may claim, for an accounting period, an additional deduction in relation to the production. The deduction is made in calculating the profit or loss of the separate exhibition trade.

  For the first period of account during which the separate exhibition trade is carried on, the amount of the additional deduction is E, where E is: (a) so much of the qualifying expenditure (see below) incurred to date as is EEA expenditure, or (b) if less, 80% of the total amount of qualifying expenditure incurred to date (CTA 2009 s 1218ZCF(2)).

  For later periods the amount of the additional deduction is E − P where E is: (a) so much of the qualifying expenditure incurred to date as is EEA expenditure, or (b) if less, 80% of the total amount of qualifying expenditure incurred to date, and P is the total amount of additional deductions given for previous periods (CTA 2009 s 1218ZCF(3)). The 80% limit may be varied by means of regulations.

- Qualifying expenditure is "core expenditure" (see below) that: (a) falls to be taken into account in calculating the profit or loss of the separate exhibition trade, (b) is not otherwise relievable, and (c) is incurred on or before 31 March 2022. (This time limit may be extended by means of regulations.) Expenditure is "otherwise relievable" if, in the event of a claim, the company would be entitled to an R&D tax credit or additional relief for R&D expenditure; film, TV, or video games tax relief; a credit or additional deduction for theatrical productions; or orchestra tax relief.

- "Core expenditure" is expenditure on the activities involved in producing, de-installing and closing the exhibition at every relevant venue, as set out in CTA 2009 s 1218ZCD. De-installing and closing expenditure is core expenditure only if the exhibition is open for 12 months or less. Several kinds of expenditure are excluded.

- **Museums and galleries exhibition tax credits** (CTA 2009 ss 1218ZCH to 1218ZCL). A qualifying company may claim a tax credit in relation to the production for an accounting period in which it has a surrenderable loss. The company may surrender the whole or part of its surrenderable loss in the accounting period.

  Subject to the limits set out below, the tax credit is 25% of the loss surrendered if the exhibition is a touring exhibition (see CTA 2009 s 1218ZAB) or 20% if it is not a touring exhibition. The company's available loss (see below) is reduced by the amount surrendered.

- The surrenderable loss is the company's available loss for the accounting period in the separate exhibition trade or, if less, the available qualifying expenditure (see below) for that period. The "available loss" is L + RUL where L is the company's loss for the period in the separate exhibition trade and RUL is the amount of any relevant unused loss, ie. so much of any available loss for the previous accounting period as has not been surrendered under CTA 2009 s 1218ZCH or carried forward under CTA 2010 s 45 or 45B and set against profits of the separate exhibition trade. (CTA 2010 s 45B was introduced by F(No 2)A 2017 s 18 and Sch 4.)

- For the first period of account during which the separate exhibition trade is carried on, the available qualifying expenditure is the amount that is E for the first period for the purpose of s 1218CF(2) (see above in relation to the additional deduction). For later periods the available qualifying expenditure is E − S where E is the amount that is E for that period for the purposes of CTA 2009 s 1218ZCF(3), and S is the total amount previously surrendered under CTA 2009 s 1218ZCH (see above).

- If a company is entitled to a tax credit and makes a claim, HMRC must pay the amount of the credit to the company. The amount payable and any interest may be applied in discharging a corporation tax liability. In the event of HMRC enquiries into the company's tax return, the credit need not be paid before the enquiries are completed but HMRC may make a provisional payment. Payment of the tax credit may be withheld if the company has outstanding PAYE and NIC liabilities (CTA 2009 s 1218ZCJ).

- The maximum tax credit is £100,000 in relation to a touring exhibition and £80,000 in relation to an exhibition that is not a touring exhibition. In order to comply with

EU state aid rules, the total amount of tax credits payable under section 1218ZCJ in the case of any undertaking cannot exceed €75m per year (CTA 2009 s 1218ZCK).

- **Anti-avoidance** (CTA 2009 ss 1218ZCM ,1218ZCN). Relief is denied if there are any tax avoidance arrangements relation to the production of the exhibition. Arrangements are "tax avoidance arrangements" if their main purpose, or one of their main purposes, is the obtaining of a tax advantage. "Arrangements" includes any scheme, agreement or understanding, and "tax advantage" is defined in CTA 2010 s 1139 (CTA 2009 s 1218ZCM). A transaction is ignored so far as it is attributable to arrangements entered into otherwise than for genuine commercial reasons (CTA 2009 s 1218ZCN).
- In calculating for the purpose of CTA 2009 Pt 15E Ch 3 the costs incurred on a production of an exhibition at the end of a period of account, any amount that has not been paid four months after the end of that period is ignored (CTA 2009 s 1218ZCL).

Losses of separate exhibition trade

CTA 2009 Pt 15E Ch 4 (ss 1218ZD to 1218ZDC) deals with losses of the separate exhibition trade.

- A loss made in the separate exhibition trade in an accounting period preceding the "completion period" (i.e. the accounting period in which the company ceases to carry on the separate exhibition trade) is not available for loss relief except to the extent that it may be carried forward under CTA 2010 s 45 or 45B to be deducted from profits of the separate exhibition trade in a subsequent period. If a loss is carried forward and deducted in this way, the deduction is ignored for the purposes of CTA 2010 s 269ZB (restriction on deductions from trading profits) (CTA 2009 s 1218ZDA). (CTA 2010 ss 45B and 269ZB were introduced by F(No 2)A 2017 s 18 and Sch 4.)
- If a loss made in the separate exhibition trade is carried forward under CTA 2010 s 45 or 45B to the completion period, so much of the loss as is not attributable to museums and galleries exhibition tax relief may be treated for the purposes of CTA 2010 s 37 (relief for trade losses against total profits) and CTA 2010 Pt 5 (group relief) as if it were a loss made in the completion period.

  If a loss is made in the separate exhibition trade in the completion period, the amount of the loss that may be deducted from total profits under CTA 2010 s 37, or surrendered as group relief, is restricted to the amount not attributable to museums and galleries exhibition tax relief. This amount is found by deducting, from the total loss, the amount of the loss that there would have been in the absence of any additional deduction in that or any earlier period (CTA 2009 s 1218ZDB).

- A "terminal loss" arises if the company (referred to below as "company A") ceases to carry on the separate exhibition trade ("trade 1") and, if it had not done so, it could have carried forward an amount under CTA 2010 s 45 or 45B. If company A is treated under CTA 2009 s 1218ZB(2) as carrying on a separate trade in relation to the production of another exhibition ("trade 2"), and is carrying on trade 2 when it ceases to carry on trade 1, it may (on making a claim) elect to have the terminal loss treated:
  - (a) where the loss could have been carried forward under CTA 2010 s 45 had trade 1 not ceased, as if it were a loss carried forward under that section to be set against the profits of trade 2 of the first accounting period beginning after the cessation and so on, and
  - (b) where the loss could have been carried forward under CTA 2010 s 45 had trade 1 not ceased, as if it were a loss made in trade 2 which has been carried forward to the first accounting period beginning after the cessation.

  If another company ("company B") is treated as carrying on a separate trade ("company B's trade") in relation to the production of the exhibition which is the subject of trade 1 or another exhibition, company B is carrying on company B's trade when company A ceases to carry on trade 1, and company B is in the same group as company A for group relief purposes, then company A may surrender the loss of a part of it to company B. On company B's claim the amount surrendered is treated:
  - (a) where the amount could have been carried forward under CTA 2010 s 45 had trade 1 not ceased, as if it were a loss carried forward by company B under that section to be set against the profits of company B's trade of the first accounting period beginning after the cessation and so on, and

(b) where the amount could have been carried forward under CTA 2010 s 45B had trade 1 not ceased, as if it were a loss made in company B's trade which has been carried forward under that section to the first accounting period beginning after the cessation (CTA 2009 s 1218ZDC).

Provisional entitlement to relief

CTA 2009 Pt 15E Ch 5 (ss 1218ZE to 1218ZEA) provides for relief to be given on a provisional basis, and for that relief to be withdrawn if it turns out that the conditions are not met.

Interpretation

CTA 2009 Pt 15E Ch 6 (ss 1218ZF to 1218ZFA) enables HM Treasury to amend CTA 2009 s 1218ZBC (costs of the production) or CTA 2009 s 1218ZCD (core expenditure) and sets out the interpretation of several expressions.

Schedule 6 Part 2

Schedule 6 Part 2 makes consequential amendments to:
- ICTA 1988 s 826 (interest on tax overpaid);
- FA 1998 Sch 18 (company tax returns, assessments and related matters);
- CAA 2001 Sch A1 (first-year tax credits);
- FA 2007 Sch 24 (penalties for errors);
- CTA 2009 s 104BA (restriction on claiming other tax reliefs); Pt 8 Ch 10 (excluded assets – a new s 808E is inserted); s 1040ZA (restriction on claiming other tax reliefs); s 1310 (orders and regulations); and Sch 4 (index of defined expressions);
- FA 2009 Sch 54A (further provision as to late payment interest and repayment interest, which is to be inserted with effect from a day to be appointed by Treasury order)
- CTA 2010 Pt 8B (taxable profits taxable at the Northern Ireland rate, which is to be inserted by Corporation Tax (Northern Ireland) Act 2015 s 1 in relation to accounting periods beginning on or after the first day of the financial year to be appointed by the Treasury);
- FA 2016 Sch 24 (tax advantages constituting the grant of state aid).

Schedule 6 Part 3

The amendments made by Sch 6 Pt 1, and Pt 2 paras 2–15 and 19, have effect for accounting periods beginning on or after 1 April 2017. Provision is made for appointment of profits where an accounting period straddles that date. Sch 6 para 2 sets out separate commencement provisions for the amendments in respect of the Northern Ireland rate of corporation tax.

SCHEDULE 7

TRADING PROFITS TAXABLE AT THE NORTHERN IRELAND RATE

Section 25

PART 1

AMENDMENTS RELATING TO SMES

Amendments of CTA 2010

1 CTA 2010 is amended as follows.

2 (1) Section 357H (introduction) is amended as follows.

(2) In subsection (5)—

(a) after "that is an SME" insert "and is a Northern Ireland employer";

(b) for "that is not an SME" substitute "that—

(a) is an SME that is not a Northern Ireland employer and has made the requisite election, or

(b) is not an SME."

3 (1) Section 357KA (meaning of "Northern Ireland company") is amended as follows.

(2) In subsection (1)(b), for "the SME condition" substitute "the SME (Northern Ireland employer) condition, the SME (election) condition".

(3) In subsection (2), for "SME condition" substitute "SME (Northern Ireland employer) condition".

(4) After subsection (2) insert—

"(2A) The "SME (election) condition" is that—

(a) the company is an SME in relation to the period,

(b) the company is not a Northern Ireland employer in relation to the period,

(c) the company has a NIRE in the period,

(d) the company is not a disqualified close company in relation to the period, and

(e) an election by the company for the purposes of this subsection has effect in relation to the period."

(5) In subsection (4), after the definition of "Northern Ireland employer" insert—

""disqualified close company", see section 357KEA;".

(6) After subsection (3) insert—

"(3A) An election for the purposes of subsection (2A)—

(a) must be made by notice to an officer of Revenue and Customs,

(b) must specify the accounting period in relation to which it is to have effect ("the specified accounting period"),

(c) must be made before the end of the period of 12 months beginning with the end of the specified accounting period, and

(d) if made in accordance with paragraphs (a) to (c) has effect in relation to the specified accounting period."

4 (1) Section 357KE (Northern Ireland workforce conditions) is amended as follows.

(2) In subsection (2)—

(a) omit the "and" at the end of paragraph (b), and

(b) at the end of paragraph (c) insert ", and

(d) in the case of a close company, or of a company which would be a close company if it were UK resident, individuals who are participators in the company."

(3) After subsection (7) insert—

"(7A) In this section "participator" has the same meaning as in sections 1064 to 1067 (see sections 1068 and 1069).

(7B) In determining for the purposes of this section the amount of working time that is spent in any place by a participator in the company, time spent by the participator in that place is to be included where—

(a) the time is spent by the participator in providing services to a person other than the company ("the third party"), and

(b) condition A or B is met.

(7C) Condition A is that the provision of the services results in a payment being made (whether directly or indirectly) to the company by—

(a) the third party, or

(b) a person connected with the third party.

(7D) Condition B is that—

(a) the company holds a right that it acquired (whether directly or indirectly) from the participator, and

(b) any payment in connection with that right is made (whether directly or indirectly) to the company by—

(i) the third party, or

(ii) a person connected with the third party.

(7E) Section 1122 (connected persons) applies for the purposes of this section."

5 After section 357KE insert—

"Meaning of "disqualified close company"

357KEA "Disqualified close company"

(1) A company is a "disqualified close company" in relation to a period if—

(a) the company is a close company, or would be a close company if it were UK resident, at any time in the period, and

(b) conditions A and B are met.

(2) Condition A is that the company has a NIRE in the period as a result of tax-avoidance arrangements.

(3) Condition B is that—

(a) 50% or more of the working time that is spent in the United Kingdom during the period by members of the company's workforce is working time spent by participators in the company otherwise than in Northern Ireland, or

(b) 50% or more of the company's workforce expenses that are attributable to working time spent in the United Kingdom during the period by members of the company's workforce are attributable to working time spent by participators in the company otherwise than in Northern Ireland.

(4) For the purposes of this section "tax avoidance arrangements" means arrangements the sole or main purpose of which is to secure that any profits or losses of the company for the period are Northern Ireland profits or losses.

(5) In subsection (4) "arrangements" includes any agreement, understanding, scheme, transaction or series of transactions (whether or not legally enforceable).

(6) The following provisions apply for the purposes of this section as they apply for the purposes of section 357KE (Northern Ireland workforce conditions)—

(a) subsections (2) to (5) and (7A) to (7E) of that section;

(b) regulations made under that section.

(7) In its application by virtue of subsection (6), subsection (5) of section 357KE has effect as if the reference in it to subsection (1)(b) of that section were to subsection (3)(b) of this section."

6 In the heading of Chapter 6 of Part 8B, at the end insert "that are Northern Ireland employers".

7 In section 357M (Chapter 6: introductory), in subsection (1), for "SME condition" substitute "SME (Northern Ireland employer) condition".

8 In the heading of Chapter 7 of Part 8B, after "losses etc:" insert "SMEs that are not Northern Ireland employers and".

9 In section 357N (Chapter 7: introductory), in subsection (1), after "by virtue of" insert "the SME (election) condition or".

10 (1) Section 357OB (Northern Ireland intangibles credits and debits: SMEs) is amended as follows.

(2) In the heading, at the end, insert "that are Northern Ireland employers".

(3) In subsection (1)(a), for "SME condition" substitute "SME (Northern Ireland employer) condition".

11 (1) Section 357OC (Northern Ireland intangibles credits and debits: large companies) is amended as follows.

(2) In the heading, after "debits:" insert "SMEs that are not Northern Ireland employers and".

(3) In subsection (1), after "by virtue of" insert "the SME (election) condition or".

12 (1) Section 357VB (relevant Northern Ireland IP profits: SMEs) is amended as follows.

(2) In the heading, at the end, insert "that are Northern Ireland employers".

(3) In subsection (1)(a), for "SME condition" substitute "SME (Northern Ireland employer) condition".

13 (1) Section 357VC (relevant Northern Ireland IP profits: large companies) is amended as follows.

(2) In the heading, after "profits:" insert "SMEs that are not Northern Ireland employers and".

(3) In subsection (1)(a), after "by virtue of" insert "the SME (election) condition or".

14 (1) Section 357WA (meaning of "Northern Ireland firm") is amended as follows.

(2) In subsection (1)(b), for "SME partnership condition" substitute "SME (Northern Ireland employer) partnership condition, the SME (election) partnership condition".

(3) In subsection (2), for "SME partnership condition" substitute "SME (Northern Ireland employer) partnership condition".

(4) After subsection (2) insert—

"(2A) The "SME (election) partnership condition" is that—

(a) the firm is an SME in relation to the firm's accounting period,

(b) the firm is not a Northern Ireland employer in relation to that period,

(c) the firm has a NIRE in that period,

(d) the firm is not a disqualified firm in relation to the period, and

(e) an election by the firm for the purposes of this subsection has effect in relation to that period."

(5) After subsection (3) insert—

"(3A) An election for the purposes of subsection (2A)—

(a) must be made by notice to an officer of Revenue and Customs,

(b) must specify the accounting period in relation to which it is to have effect ("the specified accounting period"),

(c) must be made before the end of the period of 12 months beginning with the end of the specified accounting period, and

(d) if made in accordance with paragraphs (a) to (c) has effect in relation to the specified accounting period."

(6) In subsection (4)—

(a) in the opening words, for "to subsections (2) and (3)" substitute "in relation to a firm";

(b) for paragraph (b) substitute—

"(b) references to the Northern Ireland workforce conditions were to the Northern Ireland workforce partnership conditions (see section 357WBA)."

(7) In subsection (5) omit paragraph (c).

15 After section 357WB, insert—

"357WBA Northern Ireland workforce partnership conditions

(1) The Northern Ireland workforce partnership conditions, in relation to a period, are—

(a) that 75% or more of the working time that is spent in the United Kingdom during the period by members of the firm's workforce is spent in Northern Ireland, and

(b) that 75% or more of the firm's workforce expenses that are attributable to working time spent in the United Kingdom during the period by members of the firm's workforce are attributable to time spent in Northern Ireland.

(2) References in this section to members of the firm's workforce are to—

(a) employees of the firm,

(b) externally provided workers in relation to the firm, and

(c) individuals who are partners in the firm.

(3) In subsection (2) "externally provided worker", in relation to a firm, has the same meaning as in Part 13 of CTA 2009 (see section 1128 of that Act).

In the application of section 1128 of that Act for the purposes of subsection (2), references to a company are to be read as references to a firm and references to a director are to be treated as omitted.

(4) References in this section to the working time spent by members of the firm's workforce in a place are to the total time spent by those persons in that place while providing services to the firm.

(5) References in this section to "the firm's workforce expenses" are, where the period is an accounting period of the firm, to the total of the deductions made by the firm in the period in respect of members of the firm's workforce in calculating the profits of the firm's trade.

(6) References in this section to "the firm's workforce expenses" are, where the period is not an accounting period of the firm, to the total of—

(a) the deductions made by the firm in any accounting period falling wholly within the period, and

(b) the appropriate proportion of the deductions made by the firm in any accounting period falling partly within the period,

in respect of members of the firm's workforce in calculating the profits of the firm's trade.

(7) For the purposes of subsection (6)(b), "the appropriate proportion" is to be determined by reference to the number of days in the periods concerned.

(8) The Commissioners for Her Majesty's Revenue and Customs may by regulations specify descriptions of deduction that are, or are not, to be regarded for the purposes of this section as made in respect of members of a firm's workforce.

(9) Regulations under this section—

(a) may make different provision for different purposes;

(b) may make incidental, supplemental, consequential and transitional provision and savings.

(10) Section 357WBB contains supplementary provision applying for the purposes of this section.

357WBB Section 357WBA: supplementary

(1) References in section 357WBA or this section to a partner in the firm include any person entitled to a share of income of the firm.

(2) In determining for the purposes of section 357WBA the amount of working time that is spent in any place by a partner in the firm, time spent by the partner in that place is to be included where—

(a) the time is spent by the partner in providing services to a person other than the firm ("the third party"), and
(b) condition A or B is met.

(3) Condition A is that the provision of the services results in a payment being made (whether directly or indirectly) to the firm by—

(a) the third party, or
(b) a person connected with the third party.

(4) Condition B is that—

(a) the firm holds a right that it acquired (whether directly or indirectly) from the partner, and
(b) any payment in connection with that right is made (whether directly or indirectly) to the firm by—

(i) the third party, or
(ii) a person connected with the third party.

(5) Section 1122 (connected persons) applies for the purposes of this section.

(6) References in section 357WBA to deductions made in respect of the members of the firm's workforce in calculating profits of the firm's trade include, in relation to a partner in the firm, the appropriate notional consideration for services provided by the partner (see subsections (7) and (8)).

(7) For the purposes of subsection (6), "the appropriate notional consideration for services" provided by a partner is—

(a) the amount which the partner would receive in consideration for services provided to the firm by the partner during the period in question, were the consideration to be calculated on the basis mentioned in subsection (8), less
(b) any amount actually received in consideration for such services which is not included in the partner's profit share.

(8) The consideration mentioned in subsection (7)(a) is to be calculated on the basis that the partner is not a partner in the firm and is acting at arm's length from the firm.

357WBC "Disqualified firm"

(1) For the purposes of this Chapter, a firm is a "disqualified firm" in relation to a period if conditions A and B are met.

(2) Condition A is that the firm has a NIRE in the period as a result of tax-avoidance arrangements.

(3) Condition B is that—

(a) 50% or more of the working time that is spent in the United Kingdom during the period by members of the firm's workforce is working time spent by partners otherwise than in Northern Ireland, or
(b) 50% or more of the firm's workforce expenses that are attributable to working time spent in the United Kingdom during the period by members of the firm's workforce are attributable to working time spent by partners otherwise than in Northern Ireland.

(4) For the purposes of this section "tax avoidance arrangements" means arrangements the sole or main purpose of which is to secure that any profits or losses of the firm for the period are Northern Ireland profits or losses.

(5) In subsection (4) "arrangements" includes any agreement, understanding, scheme, transaction or series of transactions (whether or not legally enforceable).

(6) The following provisions apply for the purposes of this section as they apply for the purposes of section 357WBA (Northern Ireland workforce partnership conditions)—

(a) subsections (2) to (5) of that section;
(b) regulations made under that section;
(c) section 357WBB."

16 In section 357WC (Northern Ireland profits etc of firm determined under Chapter 6), in subsection (2), for "SME partnership condition" substitute "SME (Northern Ireland employer) partnership condition".

17 (1) Section 357WD (Northern Ireland profits etc of firm determined under Chapter 7) is amended as follows.

(2) For subsections (1) to (3) substitute—

"(1) This section applies where—

(a) a company ("the corporate partner") is a partner in a firm at any time during an accounting period of the firm ("the firm's accounting period") and is within the charge to corporation tax in relation to the firm's trade, and

(b) condition A or B is met.

(2) Condition A is that the firm is a Northern Ireland firm in the firm's accounting period by virtue of the SME (election) partnership condition or the large partnership condition in section 357WA.

(3) Condition B is that—

(a) the firm is a Northern Ireland firm in the firm's accounting period by virtue of the SME (Northern Ireland employer) partnership condition in section 357WA, and

(b) the corporate partner is not an SME in relation to an accounting period of the corporate partner which is the same as, or overlaps (to any extent), the firm's accounting period."

(3) In subsection (4), after "losses etc:" insert "SMEs that are not Northern Ireland employers and".

18 In section 357WE (sections 357WC and 357WD: interpretation), omit subsection (2).

19 (1) Section 357WF (application of section 747 of CTA 2009 to Northern Ireland firm) is amended as follows.

(2) In paragraph (e)—

(a) for "SME condition" substitute "SME (Northern Ireland employer) condition";

(b) for "SME partnership condition" substitute "SME (Northern Ireland employer) partnership condition".

(3) After paragraph (e) insert—

"(ea) references to the SME (election) condition in section 357KA were to the SME (election) partnership condition in section 357WA;".

20 (1) Section 357WG (application of Part 8A to Northern Ireland firm) is amended as follows.

(2) In paragraph (g)—

(a) for "SME condition" (in the first place it appears) substitute "SME (Northern Ireland employer) condition";

(b) for "SME condition" (in the second place it appears) substitute "SME (Northern Ireland employer) partnership condition".

(3) For paragraph (h) substitute—

"(h) references in section 357VC to—

(i) the SME (election) condition in section 357KA were to the SME (election) partnership condition in section 357WA;

(ii) the large company condition in section 357KA were to the large partnership condition in section 357WA;

(iii) a qualifying trade by virtue of section 357KB(1) were to a qualifying partnership trade by virtue of section 357WB(1)."

21 In Schedule 4 (index of defined expressions)—

(a) omit the entry for "SME condition (in Part 8B)";

(b) at the appropriate places, insert—

"disqualified close company (in Part 8B)	section 357KEA"
"SME (Northern Ireland employer) condition (in Part 8B)	section 357KA"
"SME (election) condition (in Part 8B)	section 357KA"

Amendments relating to capital allowances

22 CAA 2001 is amended in accordance with paragraphs 23 and 24.

23 (1) Section 6A ("NIRE company" and "Northern Ireland SME company") is amended as follows.

(2) In the heading, for "Northern Ireland SME company" substitute "SME (Northern Ireland employer) company".

(3) In the definition of "NIRE company", after "by virtue of" insert "the SME (election) condition or".

(4) For "Northern Ireland SME company" substitute "SME (Northern Ireland employer) company".

(5) For "SME condition" substitute "SME (Northern Ireland employer) condition".

24 In the following provisions, for "a Northern Ireland SME company" substitute "an SME (Northern Ireland employer) company"—

    (a) section 6C(1)(a) and (c);
    (b) section 6D(1);
    (c) section 6E(1);
    (d) section 61(4B)(a);
    (e) section 66B(1)(a), (b) and (c);
    (f) section 66C(b);
    (g) section 66D(1)(a) and (b);
    (h) section 66E(b);
    (i) section 212ZE(b);
    (j) Schedule 1.

25 In CT(NI)A 2015, in Schedule 1, in Part 6 (capital allowances: transitional provision), in paragraphs 20(1)(a) and 21(1)(a), for "a Northern Ireland SME company" substitute "an SME (Northern Ireland employer) company".

PART 2
MINOR AMENDMENTS

26 In section 357IA of CTA 2010 (power of Northern Ireland Assembly to set Northern Ireland rate), for "Minister of Finance and Personnel" substitute "Minister of Finance".

27 In section 357QB(5)(b) of that Act (tax credit: entitlement) , for "Chapter 2" substitute "land remediation".

28 (1) Paragraph 2 of Schedule A1 to CAA 2001 (amount of first-year tax credit) is amended as follows.

(2) For sub-paragraphs (3A) and (4) substitute—

    "(4) The Treasury may by regulations amend sub-paragraph (1)—

        (a) so as to provide for a different percentage to apply where the surrenderable loss relates to a qualifying activity that is an NI rate activity, or
        (b) so as to substitute for any percentage for the time being specified in that sub-paragraph such other percentage as the Treasury thinks fit."

(3) In sub-paragraph (5), for "An order" substitute "Regulations".

29 In consequence of paragraph 28, in the Corporation Tax (Northern Ireland) Act 2015, in Schedule 1, omit paragraph 10.

PART 3
COMMENCEMENT ETC

30 (1) Any power to make regulations under Part 8B of CTA 2010 by virtue of Part 1 or 2 of this Schedule may be exercised on or after the day on which this Act is passed.

(2) Section 4 of CT(NI)A 2015 (power to make consequential amendments) has effect as if Parts 1 and 2 of this Schedule were contained in that Act.

(3) Section 5(4) to (6) of CT(NI)A 2015 (commencement) has effect as if—

    (a) references to Part 8B of CTA 2010 were to that Part as amended by Parts 1 and 2 of this Schedule, and
    (b) references to the amendments made by Schedules 1 and 2 to CT(NI)A 2015 included the amendments made by paragraphs 21 to 24 of this Schedule.

GENERAL NOTE

Schedule 7 Pt 1 (paras 1–25) introduces amendments in relation to SMEs. Broadly, the effect of the amendments is that an SME which does not meet the employment test but has a trading presence in Northern Ireland may elect to be a "Northern Ireland company" on the basis of a new "SME (election) condition".

Paragraph 1 introduces amendments to CTA 2010 and para 2 makes a consequential amendment to CTA 2010 s 357H (introduction).

Paragraph 3 amends CTA 2010 s 357KA ("Northern Ireland company"). It renames the SME condition, which becomes the "SME (Northern Ireland employer) condition", and that condition is met if the SME is a Northern Ireland employer as defined in CTA 2010 s 357KD. In addition, a company that is an SME but is not a Northern Ireland employer, and has a Northern Ireland regional establishment (NIRE), may elect (so long as it is not a "disqualified close company" – see para 5 below) to use the large company rules and allocate profits to the NIRE. A company making a valid election (see para 3(6)) will meet the new "SME (election) condition" in CTA 2010 s 357KA(1)(b).

Paragraph 4 amends CTA 2010 s 357KE (Northern Ireland workforce conditions) so that members of a company's workforce include individual participators in the company where the company is a close company or would be a close company if it were UK resident. "Participator" is defined for this purpose by CTA 2010 ss 1068 and 1069. Para 4(3) introduces new rules to determine the amount of working time spent by a participator. Where certain conditions are met, time spent in providing services to a person other than the company may be included.

Paragraph 5 inserts a new CTA 2010 s 357KEA ("disqualified close company"). A company is a "disqualified close company" in relation to a period if: (a) the company is a close company, or would be a close company if it were UK resident, at any time in the period, and (b) conditions A and B are met. Condition A is that the company has an NIRE in the period as a result of tax-avoidance arrangements, defined as arrangements the sole or main purpose of which is to secure that any profits or losses of the company for the period are Northern Ireland profits or losses. Condition B is that either: (a) 50% or more of the working time that is spent in the UK during the period by members of the company's workforce is working time spent by participators in the company otherwise than in Northern Ireland, or (b) 50% or more of the company's workforce expenses that are attributable to working time spent in the UK during the period by members of the company's workforce are attributable to working time spent by participators in the company otherwise than in Northern Ireland.

Paragraphs 6 and 7 make consequential amendments to CTA 2010 Pt 8B Ch 6 (Northern Ireland profits and losses etc: SMEs).

Paragraphs 8 and 9 extend the scope of CTA 2010 Pt 8B Ch 6 (Northern Ireland profits and losses etc: large companies) to a company that is a Northern Ireland company because it meets the new "SME (election) condition".

Paragraphs 10–13 make consequential amendments to CTA 2010 ss 357OB (Northern Ireland intangibles credits and debits: SMEs), 357OC (Northern Ireland intangibles credits and debits: large companies), 357VB (relevant Northern Ireland IP profits: SMEs) and 357VC (relevant Northern Ireland IP profits: large companies).

Paragraphs 14 to 21 make corresponding changes to the rules for partnerships.

Paragraph 14 amends CTA 2010 s 357WA (meaning of "Northern Ireland firm") and introduces a new "SME (election) partnership condition" which is broadly based on the SME (election) condition for a company.

Paragraph 15 inserts a new CTA 2010 s 357WBA (Northern Ireland workforce partnership conditions) to provide a standalone test for partnerships. Broadly, the workforce partnership conditions in relation to a period are: (a) that 75% or more of the working time that is spent in the UK during the period by members of the firm's workforce is spent in Northern Ireland, and (b) that 75% or more of the firm's workforce expenses that are attributable to working time spent in the UK during the period by members of the firm's workforce are attributable to time spent in Northern Ireland. Para 15 also inserts a new CTA 2010 s 357WBB which makes supplementary provisions in relation to the workforce conditions, and a new s 357WBC which defines a "disqualified firm" for the purpose of the new "SME (election) partnership condition" introduced by para 14.

Paragraphs 16–21 make consequential amendments to CTA 2010 ss 357WC (Northern Ireland profits etc of firm determined under Chapter 6), 357WD (Northern Ireland profits etc. of firm determined under Chapter 7), 357WE (sections 357WC and 357WD: interpretation), 357WF (application of CTA 2009 s 747 to Northern Ireland firm), 357WG (application of Part 8A to Northern Ireland firm) and Sch 4 (index of defined expressions),

Paragraphs 22–25 make consequential amendments to CAA 2001 (capital allowances).

Schedule 7 Part 2 (paragraphs 26–29) makes minor amendments to CTA 2010, CAA 2001 and CTNIA 2015.

The commencement rules in Sch 7 Pt 3 (para 30) provide for these changes to be treated as made in CTNIA 2015.

SCHEDULE 8

DEEMED DOMICILE: INCOME TAX AND CAPITAL GAINS TAX

Section 29

PART 1

APPLICATION OF DEEMED DOMICILE RULE

ICTA

1 (1) In section 266A of ICTA (life assurance premiums paid by employer), after subsection (8) insert—

"(8A) Section 835BA of ITA 2007 (deemed domicile) applies for the purposes of subsection (6)(b)."

(2) The amendment made by this paragraph has effect in relation to the tax year 2017–18 and subsequent tax years.

TCGA 1992

2 TCGA 1992 is amended as follows.

3 (1) Section 16ZA (losses: non-UK domiciled individuals) is amended as follows.

(2) For subsections (1) to (3) substitute—

"(1) An individual may make an election under this section in respect of—

(a) the first tax year in which section 809B of ITA 2007 (claim for remittance basis) applies to the individual, or

(b) the first tax year in which that section applies to the individual following a period in which the individual has been domiciled in the United Kingdom.

(2) Where an individual makes an election under this section in respect of a tax year, the election has effect in relation to the individual for—

(a) that tax year, and

(b) all subsequent tax years.

(2A) But if after making an election under this section an individual becomes domiciled in the United Kingdom at any time in a tax year, the election does not have effect in relation to the individual for—

(a) that tax year, or

(b) any subsequent tax year.

(2B) Where an election made by an individual under this section in respect of a tax year ceases to have effect by virtue of subsection (2A), the fact that it has ceased to have effect does not prevent the individual from making another election under this section in respect of a later tax year.

(3) If an individual does not make an election under this section in respect of a year referred to in subsection (1)(a) or (b), foreign losses accruing to the individual in—

(a) that tax year, or

(b) any subsequent tax year except one in which the individual is domiciled in the United Kingdom,

are not allowable losses."

(3) After subsection (6) insert—

"(7) Section 835BA of ITA 2007 (deemed domicile) applies for the purposes of this section."

(4) The amendments made by this paragraph have effect in relation to the tax year 2017–18 and subsequent tax years.

(5) Where—

(a) an individual makes an election under section 16ZA of TCGA 1992 as originally enacted for a tax year before the tax year 2017–18, but

(b) after making the election the individual becomes domiciled in the United Kingdom at any time in a tax year,

sections 16ZB and 16ZC of that Act do not have effect in relation to the individual by virtue of that election for that tax year or any subsequent tax year.

(6) Section 835BA of ITA 2007 (deemed domicile) applies for the purposes of sub-paragraph (5).

4 (1) In section 16ZB (election under section 16ZA: foreign chargeable gains remitted in the tax year after that in which they accrue), in subsection (1), for paragraphs (a) and (b) substitute—

"(a) the individual has made an election under section 16ZA in respect of a tax year before the applicable year,

(aa) the election has effect in relation to the individual for the applicable year,

(b) foreign chargeable gains accrued to the individual in or after the tax year in respect of which the election was made but before the applicable year, and".

(2) The amendment made by this paragraph has effect in relation to the tax year 2017–18 and subsequent tax years.

5 (1) In section 16ZC (election under section 16ZA by individual to whom remittance basis applies), in subsection (1), for paragraphs (a) to (c) substitute—

"(a) the individual has made an election under section 16ZA in respect of the tax year or any earlier tax year,

(b) the election has effect in relation to the individual for the tax year, and

(c) section 809B, 809D or 809E of ITA 2007 (remittance basis) applies to the individual for the tax year."

(2) The amendment made by this paragraph has effect in relation to the tax year 2017–18 and subsequent tax years.

6 (1) In section 69 (trustees of settlements), after subsection (2E) insert—

"(2F) Section 835BA of ITA 2007 (deemed domicile) applies for the purposes of subsection (2B)(c)."

(2) The amendment made by this paragraph has effect in relation to a settlement—

(a) in a case where the settlement arose on the settlor's death (whether by will, intestacy or otherwise), where the settlor died on or after 6 April 2017;

(b) in any other case, where the settlor made the settlement (or was treated for the purposes of TCGA 1992 as making the settlement) on or after 6 April 2017.

7 (1) In section 86 (attribution of gains to settlors with interest in non-resident or dual resident settlements), after subsection (3) insert—

"(3A) Section 835BA of ITA 2007 (deemed domicile) applies for the purposes of subsection (1)(c)."

(2) The amendment made by this paragraph has effect in relation to the tax year 2017–18 and subsequent tax years.

8 (1) In section 275 (location of assets), after subsection (3) insert—

"(3A) Section 835BA of ITA 2007 (deemed domicile) applies for the purposes of subsection (1)(l)(iii)."

(2) The amendment made by this paragraph has effect for the purposes of determining for the purposes of TCGA 1992 the situation of any asset, or whether the situation of any asset is in the United Kingdom, at any time on or after 6 April 2017 (irrespective of when the asset was acquired by the person holding it).

9 (1) In Schedule 5A (settlements with foreign element: information), in paragraph 3, after sub-paragraph (3) insert—

"(3A) Section 835BA of ITA 2007 (deemed domicile) applies for the purposes of sub-paragraph (3)."

(2) The amendment made by this paragraph has effect in relation to settlements created on or after 6 April 2017.

ITEPA 2003

10 (1) ITEPA 2003 is amended as follows.

(2) In section 355 (deductions for corresponding payments by non-domiciled employees with foreign employers), in subsection (2), at the end insert "(and section 835BA of ITA 2007 (deemed domicile) applies for the purposes of this subsection)".

(3) In section 373 (non-domiciled employee's travel costs and expenses where duties performed in UK), at the end insert—

"(7) Section 835BA of ITA 2007 (deemed domicile) applies for the purposes of subsection (1)."

(4) In section 374 (non-domiciled employee's spouse's etc travel costs and expenses where duties performed in UK), at the end insert —

"(10) Section 835BA of ITA 2007 (deemed domicile) applies for the purposes of subsection (1)."

(5) In section 376 (foreign accommodation and subsistence costs and expenses (overseas employment)), at the end insert —

"(6) Section 835BA of ITA 2007 (deemed domicile) applies for the purposes of subsection (1)(c)."

(6) The amendments made by this paragraph have effect in relation to the tax year 2017–18 and subsequent tax years.

ITA 2007

11 ITA 2007 is amended as follows.

12 (1) In section 476 (how to work out whether settlor meets condition C in section 475), after subsection (3) insert—

"(3A) Section 835BA (deemed domicile) applies for the purposes of subsections (2)(b) and (3)(b)."

(2) The amendment made by this paragraph has effect—

(a) so far as relating to section 476(2)(b) of ITA 2007, in relation to a settlor who dies on or after 6 April 2017;
(b) so far as relating to section 476(3)(b) of ITA 2007, in relation to a settlement made on or after 6 April 2017.

13 (1) In section 718 (meaning of "person abroad" etc), after subsection (2) insert—

"(3) Section 835BA (deemed domicile) applies for the purposes of subsection (1)(b)."

(2) The amendment made by this paragraph has effect in relation to the tax year 2017–18 and subsequent tax years.

14 (1) Chapter A1 of Part 14 (remittance basis) is amended as follows.

(2) In section 809B (claim for remittance basis to apply), after subsection (1) insert—

"(1A) Section 835BA (deemed domicile) applies for the purposes of subsection (1)(b)."

(3) In section 809C (claim for remittance basis by long-term UK resident: nomination) omit the following—

(a) in subsection (1)(b), "the 17-year residence test,";
(b) subsection (1ZA);
(c) subsection (1A)(a);
(d) in subsection (1B)(a), "the 17-year residence test or";
(e) subsection (4)(za).

(4) In section 809E (application of remittance basis without claim: other cases), after subsection (1) insert—

"(1A) Section 835BA (deemed domicile) applies for the purposes of subsection (1)(b)."

(5) In section 809H (claim for remittance basis by long-term UK resident: charge) omit the following—

(a) in subsection (1)(c), "the 17-year residence test,";
(b) in subsection (1A)—
    (i) "(1ZA)";
    (ii) "the 17-year residence test,";
(c) subsection (5B)(za).

(6) The amendments made by this paragraph have effect in relation to the tax year 2017–18 and subsequent tax years.

This is subject to paragraphs 15 and 16.

15 (1) This paragraph applies in a case where—

(a) section 10A of TCGA 1992 (temporary non-residents) as originally enacted applies in relation to an individual, and
(b) the year of return is 2017–18.

(2) For the purposes of capital gains tax in respect of foreign chargeable gains accruing to the individual during an intervening year, the amendment made by paragraph 14(2) does not have effect in relation to the year of return.

(3) Where by virtue of sub-paragraph (2) an individual makes a claim under section 809B of ITA 2007 for the tax year 2017–18, sections 809C, 809G and 809H of ITA 2007 do not apply to the individual for that tax year.

(4) In this paragraph—

"intervening year" and "year of return" have the same meanings as in section 10A of TCGA 1992 as originally enacted;

"foreign chargeable gain" has the meaning given by section 12(4) of TCGA 1992.

16 (1) This paragraph applies in a case where section 10A of TCGA 1992 as substituted by paragraph 119 of Schedule 45 to FA 2013 applies in relation to an individual.

(2) For the purposes of capital gains tax in respect of foreign chargeable gains accruing to the individual during a temporary period of non-residence beginning before 8 July 2015, the amendment made by paragraph 14(2) does not have effect in relation to the tax year which consists of or includes the period of return.

(3) Where by virtue of sub-paragraph (2) an individual makes a claim under section 809B of ITA 2007 for any of the tax years 2017–18 to 2020–21 inclusive, sections 809C, 809G and 809H of ITA 2007 do not apply to the individual for that tax year.

(4) In this paragraph, "foreign chargeable gain" has the meaning given by section 12(4) of TCGA 1992.

(5) Part 4 of Schedule 45 to FA 2013 explains what "temporary period of non-residence" and "period of return" mean.

17 (1) In section 834 (residence of personal representatives), at the end insert—

"(5) Section 835BA (deemed domicile) applies for the purposes of subsection (3)."

(2) The amendment made by this paragraph has effect in relation to the tax year 2017–18 and subsequent tax years.

PART 2

PROTECTION OF OVERSEAS TRUSTS

TCGA 1992

18 In Schedule 5 to TCGA 1992 (provisions supplementing section 86 of TCGA 1992), after paragraph 5 insert—

"**5A** (1) Section 86 does not apply in relation to a year ("the particular year") if Conditions A to D are met.

(2) Condition A is that the particular year is—

    (a) the tax year 2017–18, or

    (b) a later tax year.

(3) Condition B is that when the settlement is created the settlor—

    (a) is not domiciled in the United Kingdom, and

    (b) if the settlement is created on or after 6 April 2017, is not deemed domiciled in the United Kingdom.

(4) Condition C is that there is no time in the particular year when the settlor is—

    (a) domiciled in the United Kingdom, or

    (b) deemed domiciled in the United Kingdom by virtue of Condition A in section 835BA of ITA 2007.

(5) Condition D is that no property or income is provided directly or indirectly for the purposes of the settlement by the settlor, or by the trustees of another settlement of which the settlor is the settlor or a beneficiary, at a time in the relevant period when the settlor is—

    (a) domiciled in the United Kingdom, or

    (b) deemed domiciled in the United Kingdom.

(6) In sub-paragraph (5) "relevant period" means the period—

    (a) beginning with the start of 6 April 2017 or, if later, the creation of the settlement, and

    (b) ending with the end of the particular year.

(7) For the purposes of Condition D, the addition of value to property comprised in the settlement is to be treated as the direct provision of property for the purposes of the settlement.

(8) Paragraph 5B contains further provision for the purposes of Condition D.

(9) In this paragraph "deemed domiciled" means regarded for the purposes of section 86(1)(c) as domiciled in the United Kingdom as a result of section 835BA of ITA 2007 having effect.

5B (1) This paragraph applies for the purposes of Condition D in paragraph 5A.

(2) Ignore—

    (a) property or income provided under a transaction, other than a loan, where the transaction is entered into on arm's length terms,

(b) property or income provided, otherwise than under a loan, without any intention by the person providing it to confer a gratuitous benefit on any person,

(c) the principal of a loan which is made to the trustees of the settlement on arm's length terms,

(d) the payment of interest to the trustees of the settlement under a loan made by them on arm's length terms,

(e) repayment to the trustees of the settlement of the principal of a loan made by them,

(f) property or income provided in pursuance of a liability incurred by any person before 6 April 2017, and

(g) where the settlement's expenses relating to taxation and administration for a tax year exceed its income for that year, property or income provided towards meeting that excess if the value of any such property and income is not greater than the amount of—

    (i) the excess, or

    (ii) if greater, the amount by which such expenses exceed the amount of such expenses which may be paid out of the settlement's income.

(3) Where—

(a) a loan is made to the trustees of the settlement by the settlor or the trustees of a settlement connected with the settlor, and

(b) the loan is on arm's length terms, but

(c) a relevant event occurs,

the principal of the loan is to be regarded as having been provided to the trustees at the time of that event (despite sub-paragraph (2)).

(4) In sub-paragraph (3) "relevant event" means—

(a) capitalisation of interest payable under the loan,

(b) any other failure to pay interest in accordance with the terms of the loan, or

(c) variation of the terms of the loan such that they cease to be arm's length terms.

(5) Sub-paragraph (6) applies (subject to sub-paragraph (7)) where—

(a) the settlor becomes deemed domiciled in the United Kingdom on or after 6 April 2017,

(b) before the date on which the settlor becomes deemed domiciled in the United Kingdom ("the deemed domicile date"), a loan has been made to the trustees of the settlement by—

    (i) the settlor, or

    (ii) the trustees of a settlement connected with the settlor,

(c) the loan is not entered into on arm's length terms, and

(d) any amount that is outstanding under the loan on the deemed domicile date ("the outstanding amount") is payable or repayable on demand on or after that date.

(6) Where this sub-paragraph applies, the outstanding amount is to be regarded as property directly provided on the deemed domicile date by the lender for the purposes of the settlement (despite sub-paragraph (2)).

(7) But if the deemed domicile date is 6 April 2017, sub-paragraph (6) does not apply if—

(a) the principal of the loan is repaid, and all interest payable under the loan is paid, before 6 April 2018, or

(b) the loan becomes a loan on arm's length terms before 6 April 2018 and—

    (i) before that date interest is paid to the lender in respect of the period beginning with 6 April 2017 and ending with 5 April 2018 as if those arm's length terms had been terms of the loan in relation to that period, and

    (ii) interest continues to be payable from 6 April 2018 in accordance with those terms.

(8) For the purposes of this paragraph a loan is on "arm's length terms"—

(a) in the case of a loan made to the trustees of a settlement, only if interest at the official rate or more is payable at least annually under the loan;

(b) in the case of a loan made by the trustees of a settlement, only if any interest payable under the loan is payable at no more than the official rate.

(9) For the purposes of this paragraph—

a settlement is "connected" with a person if the person is the settlor or a beneficiary of it;

"deemed domiciled" has the same meaning as in paragraph 5A;

"official rate", in relation to interest, means the rate of interest applicable from time to time under section 178 of the Finance Act 1989 for the purposes of Chapter 7 of Part 3 of ITEPA 2003."

FA 2004

19 In paragraph 8 of Schedule 15 to FA 2004 (income tax on benefits received by former owner of property: intangible property comprised in settlement where settlor retains an interest), after sub-paragraph (3) insert—

"(4) For the purpose of deciding whether the condition in sub-paragraph (1)(a) is met, ignore section 628A of ITTOIA 2005 (which provides for section 624 of that Act not to apply to certain foreign income arising under a settlement)."

ITTOIA 2005

20 Chapter 5 of Part 5 of ITTOIA 2005 (settlements) is amended as follows.

21 In section 624 (income under a settlement where settlor retains an interest), in subsection (3) (which lists provisions containing exceptions)—

(a) omit the "and" at the end of the entry for section 627, and
(b) after the entry for section 628 insert ", and
    section 628A (exception for protected foreign-source income)."

22 After section 628 insert—

"628A Exception for protected foreign-source income

(1) The rule in section 624(1) does not apply to income which arises under a settlement if it is protected foreign-source income for a tax year.

(2) For this purpose, income arising under a settlement in a tax year is "protected foreign-source income" for the tax year if Conditions A to F are met.

(3) Condition A is that the income would be relevant foreign income if it were income of a UK resident individual.

(4) Condition B is that the income is from property originating from the settlor (see section 645).

(5) Condition C is that when the settlement is created the settlor—

(a) is not domiciled in the United Kingdom, and
(b) if the settlement is created on or after 6 April 2017, is not deemed domiciled in the United Kingdom.

(6) Condition D is that there is no time in the tax year when the settlor is—

(a) domiciled in the United Kingdom, or
(b) deemed domiciled in the United Kingdom by virtue of Condition A in section 835BA of ITA 2007.

(7) Condition E is that the trustees of the settlement are not UK resident for the tax year.

(8) Condition F is that no property or income is provided directly or indirectly for the purposes of the settlement by the settlor, or by the trustees of any other settlement of which the settlor is a beneficiary or settlor, at a time in the relevant period when the settlor is—

(a) domiciled in the United Kingdom, or
(b) deemed domiciled in the United Kingdom.

(9) In subsection (8) "relevant period" means the period—

(a) beginning with the start of 6 April 2017 or, if later, the creation of the settlement, and
(b) ending with the end of the tax year.

(10) For the purposes of Condition F, the addition of value to property comprised in the settlement is to be treated as the direct provision of property for the purposes of the settlement.

(11) Section 628B (tainting) contains further provision for the purposes of Condition F.

(12) In this section "deemed domiciled" means regarded for the purposes of section 809(1)(b) of ITA 2007 as domiciled in the United Kingdom as a result of section 835BA of ITA 2007 having effect.

(13) Section 648(3) to (5) (relevant foreign income treated as arising under settlement only if and when remitted) do not apply for the purposes of this section.

628B Section 628A: tainting

(1) This section applies for the purposes of Condition F in section 628A.

(2) Ignore—

(a) property or income provided under a transaction, other than a loan, where the transaction is entered into on arm's length terms,

(b) property or income provided, otherwise than under a loan, without any intention by the person providing it to confer a gratuitous benefit on any person,

(c) the principal of a loan which is made to the trustees of the settlement on arm's length terms,

(d) the payment of interest to the trustees of the settlement under a loan made by them on arm's length terms,

(e) repayment to the trustees of the settlement of the principal of a loan made by them,

(f) property or income provided in pursuance of a liability incurred by any person before 6 April 2017, and

(g) where the settlement's expenses relating to taxation and administration for a tax year exceed its income for that year, property or income provided towards meeting that excess if the value of any such property and income is not greater than the amount of—

(i) the excess, or

(ii) if greater, the amount by which such expenses exceed the amount of such expenses which may be paid out of the settlement's income.

(3) Where—

(a) a loan is made to the trustees of the settlement by the settlor or the trustees of a settlement connected with the settlor, and

(b) the loan is on arm's length terms, but

(c) a relevant event occurs,

the principal of the loan is to be regarded as having been provided to the trustees at the time of that event (despite subsection (2)).

(4) In subsection (3) "relevant event" means—

(a) capitalisation of interest payable under the loan,

(b) any other failure to pay interest in accordance with the terms of the loan, or

(c) variation of the terms of the loan such that they cease to be arm's length terms.

(5) Subsection (6) applies (subject to subsection (7)) where—

(a) the settlor becomes deemed domiciled in the United Kingdom on or after 6 April 2017,

(b) before the date on which the settlor becomes deemed domiciled in the United Kingdom ("the deemed domicile date"), a loan has been made to the trustees of the settlement by—

(i) the settlor, or

(ii) the trustees of a settlement connected with the settlor,

(c) the loan is not entered into on arm's length terms, and

(d) any amount that is outstanding under the loan on the deemed domicile date ("the outstanding amount") is payable or repayable on demand on or after that date.

(6) Where this subsection applies, the outstanding amount is to be regarded as property directly provided on the deemed domicile date by the lender for the purposes of the settlement (despite subsection (2)).

(7) But if the deemed domicile date is 6 April 2017, subsection (6) does not apply if—

(a) the principal of the loan is repaid, and all interest payable under the loan is paid, before 6 April 2018, or

(b) the loan becomes a loan on arm's length terms before 6 April 2018 and—

(i) before that date interest is paid to the lender in respect of the period beginning with 6 April 2017 and ending with 5 April 2018 as if those arm's length terms had been terms of the loan in relation to that period, and

(ii) interest continues to be payable from 6 April 2018 in accordance with those terms.

(8) For the purposes of this section, a loan is on "arm's length terms"—

(a) in the case of a loan made to the trustees of a settlement, only if interest at the official rate or more is payable at least annually under the loan;

(b) in the case of a loan made by the trustees of a settlement, only if any interest payable under the loan is payable at no more than the official rate.

(9) For the purposes of this section—

a settlement is "connected" with a person if the person is the settlor or a beneficiary of it;

"deemed domiciled" has the same meaning as in section 628A;

"official rate", in relation to interest, means the rate of interest applicable from time to time under section 178 of FA 1989 for the purposes of Chapter 7 of Part 3 of ITEPA 2003.

628C Foreign income arising before, but remitted on or after, 6 April 2017

(1) For the purposes of applying section 809L of ITA 2007 (meaning of remitted to the UK) in relation to transitional trust income, "relevant person" in that section does not include the trustees of the settlement concerned.

(2) "Transitional trust income" means income—

(a) that arises under a settlement in the period beginning with the tax year 2008–09 and ending with the tax year 2016–17 ("the protection period"),

(b) that would be protected foreign-source income for the purposes of section 628A(1) if section 628A(2)—

(i) had effect for the protection period, and

(ii) so had effect with a reference to conditions A to E (instead of A to F),

(c) that prior to 6 April 2017 has neither been distributed by the trustees of the settlement nor treated under section 624(1) as income of the settlor, and

(d) that would for the tax year in which it arose under the settlement have been treated under section 624(1) as income of the settlor if the settlor had been domiciled in the United Kingdom for that year.

(3) Section 648(3) to (5) (relevant foreign income treated as arising under settlement only if and when remitted), and corresponding earlier enactments, do not apply for the purposes of subsection (2)(a) and (d)."

23 (1) In section 629(5) (list of exceptions), at the end insert "or section 630A (exception for protected foreign-source income)."

(2) After section 630 insert—

"630A Exception for protected foreign-source income

(1) The rule in section 629(1) does not apply to income which arises under a settlement if it is protected foreign-source income for a tax year.

(2) Sections 628A(2) to (12) and 628B (meaning of "protected foreign-source income") have effect also for this purpose.

(3) Section 648(3) to (5) (relevant foreign income treated as arising under settlement only if and when remitted) do not apply for the purposes of this section."

24 (1) Section 635 (capital sums treated under section 633 as income: meaning of "available income") is amended as follows.

(2) In subsection (2), before "income" insert "unprotected".

(3) After subsection (4) insert—

"(5) In subsection (2) "unprotected income" means income which is not protected foreign-source income, and sections 628A(2) to (13) and 628B (meaning of "protected foreign-source income") have effect also for this purpose."

25 In section 636(1) (meaning in section 635 of "undistributed"), before "income", in both places it occurs, insert "unprotected".

26 In section 645(1) (meaning of property originating from the settlor), for "section" substitute "sections 628A and".

ITA 2007

27 Chapter 2 of Part 13 of ITA 2007 (transfer of assets abroad) is amended as follows.

28 In section 721 (income of a person abroad that is treated as arising to a UK resident individual), for subsection (3B) (amount treated as arising) substitute—

"(3B) The amount of the income treated as arising under subsection (1) is (subject to sections 724 and 725) given by the following rules—

Rule 1

The amount is equal to the amount of the income of the person abroad if the individual—

(a) is domiciled in the United Kingdom at any time in the tax year, or

(b) is at any time in the tax year regarded for the purposes of section 718(1)(b) as domiciled in the United Kingdom as a result of section 835BA having effect because of Condition A in that section being met.

Rule 2

In any other case, the amount is equal to so much of the income of the person abroad as is not protected foreign-source income (see section 721A).

(3BA) In a case in which rule 2 of subsection (3B) applies, so much of the income of the person abroad as is protected foreign-source income for the purposes of that rule counts as "protected income" for the purposes of section 733A(1)(b)(i)."

29 After section 721 insert—

"721A Meaning of "protected foreign-source income" in section 721

(1) This section has effect for the purposes of rule 2 of section 721(3B) (cases where the individual is not UK domiciled and is not deemed domiciled by virtue of Condition A in section 835BA).

(2) The income of the person abroad is "protected foreign-source income" so far as it is within subsection (3) or (4).

(3) Income is within this subsection if—

(a) it would be relevant foreign income if it were the individual's,
(b) the person abroad is the trustees of a settlement,
(c) the trustees are non-UK resident for the tax year,
(d) when the settlement is created, the individual is—

(i) not domiciled in the United Kingdom, and
(ii) if the settlement is created on or after 6 April 2017, not deemed domiciled in the United Kingdom, and

(e) no property or income is provided directly or indirectly for the purposes of the settlement by the individual, or by the trustees of any other settlement of which the individual is a beneficiary or settlor, at a time in the period—

(i) beginning with the start of 6 April 2017 or, if later, the creation of the settlement, and
(ii) ending with the end of the tax year,

when the individual is domiciled or deemed domiciled in the United Kingdom.

(4) Income is within this subsection if—

(a) it would be relevant foreign income if it were the individual's,
(b) the person abroad is a company,
(c) the trustees of a settlement—

(i) are participators in the person abroad, or
(ii) are participators in the first in a chain of two or more companies where the last company in the chain is the person abroad and where each company in the chain (except the last) is a participator in the next company in the chain,

(d) the individual's power to enjoy the income results from the trustees being participators as mentioned in paragraph (c)(i) or (ii),
(e) the trustees are not UK resident for the tax year,
(f) when the settlement is created, the individual is—

(i) not domiciled in the United Kingdom, and
(ii) if the settlement is created on or after 6 April 2017, not deemed domiciled in the United Kingdom, and

(g) no property or income is provided directly or indirectly for the purposes of the settlement by the individual, or by the trustees of any other settlement of which the individual is a beneficiary or settlor, at a time in the period—

(i) beginning with the start of 6 April 2017 or, if later, the creation of the settlement, and
(ii) ending with the end of the tax year,

when the individual is domiciled or deemed domiciled in the United Kingdom.

(5) For the purposes of subsections (3)(e) and (4)(g), the addition of value to property comprised in the settlement is to be treated as the direct provision of property for the purposes of the settlement.

(6) Section 721B (tainting) contains further provision for the purposes of subsections (3)(e) and (4)(g).

(7) In this section—

"participator", in relation to a company, has the meaning given by section 454 of CTA 2010;

"deemed domiciled" means regarded for the purposes of section 718(1)(b) as domiciled in the United Kingdom as a result of section 835BA of ITA 2007 having effect.

721B Section 721A: tainting

(1) This section applies for the purposes of subsections (3)(e) and (4)(g) of section 721A.

(2) Ignore—

(a) property or income provided under a transaction, other than a loan, where the transaction is entered into on arm's length terms,

(b) property or income provided, otherwise than under a loan, without any intention by the person providing it to confer a gratuitous benefit on any person,

(c) the principal of a loan which is made to the trustees of the settlement on arm's length terms,

(d) the payment of interest to the trustees of the settlement under a loan made by them on arm's length terms,

(e) repayment to the trustees of the settlement of the principal of a loan made by them,

(f) property or income provided in pursuance of a liability incurred by any person before 6 April 2017, and

(g) where the settlement's expenses relating to taxation and administration for a tax year exceed its income for that year, property or income provided towards meeting that excess if the value of any such property and income is not greater than the amount of—

(i) the excess, or

(ii) if greater, the amount by which such expenses exceed the amount of such expenses which may be paid out of the settlement's income.

(3) Where—

(a) a loan is made to the trustees of the settlement by the settlor or the trustees of a settlement connected with the settlor, and

(b) the loan is on arm's length terms, but

(c) a relevant event occurs,

the principal of the loan is to be regarded as having been provided to the trustees at the time of that event (despite subsection (2)).

(4) In subsection (3) "relevant event" means—

(a) capitalisation of interest payable under the loan,

(b) any other failure to pay interest in accordance with the terms of the loan, or

(c) variation of the terms of the loan such that they cease to be arm's length terms.

(5) Subsection (6) applies (subject to subsection (7)) where—

(a) the settlor becomes deemed domiciled in the United Kingdom on or after 6 April 2017,

(b) before the date on which the settlor becomes deemed domiciled in the United Kingdom ("the deemed domicile date"), a loan has been made to the trustees of the settlement by—

(i) the settlor, or

(ii) the trustees of a settlement connected with the settlor,

(c) the loan is not entered into on arm's length terms, and

(d) any amount that is outstanding under the loan on the deemed domicile date ("the outstanding amount") is payable or repayable on demand on or after that date.

(6) Where this subsection applies, the outstanding amount is to be regarded as property directly provided on the deemed domicile date by the lender for the purposes of the settlement (despite subsection (2)).

(7) But if the deemed domicile date is 6 April 2017, subsection (6) does not apply if—

(a) the principal of the loan is repaid, and all interest payable under the loan is paid, before 6 April 2018, or

(b) the loan becomes a loan on arm's length terms before 6 April 2018 and—

(i) before that date interest is paid to the lender in respect of the period beginning with 6 April 2017 and ending with 5 April 2018 as if those arm's length terms had been terms of the loan in relation to that period, and

(ii) interest continues to be payable from 6 April 2018 in accordance with those terms.

(8) For the purposes of this section, a loan is on "arm's length terms"—

(a) in the case of a loan made to the trustees of a settlement, only if interest at the official rate or more is payable at least annually under the loan;

(b) in the case of a loan made by the trustees of a settlement, only if any interest payable under the loan is payable at no more than the official rate.

(9) For the purposes of this section—

a settlement is "connected" with a person if the person is the settlor or a beneficiary of it;

"deemed domiciled" has the same meaning as in section 721A;

"official rate", in relation to interest, means the rate of interest applicable from time to time under section 178 of FA 1989 for the purposes of Chapter 7 of Part 3 of ITEPA 2003."

30 In section 726 (individuals to whom remittance basis applies), after subsection (5) insert—

"(6) In addition, where the tax year in which any foreign deemed income arises is earlier than the tax year 2017–18, section 832 of ITTOIA 2005 does not apply to the foreign deemed income so far as it—

(a) is remitted to the United Kingdom in the tax year 2017–18 or a later tax year, and

(b) is transitionally protected income.

(7) In subsection (6)—

"remitted to the United Kingdom" is to be read in accordance with Chapter A1 of Part 14, and

"transitionally protected income" means any foreign deemed income where the income mentioned in section 721(2)—

(a) arises in a tax year earlier than the tax year 2017–18,

(b) would be protected foreign-source income as defined by section 721A if section 721A—

(i) had effect for tax years earlier than the tax year 2017–18, and

(ii) so had effect with the omission of its subsections (3)(e), (4)(g), (5) and (6), and

(c) has not prior to 6 April 2017 been distributed by the trustees of the settlement concerned."

31 In section 728 (income of a person abroad that is treated as arising to a UK resident individual), for subsection (1A) (amount treated as arising) substitute—

"(1A) The amount of the income treated as arising under subsection (1) is (subject to subsection (2)) given by the following rules—

Rule 1

The amount is equal to the amount of the income of the person abroad if the individual—

(a) is domiciled in the United Kingdom at any time in the tax year, or

(b) is at any time in the tax year regarded for the purposes of section 718(1)(b) as domiciled in the United Kingdom as a result of section 835BA having effect because of Condition A in that section being met.

Rule 2

In any other case, the amount is equal to so much of the income of the person abroad as is not protected foreign-source income (see section 729A).

(1B) In a case in which rule 2 of subsection (1A) applies, so much of the income of the person abroad as is protected foreign-source income for the purposes of that rule counts as "protected income" for the purposes of section 733A(1)(b)(i)."

32 After section 729 insert—

"729A Meaning of "protected foreign-source income" in section 728

(1) This section has effect for the purposes of rule 2 of section 728(1A) (cases where the individual is not UK domiciled and is not deemed domiciled by virtue of Condition A in section 835BA).

(2) The income of the person abroad is "protected foreign-source income" so far as it is within subsection (3) or (4).

(3) Income is within this subsection if—

(a) it would be relevant foreign income if it were the individual's,

(b) the person abroad is the trustees of a settlement,

(c) the trustees are non-UK resident for the tax year,

(d) when the settlement is created, the individual is—

    (i) not domiciled in the United Kingdom, and
    (ii) if the settlement is created on or after 6 April 2017, not deemed domiciled in the United Kingdom, and

(e) no property or income is provided directly or indirectly for the purposes of the settlement by the individual, or by the trustees of any other settlement of which the individual is a beneficiary or settlor, at a time in the period—

    (i) beginning with the start of 6 April 2017 or, if later, the creation of the settlement, and
    (ii) ending with the end of the tax year,

when the individual is domiciled or deemed domiciled in the United Kingdom.

(4) Income is within this subsection if—

(a) it would be relevant foreign income if it were the individual's,
(b) the person abroad is a company,
(c) the trustees of a settlement—

    (i) are participators in the person abroad, or
    (ii) are participators in the first in a chain of two or more companies where the last company in the chain is the person abroad and where each company in the chain (except the last) is a participator in the next company in the chain,

(d) the condition in paragraph (c) is met as a result of a relevant transaction (whether or not it is also met otherwise than as a result of a relevant transaction),
(e) the income has become the income of the person abroad as a result of that relevant transaction,
(f) the trustees are not UK resident for the tax year,
(g) when the settlement is created, the individual is—

    (i) not domiciled in the United Kingdom, and
    (ii) if the settlement is created on or after 6 April 2017, not deemed domiciled in the United Kingdom, and

(h) no property or income is provided directly or indirectly for the purposes of the settlement by the individual, or by the trustees of any other settlement of which the individual is a beneficiary or settlor, at a time in the period—

    (i) beginning with start of 6 April 2017 or, if later, the creation of the settlement, and
    (ii) ending with the end of the tax year,

when the individual is domiciled or deemed domiciled in the United Kingdom.

(5) For the purposes of subsections (3)(e) and (4)(h), the addition of value to property comprised in the settlement is to be treated as the direct provision of property for the purposes of the settlement.

(6) Section 721B (tainting) applies for the purposes of subsections (3)(e) and (4)(h) as it applies for the purposes of section 721A(3)(e) and (4)(g).

(7) In this section—

"participator", in relation to a company, has the meaning given by section 454 of CTA 2010, and
"deemed domiciled" means regarded for the purposes of section 718(1)(b) as domiciled in the United Kingdom as a result of section 835BA of ITA 2007 having effect."

33 In section 730 (individuals to whom remittance basis applies), after subsection (5) insert—

"(6) In addition, where the tax year in which any foreign deemed income arises is earlier than the tax year 2017–18, section 832 of ITTOIA 2005 does not apply to the foreign deemed income so far as it—

(a) is remitted to the United Kingdom in the tax year 2017–18 or a later tax year, and
(b) is transitionally protected income.

(7) In subsection (6)—

"remitted to the United Kingdom" is to be read in accordance with Chapter A1 of Part 14, and
"transitionally protected income" means any foreign deemed income where the income mentioned in section 728(1)(a)—

(a) arises in a tax year earlier than the tax year 2017–18,
(b) would be protected foreign-source income as defined by section 729A if section 729A—

    (i) had effect for tax years earlier than the tax year 2017–18, and

(ii) so had effect with the omission of its subsections (3)(e), (4)(h), (5) and (6), and

(c) has not prior to 6 April 2017 been distributed by the trustees of the settlement concerned."

34 (1) Section 731 (charge to tax on income treated as arising under section 732) is amended as follows.

(2) In subsection (1), for "non-transferors" substitute "individuals".

(3) After subsection (1) insert—

"(1A) But where the individual is non-UK resident for the tax year in which a benefit is received, there is a charge to tax under this section on any matched deemed income—

(a) only so far as that matched deemed income would under section 735A (if it applied also for this purpose) be matched with an amount of relevant income that is protected income for the purposes of section 733A(1)(b)(i) (see sections 721(3BA) and 728(1B)), and

(b) only if—

(i) the individual is the settlor of the settlement concerned, or

(ii) the benefit is received by the individual at a time when the individual is a close member of the family of the settlor of that settlement.

(1B) For the purposes of subsection (1A)—

(a) "matched deemed income" means income which—

(i) is treated by section 732 as arising to the individual, and

(ii) would, if section 735A applied also for this purpose, be matched under that section with the benefit, and

(b) a person is a close member of the family of the settlor of a settlement if the person is—

(i) the settlor's spouse or civil partner, or

(ii) a child of the settlor, or of a person within sub-paragraph (i), if the child has not reached the age of 18;

and section 733A(7) (persons living together) applies also for the purposes of paragraph (b)."

(4) In subsection (3) (person liable for tax is person to whom income is treated as arising), at the end insert ", but this is subject to section 733A."

35 (1) Section 732 (when income is treated as arising for the purposes of the charge under section 731) is amended in accordance with sub-paragraphs (2) to (4).

(2) In subsection (1) (cases in which tax can be charged under section 731)—

(a) in paragraph (b), for "who is UK resident for a tax year receives a benefit in that tax year" substitute "receives a benefit in a tax year", and

(b) for paragraph (d) substitute—

"(d) where there is a time in the year when the individual is relevantly domiciled, the individual is not liable to income tax under section 720 or 727 by reference to the transfer, and".

(3) After subsection (3) insert—

"(4) For the purposes of subsection (1)(d), the individual is "relevantly domiciled" at any time if at that time—

(a) the individual is domiciled in the United Kingdom, or

(b) the individual is regarded for the purposes of section 718(1)(b) as domiciled in the United Kingdom as a result of section 835BA having effect because of Condition A in that section being met."

(4) In the heading, for "Non-transferors" substitute "Individuals".

(5) In section 733(1) (income charged under section 731), in the first sentence of Step 2, at the end insert "except that, where any of that income is matched deemed income for the purposes of section 731(1A), that matched deemed income is to be deducted only so far as it is matched deemed income on which tax has been charged under section 731 for an earlier tax year."

36 After section 733 insert—

"733A Settlor liable for section 731 charge on closely-related beneficiary

(1) Subsections (2) and (3) apply if—

(a) an amount of income is treated as arising to an individual under section 732 for a tax year,

(b) under section 735A (if it applied also for this purpose) that amount would be matched—

    (i) with an amount of relevant income that is protected income for the purposes of this sub-paragraph (see sections 721(3BA) and 728(1B)), and

    (ii) with a benefit received by the individual at a time when the individual was a close member (see subsection (7)) of the family of the settlor of the settlement concerned,

(c) there is no time in the year when the trustees of the settlement are resident in the United Kingdom,

(d) there is a time in the year when the settlor is resident in the United Kingdom,

(e) there is no time in the year when the settlor is domiciled in the United Kingdom, and

(f) there is no time in the year when the settlor is regarded for the purposes of section 718(1)(b) as domiciled in the United Kingdom as a result of section 835BA having effect because of Condition A in that section being met.

(2) If—

(a) the individual is not resident in the United Kingdom at any time in the year, or

(b) section 809B, 809D or 809E (remittance basis) applies to the individual for the year and none of the amount mentioned in subsection (1)(a) of this section is remitted to the United Kingdom in the year,

the settlor is liable for the tax charged under section 731 on that amount as if that amount were income arising to the settlor in the year (and the individual is not liable in any later year for income tax on that amount).

(3) If—

(a) section 809B, 809D or 809E (remittance basis) applies to the individual for the year, and

(b) part only of the amount mentioned in subsection (1)(a) of this section is remitted to the United Kingdom in the year,

the settlor is liable for the tax charged under section 731 on the remainder of that amount as if that remainder were income arising to the settlor in the year (and the individual is not liable in any later year for income tax on that remainder).

(4) The amount mentioned in subsection (1)(a) may be the whole, or part only, of the amount treated as arising to the individual under section 732 for the year in the case of the relevant transfer and its associated operations.

(5) Where any tax for which the settlor is liable as a result of subsection (2) or (3) is paid, the settlor is entitled to recover the amount of the tax from the individual.

(6) For the purpose of recovering that amount, the settlor is entitled to require an officer of Revenue and Customs to give the settlor a certificate specifying—

(a) the amount of the income concerned, and

(b) the amount of tax paid,

and any such certificate is conclusive evidence of the facts stated in it.

(7) For the purposes of subsection (1)(b)(ii), a person is a close member of the family of the settlor if the person is—

(a) the settlor's spouse or civil partner, or

(b) a child of the settlor, or of a person within paragraph (a), if the child has not reached the age of 18.

(8) For the purposes of subsection (7)—

(a) two people living together as if they were spouses of each other are treated as if they were spouses of each other, and

(b) two people of the same sex living together as if they were civil partners of each other are treated as if they were civil partners of each other.

(9) Sections 809L to 809Z6 (remittance basis: rules about when income is remitted, including rule treating pre-arising remittances of deemed income as made when the income arises) apply for the purposes of this section."

37 In section 735A(6) (matching of income on which individual charged under section 731), after "individual" insert ", or as a result of section 733A another person,".

38 After section 735A insert—

"735B Settlor liable under section 733A and remittance basis applies

    (1) This section applies in relation to income if—

        (a) the income is treated by section 732 as arising to an individual ("the beneficiary") for a tax year,

(b) another individual ("the settlor") is under section 733A(2) or (3) liable for tax on the income, and

(c) section 809B, 809D or 809E (remittance basis) applies to the settlor for that year.

(2) The income ("the transferred-liability deemed income") is treated as relevant foreign income of the settlor.

(3) If, for the purposes of section 735 as it applies in relation to the beneficiary, any benefit or relevant income relates to any part of the transferred-liability deemed income then, for the purposes of Chapter A1 of Part 14 as it applies in relation to the settlor, that benefit or relevant income is to be treated as deriving from that part of the transferred-liability deemed income.

(4) In the application of section 832 of ITTOIA 2005 in relation to the income, subsection (2) of that section has effect with the omission of its paragraph (b)."

Commencement of amendments in FA 2004, ITTOIA 2005 and ITA 2007

39 The amendments made by paragraphs 19 to 38 have effect for the tax year 2017–18 and subsequent tax years.

FA 2008

40 In Part 2 of Schedule 7 to FA 2008 (remittance basis: trusts etc), after paragraph 171 insert—

"**172** (1) Sub-paragraph (2) has effect for the purposes of—

paragraphs 100(1)(b), 101(1)(c) and 102(1)(e),

paragraph (b) of paragraph 118(3) so far as having effect for the purposes of paragraph 118(1)(d), and

paragraphs 124(1)(b), 126(7)(b), 127(1)(e) and 151(1)(b).

(2) An individual not domiciled in the United Kingdom at a time in the tax year 2017–18, or a later tax year, is to be regarded as domiciled in the United Kingdom at that time if—

(a) the individual was born in the United Kingdom,

(b) the individual's domicile of origin was in the United Kingdom, and

(c) the individual is resident in the United Kingdom for the tax year concerned."

PART 3

CAPITAL GAINS TAX REBASING

41 (1) This paragraph applies to the disposal of an asset by an individual ("P") where—

(a) the asset was held by P on 5 April 2017,

(b) the disposal is made on or after 6 April 2017,

(c) the asset was not situated in the United Kingdom at any time in the relevant period, and

(d) P is a qualifying individual.

(2) The relevant period is the period which—

(a) begins with 16 March 2016 or, if later, the date on which P acquired the asset, and

(b) ends with 5 April 2017.

(3) P is a qualifying individual if—

(a) section 809H of ITA 2007 (claim for remittance basis by long-term UK resident: charge) applied in relation to P for any tax year before the tax year 2017–18,

(b) P is not an individual—

(i) who was born in the United Kingdom, and

(ii) whose domicile of origin was in the United Kingdom,

(c) P was not domiciled in the United Kingdom at any time in a relevant tax year, and

(d) P met condition B in section 835BA of ITA 2007 in relation to each relevant tax year.

(4) The relevant tax years are—

(a) the tax year 2017–18, and

(b) if the disposal was made after that tax year, all subsequent tax years up to and including that in which the disposal was made.

(5) In computing, for the purpose of TCGA 1992, the gain or loss accruing on the disposal, it is to be assumed that P acquired the asset on 5 April 2017 for a consideration equal to its market value on that date.

(6) Sub-paragraph (5) applies notwithstanding section 58(1) of TCGA 1992 (disposals between spouses).

(7) Where under section 127 of TCGA 1992 (including that section as applied by sections 132, 135 and 136 of that Act) an original and a new holding of shares or other securities are treated as the same asset, the condition in sub-paragraph (1)(c) applies to both the original and the new holding.

(8) This Part of this Schedule has effect as if it were included in TCGA 1992.

42 (1) This paragraph applies for the purposes of paragraph 41(1)(c) in the case of an asset which, having been situated outside the United Kingdom, becomes situated in the United Kingdom before the end of the relevant period.

(2) The asset is to be regarded as not situated in the United Kingdom at a time in the relevant period when—

(a) it meets the condition in section 809Z(3)(a), (b) or (c) of ITA 2007 (public access),

(b) it meets the condition in section 809Z3(3)(a), (b) or (c) of ITA 2007 (repairs),

(c) the sole or principal purpose of its being situated in the United Kingdom is to sell it or put it up for sale, or

(d) in the case of clothing, footwear, jewellery or a watch, it is for the personal use of—

(i) P or a husband, wife or civil partner of P, or

(ii) a child or grandchild of a person within sub-paragraph (i), if the child or grandchild has not reached the age of 18.

(3) The asset is to be regarded as not situated in the United Kingdom at any time in the relevant period if it is brought to, or received or used in, the United Kingdom in circumstances in which section 809L(2)(a) of ITA 2007 applies but—

(a) by virtue of section 809X(5)(c) of ITA 2007 (notional remitted amount less than £1000) it is treated as not remitted to the United Kingdom, or

(b) by the end of the relevant period it has not failed to meet the temporary importation rule in section 809Z4 of ITA 2007.

(4) Section 809M(3)(a) and (b) of ITA 2007 (persons living together) apply for the purposes of sub-paragraph (2)(d)(i).

43 (1) An individual may make an election for paragraph 41 not to apply to a disposal made by the individual.

(2) Sections 42 and 43 of TMA 1970 (procedure and time limit for claims), except section 42(1A) of that Act, apply in relation to an election under this paragraph as they apply in relation to a claim for relief.

(3) An election under this paragraph is irrevocable.

(4) All such adjustments are to be made, whether by way of discharge or repayment of tax, the making of assessments or otherwise, as are required to give effect to an election under this paragraph.

PART 4

CLEANSING OF MIXED FUNDS

44 (1) This paragraph applies for the purposes of the application of section 809Q(3) of ITA 2007 in relation to an individual ("P").

(2) Section 809R(4) of ITA 2007 does not apply to an offshore transfer from a mixed fund where—

(a) the transfer is made in the tax year 2017–18 or the tax year 2018–19,

(b) the transfer is a transfer of money,

(c) the mixed fund from which the transfer is made is an account (account A) and the transfer is made to another account (account B),

(d) the transfer is nominated by P for the purposes of this sub-paragraph,

(e) at the time of the nomination no other transfer from account A to account B has been so nominated, and

(f) P is a qualifying individual.

(3) P is a qualifying individual if—

(a) section 809B, 809D or 809E of ITA 2007 (remittance basis) applied in relation to P for any tax year before the tax year 2017–18, and

(b) P is not an individual—

(i) who was born in the United Kingdom, and

(ii) whose domicile of origin was in the United Kingdom.

(4) An offshore transfer to which sub-paragraph (2) applies is to be treated as containing such amount of such kind or kinds of income and capital in the mixed fund immediately before the transfer as may be specified in the nomination under sub-paragraph (2)(d).

(5) An amount of a kind of income or capital specified under sub-paragraph (4) may not exceed the amount of that kind which is in the mixed fund immediately before the transfer.

(6) In this paragraph "mixed fund" and "offshore transfer" have the same meanings as in section 809R(4) of ITA 2007.

45 (1) This paragraph applies to a transfer made by a person ("P") from a mixed fund where—

(a) the transfer is made in the tax year 2017–18 or the tax year 2018–19,

(b) the transfer is a transfer of money,

(c) the mixed fund from which the transfer is made is an overseas account (account A) containing pre-6 April 2008 income or chargeable gains,

(d) the transfer is made to another overseas account (account B),

(e) the transfer is nominated by the person for the purposes of this sub-paragraph,

(f) at the time of the nomination no other transfer from account A to account B has been so nominated, and

(g) P is a qualifying individual.

(2) P is a qualifying individual if—

(a) section 809B, 809D or 809E of ITA 2007 (remittance basis) applied in relation to P for any tax year before the tax year 2017–18, and

(b) P is not an individual—

  (i) who was born in the United Kingdom, and

  (ii) whose domicile of origin was in the United Kingdom.

(3) A transfer to which this paragraph applies is to be treated as containing such amount of such kind or kinds of income or capital in the mixed fund immediately before the transfer (for example, income or chargeable gains for a particular tax year) as may be specified in the nomination under sub-paragraph (1)(e).

(4) An amount of a kind of income or capital specified under sub-paragraph (3) may not exceed the amount of that kind which is in the mixed fund immediately before the transfer.

(5) In this paragraph and paragraph 46—

"mixed fund" has the same meaning as in section 809R(4) of ITA 2007;

"overseas account" means an account situated outside the United Kingdom;

"pre-6 April 2008 income or chargeable gains" means income or chargeable gains for the tax year 2007–8 or any earlier tax year.

46 (1) This paragraph applies to determine, for the purposes of paragraph 45, the composition of the mixed fund referred to in paragraph 45(1).

(2) Sub-paragraphs (3) to (5) apply where a transfer of money is made before 6 April 2008 from the mixed fund to another overseas account.

(3) Take the following Steps—

Step 1. Calculate the total amount of income and chargeable gains in the mixed fund immediately before the transfer ("the total income and gains").

Step 2. Calculate what proportion of the total income and gains is income and what proportion is chargeable gains.

(4) If the amount transferred does not exceed the total income and gains, the transfer is to be treated as if it consisted of income and chargeable gains in the proportions found under Step 2 in sub-paragraph (3).

(5) If the amount transferred exceeds the total income and gains, the transfer is to be treated as if it consisted of—

(a) all the income and chargeable gains that were in the mixed fund immediately before the transfer, and

(b) in respect of the balance, other capital from the mixed fund.

(6) Sub-paragraphs (7) and (8) apply where—

(a) a transfer of money is made before 6 April 2008 from another overseas account to the mixed fund, and

(b) there is insufficient evidence to determine the composition of the transfer.

(7) Take the following Steps—

Step 1. Calculate the total amount of income and chargeable gains in the other overseas account immediately before the transfer ("the total income and gains").

Step 2. Calculate what proportion of the total income and gains is income and what proportion is chargeable gains.

(8) The transfer is to be presumed to consist of income and chargeable gains in the proportions found under Step 2 in sub-paragraph (7).

(9) For the purposes of Steps 1 and 2 in sub-paragraph (7), if there is insufficient evidence to say that an amount is income or that it is chargeable gains, treat it as income.

GENERAL NOTE

Schedule 8 is divided into four parts. All paragraph references are to Schedule 8.

Schedule 8 Part 1 – Application of deemed domicile rule

Part 1 amends various parts of the tax legislation which hinge on the domicile status of the taxpayer. The broad effect is to treat the person who becomes deemed domiciled under the new section 835BA of ITA 2007 as being UK domiciled for those provisions.

TA 1988 s 266A

The existing rules for non-domiciled individuals received employer paid life assurance premiums will also apply to individuals who are deemed domiciled under the new provisions.

TCGA 1992 ss 16ZA–16ZC

Paragraphs 2–5 provide that where an individual becomes deemed domiciled in the UK, any previous TCGA 1992 s 16ZA election (remittance of foreign losses) no longer applies for that tax year or any future tax year. It will, however, still be possible to make a new election for losses and gains will be calculated on the arising basis. In the absence of such an election any foreign losses made by the individual in the year of making the election or any subsequent year in which the individual is not domiciled in the UK will not be allowable losses.

If the individual subsequently loses their deemed domicile status and returns to the UK as a non-dom, they can make another election at the appropriate time. The previous election does not revive.

TCGA 1992 s 69

Trustees of settlements are treated as a single body of persons for the purpose of determining the residence of the settlement. If at least one trustee is UK resident and at least one trustee is non-UK resident, the domicile of the settlor when the trust is created will determine the residence of the trust. Paragraph 6 provides that a settlor who is deemed domiciled when the trust is created will have the same effect on the residence of the trust

TCGA 1992 s 86

A UK domiciled settlor is charged to capital gains tax on gains arising in a non-resident trust which he created, whereas a non-UK domiciled settlor may claim the remittance basis. Paragraph 7 applies this attribution rule to settlors who become deemed domiciled. However, for those who become deemed domiciled under Condition B, there is a set of reliefs to exempt them in certain circumstances. These are covered in Part 2 of Schedule 8 under the heading, Protection of overseas trusts and described below.

TCGA 1992 s 275

Paragraph 8 amends the capital gains reliefs for foreign currency bank accounts held by a non-domiciled individual. If that individual becomes deemed domiciled the foreign currency bank account will be treated as located in the UK from 6 April 2017 regardless of when the asset was originally acquired.

TCGA 1992 Sch 5A

Schedule 5A imposes reporting requirements on UK domiciled settlors in relation to non-resident trusts. Paragraph 9 extends these obligations to those who satisfy the new deemed domicile test.

ITEPA 2003

Paragraph 10 removes the relief for certain travel costs and overseas employment expenses for non-domiciled employees once they become deemed domiciled.

ITA 2007 s 476

This section of ITA 2007 applies the same rule for income tax that TCGA 1992, s 69 (see above) applies for capital gains tax for determining the residence of trustees. Paragraph 12 provides that a settlor who becomes deemed domiciled under the new rules will have the same consequential effect on the residence of the trust.

ITA 2007, s 834 applies a similar rule to determine the residence of personal representatives for income tax purposes which is now amended by paragraph 17 to take account of the deemed domicile provisions.

ITA 2007 s 718

The transfer of assets abroad legislation is amended to ensure that individuals who are deemed domiciled under the new rules are treated in the same way as other UK domiciled individuals.

ITA 2007 s 809B et seq

These sections of ITA 2007 make provisions for the application of the remittance basis to non-UK domiciled individuals. Paragraph 14 applies the new deemed domicile rules to those provisions so that all individuals who qualify under Condition A or Condition B now lose their entitlement to claim the remittance basis. All their income and gains will be taxed on the arising basis.

References to the "17-year residence test" which allowed for the highest remittance basis charge of £90,000 are removed since those individuals will now become deemed domiciled. The remittance basis charges of £30,000 and £60,000 for individuals who have been resident in the UK for seven of the last nine years or 12 of the last 14 years respectively remain in place as these individuals will not be caught by the new deemed domicile rules.

TCGA 1992

Paragraphs 15 and 16 amend the effects of paragraph 14 in relation to the capital gains temporary non-resident rules in TCGA 1992 s10A.

Individuals who left the UK prior to 2017/18 and return within five years triggering the temporary non-residence rules of TCGA 1992 s 10A are charged to capital gains tax on their return for gains realised during the intervening years of absence provided that the asset was owned at the time they left the UK. However, since the gains are deemed to arise in the year of return, a non-domiciled individual could claim the remittance basis in the year of return to mitigate a UK CGT liability. However, such individuals may now be caught by the 15/20-year rule. The new deemed domicile rules are disapplied for the year of return to enable a remittance basis claim to be made.

Paragraph 15 applies to those who fall under the original temporary non-resident rules in TCGA 1992, s 10A. Paragraph 16 applies to those who fall under the rules as amended by FA2013. The distinction relates to the dates of departure and return.

Schedule 8 Part 2 – Protection of overseas trusts

TCGA 1992 s 86 protection

TCGA 1992 s 86 attributes gains in non-UK trusts with UK domiciled settlors the settlor when the settlor has an interest in the trust.

Where a settlor was not domiciled when they settled assets into trust but at a later date becomes deemed domiciled for income tax and CGT purposes, as a result of the F(No 2)A 2017 provisions, they would without any additional rules become taxable on the trust gains as they arose unless they excluded themselves and (broadly) their family (including grandchildren) from benefit in the trust.

The protection provisions of TCGA 1992 s 8 are amended to extend the protection on such settlors who become deemed domiciled under the new Condition B rules as long as no additional property is settled into the trust.

Paragraph 18 inserts a new TCGA 1992 s 86(5A). This new sub-section disapplies the usual TCGA 1992 s 86 rule where four conditions are met:

A. The tax year is 2017/18 tax year onwards (prior to that it is anyway irrelevant).
B. The settlor was not domiciled (or deemed domiciled under the F(No 2)A 2017 rules) in the UK when the property was settled into trust.
C. The settlor is not domiciled in the UK under general law in the relevant year (i.e. the year of the disposal by the trustees), and is not a Condition A non-dom by virtue of having been born in the UK with a UK domicile of origin.
D. No property or income is provided directly or indirectly for the purposes of the settlement by the settlor, or by the trustees of another settlement of which the settlor is the settlor or a beneficiary when the settlor is either domiciled or a Condition A or Condition B deemed UK domiciled individual.

Condition D is then further provided for in a new TCGA 1992 s 86(5B) and gives instances where the provision of property to the settlement can be ignored for the purposes of the s 86 rules. These situations are:

- transactions at arm's length (e.g. purchase at market value);
- provision of property without intention to confer gratuitous benefit;
- a loan made on arm's length terms;
- interest on an arm's length loan;
- repayment of a loan made by the trustees;
- property or income in pursuance of a liability incurred by any person before 6 April 2017;
- provision of property or income to settle a trust liability in respect of tax or administrative expense and where income in the trust is insufficient to meet this expense.

This final exception will save many trusts holding non-income producing assets from losing their protected status by virtue of the settlor or another individual settling the accountancy and trustee fees.

There are certain conditions for a loan by the settlor to the trustees (or by the trustees of another settlement with the same settlor) so that it is not considered an addition of property to the settlement. The loan must be on arm's length terms and there must be no "relevant event" to trigger a deemed settlement of assets. A "relevant event" for this purpose means:

(a) capitalisation of interest payable under the loan;
(b) failure to pay interest in accordance with the terms of the loan; or
(c) variation of the terms of the loan such that they cease to be arm's length.

There are transitional rules for settlors becoming deemed domiciled on 6 April 2017 by virtue of the 15/20-year rule where a non-arm's length loan was already in place. There will not be a deemed settlement into the trust where the loan is repaid, or changed to be an arm's length loan if this is done before 6 April 2018. This essentially gives individuals and trustees a year to ensure that such loans are either repaid or changed to comply with the new legislation. Note that interest must be calculated and paid on arm's length terms from 6 April 2017 even if the new terms are not finalised until after that date (but before 6 April 2018).

For the loan to be considered at arm's length, a loan to the trustees of a settlement where the interest charged is equal to or greater than the official rate of interest, and interest is payable at least annually. A loan by the trustees of the settlement is considered arm's length if interest is payable at no more than the official rate.

If the conditions of contributing to the settlement are breached, then TCGA 1992 s 86 will apply to the whole of the trust and not just the portion of the trust affected by the additional settlement. It is therefore vital to ensure that, once a settlor becomes deemed domicile for income tax and capital gains tax purposes, all transactions and loans are carefully monitored in order to retain the protected status of the trust.

FA 2004

A consequential amendment is made to ensure that the new rules on deemed domicile do not affect the operation of the pre-owned assets regime.

ITTOIA 2005 s 624 protection

The provisions for protecting foreign source income from a settlement where the settlor retains an interest mirror the capital gains tax protection in TCGA 1992 s 86 as outlined above

ITTOIA 2005 s 624 deems income arising in a settlor-interested settlement to be treated as arising on the settlor and taxed accordingly. Settlements are caught where the settlor (or their spouse) retains an interest in the property. However, where the settlor is non-UK domiciled and the trust income is foreign income, then the settlor would generally be within the remittance basis provisions and would not be taxed on non-remitted income.

Potentially individuals affected by the new deemed domicile rules would then also be subject to the settlor income attribution rules in ITTOIA 2005 s 624. Again, the Government has introduced a measure of relief for the Condition B non-doms through the concept of a protected settlement.

ITTOIA 2005 s 628A, inserted by para 22, disapplies the normal rule attributing income to the settlor when the settlement is a protected settlement. For the protection to apply, seven conditions must be met:

A. The income would be relevant foreign income if it were income of a UK resident individual.
B. The income is from property originating from the settlor (as defined in ITTOIA 2005 s 645).
C. The settlor was not domiciled (or deemed domiciled) in the UK when the property was settled into trust.
D. The settlor is neither domiciled in the UK under general law in the relevant year (i.e. the year of the disposal by the trustees) nor a Category A deemed domicile.
E. The trustees are not UK resident in the tax year.
F. No property or income is provided directly or indirectly for the purposes of the settlement by the settlor, or by the trustees of another settlement of which the settlor is the settlor or a beneficiary when the settlor is either domiciled or deemed domiciled in the UK.

A newly-inserted ITTOIA 2005 s 628B then goes on to provide for situations where a transaction is not treated as the provision of income or property to the settlement. These circumstances mirror the exceptions in TCGA 1992 s 86(5A) as set out above under **TCGA 1992 s 86 protection**.

Also, the same transitional rules apply where a non-arm's length loan was already in place.

If the conditions of contributing to the settlement are breached, then ITTOIA 2005 s 624 will apply to the whole of the trust and not just the portion of the trust affected by the additional settlement.

New ITTOIA 2005 s 628C ensures that trustees of an ITTOIA 2005 s 624 settlement are not considered to be "relevant persons" (for the purposes of ITA 2007 s 809L) in respect of trust income which:

– arose between 6 April 2008 and 5 April 2017;
– arose in a tax year where the settlor claimed the remittance basis;
– is foreign source income;
– has not been distributed prior to 6 April 2017 nor treated as the income of the settlor; and
– would otherwise have been caught by ITTOIA 2005 s 624.

This means that where the above conditions are met, actions of the trustees of a protected trust will not create a remittance to the UK. In other words such income can be remitted to the UK without a tax charge arising. Note however that this only applies to "transitional trust income", i.e. trust income up to 2016/17.

Transfer of assets abroad and protected trusts

To the extent that trust income isn't caught by ITTOIA 2005 s 624, potentially the transfer of assets abroad legislation can still cause a problem (ITA 2007 s 720 et seq). Again, these provisions can deem income arising within an offshore structure (particularly underlying companies of offshore trusts or stand-alone companies) to be attributed to – and taxed on – the "transferor".

Individuals who are within the new deemed domicile rules would, without special rules, be subject to the income attribution rules under the transfer of assets abroad legislation under the arising basis without the potential relief of a remittance basis claim. Again, there is a measure of relief for for Condition B non-doms.

Paragraphs 27–38 of Schedule 8 insert this relief into the Transfer of Assets Abroad Code. A new sub-s (3B) is inserted into ITA 2007 s 721 which gives relief for Condition B non-doms against the attribution provisions of the transfer of assets abroad rules where the income concerned is "protected foreign source income" (as defined by a newly inserted ITA 2007 s 721A).

"Protected foreign source income" is broadly foreign income arising in a non-resident trust which was created when the settlor was neither non-domiciled nor deemed domiciled and none of the trust property or income derives from the settlor after he became deemed domiciled.

Newly inserted ITA 2007 s 721B then goes on to provide some relief from the situations where added property would cause a problem or where a loan was already in place. Essentially these are the same tainting rules as for protected settlements under the TCGA 1992 s 86 and the ITTOIA 2005 s 624 rules described above.

The protected income provisions in ITA 2007 s 721A are then mirrored in the capital payments provisions of ITA 2007 s 728.

Similarly the "non-transferor" provisions of ITA 2007 s 731 are amended to create protected income provisions.

Paragraph 36 inserts new ITA 2007, s 733A which removes the protected income relief from Condition B non-doms if income is paid to close family members (generally, spouses and children) who will not be taxed on it either because they are non-resident beneficiaries, or they are UK resident beneficiaries taxable on the remittance basis.

Schedule 8 Part 3 – CGT rebasing

An individual who becomes deemed domiciled under the new rules will no longer be able to shelter capital gains on offshore assets by claiming the remittance basis. Paragraphs 41–43 introduce provisions to enable certain individuals to "rebase" their assets to their 6 April 2017 value such that the taxable gain will be limited to that arising after the change in law.

The conditions for this rebasing relief relate both to the status of the asset and to the status of the individual. They can be summarised as follows.

Conditions relating to the asset
- the asset must have been held by the individual taxpayer on 5 April 2017;
- the asset is disposed of on or after 6 April 2017;
- the asset must not have been situated in the UK at any time in the "relevant period".

The "relevant period" in this context started on 16 March 2016 or, if later, the date on which the individual taxpayer acquired the asset, and ends on 5 April 2017. This is in effect an anti-forestalling provision to prevent individuals transferring assets overseas after the budget was announced. Essentially this applies the usual exemptions in ITA 2007 809Z such that if the asset is in the UK by reason of public access or repairs then it is not considered to be in the UK. Additionally, clothing, footwear, jewellery and watches for personal use is not considered to be in the UK. Money remitted to the UK of less than £1,000 but kept in the UK for less than 275 days is also not considered remitted to the UK.

Conditions relating to the Individual

In order for the individual to qualify for rebasing, they must meet the following conditions (para 41):
- they must have paid the remittance basis charge in a year before 2017/18;
- they must meet the Condition B 15/20-year rule for 2017/18 and all subsequent years up to and including the year of disposal;

Condition A non-doms do not benefit from this rebasing and there is no further rebasing opportunity available for individuals who subsequently become deemed domiciled.

Disapplication of the rebasing

The capital gains tax rebasing applies automatically to all eligible assets for eligible individuals as defined by the legislation. It is possible to make an election to disapply the rebasing on an asset-by-asset basis (para 43) as the disposals occur. This would clearly be of benefit to the individual if the asset has decreased in value from the date of acquisition to 5 April 2017.

TMA 1970 ss 42 and 43 apply for the making of the claim which means that it should be made within four years of the end of the tax year in which the disposal takes place.

Schedule 8 Part 4 – cleansing of mixed funds

The mixed fund rules are complex. Broadly, though, if an individual has a mixed fund offshore account containing income, gains and clean capital, a transfer of funds to the UK would first be treated as a remittance income, then gains and then capital. It would therefore only be possible to remit non-taxable capital (such as pre-arrival funds) once all other income and gains are remitted.

If an individual (without the mixed fund cleansing provisions) sought to separate out mixed funds by making a transfer to offshore accounts, the transfer would be deemed to be a pro-rata amount of each type of fund (income, gains and capital) and as such it was not possible to create a pot of clean capital from a mixed fund without remitting the whole amount to the UK.

The mixed fund cleansing rules allow for an individual (in the 2017/18 or 2018/19 tax years only) to make an offshore-to-offshore transfer that is not a pro-rata amount of income, gains and capital. The transfer made under these provisions is treated as comprising the income/gains/capital as nominated by the individual at the time of the transfer (although the allocation must be based on the actual proportions of income/gains/capital in the account).

Paragraph 44 disapplies the standard rules in ITA 2007 s 809R(4) under the following conditions:

– the transfer is made in 2017/18 or 2018/19;
– the transfer is a transfer of money (from account A to account B);
– the transfer must be between two offshore accounts;
– there must be a nomination made with respect to the transfer;
– there must be no other nominated funds transferred from account A to account B;
– the taxpayer concerned must be a *qualifying individual*.

It may be the case that an individual has mixed funds within an asset (for example a shareholding, or a tangible asset such as a painting). In this case, the individual will have to sell the asset in order to cleanse the funds within the asset. Cleansing only operates through actual cash funds in bank accounts. An investment portfolio would not qualify.

The taxpayer will be a "qualifying individual" for mixed fund cleansing if they were a remittance basis user in a tax year prior to 2017/18 and they have now become deemed domiciled under Condition B. Paragraph 44 identifies individuals to whom ITA 2007 ss 809B, 809D or 809E applied, so the relief applies not only to those who paid the Remittance Basis Charge, but also those who qualified for the remittance basis under the low income de minimis provisions

There is no requirement for the income in a mixed fund to be transferred out before the gains, or gains before capital. Indeed, it would appear that a full analysis of the mixed fund is not required to benefit at least in part from the mixed account cleansing.

For example, consider a taxpayer who had an overseas account which held £100,000 at the time of their arrival in the UK but due to lack of advice, the money was invested in stocks and shares rather than placed in a bank account. Assume the individual claimed the remittance basis in all relevant years, and liquidates the assets with the result that there is £180,000 cash in the overseas account. The individual can be certain that £100,000 is clean (pre-arrival) capital, but is not sure without detailed analysis how much of the £80,000 relates to income and how much relates to capital gains. The individual could transfer £100,000 to a new offshore account and make a nomination to the effect that the funds transferred are clean capital. This account can then be used to transfer funds to the UK without a further charge to tax.

Prior to 6 April 2008 there were no statutory ordering rules for the transfer of mixed funds. Paragraphs 45 and 46 apply the mixed fund cleansing rules to pre- 6 April 2008 funds. The original composition of the fund is calculated and the transfer deemed to be comprised of income and gains in the same proportion.

SCHEDULE 9

SETTLEMENTS AND TRANSFER OF ASSETS ABROAD: VALUE OF BENEFITS

Section 31

Capital gains tax: settlements: value of benefit conferred by certain capital payments
1 (1) In section 97(4) of TCGA 1992 (supplementary provisions in relation to settlements), at the end insert "(see sections 97A to 97C for the value of benefits conferred by a capital payment made by way of loan or by way of making movable property or land available)".

(2) After section 97 of TCGA 1992 insert—

"97A Value of benefit conferred by capital payment made by way of loan

(1) For the purposes of section 97(4), the value of the benefit conferred on a person (P) by a capital payment made by way of loan to P is, for each tax year in which the loan is outstanding, the amount (if any) by which—

(a) the amount of interest that would have been payable in that year on the loan if interest had been payable on the loan at the official rate, exceeds

(b) the amount of interest (if any) actually paid by P in that year on the loan.

(2) In this section and section 97B the "official rate", in relation to interest, means the rate applicable from time to time under section 178 of the Finance Act 1989 for the purposes of Chapter 7 of Part 3 of ITEPA 2003.

97B Value of benefit conferred by capital payment made by way of making movable property available

(1) For the purposes of section 97(4), the value of the benefit conferred by a capital payment consisting of making movable property available, without any transfer of the property in it, to a person (P) is, for each tax year in which the benefit is conferred on P—

$$((CC \times R \times D) / Y) - T$$

where—

CC is the capital cost of the movable property on the date when the property is first made available to P in the tax year,

D is the number of days in the tax year on which the property is made available to P (the relevant period),

R is the official rate of interest for the relevant period (but see subsection (3)),

T is the total of the amounts (if any) paid in the tax year by P—

(a) to the person conferring the benefit, in respect of the availability of the movable property, or

(b) so far as not within paragraph (a), in respect of the repair, insurance, maintenance or storage of the movable property, and

Y is the number of days in the tax year.

(2) In subsection (1), in the meaning of CC, the "capital cost" of movable property means an amount equal to the total of—

(a) the amount which is the greater of—

(i) the amount or value of the consideration given for the acquisition of the movable property by, or on behalf of, the person (A) conferring the benefit, and

(ii) its market value at the time of that acquisition, and

(b) the amount of any expenditure wholly and exclusively incurred by, or on behalf of, A for the purpose of enhancing the value of the movable property.

(3) If the official rate of interest changes during the relevant period, then in subsection (1) R is the average official rate of interest for the period calculated as follows.

Step 1

Multiply each official rate of interest in force during the relevant period by the number of days when it is in force.

Step 2

Add together the products found in Step 1.

Step 3

Divide the total found in Step 2 by the number of days in the relevant period.

(4) In subsections (1) and (2), "movable property" means any tangible movable property other than money.

97C Value of benefit conferred by capital payment made by way of making land available

(1) For the purposes of section 97(4), the value of the benefit conferred by a capital payment consisting of making land available for the use of a person (P) is, for each tax year in which the benefit is conferred on P, the amount by which—

(a) the rental value of the land for the period of the tax year during which the land is made available to P, exceeds

(b) the total of the amounts (if any) paid in the tax year by P—

(i) to the person conferring the benefit, in respect of the availability of the land, or

(ii) so far as not within sub-paragraph (i), in respect of costs of repair, insurance or maintenance relating to the land.

(2) Subsection (1) does not apply in the case where the person conferring the benefit transfers the whole of the person's interest in the land to P.

(3) In subsection (1) "the rental value" of the land for a period means the rent which would have been payable for the period if the land had been let to P at an annual rent equal to the annual value.

(4) For the purposes of subsection (3) "the annual value" of land is the rent that might reasonably be expected to be obtained on a letting from year to year if—

(a) the tenant undertook to pay all taxes, rates and charges usually paid by a tenant, and

(b) the landlord undertook to bear the costs of the repairs and insurance and the other expenses (if any) necessary for maintaining the property in a state to command that rent.

(5) For the purposes of subsection (4) that rent—

(a) is to be taken to be the amount that might reasonably be expected to be so obtained in respect of a letting of the land, and

(b) is to be calculated on the basis that the only amounts that may be deducted in respect of services provided by the landlord are amounts in respect of the costs to the landlord of providing any relevant services.

(6) In subsection (5) "relevant service" means a service other than the repair, insurance or maintenance of the property."

Income tax: transfer of assets abroad: value of certain benefits

2 After section 742A of ITA 2007 insert—

"Value of certain benefits

742B Value of certain benefits

Sections 742C to 742E apply where it is necessary, for the purpose of calculating a charge to income tax under the preceding provisions of this Chapter, to determine the value of a benefit provided to a person by way of—

(a) a payment by way of loan (see section 742C),

(b) making available movable property without any transfer of the property in it (see section 742D), or

(c) making available land for use without transferring the whole interest in it (see section 742E).

742C Value of benefit provided by a payment by way of loan

(1) The value of the benefit provided to a person (P) by a payment by way of loan to P is, for each tax year in which the loan is outstanding, the amount (if any) by which—

(a) the amount of interest that would have been payable in that year on the loan if interest had been payable on the loan at the official rate, exceeds

(b) the amount of interest (if any) actually paid by P in that year on the loan.

(2) In this section and section 742D the "official rate", in relation to interest, means the rate applicable from time to time under section 178 of the Finance Act 1989 for the purposes of Chapter 7 of Part 3 of ITEPA 2003.

742D Value of benefit provided by making movable property available

(1) The value of the benefit provided by making movable property available, without any transfer of the property in it, to a person (P) is, for each tax year in which the benefit is provided to P—

$$((CC \times R \times D)/Y) - T$$

where—

CC is the capital cost of the movable property on the date when the property is first made available to P in the tax year,

D is the number of days in the tax year on which the property is made available to P (the relevant period),

R is the official rate of interest for the relevant period (but see subsection (3)),

T is the total of the amounts (if any) paid in the tax year by P—

(a) to the person providing the benefit, in respect of the availability of the movable property, or

(b) so far as not within paragraph (a), in respect of the repair, insurance, maintenance or storage of the movable property, and

Y is the number of days in the tax year.

(2) In subsection (1), in the meaning of CC, the "capital cost" of the movable property means an amount equal to the total of—

(a) the amount which is the greater of—

(i) the amount or value of the consideration given for the acquisition of the movable property by, or on behalf of, the person (A) providing the benefit, and

(ii) its market value at the time of that acquisition, and

(b) the amount of any expenditure wholly and exclusively incurred by, or on behalf of, A for the purpose of enhancing the value of the movable property.

(3) If the official rate of interest changes during the relevant period, then in subsection (1) R is the average official rate of interest for the period calculated as follows.

Step 1

Multiply each official rate of interest in force during the relevant period by the number of days when it is in force.

Step 2

Add together the products found in Step 1.

Step 3

Divide the total found in Step 2 by the number of days in the relevant period.

(4) In subsections (1) and (2), "movable property" means any tangible movable property other than money.

742E Value of benefit provided by making land available

(1) The value of the benefit provided by making land available for the use of a person (P) is, for each tax year in which the benefit is provided to P, the amount by which—

(a) the rental value of the land for the period of the tax year during which the land is made available to P, exceeds

(b) the total of the amounts (if any) paid in the tax year by P—

(i) to the person providing the benefit, in respect of the availability of the land, or

(ii) so far as not within sub-paragraph (i), in respect of costs of repair, insurance or maintenance relating to the land.

(2) Subsection (1) does not apply in the case where the person providing the benefit transfers the whole of the person's interest in the land to P.

(3) In subsection (1) "the rental value" of the land for a period means the rent which would have been payable for the period if the land had been let to P at an annual rent equal to the annual value.

(4) For the purposes of subsection (3) "the annual value" of land is the rent that might reasonably be expected to be obtained on a letting from year to year if—

(a) the tenant undertook to pay all taxes, rates and charges usually paid by a tenant, and

(b) the landlord undertook to bear the costs of the repairs and insurance and the other expenses (if any) necessary for maintaining the property in a state to command that rent.

(5) For the purposes of subsection (4) that rent—

(a) is to be taken to be the amount that might reasonably be expected to be so obtained in respect of a letting of the land, and

(b) is to be calculated on the basis that the only amounts that may be deducted in respect of services provided by the landlord are amounts in respect of the costs to the landlord of providing any relevant services.

(6) In subsection (5) "relevant service" means a service other than the repair, insurance or maintenance of the property."

Commencement

3 The amendments made by this Schedule have effect in relation to capital payments or benefits received in the tax year 2017–18 and subsequent tax years.

GENERAL NOTE

The introduction to this legislation is given in the commentary to section 31 "Settlements and transfer of assets abroad: value of benefits". As stated therein the legislation provides statutory rules for valuing certain non-monetary capital payments/benefits for the purposes of the Capital Gains Tax (CGT) settlements anti-avoidance legislation (TCGA 1992 s 86A to s 96 and Sch 4C) and the Income Tax Transfer of Assets Abroad (ToAA) legislation (ITA 2007 Pt 13, Ch 2). The capital payments/benefits considered are loans, use of movable property and use of land.

Paragraph 1 inserts statutory valuation rules into TCGA 1992 for the purposes of the CGT settlements anti-avoidance provisions (TCGA 1992 s 86A to s 96 and TCGA 1992 Sch 4C) and paragraph 2 inserts wording into ITA 2007 for the purposes of the ToAA regime. The valuation rules are aligned so the value of the benefit will be the same whichever charging provision applies.

Throughout the new CGT and income tax legislation the individual who is provided with the capital payment or benefit is referred to as "P" (for person).

Commencement provisions provide that the legislation will be effective from 6 April 2017.

Capital Gains Tax (CGT) settlements legislation: value of benefits conferred by capital payments

TCGA 1992 s 97 sets down various supplementary provisions that apply to TCGA 1992 s 86A to s 96 and Sch 4C.

TCGA 1992 s 97(4) covers the valuation of non-monetary capital payments. Prior to these changes it just stated that, for the purposes of TCGA 1992 s 86A to s 96 and TCGA 1992, Sch 4C, the amount of a capital payment by way of a loan or any other capital payment which was not an outright monetary payment was determined to be equal to the value of the benefit conferred.

Paragraph 1(1) adjusts TCGA 1992 s 97(4) so that at the end it refers to the three new sections that Sch 9, para 1 is inserting after TCGA 1992 s 97, these being:

- new TCGA 1992 s 97A to value benefits conferred by a capital payment made by way of a loan;
- new TCGA 1992 s 97B to value benefits conferred by a capital payment made by way of making movable property available without any transfer of the property; and
- new TCGA 1992 s 97C to value benefits conferred by a capital payment made by way of making land available without any transfer of the whole of the interest in the property.

Benefits conferred by a capital payment made by way of a loan

For a tax year, new TCGA 1992 s 97A establishes that the amount of the capital payment conferred when an interest free or low interest loan is made to P is determined by:

(a) Establishing the amount of interest that would have been payable on the loan for the tax year if the "official rate" of interest had been charged;

(a) Subtracting from the answer at (a) the amount of interest (if any) actually paid by P in that tax year on the loan.

The "official rate" is defined as the rate applicable from time to time under Finance Act 1989 s 178 for the purposes of ITEPA 2003 Pt 3, Ch 7. This legislation allows the Treasury to provide for the rate of interest in regulations.

From 6 April 2017 to the date of writing the official interest rate is 2.5%. The relevant Regulations introducing this rate are referred to as the Taxes (Interest Rate) (Amendment) Regulations 2017, SI 2017/305.

It is important to note that the legislation refers to interest actually paid in the tax year. Rolling up interest or using a deep discounted security will not meet this requirement.

Example 1

The Unicorn Offshore Discretionary Settlement was settled by Mrs Rainbow who died in 2000.

Miss Pink (UK resident and UK domiciled) had a £5 million loan outstanding with The Unicorn Offshore Discretionary Settlement for the whole of the tax year 2017/18.

Assume that the official rate of interest remains at 2.5% for the entire year.

At the official rate of interest the amount of interest due is £125,000.

Miss Pink pays the £125,000 due on 16 April 2018. The new rules mean that she is still deemed to have received a capital payment of £125,000 for 2017/18, as the payment is not made prior to 6 April 2018 (so is not actually paid in 2017/18).

If we assume the official rate of interest remains the same for 2018/19 and the loan also remains the same Miss Pink's £125,000 payment on 16 April 2018 will mean that she is not seen as receiving a capital payment in 2018/19.

Benefits conferred by a capital payment made by way of making movable property available

Moveable property is defined as "any tangible movable property other than money". Most commonly in these situations the asset being provided will be valuable paintings or antiques.

For a tax year, the value of a capital payment conferred by way of making movable property available to P is determined by applying the formula set down in new TCGA 1992 s 97B.

The formula is as follows:

$$\frac{CC \times R \times D}{Y} - D$$

CC is the capital cost of the movable property on the date in the tax year when it is first made available to P. The capital cost of the movable property is determined by adding together the amounts determined by bullets (a) and (b) below:

(a) The greater of:
(i) the actual consideration given for the movable property by the person conferring the benefit ("A"); and
(ii) the market value of the movable property at the date of acquisition.
(b) The total expenditure incurred, by or on behalf of A, wholly and exclusively for the purposes of enhancing the movable property's value.

D is the number of days in the tax year (the relevant period) that the property has been available to P.

R is the official rate of interest (same basic definition as for new TCGA 1992 s 97A). If the official rate of interest changes during the relevant period then R becomes the average official rate for the period with the following three steps being specified to determine the amount: (Step 1) multiply each official rate of interest in force during the relevant period by the number of days when it is in force; (Step 2) add together the results found in step 1; and (step 3) divide the answer from step 2 by the number of days in the relevant period.

Y is the number of days in the tax year as a whole, so 365 or 366 (for a tax year where February has 29 days).

T is the total of the amounts (if any) paid in the tax year by P to:

(a) The person conferring the benefit. Payments must be made in respect of the availability of the movable property.
(b) Payments not within paragraph (a) that are for: the repair, insurance, maintenance or storage of the moveable property.

Example 2

The Unicorn Offshore Discretionary Settlement was settled by Mrs Rainbow who died in 2000.

Throughout the whole of 2017/18 The Unicorn Offshore Discretionary Settlement provides Miss Purple (a UK resident foreign domiciliary) with a Monet painting that she keeps in her London home.

The Unicorn Offshore Discretionary Settlement acquired it for £11.5 million at an auction in 2011. The auction price is agreed to be the market value at the date of acquisition. There are no payments made for the purposes of enhancing the value of the Monet.

In 2017/18 Miss Purple did not pay The Unicorn Offshore Discretionary Settlement anything for the use of the Monet. She did, however, pay £215,750 in the year with respect to insurance, maintenance and storage costs (there were no repair costs).

In terms of the formula:

$$\frac{CC \times R \times D}{Y} - T$$

CC = £11.5 million
R =2.5% (assuming the rate does not change for the rest of 2017/18)
D = 365
Y = 365
T = £215,750
Miss Purple has a capital payment of £71,750 for 2017/18.

Benefits conferred by a capital payment made by way of making land available

New TCGA 1992 s 97C applies in all cases where land is made available to an individual except where the person conferring the benefit transfers the whole of their interest in the land.

The value of the benefit is determined by applying the statutory rules set down in new TCGA 1992, s 97C.

For a tax year, the value of a capital payment conferred by way of making land available to an individual is found by:

(a) Determining the rental value of the land for the part of the tax year that the land is made available to P.

(b) Subtracting from the answer at (a) the total of the amounts (if any) paid in the tax year by P to:

  (i) The person conferring the benefit. Payments must be made in respect of the availability of the land.

  (ii) Payments not within paragraph (a) that are in respect of costs of repair, insurance or maintenance relating to the land.

Arriving at the "rental value of the land" is a somewhat protracted process as one has to go through various definitions within sub-sections (3) to (6).

"The rental value" of the land is initially defined by new TCGA 1992 s 97C(3). Rather than providing a definition that can be readily applied the sub-section states that the "rental value" is the rent which would have been payable if the land had been rented out to P at an annual rent equal to "the annual value".

The definition of "the annual value" can be found at new TCGA 1992 s 97C(4). Sub-section (4) provides that "the annual value" of land is the rent reasonably expected to be obtained on a letting year to year where:

– the tenant undertakes to pay all taxes, rates and charges usually suffered by a tenant; and

– the landlord undertakes to pay the costs of repairs, insurance and other expenses (if any) required to maintain the property in a state fit to command "that rent" (this is defined by new TCGA 1992 s 97C(5)).

Sub-section 5 defines "that rent" as the amount that might reasonably be expected to be obtained in respect of the letting of the land. It is to be determined on the basis that the only amounts that may be deducted in respect of services provided by the landlord are amounts in respect of the costs to the landlord of providing "relevant services" (defined by sub-section (6) as a service other than the repair, insurance or maintenance of the property).

Example 3

The Unicorn Offshore Discretionary Settlement was settled by Mrs Rainbow who died in 2000.

Throughout the whole of 2017/18 The Unicorn Offshore Discretionary Settlement allows Miss Red (UK resident and foreign domiciled) to use a three-bedroom duplex penthouse flat in central London.

The rental value of the land for the tax year was £120,000.

Miss Red does not pay The Unicorn Offshore Discretionary Settlement anything for the use of the flat. She did, however, pay £4,300 in the year with respect to repair costs.

Miss Red has a capital payment of £115,700 for 2017/18.

Income tax: transfer of assets abroad: value of certain benefits

Paragraph 2 inserts new ITA 2007 ss 742B–742E into the transfer of assets abroad legislation. The new legislation is inserted after s 742A with the sub-heading "Value of certain benefits" preceding the introductory section (new ITA 2007 s 742B).

New section 742B states that new sections 742C to 742E apply where necessary for the purposes of calculating the income tax charge under the preceding provisions of ITA 2007 Pt 13, Ch 2 where it is necessary to value a benefit provided by:

- A payment by way of a loan (new ITA 2007 s 742C).
- Making available movable property without any transfer of the property (new ITA 2007 s 742D).
- Making land available for use without a transfer of the whole interest in it (new ITA 2007 s 742E).

As mentioned above new sections ITA 2007 ss 742C–742E are very similar to the CGT provisions. The changes to the wording are to take account of the differences in the anti-avoidance legislation. The CGT provisions refer to capital payments and benefits conferred. The income tax provisions refer to benefit provided and make no reference to capital payments as that is a CGT anti-avoidance term.

The substance of the two sets of provisions is identical. As such, apart from legislative references and replacing references to capital payments by references to benefits, the commentary above for the new CGT capital payment valuation rules all applies to the new transfer of assets benefit valuation rules.

Paragraph 3 is the commencement provision for the legislation. It states that Sch 9 has effect in relation to capital payments and/or benefits received in the tax year 2017/18 and subsequent tax years.

SCHEDULE 10

INHERITANCE TAX ON OVERSEAS PROPERTY REPRESENTING UK RESIDENTIAL PROPERTY

Section 33

Non-excluded overseas property

1 In IHTA 1984, before Schedule 1 insert—

"SCHEDULE A1

NON-EXCLUDED OVERSEAS PROPERTY

PART 1

OVERSEAS PROPERTY WITH VALUE ATTRIBUTABLE TO UK

RESIDENTIAL PROPERTY

Introductory

1 Property is not excluded property by virtue of section 6(1) or 48(3)(a) if and to the extent that paragraph 2 or 3 applies to it.

Close company and partnership interests

2 (1) This paragraph applies to an interest in a close company or in a partnership, if and to the extent that the interest meets the condition in sub-paragraph (2).

(2) The condition is that the value of the interest is—

(a) directly attributable to a UK residential property interest, or
(b) attributable to a UK residential property interest by virtue only of one or more of the following—

(i) an interest in a close company;
(ii) an interest in a partnership;
(iii) property to which paragraph 3 (loans) applies.

(3) For the purposes of sub-paragraphs (1) and (2) disregard—

(a) an interest in a close company, if the value of the interest is less than 5% of the total value of all the interests in the close company;
(b) an interest in a partnership, if the value of the interest is less than 5% of the total value of all the interests in the partnership.

(4) In determining under sub-paragraph (3) whether to disregard a person's interest in a close company or partnership, treat the value of the person's interest as increased by the value of any connected person's interest in the close company or partnership.

(5) In determining whether or to what extent the value of an interest in a close company or in a partnership is attributable to a UK residential property interest for the purposes of sub-paragraph (1), liabilities of a close company or partnership are to be attributed rateably to all of its property, whether or not they would otherwise be attributed to any particular property.

Loans

3 This paragraph applies to—

(a) the rights of a creditor in respect of a loan which is a relevant loan (see paragraph 4), and

(b) money or money's worth held or otherwise made available as security, collateral or guarantee for a loan which is a relevant loan, to the extent that it does not exceed the value of the relevant loan.

4 (1) For the purposes of this Schedule a loan is a relevant loan if and to the extent that money or money's worth made available under the loan is used to finance, directly or indirectly—

(a) the acquisition by an individual, a partnership or the trustees of a settlement of—

(i) a UK residential property interest, or

(ii) property to which paragraph 2 to any extent applies, or

(b) the acquisition by an individual, a partnership or the trustees of a settlement of an interest in a close company or a partnership ("the intermediary") and the acquisition by the intermediary of property within paragraph (a)(i) or (ii).

(2) In this paragraph references to money or money's worth made available under a loan or sale proceeds being used "indirectly" to finance the acquisition of something include the money or money's worth or sale proceeds being used to finance—

(a) the acquisition of any property the proceeds of sale of which are used directly or indirectly to finance the acquisition of that thing, or

(b) the making, or repayment, of a loan to finance the acquisition of that thing.

(3) In this paragraph references to the acquisition of a UK residential property interest by an individual, a partnership, the trustees of a settlement or a close company include the maintenance, or an enhancement, of the value of a UK residential property interest which is (as the case may be) the property of the individual, property comprised in the settlement or property of the partnership or close company.

(4) Where the UK residential property interest by virtue of which a loan is a relevant loan is disposed of, the loan ceases to be a relevant loan.

(5) Where a proportion of the UK residential property interest by virtue of which a loan is a relevant loan is disposed of, the loan ceases to be a relevant loan by the same proportion.

(6) In this Schedule, references to a loan include an acknowledgment of debt by a person or any other arrangement under which a debt arises; and in such a case references to money or money's worth made available under the loan are to the amount of the debt.

PART 2

SUPPLEMENTARY

Disposals and repayments

5 (1) This paragraph applies to—

(a) property which constitutes consideration in money or money's worth for the disposal of property to which paragraph 2 or paragraph 3(a) applies;

(b) any money or money's worth paid in respect of a creditor's rights falling within paragraph 3(a);

(c) any property directly or indirectly representing property within paragraph (a) or (b).

(2) If and to the extent that this paragraph applies to any property—

(a) for the two-year period it is not excluded property by virtue of section 6(1), (1A) or (2) or 48(3)(a), (3A) or (4), and

(b) if it is held in a qualifying foreign currency account within the meaning of section 157 (non-residents' bank accounts), that section does not apply to it for the two-year period.

(3) The two-year period is the period of two years beginning with the date of—

    (a) the disposal referred to in sub-paragraph (1)(a), or

    (b) the payment referred to in sub-paragraph (1)(b).

(4) The value of any property within sub-paragraph (1)(c) is to be treated as not exceeding the relevant amount.

(5) The relevant amount is—

    (a) where the property within sub-paragraph (1)(c) directly or indirectly represents property within sub-paragraph (1)(a) ("the consideration"), the value of the consideration at the time of the disposal referred to in that sub-paragraph, and

    (b) where the property within sub-paragraph (1)(c) directly or indirectly represents property within sub-paragraph (1)(b), the amount of the money or money's worth paid as mentioned in that sub-paragraph.

Tax avoidance arrangements

6 (1) In determining whether or to what extent property situated outside the United Kingdom is excluded property, no regard is to be had to any arrangements the purpose or one of the main purposes of which is to secure a tax advantage by avoiding or minimising the effect of paragraph 1 or 5.

(2) In this paragraph—

"tax advantage" has the meaning given in section 208 of the Finance Act 2013;

"arrangements" includes any scheme, transaction or series of transactions, agreement or understanding (whether or not legally enforceable and whenever entered into) and any associated operations.

Double taxation relief arrangements

7 (1) Nothing in any double taxation relief arrangements made with the government of a territory outside the United Kingdom is to be read as preventing a person from being liable for any amount of inheritance tax by virtue of paragraph 1 or 5 in relation to any chargeable transfer if under the law of that territory—

    (a) no tax of a character similar to inheritance tax is charged on that chargeable transfer, or

    (b) a tax of a character similar to inheritance tax is charged in relation to that chargeable transfer at an effective rate of 0% (otherwise than by virtue of a relief or exemption).

(2) In this paragraph—

"double taxation relief arrangements" means arrangements having effect under section 158(1);

"effective rate" means the rate found by expressing the tax chargeable as a percentage of the amount by reference to which it is charged.

PART 3

INTERPRETATION

UK residential property interest

8 (1) In this Schedule "UK residential property interest" means an interest in UK land—

    (a) where the land consists of a dwelling,

    (b) where and to the extent that the land includes a dwelling, or

    (c) where the interest subsists under a contract for an off-plan purchase.

(2) For the purposes of sub-paragraph (1)(b), the extent to which land includes a dwelling is to be determined on a just and reasonable basis.

(3) In this paragraph—

"interest in UK land" has the meaning given by paragraph 2 of Schedule B1 to the 1992 Act (and the power in sub-paragraph (5) of that paragraph applies for the purposes of this Schedule);

"the land", in relation to an interest in UK land which is an interest subsisting for the benefit of land, is a reference to the land for the benefit of which the interest subsists;

"dwelling" has the meaning given by paragraph 4 of Schedule B1 to the 1992 Act (and the power in paragraph 5 of that Schedule applies for the purposes of this Schedule);

"contract for an off-plan purchase" has the meaning given by paragraph 1(6) of Schedule B1 to the 1992 Act.

Close companies

9 (1) In this Schedule—

"close company" means a company within the meaning of the Corporation Tax Acts which is (or would be if resident in the United Kingdom) a close company for the purposes of those Acts;

references to an interest in a close company are to the rights and interests that a participator in a close company has in that company.

(2) In this paragraph—

"participator", in relation to a close company, means any person who is (or would be if the company were resident in the United Kingdom) a participator in relation to that company within the meaning given by section 454 of the Corporation Tax Act 2010;

references to rights and interests in a close company include references to rights and interests in the assets of the company available for distribution among the participators in the event of a winding-up or in any other circumstances.

Partnerships

10 In this Schedule "partnership" means—

(a) a partnership within the Partnership Act 1890,
(b) a limited partnership registered under the Limited Partnerships Act 1907,
(c) a limited liability partnership formed under the Limited Liability Partnerships Act 2000 or the Limited Liability Partnerships Act (Northern Ireland) 2002, or
(d) a firm or entity of a similar character to either of those mentioned in paragraph (a) or (b) formed under the law of a country or territory outside the United Kingdom."

Consequential and supplementary amendments

2 IHTA 1984 is amended as follows.

3 In section 6 (excluded property), at the end insert—

"(5) This section is subject to Schedule A1 (non-excluded overseas property)."

4 In section 48 (excluded property)—

(a) in subsections (3) and (3A), at the end insert "and to Schedule A1";
(b) in subsection (4), at the end (but on a new line) insert "This subsection is subject to Schedule A1."

5 In section 65 (charge at other times), after subsection (7B) (as inserted by section 30) insert—

"(7C) Tax shall not be charged under this section by reason only that property comprised in a settlement ceases to any extent to be property to which paragraph 2 or 3 of Schedule A1 applies and thereby becomes excluded property by virtue of section 48(3)(a) above.

(7D) Tax shall not be charged under this section where property comprised in a settlement or any part of that property—

(a) is, by virtue of paragraph 5(2)(a) of Schedule A1, not excluded property for the two year period referred to in that paragraph, but
(b) becomes excluded property at the end of that period."

6 In section 157 (non-residents' bank accounts), after subsection (3) insert—

"(3A) This section is subject to paragraph 5 of Schedule A1 (non-excluded overseas property)."

7 In section 237 (imposition of charge), after subsection (2) insert—

"(2A) Where tax is charged by virtue of Schedule A1 on the value transferred by a chargeable transfer, the reference in subsection (1)(a) to property to the value of which the value transferred is wholly or partly attributable includes the UK residential property interest (within the meaning of that Schedule) to which the charge to tax relates."

8 In section 272 (general interpretation), in the definition of "excluded property", after "above" insert "and Schedule A1".

Commencement

9 (1) The amendments made by this Schedule have effect in relation to times on or after 6 April 2017.

(2) But for the purposes of paragraph 5(1) of Schedule A1 to IHTA 1984 as inserted by this Schedule—

(a) paragraph (a) of that paragraph does not apply in relation to a disposal of property occurring before 6 April 2017, and

(b) paragraph (b) of that paragraph does not apply in relation to a payment of money or money's worth occurring before 6 April 2017.

Transitional provision

10 (1) Sub-paragraphs (2) and (3) apply if an amount of inheritance tax—

(a) would not be charged but for the amendments made by this Schedule, or

(b) is, because of those amendments, greater than it would otherwise have been.

(2) Section 233 of IHTA 1984 (interest on unpaid inheritance tax) applies in relation to the amount of inheritance tax as if the reference, in the closing words of subsection (1) of that section, to the end of the period mentioned in paragraph (a), (aa), (b) or (c) of that subsection were a reference to—

(a) the end of that period, or

(b) if later, the end of the month immediately following the month in which this Act is passed.

(3) Subsection (1) of section 234 of IHTA 1984 (cases where inheritance tax payable by instalments carries interest only from instalment dates) applies in relation to the amount of inheritance tax as if the reference, in the closing words of that subsection, to the date at which an instalment is payable were a reference to—

(a) the date at which the instalment is payable, or

(b) if later, the end of the month immediately following the month in which this Act is passed.

11 (1) Sub-paragraph (2) applies if—

(a) a person is liable as mentioned in section 216(1)(c) of IHTA 1984 (trustee liable on 10-year anniversary, and other trust cases) for an amount of inheritance tax charged on an occasion, and

(b) but for the amendments made by this Schedule—

(i) no inheritance tax would be charged on that occasion, or

(ii) a lesser amount of inheritance tax would be charged on that occasion.

(2) Section 216(6)(ad) of IHTA 1984 (delivery date for accounts required by section 216(1)(c)) applies in relation to the account to be delivered in connection with the occasion as if the reference to the expiration of the period of 6 months from the end of the month in which the occasion occurs were a reference to—

(a) the expiration of that period, or

(b) if later, the end of the month immediately following the month in which this Act is passed.

GENERAL NOTE

The introduction to this legislation is given in the commentary to section 33 "Inheritance tax on overseas property representing UK residential property". As stated therein Schedule 10 extends the scope of inheritance tax (IHT), so that IHT will apply to:

- UK residential property owned by foreign domiciliaries (or trusts settled by foreign domiciliaries) through a foreign company or partnership;
- relevant loans (broadly a loan where the funds are used for the acquisition, maintenance or enhancement of an interest in UK residential property); and
- security, collateral or a guarantee given in connection with a relevant loan.

Paragraph 1 inserts into IHTA 1984 new "Sch A1 Non-Excluded Overseas Property". Commencement provisions (Sch 10, para 9(1)) provide that the legislation will be effective from 6 April 2017.

New IHTA 1984 Sch A – Non-Excluded Overseas Property

The new schedule is divided into three parts as follows:

- Part 1 – Overseas property with value attributable to UK residential property.
- Part 2 – Supplementary.

– Part 3 – Interpretation.

Overview

To the extent to which either IHTA 1984 Sch A1 para 2 or para 3 applies para 1 overrides IHTA 1984 s 6(1) and IHTA 1984 s 48(3)(a). This means that the new legislation has priority over both:

– the general excluded property rule, which provides that overseas property is not subject to IHT if the individual beneficially entitled to it is a foreign domiciliary; and
– the excluded property provision for a trust, which provides that overseas property comprised in a settlement (but not a reversionary interest in the property) will be excluded property provided the settlor was foreign domiciled when the settlement was made.

IHTA 1984 Sch A1 para 2 deals with close company and partnership interests in UK residential property.

IHTA 1984 Sch A1 para 3 deals with:

– relevant loans (broadly a loan where the funds are used for the acquisition, maintenance or enhancement of an interest in UK residential property); and
– money or money's worth given as security, collateral or a guarantee in connection with a relevant loan.

IHTA 1984 Sch A1 para 4 contains supplementary provisions in connection with para 3 (defining relevant loan and when a loan ceases to be a relevant loan).

Where, after 5 April 2017, there are disposals of UK residential property or a relevant loan is repaid IHTA 1984 Sch A1 para 5 extends the IHT charges further by introducing a "tail", so that IHT will still be due on the consideration or loan repayment if the disposal or repayment occurs within two years of a subsequent IHT chargeable event.

IHTA 1984 Sch A1 para 6 is a wide anti-avoidance provision introduced to counter any arrangements to mitigate or avoid IHT under Sch A1.

IHTA 1984 Sch A1 para 7 is concerned with double tax arrangements.

IHTA 1984 Sch A1 paras 8 to 10 collectively form Part 3 of the Schedule and provide interpretations for "UK residential property interest ", "close companies" and "partnerships"

Definitions

"UK residential property interest" is defined by new para 8. It means an "interest in UK land":

– where the land consists of a "dwelling";
– where and to the extent that the land includes a dwelling (the extent to which land includes a dwelling is to be determined on a just and reasonable basis); or
– where an interest subsists under a "contract for off plan purchase".

The meanings for "interest in UK land", "dwelling" and "contract for an off plan purchase" are taken from the legislation governing the charge to CGT on non-UK residents (TCGA 1992 Sch B1.

"Close companies" are defined by IHTA 1984 Sch A1 para 9. Close company means a company which is, *or would be if resident in the UK*, close for the purposes of the Corporation Tax Acts. References in the legislation to an interest in a close company are to the "rights and interests" that a "participator" in a close company has in that company.

"Participator", in relation to a close company, means any person who is (or would be if the company were UK resident) a participator in that company within the meaning given by CTA 2010 s 454. That is a "participator" is a person having a share or interest in the capital or income of the company. Examples of participator are:

(a) a person who possesses, or is entitled to acquire, share capital or voting rights in the company;
(b) a loan creditor of the company;
(c) a person who possesses a right to receive or participate in distributions of the company (disregarding the wider definition of distribution at CTA 2010 s 1000(2));
(d) a person who possesses a right to receive any amount payable by the company (in cash or in kind) to loan creditors by way of premium upon redemption;
(e) a person who is entitled to acquire such right as is mentioned in (c) and/or (d); and
(f) a person who is entitled to secure that income or assets (whether present or

future) of the company will be applied directly or indirectly for their benefit (investment bond arrangements are to be ignored).

For the purposes of determining whether a person is a participator they are treated as entitled to do anything which they will be entitled to do in the future.

References to "rights and interests" in a close company include references to rights and interests in the assets of the company available for distribution among the participators in the event of a winding-up or in any other circumstances.

"Partnerships" are defined by IHTA 1984 Sch A1 para 10. The definition includes any entity which is:

(a) within the Partnership Act 1890;
(b) a limited partnership registered under the Limited Partnerships Act 1907;
(c) a limited liability partnership formed under the Limited Liability Partnerships Act 2000 or the Limited Liability Partnerships Act (Northern Ireland) 2002; or
(d) a firm or entity of a similar character to either of those mentioned in (a) or (b) formed under the law of a country or territory outside of the UK.

Close company and partnership interests

IHTA 1984 Sch A1 para 2 (when combined with para 1) is the provision that, if and to the extent that the value of the interest in the shares, capital or partnership is attributable to a UK residential property interest, brings within the IHT charge:

− shares in offshore companies that would be close companies if UK resident; and
− interests in overseas partnerships.

The specific conditions that must be met for the extended IHT charge over a UK residential property interest to be met are set down at sub-para (2). The value of the interest must be either:

− directly attributable to a UK residential property interest; or
− attributable to a UK residential property interest by virtue only of one or more of the following:
  i. an interest in a close company;
  ii. an interest in a partnership;
  iii. property to which para 3 (relevant loans and security, collateral or guarantees connected to the relevant loans) applies.

There is a 5% de minimis exemption set down in sub-para (3) which provides that interests will be disregarded where:

− the value of the person's interest in the close company is less than 5% of the total value of all the interests in the close company; or
− the value of the person's interest in the partnership is less than 5% of the total value of all the interests in the partnerships.

In determining whether the 5% de minimis limit is breached it is necessary to identify all connected persons with interests in the close company or partnership and then treat the value of the person's interest as increased by the aggregate value of the connected persons' interests (see sub-para (4)).

Where there is just UK residential property within the owning entity, debts can be offset for IHT purposes in determining the value of participations deriving from UK residential property. There is, however, a special rule (sub-para (5)) for the attribution of liabilities where the owning entity has other assets. In such a case, even if the debt is secured against the UK residential property, for the purposes of calculating this IHT charge the debt has to be allocated across all the assets in proportion to the market value at the time of the chargeable event.

Example 1

The Pegasus Overseas Discretionary Trust was settled by a foreign domiciliary (who is not deemed UK domiciled). The trust owns all of Unicorn Overseas Ltd. In turn at the time of the decennial charge the company owns:

-all of Unicorn Mews a UK residential property worth £20 million at the time of the chargeable event; and
-an offshore share portfolio worth £100 million at the time of the chargeable event.

A mortgage of £12 million was taken out by the company to acquire Unicorn Mews and is secured on the property.

The total value of all the assets within Unicorn Overseas Ltd is £120 million. The provisions mean that only one sixth of the £12 million mortgage can be deducted in calculating the value attributable to UK residential property. That is only £2 million can be deducted.

Loans, security, collateral and guarantees

IHTA 1984 Sch A1 para 3 (when combined with new para 1) is the provision that brings within the scope of IHT:

- The rights of a creditor in connection with a loan which meets the "relevant loan" definition.
- Money or money's worth held or made available as security, collateral or a guarantee given in connection with a relevant loan. Where the security, collateral or guarantee is in excess of the relevant loan the excess is not caught by Sch A1.

IHTA 1984 Sch A1 para 4 provides the relevant loan definition. A loan is a relevant loan if and to the extent that money or money's worth is made available to finance the acquisition (directly or indirectly):

(1) by an individual, a partnership or the trustees of a settlement of:
   (a) a UK residential property interest; or
   (b) property to which para 2 (see commentary above) applies
(2) by an individual, a partnership or the trustees of a settlement of an interest in either a close company or a partnership (referred to in the legislation as "the intermediary") and the acquisition by the intermediary of property within (a) or (b) above.

There is a relevant loan as a result of "indirect" provision of finance where:

- the loan was originally made to acquire a property that was sold and the sales proceeds are used to acquire the UK residential property interest; and
- the loan is taken out to make or repay an initial loan taken out to acquire the UK residential property interest.

The scope of IHTA 1984 Sch A1 para 3 is widened by para 4(3), which states that references to the acquisition of a UK residential property interest include the maintenance or an enhancement of the value of that UK residential property interest.

A loan ceases to be a relevant loan where the UK residential property interest is disposed of (para 4(4)). If there is only a partial disposal of the UK residential property interest the relevant loan will be proportionately reduced in line with the percentage reduction in the UK residential property holding (para 4(5)).

The definition of loan in Sch A1 includes (see para 4(6)):

- an acknowledgment of a debt by a person; or
- any other arrangement under which a debt arises.

Disposals and repayments

Additional charging provisions (IHTA 1984 Sch A1 para 5) apply where, after 5 April 2017, property within para 2 is sold or a relevant loan is repaid within two years of a subsequent chargeable event.

The disposal provisions apply:

(1) to property which constitutes consideration in money or money's worth for the disposal of property falling within para 2 (see commentary above);
(2) to property which constitutes consideration in money or money's worth for the disposal of a relevant loan; and
(3) to any property directly or indirectly representing property within 1 or 2 above.

The repayment provisions apply:

(1) to money or money's worth that constitutes repayment of a relevant loan; and
(2) to any property directly or indirectly representing property within 1 above.

During the two-year period the property will continue to be subject to IHT. Where there is a disposal the two-year period runs from the disposal date. Where there is a loan repayment the two-year period runs from that date.

Example 2

> The Unicorn Overseas Discretionary Trust was settled by a foreign domiciliary (who is not deemed UK domiciled) on 17 June 2008. In December 2010 it lent a beneficiary £15 million to acquire a UK residential property and carry out enhancement work. The loan is repaid by way of a direct transfer to the trust's Jersey account on 30 November 2017.
>
> The £15 million loan was a relevant loan (since it was used to acquire UK residential property) and the decennial charge is within two years of the loan being repaid so it is still deemed to be relevant property for the purposes of the IHTA 1984 Sch A1 para 5 charge. Since 6 April 2017 is the effective date for the legislation quarters will only be counted from then.

The commencement provisions include transitional provisions (Sch 10, para 9(2)) such that IHT does not apply where:
- the disposal of the UK residential property occurred prior to 6 April 2017; or
- the relevant loan was repaid in money or money's worth prior to 6 April 2017.

Example 3

The Pegasus Overseas Discretionary Trust was settled by a foreign domiciliary (who is not deemed UK domiciled) on 17 June 2008. In December 2010 it lent a beneficiary £15 million to acquire a UK residential property and carry out enhancement work. The loan is repaid by way of a direct transfer to the trust's Jersey account on 30 November 2016.

The loan is repaid within two years of the decennial charge but since the repayment date is prior to 6 April 2017 it is not within the IHTA 1984 Sch A1 para 5 charging provisions.

Tax avoidance arrangements

The Government was keen that the extension of IHT should not be circumvented. As such, para 6 (tax avoidance arrangements) is included within IHTA 1984 Sch A1.

IHTA 1984 Sch A1 para 6(1) states that in determining whether overseas property is regarded as excluded property "arrangements" will be disregarded where their purpose or one of their main purposes is to secure a "tax advantage" by avoiding or minimising the effect of the new IHT provisions.

"Arrangements" are defined as including any scheme, transaction or series of transactions, agreement or understanding (whether or not legally enforceable and whenever entered into) and any associated operations.

"Tax advantage" is given the same meaning as FA 2013 s 208. That is:
- relief or increased relief from tax;
- repayment or increased repayment of tax;
- avoidance or reduction of a charge to tax or an assessment to tax;
- deferral of a payment of tax or advancement of a payment of tax; and
- avoidance of an obligation to deduct or account for tax.

Double taxation relief arrangements

IHTA 1984 Sch A1 para 7 is concerned with double taxation relief arrangements (as per IHTA 1984 s 158(1)) under international tax treaties.

It is intended to be a treaty override provision, so that the UK IHT charge as per paras 1 or 5 can still apply in relation to any chargeable event, where under the law of the territory with whom the UK has concluded the agreement:
- no tax of a character similar to IHT is charged on the chargeable IHT event; or
- a tax of a character similar to IHT is charged in relation to that chargeable transfer but at an "effective rate" of 0% (otherwise than by virtue of relief or exemption).

"Effective rate" is defined as the rate found by expressing the tax payable as a percentage of the transfer amount.

The effectiveness of IHTA 1984 Sch A1 para 7 will depend on the precise terms of the treaty.

Consequential and supplementary amendments

Schedule 10 makes various consequential and supplementary amendments to IHTA 1984 to tie it in with new IHTA 1984 Sch A1.

Paragraph 3 provides for a new sub-section (5) to be inserted at the end of IHTA 1984 s 6 (excluded property) giving Sch A1 priority over the standard excluded property provisions for individuals. Para 4 does the same thing for IHTA 1984 s 48 (the trust excluded property provision). Para 6 does a similar thing for IHTA 1984 s 157 (non-residents' foreign currency bank accounts: excluded property when for the purposes of valuing an estate immediately before the death of a foreign domiciliary). For IHTA 1984 s 157 it is only necessary to provide that Sch A1 para 5 has priority since only disposal proceeds and loan repayments could be within the foreign currency bank account.

Paragraph 5 inserts provisions into IHTA 1984 s 65 (the relevant property exit charge) that prevent an exit charge arising where any property that was caught by Sch A1 ceases to be so caught and becomes excluded property. For example, there will be no exit charge where a trust had a relevant debt which is repaid with funds going into a Jersey bank account and the two year period set down in IHTA 1984 Sch A1 para 5 has elapsed.

Paragraph 7 inserts a new sub-section into IHTA 1984 s 237 (imposition of charge) to specify that where there is a chargeable transfer resulting in an IHT charge under Sch A1 there will be a charge on the UK residential property interest (with the definition being that set down in Sch A1) to the value of the unpaid tax.

Paragraph 8 adjusts the definition of excluded property given at IHTA 1984 s 272 (general interpretation) so that in addition to IHTA 1984 s 6 and s 48 it also refers to Sch A1.

Commencement

There is one general commencement provision (Sch 10 para 9(1)) and one transitional provision (Sch 10 para 9(2)).

The general provision provides that the legislation within Sch 10 has effect in relation to times on or after 6 April 2017. The transitional provision relates to IHTA 1984 Sch A1 para 5 and has been discussed above.

Transitional provisions

Finance (No 2) Act 2017 received Royal Assent on 16 November 2017 (in excess of seven months into the tax year). This late date for Royal Assent combined with the retrospective commencement date would, without transitional relief, have been an issue for some personal representatives and trustees. This is because assets that were excluded property under the law in force at the time of a chargeable event will retrospectively become chargeable.

Example 4

An individual who is a foreign domiciliary dies on 11 April 2017 owning all the shares in a foreign company. The only asset of the foreign company is a UK residential property. At the date of death the foreign company shares were excluded property. However, when Finance (No 2) Act 2017 becomes law, the foreign company shares will retrospectively become chargeable.

Example 5

A relevant property trust settled by a foreign domiciliary has as its only property all the shares in a foreign company. The only asset of the foreign company is a UK residential property. The decennial anniversary of the trust is 11 April 2017. At the date of the decennial charge the foreign company shares were excluded property. However, when Finance (No 2) Act 2017 becomes law, the foreign company shares will retrospectively become chargeable.

Paragraphs 10 and 11 provide relief such that where the date is later:
- interest on underpaid tax will only run from the end of the month immediately following the month in which Royal Assent occurs;
- interest on an instalment payment will only run from the end of the month immediately following the month in which Royal Assent occurs; and
- the delivery date for IHT accounts due from trustees will be extended such that it runs from the end of the month immediately following the month in which Royal Assent occurs.

SCHEDULE 11

EMPLOYMENT INCOME PROVIDED THROUGH THIRD PARTIES: LOANS ETC OUTSTANDING ON 5 APRIL 2019

Section 34

PART 1

APPLICATION OF PART 7A OF ITEPA 2003

Relevant step

1 (1) A person ("P") is treated as taking a relevant step for the purposes of Part 7A of ITEPA 2003 if—

(a) P has made a loan, or a quasi-loan, to a relevant person,

(b) the loan or quasi-loan was made on or after 6 April 1999, and

(c) an amount of the loan or quasi-loan is outstanding immediately before the end of 5 April 2019.

(2) P is treated as taking the step immediately before—

(a) the end of the approved repayment date, if P has made a loan which is an approved fixed term loan on 5 April 2019, or

(b) the end of 5 April 2019, in any other case.

(3) Where P is treated by this paragraph as taking a relevant step, references to "the relevant step" in section 554A(1)(e)(i) and (ii) of ITEPA 2003 have effect as if they were references to the step of making the loan or, as the case may be, quasi-loan.

(4) For the purposes of section 554Z3(1) of ITEPA 2003 (value of relevant step), the step is to be treated as involving a sum of money equal to the amount of the loan or quasi-loan that is outstanding at the time P is treated as taking the step.

(5) Subsections (2) and (3) of section 554C of ITEPA 2003 ("relevant person") apply for the purposes of this Schedule as they apply for the purposes of that section.

(6) Sub-paragraph (1) is subject to paragraphs 23 and 24 (accelerated payments).

(7) For the purposes of this paragraph, whether an amount of a loan or quasi-loan is outstanding at a particular time—

(a) is to be determined in accordance with the following provisions of this Schedule, and

(b) does not depend on the loan or quasi-loan subsisting at that time.

(8) References in this Schedule and in Part 7A of ITEPA 2003 to a relevant step within paragraph 1 of this Schedule are to be read as references to a relevant step which a person is treated by this paragraph as taking.

Meaning of "loan", "quasi-loan" and "approved repayment date"

2 (1) In this Part of this Schedule "loan" includes—

(a) any form of credit;

(b) a payment that is purported to be made by way of a loan.

(2) For the purposes of paragraph 1, P makes a "quasi-loan" to a relevant person if (and when) P acquires a right (the "acquired debt")—

(a) which is a right to a payment or a transfer of assets, and

(b) in respect of which the condition in sub-paragraph (3) is met.

(3) The condition is met in relation to a right if there is a connection (direct or indirect) between the acquisition of the right and—

(a) a payment made, by way of a loan or otherwise, to the relevant person, or

(b) a transfer of assets to the relevant person.

(4) Where a quasi-loan or a loan made by P to a relevant person is replaced, directly or indirectly, by a loan or another loan (the "replacement loan"), references in paragraph 1 to the loan are references to the replacement loan.

(5) Where a loan or a quasi-loan made by P to a relevant person is replaced, directly or indirectly, by a quasi-loan or another quasi-loan (the "replacement quasi-loan"), references in paragraph 1 to the quasi-loan are references to the replacement quasi-loan.

(6) In this Part of this Schedule, "approved repayment date", in relation to an approved fixed term loan, means the date by which, under the terms of the loan at the time of making the application for approval under paragraph 20, the whole of the loan must be repaid.

Meaning of "outstanding": loans

3 (1) An amount of a loan is "outstanding" for the purposes of paragraph 1 if the relevant principal amount exceeds the repayment amount.

(2) In sub-paragraph (1) "relevant principal amount", in relation to a loan, means the total of—

(a) the initial principal amount lent, and

(b) any sums that have become principal under the loan, otherwise than by capitalisation of interest.

(3) In sub-paragraph (1) "repayment amount", in relation to a loan, means the total of—

(a) the amount of principal under the loan that has been repaid before 17 March 2016, and

(b) payments in money made by the relevant person on or after 17 March 2016 by way of repayment of principal under the loan.

4 (1) A payment is to be disregarded for the purposes of paragraph 3(3)(b) if—

(a) there is any connection (direct or indirect) between the payment and a tax avoidance arrangement (other than the arrangement under which the loan was made), or

(b) the payment, or a sum or asset directly or indirectly representing the payment, is the subject of a relevant step (as defined in section 554A(2) of ITEPA 2003) that is taken—

    (i) after the payment is made, but
    (ii) before the end of the relevant date.

(2) But a payment is not to be disregarded under sub-paragraph (1)(b) if, by the end of the relevant date, each relevant tax liability has been paid in full.

(3) For the purposes of this paragraph, each of the following is a "relevant tax liability"—

(a) any liability for income tax arising by virtue of the application of Chapter 2 by reason of the relevant step mentioned in sub-paragraph (1)(b), and

(b) where section 554Z6 of ITEPA 2003 (overlap with certain earnings) applies because that relevant step gives rise to relevant earnings for the purposes of that section, any liability for income tax in respect of those relevant earnings.

(4) In this paragraph, "relevant date" means—

(a) the approved repayment date, if P has made a loan which is an approved fixed term loan on 5 April 2019, or

(b) 5 April 2019, in any other case.

(5) Sub-paragraph (6) applies if a payment is disregarded under sub-paragraph (1)(b).

(6) The value of the relevant step treated as taken by paragraph 1 is not reduced under section 554Z5(3) of ITEPA 2003 (overlap with money or asset subject to earlier tax liability) by the amount of the sum, or the value of the asset, which is the subject of the relevant step mentioned in sub-paragraph (1)(b) unless the payment condition is met by reason of section 554Z5(4)(a) and (b)(ii) being met.

5 (1) This paragraph applies where—

(a) a person ("P") has made a loan to a relevant person,

(b) the loan was made on or after 6 April 1999, and

(c) before the end of 5 April 2019, A or B acquires (whether or not for consideration) a right to payment of the whole or part of the loan.

(2) The amount of the loan in respect of which A or B acquires a right to payment is to be treated—

(a) for the purposes of paragraph 1(1) as an amount, of the loan made by P to the relevant person, that is outstanding immediately before the end of 5 April 2019;

(b) for the purposes of paragraph 1(4) and section 554Z3(1) of ITEPA 2003, as an amount of the loan that is outstanding at the time P is treated as taking the relevant step under paragraph 1(1).

(3) Where a quasi-loan or a loan made by P to a relevant person is replaced, directly or indirectly, by a loan or another loan (the "replacement loan"), references in sub-paragraphs (1) and (2) to the loan are references to the replacement loan.

Meaning of "outstanding": loans in currencies other than sterling

6 (1) In paragraphs 7 to 10 "the loan currency", in relation to a loan, means the currency in which the initial principal amount of the loan is denominated (whether or not that amount is paid in that currency).

(2) For the purposes of paragraphs 7 to 10, the value of an amount in a particular currency is to be determined by reference to an appropriate spot rate of exchange.

7 (1) This paragraph applies in relation to a loan where the loan currency is a currency other than sterling.

(2) But this paragraph does not apply if paragraph 10 applies in relation to the loan.

(3) The amount of the loan that is outstanding, at the time P is treated as taking the relevant step, is to be calculated in sterling as follows—

Step 1

Calculate, in the loan currency, the amount that is outstanding at that time.

Step 2

Take the value in sterling, at that time, of that amount.

(4) See paragraph 8 for provision about repayments made in a currency other than the loan currency.

Repayments in currencies other than the loan currency

8 (1) This paragraph applies in relation to a loan where—

(a) payments in money are made by way of repayment of principal under the loan, and

(b) some or all of the payments are made in a currency other than the loan currency.

(2) But this paragraph does not apply if paragraph 10 applies in relation to the loan.

(3) For the purposes of calculating the repayment amount in relation to the loan, the amount of each of the payments referred to in sub-paragraph (1)(b) is an amount equal to its value in the loan currency on the date it is made.

Loans made in a depreciating currency

9 (1) Paragraph 10 applies in relation to a loan where—

(a) the loan currency is a currency other than sterling, and

(b) it is reasonable to suppose that the main reason, or one of the main reasons, for the loan being made in that currency is that the loan currency is expected to depreciate as against sterling during the loan period.

(2) The "loan period", in relation to a loan, is the period—

(a) beginning at the time the loan is made, and

(b) ending with the time by which, under the terms of the loan, the whole of the loan is to be repaid.

10 (1) Where this paragraph applies in relation to a loan—

(a) paragraphs 7 and 8 do not apply in relation to the loan, and

(b) sub-paragraphs (2) to (5) apply for the purposes of calculating the amount of the loan that is outstanding at the time P is treated as taking the relevant step.

(2) The relevant principal amount, in relation to the loan, is an amount equal to the total of—

(a) the value in sterling, at the reference date, of the initial principal amount lent, and

(b) the value in sterling, at the reference date, of any sums that become principal under the loan, otherwise than by capitalisation of interest.

(3) The "reference date"—

(a) in relation to an amount within sub-paragraph (2)(a), means the date on which the loan is made, and

(b) in relation to a sum within sub-paragraph (2)(b), means the date on which the sum becomes principal.

(4) The repayment amount, in relation to the loan, is an amount equal to the total of—

(a) the amount of principal under the loan that has been repaid in sterling, and

(b) where payments are made, in a currency other than sterling, by way of repayment of principal under the loan, the amount equal to the sterling value of the payments.

(5) The "sterling value" of a payment is its value in sterling on the date it is made.

Meaning of "outstanding": quasi-loans

11 (1) An amount of a quasi-loan is outstanding for the purposes of paragraph 1 if the initial debt amount exceeds the repayment amount.

(2) In sub-paragraph (1) "initial debt amount", in relation to a quasi-loan, means the total of—

(a) an amount equal to the value of the acquired debt (see paragraph 2(2)), and

(b) where P subsequently acquires a further right (an "additional debt") to a payment, or transfer of assets, in connection with the payment mentioned in paragraph 2(3)(a) or (as the case may be) the transfer mentioned in paragraph 2(3)(b), an amount equal to the value of the additional debt.

(3) For the purposes of sub-paragraph (2)—

(a) where the acquired debt is a right to payment of an amount, the "value" of the debt is that amount,

(b) where the additional debt is a right to payment of an amount, the "value" of the debt is that amount, but is nil if the additional debt accrued to P by the capitalisation of interest on the acquired debt or another additional debt, and

(c) where the acquired debt or additional debt is a right to a transfer of assets, the "value" of the debt is an amount equal to—

   (i) the market value of the assets at the time the right is acquired (or the value of the right at that time if the assets are non-fungible and not in existence at that time), or
   (ii) if higher, the cost of the assets at that time.

(4) In sub-paragraph (1) "repayment amount", in relation to a quasi-loan, means the total of—

   (a) the amount (if any) by which the initial debt amount has been reduced (by way of repayment) before 17 March 2016,
   (b) payments in money (if any) made by the relevant person on or after 17 March 2016 by way of repayment of the initial debt amount, and
   (c) if the acquired debt or an additional debt is a right to a transfer of assets, and the assets have been transferred, an amount equal to the market value of the assets at the time of the transfer.

12 (1) A payment or transfer is to be disregarded for the purposes of paragraph 11(4)(b) or (c) if—

   (a) there is any connection (direct or indirect) between the payment or transfer and a tax avoidance arrangement (other than the arrangement under which the quasi-loan was made), or
   (b) the payment or the asset transferred, or a sum or asset directly or indirectly representing the payment or asset, is the subject of a relevant step (as defined in section 554A(2) of ITEPA 2003) that is taken—
      (i) after the payment is made or the asset transferred, but
      (ii) before the end of 5 April 2019.

(2) But a payment or transfer is not to be disregarded under sub-paragraph (1)(b) if, by the end of 5 April 2019, each relevant tax liability has been paid in full.

(3) For the purposes of this paragraph, each of the following is a "relevant tax liability"—

   (a) any liability for income tax arising by virtue of the application of Chapter 2 by reason of the relevant step mentioned in sub-paragraph (1)(b), and
   (b) where section 554Z6 of ITEPA 2003 (overlap with certain earnings) applies because that relevant step gives rise to relevant earnings for the purposes of that section, any liability for income tax in respect of those relevant earnings.

(4) Sub-paragraph (5) applies if a payment is disregarded under sub-paragraph (1)(b).

(5) The value of the relevant step treated as taken by paragraph 1 is not reduced under section 554Z5(3) of ITEPA 2003 (overlap with money or asset subject to earlier tax liability) by the amount of the sum, or the value of the asset, which is the subject of the relevant step mentioned in sub-paragraph (1)(b) unless the payment condition is met by reason of section 554Z5(4)(a) and (b)(ii) being met.

13 (1) This paragraph applies where—

   (a) a person ("P") has made a quasi-loan to a relevant person,
   (b) the quasi-loan was made on or after 6 April 1999, and
   (c) before the end of 5 April 2019, A or B acquires (whether or not for consideration) a right to the payment or transfer of assets mentioned in paragraph 2(2)(a).

(2) The amount equal to the value of the right acquired by A or B is to be treated—

   (a) for the purposes of paragraph 1(1) as an amount, of the quasi-loan made by P to the relevant person, that is outstanding immediately before the end of 5 April 2019;
   (b) for the purposes of paragraph 1(4) and section 554Z3(1) of ITEPA 2003, as an amount of the quasi-loan that is outstanding at the time P is treated as taking the relevant step under paragraph 1(1).

(3) For the purposes of sub-paragraph (2)—

   (a) where the right acquired by A or B is a right to payment of an amount, the "value" of the right is that amount;
   (b) where the right acquired by A or B is a right to a transfer of assets, the "value" of the right is an amount equal to—
      (i) the market value of the assets at the time the right is acquired (or the value of the right at that time if the assets are non-fungible and not in existence at that time), or
      (ii) if higher, the cost of the assets at that time.

(4) Where a loan or a quasi-loan made by P to a relevant person is replaced, directly or indirectly, by a quasi-loan or another quasi-loan (the "replacement quasi-loan"), references in sub-paragraphs (1) and (2) to the quasi-loan are references to the replacement quasi-loan.

Meaning of "outstanding": quasi-loans in currencies other than sterling

14 (1) Paragraphs 15 to 18 apply where P makes a quasi-loan to a relevant person by reason of acquiring a right to a payment in a particular currency (the "quasi-loan currency").

(2) For the purposes of paragraphs 15 to 18, the value of an amount in a particular currency is to be determined by reference to an appropriate spot rate of exchange.

15 (1) This paragraph applies in relation to the quasi-loan if the quasi-loan currency is a currency other than sterling.

(2) But this paragraph does not apply if paragraph 18 applies in relation to the quasi-loan.

(3) The amount of the quasi-loan that is outstanding, at the time P is treated as taking the relevant step, is to be calculated in sterling as follows—

Step 1

Calculate, in the quasi-loan currency, the amount that is outstanding at that time.

Step 2

Take the value in sterling, at that time, of that amount.

(4) See paragraph 16 for provision about repayments made in a currency other than the quasi-loan currency.

Repayments in currencies other than the quasi-loan currency

16 (1) This paragraph applies in relation to the quasi-loan if—

(a) payments in money are made by way of repayment of the initial debt amount, and
(b) some or all of the payments are made in a currency other than the quasi-loan currency.

(2) But this paragraph does not apply if paragraph 18 applies in relation to the quasi-loan.

(3) For the purposes of calculating the repayment amount in relation to the quasi-loan, the amount of each of the payments referred to in sub-paragraph (1)(b) is an amount equal to its value in the quasi-loan currency on the date it is made.

Quasi-loans made in a depreciating currency

17 (1) Paragraph 18 applies in relation to the quasi-loan if—

(a) the quasi-loan currency is a currency other than sterling, and
(b) it is reasonable to suppose that the main reason, or one of the main reasons, for the quasi-loan being made in that currency is that the quasi-loan currency is expected to depreciate during the quasi-loan period.

(2) The "quasi-loan period", in relation to a quasi-loan, is the period—

(a) beginning at the time the quasi-loan is made, and
(b) ending with the time by which, under the terms of the quasi-loan, the whole of the quasi-loan is to be repaid.

18 (1) Where this paragraph applies in relation to the quasi-loan—

(a) paragraphs 15 and 16 do not apply in relation to the quasi-loan, and
(b) sub-paragraphs (2) to (5) apply for the purposes of calculating the amount of the quasi-loan that is outstanding at the time P is treated as taking the relevant step.

(2) The initial debt amount, in relation to the quasi-loan, is an amount equal to the total of—

(a) the value in sterling, at the reference date, of the acquired debt, and
(b) the value in sterling, at the reference date, of any additional debt.

(3) The "reference date"—

(a) in relation to a right within sub-paragraph (2)(a), means the date on which P acquires it, and
(b) in relation to a right within sub-paragraph (2)(b), means the date on which P acquires it.

(4) The repayment amount, in relation to the quasi-loan, is an amount equal to the total of—

(a) the amount of the initial debt amount that has been repaid in sterling, and
(b) where payments are made, in a currency other than sterling, by way of repayment of the initial debt amount, the amount equal to the sterling value of the payments.

(5) The "sterling value" of a payment is its value in sterling on the date it is made.

Meaning of "approved fixed term loan"

19 (1) A loan is an "approved fixed term loan" on 5 April 2019 if, at any time on that day, it is a qualifying loan which has been approved by an officer of Revenue and Customs in accordance with paragraph 20.

(2) A loan is a "qualifying loan" if—

    (a) the loan was made before 9 December 2010,

    (b) the term of the loan cannot exceed 10 years, and

    (c) it is not an excluded loan under sub-paragraph (3).

(3) A loan is an excluded loan if, at any time after the loan was made—

    (a) the loan has been replaced, directly or indirectly, by another loan, or

    (b) the terms of the loan have been altered so as—

        (i) to meet the condition in sub-paragraph (2)(b), or

        (ii) to postpone the date by which, under the terms of the loan, the whole of the loan must be repaid.

PART 2
APPROVAL OF A QUALIFYING LOAN ETC.

Application to HMRC

20 (1) The liable person in relation to a qualifying loan may make an application to the Commissioners for Her Majesty's Revenue and Customs for approval of the loan.

(2) An officer of Revenue and Customs may grant such an application if satisfied that, in relation to the loan—

    (a) the qualifying payments condition is met (see paragraph 21), or

    (b) the commercial terms condition is met (see paragraph 22).

(3) Subject to sub-paragraph (4), an application may be made in 2018.

(4) An application may be made after 2018 if an officer of Revenue and Customs considers it is reasonable in all the circumstances for the liable person to make a late application.

(5) An application for an approval must be made in such form and manner, and contain such information, as may be specified by, or on behalf of, the Commissioners for Her Majesty's Revenue and Customs.

(6) An officer of Revenue and Customs must notify the applicant of the decision on an application.

(7) Where on an application under this paragraph a loan is approved, the approval may be revoked by an officer of Revenue and Customs if the officer considers that—

    (a) information provided in making the application contained an inaccuracy, and

    (b) the inaccuracy was deliberate on the applicant's part.

(8) Where approval is revoked under sub-paragraph (7), approval is to be treated as having been refused at the outset.

(9) In this paragraph "liable person", in relation to a loan, means the person who is liable for any tax on the value of the relevant step in relation to the loan under paragraph 1.

Qualifying payments condition

21 (1) The qualifying payments condition is met in relation to a qualifying loan if, during the relevant period—

    (a) payments have been made to the lender in respect of the repayment of the principal of the loan, and

    (b) the payments have been made at intervals not exceeding 53 weeks.

(2) The "relevant period" in relation to a loan is the period beginning with the making of the loan and ending with the making of the application.

Commercial terms condition

22 (1) The commercial terms condition is met in relation to a qualifying loan if—

    (a) either—

        (i) it is reasonable to assume that, had the qualifying loan been made in the ordinary course of a lending business, loans on terms comparable to those of the qualifying loan would have been available to members of the public, or

        (ii) the qualifying loan was made in the ordinary course of a lending business, and

(b) the borrower has, in all material respects, complied with the terms of the loan.

(2) For the purposes of sub-paragraph (1), a loan is made in the ordinary course of a lending business if it is made by a person in the ordinary course of a business carried on by the person which includes—

(a) the lending of money, or

(b) the supplying of goods or services on credit.

Accelerated payments

23 (1) Paragraph 24(1) applies where—

(a) a person ("P") would (ignoring paragraph 24) be treated as taking a relevant step within paragraph 1 by reason of making a loan, or a quasi-loan, to a relevant person,

(b) an accelerated payment notice, or a partner payment notice, relating to a relevant charge (the "accelerated payment notice") has been given under Chapter 3 of Part 4 of FA 2014,

(c) the relevant person makes a payment (the " accelerated payment") in respect of the understated or disputed tax to which the notice relates,

(d) the accelerated payment is made on or before the relevant date, and

(e) the amount of the loan or quasi-loan that, at the end of the relevant date, is outstanding for the purposes of paragraph 1 (see paragraphs 3 to 18) is equal to or less than the amount of the accelerated payment.

(2) In sub-paragraph (1)(b), "relevant charge" means a charge to tax arising by reason of a step taken pursuant to the relevant arrangement concerned.

(3) The reference in sub-paragraph (2) to the relevant arrangement concerned is a reference to the relevant arrangement in pursuance of which, or in connection with which, the loan or quasi-loan mentioned in sub-paragraph (1)(a) is made.

(4) In sub-paragraph (1)(d) and (e), " the relevant date" means—

(a) the approved repayment date, if P has made a loan which is an approved fixed term loan on 5 April 2019, or

(b) 5 April 2019, in any other case.

(5) In sub-paragraphs (1)(c) and (2)—

(a) the reference to tax includes a reference to relevant contributions, and

(b) the reference to a charge to tax includes a reference to a liability to pay relevant contributions;

and for those purposes "relevant contributions" has the same meaning as in Schedule 2 to the National Insurance Contributions Act 2015 (application of Part 4 of FA 2014 to national insurance contributions).

(6) If more than one notice relating to a particular relevant charge has been given—

(a) the reference in sub-paragraph (1)(e) to the amount of the accelerated payment is to be treated as a reference to the aggregate of the amounts of each accelerated payment in respect of which the conditions in sub-paragraph (1)(c) and (d) are met, and

(b) the reference in paragraph 24(2) to the accelerated payment notice is to be treated as a reference to the accelerated payment notices or any of them.

24 (1) The relevant person may make an application to the Commissioners for Her Majesty's Revenue and Customs for P to be treated—

(a) as taking the relevant step only if the condition in sub-paragraph (2) is met, and

(b) as doing so not at the time given by paragraph 1(2) but immediately before—

(i) the end of the 30 days beginning with the date on which the condition in sub-paragraph (2) becomes met, or

(ii) if later, the end of 5 April 2019.

(2) The condition is that, on the withdrawal of the accelerated payment notice or on the determination of an appeal, any part of the accelerated payment is repaid.

(3) Subject to sub-paragraph (4), an application under sub-paragraph (1) may be made in 2018.

(4) An application may be made after 2018 if an officer of Revenue and Customs considers it is reasonable in all the circumstances for the relevant person to make a late application.

(5) An application must be made in such form and manner, and contain such information, as may be specified by, or on behalf of, the Commissioners for Her Majesty's Revenue and Customs.

(6) An officer of Revenue and Customs must notify the applicant of the decision on an application under this paragraph.

(7) A favourable decision on an application under this paragraph may be revoked by an officer of Revenue and Customs if the officer considers that—

(a) information provided in making the application contained an inaccuracy, and

(b) the inaccuracy was deliberate on the applicant's part.

(8) Where the decision on an application is revoked under sub-paragraph (7), the application is to be treated as having been refused at the outset.

PART 3
EXCLUSIONS

Commercial transactions

25 Chapter 2 of Part 7A of ITEPA 2003 does not apply by reason of a relevant step within paragraph 1 which is treated as being taken by a person ("P") if—

(a) P is treated as taking a relevant step by that paragraph by reason of the payment of a sum of money by way of a loan,

(b) the loan is (at the time it is made) a loan on ordinary commercial terms within the meaning of section 176 of ITEPA 2003, ignoring conditions B and C in that section, and

(c) there is no connection (direct or indirect) between the relevant step and a tax avoidance arrangement.

26 In section 554F of ITEPA 2003 (exclusions: commercial transactions), at the end insert—

"(6) See paragraph 25 of Schedule 11 to F(No. 2)A 2017 for provision about exclusions where a loan is made on ordinary commercial terms and the relevant step is within paragraph 1 of that Schedule."

Transfer of employment-related loans

27 (1) Chapter 2 of Part 7A of ITEPA 2003 does not apply by reason of a relevant step within paragraph 1 which is treated as being taken by a person ("P") if—

(a) P is treated as taking a relevant step within that paragraph by reason of making a quasi-loan by acquiring a right to payment of an amount equal to the whole or part of a payment made by way of a loan to a relevant person (the "borrower"),

(b) the loan, at the time it was made, was an employment-related loan,

(c) at the time the right is acquired, the section 180 threshold is not exceeded in relation to the loan,

(d) at the time the right is acquired, the borrower is an employee, or a prospective employee, of P, and

(e) there is no connection (direct or indirect) between the acquisition of the right and a tax avoidance arrangement.

(2) Subsections (2) to (5) of section 554OA of ITEPA 2003 (section 180 threshold) apply for the purposes of this paragraph as they apply for the purposes of that section.

(3) In this paragraph, "employment-related loan" has the same meaning as it has for the purposes of Chapter 7 of Part 3.

28 In section 554OA of ITEPA 2003 (exclusions: transfer of employment-related loans), at the end insert—

"(6) See paragraph 27 of Schedule 11 to F(No. 2)A 2017 for provision about exclusions where a loan is an employment-related loan and the relevant step is within paragraph 1 of that Schedule."

Transactions under employee benefit packages

29 (1) Chapter 2 of Part 7A of ITEPA 2003 does not apply by reason of a relevant step within paragraph 1 which is treated as being taken by a person ("P") if—

(a) P is treated as taking a relevant step by that paragraph by reason of the payment of a sum of money by way of a loan,

(b) the step is not taken under a pension scheme,

(c) the loan was made for the sole purpose of a transaction of P's with A and which P entered into in the ordinary course of P's business,

(d) at the time the loan was made (the "relevant time")—

(i) a substantial proportion of P's business involved making similar loans to members of the public,

(ii) the transaction with A was part of a package of benefits which was available to a substantial proportion of B's employees, and

(iii) sub-paragraph (3) does not apply,

(e) the terms on which similar transactions were offered by P under the package of benefits mentioned in paragraph (d)(ii) were generous enough to enable substantially all of the employees of B to whom the package was available at or around the relevant time to take advantage of what was offered (if they wanted to),

(f) the terms on which P entered into the transaction with A were substantially the same as the terms on which at or around the relevant time P normally entered into similar transactions with employees of B under the package of benefits,

(g) if B is a company, a majority of B's employees to whom the package of benefits was available at the relevant time did not have a material interest (as defined in section 68 of ITEPA 2003) in B, and

(h) there is no connection (direct or indirect) between the relevant step and a tax avoidance arrangement.

(2) For the purposes of sub-paragraph (1)(d)(i)—

(a) a loan is "similar" if it is made for the same or similar purposes as the loan which is the subject of the relevant step, and

(b) "members of the public" means members of the public at large with whom P deals at arm's length.

(3) This sub-paragraph applies if any feature of the package of benefits mentioned in sub-paragraph (1)(d)(ii) had or would have been likely to have had the effect that, of the employees of B to whom the package was available, it is employees within sub-paragraph (4) on whom benefits under the package will be wholly or mainly conferred.

(4) The employees within this sub-paragraph are—

(a) directors,

(b) senior employees,

(c) employees who at the relevant time received, or as a result of the package of benefits would have been likely to have received, the higher or highest levels of remuneration, and

(d) if, at the relevant time, B was a company and was a member of a group of companies, any employees not within paragraph (b) or (c) who—

(i) were senior employees in the group, or

(ii) received, or as a result of the package of benefits would have been likely to have received, the higher or highest levels of remuneration in the group.

(5) For the purposes of sub-paragraph (1)(d) and (e) a transaction is "similar" if it is of the same or a similar type to the transaction which P has or had with A.

(6) In this paragraph references to A include references to any person linked with A.

(7) In this paragraph "pension scheme" has the same meaning as in Part 4 of FA 2004 (see section 150(1) of that Act).

30 In section 554G of ITEPA 2003 (exclusions: transactions under employee benefit packages), at the end insert—

"(8) See paragraph 29 of Schedule 11 to F(No. 2)A 2017 for provision about exclusions for transactions under employee benefit packages in a case in which the relevant step is within paragraph 1 of that Schedule."

Cases involving employment-related securities

31 Chapter 2 of Part 7A of ITEPA 2003 does not apply by reason of a relevant step within paragraph 1 which is treated as being taken by a person ("P") if—

(a) P is treated as taking a relevant step by that paragraph by reason of the payment of a sum of money by way of a loan (the "relevant loan"),

(b) the relevant loan is made and used solely for the purpose of enabling A to exercise an employment-related securities option (within the meaning of Chapter 5 of Part 7 of ITEPA 2003),

(c) the exercise of the option by A gives rise to employment income of A in respect of A's employment with B—

(i) which is chargeable to income tax or would be chargeable apart from Chapter 5B of Part 2 of ITEPA 2003, or

(ii) which is exempt income, and

(d) there is no connection (direct or indirect) between the relevant step and a tax avoidance arrangement.

32 In section 554N of ITEPA 2003 (exclusions: other cases involving employment-related securities etc.), at the end insert—

"(17) See paragraph 31 of Schedule 11 to F(No. 2)A 2017 for provision about exclusions where a loan is made for the purpose of enabling the exercise of an employment-related securities option and the relevant step is within paragraph 1 of that Schedule."

Employee car ownership schemes

33 (1) This paragraph applies if—

(a) there is an arrangement ("the car ownership arrangement") which—

(i) provides for A to purchase a new car from another person ("S") using a loan ("the car loan") to be made to A by an authorised lender,

(ii) specifies the date ("the repayment date") by which the car loan must be fully repaid which must be no later than four years after the date on which the car loan is made, and

(iii) permits A, in order to obtain funds to repay the car loan, to sell the car back to S on a specified date at a specified price based on an estimate (made at the time the car ownership arrangement is made) of the likely outstanding amount of the car loan on the specified date, and

(iv) as provided for by the car ownership arrangement, A purchases the car using the car loan.

(2) Chapter 2 does not apply by reason of a relevant step within paragraph 1 which is treated as being taken by a person if—

(a) the person is treated as taking a relevant step by that paragraph by reason of making the car loan, and

(b) the car ownership arrangement is not a tax avoidance arrangement and there is no other connection (direct or indirect) between the relevant step and a tax avoidance arrangement.

(3) In this paragraph—

"car" has the meaning given by section 235(2) of ITEPA 2003, and

"authorised lender" means a person who—

(a) has permission under Part 4A of the Financial Services and Markets Act 2000 to enter into, or to exercise or have the right to exercise rights and duties under, a contract of the kind mentioned in paragraph 23 of Schedule 2 to that Act, and

(b) is not acting as a trustee.

(4) The definition of "authorised lender" must be read with—

(a) section 22 of the Financial Services and Markets Act 2000,

(b) any relevant order under that section, and

(c) Schedule 2 to that Act.

34 In section 554O of ITEPA 2003 (exclusions: employee car ownership schemes), at the end insert—

"(7) See paragraph 33 of Schedule 11 to F(No. 2)A 2017 for provision about exclusions for car loans in a case in which the relevant step is within paragraph 1 of that Schedule."

Acquisition of unlisted employer shares

35 (1) Chapter 2 of Part 7A of ITEPA 2003 does not apply by reason of a relevant step within paragraph 1 which is treated as being taken by a person ("P") if the conditions in sub-paragraph (2) are met.

(2) The conditions are that—

(a) the loan or quasi-loan concerned was made before 9 December 2010,

(b) if P is treated as taking a relevant step by paragraph 1 by reason of the payment of a sum of money by way of loan, the sum is used by A solely to acquire employer shares,

(c) if P is treated as taking a relevant step by paragraph 1 by reason of making a quasi-loan, the transfer of assets mentioned in paragraph 2(3)(b) is the transfer of employer shares to A,

(d) the employer shares are acquired, or transferred, before the end of the period of one year beginning with the day on which the loan, or quasi-loan, is made, and

(e) the employer shares are not listed on a recognised stock exchange at any time during the period beginning with the day on which the loan, or quasi-loan, is made and ending with the earlier of—

(i) the day on which A ceases to hold the shares, or

(ii) the day on which the loan, or quasi-loan, is repaid.

(3) In this paragraph "employer shares" means shares that form part of the ordinary share capital of—

(a) B, or

(b) if B is a company and is a member of a group of companies at the time the shares are acquired, any other company which is a member of that group at that time.

(4) Sub-paragraph (6) applies if—

(a) apart from sub-paragraph (1), Chapter 2 of Part 7A would apply by reason of the relevant step mentioned in sub-paragraph (1), and

(b) at the end of the relevant period, an amount of the loan, or quasi-loan, is outstanding.

(5) In this paragraph "the relevant period" means the period of 12 months beginning with the day on which A ceases to hold the shares.

(6) Part 7A of ITEPA 2003 has effect as if—

(a) a relevant step within paragraph 1 were taken by reason of making a loan, or quasi-loan, of an amount equal to the amount of the loan, or quasi-loan, outstanding at the end of the relevant period, and

(b) the relevant step were taken on the day after the end of the relevant period.

PART 4

SUPPLEMENTARY PROVISION

Duty to provide loan balance information to B

36 (1) This paragraph applies where—

(a) a person ("P") has made a loan, or a quasi-loan, to a relevant person,

(b) the loan or quasi-loan was made on or after 6 April 1999, and

(c) an amount of the loan or quasi-loan is outstanding at any time—

(i) on or after 17 March 2016, and

(ii) before the end of 5 April 2019.

(2) Each of A and P must ensure that the loan balance information in relation to the loan or quasi-loan is provided to B before the end of the period of 10 days beginning with the day after the loan charge date.

(3) The "loan balance information" is—

(a) the information that is necessary for B to ascertain the amount of the loan or quasi-loan concerned that is outstanding immediately before the end of the loan charge date, and

(b) such other information about the loan or quasi-loan as B may reasonably require for the purpose of compliance with B's obligations under PAYE regulations.

(4) In this paragraph "loan charge date" means—

(a) the approved repayment date, if the loan is an approved fixed term loan on 5 April 2019, or

(b) 5 April 2019, in any other case.

(5) If, despite taking reasonable steps, A and P have failed to contact B to provide the loan balance information, each of them is responsible for ensuring that the Commissioners for Her Majesty's Revenue and Customs are notified of that fact.

(6) A notification under sub-paragraph (5) must be made in such form and manner, and contain such information, as may be specified by, or on behalf of, the Commissioners for Her Majesty's Revenue and Customs.

(7) "Loan", "quasi-loan" and "outstanding" have the same meaning for the purposes of this paragraph as they have for the purposes of paragraph 1.

Double taxation

37 (1) Sub-paragraph (2) applies where—

(a) P is treated as taking a relevant step by paragraph 1 by reason of a loan made to a relevant person, and

(b) the loan is an employment-related loan (within the meaning of Chapter 7 of Part 3 of ITEPA 2003).

(2) The effect of section 554Z2(2)(a) of ITEPA 2003 (value of relevant step to count as employment income: application of Part 7A instead of the benefits code) is that the loan is not be treated as a taxable cheap loan for the purposes of Chapter 7 of Part 3 of that Act for—

(a) the tax year in which the relevant step is treated as being taken, and

(b) any subsequent tax year.

38 In section 554Z2 of ITEPA 2003, at the end insert—

"(4) See paragraph 37 of Schedule 11 to F(No. 2)A 2017 for provision about the effect of subsection (2)(a) in a case in which the relevant step is within paragraph 1 of that Schedule."

Remittance basis

39 Part 7A of ITEPA 2003 is amended as follows.

40 (1) Section 554Z9 (remittance basis: A does not meet section 26A requirement) is amended in accordance with this paragraph.

(2) In subsection (1), for "Subsection (2) applies" substitute "Subsections (2) and (2A) apply".

(3) In subsection (1A), for "subsection (2) does not apply" substitute "subsections (2) and (2A) do not apply".

(4) At the beginning of subsection (2) insert "Except in a case within subsection (2A),".

(5) After subsection (2) insert—

"(2A) Where the relevant step is within paragraph 1 of Schedule 11 to F(No. 2)A 2017, A's employment income by virtue of section 554Z2(1), or the relevant part of it, is "taxable specific income" in the tax year in which the relevant step is treated as being taken so far as the income is remitted to the United Kingdom in that tax year or in any previous tax year."

(6) In subsection (3) for "this purpose" substitute "the purposes of subsections (2) and (2A)".

(7) In subsection (5)—

(a) in the words before paragraph (a), for "subsection (2)" substitute "subsection (2) or (2A)";

(b) in the words after paragraph (d)—

(i) for "subsection (2)" substitute "subsection (2) or (2A)";

(ii) for "that subsection" substitute "subsection (2) or (2A) (as the case may be)".

41 (1) Section 554Z10 (remittance basis: A meets section 26A requirement) is amended in accordance with this paragraph.

(2) In subsection (1) for "Subsection (2) applies" substitute "Subsections (2) and (2A) apply".

(3) At the beginning of subsection (2) insert "Except in a case within subsection (2AA),".

(4) After subsection (2) insert—

"(2AA) Where the relevant step is within paragraph 1 of Schedule 11 to F(No. 2)A 2017, the overseas portion of (as the case may be)—

(a) A's employment income by virtue of section 554Z2(1), or

(b) the relevant part of A's employment income by virtue of that section,

is "taxable specific income" in the tax year in which the relevant step is treated as being taken so far as the overseas portion is remitted to the United Kingdom in that tax year or in any previous tax year."

42 (1) Section 554Z11 (remittance basis: supplementary) is amended in accordance with this paragraph.

(2) In subsection (4), for "554Z9(2) or 554Z10(2)" substitute "554Z9(2) or (2A) or 554Z10(2) or (2AA)".

(3) In subsection (5), for "554Z9(2) or 554Z10(2)" substitute "554Z9(2) or (2A) or 554Z10(2) or (2AA)".

(4) In subsection (6), for "554Z9(2) or 554Z10(2)" substitute "554Z9(2) or (2A) or 554Z10(2) or (2AA)".

43 (1) Section 554Z11A (temporary non-residents) is amended in accordance with this paragraph.

(2) In subsection (2)—

(a) after "554Z9(2)" insert "or (2A)";

(b) after "554Z10(2)" insert "or (2AA)".

(3) In subsection (3)(d)(i), for "554Z9(2) or 554Z10(2)" substitute "554Z9(2) or (2A) or 554Z10(2) or (2AA)".

Interpretation

44 (1) In this Schedule, "tax avoidance arrangement" has the same meaning as it has for the purposes of Part 7A of ITEPA 2003 (see section 554Z(13) to (15) of that Act).

(2) Section 554Z(16) (determining whether a step is connected with a tax avoidance arrangement) applies for the purposes of this Schedule as it applies for the purposes of Part 7A of ITEPA 2003.

45 See section 554A(1)(a) of ITEPA 2003 for the meaning of "A" and "B".

PART 5
CONSEQUENTIAL AMENDMENTS

ITEPA 2003

46 (1) ITEPA 2003 is amended in accordance with this paragraph.

(2) In section 554A(2) (meaning of "relevant step"), after "or 554D" insert ", or paragraph 1 of Schedule 11 to F(No. 2)A 2017".

(3) In section 554A(4) (relevant step taken on or after A's death), in paragraph (a) after "section 554B taken" insert ", or a relevant step within paragraph 1 of Schedule 11 to F(No. 2)A 2017 which is treated as being taken,".

(4) In section 554Z(9) (interpretation: reference to definition of "relevant step"), at the end insert ", but see also Schedule 11 to F(No. 2)A 2017".

(5) In section 554Z(10) (interpretation: relevant step which involves a sum of money) omit "or" at the end of paragraph (b) and after paragraph (c) insert ", or

(d) a step within paragraph 1 of Schedule 11 to F(No. 2)A 2017."

(6) In section 554Z5 of ITEPA 2003 (overlap with money or asset subject to earlier tax liability), at the end insert—

"(12) See paragraphs 4(5) and (6) and 12(4) and (5) of Schedule 11 of F(No. 2)A 2017 for provision about the effect of subsection (3) in certain cases where the relevant step is within paragraph 1 of that Schedule."

FA 2011

47 In paragraph 59 of Schedule 2 to FA 2011 (transitional provision relating to Part 7A of ITEPA 2003), in sub-paragraph (1)(a), after "ITEPA 2003" insert "or paragraph 1 of Schedule 11 to F(No. 2)A 2017".

GENERAL NOTE

Part One

Relevant Step

Under paragraph 1(1) a person (P) (which will normally be an employee benefit trust or similar) is treated as taking a relevant step under ITEPA 2003 Pt 7A where it has made a loan to a relevant person (broadly the employee) on or after 6 April 1999 and the loan is still outstanding at the end of 5 April 2019. The provision also applies to quasi-loans as defined.

Paragraph 1(2) states that the relevant step will generally be treated as having been made on 5 April 2019. For approved fixed terms loans (as defined) the relevant step is taken at the end of the approved repayment date.

Paragraph 1(3) is a consequential drafting amendment.

Paragraph 1(4) explains that the value of the relevant step is taken to be the amount of loan which is outstanding on 5 April 2019 (or for fixed term loans the later date given in (2) above). Note that it is the amount of the loan which is relevant – not its value. There is therefore no discounting for the risk that the loan may not be repaid.

Paragraph 1(5) imports the definition of relevant person in ITEPA 2003 s 554C (2) and (3).

Paragraph 1(6) states that (1) above is subject to paras 23 and 24, which deal with accelerated payments. In some circumstances the charge does not apply where an accelerated payment notice (APN) has been paid.

Paragraph 1(7) states that determination of whether a loan is outstanding at any time is to be made by reference to the rules in this Schedule and does not depend on whether the loan is actually outstanding at that time. This is important, because there will be some cases where a loan which is no longer in existence on 5 April 2019 can still trigger a liability under the loan charge provisions of this Schedule.

Paragraph 1(8) is a consequential drafting amendment.

Meaning of loan, quasi-loan and approved repayment date

Paragraph 2(1) states that loan includes any form of credit or payment purported to be by way of loan.

Paragraph 2(2) deals with quasi-loans. The intention here is to combat arrangements where debts are transferred between parties so that an individual ends up owing money to an EBT but where the EBT has not actually made a loan to that individual. A person (i.e. the EBT) makes a quasi-loan when it acquires a right to payment or to a transfer of assets in circumstances where the conditions in (3) below are met.

Paragraph 2(3) states that the conditions are met where there is a direct or indirect connection between the acquisition of the right and a payment made, or a transfer of assets to, the relevant person (i.e. the employee). For example, a company might make a loan to an individual and then transfer the benefit of the repayment of the loan to the EBT trustees. The individual would end up indebted to the EBT even though the EBT had not actually made a loan to him or her.

Paragraph 2(4) provides that references to loans and quasi-loans also include replacement loans and paragraph 2(5) that references to loans and quasi-loans also refer to replacement quasi-loans.

Paragraph 2(6) states that approved repayment date refers to the date specified in para 20 below.

Meaning of outstanding loans

Paragraph 3(1) creates a freestanding test of whether a loan is outstanding. It may result in a loan being treated as outstanding for the purposes of ITEPA 2003 Pt 7A even though in fact it is no longer outstanding. A loan, or amount of a loan, is outstanding if the relevant principal amount exceeds the repayment amount. In other words the test requires a simple arithmetical comparison.

Paragraph 3(2) provides that the relevant principal amount is the initial amount lent plus any sums which have become principal under the loan (for example additional amounts advanced) other than by capitalisation of interest.

Paragraph 3(3) explains that "repayment amount" is the total amount of principal repaid before 17 March 2016 and repayments in money by the relevant person on or after that date. This means that repayments in non-monetary form are treated as repayments only if they are made before 17 March 2016 (the date on which the loan charge was first announced). Repayments on or after that date have to be made in cash by the person to whom the loan was paid. This means that although a person could have actually repaid the whole of their outstanding loan on 1 January 2017 in kind (say by the transfer of an asset) the loan would still fall within the loan charge on 5 April 2019.

Paragraph 4(1) states that repayments in money after 17 March 2016 are to be ignored if there is a connection between the repayment and a tax avoidance arrangement, or if they are the subject of a relevant step after the repayment but before the relevant date. This for example would mean that a repayment by a further advance from the trust would not be treated as a repayment of the loan.

Paragraph 4(2) provides that the exception for further relevant steps in (1) above does not apply if tax is paid in full on the relevant step by the relevant date.

Paragraph 4(3) explains that a relevant tax liability for the purposes of (2) above is a liability triggered by a relevant step or under an earnings charge.

Paragraph 4(4) defines relevant date as 5 April 2019, or the approved repayment date for fixed term loans if later.

Paragraph 4(5) introduces (6) below which applies if a payment is disregarded under 4(1)(b) as being the subject of a relevant step.

Paragraph 4(6) ensures that there is no overlap relief under ITEPA 2003 s 554Z5(3) unless the amount of tax due on the relevant step is actually paid.

Paragraph 5(1) applies where the employer or employee acquires the right to repayment of a loan made on or after 6 April 1999. It does not matter whether the acquisition was for consideration or not.

Paragraph 5(2) explains that the amount of the loan which is acquired under (1) above is subject to the charge under this Schedule.

Paragraph 5(3) states that the rules about replacement loans also apply to loans within 5(1) above.

Meaning of "outstanding" loans in currencies other than sterling

Paragraph 6(1) introduces paras 7 to 10 which deal with loans denominated other than in sterling.

Paragraph 6(2) provides that the value of a currency is to be determined by reference to the appropriate spot rate of exchange.

Paragraph 7(1) and (2) state that this paragraph applies where the loan currency is not sterling but it does not apply in cases of loans in depreciating currencies dealt with under paragraph 10.

Paragraph 7(3) explains that to calculate the amount of loan which is outstanding at the date of the relevant step it is necessary to compute in the foreign currency the amount of the loan outstanding at that date and then convert it into sterling at that date.

Paragraph 7(4) states that if there is a provision for payment in a currency other than that the loan was made in para 8 below applies.

Repayments in currencies other than the loan currency

Paragraph 8(1) applies where loan repayments are made in a currency other than the loan currency.

Paragraph 8(2) states that this paragraph does not apply in cases of loans in depreciating currencies dealt with under paragraph 10.

Paragraph 8(3) states that for the purpose of calculating the repayment amounts each payment is treated as being made by reference to its value in the loan currency on the date it was made. This is a necessary rule because otherwise a loan charge could arise even though a loan had been repaid in full, simply because of subsequent exchange-rate movements.

Example

> Mr X was provided with a loan of £1m in 2008 by an EBT. He repaid it in 2018 in dollars where the exchange rate was $1 = £0.75. He therefore repaid $1,333,333 in full satisfaction of the loan. If on 5 April 2019 the rate was $1 = £0.70 without this special rule he would have been treated as having paid only £933,333 of the loan and therefore a Part 7A charge would arise on the £66,667 deemed to have been unpaid.

Loans made in a depreciating currency

Paragraph 9(1) introduces paragraph 10 and states that it applies where the loan is made in a non-sterling currency and it is reasonable to suppose that the reason, or one of the main reasons, for the loan to be made in that currency is that the currency is expected to depreciate against sterling during the loan period.

Paragraph 9(2) states that the loan period is the period from the time the loan is made to the time specified in the loan agreement for the whole of the loan to be repaid.

Paragraph 10(1) explains that where para 9 applies the rules in paras 7 and 8 dealing with loan repayments do not apply and instead the rules in sub-paras (2) to (5) below are to be used.

Paragraph 10(2) provides that the principal amount of the loan is its sterling value at the date it was made plus the value in sterling of any other amounts (other than capitalised interest) that become amounts of principal.

Paragraph 10(3) defines the reference date.

Paragraph 10(4) states that the repayment amount is amount of principal repaid in sterling and, where payments are made in a non-sterling currency, the amount equal to the sterling value of the payments.

Paragraph 10(5) states that the sterling value of the payment is its sterling value on the date it is made. The effect of this is that the loan and any repayment are both computed on a sterling basis, and therefore the taxpayer does not get the benefit of the reduction in liability caused by the depreciation in the value of the currency in which the loan is actually denominated.

Meaning of outstanding quasi-loans

Paragraph 11(1) specifies the way in which the outstanding amount of a quasi-loan is to be determined. The initial debt amount is compared to the repayment amount.

Paragraph 11(2) states that the initial debt amount for a quasi-loan is the value of the acquired debt (as defined in para 2(2)) and the value of any additional acquired debt.

Paragraph 11(3) sets out rules for the determination of the value of the acquired debt. The normal rule is that the value is the right to the repayment of the acquired amount. Where the additional debt is the right to repayment of an amount the value of the debt is that amount, but if the amount is capitalised interest on the accrued debt the value is Nil. This reflects the basic principle of this Schedule, that capitalised interest is ignored. Where the acquired debt is a right to transfer of assets the value is the market value of the assets at the time the right is acquired, or, if higher the cost of the assets at that time. Where the assets are non-fungible and not in existence at the time that the right is acquired the value is the value of the right at that time.

Paragraph 11(4) provides that the repayment amount in relation to a quasi-loan is the total by which the initial debt amount has been reduced by repayment before 17 March 2016, plus payment in money on or after 17 March 2016. If the acquired debt is a right to a transfer of assets and the assets have been transferred the repayment amount is an amount equal to the market value of the assets at the time of the transfer.

Paragraph 12 (1)–(5) repeat the provisions of para (4) more or less identically other than referring to quasi-loans rather than loans. For commentary see above.

Paragraph 13 (1)–(4) repeat the provision of para (5) more or less identically other than referring to quasi-loans rather than loans. For commentary see above.

Paragraph 14 (1)–(2) repeat the provisions of para (6) more or less identically other than referring to quasi-loans rather than loans. For commentary see above.

Paragraph 15(1)–(4) repeat the provisions of para (7) more or less identically other than referring to quasi-loans rather than loans. For commentary see above.

Paragraph 16(1)–(3) repeat the provision of para (8) more or less identically other than referring to quasi-loans rather loans. For commentary see above.

Paragraph 17 (1)–(2) repeat the provisions of para (9) more or less identically other than referring to quasi-loans rather than loans. For commentary see above.

Paragraph 18(1)–(5) repeat the provisions of para (10) more or less identically other than referring to quasi-loans rather than loans. For commentary see above.

Meaning of approved fixed-term loan

Paragraph 19(1) sets out the conditions for a loan to be treated as a fixed term loan on 5 April 2019. It must be a qualifying loan which has been approved by an HMRC officer under para 20.

Paragraph 19(2) provides that a loan is a qualifying loan if it was made before 9 December 2010, the term of the loan cannot exceed ten years, and it is not an excluded loan.

Paragraph 19(3) states that a loan is an excluded loan if, at any time after it is made, it has been replaced directly or indirectly by another loan, or if its terms have been altered to meet the maximum 10-year condition, or to postpone the date on which it must be repaid.

Part 2: Approval of a qualifying loan etc.

Part 2 of Schedule 11 sets out the procedure for HMRC to approve a loan as meeting the qualifying conditions.

Application to HMRC

Paragraph 20(1) states that an application may be made to HMRC for approval of the loan. This must be done by the liable person in relation to the loan (as defined).

Paragraph 20(2) provides that the officer may approve the loan if the qualifying payment and commercial terms conditions are both met.

Paragraph 20(3) states that application for approval may be made in 2018.

Paragraph 20(4) provides that an application may be made after 2018 if the officer considers it reasonable in all of the circumstances for the application to have been made late.

Paragraph 20(5) states that an application must be made in the form approved by HMRC and paragraph 20(6) that the officer must notify the applicant of the decision.

Paragraph 20(7) provides that if an application has been approved the approval can be revoked by HMRC if the officer considers that the application included a deliberate inaccuracy.

Paragraph 20(8) states that if approval is revoked the loan is treated as having been non-approved from the outset.

Paragraph 20(9) explains that a liable person is the person who is liable for tax on the relevant step in relation to the loan.

Qualifying payments condition

Paragraph 21(1) states that the condition is met if payments have been made to the lender during the relevant period at intervals not exceeding 53 weeks.

Paragraph 21(2) states that the relevant period is the period from the making of the loan to the date of making the application. Note that this means that the repayment condition must have been met before the application is made. It is not possible to make an application in circumstances where no repayments have been made prior to the application but there is an intention to make repayments after the application has been approved.

Commercial terms condition

Paragraph 22(1) provides that this is met either where it is reasonable to assume that the loan was made on terms which would be comparable to those made available to the public by a lending business in the ordinary course of its business, or the loan was actually made in the ordinary course of a lending business. Provided that, in both cases, the borrower has complied in all material respects with the terms of the loan.

Paragraph 22(2) states that a loan is made in the ordinary course of business if it is made in the course of a business of lending money or supplying goods and services on credit.

Accelerated payments

In many cases accelerated payment notices will have been issued in EBT cases, largely on the grounds that the initial transfer of funds to the EBT (or the allocation of funds to a sub trust of the EBT) creates an earnings charge. In most cases the APN will have been issued to the employing company rather than the individual recipient. Paragraph 23 deals with the interaction of APNs and the loan charge and is broadly intended to allow a measure of relief against the loan charge when an APN has already been paid. It does not however entirely prevent double taxation.

Paragraph 23(1) sets out the basic conditions under which the exclusion in para 24 below will apply. These are:

– a person is treated as taking a relevant step within para 1 – i.e. a loan charge arises;
– an accelerated payment notice (APN) or partner payment notice has been given in respect of a relevant charge; note that the legislation does not specify to whom the APN has been given;
– the APN is paid;
– the payment is made before the relevant date;
– the amount of the loan which is outstanding on 5 April 2019 (or the later date for approved fixed term loans) is equal to or less than the amount of the accelerated payment.

Paragraph 23(2) states that a relevant charge is a charge to tax arising by reason of a step taken pursuant to the relevant arrangement.

Paragraph 23(3) explains that the relevant arrangement is the whole of the EBT structure from its initial setting up and not just the loan itself.

Paragraph 23(4) defines the relevant date in the same way as elsewhere in this Schedule.

Paragraph 23(5) extends the provisions of this paragraph to APNs in respect of National Insurance Contributions.

Paragraph 23(6) allows all of the APNs in relation to a single charge to be treated as one notice.

Paragraph 24(1) is the relieving provision. A relevant person may apply to HMRC to treat the relevant step as occurring only after the condition in sub-para (2) is met.

Where this applies the relevant step is taken as occurring 30 days after the paragraph 24(2) condition is met or, if later, on 5 April 2019. If the condition is never met there is no relevant charge.

Paragraph 24(2) explains that the condition is that the accelerated payment is withdrawn or repaid on the determination of an appeal. In other words, while HMRC hold the amount paid under the APN the loan charge, assuming that the test in para 23(1) is met is postponed, so there is no question of the same amount being taxed twice. If the accelerated payment is repaid (because, say, there is an agreement that no PAYE is triggered on the setting up of the trust) the loan charge then becomes payable.

Paragraph 24(3) states that an application must be made for relief under this paragraph in 2018.

Paragraph 24(4) provides that a late application may be made if HMRC considerers in all of the circumstances that it is reasonable for the application to be made late.

Paragraph 24(5) states that an application must be made in the form prescribed by HMRC and para 24(6) that an officer must notify the applicant of the outcome of the application.

Paragraph 24(7) provides that a decision may be revoked if the officer considers that the application contained a deliberate inaccuracy.

Paragraph 24(8) states that where an application is revoked it is treated as having been refused at the outset.

Example

A Ltd made a contribution to an EBT of £1m in 2009 and the trustees of the EBT loaned the whole amount to Mrs B a few days later. HMRC believe that the arrangement creates an earnings charge and issue an accelerated payment notice to A Ltd, charging £400,000, being 40% of £1m. The loan is still outstanding at 5 April 2019.

The comparison to be made under para 23(1) is between the amount of the loan outstanding and the amount of tax paid under the APN: not, as might be expected, between the amount of the loan and the gross amount used to calculate the APN. The amount of the loan outstanding on 5 April 2019 is £1m. As this is greater than the amount of APN the conditions are not met and a loan charge will arise, even though tax has already been paid under an APN on what is essentially the same £1m. In order to avoid the loan charge Mrs B would have had to repay at least £600,000 of the loan before 5 April 2019. If she did the amount of the outstanding loan would be £400,000. This is equal to the amount paid under the APN and therefore the loan charge could be postponed. However if she had only repaid £599,999 of the loan the conditions would not be met as the outstanding amount of the loan, £400,001 would be greater than the amount of the APN and therefore the loan charge could not be postponed.

This is a counter intuitive outcome but the explanatory notes make it clear that this is how the provisions are intended to operate.

Part 3: exclusions

Part 3 of Schedule 11 is concerned with exclusions from the loan charge imposed at para 1 above. In the main these reflect the existing exclusions within ITEPA 2003 Pt 7A itself and are designed to ensure that loans related to transactions which themselves are not taxable do not inadvertently attract the loan charge if they are outstanding on 5 April 2019.

Paragraph 25 exempts ordinary commercial loans, using the existing Part 7A definition, from the loan charge provided there is no connection between the relevant step and a tax avoidance arrangement.

Paragraph 26 is a consequential drafting amendment.

Transfer of employment-related loans

Paragraph 27(1) preserves the existing exemption for employment-related loans where loans are transferred between employers. It does not apply where there are tax avoidance arrangements.

Paragraph 27(2) is a minor drafting amendment.

Paragraph 27(3) imports the existing ITEPA 2003 Pt 7A definition of employment-related loans into this Schedule.

Paragraph 28 is a consequential drafting amendment.

Transactions under employee-benefit packages

Paragraph 29(1) exempts loans related to defined employee benefit packages from the loan charge. Conditions (a) to (h) mirror almost exactly the terms of the existing exclusion within ITPEA 2003 ss 203, 554G(1).

Paragraph 29(2) defines "similar" and "member of the public" in the same way as the existing provision in ITPEA 2003 ss 203, 554G(2).

Paragraph 29(3) and (4) require that, in order to qualify for the exemption, the loan was not restricted to senior employees. The test is the same test as in ITEPA 2003 ss 203, 554G(3) and (4).

Paragraph 29(5) specifies what is a similar transaction.

Paragraph 29(6) states that references to A include references to any person linked with A.

Paragraph 29(7) imports the FA 2004 s 150(1) definition of a pension scheme.

Paragraph 30 is a consequential drafting amendment.

Cases involving employment-related securities

Paragraph 31(a) and (b) mirror the exemption in ITEPA 2003 s 554N(13) for loans used to enable a person to exercise share options.

Paragraph 31(c) states that the exercise of the option must either be employment income or within a specific exemption.

Paragraph 31(d) provides that there must be no connection between the relevant step and the tax avoidance arrangement.

Paragraph 32 is a consequential drafting amendment.

Employee car ownership schemes

Paragraph 33(1) defines car ownership arrangements in similar terms to ITEPA 2003 s 554O(1).

Paragraph 33(2) exempts loans relating to car ownership arrangements from the loan charge provided there is no connection with a tax avoidance arrangement.

Paragraph 33(3) defines car and authorised lender.

Paragraph 33(4) supplements the definition of authorised lender.

Paragraph 34 is a consequential drafting amendment.

Acquisition of unlisted employer shares

Paragraph 35(1) introduces the exemption for the acquisition of unlisted employer shares. Unlike all of the other exclusions within Part 3 of this Schedule this exemption is new and is not derived from the existing Part 7A exclusions.

Paragraph 35(2) sets out the conditions for the exemption:
(a) The loan (or quasi-loan) must have been made before 9 December 2010.
(b) The loan is used solely to purchase employer shares.
(c) Where the relevant step is a quasi-loan the transfer of assets in para 2(3)(b) of this Schedule is the transfer of shares in the employer.
(d) The shares are acquired or transferred within one year of the loan (or quasi-loan) being made.
(e) The shares are unlisted between the date the loan was made and the earlier of the date on which the loan is repaid and the employee ceasing to own the shares.

Paragraph 35(3) defines employer shares as being shares that form the ordinary share capital of the company which employs the individual to whom the loan is made, or of any other company in the same group.

Paragraph 35(4) sets out the conditions for the exemption in sub paragraph (6) to apply. The loan must be one which would have been chargeable under ITEPA 2003 Pt 7A had it not been for the exemption in sub paragraph (1) above and an amount of the loan is outstanding at the end of the relevant period.

Paragraph 35(5) states that the relevant period is 12 months from the day on which the individual ceased to hold the shares.

Paragraph 35(6) states that the loan charge will apply after the relevant period has come to an end.

The effect of these provisions is that where an employee had a pre 9 December 2010 loan which was used to purchase shares in his or her employer the loan charge will not arise if the loan is repaid within 12 months of the date on which the employee sold the shares. If however the loan is still outstanding 12 months after the shares have been sold the loan charge will arise.

Part 4: Supplementary Provision

Duty to provide loan balance information to B

The obligation to account for PAYE on the loan charge falls primarily on the employer. However, if the employer was not party to the making of the loan because it was made by a third party the employer may have no knowledge of what loans have been made or repaid. Indeed, in some instances the employee may have left the employing company many years ago, perhaps in difficult circumstances, and there is no longer any communication between them. Part 4 is therefore intended to provide a mechanism under which information is made available to the employer to enable it to account for PAYE.

Paragraph 36(1) sets out the conditions which must be met for the reporting obligation to subsist. P (i.e. the third party, generally an EBT) must have made a loan or quasi-loan to a relevant person (i.e. an employee) on or after 6 April 1999 and the loan is outstanding at any time between 17 March 2016 and 5 April 2019. Note therefore that the obligation will exist not only for loans outstanding at the date the loan charge is triggered but for loans which may have been repaid before that date. This is to enable the employer to be satisfied that existing loans have been repaid.

Paragraph 36(2) states that the employee (A) and the third party (P) each have an obligation to provide loan balance information (as defined) to the employer within ten days of the date on which the loan charge is triggered.

Paragraph 36(3) explains that the loan balance information is the information necessary for the employer to be able to ascertain the amount of loan outstanding at the loan charge date and such other information as the employer may reasonably require to enable it to comply with its PAYE obligations.

Paragraph 36(4) states that the loan charge date is 5 April 2019, unless the loan is an approved fixed term loan in which case it is the approved repayment date.

Paragraph 36(5) provides that A and P must take reasonable steps to contact the employer in order to provide it with the information. If after taking those steps they have been unable to contact the employer they both have an obligation to notify HMRC of the fact that they have been unable to make contact. Note that they do not have an obligation to give HMRC the loan charge information itself, only the fact that they have not been able to make contact.

Paragraph 36(6) states that the notification under (5) above must be in a form and manner specified by HMRC.

Paragraph 36(7) imports the existing definitions of loan, quasi-loan, and outstanding into this part of the Schedule.

Double Taxation

Paragraph 37(1) introduces the paragraph. It applies where the loan charge has arisen on a loan which is an employment related loan.

Paragraph 37(2) states that once the loan charge has been triggered the loan is not treated as a taxable cheap loan for that or any subsequent year. In other words, no future taxable benefit will be due on the benefit of the cheap loan.

Paragraph 38 is a consequential drafting amendment.

Remittance basis

Paragraph 39 introduces amendments to ITEPA 2003 Pt 7A.

Paragraph 40(1) deals with remittance basic cases where the employee does not meet the ITEPA 2003 s 26A requirement (broadly this requires there to be three prior years of non-residence).

Paragraph 40(2)–(4) are minor drafting amendments.

Paragraph 40(5) is the substantive provision. It introduces a new ITEPA 2003 s 554Z9(2A). In cases where the relevant step is within F(No 2)A 2017 Sch 11 it is treated as "taxable specific income" in the year in which the relevant step is taken if the income is remitted to the UK in that tax year or any previous tax year.

Paragraph 40(6) and (7) are minor drafting amendments.

Paragraph 41(1) deals with remittance basis when A does meet the ITEPA 2003 s 26A test.

Paragraph 41(2)–(3) are minor drafting amendments.

Paragraph 41(4) is the substantive provision. It introduces a new ITEPA 2003 s 554Z10(2AA) which states that the overseas proportion of the individual's income is "taxable specific income" in the year in which the relevant step is taken so far as the overseas portion is remitted to the UK in that tax year or any previous tax year.

Paragraphs 42 and 43 contain minor drafting amendments.

Paragraph 44 imports the existing ITEPA 2003 Pt 7A definitions of tax avoidance arrangements and steps connected with tax avoidance arrangements into these provisions.

Paragraph 45 imports the existing definition of "A" and "B" from ITEPA 2003 s 554A(1)(a) into these provisions.

Part 5: consequential amendments

Paragraph 46 makes minor drafting amendments to ITEPA 2003.

Paragraph 47 amends FA 2011 Sch 2 para 59 to ensure that the relief afforded by that paragraph (which broadly speaking gives a credit for tax already paid against Part 7A charges) is extended to tax payable under the loan charge.

SCHEDULE 12

TRADING INCOME PROVIDED THROUGH THIRD PARTIES: LOANS ETC OUTSTANDING ON 5 APRIL 2019

Section 35

Application of sections 23A to 23H of ITTOIA 2005 in relation to loans etc. outstanding on 5 April 2019

1 (1) A loan or quasi-loan in relation to which sub-paragraph (2) applies is to be treated as a "relevant benefit" for the purposes of sections 23A to 23H of ITTOIA 2005.

(2) This sub-paragraph applies in relation to a loan or a quasi-loan if—

    (a) the loan or quasi-loan was made—

        (i) on or after 6 April 1999, and

        (ii) before 6 April 2017, and

    (b) an amount of the loan or quasi-loan is outstanding immediately before the end of 5 April 2019.

(3) Where section 23E of ITTOIA 2005 applies in relation to a relevant benefit which is a loan or quasi-loan in relation to which sub-paragraph (2) applies, section 23E has effect—

    (a) as if the "relevant benefit amount" were the amount of the loan or quasi-loan that is outstanding immediately before—

        (i) the end of the approved repayment date, if the relevant benefit is an approved fixed term loan on 5 April 2019, or

        (ii) the end of 5 April 2019 in any other case,

    (b) as if section 23E(1)(a) specified—

        (i) the tax year in which the approved repayment date falls, if the relevant benefit is an approved fixed term loan on 5 April 2019, or

        (ii) the tax year 2018–2019 in any other case, and

    (c) where T ceases to carry on the relevant trade in a tax year before the tax year so specified in section 23E(1)(a), as if section 23E(1)(b) were omitted and as if section 23E(1) provided that the relevant benefit amount is to be treated for income tax purposes as a post-cessation receipt of the trade received in the tax year so specified in section 23E(1)(a).

(4) This paragraph is subject to paragraphs 19 and 20 (accelerated payments).

(5) For the purposes of this paragraph, whether an amount of a loan or quasi-loan is outstanding at a particular time—

    (a) is to be determined in accordance with the following provisions of this Schedule, and

    (b) does not depend on the loan or quasi-loan subsisting at that time.

Meaning of "loan", "quasi-loan" and "approved repayment date"

2 (1) In this Schedule "loan" includes—

(a) any form of credit;

(b) a payment that is purported to be made by way of a loan.

(2) For the purposes of paragraph 1, a person ("P") makes a "quasi-loan" to T if (and when) P acquires a right (the "acquired debt")—

(a) which is a right to a payment or a transfer of assets, and

(b) in respect of which the condition in sub-paragraph (3) is met.

(3) The condition is met in relation to a right if there is a connection (direct or indirect) between the acquisition of the right and—

(a) a payment made, by way of a loan or otherwise, to T, or

(b) a transfer of assets to T.

(4) Where a loan or a quasi-loan made to T is replaced, directly or indirectly, by another loan (the "replacement loan"), references in paragraph 1 to the loan are references to the replacement loan.

(5) Where a loan or a quasi-loan made to T is replaced, directly or indirectly, by another quasi-loan (the "replacement quasi-loan"), references in paragraph 1 to the quasi-loan are references to the replacement quasi-loan.

(6) In this Schedule, "approved repayment date", in relation to an approved fixed term loan, means the date by which, under the terms of the loan at the time of making the application for approval under paragraph 16, the whole of the loan must be repaid.

(7) In this paragraph and in paragraphs 3, 9, 10, 19 and 20—

(a) "T" is the person mentioned in section 23A(2) of ITTOIA 2005,

(b) references to T include references to a person who is or has been connected with T, and

(c) for that purpose, section 993 of ITA 2007 (meaning of "connected") applies for the purposes of this Schedule but as if subsection (4) of that section were omitted.

Meaning of "outstanding": loans

3 (1) An amount of a loan is "outstanding" for the purposes of paragraph 1 if the relevant principal amount exceeds the repayment amount.

(2) In sub-paragraph (1) "relevant principal amount", in relation to a loan, means the total of—

(a) the initial principal amount lent, and

(b) any sums that have become principal under the loan, otherwise than by capitalisation of interest.

(3) In sub-paragraph (1) "repayment amount", in relation to a loan, means the total of—

(a) the amount of principal under the loan that has been repaid before 5 December 2016, and

(b) payments in money made by T on or after 5 December 2016 by way of repayment of principal under the loan.

(4) A payment is to be disregarded for the purposes of sub-paragraph (3)(b) if there is any connection (direct or indirect) between the payment and a tax avoidance arrangement (other than the arrangement in pursuance of which the loan was made).

(5) In this paragraph and in paragraph 9, "tax avoidance arrangement" means an arrangement which has a tax avoidance purpose.

(6) For the purposes of sub-paragraph (5), an arrangement has a tax avoidance purpose if sub-paragraph (7) applies to a person who is a party to the arrangement.

(7) This sub-paragraph applies to a person if the main purpose, or one of the main purposes, of the person entering into the arrangement is the avoidance of tax.

(8) The following paragraphs apply for the purpose of determining whether any payment is connected with a tax avoidance arrangement—

(a) a payment is connected with a tax avoidance arrangement if (for example) the payment is made (wholly or partly) in pursuance of—

(i) the tax avoidance arrangement, or

(ii) an arrangement at one end of a series of arrangements with the tax avoidance arrangement being at the other end, and

(b) it does not matter whether the person making the payment is unaware of the tax avoidance arrangement.

Meaning of "outstanding": loans in currencies other than sterling

4 (1) In paragraphs 5 to 8 "the loan currency", in relation to a loan, means the currency in which the initial principal amount of the loan is denominated (whether or not that amount is paid in that currency).

(2) For the purposes of paragraphs 5 to 8, the value of an amount in a particular currency is to be determined by reference to an appropriate spot rate of exchange.

5 (1) This paragraph applies in relation to a loan where the loan currency is a currency other than sterling.

(2) But this paragraph does not apply if paragraph 8 applies in relation to the loan.

(3) The amount of the loan that is outstanding, at the relevant time, is to be calculated in sterling as follows—

Step 1

Calculate, in the loan currency, the amount that is outstanding at that time.

Step 2

Take the value in sterling, at that time, of that amount.

(4) For the purposes of this paragraph and paragraph 8, the "relevant time" in relation to a loan is the time immediately before—

(a) the end of the approved repayment date, if the loan is an approved fixed term loan on 5 April 2019, or

(b) the end of 5 April 2019 in any other case.

(5) See paragraph 6 for provision about repayments made in a currency other than the loan currency.

Repayments in currencies other than the loan currency

6 (1) This paragraph applies in relation to a loan where—

(a) payments in money are made by way of repayment of principal under the loan, and

(b) some or all of the payments are made in a currency other than the loan currency.

(2) But this paragraph does not apply if paragraph 8 applies in relation to the loan.

(3) For the purposes of calculating the repayment amount in relation to the loan, the amount of each of the payments referred to in sub-paragraph (1)(b) is an amount equal to its value in the loan currency on the date it is made.

Loans made in a depreciating currency

7 (1) Paragraph 8 applies in relation to a loan where—

(a) the loan currency is a currency other than sterling, and

(b) it is reasonable to suppose that the main reason, or one of the main reasons, for the loan being made in that currency is that the loan currency is expected to depreciate as against sterling during the loan period.

(2) The "loan period", in relation to a loan, is the period—

(a) beginning at the time the loan is made, and

(b) ending with the time by which, under the terms of the loan, the whole of the loan is to be repaid.

8 (1) Where this paragraph applies in relation to a loan—

(a) paragraphs 5 and 6 do not apply in relation to the loan, and

(b) sub-paragraphs (2) to (5) apply for the purposes of calculating the amount of the loan that is outstanding at the relevant time (as defined in paragraph 5(4)).

(2) The relevant principal amount, in relation to the loan, is an amount equal to the total of—

(a) the value in sterling, at the reference date, of the initial principal amount lent, and

(b) the value in sterling, at the reference date, of any sums that become principal under the loan, otherwise than by capitalisation of interest.

(3) The "reference date"—

(a) in relation to an amount within sub-paragraph (2)(a), means the date on which the loan is made, and

(b) in relation to a sum within sub-paragraph (2)(b), means the date on which the sum becomes principal.

(4) The repayment amount, in relation to the loan, is an amount equal to the total of—

(a) the amount of principal under the loan that has been repaid in sterling, and

(b) where payments are made, in a currency other than sterling, by way of repayment of principal under the loan, the amount equal to the sterling value of the payments.

(5) The "sterling value" of a payment is its value in sterling on the date it is made.

Meaning of outstanding: "quasi-loans"

9 (1) An amount of a quasi-loan is outstanding for the purposes of paragraph 1 if the initial debt amount exceeds the repayment amount.

(2) In sub-paragraph (1), "initial debt amount" means the total of—

    (a) an amount equal to the value of the acquired debt (see paragraph 2(2)), and

    (b) where P subsequently acquires a further right (the "additional debt") to a payment, or transfer of assets, in connection with the payment mentioned in paragraph 2(3)(a) or (as the case may be) the transfer mentioned in paragraph 2(3)(b), an amount equal to the value of the additional debt.

(3) For the purposes of sub-paragraph (2)—

    (a) where the acquired debt is a right to payment of an amount, the "value" of the debt is that amount,

    (b) where the additional debt is a right to payment of an amount, the "value" of the debt is that amount, but is nil if the additional debt accrued to P by the capitalisation of interest on the acquired debt or another additional debt, and

    (c) where the acquired debt or additional debt is a right to a transfer of assets, the "value" of the debt is an amount equal to—

        (i) the market value of the assets at the time the right is acquired (or the value of the right at that time if the assets are non-fungible and not in existence at that time), or

        (ii) if higher, the cost of the assets at that time.

(4) In sub-paragraph (1), "repayment amount", in relation to a quasi-loan, means the total of—

    (a) the amount (if any) by which the initial debt amount has been reduced (by way of repayment) before 5 December 2016,

    (b) payments in money (if any) made by T on or after 5 December 2016 by way of repayment of the initial debt amount, and

    (c) if the acquired debt or additional debt is a right to a transfer of assets, and the assets have been transferred, an amount equal to the market value of the assets at the time of the transfer.

(5) A payment or transfer is to be disregarded for the purposes of sub-paragraph (4)(b) or (c) if there is any connection (direct or indirect) between the payment or transfer and a tax avoidance arrangement (other than the arrangement under which the quasi-loan was made).

(6) In this paragraph, "market value" has the same meaning as it has for the purposes of TCGA 1992 by virtue of Part 8 of that Act.

Meaning of "outstanding": quasi-loans in currencies other than sterling

10 (1) Paragraphs 11 to 14 apply where P makes a quasi-loan to T by reason of acquiring a right to a payment in a particular currency (the "quasi-loan currency").

(2) For the purposes of paragraphs 11 to 14, the value of an amount in a particular currency is to be determined by reference to an appropriate spot rate of exchange.

11 (1) This paragraph applies in relation to the quasi-loan if the quasi-loan currency is a currency other than sterling.

(2) But this paragraph does not apply if paragraph 14 applies in relation to the quasi-loan.

(3) The amount of the quasi-loan that is outstanding, at the relevant time, is to be calculated in sterling as follows—

Step 1

Calculate, in the quasi-loan currency, the amount that is outstanding at that time.

Step 2

Take the value in sterling, at that time, of that amount.

(4) For the purposes of this paragraph and paragraph 14, the "relevant time" in relation to a quasi-loan is the time immediately before the end of 5 April 2019.

(5) See paragraph 12 for provision about repayments made in a currency other than the quasi-loan currency.

Repayments in currencies other than the quasi-loan currency

12 (1) This paragraph applies in relation to the quasi-loan if—

    (a) payments in money are made by way of repayment of the initial debt amount, and

(b) some or all of the payments are made in a currency other than the quasi-loan currency.

(2) But this paragraph does not apply if paragraph 14 applies in relation to the quasi-loan.

(3) For the purposes of calculating the repayment amount in relation to the quasi-loan, the amount of each of the payments referred to in sub-paragraph (1)(b) is an amount equal to its value in the quasi-loan currency on the date it is made.

Quasi-loans made in a depreciating currency

13 (1) Paragraph 14 applies in relation to the quasi-loan if—

(a) the quasi-loan currency is a currency other than sterling, and
(b) it is reasonable to suppose that the main reason, or one of the main reasons, for the quasi-loan being made in that currency is that the quasi-loan currency is expected to depreciate as against sterling during the quasi-loan period.

(2) The "quasi-loan period", in relation to a quasi-loan, is the period—

(a) beginning at the time the quasi-loan is made, and
(b) ending with the time by which, under the terms of the quasi-loan, the whole of the quasi-loan is to be repaid.

14 (1) Where this paragraph applies in relation to the quasi-loan—

(a) paragraphs 11 and 12 do not apply in relation to the quasi-loan, and
(b) sub-paragraphs (2) to (5) apply for the purposes of calculating the amount of the quasi-loan that is outstanding at the relevant time (as defined in paragraph 11(4)).

(2) The initial debt amount, in relation to the quasi-loan, is an amount equal to the total of—

(a) the value in sterling, at the reference date, of the acquired debt, and
(b) the value in sterling, at the reference date, of any additional debt.

(3) The "reference date", in relation to a right within sub-paragraph (2)(a) or (2)(b), means the date on which P acquires it.

(4) The repayment amount, in relation to the quasi-loan, is an amount equal to the total of—

(a) the amount of the initial debt amount that has been repaid in sterling, and
(b) where payments are made, in a currency other than sterling, by way of repayment of the initial debt amount, the amount equal to the sterling value of the payments.

(5) The "sterling value" of a payment is its value in sterling on the date it is made.

Meaning of "approved fixed term loan"

15 (1) A loan is an "approved fixed term loan" on 5 April 2019 if, at any time on that day, it is a qualifying loan which has been approved by an officer of Revenue and Customs in accordance with paragraph 16.

(2) A loan is a "qualifying loan" if—

(a) the loan was made before 9 December 2010,
(b) the term of the loan cannot exceed 10 years, and
(c) it is not an excluded loan under sub-paragraph (3).

(3) A loan is an excluded loan if, at any time after the loan was made—

(a) the loan has been replaced, directly or indirectly, by another loan, or
(b) the terms of the loan have been altered so as—
    (i) to meet the condition in sub-paragraph (2)(b), or
    (ii) to postpone the date by which, under the terms of the loan, the whole of the loan must be repaid.

Approval: application to HMRC

16 (1) A person may make an application to the Commissioners for Her Majesty's Revenue and Customs for approval of a qualifying loan made to T.

(2) An officer of Revenue and Customs may grant such an application if satisfied that, in relation to the loan—

(a) the qualifying payments condition is met (see paragraph 17), or
(b) the commercial terms condition is met (see paragraph 18).

(3) Subject to sub-paragraph (4), an application may be made in 2018.

(4) An application may be made after 2018 if an officer of Revenue and Customs considers it reasonable in all the circumstances for a late application to be made.

(5) An application for an approval must be made in such form and manner, and contain such information, as may be specified by, or on behalf of, the Commissioners for Her Majesty's Revenue and Customs.

(6) An officer of Revenue and Customs must notify the applicant of the decision on an application.

Approval: qualifying payments condition

17 (1) The qualifying payments condition is met in relation to a qualifying loan if, during the relevant period—

(a) payments have been made in respect of the repayment of the principal of the loan, and

(b) the payments have been made at intervals not exceeding 53 weeks.

(2) The "relevant period" in relation to a loan is the period beginning with the making of the loan and ending with the making of the application.

Approval: commercial terms condition

18 (1) The commercial terms condition is met in relation to a qualifying loan if—

(a) either—

(i) it is reasonable to assume that, had the qualifying loan been made in the ordinary course of a lending business, loans on terms comparable to those of the qualifying loan would have been available to members of the public, or

(ii) the qualifying loan was made in the ordinary course of a lending business; and

(b) the borrower has, in all material respects, complied with the terms of the loan.

(2) For the purposes of sub-paragraph (1), a loan is made in the ordinary course of a lending business if it is made by a person in the ordinary course of a business carried on by the person which includes—

(a) the lending of money, or

(b) the supplying of goods or services on credit.

Accelerated payments

19 (1) Paragraph 20(1) applies where—

(a) section 23E of ITTOIA 2005 would (ignoring paragraph 20) apply in relation to a relevant benefit arising to T,

(b) the relevant benefit is a loan or quasi-loan in relation to which paragraph 1(2) applies,

(c) an accelerated payment notice, or a partner payment notice, relating to a relevant charge (the "accelerated payment notice") has been given under Chapter 3 of Part 4 of FA 2014,

(d) T makes a payment (the " accelerated payment") in respect of the understated or disputed tax to which the notice relates,

(e) the accelerated payment is made on or before the relevant date, and

(f) the amount of the loan or quasi-loan that, at the end of the relevant date, is outstanding for the purposes of paragraph 1 (see paragraphs 3 to 14) is equal to or less than the amount of the accelerated payment.

(2) In sub-paragraph (1)(c), "relevant charge" means a charge to tax under section 23E of ITTOIA 2005 arising by reason of a relevant benefit which arises to T in pursuance of the relevant arrangement in pursuance of which the relevant benefit mentioned in sub-paragraph (1)(a) and (b) arises.

(3) In sub-paragraph (1)(e) and (f), " the relevant date" means—

(a) the approved repayment date, if the relevant benefit is an approved fixed term loan on 5 April 2019, or

(b) 5 April 2019, in any other case.

20 (1) T may make an application to the Commissioners for Her Majesty's Revenue and Customs to be treated—

(a) as if the relevant benefit mentioned in paragraph 19(1)(a) and (b) arises only if the condition in sub-paragraph (2) is met, and

(b) as if it arises immediately before the end of the 30 days beginning with the date on which the condition in sub-paragraph (2) becomes met.

(2) The condition is that, on the withdrawal of the accelerated payment notice or on the determination of an appeal, any part of the accelerated payment is repaid.

(3) Subject to sub-paragraph (4), an application under sub-paragraph (1) may be made in 2018.

(4) An application may be made after 2018 if an officer of Revenue and Customs considers it reasonable in all the circumstances for a late application to be made.

(5) An application must be made in such form and manner, and contain such information, as may be specified by, or on behalf of, the Commissioners for Her Majesty's Revenue and Customs.

(6) An officer of Revenue and Customs must notify the applicant of the decision on an application under this paragraph.

GENERAL NOTE

This Schedule, which applies to sole traders and partnerships, closely mirrors the provisions in Schedule 11 which impose a tax charge on loans outstanding on 5 April 2019. This commentary refers back to the commentary on Schedule 11 where appropriate and only looks in detail at those parts of the Schedule which do not directly use the concepts and definitions in Schedule 11.

Application of ITTOIA 2005 ss 23A–23H in relation to loans etc. outstanding on 5 April 2019

Paragraph 1(1) treats certain loans or quasi-loans as relevant benefits.

Paragraph 1(2) states that the paragraph applies where the loan (or quasi-loan) was made between 6 April 1999 and 5 April 2017 and an amount of the loan is outstanding (as defined) at the end of 5 April 2019.

Paragraph 1(3)(a) explains that the amount of the loan outstanding on 5 April 2019 is treated as a relevant benefit under ITTOIA 2005 s 23E. The benefit arises on 5 April 2019 unless the loan is an approved fixed term loan, in which case the benefit arises on the approved repayment date.

Paragraph 1(3)(b) provides that the liability is for the tax year 2018/19, unless the loan is an approved fixed term loan, in which case the liability is for the tax year in which the approved repayment date falls.

Paragraph 1(3)(c) explains that If the trade has ceased before the commencement of the tax year above the relevant benefit is treated as a post-cessation receipt in the year given by (1)(3)(b) above – i.e. it is not treated as a receipt of the final year of trading.

Paragraph 1(4) states that para 1 is subject to paras 19 and 20, which deal with accelerated payment notices.

Paragraph 1(5) provides that in determining whether a loan is outstanding at any point the tests in this Schedule are to be used, even though as a matter of fact the loan may not actually be outstanding at that point.

Meaning of loan, quasi-loan, and approved repayment date

Paragraph 2 repeats, with only minor drafting changes, Sch 11 para 2.

Meaning of outstanding loans

Paragraph 3(1), (2) repeat Sch 11 paras 3(1) and (2).

Paragraph 3(3) defines repayment amount. This is: (a) the amount of principal under the loan which has been repaid before 5 December 2016, and (b) payment made in money by the trader on or after 5 December 2016 by way of repayment of principal. Note that these dates are different to those in the equivalent provisions in Sch 11 para 3(3).

Paragraph 3(4) states that a payment is to be disregarded for the purposes of 3(b) above if there is a connection between the payment (directly or indirectly) and a tax avoidance arrangement. The arrangement under which the loan itself was provided is ignored for this purpose.

Paragraph 3(5) explains that a tax avoidance arrangement is defined as an arrangement which has a tax avoidance purpose.

Paragraph 3(6) states that an arrangement has a tax avoidance purpose if sub-para (7) applies to a person who is party to the arrangement.

Paragraph 3(7) applies to a person if the main purpose, or one of the main purposes, of the person entering the arrangement is the avoidance of tax.

Paragraph 3(8) sets out a test for determining whether a payment is connected with a tax avoidance arrangement. It covers not only payments made in pursuance of tax avoidance arrangements but also payments at what the draftsman calls rather inelegantly "one end of a series of arrangements" with the tax avoidance arrangement being at the other end. It also applies even if the person making the payment is unaware of the tax avoidance arrangement. This is an extremely wide test and is clearly designed to enable HMRC to stop people arguing that a particular payment was not itself a tax avoidance arrangement because the person making the payment did not know how it was going to be used as part of a tax avoidance arrangement. Whether in practice the definition will be workable is something which will need to be tested through litigation.

Meaning of "outstanding": loans in currencies other than sterling
Paragraph 4 repeats, with minor drafting amendments, Sch 11 para 6.
Paragraph 5 repeats, with minor drafting amendments, Sch 11 para 7.

Repayments in currencies other than the loan currency
Paragraph 6 repeats, with minor drafting amendments, Sch 11 para 8.

Loans made in a depreciating currency
Paragraph 7 repeats, with minor drafting amendments, Sch 11 para 9.
Paragraph 8 repeats, with minor drafting amendments, Sch 11 para 10.

Meaning of outstanding quasi-loans
Paragraph 9(1) to (3) repeat, with minor drafting amendments, Sch 11 para 11.
Paragraph 9(4) states that the repayment amount in relation to a quasi-loan is the amount (if any) by which:
(a) the initial debt has been reduced by way of repayment before 5 December 2016;
(b) and any payments in money made by the trade on or after 5 December 2016 by way of repayment of the original debt amount. Note again that these dates are different to those in the equivalent provision in the loan charge under ITEPA 2003 Pt 7A;
(c) if the acquired debt or additional debt is the right to a transfer of assets, and the assets have been transferred, the repayment amount is an amount equal to the market value of the assets at the time of transfer.
Paragraph 9(5) explains that a payment is to be disregarded for the purposes of (4)(b) or (c) above if there is any connection, direct or indirect, between the payment or transfer and a tax avoidance arrangement. The original loan itself is ignored in the test. This definition is different to the equivalent provision in Sch 11 para 11.
Paragraph 9(6) provides that "market value" uses the same definition as TCGA 1992 Pt 8.

Meaning of "outstanding" quasi-loans in currencies other than sterling
Paragraph 10 repeats, with minor drafting amendments, Sch 11 para 14.
Paragraph 11 repeats, with minor drafting amendments, Sch 11 para 15. The only material difference is that para 15 is written in terms of the date of the relevant step whereas this paragraph is written in terms of the relevant time, which is defined as the time immediately before the end of 5 April 2019.

Repayments in currencies other than the quasi-loan currency
Paragraph 12 repeats, with minor drafting amendments, Sch 11 para 16.

Quasi-loans made in a depreciating currency
Paragraph 13 repeats, with minor drafting amendments, Sch 11 para 17.
Paragraph 14 repeats, with minor drafting amendments, Sch 11 para 18.

Meaning of "approved fixed-term loan"
Paragraph 15 repeats, with minor drafting amendments, Sch 11 para 19.

Approval: application to HMRC

Paragraph 16 repeats, with minor drafting amendments, Sch 11 para 20(1)–(6). Note that the additional paragraphs (7) to (9) in para 20, which deal with revocations of loan approvals, are not included within this paragraph.

Approval: qualifying payment conditions

Paragraph 17 repeats, with minor drafting amendments, Sch 11 para 21.

Approval: commercial terms condition

Paragraph 18 repeats, with minor drafting amendments, Sch 11 para 22.

Accelerated payments

Paragraph 19(1) sets outs the conditions for para 20 below, which gives relief where an accelerated payment notice (APN) has been given, to apply:

(a) a charge under s 23E above (the principal charging provision) would arise on a relevant benefit;
(b) the relevant benefit is a loan or quasi-loan which attracts a charge under para 1(2) of this Schedule;
(c) an APN or partner payment notice has been given;
(d) the trader makes a payment under the APN;
(e) the payment is made on or before the relevant date (as defined below);
(f) the amount of the loan (or quasi-loan) which is outstanding at the end of relevant date is equal to or less than the amount of the accelerated payment.

Paragraph 19(2) states that the relevant charge is a charge under s 23E by reason of a relevant benefit arising to T in respect of the relevant arrangement.

Paragraph 19(3) provides that the relevant date is 5 April 2019 except in the case of an approved fixed term loan, in which case the relevant date is the approved repayment date.

Paragraph 20(1) explains that the trader may make an application to HMRC to be treated as if the relevant benefit only arises if the condition in (2) below is met, and if this applies, the benefit arises 30 days after that condition is met.

Paragraph 20(2) states that the condition is that the accelerated payment is repaid either because of the determination of an appeal or the withdrawal of the APN.

Paragraph 20(3) states that the application must be made in 2018.

Paragraph 20(4) provides that a late application may be made if an officer of HMRC considers it reasonable in all of the circumstances for a late application to be made.

Paragraph 20(5) stipulates that an application must be made in the form and manner prescribed by HMRC.

Paragraph 20(6) specifies that an officer of HMRC must notify the applicant of a decision on an application under this paragraph.

The effect of this paragraph is that if an APN has been paid the trader may apply to HMRC for agreement not to pay the loan charge, provided that the APN relates to the same arrangement, and the same amount, as the loan charge. If the APN is for any reason repaid then the loan charge becomes payable. However this is not retrospective – the charge only arises 30 days after the APN has been repaid.

SCHEDULE 13

THIRD COUNTRY GOODS FULFILMENT BUSINESSES: PENALTY

Section 55

Liability to penalty

1 (1) A penalty is payable by a person ("P") who—

(a) carries on a third country goods fulfilment business, and
(b) is not an approved person.

(2) In this Schedule references to a "contravention" are to acting as mentioned in sub-paragraph (1).

Amount of penalty

2 (1) If the contravention is deliberate and concealed, the amount of the penalty is the maximum amount (see paragraph 10).

(2) If the contravention is deliberate but not concealed, the amount of the penalty is 70% of the maximum amount.

(3) In any other case, the amount of the penalty is 30% of the maximum amount.

(4) The contravention is—

(a) "deliberate and concealed" if the contravention is deliberate and P makes arrangements to conceal the contravention, and

(b) "deliberate but not concealed" if the contravention is deliberate but P does not make arrangements to conceal the contravention.

Reductions for disclosure

3 (1) Paragraph 4 provides for reductions in penalties under this Schedule where P discloses a contravention.

(2) P discloses a contravention by—

(a) telling the Commissioners about it,

(b) giving the Commissioners reasonable help in identifying any other contraventions of which P is aware, and

(c) allowing the Commissioners access to records for the purpose of identifying such contraventions.

(3) Disclosure of a contravention—

(a) is "unprompted" if made at a time when P has no reason to believe that the Commissioners have discovered or are about to discover the contravention, and

(b) otherwise, is "prompted".

(4) In relation to disclosure, "quality" includes timing, nature and extent.

4 (1) Where P discloses a contravention, the Commissioners must reduce the penalty to one that reflects the quality of the disclosure.

(2) If the disclosure is prompted, the penalty may not be reduced below—

(a) in the case of a contravention that is deliberate and concealed, the maximum amount,

(b) in the case of a contravention that is deliberate but not concealed, 35% of the maximum amount, and

(c) in any other case, 20% of the maximum amount.

(3) If the disclosure is unprompted, the penalty may not be reduced below—

(a) in the case of a contravention that is deliberate and concealed, 30% of the maximum amount,

(b) in the case of a contravention that is deliberate but not concealed, 20% of the maximum amount, and

(c) in any other case, 10% of the maximum amount.

Special reduction

5 (1) If the Commissioners think it right because of special circumstances, they may reduce a penalty under this Schedule.

(2) In sub-paragraph (1) "special circumstances" does not include ability to pay.

(3) In sub-paragraph (1) the reference to reducing a penalty includes a reference to—

(a) staying a penalty, and

(b) agreeing a compromise in relation to proceedings for a penalty.

Assessment

6 (1) Where P becomes liable for a penalty under this Schedule, the Commissioners must—

(a) assess the penalty,

(b) notify P, and

(c) state in the notice the contravention in respect of which the penalty is assessed.

(2) A penalty under this Schedule must be paid before the end of the period of 30 days beginning with the day on which notification of the penalty is issued.

(3) A penalty under this Schedule is recoverable as a debt due to the Crown.

(4) An assessment of a penalty under this Schedule may not be made later than one year after evidence of facts sufficient in the opinion of the Commissioners to indicate the contravention comes to their knowledge.

(5) Two or more contraventions may be treated by the Commissioners as a single contravention for the purposes of assessing a penalty under this Schedule.

Reasonable excuse

7 (1) Liability to a penalty does not arise under this Schedule in respect of a contravention which is not deliberate if P satisfies the Commissioners or (on an appeal made to the appeal tribunal) the tribunal that there is a reasonable excuse for the contravention.

(2) For the purposes of sub-paragraph (1), where P relies on any other person to do anything, that is not a reasonable excuse unless P took reasonable care to avoid the contravention.

Companies: officer's liability

8 (1) Where a penalty under this Schedule is payable by a company in respect of a contravention which was attributable to an officer of the company, the officer is liable to pay such portion of the penalty (which may be 100%) as the Commissioners may specify by written notice to the officer.

(2) Sub-paragraph (1) does not allow the Commissioners to recover more than 100% of a penalty.

(3) In the application of sub-paragraph (1) to a body corporate other than a limited liability partnership, "officer" means—

(a) a director (including a shadow director within the meaning of section 251 of the Companies Act 2006),
(b) a manager, and
(c) a secretary.

(4) In the application of sub-paragraph (1) to a limited liability partnership, "officer" means a member.

(5) In the application of sub-paragraph (1) in any other case, "officer" means—

(a) a director,
(b) a manager,
(c) a secretary, and
(d) any other person managing or purporting to manage any of the company's affairs.

(6) Where the Commissioners have specified a portion of a penalty in a notice given to an officer under sub-paragraph (1)—

(a) paragraph 5 applies to the specified portion as to a penalty,
(b) the officer must pay the specified portion before the end of the period of 30 days beginning with the day on which the notice is given,
(c) sub-paragraphs (3) to (5) of paragraph 6 apply as if the notice were an assessment of a penalty, and
(d) paragraph 9 applies as if the officer were liable to a penalty.

(7) In this paragraph "company" means any body corporate or unincorporated association, but does not include a partnership.

Double jeopardy

9 P is not liable to a penalty under this Schedule in respect of a contravention in respect of which P has been convicted of an offence.

The maximum amount

10 (1) In this Schedule "the maximum amount" means £10,000.

(2) If it appears to the Treasury that there has been a change in the value of money since the last relevant date, they may by regulations substitute for the sum for the time being specified in sub-paragraph (1) such other sum as appears to them to be justified by the change.

(3) In sub-paragraph (2), "relevant date" means—

(a) the date on which this Act is passed, and
(b) each date on which the power conferred by that sub-paragraph has been exercised.

(4) Regulations under this paragraph do not apply to any contravention which occurs wholly before the date on which they come into force.

Appeal tribunal

11 In this Schedule "appeal tribunal" has the same meaning as in Chapter 2 of Part 1 of the Finance Act 1994.

GENERAL NOTE

Paragraph 1 – liability to penalty

Paragraph 1(1)

This paragraph contemplates the imposition of a penalty on a person (identified as "P") if "P" carries on a third country goods fulfilment business and "P" is not an approved person (as defined in section 49(5)).

Paragraph 1(2)

This paragraph stipulates that where the word "contravention" is used within the Schedule it should mean that "P" acts as mentioned in section 1(1) above (i.e. "P" carries on a third country fulfilment business without the requisite approval).

Paragraph 2 – amount of penalty

Paragraph 2(1)

This paragraph stipulates that if a contravention is deliberate and concealed, the amount of the penalty will be the maximum amount (set at £10,000 by paragraph 10 – see below).

Paragraph 2(2)

This paragraph stipulates that if a contravention is deliberate but not concealed, the amount of the penalty will be 70% of the maximum amount.

Paragraph 2(3)

In any other case, the amount of the penalty will be 30% of the maximum amount.

Paragraph 2(4)

This paragraph defines when a contravention is regarded as deliberate and concealed and deliberate but not concealed.

(a) a contravention is deliberate and concealed if the contravention is deliberate and "P" makes arrangements to conceal the contravention; and

(b) a contravention is deliberate but not concealed if the contravention is deliberate but "P" does not make arrangements to conceal the contravention.

Paragraph 3 – reductions for disclosure

Paragraph 3(1)

This paragraph announces that a penalty contemplated by this Schedule can be reduced under section 4 if "P" makes a disclosure in relation to a contravention.

Paragraph 3(2)

A disclosure is made by "P" if he:

(a) tells the Commissioners about the contravention;

(b) gives the Commissioners reasonable help in identifying any other contraventions of which "P" is aware; and

(c) allows the Commissioners access to records to help them to identify such contraventions.

Paragraph 3(3)

This paragraph defines what constitutes an "unprompted" disclosure.

A disclosure is unprompted if:

(a) it is made at a time when "P" has no reason to believe that the Commissioners have discovered or are about to discover the contravention; but

(b) otherwise than as in (a) above the disclosure of a contravention by "P" will be regarded as prompted.

Paragraph 3(4)

This paragraph stipulates that use of the term "quality" in paragraph 4 in relation to disclosures includes reference to the timing of a disclosure, the nature of the disclosure and the extent of the disclosure.

Paragraph 4(1)

This provision makes it mandatory that the Commissioners allow a reduction in the amount of any penalty to reflect the "quality of the disclosure made by 'P'".

Paragraph 4(2)

Deals with prompted disclosures and stipulates that the penalty cannot be reduced below:
(a) the maximum amount (in the case of deliberate and concealed contraventions);
(b) 35% of the maximum amount (in the case of deliberate but not concealed contraventions); and
(c) 20% of the maximum amount in all other cases.

Paragraph 4(3)

Deals with un-prompted disclosures and stipulates that that the penalty cannot be reduced below:
(a) 30% of the maximum account in the case of a deliberate and concealed contravention;
(b) 20% of the maximum amount in the case of a deliberate but not concealed contravention; and
(c) 10% in all other cases.

Paragraph 5 – special reduction

Paragraph 5(1)

This paragraph gives the Commissioners power to reduce a penalty if they consider that it is right to do so because there are "special circumstances" prevailing.

Paragraph 5(2)

What constitutes "special circumstances" is left open with the exception of P's ability to pay any penalty. In other words, P's inability to pay a penalty will not be regarded as a "special circumstance" in relation to any reduction being considered by the Commissioners.

Paragraph 5(3)

This paragraph stipulates that in relation to paragraph 5(1) the term "reduction" in penalty includes a reference to either "staying" a penalty or agreeing a compromise in relation to proceedings for a penalty.

Paragraph 6 – assessment

Paragraph 6(1)

This paragraph stipulates that where "P" has become liable to a penalty under this Schedule, the Commissioners must follow a process. That is:
(a) the penalty must be assessed;
(b) "P" must be notified (of the assessment); and
(c) The particular contravention giving rise to the penalty must be identified.

Paragraph 6(2)

Stipulates that any penalty imposed must be paid within 30 days of the penalty notification being issued.

Paragraph 6(3)

A penalty imposed under this Schedule is recoverable as a debt due to the Crown.

Paragraph 6(4)

This paragraph imposes a time limit by which an assessment for a penalty can be issued. A penalty may not be made more than one year after evidence of facts sufficient in the opinion of the Commissioners to indicate the contravention comes to their knowledge.

Paragraph 6(5)

This paragraph allows the Commissioners to treat two or more contraventions (under paragraph 1(1)) as a single contravention for the purposes of assessing a penalty under this Schedule.

Paragraph 7 – reasonable excuse

Paragraph 7(1)

This paragraph stipulates that no penalty will be imposed if "P" can satisfy the Commissioners or a Tribunal (on appeal) that he has a reasonable excuse for the contravention.

Paragraph 7(2)

In relation to paragraph 7(1), a reasonable excuse does not subsist if "P" relies on any other person to do anything unless "P" took reasonable care to avoid the contravention.

Paragraph 8 – companies: officer's liability

Paragraph 8(1)

This paragraph allows for any penalties imposed against a company to be payable by an officer of the company in circumstances where the contravention has occurred as a result of that officer's conduct. The officer can be liable to all or a portion of the penalty as specified to him by the Commissioners in writing.

Paragraph 8(2)

Sub-paragraph (2) makes it clear that the Commissioners may not recover more than 100% of the penalty imposed on the company.

Paragraph 8(3)

This paragraph defines what is meant by an "officer" of a body corporate (other than a limited liability partnership). An officer includes:
(a) a director (including a shadow director within the meaning of section 251 of the Companies Act 2006),
(b) a manager, and
(c) a secretary.

Paragraph 8(4)

As far as limited liability partnerships are concerned, an "officer" means a "member" of the LLP.

Paragraph 8(5)

In all other cases (than those covered in paragraphs 8(3) and 8(4)), an "officer" includes:
(a) a director,
(b) a manager,
(c) a secretary, and
(d) any other person managing or purporting to manage any of the company's affairs.

Paragraph 8(6)

This paragraph makes it clear that where (under paragraph 8(1)) the Commissioners have specified a portion of the penalty in a notice as being payable by an officer, paragraph 5 (special reductions) can apply to the portion in question. In addition, the officer must pay the portion specified within 30 days of the notice being given.

Paragraphs 6(3) to 6(5) shall apply equally to any notice issued by the Commissioners as if the notice were an assessment of a penalty and the double jeopardy rule contained in paragraph 9 (see below) applies to an officer as it does to "P".

Paragraph 8(7)

"Company" includes any body corporate or unincorporated association, but does not include a partnership.

Paragraph 9 – double jeopardy

Paragraph 9(1)

This paragraph stipulates that "P" (and, by virtue of paragraph 8(7), an officer) is not liable to a penalty under this Schedule if he has been convicted of an offence in relation to a contravention.

Paragraph 10 – the maximum amount

Paragraph 10(1)

The maximum amount is defined as £10,000.

Paragraph 10(2)

This paragraph allows the Commissioners to alter the maximum amount specified in paragraph 10(1) if the value of money is perceived by them to have changed from a "relevant date".

Paragraph 10(3)

"Relevant date" in this context means either the date of the coming into force of the Act or each date subsequently on which the power to amend the maximum amount was exercised.

Paragraph 10(4)

This paragraph makes it clear that the maximum amount applicable to a penalty can only be that amount applicable at the date of the contravention.

Paragraph 11 – appeal tribunal

Paragraph 11(1)

This paragraph makes it clear that the reference to an "appeal tribunal" in paragraph 7 of Schedule 13 has the same meaning as in FA 1994 Pt 1 Ch 2.

SCHEDULE 14

DIGITAL REPORTING AND RECORD-KEEPING FOR INCOME TAX ETC: FURTHER AMENDMENTS

Section 61

PART 1

AMENDMENTS OF TMA 1970

1 TMA 1970 is amended as follows.

2 (1) Section 7 (notice of liability) is amended as follows.

(2) In subsection (1A) for the words from "under section 8" to the end substitute "to file under section 8 for the year of assessment".

(3) In subsection (1B)(a) for the words from "under section 8" to "gains" substitute "to file under section 8 for the year of assessment".

(4) In subsection (7) for "section 9" substitute "section 8 or 8A".

3 (1) Section 8 (personal return) is amended as follows.

(2) For the heading substitute "Notices to file: persons other than trustees".

(3) For subsection (1) substitute—

"(1) For the purpose of establishing—

(a) the amounts in which a person is chargeable to income tax and capital gains tax for a year of assessment, and

(b) the amount payable by the person by way of income tax for the year,

an officer of Revenue and Customs may give the person a notice to file for the year of assessment."

(4) In subsection (1AA)(a) for "return" substitute "information filed in response to the notice to file or in any end of period statement for the year of assessment provided to HMRC by the person".

(5) After subsection (1AA) insert—

"(1AB) A notice to file for a year of assessment is a notice requiring the person concerned—

(a) to file the following for that year (in addition to any end of period statement for the year that may be required by regulations under paragraph 8 of Schedule A1)—

(i) such information as may reasonably be required in pursuance of the notice for the purpose mentioned in subsection (1),

(ii) a self-assessment (but see section 9(2)), and

(iii) a final declaration, and

(b) to deliver to HMRC such accounts, statements, or other documents (relating to the information filed as mentioned in paragraph (a)(i) and (ii)) as may reasonably be required for the purpose mentioned in subsection (1).

(1AC) The duty to file the things mentioned in subsection (1AB)(a) is to be complied with—

(a) where the person is not required to provide an end of period statement for the year, by making and delivering to HMRC a return containing those things, and

(b) where the person is required to provide such a statement, by—

(i) making and delivering to HMRC a return containing those things, or

(ii) providing those things to HMRC using the facility to file mentioned in paragraph 9 of Schedule A1.

(1AD) It is immaterial that any of the information required as mentioned in subsection (1AB)(a)(i) in response to a notice to file has been provided to HMRC before the date of the notice."

(6) In subsection (1B)—

(a) for "a return under this section" substitute "the information filed in response to a notice to file";

(b) after "relevant" insert "partnership".

(7) In subsection (1C)—

(a) after ""relevant" insert "partnership";

(b) after "means a" insert "partnership";

(c) for "of this Act" substitute ", or under regulations under paragraph 10 of Schedule A1,".

(8) For subsection (1D) substitute—

"(1D) Where the method to be used for complying with a notice to file for a year of assessment (Year 1) is filing a return—

(a) if the return is a non-electronic return, the person must comply with the notice on or before 31 October in Year 2, and

(b) if the return is an electronic return, the person must comply with the notice on or before 31 January in Year 2."

(9) In subsection (1F) for "a return" substitute "the return".

(10) In subsection (1G) for "a return" substitute "the return".

(11) After subsection (1H) insert—

"(1HA) Where the method to be used for complying with a notice to file for a year of assessment (Year 1) is using the facility mentioned in paragraph 9 of Schedule A1, the person must comply with the notice on or before—

(a) 31 January in Year 2, or

(b) if later, the last day of the period of 3 months beginning with the date of the notice."

(12) For subsection (2) substitute—

"(2) The final declaration required by a notice to file is a declaration by the person concerned to the effect that to the best of the person's knowledge the information and self-assessment filed in response to the notice are (taken together) correct and complete."

(13) In subsections (3), (4) and (4A) for "under this section" substitute "to file".

(14) In subsection (4B) for the words from "may" to "income" substitute "to file may require the information filed in response".

(15) After subsection (5) insert—

"(6) In this section "notice to file" means a notice to file under this section.

(7) In the Taxes Acts, unless the contrary intention appears, a reference (whether specific or general)—

(a) to a return under this section for a year of assessment, is to—

(i) the information, self-assessment and final declaration filed for the year under this section, and

(ii) any end of period statement for the year provided to HMRC;

(b) to anything required to be included in a return under this section for a year of assessment, is to—

(i) the information, self-assessment and final declaration required to be filed for the year under this section, and

(ii) any end of period statement for the year required to be provided to HMRC, and

(c) to making or delivering a return under this section, is to—

(i) making or delivering a return as mentioned in subsection (1AC)(a) or (b)(i), or

(ii) if the response to a notice to file is made using the facility mentioned in paragraph 9 of Schedule A1, making the final declaration required by the notice."

4 (1) Section 8A (trustee's return) is amended as follows.

(2) For the heading substitute "Notices to file: trustees".

(3) For subsection (1) substitute—

"(1) For the purpose of establishing—

(a) the amounts in which the relevant trustees of a settlement, and the settlors and beneficiaries, are chargeable to income tax and capital gains tax for a year of assessment, and

(b) the amount payable by them by way of income tax for the year,

an officer of Revenue and Customs may give any relevant trustee a notice to file for the year of assessment.

(1ZA) A notice to file may be given to any one trustee or separate notices may be given to each trustee or to such trustees as the officer giving the notice thinks fit."

(4) In subsection (1AA)(a) for "return" substitute "information filed in response to the notice to file or in any end of period statement for the year of assessment provided to HMRC by the relevant trustees".

(5) After subsection (1AA) insert—

"(1AB) A notice to file for a year of assessment is a notice requiring the trustee to whom it is given—

(a) to file the following for that year (in addition to any end of period statement for the year that may be required by regulations under paragraph 8 of Schedule A1)—

(i) such information as may reasonably be required in pursuance of the notice for the purpose mentioned in subsection (1),

(ii) a self-assessment (but see section 9(2)), and

(iii) a final declaration, and

(b) to deliver to HMRC such accounts, statements, or other documents (relating to the information filed as mentioned in paragraph (a)(i) and (ii)) as may reasonably be required for the purpose mentioned in subsection (1).

(1AC) The duty to file the things mentioned in subsection (1AB)(a) is to be complied with—

(a) where the relevant trustees are not required to provide an end of period statement for the year, by the trustee making and delivering to HMRC a return containing those things, and

(b) where the relevant trustees are required to provide such a statement, by the trustee—

(i) making and delivering to HMRC a return containing those things, or

(ii) providing those things to HMRC using the facility to file mentioned in paragraph 9 of Schedule A1.

(1AD) It is immaterial that any of the information required as mentioned in subsection (1AB)(a)(i) in response to a notice to file has been provided to HMRC before the date of the notice."

(6) For subsection (1B) substitute—

"(1B) Where the method to be used by the trustee for complying with a notice to file for a year of assessment (Year 1) is filing a return—

(a) if the return is a non-electronic return, the trustee must comply with the notice on or before 31 October in Year 2, and

(b) if the return is an electronic return, the trustee must comply with the notice on or before 31 January in Year 2."

(7) In subsection (1D) for "a return" substitute "the return".

(8) In subsection (1E) for "a return" substitute "the return".

(9) After subsection (1F) insert—

"(1FA) Where the method to be used for complying with a notice to file for a year of assessment (Year 1) is using the facility mentioned in paragraph 9 of Schedule A1, the trustee must comply with the notice on or before—

(a) 31 January in Year 2, or

(b) if later, the last day of the period of 3 months beginning with the date of the notice."

(10) For subsection (2) substitute—

"(2) The final declaration required by a notice to file is a declaration by the trustee to the effect that to the best of the trustee's knowledge the information and self-assessment filed in response to the notice are (taken together) correct and complete."

(11) In subsections (3) and (4) for "under this section" substitute "to file".

(12) After subsection (5) insert—

"(6) In this section "notice to file" means a notice to file under this section.

(7) In the Taxes Acts, unless the contrary intention appears, a reference (whether specific or general)—

(a) to a return under this section for a year of assessment, is to—

(i) the information, self-assessment and final declaration filed for the year under this section, and

(ii) any end of period statement for the year provided to HMRC,

(b) to anything required to be included in a return under this section for a year of assessment, is to—

(i) the information, self-assessment and final declaration required to be filed for the year under this section, and

(ii) any end of period statement for the year required to be provided to HMRC, and

(c) to making or delivering a return under this section, is to—

(i) making or delivering a return as mentioned in subsection (1AC)(a) or (b)(i), or

(ii) if the response to a notice to file is made using the facility mentioned in paragraph 9 of Schedule A1, making the final declaration required by the notice."

5 In section 8B (withdrawal of notice under section 8 or 8A)—

(a) in the heading after "notice" insert "to file";

(b) in subsection (1) after "notice" insert "to file".

6 (1) Section 9 (returns to include self-assessment) is amended as follows.

(2) For the heading substitute "Self-assessment required by a notice to file".

(3) In subsection (1) for the words from the beginning to "say—" substitute "Subject to subsection (1A), the self-assessment required by virtue of subsection (1AB)(a) of section 8 or 8A from a person given a notice to file for a year of assessment is—".

(4) In subsection (2) for "to comply with subsection (1) above" substitute "by virtue of section 8 or 8A to make and file a self-assessment".

(5) In subsection (3) for the words from ", a person" to "above" substitute "required by virtue of section 8 or 8A, a person does not include a self-assessment".

(6) In subsection (3A) after "self-assessment" insert "under section 8 or 8A".

7 (1) Section 12ZH (NRCGT returns and self-assessment: section 8) is amended as follows.

(2) In subsection (3) for the words from "required" to "return" substitute "given a notice to file".

(3) In subsection (4) after "(1G)" insert "and (1HA)".

(4) In subsections (5) and (6) omit ", for the purposes set out in section 9(1),".

(5) In subsection (8)(b) for "section 9" substitute "section 8".

(6) In subsection (10) for "section 9" substitute "section 8".

(7) In subsection (11) for "section 9" substitute "section 8".

8 (1) Section 12ZI (NRCGT returns and self-assessment: section 8A) is amended as follows.

(2) In subsection (3) for the words from "required" to "return" substitute "given a notice to file".

(3) In subsection (4)(b) after "(1E)" insert "and (1FA)".

(4) In subsections (5) and (6) omit ", for the purposes set out in section 9(1),".

(5) In subsection (8)(b) for "section 9" substitute "section 8A".

(6) In subsection (10) for "section 9" substitute "section 8A".

(7) In subsection (11) for "section 9" substitute "section 8A".

9 In section 12AA(10A) (definitions) for ""partnership return"" substitute ""section 12AA partnership return"".

10 In section 12AB(1) (partnership return to include partnership statement) in the words before paragraph (a) after "Every" insert "section 12AA".

11 (1) Section 12ABA (amendment of partnership return by taxpayer) is amended as follows.

(2) In subsection (1)—

    (a) omit the words from "by the" to "successor,";

    (b) at the end insert "given by—

        (a) in the case of a section 12AA partnership return, the partner who made and delivered the return or his successor, and

        (b) in the case of a Schedule A1 partnership return, the nominated partner."

(3) In subsection (4) after "date"" insert ", in relation to a section 12AA partnership return,".

(4) After subsection (4) insert—

    "(5) In this section "the filing date", in relation to a Schedule A1 partnership return for a year of assessment (Year 1), means 31 January of Year 2."

12 (1) Section 12ABB (HMRC power to correct partnership return) is amended as follows.

(2) In subsection (2), for the words from "by notice" to the end substitute—

    "(a) in the case of a section 12AA partnership return, by notice to the partner who made and delivered the return, or his successor, and

    (b) in the case of a Schedule A1 partnership return, by notice to the nominated partner."

(3) In subsection (4) for the words from "the person" to the end substitute "notice rejecting the correction is given—

    (a) in the case of a section 12AA partnership return, by the person to whom the notice of correction was given or his successor, and

    (b) in the case of a Schedule A1 partnership return, by the nominated partner."

13 (1) Section 12AC (notice of enquiry into partnership return) is amended as follows.

(2) In subsection (1)—

    (a) after "return if" insert ", within the time allowed,";

    (b) at the beginning of paragraph (a) insert "in the case of a section 12AA partnership return,";

    (c) after that paragraph insert—

    "(aa) in the case of a Schedule A1 partnership return, to the nominated partner.";

    (d) omit paragraph (b).

(3) In subsection (7)—

    (a) the words from "the day" to the end become paragraph (a);

    (b) at the beginning of that paragraph insert "in relation to a section 12AA partnership return,";

    (c) after that paragraph insert—

"(b) in relation to a Schedule A1 partnership return for a year of assessment (Year 1), means 31 January of Year 2."

14 (1) Section 12B (records to be kept for purposes of returns) is amended as follows.

(2) For subsection (1) substitute—

"(1) This section applies to any person who may—

(a) be given a notice to file under section 8 or 8A in respect of a year of assessment,

(b) be required by a notice under section 12AA to make and deliver a partnership return in respect of a year of assessment or other period, or

(c) be required by regulations under paragraph 10 of Schedule A1 to provide a partnership return for a year of assessment.

(1A) The person must—

(a) keep all such records as may be requisite for the purpose of enabling the person to make and deliver a correct and complete return, under that section or those regulations, for that year of assessment or period, and

(b) preserve those records until the end of the relevant day (see subsections (2) to (2ZB))."

(3) In subsection (2) for "day referred to in subsection (1) above is" substitute "relevant day is (subject to subsection (2ZB))".

(4) After subsection (2) insert—

"(2ZA) Subsection (2ZB) applies where, before the day mentioned in subsection (2), the person—

(a) is given a notice under section 8, 8A or 12AA, or

(b) becomes subject to a requirement imposed by regulations under paragraph 10 of Schedule A1.

(2ZB) Where this subsection applies the relevant day is the later of the day mentioned in subsection (2), and—

(a) if enquiries are made into the return, the day on which under section 28A(1B) or 28B(1B) those enquiries are completed, or

(b) if no such enquiries are made, the day on which an officer no longer has power to make them."

(5) In subsection (2A)—

(a) in paragraph (a) for "(1)" substitute "(1)(a) or (b)";

(b) in the words after paragraph (b)—

(i) omit "the relevant day, that is to say,";

(ii) for "(1)" substitute "(1A)".

(6) In subsection (3)(a) for "(1)" substitute "(1A)".

(7) In subsection (4)—

(a) for "(1)" substitute "(1A)";

(b) at the end insert "and regulations under paragraph 11 of Schedule A1".

(8) In subsection (5) for "(1)" substitute "(1A)".

15 In section 28ZA(6) (referral of questions during enquiry)—

(a) in paragraph (b) after "of this Act" insert "into a section 12AA partnership return";

(b) after paragraph (b) insert—

"(c) in relation to an enquiry under section 12AC(1) of this Act into a Schedule A1 partnership return, the nominated partner."

16 In section 28B(8) (completion of enquiry into partnership return) for the words from "the person" to the end substitute—

"(a) in relation to a section 12AA partnership return, the person to whom notice of enquiry was given or his successor, and

(b) in relation to a Schedule A1 partnership return, the nominated partner."

17 In section 28C(3) (determination of tax where no return delivered) for "section 9" substitute "section 8 or 8A".

18 In section 28H(2)(b) (simple assessments)—

(a) for the words "to make and deliver such a return" substitute "imposed";

(b) after "notice" insert "to file".

19 In section 28I(2)(b) (simple assessments for trustees)—

(a) for the words "to make and deliver such a return" substitute "imposed";

(b) after "notice" insert "to file".

20 (1) Section 29 (assessment where loss of tax discovered) is amended as follows.

(2) In subsection (2) at the end insert "(or, where the error or mistake is in an end of period statement forming part of the return, if that statement was provided on the basis of or in accordance with the practice generally prevailing at the time when it was provided)."

(3) In subsection (6) after paragraph (a) insert—

"(aa) it is contained in any information provided by the taxpayer to HMRC under regulations under paragraph 7 of Schedule A1 (periodic updates);".

21 In section 30B(10) (amendment of partnership statement where loss of tax discovered) at the end insert "or (in relation to a Schedule A1 partnership return) the nominated partner".

22 (1) Section 42 (procedure for making claims) is amended as follows.

(2) In subsection (2)—

(a) after "of this Act" insert ", or where a partnership is required to provide a return by regulations under paragraph 10 of Schedule A1,";
(b) after "that section" insert "or those regulations".

(3) In subsection (9) after "of this Act" insert "or a Schedule A1 partnership return".

(4) In subsection (11)(a) after "of this Act" insert "or a Schedule A1 partnership return".

23 (1) Section 59A (payments on account of income tax) is amended as follows.

(2) In subsection (1)(a) for "section 9" substitute "section 8 or 8A".

(3) In subsection (4A)(a) for "section 9" substitute "section 8 or 8A".

24 (1) Section 59B (payment of income tax and capital gains tax: assessments other than simple assessments) is amended as follows.

(2) In subsection (1)(a) for "section 9" substitute "section 8 or 8A".

(3) In subsection (4A) for "section 9" substitute "section 8 or 8A".

(4) In subsection (5A) for "section 9" substitute "section 8 or 8A".

(5) In subsection (6) for "section 9" substitute "section 8 or 8A".

25 (1) Section 106C (offence of failing to deliver a return) is amended as follows.

(2) In subsection (1)—

(a) for "required by a notice under section 8 to make and deliver a return" substitute "given a notice to file under section 8";
(b) in paragraph (a) for "the return" substitute "a return under that section".

(3) In subsection (2) for "the return" substitute "a return under section 8".

26 In section 106D(1) (offence of making inaccurate return)—

(a) for "required by a notice under section 8 to make and deliver a return" substitute "given a notice to file under section 8";
(b) in paragraph (a) after "return" insert "under that section".

27 In section 106E (exclusions from offences under sections 106B to 106D) for "or make and deliver the return" substitute "under section 7, or is given the notice to file under section 8,".

28 In section 107A(2)(a) (trustee liability for penalties) after "section 12B of this Act" insert "or paragraph 12 of Schedule A1 to this Act".

29 In section 118(1) (interpretation)—

(a) after the definition of "CTA 2010" insert—
""end of period statement" has the meaning given by paragraph 8(6) of Schedule A1, and references to an end of period statement for a tax year are to be read in accordance with that paragraph;";
(b) after the definition of "ITA 2007" insert—
""nominated partner" has the meaning given by paragraph 5(5) of Schedule A1;"
(c) in the definition of "partnership return" for the words from "has the" to the end substitute "means (unless the context otherwise requires)—
(a) a section 12AA partnership return, or
(b) a Schedule A1 partnership return;";
(d) after the definition of "partnership return" insert—
""partnership statement"—
(a) in relation to a section 12AA partnership return, means the statement required by section 12AB;
(b) in relation to a Schedule A1 partnership return, has the meaning given by paragraph 10(6) of that Schedule;"

(e) after the definition of "return" insert—
    ""Schedule A1 partnership return" has the meaning given by paragraph 10(6) of Schedule A1;
    "section 12AA partnership return" has the meaning given by section 12AA(10A) of this Act;";
  (f) in the definition of "successor" after "delivered, a" insert "section 12AA".

30 (1) Paragraph 3 of Schedule 1AB (recovery of overpaid tax) is amended as follows.

(2) In sub-paragraph (2)(a) after "of this Act" insert "or a Schedule A1 partnership return".

(3) In sub-paragraph (3)(a) after "12AA" insert "or a Schedule A1 partnership return".

(4) In sub-paragraph (4) at the end insert "or a Schedule A1 partnership return".

PART 2

AMENDMENTS OF OTHER ACTS

TCGA 1992

31 In section 188J(2) of TCGA 1992 (the representative company of an NRCGT group) for "section 9(2)" substitute "section 8(1AB)(a)(iii)".

FA 1998

32 In paragraph 12(2) of Schedule 18 to FA 1998 (information about business carried on in partnership) for "statement under section 12AB of" substitute "partnership statement within the meaning of".

CAA 2001

33 In section 201(6) of CAA 2001 (elections) after "section 12AA of" insert "or regulations under paragraph 10 of Schedule A1 to".

Tax Credits Act 2002

34 In section 19(4)(a) of the Tax Credits Act 2002 (power to enquire) for "by section 8 of the Taxes Management Act 1970 (c. 9) to make a return" substitute "to make a return under section 8 of the Taxes Management Act 1970".

ITTOIA 2005

35 In section 217(2) of ITTOIA 2005 (conditions for basis period to end with new accounting date)—
  (a) in paragraph (a)—
    (i) after "TMA 1970" insert ", or of regulations under that Act," and
    (ii) after "or 12AA of" insert ", or regulations under paragraph 10 of Schedule A1 to,";
  (b) in paragraph (b) for "provision" substitute "section or paragraph".

ITA 2007

36 In section 964(4)(b) (collection through self-assessment return) for "section 9 of that Act" substitute "that section".

Crossrail Act 2008

37 In paragraph 44(1)(a) of Schedule 13 to the Crossrail Act 2008 (modification of transfer schemes: other persons and partnerships) after "12AA of" insert ", or regulations under paragraph 10 of Schedule A1 to,".

FA 2008

38 (1) Schedule 36 to FA 2008 (information and inspection powers) is amended as follows.

(2) In paragraph 21(1) (taxpayer notices) after "12AA of" insert ", or regulations under paragraph 10 of Schedule A1 to,".

(3) In paragraph 37(2)(a) (partnerships) after "section 12AA of" insert ", or regulations under paragraph 10 of Schedule A1 to,".

TIOPA 2010

39 TIOPA 2010 is amended as follows.

40 In section 94(3) (information made available) in each of paragraphs (a) and (b) after "section 12AA of" insert ", or regulations under paragraph 10 of Schedule A1 to,".

41 In section 95(8)(a) (interpretation of "tax return") after "12AA of" insert ", or regulations under paragraph 10 of Schedule A1 to,".

42 In section 171(5) (tax returns where transfer pricing notice given), in paragraph (a) of the definition of "tax return", after "12AA of" insert ", or regulations under paragraph 10 of Schedule A1 to,".

FA 2014

43 FA 2014 is amended as follows.

44 In section 253(6)(c) (definition of "tax return") after "section 12AA of" insert ", or regulations under paragraph 10 of Schedule A1 to,".

45 (1) Schedule 31 (follower notices and partnerships) is amended as follows.

(2) In paragraph 2 (interpretation)—

  (a) in sub-paragraph (3)—

    (i) the words from "in pursuance" to the end become paragraph (a);

    (ii) at the end of that paragraph insert "(a "section 12AA partnership return"), or";

    (iii) after that paragraph insert—

      "(b) required by regulations under paragraph 10 of Schedule A1 to TMA 1970 (a "Schedule A1 partnership return").";

  (b) in sub-paragraph (4) after "in relation to a" insert "section 12AA";

  (c) after sub-paragraph (4) insert—

    "(4A) "The nominated partner", in relation to a Schedule A1 partnership return, has the meaning given by paragraph 5 of Schedule A1 to TMA 1970."

(3) In paragraph 3 (giving of follower notices in relation to partnership returns)—

  (a) in sub-paragraph (1), after "in relation to a" insert "section 12AA";

  (b) after sub-paragraph (1) insert—

    "(1A) For the purposes of section 204 a Schedule A1 partnership return, or an appeal in respect of the return, is to be regarded as made by the person who is for the time being the nominated partner (if that would not otherwise be the case).";

  (c) in sub-paragraph (2), at the end insert ", or the nominated partner (as the case may be).";

  (d) in sub-paragraph (4)—

    (i) in paragraph (a), after "or a successor of that partner," insert "or as the nominated partner of a partnership,";

    (ii) in paragraph (b) after "successors of that partner" insert "or to a nominated partner".

(4) In paragraph 5 (calculation of penalty etc) in sub-paragraph (10)—

  (a) the words from "the representative partner" to the end become paragraph (a);

  (b) at the end of that paragraph insert "(in relation to a section 12AA partnership return), or";

  (c) after that paragraph insert—

    "(b) the nominated partner (in relation to a Schedule A1 partnership return)."

46 (1) Schedule 32 (accelerated payments and partnerships) is amended as follows.

(2) In paragraph 1 (interpretation)—

  (a) in sub-paragraph (2)—

    (i) the words from "in pursuance" to the end become paragraph (a);

    (ii) at the end of that paragraph insert "(a "section 12AA partnership return"), or";

    (iii) after that paragraph insert—

      "(b) required by regulations under paragraph 10 of Schedule A1 to TMA 1970 (a "Schedule A1 partnership return").";

  (b) in sub-paragraph (3) after "in relation to a" insert "section 12AA";

  (c) after sub-paragraph (3) insert—

    "(3A) "The nominated partner", in relation to a Schedule A1 partnership return, has the meaning given by paragraph 5 of Schedule A1 to TMA 1970."

(3) In paragraph 2(2) (restriction on circumstances when accelerated payment notices can be given) after "a successor of that partner" insert "(in relation to a section 12AA partnership return), or to the nominated partner of the partnership (in relation to a Schedule A1 partnership return)".

(4) In paragraph 3(5)(a) (circumstances in which partner payment notices can be given) after "or a successor of that partner" insert "(in relation to a section 12AA partnership return), or the nominated partner (in relation to a Schedule A1 partnership return)".

FA 2016

47 FA 2016 is amended as follows.

48 (1) Schedule 18 (serial tax avoidance) is amended as follows.

(2) In paragraph 51(8)(b) (partnerships: information) after "TMA 1970" insert ", or under equivalent provision made by regulations under paragraph 10 of Schedule A1 to that Act,".

(3) In paragraph 52 (partnerships: special provision about taxpayer emendations)—

(a) in sub-paragraph (1) for "subsection (1)(b) of section 12AB of that Act (partnership statement)" substitute "section 12AB(1)(b) of that Act or under equivalent provision made by regulations under paragraph 10 of Schedule A1 to that Act (partnership statement)";
(b) in sub-paragraph (3)—

(i) in the words before paragraph (a), after "that person's successor" insert "(in the case of a section 12AA partnership return) or the nominated partner (in the case of a Schedule A1 partnership return)";
(ii) for "subsection (1)(b) of section 12AB of TMA 1970 (partnership statement)" substitute "section 12AB(1)(b) of TMA 1970 or under equivalent provision made by regulations under paragraph 10 of Schedule A1 to that Act (partnership statement)".

(4) In paragraph 53(1) (supplementary provision relating to partnerships)—

(a) in the definition of "the representative partner" after "in relation to a" insert "section 12AA";
(b) after the definition of "successor" insert—
""the nominated partner", in relation to a Schedule A1 partnership return, has the meaning given by paragraph 5 of Schedule A1 to TMA 1970."

(5) In paragraph 58(1) (general interpretation), for the definition of "partnership return" substitute—

""partnership return" means a return—

(a) under section 12AA of TMA 1970 (a "section 12AA partnership return"), or
(b) required by regulations made under paragraph 10 of Schedule A1 to TMA 1970 (a "Schedule A1 partnership return");".

49 (1) Schedule 19 (large businesses: tax strategies and sanctions) is amended as follows.

(2) In paragraph 12(5) (definition of "representative partner")—

(a) the words from "the partner" to the end become paragraph (a);
(b) at the end of that paragraph insert ", or";
(c) after that paragraph insert—
"(b) the nominated partner within the meaning of paragraph 5 of Schedule A1 to TMA 1970."

(3) In paragraph 13 (definition of "financial year") in paragraph (c) for "under a return issued under section 12AB" substitute "within the meaning of".

GENERAL NOTE

The modifications to the requirement to make a return change the phraseology to "information filed in response to a notice to file" so that as individuals come within Making Tax Digital they may have to meet their obligations under a notice to file by making the electronic submissions required by Schedule A1, together with other information. The terms are flexible enough to cover those who are not within the obligations under Schedule A1, and still include the possibility of making a formal return.

The existing deadlines for making a self-assessment return are retained, but the wording is amended to recognise that the obligation may be met by providing "information" rather than a return. The requirement for a declaration is also expanded so that it covers a return and/or information provided. Finally, all references to a return are now to be taken (unless specified to the contrary) as a reference to:

– the information, self-assessment and final declaration filed for the year ..., and
– any end of period statement for the year provided to HMRC.

Consequential changes flow through to legislation on determinations, penalties for late filing, accelerated payment notices and similar. The main source of amendment is the renaming of a partnership return which can now be a return under TMA 1970 s 12AA or a return under Schedule A1 of the same.

SCHEDULE 15
PARTIAL CLOSURE NOTICES
Section 63

TMA 1970

1 TMA 1970 is amended as follows.

2 In section 9A (notice of enquiry), in subsection (5)—

(a) in paragraph (a), omit the final "or";

(b) for paragraph (b) substitute—

"(b) after a final closure notice has been issued in relation to an enquiry into the return, or

(c) after a partial closure notice has been issued in such an enquiry in relation to the matters to which the amendment relates or which are affected by the amendment,".

3 (1) Section 9B (amendment of return by taxpayer during enquiry) is amended as follows.

(2) In subsection (1), for "is in progress into the return" substitute "into the return is in progress in relation to any matter to which the amendment relates or which is affected by the amendment".

(3) In subsection (3)—

(a) after "in progress" insert "in relation to any matter to which the amendment relates or which is affected by the amendment";

(b) in paragraph (a), for "the closure notice" substitute "a partial or final closure notice";

(c) in paragraph (b), for "the closure notice is issued" substitute "a partial closure notice is issued in relation to the matters to which the amendment relates or which are affected by the amendment or, if no such notice is issued, a final closure notice is issued".

(4) In subsection (4)—

(a) after "in progress" insert "in relation to any matter";

(b) for "the enquiry is completed" substitute "a partial closure notice is issued in relation to the matter or, if no such notice is issued, a final closure notice is issued".

4 (1) Section 9C (amendment of self-assessment during enquiry to prevent loss of tax) is amended as follows.

(2) In subsection (1), for "is in progress into a return" substitute "into a return is in progress in relation to any matter".

(3) In subsection (2), after "deficiency" insert "so far as it relates to the matter".

(4) In subsection (4)—

(a) after "in progress" insert "in relation to any matter";

(b) for "the enquiry is completed" substitute "a partial closure notice is issued in relation to the matter or, if no such notice is issued, a final closure notice is issued".

5 In section 12ZM (NRCGT returns: notice of enquiry), in subsection (4)—

(a) in paragraph (a), omit the final "or";

(b) for paragraph (b) substitute—

"(b) after a final closure notice has been issued in relation to an enquiry into the return, or

(c) after a partial closure notice has been issued in such an enquiry in relation to the matters to which the amendment relates or which are affected by the amendment,".

6 (1) Section 12ZN (NRCGT returns: amendment of return by taxpayer during enquiry) is amended as follows.

(2) In subsection (1), for "is in progress into the return" substitute "into the return is in progress in relation to any matter to which the amendment relates or which is affected by the amendment".

(3) In subsection (3)—

(a) after "in progress" insert "in relation to any matter to which the amendment relates or which is affected by the amendment";

(b) in paragraph (a), for "the closure notice" substitute "a partial or final closure notice";

(c) in paragraph (b), for "the closure notice is issued" substitute "a partial closure notice is issued in relation to the matters to which the amendment relates or which are affected by the amendment or, if no such notice is issued, a final closure notice is issued".

(4) In subsection (4)—

(a) after "in progress" insert "in relation to any matter";

(b) for "the enquiry is completed" substitute "a partial closure notice is issued in relation to the matter or, if no such notice is issued, a final closure notice is issued".

7 In section 12AC (partnership return: notice of enquiry), in subsection (5)—

(a) in paragraph (a), omit the final "or";

(b) for paragraph (b) substitute—

"(b) after a final closure notice has been issued in relation to an enquiry into the return, or

(c) after a partial closure notice has been issued in such an enquiry in relation to the matters to which the amendment relates or which are affected by the amendment,".

8 (1) Section 12AD (amendment of partnership return by taxpayer during enquiry) is amended as follows.

(2) In subsection (1), for "is in progress into the return" substitute "into the return is in progress in relation to any matter to which the amendment relates or which is affected by the amendment".

(3) In subsection (3)—

(a) after "in progress" insert "in relation to any matter to which the amendment relates or which is affected by the amendment";

(b) in paragraph (a), for "the closure notice" substitute "a partial or final closure notice";

(c) in paragraph (b), for "the closure notice is issued" substitute "a partial closure notice is issued in relation to the matters to which the amendment relates or which are affected by the amendment or, if no such notice is issued, a final closure notice is issued".

(4) In subsection (4)(a), after "in progress" insert "in relation to any matter to which the amendment relates or which is affected by the amendment".

(5) In subsection (5)—

(a) after "in progress" insert "in relation to any matter";

(b) for "the enquiry is completed" substitute "a partial closure notice is issued in relation to the matter or, if no such notice is issued, a final closure notice is issued".

9 In section 12B (records), in subsection (1)(b)(i), for "28A(1) or 28B(1)" substitute "28A(1B) or 28B(1B)".

10 (1) Section 28ZA (referral of questions during enquiry) is amended as follows.

(2) In subsection (1), after "of this Act" insert "in relation to any matter".

(3) In subsection (5)—

(a) after "in progress" insert "in relation to any matter";

(b) for "the enquiry is completed" substitute "a partial closure notice is issued in relation to the matter or, if no such notice is issued, a final closure notice is issued".

11 In section 28ZD (effect of referral on enquiry), in subsection (1)—

(a) for paragraph (a) substitute—

"(a) no partial closure notice relating to the question referred shall be given,

(aa) no final closure notice shall be given in relation to the enquiry, and";

(b) in paragraph (b), for "such a notice" substitute "a notice referred to in paragraph (a) or (aa)".

12 (1) Section 28A (completion of enquiry into personal, trustee or NRCGT return) is amended as follows.

(2) For subsection (1) substitute—

"(1) This section applies in relation to an enquiry under section 9A(1) or 12ZM of this Act.

(1A) Any matter to which the enquiry relates is completed when an officer of Revenue and Customs informs the taxpayer by notice (a "partial closure notice") that the officer has completed his enquiries into that matter.

(1B) The enquiry is completed when an officer of Revenue and Customs informs the taxpayer by notice (a "final closure notice") —

  (a) in a case where no partial closure notice has been given, that the officer has completed his enquiries, or

  (b) in a case where one or more partial closure notices have been given, that the officer has completed his remaining enquiries."

(3) In subsection (2)—

  (a) for "closure notice" substitute "partial or final closure notice";

  (b) for "either" substitute "state the officer's conclusions and".

(4) In subsections (3) and (4), for "closure notice" substitute "partial or final closure notice".

(5) In subsection (6), for "a closure notice" substitute "the partial or final closure notice".

(6) After subsection (6) insert—

  "(7) In this section "the taxpayer" means the person to whom notice of enquiry was given.

  (8) In the Taxes Acts, references to a closure notice under this section are to a partial or final closure notice under this section."

13 (1) Section 28B (completion of enquiry into partnership return) is amended as follows.

(2) For subsection (1) substitute—

  "(1) This section applies in relation to an enquiry under section 12AC of this Act.

  (1A) Any matter to which the enquiry relates is completed when an officer of Revenue and Customs informs the taxpayer by notice (a "partial closure notice") that the officer has completed his enquiries into that matter.

  (1B) The enquiry is completed when an officer of Revenue and Customs informs the taxpayer by notice (a "final closure notice")—

  (a) in a case where no partial closure notice has been given, that the officer has completed his enquiries, or

  (b) in a case where one or more partial closure notices have been given, that the officer has completed his remaining enquiries."

(3) In subsection (2)—

  (a) for "closure notice" substitute "partial or final closure notice";

  (b) for "either" substitute "state the officer's conclusions and".

(4) In subsections (3) and (5), for "closure notice" substitute "partial or final closure notice".

(5) In subsection (7), for "a closure notice" substitute "the partial or final closure notice".

(6) After subsection (7) insert—

  "(8) In this section "the taxpayer" means the person to whom notice of enquiry was given or his successor.

  (9) In the Taxes Acts, references to a closure notice under this section are to a partial or final closure notice under this section."

14 In section 29 (assessment where loss of tax discovered), in subsection (5), for paragraph (b) substitute—

  "(b) in a case where a notice of enquiry into the return was given—

    (i) issued a partial closure notice as regards a matter to which the situation mentioned in subsection (1) above relates, or

    (ii) if no such partial closure notice was issued, issued a final closure notice,".

15 In section 29A (NRCGT disposals: determination of amount which should have been assessed), in subsection (5), for paragraph (b) substitute—

  "(b) in a case where a notice of enquiry into the return was given—

    (i) issued a partial closure notice as regards a matter to which the situation mentioned in subsection (1) relates, or

    (ii) if no such partial closure notice was issued, issued a final closure notice,".

16 In section 30 (recovery of overpayment of tax etc), in subsection (5)(b), for "28A(1)" substitute "28A(1B)".

17 In section 30B (amendment of partnership statement where loss of tax discovered), in subsection (6), for paragraph (b) substitute—

  "(b) in a case where a notice of enquiry into that return was given—

(i) issued a partial closure notice as regards a matter to which the situation mentioned in subsection (1) above relates, or

(ii) if no such partial closure notice was issued, issued a final closure notice,".

18 In section 31 (appeals: right of appeal), in subsection (2)—

(a) after "in progress" insert "in relation to any matter to which the amendment relates or which is affected by the amendment";

(b) for "the enquiry is completed" substitute "a partial closure notice is issued in relation to the matter or, if no such notice is issued, a final closure notice is issued".

19 In section 59AA (NRCGT disposals: payments on account of CGT), in subsection (8)(a), for "28A(1)" substitute "28A(1B)".

20 In section 59B (payment of income tax and capital gains tax), in subsection (4A)(a), for "28A(1)" substitute "28A(1B)".

21 (1) In Schedule 3ZA (date by which payment to be made after amendment etc of self-assessment), paragraph 2 is amended as follows.

(2) In sub-paragraph (3)(b)—

(a) for the first "the closure notice" substitute "a partial or final closure notice";

(b) for "the day on which the closure notice was given" substitute "the relevant day".

(3) After sub-paragraph (3) insert—

"(4) In sub-paragraph (3)(b), "the relevant day" means—

(a) in the case of an amount of tax that is payable, the day on which the partial or final closure notice was given;

(b) in the case of an amount of tax that is repayable—

(i) if the closure notice was a final closure notice, the day on which that notice was given, and

(ii) if the closure notice was a partial closure notice, the day on which the final closure notice relating to the enquiry was given."

TCGA 1992

22 (1) Section 184I of TCGA 1992 (notices under sections 184G and 184H) is amended as follows.

(2) In subsection (4)—

(a) after "completed" insert "in relation to any matters";

(b) after "relevant notice" insert "relating to those matters".

(3) In subsection (5), for "into the return" substitute "referred to in subsection (4)".

(4) In subsection (7)(a), after "period" insert "(so far as relating to the matters in question)".

(5) After subsection (9) insert—

"(9A) Subsection (9) does not apply to a partial closure notice which does not relate to any matter to which the relevant notice relates."

(6) In subsection (10), after "completed," insert "so far as relating to the matters to which the relevant notice relates,".

FA 1998

23 Schedule 18 to FA 1998 (company tax returns, assessments and related matters) is amended as follows.

24 (1) Paragraph 30 (amendment of self-assessment during enquiry to prevent loss of tax) is amended as follows.

(2) In sub-paragraph (1)—

(a) for "before the enquiry is completed" substitute "while the enquiry is in progress in relation to a matter";

(b) after "deficiency" insert "so far as it relates to the matter".

(3) After sub-paragraph (5) insert—

"(6) For the purposes of this paragraph, the period during which an enquiry is in progress in relation to any matter is the whole of the period—

(a) beginning with the day on which notice of enquiry is given, and

(b) ending with the day on which a partial closure notice is issued in relation to the matter or, if no such notice is issued, a final closure notice is issued."

25 (1) Paragraph 31 (amendment of return by company during enquiry) is amended as follows.

(2) In sub-paragraph (1), for "is in progress into the return" substitute "into the return is in progress in relation to any matter to which the amendment relates or which is affected by the amendment".

(3) In sub-paragraph (3) for "until after the enquiry is completed" substitute "while the enquiry is in progress in relation to any matter to which the amendment relates or which is affected by the amendment".

(4) In sub-paragraph (4)(a)—

(a) for "the closure notice" substitute "a partial or final closure notice";
(b) for "on the completion of the enquiry" substitute "when a partial closure notice is issued in relation to the matters to which the amendment relates or which are affected by the amendment or, if no such notice is issued, a final closure notice is issued".

(5) In sub-paragraph (5)—

(a) after "in progress" insert "in relation to any matter";
(b) for "the enquiry is completed" substitute "a partial closure notice is issued in relation to the matter or, if no such notice is issued, a final closure notice is issued".

26 (1) Paragraph 31A (referral of questions to the tribunal during enquiry) is amended as follows.

(2) In sub-paragraph (1), for "into" substitute "in relation to any matter relating to".

(3) In sub-paragraph (5)—

(a) after "in progress" insert "in relation to any matter";
(b) for "the enquiry is completed" substitute "a partial closure notice is issued in relation to the matter or, if no such notice is issued, a final closure notice is issued".

27 In paragraph 31C (effect of referral on enquiry), in sub-paragraph (1)—

(a) for paragraph (a) substitute—
"(a) no partial closure notice relating to the question referred shall be given,
(aa) no final closure notice shall be given in relation to the enquiry, and";
(b) in paragraph (b), for "such a notice" substitute "a notice referred to in paragraph (a) or (aa)".

28 (1) Paragraph 32 (completion of enquiry) is amended as follows.

(2) For sub-paragraph (1) substitute—

"(1) Any matter to which an enquiry relates is completed when an officer of Revenue and Customs informs the company by notice (a "partial closure notice") that they have completed their enquiries into that matter.

(1A) An enquiry is completed when an officer of Revenue and Customs informs the company by notice (a "final closure notice")—

(a) in a case where no partial closure notice has been given, that they have completed their enquiries, or
(b) in a case where one or more partial closure notices have been given, that they have completed their remaining enquiries.

(1B) A partial or final closure notice takes effect when it is issued."

(3) In subsection (2), after "concludes" insert "in a partial or final closure notice".

(4) After sub-paragraph (3) insert—

"(4) In the Taxes Acts, references to a closure notice under this paragraph are to a partial or final closure notice under this paragraph."

29 In paragraph 33 (direction to complete enquiry), in sub-paragraphs (1) and (3), for "closure notice" substitute "partial or final closure notice".

30 (1) Paragraph 34 (amendment of return after enquiry) is amended as follows.

(2) In sub-paragraph (1), for "closure notice" substitute "partial or final closure notice".

(3) In sub-paragraph (2)—

(a) for "closure notice" substitute "partial or final closure notice";
(b) after "must" insert "state the officer's conclusions and".

(4) In sub-paragraphs (2A), (4)(c) and (5), for "closure notice" substitute "partial or final closure notice".

31 In paragraph 42 (restriction on power to make discovery assessment or determination), in sub-paragraph (2A), for the words from "after any" to the end substitute "a notice within sub-paragraph (4) after any enquiries have been completed into the return (so far as relating to the matters to which the notice relates)".

32 In paragraph 44 (situation not disclosed by return or related document etc), in sub-paragraph (1), for paragraph (b) substitute—

"(b) in a case where a notice of enquiry into the return was given—

(i) issued a partial closure notice as regards a matter to which the situation mentioned in paragraph 41(1) or (2) relates, or

(ii) if no such partial closure notice was issued, issued a final closure notice,".

33 In paragraph 61 (consequential claims etc), in sub-paragraphs (1)(a) and (3)(a), for "closure notice" substitute "partial or final closure notice".

34 (1) Paragraph 88 (conclusiveness) is amended as follows.

(2) In sub-paragraph (3)(b), at the end insert "(or is completed so far as relating to the matters to which the amount relates by the issue of a partial closure notice)".

(3) In sub-paragraph (4)(b), at the end insert "(or the completion of the enquiry so far as relating to the matters to which the amount relates by the issue of a partial closure notice)".

Tax Credits Act 2002

35 (1) Section 20 of the Tax Credits Act 2002 (decisions on discovery) is amended as follows.

(2) In subsection (2)(f), for "a closure notice" substitute "a partial or final closure notice".

(3) In subsection (3)(b), at the end insert "as specified in subsection (1)".

FA 2008

36 In Schedule 36 to FA 2008 (information and inspection powers), in paragraphs 21(4) and 21ZA(3), at the end insert "so far as relating to the matters to which the taxpayer notice relates".

TIOPA 2010

37 TIOPA 2010 is amended as follows.

38 (1) Section 92 (counteraction notices given after tax return made) is amended as follows.

(2) In subsection (3)—

  (a) after "completed" insert "in relation to any matters";
  (b) after "counteraction notice" insert "relating to those matters".

(3) In subsection (4), after "enquiries" insert "referred to in subsection (3)".

(4) In subsection (5)(a), after "return" insert "(so far as relating to the matters in question)".

39 (1) Section 93 (amendment, closure notices and discovery assessments in section 92 cases) is amended as follows.

(2) After subsection (3) insert—

"(3A) Subsection (3) does not apply to a partial closure notice which does not relate to any matter to which the counteraction notice relates."

(3) In subsection (4), after "completed," insert "so far as relating to the matters to which the counteraction notice relates,".

40 In section 171 (tax returns where transfer pricing notice given), after subsection (2) insert—

"(2A) Subsection (2) does not apply to a partial closure notice which does not relate to any matter to which the transfer pricing notice relates."

41 (1) Section 256 (notices given after tax return made), so far as continuing to have effect, is amended as follows.

(2) In subsection (2)—

  (a) after "completed" insert "in relation to any matters";
  (b) after "receipt notice" insert "relating to those matters".

(3) In subsection (6)(a), after "return" insert "(so far as relating to the matters in question)".

42 (1) Section 257 (amendments, closure notices etc), so far as continuing to have effect, is amended as follows.

(2) After subsection (4) insert—

"(4A) Subsection (4) does not apply to a partial closure notice which does not relate to any matter to which the Part 6 notice relates."

(3) In subsection (5), after "completed," insert "so far as relating to the matters to which the Part 6 notice relates,".

43 In section 371IJ (claims), in subsection (4)(b), after "completed" insert "so far as relating to the matters to which the claim relates".

Commencement

44 The amendments made by this Schedule have effect in relation to an enquiry under section 9A, 12ZM or 12AC of TMA 1970 or Schedule 18 to FA 1998 where—

    (a) notice of the enquiry is given on or after the day on which this Act is passed, or

    (b) the enquiry is in progress immediately before that day.

GENERAL NOTE

Paragraph 1 introduces amendments to the Taxes Management Act 1970 (TMA) to effect the operation of a partial closure notice similar to a full closure notice although limited to the subject of the notice.

Paragraph 2 to 11 make amendments to facilitate that operation, including:

- limiting the scope of notices of enquiries where a Partial Closure Notice is issued;
- permitting any taxpayer amendment relating to matters in an open enquiry to be concluded by Partial of Final Closure Notices and restricting enquiries to matters to which the taxpayer amendment relates;
- allowing amendments to a self-assessment during an enquiry in relation to matters not concluded by a Partial Closure Notice;
- preserving records to the date on which a Final Closure Notice is issued, even if a Partial Closure Notice has been issued;
- any question relating to a matter in an enquiry under TMA 1970 ss 9A(1) or 12AC(1) may be referred jointly to the tribunal;
- neither a Partial nor Final Closure Notices may be issued relating to questions referred under TMA 1970 s 28ZA (Effect of referral on enquiry).

Paragraph 12 amends TMA 1970 s 28A (Completion of enquiry into personal or trustee return or NRCGT return) to take into account whether a Partial Closure Notice has been issued.

Similarly, paragraph 13 amends TMA 1970 s 28B for the closure of enquiries into partnership returns and extends the right to the taxpayer to apply to the tribunal for a direction.

Paragraph 14 amends TMA 1970 s 29 (Assessment where loss of tax discovered) to incorporate Partial and Final closure notices. The amendment permits discovery assessments where an officer could not have been reasonably expected, on the basis of the information made available to him, to be aware of the situation when a Partial or Final Closure Notice was issued.

Paragraph 15 makes similar amendments (as para 14) to TMA 1970 s 29A for Non-Resident Capital Gains Tax disposals.

Paragraph 16 amends TMA 1970 s 30 (Recovery of overpayment of tax). The amendment concerns one of the dates by which the time limit for an assessment under section 30 to recover overpayment of tax is determined. The effect is that the date in subsection (5)(b) is determined by reference to the issue of a Final Closure Notice.

Paragraph 17 makes similar amendments (as para 14) to TMA 1970 s 30B (Amendment of partnership statement where loss of tax discovered).

Paragraph 18 amends TMA 1970 s 31 so that where there is an appeal in an open enquiry against a TMA 1970 s 9C amendment, the appeal cannot proceed further until a Partial or Final Closure Notice has been issued relating to the amendment.

Paragraph 19 amends TMA 1970 s 59AA (Non-resident CGT disposals: payments on account of capital gains tax). The amendment has the effect that the repayment need not be made before a Final Closure Notice is issued. TMA 1970 s 59AA(8)(b) remains unchanged and an officer, should they see fit, may make a provisional repayment.

Paragraph 20 makes similar (as para 19) amendments to TMA 1970 s 59B (Payment of income tax and capital gains tax: assessments other than simple assessments).

Paragraph 21 amends TMA 1970 Sch 3ZA concerning the dates when an amount is payable or repayable where a self-assessment is amended by the taxpayer during an enquiry. The amendments have the effect that any amount repayable would not be due for repayment until the issuing of a Final Closure Notice.

Paragraph 22 amends TCGA 1992 s 184I, which relate to notices (under section 184G and 184H) and avoidance schemes. The amendments relate to the restrictions on giving notices after completion of an enquiry and the restriction on discovery assessments following a relevant notice given after completion of an enquiry.

Finance Act 1998 Schedule 18

FA 1998 Sch 18 (Company tax returns, assessments and related matters) has been amended to reflect the introduction of the Partial Closure Notice, including:

- amendments to protect HMRC's right to seek tax in relation to matters not the subject of a Partial Closure Notice;
- amendments to tax are effective on conclusion by Partial or Final Closure Notice;
- a referral to a tribunal on a matter in an enquiry is permitted until either a Partial or Final Closure Notice is issued in relation to the matter;
- neither Partial or Final Closure Notices may be issued in relation to a matter that is the subject of appeal;
- the procedure for closure of enquiries is amended to take into account Partial Closure Notices;
- a company has the right to apply to the tribunal for a direction to issue a Partial Closure Notice;
- the Partial or Final Closure Notice must state the officer's conclusions, amendments to the discovery provisions;
- after the completion of an enquiry, the giving of a counteraction notice is restricted and the ability to raise a discovery assessment is also restricted;
- where a transfer pricing notice has been given after an enquiry opened and not completed, a Partial Closure Notice may be given on unconnected matters.

SCHEDULE 16

PENALTIES FOR ENABLERS OF DEFEATED TAX AVOIDANCE

Section 65

PART 1

LIABILITY TO PENALTY

1 Where—

(a) a person ("T") has entered into abusive tax arrangements, and
(b) T incurs a defeat in respect of the arrangements,

a penalty is payable by each person who enabled the arrangements.

2 (1) Parts 2 to 4 of this Schedule define—

"abusive tax arrangements";
a "defeat in respect of the arrangements";
a "person who enabled the arrangements".

(2) The other Parts of this Schedule make provision supplementing paragraph 1 as follows—

(a) Part 5 makes provision about the amount of a penalty;
(b) Parts 6 to 8 provide for the assessment of penalties, referrals to the GAAR Advisory Panel and appeals against assessments;
(c) Part 9 applies information and inspection powers, and makes provision about declarations relating to legally privileged communications;
(d) Part 10 confers power to publish details of persons who have incurred penalties;
(e) Parts 11 and 12 contain miscellaneous and general provisions.

PART 2

"ABUSIVE" AND "TAX ARRANGEMENTS": MEANING

3 (1) Arrangements are "tax arrangements" for the purposes of this Schedule if, having regard to all the circumstances, it would be reasonable to conclude that the obtaining of a tax advantage was the main purpose, or one of the main purposes, of the arrangements.

(2) Tax arrangements are "abusive" for the purposes of this Schedule if they are arrangements the entering into or carrying out of which cannot reasonably be regarded as a reasonable course of action in relation to the relevant tax provisions, having regard to all the circumstances.

(3) The circumstances to which regard must be had under sub-paragraph (2) include—

(a) whether the substantive results, or the intended substantive results, of the arrangements are consistent with any principles on which the relevant tax provisions are based (whether express or implied) and the policy objectives of those provisions,

(b) whether the means of achieving those results involves one or more contrived or abnormal steps, and

(c) whether the arrangements are intended to exploit any shortcomings in those provisions.

(4) Where the tax arrangements form part of any other arrangements regard must also be had to those other arrangements.

(5) Each of the following is an example of something which might indicate that tax arrangements are abusive—

(a) the arrangements result in an amount of income, profits or gains for tax purposes that is significantly less than the amount for economic purposes;

(b) the arrangements result in deductions or losses of an amount for tax purposes that is significantly greater than the amount for economic purposes;

(c) the arrangements result in a claim for the repayment or crediting of tax (including foreign tax) that has not been, and is unlikely to be, paid;

but a result mentioned in paragraph (a), (b) or (c) is to be taken to be such an example only if it is reasonable to assume that such a result was not the anticipated result when the relevant tax provisions were enacted.

(6) The fact that tax arrangements accord with established practice, and HMRC had, at the time the arrangements were entered into, indicated their acceptance of that practice, is an example of something which might indicate that the arrangements are not abusive.

(7) The examples given in sub-paragraphs (5) and (6) are not exhaustive.

(8) In sub-paragraph (5) the reference to income includes earnings, within the meaning of Part 1 of the Social Security Contributions and Benefits Act 1992 or Part 1 of the Social Security Contributions and Benefits (Northern Ireland) Act 1992.

PART 3
"DEFEAT" IN RESPECT OF ABUSIVE TAX ARRANGEMENTS

"Defeat" in respect of abusive tax arrangements

4 T (within the meaning of paragraph 1) incurs a "defeat" in respect of abusive tax arrangements entered into by T ("the arrangements concerned") if—

(a) Condition A (in paragraph 5) is met, or

(b) Condition B (in paragraph 6) is met.

Condition A

5 (1) Condition A is that—

(a) T, or a person on behalf of T, has given HMRC a document of a kind listed in the Table in paragraph 1 of Schedule 24 to FA 2007 (returns etc),

(b) the document was submitted on the basis that a tax advantage ("the relevant tax advantage") arose from the arrangements concerned,

(c) the relevant tax advantage has been counteracted, and

(d) the counteraction is final.

(2) For the purposes of this paragraph the relevant tax advantage has been "counteracted" if adjustments have been made in respect of T's tax position on the basis that the whole or part of the relevant tax advantage does not arise.

(3) For the purposes of this paragraph a counteraction is "final" when the adjustments in question, and any amounts arising from the adjustments, can no longer be varied, on appeal or otherwise.

(4) In this paragraph "adjustments" means any adjustments, whether by way of an assessment, the modification of an assessment or return, the amendment or disallowance of a claim, a payment, the entering into of a contract settlement or otherwise.

Accordingly, references to "making" adjustments include securing that adjustments are made by entering into a contract settlement.

(5) Any reference in this paragraph to giving HMRC a document includes—

(a) communicating information to HMRC in any form and by any method;

(b) making a statement or declaration in a document.

(6) Any reference in this paragraph to a document of a kind listed in the Table in paragraph 1 of Schedule 24 to FA 2007 includes—

(a) a document amending a document of a kind so listed, and
(b) a document which—
    (i) relates to national insurance contributions, and
    (ii) is a document in relation to which that Schedule applies.

Condition B

6 (1) Condition B is that (in a case not falling within Condition A)—
(a) HMRC have made an assessment in relation to tax,
(b) the assessment counteracts a tax advantage that it is reasonable to assume T expected to obtain from the arrangements concerned ("the expected tax advantage"), and
(c) the counteraction is final.

(2) For the purposes of this paragraph an assessment "counteracts" the expected tax advantage if the assessment is on a basis which prevents T from obtaining (or obtaining the whole of) the expected tax advantage.

(3) For the purposes of this paragraph a counteraction is "final"—
(a) when a relevant contract settlement is made, or
(b) if no contract settlement has been made, when the assessment in question and any amounts arising from the assessment can no longer be varied, on appeal or otherwise.

(4) In sub-paragraph (3) a "relevant contract settlement" means a contract settlement on a basis which prevents T from obtaining (or obtaining the whole of) the expected tax advantage.

PART 4
PERSONS WHO "ENABLED" THE ARRANGEMENTS

Persons who "enabled" the arrangements

7 (1) A person is a person who "enabled" the arrangements mentioned in paragraph 1 if that person is—
(a) a designer of the arrangements (see paragraph 8),
(b) a manager of the arrangements (see paragraph 9),
(c) a person who marketed the arrangements to T (see paragraph 10),
(d) an enabling participant in the arrangements (see paragraph 11), or
(e) a financial enabler in relation to the arrangements (see paragraph 12).

(2) This paragraph is subject to paragraph 13 (excluded persons).

Designers of arrangements

8 (1) For the purposes of paragraph 7 a person is a "designer" of the arrangements if that person was, in the course of a business carried on by that person, to any extent responsible for the design of—
(a) the arrangements, or
(b) a proposal which was implemented by the arrangements;
but this is subject to sub-paragraph (2).

(2) Where a person would (in the absence of this sub-paragraph) fall within sub-paragraph (1) because of having provided advice which was used in the design of the arrangements or of a proposal, that person does not because of that advice fall within that sub-paragraph unless—
(a) the advice is relevant advice, and
(b) the knowledge condition is met.

(3) Advice is "relevant advice" if—
(a) the advice or any part of it suggests arrangements or an alteration of proposed arrangements, and
(b) it is reasonable to assume that the suggestion was made with a view to arrangements being designed in such a way that a tax advantage (or a greater tax advantage) might be expected to arise from them.

(4) The knowledge condition is that, when the advice was provided, the person providing it knew or could reasonably be expected to know—
(a) that the advice would be used in the design of abusive tax arrangements or of a proposal for such arrangements, or
(b) that it was likely that the advice would be so used.

(5) For the purposes of sub-paragraph (3), advice is not to be taken to "suggest" anything—

(a) which is put forward by the advice for consideration, but

(b) which the advice can reasonably be read as recommending against.

(6) In sub-paragraph (3)—

(a) the reference in paragraph (a) to arrangements or an alteration of proposed arrangements includes a proposal for arrangements or an alteration of a proposal for arrangements, and

(b) the reference in paragraph (b) to arrangements includes arrangements proposed by a proposal.

(7) For the purposes of this paragraph—

(a) references to advice include an opinion;

(b) advice is "used" in a design if the advice is taken account of in that design.

Managers of arrangements

9 (1) For the purposes of paragraph 7 a person is a "manager" of the arrangements if that person—

(a) was, in the course of a business carried on by that person, to any extent responsible for the organisation or management of the arrangements, and

(b) when carrying out any functions in relation to the organisation or management of the arrangements, knew or could reasonably be expected to know that the arrangements involved were abusive tax arrangements.

(2) Where—

(a) a person is, in the course of a business carried on by the person, to any extent responsible for facilitating T's withdrawal from the arrangements, and

(b) it is reasonable to assume that the obtaining of a tax advantage is not T's purpose (or one of T's purposes) in withdrawing from the arrangements,

that person is not because of anything done in the course of facilitating that withdrawal to be regarded as to any extent responsible for the organisation or management of the arrangements.

Marketers of arrangements

10 For the purposes of paragraph 7 a person "marketed" the arrangements to T if, in the course of a business carried on by that person—

(a) that person made available for implementation by T a proposal which has since been implemented, in relation to T, by the arrangements, or

(b) that person—

(i) communicated information to T or another person about a proposal which has since been implemented, in relation to T, by the arrangements, and

(ii) did so with a view to T entering into the arrangements or transactions forming part of the arrangements.

Enabling participants

11 For the purposes of paragraph 7 a person is "an enabling participant" in the arrangements if—

(a) that person is a person (other than T) who enters into the arrangements or a transaction forming part of the arrangements,

(b) without that person's participation in the arrangements or transaction (or the participation of another person in the arrangements or transaction in the same capacity as that person), the arrangements could not be expected to result in a tax advantage for T, and

(c) when that person entered into the arrangements or transaction, that person knew or could reasonably be expected to know that what was being entered into was abusive tax arrangements or a transaction forming part of such arrangements.

Financial enablers

12 (1) For the purposes of paragraph 7 a person is a "financial enabler" in relation to the arrangements if—

(a) in the course of a business carried on by that person, that person provided a financial product (directly or indirectly) to a relevant party,

(b) it is reasonable to assume that the purpose (or a purpose) of the relevant party in obtaining the financial product was to participate in the arrangements, and

(c) when the financial product was provided, the person providing it knew or could reasonably be expected to know that the purpose (or a purpose) of obtaining it was to participate in abusive tax arrangements.

(2) In this paragraph "a relevant party" means T or an enabling participant in the arrangements within the meaning given by paragraph 11.

(3) Any reference in this paragraph to a person's providing a financial product to a relevant party includes (but is not limited to) the person's doing any of the following—

(a) providing a loan to a relevant party;
(b) issuing or transferring a share to a relevant party;
(c) entering into arrangements with a relevant party such that—

    (i) the person becomes a party to a relevant contract within the meaning of section 577 of CTA 2009 (derivative contracts);
    (ii) there is a repo in respect of securities within the meaning of section 263A(A1) of TCGA 1992;
    (iii) the person or the relevant party has a creditor repo, creditor quasi-repo, debtor repo or debtor quasi-repo within the meaning of sections 543, 544, 548 and 549 of CTA 2009;

(d) entering into a stock lending arrangement, within the meaning of section 263B(1) of TCGA 1992, with a relevant party;
(e) entering into an alternative finance arrangement, within the meaning of Chapter 6 of Part 6 of CTA 2009 or Part 10A of ITA 2007, with a relevant party;
(f) entering into a contract with a relevant party which, whether alone or in combination with one or more other contracts—

    (i) is in accordance with generally accepted accounting practice required to be treated as a loan, deposit or other financial asset or obligation, or
    (ii) would be required to be so treated by the person if the person were a company to which the Companies Act 2006 applies;

and references to obtaining a financial product are to be read accordingly.

(4) The Treasury may by regulations amend sub-paragraph (3).

Excluded persons

13 (1) A person who—

(a) would (in the absence of this paragraph) be regarded for the purposes of this Schedule as having enabled particular arrangements mentioned in paragraph 1, but
(b) is a person within sub-paragraph (2),

is not to be regarded as having enabled those arrangements.

(2) The persons within this sub-paragraph are—

(a) T;
(b) where T is a company, any company in the same group as T.

Powers to add categories of enabler and to provide exceptions

14 (1) The Treasury may by regulations add to the categories of persons who, in relation to arrangements mentioned in paragraph 1, are for the purposes of this Schedule persons who enabled the arrangements.

(2) The Treasury may by regulations provide that a person who would otherwise be regarded for the purposes of this Schedule as having enabled arrangements is not to be so regarded where conditions prescribed by the regulations are met.

(3) Regulations under this paragraph may—

(a) amend this Part of this Schedule;
(b) make supplementary, incidental, and consequential provision, including provision amending any other Part of this Schedule;
(c) make transitional provision.

PART 5

AMOUNT OF PENALTY

Amount of penalty

15 (1) For each person who enabled the arrangements mentioned in paragraph 1, the penalty payable under paragraph 1 is the total amount or value of all the relevant consideration received or receivable by that person ("the person in question").

(2) Particular consideration is "relevant" for the purposes of this paragraph if—

(a) it is consideration for anything done by the person in question which enabled the arrangements mentioned in paragraph 1, and

(b) it has not previously been taken into account in calculating the amount of a penalty payable under paragraph 1.

(3) For the purposes of this paragraph a thing done by a person "enabled" the arrangements mentioned in paragraph 1 if, by doing that thing (alone or with anything else), the person fell within the definition in Part 4 of this Schedule of a person who enabled those arrangements.

16 (1) This paragraph applies for the purposes of paragraph 15.

(2) Where consideration for anything done by a person ("A") is, under any arrangements with A, paid or payable to a person other than A, it is to be taken to be received or receivable by A.

(3) The "consideration" for anything done by a person does not include any amount charged by that person in respect of value added tax.

(4) Consideration attributable to two or more transactions is to be apportioned on a just and reasonable basis.

(5) Any consideration given for what is in substance one bargain is to be treated as attributable to all elements of the bargain, even though—

(a) separate consideration is, or purports to be, given for different elements of the bargain, or

(b) there are, or purport to be, separate transactions in respect of different elements of the bargain.

Reduction of penalty where other penalties incurred

17 (1) The amount of a penalty for which a person is liable under paragraph 1 is to be reduced by the amount of any other penalty incurred by the person in respect of conduct for which the person is liable to the penalty under paragraph 1.

(2) In this paragraph "any other penalty" means a penalty—

(a) which is a penalty under a provision other than paragraph 1, and

(b) which has been assessed.

Mitigation of penalty

18 (1) HMRC may in their discretion reduce a penalty under paragraph 1.

(2) In this paragraph the reference to reducing a penalty includes a reference to—

(a) entirely remitting the penalty, or

(b) staying, or agreeing a compromise in relation to, proceedings for the recovery of a penalty.

PART 6

ASSESSMENT OF PENALTY

Assessment of penalty

19 (1) Where a person is liable for a penalty under paragraph 1 HMRC must—

(a) assess the penalty, and

(b) notify the person.

(2) If—

(a) HMRC do not have all the information required to determine the amount or value of the relevant consideration within the meaning of paragraph 15, and

(b) HMRC have taken all reasonable steps to obtain that information,

HMRC may assess the penalty on the basis of a reasonable estimate by HMRC of that consideration.

(3) This paragraph is subject to—

(a) paragraphs 21 and 22 (limits on when penalty may be assessed); and

(b) Part 7 of this Schedule (requirement for opinion of GAAR Advisory Panel before penalty may be assessed).

20 (1) A penalty under paragraph 1 must be paid before the end of the period of 30 days beginning with the day on which notification of the penalty is issued.

(2) An assessment of a penalty under paragraph 1—

(a) is to be treated for procedural purposes in the same way as an assessment to tax (except in respect of a matter expressly provided for by this Schedule), and

(b) may be enforced as if it were an assessment to tax.

Special provision about assessment for multi-user schemes

21 (1) This paragraph applies where—

(a) a proposal for arrangements is implemented more than once, by a number of tax arrangements which are substantially the same as each other ("related arrangements"),

(b) paragraph 1 applies in relation to particular arrangements ("the arrangements concerned") which are one of the number of related arrangements implementing the proposal, and

(c) at the time when the person who entered into the arrangements concerned incurs a defeat in respect of them, the required percentage of relevant defeats has not been reached.

(2) HMRC may not assess any penalty payable under paragraph 1 in respect of the arrangements concerned until the required percentage of relevant defeats is reached.

(3) For the purposes of this paragraph the "required percentage of relevant defeats" is reached when HMRC reasonably believe that defeats have been incurred in the case of more than 50% of the related arrangements implementing the proposal.

(4) Sub-paragraph (2) does not apply in relation to a penalty if the person liable to the penalty requests assessment of the penalty sooner than the time allowed by sub-paragraph (2).

Time limit for assessment

22 (1) An assessment of a person as liable to a penalty under paragraph 1 may not take place after the relevant time.

(2) In this paragraph "the relevant time" means, subject to sub-paragraphs (3) to (6)—

(a) where a GAAR final decision notice within the meaning of paragraph 24(1) has been given in relation to the arrangements to which the penalty relates, the end of 12 months beginning with the date on which T incurs the defeat mentioned in paragraph 1;

(b) where a notice under paragraph 25 has been given to the person mentioned in sub-paragraph (1) above in respect of the arrangements to which the penalty relates, the end of 12 months beginning with the end of the time allowed for making representations in respect of that notice;

(c) where—

(i) a referral has been made under paragraph 26 in respect of the arrangements to which the penalty relates, and

(ii) paragraph (d) does not apply,

the end of 12 months beginning with the date on which the opinion of the GAAR Advisory Panel is given on the referral (within the meaning given by paragraph 34(6));

(d) where a notice under paragraph 35 has been given to the person mentioned in sub-paragraph (1) above in respect of the arrangements to which the penalty relates, the end of 12 months beginning with the end of the time allowed for making representations in respect of that notice.

(3) Where—

(a) paragraph 21 prevented a penalty from being assessed before the required percentage of relevant defeats was reached, and

(b) the required percentage of relevant defeats (within the meaning of paragraph 21) has been reached,

the relevant time in relation to that penalty is whichever is the later of—

(i) the relevant time given by sub-paragraph (2), and

(ii) the end of 12 months beginning with the date on which that required percentage was reached.

(4) Where under paragraph 21(4) a person requests assessment of a penalty, the relevant time in relation to that penalty is whichever is the later of—

(a) the relevant time given by sub-paragraph (2), and

(b) the end of 12 months beginning with the date on which the request is made,

and sub-paragraph (3) does not apply to the penalty even if the required percentage of relevant defeats is reached.

(5) Sub-paragraph (6) applies where—

(a) at any time a declaration has been made under paragraph 44 for the purposes of any determination of whether a person is liable to a penalty under paragraph 1 in relation to particular arrangements ("the arrangements concerned"), and

(b) subsequently, facts that in the Commissioners' opinion are sufficient to indicate that the declaration contains a material inaccuracy have come to the Commissioners' knowledge.

(6) The relevant time in respect of any penalty under paragraph 1 payable by that person in relation to the arrangements concerned is whichever is the later of—

(a) the relevant time given by the preceding provisions of this paragraph, and
(b) the end of 12 months beginning with the date on which such facts came to the Commissioners' knowledge.

PART 7
GAAR ADVISORY PANEL OPINION, AND REPRESENTATIONS

Requirement for opinion of GAAR Advisory Panel

23 (1) A penalty under paragraph 1 may not be assessed unless—

(a) the decision that it should be assessed is taken by a designated HMRC officer, and
(b) either the condition in sub-paragraph (2) or the condition in sub-paragraph (3) is met.

(2) The condition in this sub-paragraph is that, when the assessment is made—

(a) a GAAR final decision notice has been given in relation to—

(i) the arrangements to which the penalty relates ("the relevant arrangements"), or
(ii) arrangements that are equivalent to the relevant arrangements,

(b) where a notice is required by paragraph 25 to be given to the person liable to the penalty, that notice has been given and the time allowed for making representations under that paragraph has expired, and
(c) a designated HMRC officer has, in deciding whether the penalty should be assessed, considered—

(i) the opinion of the GAAR Advisory Panel which was considered by HMRC in preparing that GAAR final decision notice, and
(ii) any representations made under paragraph 25.

(3) The condition in this sub-paragraph is that, when the assessment is made—

(a) an opinion of the GAAR Advisory Panel which applies to the relevant arrangements has been given on a referral under paragraph 26,
(b) where a notice is required by paragraph 35 to be given to the person liable to the penalty, that notice has been given and the time allowed for making representations under that paragraph has expired, and
(c) a designated HMRC officer has, in deciding whether the penalty should be assessed, considered—

(i) that opinion of the GAAR Advisory Panel, and
(ii) any representations made under paragraph 35.

(4) Where a notification of a penalty under paragraph 1 is given, the notification must be accompanied by a report prepared by HMRC of—

(a) if the condition in sub-paragraph (2) is met, the opinion of the GAAR Advisory Panel which was considered by HMRC in preparing the GAAR final decision notice;
(b) if the condition in sub-paragraph (3) is met, the opinion of the GAAR advisory panel mentioned in that sub-paragraph.

(5) Paragraph 24 contains definitions of terms used in this paragraph.

24 (1) In this Schedule a "GAAR final decision notice" means a notice under—

(a) paragraph 12 of Schedule 43 to FA 2013 (notice of final decision after considering opinion of GAAR Advisory Panel on referral under Schedule 43),
(b) paragraph 8 or 9 of Schedule 43A to FA 2013 (notice of final decision after considering opinion of GAAR Advisory Panel), or
(c) paragraph 8 of Schedule 43B to FA 2013 (notice of final decision after considering opinion of GAAR Advisory Panel on referral under Schedule 43B).

(2) For the purposes of this Part of this Schedule, where the GAAR Advisory Panel gives an opinion on a referral under paragraph 26 the arrangements to which the opinion "applies" are—

(a) the arrangements in respect of which the referral was made (that is, "the arrangements in question" within the meaning given by paragraph 26(1)), and
(b) any arrangements that are equivalent to those arrangements.

(3) For the purposes of this Part of this Schedule, arrangements are "equivalent" to one another if they are substantially the same as one another having regard to—

(a) their substantive results or intended substantive results,
(b) the means of achieving those results, and

(c) the characteristics on the basis of which it could reasonably be argued, in each case, that the arrangements are abusive tax arrangements.

Notice where Panel opinion already obtained in relation to equivalent arrangements

25 (1) This paragraph applies where a designated HMRC officer is of the view that—

(a) a person is liable to a penalty under paragraph 1 in relation to particular arrangements ("the arrangements concerned"),

(b) no GAAR final decision notice has been given in relation to those arrangements, but those arrangements are equivalent to arrangements in relation to which a GAAR final decision notice has been given ("the GAAR decision arrangements"), and

(c) accordingly, the opinion of the GAAR Advisory Panel which was considered by HMRC in preparing that GAAR final decision notice is relevant to the arrangements concerned.

(2) A designated HMRC officer must give the person mentioned in sub-paragraph (1) a notice in writing—

(a) explaining that the officer is of the view mentioned there,

(b) specifying the arrangements concerned,

(c) describing the material characteristics of the GAAR decision arrangements,

(d) setting out a report prepared by HMRC of the opinion of the GAAR Advisory Panel which was considered by HMRC in preparing the GAAR final decision notice, and

(e) explaining the effect of sub-paragraphs (3) and (4).

(3) A person to whom a notice under this paragraph is given has 30 days, beginning with the day on which the notice is given, to send to the designated HMRC officer (in writing) any representations that that person wishes to make as to why the arrangements concerned are not equivalent to the GAAR decision arrangements.

(4) A designated HMRC officer may, on a written request by that person, extend the period during which representations may be made by that person.

(5) Paragraph 24 contains definitions of the following terms used in this paragraph—

"GAAR final decision notice";

"equivalent", in relation to arrangements.

Referral to GAAR Advisory Panel

26 (1) A designated HMRC officer may make a referral under this paragraph if—

(a) the officer considers that a person is liable to a penalty under paragraph 1 in relation to particular arrangements ("the arrangements in question"), and

(b) the requirements of paragraph 28 (procedure before making of referral) have been complied with.

(2) But a referral may not be made under this paragraph if a GAAR final decision notice (within the meaning of paragraph 24(1)) has already been given in relation to—

(a) the arrangements in question, or

(b) arrangements that are equivalent to those arrangements.

(3) A referral under this paragraph is a referral to the GAAR Advisory Panel of the question whether the entering into and carrying out of tax arrangements such as are described in the referral statement (see paragraph 27) is a reasonable course of action in relation to the relevant tax provisions.

27 (1) In this Part of this Schedule "the referral statement", in relation to a referral under paragraph 26, means a statement made by a designated HMRC officer which—

(a) accompanies the referral,

(b) is a general statement of the material characteristics of the arrangements in question (within the meaning given by paragraph 26(1)), and

(c) complies with sub-paragraph (2).

(2) A statement under this paragraph must—

(a) contain a factual description of the arrangements in question,

(b) set out HMRC's view as to whether those arrangements accord with established practice (as it stood when those arrangements were entered into),

(c) explain why it is the designated HMRC officer's view that a tax advantage of the nature described in the statement and arising from tax arrangements having the characteristics described in the statement would be a tax advantage arising from arrangements that are abusive,

(d) set out any matters the designated HMRC officer is aware of which may suggest that any view of HMRC or the designated HMRC officer expressed in the statement is not correct, and

(e) set out any other matters which the designated HMRC officer considers are required for the purposes of the exercise of the GAAR Advisory Panel's functions under paragraphs 33 and 34.

Notice before decision whether to refer

28 (1) A referral must not be made under paragraph 26 unless—

(a) a designated HMRC officer has given each relevant person a notice under this paragraph,

(b) in the case of each relevant person, the time allowed for making representations has expired, and

(c) in deciding whether to make the referral, a designated HMRC officer has considered any representations made by a relevant person within the time allowed.

(2) In this paragraph a "relevant person" means any person who at the time of the referral is considered by the officer making the referral to be liable to a penalty under paragraph 1 in relation to the arrangements in question (within the meaning given by paragraph 26(1)).

(3) A notice under this paragraph is a notice in writing which—

(a) explains that the officer giving the notice considers that the person to whom the notice is given is liable to a penalty under paragraph 1 in relation to the arrangements in question (specifying those arrangements),

(b) explains why the officer considers those arrangements to be abusive tax arrangements,

(c) explains that HMRC are proposing to make a referral under paragraph 26 of the question whether the entering into and carrying out of tax arrangements that have the characteristics of the arrangements in question is a reasonable course of action in relation to the relevant tax provisions, and

(d) explains the effect of sub-paragraphs (4) and (5).

(4) Each person to whom a notice under this paragraph is given has 45 days, beginning with the day on which the notice is given to that person, to send written representations to the designated HMRC officer in response to the notice.

(5) A designated HMRC officer may, on a written request by a person to whom a notice is given, extend the period during which representations may be made by that person.

Notice of decision whether to refer

29 Where a designated HMRC officer decides whether to make a referral under paragraph 26, the officer must, as soon as reasonably practicable, give written notice of that decision to each person to whom notice under paragraph 28 was given.

Information to accompany referral

30 A referral under paragraph 26 must (as well as being accompanied by the referral statement under paragraph 27) be accompanied by—

(a) a declaration that, as far as HMRC are aware, nothing which is material to the GAAR Advisory Panel's consideration of the matter has been omitted from that statement,

(b) a copy of each notice given under paragraph 28 by HMRC in relation to the referral,

(c) a copy of any representations received under paragraph 28 and any comments that HMRC wish to make in respect of those representations, and

(d) a copy of each notice given under paragraph 31 by HMRC.

Notice on making of referral

31 (1) Where a referral is made under paragraph 26, a designated HMRC officer must at the same time give to each relevant person a notice in writing which—

(a) notifies the person of the referral,

(b) is accompanied by a copy of the referral statement,

(c) is accompanied by a copy of any comments provided to the GAAR Advisory Panel under paragraph 30(c) in respect of representations made by the person,

(d) notifies the person of the period under paragraph 32 for making representations, and

(e) notifies the person of the requirement under that paragraph to send any representations to the officer.

(2) In this paragraph "relevant person" has the same meaning as in paragraph 28 (see sub-paragraph (2) of that paragraph).

Right to make representations to GAAR Advisory Panel

32 (1) A person who has received a notice under paragraph 31 has 21 days, beginning with the day on which that notice is given, to send to the GAAR Advisory Panel written representations about—

(a) the notice given to the person under paragraph 28, or

(b) any comments provided to the GAAR Advisory Panel under paragraph 30(c) in respect of representations made by the person.

(2) The GAAR Advisory Panel may, on a written request made by the person, extend the period during which representations may be made.

(3) If a person sends representations to the GAAR Advisory Panel under this paragraph, the person must at the same time send a copy of the representations to the designated HMRC officer.

(4) If a person sends representations to the GAAR Advisory Panel under this paragraph and that person made no representations under paragraph 28, a designated HMRC officer—

(a) may provide the GAAR Advisory Panel with comments on that person's representations under this paragraph, and

(b) if such comments are provided, must at the same time send a copy of them to that person.

Decision of GAAR Advisory Panel and opinion notices

33 (1) Where a referral is made to the GAAR Advisory Panel under paragraph 26, the Chair must arrange for a sub-panel consisting of 3 members of the GAAR Advisory Panel (one of whom may be the Chair) to consider it.

(2) The sub-panel may invite—

(a) any person to whom notice under paragraph 28 was given, or

(b) the designated HMRC officer,

(or both) to supply the sub-panel with further information within a period specified in the invitation.

(3) Invitations must explain the effect of sub-paragraph (4) or (5) (as appropriate).

(4) If a person invited under sub-paragraph (2)(a) supplies information to the sub-panel under this paragraph, that person must at the same time send a copy of the information to the designated HMRC officer.

(5) If a designated HMRC officer supplies information to the sub-panel under this paragraph, the officer must at the same time send a copy of the information to each person to whom notice under paragraph 28 was given.

34 (1) The sub-panel must produce—

(a) one opinion notice stating the joint opinion of all the members of the sub-panel, or

(b) two or three opinion notices which taken together state the opinions of all the members.

(2) The sub-panel must give a copy of the opinion notice or notices to the designated HMRC officer.

(3) An opinion notice is a notice which states that in the opinion of the members of the sub-panel, or one or more of those members—

(a) the entering into and carrying out of tax arrangements such as are described in the referral statement is a reasonable course of action in relation to the relevant tax provisions,

(b) the entering into or carrying out of such tax arrangements is not a reasonable course of action in relation to the relevant tax provisions, or

(c) it is not possible, on the information available, to reach a view on that matter,

and the reasons for that opinion.

(4) In forming their opinions for the purposes of sub-paragraph (3) members of the sub-panel must—

(a) have regard to all the matters set out in the referral statement,

(b) have regard to the matters mentioned in paragraphs (a) to (c) of paragraph 3(3) and paragraph 3(4), and

(c) take account of paragraph 3(5) to (7).

(5) For the purposes of the giving of an opinion under this paragraph, the arrangements are to be assumed to be tax arrangements.

(6) For the purposes of this Schedule—

(a) an opinion of the GAAR Advisory Panel is to be treated as having been given on a referral under paragraph 26 when an opinion notice (or notices) has been given under this paragraph in respect of the referral, and

(b) any requirement to consider the opinion of the GAAR Advisory Panel given on such a referral is a requirement to consider the contents of the opinion notice (or notices) given on the referral.

Notice before deciding that arrangements are ones to which Panel opinion applies

35 (1) This paragraph applies where—

(a) an opinion of the GAAR Advisory Panel has been given on a referral under paragraph 26,

(b) a designated HMRC officer is of the view that a person is liable to a penalty under paragraph 1 in relation to particular arrangements ("the arrangements concerned") and that that opinion of the GAAR Advisory Panel applies to those arrangements, and

(c) that person is not a person to whom notice under paragraph 28 was given in connection with the referral.

(2) A designated HMRC officer must give the person mentioned in sub-paragraph (1)(b) a notice in writing—

(a) explaining that the officer is of the view mentioned in that paragraph,

(b) specifying the arrangements concerned,

(c) setting out a report prepared by HMRC of the opinion mentioned in sub-paragraph (1)(a), and

(d) explaining the effect of sub-paragraphs (3) and (4).

(3) A person to whom a notice under this paragraph is given has 30 days, beginning with the day on which the notice is given, to send the designated HMRC officer (in writing) any representations as to why the opinion does not apply to the arrangements concerned.

(4) A designated HMRC officer may, on a written request by that person, extend the period during which representations may be made by that person.

(5) Paragraph 24(2) defines the arrangements that an opinion given on a referral under paragraph 26 "applies to".

Requirement for court or tribunal to take Panel opinion into account

36 (1) In this paragraph "enabler penalty proceedings" means proceedings before a court or tribunal in connection with a penalty under paragraph 1.

(2) In determining in enabler penalty proceedings any question whether tax arrangements to which the penalty relates were abusive, the court or tribunal—

(a) must take into account the relevant Panel opinion, and

(b) may also take into account any matter mentioned in sub-paragraph (4).

(3) In sub-paragraph (2)(a) "the relevant Panel opinion" means the opinion of the GAAR Advisory Panel which under this Part of this Schedule was required to be considered by a designated HMRC officer in deciding whether the penalty should be assessed.

(4) The matters mentioned in sub-paragraph (2)(b) are—

(a) guidance, statements or other material (whether of HMRC, a Minister of the Crown or anyone else) that was in the public domain at the time the arrangements were entered into, and

(b) evidence of established practice at that time.

PART 8

APPEALS

37 A person may appeal against—

(a) a decision of HMRC that a penalty under paragraph 1 is payable by that person, or

(b) a decision of HMRC as to the amount of a penalty under paragraph 1 payable by the person.

38 (1) An appeal under paragraph 37 is to be treated in the same way as an appeal against an assessment to the tax to which the arrangements concerned relate (including by the application of any provision about bringing the appeal by notice to HMRC, about HMRC review of the decision or about determination of the appeal by the First-tier Tribunal or Upper Tribunal).

(2) Sub-paragraph (1) does not apply—

(a) so as to require a person to pay a penalty under paragraph 1 before an appeal against the assessment of the penalty is determined;

(b) in respect of any other matter expressly provided for by this Schedule.

(3) In this paragraph "the arrangements concerned" means the arrangements to which the penalty relates.

39 (1) On an appeal under paragraph 37(a) that is notified to the tribunal, the tribunal may affirm or cancel HMRC's decision.

(2) On an appeal under paragraph 37(b) that is notified to the tribunal, the tribunal may—

(a) affirm HMRC's decision, or

(b) substitute for that decision another decision that HMRC had power to make.

(3) If the tribunal substitutes its decision for HMRC's, the tribunal may rely on paragraph 18—

(a) to the same extent as HMRC (which may mean applying the same percentage reduction as HMRC to a different starting point), or

(b) to a different extent, but only if the tribunal thinks that HMRC's decision in respect of the application of paragraph 18 was flawed.

(4) In sub-paragraph (3)(b) "flawed" means flawed when considered in the light of the principles applicable in proceedings for judicial review.

(5) In this paragraph "tribunal" means the First-tier Tribunal or Upper Tribunal (as appropriate by virtue of paragraph 38(1)).

PART 9
INFORMATION

Information and inspection powers: application of Schedule 36 to FA 2008

40 (1) Schedule 36 to FA 2008 (information and inspection powers) applies for the purpose of checking a relevant person's position as regards liability for a penalty under paragraph 1 as it applies for checking a person's tax position, subject to the modifications in paragraphs 41 to 43.

(2) In this paragraph and paragraphs 41 to 43—

"relevant person" means a person an officer of Revenue and Customs has reason to suspect is or may be liable to a penalty under paragraph 1;

"the Schedule" means Schedule 36 to FA 2008.

General modifications of Schedule 36 to FA 2008 as applied

41 In its application for the purpose mentioned in paragraph 40(1) above, the Schedule has effect as if—

(a) any provisions which can have no application for that purpose were omitted,

(b) references to "the taxpayer" were references to the relevant person whose position as regards liability for a penalty under paragraph 1 is to be checked, and references to "a taxpayer" were references to a relevant person,

(c) references to a person's "tax position" were to the relevant person's position as regards liability for a penalty under paragraph 1,

(d) references to prejudice to the assessment or collection of tax included prejudice to the investigation of the relevant person's position as regards liability for a penalty under paragraph 1, and

(e) references to a pending appeal relating to tax were to a pending appeal relating to an assessment of liability for a penalty under paragraph 1.

Specific modifications of Schedule 36 to FA 2008 as applied

42 (1) The Schedule as it applies for the purpose mentioned in paragraph 40(1) above has effect with the modifications in sub-paragraphs (2) to (6).

(2) Paragraph 10A (power to inspect business premises of involved third parties) has effect as if the reference in sub-paragraph (1) to the position of any person or class of persons as regards a relevant tax were to the position of a relevant person as regards liability for a penalty under paragraph 1.

(3) Paragraph 47 (right to appeal against penalties under the Schedule) has effect as if after paragraph (b) (but not as part of that paragraph) there were inserted the words "but paragraph (b) does not give a right of appeal against the amount of an increased daily penalty payable by virtue of paragraph 49A."

(4) Paragraph 49A (increased daily default penalty) has effect as if—

(a) in sub-paragraphs (1)(c) and (2) for "imposed" there were substituted "assessable";
(b) for sub-paragraphs (3) and (4) there were substituted—

"(3) If the tribunal decides that an increased daily penalty should be assessable—

(a) the tribunal must determine the day from which the increased daily penalty is to apply and the maximum amount of that penalty ("the new maximum amount");
(b) from that day, paragraph 40 has effect in the person's case as if "the new maximum amount" were substituted for "£60".

(4) The new maximum amount may not be more than £1,000.";

(c) in sub-paragraph (5) for "the amount" there were substituted "the new maximum amount".

(5) Paragraph 49B (notification of increased daily default penalty) has effect as if—

(a) in sub-paragraph (1) for "a person becomes liable to a penalty" there were substituted "the tribunal makes a determination";
(b) in sub-paragraph (2) for "the day from which the increased penalty is to apply" there were substituted "the new maximum amount and the day from which it applies";
(c) sub-paragraph (3) were omitted.

(6) Paragraph 49C is treated as omitted.

43 Paragraphs 50 and 51 are excluded from the application of the Schedule for the purpose mentioned in paragraph 40(1) above.

Declarations about contents of legally privileged communications

44 (1) Subject to sub-paragraph (5), a declaration under this paragraph is to be treated by—

(a) HMRC, or
(b) in any proceedings before a court or tribunal in connection with a penalty under paragraph 1, the court or tribunal,

as conclusive evidence of the things stated in the declaration.

(2) A declaration under this paragraph is a declaration which—

(a) is made by a relevant lawyer,
(b) relates to one or more communications falling within sub-paragraph (3), and
(c) meets such requirements as may be prescribed by regulations under sub-paragraph (4).

(3) A communication falls within this sub-paragraph if—

(a) it was made by a relevant lawyer (whether or not the one making the declaration),
(b) it is legally privileged, and
(c) if it were not legally privileged, it would be relied on by a person for the purpose of establishing that that person is not liable to a penalty under paragraph 1 (whether or not that person is the person who made the communication or is making the declaration).

(4) The Treasury may by regulations impose requirements as to the form and contents of declarations under this paragraph.

(5) Sub-paragraph (1) does not apply where HMRC or (as the case may be) the court or tribunal is satisfied that the declaration contains information which is incorrect.

(6) In this paragraph "a relevant lawyer" means a barrister, advocate, solicitor or other legal representative communications with whom may be the subject of a claim to legal professional privilege or, in Scotland, protected from disclosure in legal proceedings on the grounds of confidentiality of communication.

(7) For the purpose of this paragraph, a communication is "legally privileged" if it is a communication in respect of which a claim to legal professional privilege, or (in Scotland) to confidentiality of communications as between client and professional legal adviser, could be maintained in legal proceedings.

45 (1) Where a person carelessly or deliberately gives any incorrect information in a declaration under paragraph 44, the person is liable to a penalty not exceeding £5,000.

(2) For the purposes of this paragraph, incorrect information is carelessly given by a person if the information is incorrect because of a failure by the person to take reasonable care.

(3) Paragraphs 19(1), 20, 22(1), 37, 38 and 39(1), (2) and (5) apply in relation to a penalty under this paragraph as they apply in relation to a penalty under paragraph 1, subject to the modifications in sub-paragraphs (4) and (5).

(4) In its application to a penalty under this paragraph, paragraph 22(1) has effect as if for "the relevant time" there were substituted "the end of 12 months beginning with the date on which facts sufficient to indicate that the person is liable to the penalty came to the Commissioners' knowledge".

(5) In its application to a penalty under this paragraph, paragraph 38(3) has effect as if the reference to the arrangements to which the penalty relates were to the arrangements to which the declaration under paragraph 44 relates.

(6) In paragraph 44 any reference to a penalty under paragraph 1 includes a reference to a penalty under this paragraph.

PART 10
PUBLISHING DETAILS OF PERSONS WHO HAVE INCURRED PENALTIES

Power to publish details

46 (1) The Commissioners may publish information about a person where—

    (a) the person has incurred a penalty under paragraph 1,

    (b) the penalty has become final, and

    (c) either the condition in sub-paragraph (2) or the condition in sub-paragraph (3) is met.

(2) The condition in this sub-paragraph is that, at the time when the penalty mentioned in sub-paragraph (1) becomes final, 50 or more other penalties which are reckonable penalties have been incurred by the person.

(3) The condition in this sub-paragraph is that—

    (a) the amount of the penalty mentioned in sub-paragraph (1), or

    (b) the total amount of that penalty and any other penalties incurred by that person which are reckonable penalties,

is more than £25,000.

(4) The information that may be published under this paragraph is—

    (a) the person's name (including any trading name, previous name or pseudonym),

    (b) the person's address (or registered office),

    (c) the nature of any business carried on by the person,

    (d) the total number of the penalties in question (that is, the penalty mentioned in sub-paragraph (1) and any penalties that are reckonable penalties in relation to that penalty),

    (e) the total amount of the penalties in question, and

    (f) any other information that the Commissioners consider it appropriate to publish in order to make clear the person's identity.

(5) The information may be published in any way that the Commissioners consider appropriate.

(6) For the purposes of this Part of this Schedule a penalty becomes "final"—

    (a) if the penalty has been assessed and paragraph (b) does not apply, at the time when the period for any appeal or further appeal relating to the penalty expires or, if later, when any appeal or final appeal relating to it is finally determined;

    (b) if a contract settlement has been made in relation to the penalty, at the time when the contract is made;

and "contract settlement" here means a contract between the Commissioners and the person under which the Commissioners undertake not to assess the penalty or (if it has been assessed) not to take proceedings to recover it.

(7) "Reckonable penalty" has the meaning given by paragraph 47.

(8) This paragraph is subject to paragraphs 48 to 50.

47 (1) A penalty is a "reckonable penalty" for the purposes of paragraph 46 if—

    (a) it is a penalty under paragraph 1 which becomes final at the same time as, or before, the penalty mentioned in paragraph 46(1),

    (b) its entry date and the entry date of the penalty mentioned in paragraph 46(1) are not more than 12 months apart, and

    (c) it is not a penalty which under paragraph 48(1) is to be disregarded.

(2) For the purposes of this paragraph the "entry date" of a penalty under paragraph 1 is the date (or, if more than one, the latest date) on which the arrangements concerned or any agreement or transaction forming part of those arrangements was entered into by the taxpayer.

(3) In sub-paragraph (2)—

"the arrangements concerned" means the arrangements to which the penalty relates, and

"the taxpayer" means the person whose defeat in respect of those arrangements resulted in the penalty being payable.

(4) For the purposes of this paragraph, the entry date of a penalty is not more than 12 months apart from the entry date of another penalty if—

    (a) the entry dates of those penalties are the same, or

    (b) the period beginning with whichever of the entry dates is the earlier and ending with whichever of the entry dates is the later is 12 months or less.

Restrictions on power

48 (1) In determining at any time whether or what information may be published in relation to a person under paragraph 46, the following penalties incurred by the person are to be disregarded—

    (a) a penalty which has been reduced to nil or stayed;

    (b) a penalty by reference to which information has previously been published under paragraph 46;

    (c) a penalty where—

        (i) the arrangements to which the penalty relates ("the arrangements concerned") are related to other arrangements, and

        (ii) the condition in sub-paragraph (3) is not met;

    (d) a penalty that relates to arrangements which are related to arrangements that have already been dealt with (within the meaning given by sub-paragraph (4)).

(2) For the purposes of sub-paragraph (1)(c) and (d) arrangements are "related to" each other if they—

    (a) implement the same proposal for tax arrangements, and

    (b) are substantially the same as each other.

(3) The condition referred to in sub-paragraph (1)(c) is that HMRC reasonably believe that—

    (a) defeats have been incurred in the case of all the arrangements that are related to the arrangements concerned ("the related arrangements"), and

    (b) each penalty under paragraph 1 which relates to the arrangements concerned or to any of the related arrangements has become final.

(4) For the purposes of sub-paragraph (1)(d) arrangements have "already been dealt with" if information about the person has already been published under paragraph 46 by reference to a penalty that relates to those arrangements.

49 (1) Publication of information under paragraph 46 on the basis of a penalty or penalties incurred by a person may not take place after the relevant time.

(2) In this paragraph "the relevant time" means the end of 12 months beginning with the date on which the penalty became final or, where more than one penalty is involved, the latest date on which any of them became final.

(3) Sub-paragraph (1) is not to be taken to prevent the re-publishing, or continued publishing, after the relevant time of a set of information published under paragraph 46 before that time.

(4) Information published under paragraph 46 may not be re-published, or continue to be published, after the end of 12 months beginning with the date on which it was first published.

(5) Nothing in paragraph 48 applies in relation to determining whether to re-publish (or continue to publish) a set of information already published under paragraph 46.

50 Before publishing information under paragraph 46 the Commissioners must—

    (a) inform the person that they are considering doing so, and

    (b) afford the person the opportunity to make representations about whether it should be published.

Power to amend

51 The Treasury may by regulations amend this Part of this Schedule so as to alter any of the following—

    (a) the figure for the time being specified in paragraph 46(2);

    (b) the sum for the time being specified in paragraph 46(3);

    (c) any period for the time being specified in paragraph 47(1)(b) or (4).

PART 11
MISCELLANEOUS

Double jeopardy

52 A person is not liable to a penalty under paragraph 1 in respect of conduct for which the person has been convicted of an offence.

Application of provisions of TMA 1970

53 Subject to the provisions of this Schedule, the following provisions of TMA 1970 apply for the purposes of this Schedule as they apply for the purposes of the Taxes Acts—

   (a) section 108 (responsibility of company officers),
   (b) section 114 (want of form), and
   (c) section 115 (delivery and service of documents).

PART 12
GENERAL

Meaning of "tax"

54 (1) In this Schedule "tax" includes any of the following taxes—

   (a) income tax,
   (b) corporation tax, including any amount chargeable as if it were corporation tax or treated as if it were corporation tax,
   (c) capital gains tax,
   (d) petroleum revenue tax,
   (e) diverted profits tax,
   (f) apprenticeship levy,
   (g) inheritance tax,
   (h) stamp duty land tax, and
   (i) annual tax on enveloped dwellings,

and also includes national insurance contributions.

(2) The Treasury may by regulations amend sub-paragraph (1) so as to—

   (a) add a tax to the list of taxes for the time being set out in that sub-paragraph;
   (b) remove a tax for the time being set out in that sub-paragraph;
   (c) remove the reference to national insurance contributions;
   (d) substitute for that reference a reference to national insurance contributions of a particular class or classes;
   (e) where provision has been made under paragraph (d)—
      (i) add a class or classes of national insurance contributions to those for the time being specified in that sub-paragraph;
      (ii) remove a class or classes of national insurance contributions for the time being so specified.

(3) Regulations under this paragraph may—

   (a) make supplementary, incidental, and consequential provision, including provision amending or repealing any provision of this Schedule;
   (b) make transitional provision.

Meaning of "tax advantage"

55 In this Schedule "tax advantage" includes—

   (a) relief or increased relief from tax,
   (b) repayment or increased repayment of tax,
   (c) receipt, or advancement of a receipt, of a tax credit,
   (d) avoidance or reduction of a charge to tax, an assessment of tax or a liability to pay tax,
   (e) avoidance of a possible assessment to tax or liability to pay tax,
   (f) deferral of a payment of tax or advancement of a repayment of tax, and
   (g) avoidance of an obligation to deduct or account for tax.

Other definitions

56 (1) In this Schedule—

"abusive tax arrangements" has the meaning given by paragraph 3;

"arrangements" includes any agreement, understanding, scheme, transaction or series of transactions (whether or not legally enforceable);

"business" includes any trade or profession;

"the Commissioners" means the Commissioners for Her Majesty's Revenue and Customs;

"company" has the same meaning as in the Corporation Tax Acts (see section 1121 of CTA 2010);

"contract settlement" (except in paragraph 46(6)) means an agreement in connection with a person's liability to make a payment to the Commissioners under or by virtue of an enactment;

"a defeat", in relation to arrangements, is to be read in accordance with paragraph 4;

a "designated HMRC officer" means an officer of Revenue and Customs who has been designated by the Commissioners for the purposes of this Schedule;

"the GAAR Advisory Panel" has the meaning given by paragraph 1 of Schedule 43 to FA 2013;

"group" is to be read in accordance with sub-paragraph (2);

"HMRC" means Her Majesty's Revenue and Customs;

"national insurance contributions" means contributions under Part 1 of the Social Security Contributions and Benefits Act 1992 or Part 1 of the Social Security Contributions and Benefits (Northern Ireland) Act 1992;

a "NICs decision" means a decision under section 8 of the Social Security Contributions (Transfer of Functions, etc.) Act 1999 or Article 7 of the Social Security Contributions (Transfer of Functions, etc.) (Northern Ireland) Order 1999 (SI 1999/671) relating to a person's liability for relevant contributions;

"relevant contributions" means any of the following contributions under Part 1 of the Social Security Contributions and Benefits Act 1992 or Part 1 of the Social Security Contributions and Benefits (Northern Ireland) Act 1992—

    (a) Class 1 contributions;

    (b) Class 1A contributions;

    (c) Class 1B contributions;

    (d) Class 2 contributions which must be paid but in relation to which section 11A of the Act in question (application of certain provisions of the Income Tax Acts) does not apply;

"tax" is to be read in accordance with paragraph 54;

"tax advantage" is to be read in accordance with paragraph 55.

(2) For the purposes of this Schedule two companies are members of the same group if—

    (a) one is a 75% subsidiary of the other, or

    (b) both are 75% subsidiaries of a third company;

and in this paragraph "75% subsidiary" has, subject to sub-paragraph (3), the meaning given by section 1154 of CTA 2010.

(3) So far as relating to 75% subsidiaries, section 151(4) of CTA 2010 (requirements relating to beneficial ownership) applies for the purposes of this Schedule as it applies for the purposes of Part 5 of that Act.

(4) In this Schedule references to an assessment to tax, however expressed—

    (a) in relation to inheritance tax and petroleum revenue tax, include a determination;

    (b) in relation to relevant contributions, include a NICs decision.

Regulations

57 (1) Any regulations under this Schedule must be made by statutory instrument.

(2) A statutory instrument which contains (alone or with other provision) any regulations within sub-paragraph (3) may not be made unless a draft of the instrument has been laid before, and approved by a resolution of, the House of Commons.

(3) Regulations within this sub-paragraph are—

    (a) regulations under paragraph 12;

    (b) regulations under paragraph 14(1);

    (c) regulations under paragraph 14(2) which amend or repeal any provision of this Schedule;

    (d) regulations under paragraph 51;

    (e) regulations under paragraph 54.

(4) A statutory instrument containing only—

    (a) regulations under paragraph 14(2) which do not amend or repeal any provision of this Schedule, or

    (b) regulations under paragraph 44,

is subject to annulment in pursuance of a resolution of the House of Commons.

Consequential amendments

58 In section 103ZA of TMA 1970 (disapplication of sections 100 to 103 of that Act in the case of certain penalties)—

(a) omit "or" at the end of paragraph (i), and

(b) after paragraph (j) insert "or

"(k) paragraph 1 or 45 of Schedule 16 to the Finance (No. 2) Act 2017 (enablers of defeated tax avoidance etc)."

59 In section 54 of ITTOIA 2005 (no deduction allowed for certain penalties etc) at the end of the table in subsection (2) insert—

"Penalty under Schedule 16 to F(No. 2)A 2017	Various taxes"

60 In section 1303 of CTA 2009 (no deduction allowed for certain penalties etc) at the end of the table in subsection (2) insert—

"Penalty under Schedule 16 to F(No. 2)A 2017	Various taxes"

61 In Schedule 34 to FA 2014 (promoters of tax avoidance schemes: threshold conditions), in paragraph 7—

(a) in paragraph (a), for the words after "promoter" substitute "—

(i) have been referred to the GAAR Advisory Panel under Schedule 43 to FA 2013 (referrals of single schemes),

(ii) are in a pool in respect of which a referral has been made to that Panel under Schedule 43B to that Act (generic referrals), or

(iii) have been referred to that Panel under paragraph 26 of Schedule 16 to F(No. 2)A 2017 (referrals in relation to penalties for enablers of defeated tax avoidance),";

(b) in paragraph (b), for the words after "referral" substitute "under (as the case may be)—

(i) paragraph 11(3)(b) of Schedule 43 to FA 2013,

(ii) paragraph 6(4)(b) of Schedule 43B to that Act, or

(iii) paragraph 34(3)(b) of Schedule 16 to F(No. 2)A 2017,

(opinion of sub-panel of GAAR Advisory Panel that arrangements are not reasonable), and".

Commencement

62 (1) Subject to sub-paragraphs (2) and (3), paragraphs 1 to 61 of this Schedule have effect in relation to arrangements entered into on or after the day on which this Act is passed.

(2) In determining in relation to any particular arrangements whether a person is a person who enabled the arrangements, any action of the person carried out before the day on which this Act is passed is to be disregarded.

(3) The amendments made by paragraph 61 do not apply in relation to a person who is a promoter in relation to arrangements if by virtue of sub-paragraph (2) above that person is not a person who enabled the arrangements.

GENERAL NOTE

Schedule 16 makes provision for penalties for persons who enable the use of abusive tax avoidance arrangements which are later defeated.

PART 1 Liability to penalty (paras 1–2)

Paragraph 1 explains that a penalty is payable where a person ("T") has entered into abusive tax arrangements (defined in Part 2) and T has incurred a defeat in respect of those arrangements (defined in Part 3) and that the penalty is payable by each person who enabled the arrangements (defined in Part 4).

Paragraph 2 explains what is provided for in the rest of the Schedule.

PART 2 "Abusive" and "tax arrangements": meaning (para 3)

Paragraph 3(1) defines "tax arrangements" and paragraph 3(2) defines when tax arrangements are "abusive". Both definitions replicate the wording in FA 2013 s 207 applying to the GAAR.

Arrangements are "tax arrangements" if, "having regard to all the circumstances, it would be reasonable to conclude that the obtaining of a tax advantage was the main purpose, or one of the main purposes, of the arrangements". This is the familiar broad purpose test used in most anti-avoidance legislation. It sets an initially low threshold for determining whether the GAAR might apply to the arrangements.

A second higher threshold confines the application of the GAAR only to arrangements that are "abusive". Tax arrangements are "abusive" if "they are arrangements the entering into or carrying out of which cannot reasonably be regarded as a reasonable course of action in relation to the relevant tax provisions, having regard to all the circumstances". This is the so-called GAAR "double reasonableness" test.

The enablers' penalty will apply where the defeated arrangements meet this test, regardless of whether they are notifiable under DOTAS or whether they are defeated or counteracted by a targeted anti-avoidance rule, unallowable purpose test, the GAAR or any other statutory rule. The intention is that, by applying the penalty only to abusive arrangements that fail the GAAR double reasonableness test, bona fide commercial transactions should not be affected.

The rest of paragraph 3 goes on to explain the circumstances to which regard must be had in determining whether arrangements are abusive or not, and provides examples of things which might indicate that tax arrangements are abusive. There is an "accepted established practice" let-out. Again, this largely replicates the wording of FA 2013 s 207.

The definition of "tax, "tax advantage", and "arrangements" are in Part 12 paras 54(1), 55 and 56(1). They are the definitions that are commonly found in anti-avoidance legislation.

"Tax" includes national insurance contributions.

"Tax advantage" includes relief or increased relief from tax and the other familiar circumstances.

"Arrangements" includes any agreement, understanding, scheme, transaction or series of transactions (whether or not legally enforceable).

PART 3 "Defeat" in respect of abusive tax arrangements (paras 4–6)

The approach followed is the same as that used in FA 2014 Sch 34A in relation to Promoters of Tax Avoidance Schemes and in FA 2016 Sch 18 in relation to the Serial Tax Avoidance Regime. This treats arrangements as being defeated when there is a final determination of a tribunal or court that the arrangements do not achieve their purported tax advantage, or, in the absence of such a decision, there is an agreement between the taxpayer and HMRC that the arrangements do not work.

Paragraph 4 sets out that "T" incurs a "defeat" in respect of abusive tax arrangements ("the arrangements concerned") entered into by T if either Condition A or Condition B is met.

Condition A (giving HMRC a document) is defined by Paragraph 5. Condition A is met where:

(a) T, or a person on T's behalf, has given HMRC a document, such those listed in the Table in FA 2007, Sch 24 para 1 (i.e. returns);

(b) It was submitted on the basis that a tax advantage ("the relevant tax advantage") arose from the arrangements concerned;

(c) The relevant tax advantage has been counteracted, ie that adjustments have been made on the basis that the whole or part of the relevant tax advantage does not arise; and

(d) The counteraction is final, ie when the adjustments can no longer be varied, on appeal or otherwise.

Adjustments include the entering into of a contract settlement.

Condition B (HMRC assessment) is defined by paragraph 6, and refers to cases not falling with Condition A. Condition B is met where:

(a) HMRC have made an assessment in relation to tax;

(b) The assessment counteracts a tax advantage that it is reasonable to assume T expected to obtain from the arrangements concerned ("the expected tax advantage"), i.e. it is made on a basis which prevents T from obtaining the expected tax advantage, and

(c) The counteraction is final, ie when a contract settlement is made or when the assessment can no longer be varied on appeal or otherwise.

In cases where counteraction become final because there is agreement between T and HMRC that their arrangements do not work, paragraph 21 sets out that HMRC will not issue enabler penalties until all or most of the users of the same scheme have agreed that it does not work.

PART 4 Persons who "enabled" the arrangements (paras 7–14)

Paragraph 7 sets out five categories of enablers, but paragraph 13 clarifies that neither T nor (where T is a company) any company in the same group as T are to be regarded as enablers, regardless of whether they otherwise meet the definition of enabler.

Paragraph 8 – a "designer" of the arrangements is a person who, in the course of a business carried on by that person (so this will exclude an employee of a business), is to any extent responsible for the design of the arrangements or a proposal that was implemented by the arrangements, *but* the person is not an enabler unless the advice they provided is "relevant advice" and the "knowledge condition" is met.

Paragraph 8(3) explains when advice is "relevant advice" but para 8(5) clarifies that advice will not be taken to "suggest" anything which is put forward by the advice for consideration but which the advice can reasonably be read as recommending against.

It is important to note that advice includes an opinion (para 8(7)(a)).

HMRC recognised during the consultation process that the regime needed to distinguish "enablers" from those who simply provide second opinion advice to clients on arrangements designed or enabled by others, but who do not contribute to the design of the arrangements themselves.

The legislation provides that an adviser who merely gives a client a second opinion on abusive arrangements, where that opinion contains no suggestion for any alteration of those proposed arrangements, is not an enabler by virtue of having given that second opinion.

Advice or an opinion which suggests how the arrangements can be modified or adapted to achieve the intended or other tax advantages would constitute enabling unless one can draw a conclusion from reading the advice or opinion that it is clearly recommending against the arrangements (for example because there is a high risk they will be considered abusive and setting out those risks). This is provided for in para 8(5).

HMRC also recognised that the definition of an enabler needed to be well-targeted to ensure those who are unwittingly within the meaning of enabler are also excluded.

Paragraph 8(4) defines the "knowledge condition". Broadly this is where the person providing the advice knew or could reasonably be expected to know that the advice would be (or it was likely it would be) used in the design of abusive tax arrangements.

This ensures that a person, such as a company formation agent, will not be caught so long as they had no knowledge that the services they provided were being used in the design of abusive tax arrangements.

Paragraph 9 – a "manager" of the arrangements is a person who, in the course of a business carried on by that person, to any extent responsible for the organisation or management of the arrangements, and when carrying out any functions in relation to the organisation or management of the arrangements, knew or could reasonably be expected to know that the arrangements involved were abusive tax arrangements.

Paragraph 9(2) explains that a person who, in the course of their business, facilitates T's withdrawal from the arrangements is not to be regarded as a manager of the arrangements because of anything done in the course of facilitating that withdrawal, but only if it is reasonable to assume that the obtaining of a tax advantage is not T's purpose in withdrawing from them. An adviser who is merely assisting a client in unwinding abusive tax arrangements they previously implemented is not an enabler, so long as the purpose in exiting the arrangements is not to seek a further tax advantage.

Paragraph 10 – a person who "marketed" the arrangements is broadly someone who, in the course of a business carried on by them, makes available for implementation by T a proposal, which has since been implemented, or has communicated information to T about a proposal which has since been implemented and did so with a view to T entering the arrangements. Note that there is no 'knowledge condition" as it is assumed that a marketer of arrangements would be fully aware of what it is they are marketing.

Paragraph 11 – an "enabling participant" in the arrangements is a person (not T) who enters into the arrangements, without that person's participation in the arrangements the arrangements could not be expected to result in a tax advantage for T and, when that person entered into the arrangements, that person knew or could reasonably be expected to know that what was being entered into was abusive tax arrangements.

Paragraph 12 – a "financial enabler" in relation to the arrangements is a person if in the course of their business they provide a financial product (directly or indirectly), to T (or an enabling participant), it is reasonable to assume that the purpose in obtaining the financial product was to participate in the arrangements and when the product was provided the person providing it knew of could reasonably be expected to know that the purpose of obtaining it was to participate in abusive tax arrangements.

There is a non-exhaustive list of what "providing a financial product" includes in para 12(3). The list can be amended by regulations.

Paragraph 14 allows the Treasury to add to the categories of persons who can "enable" arrangements by regulations. Likewise, they may provide for exemptions from the definition by Regulations.

PART 5 Amount of penalty (paras 15–18)

Paragraph 15 explains that a penalty is payable by each person who enabled the abusive tax arrangements. The amount of the penalty is the total amount or value of all the consideration received or receivable by that person for enabling the arrangements. Setting the penalty at the level of the enabler's fee reflects the level of the enabler's involvement. It should also act as a very strong deterrent to anyone considering enabling abusive tax avoidance schemes after the legislation comes into effect.

Paragraph 16 goes on to specify, among other things, how the consideration will be computed if there are two or more transactions, or where consideration is given for what is in substance one bargain. This provision is to deal with any complex or less than transparent fee arrangements.

Paragraph 17 provides that the penalty will be reduced where other penalties have been assessed in relation to the same conduct which triggered the enabling penalty. This would, for example, include a penalty for enabling offshore tax evasion (or non-compliance) under FA 2016 Sch 20.

Paragraph 18 specifies that HMRC may in their discretion reduce an enabling penalty, which could include remitting the penalty completely, or staying proceedings for the recovery of the penalty. It is hoped that HMRC's guidance will specify in what circumstances HMRC might consider exercising this discretion.

PART 6 Assessment of penalty (paragraphs 19–22)

Paragraph 19 explains how HMRC will assess the penalty and notify the enabler. In particular, it explains what the position is if HMRC do not have sufficient information to work out the amount of the consideration received or receivable by the enabler. In this situation they are permitted to make a reasonable estimate. Importantly, a penalty cannot be assessed until the GAAR Advisory Panel has given its opinion on the arrangements.

Paragraph 20 specifies the payment period as 30 days beginning with the day on which the penalty notification is issued.

Paragraph 21 explains what will happen where there are multi-users of what are substantially the same tax arrangements ("related arrangements"), i.e. where, typically, an avoidance scheme has been marketed and sold to multiple users who have implemented the arrangements. HMRC cannot assess a penalty until "the required percentage of relevant defeats" has been reached. This is reached when HMRC reasonably believe that defeats have been incurred in the case of more than 50% of the related arrangements implementing the proposal.

This approach is similar to that used in FA 2014 Sch 34A in relation to Promoters of Tax Avoidance Schemes, although there the proportion is higher at 75%.

Paragraph 22 contains information about the assessing time limits, which will vary depending upon whether a GAAR final opinion notice has been given or not, and when (see Part 7).

PART 7 GAAR Advisory Panel opinion, and representations (paras 23–36)

These paragraphs set out the role of the GAAR and the GAAR Advisory Panel, and the procedures that must be followed by HMRC before they can assess a penalty. A penalty can only be assessed if a designated HMRC officer decides that it should be assessed having considered a Panel opinion that is relevant to the arrangements in question.

Broadly speaking, if a GAAR final decision notice has already been given in relation to the arrangements in question – or arrangements equivalent to the defeated arrangements – then there is no need for another referral to be made to the Panel before an enabling penalty can be assessed (para 23).

Once the enabling penalty measures take effect, every adverse opinion of the Panel can therefore potentially be used to trigger the assessment of an enabling penalty. The first Panel opinion notice was issued on 18 July 2017. There is every reason to think that more referrals will be made by HMRC once the enabling penalty comes into effect.

However, where a GAAR final decision notice has not already been given in relation to the arrangements in question, or arrangements equivalent to the defeated arrangements, then HMRC may make a referral under paragraph 26 to the Panel of the question whether the entering into and carrying out of tax arrangements is a reasonable course of action in relation to the relevant tax provisions.

Paragraphs 27–31 set out the procedures that must be followed by HMRC when making a referral.

Paragraph 32 explains that representations can be sent to the Panel once a referral has been made.

Paragraphs 33 and 34 set out the procedures that must be followed by the Panel following the referral and that it must produce an opinion notice or notices that either:

(a) the entering into and carrying out of tax arrangements as described in the referral statement is a reasonable course of action in relation to the relevant tax provisions,

(b) the entering into or carrying out of such tax arrangements is not a reasonable course of action in relation to the relevant tax provisions, or

(c) it is not possible, on the information available, to reach a view on that matter, and the reasons for that opinion.

The resulting Panel opinion is not binding on HMRC or the enabler, but must be taken into account in determining whether those arrangements or any equivalent tax arrangements are abusive for the purposes of the enablers' legislation.

It is expected that HMRC's guidance on the enabling penalty will provide details of the procedures that must be followed. The existing GAAR Guidance, which will be updated following enactment of the enabling penalty legislation, will also be relevant.

PART 8 Appeals (paras 37–39)

An appeal may be made to the Tribunal against HMRC's decision to charge an enabling penalty or the amount of the penalty. Paragraph 39 allows the Tribunal to substitute its decision for HMRC's by using its discretion to mitigate a penalty in the same way that HMRC can under para 18, but where it thinks that HMRC's decision was flawed it may rely on para 18 to a different extent.

PART 9 Information (paras 40–45)

HMRC's information and inspection powers in FA 2008 Sch 36 are applied for the purposes of checking a person's liability to an enabling penalty, as modified by paras 41 to 43.

Paragraph 44 contains provisions applying specifically to legally privileged communications. The government recognises that the information sought under Sch 36 powers might contain items protected by legal professional privilege (LPP) (in Scotland, protected from disclosure in legal proceedings on the grounds of confidentiality of communications as between client and professional legal adviser), which cannot therefore be provided. In its response to the 2016 consultation HMRC said the following (at paras 2.14 and 2.15):

> "The government recognises that, in order to demonstrate that they have not acted as an enabler of a defeated avoidance scheme, lawyers bound by LPP might not be able to provide evidence of the advice they gave, as LPP will remain with the client who may be unwilling to waive this right. Whilst the

government recognises that there are ways in which the terms and conditions under which advice may be given could be drafted to remove this issue, it is appropriate to provide a way in which the lawyer could, in appropriate cases, show that they do not fall within the scope of the penalty provisions without disturbing LPP rights. This will involve them making a declaration. HMRC will consult on the wording of the declaration to ensure it is both robust and compliant with LPP. The declaration will be subject to a penalty for making a misdeclaration".

Paragraph 44 allows a lawyer to make a declaration in connection with an enabling penalty where legally privileged communications with a person would otherwise be relied upon to establish that the person is not liable to an enabling penalty. Lawyer includes a barrister, advocate, solicitor or other legal representative. The declaration must be treated by HMRC and the courts or tribunals as conclusive evidence of the matters stated in the declaration, unless they are satisfied that the declaration contains information that is incorrect, for example based on evidence which has come to light during the course of an enquiry. A penalty not exceeding £5,000 can be levied if a person deliberately or carelessly gives incorrect information in a declaration.

Further requirements as to the content and form of the declaration will be specified in regulations.

In the explanatory notes to the Finance Bill, it states the following (page 315 paragraph 82):

"Regulations will only be able to provide for a declaration that does not in itself breach legal professional privilege. It is intended that a declaration will consist of a list of the exemptions from being within the meaning of an enabler provided in paragraphs 8 to 12. The relevant lawyer who signs the declaration on behalf of the person will indicate that at least one of those exemptions applies to prevent that person being an enabler for the purposes of this Schedule but will not specify which. The declaration will not specify the name of the client, or what the communications were to ensure that it does not contain information which would breach legal professional privilege".

If there is non-privileged information that would establish that the person is not an enabler, the person should rely on that information rather than making a declaration.

It is expected that further information will be provided in HMRC's guidance.

PART 10 Publishing details of persons who have incurred penalties (paras 46–51)

In common with other recent anti-avoidance measures, HMRC have the power to publish information about a person who incurs an enabling penalty which has become final, but only where, over a period of 12 months, either the person has incurred 50 or more other penalties which are "reckonable penalties", or the total amount of all the penalties incurred is more than £25,000. Both thresholds can be altered by regulations.

Paragraph 46 specifies what details may be published.

Paragraph 47 defines reckonable penalty, and paragraph 48 explains when a penalty is not a reckonable penalty.

Paragraphs 49 and 50 explain the manner of publication and time restrictions on the length of publication.

PART 11 Miscellaneous (paras 52–53)

Paragraph 52 specifies that a person is not liable to an enabling penalty if they have been convicted of a criminal offence for the same conduct.

PART 12 General (paras 54–62)

Paragraphs 54 to 56 contain definitions of words and phrases used in the Schedule.

Paragraph 57 provides for regulations to be made by statutory instrument.

Paragraph 58 makes consequential amendments to TMA 1970 s 103ZA.

Paragraphs 59 to 60 specify that an enabling penalty is not an allowable deduction for income tax or corporation tax.

Paragraph 61 provides that an adverse opinion of the GAAR Advisory Panel given under para 34 is to be added to the list of threshold conditions which can attract a conduct notice under the POTAS regime.

Paragraph 62 provides that the Schedule takes effect from Royal Assent to the Finance (No 2) Act 2017 in relation to actions carried out after that date and arrangements entered into on or after that date.

This suggests that a person can be an enabler if they modify or otherwise amend an arrangement that is already in existence, or has already been entered into, before Royal Assent is given.

SCHEDULE 17

DISCLOSURE OF TAX AVOIDANCE SCHEMES: VAT AND OTHER INDIRECT TAXES

Section 66

PART 1

DUTIES TO DISCLOSE AVOIDANCE SCHEMES ETC

Preliminary: application of definitions

1 The definitions in paragraphs 2, 3, and 7 to 10 apply for the purposes of this Schedule.

"Indirect tax"

2 (1) "Indirect tax" means any of the following—

VAT
insurance premium tax
general betting duty
pool betting duty
remote gaming duty
machine games duty
gaming duty
lottery duty
bingo duty
air passenger duty
hydrocarbon oils duty
tobacco products duty
duties on spirits, beer, wine, made-wine and cider
soft drinks industry levy
aggregates levy
landfill tax
climate change levy
customs duties.

(2) The Treasury may by regulations amend the list in sub-paragraph (1) by adding, varying or omitting an entry for a tax.

"Notifiable arrangements" and "notifiable proposal"

3 (1) "Notifiable arrangements" means any arrangements not excluded by sub-paragraph (2) which—

(a) fall within any description prescribed by the Treasury by regulations,

(b) enable, or might be expected to enable, any person to obtain a tax advantage in relation to any indirect tax that is so prescribed in relation to arrangements of that description, and

(c) are such that the main benefit, or one of the main benefits, that might be expected to arise from the arrangements is the obtaining of that tax advantage.

(2) Arrangements that meet the requirements in paragraphs (a) to (c) of sub-paragraph (1) are not notifiable arrangements if they implement a proposal which is excluded from being a notifiable proposal by sub-paragraph (4).

(3) "Notifiable proposal" means a proposal for arrangements which, if entered into, would be notifiable arrangements (whether the proposal relates to a particular person or to any person who may seek to take advantage of it).

(4) A proposal is not a notifiable proposal if any of the following occur before 1 January 2018—

(a) a promoter first makes a firm approach to another person in relation to the proposal,

(b) a promoter makes the proposal available for implementation by any other person, or

(c) a promoter first becomes aware of any transaction forming part of arrangements implementing the proposal.

4 (1) HMRC may apply to the tribunal for an order that—

(a) a proposal is notifiable, or

(b) arrangements are notifiable.

(2) An application must specify—

(a) the proposal or arrangements in respect of which the order is sought, and

(b) the promoter.

(3) On an application the tribunal may make the order only if satisfied that paragraph 3(1)(a) to (c) applies to the relevant arrangements and that they are not excluded from being notifiable by paragraph 3(2).

5 (1) HMRC may apply to the tribunal for an order that—

(a) a proposal is to be treated as notifiable, or

(b) arrangements are to be treated as notifiable.

(2) An application must specify—

(a) the proposal or arrangements in respect of which the order is sought, and

(b) the promoter.

(3) On an application the tribunal may make the order only if satisfied that HMRC—

(a) have taken all reasonable steps to establish whether the proposal or arrangements are notifiable, and

(b) have reasonable grounds for suspecting that the proposal or arrangements may be notifiable.

(4) Reasonable steps under sub-paragraph (3)(a) may (but need not) include taking action under paragraph 29 or 30.

(5) Grounds for suspicion under sub-paragraph (3)(b) may include—

(a) the fact that the relevant arrangements fall within a description prescribed under paragraph 3(1)(a),

(b) an attempt by the promoter to avoid or delay providing information or documents about the proposal or arrangements under or by virtue of paragraph 29 or 30,

(c) the promoter's failure to comply with a requirement under or by virtue of paragraph 29 or 30 in relation to another proposal or other arrangements.

(6) Where an order is made under this paragraph in respect of a proposal or arrangements, the relevant period for the purposes of sub-paragraph (1) of paragraph 11 or 12 in so far as it applies by virtue of the order is the period of 11 days beginning with the day on which the order is made.

(7) An order under this paragraph in relation to a proposal or arrangements is without prejudice to the possible application of any of paragraphs 11 to 15, other than by virtue of this paragraph, to the proposal or arrangements.

"Tax advantage" in relation to VAT

6 (1) A person (P) obtains a tax advantage in relation to VAT if—

(a) in any prescribed accounting period, the amount by which the output tax accounted for by P exceeds the input tax deducted by P is less than it would otherwise be;

(b) P obtains a VAT credit when P would otherwise not do so, or obtains a larger credit or obtains a credit earlier than would otherwise be the case;

(c) in a case where P recovers input tax as a recipient of a supply before the supplier accounts for the output tax, the period between the time when the input tax is recovered and the time when the output tax is accounted for is greater than would otherwise be the case;

(d) in any prescribed accounting period, the amount of P's non-deductible tax is less than it otherwise would be;

(e) P avoids an obligation to account for tax.

(2) In sub-paragraph (1)(d) "non-deductible tax", in relation to a taxable person, means—

(a) input tax for which the person is not entitled to credit under section 25 of VATA 1994,

(b) any VAT incurred by the person which is not input tax and in respect of which the person is not entitled to a refund from the Commissioners by virtue of any provision of VATA 1994.

(3) For the purposes of sub-paragraph (2)(b), the VAT "incurred" by a taxable person is—

    (a) VAT on the supply to the person of any goods or services,
    (b) VAT on the acquisition by the person from another member State of any goods,
    (c) VAT paid or payable by the person on the importation of any goods from a place outside the member States.

(4) A person who is not a taxable person obtains a tax advantage in relation to VAT if that person's non-refundable tax is less that it otherwise would be.

(5) In sub-paragraph (4) "non-refundable tax" means—

    (a) VAT on the supply to the person of any goods or services,
    (b) VAT on the acquisition by the person from another member State of goods,
    (c) VAT paid or payable by the person on the importation of any goods from a place outside the member States,

but excluding (in each case) any VAT in respect of which the person is entitled to a refund from the Commissioners by virtue of any provision of VATA 1994.

(6) Terms used in this paragraph which are defined in section 96 of VATA 1994 have the meanings given by that section.

"Tax advantage" in relation to taxes other than VAT

7 "Tax advantage", in relation to an indirect tax other than VAT, means—

    (a) relief or increased relief from tax,
    (b) repayment or increased repayment of tax,
    (c) avoidance or reduction of a charge to tax, an assessment of tax or a liability to pay tax,
    (d) avoidance of a possible assessment to tax or liability to pay tax,
    (e) deferral of a payment of tax or advancement of a repayment of tax, or
    (f) avoidance of an obligation to deduct or account for tax.

"Promoter"

8 (1) This paragraph describes when a person (P) is a promoter in relation to a notifiable proposal or notifiable arrangements.

(2) P is a promoter in relation to a notifiable proposal if, in the course of a relevant business, P—

    (a) is to any extent responsible for the design of the proposed arrangements,
    (b) makes a firm approach to another person (C) in relation to the proposal with a view to P making the proposal available for implementation by C or any other person, or
    (c) makes the proposal available for implementation by other persons.

(3) P is a promoter in relation to notifiable arrangements if—

    (a) P is by virtue of sub-paragraph (2)(b) or (c) a promoter in relation to a notifiable proposal which is implemented by the arrangements, or
    (b) if in the course of a relevant business, P is to any extent responsible for—

        (i) the design of the arrangements, or
        (ii) the organisation or management of the arrangements.

(4) In this paragraph "relevant business" means any trade, profession or business which—

    (a) involves the provision to other persons of services relating to taxation, or
    (b) is carried on by a bank or securities house.

(5) In sub-paragraph (4)(b)—

    "bank" has the meaning given by section 1120 of CTA 2010, and
    "securities house" has the meaning given by section 1009(3) of that Act.

(6) For the purposes of this paragraph anything done by a company is to be taken to be done in the course of a relevant business if it is done for the purposes of a relevant business falling within sub-paragraph (4)(b) carried on by another company which is a member of the same group.

(7) Section 170 of the TCGA 1992 has effect for determining for the purposes of sub-paragraph (6) whether two companies are members of the same group, but as if in that section—

    (a) for each of the references to a 75 per cent subsidiary there were substituted a reference to a 51 per cent subsidiary, and
    (b) subsection (3)(b) and subsections (6) to (8) were omitted.

(8) A person is not to be treated as a promoter by reason of anything done in prescribed circumstances.

(9) In the application of this Schedule to a proposal or arrangements which are not notifiable, a reference to a promoter is a reference to a person who would be a promoter under this paragraph if the proposal or arrangements were notifiable.

"Introducer"

9 (1) A person is an introducer in relation to a notifiable proposal if the person makes a marketing contact with another person in relation to the proposal.

(2) A person is not to be treated as an introducer by reason of anything done in prescribed circumstances.

(3) In the application of this Schedule to a proposal or arrangements which are not notifiable, a reference to an introducer is a reference to a person who would be an introducer under this paragraph if the proposal or arrangements were notifiable.

"Makes a firm approach" and "marketing contact"

10 (1) A person makes a firm approach to another person in relation to a notifiable proposal if the person makes a marketing contact with the other person in relation to the proposal at a time when the proposed arrangements have been substantially designed.

(2) A person makes a marketing contact with another person in relation to a notifiable proposal if—

  (a) the person communicates information about the proposal to the other person,
  (b) the communication is made with a view to that other person, or any other person, entering into transactions forming part of the proposed arrangements, and
  (c) the information communicated includes an explanation of the tax advantage that might be expected to be obtained from the proposed arrangements.

(3) For the purposes of sub-paragraph (1) proposed arrangements have been substantially designed at any time if by that time the nature of the transactions to form part of them has been sufficiently developed for it to be reasonable to believe that a person who wished to obtain the tax advantage mentioned in sub-paragraph (2)(c) might enter into—

  (a) transactions of the nature developed, or
  (b) transactions not substantially different from transactions of that nature.

Duties of promoter in relation to notifiable proposals or notifiable arrangements

11 (1) A person who is a promoter in relation to a notifiable proposal must, within the relevant period, provide HMRC with prescribed information relating to the proposal.

(2) In sub-paragraph (1) "the relevant period" is the period of 31 days beginning with the relevant date.

(3) In sub-paragraph (2) "the relevant date" is the earliest of the following—

  (a) the date on which the promoter first makes a firm approach to another person in relation to the proposal,
  (b) the date on which the promoter makes the proposal available for implementation by any other person, or
  (c) the date on which the promoter first becomes aware of any transaction forming part of notifiable arrangements implementing the proposal.

12 (1) A person who is a promoter in relation to notifiable arrangements must, within the relevant period after the date on which the person first becomes aware of any transaction forming part of the arrangements, provide HMRC with prescribed information relating to the arrangements.

(2) In sub-paragraph (1) "the relevant period" is the period of 31 days beginning with that date.

(3) The duty under sub-paragraph (1) does not apply if the notifiable arrangements implement a proposal in respect of which notice has been given to HMRC under paragraph 11(1).

13 (1) This paragraph applies where a person complies with paragraph 11(1) in relation to a notifiable proposal for arrangements and another person is—

  (a) also a promoter in relation to the proposal or is a promoter in relation to a notifiable proposal for arrangements which are substantially the same as the proposed arrangements (whether they relate to the same or different parties), or
  (b) a promoter in relation to notifiable arrangements implementing the proposal or notifiable arrangements which are substantially the same as notifiable arrangements implementing the proposal (whether they relate to the same or different parties).

(2) Any duty of the other person under paragraph 11(1) or 12(1) in relation to the notifiable proposal or notifiable arrangements is discharged if—

(a) the person who complied with paragraph 11(1) has notified the identity and address of the other person to HMRC or the other person holds the reference number allocated to the proposed notifiable arrangements under paragraph 22(1), and

(b) the other person holds the information provided to HMRC in compliance with paragraph 11(1).

14 (1) This paragraph applies where a person complies with paragraph 12(1) in relation to notifiable arrangements and another person is—

(a) a promoter in relation to a notifiable proposal for arrangements which are substantially the same as the notifiable arrangements (whether they relate to the same or different parties), or

(b) also a promoter in relation to the notifiable arrangements or notifiable arrangements which are substantially the same (whether they relate to the same or different parties).

(2) Any duty of the other person under paragraph 11(1) or 12(1) in relation to the notifiable proposal or notifiable arrangements is discharged if—

(a) the person who complied with paragraph 12(1) has notified the identity and address of the other person to HMRC or the other person holds the reference number allocated to the notifiable arrangements under paragraph 22(1), and

(b) the other person holds the information provided to HMRC in compliance with paragraph 12(1).

15 Where a person is a promoter in relation to two or more notifiable proposals or sets of notifiable arrangements which are substantially the same (whether they relate to the same parties or different parties) the person need not provide information under paragraph 11(1) or 12(1) if the person has already provided information under either of those paragraphs in relation to any of the other proposals or arrangements.

Duty of promoter: supplemental information

16 (1) This paragraph applies where—

(a) a promoter (P) has provided information in purported compliance with paragraph 11(1) or 12(1), but

(b) HMRC believe that P has not provided all the prescribed information.

(2) HMRC may apply to the tribunal for an order requiring P to provide specified information about, or documents relating to, the notifiable proposal or arrangements.

(3) The tribunal may make an order under sub-paragraph (2) in respect of information or documents only if satisfied that HMRC have reasonable grounds for suspecting that the information or documents—

(a) form part of the prescribed information, or

(b) will support or explain the prescribed information.

(4) A requirement by virtue of sub-paragraph (2) is to be treated as part of P's duty under paragraph 11(1) or 12(1).

(5) In so far as P's duty under sub-paragraph (1) of paragraph 11 or 12 arises out of an order made by virtue of sub-paragraph (2) above the relevant period for the purposes of that sub-paragraph (1) is—

(a) the period of 11 days beginning with the date of the order, or

(b) such longer period as HMRC may direct.

Duty of person dealing with promoter outside United Kingdom

17 (1) This paragraph applies where a person enters into any transaction forming part of any notifiable arrangements in relation to which—

(a) a promoter is resident outside the United Kingdom, and

(b) no promoter is resident in the United Kingdom.

(2) The person must, within the relevant period, provide HMRC with prescribed information relating to the arrangements.

(3) In sub-paragraph (2) "the relevant period" is the period of 6 days beginning with the day on which the person enters into the first transaction forming part of the arrangements.

(4) Compliance with paragraph 11(1) or 12(1) by any promoter in relation to the arrangements discharges the person's duty under sub-paragraph (1).

Duty of parties to notifiable arrangements not involving promoter

18 (1) This paragraph applies to any person who enters into any transaction forming part of notifiable arrangements as respects which neither that person nor any other person in the United Kingdom is liable to comply with paragraph 11(1), 12(1) or 17(2).

(2) The person must at the prescribed time provide HMRC with prescribed information relating to the arrangements.

Duty to provide further information requested by HMRC

19 (1) This paragraph applies where—

(a) a person has provided the prescribed information about notifiable proposals or arrangements in compliance with paragraph 11(1), 12(1), 17(2) or 18(2), or

(b) a person has provided information in purported compliance with paragraph 17(2) or 18(2) but HMRC believe that the person has not provided all the prescribed information.

(2) HMRC may require the person to provide—

(a) further specified information about the notifiable proposals or arrangements (in addition to the prescribed information under paragraph 11(1), 12(1), 17(2) or 18(2));

(b) documents relating to the notifiable proposals or arrangements.

(3) Where HMRC impose a requirement on a person under this paragraph, the person must comply with the requirement within—

(a) the period of 10 working days beginning with the day on which HMRC imposed the requirement, or

(b) such longer period as HMRC may direct.

20 (1) This paragraph applies where HMRC—

(a) have required a person to provide information or documents under paragraph 19, but

(b) believe that the person has failed to provide the information or documents required.

(2) HMRC may apply to the tribunal for an order requiring the person to provide the information or documents required.

(3) The tribunal may make an order imposing such a requirement only if satisfied that HMRC have reasonable grounds for suspecting that the information or documents will assist HMRC in considering the notifiable proposals or arrangements.

(4) Where the tribunal makes an order imposing such a requirement, the person must comply with the requirement within—

(a) the period of 10 working days beginning with the day on which the tribunal made the order, or

(b) such longer period as HMRC may direct.

Duty of promoters to provide updated information

21 (1) This paragraph applies where—

(a) information has been provided under paragraph 11(1), or 12(1) about any notifiable arrangements, or proposed notifiable arrangements, to which a reference number is allocated under paragraph 22, and

(b) after the provision of the information, there is a change in relation to the arrangements of a kind mentioned in sub-paragraph (2).

(2) The changes referred to in sub-paragraph (1)(b) are—

(a) a change in the name by which the notifiable arrangements, or proposed notifiable arrangements, are known;

(b) a change in the name or address of any person who is a promoter in relation to the arrangements or, in the case of proposed arrangements, the notifiable proposal.

(3) A person who is a promoter in relation to the notifiable arrangements or, in the case of proposed notifiable arrangements, the notifiable proposal must inform HMRC of the change mentioned in sub-paragraph (1)(b) within 30 days after it is made.

(4) Sub-paragraphs (5) and (6) apply for the purposes of sub-paragraph (3) where there is more than one person who is a promoter in relation to the notifiable arrangements or proposal.

(5) If the change in question is a change in the name or address of a person who is a promoter in relation to the notifiable arrangements or proposal, it is the duty of that person to comply with sub-paragraph (3).

(6) If a person provides information in compliance with sub-paragraph (3), the duty imposed by that sub-paragraph on any other person, so far as relating to the provision of that information, is discharged.

Arrangements to be given reference number

22 (1) Where a person (P) complies or purports to comply with paragraph 11(1), 12(1), 17(2) or 18(2) in relation to any notifiable proposal or notifiable arrangements, HMRC may within 90 days allocate a reference number to the notifiable arrangements or, in the case of a notifiable proposal, to the proposed notifiable arrangements.

(2) If HMRC do so it must notify the number to P and (where the person is one who has complied or purported to comply with paragraph 11(1) or 12(1)), to any other person—

    (a) who is a promoter in relation to—

        (i) the notifiable proposal (or arrangements implementing the notifiable proposal), or

        (ii) the notifiable arrangements (or proposal implemented by the notifiable arrangements), and

    (b) whose identity and address has been notified to HMRC by P.

(3) The allocation of a reference number to any notifiable arrangements (or proposed notifiable arrangements) is not to be regarded as constituting any indication by HMRC that the arrangements would or could as a matter of law result in the obtaining by any person of a tax advantage.

(4) In this Part of this Schedule "reference number", in relation to any notifiable arrangements, means the reference number allocated under this paragraph.

Duty of promoter to notify client of number

23 (1) This paragraph applies where a person who is a promoter in relation to notifiable arrangements is providing (or has provided) services to any person ("the client") in connection with the arrangements.

(2) The promoter must, within 30 days after the relevant date, provide the client with prescribed information relating to any reference number (or, if more than one, any one reference number) that has been notified to the promoter (whether by HMRC or any other person) in relation to—

    (a) the notifiable arrangements, or

    (b) any arrangements substantially the same as the notifiable arrangements (whether involving the same or different parties).

(3) In sub-paragraph (2) "the relevant date" means the later of—

    (a) the date on which the promoter becomes aware of any transaction which forms part of the notifiable arrangements, and

    (b) the date on which the reference number is notified to the promoter.

(4) But where the conditions in sub-paragraph (5) are met the duty imposed on the promoter under sub-paragraph (2) to provide the client with information in relation to notifiable arrangements is discharged

(5) Those conditions are—

    (a) that the promoter is also a promoter in relation to a notifiable proposal and provides services to the client in connection with them both,

    (b) the notifiable proposal and the notifiable arrangements are substantially the same, and

    (c) the promoter has provided to the client, in a form and manner specified by HMRC, prescribed information relating to the reference number that has been notified to the promoter in relation to the proposed notifiable arrangements.

(6) HMRC may give notice that, in relation to notifiable arrangements specified in the notice, promoters are not under the duty under sub-paragraph (2) after the date specified in the notice.

Duty of client to notify parties of number

24 (1) In this paragraph "client" means a person to whom a person who is a promoter in relation to notifiable arrangements or a notifiable proposal is providing (or has provided) services in connection with the arrangements or proposal.

(2) Sub-paragraph (3) applies where the client receives prescribed information relating to the reference number allocated to the arrangements or proposed arrangements,

(3) The client must, within the relevant period, provide prescribed information relating to the reference number to any other person—

(a) who the client might reasonably be expected to know is or is likely to be a party to the arrangements or proposed arrangements, and

(b) who might reasonably be expected to gain a tax advantage in relation to any relevant tax by reason of the arrangements or proposed arrangements.

(4) In sub-paragraph (3) "the relevant period" is the period of 30 days beginning with the later of—

(a) the day on which the client first becomes aware of any transaction forming part of the notifiable arrangements or proposed notifiable arrangements, and

(b) the day on which the prescribed information is notified to the client by the promoter under paragraph 23.

(5) HMRC may give notice that, in relation to notifiable arrangements or a notifiable proposal specified in the notice, persons are not under the duty under sub-paragraph (3) after the date specified in the notice.

(6) The duty under sub-paragraph (3) does not apply in prescribed circumstances.

(7) For the purposes of this paragraph a tax is a "relevant tax", in relation to arrangements or arrangements proposed in a proposal of any description, if it is prescribed in relation to arrangements or proposals of that description by regulations under paragraph 3(1).

Duty of client to provide information to promoter

25 (1) This paragraph applies where a person who is a promoter in relation to notifiable arrangements has provided a person ("the client") with the information prescribed under paragraph 23(2).

(2) The client must, within the relevant period, provide the promoter with prescribed information relating to the client.

(3) In sub-paragraph (2) "the relevant period" is the period of 11 days beginning with the later of—

(a) the date the client receives the reference number for the arrangements, and

(b) the date the client first enters into a transaction which forms part of the arrangements.

(4) The duty under sub-paragraph (2) is subject to any exceptions that may be prescribed.

Duty of parties to notifiable arrangements to notify HMRC of number, etc

26 (1) Any person (P) who is a party to any notifiable arrangements must provide HMRC with prescribed information relating to—

(a) any reference number notified to P under paragraph 23 or 24, and

(b) the time when P obtains or expects to obtain by virtue of the arrangements a tax advantage in relation to any relevant tax.

(2) For the purposes of sub-paragraph (1) a tax is a "relevant tax" in relation to any notifiable arrangements if it is prescribed in relation to arrangements of that description by regulations under paragraph 3(1).

(3) Regulations made by the Commissioners may—

(a) in prescribed cases, require the information prescribed under sub-paragraph (1) to be given to HMRC—

   (i) in the prescribed manner,

   (ii) in the prescribed form,

   (iii) at the prescribed time, and

(b) in prescribed cases, require the information prescribed under sub-paragraph (1) and such other information as is prescribed to be provided separately to HMRC at the prescribed time or times.

(4) In sub-paragraph (3) "prescribed" includes being prescribed in a document made under a power conferred by regulations made by the Commissioners.

(5) HMRC may give notice that, in relation to notifiable arrangements specified in the notice, persons are not under the duty under sub-paragraph (1) after the date specified in the notice.

(6) The duty under sub-paragraph (1) does not apply in prescribed circumstances.

Duty of promoter to provide details of clients

27 (1) This paragraph applies where a person who is a promoter in relation to notifiable arrangements is providing (or has provided) services to any person ("the client") in connection with the arrangements and either—

(a) the promoter is subject to the reference number information requirement, or

(b) the promoter has failed to comply with paragraph 11(1) or 12(1) in relation to the arrangements (or the notifiable proposal for them) but would be subject to the reference number information requirement if a reference number had been allocated to the arrangements.

(2) For the purposes of this paragraph "the reference number information requirement" is the requirement under paragraph 23(2) to provide to the client prescribed information relating to the reference number allocated to the notifiable arrangements.

(3) The promoter must, within the prescribed period after the end of the relevant period, provide HMRC with prescribed information in relation to the client.

(4) In sub-paragraph (3) "the relevant period" means such period (during which the promoter is or would be subject to the reference number information requirement) as is prescribed.

(5) The promoter need not comply with sub-paragraph (3) in relation to any notifiable arrangements at any time after HMRC have given notice under paragraph 23(6) in relation to the arrangements.

Enquiry following disclosure of client details

28 (1) This paragraph applies where—

(a) a person who is a promoter in relation to notifiable arrangements has provided HMRC with information in relation to a person ("the client") under paragraph 27(3) (duty to provide client details), and

(b) HMRC suspect that a person other than the client is or is likely to be a party to the arrangements.

(2) HMRC may by written notice require the promoter to provide prescribed information in relation to any person other than the client who the promoter might reasonably be expected to know is or is likely to be a party to the arrangements.

(3) The promoter must comply with a requirement under or by virtue of sub-paragraph (2) within—

(a) the relevant period, or

(b) such longer period as HMRC may direct.

(4) In sub-paragraph (3) "the relevant period" is the period of 11 days beginning with the day on which the promoter receives the notice under sub-paragraph (2).

Pre-disclosure enquiry

29 (1) Where HMRC suspect that a person (P) is the promoter or introducer of a proposal, or the promoter of arrangements, which may be notifiable, they may by written notice require P to state—

(a) whether in P's opinion the proposal or arrangements are notifiable by P, and

(b) if not, the reasons for P's opinion.

(2) The notice must specify the proposal or arrangements to which it relates.

(3) For the purposes of sub-paragraph (1)(b)—

(a) it is not sufficient to refer to the fact that a lawyer or other professional has given an opinion,

(b) the reasons must show, by reference to this Part of this Schedule and regulations under it, why P thinks the proposal or arrangements are not notifiable by P, and

(c) in particular, if P asserts that the arrangements do not fall within any description prescribed under paragraph 3(1)(a), the reasons must provide sufficient information to enable HMRC to confirm the assertion.

(4) P must comply with a requirement under or by virtue of sub-paragraph (1) within—

(a) the relevant period, or

(b) such longer period as HMRC may direct.

(5) In sub-paragraph (4) "the relevant period" is the period of 11 days beginning with the day on which the notice under sub-paragraph (1) is issued.

Reasons for non-disclosure: supporting information

30 (1) Where HMRC receive from a person (P) a statement of reasons why a proposal or arrangements are not notifiable by P, HMRC may apply to the tribunal for an order requiring P to provide specified information or documents in support of the reasons.

(2) P must comply with a requirement under or by virtue of sub-paragraph (1) within—

(a) the relevant period, or

(b) such longer period as HMRC may direct.

(3) In sub-paragraph (2) "the relevant period" is the period of 15 days beginning with the day on which the order concerned is made.

(4) The power under sub-paragraph (1)—

(a) may be exercised more than once, and

(b) applies whether or not the statement of reasons was received under paragraph 29(1)(b).

Provision of information to HMRC by introducers

31 (1) This paragraph applies where HMRC suspect—

(a) that a person (P) is an introducer in relation to a proposal, and

(b) that the proposal may be notifiable.

(2) HMRC may by written notice require P to provide HMRC with one or both of the following—

(a) prescribed information in relation to each person who has provided P with any information relating to the proposal,

(b) prescribed information in relation to each person with whom P has made a marketing contact in relation to the proposal.

(3) A notice must specify the proposal to which it relates.

(4) P must comply with a requirement under or sub-paragraph(2) within—

(a) the relevant period, or

(b) such longer period as HMRC may direct.

(5) In sub-paragraph (4) "the relevant period" is the period of 11 days beginning with the day on which the notice under sub-paragraph (2) is given.

Legal professional privilege

32 (1) Nothing in this Part of this Schedule requires any person to disclose to HMRC any privileged information.

(2) In this Part of this Schedule "privileged information" means information with respect to which a claim to legal professional privilege, or, in Scotland, to confidentiality of communications, could be maintained in legal proceedings.

Information

33 (1) This paragraph applies where a person is required to provide information under paragraph 23(2) or 24(3).

(2) HMRC may specify additional information which must be provided by that person to the recipients under paragraph 23(2) or 24(3) at the same time as the information referred to in sub-paragraph (1).

(3) HMRC may specify the form and manner in which the additional information is to be provided.

(4) For the purposes of this paragraph "additional information" means information supplied by HMRC which relates to notifiable proposals or notifiable arrangements in general.

34 (1) HMRC may specify the form and manner in which information required to be provided by or under any of the information provisions must be provided if the provision is to be complied with.

(2) The "information provisions" are paragraphs 11(1), 12(1), 17(2), 18(2), 19(2), 21(3), 23(2), 24(3), 26(1) and (3), 27(3), 28(2), 29(1), 31(2) and 33(2).

35 No duty of confidentiality or other restriction on disclosure (however imposed) prevents the voluntary disclosure by any person to HMRC of information or documents which the person has reasonable grounds for suspecting will assist HMRC in determining whether there has been a breach of any requirement imposed by or under this Part of this Schedule.

36 (1) HMRC may publish information about—

(a) any notifiable arrangements, or proposed notifiable arrangements, to which a reference number is allocated under paragraph 22;

(b) any person who is a promoter in relation to the notifiable arrangements or, in the case of proposed notifiable arrangements, the notifiable proposal.

(2) The information that may be published is (subject to sub-paragraph (4))—

(a) any information relating to arrangements within sub-paragraph (1)(a), or a person within sub-paragraph (1)(b), that is prescribed information for the purposes of paragraph 11, 12, 17 or 18;

(b) any ruling of a court or tribunal relating to any such arrangements or person (in that person's capacity as a promoter in relation to a notifiable proposal or arrangements);

(c) the number of persons in any period who enter into transactions forming part of notifiable arrangements within sub-paragraph (1)(a);

(d) any other information that HMRC considers it appropriate to publish for the purpose of identifying arrangements within sub-paragraph (1)(a) or a person within sub-paragraph (1)(b).

(3) The information may be published in any manner that HMRC considers appropriate.

(4) No information may be published under this paragraph that identifies a person who enters into a transaction forming part of notifiable arrangements within sub-paragraph (1)(a).

(5) But where a person who is a promoter within sub-paragraph (1)(b) is also a person mentioned in sub-paragraph (4), nothing in sub-paragraph (4) is to be taken as preventing the publication under this paragraph of information so far as relating to the person's activities as a promoter.

(6) Before publishing any information under this paragraph that identifies a person as a promoter within sub-paragraph (1)(b), HMRC must—

(a) inform the person that they are considering doing so, and

(b) give the person reasonable opportunity to make representations about whether it should be published.

37 (1) This paragraph applies if—

(a) information about notifiable arrangements, or proposed notifiable arrangements, is published under paragraph 36,

(b) at any time after the information is published, a ruling of a court or tribunal is made in relation to tax arrangements, and

(c) HMRC is of the opinion that the ruling is relevant to the arrangements mentioned in paragraph (a)

(2) A ruling is "relevant" to the arrangements if—

(a) the principles laid down, or reasoning given, in the ruling would, if applied to the arrangements, allow the purported advantage arising from the arrangements in relation to tax, and

(b) the ruling is final.

(3) HMRC must publish information about the ruling.

(4) The information must be published in the same manner as HMRC published the information mentioned in sub-paragraph (1)(a) (and may also be published in any other manner that HMRC considers appropriate).

(5) A ruling is "final" if it is—

(a) a ruling of the Supreme Court, or

(b) a ruling of any other court or tribunal in circumstances where—

(i) no appeal may be made against the ruling,

(ii) if an appeal may be made against the ruling with permission, the time limit for applications has expired and either no application has been made or permission has been refused,

(iii) if such permission to appeal against the ruling has been granted or is not required, no appeal has been made within the time limit for appeals, or

(iv) if an appeal was made, it was abandoned or otherwise disposed of before it was determined by the court or tribunal to which it was addressed.

(6) Where a ruling is final by virtue of sub-paragraph (ii), (iii) or (iv) of sub-paragraph (5)(b), the ruling is to be treated as made at the time when the sub-paragraph in question is first satisfied.

(7) In this paragraph "tax arrangements" means arrangements in respect of which it would be reasonable to conclude (having regard to all the circumstances) that the main purpose, or one of the main purposes, was the obtaining of a tax advantage.

Power to vary certain relevant periods

38 The Commissioners may by regulations amend this Part of this Schedule with a view to altering the definition of "the relevant period" for the purposes of—

paragraph 5(6)
paragraph 11(1)
paragraph 12(1)
paragraph 16(5)
paragraph 17(2)

paragraph 24(3)
paragraph 25(2)
paragraph 27(3)
paragraph 28(3)
paragraph 29(4)
paragraph 30(2))
paragraph 31(4).

PART 2

PENALTIES

Penalty for failure to comply with duties under Part 1 (apart from paragraph 26)

39 (1) A person who fails to comply with any of the provisions of Part 1 of this Schedule mentioned in sub-paragraph (2) is liable—

(a) to a penalty not exceeding—

(i) in the case of a failure to comply with paragraph 11(1), 12(1), 17(2), 18(2) or 19, £600 for each day during the initial period for which the failure continues (but see also paragraphs 40(4) and 41), and

(ii) in any other case, £5,000, and

(b) if the failure continues after a penalty is imposed under paragraph (a), to a further penalty or penalties not exceeding £600 for each day on which the failure continues after the day on which the penalty under paragraph (a) was imposed (but excluding any day for which a penalty under this paragraph has already been imposed).

(2) Those provisions are—

(a) paragraph 11(1) (duty of promoter in relation to notifiable proposal),

(b) paragraph 12(1) (duty of promoter in relation to notifiable arrangements),

(c) paragraph 17(2) (duty of person dealing with promoter outside United Kingdom),

(d) paragraph 18(2) (duty of parties to notifiable arrangements not involving promoter),

(e) paragraph 19 (duty to provide further information requested by HMRC),

(f) paragraph 21 (duty of promoters to provide updated information),

(g) paragraph 23(2) (duty of promoter to notify client of reference number),

(h) paragraph 24(3) (duty of client to notify parties of reference number),

(i) paragraph 25(2) (duty of client to provide information to promoter),

(j) paragraph 27(3) (duty of promoter to provide details of clients),

(k) paragraph 28(3) (enquiry following disclosure of client details),

(l) paragraphs 29(4) and 30(2) (duty of promoter to respond to inquiry)

(m) paragraph 31(4) (duty of introducer to give details of persons who have provided information or have been provided with information, and

(n) paragraph 33 (duty to provide additional information).

(3) In this paragraph "the initial period" means the period—

(a) beginning with the relevant day, and

(b) ending with the earlier of the day on which the penalty under sub-paragraph (1)(a)(i) is determined and the last day before the failure ceases.

(4) For the purposes of sub-paragraph (3)(a) "the relevant day" is the day specified in relation to the failure in the following table—

Failure	Relevant day
A failure to comply with paragraph 11(1) or 12(1) in so far as it applies by virtue of an order under paragraph 5	The first day after the end of the relevant period described in paragraph 5(6)
A failure to comply with paragraph 11(1) or 12(1) in so far as it applies by virtue of an order under paragraph 16(2)	The first day after the end of the relevant period (whether that is the period described in sub-paragraph 16(5)(a) or that period as extended by a direction under paragraph 16(5)(b))
Any other failure to comply with sub-paragraph (1) of paragraph 11	The first day after the end of the relevant period described in paragraph 11(2)
Any other failure to comply with sub-paragraph (1) of paragraph 12	The first day after the end of the relevant period described in paragraph 12(2)
A failure to comply with paragraph 17(2)	The first day after the end of the relevant period described in paragraph 17(3)

| A failure to comply with paragraph 18(2) | The first day after the latest time by which paragraph 18(2) should have been complied with in the case concerned |
| A failure to comply with paragraph 19 | The first day after the end of the period within which the person must comply with paragraph 19 |

40 (1) In the case of a failure to comply with paragraph 11(1), 12(1), 17(2), 18(2) or 19, the amount of the penalty under paragraph 39(1)(a)(i) is to be arrived at after taking account of all relevant considerations.

(2) Those considerations include the desirability of the penalty being set at a level which appears appropriate for deterring the person, or other persons, from similar failures to comply on future occasions having regard (in particular)—

(a) in the case of a penalty for a promoter's failure to comply with paragraph 11(1), 12(1) or 19, to the amount of any fees received, or likely to have been received, by the promoter in connection with the notifiable proposal (or arrangements implementing the notifiable proposal), or with the notifiable arrangements, and

(b) in the case of a penalty for a relevant person's failure to comply with paragraph 17(2), 18(2) or 19, to the amount of any advantage gained, or sought to be gained, by the person in relation to any tax prescribed under paragraph 3(1)(b) in relation to the notifiable arrangements

(3) In sub-paragraph (2)(b) "relevant person" means a person who enters into any transaction forming part of notifiable arrangements.

(4) If the maximum penalty under paragraph 39(1)(a)(i) appears inappropriately low after taking account of all relevant considerations, the penalty is to be of such amount not exceeding £1 million as appears appropriate having regard to those considerations.

41 (1) This paragraph applies where a failure to comply with a provision mentioned in paragraph 39(2) concerns a proposal or arrangements in respect of which an order has been made under paragraph 4 or 5.

(2) The amounts specified in paragraph 39(1)(a)(i) and (b) are increased to £5,000 in relation to days falling after the end of the period of 11 days beginning with the day on which the order is made.

42 (1) The Treasury may by regulations vary—

(a) any of the sums for the time being specified in paragraph 39(1);
(b) the sum for the time being specified in paragraph 40(4);
(c) the period for the time being specified in paragraph 41(2);
(d) the sum for the time being specified in paragraph 41(2).

(2) Regulations under this paragraph may include incidental or transitional provision.

43 Where it appears to an officer of Revenue and Customs that—

(a) a penalty under paragraph 39(1)(a) has been imposed in a case where the maximum penalty is set by paragraph 39(1)(a)(i), and

(b) the maximum penalty was calculated on the basis that the initial period began with a day later than that which the officer considers to be the relevant day,

an officer of Revenue and Customs may commence proceedings for a re-determination of the penalty.

Penalty for failure to comply with duties under paragraph 26

44 (1) A person who fails to comply with—

(a) paragraph 26(1), or
(b) regulations under paragraph 26(3),

is liable to a penalty not exceeding the relevant sum.

(2) The relevant sum is £5,000 in respect of each scheme to which the failure relates unless the person falls within sub-paragraph (3) or (4).

(3) If the person has previously failed to comply with paragraph 26(1) or regulations under paragraph 26(3) on one (and only one) occasion during the period of 36 months ending with the date on which the current failure began, the relevant sum is £7,500 in respect of each scheme to which the current failure relates (whether or not the same as any scheme to which the previous failure relates).

(4) If the person has previously failed to comply with paragraph 26(1) or regulations under paragraph 26(3) on two or more occasions during the period of 36 months ending with the date on which the current failure began, the relevant sum is £10,000 in respect of each scheme to which the current failure relates (whether or not the same as any scheme to which any of the previous failures relates).

(5) In this paragraph "scheme" means any notifiable arrangements.

Penalty proceedings before First-tier tribunal

45 (1) An authorised officer may commence proceedings before the First-tier Tribunal for any penalty under paragraph 39(1)(a).

(2) In sub-paragraph (1) "authorised officer" means an officer of Revenue and Customs authorised by HMRC for the purposes of this paragraph.

(3) Proceedings for a penalty may not be commenced more than 12 months after evidence of facts sufficient to justify the bringing of proceedings comes to the knowledge of HMRC.

(4) If the First-tier Tribunal decide that the penalty is payable by the person—

(a) the penalty is for all purposes to be treated as if it were tax charged in an assessment and due and payable,

(b) the person may appeal to the Upper Tribunal against the decision that the penalty is payable, and

(c) the person may appeal to the Upper Tribunal against the decision as to the amount of the penalty.

(5) On an appeal under sub-paragraph (4)(b) the Upper Tribunal may, if it appears that no penalty has been incurred, cancel the decision of the First-tier Tribunal.

(6) On an appeal under sub-paragraph (4)(c) the Upper Tribunal may—

(a) affirm the decision of the First-tier Tribunal as to the amount of the penalty, or

(b) substitute for that decision a decision that the First-tier Tribunal had power to make.

Assessment of penalties under paragraph 39(1)(b) or 44

46 (1) Where a person is liable to a penalty under paragraph 39(1)(b) or 44 an authorised officer may assess the amount due by way of a penalty.

(2) An assessment may not be made more than 12 months after evidence of facts sufficient to justify the making of the assessment first comes to the knowledge of HMRC.

(3) A notice of an assessment under sub-paragraph (1) stating—

(a) the date on which it is issued, and

(b) the time within which an appeal against the assessment may be made,

must be served on the person liable to the penalty.

(4) After the notice has been served the assessment may not be altered except in accordance with this paragraph or on appeal.

(5) If it is discovered by an authorised officer that the amount of a penalty assessed under this paragraph is or has become insufficient the officer may make an assessment in a further amount so that the penalty is set at the amount which, in the officer's opinion, is correct or appropriate.

(6) A penalty imposed by a decision under this paragraph—

(a) is due and payable at the end of the period of 30 days beginning with the date of the issue of the notice of the decision, and

(b) is to be treated for all purposes as if it were tax charged in an assessment and due and payable.

(7) In this paragraph "authorised officer" means an officer of Revenue and Customs authorised by HMRC for the purposes of this paragraph.

47 (1) Where a person (P) is served with notice of an assessment under paragraph 46—

(a) P may appeal against the decision that a penalty is payable by P, and

(b) P may appeal against the decision as to the amount of the penalty.

(2) An appeal under sub-paragraph (1) is to be treated for procedural purposes in the same way as an appeal against an assessment to the relevant tax (including by the application of any provision about the bringing of an appeal by notice to HMRC, about HMRC review of the decision or about determination of the appeal by the First-tier Tribunal or Upper Tribunal)

(3) Sub-paragraph (2) does not apply—

(a) so as to require P to pay a penalty before an appeal under sub-paragraph (1) is determined, or

(b) in respect of any other matter expressly provided for by this Schedule.

(4) On an appeal under sub-paragraph (1)(a) the tribunal may affirm or cancel the decision that a penalty is payable by P.

(5) On an appeal under sub-paragraph (1)(b) the tribunal may—

(a) affirm the decision as to the amount of the penalty, or

(b) substitute for that decision another decision that the authorised officer had power to make.

(6) In this paragraph "tribunal" means the First-tier Tribunal or Upper Tribunal (as appropriate by virtue of sub-paragraph (2)).

Reasonable excuse

48 (1) Liability to a penalty under this Part of this Schedule does not arise in relation to a particular failure to comply if the person concerned (P) satisfies HMRC or the relevant tribunal (as the case may be) that there is a reasonable excuse for the failure.

(2) For this purpose—

(a) an insufficiency of funds is not a reasonable excuse, unless attributable to events outside P's control,

(b) where P relied on any other person to do anything, that cannot be a reasonable excuse unless P took reasonable care to avoid the failure,

(c) where P had a reasonable excuse but the excuse has ceased, P is to be treated as continuing to have the excuse if the failure is remedied without unreasonable delay after the excuse ceased, and

(d) reliance on advice is to be taken automatically not to be a reasonable excuse if the advice was addressed to, or was given to, a person other than P or takes no account of P's individual circumstances.

49 (1) The making of an order under paragraph 4 or 5 against P does not of itself mean that P either did or did not have a reasonable excuse for non- compliance before the order was made.

(2) Where an order is made under paragraph 4 or 5 then for the purposes of paragraph 48—

(a) the person identified in the order as the promoter of the proposal or arrangements cannot, in respect of any time after the end of the prescribed period mentioned in paragraph 41, rely on doubt as to notifiability as a reasonable excuse for failure to comply with paragraph 11(1) or 12(1), and

(b) any delay in compliance with that provision after the end of that period is not capable of being a reasonable excuse unless attributable to something other than doubt as to notifiability.

50 (1) Where a person fails to comply with—

(a) paragraph 17(2) and the promoter for the purposes of paragraph 17 is a monitored promoter, or

(b) paragraph 18(2) and the arrangements for the purposes of paragraph 18 are arrangements of a monitored promoter,

then for the purposes of paragraph 48 legal advice which the person took into account is to be disregarded in determining whether the person had a reasonable excuse, if the advice was given or procured by that monitored promoter.

(2) In determining for the purpose of paragraph 48 whether or not a person who is a monitored promoter had a reasonable excuse for a failure to do something, reliance on legal advice is to be taken automatically not to constitute a reasonable excuse if either—

(a) the advice was not based on a full and accurate description of the facts, or

(b) the conclusions in the advice that the person relied on were unreasonable.

(3) In this paragraph "monitored promoter" means a person who is a monitored promoter for the purposes of Part 5 of FA 2014

PART 3

CONSEQUENTIAL AMENDMENTS

VATA 1994

51 In section 77(4A) of VATA 1994 (cases in which the time allowed for assessment is 20 years), in paragraph (d) after "11A" insert "or an obligation under paragraph 17(2) or 18(2) of Schedule 17 to FA 2017".

Promoters of tax avoidance schemes

52 Part 5 of FA 2014 (promoters of tax avoidance schemes) is amended as follows.

53 (1) Section 281A (VAT: meaning of "tax advantage") is amended as follows.

(2) In the heading after "VAT" insert "and other indirect taxes".

(3) In subsection (1)—

(a) in paragraph (a) after "VAT" insert "and other indirect taxes", and

(b) in paragraph (b) for the words from "in paragraph 1" to the end substitute "for VAT in paragraph 6, and for other indirect taxes in paragraph 7, of Schedule 17 to FA 2017 (disclosure of tax avoidance schemes: VAT and other indirect taxes)."

(4) In subsection (3) after "value added tax" (in both places) insert "or other indirect taxes".

(5) After subsection (3) insert—

"(4) In this section "indirect tax" has the same meaning as in Schedule 17 to FA 2017."

54 (1) Schedule 34A (defeated arrangements) is amended as follows.

(2) In paragraph 2(4) after ""schemes)" insert "or paragraph 22 of Schedule 17 to FA 2017 (disclosure of avoidance schemes: VAT and other indirect taxes).

(3) In paragraph 14—

(a) in sub-paragraph (1)(a) after "VAT" insert "or other indirect tax", and
(b) in sub-paragraphs (1)(a) and (b), (2) and (3) omit "taxable".

(4) After paragraph 26 insert—

"Disclosable VAT or other indirect tax arrangements"

26A (1) For the purposes of this Schedule arrangements are "disclosable VAT or other indirect tax arrangements" at any time if at that time—

(a) the arrangements are disclosable Schedule 11A arrangements, or
(b) sub-paragraph (2) applies.

(2) This sub-paragraph applies if a person—

(a) has provided information in relation to the arrangements under paragraph 12(1), 17(2) or 18(2) of Schedule 17 to FA 2017, or
(b) has failed to comply with any of those provisions in relation to the arrangements.

(3) But for the purposes of this Schedule arrangements in respect of which HMRC have given notice under paragraph 23(6) of that Schedule (notice that promoters not under duty to notify client of reference number) are not to be regarded as disclosable VAT or other indirect tax arrangements.

(4) For the purposes of sub-paragraph (2) a person who would be required to provide information under paragraph 12(1) of that Schedule—

(a) but for the fact that the arrangements implement a proposal in respect of which notice has been given under paragraph 11(1) of that Schedule, or
(b) but for paragraph 13, 14 or 15 of that Schedule,

is treated as providing the information at the end of the period referred to in paragraph 12(1)."

(5) In the heading before paragraph 27, after ""disclosable" insert "Schedule 11A".

(6) In paragraph 27—

(a) for "this Schedule" substitute "paragraph 26A", and
(b) after ""disclosable" insert "Schedule 11A".

(7) In the heading before paragraph 28 for "and 27" substitute "to 27".

(8) In paragraph 28(1) after "26(1)(a)" insert "26A(2)(a)

Serial tax avoidance

55 (1) Schedule 18 to FA 2016 (serial tax avoidance) is amended as follows.

(2) In paragraph 4 (meaning of "tax")—

(a) number the current text as sub-paragraph (1) of that paragraph,
(b) in that sub-paragraph (1), in paragraph (j) after "VAT" insert" "and indirect taxes", and
(c) after that sub-paragraph (1) insert—

"(2) For the purposes of this Schedule "indirect tax" means any of the following—

insurance premium tax
general betting duty
pool betting duty
remote gaming duty
machine games duty
gaming duty
lottery duty
bingo duty
air passenger duty

hydrocarbon oils duty
tobacco products duty
duties on spirits, beer, wine, made-wine and cider
soft drinks industry levy
aggregates levy
landfill tax
climate change levy
customs duties.

(3) Before paragraph 9 (meaning of "disclosable VAT arrangements") insert—

"**8A** (1) For the purposes of this Schedule arrangements are "disclosable VAT arrangements" at any time if at that time sub-paragraph (2) or (3) applies.

(2) This sub-paragraph applies if the arrangements are disclosable Schedule 11A VAT arrangements (see paragraph 9).

(3) This paragraph applies if—

(a) the arrangements are notifiable arrangements for the purposes of Schedule 17 to FA 2017,
(b) the main benefit, or one of the main benefits that might be expected to arise from the arrangements is the obtaining of a tax advantage in relation to VAT (within the meaning of paragraph 6 of that Schedule), and
(c) a person—

(i) has provided information about the arrangements under paragraph 12(1), 17(2) or 18(2) of that Schedule, or
(ii) has failed to comply with any of those provisions in relation to the arrangements.

(4) But for the purposes of this Schedule arrangements in respect of which HMRC have given notice under paragraph 23(6) of Schedule 17 (notice that promoters not under duty to notify client of reference number) are not to be regarded as "disclosable VAT arrangements".

(5) For the purposes of sub-paragraph (3)(c) a person who would be required to provide information under paragraph 12(1) of Schedule 17 to FA 2017—

(a) but for the fact that the arrangements implement a proposal in respect of which notice has been given under paragraph 11(1) of that Schedule, or
(b) but for paragraph 13, 14 or 15 of that Schedule,

is treated as providing the information at the end of the period referred to in paragraph 12(1)."

(4) In the heading before paragraph 9 after ""Disclosable" insert "Schedule 11A".

(5) In paragraph 9—

(a) for "this Schedule" substitute "paragraph 8A", and
(b) after ""disclosable" insert "Schedule 11A".

(6) After paragraph 9 insert—

"Disclosable indirect tax arrangements"

"**9A** (1) For the purposes of this Schedule arrangements are "disclosable indirect tax arrangements" at any time if at that time—

(a) the arrangements are notifiable arrangements for the purposes of Schedule 17 to FA 2017,
(b) the main benefit, or one of the main benefits that might be expected to arise from the arrangements is the obtaining of a tax advantage in relation to an indirect tax other than VAT (within the meaning of paragraph 7 of that Schedule), and
(c) a person—

(i) has provided information about the arrangements under paragraph 12(1), 17(2) or 18(2) of that Schedule, or
(ii) has failed to comply with any of those provisions in relation to the arrangements.

(2) But for the purposes of this Schedule arrangements in respect of which HMRC have given notice under paragraph 23(6) of Schedule 17 to FA 2016 (notice that promoters not under duty to notify client of reference number) are not to be regarded as "disclosable indirect tax arrangements".

(3) For the purposes of sub-paragraph (1)(c) a person who would be required to provide information under paragraph 12(1) of Schedule 17—

(a) but for the fact that the arrangements implement a proposal in respect of which notice has been given under paragraph 11(1) of that Schedule, or

(b) but for paragraph 13, 14 or 15 of that Schedule,

is treated as providing the information at the end of the period referred to in paragraph 12(1)."

(7) In the heading before paragraph 10 (meaning of "failure to comply") for "and 9" substitute "to 9A".

(8) In paragraph 10(1) for "or 9(a)" substitute ", 8A(2)(c), 9(a) or 9A(1)(c)".

(9) In paragraph 11(1) (meaning of "relevant defeat") for "E" substitute "F".

(10) After paragraph 16 (condition E) insert—

"Condition F

16A (1) Condition F is that—

(a) the arrangements are indirect tax arrangements,

(b) P has relied on the arrangements (see sub-paragraph (2),

(c) the arrangements have been counteracted, and

(d) the counteraction is final.

(2) For the purpose of sub-paragraph (1) P relies on the arrangements if—

(a) P makes a return, claim, declaration or application for approval on the basis that a relevant tax advantage arises, or

(b) P fails to discharge a relevant obligation ("the disputed obligation") and there is reason to believe that P's failure to discharge that obligation is connected with the arrangements.

(3) For the purposes of sub-paragraph (2) "relevant tax advantage" means a tax advantage which the arrangements might be expected to enable P to obtain.

(4) For the purposes of sub-paragraph (2) an obligation is a relevant obligation if the arrangements might be expected to have the result that the obligation does not arise.

(5) For the purposes of this paragraph the arrangements are "counteracted" if—

(a) adjustments, other than taxpayer emendations, are made in respect of P's tax position —

(i) on the basis that the whole or part of the relevant tax advantage mentioned in sub-paragraph (2)(a) does not arise, or

(ii) on the basis that the disputed obligation does (or did) arise, or

(b) an assessment to tax is made, or any other action is taken by HMRC, on the basis mentioned in paragraph (a)(i) or (ii) (otherwise than by way of an adjustment).

(6) For the purposes of this paragraph a "counteraction" is final when the adjustments, assessment or action in question, and any amounts arising from the adjustments, assessment or action, can no longer be varied, on appeal or otherwise.

(7) For the purposes of sub-paragraph (1) the time at which it falls to be determined whether or not the arrangements are disclosable indirect tax arrangements is when the counteraction becomes final.

(8) The following are "taxpayer emendations" for the purposes of sub-paragraph (5)—

(a) an adjustment made by P at a time when P had no reason to believe that HMRC had begun or were about to begin enquiries into P's affairs in relation to the tax in question;

(b) an adjustment made by HMRC with respect to P's tax position (whether by way of an assessment or otherwise) as a result of a disclosure by P which meets the conditions in sub-paragraph (9).

(9) The conditions are that the disclosure—

(a) is a full and explicit disclosure of an inaccuracy in a return or other document or of a failure to comply with an obligation, and

(b) was made at a time when P had no reason to believe that HMRC were about to begin enquiries into P's affairs in relation to the tax in question."

(11) In paragraph 17 (annual information notices)—

(a) in sub-paragraph (3)(a) for "or election," insert "election, declaration or application for approval,",

(b) in sub-paragraphs (3)(b), (4) and (5)(a) for "DOTAS arrangements or VAT" substitute "disclosable",

(c) in sub-paragraph (5) for "or election" insert "election, declaration or application for approval", and

(d) after sub-paragraph (11) insert—

"(12) In this paragraph "disclosable arrangements" means any of the following—

    (a) DOTAS arrangements,
    (b) disclosable VAT arrangements, and
    (c) disclosable indirect tax arrangements.

(12) In the heading before paragraph 28 (exclusion of VAT from Part 4 of Schedule) after "VAT" insert "and indirect taxes".

(13) In paragraph 28 after "VAT" insert "or any other indirect tax".

(14) In paragraph 32 (value of counteracted advantage: basic rule for taxes other than VAT)—

    (a) in sub-paragraph (1) for "or C" substitute "C or F" and after paragraph (c) insert ";

        (d) in the case of a relevant defeat incurred by virtue of Condition F, the additional amount due or payable in respect of tax as a result of the counteraction mentioned in paragraph 16A(1)(d).", and
    (b) in sub-paragraph (2)(b) for "or (c)" substitute "(c) or (d)".

(15) In paragraph 35 (meaning of "the counteracted advantage" in paragraphs 33 and 34) in sub-paragraph (1) after paragraph (c) insert ";

    "(d) in relation to a relevant defeat incurred by virtue of Condition F, means any tax advantage in respect of which the counteraction mentioned in paragraph 16A(1)(c) is made."

(16) In paragraph 43 (paragraph 42: meaning of "the relevant failure") after sub-paragraph (7) insert—

    "(8) In relation to a relevant defeat incurred by virtue of Condition F, "the relevant failure" means the failures or inaccuracies as a result of which the adjustments, assessments, or other actions mentioned in paragraph 16A(5) are required."

(17) In paragraph 55 (time of "use" of defeated arrangements) after sub-paragraph (8) insert—

    "(8A) If the person incurs the relevant defeat by virtue of Condition F, the person is treated as having "used" the arrangements on the following dates—

        (a) the filing date of any return made by the person on the basis mentioned in paragraph 16A(2)(a);
        (b) the date on which the person makes any claim, declaration or application for approval;
        (c) the date of any failure by the person to comply with a relevant obligation (as defined in paragraph 16A(4))."

(18) In paragraph 58(1) (interpretation)—
    (a) after the definition of "contract settlement" insert—
    ""disclosable indirect tax arrangements" is to be interpreted in accordance with paragraph 9A;
    "disclosable Schedule 11A VAT arrangements is to be interpreted in accordance with paragraph 9;",
    (b) after the definition of "HMRC" insert—
    ""indirect tax" has the meaning given by paragraph 4(2);",
    (c) in the definition of "disclosable VAT arrangements" for "9" substitute "8A", and
    (d) in the definition of "tax" for "4" substitute "4(1)".

PART 4

SUPPLEMENTAL

Regulations

56 (1) Any power of the Treasury or the Commissioners to make regulations under this Schedule is exercisable by statutory instrument.

(2) Regulations made under any such power may make different provision for different cases and may contain transitional provisions and savings.

(3) A statutory instrument containing regulations made by the Treasury under paragraph 2(2) or 42(1) may not be made unless a draft of the instrument has been laid before and approved by a resolution of the House of Commons.

(4) Any other statutory instrument containing regulations made under this Schedule, if made without a draft having been approved by a resolution of the House of Commons, is subject to annulment in pursuance of a resolution of the House of Commons.

Interpretation

57 In this Schedule—

"arrangements" includes any scheme, transaction or series of transactions;

"the Commissioners" means the Commissioners for Her Majesty's Revenue and Customs;

"company" has the meaning given by section 1121 of the Corporation Tax Act 2010;

"HMRC" means Her Majesty's Revenue and Customs;

"indirect tax" has the meaning given by paragraph 2(1);

"introducer" is to be construed in accordance with paragraph 9;

"makes a firm approach" has the meaning given by paragraph 10(1);

"makes a marketing contact" has the meaning given by paragraph 10(2);

"marketing contact" has the meaning give by paragraph 10(2);

"notifiable arrangements" has the meaning given by paragraph 3(1);

"notifiable proposal" has the meaning given by paragraph 3(3);

"prescribed" (except in or in references to paragraph 3(1)(a)), means prescribed by regulations made by HMRC;

"promoter" is to be construed in accordance with paragraph 8;

"reference number", in relation to notifiable arrangements, has the meaning given by paragraph 22(4);

"TCEA 2007" means the Tribunals, Courts and Enforcement Act 2007;

"tax advantage" means a tax advantage within the meaning of—

    (a) paragraph 6 (in relation to VAT), or

    (b) paragraph 7 (in relation to indirect taxes other than VAT);

"trade" includes every venture in the nature of a trade;

"tribunal" means the First-tier tribunal, or where determined by or under Tribunal Procedure Rules, the Upper Tribunal;

"working day" means a day which is not a Saturday or a Sunday, Christmas Day, Good Friday or a bank holiday under the Banking and Financial Dealings Act 1971 in any part of the United Kingdom.

BACKGROUND NOTE

Schedule 17 replaces the previous legislation in VATA 1994 s 58A and Sch 11A, with effect in relation to any scheme entered into by a person on or after 1 January 2018.

The new legislation also extends the disclosure regime to all indirect taxes including the Soft Drinks Industry Levy.

The new legislation has shifted the responsibility for disclosing an avoidance scheme from the scheme user to the scheme promoter.

GENERAL NOTE

Overview of disclosure regime

The disclosure of indirect tax avoidance schemes (DOITAS) requires certain persons, usually promoters of schemes, but also users in certain circumstances, to provide HMRC with information about "notifiable arrangements" and "notifiable proposals" (broadly, tax planning arrangements).

An overview of the scheme is as follows—

- The fundamental requirement of DOITAS is the obligation to make a disclosure to HMRC of information relating to "notifiable arrangements" and "notifiable proposals".
- Schemes developed offshore, if not disclosed by the promoter, must be disclosed by the user.
- A scheme reference number ("SRN") system enables HMRC to identify the users of schemes. When a scheme is disclosed, HMRC allocate a SRN and notify it to the promoter. The promoter must pass the SRN to their clients who in turn must use it to identify themselves to HMRC.
- There are information powers enabling HMRC to investigate cases of suspected non-compliance and penalties for failing to disclose a scheme and for failing to pass on or report a SRN.

Regulations

At the time of writing, the following regulations had been published in draft—

- the Indirect Taxes (Notifiable Arrangements) Regulations 2017 – which will prescribe the hallmark tests for notifiable arrangements under the new DOITAS regime; and
- the Indirect Taxes (Disclosure of Avoidance Schemes) Regulations 2017 – which will prescribe information to be disclosed, and define those persons not to be treated as promoters, under the new rules.

Definitions

Paragraphs 1 to 10 of Sch 17 set out the key terms for the operation of the new regime, including—

- the arrangements and proposals which must be disclosed to HMRC (para 3);
- the circumstances in which a person obtains a "tax advantage" in relation to VAT and other indirect taxes (paras 6, 7);
- "promoters" (para 8); and
- "introducers" (para 9).

Duty of promoter in relation to a notifiable proposal or notifiable arrangements

Promoters (paras 11, 12)

The promoter of a notifiable proposal must, within a period of 31 days ("the relevant period") of the "relevant date", provide HMRC with prescribed information relating to the proposal.

The promoter of notifiable arrangements must, within 31 days after the date on which he first becomes aware of any transaction forming part of the arrangements, provide HMRC with prescribed information relating to the arrangements. However, this does not apply if the notifiable arrangements implement a proposal in respect of which notice has already been given to HMRC.

Multiple promoters (paras 13, 14)

Where a promoter ("P") has provided HMRC with the prescribed information as required above, another promoter of a notifiable proposal or notifiable arrangements which is/are substantially the same is not required to provided HMRC with the same information again, provided that:

(a) P gives HMRC the name and address of any such promoter, or
(b) any such a promoter holds the Reference Number (see below),

and (in either case) such a promoter holds the information provided to HMRC.

Multiple proposals/arrangements (para 15)

Where a promoter has already notified HMRC about a proposal or arrangements, he need not make a further notification in respect of a proposal or arrangements which are substantially the same as those already notified.

Supplemental information (para 16)

Where HMRC believe that a promoter ("P") has not provided all the prescribed information, they may apply to the tribunal for an order requiring P to provide specified information about, or documents relating to, the notifiable proposal or arrangements. The tribunal may only make such an order if it is satisfied that HMRC have reasonable grounds for suspecting that the information or documents form part of, or will support or explain, the prescribed information.

Duty of person dealing with non-UK promoter (para 17)

Where the only promoter or promoters of any notifiable arrangements are resident outside the UK, the responsibility for providing HMRC with the prescribed information falls upon any person who enters into any transaction forming part of those arrangements. The information must be provided within six days of the day on which the person enters into the first such transaction.

Duty of parties to notifiable arrangements not involving a promoter (para 18)

Where there is no promoter of notifiable arrangements in the UK, the liability for providing HMRC with the prescribed information falls upon any person who enters into any transaction forming part of those arrangements. The information must be provided at the prescribed time.

Duty to provide further information (paras 19, 20)

Where HMRC believe that a person has not provided all the prescribed information, they may require that person to provide, within ten working days of the requirement or such longer period as HMRC may direct, further specified information or documents. Where, despite such a requirement, HMRC believe that the person ("P") has failed to comply, they may apply to the tribunal for an order requiring P to provide specified information about, or documents relating to, the notifiable proposal or arrangements. The tribunal may only make such an order if it is satisfied that HMRC have reasonable grounds for suspecting that the information or documents form part of, or will support or explain, the prescribed information. Where such an order is made, it must be complied with within 10 working days of the requirement or such longer period as HMRC may direct.

Duty of promoter to provide updated information (para 21)

Where prescribed information in relation to notifiable arrangements or proposed notifiable arrangements has been provided to HMRC and a Reference Number has been allocated, any change in the name by which those arrangements are known, or any change of name or address of any promoter must be notified to HMRC by the promoter within 30 days of the change. If, where there is more than one promoter, the change relates to the name or address of a promoter, it is the duty of that promoter to notify HMRC.

Reference numbers

Notification of promoter by HMRC (para 22)

Where a person ("P") has provided HMRC with prescribed information as described above, HMRC may within 90 days allocate a reference number to the notifiable (or proposed notifiable) arrangements. They must then notify P, and any other promoter whose identity and address has been notified to them by P, of that number.

The allocation of a reference number does not indicate that HMRC consider that a tax advantage exists as a result of the arrangements.

Duty of promoter to notify client; duty of client to notify promoter; duty of promoter to provide client details to HMRC (paras 23, 25, 27–28)

Where a promoter has been notified of a reference number, he must notify any person to whom he is providing services ("the client") in connection with the arrangements (or any arrangements which are substantially the same) to which the number relates of the prescribed information (and such additional information as HMRC may specify) relating to that number. It would appear, although it is not currently specified, that the information provided includes the reference number itself. Such notification must be made within 30 days of the later of—

(a) the date on which the promoter becomes aware of any transaction which forms part of the notifiable arrangements, and
(b) the date on which the reference number is notified to the promoter.

Notification is not necessary if it has already been made in relation to services provided by the same promoter to the same client in respect of arrangements which are substantially the same.

Within 11 days of the later of—

(a) the date the client receives the reference number for the arrangements, and
(b) the date the client first enters into a transaction which forms part of the arrangements,

the client must provide prescribed information to the promoter.

In such circumstances, the promoter is also required to provide HMRC with prescribed information relating to clients within a prescribed period. This requirement also applies if he was required to notify prescribed information to the client but failed to do so. Following such notification, if HMRC consider that a person other than the client is likely to be party to the arrangements, they may, by written notice, require the promoter to provide prescribed information relating to that person within 11 days of the notice or such longer period as they may direct.

Duty of client to notify interested parties (para 24)

Where the client receives prescribed information from the promoter as described above, he must, unless HMRC otherwise allow, provide that information (and such additional information as HMRC may specify) to any other person who he (the client) might reasonably be expected to know is, or is likely to be, a party to the arrangements and who might reasonably be expected to gain a tax advantage in relation to any relevant tax by reason of the arrangements. The information must be provided within 30 days beginning with the later of—

(a) the day on which the client first becomes aware of any transaction forming part of the arrangements, and
(b) the day on which the prescribed information is notified to the client by the promoter.

Notification of HMRC by party to notifiable arrangements (para 26)

Any party ("P") to notified arrangements must inform HMRC of the fact by advising them of the reference number and the time at which P obtains or expects to obtain by virtue of the arrangements a tax advantage in relation to any relevant tax. The time of notification and the extent of the information provided is to be specified by regulations.

Duty of introducers to provide information (para 31)

Where HMRC suspect that a person ("P") is an introducer in relation to a proposal, and that the proposal may be notifiable, they may by written notice require P to provide HMRC with one or both of the following—

(a) prescribed information in relation to each person who has provided P with any information relating to the proposal,
(b) prescribed information in relation to each person with whom P has made a marketing contact in relation to the proposal.

The notice must specify the proposal to which it relates. P must comply with such a requirement within eleven days of the notice or such longer period as HMRC may direct.

Publication of information by HMRC

Publication in respect of promoters or arrangements (para 36)

HMRC may publish the following information in relation to notifiable arrangements or proposed notifiable arrangements in respect of which a reference number has been allocated, or in relation to a person who is a promoter in relation to those arrangements—

(a) any information relating to such arrangements or such a promoter that is prescribed information;
(b) any ruling of a court or tribunal relating to any such arrangements or promoter (in his capacity as a promoter in relation to a notifiable proposal or arrangements);
(c) the number of persons in any period who enter into transactions forming part of such notifiable arrangements;
(d) any other information that HMRC consider it appropriate to publish for the purpose of identifying such arrangements or promoter.

The information may be published in any form which HMRC consider appropriate. It may not include details of a person who enters into a transaction forming part of the arrangements unless that person is also a promoter in relation to those arrangements, in which cause information may be published so far as relating to his activities as promoter.

Before publication of information relating to a promoter, HMRC must inform the promoter and give him reasonable opportunity to make representations regarding the decision to publish.

Publication in respect of rulings (para 37)

Where—

(a) information concerning notifiable arrangements or proposed notifiable arrangements is published in accordance with the above provisions;
(b) a ruling of a court or tribunal is made in relation to tax arrangements;
(c) HMRC consider that the principles laid down, or reasoning given, in the ruling would, if applied to the arrangements, allow the purported advantage arising from the arrangements in relation to tax.

HMRC must publish information about the ruling. This only applies, however, where the ruling is final, i.e.:

(a) it is a ruling of the Supreme Court, or

(b) it is a ruling of any other court or tribunal in circumstances where:

    (i) no appeal may be made against the ruling;

    (ii) if an appeal may be made against the ruling with permission, the time limit for applications has expired and either no application has been made or permission has been refused;

    (iii) if such permission to appeal against the ruling has been granted or is not required, no appeal has been made within the time limit for appeals; or

    (iv) if an appeal was made, it was abandoned or otherwise disposed of before it was determined by the court or tribunal to which it was addressed.

Penalties

Penalty for non-compliance with certain duties ("initial penalty") (paras 39, 40)

A person who fails to comply with the following paragraphs of Sch 17 is liable to a penalty:

(a) paragraph 11(1) (duty of promoter in relation to notifiable proposal),

(b) paragraph 12(1) (duty of promoter in relation to notifiable arrangements),

(c) paragraph 17(2) (duty of person dealing with promoter outside United Kingdom),

(d) paragraph 18(2) (duty of parties to notifiable arrangements not involving promoter),

(e) paragraph 19 (duty to provide further information requested by HMRC),

(f) paragraph 21 (duty of promoters to provide updated information),

(g) paragraph 23(2) (duty of promoter to notify client of reference number),

(h) paragraph 24(3) (duty of client to notify parties of reference number),

(i) paragraph 25(2) (duty of client to provide information to promoter),

(j) paragraph 27(3) (duty of promoter to provide details of clients),

(k) paragraph 28(3) (enquiry following disclosure of client details),

(l) paragraphs 29(4) and 30(2) (duty of promoter to respond to inquiry),

(m) paragraph 31(4) (duty of introducer to give details of persons who have provided information or have been provided with information), and

(n) paragraph 33 (duty to provide additional information).

Amount of penalty relating to a failure under (a)–(e) above

The maximum penalty in respect of a failure to comply with these provisions is £600 for each day during the "initial period" for which the failure continues. The "initial period" is the period beginning with the "relevant day" and ending with the earlier of the day on which the penalty is determined and the last day before the failure ceases. The "relevant day" is the day after the end of the period during which compliance with any of the above provisions was required. However, the maximum figure of £600, if it appears inappropriately low, may be replaced by a figure not exceeding £1 million.

In determining the appropriateness of any penalty figure, the need for the penalty to act as a deterrent against future failures is taken into account, having regard to—

 (i) in the case of a failure relating to heads (a), (b) or (e), the amount of any fees relating to the underlying arrangements;

 (ii) in the case of a failure relating to heads (c), (d) or (e), the amount of any tax advantage gained or sought to be gained.

Amount of penalty relating a failure under (f)–(n) above

The maximum penalty in respect of a failure to comply with these provisions is £5,000.

Continuing failure after imposition of penalty ("further penalty")

If the failure continues after the initial penalty is imposed, the person is liable to a further penalty or penalties not exceeding £600 for each day on which the failure continues after the day on which the initial penalty. Any day for which a penalty has already been imposed is excluded.

Increase of daily penalties where an order has been made (para 41)

Where the failure concerns a proposal or arrangements in respect of which an order has been made (under Sch 17 paras 4 or 5) by the tribunal following an application by HMRC that a proposal or arrangements are, or are to be treated as, notifiable, the daily penalty rates are increased to £5,000 in relation to days falling after the end of the period of 11 days beginning with the day on which the order is made. In such a case the promoter cannot rely on doubt as to notifiability as a reasonable excuse after the end of that period.

Penalty for failing to notify HMRC of information regarding a reference number (para 44)

A person ("P") who is a party to any notifiable arrangements and consequently is required to notify HMRC of prescribed information relating to a reference number, or the time when P expects to obtain a tax advantage by reference to those arrange-ments, is liable to a penalty not exceeding £5,000 ("the prescribed sum") if—
(a) he fails to notify HMRC, or
(b) fails to notify HMRC in the time, manner and form prescribed by regulations.
For a second failure within a 36-month period (ending on the date on which the current failure began), the prescribed sum is £7,500. For the third or further failure within that period, the prescribed sum is £10,000.

Proceedings for initial penalty (para 45)

An HMRC officer authorised by HMRC may commence proceedings before the First-tier Tribunal for an initial penalty. Commencement must be made within 12 months after evidence of facts sufficient to justify the bringing of proceedings comes to the knowledge of HMRC. If the Tribunal decides that a penalty is payable, the penalty is for all purposes to be treated as if it were tax charged in an assessment and due and payable.

Assessment (paras 46, 47)

HMRC may assess the amount due in respect of a further penalty or a penalty for failing to notify HMRC of information regarding a reference number, etc. The assessment must be made within 12 months after evidence of facts sufficient to justify the making of the assessment comes to the knowledge of HMRC. It must be served upon the person liable to the penalty, and state the date of issue and the time within which an appeal must be made. A further assessment may be made if the initially assessed amount.

The assessment must be paid within 30 days of the date of the assessment notice.

Exception for reasonable excuse (paras 48, 49)

A failure to comply with a requirement described above does not give rise to a penalty if the person concerned ("P") satisfies HMRC (or the Tribunal, as appropriate) that there is a reasonable excuse for the failure. This is subject to the following provisos:
(a) an insufficiency of funds is not a reasonable excuse, unless attributable to events outside P's control;
(b) where P relied on any other person to do anything, that cannot be a reasonable excuse unless P took reasonable care to avoid the failure;
(c) where P had a reasonable excuse but the excuse has ceased, P is to be treated as continuing to have the excuse if the failure is remedied without unreasonable delay after the excuse ceased;
(d) reliance on advice is to be taken automatically not to be a reasonable excuse if the advice was addressed to, or was given to, a person other than P or takes no account of P's individual circumstances;
(e) where an order has been made by the tribunal following an application by HMRC that a proposal/arrangements are, or are to be regarded as notifiable, that does not mean that P did or did not have a reasonable excuse for non-compliance before the order was made;
(f) where the failure to notify arises in circumstances where there is no UK promoter, any legal advice relied upon by P is to be disregarded for reasonable excuse purposes if the advice was given or obtained by a monitored promoter, and in determining whether or not a person who is a monitored promoter had a reasonable excuse for a failure to do something, reliance on legal advice is to be taken automatically not to constitute a reasonable excuse if either—
   (i) the advice was not based on a full and accurate description of the facts, or
   (ii) the conclusions in the advice that the person relied on were unreasonable.

SCHEDULE 18

REQUIREMENT TO CORRECT CERTAIN OFFSHORE TAX NON-COMPLIANCE

Section 67

PART 1

LIABILITY FOR PENALTY FOR FAILURE TO CORRECT

Failure to correct relevant offshore tax non-compliance

1 A penalty is payable by a person who—

(a) has any relevant offshore tax non-compliance to correct at the end of the tax year 2016–17, and

(b) fails to correct the relevant offshore tax non-compliance within the period beginning with 6 April 2017 and ending with 30 September 2018 (referred to in this Schedule as "the RTC period").

Main definitions: general

2 Paragraphs 3 to 13 have effect for the purposes of this Schedule.

"Relevant offshore tax non-compliance"

3 (1) At the end of the 2016–17 tax year a person has "relevant offshore tax non-compliance" to correct if—

(a) Conditions A and B are satisfied in respect of any offshore tax non-compliance committed by that person on or before 5 April 2017 ("the original offshore tax non-compliance"), and

(b) Condition C will be satisfied on the relevant date (see paragraph 6).

(2) Where the original offshore tax non-compliance committed by a person has been corrected in part by the end of the tax year 2016–17, the person's "relevant offshore tax non-compliance" is the uncorrected part of the original offshore tax non-compliance.

4 Condition A is that the original offshore tax non-compliance has not been fully corrected before the end of the tax year 2016–17 (see paragraph 13).

5 Condition B is that—

(a) the original offshore tax non-compliance involved a potential loss of revenue when it was committed, and

(b) if the original offshore tax non-compliance has been corrected in part by the end of the tax year 2016–17, the uncorrected part at that time involved a potential loss of revenue.

6 (1) Condition C is that on the relevant date it is lawful, on the assumptions set out in sub-paragraph (2), for HMRC to assess the person concerned to any tax the liability to which would have been disclosed to or discovered by HMRC if on that date—

(a) where none of the original offshore tax non-compliance was corrected before the end of the 2016–17 tax year, HMRC were aware of the information missing as a result of the failure to correct that tax non-compliance, or

(b) where the original offshore tax non compliance was corrected in part before that time, HMRC were aware of the information missing as a result of the failure to correct the rest of that tax non-compliance.

(2) The assumptions are—

(a) that paragraph 26 is to be disregarded, and

(b) where the tax at stake is inheritance tax, that the relevant offshore tax non-compliance is not corrected before the relevant date

(3) In this paragraph "the relevant date" is—

(a) where the tax at stake is income tax or capital gains tax, 6 April 2017, and

(b) where the tax at stake is inheritance tax, the day after the day on which this Act is passed.

"Offshore tax-non compliance" etc

7 (1) "Offshore tax non-compliance" means tax non-compliance which involves an offshore matter or an offshore transfer, whether or not it also involves an onshore matter.

(2) Tax non-compliance "involves an onshore matter" if and to the extent that it does not involve an offshore matter or an offshore transfer.

(3) For the meaning of "involves an offshore matter or an offshore transfer" (in relation to the different descriptions of tax non-compliance) see paragraphs 9 to 11.

"Tax non-compliance"

8 (1) "Tax non-compliance" means any of the following—

(a) a failure to comply on or before the filing date with an obligation under section 7 of TMA 1970 to give notice of chargeability to income tax or capital gains tax,

(b) a failure to comply on or before the filing date with an obligation to deliver to HMRC a return or other document which is listed in sub-paragraph (3), or

(c) delivering to HMRC a return or other document which is listed in sub-paragraph (3) or (4) and contains an inaccuracy which amounts to, or leads to—

(i) an understatement of a liability to tax,

(ii) a false or inflated statement of a loss, or

(iii) a false or inflated claim to repayment of tax.

(2) In sub-paragraph (1)—

(a) "filing date", in relation to a notice of chargeability or a return or other document, means the date by which it is required to be given, made or delivered to HMRC,

(b) "loss" includes a charge, expense, deficit and any other amount which may be available for, or relied on to claim, a deduction or relief, and

(c) "repayment of tax" includes a reference to allowing a credit against tax.

(3) The documents relevant for the purposes of both of paragraphs (b) and (c) of sub-paragraph (1) are (so far as they relate to the tax or taxes shown in the first column)—

Tax to which document relates	Document
Income tax or capital gains tax	Return, accounts, statement or document required under section 8(1) of TMA 1970 (personal return)
Income tax or capital gains tax	Return, accounts, statement or document required under section 8A(1) of TMA 1970 (trustee's return)
Income tax	Return, accounts, statement or document required under section 12AA(2) or (3) of TMA 1970 (partnership return)
Income tax	Return under section 254 of FA 2004 (pension schemes)
Income tax	Particulars or documents required under regulation 12 of the Retirement Benefits Schemes (Information Powers) Regulations 1995 (SI 1995/3101) (information relating to pension schemes)
Capital gains tax	NRCGT return under section 12ZB of TMA 1970
Inheritance tax	Account under section 216 or 217 of IHTA 1984.

(4) The documents relevant for the purposes only of paragraph (c) of sub-paragraph (1) are (so far as they relate to the tax or taxes shown in the first column)—

Tax to which document relates	Document
Income tax or capital gains tax	Return, statement or declaration in connection with a claim for an allowance, deduction or relief
Income tax or capital gains tax	Accounts in connection with ascertaining liability to tax
Income tax or capital gains tax	Statement or declaration in connection with a partnership return
Income tax or capital gains tax	Accounts in connection with a partnership return
Inheritance tax	Information or document under regulations under section 256 of IHTA 1984
Inheritance tax	Statement or declaration in connection with a deduction, exemption or relief.
Income tax, capital gains tax or inheritance tax	Any other document given to HMRC by a person ("P") which is likely to be relied on by HMRC to determine, without further inquiry, a question about— (a)P's liability to tax; (b)payments by P by way of or in connection with tax; (c)any other payment by P (including penalties); (d)repayments, or any other kind of payment or credit, to P.

"Involves an offshore matter" and "involves an offshore transfer"

9 (1) This paragraph applies to any tax non-compliance consisting of a failure to comply with an obligation under section 7 of TMA 1970 to notify chargeability to income tax or capital gains tax.

(2) The tax non-compliance "involves an offshore matter" if the potential loss of revenue is charged on or by reference to—

    (a) income arising from a source in a territory outside the UK,

    (b) assets situated or held in a territory outside the UK,

    (c) activities carried on wholly or mainly in a territory outside the UK, or

    (d) anything having effect as if it were income, assets or activities of a kind described above.

(3) The tax non-compliance "involves an offshore transfer" if—

    (a) it does not involve an offshore matter, and

    (b) the applicable condition is satisfied (see sub-paragraphs (4) and (5)).

(4) Where the tax at stake is income tax the applicable condition is satisfied if the income on or by reference to which tax is charged, or any part of the income—

    (a) was received in a territory outside the UK, or

    (b) was transferred on or before 5 April 2017 to a territory outside the UK.

(5) Where the tax at stake is capital gains tax, the applicable condition is satisfied if the proceeds of the disposal on or by reference to which the tax is charged, or any part of the proceeds—

    (a) were received in a territory outside the UK, or

    (b) were transferred on or before 5 April 2017 to a territory outside the UK.

(6) In the case of a transfer falling within sub-paragraph (4)(b) or (5)(b), references to the income or proceeds transferred are to be read as including references to any assets derived from or representing the income or proceeds.

(7) In this paragraph and paragraphs 10 and 11 "assets" has the meaning given in section 21(1) of TCGA 1992, but also includes sterling.

10 (1) This paragraph applies where—

    (a) any tax non-compliance by a person consists of a failure to comply with an obligation to deliver a return or other document, and

    (b) a complete and accurate return or other document would have included information that would have enabled or assisted HMRC to assess the person's liability to tax.

(2) The tax non-compliance "involves an offshore matter" if the liability to tax that would have been shown in the return or other document is or includes a liability to tax charged on or by reference to—

    (a) income arising from a source in a territory outside the UK,

    (b) assets situated or held in a territory outside the UK,

    (c) activities carried on wholly or mainly in a territory outside the UK, or

    (d) anything having effect as if it were income, assets or activities of a kind described above.

(3) Where the tax at stake is inheritance tax, assets are treated for the purposes of sub-paragraph (2) as situated or held in a territory outside the UK if they are so situated or held immediately after the transfer of value by reason of which inheritance tax becomes chargeable.

(4) The tax non-compliance "involves an offshore transfer" if—

    (a) it does not involve an offshore matter, and

    (b) the applicable condition is satisfied in respect of the liability to tax that would have been shown by the return or other document (see sub-paragraphs (5) to (7)).

(5) Where the tax at stake is income tax the applicable condition is satisfied if the income on or by reference to which tax is charged, or any part of the income—

    (a) was received in a territory outside the UK, or

    (b) was transferred on or before 5 April 2017 to a territory outside the UK.

(6) Where the tax at stake is capital gains tax, the applicable condition is satisfied if the proceeds of the disposal on or by reference to which the tax is charged, or any part of the proceeds—

    (a) was received in a territory outside the UK, or

    (b) was transferred on or before 5 April 2017 to a territory outside the UK.

(7) Where the liability to tax which would have been shown in the document is a liability to inheritance tax, the applicable condition is satisfied if—

    (a) the disposition that gives rise to the transfer of value by reason of which the tax becomes chargeable involves a transfer of assets, and

(b) after that disposition but on or before 5 April 2017 the assets, or any part of the assets, are transferred to a territory outside the UK.

(8) In the case of a transfer falling within sub-paragraph (5)(b), (6)(b) or (7)(b), references to the income or proceeds transferred are to be read as including references to any assets derived from or representing the income or proceeds.

11 (1) This paragraph applies to any tax non-compliance by a person if—

(a) the tax non-compliance consists of delivering or giving HMRC a return or other document which contains an inaccuracy, and

(b) the inaccuracy relates to information that would have enabled or assisted HMRC to assess the person's liability to tax.

(2) The tax non-compliance to which this paragraph applies "involves an offshore matter" if the information that should have been given in the tax document relates to—

(a) income arising from a source in a territory outside the UK,

(b) assets situated or held in a territory outside the UK,

(c) activities carried on wholly or mainly in a territory outside the UK, or

(d) anything having effect as if it were income, assets or activities of a kind described above.

(3) Where the tax at stake is inheritance tax, assets are treated for the purposes of sub-paragraph (2) as situated or held in a territory outside the UK if they are so situated or held immediately after the transfer of value by reason of which inheritance tax becomes chargeable.

(4) Tax non-compliance to which this paragraph applies "involves an offshore transfer" if—

(a) it does not involve an offshore matter, and

(b) the applicable condition is satisfied in respect of the liability to tax that would have been shown by the return or other document (see sub-paragraphs (5) to (7)).

(5) Where the tax at stake is income tax the applicable condition is satisfied if the income on or by reference to which the tax is charged, or any part of the income—

(a) was received in a territory outside the UK, or

(b) was transferred on or before 5 April 2017 to a territory outside the UK.

(6) Where the tax at stake is capital gains tax, the applicable condition is satisfied if—

(a) the information that should have been given in the tax document relates to the proceeds of the disposal on or by reference to which the tax is charged, and

(b) the proceeds, or any part of the proceeds—

(i) were received in a territory outside the UK, or

(ii) were transferred on or before 5 April 2017 to a territory outside the UK.

(7) Where the tax at stake is inheritance tax, the applicable condition is satisfied if—

(a) the information that should have been given in the tax document relates to the disposition that gives rise to the transfer of value by reason of which the tax becomes payable relates to a transfer of assets, and

(b) after that disposition but on or before 5 April 2017 the assets or any part of the assets are transferred to a territory outside the UK.

(8) In the case of a transfer falling within sub-paragraph (5)(b), (6)(b) or (7)(b), references to the income, proceeds or assets transferred are to be read as including references to any assets derived from or representing the income, proceeds or assets.

"Tax"

12 (1) References to "tax" are (unless in the context the reference is more specific) to income tax, capital gains tax or inheritance tax.

(2) References to "capital gains tax" do not include capital gains tax payable by companies in respect of chargeable gains accruing to them to the extent that those gains are NRCGT gains in respect of which the companies are chargeable to capital gains tax under section 14D or 188D of TCGA 1992 (see section 1(2A)(b) of that Act).

(3) In sub-paragraph (2) "company" has the same meaning as in TCGA 1992.

Correcting offshore tax non-compliance

13 (1) This paragraph sets out how offshore tax non-compliance may be corrected.

(2) References to the correction of offshore tax non-compliance of any description are to the taking of any action specified in this paragraph as a means of correcting offshore tax non-compliance of that description.

(3) Offshore tax non-compliance consisting of a failure to notify chargeability may be corrected by—

(a) giving the requisite notice to HMRC (unless before doing so the person has received a notice requiring the person to make and deliver a tax return) and giving HMRC the relevant information by any means mentioned in paragraph (b),

(b) giving HMRC the relevant information—

(i) by making and delivering a tax return,

(ii) using the digital disclosure service or any other service provided by HMRC as a means of correcting tax non-compliance,

(iii) communicating it to an officer of Revenue and Customs in the course of an enquiry into the person's tax affairs, or

(iv) using a method agreed with an officer of Revenue and Customs.

(4) In sub-paragraph (3) "relevant information" means information relating to offshore tax that—

(a) had the requisite notice been given in time and the person given a notice to make and deliver a tax return, would have been required to be included in the tax return, and

(b) would have enabled or assisted HMRC to calculate the offshore tax due.

(5) Offshore tax non-compliance consisting of a failure to make or deliver a return or other document may be corrected by giving HMRC the relevant information by—

(a) making or delivering the requisite return or document,

(b) using the digital disclosure service or any other service provided by HMRC as a means of correcting tax non-compliance,

(c) communicating it to an officer of Revenue and Customs in the course of an enquiry into the person's tax affairs, or

(d) using a method agreed with an officer of Revenue and Customs.

(6) In subsection (5) "relevant information" means information relating to offshore tax that—

(a) should have been included in the return or other document, and

(b) would have enabled or assisted HMRC to calculate the offshore tax due.

(7) Offshore tax non-compliance consisting of making and delivering a return or other document containing an inaccuracy may be corrected by giving HMRC the relevant information by—

(a) in the case of an inaccurate tax document, amending the document or delivering a new document,

(b) using the digital disclosure service or any other service provided by HMRC as a means of correcting tax non-compliance,

(c) communicating it to an officer of Revenue and Customs in the course of an enquiry into the person's tax affairs, or

(d) using a method agreed with an officer of Revenue and Customs.

(8) In sub-paragraph (7) "relevant information" means information relating to offshore tax that—

(a) should have been included in the return but was not (whether due to an omission or the giving of inaccurate information), and

(b) would have enabled or assisted HMRC to calculate the offshore tax due.

(9) In this paragraph "offshore tax", in relation to any offshore tax non-compliance, means tax corresponding to the offshore PLR in respect of the non-compliance.

PART 2

AMOUNT OF PENALTY

Amount of penalty

14 (1) The penalty payable under paragraph 1 is 200% of the offshore PLR attributable to the uncorrected offshore tax non-compliance (subject to any reduction under a provision of this Part of this Schedule).

(2) In this Part of this Schedule "the uncorrected offshore tax non-compliance" means—

(a) the relevant offshore tax non-compliance, in a case where none of it is corrected within the RTC period, or

(b) so much of the relevant offshore tax non-compliance as has not been corrected within the RTC period, in a case where part of it is corrected within that period.

Offshore PLR

15 (1) In this Schedule "offshore PLR", in relation to any offshore tax non-compliance means the potential loss of revenue attributable to that non-compliance, to be determined as follows.

(2) The potential lost revenue attributable to any offshore tax non-compliance is (subject to sub-paragraphs (5) and (6)) —

(a) if the non-compliance is a failure to notify chargeability, the potential lost revenue under the applicable provisions of paragraph 7 of Schedule 41 to FA 2008 (or, where the original offshore tax non-compliance took place before 1 April 2010, the amount referred to in section 7(8) of TMA 1970),

(b) if the non-compliance is a failure to deliver a return or other document, the amount of the liability to tax under the applicable provisions of paragraph 24 of Schedule 55 to FA 2009 (or, where the original offshore tax non-compliance took place before 1 April 2011, the amount of liability to tax that would have been shown in the return as defined in section 93(9) of TMA 1970), and

(c) if the non-compliance is delivering a return or other document containing an inaccuracy, the potential lost revenue under the applicable provisions of paragraphs 5 to 8 of Schedule 24 to FA 2007 (or, where the original offshore tax non-compliance took place before 1 April 2008, the difference described in section 95(2) of TMA 1970).

(3) In its application for the purposes of sub-paragraph (2)(c) above, paragraph 6 of Schedule 24 to FA 2007 has effect as if—

(a) for sub-paragraph (1) there were substituted—

"(1) Where—

(a) P is liable to a penalty in respect of two or more inaccuracies (each being an inaccuracy in a return or other document listed in paragraph 8(3) or (4) of Schedule 18) to F(No 2)A 2017) in relation to a tax year or, in the case of inheritance tax, a single transfer of value,

(b) in relation to any one (or more than one) of those inaccuracies, the delivery of the return or other document containing it constitutes offshore tax non-compliance, and

(c) the calculation of potential lost revenue attributable to each of those inaccuracies depends on the order in which they are corrected,

the potential lost revenue attributable to any offshore tax non-compliance constituted by any one of those inaccuracies is to be taken to be such amount as is just and reasonable.

(1A) In sub-paragraph (1) "offshore tax non-compliance" has the same meaning as in Schedule 18 to F(No2)A 2017."; and

(b) in sub-paragraph (4), for paragraphs (b) to (d) there were substituted—
"(b) other understatements."

(4) In sub-paragraphs (5) and (6) "combined tax non-compliance" is tax non-compliance that—

(a) involves an offshore matter or an offshore transfer, but

(b) also involves an onshore matter.

(5) Any combined tax non-compliance is to be treated for the purposes of this Schedule as if it were two separate acts of tax non-compliance, namely—

(a) the combined tax non-compliance so far as it involves an offshore matter or an offshore transfer (which is then offshore tax non-compliance within the meaning of this Schedule), and

(b) the combined tax non-compliance so far as it involves an onshore matter.

(6) The potential lost revenue attributable to the offshore tax non-compliance referred to in sub-paragraph (5)(a) is to be taken to be such share of the potential lost revenue attributable to the combined tax non-compliance as is just and reasonable.

Reduction of penalty for disclosure etc by person liable to penalty

16 (1) This paragraph provides for a reduction in a penalty under paragraph 1 for any uncorrected relevant offshore tax non-compliance if the person ("P") who is liable to the penalty discloses any matter mentioned in sub-paragraph (2) that is relevant to the non-compliance or its correction or to the assessment or enforcement of the offshore tax attributable to it.

(2) The matters are—

(a) chargeability to income tax or capital gains tax (where the tax non-compliance is a failure to notify chargeability),

(b) a missing tax return,

(c) an inaccuracy in a document,

(d) a supply of false information or a withholding of information, or

(e) a failure to disclose an under-assessment.

(3) A person discloses a matter for the purposes of this paragraph only by—

(a) telling HMRC about it,

(b) giving HMRC reasonable help in relation to the matter (for example by quantifying an inaccuracy in a document),

(c) informing HMRC of any person who acted as an enabler of the relevant offshore tax non-compliance or the failure to correct it, and

(d) allowing HMRC access to records—

(i) for any reasonable purpose connected with resolving the matter (for example for the purpose of ensuring that an inaccuracy in a document is fully corrected), and

(ii) for the purpose of ensuring that HMRC can identify all persons who may have acted as an enabler of the relevant offshore tax non-compliance or the failure to correct it.

(4) Where a person liable to a penalty under paragraph 1 discloses a matter HMRC must reduce the penalty to one that reflects the quality of the disclosure.

(5) But the penalty may not be reduced below 100% of the offshore PLR.

(6) In relation to disclosure or assistance, "quality" includes timing, nature and extent.

(7) For the purposes of sub-paragraph (3) a person "acted as an enabler" of relevant offshore tax non-compliance by another if the person encouraged, assisted or otherwise facilitated the conduct by the other person that constituted the offshore tax non-compliance.

17 (1) If they think it right because of special circumstances, HMRC may reduce a penalty under paragraph 1.

(2) In sub-paragraph (1) "special circumstances" does not include—

(a) ability to pay, or

(b) the fact that a potential loss of revenue from one taxpayer is balanced by a potential overpayment by another.

(3) In sub-paragraph (1) the reference to reducing a penalty includes a reference to—

(a) staying a penalty, or

(b) agreeing a compromise in relation to proceedings for a penalty.

Procedure for assessing penalty, etc

18 (1) Where a person is found liable for a penalty under paragraph 1 HMRC must—

(a) assess the penalty,

(b) notify the person, and

(c) state in the notice—

(i) the uncorrected relevant offshore tax non-compliance to which the penalty relates, and

(ii) the tax period to which that offshore tax non-compliance relates.

(2) A penalty must be paid before the end of the period of 30 days beginning with the day on which notification of the penalty is issued.

(3) An assessment of a penalty—

(a) is to be treated for procedural purposes in the same way as an assessment to tax (except in respect of a matter expressly provided for by this Schedule),

(b) may be enforced as if it were an assessment to tax, and

(c) may be combined with an assessment to tax.

(4) A supplementary assessment may be made in respect of a penalty if an earlier assessment operated by reference to an underestimate of the liability to tax that would have been shown in a return.

(5) Sub-paragraph (6) applies if—

(a) an assessment in respect of a penalty is based on a liability to offshore tax that would have been shown on a return, and

(b) that liability is found by HMRC to have been excessive.

(6) HMRC may amend the assessment so that it is based upon the correct amount.

(7) But an amendment under sub-paragraph (6)—

(a) does not affect when the penalty must be paid, and

(b) may be made after the last day on which the assessment in question could have been made under paragraph 19.

19 (1) An assessment of a penalty under paragraph 1 in respect of uncorrected relevant offshore tax non-compliance must be made before the end of the relevant period for that non-compliance.

(2) If the non-compliance consists of a failure to notify chargeability, the relevant period is the period of 12 months beginning with—

(a) the end of the appeal period for the assessment of tax unpaid by reason of the failure, or

(b) if there is no such assessment, the date on which the amount of tax unpaid by reason of the failure is ascertained.

(3) If the non-compliance consists of a failure to submit a return or other document, the relevant period is the period of 12 months beginning with—

(a) the end of the appeal period for the assessment of the liability to tax which would have been shown in the return, or

(b) if there is no such assessment, the date on which that liability is ascertained.

(4) If the non-compliance consists of making and delivering a tax document containing an inaccuracy, the relevant period is the period of 12 months beginning with—

(a) the end of the appeal period for the decision correcting the inaccuracy, or

(b) if there is no assessment to the tax concerned within paragraph (a), the date on which the inaccuracy is corrected.

(5) In this paragraph references to the appeal period are to the period during which—

(a) an appeal could be brought, or

(b) an appeal that has been brought has not been finally determined or withdrawn.

Appeals

20 A person may appeal against—

(a) a decision of HMRC that a penalty under paragraph 1 is payable by that person, or

(b) a decision of HMRC as to the amount of a penalty under paragraph 1 payable by the person.

21 (1) An appeal under paragraph 20 is to be treated in the same way as an appeal against an assessment to the tax at stake (including by the application of any provision about bringing the appeal by notice to HMRC, about HMRC review of the decision or about determination of the appeal by the First-tier Tribunal or Upper Tribunal).

(2) Sub-paragraph (1) does not apply—

(a) so as to require the person bringing the appeal to pay a penalty before an appeal against the assessment of the penalty is determined,

(b) in respect of any other matter expressly provided for by this Schedule.

22 (1) On an appeal under paragraph 20(a) that is notified to the tribunal, the tribunal may affirm or cancel HMRC's decision.

(2) On an appeal under paragraph 20(b) that is notified to the tribunal, the tribunal may—

(a) affirm HMRC's decision, or

(b) substitute for that decision another decision that HMRC had power to make.

(3) If the tribunal substitutes its own decision for HMRC's, the tribunal may rely on paragraph 16 or 17 (or both)—

(a) to the same extent as HMRC (which may mean applying the same percentage reduction as HMRC to a different starting point),

(b) to a different extent, but only if the tribunal thinks that HMRC's decision in respect of the application of that paragraph was flawed.

(4) In sub-paragraph (3)(b) "flawed" means flawed when considered in the light of the principles applicable in proceedings for judicial review.

(5) In this paragraph "tribunal" means the First-tier Tribunal or Upper Tribunal (as appropriate by virtue of paragraph 21(1)).

Reasonable excuse

23 (1) Liability to a penalty under paragraph 1 does not arise in relation to a particular failure to correct any relevant offshore tax non-compliance within the RTC period if the person concerned (P) satisfies HMRC or the relevant tribunal (as the case may be) that there is a reasonable excuse for the failure.

(2) For this purpose—

(a) an insufficiency of funds is not a reasonable excuse, unless attributable to events outside P's control,

(b) where P relied on any other person to do anything, that cannot be a reasonable excuse unless P took reasonable care to avoid the failure,

(c) where P had a reasonable excuse but the excuse has ceased, P is to be treated as continuing to have the excuse if the failure is remedied without unreasonable delay after the excuse ceased, and

(d) reliance on advice is to be taken automatically not to be a reasonable excuse if it is disqualified under sub-paragraph (3).

(3) Advice is disqualified (subject to sub-paragraph (4)) if—

(a) the advice was given to P by an interested person,

(b) the advice was given to P as a result of arrangements made between an interested person and the person who gave the advice,

(c) the person who gave the advice did not have appropriate expertise for giving the advice,

(d) the advice failed to take account of all P's individual circumstances (so far as relevant to the matters to which the advice relates), or

(e) the advice was addressed to, or was given to, a person other than P.

(4) Where advice would otherwise be disqualified under any of paragraphs (a) to (d) of sub-paragraph (3) the advice is not disqualified if at the end of the RTC period P—

(a) has taken reasonable steps to find out whether or not the advice falls within that paragraph, and

(b) reasonably believes that it does not.

(5) In sub-paragraph (3) "an interested person" means, in relation to any relevant offshore tax non-compliance—

(a) a person (other than P) who participated in relevant avoidance arrangements or any transaction forming part of them, or

(b) a person who for any consideration (whether or not in money) facilitated P's entering into relevant avoidance arrangements.

(6) In this paragraph "avoidance arrangements" means arrangements as respects which, in all the circumstances, it would be reasonable to conclude that their main purpose, or one of their main purposes, is the obtaining of a tax advantage.

(7) But arrangements are not avoidance arrangements for the purposes of this paragraph if (although they fall within sub-paragraph (6))—

(a) they are arrangements which accord with established practice, and

(b) HMRC had, at the time the arrangements were entered into, indicated its acceptance of that practice.

(8) Where any relevant offshore tax non-compliance arose originally because information was submitted to HMRC on the basis that particular avoidance arrangements had an effect which they did not have, those avoidance arrangements are "relevant avoidance arrangements" in relation to that tax non-compliance.

(9) In sub-paragraph (6)—

(a) "arrangements" includes any agreement, understanding, scheme, transaction or series of transactions (whether or not legally enforceable), and

(b) a "tax advantage" includes—

(i) relief or increased relief from tax,

(ii) repayment or increased repayment of tax,

(iii) avoidance or reduction of a charge to tax or an assessment to tax,

(iv) avoidance of a possible assessment to tax,

(v) deferral of a payment of tax or advancement of a repayment of tax.

Double jeopardy

24 (1) Where by reason of any conduct a person—

(a) has been convicted of an offence, or

(b) is liable to a penalty otherwise than under paragraph 1 for which the person has been assessed (and the assessment has not been successfully appealed against or withdrawn),

that conduct does not give rise to liability to a penalty under paragraph 1.

(2) In sub-paragraph (1) the reference to a penalty otherwise than under paragraph 1—

(a) includes a penalty under paragraph 6 of Schedule 55 to FA 2009, but does not include penalties under any other provision of that Schedule, and

(b) includes a penalty under subsection (5) of section 93 of TMA 1970 but, does not include penalties under any other provision of that section.

(3) But the aggregate of—

(a) the amount of a penalty under paragraph 1, and

(b) the amount of a penalty under paragraph 5 of Schedule 55 which is determined by reference to a liability to tax,

must not exceed 200% of that liability to tax.

(4) In sub-paragraph (1) "conduct" includes a failure to act.

Application of provisions of TMA 1970

25 Subject to the provisions of this Part of this Schedule, the following provisions of TMA 1970 apply for the purposes of this Part of this Schedule as they apply for the purposes of the Taxes Acts—

(a) section 108 (responsibility of company officers),
(b) section 114 (want of form), and
(c) section 115 (delivery and service of documents).

PART 3
FURTHER PROVISIONS RELATING TO THE REQUIREMENT TO CORRECT

Extension of period for assessment etc of offshore tax

26 (1) This paragraph applies where—

(a) at the end of the tax year 2016–17 a person has relevant offshore tax non-compliance to correct, and
(b) the last day on which it would (disregarding this paragraph) be lawful for HMRC to assess the person to any offshore tax falls within the period beginning with 6 April 2017 and ending with 4 April 2021.

(2) The period in which it is lawful for HMRC to assess the person to the offshore tax is extended by virtue of this paragraph to end with 5 April 2021.

(3) In this paragraph "offshore tax", in relation to any relevant offshore tax non-compliance, means tax corresponding to the offshore PLR in respect of the non-compliance.

Further penalty in connection with offshore asset moves

27 (1) Schedule 21 to FA 2015 (penalties in connection with offshore asset moves) is amended as follows.

(2) In paragraph 2 (original penalties triggering penalties under Schedule 21) omit "and" after paragraph (b) and after paragraph (c) insert ", and

"(d) a penalty under paragraph 1 of Schedule 18 to FA 2017 (requirement to correct relevant offshore tax non-compliance)."

(3) In paragraph 3 (meaning of deliberate failure) after paragraph (c) insert—

"(d) in the case of a penalty within paragraph 2(d), P was aware at any time during the RTC period that at the end of the 2016–17 tax year P had relevant offshore tax non-compliance to correct;

and terms used in paragraph (d) have the same meaning as in Schedule 18 to FA 2017."

(4) In paragraph 5 (meaning of "relevant time") after sub-paragraph (4) insert—

"(5) Where the original penalty is under paragraph 1 of Schedule 18 to FA 2017, the relevant time is the time when that Schedule comes into force."

Asset-based penalty in addition to penalty under paragraph 1

28 (1) Schedule 22 to FA 2016 (asset-based penalty for offshore inaccuracies and failures) is amended as follows.

(2) In paragraph 2 (meaning of standard offshore penalty)—

(a) in sub-paragraph (1) for "or (4)" substitute "(4) or (4A)",
(b) after sub-paragraph (4) insert—

"(4A) A penalty falls within this paragraph if—

(a) it is imposed on a person under paragraph 1 of Schedule 18 to FA 2017 (requirement to correct relevant offshore tax non-compliance),
(b) the person was aware at any time during the RTC period that at the end of the 2016–17 tax year P had relevant offshore tax non-compliance to correct, and
(c) the tax at stake is (or includes) capital gains tax, inheritance tax or asset-based income tax.", and

(c) after sub-paragraph (5) insert—

"(5A) Sub-paragraph (5) does not apply to a penalty imposed under paragraph 1 of Schedule 18 to FA 2017."

(3) In paragraph 3 (tax year to which standard offshore penalty relates) after sub-paragraph (3) insert—

"(4) Where a standard offshore penalty is imposed under paragraph 1 of Schedule 18 to FA 2017, the tax year to which that penalty relates is—

(a) if the tax at stake in relation to the uncorrected relevant offshore tax non-compliance is income tax or capital gains tax, the tax year or years to which the failure or inaccuracy constituting the relevant offshore tax non-compliance in question relates;

(b) if the tax at stake in relation to the uncorrected relevant offshore tax non-compliance is inheritance tax, the year, beginning on 6 April and ending on the following 5 April, in which the liability to tax first arose.

(5) In sub-paragraph (4) references to uncorrected relevant offshore tax non-compliance are to the relevant offshore tax non-compliance in respect of which the standard offshore penalty is imposed."

(4) In paragraph 5 (meaning of offshore PLR), in sub-paragraph (1)(a) after "FA 2008" insert "or Schedule 18 to FA 2017".

(5) In paragraph 6 (restriction on imposition of multiple asset-based penalties for same asset), in sub-paragraph (1)(a) after "penalty" insert "(other than one imposed under paragraph 1 of Schedule 18 to FA 2017)".

(6) After paragraph 6 insert—

"**6A** Where—

(a) a penalty has been imposed on a person under paragraph 1 of Schedule 18 to FA 2017, and

(b) the potential loss of revenue threshold has been met,

only one asset-based penalty is payable by the person in relation to any given asset."

(7) In paragraph 13 (asset-based income tax) after sub-paragraph (2) insert—

"(2A) In relation to cases where the standard offshore penalty is a penalty falling within paragraph 2(4A), each reference to provisions of ITTOIA 2005 in column 1 of the Table in sub-paragraph (2) includes a reference—

(a) to the corresponding provisions of the legislation in force immediately before those provisions of ITTOIA 2005 came into force (and to any previous text of those corresponding provisions), and

(b) to any other provision that had the same purpose as, or a similar purpose to, any of those corresponding provisions (or any earlier text mentioned in paragraph (a)), if and so far as that other provision was in force—

(i) on or after 6 April 1997, but

(ii) before the corresponding provisions (or the earlier text mentioned in paragraph (a)) came into force.""

(8) In paragraph 19(2) (interpretation: incorporation of definitions from other legislation for "or Schedule 55 to FA 2009" substitute "Schedule 55 to FA 2009 or Part 1 of Schedule 18 to FA 2017".

29 (1) TMA 1970 is amended as follows.

(2) In section 103ZA (disapplication of sections 100 to 103 in the case of certain penalties) omit the "or" after paragraph (j) and after paragraph (k) insert ", or

(l) Schedule 18 to the Finance Act 2017."

(3) In section 107A (relevant trustees)—

(a) in subsection (2)(a) after "Finance Act 2009" insert or Schedule 18 to the Finance Act 2017", and

(b) in subsection (3), after paragraph (c) insert—

"(d) in relation to—

(i) a penalty under Schedule 18 to the Finance Act 2017, or

(ii) interest under section 101 of the Finance Act 2009 on a penalty within sub-paragraph (i),

the end of the RTC period (within the meaning of Schedule 18 to the Finance Act 2017);".

Publishing details of persons assessed to penalty or penalties under paragraph 1

30 (1) The Commissioners for Her Majesty's Revenue and Customs ("the Commissioners") may publish information about a person (P) if in consequence of an investigation they consider that sub-paragraph (2) or (3) applies in relation to P.

(2) This sub-paragraph applies if—

(a) P has been found to have incurred one or more relevant penalties under paragraph 1 (and has been assessed or is the subject of a contract settlement), and
(b) the offshore potential lost revenue in relation to the penalty, or the aggregate of the offshore potential lost revenue in relation to each of the penalties, exceeds £25,000.

(3) This sub-paragraph applies if P has been found to have incurred 5 or more relevant penalties under paragraph 1.

(4) A penalty incurred by P under paragraph 1 is "relevant" if —

(a) P was aware at any time during the RTC period that at the end of the 2016–17 tax year the person had relevant offshore tax non-compliance to correct, and
(b) the penalty relates to the failure to correct that non-compliance.

(5) The information that may be published is—

(a) P's name (including any trading name, previous name or pseudonym),
(b) P's address (or registered office),
(c) the nature of any business carried on by P,
(d) the amount of the penalty or penalties,
(e) the offshore potential lost revenue in relation to the penalty or the aggregate of the offshore potential lost revenue in relation to each of the penalties,
(f) the periods or times to which the uncorrected relevant offshore tax non-compliance relates,
(g) any other information that the Commissioners consider it appropriate to publish in order to make clear the person's identity.

(6) In sub-paragraph (5)(f) the reference to the uncorrected relevant offshore tax non-compliance is to so much of P's relevant offshore tax non-compliance at the end of the 2016–17 tax year as P failed to correct within the RTC period.

(7) The information may be published in any manner that the Commissioners consider appropriate.

(8) Before publishing any information the Commissioners must—

(a) inform P that they are considering doing so, and
(b) afford P the opportunity to make representations about whether it should be published.

(9) No information may be published before the day on which the penalty becomes final or, where more than one penalty is involved, the latest day on which any of the penalties becomes final.

(10) No information may be published for the first time after the end of the period of one year beginning with that day.

(11) No information may be published (or continue to be published) after the end of the period of one year beginning with the day on which it is first published.

(12) No information may be published if the amount of the penalty—

(a) is reduced under paragraph 16 to the minimum permitted amount (being 100% of the offshore PLR), or
(b) is reduced under paragraph 17 to nil or stayed.

(13) For the purposes of this paragraph a penalty becomes final—

(a) if it has been assessed, when the time for any appeal or further appeal relating to it expires or, if later, any appeal or final appeal relating to it is finally determined, and
(b) if a contract settlement has been made, at the time when the contract is made.

(14) In this paragraph "contract settlement", in relation to a penalty, means a contract between the Commissioners and the person under which the Commissioners undertake not to assess the penalty or (if it has been assessed) not to take proceedings to recover it.

31 (1) The Treasury may by regulations amend paragraph 30(2) to vary the amount for the time being specified in paragraph (b).

(2) Regulations under this paragraph are to be made by statutory instrument.

(3) A statutory instrument under this paragraph is subject to annulment in pursuance of a resolution of the House of Commons.

PART 4

SUPPLEMENTARY

Interpretation: minor

32 (1) In this Schedule (apart from the amendments made by Part 3)—

"HMRC" means Her Majesty's Revenue and Customs;

"tax period" means a tax year or other period in respect of which tax is charged (or in the case of inheritance tax, the year beginning with 6 April and ending on the following 5 April in which the liability to tax first arose);

"tax year", in relation to inheritance tax, means a period of 12 months beginning on 6 April and ending on the following 5 April;

"UK" means the United Kingdom, including its territorial sea.

(2) A reference to making a return or doing anything in relation to a return includes a reference to amending a return or doing anything in relation to an amended return.

(3) References to delivery (of a document) include giving, sending and any other similar expressions.

(4) A reference to delivering a document to HMRC includes—

(a) a reference to communicating information to HMRC in any form and by any method (whether by post, fax, email, telephone or otherwise, and

(b) a reference to making a statement or declaration in a document.

(5) References to an assessment to tax, in relation to inheritance tax, are to a determination.

(6) An expression used in relation to income tax has the same meaning as in the Income Tax Acts.

(7) An expression used in relation to capital gains tax has the same meaning as in the enactments relating to that tax.

(8) An expression used in relation to inheritance tax has the same meaning as in IHTA 1984.

Terms defined or explained for purposes of more than one paragraph of this Schedule

Term	Paragraph
assets (in paragraphs 8 to 10)	paragraph 9(7)
capital gains tax	paragraph 12(2)
HMRC	paragraph 32(1)
involves an offshore matter (in relation to failure to notify chargeability)	paragraph 9(2)
involves an offshore matter (in relation to failure to deliver a return or other document)	paragraph 10(2) and (3)
involves an offshore matter (in relation to delivery of a return or other document containing an inaccuracy)	paragraph 11(2) and (3)
involves an offshore transfer (in relation to failure to notify chargeability)	paragraph 9(3) to (6)
involves an offshore transfer (in relation to failure to deliver a return or other document)	paragraph 10(4) to (8)
involves an offshore transfer (in relation to delivery of a return or other document containing an inaccuracy)	paragraph 11(4) to (8)
involves an onshore matter (in relation to any tax non-compliance)	paragraph 7(2)
offshore tax non-compliance	paragraph 7(1)
offshore PLR	paragraph 15(1)
potential lost revenue	paragraph 15(2)
RTC period	paragraph 1(b)
relevant offshore tax non-compliance	paragraph 3
tax non-compliance	paragraph 8(1)
tax period	paragraph 32(1)

tax year (in relation to inheritance tax)	paragraph 32(1)
tax	paragraph 12(1)
UK	paragraph 32(1)
uncorrected offshore tax non-compliance (in Part 2)	paragraph 14(2)

GENERAL NOTE

Part 1

Paragraphs 1–2 require a penalty to be payable by a person who has relevant offshore tax non-compliance at the end of tax year 2016/17 and who fails to correct it within the requirement to correct ("RTC") period. The RTC period is 6 April 2017 to 30 September 2018.

The conditions to determine whether a person has "relevant offshore tax non-compliance" at the end of the 2016/17 tax year are:

– Condition A: offshore tax non-compliance has not been fully corrected before the end of the tax year 2016/17;
– Condition B: the offshore tax non-compliance that has not been fully corrected by that time involves a potential loss of revenue; and
– Condition C: on the relevant date (6 April 2017 for income tax and capital gains tax and the day after the Act is passed for inheritance tax), HMRC would have been able to assess the person concerned to the tax liability which should have otherwise been disclosed and corrected.

Offshore tax non-compliance is tax non-compliance involving an offshore matter or an offshore transfer.

Tax non-compliance means:

– a failure to notify chargeability to income tax or capital gains tax before the required date;
– a failure to deliver a return, or any other document required to establish a person's liability to tax, before the required date; or
– delivering a return or any other document to HMRC that contains an inaccuracy causing an understatement of tax liability, a false or inflated statement of loss or an inflated claim to a repayment of loss.

Tax non-compliance as listed above involves an offshore matter if the tax at stake relates to income arising outside the UK, assets situated outside the UK, activities carried out wholly or mainly outside the UK, or anything that has the effect of any of these. It involves an offshore transfer if it is not an offshore matter and the applicable condition conditions set out at paras 9(5), 10(5) and 11(5), are met, i.e. if the tax at stake is income tax (capital gains tax) and the income (gain) is received in a territory outside the UK or before 5 April 2017 that income (gain) was transferred to a territory outside the UK. Paragraphs 10 and 11 can apply to IHT.

References to "tax" are to income tax, capital gains tax, and inheritance tax, but exclude capital gains tax on certain capital gains payable by companies as part of their corporation tax liability.

Paragraph 13 sets out the manner in which the failures can be corrected and includes providing relevant information to HMRC by delivering the document/notice of chargeability/tax return as well as using a facility provided for the purpose; or telling an officer in the course of an enquiry, or another method agreed with HMRC. Basically, making a disclosure of the irregularities.

Those professionals who have advised on offshore structures will be familiar with the complexities of the legislation giving rise to a tax charge and the exemptions from those charges. If it is determined that, contrary to professional advice, there was a RTC, an exposure to a penalty could arise, although subject to any reasonable excuse, see below.

Part 2

The amount of penalty is 200% of the potential lost revenue (PLR) relating to the relevant offshore tax non-compliance that has not been corrected within the RTC period.

The penalty can be reduced if the person makes an appropriate disclosure (para 16). The amount of the reduction should reflect the quality of the disclosure (timing, nature and extent). The penalty cannot be reduced below 100% of the PLR.

HMRC may, in special circumstances, reduce or stay a penalty, or agree a compromise in relation to penalty proceedings. Special circumstances do not include ability to pay, or that loss of revenue due to underpayment by one taxpayer is balanced by overpayment by another.

PLR is calculated by reference to the rules for calculating PLR in the corresponding circumstances in:

- Paragraph 8(1)(a): Finance Act 2008 Sch 41;
- Paragraph 8(1)(b): Finance Act 2009 Sch 55; and
- Paragraph 8(1)(c): Finance Act 2007 Sch 24.

Where the taxpayer is liable to a penalty in respect of two or more inaccuracies in a return or other document and at least one constitutes offshore tax non-compliance, the calculation of the PLR attributable to each inaccuracy depends on the order they are corrected. The PLR attributable to the offshore tax non-compliance is to be calculated on a just and reasonable basis (see FA 2007 Sch 24 para 6).

An apportionment must also be made on a just and reasonable basis to identify the PLR relating to offshore tax non-compliance and the PLR relating to tax non-compliance involving onshore matters

The statutory procedure for assessing the penalty (para 18) provides a deadline of 30 days from the notification to the taxpayer for payment of the penalty. HMRC may make supplementary assessments if a previous penalty assessment is found insufficient due to an underestimate of liability to tax and an assessment may be amended although it does not affect the original penalty payment deadline.

A penalty must be made within the period of 12 months beginning with the relevant period, which is broadly the end of the appeal period or the date on which that failure/liability is ascertained or the date on which the inaccuracy is corrected.

There is a right of appeal against the decision to charge a penalty, or the amount of the penalty (para 20). Penalty appeals are to be treated in the same way as appeals against an assessment to tax. A person cannot be required to pay a penalty before an appeal against it is determined.

The penalty may be fully mitigated where the Tribunal or HMRC are satisfied there is a reasonable excuse. When considering reasonable excuse through reliance on a professional, it will be necessary to consider whether that professional was unconnected to the structure (i.e. not a provider or remunerated by the provider), whether an appropriately qualified expert to provide the advice and whether the facts opined on were correct or whether generic advice was relied upon. Furthermore, independent professionals advising on complicated offshore structures will often set out the risks involved and a person in possession of knowing these risks may be regarded as acting in acceptance of them and not able to rely on a reasonable excuse.

Measures prevent duplication of penalties arising under different provisions.

Part 3

The period in which HMRC may assess tax in respect of relevant offshore tax non-compliance is extended where the normal assessment period expires during the period beginning with 6 April 2017 and ending with 4 April 2021, to 5 April 2021.

Paragraph 27 amends FA 2015 Sch 21 (penalties in connection with offshore asset moves) to ensure liability to a penalty under Schedule 21 to the Finance Act 2015 if the person is aware that there is relevant offshore tax non-compliance in relation to their affairs and moves an asset between territories before the end of the RTC period intending to escape the RTC penalty.

Paragraph 28 amends FA 2016 Sch 22 (asset-based penalty for offshore inaccuracies and failures) so that a person may also be subject to the asset-based penalty. They are subject to the penalty if during the RTC period, the person was aware that at the end of the 2016/17 tax year they had relevant offshore tax non-compliance to correct. Only one asset-based penalty may be imposed in relation to an asset by reference to a RTC penalty.

HMRC may publish information about a person who incurs one or more relevant FTC penalties involving PLR exceeding £25,000 or if the person incurs five or more FTC penalties. A penalty is relevant if the person was aware they had a relevant offshore tax non-compliance to correct during the RTC period and that at the end of the 2016/17 tax year the person had relevant offshore tax non-compliance to correct.

The threshold of £25,000 may be amended by statutory instrument.

Information cannot be published:
- before the time to appeal the penalty has expired;
- until an appeal is finally determined;
- for the first time more than one year after those times.

Publication must stop after one year from the date of first publication. No publication can be made in relation to FTC penalties that are reduced to the minimum permitted or reduced to nil.

HMRC must advise a taxpayer that publication is being considered and allow the person to make representations. HMRC may publish:
- name and address (or registered office);
- nature of any business carried on by the person;
- amount of penalty/penalties and the PLR in question;
- when the offshore non-compliance occurred;
- any other information to make the person's identity clear.

INDEX